Cambridge IGCSE® International Mathematics

(0607) Core

Keith Black
Alison Ryan
Michael Haese
Robert Haese
Sandra Haese
James Foley

Endorsed by Cambridge Inter

Haese and Harris P
specialists in mathe

CAMBRIDGE IGCSE INTERNATIONAL MATHEMATICS (0607) CORE

Keith Black   B.Sc.(Hons.), Dip.Ed.
Alison Ryan   B.Sc., M.Ed.
Michael Haese   B.Sc.(Hons.), Ph.D.
Robert Haese   B.Sc.
Sandra Haese   B.Sc.
James Foley   B.Ma.Comp.Sc.(Hons.)

Haese Mathematics
152 Richmond Road, Marleston, SA 5033, AUSTRALIA
Telephone: +61 8 8210 4666, Fax: + 61 8 8354 1238
Email: info@haesemathematics.com.au
Web: www.haesemathematics.com.au

National Library of Australia Card Number & ISBN 978-1-921500-22-0

© Haese & Harris Publications 2011

Published by Haese Mathematics
152 Richmond Road, Marleston, SA 5033, AUSTRALIA

First Edition   2011
Reprinted   2014

Cartoon artwork by John Martin. Artwork by Piotr Poturaj.

Cover design by Piotr Poturaj.

Fractal artwork on the cover copyright by Jaroslaw Wierny, www.fractal.art.pl

Computer software by David Purton, Troy Cruickshank, Thomas Jansson, Adrian Blackburn, Andi Raicu, Ashvin Narayanan, and Ben Fitzgerald.

Typeset in Australia by Susan Haese and Charlotte Frost (Raksar Nominees). Typeset in Times Roman 10/11.

This textbook and its accompanying CD have been endorsed by Cambridge International Examinations.

Printed in China by Prolong Press Limited.

This book is copyright. Except as permitted by the Copyright Act (any fair dealing for the purposes of private study, research, criticism or review), no part of this publication may be reproduced, stored in a retrieval system, or transmitted in any form or by any means, electronic, mechanical, photocopying, recording or otherwise, without the prior permission of the publisher. Enquiries to be made to Haese Mathematics.

Copying for educational purposes: Where copies of part or the whole of the book are made under Part VB of the Copyright Act, the law requires that the educational institution or the body that administers it has given a remuneration notice to Copyright Agency Limited (CAL). For information, contact the Copyright Agency Limited.

Acknowledgements: The publishers acknowledge the cooperation of Oxford University Press, Australia, for the reproduction of material originally published in textbooks produced in association with Haese Mathematics. While every attempt has been made to trace and acknowledge copyright, the authors and publishers apologise for any accidental infringement where copyright has proved untraceable. They would be pleased to come to a suitable agreement with the rightful owner.

Disclaimer: All the internet addresses (URLs) given in this book were valid at the time of printing. While the authors and publisher regret any inconvenience that changes of address may cause readers, no responsibility for any such changes can be accepted by either the authors or the publisher.

® IGCSE is the registered trademark of Cambridge International Examinations

FOREWORD

This book has been written to cover the '*Cambridge IGCSE International Mathematics (0607) Core*' course over a two-year period.

Following the release of our IGCSE Extended textbook, this book has been written at the request of and with interest from teachers.

The new course was developed by Cambridge International Examinations in consultation with teachers in international schools around the world. It has been designed for schools that want their mathematics teaching to focus more on investigations and modelling, and to utilise the powerful technology of graphics calculators.

The course springs from the principles that students should develop a good foundation of mathematical skills and that they should learn to develop strategies for solving open-ended problems. It aims to promote a positive attitude towards Mathematics and a confidence that leads to further enquiry. Some of the schools consulted by Cambridge were IB schools and as a result, Cambridge International Mathematics integrates exceptionally well with the approach to the teaching of Mathematics in IB schools.

This book is an attempt to cover, in one volume, the content outlined in the Cambridge International Mathematics (0607) syllabus. References to the syllabus are made throughout but the book can be used as a full course in its own right. It reinforces basic mathematical concepts and prepares students for the IB Mathematical Studies Standard Level course and other courses that do not require in-depth algebraic manipulation. It also contains the presumed knowledge for the IB Mathematics Standard Level course. The book has been endorsed by Cambridge but it has been developed independently of the International Baccalaureate Organization and is not connected with, or endorsed by, the IBO.

To reflect the principles on which the new course is based, we have attempted to produce a book and CD package that embraces technology, problem solving and investigating, in order to give students different learning experiences. An introductory section 'Graphics calculator instructions' appears on p. 11. It is intended as a basic reference to help students who may be unfamiliar with graphics calculators. The use of graphics calculators and computer packages throughout the book enables students to realise the importance, application and appropriate use of technology. There are non-calculator sections as well as traditional areas of mathematics. To reflect one of the main aims of the new course, the last two chapters in the book are devoted to multi-topic questions, and investigation questions. Each chapter begins with an opening problem and ends with review sets. 'Challenge', 'Discovery' and 'Activity' exercises appear throughout the text to build knowledge and understanding through a variety of approaches. Answers are given at the end of the book, followed by an index.

The interactive CD contains ◉ *Self Tutor* software (see p. 5), geometry and graphics software, demonstrations and simulations. The CD also contains the text of the book so that students can load it on a home computer and keep the textbook at school.

The Cambridge International Mathematics examinations are in the form of three papers: one a non-calculator paper, another requiring the use of a graphics calculator, and a third paper containing an investigation question. All of these aspects of examining are addressed in the book.

The book can be used as a scheme of work but it is expected that the teacher will choose the order of topics. There are a few occasions where a question in an exercise may require something done later in the book but this has been kept to a minimum. Exercises in the book range from routine practice and consolidation of basic skills, to problem solving exercises.

In this changing world of mathematics education, we believe that the contextual approach shown in this book, with the associated use of technology, will enhance the students' understanding, knowledge and appreciation of mathematics, and its universal application.

We welcome your feedback.

Email: info@haesemathematics.com.au
Web: www.haesemathematics.com.au

KB, AR, PMH, RCH, SHH, JMF

USING THE INTERACTIVE CD

The interactive Student CD that comes with this book is designed for those who want to utilise technology in teaching and learning Mathematics.

The CD icon that appears throughout the book denotes an active link on the CD. Simply click on the icon when running the CD to access a large range of interactive features that includes:

- spreadsheets
- printable worksheets
- graphing packages
- geometry software
- demonstrations
- simulations
- printable chapters
- SELF TUTOR

INTERACTIVE LINK

SELF TUTOR is an exciting feature of this book.

The **Self Tutor** icon on each worked example denotes an active link on the CD.

Simply 'click' on the **Self Tutor** (or anywhere in the example box) to access the worked example, with a teacher's voice explaining each step necessary to reach the answer. Play any line as often as you like. See how the basic processes come alive using movement and colour on the screen.

Ideal for students who have missed lessons or need extra help.

Example 2

 **Self Tutor**

Make y the subject of $2x + 3y = 12$.

$2x + 3y = 12$

$\therefore \quad 2x + 3y - 2x = 12 - 2x$ { $-2x$ from both sides}

$\therefore \quad 3y = 12 - 2x$

$\therefore \quad \dfrac{3y}{3} = \dfrac{12 - 2x}{3}$ { $\div$ both sides by 3}

$\therefore \quad y = \dfrac{12}{3} - \dfrac{2x}{3}$

$= 4 - \dfrac{2}{3}x$

See Chapter 8, **Formulae and inequalities**, p. 173.

GRAPHICS CALCULATORS

The course assumes that each student will have a graphics calculator. An introductory section 'Graphics calculator instructions' appears on p. 11. To help get students started, the section includes some basic instructions for the Texas Instruments TI-84 Plus and the Casio fx-9860G calculators.

SYMBOLS AND NOTATION USED IN THIS BOOK

$\mathbb{N}$	the set of positive integers and zero, $\{0, 1, 2, 3, \ldots\}$
$\mathbb{Z}$	the set of integers, $\{0, \pm 1, \pm 2, \pm 3, \ldots\}$
$\mathbb{Z}^+$	the set of positive integers, $\{1, 2, 3, \ldots\}$
$\mathbb{Q}$	the set of rational numbers
$\mathbb{Q}^+$	the set of positive rational numbers, $\{x \mid x > 0, \, x \in \mathbb{Q}\}$
$\mathbb{R}$	the set of real numbers
$\mathbb{R}^+$	the set of positive real numbers, $\{x \mid x > 0, \, x \in \mathbb{R}\}$
$\{x_1, x_2, \ldots\}$	the set with elements $x_1, x_2, \ldots$
$n(A)$	the number of elements in the finite set A
$\{x \mid \ldots\}$	the set of all x such that
$\in$	is an element of
$\notin$	is not an element of
$\varnothing$ or $\{\ \}$	the empty (null) set
$\mathscr{E}$	the universal set
$\cup$	union
$\cap$	intersection
$\subseteq$	is a subset of
$\subset$	is a proper subset of
A'	the complement of the set A
$a^{\frac{1}{n}}, \sqrt[n]{a}$	a to the power of $\frac{1}{n}$, nth root of a (if $a \geq 0$ then $\sqrt[n]{a} \geq 0$)
$a^{\frac{1}{2}}, \sqrt{a}$	a to the power $\frac{1}{2}$, square root of a (if $a \geq 0$ then $\sqrt{a} \geq 0$)
$\|x\|$	the modulus or absolute value of x, that is $\begin{cases} x \text{ for } x \geq 0, \, x \in \mathbb{R} \\ -x \text{ for } x < 0, \, x \in \mathbb{R} \end{cases}$
$\equiv$	identity or is equivalent to
$\approx$	is approximately equal to
$\cong$	is congruent to
$\parallel$	is parallel to
$\perp$	is perpendicular to

$>$	is greater than
$\geq$ or $\geqslant$	is greater than or equal to
$<$	is less than
$\leq$ or $\leqslant$	is less than or equal to
u_n	the nth term of a sequence or series
$f : x \mapsto y$	f is a function under which x is mapped to y
$f(x)$	the image of x under the function f
f^{-1}	the inverse function of the function f
$\log_a x$	logarithm to the base a of x
sin, cos, tan	the circular functions
$A(x, y)$	the point A in the plane with Cartesian coordinates x and y
AB	the line segment with end points A and B the distance from A to B the line containing points A and B
$\hat{A}$	the angle at A
$\hat{CAB}$	the angle between CA and AB
$\triangle ABC$	the triangle whose vertices are A, B and C
$\mathbf{v}$	the vector $\mathbf{v}$
$\overrightarrow{AB}$	the vector represented in magnitude and direction by the directed line segment from A to B
$\|\mathbf{a}\|$	the magnitude of vector $\mathbf{a}$
$\|\overrightarrow{AB}\|$	the magnitude of $\overrightarrow{AB}$
$P(A)$	probability of event A
$P(A')$	probability of the event "not A"
$x_1, x_2, \ldots$	observations of a variable
$f_1, f_2, \ldots$	frequencies with which the observations $x_1, x_2, x_3, \ldots$ occur
$\bar{x}$	mean of the values $x_1, x_2, \ldots$
Σf	sum of the frequencies $f_1, f_2, \ldots$
r	Pearson's correlation coefficient
r^2	coefficient of determination

TABLE OF CONTENTS

SYMBOLS AND NOTATION USED IN THIS BOOK 6

1 NUMBER 27

- A Number types 28
- B Operations and brackets 30
- C HCF and LCM 33
- D Fractions 35
- E Powers and roots 39
- F Ratio and proportion 40
- G Number equivalents 47
- H Percentage 48
- I Rounding numbers 49
- J Time 54
- Review set 1A 57
- Review set 1B 58

2 SETS 59

- A Set notation 59
- B Special number sets 62
- C Interval notation 64
- D Venn diagrams 65
- E Union and intersection 68
- F Problem solving 72
- Review set 2A 74
- Review set 2B 75

3 ALGEBRA (EXPRESSIONS AND EQUATIONS) 77

- A Basic problem solving 77
- B Introduction to algebra 78
- C Evaluating expressions 80
- D Algebraic expressions 80
- E Linear equations 84
- F Equations of the form $x^2 = k$ 88
- G Forming equations 89
- H Problem solving using equations 91
- Review set 3A 93
- Review set 3B 94

4 LINES, ANGLES, AND POLYGONS 95

- A Angles 96
- B Lines and line segments 97
- C Polygons 98
- D Symmetry 101
- E Congruence 103
- F Angle properties 104
- G Triangles 108
- H Isosceles triangles 111
- I The interior angles of a polygon 114
- J The exterior angles of a polygon 117
- Review set 4A 118
- Review set 4B 120

5 ALGEBRA (EXPANSION AND FACTORISATION) 123

- A The distributive law 123
- B Equations containing brackets 125
- C Equations containing fractions 126
- D The product $(a+b)(c+d)$ 128
- E Difference of two squares 130
- F Algebraic common factors 132
- G Factorising with common factors 134
- Review set 5A 137
- Review set 5B 137
- Review set 5C 138

6 GRAPHS, CHARTS, AND TABLES 139

- A Interpreting graphs and tables 140
- B Types of graphs 143
- C Graphs which compare data 147
- D Using technology to graph data 150
- Review set 6A 152
- Review set 6B 153

7 EXPONENTS 155

- A Exponent or index notation 155
- B Exponent or index laws 158
- C Zero and negative indices 161
- D Standard form 162
- Review set 7A 166
- Review set 7B 167

8 FORMULAE AND INEQUALITIES 169

- A Formula substitution 169
- B Formula rearrangement 172

GRAPHICS CALCULATOR INSTRUCTIONS 11

- A Basic calculations 12
- B More calculations 14
- C Secondary function and alpha keys 17
- D Memory 17
- E Lists 19
- F Statistics 21
- G Working with functions 23

Table of Contents

C	Formula derivation	175
D	Interpreting linear inequalities	177
E	Solving linear inequalities	179
	Review set 8A	181
	Review set 8B	182

9 SIMULTANEOUS EQUATIONS 183

A	Equating values of y	185
B	Solution by substitution	186
C	Solution by elimination	187
D	Problem solving	190
	Review set 9A	192
	Review set 9B	193

10 THE THEOREM OF PYTHAGORAS 195

A	Pythagoras' theorem	196
B	Problem solving	202
C	Circle problems	206
	Review set 10A	209
	Review set 10B	210

11 MENSURATION (LENGTH AND AREA) 213

A	Length	214
B	Perimeter	216
C	Area	218
D	Circles and sectors	223
	Review set 11A	227
	Review set 11B	228

12 TOPICS IN ARITHMETIC 231

A	Percentage	231
B	Profit and loss	233
C	Simple interest	236
D	Multipliers and chain percentage	239
E	Compound growth	243
F	Speed, distance and time	245
G	Travel graphs	247
	Review set 12A	249
	Review set 12B	250

13 MENSURATION (SOLIDS AND CONTAINERS) 251

A	Surface area	251
B	Volume	259
C	Capacity	265
D	Mass	268
E	Compound solids	270
	Review set 13A	273
	Review set 13B	275

14 COORDINATE GEOMETRY 277

A	Plotting points	278
B	Distance between two points	280
C	Midpoint of a line segment	282
D	Gradient of a line segment	284
E	Parallel lines	289
F	Using coordinate geometry	291
	Review set 14A	293
	Review set 14B	294

15 ANALYSIS OF DISCRETE DATA 295

A	Variables used in statistics	297
B	Organising and describing discrete data	298
C	The centre of a discrete data set	302
D	Measuring the spread of discrete data	305
E	Data in frequency tables	308
F	Grouped discrete data	310
G	Statistics from technology	312
	Review set 15A	313
	Review set 15B	315

16 STRAIGHT LINES 317

A	Vertical and horizontal lines	318
B	Graphing from a table of values	319
C	Equations of lines	321
D	Graphing lines from equations	325
E	Lines of symmetry	326
	Review set 16A	328
	Review set 16B	328

17 TRIGONOMETRY 331

A	Labelling sides of a right angled triangle	332
B	The trigonometric ratios	333
C	Problem solving	340
D	True bearings	345
	Review set 17A	347
	Review set 17B	348

18 ALGEBRAIC FRACTIONS 351

A	Simplifying algebraic fractions	351
B	Multiplying and dividing algebraic fractions	355
C	Adding and subtracting algebraic fractions	357
	Review set 18A	359
	Review set 18B	360

19 CONTINUOUS DATA 361

A	The mean of continuous data	362
B	Cumulative frequency	364
	Review set 19A	369
	Review set 19B	370

Table of Contents

20 SIMILARITY — 373

A	Similarity	373
B	Similar triangles	376
C	Problem solving	380
	Review set 20A	383
	Review set 20B	384

21 INTRODUCTION TO FUNCTIONS — 387

A	Mapping diagrams	387
B	Functions	390
C	Function notation	394
D	Reciprocal functions	398
	Review set 21A	400
	Review set 21B	401

22 TRANSFORMATION GEOMETRY — 403

A	Directed line segments	404
B	Component form	406
C	Translations	408
D	Rotations	410
E	Reflections	411
F	Enlargements and reductions	413
G	Transforming functions	416
H	Miscellaneous transformations	420
	Review set 22A	422
	Review set 22B	423

23 TWO VARIABLE ANALYSIS — 425

A	Correlation	426
B	Line of best fit by eye	429
	Review set 23A	434
	Review set 23B	435

24 FURTHER FUNCTIONS — 437

A	Unfamiliar functions	438
B	Solving equations graphically	441
C	Problem solving	445
	Review set 24A	447
	Review set 24B	447

25 PROBABILITY — 449

A	Introduction to probability	450
B	Estimating probability	451
C	Probabilities from two-way tables	454
D	Expectation	456
E	Representing combined events	457
F	Theoretical probability	459
G	Compound events	463
H	Using tree diagrams	467
I	Sampling with and without replacement	469
J	Mutually exclusive and non-mutually exclusive events	471
K	Miscellaneous probability questions	472
	Review set 25A	474
	Review set 25B	475

26 SEQUENCES — 477

A	Number sequences	478
B	Algebraic rules for sequences	480
C	The difference method for sequences	482
	Review set 26A	486
	Review set 26B	487

27 CIRCLE GEOMETRY — 489

A	Circle theorems	489
B	Miscellaneous right angle problems	494
	Review set 27A	496
	Review set 27B	498

28 MULTI-TOPIC QUESTIONS — 501

29 INVESTIGATION QUESTIONS — 517

ANSWERS — 542

INDEX — 600

Graphics calculator instructions

Contents:

- **A** Basic calculations
- **B** More calculations
- **C** Secondary function and alpha keys
- **D** Memory
- **E** Lists
- **F** Statistics
- **G** Working with functions

In this course it is assumed that you have a **graphics calculator**. If you learn how to operate your calculator successfully, you should experience little difficulty with future arithmetic calculations.

There are many different brands (and types) of calculators. Different calculators do not have exactly the same keys. It is therefore important that you have an instruction booklet for your calculator, and use it whenever you need to.

However, to help get you started, we have included here some basic instructions for the **Texas Instruments TI-84 Plus** and the **Casio fx-9860G** calculators. Note that instructions given may need to be modified slightly for other models.

GETTING STARTED

Texas Instruments TI-84 Plus

The screen which appears when the calculator is turned on is the **home screen**. This is where most basic calculations are performed.

You can return to this screen from any menu by pressing [2nd] [MODE].

When you are on this screen you can type in an expression and evaluate it using the [ENTER] key.

Casio fx-9860g

Press [MENU] to access the **Main Menu**, where you can choose what type of task you wish the calculator to do.

Select **RUN·MAT**. This takes you to where most of the basic calculations are performed.

When you are on this screen you can type in an expression and evaluate it using the [EXE] key.

A BASIC CALCULATIONS

Most modern calculators have the rules for **Order of Operations** built into them. This order is sometimes referred to as BEDMAS.

This section explains how to use grouping symbols (brackets), and how to enter different types of numbers such as negative numbers, fractions, and time.

GROUPING SYMBOLS (BRACKETS)

Both the **TI-84 Plus** and **Casio** have bracket keys that look like $\boxed{(}$ and $\boxed{)}$.

Brackets are regularly used in mathematics to indicate an expression which needs to be evaluated before other operations are carried out.

For example, to enter $2 \times (4 + 1)$ we type $2 \boxed{\times} \boxed{(} 4 \boxed{+} 1 \boxed{)}$.

We also use brackets to make sure the calculator understands the expression we are typing in.

For example, to enter $\frac{2}{4+1}$ we type $2 \boxed{\div} \boxed{(} 4 \boxed{+} 1 \boxed{)}$. If we typed $2 \boxed{\div} 4 \boxed{+} 1$ the calculator would think we meant $\frac{2}{4} + 1$.

In general, it is a good idea to place brackets around any complicated expressions which need to be evaluated separately.

NEGATIVE NUMBERS

To enter negative numbers we use the **sign change** key. On both the **TI-84 Plus** and **Casio** this looks like $\boxed{(-)}$. Simply press the sign change key and then type in the number.

For example, to enter -7, press $\boxed{(-)}$ 7.

FRACTIONS

On most scientific calculators and also the **Casio** graphics calculator there is a special key for entering fractions. No such key exists for the **TI-84 Plus**, so we use a different method.

Texas Instruments TI-84 Plus

To enter common fractions, we enter the fraction as a division.

For example, we enter $\frac{3}{4}$ by typing $3 \boxed{\div} 4$. If the fraction is part of a larger calculation, it is generally wise to place this division in brackets, like this: $\boxed{(} 3 \boxed{\div} 4 \boxed{)}$.

To enter mixed numbers, either convert the mixed number to an improper fraction and enter as a common fraction *or* enter the fraction as a sum.

For example, we can enter $2\frac{3}{4}$ as $\boxed{(} 11 \boxed{\div} 4 \boxed{)}$ or $\boxed{(} 2 \boxed{+} 3 \boxed{\div} 4 \boxed{)}$.

Graphics calculator instructions

Casio fx-9860g

To enter fractions we use the **fraction** key [a b/c].

For example, we enter $\frac{3}{4}$ by typing 3 [a b/c] 4 and $2\frac{3}{4}$ by typing 2 [a b/c] 3 [a b/c] 4.

Press [SHIFT] [F↔D] ($a\frac{b}{c} \leftrightarrow \frac{d}{c}$) to convert between mixed numbers and improper fractions.

SIMPLIFYING FRACTIONS & RATIOS

Graphics calculators can *sometimes* be used to express fractions and ratios in simplest form.

Texas Instruments TI-84 Plus

To express the fraction $\frac{35}{56}$ in simplest form, press 35 [÷] 56 [MATH] **1:▶Frac** [ENTER]. The result is $\frac{5}{8}$.

To express the ratio $\frac{2}{3} : 1\frac{1}{4}$ in simplest form, press [(] 2 [÷] 3 [)] [÷] [(] 1 [+] 1 [÷] 4 [)] [MATH] **1:▶Frac** [ENTER].

The ratio is 8 : 15.

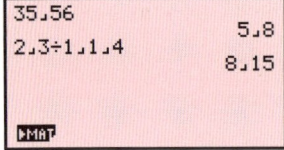

Casio fx-9860g

To express the fraction $\frac{35}{56}$ in simplest form, press 35 [a b/c] 56 [EXE]. The result is $\frac{5}{8}$.

To express the ratio $\frac{2}{3} : 1\frac{1}{4}$ in simplest form, press 2 [a b/c] 3 [÷] 1 [a b/c] 1 [a b/c] 4 [EXE]. The ratio is 8 : 15.

ENTERING TIMES

In questions involving time, it is often necessary to be able to express time in terms of hours, minutes, and seconds.

Texas Instruments TI-84 Plus

To enter 2 hours 27 minutes, press 2 [2nd] [APPS] (ANGLE) **1:°** 27 [2nd] [APPS] **2:'**. This is equivalent to 2.45 hours.

To express 8.17 hours in terms of hours, minutes, and seconds, press 8.17 [2nd] [APPS] **4:▶DMS** [ENTER].
This is equivalent to 8 hours, 10 minutes, and 12 seconds.

Casio fx-9860g

To enter 2 hours 27 minutes, press [OPTN] [F6] [F5] (ANGL) 2 [F4] (°'") 27 [F4] (°'") [EXE]. This is equivalent to 2.45 hours.

To express 8.17 hours in terms of hours, minutes, and seconds, press 8.17 [OPTN] [F6] [F5] (ANGL) [F6] [F3] (▶DMS) [EXE]. This is equivalent to 8 hours, 10 minutes, and 12 seconds.

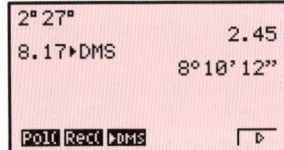

B MORE CALCULATIONS

POWER KEYS

Both the **TI-84 Plus** and **Casio** have power keys that look like $\boxed{\wedge}$. We type the base first, press the power key, then enter the index or exponent.

For example, to enter 25^3 we type 25 $\boxed{\wedge}$ 3.

Note that there are special keys which allow us to quickly evaluate squares.

Numbers can be squared on both the **TI-84 Plus** and **Casio** using the special key $\boxed{x^2}$.

For example, to enter 25^2 we type 25 $\boxed{x^2}$.

ROOTS

To enter roots on either calculator we need to use a secondary function (see **Secondary Function and Alpha Keys**).

Texas Instruments TI-84 Plus

The **TI-84 Plus** uses a secondary function key $\boxed{\text{2nd}}$.

We enter square roots by pressing $\boxed{\text{2nd}}$ $\boxed{x^2}$.

For example, to enter $\sqrt{36}$ we press $\boxed{\text{2nd}}$ $\boxed{x^2}$ 36 $\boxed{)}$.

The end bracket is used to tell the calculator we have finished entering terms under the square root sign.

Cube roots are entered by pressing $\boxed{\text{MATH}}$ **4:** $\sqrt[3]{\ }$ (.

For example, to enter $\sqrt[3]{8}$ we press $\boxed{\text{MATH}}$ 4 8 $\boxed{)}$.

Higher roots are entered by pressing $\boxed{\text{MATH}}$ **5:** $\sqrt[x]{\ }$.

For example, to enter $\sqrt[4]{81}$ we press 4 $\boxed{\text{MATH}}$ 5 81 .

Casio fx-9860g

The Casio uses a shift key $\boxed{\text{SHIFT}}$ to get to its second functions.

We enter square roots by pressing $\boxed{\text{SHIFT}}$ $\boxed{x^2}$.

For example, to enter $\sqrt{36}$ we press $\boxed{\text{SHIFT}}$ $\boxed{x^2}$ 36.

If there is a more complicated expression under the square root sign you should enter it in brackets.

For example, to enter $\sqrt{18 \div 2}$ we press $\boxed{\text{SHIFT}}$ $\boxed{x^2}$ $\boxed{(}$ 18 $\boxed{\div}$ 2 $\boxed{)}$.

Cube roots are entered by pressing $\boxed{\text{SHIFT}}$ $\boxed{(}$. For example, to enter $\sqrt[3]{8}$ we press $\boxed{\text{SHIFT}}$ $\boxed{(}$ 8.

Higher roots are entered by pressing $\boxed{\text{SHIFT}}$ $\boxed{\wedge}$. For example, to enter $\sqrt[4]{81}$ we press 4 $\boxed{\text{SHIFT}}$ $\boxed{\wedge}$ 81.

Graphics calculator instructions

ROUNDING OFF

You can use your calculator to round off answers to a fixed number of decimal places.

Texas Instruments TI-84 Plus

To round to 2 decimal places, press MODE then ▼ to scroll down to Float.

Use the ▶ button to move the cursor over the 2 and press ENTER. Press 2nd MODE to return to the home screen.

If you want to unfix the number of decimal places, press MODE ▼ ENTER to highlight Float.

Casio fx-9860g

To round to 2 decimal places, select **RUN·MAT** from the Main Menu, and press SHIFT MENU to enter the setup screen. Scroll down to Display, and press F1 (**Fix**). Press 2 EXE to select the number of decimal places. Press EXIT to return to the home screen.

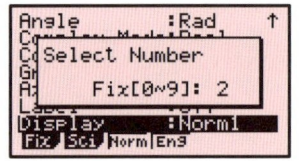

To unfix the number of decimal places, press SHIFT MENU to return to the setup screen, scroll down to Display, and press F3 (**Norm**).

STANDARD FORM

If a number is too large or too small to be displayed neatly on the screen, it will be expressed in standard form, which is the form $a \times 10^n$ where $1 \leqslant a < 10$ and n is an integer.

Texas Instruments TI-84 Plus

To evaluate 4700^3, press 4700 ^ 3 ENTER.
The answer displayed is $1.038\,23\text{E}11$, which means $1.038\,23 \times 10^{11}$.

To evaluate $\dfrac{3}{20\,000}$, press 3 ÷ 20 000 ENTER.
The answer displayed is $1.5\text{E}-4$, which means 1.5×10^{-4}.

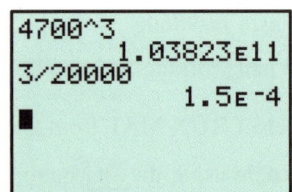

You can enter values in standard form using the EE function, which is accessed by pressing 2nd , .

For example, to evaluate $\dfrac{2.6 \times 10^{14}}{13}$, press 2.6 2nd , 14 ÷ 13 ENTER.
The answer is 2×10^{13}.

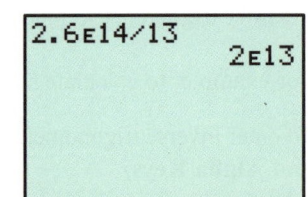

Casio fx-9860g

To evaluate 4700^3, press 4700 ^ 3 EXE.
The answer displayed is $1.038\,23\text{E}+11$, which means $1.038\,23 \times 10^{11}$.

To evaluate $\dfrac{3}{20\,000}$, press 3 ÷ 20 000 EXE.

The answer displayed is $1.5\text{E}-04$, which means 1.5×10^{-4}.

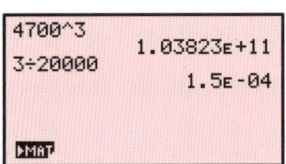

You can enter values in standard form using the [EXP] key. For example, to evaluate $\frac{2.6 \times 10^{14}}{13}$, press 2.6 [EXP] 14 [÷] 13 [EXE].

The answer is 2×10^{13}.

TRIGONOMETRIC FUNCTIONS

Texas Instruments TI-84 Plus

When working with angles, make sure your calculator is in degrees mode.

Press [MODE]. On the third line, **DEGREE** should be in a black box. If not, scroll down to that line using [▼]. Move the cursor over **DEGREE** using [▶] and press [ENTER]. Press [2nd] [MODE] to return to the home screen.

To enter trigonometric functions, use the [SIN], [COS], and [TAN] buttons.

For example, to calculate $\sin 30°$, press [SIN] 30 [)].

To enter inverse trigonometric functions, you will need to use a secondary function (see **Secondary Function and Alpha Keys**).

The inverse trigonometric functions $\sin^{-1}$, $\cos^{-1}$, and $\tan^{-1}$ are the secondary functions of [SIN], [COS], and [TAN] respectively. They are accessed by using the secondary function key [2nd].

For example, if $\cos x = \frac{3}{5}$, then $x = \cos^{-1}\left(\frac{3}{5}\right)$.

To calculate this, press [2nd] [COS] 3 [÷] 5 [)] [ENTER].

Casio fx-9860g

When working with angles, make sure your calculator is in degrees mode.

Select **RUN·MAT** from the Main Menu, and press [SHIFT] [MENU] to enter the setup screen. Scroll down to **Angle** using the [▼] button, and press [F1] **(Deg)**. Press [EXIT].

To enter trigonometric functions, use the [sin], [cos], and [tan] buttons.

For example, to calculate $\sin 30°$, press [sin] 30.

To enter inverse trigonometric functions, you will need to use a secondary function (see **Secondary Function and Alpha Keys**).

The inverse trigonometric functions $\sin^{-1}$, $\cos^{-1}$, and $\tan^{-1}$ are the secondary functions of [sin], [cos], and [tan] respectively. They are accessed by using the secondary function key [SHIFT].

For example, if $\cos x = \frac{3}{5}$, then $x = \cos^{-1}\left(\frac{3}{5}\right)$.

To calculate this, press [SHIFT] [cos] [(] 3 [a b/c] 5 [)] [EXE].

Graphics calculator instructions

C SECONDARY FUNCTION AND ALPHA KEYS

Texas Instruments TI-84 Plus

The **secondary function** of each key is displayed in blue above the key. It is accessed by pressing the [2nd] key, followed by the key corresponding to the desired secondary function. For example, to calculate $\sqrt{36}$, press [2nd] [x^2] 36 [)] [ENTER].

The **alpha function** of each key is displayed in green above the key. It is accessed by pressing the [ALPHA] key followed by the key corresponding to the desired letter. The main purpose of the alpha keys is to store values into memory which can be recalled later. Refer to the **Memory** section.

Casio fx-9860g

The **shift function** of each key is displayed in yellow above the key. It is accessed by pressing the [SHIFT] key followed by the key corresponding to the desired shift function. For example, to calculate $\sqrt{36}$, press [SHIFT] [x^2] 36 [EXE].

The **alpha function** of each key is displayed in red above the key. It is accessed by pressing the [ALPHA] key followed by the key corresponding to the desired letter. The main purpose of the alpha keys is to store values into memory which can be recalled later. Refer to the **Memory** section.

D MEMORY

Utilising the memory features of your calculator allows you to recall calculations you have performed previously. This not only saves time, but also enables you to maintain accuracy in your calculations.

SPECIFIC STORAGE TO MEMORY

Values can be stored into the variable letters A, B, ..., Z using either calculator. Storing a value in memory is useful if you need that value multiple times.

Texas Instruments TI-84 Plus

Suppose we wish to store the number 15.4829 for use in a number of calculations. Type in the number then press [STO▶] [ALPHA] [MATH] (A) [ENTER].

We can now add 10 to this value by pressing [ALPHA] [MATH] [+] 10 [ENTER], or cube this value by pressing [ALPHA] [MATH] [^] 3 [ENTER].

```
15.4829→A
            15.4829
A+10
            25.4829
A^3
         3711.563767
```

Casio fx-9860g

Suppose we wish to store the number 15.4829 for use in a number of calculations. Type in the number then press [→] [ALPHA] [X,θ,T] (A) [EXE].

We can now add 10 to this value by pressing [ALPHA] [X,θ,T] [+] 10 [EXE], or cube this value by pressing [ALPHA] [X,θ,T] [^] 3 [EXE].

Both calculators allow you to recall values from other screen types. For example, after finding the intersection of two graphs, the variable **X** will hold the x-coordinate you just found.

ANS VARIABLE

Texas Instruments TI-84 Plus

The variable **Ans** holds the most recent evaluated expression, and can be used in calculations by pressing [2nd] [(−)].

For example, suppose you evaluate 3×4, and then wish to subtract this from 17. This can be done by pressing 17 [−] [2nd] [(−)] [ENTER].

If you start an expression with an operator such as [+], [−], etc., the previous answer **Ans** is automatically inserted ahead of the operator. For example, the previous answer can be halved simply by pressing [÷] 2 [ENTER].

If you wish to view the answer in fractional form, press [MATH] 1 [ENTER].

Casio fx-9860g

The variable **Ans** holds the most recent evaluated expression, and can be used in calculations by pressing [SHIFT] [(−)]. For example, suppose you evaluate 3×4, and then wish to subtract this from 17. This can be done by pressing 17 [−] [SHIFT] [(−)] [EXE].

If you start an expression with an operator such as [+], [−], etc., the previous answer **Ans** is automatically inserted ahead of the operator. For example, the previous answer can be halved simply by pressing [÷] 2 [EXE].

If you wish to view the answer in fractional form, press [F↔D].

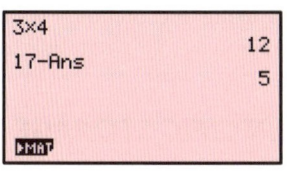

RECALLING PREVIOUS EXPRESSIONS

Texas Instruments TI-84 Plus

The **ENTRY** function recalls previously evaluated expressions, and is used by pressing [2nd] [ENTER].

This function is useful if you wish to repeat a calculation with a minor change, or if you have made an error in typing.

Suppose you have evaluated $100 + \sqrt{132}$. If you now want to evaluate $100 + \sqrt{142}$, instead of retyping the command, it can be recalled by pressing [2nd] [ENTER].

Graphics calculator instructions

The change can then be made by moving the cursor over the 3 and changing it to a 4, then pressing ENTER.

If you have made an error in your original calculation, and intended to calculate $1500 + \sqrt{132}$, again you can recall the previous command by pressing 2nd ENTER.

Move the cursor to the first 0.

You can insert the digit 5, rather than overwriting the 0, by pressing 2nd DEL (INS) 5 ENTER.

Pressing 2nd ENTER (ENTRY) multiple times allows you to scroll through many recently evaluated expressions.

Casio fx-9860g

Pressing the left cursor key allows you to edit the most recently evaluated expression, and is useful if you wish to repeat a calculation with a minor change, or if you have made an error in typing.

Suppose you have evaluated $100 + \sqrt{132}$.

If you now want to evaluate $100 + \sqrt{142}$, instead of retyping the command, it can be recalled by pressing the left cursor key.

Move the cursor between the 3 and the 2, then press DEL 4 to remove the 3 and replace it with a 4. Press EXE to re-evaluate the expression.

After clearing the screen using AC/ON, pressing the up and down cursor keys allows you to scroll through many recently evaluated expressions. When you reach the one you want, press the left or right cursor keys to edit the expression.

E LISTS

Lists are used for a number of purposes on the calculator. They enable us to enter sets of numbers, and we use them to generate number sequences using algebraic rules.

CREATING A LIST

Texas Instruments TI-84 Plus

Press STAT 1: Edit... to take you to the **list editor** screen.

To enter the data {2, 5, 1, 6, 0, 8} into **List 1**, start by moving the cursor to the first entry of L_1. Press 2 ENTER 5 ENTER .... and so on until all the data is entered.

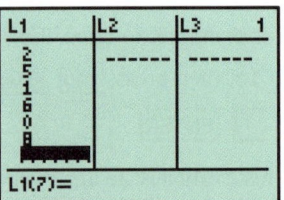

Casio fx-9860g

Selecting **STAT** from the Main Menu takes you to the **list editor** screen.

To enter the data {2, 5, 1, 6, 0, 8} into **List 1**, start by moving the cursor to the first entry of **List 1**. Press 2 EXE 5 EXE .... and so on until all the data is entered.

DELETING LIST DATA

Texas Instruments TI-84 Plus

In the **list editor** screen, move the cursor to the heading of the list you want to delete, then press CLEAR ENTER.

Casio fx-9860g

In the **list editor** screen, move the cursor to anywhere on the list you wish to delete, then press F6 (▷) F4 (DEL-A) F1 (Yes).

REFERENCING LISTS

Texas Instruments TI-84 Plus

Lists can be referenced by using the secondary functions of the keypad numbers 1 - 6.

For example, suppose you want to add 2 to each element of **List 1** and display the results in **List 2**. To do this, move the cursor to the heading of L_2 and press 2nd 1 (L_1) + 2 ENTER.

Casio fx-9860g

Lists can be referenced using the List function, which is accessed by pressing SHIFT 1.

For example, if you want to add 2 to each element of **List 1** and display the results in **List 2**, move the cursor to the heading of **List 2** and press SHIFT 1 (List) 1 + 2 EXE.

For Casio models without the List function, you can do this by pressing OPTN F1 (LIST) F1 (List) 1 + 2 EXE.

NUMBER SEQUENCES

Texas Instruments TI-84 Plus

You can create a sequence of numbers defined by a certain rule using the **seq** command.

This command is accessed by pressing 2nd STAT ▶ to enter the **OPS** section of the List menu, then selecting **5:seq(**.

For example, to store the sequence of even numbers from 2 to 8 in **List 3**, move the cursor to the heading of L_3, then press 2nd STAT ▶ 5 to enter the **seq** command, followed by 2 X,T,θ,n , X,T,θ,n , 1 , 4) ENTER.

This evaluates $2x$ for every value of x from 1 to 4, putting the values in **List 3**.

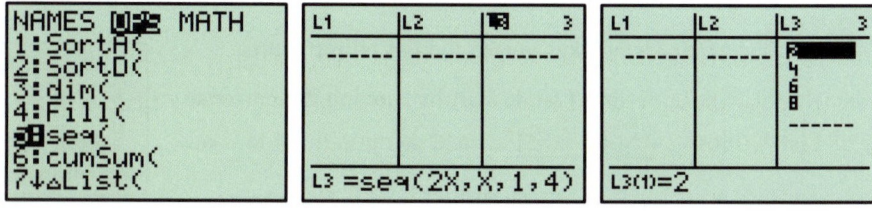

Graphics calculator instructions

Casio fx-9860g

You can create a sequence of numbers defined by a certain rule using the **Seq** command.

This command is accessed by pressing OPTN F1 **(LIST)** F5 **(Seq)**.

For example, to store the sequence of even numbers from 2 to 8 in **List 3**, move the cursor to the heading of **List 3**, then press OPTN F1 F5 to enter the **Seq** command, followed by 2 X,θ,T , X,θ,T , 1 , 4 , 1) EXE .

This evaluates $2x$ for every value of x from 1 to 4 with an increment of 1.

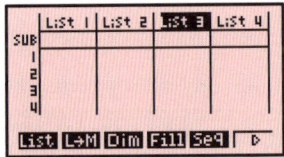 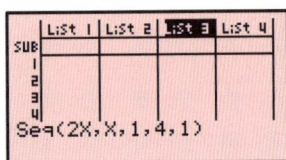 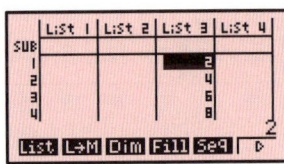

F STATISTICS

Your graphics calculator is a useful tool for analysing data and creating statistical graphs.

In this section we produce graphs and descriptive statistics for the data set: 5 2 3 3 6 4 5 3 7 5 7 1 8 9 5.

STATISTICAL GRAPHS

Texas Instruments TI-84 Plus

Enter the data into **List 1** using the instructions on page **19**.

To obtain a vertical bar chart of the data, press 2nd Y= 1, and set up **Statplot1** as shown. Press ZOOM 9:ZoomStat to draw the bar chart. Press WINDOW and set the **Xscl** to 1, then GRAPH to redraw the bar chart.

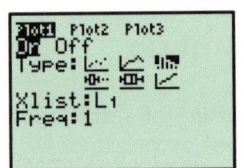 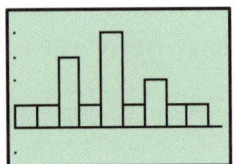

You can experiment with other types of graphs from the **STATPLOT** window.

Casio fx-9860g

Enter the data into **List 1** using the instructions on page **19**.

To obtain a vertical bar chart of the data, press F1 **(GRPH)** F6 **(SET)**, and set up **StatGraph1** as shown. Press EXIT F1 **(GPH1)** to draw the bar chart (set Start to 0, and Width to 1).

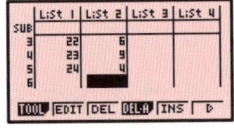 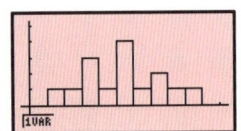

You can experiment with other types of graphs from the **SET** window.

DESCRIPTIVE STATISTICS

Texas Instruments TI-84 Plus

Enter the data into **List 1** using the instructions on page **19**.
To obtain descriptive statistics of the data set, press [STAT]
▶ **1:1-Var Stats** [2nd] 1 (L₁) [ENTER] .

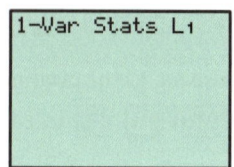 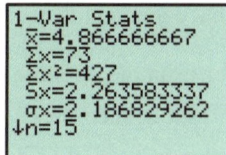

Say instead we had the *grouped* data below:

Data value	20	21	22	23	24
Frequency	2	5	6	9	4

Clear the current values in **List 1** and **List 2**, if necessary.

Enter the data values into **List 1** and the frequencies into **List 2**.

To obtain descriptive statistics of the data set, press [STAT]
▶ **1:1-Var Stats** [(] [2nd] 1 (L₁) [,] [2nd] 2 (L₂) [)]
[ENTER] .

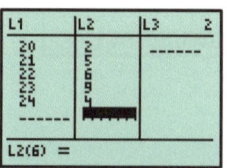 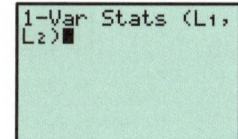

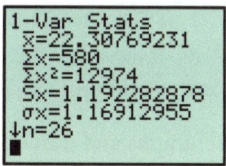

Casio fx-9860g

Enter the data into **List 1** using the instructions on page **19**.
To obtain the descriptive statistics, press [F6] (▷) until the **GRPH** icon is in the bottom left corner of the screen, then press [F2] (**CALC**) [F1] (**1VAR**).

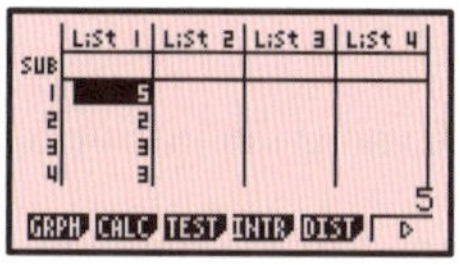

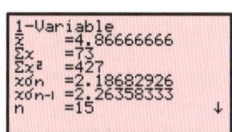

To obtain descriptive statistics of a different data set, press [F6] (**SET**).

Say instead we had the *grouped* data below:

Data value	20	21	22	23	24
Frequency	2	5	6	9	4

Clear the current values in **List 1** and **List 2**, if necessary.
Enter the data values into **List 1** and the frequencies into **List 2**.

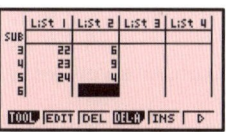

To obtain descriptive statistics of the data set, press [F2] (**CALC**) [F6] (**SET**), and set up **1Var** as shown. Then press [EXIT] [F1] (**1VAR**).

 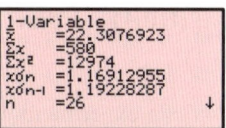

G WORKING WITH FUNCTIONS

GRAPHING FUNCTIONS

Texas Instruments TI-84 Plus

Pressing Y= selects the **Y=** editor, where you can store functions to graph. Delete any unwanted functions by scrolling down to the function and pressing CLEAR .

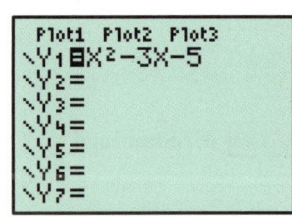

To graph the function $y = x^2 - 3x - 5$, move the cursor to **Y1**, and press X,T,θ,n x^2 − 3 X,T,θ,n − 5 ENTER . This stores the function into **Y1**. Press GRAPH to draw a graph of the function.

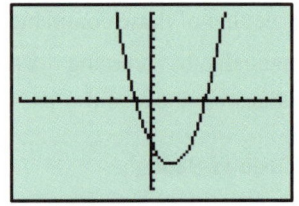

To view a table of values for the function, press 2nd GRAPH (**TABLE**). The starting point and interval of the table values can be adjusted by pressing 2nd WINDOW (**TBLSET**).

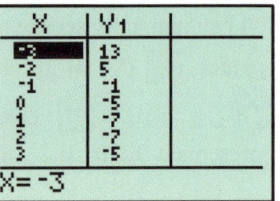

Casio fx-9860g

Selecting **GRAPH** from the Main Menu takes you to the Graph Function screen, where you can store functions to graph. Delete any unwanted functions by scrolling down to the function and pressing DEL F1 (**Yes**).

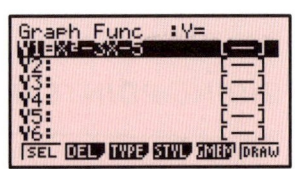

To graph the function $y = x^2 - 3x - 5$, move the cursor to **Y1** and press X,θ,T x^2 − 3 X,θ,T − 5 EXE . This stores the function into **Y1**. Press F6 (**DRAW**) to draw a graph of the function.

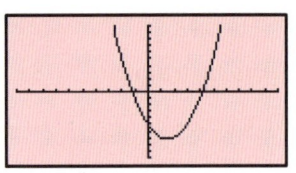

To view a table of values for the function, press MENU and select **TABLE**. The function is stored in **Y1**, but not selected. Press F1 (**SEL**) to select the function, and F6 (**TABL**) to view the table. You can adjust the table settings by pressing EXIT and then F5 (**SET**) from the Table Function screen.

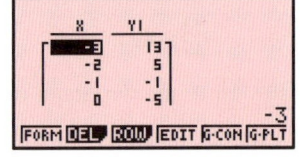

ADJUSTING THE VIEWING WINDOW

When graphing functions it is important that you are able to view all the important features of the graph. As a general rule it is best to start with a large viewing window to make sure all the features of the graph are visible. You can then make the window smaller if necessary.

Texas Instruments TI-84 Plus

Some useful commands for adjusting the viewing window include:

ZOOM **0:ZoomFit** : This command scales the y-axis to fit the minimum and maximum values of the displayed graph within the current x-axis range.

ZOOM **6:ZStandard** : This command returns the viewing window to the default setting of $-10 \leqslant x \leqslant 10$, $-10 \leqslant y \leqslant 10$.

If neither of these commands are helpful, the viewing window can be adjusted manually by pressing WINDOW and setting the minimum and maximum values for the x and y axes.

Casio fx-9860g

The viewing window can be adjusted by pressing SHIFT F3 (**V-Window**). You can manually set the minimum and maximum values of the x and y axes, or press F3 (**STD**) to obtain the standard viewing window $-10 \leqslant x \leqslant 10$, $-10 \leqslant y \leqslant 10$. F1 (**INIT**) gives a viewing window where each dot represents a 0.1 by 0.1 square.

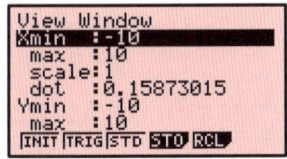

While viewing a graph, pressing F2 (**ZOOM**) presents some useful commands for adjusting the viewing window. For example, F5 (**AUTO**) scales the y-axis to fit the minimum and maximum values of the displayed graph within the current x-axis range.

FINDING POINTS OF INTERSECTION

It is often useful to find the points of intersection of two graphs, for instance, when you are trying to solve simultaneous equations.

Texas Instruments TI-84 Plus

We can solve $y = 11 - 3x$ and $y = \dfrac{12 - x}{2}$ simultaneously by finding the point of intersection of these two lines.

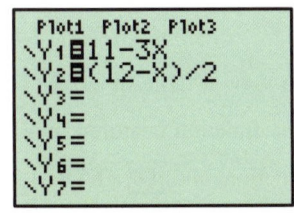

Press Y=, then store $11 - 3x$ into Y_1 and $\dfrac{12 - x}{2}$ into Y_2. Press GRAPH to draw a graph of the functions.

To find their point of intersection, press 2nd TRACE (**CALC**) **5:intersect**. Press ENTER twice to specify the functions Y_1 and Y_2 as the functions you want to find the intersection of, then use the arrow keys to move the cursor close to the point of intersection and press ENTER once more.

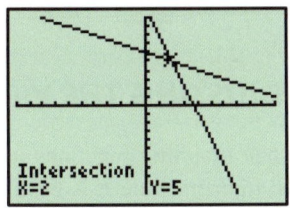

The solution $x = 2$, $y = 5$ is given. Other points of intersection (if they exist) can be found by moving the cursor close to them.

Casio fx-9860g

We can solve $y = 11 - 3x$ and $y = \dfrac{12 - x}{2}$ simultaneously by finding the point of intersection of these two lines. Select **GRAPH** from the Main Menu, then store $11 - 3x$ into **Y1** and $\dfrac{12 - x}{2}$ into **Y2**. Press F6 **(DRAW)** to draw a graph of the functions.

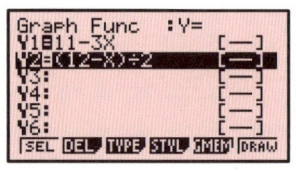

To find their point of intersection, press F5 **(G-Solv)** F5 **(ISCT)**. The solution $x = 2$, $y = 5$ is given.

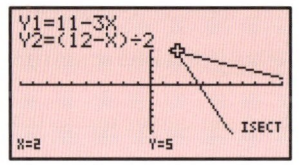

Notes: 1 If there is more than one point of intersection, you can move between the points of intersection by pressing ◀ and ▶.

2 Only points of intersection with an x-coordinate in the current viewing window will be found.

SOLVING $f(x) = 0$

In the special case when you wish to solve an equation of the form $f(x) = 0$, this can be done by graphing $y = f(x)$ and then finding when this graph cuts the x-axis.

Texas Instruments TI-84 Plus

To solve $x^3 - 3x^2 + x + 1 = 0$, press Y= and store $x^3 - 3x^2 + x + 1$ into **Y1**. Press GRAPH to draw the graph.

To find where this function first cuts the x-axis, press 2nd TRACE **(CALC)** **2:zero**. Move the cursor to the left of the first zero and press ENTER, then move the cursor to the right of the first zero and press ENTER. Finally, move the cursor close to the first zero and press ENTER once more. The solution $x \approx -0.414$ is given.

Repeat this process to find the remaining solutions $x = 1$ and $x \approx 2.414$.

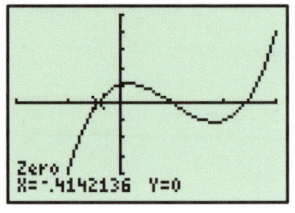

Casio fx-9860g

To solve $x^3 - 3x^2 + x + 1 = 0$, select **GRAPH** from the Main Menu and store $x^3 - 3x^2 + x + 1$ into **Y1**. Press F6 **(DRAW)** to draw the graph.

To find where this function cuts the x-axis, press F5 **(G-Solv)** F1 **(ROOT)**. The first solution $x \approx -0.414$ is given.

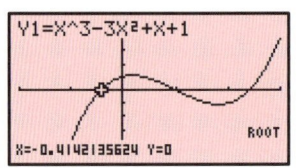

Press ▶ to find the remaining solutions $x = 1$ and $x \approx 2.414$.

TURNING POINTS

Texas Instruments TI-84 Plus

To find the turning point (vertex) of $y = -x^2 + 2x + 3$, press Y= and store $-x^2 + 2x + 3$ into **Y**₁. Press GRAPH to draw the graph.

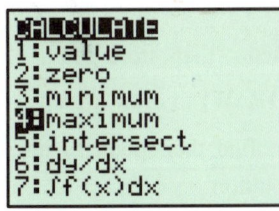

From the graph, it is clear that the vertex is a maximum, so press 2nd TRACE (CALC) **4:maximum**.

Move the cursor to the left of the vertex and press ENTER, then move the cursor to the right of the vertex and press ENTER. Finally, move the cursor close to the vertex and press ENTER once more. The vertex is $(1, 4)$.

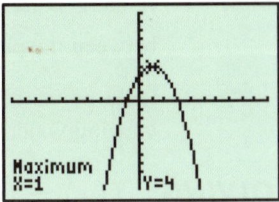

Casio fx-9860g

To find the turning point (vertex) of $y = -x^2 + 2x + 3$, select **GRAPH** from the Main Menu and store $-x^2 + 2x + 3$ into **Y1**. Press F6 **(DRAW)** to draw the graph.

From the graph, it is clear that the vertex is a maximum, so to find the vertex press F5 **(G-Solv)** F2 **(MAX)**.

The vertex is $(1, 4)$.

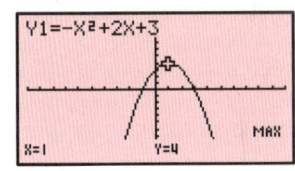

Number

Contents:

A	Number types	[1.1]
B	Operations and brackets	[1.2]
C	HCF and LCM	[1.3]
D	Fractions	
E	Powers and roots	[1.4]
F	Ratio and proportion	[1.5]
G	Number equivalents	[1.7]
H	Percentage	[1.8]
I	Rounding numbers	[1.11]
J	Time	[1.12]

People use numbers to describe the world around them every day. We count everything from sheep to the stars. We use numbers to measure size, weight, and temperature, and to tell the time and handle money. You probably have a student number, bank card number, and telephone number. Dealing with numbers is a necessary part of daily life.

Opening problem

A milkshake machine makes small or large milkshakes. A small milkshake takes 45 seconds to make, and a large one takes 80 seconds. On a certain day, the machine makes 117 small milkshakes and 162 large milkshakes.

a How long did the machine spend making:
  i small milkshakes **ii** large milkshakes?

b Write, in hours, minutes and seconds, the total length of time the machine was at work that day.

c Compare the time taken for a small milkshake with the time taken for a large milkshake, using a ratio in simplest form.

d What percentage of the milkshakes made were small? Round off your answer to:
  i 2 decimal places **ii** 3 significant figures.

A NUMBER TYPES [1.1]

The simplest numbers are those we use to count: 0, 1, 2, 3, ... We call these the **natural** numbers.

We often write collections of numbers in **sets** by putting curly braces around them. Some collections of numbers have special names and labels. For example,

the set of **natural** or **counting** numbers is $\mathbb{N} = \{0, 1, 2, 3, 4, 5, 6, ...\}$.

The set of natural numbers is endless, so we call it an **infinite set**.

The set of **integers** or whole numbers is $\mathbb{Z} = \{...., -4, -3, -2, -1, 0, 1, 2, 3, 4, ...\}$.

The set $\mathbb{Z}$ includes $\mathbb{N}$ as well as all negative whole numbers.

For example: 0, 127, -15, 10 000 and $-34\,618$ are all members of $\mathbb{Z}$.

$\mathbb{Z}$ is from the German word *Zahlen*, which means "numbers".

OTHER CLASSIFICATIONS

The **square** of a number is that number multiplied by itself.

For example, 5 squared is 5×5 which is 25. We write $5^2 = 25$.

The **cube** of a number is that number multiplied by itself twice.

For example, 2 cubed is $2 \times 2 \times 2$ which is 8. We write $2^3 = 8$.

The **square root** of a number is multiplied by itself to give the number.

For example, $3 \times 3 = 9$ so the square root of 9 is 3. We write $\sqrt{9} = 3$.

A **perfect square** or **square number** is an integer which can be written as the square of another integer.

For example, 4 and 25 are both perfect squares since $4 = 2^2$ and $25 = 5^2$.

A **perfect cube** is an integer which can be written as the cube of another integer.

For example, 8 and -125 are perfect cubes since $8 = 2^3$ and $-125 = (-5)^3$.

RATIONAL AND IRRATIONAL NUMBERS

The set of **rational** numbers, denoted $\mathbb{Q}$, is the set of all numbers of the form $\dfrac{a}{b}$ where a and b are integers and $b \neq 0$.

For example:
- $\frac{1}{3}, \frac{15}{32}, \frac{-5}{4}$ are all rational
- $-2\frac{1}{4}$ is rational as $-2\frac{1}{4} = \frac{-9}{4}$
- 5 is rational as $5 = \frac{5}{1}$ or $\frac{20}{4}$
- 0.431 is rational as $0.431 = \frac{431}{1000}$
- $0.\overline{8}$ is rational as $0.\overline{8} = \frac{8}{9}$

l decimal numbers that terminate or recur are rational numbers.

Number (Chapter 1)

The set of **real** numbers, denoted $\mathbb{R}$, consists of all numbers which can be located on a number line.

$\frac{2}{0}$ and $\sqrt{-5}$ cannot be placed on a number line, and so are not real.

The set of **irrational** numbers is made of all real numbers which cannot be written in the form $\frac{a}{b}$ where a and b are integers and $b \neq 0$.

For example: $\sqrt{2}$, $\sqrt{3}$ and π are all irrational.
However, $\sqrt{9}$ and $\sqrt{1.21}$ are rational since $\sqrt{9} = 3 = \frac{3}{1}$ and $\sqrt{1.21} = 1.1 = \frac{11}{10}$.

PRIMES AND COMPOSITES

The **factors** of a positive integer are the positive integers which divide exactly into it, leaving no remainder.

For example, the factors of 10 are: 1, 2, 5 and 10.

A positive integer is a **prime** number if it has exactly two factors, 1 and itself.

A positive integer is a **composite** number if it has more than two factors.

For example: 3 is prime as it has two factors: 1 and 3.
6 is composite as it has four factors: 1, 2, 3 and 6.
1 is neither prime nor composite.

If we are given a positive integer, we can use the following procedure to see if it is prime:

Step 1: Find the square root of the number.
Step 2: Divide the whole number, in turn, by all known primes less than its square root. If the division is never exact, the number is a prime.

The first few prime numbers are 2, 3, 5, 7, 11, 13, 17, 19, ...

Example 1   ◀) Self Tutor

Is 131 a prime number?

$\sqrt{131} = 11.445....$, so we divide 131 by 2, 3, 5, 7 and 11.
$131 \div 2 = 65.5$
$131 \div 3 = 43.66....$
$131 \div 5 = 26.2$
$131 \div 7 = 18.7142....$
$131 \div 11 = 11.9090....$
None of the divisions is exact, so 131 is a prime number.

EXERCISE 1A

1 Copy and complete the table given.

Number	$\mathbb{N}$	$\mathbb{Z}$	$\mathbb{Q}$	$\mathbb{R}$
19	✓	✓	✓	✓
$-\frac{2}{3}$				
$\sqrt{7}$				
5.6389				
$\sqrt{16}$				
2π				
-11				
$\frac{6}{0}$				
$\sqrt{-2}$				

2 List the factors of:
   a 10   **b** 16   **c** 12   **d** 18   **e** 17   **f** 20
   g 32   **h** 63   **i** 36   **j** 42   **k** 64   **l** 100

3 Find:
   a 7^2 **b** 5^3 **c** $\sqrt{121}$ **d** 13^2 **e** $\sqrt{169}$ **f** 6^3

4 Show that:
   a 16, 529 and 20 802 721 are square numbers   **b** 27, 343 and 13 824 are cube numbers
   c 11, 17 and 97 are prime numbers   **d** 64 and 729 are both squares and cubes.

5 List all prime numbers between 50 and 70.

6 Explain why 1 is not a prime number.

7 Is 263 a prime number? Show all working.

B   OPERATIONS AND BRACKETS   [1.2]

RULES FOR THE ORDER OF OPERATIONS

- Perform the operations within **brackets** first.
- Calculate any part involving **exponents**.
- Starting from the left, perform all **divisions** and **multiplications** as you come to them.
- Starting from the left, perform all **additions** and **subtractions** as you come to them.

Brackets are **grouping symbols** that tell us what to evaluate first.

You can remember this using the word **BEDMAS**.

      Brackets
      Exponents
      Division
      Multiplication
      Addition
      Subtraction

Number (Chapter 1)

RULES FOR THE USE OF BRACKETS

- If an expression contains *one set* of brackets or grouping symbols, work that part first.
- If an expression contains *two or more sets* of grouping symbols one inside the other, work the innermost first.
- The division line of fractions also behaves as a grouping symbol. This means that the numerator and the denominator must be found separately before doing the division.

Example 2

Simplify: **a** $3 + 7 - 5$ **b** $6 \times 3 \div 2$

a $3 + 7 - 5$
   $= 10 - 5$ {Work left to right as only $+$ and $-$ are involved.}
   $= 5$

b $6 \times 3 \div 2$
   $= 18 \div 2$ {Work left to right as only $\times$ and $\div$ are involved.}
   $= 9$

Example 3

Simplify: **a** $23 - 10 \div 2$ **b** $3 \times 8 - 6 \times 5$

a $23 - 10 \div 2$ **b** $3 \times 8 - 6 \times 5$
   $= 23 - 5$ {$\div$ before $-$} $= 24 - 30$ {$\times$ before $-$}
   $= 18$ $= -6$

EXERCISE 1B

1 Simplify:

   a $6 + 9 - 5$ **b** $6 - 9 + 5$ **c** $6 - 9 - 5$ **d** $9 - 5 + 6$

   e $3 \times 12 \div 6$ **f** $12 \div 6 \times 3$ **g** $6 \times 12 \div 3$ **h** $12 \div 3 \times 6$

2 Simplify:

   a $5 + 8 \times 4$ **b** $9 \times 4 + 7$ **c** $17 - 7 \times 2$ **d** $6 \times 7 - 18$

   e $36 - 6 \times 5$ **f** $19 - 7 \times 0$ **g** $3 \times 6 - 6$ **h** $70 - 5 \times 4 \times 3$

   i $45 \div 3 - 9$ **j** $8 \times 5 - 6 \times 4$ **k** $7 + 3 + 5 \times 2$ **l** $17 - 6 \times 4 + 9$

Example 4

Simplify: $3 + (11 - 7) \times 2$

$3 + (11 - 7) \times 2$
$= 3 + 4 \times 2$ {evaluating the brackets first}
$= 3 + 8$ {$\times$ before $+$}
$= 11$

3 Simplify:

   a $14 + (8 - 5)$ **b** $(19 + 7) - 13$ **c** $(18 \div 6) - 2$ **d** $18 \div (6 - 4)$

   e $72 - (18 \div 6)$ **f** $(72 - 18) \div 6$ **g** $36 + (14 \div 2)$ **h** $36 - (7 + 13) - 9$

   i $(22 - 5) + (15 - 7)$ **j** $(18 \div 3) \div 2$ **k** $32 \div (4 \div 2)$ **l** $28 - (7 \times 3) - 9$

Example 5   ◀) *Self Tutor*

Simplify: $[12 + (9 \div 3)] - 11$

$[12 + (9 \div 3)] - 11$
$= [12 + 3] - 11$ {evaluating the inner brackets first}
$= 15 - 11$ {outer brackets next}
$= 4$

---

4 Simplify:

   a $8 - [(4 - 6) + 3 \times 2]$ **b** $[22 - (11 + 4)] \times 3$ **c** $25 - [(11 - 7) + 8]$

   d $[28 - (15 \div 3)] \times 4$ **e** $300 \div [6 \times (15 \div 3)]$ **f** $[(14 \times 5) \div (28 \div 2)] \times 3$

   g $[24 \div (8 - 6) \times 9]$ **h** $18 - [(1 + 6) \times 2]$ **i** $[(14 \div 2) \times (14 \div 7)] \div 2$

Example 6   ◀) *Self Tutor*

Simplify: $\dfrac{12 + (5 - 7)}{18 \div (6 + 3)}$

$\dfrac{12 + (5 - 7)}{18 \div (6 + 3)}$

$= \dfrac{12 + (-2)}{18 \div 9}$ {evaluating the brackets first}

$= \dfrac{10}{2}$ {simplifying the numerator and denominator}

$= 5$

---

5 Simplify:

   a $\dfrac{240}{8 \times 6}$ **b** $\dfrac{27}{17 - 8}$ **c** $\dfrac{39 \div 3}{14 + 12}$ **d** $\dfrac{18 + 7}{7 - 2}$

   e $\dfrac{6 \times 7 + 7}{7}$ **f** $\dfrac{54}{11 - (2 \times 4)}$ **g** $\dfrac{(6 + 9) - 5}{7 + (9 - 6)}$ **h** $\dfrac{2 - 2 \times 2}{2 \times (2 + 2)}$

6 Find:

   a $7 - -8$ **b** $10 - (2 + 5)$ **c** 6×-7 **d** $\dfrac{-4}{8}$

   e $(-2) \times (-2)$ **f** $4 - (-3)$ **g** $(-3) \times (-7)$ **h** $\dfrac{-24}{-6}$

   i $2 - 5 \times (-3)$ **j** $2 \times 5 - (-3)$ **k** $\dfrac{-2 \times 3}{-4}$ **l** $\dfrac{2 \times (-3)}{-4 \times 6}$

Example 7

Use your calculator to evaluate: **a** $12 + 32 \div (8 - 6)$ **b** $\dfrac{75}{7+8}$

a Key in 12 [+] 32 [÷] [(] 8 [−] 6 [)] [ENTER]   *Answer:* 28

b Key in 75 [÷] [(] 7 [+] 8 [)] [ENTER]   *Answer:* 5

For help using your calculator, refer to the **graphics calculator instructions** on page **12**.

Example 8

Calculate: **a** 41×-7 **b** -18×23

a Key in 41 [×] [(−)] 7 [ENTER]   *Answer:* -287

b Key in [(−)] 18 [×] 23 [ENTER]   *Answer:* -414

7 Evaluate each of the following using your calculator:

   a $87 + 27 \times 13$ **b** $(29 + 17) \times 19$ **c** $136 \div 8 + 16$

   d $136 \div (8 + 9)$ **e** 39×-27 **f** $-128 \div -32$

   g $\dfrac{97 + -7}{-5 \times 3}$ **h** $-67 + 64 \div -4$ **i** $\dfrac{-25 - 15}{9 - (16 \div 4)}$

8 Use a calculator to answer the following questions:

   a Kevin can throw a tennis ball 47.55 m, and Dean can throw a tennis ball 42.8 m. How much further than Dean can Kevin throw?

   b Find the cost of purchasing 2.7 kg of bananas at £2.45 per kilogram.

   c Chen travels 11 km on the bus to school each day, and the same distance home. He goes to school on 205 days in one year. Find the total distance Chen travels on the bus to and from school for the year.

   d June buys 3 packets of sugar weighing 1.2 kg each, 4 packets of cereal weighing 1.3 kg each, and 2 containers of ice cream weighing 1.5 kg each. Find the total weight of these items.

   e Jordan is paid €15.60 per hour to work at a petrol station. He wants to save €1170 to buy a car. How many hours will he need to work?

C HCF AND LCM [1.3]

Numbers can be expressed as products of their factors.

Factors that are prime numbers are called **prime factors**. The prime factors of any number can be found by repeated division.

For example:

2	24
2	12
2	6
3	3
	1

∴ $24 = 2 \times 2 \times 2 \times 3$

2	42
3	21
7	7
	1

∴ $42 = 2 \times 3 \times 7$

COMMON FACTORS AND HCF

Notice that 2 is a factor of both 24 and 42. We say that 2 is a **common factor** of 24 and 42.

3 is also a common factor of 24 and 42, which means the product $2 \times 3 = 6$ is another common factor.

> A **common factor** is a number that is a factor of two or more other numbers.
>
> The **highest common factor (HCF)** is the largest factor that is common to two or more numbers.

To find the highest common factor of a group of numbers it is often best to express the numbers as products of prime factors. The common prime factors can then be found, and multiplied to give the HCF.

Example 9 ◀) Self Tutor

Find the highest common factor of 36 and 81.

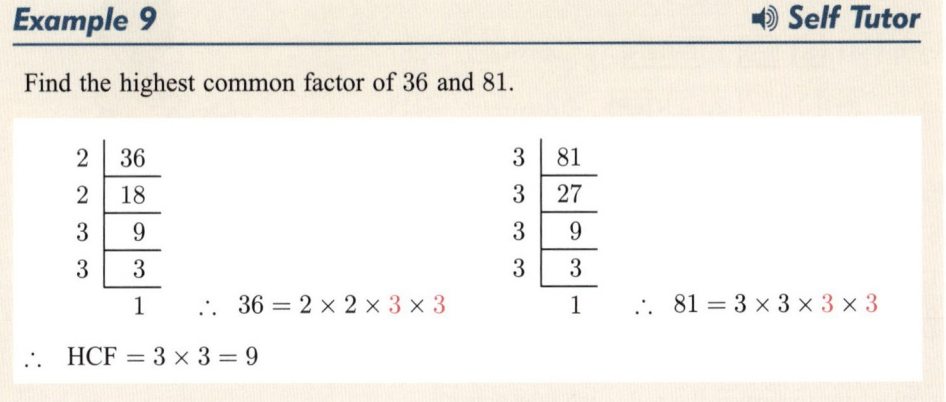

$\therefore$ HCF $= 3 \times 3 = 9$

MULTIPLES

> A **multiple** of any positive integer is obtained by multiplying it by another positive integer.

For example, the multiples of 7 are $7 \times 1 = 7$, $7 \times 2 = 14$, $7 \times 3 = 21$, $7 \times 4 = 28$, ...
so we can list them as 7, 14, 21, 28, 35, ...

Example 10 ◀) Self Tutor

Find: **a** the largest multiple of 7 which is less than 300
b the smallest multiple of 7 which is greater than 500.

a $7 \overline{| 3 \; 0 \; {}^20}$
   $ 4 \; 2 \quad$ with remainder 6
   So, the largest multiple is
   $7 \times 42 = 294$.

b $7 \overline{| 5 \; 0 \; {}^10}$
   $ 7 \; 1 \quad$ with remainder 3
   So, the smallest multiple is
   $7 \times 72 = 504$.

> The **lowest common multiple** or **LCM** of two or more positive integers is the smallest multiple which all of them have in common.

Number (Chapter 1)

Example 11

Find the LCM of: **a** 3 and 4   **b** 3, 4 and 8

a The multiples of 3 are: 3, 6, 9, 12, 15, 18, 21, 24, 27, ...
    The multiples of 4 are: 4, 8, 12, 16, 20, 24, 28, 32, ...
    ∴ the common multiples of 3 and 4 are: 12, 24, 36, ... of which 12 is the LCM.

b The multiples of 3 are: 3, 6, 9, 12, 15, 18, 21, 24, 27, ...
    The multiples of 4 are: 4, 8, 12, 16, 20, 24, 28, 32, ...
    The multiples of 8 are: 8, 16, 24, 32, 40, ...
    So, the LCM is 24.

EXERCISE 1C

1 List the first *five* multiples of:
    a 6   **b** 11   **c** 13   **d** 29

2 Find the HCF of:
    a 3, 12   **b** 8, 12   **c** 18, 24   **d** 13, 52
    e 3, 5, 6   **f** 15, 20, 30   **g** 27, 36, 45   **h** 24, 48, 120

3 Find the largest multiple of:
    a 11 which is less than 200   **b** 17 which is less than 500.

4 Find the smallest multiple of:
    a 9 which is more than 300   **b** 23 which is more than 8000.

5 Find the LCM of:
    a 3, 8   **b** 6, 8   **c** 14, 21   **d** 9, 24
    e 2, 3, 5   **f** 2, 4, 7   **g** 3, 5, 10   **h** 9, 12, 18

6 Find the highest common multiple of:
    a 9 and 12 that is less than 40   **b** 5 and 15 that is less than 80.

7 Three bells chime once at intervals of 3, 5 and 12 seconds respectively. They first chime at exactly the same instant. After how many seconds will all three again chime simultaneously?

8 If a and b are positive integers, the LCM of a and b can be found by multiplying a and b and then dividing the result by their HCF. Check your answers to **5** using this method.

D   FRACTIONS

A **common fraction** consists of two whole numbers, a **numerator** and a **denominator**, separated by a bar symbol.

$$\frac{4}{5} \begin{matrix} \leftarrow \text{numerator} \\ \leftarrow \text{bar (which also means } divide\text{)} \\ \leftarrow \text{denominator} \end{matrix}$$

TYPES OF FRACTIONS

$\frac{4}{5}$ is a **proper fraction** since the numerator is less than the denominator.

$\frac{7}{6}$ is an **improper fraction** since the numerator is greater than the denominator.

$2\frac{3}{4}$ is a **mixed number** which really means $2 + \frac{3}{4}$.

$\frac{1}{2}, \frac{3}{6}$ are **equivalent fractions** since both fractions represent equivalent portions.

LOWEST COMMON DENOMINATOR

The **lowest common denominator (LCD)** of two or more numerical fractions is the lowest common multiple of their denominators.

ADDITION AND SUBTRACTION

To **add** (or **subtract**) two fractions we convert them to equivalent fractions with a common denominator. We then add (or subtract) the new numerators.

Example 12　　　🔊 *Self Tutor*

Find:　　$\frac{3}{4} + \frac{5}{6}$

$\frac{3}{4} + \frac{5}{6}$　　　　{LCD = 12}

$= \frac{3\times3}{4\times3} + \frac{5\times2}{6\times2}$　　{to achieve a common denominator of 12}

$= \frac{9}{12} + \frac{10}{12}$

$= \frac{19}{12}$

$= 1\frac{7}{12}$

We can multiply both the numerator and denominator of a fraction by the same number to generate an equivalent fraction.

Example 13　　　🔊 *Self Tutor*

Find:　　$1\frac{2}{3} - 1\frac{2}{5}$

$1\frac{2}{3} - 1\frac{2}{5} = \frac{5}{3} - \frac{7}{5}$　　{write as improper fractions}

$= \frac{5\times5}{3\times5} - \frac{7\times3}{5\times3}$　　{to achieve a common denominator of 15}

$= \frac{25}{15} - \frac{21}{15}$

$= \frac{4}{15}$

MULTIPLICATION

To **multiply** two fractions, we first cancel any common factors in the numerators and denominators. We then multiply the numerators together and the denominators together.

Example 14　　　🔊 *Self Tutor*

Find:　　**a** $\frac{1}{4} \times \frac{2}{3}$　　　**b** $(3\frac{1}{2})^2$

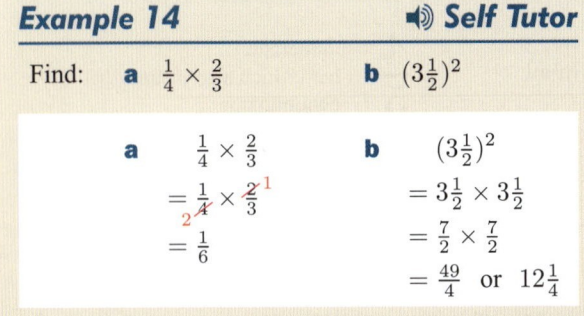

Cancel any common factors before completing the multiplication.

Number (Chapter 1) 37

DIVISION

To **divide** by a fraction, we multiply the number by the reciprocal of the fraction we are dividing by.

Example 15 — Self Tutor

Find: **a** $3 \div \frac{2}{3}$ **b** $2\frac{1}{3} \div \frac{2}{3}$

a $\quad 3 \div \frac{2}{3}$
$\quad = \frac{3}{1} \div \frac{2}{3}$
$\quad = \frac{3}{1} \times \frac{3}{2}$
$\quad = \frac{9}{2}$
$\quad = 4\frac{1}{2}$

b $\quad 2\frac{1}{3} \div \frac{2}{3}$
$\quad = \frac{7}{3} \div \frac{2}{3}$
$\quad = \frac{7}{\underset{1}{3}} \times \frac{\overset{1}{3}}{2}$
$\quad = \frac{7}{2}$
$\quad = 3\frac{1}{2}$

The reciprocal of $\dfrac{c}{d}$ is $\dfrac{d}{c}$.

EXERCISE 1D

1 Find:
  a $\frac{5}{13} + \frac{7}{13}$
  b $\frac{9}{16} + \frac{2}{16}$
  c $\frac{3}{8} + \frac{1}{4}$
  d $\frac{2}{5} + \frac{1}{6}$
  e $\frac{3}{7} + 4$
  f $1\frac{1}{3} + \frac{5}{6}$
  g $2\frac{1}{3} + 1\frac{1}{6}$
  h $1\frac{1}{2} + 4\frac{2}{3}$

2 Find:
  a $\frac{7}{11} - \frac{3}{11}$
  b $\frac{5}{6} - \frac{2}{3}$
  c $\frac{4}{9} - \frac{1}{3}$
  d $1 - \frac{3}{8}$
  e $4 - 2\frac{1}{4}$
  f $2\frac{3}{5} - 1\frac{1}{2}$
  g $3\frac{1}{3} - 1\frac{1}{2}$
  h $4\frac{3}{7} - 2\frac{1}{3}$

3 Calculate:
  a $\frac{2}{15} \times \frac{5}{6}$
  b $\frac{6}{7} \times \frac{1}{3}$
  c $3 \times \frac{3}{6}$
  d $\frac{2}{3} \times 7$
  e $1\frac{1}{3} \times \frac{6}{7}$
  f $1\frac{1}{8} \times \frac{4}{9}$
  g $(2\frac{1}{2})^2$
  h $(1\frac{1}{3})^3$

4 Evaluate:
  a $\frac{3}{5} \div \frac{7}{10}$
  b $\frac{3}{8} \div \frac{6}{11}$
  c $\frac{4}{15} \div \frac{2}{5}$
  d $\frac{2}{5} \div 4$
  e $1 \div \frac{3}{5}$
  f $1\frac{1}{3} \div \frac{3}{8}$
  g $\frac{2}{3} \div 1\frac{1}{2}$
  h $2\frac{1}{4} \div 1\frac{2}{3}$

5 Calculate:
  a $3\frac{3}{7} + 1\frac{4}{5}$
  b $4\frac{1}{2} - 2\frac{2}{3}$
  c $7 - 6 \times \frac{3}{4}$
  d $\frac{4}{5} \times 1\frac{1}{2} \div 3$
  e $\dfrac{8 \times 3 \times \frac{1}{3}}{\frac{2}{3}}$
  f $1 \div (\frac{1}{4} + \frac{2}{3})$
  g $1 \div \frac{1}{4} + \frac{2}{3}$
  h $\dfrac{3 - \frac{1}{2}}{3 \times \frac{5}{3}}$
  i $\frac{2}{3} + \frac{1}{3} \times 1\frac{1}{2}$
  j $\frac{5}{6} \times \frac{4}{5} - \frac{1}{15}$
  k $\frac{1}{3} + \frac{1}{3} \div \frac{1}{5} + \frac{3}{5}$
  l $1\frac{1}{2} - 2\frac{1}{3} \div 1\frac{2}{3}$
  m $12 - \frac{2}{7} \times 3\frac{1}{2}$
  n $1\frac{1}{3} + \frac{5}{6} - \frac{11}{12}$
  o $6\frac{2}{5} - \frac{1}{4} \times 1\frac{1}{3} \div \frac{1}{6}$

Example 16

Anna scores $\frac{3}{5}$ of her team's goals in a netball match.

How many goals did she shoot if the team shot 70 goals?

Anna shot $\frac{3}{5}$ of $70 = \frac{3}{5} \times 70$

$= \dfrac{3 \times \cancel{70}^{14}}{_{1}\cancel{5}}$

$= 42$ goals.

The word 'of' means '×'.

6 **a** During a full season a football team scored 84 goals. If William scored $\frac{5}{12}$ of the goals, how many goals did William score?

b $\frac{2}{7}$ of my weekly earnings must be paid as tax to the government. If I earn £840.00 in one week, how much tax needs to be paid?

c Jade drinks $\frac{1}{4}$ of a full bottle of water. An hour later she drinks $\frac{1}{6}$ of the original volume. What fraction remains?

d Sally was paid €1830.00 as an end of year bonus for doing well at her job. She spent $\frac{1}{3}$ of it on clothing, $\frac{1}{4}$ on sporting goods, and $\frac{1}{12}$ on jewellery.
   i What fraction did she spend?   **ii** How much of the money was left?

e Carli ate $\frac{1}{4}$ of a chocolate bar and later ate $\frac{2}{3}$ of what remained. What fraction of the original bar does she have left?

Example 17

May ate 18 jelly beans. This was $\frac{2}{5}$ of the jelly beans in the packet. How many jelly beans remained?

$\frac{2}{5}$ of the jelly beans $= 18$

$\therefore$ $\frac{1}{5}$ of the jelly beans $= 9$

$\therefore$ $\frac{3}{5}$ of the jelly beans $= 27$ So, 27 jelly beans remained.

7 **a** In the first half of a basketball game one team scored 45 points. This was $\frac{5}{9}$ of their score for the whole game. How many points did the team score in the second half?

b $\frac{3}{7}$ of Fred's fortune is ¥3 240 000. How much money does Fred have in total?

FRACTIONS ON A CALCULATOR

Most scientific calculators and the **Casio fx-9860G** have a fraction key $\boxed{a\,b/c}$ that is used to enter common fractions.

There is no such key for the **TI-84 Plus**, so fractions need to be entered differently. You should consult the calculator section on page **12**.

Number (Chapter 1)

Remember that although you may perform operations on fractions using your calculator, you **must not rely** on your calculator and forget how to manually perform operations with fractions.

Example 18 — Self Tutor

Find, using your calculator: a $\frac{1}{4} - \frac{2}{3}$ b $1\frac{1}{12} + 2\frac{1}{4}$ c $\frac{1}{4} \div \frac{2}{3}$

Note the solution given is for a scientific calculator or the **Casio fx-9860G**.

a $\frac{1}{4} - \frac{2}{3}$ Key in 1 [a b/c] 4 [−] 2 [a b/c] 3 [EXE]

Display $1 \lrcorner 4 - 2 \lrcorner 3$ ⟶ $-5 \lrcorner 12$ Answer: $-\frac{5}{12}$

b $1\frac{1}{12} + 2\frac{1}{4}$ Key in 1 [a b/c] 1 [a b/c] 12 [+] 2 [a b/c] 1 [a b/c] 4 [EXE] [SHIFT] [F↔D]

Display $1 \lrcorner 1 \lrcorner 12 + 2 \lrcorner 1 \lrcorner 4$ ⟶ $3 \lrcorner 1 \lrcorner 3$ Answer: $3\frac{1}{3}$

c $\frac{1}{4} \div \frac{2}{3}$ Key in 1 [a b/c] 4 [÷] 2 [a b/c] 3 [EXE]

Display $1 \lrcorner 4 \div 2 \lrcorner 3$ ⟶ $3 \lrcorner 8$ Answer: $\frac{3}{8}$

8 Find, using your calculator:

a $\frac{1}{5} + \frac{1}{3}$ b $\frac{1}{3} + \frac{2}{7}$ c $\frac{5}{8} - \frac{2}{7}$ d $\frac{3}{4} - \frac{1}{3}$

e $\frac{2}{5} \times \frac{3}{2}$ f $\frac{4}{7} \times \frac{2}{3}$ g $\frac{6}{7} \times \frac{2}{5}$ h $\frac{3}{5} \div \frac{2}{9}$

i $2\frac{1}{4} + 2\frac{1}{2} \times \frac{3}{4}$ j $1\frac{3}{7} \times 2\frac{1}{8} + 1\frac{1}{7}$ k $2\frac{3}{7} \div (2\frac{3}{4} \times \frac{4}{7})$

E POWERS AND ROOTS   [1.4]

Rather than writing $3 \times 3 \times 3 \times 3$, we can write such a product as 3^4. We call this **power** or **index notation**.

3^4 reads "three to the power of four" or "three to the fourth".

3^4 — power, index or exponent
— base

The **square root** of a number a is the positive number that when squared is a. We write this number as $\sqrt{a}$.

Since $7^2 = 49$, we write $\sqrt{49} = 7$.

We can also find the **cube root** of a, the number that when cubed is a. We write this number as $\sqrt[3]{a}$.

Since $2^3 = 8$, we write $\sqrt[3]{8} = 2$.

In general,   if $a^n = b$ then $\sqrt[n]{b} = a$ and we say that "b is the nth root of a".

For example, $2^7 = 128$ so $\sqrt[7]{128} = 2$.

For help with calculating powers and roots, refer to the **graphics calculator instructions** on page **14**.

EXERCISE 1E

1 Write down:
   a the first 8 powers of 2
   b the first 5 powers of 3
   c the first 4 powers of 4
   d the first 4 powers of 5.

The powers of 2, 3, 4, and 5 are worth memorising.

2 Find without using a calculator:
   a $\sqrt{25}$
   b $\sqrt[3]{8}$
   c $\sqrt[5]{32}$
   d $\sqrt[3]{27}$
   e $\sqrt[4]{81}$
   f $\sqrt[3]{125}$
   g $\sqrt[3]{64}$
   h $\sqrt[4]{625}$
   i $\sqrt[3]{1000}$
   j $\sqrt{2\frac{1}{4}}$

3 Use your calculator to find the exact value of:
   a $\sqrt[5]{1024}$
   b 7^4
   c 4^7
   d $\sqrt[3]{729}$
   e $\sqrt{6.76}$
   f $\sqrt{16.81}$
   g $(0.83)^3$
   h $\sqrt{0.5041}$
   i $\sqrt[3]{1.157\,625}$
   j $\sqrt{7163.9296}$
   k $(1.04)^4$
   l $(2.3)^5$
   m $(-3)^4$
   n -3^4
   o $(-1.4)^3 \times -2.7^2$

F RATIO AND PROPORTION [1.5]

A **ratio** is a way of comparing two quantities.

If we have 6 apples and 4 bananas, the ratio of the number of apples to the number of bananas is 6 to 4.

We write this as   apples : bananas $= 6 : 4$
           or   bananas : apples $= 4 : 6$

If measurements are involved we must use the **same units** for each quantity.

For example, the ratio of lengths shown is $20 : 7$ {20 mm : 7 mm} and **not** $2 : 7$.

2 cm   7 mm

Example 19   ◀)) Self Tutor

Find the ratio of the number of squares to the number of triangles.

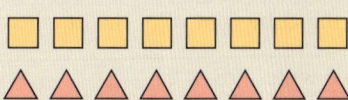

number of squares : number of triangles $= 8 : 11$

Example 20

Write as a ratio, without simplifying your answer:
- **a** Jack has $5 and Jill has 50 cents.
- **b** Mix 200 ml of cordial with 1 litre of water.

a Jack : Jill = $5 : 50 cents   {write in the correct order}
             = 500 cents : 50 cents   {write in the same units}
             = 500 : 50   {express without units}

b cordial : water = 200 ml : 1 litre   {write in the correct order}
                      = 200 ml : 1000 ml   {write in the same units}
                      = 200 : 1000   {express without units}

EXERCISE 1F.1

1
  a Find the ratio of circles to squares in:

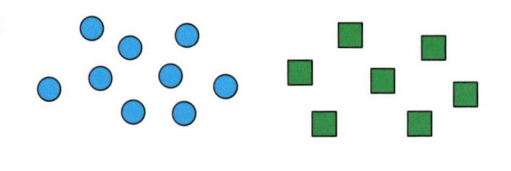

  b Find the ratio of ♣s to ♦s in:

  c Find the ratio of:
   i ♯s to ♭s
   ii ♯s to ♪s
   iii ♪s to ♭s
   iv ♭s to ♪s.

2 Write as a ratio, without simplifying your answer:
  a $8 is to $3
  b 3 litres is to 7 litres
  c 35 kg is to 45 kg
  d £3 is to 50 pence
  e 500 ml is to 3 litres
  f 400 m is to 2.5 km
  g 9 km is to 150 m
  h 12 m is to 8 km
  i 4 h is to 40 min

SIMPLIFYING RATIOS

If we have 6 apples and 4 bananas, we have 3 apples for every 2 bananas.

So, 6 : 4 is the same as 3 : 2.

We say that 6 : 4 and 3 : 2 are **equal ratios**.

Notice that to get from 6 : 4 to 3 : 2 we can divide each number in the first ratio by 2.

Also, to get from 3 : 2 to 6 : 4 we can multiply each number in the first ratio by 2.

> To **simplify a ratio** we can multiply or divide each part by the same non-zero number.

Example 21

Express $45:10$ in simplest form.

$45:10$
$= 45 \div 5 : 10 \div 5$ {5 is the HCF of 45 and 10}
$= 9:2$

Example 22

Express in simplest form:

a $0.4:1.4$ **b** $2\tfrac{1}{2}:\tfrac{1}{2}$

a $0.4:1.4$
$= 0.4 \times 10 : 1.4 \times 10$
$= 4:14$
$= 4 \div 2 : 14 \div 2$
$= 2:7$

b $2\tfrac{1}{2}:\tfrac{1}{2}$
$= \tfrac{5}{2}:\tfrac{1}{2}$
$= \tfrac{5}{2} \times 2 : \tfrac{1}{2} \times 2$
$= 5:1$

EXERCISE 1F.2

1 Express as a ratio in simplest form:
  a $6:8$
  b $8:4$
  c $4:12$
  d $9:15$
  e $3:6$
  f $14:8$
  g $8:16$
  h $18:24$
  i $125:100$
  j $2:4:6$
  k $1000:50$
  l $6:12:24$

2 Express as a ratio in simplest form:
  a $0.5:0.2$
  b $0.3:0.7$
  c $0.6:0.4$
  d $0.4:0.2$
  e $0.7:1.2$
  f $0.03:0.12$
  g $2:0.5$
  h $0.05:1$

3 Express as a ratio in simplest form:
  a $\tfrac{1}{3}:\tfrac{2}{3}$
  b $\tfrac{3}{4}:\tfrac{1}{4}$
  c $1\tfrac{1}{2}:\tfrac{1}{2}$
  d $1\tfrac{1}{2}:2\tfrac{1}{2}$
  e $\tfrac{1}{3}:\tfrac{1}{2}$
  f $1\tfrac{1}{3}:2\tfrac{1}{2}$
  g $\tfrac{2}{3}:3\tfrac{1}{4}$
  h $1\tfrac{3}{10}:1\tfrac{2}{3}$
  i $1\tfrac{1}{3}:\tfrac{2}{3}$
  j $\tfrac{3}{4}:1\tfrac{1}{2}$
  k $6:1\tfrac{1}{2}$
  l $\tfrac{1}{2}:\tfrac{1}{3}:\tfrac{1}{4}$

4 Write the following comparisons as ratios in simplest form. Compare the first quantity mentioned with the second quantity mentioned:
  a a bag of peanuts costing £15 to a bag of pistachios costing £60
  b a bus 9 minutes late to a train 3 minutes late
  c the length of a 40 km cycling time trial to a 200 km mountain stage
  d a snooker player's break of 45 points to his opponent's break of 63 points
  e a tom cat weighing 7.2 kg to a kitten weighing 0.9 kg
  f a shelf 30 cm high to a bookcase 1.5 m high
  g a road 2.4 km long to a road 900 m long.

Number (Chapter 1)

EQUAL RATIOS

> Ratios are **equal** if they can be expressed in the same simplest form.

For example, $6:4$ and $9:6$ are equal as they are both expressed in simplest form as $3:2$.

> A **proportion** is a statement that two ratios are equal.

For example, $6:4=9:6$ is a proportion.

Sometimes we need to find one quantity given another quantity and the ratio which compares them. To do this we use equal ratios.

Example 23

Find x if: **a** $3:5=6:x$ **b** $15:20=x:16$

a $3:5=6:x$ (×2)
$\therefore\ x=5\times 2$
$\therefore\ x=10$

b $15:20=15\div 5:20\div 5$
$=3:4$
$\therefore\ 3:4=x:16$ (×4)
$\therefore\ x=3\times 4=12$

Example 24

The ratio of walkers to guides on the Milford Track walk was $9:2$. How many guides were needed if there were 27 walkers?

Let the number of guides be x.

walkers : guides $= 27:x$
$\therefore\ 9:2=27:x$ (×3)
$\therefore\ x=2\times 3$
$\therefore\ x=6$
$\therefore\ $ 6 guides were needed.

EXERCISE 1F.3

1 Find x if:
  a $2:3=8:x$
  b $1:4=x:12$
  c $3:2=15:x$
  d $4:3=x:21$
  e $5:7=25:x$
  f $6:11=x:77$
  g $5:12=40:x$
  h $7:10=x:80$
  i $4:5=x:45$

2 Find x if:
  a $4:5=12:x$
  b $3:9=x:18$
  c $2:3=10:x$
  d $5:10=x:18$
  e $16:4=12:x$
  f $21:28=12:x$

3 The capacities of two bowls are in the ratio $2:3$. If the smaller bowl holds 12 litres, what is the capacity of the bigger bowl?

4 Liquid hand soap is mixed in a ratio of water to soap of $5:2$. If I have a 400 g block of soap, how much water do I need?

5 A hairdressing salon increases the price of a men's cut from €36 to €39. If the €48 ladies' cut is increased in the same ratio, how much does a ladies' cut cost now?

6 A stationer stocks pencils and pens in the ratio $7:11$. If the stationer has 550 pens, how many pencils are there?

7 A recipe for chocolate ice cream uses melted chocolate and cream in the ratio $3:25$. If 150 ml of melted chocolate is used, how much cream is needed?

8   **a** Increase £240 in the ratio:
     i $2:1$ **ii** $5:4$ **iii** $10:3$
  b Decrease 18 m in the ratio:
     i $1:6$ **ii** $5:9$ **iii** $1:20$

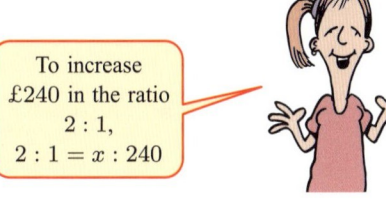

> To increase £240 in the ratio $2:1$,
> $2:1 = x:240$

THE UNITARY METHOD FOR RATIOS

Some ratio problems are best handled using the **unitary method**.

Consider **Example 24** where walkers : guides $= 9:2$.
There are 27 walkers, so $9:2 = 27:x$.

To use the unitary method, we note that 9 parts is 27, and ask what 1 part is worth. When we know the worth of 1 part, we can find the worth of any other number of parts.

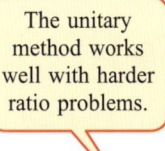

So, for this problem: 9 parts is   27
                        $\therefore$ 1 part is $27 \div 9 = 3$
                        $\therefore$ 2 parts is $3 \times 2 = 6$
                        $\therefore$ 6 guides were needed.

We can also use fractions to solve ratio problems.

> The unitary method works well with harder ratio problems.

Example 25   Self Tutor

The ratio of Pam's height to Sam's height is $7:6$. If Pam is 1.63 m tall, how tall is Sam?

Let Sam's height be x m.
Pam : Sam $= 7:6$
$\therefore \quad 1.63 : x = 7:6$

So, 7 parts is   1.63 m
$\therefore$ 1 part is $1.63 \div 7$ m
$\therefore$ 6 parts is $1.63 \div 7 \times 6$ m
$\therefore$ Sam's height is ≈ 1.40 m.

or

Let Sam's height be x m.
Pam : Sam $= 7:6$
$\therefore \quad 1.63 : x = 7:6$
$\therefore \quad \dfrac{x}{1.63} = \dfrac{6}{7}$
$\therefore \quad x = \tfrac{6}{7} \times 1.63$
$\therefore \quad x \approx 1.40$
$\therefore$ Sam's height is ≈ 1.40 m.

Example 26

In one year, Maria's height increases from 150 cm in the ratio 31 : 30. Find Maria's new height.

The second number in the ratio represents the original quantity. The first number represents the final quantity.

Maria's original height = 30 parts = 150 cm
$\therefore$ 1 part = 5 cm

Maria's new height = 31 parts
$= 31 \times 5$ cm
$= 155$ cm

Example 27

On a particular day, 1 Australian dollar is worth 0.94 US dollars. How many Australian dollars can be exchanged for $20 US?

Suppose $20 US is worth x Australian dollars.
$\therefore$ $1 : 0.94 = x : 20$
$\therefore$ $100 : 94 = x : 20$
If 94 parts = 20
then 1 part = $\frac{20}{94}$
$\therefore$ 100 parts = $\frac{20}{94} \times 100 \approx 21.28$
$\therefore$ $20 US can be exchanged for $21.28 AUD.

EXERCISE 1F.4

Use the *unitary method* to solve these problems:

1 The ratio of Terry's handspan to Gary's handspan is 5 : 6. If Terry's handspan is 19.2 cm, what is Gary's handspan?

2 Mary has left money in her will for her daughters, Elizabeth and Anne, in the ratio 9 : 8. If Elizabeth receives £20 115, how much does Anne receive?

3 On his drive to work, Hans has an average speed of 26.3 km/h. The ratio of Hans' speed to Klaus' speed is 1 : 1.17. Find Klaus' average speed on his way to work.

4 The diameters of a planet and its moon are in the ratio 16 : 5. The larger planet has a diameter of 2272 km. What is the diameter of its moon?

5 On a particular day, one Hong Kong dollar is worth 11.3 Japanese yen. How many dollars can be exchanged for 25 000 yen? Give your answer to the nearest dollar.

6 The car shown alongside is a 1 : 60 scale model.
   a What is the   **i** length   **ii** height
   of the full-size car?
   b The latest model of the car now has a 213 mm wide spoiler on the back. If this were added to the model how wide would it be?

7 Jillian is watching a group of protesters. She decides to donate $1.75 to charity for every hour that the protest lasts. If the protest goes on for 5 hours and 40 minutes, how much will Jillian donate to charity?

8 A quantity is increased in the ratio 5 : 4, and then decreased in the ratio 3 : 4. Find, in simplest form, the ratio of the final quantity to the original quantity.

USING RATIOS TO DIVIDE QUANTITIES

Quantities can be divided in a particular ratio by considering the **number of parts** the whole is divided into.

Example 28   ◀)) Self Tutor

An inheritance of $60 000 is to be divided between Donny and Marie in the ratio 2 : 3. How much does each receive?

There are $2 + 3 = 5$ parts.

$\therefore$ Donny gets $\frac{2}{5}$ of $60 000   and Marie gets $\frac{3}{5}$ of $60 000
$= \frac{2}{5} \times 60\,000$ $= \frac{3}{5} \times 60\,000$
$= \$24\,000$ $= \$36\,000$

EXERCISE 1F.5

1 Find the total number of parts represented in each of the following ratios:
   a 2 : 3   **b** 4 : 1   **c** 7 : 9   **d** 12 : 5
   e 10 : 3   **f** 3 : 16   **g** 7 : 4   **h** 9 : 10

2 Divide a 120 m length of fishing line in the following ratios:
   a 1 : 1   **b** 3 : 1   **c** 2 : 3   **d** 13 : 17

3 Divide:
   a £60 in the ratio 1 : 5   **b** $65 in the ratio 6 : 7   **c** €36 in the ratio 3 : 2

4 The winning pilot from an air race shares his €35 000 prize with his technical crew in the ratio 4 : 3.
   a How much does the pilot receive?   **b** How much does the technical crew receive?

5 The ratio of doctors to nurses at a hospital is 3 : 8. If there are 649 doctors and nurses altogether, how many nurses are at the hospital?

Number (Chapter 1)

6 Bill and Bob buy a 10 kg bag of rice from the bulk food store. Bill pays $20.50 and Bob pays $8.20.
  a How much did the bag of rice cost?
  b Write down the ratio of Bill's contribution to Bob's contribution.
  c Bill and Bob share the rice in proportion to their contribution. How much rice does each of them get?

7 Barry, Robin, and Maurice invest in a house in the ratio $3:2:7$. It later sells for 6 million pounds. Fairly divide the revenue amongst the investors.

8 A soil mixture has the peat : compost : vermiculite ratio $2:2.4:0.5$ by mass. A gardener has 6 kg of peat, and uses it all in a batch of soil mix.
  How much   **a** compost   **b** vermiculite   is in the mix?

9 In a motor club there are three makes of car: Vauxhalls, Fords, and Audis.
  The ratio of Vauxhalls : Fords : Audis at a meeting is $6:2:3$. There are 45 vehicles at the meeting, one being the Volkswagen lunch van. How many are: **a** Vauxhalls   **b** Fords   **c** Audis?

G NUMBER EQUIVALENTS   [1.7]

Consider the decimal number 0.75.

We can write it as a fraction, since $0.75 = \frac{75}{100} = \frac{3}{4}$.

We can also write it as the ratio $3:4$, or as a percentage since $0.75 \times 100\% = 75\%$.

So, 0.75, $\frac{3}{4}$, $3:4$ and 75% are all **equivalent**.

It is important that you can convert between these different forms of numbers.

Example 29   Self Tutor

Copy and complete:

	Decimal	Fraction	Ratio	Percentage
a		$\frac{2}{5}$		
b			$3:2$	
c				68%
d	0.875			

a $\frac{2}{5} = \frac{4}{10} = 0.4$
  $\frac{2}{5}$ is the ratio $2:5$
  $\frac{2}{5} \times 100\% = 40\%$

b $3:2$ is the fraction $\frac{3}{2}$
  $\frac{3}{2} = 3 \div 2 = 1.5$
  $\frac{3}{2} \times 100\% = 150\%$

c $68\% = \frac{68}{100} = 0.68$
  $\frac{68}{100} = \frac{17}{25}$
  $\frac{17}{25}$ is the ratio $17:25$

d $0.875 = \frac{875}{1000} = \frac{7}{8}$
  $\frac{7}{8}$ is the ratio $7:8$
  $\frac{875}{1000} = \frac{87.5}{100} = 87.5\%$

	Decimal	Fraction	Ratio	Percentage
a	0.4	$\frac{2}{5}$	$2:5$	40%
b	1.5	$\frac{3}{2}$	$3:2$	150%
c	0.68	$\frac{17}{25}$	$17:25$	68%
d	0.875	$\frac{7}{8}$	$7:8$	87.5%

EXERCISE 1G

1 Convert:
   a 0.65 into an equivalent fraction, percentage and ratio
   b 60% into an equivalent fraction, decimal and ratio
   c 2 : 5 into an equivalent fraction, decimal and percentage
   d $\frac{5}{8}$ into an equivalent decimal, ratio and percentage.

2 Copy and complete:

Decimal	Fraction	Ratio	Percentage
	$\frac{1}{4}$		
			85%
0.36			
		4 : 5	
$0.\overline{2}$			
		5 : 4	
			200%
	$5\frac{1}{2}$		

H PERCENTAGE   [1.8]

The whole of a quantity is regarded as 100%. So, to find 20% of a quantity, we multiply by $\frac{20}{100}$.

To find x% of a quantity, we multiply by $\frac{x}{100}$.

Alternatively, we can multiply by the equivalent decimal number.

Example 30   ◀)) Self Tutor

The Brown family budget is £800 per week.
a The Browns spend 28% of their budget on groceries. How much money is this?
b The average weekly cost of utilities is £40. What percentage of the budget is this?

a 28% of £800 = 0.28 × £800
            = £224
   The Browns spend £224 on groceries each week.

b $\frac{40}{800} = \frac{1}{20}$
   $\frac{1}{20} \times 100\% = 5\%$
   ∴ 5% of the Browns' budget goes to utilities.

EXERCISE 1H

1 Express as a percentage:
   a 35 marks out of 50 marks   b 3 km out of 20 km
   c 27 mm out of 3 m   d 83 cents out of 6 dollars

2 Tomas reduces his weight from 85.4 kg to 78.7 kg. What is his percentage weight loss?

Number (Chapter 1)

3 If 17% of Helen's assets amount to €43 197, find:
   a 1% of her assets
   b the total value of all her assets.

4 Find:
   a 20% of 3 kg
   b 4.2% of $26 000
   c 105% of 80 kg
   d $1\frac{1}{4}$% of 2000 litres
   e 0.7% of 2670 tonnes
   f 46.7% of £35 267.20

5 Alex scored 72% for an examination out of 150 marks. How many marks did Alex score?

6 **a** A marathon runner starts a race with a mass of 72.0 kg. Despite continual rehydration he loses 3% of this mass during the race. Calculate his mass at the end of the race.
   b Another runner had a starting mass of 68.3 kg and a finishing mass of 66.9 kg. Calculate her percentage loss in mass.

7 Petra has a monthly income of £4700. She does not have to pay any tax on the first £2400 she earns, but she has to pay 15% of the remainder as tax.
   a How much tax does Petra have to pay?
   b How much does Petra have left after tax?
   c What percentage of the £4700 does Petra actually pay in tax?

8 If 3 students in a class of 24 are absent, what percentage are present?

9 After 2 hours, a walker has completed 8 km of an 11.5 km journey. Calculate the percentage of the journey which remains.

10 The side lengths of the rectangle are increased by 20%. What is the percentage increase in the area of the rectangle?

8 cm
10 cm

I ROUNDING NUMBERS [1.11]

In many situations we may be given a very precise value of a measurement. Stating the *exact* value of the measurement may not be particularly important; what we want is a good *approximation* of the measurement.

For example, since 1924 the Olympic marathon has been measured as exactly 42.195 km or 26.2187 miles. The exact value is rarely quoted, however, since most people use approximations; they commonly say 42 km, 42.2 km, 26 miles, or 26.2 miles.

There are different ways of describing the level of accuracy we need. We can round a number to:

- the **nearest integer** or **whole number**
- a certain number of **decimal places**
- a certain number of **significant figures**.

RULES FOR ROUNDING

- **Rounding to the nearest whole number**
  Look at the *first* decimal place.
  If the digit is   0, 1, 2, 3 or 4,   round **down**.
  If the digit is   5, 6, 7, 8 or 9,   round **up**.

  5.648
  — look at this
  — then round this

- **Rounding to the nearest one decimal place**
  Look at the *second* decimal place.
  If the digit is   0, 1, 2, 3 or 4,   round **down**.
  If the digit is   5, 6, 7, 8 or 9,   round **up**.

  5.648
  — look at this
  — then round this

- **Rounding to the nearest two decimal places**
  Look at the *third* decimal place.
  If the digit is   0, 1, 2, 3 or 4,   round **down**.
  If the digit is   5, 6, 7, 8 or 9,   round **up**.

  5.648
  — look at this
  — then round this

Example 31   ◀) Self Tutor

Round 39.748 to the nearest:

   a whole number   **b** one decimal place   **c** two decimal places.

   a $39.748 \approx 40$ to the nearest whole number
   b $39.748 \approx 39.7$ to one decimal place
   c $39.748 \approx 39.75$ to two decimal places

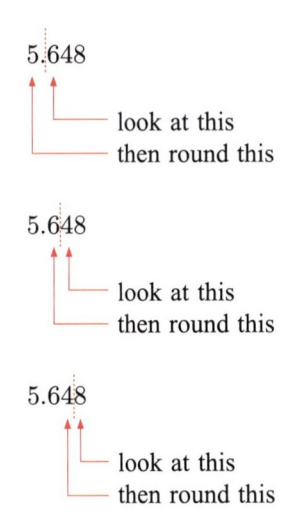

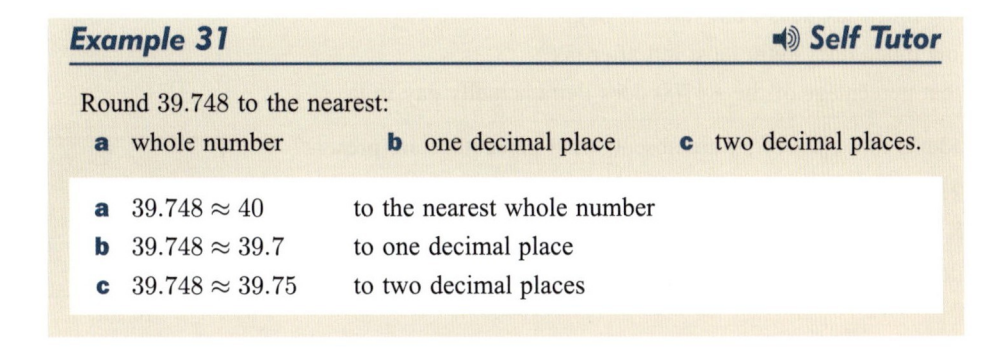

Notice that: $0.5464 \approx 0.546$ (to 3 decimal places)
                     ≈ 0.55 (to 2 decimal places)
                     ≈ 0.5 (to 1 decimal place)

EXERCISE 11.1

1 Round to the nearest whole number:
   a 0.813   **b** 7.499   **c** 7.500   **d** 11.674   **e** 128.437

2 Write these numbers correct to 1 decimal place:
   a 2.43   **b** 3.57   **c** 4.92   **d** 6.38   **e** 4.275

3 Write these numbers correct to 2 decimal places:
   a 4.236   **b** 2.731   **c** 5.625   **d** 4.377   **e** 6.5237

4 Write 0.183 75 correct to:
   a 1 decimal place   **b** 2 decimal places   **c** 3 decimal places   **d** 4 decimal places

Number (Chapter 1)

Example 32 ◀)) Self Tutor

Find $\frac{2}{7}$ correct to 3 decimal places.

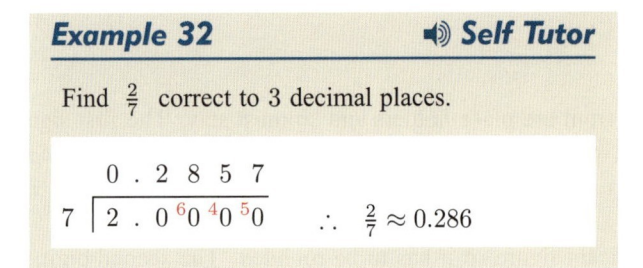

$$7 \overline{\smash{\big)}\, 2 \,.\, 0\,^{6}0\,^{4}0\,^{5}0}^{0\,.\,2\,\,8\,\,5\,\,7}$$

$\therefore \; \frac{2}{7} \approx 0.286$

5 Find the answer correct to the number of decimal places shown in square brackets:

   a $\frac{17}{4}$ [1 d.p.]   **b** $\frac{73}{8}$ [2 d.p.]   **c** 4.3×2.6 [1 d.p.]

   d 0.12×0.4 [2 d.p.]   **e** $\frac{8}{11}$ [2 d.p.]   **f** 0.08×0.31 [3 d.p.]

   g $(0.7)^2$ [1 d.p.]   **h** $\frac{37}{6}$ [2 d.p.]   **i** $\frac{17}{7}$ [3 d.p.]

6 In her maths exam Julie was asked to round 7.45 cm to one decimal place and to the nearest whole integer.

Julie's answer was that $7.45 \text{ cm} \approx 7.5 \text{ cm}$ (to one decimal place), and that $7.5 \text{ cm} \approx 8 \text{ cm}$ (to the nearest whole number).

Explain what Julie has done wrong and why we need to be careful when we make approximations.

SIGNIFICANT FIGURE ROUNDING

The first **significant figure** of a decimal number is the left-most non-zero digit.

For example:
- the first significant figure of 1234 is 1
- the first significant figure of 0.023 45 is 2.

Every digit to the right of the first significant figure is regarded as another significant figure.

Procedure for rounding off to significant figures:

> Count off the specified number of significant figures then look at the next digit.
> - If the digit is less than 5, do not change the last significant figure.
> - If the digit is 5 or more then increase the last significant figure by 1.
>
> Delete all figures following the significant figures, replacing with 0s where necessary.

Notice that if 13.238 is rounded to 13.24, then it has been rounded to 2 decimal places or to 4 significant figures.

Example 33 ◀)) Self Tutor

Round: **a** 5.371 to 2 significant figures   **b** 0.0086 to 1 significant figure
           c 423 to 1 significant figure

a $5.371 \approx 5.4$ (2 s.f.)
    ↑

This is the 2nd significant figure, so we look at the next digit which is 7.
The 7 tells us to round the 3 to a 4 and leave off the remaining digits.

b $0.0086 \approx 0.009$ (1 s.f.)

These zeros at the front are place holders and so must stay. The first significant figure is the 8. The next digit is 6, which tells us to round the 8 to a 9 and leave off the remaining digits.

c $423 \approx 400$ (1 s.f.)

4 is the first significant figure so it has to be rounded. The second digit, 2, tells us to keep the original 4. We convert the 23 into 00. These two zeros are place holders; they are not 'significant figures' but need to be there to make sure the 4 still represents 4 hundreds.

EXERCISE 11.2

1 Round correct to the number of significant figures shown in brackets.

a	42.3	[2 s.f.]	**b**	6.237	[3 s.f.]	**c**	0.0462	[2 s.f.]
d	0.2461	[2 s.f.]	**e**	437	[2 s.f.]	**f**	2064	[2 s.f.]
g	31 009	[3 s.f.]	**h**	10.27	[3 s.f.]	**i**	0.999	[1 s.f.]
j	0.999	[2 s.f.]	**k**	264 003	[4 s.f.]	**l**	0.037 642	[4 s.f.]
m	3699.231	[4 s.f.]	**n**	0.007 639	[2 s.f.]	**o**	29 999	[3 s.f.]
p	69.7003	[2 s.f.]						

2 The crowd at a football match was officially 26 247 people.

  a Round the crowd size to:

  i 1 significant figure

  ii 2 significant figures.

  b Which of these figures might be used by the media to indicate crowd size?

3 The newspaper stated that 2500 people attended a protest march in Paris.
Given that this figure had been rounded to two significant figures, what was the largest number of people that could have attended the protest?

4 During a rabbit plague there were 132 709 rabbits in South Australia. What figure would you expect to see in a newspaper headline for an article on these rabbits?

ONE FIGURE APPROXIMATIONS

A fast way of estimating a calculation is to perform a **one figure approximation**. We round each number in the calculation to one significant figure, then perform the calculation with these approximations.

Rules:
- Leave single digit numbers as they are.
- Round all other numbers to one significant figure.
- Perform the calculation.

For example, 3785×7
$\approx 4000 \times 7$
$\approx 28\,000$

Number (Chapter 1)

Example 34

Estimate the product: **a** 57×8 **b** 537×6

a Round 57 to the nearest 10.
57×8
$\approx 60 \times 8$
≈ 480

b Round 537 to the nearest 100.
537×6
$\approx 500 \times 6$
≈ 3000

Example 35

Estimate the product: 623×69

Round 623 to the nearest 100 and round 69 to the nearest 10.
623×69
$\approx 600 \times 70$
$\approx 42\,000$

The estimate tells us the correct answer should have 5 digits in it.

Example 36

Find the approximate value of $3946 \div 79$.

$3946 \div 79 \approx 4000 \div 80$
$\approx 400 \div 8$
≈ 50

EXERCISE 11.3

1 Estimate the products:
   a 79×4
   b 47×8
   c 62×7
   d 494×6
   e 817×8
   f 2094×7

2 Estimate the products using one figure approximations:
   a 57×42
   b 73×59
   c 85×98
   d 275×54
   e 389×73
   f 4971×32
   g 3079×29
   h $40\,989 \times 9$
   i 880×750

3 Estimate using one figure approximations:
   a $397 \div 4$
   b $6849 \div 7$
   c $79\,095 \div 8$
   d $6000 \div 19$
   e $80\,000 \div 37$
   f $18\,700 \div 97$
   g $2780 \div 41$
   h $48\,097 \div 243$
   i $798\,450 \div 399$

J TIME [1.12]

In early civilisations, time was measured by regular changes in the sky. The recurring period of daylight and darkness came to be called a **day**. The Babylonians divided the day into hours, minutes, and seconds. Ancient astronomers found the time taken for the Earth to complete one orbit around the Sun. This became known as a **year**.

The base unit of time in the International System of Units is the **second**, abbreviated **s**.

UNITS OF TIME

1 **minute** = 60 seconds	1 **year** = 12 months = 365 days
1 **hour** = 60 minutes = 3600 seconds	1 **decade** = 10 years
1 **day** = 24 hours	1 **century** = 100 years
1 **week** = 7 days	1 **millennium** = 1000 years

Example 37 ◀) Self Tutor

Convert 8 days, 7 hours, and 6 minutes to minutes.

$$\begin{aligned}
8 \text{ days} \times 24 \times 60 &= 11\,520 \text{ minutes} \\
7 \text{ hours} \times 60 &= 420 \text{ minutes} \\
6 \text{ minutes} &= 6 \text{ minutes} \\
\therefore \text{ total} &= 11\,946 \text{ minutes}
\end{aligned}$$

Example 38 ◀) Self Tutor

Convert 30 240 minutes to days.

$$\begin{aligned}
30\,240 &= (30\,240 \div 60) \text{ hours} \quad \{60 \text{ min in 1 hour}\} \\
&= 504 \text{ hours} \\
&= (504 \div 24) \text{ days} \quad \{24 \text{ hours in 1 day}\} \\
&= 21 \text{ days}
\end{aligned}$$

Example 39 ◀) Self Tutor

Convert 3 hours, 14 minutes to seconds.

$$\begin{aligned}
3 \text{ hours, } 14 \text{ minutes} &= (3 \times 60) \text{ min} + 14 \text{ min} \quad \{60 \text{ min in 1 hour}\} \\
&= 194 \text{ min} \\
&= (194 \times 60) \text{ s} \quad \{60 \text{ s in 1 min}\} \\
&= 11\,640 \text{ s}
\end{aligned}$$

Number (Chapter 1)

EXERCISE 1J.1

1 Convert the following times to minutes:
   - **a** 5 hours
   - **b** 3 days
   - **c** 2 days 15 hours
   - **d** 2220 seconds

2 Convert the following times to days:
   - **a** 1248 hours
   - **b** 23 040 min
   - **c** 3 years
   - **d** 6 hours

3 Convert the following times to seconds:
   - **a** 35 minutes
   - **b** 3 hours 19 min
   - **c** 5 days
   - **d** 1 week 2 days

4 Calculate the following, expressing your answers in hours, minutes and seconds:
   - **a** 1 h 19 min + 2 h 42 min + 1 h 7 min
   - **b** 4 h 51 min 16 s + 2 h 19 min 54 s
   - **c** 12 h − 7 h 55 min
   - **d** 5 h 23 min − 2 h 48 min

> The abbreviation for hours is **h** and for minutes is **min**.

5 Xani has 6 science lessons a week, each of 45 minutes duration. Find the total time spent in science lessons in a twelve week term.

Example 40   ◀) Self Tutor

What is the time difference between 9.55 am and 1.25 pm?

$$\begin{aligned}
\text{9.55 am to 10.00 am} &= 5 \text{ min} \\
\text{10.00 am to 1.00 pm} &= 3 \text{ h} \\
\text{1.00 pm to 1.25 pm} &= 25 \text{ min} \\
\hline
& 3 \text{ h } 30 \text{ min}
\end{aligned}$$

The time difference is 3 hours 30 minutes.

Example 41   ◀) Self Tutor

What is the time $3\frac{1}{2}$ hours after 10.40 am?

$$\begin{aligned}
10.40 \text{ am} + 3\tfrac{1}{2} \text{ hours} &= 10.40 \text{ am} + 3 \text{ h} + 30 \text{ min} \\
&= 1.40 \text{ pm} + 30 \text{ min} \\
&= 2.10 \text{ pm}
\end{aligned}$$

6 Find the time difference between:
   - **a** 4.30 am and 6.55 am
   - **b** 10.08 am and 5.52 pm
   - **c** 3.15 pm and 9.03 pm
   - **d** 7.54 am and 2.29 pm

7 Henry left home at 7.48 am and arrived at work at 9.02 am. How long did it take him to get to work?

8 Your time schedule shows you worked the following hours last week:

Monday	8.45 am - 5.05 pm
Tuesday	8.50 am - 5.10 pm
Wednesday	8.45 am - 4.55 pm
Thursday	8.30 am - 5.00 pm
Friday	8.35 am - 5.15 pm

a How many hours did you work last week?
b If you are paid €9.00 per hour, what was your income for the week?

9 Calculate the time:
   a 3 hours after 8.16 am
   b 3 hours before 11.45 am
   c $5\frac{1}{2}$ hours after 10.15 am
   d $3\frac{1}{2}$ hours before 1.18 pm

10 Boris caught a plane flight at 8.45 am. The flight was $6\frac{1}{2}$ hours. At what time did he arrive at his destination, assuming it was in the same time zone?

11 If a train is travelling at 36 m/s, how far will it travel in 1 hour? Give your answer in kilometres.

24-HOUR TIME

24-hour time is used by the armed forces and in train and airline timetables. It avoids the need for using **am** and **pm** to indicate morning and afternoon.

In 24-hour time, four digits are always used. For example:

- 0800 is 8.00 am

  "Oh eight hundred hours"
- 0000 is midnight
- 2359 is one minute before midnight

- 2000 is 8.00 pm

  "twenty hundred hours"
- 1200 is noon or midday

Morning times (am) are from midnight (0000) to midday (1200).

Afternoon times (pm) are from midday (1200) to midnight (0000).

Notice that:
- midnight is 0000 not 2400
- to convert afternoon 24-hour time to pm times we subtract 1200.

EXERCISE 1J.2

1 Change to 24-hour time:
   a 9.57 am
   b 11.06 am
   c 4 o'clock pm
   d 2.25 pm
   e 8 o'clock am
   f 1.06 am
   g 8.58 pm
   h noon
   i 2 minutes past midnight

2 Change to am/pm time:
   a 1140
   b 0346
   c 1634
   d 1900
   e 0800
   f 2330
   g 1223
   h 2040

Number (Chapter 1)   57

3 Copy and complete the following railway schedule:

	Departure	Travelling time	Arrival
a	0520	6 h 20 min	
b	0710		1405
c		56 min	1027
d		4 h 23 min	1652
e	2012		0447 (next day)

Review set 1A

1 Copy and complete the table given:

Number	$\mathbb{N}$	$\mathbb{Z}$	$\mathbb{Q}$	$\mathbb{R}$
17.3				
-5				
$\frac{4}{0}$				
$\sqrt{6}$				
12				

2 Evaluate: **a** $(-3)^2 + 5$ **b** $\dfrac{45 - 7 \times 6}{3 \times 4}$ **c** $27 \div 9 \times (4 - 15)$

3 Find the HCF of 28 and 42.

4 Find the largest multiple of 15 which is less than 400.

5 Calculate: **a** $\frac{4}{7} + \frac{2}{5}$ **b** $1\frac{1}{3} \div \frac{1}{6}$

6 Courtney uses $\frac{1}{3}$ of a reel of rope to make a rope ladder. She cuts off another $\frac{1}{4}$ of the remaining reel to keep in her trailer. The original reel was 90 m long. How much rope is left?

7 Find: **a** 5^3 **b** $\sqrt[4]{256}$

8 Write as a ratio in simplest form:
   a 24 : 60   **b** 300 ml : 2 litres

9   **a** Increase 70 kg in the ratio 9 : 7.   **b** Decrease 70 kg in the ratio 2 : 5.

10 A pride of lions has adults and cubs in the ratio 3 : 5. If there are 10 cubs, how many adults are there?

11 Three sisters receive an inheritance in the ratio 5 : 3 : 2. How much does each receive from $440 000?

12 Convert: **a** 0.75 into an equivalent fraction, percentage, and ratio
   b $\frac{2}{3}$ into an equivalent decimal, ratio, and percentage.

13 The average human body is 57% water. How many kg of water do you expect in a 62 kg person?

14 Find, to the accuracy given in square brackets:

    a 0.41×235 [nearest integer]   **b** $\frac{46}{17}$ [3 significant figures]

15 Nataliya arrives at a bird hide at 11.17 am. She sees a sociable lapwing at 5.03 pm. How long did she wait to see it?

Review set 1B

1 Is 47 a prime number?

2 A camping chair uses 13 metal rods, each of which costs £1.27. The other costs total £4.26 per chair. What is the cost of making a set of 4 chairs?

3 List all the factors of 45.

4 Find the LCM of 2, 5 and 6.

5 Calculate: **a** $3\frac{7}{10} - 2\frac{4}{5}$ **b** $\frac{5}{9} \times \frac{3}{10}$ **c** $8 - \frac{3}{4} \times 2\frac{2}{9}$

6 Find using a calculator: **a** 6^7 **b** $\sqrt{7.0225}$

7 Write as a ratio in simplest form: **a** $1.5 : 0.5$ **b** $8 : 6 : 18$

8 Find x if: **a** $5 : 3 = x : 12$ **b** $35 : 56 = 25 : x$

9 When Hermann goes to the exchange bureau, 1 euro is worth 1.37 Swiss francs. How many euros can he get for 50 Swiss francs?

10 Katie and Jo buy a 4.55 kg beef fillet from the butcher and share it in the ratio $4 : 3$. Find the size of Katie's share.

11 A fashion parade has an attendance of 300. If the ratio of males to females is $5 : 7$, how many males are present?

12 A school's senior football squad has 29 players. When the graduating students leave at the end of the year, only 10 footballers are left. Calculate the percentage loss.

13   **a** Write down $457.268\,113$ to 2 decimal places.

    b Estimate 489×73 using a one figure approximation.

14 What time is 3 hours and 15 minutes before 11.20 pm? Give your answer in:

    a am/pm time   **b** 24-hour time.

Sets

2

Contents:

A	Set notation	[9.1, 9.2]
B	Special number sets	[1.1, 9.2]
C	Interval notation	[9.2]
D	Venn diagrams	[9.3]
E	Union and intersection	[9.4]
F	Problem solving	[9.3, 9.4]

Opening problem

A survey of 50 tea-drinkers found that 32 people surveyed put milk in their tea, 19 put sugar in their tea, and 10 put both milk and sugar in their tea.

How many of the people surveyed have their tea with:

- milk but not sugar
- milk or sugar
- neither milk nor sugar?

A   SET NOTATION   [9.1, 9.2]

A **set** is a collection of objects or things.

A set is usually denoted by a capital letter.

For example: E is the set of all year 11 students who study English.
C is the set of all cars parked in the school's car park
P is the set of all prime numbers less than 10.

These sets could be written in the form: $E = \{$year 11 students who study English$\}$
$C = \{$cars parked in the school's car park$\}$
$P = \{2, 3, 5, 7\}$

where the curly brackets are read as 'the set of'.

> The **elements** of a set are the objects or members which make up the set.

We use $\in$ to mean '*is an element of*' or '*is a member of*'
and $\notin$ to mean '*is not an element of*' or '*is not a member of*'.

So, for $P = \{2, 3, 5, 7\}$ we can write $2 \in P$ and $6 \notin P$.

It does not matter what order we write the elements of a set in.

So, $\{7, 5, 3, 2\}$ means the same thing as $\{2, 3, 5, 7\}$.

> Two sets A and B are **equal** if their elements are exactly the same.

For example, if $A = \{$Kate, Laura, Mary$\}$ and $B = \{$Kate, Mary, Laura$\}$, $A = B$.

SIZE OF SETS

There are 4 elements in the set $P = \{2, 3, 5, 7\}$, so we write $n(P) = 4$.

> $n(A)$ reads 'the number of elements in set A'.

If a set has a finite number of elements, we call it a **finite** set.

However, consider the set of all positive integers $\{1, 2, 3, 4, ...\}$.

> These dots indicate that the set goes on forever.

The set has an infinite number of elements, so we call it an **infinite** set.

SUBSETS

Each of the elements of the set $S = \{2, 5, 7\}$ is also an element of the set $P = \{2, 3, 5, 7\}$.
We say that S is a **subset** of P, and write $S \subseteq P$.

> A is a **subset** of B if all elements of A are also elements of B.
> We write $A \subseteq B$.

For example, $\{1, 3\} \subseteq \{1, 2, 3\}$ but $\{1, 2, 3\} \not\subseteq \{1, 3\}$.

> A is a **proper subset** of B if every element of A is also an element of B, but $A \neq B$.
> We write $A \subset B$.

For example, $\{2, 6\} \subset \{2, 4, 6\}$ but $\{2, 4, 6\} \not\subset \{2, 4, 6\}$.

THE UNIVERSAL SET

We often think of a set as being within some universal set, denoted $\mathscr{E}$.

> The **universal set** $\mathscr{E}$ contains all of the elements under consideration.

For example, say P is the set of prime numbers under 20. In this case $P = \{2, 3, 5, 7, 11, 13, 17, 19\}$.
The universal set $\mathscr{E}$ could be the set of all positive integers under 20, $\mathscr{E} = \{1, 2, 3, 4, 5, 6, 7, ..., 19\}$.

> These dots indicate that the pattern continues up to the final element.

Sets (Chapter 2)

Within $\mathcal{E}$, the set of composite numbers is $Q = \{4, 6, 8, 9, 10, 12, 14, 15, 16, 18\}$.

Notice that $P \subset \mathcal{E}$ and $Q \subset \mathcal{E}$.

THE COMPLEMENT OF A SET

Suppose $\mathcal{E} = \{1, 2, 3, 4, 5, 6, 7, 8\}$ and $A = \{2, 4, 5, 7, 8\}$.

The set of elements $\{1, 3, 6\}$ includes all elements of $\mathcal{E}$ that are *not* elements of A. We call this set the *complement* of A, and denote it A'.

No element of A is in A', and no element of A' is in A.

> The **complement** of A is the set of all elements of $\mathcal{E}$ which are *not* elements of A.
> We denote the complement A'.

THE EMPTY SET

Sometimes we find that a set has no elements. Such a set is called the **empty set**, and is denoted $\varnothing$ or $\{\ \}$. The empty set $\varnothing$ is a proper subset of any other set.

EXERCISE 2A

1. F is the set of friends: $F = \{$Allan, Bob, Carlos, Dean, Edward$\}$.
    a. Find $n(F)$.
    b. True or false?　　i　Bob $\in F$　　ii　Brian $\in F$
    c. Consider $G = \{$Dean, Gordon, Carlos$\}$ and $H = \{$Edward, Allan, Dean$\}$.
       True or false?　　i　$G \subseteq F$　　ii　$H \subseteq F$　　iii　$H \subset F$　　iv　$H \subseteq G$

2. $\mathcal{E} = \{1, 2, 3, 4, 5, ..., 12\}$, $S = \{2, 4, 7, 9, 11\}$ and $T = \{4, 11\}$.
    a. Find:　　i　$n(\mathcal{E})$　　ii　$n(S)$　　iii　$n(T)$.
    b. List the sets S' and T'.
    c. True or false?　　i　$S \subseteq \mathcal{E}$　　ii　$S \subseteq T$　　iii　$T \subset S$
    d. True or false?　　i　$5 \in S$　　ii　$5 \notin T$
    e. If $R = \{4, 7, 11, 9, x\}$ and $S \subseteq R$, find x.
    f. Is S finite or infinite? Explain your answer.

3. The subsets of $\{a, b\}$ are $\varnothing$, $\{a\}$, $\{b\}$ and $\{a, b\}$.
    a. List all subsets of $\{a\}$.
    b. List all subsets of $\{a, b, c\}$.
    c. Predict the number of subsets of $\{a, b, c, d\}$ without listing them.

4. List all proper subsets of $S = \{2, 4, 7, 9\}$.

5. List the elements of the set S which contains the:
    a. factors of 6
    b. multiples of 6
    c. factors of 17
    d. multiples of 17
    e. prime numbers less than 20
    f. composite numbers between 10 and 30.

> Prime numbers have exactly two factors. Composite numbers have more than 2 factors.

6 Find $n(S)$ for each set in **5**.

7 Suppose $A = \{\text{prime numbers between 20 and 30}\}$,
$B = \{\text{even numbers between 20 and 30}\}$,
$C = \{\text{composite numbers between 20 and 30}\}$,
and $D = \{\text{multiples of 18 between 20 and 30}\}$.
  a List the elements of each set.
  b Find: **i** $n(A)$ **ii** $n(D)$.
  c Which of the sets listed are:
  i subsets of A **ii** proper subsets of C?
  d True or false?   **i** $23 \in C$ **ii** $27 \notin A$ **iii** $25 \in B$

8 a Suppose $\mathscr{E} = \{2, 3, 4, 5, 6, 7, 8\}$, $A = \{2, 3, 4, 7\}$, and $B = \{2, 5\}$. Find:
  i $n(\mathscr{E})$ **ii** $n(A)$ **iii** $n(A')$ **iv** $n(B)$ **v** $n(B')$
  b Copy and complete: For any set $S \subseteq \mathscr{E}$ when $\mathscr{E}$ is the universal set, $n(S) + n(S') = ...$

9 Find $n(\varnothing)$.

10 Set A is equal to set B. Explain why $n(A) = n(B)$.

B SPECIAL NUMBER SETS   [1.1, 9.2]

There are some number sets we refer to frequently and so we give them special symbols. We use:

- $\mathbb{N}$ to represent the set of all **natural** or **counting** numbers $\{0, 1, 2, 3, 4, 5, 6 ....\}$
  The set of natural numbers is endless, so we say $n(\mathbb{N})$ is infinite.

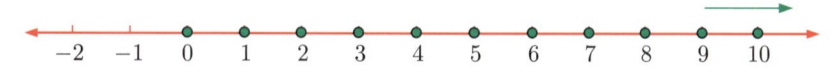

- $\mathbb{Z}$ to represent the set of all **integers** $\{...., -4, -3, -2, -1, 0, 1, 2, 3, 4, ...\}$

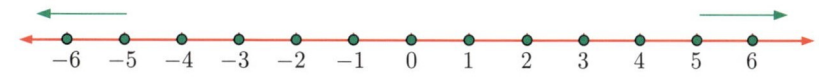

- $\mathbb{Z}^+$ to represent the set of all **positive integers** $\{1, 2, 3, 4, 5, 6, ...\}$

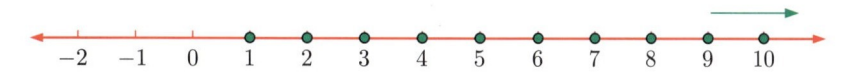

- $\mathbb{Q}$ to represent the set of all **rational numbers** which have the form $\dfrac{p}{q}$ where p and q are integers and $q \neq 0$.

- $\mathbb{R}$ to represent the set of all **real numbers**, which are numbers that can be placed on a number line.

Sets   (Chapter 2)

Example 1

True or false? Give reasons for your answers.

  a $2 \in \mathbb{Z}$ **b** $2\frac{1}{2} \in \mathbb{Q}$ **c** $5 \notin \mathbb{Q}$ **d** $\pi \in \mathbb{Q}$ **e** $-2 \notin \mathbb{R}$

  a $2 \in \mathbb{Z}$ is true as $\mathbb{Z} = \{...., -3, -2, -1, 0, 1, 2, 3, ...\}$
  b $2\frac{1}{2} \in \mathbb{Q}$ is true as $2\frac{1}{2} = \frac{5}{2}$ where 5 and 2 are integers.
  c $5 \notin \mathbb{Q}$ is false as $5 = \frac{5}{1}$ where 5 and 1 are integers.
  d $\pi \in \mathbb{Q}$ is false as π is a known irrational number.
  e $-2 \notin \mathbb{R}$ is false as -2 can be put on the number line.

Example 2

Show that $0.\overline{36}$, which is $0.36363636....$, is a rational number.

  Let $x = 0.\overline{36} = 0.36363636....$
  $\therefore$ $100x = 36.363636.... = 36 + x$
  $\therefore$ $99x = 36$ and so $x = \frac{36}{99} = \frac{4}{11}$

  So, $0.\overline{36}$ is actually the rational number $\frac{4}{11}$.

EXERCISE 2B

1 True or false?

  a $3 \in \mathbb{Z}^+$ **b** $6 \in \mathbb{Z}$ **c** $\frac{3}{4} \in \mathbb{Q}$ **d** $\sqrt{2} \notin \mathbb{Q}$

  e $-\frac{1}{4} \notin \mathbb{Q}$ **f** $2\frac{1}{3} \in \mathbb{Z}$ **g** $0.3684 \in \mathbb{R}$ **h** $\frac{1}{0.1} \in \mathbb{Z}$

2 Which of these are rational?

  a 8   **b** -8 **c** $2\frac{1}{3}$ **d** $-3\frac{1}{4}$

  e $\sqrt{3}$ **f** $\sqrt{400}$ **g** 9.176 **h** $\pi - \pi$

3 Show that these numbers are rational: **a** $0.\overline{7}$ **b** $0.\overline{41}$ **c** $0.\overline{324}$

4 **a** Explain why 0.527 is a rational number.
    b $0.\overline{9}$ is a rational number. In fact, $0.\overline{9} \in \mathbb{Z}$. Give evidence to support this statement.

5 Explain why these statements are false:
    a The sum of two irrationals is irrational.   **b** The product of two irrationals is irrational.

6 True or false?   **a** $\mathbb{N} \subseteq \mathbb{Z}$ **b** $\mathbb{R} \subseteq \mathbb{Q}$ **c** $\mathbb{Z} \subseteq \mathbb{Q}$.

7 If the universal set is the set of real numbers $\mathbb{R}$, what does $\mathbb{Q}'$ represent?

C INTERVAL NOTATION [9.2]

Interval notation allows us to quickly describe sets of numbers using mathematical symbols only.

For example: $\{x \mid -3 < x \leqslant 2, \ x \in \mathbb{R}\}$

- the set of all x
- such that
- x lies between negative 3 and 2, including 2
- and
- x is real

Unless stated otherwise, we assume we are dealing with *real* numbers. Thus, the set can simply be written as $\{x \mid -3 < x \leqslant 2\}$.

We can represent the set on a number line as:

not included — included

Sometimes we want to restrict a set to include only integers or rationals.

For example: $\{x \mid -5 < x < 5, \ x \in \mathbb{Z}\}$ is the set of all integers x such that x lies between negative 5 and 5.

We can represent the set on a number line as:

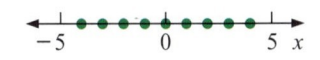

It is also common to write this as $\{x \in \mathbb{Z} \mid -5 < x < 5\}$.

Example 3   ◀)) Self Tutor

Write in interval notation:

a

b

a $\{x \mid 1 \leqslant x \leqslant 5, \ x \in \mathbb{N}\}$
or $\{x \mid 1 \leqslant x \leqslant 5, \ x \in \mathbb{Z}\}$

b $\{x \mid -3 \leqslant x < 6\}$

Example 4   ◀)) Self Tutor

a List the elements of the set:
  i $\{x \mid -2 \leqslant x \leqslant 1, \ x \in \mathbb{Z}\}$ **ii** $\{x \mid 0 \leqslant x < 4, \ x \in \mathbb{N}\}$
b Write in interval notation: $\{-3, -2, -1, 0, 1, 2, 3, 4, ...\}$

a **i** $\{x \mid -2 \leqslant x \leqslant 1, \ x \in \mathbb{Z}\}$
       $= \{-2, -1, 0, 1\}$

   ii $\{x \mid 0 \leqslant x < 4, \ x \in \mathbb{N}\}$
        $= \{0, 1, 2, 3\}$

b We first notice that the elements of the set are all integers, so we are dealing with $x \in \mathbb{Z}$.
  $\{-3, -2, -1, 0, 1, 2, ...\} = \{x \mid x \geqslant -3, \ x \in \mathbb{Z}\}$

Sets (Chapter 2)

EXERCISE 2C

1 Write a statement in words for the meaning of:
- **a** $\{x \mid x > 4\}$
- **b** $\{x \mid x \leqslant 5\}$
- **c** $\{y \mid 0 < y < 8\}$
- **d** $\{x \mid 1 \leqslant x \leqslant 4\}$
- **e** $\{t \mid 2 < t < 7\}$
- **f** $\{n \mid n \leqslant 3 \text{ or } n > 6\}$

2 List the elements of the set:
- **a** $\{x \mid 1 < x \leqslant 6, \ x \in \mathbb{N}\}$
- **b** $\{x \mid x \geqslant 5, \ x \in \mathbb{Z}\}$
- **c** $\{x \mid x < 3, \ x \in \mathbb{Z}\}$
- **d** $\{x \mid -3 \leqslant x \leqslant 5, \ x \in \mathbb{N}\}$
- **e** $\{x \mid x \geqslant -4, \ x \in \mathbb{Z}\}$
- **f** $\{x \mid x \leqslant 6, \ x \in \mathbb{Z}^+\}$

3 Write these sets in interval notation:
- **a** $\{-5, -4, -3, -2, -1\}$
- **b** $\{0, 1, 2, 3, 4, 5\}$
- **c** $\{4, 5, 6, 7, 8, ...\}$
- **d** $\{...., -3, -2, -1, 0, 1\}$
- **e** $\{-5, -4, -3, -2, -1, 0, 1\}$
- **f** $\{...., 41, 42, 43, 44\}$

4 Write in interval notation:
- **a**
- **b**
- **c**
- **d**
- **e**
- **f**

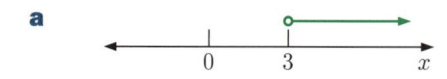

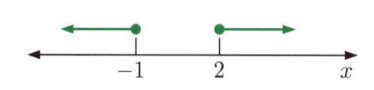

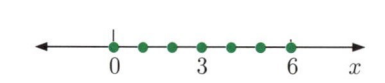

5 Sketch the following number sets:
- **a** $\{x \mid 4 \leqslant x < 8, \ x \in \mathbb{N}\}$
- **b** $\{x \mid -5 < x \leqslant 4, \ x \in \mathbb{Z}\}$
- **c** $\{x \mid -3 < x \leqslant 5, \ x \in \mathbb{R}\}$
- **d** $\{x \mid x > -5, \ x \in \mathbb{Z}\}$
- **e** $\{x \mid x \leqslant 6\}$
- **f** $\{x \mid -5 \leqslant x \leqslant 0\}$

6 Are the following sets finite or infinite?
- **a** $\{x \mid 1 \leqslant x \leqslant 10, \ x \in \mathbb{Z}\}$
- **b** $\{x \mid x < 4, \ x \in \mathbb{Z}\}$
- **c** $\{x \mid x > 5, \ x \in \mathbb{Z}^+\}$
- **d** $\{x \mid x < 7, \ x \in \mathbb{Z}^+\}$
- **e** $\{x \mid x \leqslant 9, \ x \in \mathbb{N}\}$
- **f** $\{x \mid 2 \leqslant x \leqslant 6, \ x \in \mathbb{R}\}$

D VENN DIAGRAMS   [9.3]

A **Venn diagram** consists of a universal set $\mathscr{E}$ represented by a rectangle, and sets within it that are generally represented by circles.

For example, consider the universal set $\mathscr{E} = \{x \mid x \leqslant 10, \ x \in \mathbb{Z}^+\}$.

We can display the set $S = \{2, 4, 6, 7\}$ on the Venn diagram using a circle. The elements of S are placed within the circle, while the elements of S' are placed outside the circle.

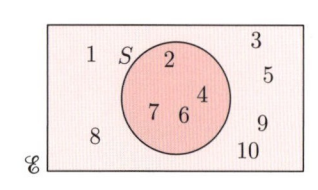

Example 5

If $\mathscr{E} = \{0, 1, 2, 3, 4, 5, 6, 7\}$ and $E = \{2, 3, 5, 7\}$, list the set E' and illustrate E and E' on a Venn diagram.

Hence find: **a** $n(E)$ **b** $n(E')$ **c** $n(\mathscr{E})$

$E' = \{0, 1, 4, 6\}$

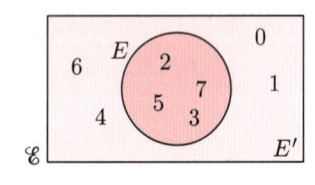

a E contains 4 elements, so $n(E) = 4$
b $n(E') = 4$ **c** $n(\mathscr{E}) = 8$

Consider the sets $\mathscr{E} = \{1, 2, 3, 4, 5, 6, 7, 8\}$, $A = \{2, 3, 5, 7\}$ and $B = \{2, 7\}$.

We notice that $B \subset A$, so the circle representing B lies entirely within the circle representing A.

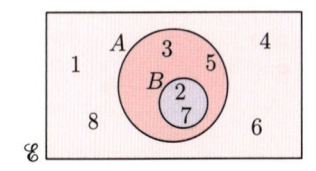

We can use this property to draw a Venn diagram for the special number sets $\mathbb{N}$, $\mathbb{Z}$, $\mathbb{Q}$ and $\mathbb{R}$. In this case $\mathbb{R}$ is the universal set, and $\mathbb{N} \subseteq \mathbb{Z} \subseteq \mathbb{Q} \subseteq \mathbb{R}$.

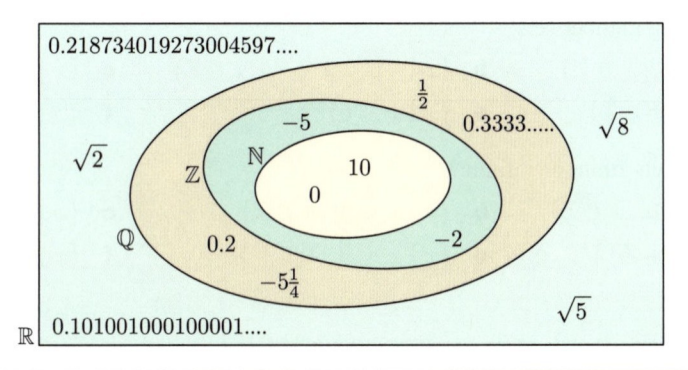

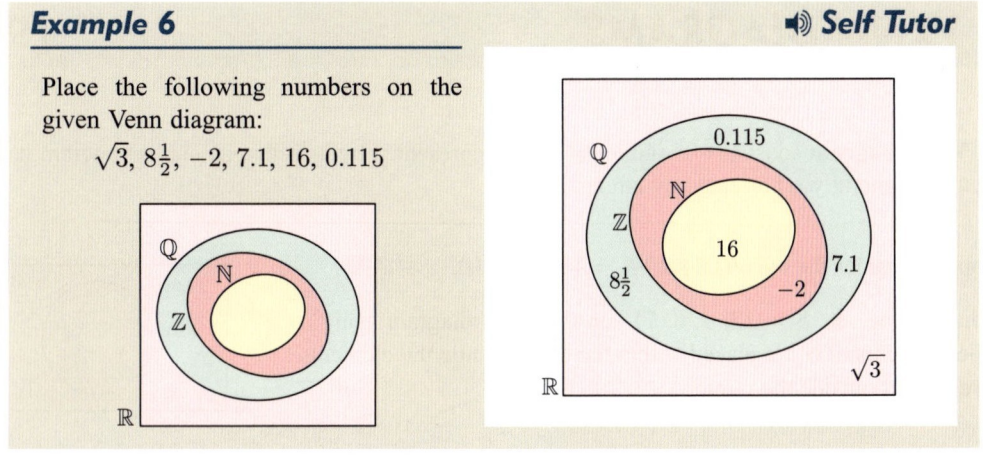

Example 6

Place the following numbers on the given Venn diagram:

$\sqrt{3}$, $8\frac{1}{2}$, -2, 7.1, 16, 0.115

Sets (Chapter 2)

If two sets A and B have elements in common, but $A \nsubseteq B$ and $B \nsubseteq A$, the circles for these sets overlap.

Example 7

Consider the sets $\mathcal{E} = \{x \mid 0 \leqslant x \leqslant 12,\ x \in \mathbb{Z}\}$, $A = \{2, 3, 5, 7, 11\}$ and $B = \{1, 3, 6, 7, 8\}$. Show A and B on a Venn diagram.

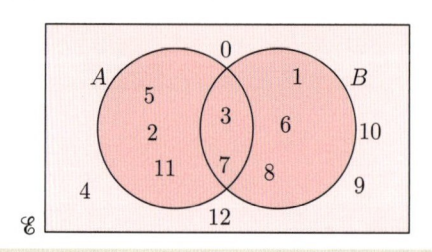

We notice that 3 and 7 are in both A and B so the circles representing A and B must overlap.

We place 3 and 7 in the overlap, then fill in the rest of A, then fill in the rest of B.

The remaining elements of $\mathcal{E}$ go outside the two circles.

EXERCISE 2D

1. Suppose $\mathcal{E} = \{x \mid x \leqslant 8,\ x \in \mathbb{Z}^+\}$ and $A = \{\text{prime numbers} \leqslant 8\}$.
   a Show set A on a Venn diagram.   b List the set A'.   c Find $n(A)$ and $n(A')$.

2. Suppose $\mathcal{E} = \{\text{letters of the English alphabet}\}$ and
   $V = \{\text{letters of the English alphabet which are vowels}\}$.
   a Show these two sets on a Venn diagram.   b List the set V'.

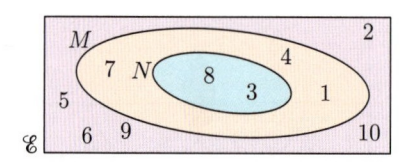

3.
   a List the elements of:
      i $\mathcal{E}$ ii N iii M
   b Find $n(N)$ and $n(M)$.
   c Is $M \subseteq N$?

4. Suppose $\mathcal{E} = \{\text{cockroaches, crocodiles, dolphins, earthworms, otters, parrots, penguins, whales}\}$,
   $S = \{\text{animals that can swim}\}$ and $L = \{\text{animals with legs}\}$.
   Illustrate these sets on a Venn diagram.

5. Show A and B on a Venn diagram if:
   a $\mathcal{E} = \{1, 2, 3, 4, 5, 6\}$, $A = \{1, 2, 3, 4\}$, $B = \{3, 4, 5, 6\}$
   b $\mathcal{E} = \{4, 5, 6, 7, 8, 9, 10\}$, $A = \{6, 7, 9, 10\}$, $B = \{5, 6, 8, 9\}$
   c $\mathcal{E} = \{3, 4, 5, 6, 7, 8, 9\}$, $A = \{3, 5, 7, 9\}$, $B = \{4, 6, 8\}$

6. Show the following information on a Venn diagram:
   a $\mathcal{E} = \{\text{triangles}\}$, $E = \{\text{equilateral triangles}\}$, $I = \{\text{isosceles triangles}\}$
   b $\mathcal{E} = \{\text{quadrilaterals}\}$, $P = \{\text{parallelograms}\}$, $R = \{\text{rectangles}\}$
   c $\mathcal{E} = \{\text{quadrilaterals}\}$, $P = \{\text{parallelograms}\}$, $T = \{\text{trapezia}\}$
   d $\mathcal{E} = \{\text{quadrilaterals}\}$, $P = \{\text{parallelograms}\}$, $H = \{\text{rhombuses}\}$

7 Suppose the universal set is $\mathcal{E} = \mathbb{R}$, the set of all real numbers.

$\mathbb{Q}$, $\mathbb{Z}$, and $\mathbb{N}$ are all subsets of $\mathbb{R}$.

  a Copy the given Venn diagram and label the sets $\mathcal{E}$, $\mathbb{Q}$, $\mathbb{Z}$, and $\mathbb{N}$ on it.

  b Place these numbers on the Venn diagram:

    $\frac{1}{2}$, $\sqrt{2}$, $0.\overline{3}$, -5, $5\frac{1}{4}$, 0, 10, and

    $0.2137005618....$ which does not terminate or recur.

  c True or false?   **i** $\mathbb{N} \subseteq \mathbb{Z}$ **ii** $\mathbb{Z} \subseteq \mathbb{Q}$ **iii** $\mathbb{N} \subseteq \mathbb{Q}$

  d Shade the region representing the set of irrationals $\mathbb{Q}'$.

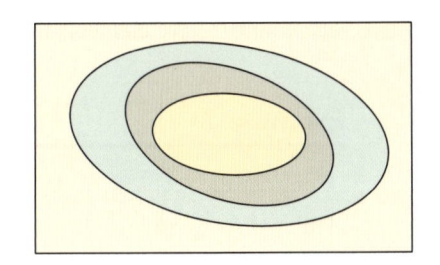

E   UNION AND INTERSECTION   [9.4]

THE UNION OF TWO SETS

$A \cup B$ denotes the **union** of sets A and B.

This set contains all elements belonging to A **or** B **or both** A and B.

$A \cup B = \{x \mid x \in A \text{ or } x \in B\}$

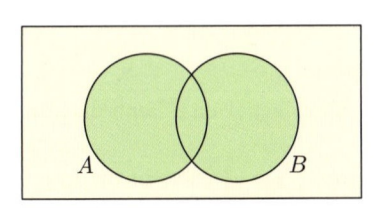

$A \cup B$ is shaded green.

THE INTERSECTION OF TWO SETS

$A \cap B$ denotes the **intersection** of sets A and B.

This is the set of all elements common to both sets.

$A \cap B = \{x \mid x \in A \text{ and } x \in B\}$

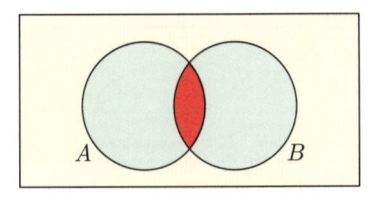

$A \cap B$ is shaded red.

In the Venn diagram alongside,

$A = \{2, 3, 4, 7\}$ and $B = \{1, 3, 7, 8, 10\}$.

We can see that $A \cap B = \{3, 7\}$

         and $A \cup B = \{1, 2, 3, 4, 7, 8, 10\}$.

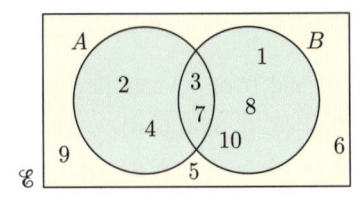

DISJOINT SETS

Two sets A and B are **disjoint** if they have no elements in common, or in other words if $A \cap B = \varnothing$.

If A and B have elements in common then they are **non-disjoint**.

Sets (Chapter 2)

Example 8

If $\mathscr{E} = \{\text{positive integers} \leq 12\}$, $A = \{\text{primes} \leq 12\}$ and $B = \{\text{factors of 12}\}$:

a List the elements of the sets A and B.
b Show the sets A, B and $\mathscr{E}$ on a Venn diagram.
c List the elements in: **i** A' **ii** $A \cap B$ **iii** $A \cup B$
d Find: **i** $n(A \cap B)$ **ii** $n(A \cup B)$ **iii** $n(B')$

a $A = \{2, 3, 5, 7, 11\}$ and $B = \{1, 2, 3, 4, 6, 12\}$

b

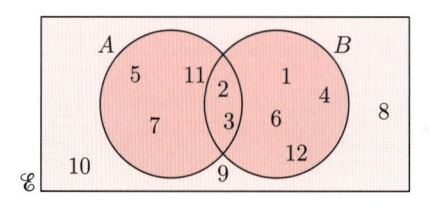

c **i** $A' = \{1, 4, 6, 8, 9, 10, 12\}$ **ii** $A \cap B = \{2, 3\}$
   iii $A \cup B = \{1, 2, 3, 4, 5, 6, 7, 11, 12\}$

d **i** $n(A \cap B) = 2$ **ii** $n(A \cup B) = 9$
   iii $B' = \{5, 7, 8, 9, 10, 11\}$, so $n(B') = 6$

EXERCISE 2E.1

1   **a** List:
   i set C **ii** set D **iii** set $\mathscr{E}$
   iv set $C \cap D$ **v** set $C \cup D$
   b Find:
   i $n(C)$ **ii** $n(D)$ **iii** $n(\mathscr{E})$
   iv $n(C \cap D)$ **v** $n(C \cup D)$

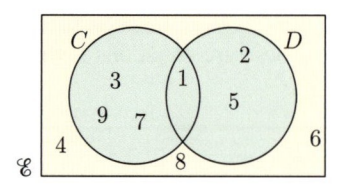

2   **a** List:
   i set A **ii** set B **iii** set $\mathscr{E}$
   iv set $A \cap B$ **v** set $A \cup B$
   b Find:
   i $n(A)$ **ii** $n(B)$ **iii** $n(\mathscr{E})$
   iv $n(A \cap B)$ **v** $n(A \cup B)$

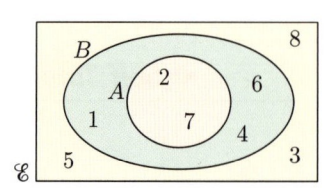

3 Consider $\mathscr{E} = \{x \mid x \leq 12, \ x \in \mathbb{Z}^+\}$,
$A = \{2, 7, 9, 10, 11\}$ and $B = \{1, 2, 9, 11, 12\}$.
   a Show these sets on a Venn diagram.
   b List the elements of: **i** $A \cap B$ **ii** $A \cup B$ **iii** B'
   c Find: **i** $n(A)$ **ii** $n(B')$ **iii** $n(A \cap B)$ **iv** $n(A \cup B)$

4 If A is the set of all factors of 36 and B is the set of all factors of 63, find:
   a $A \cap B$ **b** $A \cup B$

5 If $X = \{A, B, D, M, N, P, R, T, Z\}$ and $Y = \{B, C, M, T, W, Z\}$, find:
  a $X \cap Y$
  b $X \cup Y$

6 Suppose $\mathcal{E} = \{x \mid x \leqslant 30, \ x \in \mathbb{Z}^+\}$,
  $A = \{\text{factors of } 30\}$ and $B = \{\text{prime numbers} \leqslant 30\}$.
  a Find: **i** $n(A)$ **ii** $n(B)$ **iii** $n(A \cap B)$ **iv** $n(A \cup B)$
  b Use **a** to verify that $n(A \cup B) = n(A) + n(B) - n(A \cap B)$.

7 **a** Use the Venn diagram given to show that:
        $n(A \cup B) = n(A) + n(B) - n(A \cap B)$.
     b Suppose A and B are disjoint events.
        Explain why $n(A \cup B) = n(A) + n(B)$.

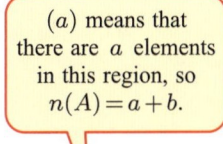

(a) means that there are a elements in this region, so $n(A) = a + b$.

8 Simplify:
  a $X \cap Y$ for $X = \{1, 3, 5, 7\}$ and $Y = \{2, 4, 6, 8\}$
  b $A \cup A'$ for any set $A \in \mathcal{E}$
  c $A \cap A'$ for any set $A \in \mathcal{E}$.

USING VENN DIAGRAMS TO ILLUSTRATE REGIONS

We can use a Venn diagram to help illustrate regions such as the union or intersection of sets.

Shaded regions of a Venn diagram can be used to verify **set identities**. These are equations involving sets which are true for *all* sets.

Examples of set identities include:

$$A \cup A' = \mathcal{E} \qquad\qquad A \cap A' = \varnothing$$
$$(A \cup B)' = A' \cap B' \qquad\qquad (A \cap B)' = A' \cup B'$$

Example 9   ◀)) Self Tutor

On separate Venn diagrams, shade the region representing:
  a in A or in B but not in both
  b $A' \cap B$

b We look for where the outside of A intersects (overlaps) with B.

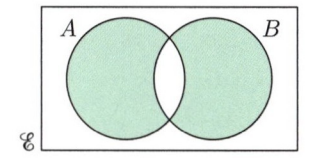

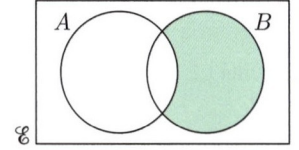

Sets (Chapter 2)

Example 10

Verify that $(A \cup B)' = A' \cap B'$.

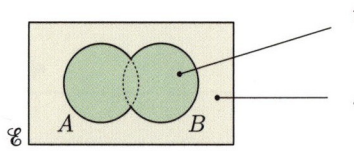

this shaded region is $(A \cup B)$

∴ this shaded region is $(A \cup B)'$

represents A'
represents B'
represents $A' \cap B'$

$(A \cup B)'$ and $A' \cap B'$ are represented by the same regions, verifying that $(A \cup B)' = A' \cap B'$.

EXERCISE 2E.2

1 On separate Venn diagrams like the one given, shade the region representing:
- **a** not in A
- **b** in both A and B
- **c** $A \cap B'$
- **d** in either A or B
- **e** $A \cup B'$
- **f** $(A \cup B)'$
- **g** $(A \cap B)'$
- **h** in exactly one of A or B.

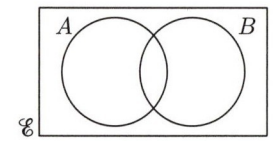

2 Describe in words, the shaded region of:
- **a**
- **b**
- **c**

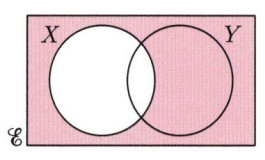

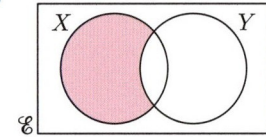

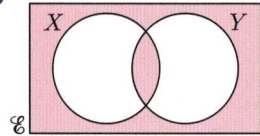

3 If A and B are two non-disjoint sets, shade the region of a Venn diagram representing:
- **a** A'
- **b** $A' \cap B$
- **c** $A' \cup B$
- **d** $A' \cap B'$

4 The Venn diagram alongside shows A and B when $B \subset A$. On diagrams like this one, shade the region representing:
- **a** A
- **b** B'
- **c** $A \cup B$
- **d** $A \cap B$

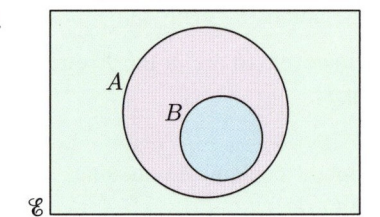

5 Verify that:
- **a** $(A \cap B)' = A' \cup B'$
- **b** $(A \cap B) \cup (A' \cap B) = B$

DEMO

F PROBLEM SOLVING   [9.3, 9.4]

When we solve problems with Venn diagrams, we generally do not deal with individual elements. Instead, we simply record the *number* of elements in each region.

Example 11   ◀)) Self Tutor

The Venn diagram alongside illustrates the number of people in a sporting club who play tennis (T) and hockey (H). Determine the number of people:

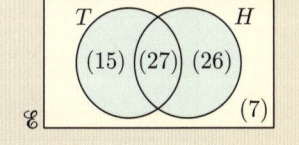

- **a** in the club
- **b** who play hockey
- **c** who play both sports
- **d** who play neither sport
- **e** who play at least one sport.

- **a** Number in the club $= 15 + 27 + 26 + 7 = 75$
- **b** Number who play hockey $= 27 + 26 = 53$
- **c** Number who play both sports $= 27$
- **d** Number who play neither sport $= 7$
- **e** Number who play at least one sport $= 15 + 27 + 26 = 68$

Example 12   ◀)) Self Tutor

In a class of 24 boys, 16 play football and 11 play baseball. If two play neither game, how many play both games?

Method 1:

Let x be the number who play both games.

$\therefore$ $16 - x$ play football and $11 - x$ play baseball.

2 boys play neither sport.

$\therefore$ $(16 - x) + x + (11 - x) + 2 = 24$

$\therefore$ $29 - x = 24$

$\therefore$ $x = 5$

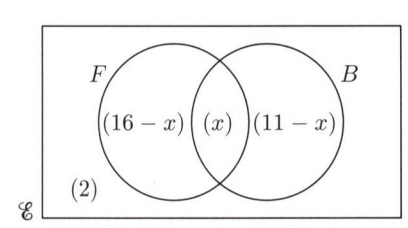

So, 5 play both games.

Method 2:

2 boys play neither game, so $24 - 2 = 22$ must be in the union $F \cup B$.

However, 16 are in the F circle, so 6 must go in the rest of B.

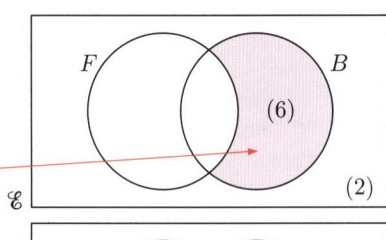

But B contains 11 in total, so 5 go in the intersection $F \cap B$.

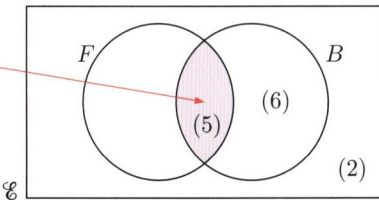

So, 5 play both games.

Sets (Chapter 2)

EXERCISE 2F

1 A survey was conducted with a group of teenagers to see how many liked going to the cinema (C) and ice-skating (I). The results are shown in the Venn diagram. Determine the number of teenagers:

   a in the group

   b who like going to the cinema

   c who like at least one of these activities

   d who only like ice-skating

   e who do not like going ice-skating.

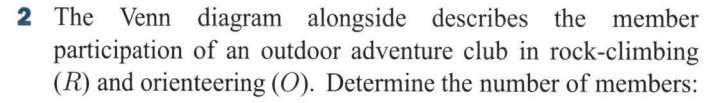

2 The Venn diagram alongside describes the member participation of an outdoor adventure club in rock-climbing (R) and orienteering (O). Determine the number of members:

   a in the club

   b who go rock-climbing

   c who do not go orienteering

   d who rock-climb but do not orienteer

   e who do exactly one of these activities.

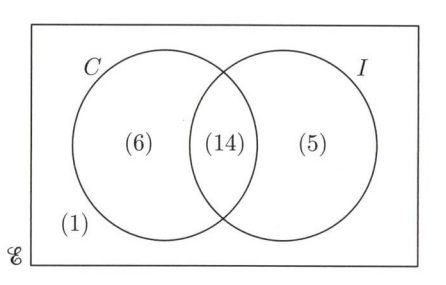

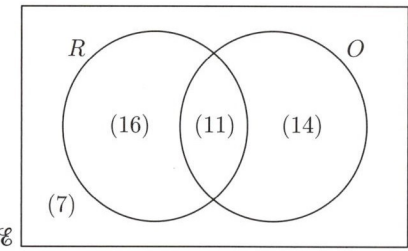

3 A team of 24 swimmers took part in a competition. 15 competed in freestyle, 11 competed in backstroke, and 6 competed in both of these strokes. Display this information on a Venn diagram, and hence determine the number of swimmers who competed in:

   a backstroke but not freestyle   **b** at least one of these strokes

   c freestyle but not backstroke   **d** neither stroke

   e exactly one of these strokes.

4 In a building with 58 apartments, 45 households have children, 19 have pets, and 5 have neither children nor pets. Draw a Venn diagram to display this information, and hence determine the number of households which:

   a do not have children   **b** have children or pets or both

   c have children or pets but not both   **d** have pets but not children

   e have children but not pets.

5 In a class of 36 girls, 18 play volleyball, 13 play badminton, and 11 play neither sport. Determine the number of girls who play both volleyball and badminton.

6 At their beachhouse, Anna and Ben have 37 books. Anna has read 21 of them and Ben has read 26 of them. 2 of the books have not been read at all. Find the number of books which have been read by:

   a both Anna and Ben   **b** Ben but not Anna.

7 On a particular day, 500 people visited a carnival. 300 people rode the ferris wheel and 350 people rode the roller coaster. Each person rode at least one of these attractions. Using a Venn diagram, find how many people rode:

   a both attractions   **b** the ferris wheel but not the roller coaster.

8 There are 46 shops in the local mall. 25 shops sell clothes, 16 sell shoes, and 34 sell at least one of these items. With the aid of a Venn diagram, determine how many shops sell:

   a both clothes and shoes   **b** neither clothes nor shoes   **c** clothes but not shoes.

9 Joe owns an automotive garage which does car services and mechanical repairs. In one week 18 cars had services or repairs, 9 had services, and 5 had both services and repairs. How many cars had repairs?

10 All the guests at a barbecue ate either sausages or chicken shashliks. 18 people ate sausages, 15 ate sausages and chicken shashliks, and 24 ate exactly one of sausages or chicken shashliks. How many guests attended the barbecue?

11 At a dance school each member studies at least one of classical ballet or modern dance. 72% study classical ballet and 35% study modern dance. What percentage of the students study both classical ballet and modern dance?

12 A group of 28 workers are repairing a road. 9 use machinery, 15 do not use shovels, and 7 do not use either machinery or shovels. How many workers use both machinery and shovels?

Review set 2A

1   **a** Explain why 1.3 is a rational number.   **b** True or false? $\sqrt{4000} \in \mathbb{Q}$
   c List the set of all prime numbers between 20 and 40.
   d Write a statement describing the meaning of $\{t \mid -1 \leq t < 3\}$.
   e Write in interval notation: 
   f Sketch the number set $\{x \mid -2 \leq x \leq 3, \ x \in \mathbb{Z}\}$.

2 Suppose $\mathcal{E} = \{x \mid x \leq 12, \ x \in \mathbb{Z}^+\}$ and $A = \{\text{multiples of } 3 \leq 12\}$.
   a Show A on a Venn diagram.   **b** List the set A'.
   c Find $n(A')$.   **d** True or false? If $C = \{1, 2, 4\}$ then $C \subseteq A$.

3 List the proper subsets of $M = \{1, 3, 6, 8\}$.

4 True or false?   **a** $\mathbb{N} \subseteq \mathbb{Z}^+$ **b** $\mathbb{Q} \subseteq \mathbb{Z}$

5   **a** List:
     i set A **ii** set B **iii** set $\mathcal{E}$
     iv set $A \cup B$ **v** set $A \cap B$
   b Find:
     i $n(A)$ **ii** $n(B)$ **iii** $n(A \cup B)$

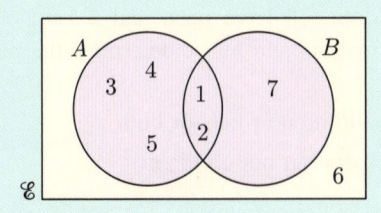

6 Consider $\mathcal{E} = \{x \mid x \leq 10, \ x \in \mathbb{Z}^+\}$, $P = \{2, 3, 5, 7\}$ and $Q = \{2, 4, 6, 8\}$.
   a Show these sets on a Venn diagram.
   b List the elements of: **i** $P \cap Q$ **ii** $P \cup Q$ **iii** Q'
   c Find: **i** $n(P')$ **ii** $n(P \cap Q)$ **iii** $n(P \cup Q)$
   d True or false? $P \cap Q \subseteq P$

7 Describe in words the shaded region of:
   a   **b** 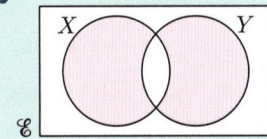   **c**

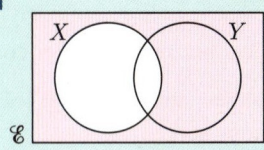

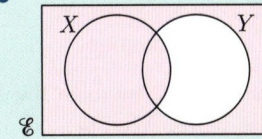

8 In a survey at an airport, 76 travellers said that last year they had been to Japan, 58 said they had visited China, and 40 had been to both. 411 had been to neither. Draw a Venn diagram to illustrate this information, and use it to find how many travellers took part in the survey.

Review set 2B

1 a True or false?   **i** $-2 \in \mathbb{Z}^+$ **ii** $\frac{1}{\sqrt{7}} \in \mathbb{Q}$

  b Show that $0.\overline{51}$ is a rational number.

  c Write in interval notation: [number line from -3 (closed) to 4 (open), variable t]

  d Sketch the number set $\{x \mid x \leqslant 3 \text{ or } x > 7, \ x \in \mathbb{R}\}$.

2 Illustrate these numbers on a Venn diagram like the one opposite:

  $-1, \ \sqrt{2}, \ 2, \ 3.1, \ \pi, \ 4.\overline{2}$

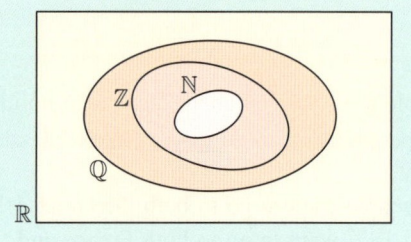

3 Show this information on a Venn diagram:

  a $\mathcal{E} = \{10, 11, 12, 13, 14, 15\}, \quad A = \{10, 12, 14\}, \quad B = \{11, 12, 13\}$

  b $\mathcal{E} = \{\text{quadrilaterals}\}, \quad S = \{\text{squares}\}, \quad R = \{\text{rectangles}\}$

  c $\mathcal{E} = \mathbb{N}, \quad A = \{\text{multiples of } 2\}, \quad B = \{\text{multiples of } 3\}$.

4 If A is the set of all factors of 24 and B is the set of all factors of 18, find:

  a $A \cap B$ **b** $A \cup B$

5 Suppose $\mathcal{E} = \{x \mid x \leqslant 10, \ x \in \mathbb{Z}^+\}$, $A = \{\text{primes less than 10}\}$, and $B = \{\text{odd numbers between 0 and 10}\}$.

  a Show these sets on a Venn diagram.

  b List: **i** A' **ii** $A \cap B$

  c True or false?   **i** $A \subset B$ **ii** $A \cap B \subseteq A$

  d Find: **i** $n(A)$ **ii** $n(B')$ **iii** $n(A \cup B)$.

6 On separate Venn diagrams like the one shown, shade the region representing:

  a B' **b** in A and in B **c** $(A \cup B)'$

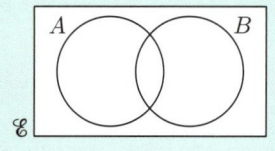

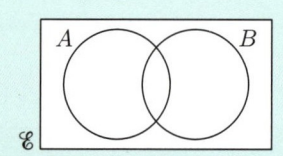

7 Using separate Venn diagrams like the one shown, shade regions to verify that

$A \cup B' = (A' \cap B)'$.

8 Participants in a survey were asked if they had done volunteer work or donated to charity in the last month. 34% had volunteered, 76% had donated to charity, and 19% had done neither. Draw a Venn diagram and use it to find what percentage of participants only volunteered.

Challenge

1 50 people were surveyed at a concert that had 3 bands: The Artists, The Brave, and The Cold, and were asked who they enjoyed listening to.

27 people said they liked listening to The Artists, 26 liked The Brave, and 35 liked The Cold. 12 people liked both The Artists and The Brave, 22 liked both The Artists and The Cold, and 18 liked The Brave and The Cold. 10 people liked all three bands.

Record this information on a Venn diagram like the one alongside, and hence find the number of people surveyed who did not like any of the three bands.

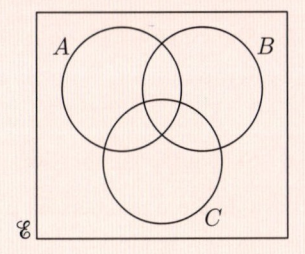

2 150 people are surveyed about their ideal holiday destination in Europe.

40% of people want to go to the Greek Islands, 42% want to go to Italy, and 48% want to go to France.

28% of people want to go to both the Greek Islands and Italy. 24% want to go to both France and Italy, and 18% want to go to both France and the Greek Islands. 16% want to go to all 3.

    a Copy the given Venn diagram and use the information above to complete it.

    b Find the number of people who want to go to:
        i the Greek Islands only
        ii Italy only
        iii Italy, given that they also want to go to France.

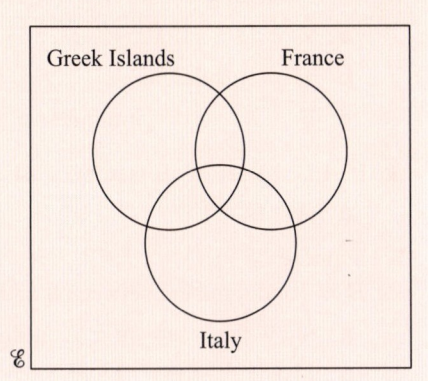

Algebra (expressions and equations)

3

Contents:

- **A** Basic problem solving
- **B** Introduction to algebra
- **C** Evaluating expressions
- **D** Algebraic expressions
- **E** Linear equations [2.3]
- **F** Equations of the form $x^2 = k$
- **G** Forming equations
- **H** Problem solving using equations

Opening problem

Flour comes in 7 kg and 10 kg sacks. A bakery has 217 kg of flour in 25 sacks. How many sacks of each weight are at the bakery?

A BASIC PROBLEM SOLVING

Some problems involving numbers we can solve in our heads. We say we are using **mental arithmetic**.

For example, "10 is 4 bigger than a certain number. What is the number?"

We know that $6 + 4 = 10$, so the number we want is 6.

EXERCISE 3A

Solve these problems using mental arithmetic:

1. 2 more than a number is 7. Find the number.
2. Which number is 3 more than 11?
3. Half of a number is 14. What is the number?

4 A number is increased by 5 to get 12. What was the number?

5 When 16 is decreased by a certain number, the answer is 4. Find the number.

6 What number is twice as big as 9?

7 8 is a quarter of which number?

8 27 is one more than double a certain number. What is the number?

9 Find two consecutive numbers that add to 19.

10 Consider this matchstick pattern:

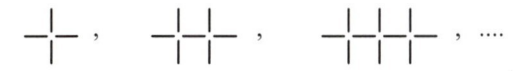

How many matchsticks are needed for the:
  a first pattern
  b second pattern
  c third pattern
  d tenth pattern?

B INTRODUCTION TO ALGEBRA

The problems we have seen so far are simple enough to solve mentally. For harder problems we use a technique called **algebra**. In the following sections we go through basic algebra techniques and then apply these to problem solving.

WORDS USED IN ALGEBRA

It is important to know the following words and their meanings.

> A **numeral** is a symbol used to represent a known number.

For example: 2, 5, 0, 1.47, -6 and $\frac{4}{7}$ are all numerals.

> A **variable** is an unknown number. We represent variables with letters called **pronumerals**.

For example: the *height of the building* is represented by h
the *number of broken watches* is represented by w.

> An **expression** is an algebraic form made up of numerals, variables, and operation signs like $+, -, \times, \div, \sqrt{\ }$.

For example: $3(y - \sqrt{7})$ and $\dfrac{-5}{4+t}$ are both expressions.

> An **equation** is an algebraic form containing the equals sign '='.

For example: $2x + 7 = 43$ and $\sqrt{x-4} = y$ are both equations.

> The parts of an expression or equation separated by the $+$, $-$ or $=$ signs are called **terms**. $-$ signs are included in the term.

For example: in $2x + 5y - 4$, the terms are $2x$, $5y$, and -4
in $-a = 2b + c$, the terms are $-a$, $2b$, and c.

Algebra (expressions and equations) (Chapter 3)

Two (or more) terms are called **like terms** if they have exactly the same combination of variables.

For example:
- $2x$ and $-5x$ are like terms {both have x}
- xy^2 and $4xy^2$ are like terms {both have xy^2}
- -3 and 6 are like terms {both have no variables}
- $3x$ and 4 are unlike terms {only one has x}
- $5x$ and $2x^2$ are unlike terms {one has x and the other x^2}
- $4xy$ and x are unlike terms {one has xy and the other only x}

A **constant term** is any term that does not contain a variable.

For example:
- in $2x + 7$, the constant term is 7
- in $3x - 5 = x + 4$, the constant terms are -5 and 4
- in $3x^2 - y + x$, there is no constant term.

The **coefficient** of any term is its numerical part, including the sign.

For example:
- in $3x - 4$, we say "the first term has coefficient 3" or "the coefficient of x is 3"
- in $5 - 8k$, we say "the second term has coefficient -8" or "the coefficient of k is -8"
- in $x + 6$, the coefficient of x is 1, as x is really $1 \times x$.

EXERCISE 3B

1 Are the following statements true or false? Correct the false statements.
   - **a** $z + 9$ is an equation
   - **b** $3t + 3$ is an expression
   - **c** $C = 8 - \frac{1}{5}p$ is an equation
   - **d** $K = 4 + 5v$ is an expression
   - **e** $5p + 5y - 5$ has 5 terms
   - **f** the coefficient of x in $2x - 4y + 7$ is 2
   - **g** the coefficient of y in $3x - 2y - 4$ is 2
   - **h** the constant term in $5a + b - 4$ is 4
   - **i** the constant term in $7 + 3s + t$ is 1.

2 Find the coefficient of x in each of the following:
   - **a** $3x$
   - **b** $2 + 5x$
   - **c** $6x + 1$
   - **d** $3y + 2x + 7$
   - **e** $x + 1$
   - **f** $z - 3x + 4$
   - **g** $4 - x$
   - **h** $x - 4$
   - **i** $-\frac{1}{2}x + 3$

3 How many terms are in each expression in question **2**?

4 Consider the expression $2y - 5z - 3 + 4y$.
   - **a** How many terms are in the expression?
   - **b** What is the constant term?
   - **c** What are the like terms?
   - **d** What is the coefficient of z?

5 State the like terms in:
   - **a** $y + x + 2z + 3x$
   - **b** $y + 2z + 4z - 5$
   - **c** $3z - y - 2x + 4y$
   - **d** $y + 2 - 3x + 8$
   - **e** $-5x + 3 + 2x - 1$
   - **f** $3xy - x + 4xy - 2$

6 Consider the expression $2 - x^2 - 3x$. Match each clue with its answer:
   - **a** number of terms
   - **b** second term
   - **c** coefficient of x
   - **d** constant term
   - **A** $-x^2$
   - **B** 2
   - **C** 3
   - **D** -3

C EVALUATING EXPRESSIONS

If we know the values of the variables in an expression, we can **evaluate** the expression. We **substitute** the known values in place of the variables, then calculate the result.

Example 1

If $r = 3$, $s = -2$, and $t = 5$, evaluate:

a $4r - s$ **b** rst **c** $(r + t)^2$

a $4r - s = 4 \times 3 - (-2)$
$= 12 + 2$
$= 14$

b $rst = 3 \times (-2) \times 5$
$= -30$

c $(r + t)^2 = (3 + 5)^2$
$= 8^2$
$= 64$

EXERCISE 3C

1 If $a = 2$ and $b = 7$, find the values of the following expressions:
- **a** $3b$
- **b** $2(a + b)$
- **c** $3 + 2b$
- **d** $7a - 2b$
- **e** $11 - b - a$
- **f** $a(b - 4)$
- **g** $10a - b$
- **h** $(a + 1)(b - 2)$
- **i** $4(b - 3a)$
- **j** $a + 3b - 8$
- **k** $8 - a$
- **l** $2(b - a) + 5$

2 If $x = 5$, $y = 1$, and $z = 3$, find the value of:
- **a** $y + 3z$
- **b** $z - 2xy$
- **c** $(x + z)(x - z)$
- **d** xyz
- **e** $x - 2y + 3z$
- **f** $x^2 - y^2$
- **g** $xz - 7y$
- **h** $3y^2$

3 If $p = -2$, $q = 0$, $r = 4$, and $s = 3$, evaluate:
- **a** $p + s^2$
- **b** $3r - 4s$
- **c** $pqrs$
- **d** $-3p^2 s$
- **e** $(pr)^2$
- **f** $p^2 + s^3$
- **g** $pr^2 s$
- **h** $p^2 r + p^2 q$

4 Given $d = -2$, $e = -3$, $f = 4$, and $g = -1$, evaluate:
- **a** $de + g$
- **b** e^2
- **c** $5d^2 - g^2$
- **d** $(f - e)^2$
- **e** $d^2 + f^2$
- **f** $de - dg$
- **g** $f - g^3$
- **h** $de + fg^2$

5 Given $m = 5$, $n = 7$, and $p = -3$, find the value of:
- **a** $m^2 - n^2$
- **b** $\sqrt{n - 3p}$
- **c** $\dfrac{mp}{n - 2}$
- **d** $p^2 m$
- **e** $\dfrac{3p - 2}{n}$
- **f** $mn - p$
- **g** $n(m + p)$
- **h** $m^2 + 2p^2$

D ALGEBRAIC EXPRESSIONS

KEY WORDS

When we are given a mathematical problem in words, we need to look for **key words** which tell us which operations to use. In particular we look for words associated with **sums**, **differences**, **products**, and **quotients**.

Algebra (expressions and equations)   (Chapter 3)

Examples of key words are shown in the table alongside.

Statement	Translation
decreased by	subtract
more than	add
double	multiply by 2
halve	divide by 2

Example 2   ◆) Self Tutor

a State the sum of 7 and x.
b Find the difference between y and 5, where $y > 5$.
c Write down the quotient of m and z.

> For a quotient we write the first number mentioned divided by the second.

a The sum of 7 and x is $7 + x$.
b The difference between y and 5 is $y - 5$
   {as y is greater than 5}.
c The quotient of m and z is $\dfrac{m}{z}$.

EXERCISE 3D.1

1 State the sum of:
  a 4 and 3   **b** 2 and x **c** y and z **d** m, n, and o

> When we write an algebraic product, we list the letters in alphabetical order.

2 Write down the product of:
  a 5 and 8   **b** a and 6   **c** $2b$ and c **d** e, i and u

3 Find the quotient of:
  a 7 and 3   **b** 5 and t **c** k and $6l$
  d the sum of f and g, and r

4 Write an expression for the difference between:
  a 6 and 9   **b** 2 and r if $2 < r$ **c** x and y if $x > y$

5 Write down algebraic expressions for:
  a the sum of a and $3k$
  b $2z$ subtract $5s$
  c the quotient of b squared, and 7
  d 6 less than three times d
  e a number x times the size of y
  f the total of l, twice m, and n
  g the product of r and half of s
  h w divided by the square root of h

WRITING EXPRESSIONS

When given a real world problem, it is often easier to think in terms of numbers before writing an algebraic expression.

For example, suppose we need to find the total cost of m melons where each melon costs $\$d$.

If there were 7 melons and each melon cost $\$4$, the total cost would be $7 \times \$4 = \$28$.

We see that to find the total cost, we multiply the number of melons by the cost of each melon. So, the total cost of m melons at $\$d$ each is $m \times \$d = \$dm$.

Example 3

Find:
a the total length of x cables, each one 15 m long
b the change from £20 when buying b bus fares at £2 each.

a If we had 8 cables, each one 15 m long,
the total length of 8 cables 15 m long would be 8×15 m.
$\therefore$ the total length of x cables 15 m long is $x \times 15 = 15x$ m.

b If we bought 3 bus fares at £2 each,
the change would be $20 - (3 \times 2)$ pounds.
$\therefore$ the change when buying b bus fares at £2 each is $20 - (b \times 2)$ pounds
$= 20 - 2b$ pounds.

EXERCISE 3D.2

1 Find the total cost, in pence, of:
  a 6 candles at 90 pence each
  b c candles at 90 pence each
  c c candles at y pence each.

2 Find the total mass of:
  a 8 tins of mass 3 kg each
  b t tins of mass 3 kg each
  c t tins of mass m kg each.

3 Find the change from ¥5000 when buying:
  a 12 pens at ¥200 each
  b p pens at ¥200 each
  c p pens at ¥q each.

4 Find the cost per mug if:
  a 8 mugs cost €40
  b a mugs cost €40
  c a mugs cost €b.

5 Danielle is 130 cm tall. How high will she be if she grows k cm?

6 An essay has a 6 line introduction, x lines in the main body, and 7 lines in the conclusion. If the bibliography is z lines, how long is the essay?

7 A saucepan of soup contains 14 litres.
  a If 8 bowls of soup are poured, each containing v litres, how much soup is left?
  b If b bowls of soup are poured, each containing v litres, how much soup is left?

8 a A hiker travels at an average speed of 4 km/h for 3 hours. How far does the hiker travel?
  b How far does the hiker travel if she walks at an average speed of k km/h for t hours?
  c What is the hiker's average speed if she walks s km in 5 hours?

9 Swimming caps cost €4 and goggles cost €7. Find the total cost of c caps and g pairs of goggles.

10 A company makes soft drinks in boxes of 12 cans. The cans cost a cents to produce, and the box costs b cents. Find the sale price for the company to make $2.50 profit per box.

11 Find the mean mass of three bricks weighing f, g and h grams.

Example 4

Convert into an algebraic expression:

a 11 greater than a number
b 4 less than a number
c half a number
d double the sum of a number and 5.

a 11 greater than a number is the number plus 11, or $x + 11$.
b 4 less than a number is the number minus 4, or $n - 4$.
c Half a number is the number divided by 2, or $\frac{k}{2}$.
d The sum of a number and 5 is $a + 5$,
so double this sum $= 2 \times (a + 5) = 2(a + 5)$.

We can use any pronumeral we choose if none is given.

12 Convert into an algebraic expression:
  a 2 more than a number
  b 6 less than a number
  c a number tripled
  d one fifth of a number
  e 7 times greater than a number
  f the sum of a number and 6
  g 3 more than twice a number
  h 9 less than a quarter of a certain number.

13 Copy and complete:
  a Two numbers have a difference of 5. If the larger one is x, the smaller one is ....
  b A runner has run y m of a 100 m sprint. The runner has .... m to go.
  c There are twice as many chickens as eggs. If there are e eggs, there are .... chickens.
  d Two numbers are in the ratio $1 : 3$. If the smaller number is a, the larger one is ....
  e Two consecutive integers in ascending order are j and ....
  f Three consecutive integers in descending order are u, ..., ...
  g The sum of two numbers is 17. One of them is m and the other is ....
  h Two consecutive odd numbers are o and ....

Example 5

Lyn goes shopping and buys 9 pieces of fruit. She buys x peaches which cost 70 pence each, and the rest nectarines which cost 55 pence each. Write an expression for the total cost of Lyn's fruit.

The numbers of peaches and nectarines add up to 9.
$\therefore$ since Lyn bought x peaches, she bought $(9 - x)$ nectarines.

The peaches cost $\quad x \times 70 = 70x\;$ pence.

The nectarines cost $\quad (9 - x) \times 55 = 55(9 - x)\;$ pence.

$\therefore\;$ the total cost $= 70x + 55(9 - x)\;$ pence.

14
  a The smallest of three consecutive numbers is s. Write an expression for the sum of the three numbers.
  b Write an expression for the sum of two consecutive odd numbers.
  c Kurt has x five cent coins and $x + 3$ twenty cent coins. Write an expression for the total value of Kurt's coins.
  d Nadia bought 20 fish for her aquarium. She bought g guppies and the rest were tetras. Guppies cost €5 each and tetras cost €4 each. Write an expression for the total amount Nadia spent on fish.
  e Mushtaq bought 17 balls. Some were basketballs and the rest were fitness balls. Basketballs cost £23 each and fitness balls cost £15 each. Write an algebraic expression for the total cost of the balls, in terms of one pronumeral.

E LINEAR EQUATIONS [2.3]

An **equation** is a statement that two expressions are equal. When we have an *equation*, we follow a formal procedure to **solve** the equation.

SIDES OF AN EQUATION

> The **left hand side** (LHS) of an equation is on the left of the $=$ sign.
> The **right hand side** (RHS) of an equation is on the right of the $=$ sign.

For example, $3x + 7 = 13$
            LHS   RHS

THE SOLUTIONS OF AN EQUATION

> The **solutions** of an equation are the values of the variable which make the equation true, which means the **left hand side** (**LHS**) is equal to the **right hand side** (**RHS**).

In the example $3x + 7 = 13$ above, the only value of the variable x which makes the equation true is $x = 2$.

Notice that when $x = 2$, LHS $= 3x + 7$
                                $= 3 \times 2 + 7$
                                $= 6 + 7$
                                $= 13$
                                $=$ RHS $\therefore$ LHS $=$ RHS

There are many types of equations, but in this course we will focus mainly on **linear** equations.

> A **linear equation** is an equation where the variables are only raised to the power of 1.

For example, $3x + 4 = 2$, $\frac{2}{3}x + 1 = 6$, and $\frac{x-1}{4} = 8 - x$ are all linear equations.

$x^2 + 4x = -5$ is not a linear equation since the variable x is raised to the power 2 in one of the terms.
$\sqrt{x} - 3 = 4x$ is not a linear equation as there is a square root of the variable x.

Algebra (expressions and equations)   (Chapter 3)

MAINTAINING BALANCE

The two sides of an equation are like the two sides of a set of scales. Just like scales, we want to keep equations in **balance**. To do this we perform the same operation on **both sides** of the equals sign.

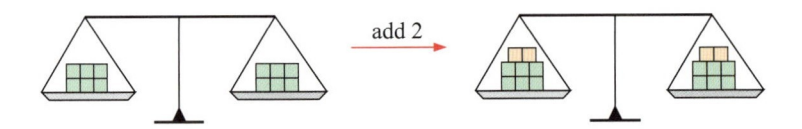

Adding to, subtracting from, multiplying by, and dividing by the same quantity on **both sides** of an equation will **maintain the balance** or **equality**.

For example, consider the linear equation $2x + 3 = 8$.
Using ▭ for x and • for the number 1, we represent $2x + 3$ on one side of a set of scales, and 8 on the other. The = tells us that the sides are balanced.

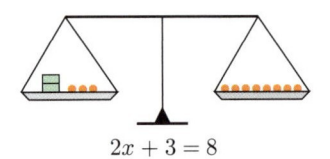

If we take 3 from both sides of the scales, the scales will still be balanced.

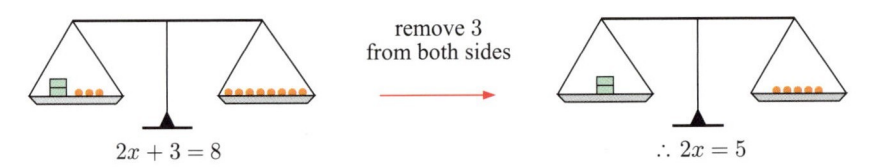

We keep performing operations on both sides of each equation in order to **isolate the unknown**. We consider how the expression has been **built up**, then **isolate the unknown** by using **inverse operations** in **reverse order**.

For example, for the equation $2x + 3 = 8$, the LHS is built up by starting with x, multiplying by 2, then adding 3.

So, to isolate x, we first subtract 3 from both sides, then divide both sides by 2.

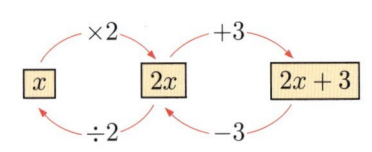

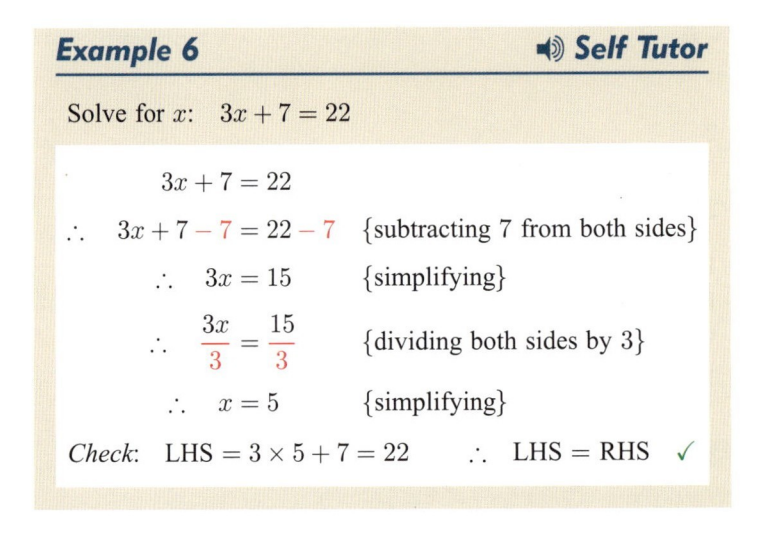

Example 6   ◀) Self Tutor

Solve for x: $3x + 7 = 22$

$3x + 7 = 22$

$\therefore \ 3x + 7 - 7 = 22 - 7$ {subtracting 7 from both sides}

$\therefore \ 3x = 15$ {simplifying}

$\therefore \ \dfrac{3x}{3} = \dfrac{15}{3}$ {dividing both sides by 3}

$\therefore \ x = 5$ {simplifying}

Check: LHS $= 3 \times 5 + 7 = 22$ $\therefore$ LHS = RHS ✓

The inverse operation for $+7$ is -7.

Example 7

Solve for x: $\quad 11 - 5x = 26$

$$11 - 5x = 26$$
$$\therefore \quad 11 - 5x - 11 = 26 - 11 \quad \text{\{subtracting 11 from both sides\}}$$
$$\therefore \quad -5x = 15 \quad \text{\{simplifying\}}$$
$$\therefore \quad \frac{-5x}{-5} = \frac{15}{-5} \quad \text{\{dividing both sides by } -5\text{\}}$$
$$\therefore \quad x = -3 \quad \text{\{simplifying\}}$$

Check: LHS $= 11 - 5 \times -3 = 11 + 15 = 26 \quad \therefore$ LHS = RHS ✓

Example 8

Solve for x: $\quad \dfrac{x}{3} + 2 = -2$

$$\frac{x}{3} + 2 = -2$$
$$\therefore \quad \frac{x}{3} + 2 - 2 = -2 - 2 \quad \text{\{subtracting 2 from both sides\}}$$
$$\therefore \quad \frac{x}{3} = -4$$
$$\therefore \quad \frac{x}{3} \times 3 = -4 \times 3 \quad \text{\{multiplying both sides by 3\}}$$
$$\therefore \quad x = -12$$

Check: LHS $= -\frac{12}{3} + 2 = -4 + 2 = -2 =$ RHS. ✓

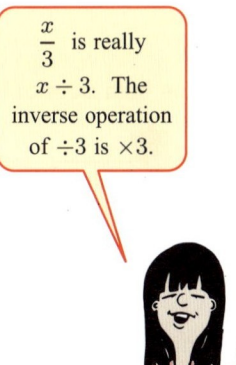

$\dfrac{x}{3}$ is really $x \div 3$. The inverse operation of $\div 3$ is $\times 3$.

Example 9

Solve for x: $\quad \dfrac{4x + 3}{5} = -2$

$$\frac{4x + 3}{5} = -2$$
$$\therefore \quad 5 \times \frac{(4x + 3)}{5} = -2 \times 5 \quad \text{\{multiplying both sides by 5\}}$$
$$\therefore \quad 4x + 3 = -10$$
$$\therefore \quad 4x + 3 - 3 = -10 - 3 \quad \text{\{subtracting 3 from both sides\}}$$
$$\therefore \quad 4x = -13$$
$$\therefore \quad \frac{4x}{4} = -\frac{13}{4} \quad \text{\{dividing both sides by 4\}}$$
$$\therefore \quad x = -3\tfrac{1}{4}$$

Algebra (expressions and equations) (Chapter 3)

EXERCISE 3E.1

1 Solve for x:
- **a** $x + 11 = 0$
- **b** $4x = -12$
- **c** $5x + 35 = 0$
- **d** $4x - 5 = -17$
- **e** $5x + 3 = 28$
- **f** $3x - 9 = 18$
- **g** $8x - 1 = 7$
- **h** $3x + 5 = -10$
- **i** $13 + 7x = -1$
- **j** $14 = 3x + 5$
- **k** $4x - 7 = -13$
- **l** $-3 = 2x + 9$

2 Solve for x:
- **a** $8 - x = -3$
- **b** $-4x = 22$
- **c** $3 - 2x = 11$
- **d** $6 - 4x = -8$
- **e** $3 - 7x = -4$
- **f** $17 - 2x = -5$
- **g** $15 = 3 - 2x$
- **h** $24 - 3x = -9$
- **i** $4 = 3 - 2x$
- **j** $13 = -1 - 7x$
- **k** $-21 = 3 - 6x$
- **l** $23 = -4 - 3x$

3 Solve for x:
- **a** $\dfrac{x}{4} = 7$
- **b** $\dfrac{2x}{5} = -6$
- **c** $\dfrac{x}{2} + 3 = -5$
- **d** $\dfrac{x}{4} - 2 = -5$
- **e** $\dfrac{x-1}{3} = 6$
- **f** $\dfrac{x+5}{6} = -1$
- **g** $4 = \dfrac{2+x}{3}$
- **h** $-1 + \dfrac{x}{3} = 7$

4 Solve for x:
- **a** $\dfrac{2x+11}{3} = 0$
- **b** $\tfrac{1}{2}(3x+1) = -4$
- **c** $\dfrac{1+2x}{5} = 7$
- **d** $\dfrac{1-2x}{5} = 3$
- **e** $\tfrac{1}{4}(1-3x) = -2$
- **f** $\tfrac{1}{4}(5-2x) = -3$

EQUATIONS WITH A REPEATED UNKNOWN

Equations where the unknown appears more than once need to be solved systematically. Generally, we:
- collect like terms
- use inverse operations to isolate the unknown.

Remember to always maintain the balance of the equation.

When the unknown appears on both sides of the equation, remove it from one side. Aim to do this so the unknown is left with a **positive** coefficient.

Example 10

Solve for x: $5x + 2 = 3x - 5$

$5x + 2 = 3x - 5$
$\therefore \; 5x + 2 - 3x = 3x - 5 - 3x$ {subtracting $3x$ from both sides}
$\therefore \; 2x + 2 = -5$
$\therefore \; 2x + 2 - 2 = -5 - 2$ {subtracting 2 from both sides}
$\therefore \; 2x = -7$
$\therefore \; \dfrac{2x}{2} = \dfrac{-7}{2}$ {dividing both sides by 2}
$\therefore \; x = -3\tfrac{1}{2}$

Example 11

Solve for x: $15 - 2x = 11 + x$

$15 - 2x = 11 + x$
$\therefore \quad 15 - 2x + 2x = 11 + x + 2x$ {adding $2x$ to both sides}
$\therefore \quad 15 = 11 + 3x$
$\therefore \quad 15 - 11 = 11 + 3x - 11$ {subtracting 11 from both sides}
$\therefore \quad 4 = 3x$
$\therefore \quad \dfrac{4}{3} = \dfrac{3x}{3}$ {dividing both sides by 3}
$\therefore \quad x = 1\tfrac{1}{3}$

EXERCISE 3E.2

1 Solve for x:
- **a** $5x + 2 = 3x + 14$
- **b** $8x + 7 = 4x - 5$
- **c** $7x + 3 = 2x + 9$
- **d** $3x - 8 = 5x - 2$
- **e** $x - 3 = 5x + 11$
- **f** $3 + x = 15 + 4x$
- **g** $2x - 9 = 4x - 3$
- **h** $7x + 8 = 4 - x$
- **i** $9x - 11 = 15x + 4$

2 Solve for x:
- **a** $6 + 2x = 15 - x$
- **b** $3x + 7 = 15 - x$
- **c** $5 + x = 11 - 2x$
- **d** $17 - 3x = 4 - x$
- **e** $8 - x = x + 6$
- **f** $9 - 2x = 3 - x$
- **g** $20 - x = 14 + 3x$
- **h** $13 + 3x = 5 - x$
- **i** $8 - 3x = 5 - 5x$

F   EQUATIONS OF THE FORM $x^2 = k$

Consider the equation $x^2 = 25$.
We know that $5^2 = 25$, so $x = 5$ is one solution.
But we also know $(-5)^2 = 25$, so $x = -5$ is *also* a solution.
So, if $x^2 = 25$, $x = \pm 5$

± 5 is read as 'plus or minus 5'

Now consider $x^2 = -9$.

We know that no real number has a negative square, so $x^2 = -9$ has **no real solutions**.

Equations of the form $x^2 = k$ are known as **quadratic equations**. They may have zero, one or two solutions.

If $x^2 = k$ then $\begin{cases} x = \pm\sqrt{k} & \text{if } k > 0 \\ x = 0 & \text{if } k = 0 \\ \text{there are } \textbf{no real solutions} \text{ if } k < 0. \end{cases}$

Algebra (expressions and equations) (Chapter 3)

Example 12
Self Tutor

Solve for x: **a** $x^2 = 13$ **b** $2x^2 = -8$ **c** $x^2 - 5 = 11$

a $x^2 = 13$
$\therefore x = \pm\sqrt{13}$

b $2x^2 = -8$
$\therefore x^2 = -4$
{dividing both sides by 2}
This has no solutions as x^2 cannot be < 0.

c $x^2 - 5 = 11$
$\therefore x^2 = 16$
{adding 5 to both sides}
$\therefore x = \pm\sqrt{16}$
$\therefore x = \pm 4$

EXERCISE 3F

1 Solve for x:
  a $x^2 = 49$
  b $x^2 = 121$
  c $x^2 = 56$
  d $x^2 = 46$
  e $x^2 = -14$
  f $x^2 = -100$
  g $x^2 = 23$
  h $x^2 = 0$
  i $x^2 = 17$

2 Solve for x:
  a $x^2 - 1 = 24$
  b $3 + x^2 = 19$
  c $5 = x^2 + 1$
  d $3x^2 = 27$
  e $-2x^2 = 32$
  f $5x^2 = 30$
  g $x^2 - 7 = -15$
  h $\frac{1}{4}x^2 = 25$
  i $6 - x^2 = 18$

G FORMING EQUATIONS

Earlier in this chapter, we practised turning sentences into algebraic expressions. Other sentences can be turned into equations that can be solved, giving the answer to a problem.

The following steps should be followed:

Step 1: Decide what the unknown quantity is and choose a variable such as x to represent it.

Step 2: Look for the operation(s) involved in the problem. We look for the same key words we used for expressions.

Step 3: Form the equation with an "=" sign. These phrases indicate equality:
"the answer is", "will be", "the result is", "is equal to", or simply "is".

Example 13
Self Tutor

Translate into an equation:
  a "When a number is added to 6, the result is 15."
  b "Twice a certain number is 7 more than the number."

a We let the number be x.
The number added to 6 is $6 + x$.
"the result is" indicates equality, so $6 + x = 15$.

b We let the number be x.
Twice the certain number is $2x$.
The "is" indicates equality: $2x =$
7 more than the number is $x + 7$. So, $2x = x + 7$.

> In the following exercise, you do not have to set out your answers like those given in the example.

With practice you will find that you can combine the steps, but you should note:
- the mathematical sentence you form must be an accurate translation of the information
- for these types of problems, you must have only one variable in your equation.

Example 14

Translate into an equation: "The sum of 2 consecutive even integers is 34."

Let the smaller even integer be x.

$\therefore$ the next even integer is $x + 2$.

So, $x + (x + 2) = 34$ is the equation.

Example 15

Apples cost 13 cents each and oranges cost 11 cents each.

I buy 5 more apples than oranges and the total cost of the apples and oranges is $2.33.

Write a linear equation involving the total cost.

Type of fruit	Number of pieces of fruit	Cost per piece of fruit	Total cost
oranges	x	11 cents	$11x$ cents
apples	$x + 5$	13 cents	$13(x + 5)$ cents
			233 cents

From the table, $11x + 13(x + 5) = 233$.

EXERCISE 3G

1 Translate into linear equations, but *do not solve*:
   a When a number is increased by 6, the answer is 13.
   b When a number is decreased by 5, the result is -4.
   c A number is doubled and 7 is added. The result is 1.
   d When a number is decreased by 1 and the resulting number is halved, the answer is 45.
   e Three times a number is equal to 17 minus the number.
   f Five times a number is 2 more than the number.

2 Translate into equations, but *do not solve*:
   a The sum of two consecutive integers is 33.
   b The sum of 3 consecutive integers is 102.
   c The sum of two consecutive odd integers is 52.
   d The sum of 3 consecutive odd integers is 69.

Algebra (expressions and equations)   (Chapter 3)   91

3 Write an equation for each of the following:

a Peter is buying some outdoor furniture for his patio. Tables cost $40 each and chairs cost $25 each. Peter buys 10 items of furniture at a total cost of $280. (Let the number of tables purchased be t.)

b Pencils cost 40 pence each and erasers cost 70 pence each. If I purchase three fewer erasers than pencils, the total cost will be £3.40. (Let the variable p represent the number of pencils purchased.)

c A group of friends went to a café for tea and coffee. Tea costs €2.50 and coffee costs €3.60. The number of people who ordered coffee was twice the number who ordered tea, and the total bill was €29.10. (Let the number of people who ordered tea be t.)

H PROBLEM SOLVING USING EQUATIONS

PROBLEM SOLVING METHOD   Exercise 3G

- Identify the unknown quantity and allocate a variable to it.
- Decide which operations are involved.
- Translate the problem into a linear equation and check that your translation is correct.
- Solve the linear equation by isolating the variable.
- Check that your solution does satisfy the original problem.
- Write your answer in sentence form.

Example 16   ◀) Self Tutor

A number is tripled and then decreased by 5, with a result of 19. Find the number.

Let x be the number.
Triple the number   is $3x$.
Triple the number, decreased by 5,   is $3x - 5$.
"with a result of 19" indicates $3x - 5 = 19$.

So, we solve: $3x - 5 = 19$ {the equation}
              $\therefore \ 3x - 5 + 5 = 19 + 5$ {adding 5 to both sides}
                    $\therefore \ 3x = 24$
                    $\therefore \ \dfrac{3x}{3} = \dfrac{24}{3}$ {dividing both sides by 3}
                    $\therefore \ x = 8$

So, the number is 8.

Example 17

The sum of 3 consecutive even integers is 132. Find the smallest integer.

Let x be the smallest even integer.

$\therefore$ the next is $x + 2$ and the largest is $x + 4$.

So, $x + (x + 2) + (x + 4) = 132$ {their sum is 132}

$\therefore \quad 3x + 6 = 132$

$\therefore \quad 3x + 6 - 6 = 132 - 6$ {subtracting 6 from both sides}

$\therefore \quad 3x = 126$

$\therefore \quad \dfrac{3x}{3} = \dfrac{126}{3}$ {dividing both sides by 3}

$\therefore \quad x = 42$ So, the smallest integer is 42.

Example 18

If twice a number is subtracted from 11, the result is 4 more than the number. What is the number?

Let x be the number.

LHS of the algebraic expression is $11 - 2x$.

RHS of the algebraic expression is $x + 4$.

$\therefore \quad 11 - 2x = x + 4$ {the equation}

$\therefore \quad 11 - 2x + 2x = x + 4 + 2x$ {adding $2x$ to both sides}

$\therefore \quad 11 = 3x + 4$

$\therefore \quad 11 - 4 = 3x + 4 - 4$ {subtracting 4 from both sides}

$\therefore \quad 7 = 3x$

$\therefore \quad \dfrac{7}{3} = \dfrac{3x}{3}$ {dividing both sides by 3}

$\therefore \quad x = 2\tfrac{1}{3}$ So, the number is $2\tfrac{1}{3}$.

EXERCISE 3H

1. Five less than a number is 8. Find the number.
2. One third of a certain number is 4. Find the number.
3. When a number is doubled and the result is increased by 6, the answer is 20. Find the number.
4. The sum of two consecutive integers is 75. Find the integers.
5. The sum of two consecutive odd integers is 68. Find the smaller integer.
6. Three consecutive numbers add up to 93. Find the middle number.

Algebra (expressions and equations) (Chapter 3)

7 The sum of three consecutive even integers is 54. Find the largest of them.

8 When a number is subtracted from 40, the result is 14 more than the original number. Find the number.

9 A number is halved, and the result is 17 less than the original number. Find the number.

Example 19 ◀》 **Self Tutor**

Yang Song buys 4 tubes of paint. He receives $6.20 change from a $20 note. What does a single paint tube cost?

Let $\$x$ be the price of a tube of paint.

4 paint tubes and $6.20 makes $20,

$$\text{so} \quad 4x + 6.2 = 20$$
$$\therefore \quad 4x + 6.2 - 6.2 = 20 - 6.2$$
$$\therefore \quad 4x = 13.8$$
$$\therefore \quad \frac{4x}{4} = \frac{13.8}{4}$$
$$\therefore \quad x = 3.45$$

So, a paint tube costs $3.45.

---

10 Tyler has to lay 40 m of pipe. After laying 4 equal lengths of pipe, he finds he has 12 m to go. How long are the pipe lengths?

11 A shop labels the selling price of a shirt at twice its cost price. A customer buys the shirt and gets €10 off in a sale. If the shop makes a €17 profit, what was the cost price of the shirt?

12 Brianna plants a 110 cm tree in her garden. After 3 years, she prunes it back, taking 35 cm off the top. Brianna notices that the tree is exactly three times as high as it was when planted. What was the growth per year?

Review set 3A

1 True or false:
   a $3x^2 + 5 - \sqrt{x}$ is an equation.
   b $4k + 3 - k + 1 - 3k$ has 2 terms.
   c The coefficient of a in $-4a + 2 - 7b$ is 4.
   d $5x + 9 = 2x - 4$ is a linear equation.

2 If $i = -3$ and $j = 2$, find:
   a $4i$
   b $3 - 7j$
   c $2i + 3j$
   d ij^2

3 Write an algebraic expression for:
   a 5 fewer than a number
   b the sum of c, d, and the square of e.

4 Solve for x:
   a $7 - 3x = 1$
   b $\dfrac{2x - 5}{3} = 4$

5 Solve for x:
   a $x^2 = 17$
   b $3x^2 = -75$

6 Write an equation to describe this situation, *but do not solve it*.

Along a street, x copies of a national newspaper are delivered, and $x + 15$ copies of the local newspaper are delivered. The national newspaper costs £1, and the local paper costs £0.80. The total takings for the street are £62.40.

7 Solve these problems:

   a When a number is halved and 7 is added to the result, the answer is the same as the original number less 12. Find the number.

   b The sum of three consecutive integers is 141. Find the integers.

   c Jillian is reading a magazine. She reads $\frac{3}{4}$ of it at breakfast, and 15 pages at morning tea. There are 16 pages left for Jillian to read. How many pages does the magazine have?

Review set 3B

1 Consider $2x + 7 - 5xy + 3x$.

   a Is it an expression or an equation?   **b** How many terms does it have?
   c What is the coefficient of xy?   **d** What is the constant term?
   e Write down any like terms.

2 If $c = 4$ and $d = 11$, evaluate:

   a $-c$ **b** $d - c$ **c** $\dfrac{d+3}{c}$ **d** $(2c + d)^2$

3 A businessman donates $\$x$ to charity for every run in a baseball match, and an extra $\$2x$ if the run was a home run. Write an expression for the amount of money donated if there were 9 runs scored, 3 of which were home runs.

4 Solve for x: **a** $2x + 15 = 7$ **b** $\frac{1}{2}(12 - x) = -1$

5 Solve for x: **a** $2x^2 - 8 = 0$ **b** $-6x^2 = 0$

6 Translate into linear equations *but do not solve*:

   a A number is tripled and the resulting number is subtracted from 53. The result is 29.

   b The sum of two consecutive odd integers is 20.

7 Solve these problems:

   a When a number is trebled and 5 is subtracted from the result, the answer is the same as the sum of the original number and 17. Find the number.

   b Arthur buys 5 music CDs. If he receives $16 change from a $50 note, find the cost of each CD if they are all the same price.

   c Katie and Toby are at a café, where all main meals are the same price. They order two main meals, and one side salad costing $7. They split the bill equally. If Katie's share of the bill is $16, how much does a main meal cost?

Lines, angles, and polygons

4

Contents:

A	Angles	[4.1, 4.3]
B	Lines and line segments	[4.1]
C	Polygons	[4.1]
D	Symmetry	[4.2]
E	Congruence	[4.1]
F	Angle properties	[4.4]
G	Triangles	[4.4]
H	Isosceles triangles	[4.4]
I	The interior angles of a polygon	[4.4]
J	The exterior angles of a polygon	[4.4]

Opening problem

On his birthday, Billy receives a cake in the shape of a regular hexagon. He divides the cake into 4 pieces by making cuts from one corner to each of the other corners as shown.

Things to think about:

a When Billy cuts the cake in this way, are the four angles at the top of the hexagon equal in size? Can you find the size of each angle?

b When a regular hexagon is cut in this way, four triangles are formed. Do any of these triangles contain right angles?

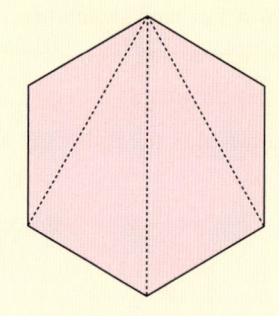

In this chapter we look at the basic components of geometry, which we will build on throughout the course. We begin by studying lines and angles, which are used to describe the world around us. In the second part of the chapter we take a more in-depth look at the properties of polygons, particularly triangles and quadrilaterals.

A ANGLES [4.1, 4.3]

Angles are described by their size or degree measure. The different types of angle are summarised in the following table:

Revolution	Straight Angle	Right Angle
 One complete turn. One revolution $= 360°$.	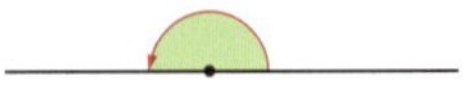 $\frac{1}{2}$ turn. 1 straight angle $= 180°$.	 $\frac{1}{4}$ turn. 1 right angle $= 90°$.
Acute Angle	**Obtuse Angle**	**Reflex Angle**
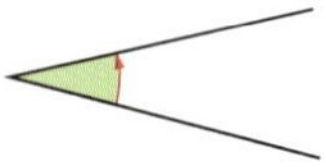 Less than a $\frac{1}{4}$ turn. An acute angle has size between $0°$ and $90°$.	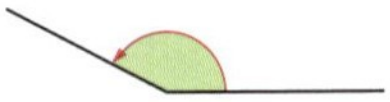 Between $\frac{1}{4}$ turn and $\frac{1}{2}$ turn. An obtuse angle has size between $90°$ and $180°$.	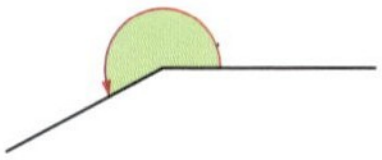 Between $\frac{1}{2}$ turn and 1 turn. A reflex angle has size between $180°$ and $360°$.

There are several ways to label angles.

We can use a small case letter or a letter of the Greek alphabet.

We can also use **three point notation** to refer to an angle.

For example, the illustrated angle θ is angle PQR or $P\hat{Q}R$.

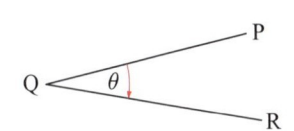

EXERCISE 4A

1 Draw a freehand sketch of:
  a an acute angle
  b an obtuse angle
  c a right angle
  d a reflex angle
  e a straight angle

2 State whether the following angles are straight, acute, obtuse or reflex:
  a **b** **c** **d**
  e **f** **g** **h**

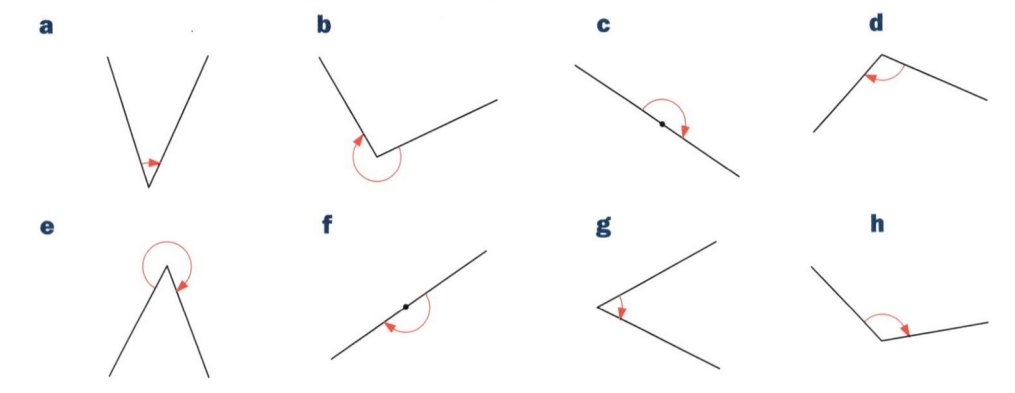

Lines, angles, and polygons (Chapter 4)

3 For the angle sizes given below, state whether the angle is a revolution, a straight angle, a right angle, an acute angle, an obtuse angle, or a reflex angle.

  a 31°   **b** 117°   **c** 360°   **d** 213°   **e** 89°   **f** 90°
  g 127° **h** 180°   **i** 358°   **j** 45°   **k** 270° **l** 150°

4 Find the measure of angle:

  a BAC   **b** DAE
  c BAD   **d** CAE
  e CAF   **f** BAE

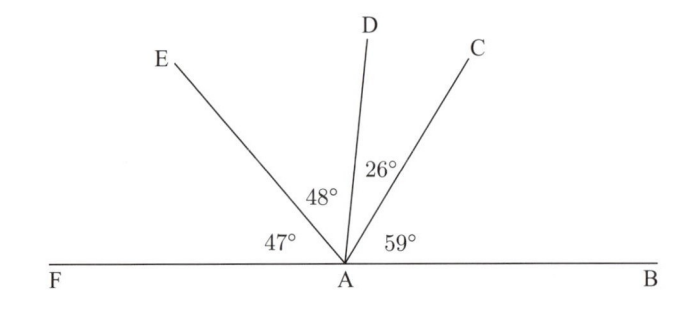

5 Which is the larger angle, $\hat{KLM}$ or $\hat{PQR}$?

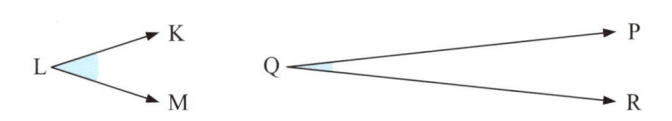

B LINES AND LINE SEGMENTS [4.1]

When we talk about lines and line segments, it is important to state exactly what we mean.

Line AB is the endless straight line passing through the points A and B.

Line segment AB is the part of the straight line AB that connects A with B.

The **distance AB** is the length of the line segment AB.

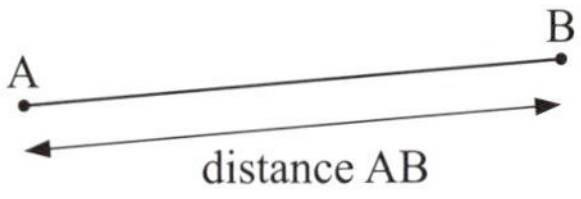

There are several other important words we use when talking about lines:

- **Concurrent lines** are three or more lines that all pass through a common point.

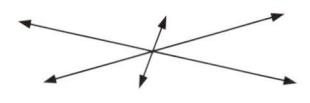

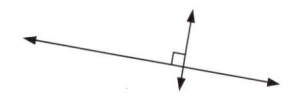

- **Collinear points** are points which lie in a straight line.

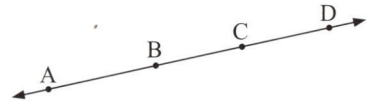

- **Perpendicular lines** intersect at right angles.

- **Parallel lines** are lines which never intersect. Arrowheads in the middle of lines indicate parallelism.

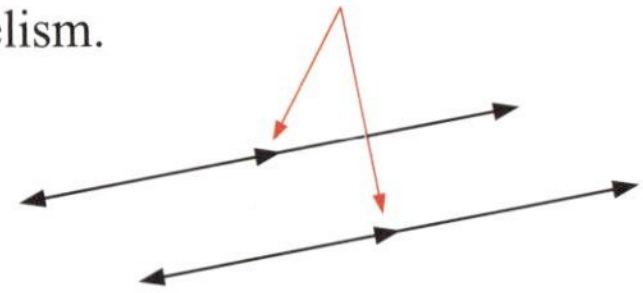

- A **transversal** is a line which crosses over two other lines.

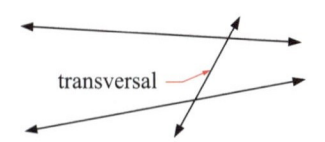

EXERCISE 4B

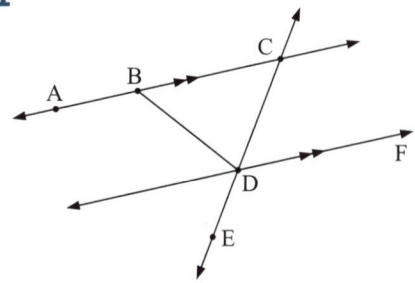

1 Copy and complete:
  a Points A, B and C are ....
  b The part of line BD we can see is ....
  c The line parallel to line BC is ....
  d The lines through B and D, C and E, and D and F, are .... at D.

2 Draw a diagram which shows:
  a line AB perpendicular to line CD
  b X, Y and Z being collinear
  c four concurrent lines
  d two lines being cut by a transversal.

3 Draw a diagram which shows parallel lines MN and PQ. Add to your diagram the transversals MP and NQ.

C POLYGONS [4.1]

A **polygon** is any closed figure with straight line sides which can be drawn on a flat surface.

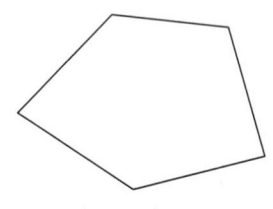

is a polygon.   are not polygons.

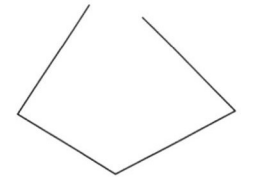

A **triangle** is a polygon with 3 sides.
A **quadrilateral** is a polygon with 4 sides.
A **pentagon** is a polygon with 5 sides.
A **hexagon** is a polygon with 6 sides.
An **octagon** is a polygon with 8 sides.

Lines, angles, and polygons (Chapter 4)

TRIANGLES

There are several types of triangle you should be familiar with:

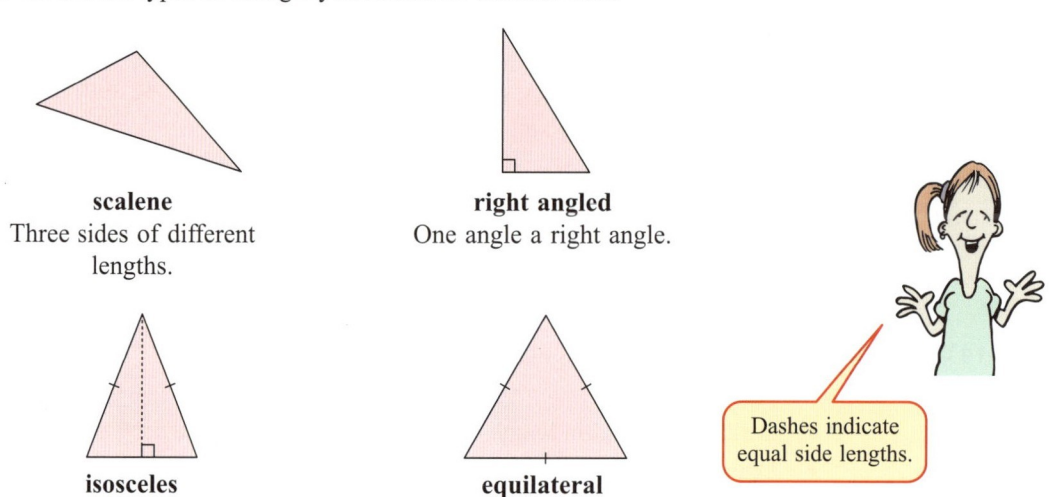

scalene
Three sides of different lengths.

right angled
One angle a right angle.

isosceles
Two sides are equal.

equilateral
Three sides are equal.

Dashes indicate equal side lengths.

REGULAR POLYGONS

A **regular polygon** is one in which all sides are equal and all angles are equal.

For example, these are all regular polygons:

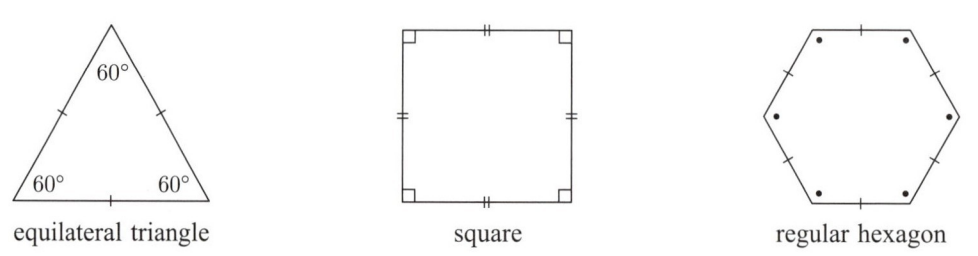

equilateral triangle (60°, 60°, 60°)

square

regular hexagon

SPECIAL QUADRILATERALS

There are six special quadrilaterals:

- A **parallelogram** is a quadrilateral which has opposite sides parallel.
- A **rectangle** is a parallelogram with four equal angles of 90°.
- A **rhombus** is a quadrilateral in which all sides are equal.
- A **square** is a rhombus with four equal angles of 90°.
- A **trapezium** is a quadrilateral which has exactly one pair of parallel sides.
- A **kite** is a quadrilateral which has two pairs of equal adjacent sides.

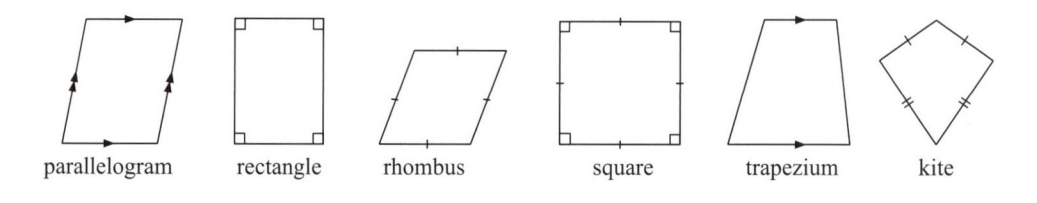

parallelogram   rectangle   rhombus   square   trapezium   kite

The following properties of quadrilaterals are useful:

PARALLELOGRAM

In any parallelogram:
- opposite sides are parallel
- opposite sides are equal in length
- opposite angles are equal in size
- diagonals bisect each other.

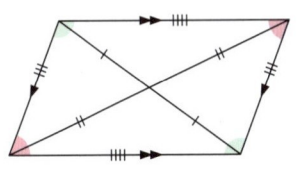

RECTANGLE

In any rectangle:
- opposite sides are parallel
- all angles are right angles
- opposite sides are equal in length
- diagonals are equal in length
- diagonals bisect each other.

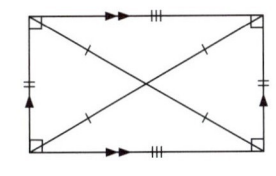

RHOMBUS

In any rhombus:
- all sides are equal in length
- opposite sides are parallel
- opposite angles are equal in size
- diagonals bisect each other at right angles
- diagonals bisect the angles at each vertex.

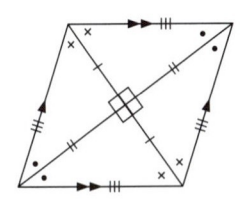

SQUARE

In any square:
- all sides are equal in length
- all angles are right angles
- opposite sides are parallel
- diagonals bisect each other at right angles
- diagonals bisect the angles at each vertex.

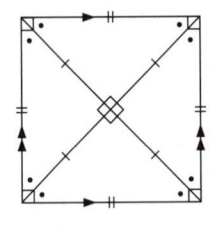

KITE

In any kite:
- two pairs of adjacent sides are equal
- the diagonals are perpendicular
- one diagonal splits the kite into two isosceles triangles.

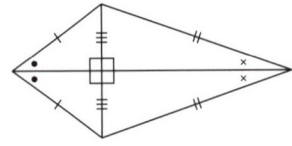

EXERCISE 4C

1 Classify these triangles:

   a 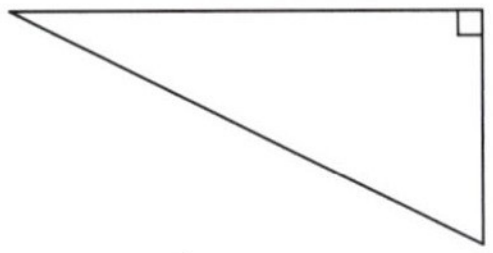   **b** 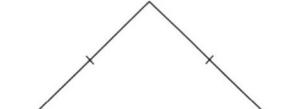   **c**

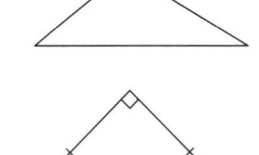

   d 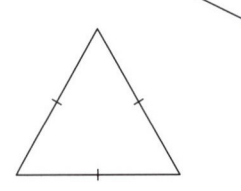   **e** 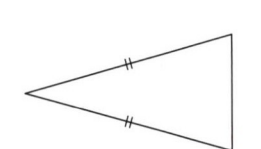   **f**

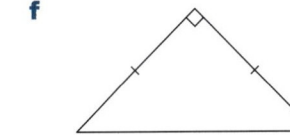

2 Draw diagrams to illustrate:

   a a quadrilateral   **b** a pentagon   **c** a hexagon

   d an octagon   **e** a regular quadrilateral   **f** a regular triangle

   g a parallelogram   **h** a rhombus   **i** a trapezium

Lines, angles, and polygons (Chapter 4) 101

3 List with illustration:

   a the *three* properties of a parallelogram   **b** the *four* properties of a rhombus.

D SYMMETRY [4.2]

LINE SYMMETRY

A figure has **line symmetry** if it can be reflected in a line so that each half of the figure is reflected onto the other half of the figure.

For example, an isosceles triangle has one line of symmetry, which is the line from its apex to the midpoint of its base.

A square has 4 lines of symmetry.

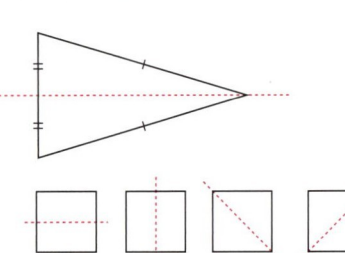

A figure has a line of symmetry if it can be folded onto itself along that line.

Example 1 ◀) Self Tutor

For the following figures, draw all lines of symmetry:

a   **b**   **c**

a 1 line of symmetry   **b** no lines of symmetry   **c** 2 lines of symmetry

ROTATIONAL SYMMETRY

A figure has **rotational symmetry** if it can be mapped onto itself more than once as it rotates through 360° about a point called the **centre of symmetry**.

The flag of the Isle of Man features a symbol called a *triskelion* which has rotational symmetry.

Every time you rotate the triskelion through 120° it fits onto itself. This is done 3 times to get back to the starting position. We say that its *order* of rotational symmetry is 3.

EXERCISE 4D

1 How many lines of symmetry do the following have?

a, b,  c,  d

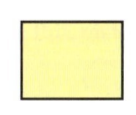

e,  f, 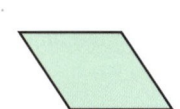 g,  h

i, 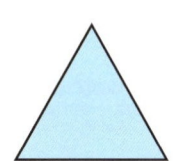 j,  k, 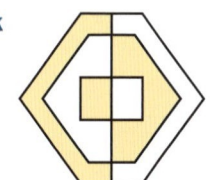 l

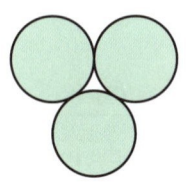

2 Which of the following alphabet letters show line symmetry?

A B C D E F G H I J K L M
N O P Q R S T U V W X Y Z

3 Draw a triangle which has:
    a no lines of symmetry   **b** one line of symmetry   **c** three lines of symmetry.

4 Draw a quadrilateral which has:
    a no lines of symmetry   **b** one line of symmetry   **c** two lines of symmetry
    d four lines of symmetry.

5 What is the order of rotational symmetry for each of these figures?

a, b, 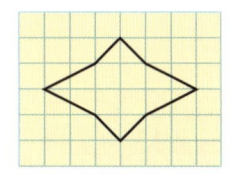 c

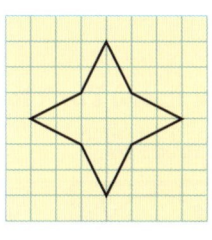

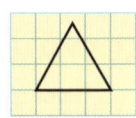

d, 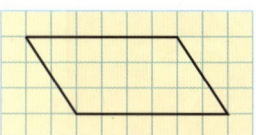 e,  f

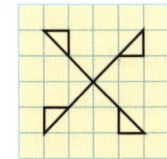

Lines, angles, and polygons (Chapter 4) 103

6 Find the order of rotational symmetry of the *Bauhinia blakeana* flower on the flag of Hong Kong.

7 Which of the following letters show rotational symmetry?

ABCDEFGHIJKLMNOPQRSTUVWXYZ

E CONGRUENCE [4.1]

In mathematics we use the term **congruent** to describe things which have the same shape and size. The closest we get to congruence in humans is identical twins.

We use the symbol $\cong$ to show things are congruent. For example, $\triangle ABC \cong \triangle XYZ$ reads 'triangle ABC is congruent to triangle XYZ'.

EXERCISE 4E

1 Which of the following figures are congruent?

A B C D E

2 Which of the following geometric figures are congruent?

A B C D E F G H

I J K L M N O

3 Here are some pairs of congruent geometric figures.

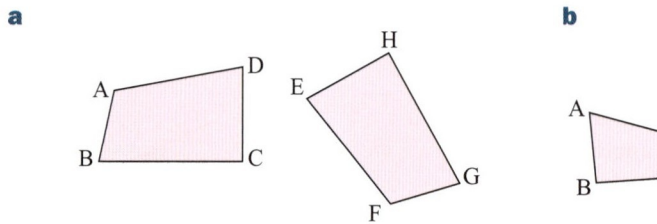

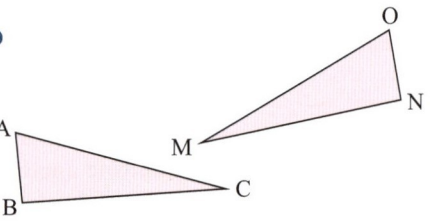

a

b

c

d

e

f

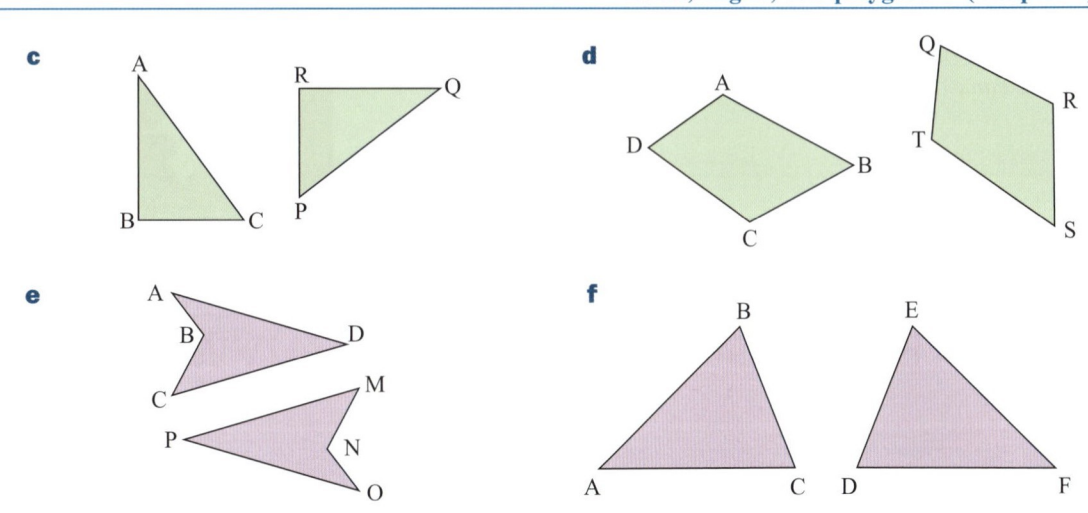

For each pair:

i Identify the side in the second figure corresponding to the side AB in the first figure.

ii Identify the angle in the second figure corresponding to $A\hat{B}C$ in the first figure.

F ANGLE PROPERTIES [4.4]

There are some key words we use when talking about how two angles are related. You should become familiar with these terms:

- Two angles with sizes which add to 90° are called **complementary angles**.
  $X\hat{P}Y$ and $Y\hat{P}Z$ are complementary angles.

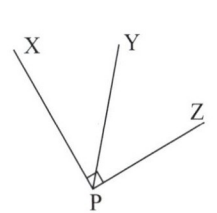

- Two angles with sizes which add to 180° are called **supplementary angles**.
  $A\hat{P}B$ and $B\hat{P}C$ are supplementary angles.

- Two angles which have the same vertex and share a common arm are called **adjacent angles**.
  $P\hat{A}Q$ and $Q\hat{A}R$ are adjacent angles.

- For intersecting lines, angles which are directly opposite each other are called **vertically opposite angles**.

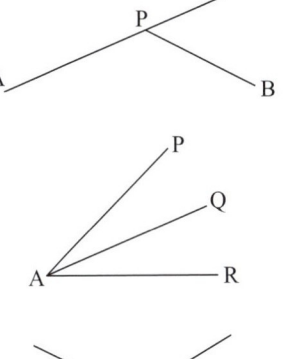

Lines, angles, and polygons (Chapter 4)

The following properties can be used to solve problems involving angles:

Title	Property	Figure
Angles centred at a point	The sum of the sizes of the angles at a point is $360°$.	$a + b + c = 360$
Adjacent angles on a straight line	The sum of the sizes of the angles on a line is $180°$. The angles are supplementary.	$a + b = 180$
Adjacent angles in a right angle	The sum of the sizes of the angles in a right angle is $90°$. The angles are complementary.	$a + b = 90$
Vertically opposite angles	Vertically opposite angles are equal in size.	$a = b$
Corresponding angles	When two *parallel* lines are cut by a third line, then angles in corresponding positions are equal in size.	$a = b$
Alternate angles	When two *parallel* lines are cut by a third line, then angles in alternate positions are equal in size.	$a = b$
Co-interior angles (also called allied angles)	When two *parallel* lines are cut by a third line, then co-interior angles are supplementary.	$a + b = 180$

Example 2

Find, giving brief reasons, the value of the unknown in:

a

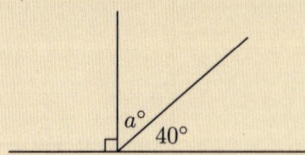

b

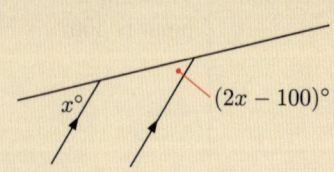

a $90 + a + 40 = 180$ {angles on a line}
$\therefore \quad a + 130 = 180$
$\therefore \quad a = 50$

b $\quad 2x - 100 = x$ {equal corresponding angles}
$\therefore \quad 2x - 100 - x = x - x$ {subtracting x from both sides}
$\therefore \quad x - 100 = 0$ {simplifying}
$\therefore \quad x = 100$

EXERCISE 4F

1 Use the figure illustrated to answer the following questions:
AB is a fixed line and OP can rotate about O between OA and OB.

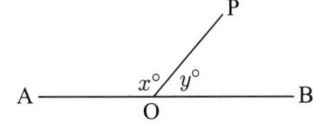

  a If $x = 136$, find y.   **b** If $y = 58$, find x.
  c What is x if y is 39?   **d** If x is 0, what is y?
  e If $x = 81$, find y.   **f** If $x = y$, what is the value of each?

2 Find the values of the unknowns, giving brief reasons. You should **not** need to set up an equation.

a

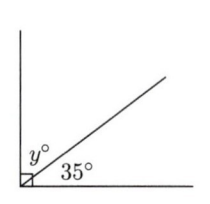

b

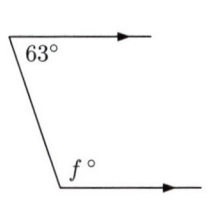

c

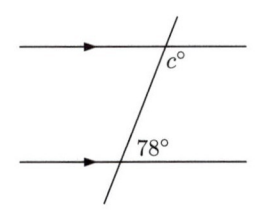

d

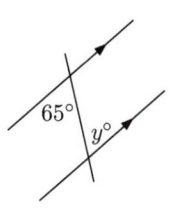

e

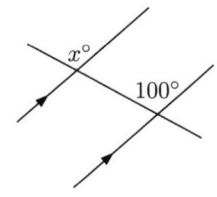

f

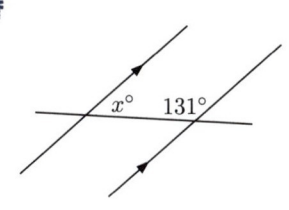

g

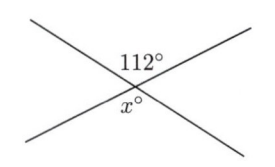

h

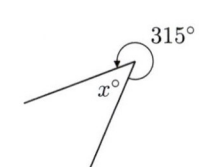

i

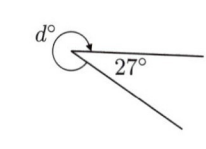

Lines, angles, and polygons (Chapter 4) 107

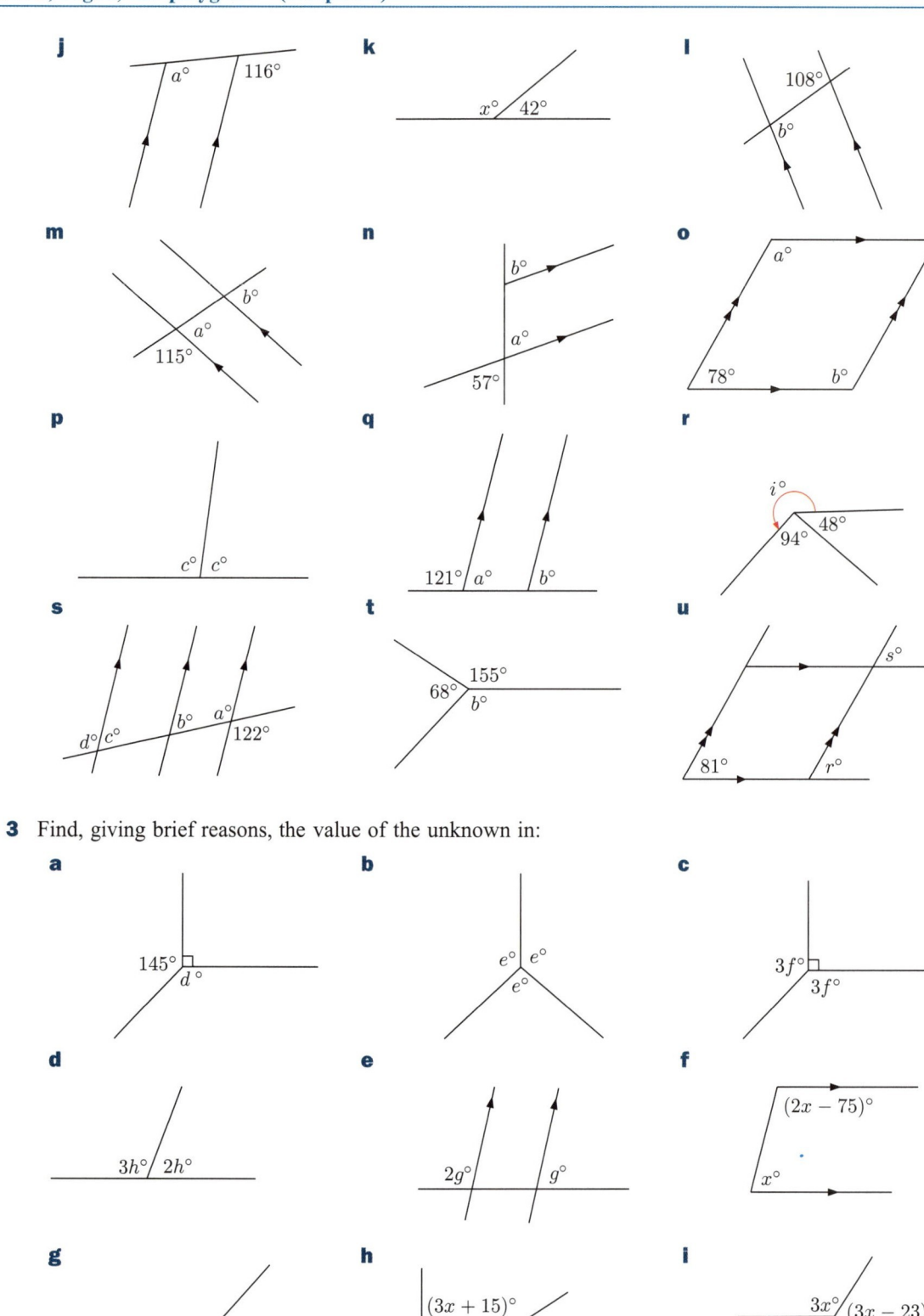

j $a°$, $116°$

k $x°$, $42°$

l $108°$, $b°$

m $115°$, $a°$, $b°$

n $b°$, $a°$, $57°$

o $a°$, $78°$, $b°$

p $c°$, $c°$

q $121°$, $a°$, $b°$

r $i°$, $94°$, $48°$

s $d°$, $c°$, $b°$, $a°$, $122°$

t $68°$, $155°$, $b°$

u $s°$, $81°$, $r°$

3 Find, giving brief reasons, the value of the unknown in:

a $145°$, $d°$

b $e°$, $e°$, $e°$

c $3f°$, $3f°$

d $3h°$, $2h°$

e $2g°$, $g°$

f $(2x-75)°$, $x°$

g $(2x+10)°$, $(x+35)°$

h $(3x+15)°$, $2x°$

i $3x°$, $(3x-23)°$, $45°$, $(x+44)°$

4 State whether KL is parallel to MN, giving a brief reason for your answer. Note that these diagrams are sketches only and have not been drawn accurately.

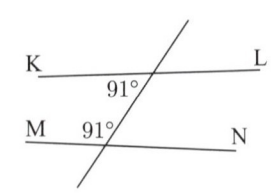

a (diagram with angles 85° and 85°, points K, L, M, N)

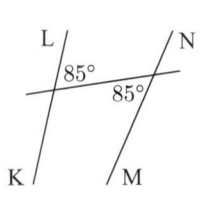

b (diagram with angles 91° and 91°, points K, L, M, N)

c (diagram with angles 96° and 96°, points K, L, M, N)

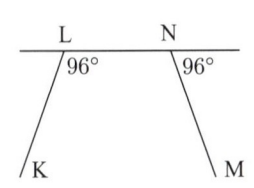

5 Find the value of the unknowns in:

a (parallelogram with angles 120°, $y°$, $x°$)

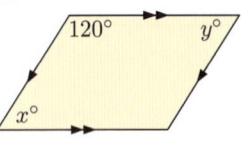

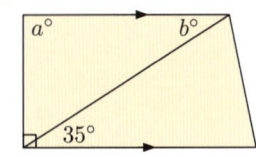

b (trapezium with angles $a°$, $b°$, 35° and a right angle)

c (parallelogram with angles $q°$, 65°, $r°$, $p°$)

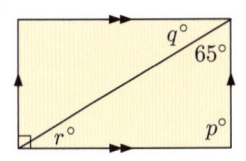

G TRIANGLES [4.4]

> A **triangle** is a polygon which has three sides.
>
> It is the only **rigid** polygon.
>
> The longest side of a triangle is opposite the largest angle.

Discussion

Bridges and other specialised structures often have triangular supports rather than rectangular ones.

The reason for this is that
"the triangle is the only rigid polygon".

1 Explain what is meant by "rigid polygon".

2 Why is this important?

PROPERTIES OF TRIANGLES

Title	Property	Figure
Angles of a triangle	The sum of the interior angles of a triangle is 180°. **DEMO**	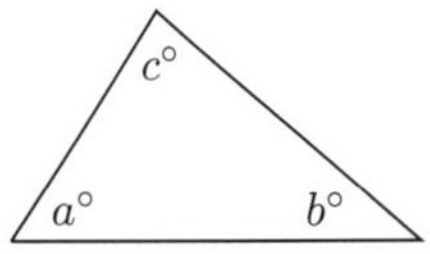 (triangle with angles $a°$, $b°$, $c°$) $a + b + c = 180$

Lines, angles, and polygons (Chapter 4) 109

Title	Property	Figure
Exterior angle of a triangle	The size of the exterior angle of a triangle is equal to the sum of the interior opposite angles. **DEMO**	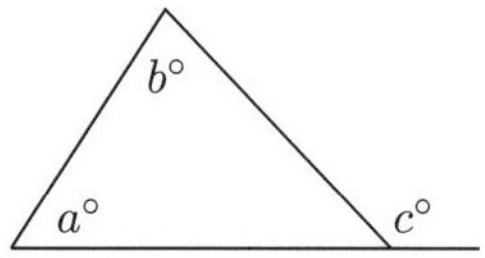 $c = a + b$

Example 3 ◀) Self Tutor

Find the unknown in the following, giving brief reasons:

a

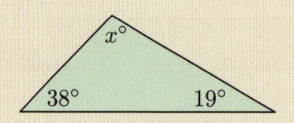

b

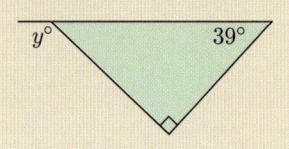

a $x + 38 + 19 = 180$ {angle sum of a triangle}
$\therefore \quad x = 180 - 38 - 19$
$\therefore \quad x = 123$

b $y = 39 + 90$ {exterior angle of a triangle}
$\therefore \quad y = 129$

Example 4 ◀) Self Tutor

Find the values of the unknowns, giving brief reasons for your answers.

a

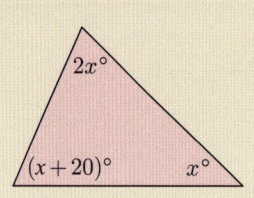

b

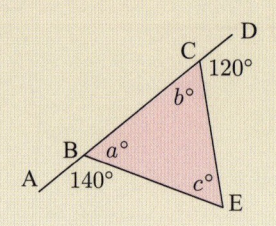

a $2x + x + (x + 20) = 180$ {angles of a triangle}
$\therefore \quad 4x + 20 = 180$
$\therefore \quad 4x = 160$
$\therefore \quad x = 40$

b $a = 180 - 140 = 40$ {angles on a line}
Likewise $b = 180 - 120 = 60$
But $a + b + c = 180$ {angles of a triangle}
$\therefore \quad 40 + 60 + c = 180$
$\therefore \quad 100 + c = 180$
$\therefore \quad c = 80$

EXERCISE 4G

1 Find the unknown in the following, giving brief reasons:

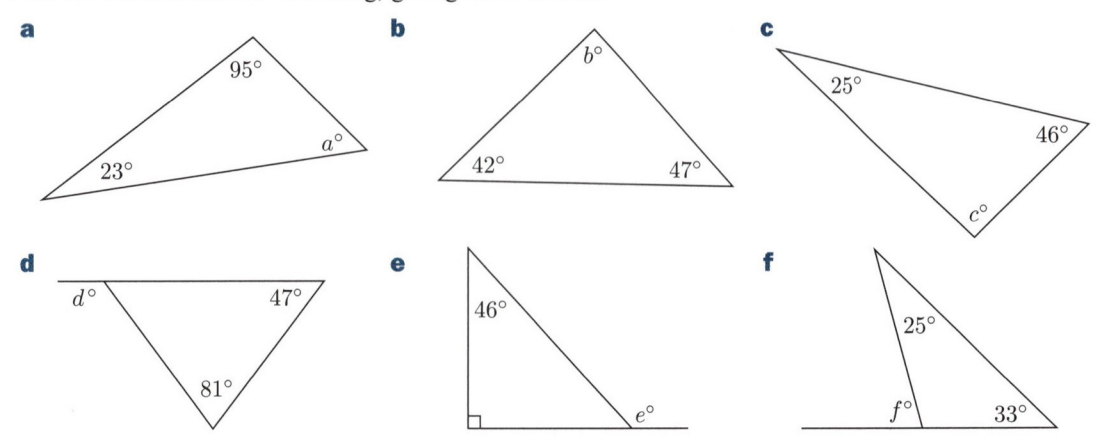

a Triangle with angles 95°, 23°, and $a°$

b Triangle with angles $b°$, 42°, and 47°

c Triangle with angles 25°, 46°, and $c°$

d Triangle with angles $d°$, 47°, and 81°

e Right-angled triangle with angles 46° and $e°$

f Triangle with angles 25°, $f°$ (exterior), and 33°

2 The following triangles are *not* drawn to scale. State the longest side of each triangle.

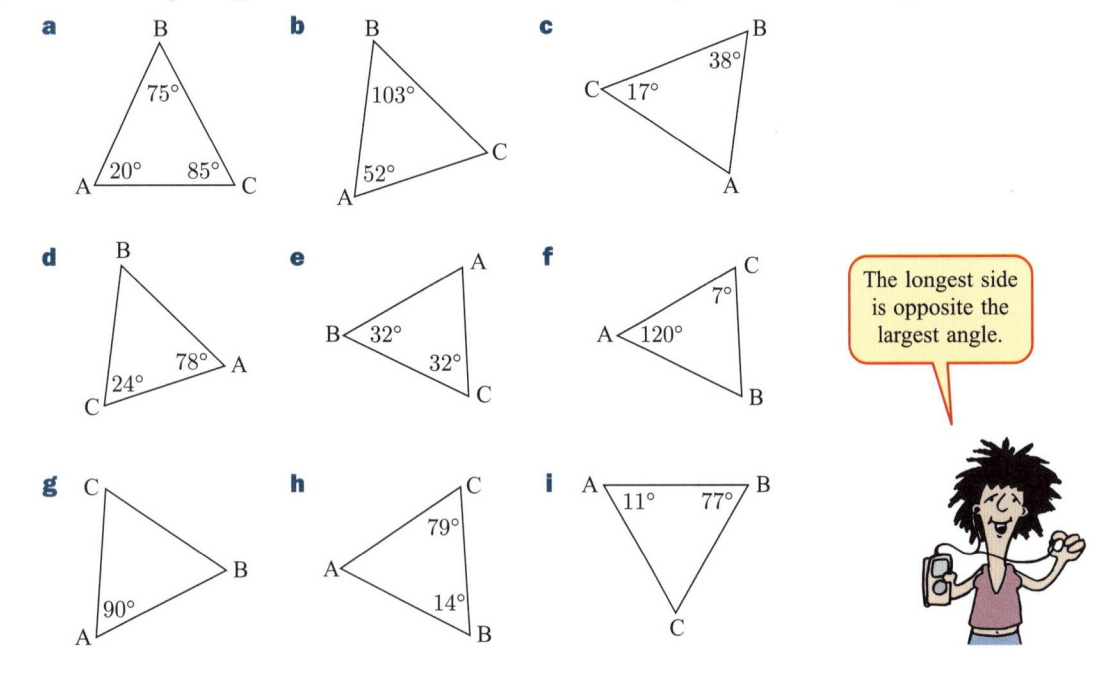

a Triangle ABC with angles A = 20°, B = 75°, C = 85°

b Triangle ABC with angles A = 52°, B = 103°

c Triangle ABC with angles B = 38°, C = 17°

d Triangle ABC with angles B = 78°, C = 24°

e Triangle ABC with angles B = 32°, C = 32°

f Triangle ABC with angles A = 120°, C = 7°

g Triangle ABC with angle A = 90°

h Triangle ABC with angles B = 14°, C = 79°

i Triangle ABC with angles A = 11°, B = 77°

The longest side is opposite the largest angle.

3 State whether the following statements are *true* or *false*:

   a The sum of the angles of a triangle is equal to two right angles.
   b A right angled triangle can contain an obtuse angle.
   c The sum of two angles of a triangle is always greater than the third angle.
   d The two smaller angles of a right angled triangle are supplementary.
   e A concave triangle is impossible.

Lines, angles, and polygons (Chapter 4)   111

4 Find the values of the unknowns in each triangle, giving a brief reason for each answer:

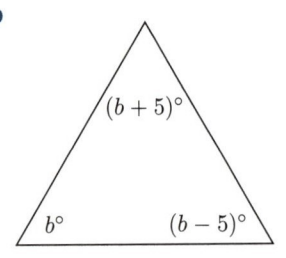

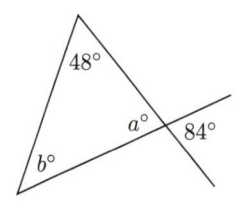

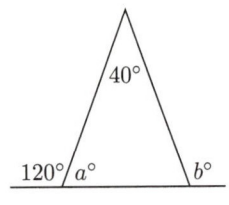

a Triangle with angles $a°$ at top, $4a°$ and $4a°$ at base.

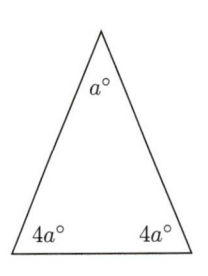

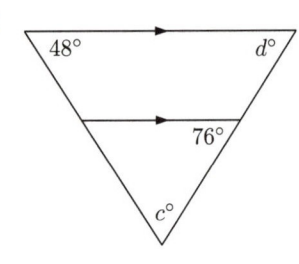

b Triangle with angles $(b+5)°$ at top, $b°$ and $(b-5)°$ at base.

c Triangle with $48°$, $d°$ (exterior with parallel line), $76°$, $c°$.

d Triangle with $48°$, $a°$, $84°$, $b°$ (intersecting lines).

e Triangle with $40°$ at top, $120°/a°$ and $b°$ at base (exterior angle).

f Triangle with $65°$, $b°$, $a°$, $72°$, $c°$, $d°$ (intersecting lines).

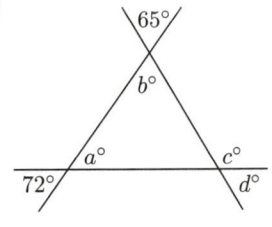

5 The three angles of a scalene triangle are $x°$, $(x-12)°$ and $(2x+6)°$. What are the sizes of these angles?

H   ISOSCELES TRIANGLES   [4.4]

An **isosceles triangle** is a triangle in which two sides are equal in length.

The angles opposite the two equal sides are called the **base angles**.

The vertex where the two equal sides meet is called the **apex**.

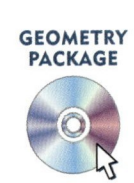

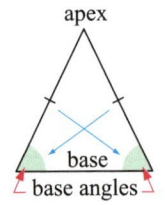

THE ISOSCELES TRIANGLE THEOREM

In an isosceles triangle:
- base angles are equal
- the line joining the apex to the midpoint of the base bisects the vertical angle and meets the base at right angles.

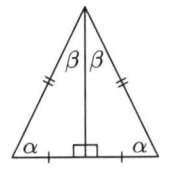

PROPERTIES

The following properties are associated with the isosceles triangle theorem:

Property 1: If a triangle has two equal angles then it is isosceles.

Property 2: The angle bisector of the apex of an isosceles triangle bisects the base at right angles.

Property 3: The perpendicular bisector of the base of an isosceles triangle passes through its apex.

- To prove *Property 1*, Sam tries to use Figure 1 and triangle congruence. Will he be successful? Why or why not? Could Sam be successful using Figure 2?
- Can you prove *Property 2* using triangle congruence?

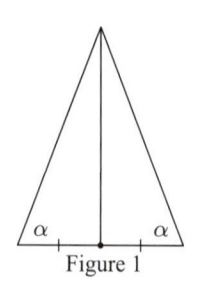

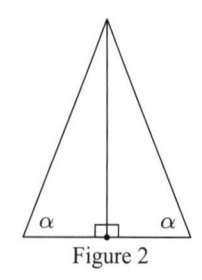

Example 5

Find x, giving brief reasons:

a

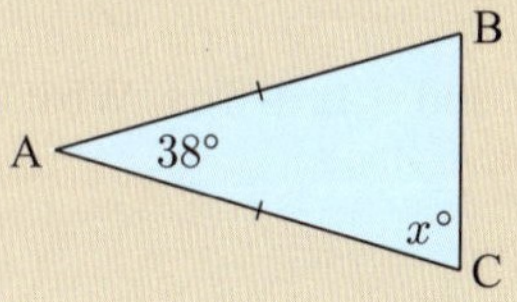

b

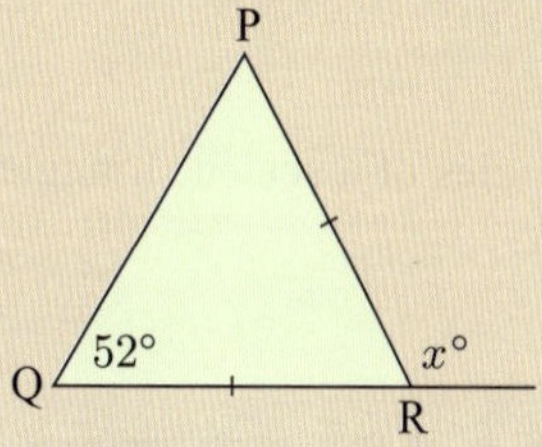

a 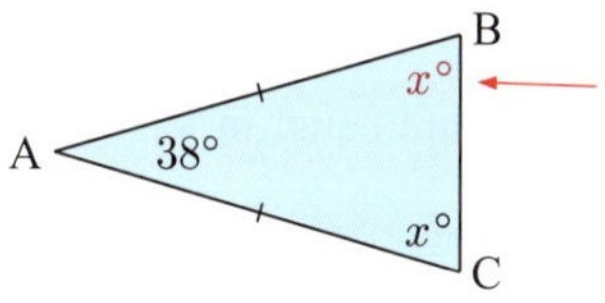 As $AB = AC$, the triangle is isosceles

$\therefore \ A\widehat{B}C = x°$ also

Now $x + x + 38 = 180$ {angles of a $\triangle$}

$\therefore \ 2x = 180 - 38$

$\therefore \ 2x = 142$

$\therefore \ x = 71$

b As $PR = QR$, the triangle is isosceles

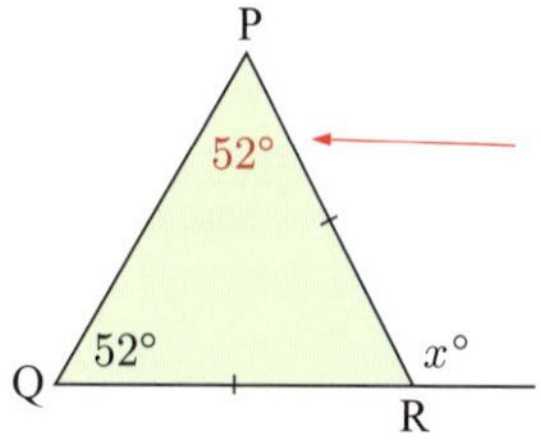

$\therefore \ Q\widehat{P}R = 52°$ {isosceles $\triangle$ theorem}

$\therefore \ x = 52 + 52$ {exterior angle theorem}

$\therefore \ x = 104$

EXERCISE 4H

1 Find x, giving reasons:

a

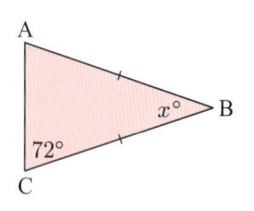

b

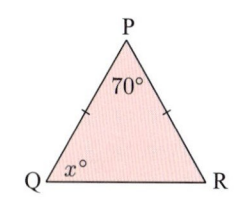

c

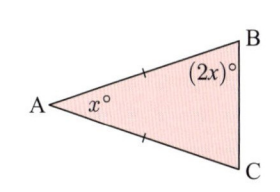

Lines, angles, and polygons (Chapter 4) 113

d Triangle PQR with angle $x°$ at P and $(146-x)°$ at Q.

e Triangle with A, angle $120°$ at B labeled, C with angle $x°$, D.

f Triangle ADC with $x°$ at D, $65°$ at B, B on AC.

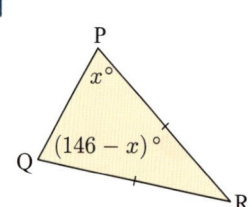

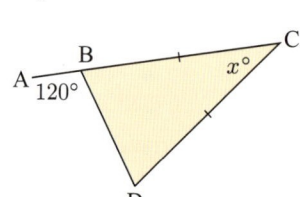

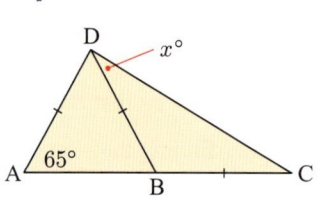

2 Find x, giving brief reasons:

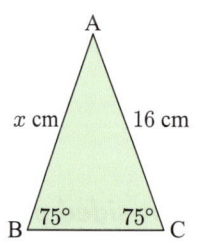

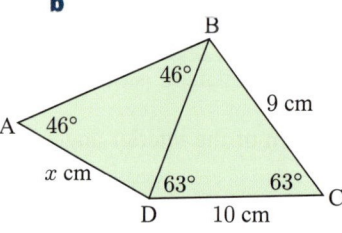

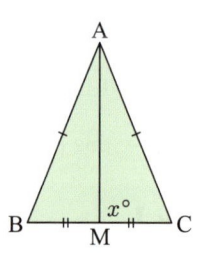

a Triangle ABC, AB = x cm, AC = 16 cm, angles $75°$ at B and $75°$ at C.

b Quadrilateral with angle $46°$ at B, $46°$ at A, BC = 9 cm, DC = 10 cm, angles $63°$ and $63°$ at D and C, AD = x cm.

c Triangle ABC with M on BC, AM drawn, angle $x°$ at M.

3 Classify the following triangles as equilateral, isosceles or scalene. They are not drawn to scale, but the information marked on them is correct.

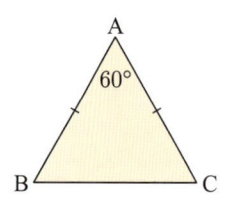

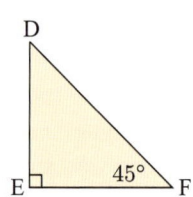

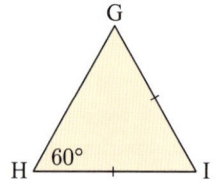

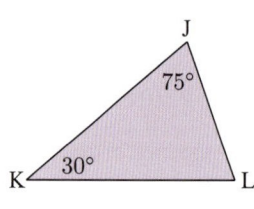

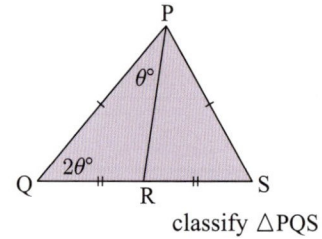

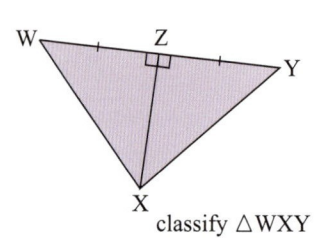

a Triangle ABC with $60°$ at A.

b Triangle DEF with right angle at E and $45°$ at F.

c Triangle GHI with $60°$ at H.

d Triangle JKL with $75°$ at J and $30°$ at K.

e Triangle PQS with R on QS, angle $\theta°$ at P, $20°$ at Q. classify △PQS

f Triangle WXY with Z on WY, right angle at Z. classify △WXY

4 The figure alongside has not been drawn to scale.
  a Find x.
  b What can be deduced about the triangle?

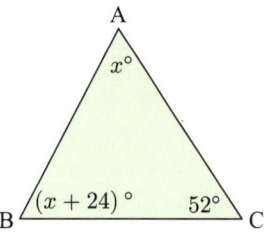

Triangle ABC with $x°$ at A, $(x+24)°$ at B, $52°$ at C.

5 Because of its symmetry, a regular pentagon can be constructed from five isosceles triangles.
  a Find the size of angle θ at the centre O.
  b Hence, find ϕ.
  c Hence, find the measure of one interior angle such as $A\hat{B}C$.

6 Repeat question **5** but use a regular decagon. Remember that a decagon has 10 sides.

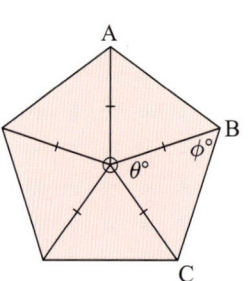

1 THE INTERIOR ANGLES OF A POLYGON [4.4]

We have already seen that the sum of the interior angles of a triangle is 180°.

Now consider finding the sum of the angles of a quadrilateral.

We can construct a diagonal of the quadrilateral as shown.

The red angles must add to 180° and so must the green angles.

But these 6 angles form the 4 angles of the quadrilateral.

So,   the sum of the interior angles of a quadrilateral is 360°.

We can generalise this process to find the sum of the interior angles of any polygon.

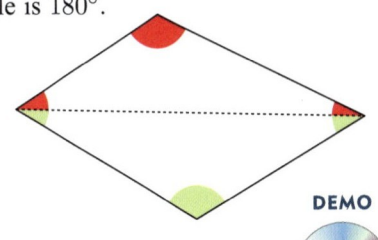

Discovery 1 — Angles of an n-sided polygon

What to do:

1. Draw any pentagon (5-sided polygon) and label one of its vertices A. Draw in all the diagonals from A.

2. Repeat **1** for a hexagon, a heptagon (7-gon), an octagon, and so on, drawing diagonals from one vertex only.

3. Copy and complete the following table:

Polygon	Number of sides	Number of diagonals from A	Number of triangles	Angle sum of polygon
quadrilateral	4	1	2	$2 \times 180° = 360°$
pentagon				
hexagon				
octagon				
20-gon				

4. Copy and complete the following statement:
   "The sum of the interior angles of any n-sided polygon is ...... $\times$ 180°."

You should have discovered that:

> The sum of the interior angles of any n-sided polygon is $(n-2) \times 180°$.

Example 6   ◀» Self Tutor

Find x, giving a brief reason:

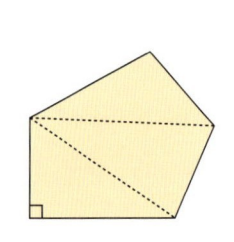

Lines, angles, and polygons (Chapter 4)

The pentagon has 5 sides

∴ the sum of interior angles is $3 \times 180° = 540°$

∴ $x + x + x + 132 + 90 = 540$
∴ $3x + 222 = 540$
∴ $3x = 318$
∴ $x = 106$

EXERCISE 4I

1 Find the sum of the interior angles of:
   a a quadrilateral   **b** a pentagon   **c** a hexagon   **d** an octagon.

2 Find the value of the unknown in:

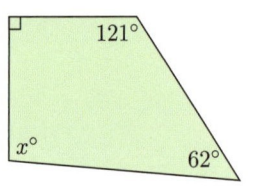

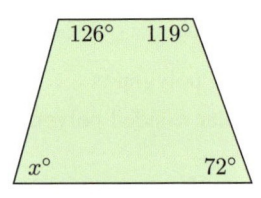

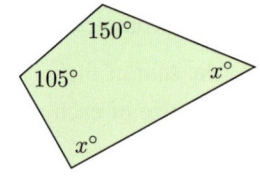

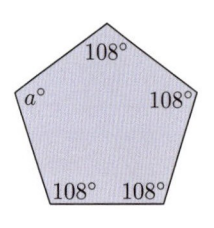

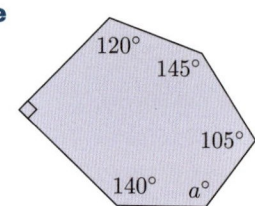

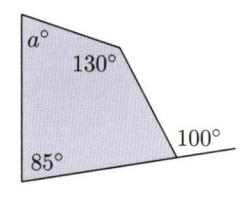

3 Find the value of x in each of the following, giving a reason:

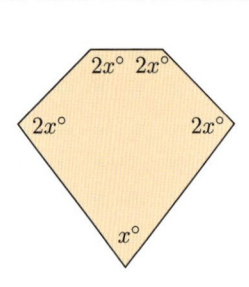

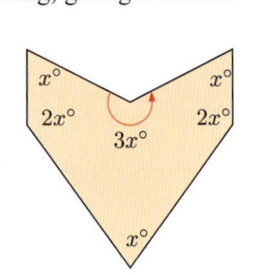

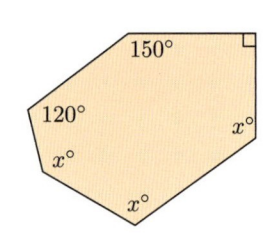

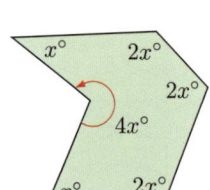

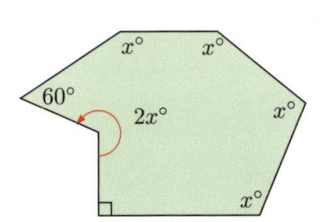

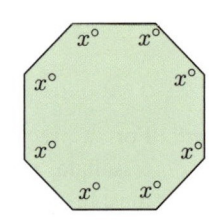

4 A pentagon has three right angles and two other equal angles.
What is the size of each of the two equal angles?

5 Find the size of each interior angle within a regular:
   a pentagon   **b** hexagon   **c** octagon   **d** decagon

6 The sum of the angles of a polygon is 1800°. How many angles has the polygon?

7 Joanna has found a truly remarkable polygon which has interior angles with a sum of 2060°. Comment on Joanna's finding.

8 Copy and complete the following table for regular polygons:

Regular polygon	Number of sides	Number of angles	Size of each angle
equilateral triangle			
square			
pentagon			
hexagon			
octagon			
decagon			

9 Copy and complete:
- the sum of the angles of an n-sided polygon is ....
- the size of each angle θ, of a regular n-sided polygon, is $\theta = ...$

10 Answer the **Opening Problem** on page **95**.

11 The figure alongside is a regular heptagon.
   a Find the size of each interior angle.
   b Hence, find the value of each of the unknowns.

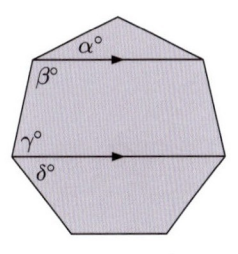

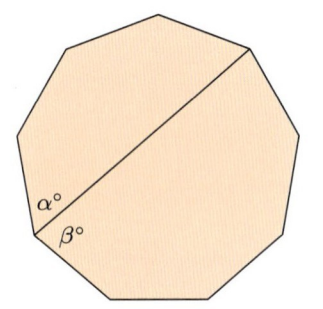

12 The figure alongside is a regular nonagon. Find α and β.

13 A **tessellation** is a pattern made with a number of objects of the same shape and size, which can cover an area without leaving any gaps. Which regular polygons tessellate?

    Hint: For a regular polygon to tessellate, copies of its shape must be able to meet at a point with no gaps. What property must the size of its interior angle have?

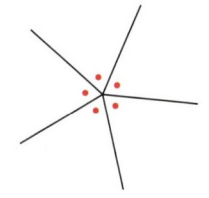

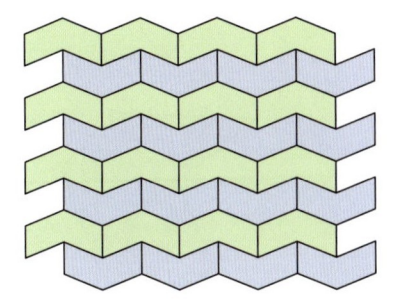

Lines, angles, and polygons (Chapter 4)

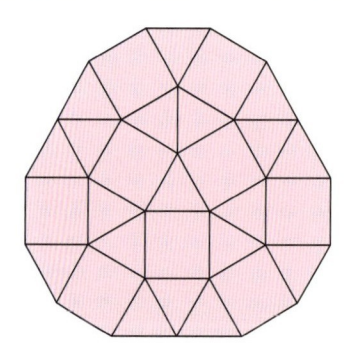

14 We can cover a region with tiles which are equilateral triangles and squares with sides of equal length.

    a Copy this pattern and add to it the next outer layer.

    b Can you construct a pattern without gaps, using a regular octagon and a square?

J THE EXTERIOR ANGLES OF A POLYGON [4.4]

The **exterior angles** of a polygon are formed by extending the sides in either direction.

Discovery 2 — Exterior angles of a polygon

The shaded angle is said to be an exterior angle of quadrilateral ABCD at vertex B.

The purpose of this Discovery is to find the sum of all exterior angles of a polygon.

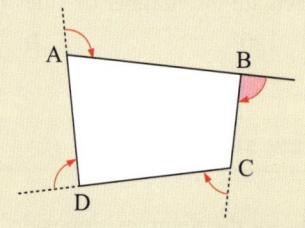

What to do:

1 In the school grounds, place four objects on the ground no more than 10 m apart, forming the vertices of an imaginary quadrilateral. Start at one vertex, and looking towards the next vertex, walk directly to it and turn to face the next vertex. Measure the angle that you have turned through.

2 Repeat this process until you are back to where you started from, and turn in the same way to face your original direction of sight, measuring each angle that you turn through.

3 Through how many degrees have you turned from start to finish?

4 Would your answer in **3** change if an extra object was included to form a pentagon?

5 Write a statement indicating what you have learnt about the sum of the exterior angles of any polygon.

From the Discovery, you should have found that:

> The sum of the exterior angles of any polygon is always $360°$.

This fact is useful for finding the size of an interior angle of a regular polygon.

Example 7   ◀) Self Tutor

A regular polygon has 15 sides. Calculate the size of each interior angle.

For a 15-sided polygon, each exterior angle is $360° \div 15 = 24°$

$\therefore$ each interior angle is $180° - 24° = 156°$ {angles on a line}

EXERCISE 4J

1 Solve for x:

   a   **b** 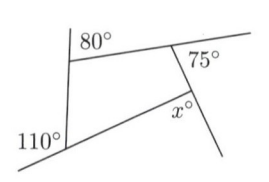   **c**

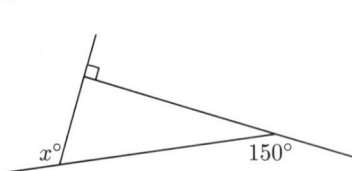

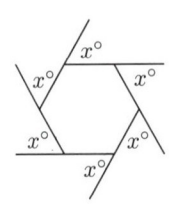

2 Calculate the size of each interior angle of these regular polygons:

   a with 5 sides   **b** with 8 sides   **c** with 10 sides

   d with 20 sides   **e** with 100 sides   **f** with n sides

3 Calculate the number of sides of a regular polygon given that an exterior angle is:

   a $45°$ **b** $15°$ **c** $2°$ **d** $\frac{1}{2}°$

4 Calculate the number of sides of a regular polygon with an interior angle of:

   a $120°$ **b** $150°$ **c** $175°$ **d** $179°$

Review set 4A

1 From the diagram alongside, name:

   a two supplementary angles

   b two complementary angles

   c a right angle

   d a pair of congruent triangles.

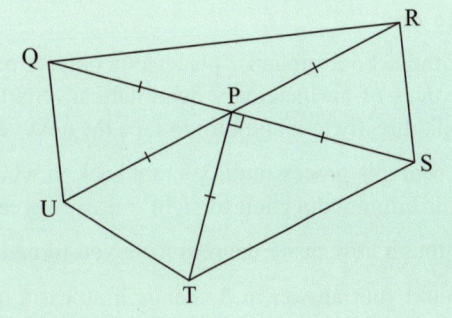

2 Classify these quadrilaterals, which are not drawn to scale:

   a   **b** 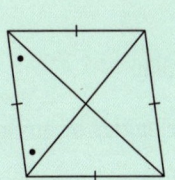   **c**

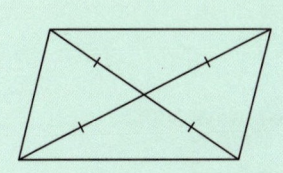

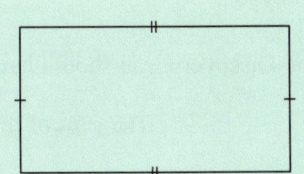

3 How many lines of symmetry do each of the following have?

   a   **b**    **c**

Lines, angles, and polygons (Chapter 4)

4 Copy and complete: If two parallel lines are cut by a third line then:
  a the alternate angles are ....
  b co-interior angles are ....

5 Find the value of the unknown, giving reasons for your answer:

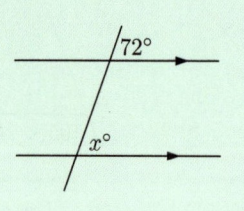

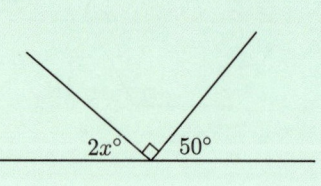

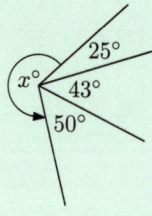

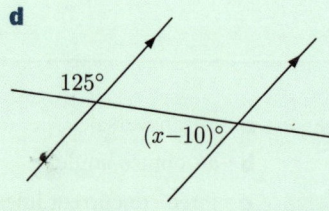

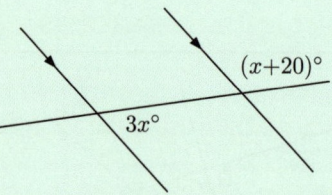

  a 72°, $x°$

  b $2x°$, 50°

  c $x°$, 25°, 43°, 50°

  d 125°, $(x-10)°$

  e $3x°$, $(x+20)°$

6 Decide if the figure contains parallel lines, giving a brief reason for your answer: 130°, 50°

7 Find the value of x in:

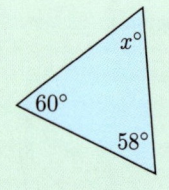

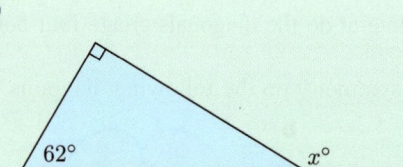

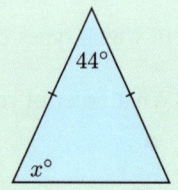

  a $x°$, 60°, 58°

  b 62°, $x°$

  c 44°, $x°$

8 What can be deduced about triangle ABC shown? Give reasons for your answer.
  A, 56°, B, 118°, C

9 Find, giving reasons, the values of the unknowns in:

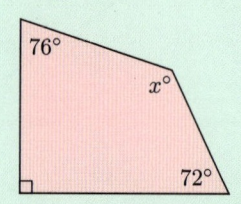

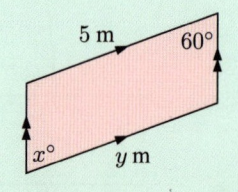

  a 76°, $x°$, 72°

  b 5 m, 60°, $x°$, y m

  c 55°, $x°$, $y°$

10 Copy and complete:

Polygon	Number of sides	Sum of interior angles
pentagon		
hexagon		
octagon		

11 Find the value of x in each of the following, giving reasons:

a (pentagon with angles 85°, 145°, $x°$, $x°$, and a right angle)

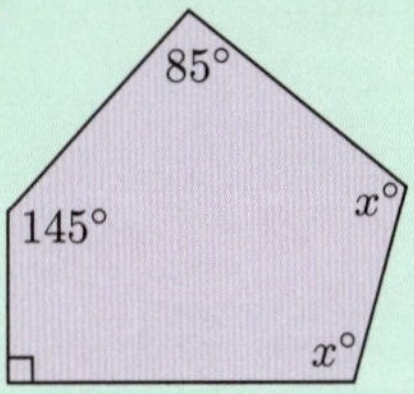

b (hexagon with four angles marked $x°$)

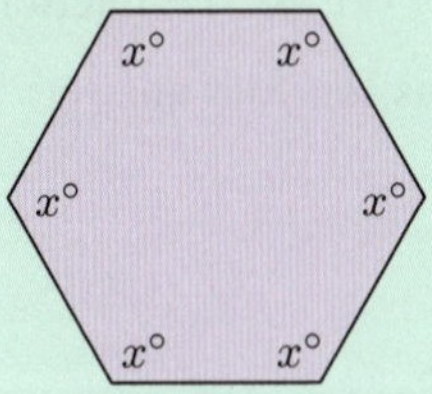

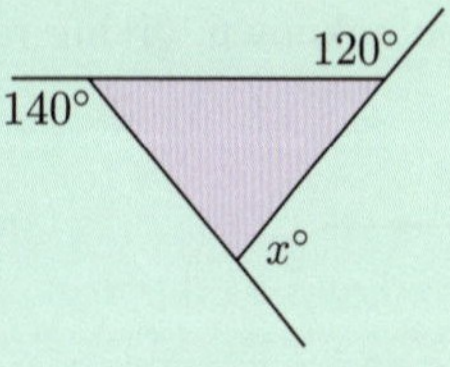

c (triangle with angles 140° (exterior), 120°, $x°$)

d (quadrilateral with two right angles, 105°, and $x°$)

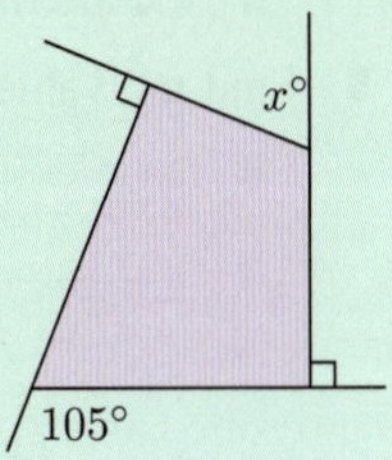

Review set 4B

1 (diagram with points A, B, C, D, E, F, G, H, I, J, K)

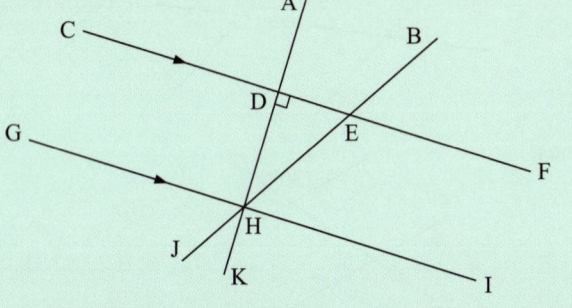

Name:
a a transversal
b an obtuse angle
c three concurrent lines
d two parallel lines
e two perpendicular lines

2 Draw a diagram of a kite, labelling all important properties.

3 In which types of quadrilateral do the diagonals create four congruent triangles?

4 What order of rotational symmetry do the following diagrams have?

a (five-pointed star)   **b** (six-petal flower)   **c** (scalene triangle)

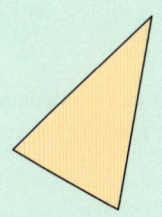

5 State the values of the unknowns in each figure, giving a brief reason for each answer:

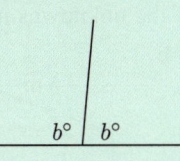

a ($a°$, 107° on a straight line)

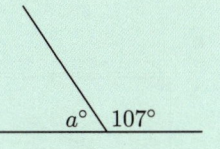

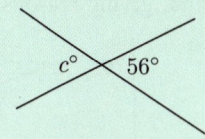

b ($b°$, $b°$ on a straight line with a vertical line)

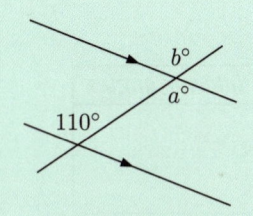

c ($c°$, 56° at intersecting lines)

d (110°, $b°$, $a°$ with parallel lines)

e $(x+15)°$ / $(4x-35)°$

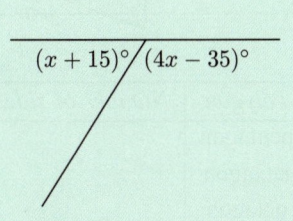

Lines, angles, and polygons (Chapter 4)

6 Find the value of the unknown in each figure, giving a brief reason for your answer:

  a   **b** 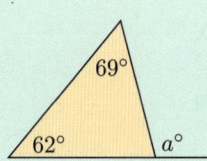   **c**

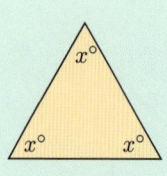

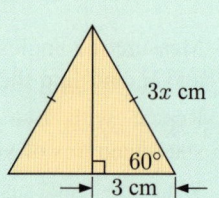

7 Find the values of x and y, giving brief reasons for your answers:

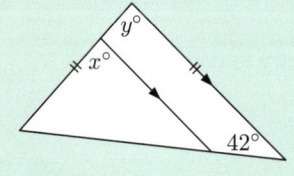

8 Classify each triangle in as much detail as possible:

  a   **b** 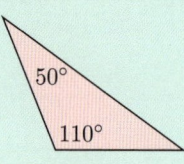   **c**

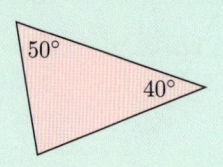

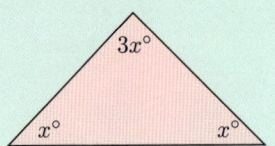

9 Find the values of the unknowns:

  a   **b**

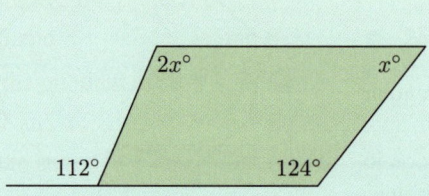

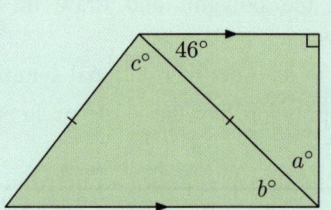

10 Calculate the size of each interior angle for a regular polygon with:

  a 12 sides   **b** 18 sides

11 Solve for x:

  a   **b**

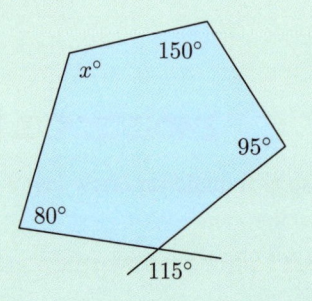

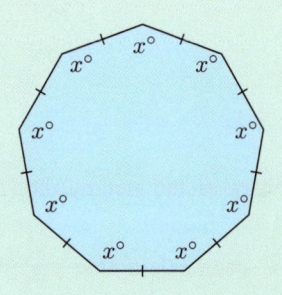

Challenge

1 **a** Measure the angles at A, B, C, D, and E, and find their sum.
   b Repeat with two other '5-point star' diagrams of your choosing.
   c What do you suspect about the angle sum for all '5-point star' diagrams?
   d Use deductive geometry to confirm your suspicion.

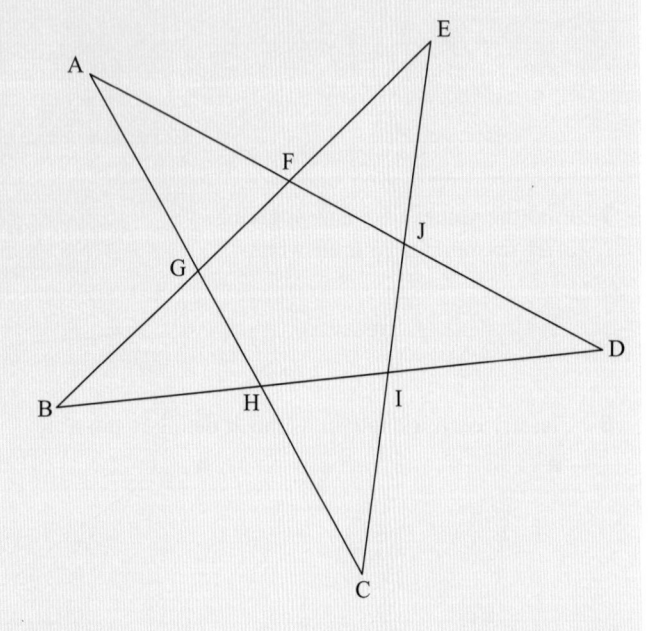

2 In the polygon alongside, every side has length 1 cm.
   a Is the polygon regular?
   b Copy the polygon and draw on it all lines of symmetry.
   c What is its order of rotational symmetry?
   d This polygon has the same perimeter as a regular hexagon with sides 2 cm.
   36 of these polygons are arranged in a tessellation in a 6 by 6 array. What is the total length of the lines in the tessellation?

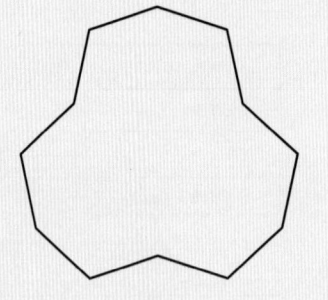

Algebra (expansion and factorisation)

5

Contents:

A	The distributive law	[2.7]
B	Equations containing brackets	
C	Equations containing fractions	[2.3]
D	The product $(a+b)(c+d)$	[2.7]
E	Difference of two squares	[2.7]
F	Algebraic common factors	
G	Factorising with common factors	[2.8]

Opening problem

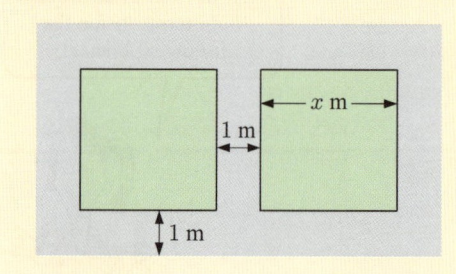

A 1 m wide path goes between and around two square garden beds. The garden beds are x m wide.

a Fill in the blanks:
  "The entire region is .... m long by .... m wide."
b Find an expression for the area of the entire region.
c Rewrite your expression in **b** without brackets.
d Show that the area of the path is $(7x+6)$ m^2.

In this chapter we will practise two important algebraic techniques: the **expansion** of expressions which involve brackets, and the reverse process, which is called **factorisation**.

A THE DISTRIBUTIVE LAW   [2.7]

Consider the expression $2(x+3)$. We say that 2 is the **coefficient** of the expression in the brackets. We can **expand** the brackets using the **distributive law**:

$$a(b+c) = ab + ac$$

The distributive law says that we must multiply the coefficient by each term within the brackets, and add the results.

Geometric Demonstration:

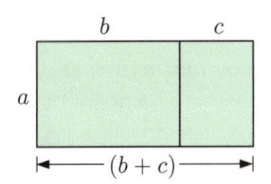

The overall area of the rectangle is found by multiplying the length $(b + c)$ by the width a.

So, the area is $a(b + c)$.

However, this area could also be found by adding the areas of the two small rectangles: $ab + ac$.

So, $a(b + c) = ab + ac$. {equating areas}

Example 1 ◀)) Self Tutor

Expand the following:

a $\quad 3(4x + 1)$ 	b $\quad 2x(5 - 2x)$ 	c $\quad -2x(x - 3)$

a $\quad 3(4x + 1)$
$= 3 \times 4x + 3 \times 1$
$= 12x + 3$

b $\quad 2x(5 - 2x)$
$= 2x(5 + -2x)$
$= 2x \times 5 + 2x \times -2x$
$= 10x - 4x^2$

c $\quad -2x(x - 3)$
$= -2x(x + -3)$
$= -2x \times x + -2x \times -3$
$= -2x^2 + 6x$

With practice, we do not need to write all of these steps.

Example 2 ◀)) Self Tutor

Expand and simplify:

a $\quad 2(3x - 1) + 3(5 - x)$ 	b $\quad x(2x - 1) - 2x(5 - x)$

a $\quad 2(3x - 1) + 3(5 - x)$
$= 6x - 2 + 15 - 3x$
$= 3x + 13$

b $\quad x(2x - 1) - 2x(5 - x)$
$= 2x^2 - x - 10x + 2x^2$
$= 4x^2 - 11x$

Notice in **b** that the minus sign in front of $2x$ affects *both* terms inside the following bracket.

EXERCISE 5A

1 Expand and simplify:

a $\quad 3(x + 1)$ 	b $\quad 2(5 - x)$ 	c $\quad -(x + 2)$ 	d $\quad -(3 - x)$
e $\quad 4(a + 2b)$ 	f $\quad 3(2x + y)$ 	g $\quad 5(x - y)$ 	h $\quad 6(-x^2 + y^2)$
i $\quad -2(x + 4)$ 	j $\quad -3(2x - 1)$ 	k $\quad x(x + 3)$ 	l $\quad 2x(x - 5)$
m $\quad -3(x + 2)$ 	n $\quad -4(x - 3)$ 	o $\quad -(7 - 2x)$ 	p $\quad -2(x - y)$
q $\quad a(a + b)$ 	r $\quad -a(a - b)$ 	s $\quad x(2x - 1)$ 	t $\quad 2x(x^2 - x - 2)$

2 Expand and simplify:

a $\quad 1 + 2(x + 2)$ 	b $\quad 13 - 4(x + 3)$ 	c $\quad 3(x - 2) + 5$
d $\quad 4(3 - x) - 10$ 	e $\quad x(x - 1) + x$ 	f $\quad 2x(3 - x) + x^2$
g $\quad 2a(b - a) + 3a^2$ 	h $\quad 4x - 3x(x - 1)$ 	i $\quad 7x^2 - 5x(x + 2)$

Algebra (expansion and factorisation) (Chapter 5)

3 Expand and simplify:

- **a** $3(x-4) + 2(5+x)$
- **b** $2a + (a - 2b)$
- **c** $2a - (a - 2b)$
- **d** $3(y+1) + 6(2-y)$
- **e** $2(y-3) - 4(2y+1)$
- **f** $3x - 4(2 - 3x)$
- **g** $2(b-a) + 3(a+b)$
- **h** $x(x+4) + 2(x-3)$
- **i** $x(x+4) - 2(x-3)$
- **j** $x^2 + x(x-1)$
- **k** $-x^2 - x(x-2)$
- **l** $x(x+y) - y(x+y)$
- **m** $-4(x-2) - (3-x)$
- **n** $5(2x-1) - (2x+3)$
- **o** $4x(x-3) - 2x(5-x)$

B EQUATIONS CONTAINING BRACKETS

When we are given a linear equation containing brackets, we:
- expand the brackets
- collect like terms
- use inverse operations to isolate the unknown.

Example 3 ◀)) Self Tutor

Solve for x: $\quad 5(x+1) - 2x = -7$

$$5(x+1) - 2x = -7$$
$$\therefore \quad 5x + 5 - 2x = -7 \qquad \{\text{expanding the brackets}\}$$
$$\therefore \quad 3x + 5 = -7 \qquad \{\text{collecting like terms}\}$$
$$\therefore \quad 3x + 5 - 5 = -7 - 5 \qquad \{\text{subtracting 5 from both sides}\}$$
$$\therefore \quad 3x = -12$$
$$\therefore \quad \frac{3x}{3} = \frac{-12}{3} \qquad \{\text{dividing both sides by 3}\}$$
$$\therefore \quad x = -4$$

EXERCISE 5B

1 Solve for x:

- **a** $3(x-2) - x = 12$
- **b** $4(x+2) - 2x = -16$
- **c** $5(x-3) + 4x = -6$
- **d** $2(3x+2) - x = -6$
- **e** $5(2x-1) - 4x = 11$
- **f** $-2(4x+3) + 2x = 12$

2 Solve for x:

- **a** $3(x+2) + 2(x+4) = -1$
- **b** $5(x+1) - 3(x+2) = 11$
- **c** $4(x-3) - 2(x-1) = -6$
- **d** $3(3x+1) - 4(x+1) = 14$
- **e** $2(3+2x) + 3(x-4) = 8$
- **f** $4(5x-3) - 3(2x-5) = 17$

3 Solve for x:

- **a** $2(x+4) - x = 8$
- **b** $5(2-3x) = -8 - 6x$
- **c** $3(x+2) - x = 12$
- **d** $2(x+1) + 3(x-4) = 5$
- **e** $4(2x-1) + 9 = 3x$
- **f** $11x - 2(x-1) = -5$
- **g** $3x - 2(x+1) = -7$
- **h** $8 - (2-x) = 2x$
- **i** $5x - 4(4-x) = x + 12$

4 Try to solve for x. In each case explain your result.

- **a** $3(x-6) + 7x = 5(2x-1)$
- **b** $3(2x-4) = 5x - (12-x)$

5 Find the number that can be decreased by 2 and then multiplied by 4, to get -16.

6 When 22 is subtracted from a number and the result is doubled, the answer is 6 more than the original number. Find the number.

7 When a number is subtracted from 21 and then multiplied by 6, the result is 8 times the original number. Find the number.

8 Find the number that can be increased by 11, and then quartered, to get 6.

Example 4   ◀)) *Self Tutor*

Cans of sardines come in two sizes. Small cans cost $2 each and large cans cost $3 each. If 15 cans of sardines are bought for a total of $38, how many small cans were purchased?

Size	Cost per can	Number bought	Value
small	$2	x	$2x$
large	$3	$15 - x$	$3(15 - x)$
		15	$38

So, $2x + 3(15 - x) = 38$

$\therefore \quad 2x + 45 - 3x = 38$ {expanding brackets}

$\therefore \quad 45 - x = 38$

$\therefore \quad 45 - x - 45 = 38 - 45$ {subtracting 45 from both sides}

$\therefore \quad -x = -7$

$\therefore \quad x = 7$ So, 7 small cans were bought.

---

9 Nick has 40 coins in his collection, all of which are either 5-cent or 10-cent coins. If the total value of his coins is $3.15, how many of each coin type does he have?

10 Roses cost £5 each and geraniums cost £3 each. Michelle bought 4 more geraniums than roses, and in total she spent £52. How many roses did she buy?

11 A store sells batteries in packets of 6 or 10. In stock they have 25 packets which contain a total of 186 batteries. How many of each packet size are in stock?

12 A petrol station sells two types of fuel, unleaded and diesel. The unleaded petrol is sold for 127 p per litre and the diesel is sold for 130 p per litre. If 1400 l of petrol is pumped in 1 hour at a total of £1797.50, how many litres of diesel petrol was pumped?

C   EQUATIONS CONTAINING FRACTIONS   [2.3]

To solve equations containing fractions, we:
- write all fractions with the **lowest common denominator (LCD)**, and then
- **equate numerators**.

In the solution process we often need to expand brackets using the distributive law.

Algebra (expansion and factorisation)   (Chapter 5)

Example 5

Solve for x: $\dfrac{x}{2} = \dfrac{3}{7}$

$\dfrac{x}{2} = \dfrac{3}{7}$ {LCD = 14}

$\therefore \dfrac{x \times 7}{2 \times 7} = \dfrac{3 \times 2}{7 \times 2}$ {to achieve a common denominator}

$\therefore 7x = 6$ {equating numerators}

$\therefore \dfrac{7x}{7} = \dfrac{6}{7}$ {dividing both sides by 7}

$\therefore x = \dfrac{6}{7}$

To solve equations involving fractions, we make the denominators the same, then equate the numerators.

Example 6

Solve for x: $\dfrac{2x+3}{4} = \dfrac{x-2}{3}$

$\dfrac{2x+3}{4} = \dfrac{x-2}{3}$ {LCD = 12}

$\therefore \dfrac{3 \times (2x+3)}{3 \times 4} = \dfrac{4 \times (x-2)}{4 \times 3}$ {to achieve a common denominator}

$\therefore 3(2x+3) = 4(x-2)$ {equating numerators}

$\therefore 6x + 9 = 4x - 8$ {expanding brackets}

$\therefore 6x + 9 - 4x = 4x - 8 - 4x$ {subtracting $4x$ from both sides}

$\therefore 2x + 9 = -8$

$\therefore 2x + 9 - 9 = -8 - 9$ {subtracting 9 from both sides}

$\therefore 2x = -17$

$\therefore \dfrac{2x}{2} = -\dfrac{17}{2}$ {dividing both sides by 2}

$\therefore x = -8\tfrac{1}{2}$

EXERCISE 5C

1 Solve for x:

   a $\dfrac{x}{5} = \dfrac{2}{3}$ **b** $\dfrac{x}{4} = 1\tfrac{1}{2}$ **c** $\dfrac{1}{5} = \dfrac{x}{2}$

   d $\dfrac{3x}{4} = \dfrac{2}{9}$ **e** $\dfrac{8}{5} = \dfrac{5x}{3}$ **f** $\dfrac{3x}{5} = \dfrac{2x}{7}$

2 Solve for x:

   a $\dfrac{2x+3}{5} = \dfrac{1}{2}$ **b** $\dfrac{x+6}{2} = \dfrac{x}{3}$ **c** $\dfrac{2x-11}{7} = \dfrac{3x}{5}$

   d $\dfrac{x+4}{2} = \dfrac{2x-3}{3}$ **e** $\dfrac{3x+2}{2} = \dfrac{x-1}{4}$ **f** $\dfrac{1-x}{2} = \dfrac{x+2}{3}$

   g $\dfrac{x+5}{2} = 1-x$ **h** $\dfrac{2x+7}{3} = x+4$ **i** $\dfrac{2x+9}{2} = x-8$

Example 7

Solve for x: $\dfrac{x}{3} - \dfrac{1-2x}{6} = -4$

$\dfrac{x}{3} - \dfrac{1-2x}{6} = -4$ {LCD = 6}

$\therefore \quad \dfrac{x}{3} \times \dfrac{2}{2} - \left(\dfrac{1-2x}{6}\right) = -4 \times \dfrac{6}{6}$ {to create a common denominator}

$\therefore \quad 2x - (1 - 2x) = -24$ {equating numerators}

$\therefore \quad 2x - 1 + 2x = -24$ {expanding}

$\therefore \quad 4x - 1 = -24$

$\therefore \quad 4x - 1 + 1 = -24 + 1$ {adding 1 to both sides}

$\therefore \quad 4x = -23$

$\therefore \quad x = -\dfrac{23}{4}$ {dividing both sides by 4}

3 Solve for x:

a $\dfrac{x}{2} - \dfrac{x}{6} = 4$

b $\dfrac{x}{4} - 3 = \dfrac{2x}{3}$

c $\dfrac{x}{8} + \dfrac{x+2}{2} = -1$

d $\dfrac{x+2}{3} + \dfrac{x-3}{4} = 1$

e $\dfrac{2x-1}{3} - \dfrac{5x-6}{6} = -2$

f $\dfrac{x}{4} = 4 - \dfrac{x+2}{3}$

g $\dfrac{2x-7}{3} - 1 = \dfrac{x-4}{6}$

h $\dfrac{x+1}{3} - \dfrac{x}{6} = \dfrac{2x-3}{2}$

i $\dfrac{x}{5} - \dfrac{2x-5}{3} = \dfrac{3}{4}$

j $\dfrac{x+1}{3} + \dfrac{x-2}{6} = \dfrac{x+4}{12}$

k $\dfrac{x-6}{5} - \dfrac{2x-1}{10} = \dfrac{x-1}{2}$

l $\dfrac{2x+1}{4} - \dfrac{1-4x}{2} = \dfrac{3x+7}{6}$

D THE PRODUCT $(a+b)(c+d)$ [2.7]

Consider the product $(a+b)(c+d)$.

It has two **factors**, $(a+b)$ and $(c+d)$.

We can evaluate this product by using the distributive law several times.

$(a+b)(c+d) = a(c+d) + b(c+d)$
$ = ac + ad + bc + bd$

So, $(a+b)(c+d) = ac + ad + bc + bd$

This is sometimes called the **FOIL** rule.

The final result contains four terms:

ac is the product of the **F**irst terms of each bracket.
ad is the product of the **O**uter terms of each bracket.
bc is the product of the **I**nner terms of each bracket.
bd is the product of the **L**ast terms of each bracket.

Algebra (expansion and factorisation) (Chapter 5)

Example 8

Expand and simplify: $(x+3)(x+2)$

$(x+3)(x+2)$
$= x \times x + x \times 2 + 3 \times x + 3 \times 2$
$= x^2 + 2x + 3x + 6$
$= x^2 + 5x + 6$

In practice we do not include the second line of these examples.

Example 9

Expand and simplify: $(2x+1)(3x-2)$

$(2x+1)(3x-2)$
$= 2x \times 3x + 2x \times -2 + 1 \times 3x + 1 \times -2$
$= 6x^2 - 4x + 3x - 2$
$= 6x^2 - x - 2$

Example 10

Expand and simplify:

a $(x+3)(x-3)$ **b** $(3x-5)(3x+5)$

a $(x+3)(x-3)$
  $= x^2 - 3x + 3x - 9$
  $= x^2 - 9$

b $(3x-5)(3x+5)$
  $= 9x^2 + 15x - 15x - 25$
  $= 9x^2 - 25$

In Examples 10 and 11, what do you notice about the two middle terms?

Example 11

Expand and simplify:

a $(3x+1)^2$ **b** $(2x-3)^2$

a $(3x+1)^2$
  $= (3x+1)(3x+1)$
  $= 9x^2 + 3x + 3x + 1$
  $= 9x^2 + 6x + 1$

b $(2x-3)^2$
  $= (2x-3)(2x-3)$
  $= 4x^2 - 6x - 6x + 9$
  $= 4x^2 - 12x + 9$

EXERCISE 5D

1 Consider the figure alongside.
Give an expression for the area of:
  a rectangle 1   **b** rectangle 2
  c rectangle 3   **d** rectangle 4
  e the overall rectangle.
What can you conclude?

2 Expand and simplify:
  a $(x+3)(x+7)$
  b $(x+5)(x-4)$
  c $(x-3)(x+6)$
  d $(x+2)(x-2)$
  e $(x-8)(x+3)$
  f $(2x+1)(3x+4)$
  g $(1-2x)(4x+1)$
  h $(4-x)(2x+3)$
  i $(3x-2)(1+2x)$
  j $(5-3x)(5+x)$
  k $(7-x)(4x+1)$
  l $(5x+2)(5x+2)$

3 Expand and simplify:
  a $(x+2)(x-2)$
  b $(a-5)(a+5)$
  c $(4+x)(4-x)$
  d $(2x+1)(2x-1)$
  e $(5a+3)(5a-3)$
  f $(4+3a)(4-3a)$

4 Expand and simplify:
  a $(x+3)^2$
  b $(x-2)^2$
  c $(3x-2)^2$
  d $(1-3x)^2$
  e $(3-4x)^2$
  f $(5x-y)^2$

5 A square photograph has sides of length x cm. It is surrounded by a wooden frame with the dimensions shown. Show that the total area of the photograph and the frame is given by $A = x^2 + 10x + 24$ cm^2.

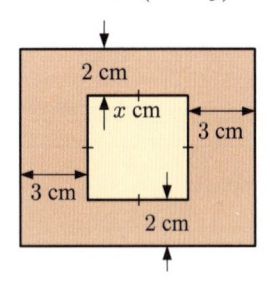

E DIFFERENCE OF TWO SQUARES [2.7]

a^2 and b^2 are perfect squares and so $a^2 - b^2$ is called the **difference of two squares**.

Notice that $(a+b)(a-b) = a^2 \underbrace{- ab + ab}_{\text{the sum of the two middle terms is zero}} - b^2 = a^2 - b^2$

Thus, $\boxed{(a+b)(a-b) = a^2 - b^2}$

Geometric Demonstration:

Consider the figure alongside:

The shaded area
= area of large square − area of small square
= $a^2 - b^2$

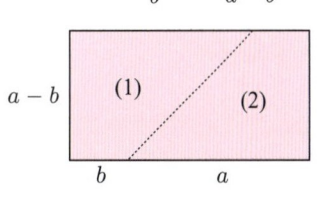

Algebra (expansion and factorisation) (Chapter 5)

Cutting along the dotted line and flipping (2) over, we can form a rectangle.

The rectangle's area is $(a+b)(a-b)$.

$\therefore \quad (a+b)(a-b) = a^2 - b^2$

Example 12 ◀) Self Tutor

Expand and simplify:

a $(x+5)(x-5)$ **b** $(3-y)(3+y)$

a $(x+5)(x-5)$
$= x^2 - 5^2$
$= x^2 - 25$

b $(3-y)(3+y)$
$= 3^2 - y^2$
$= 9 - y^2$

Example 13 ◀) Self Tutor

Expand and simplify:

a $(2x-3)(2x+3)$ **b** $(5-3y)(5+3y)$ **c** $(3x+4y)(3x-4y)$

a $(2x-3)(2x+3)$
$= (2x)^2 - 3^2$
$= 4x^2 - 9$

b $(5-3y)(5+3y)$
$= 5^2 - (3y)^2$
$= 25 - 9y^2$

c $(3x+4y)(3x-4y)$
$= (3x)^2 - (4y)^2$
$= 9x^2 - 16y^2$

EXERCISE 5E

1 Expand and simplify using the rule $(a+b)(a-b) = a^2 - b^2$:
- **a** $(x+2)(x-2)$
- **b** $(x-2)(x+2)$
- **c** $(2+x)(2-x)$
- **d** $(2-x)(2+x)$
- **e** $(x+1)(x-1)$
- **f** $(1-x)(1+x)$
- **g** $(x+7)(x-7)$
- **h** $(c+8)(c-8)$
- **i** $(d-5)(d+5)$
- **j** $(x+y)(x-y)$
- **k** $(4+d)(4-d)$
- **l** $(5+e)(5-e)$

2 Expand and simplify using the rule $(a+b)(a-b) = a^2 - b^2$:
- **a** $(2x-1)(2x+1)$
- **b** $(3x+2)(3x-2)$
- **c** $(4y-5)(4y+5)$
- **d** $(2y+5)(2y-5)$
- **e** $(3x+1)(3x-1)$
- **f** $(1-3x)(1+3x)$
- **g** $(2-5y)(2+5y)$
- **h** $(3+4a)(3-4a)$
- **i** $(4+3a)(4-3a)$

3 Expand and simplify using the rule $(a+b)(a-b) = a^2 - b^2$:
- **a** $(2a+b)(2a-b)$
- **b** $(a-2b)(a+2b)$
- **c** $(4x+y)(4x-y)$
- **d** $(4x+5y)(4x-5y)$
- **e** $(2x+3y)(2x-3y)$
- **f** $(7x-2y)(7x+2y)$

4 **a** Use the difference of two squares expansion to show that:
   i $43 \times 37 = 40^2 - 3^2$ **ii** $24 \times 26 = 25^2 - 1^2$
  b Evaluate without using a calculator:
   i 18×22 **ii** 49×51 **iii** 103×97

Discovery — The product of three consecutive integers

Con was trying to multiply $19 \times 20 \times 21$ without a calculator.

Aimee told him to 'cube the middle integer and then subtract the middle integer' to get the answer.

What to do:

1 **a** Find $19 \times 20 \times 21$ using a calculator.   **b** Find $20^3 - 20$ using a calculator.
   c Does Aimee's rule seem to work?

2 Check that Aimee's rule works for the following products:
   a $4 \times 5 \times 6$ **b** $9 \times 10 \times 11$ **c** $49 \times 50 \times 51$

3 Let the middle integer be x, so the other integers must be $(x-1)$ and $(x+1)$.
Find the product $(x-1) \times x \times (x+1)$ by expanding and simplifying. Have you proved Aimee's rule?

F ALGEBRAIC COMMON FACTORS

Algebraic products are products which contain variables.

For example, $6c$ and $4x^2y$ are both algebraic products.

In the same way that whole numbers have factors, algebraic products are also made up of factors.

For example, in the same way that we can write 60 as $2 \times 2 \times 3 \times 5$, we can write $2xy^2$ as $2 \times x \times y \times y$.

To find the **highest common factor** of a group of numbers, we express the numbers as products of prime factors. The common prime factors are then found and multiplied to give the highest common factor (HCF).

We can use the same technique to find the highest common factor of a group of algebraic products.

Example 14   ◀》 Self Tutor

a Write $20x$ as a product of prime factors.
b Hence find the missing factor: $2 \times \square = 20x$.

a $20x = 2 \times 2 \times 5 \times x$
b $2 \times \boxed{2 \times 5 \times x} = 20x$
So, the missing factor is $2 \times 5 \times x = 10x$.

Algebra (expansion and factorisation) (Chapter 5)

Example 15

Find the highest common factor of:

a $8a$ and $12b$ **b** $4x^2$ and $6xy$

a
$$8a = 2 \times 2 \times 2 \times a$$
$$12b = 2 \times 2 \times 3 \times b$$
$$\therefore \text{ HCF} = 2 \times 2$$
$$= 4$$

b
$$4x^2 = 2 \times 2 \times x \times x$$
$$6xy = 2 \times 3 \times x \times y$$
$$\therefore \text{ HCF} = 2 \times x$$
$$= 2x$$

*Write each term as a product of its **factors**!*

Example 16

Find the HCF of $3(x+3)$ and $(x+3)(x+1)$.

$$3(x+3) = 3 \times (x+3) \qquad (x+3)(x+1) = (x+3) \times (x+1)$$
$$\therefore \text{ HCF} = (x+3)$$

EXERCISE 5F

1 Write as a product of prime factors:
- **a** 15
- **b** $3x$
- **c** $2y$
- **d** xy
- **e** $39x$
- **f** a^2
- **g** $25b^2$
- **h** c^2d
- **i** $7xy$
- **j** $3m^2n$
- **k** $42pq^2$
- **l** $36ijk^2$

2 Find the missing factor:
- **a** $3 \times \square = 6a$
- **b** $3 \times \square = 15b$
- **c** $2 \times \square = 8xy$
- **d** $2x \times \square = 8x^2$
- **e** $\square \times 2x = 2x^2$
- **f** $\square \times 5x = -10x^2$
- **g** $-a \times \square = ab$
- **h** $\square \times a^2 = 4a^3$
- **i** $3x \times \square = -9x^2y$

3 Find the highest common factor of the following:
- **a** $2a$ and 6
- **b** $5c$ and $8c$
- **c** $8r$ and 27
- **d** $12k$ and $7k$
- **e** $3a$ and $12a$
- **f** $5x$ and $15x$
- **g** $25x$ and $10x$
- **h** $24y$ and $32y$
- **i** $36b$ and $54d$

4 Find the HCF of the following:
- **a** $23ab$ and $7ab$
- **b** abc and $6abc$
- **c** $36a$ and $12ab$
- **d** a^2 and a
- **e** $9r$ and r^3
- **f** $3q$ and qr
- **g** $3b^2$ and $9b$
- **h** dp^2 and pd
- **i** $4r$ and $8r^2$
- **j** $3pq$ and $6pq^2$
- **k** $2a^2b$ and $6ab$
- **l** $6xy$ and $18x^2y^2$
- **m** $15a$, $20ab$ and $30b$
- **n** $12wxz$, $12wz$, $24wxyz$
- **o** $24p^2qr$, $36pqr^2$

5 Find the HCF of:
- **a** $5(x+2)$ and $(x+8)(x+2)$
- **b** $2(x+5)^2$ and $6(x+9)(x+5)$
- **c** $3x(x+4)$ and $x^2(x+2)$
- **d** $6(x+1)^2$ and $2(x+1)(x-2)$
- **e** $2(x+3)^2$ and $4(x+3)(x-7)$
- **f** $4x(x-3)$ and $6x(x-3)^2$

Activity: Algebraic common factor maze

To find your way through this maze, follow the given instructions. After you have completed the maze you may like to construct your own maze for a friend to follow.

Instructions:

1. You can only move to an adjacent cell.
2. You are permitted to move horizontally or vertically but **not** diagonally.
3. A move to the next cell is only possible if that cell has a factor in common with the one you are presently on.
4. Start with the term 12.
5. Find your way to the exit.

$6m$	$2a$	3	$9c^2$	$3c$	c^2	8	$2p^2$
$4m$	mn	$6n$	$5c$	25	$5m$	12	$4p$
$8y$	xy	2	$6a$	$5a$	mn	$6n^2$	7
$7y$	21	$3z$	$5x$	$3y$	y^2	$3p$	p
ab	$7a$	yz	xy	$15x$	xy	p^2	7
17	pq	$3q$	q^2	63	$7b$	b^2	6
12	5	10	$10b$	12	y^2	$9b$	$3b$
$6a$	a^2	$5a$	$3a$	$4x$	xy	$2x$	x^2

start → (row 7, column 1)   → exit (row 3, right)

G FACTORISING WITH COMMON FACTORS [2.8]

Factorisation is the process of writing an expression as a **product** of its **factors**.

Factorisation is the reverse process of expansion.

In **expansions** we have to *remove brackets*, whereas in **factorisation** we have to *insert brackets*.

Consider the expression $3(x+2)$. We can expand this to $3x+6$.

The *reverse* of this process is *factorising* $3x+6$ to $3(x+2)$.

We have turned $3x+6$ into the *product of two factors*, 3 and $x+2$. Notice that we write $3(x+2)$ and not $3x+2$.

The brackets are essential, since in $3(x+2)$ the whole of $x+2$ is multiplied by 3 whereas in $3x+2$ only the x is multiplied by 3.

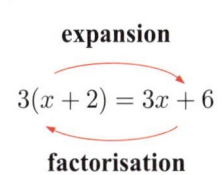

expansion

$$3(x+2) = 3x+6$$

factorisation

To factorise an algebraic expression involving a number of terms, we look for the HCF of the terms and write it in front of a set of brackets. We then find the contents of the brackets.

For example, $5x^2$ and $10xy$ have HCF $5x$.

So, $5x^2 + 10xy = 5x \times x + 5x \times 2y$
$= 5x(x+2y)$

Algebra (expansion and factorisation) (Chapter 5)

FACTORISING FULLY

Notice that $6a + 12 = 3(2a + 4)$ is not *fully* factorised. $(2a + 4)$ still has a common factor of 2 which could be removed. Although 3 is a common factor of $6a + 12$, it is not the *highest* common factor. The HCF is 6 and so

$$6a + 12 = 6(a + 2) \text{ is fully factorised.}$$

Example 17

Fully factorise: **a** $3a + 6$ **b** $ab - 2bc$

a $3a + 6$
$= 3 \times a + 3 \times 2$
$= 3(a + 2)$ {HCF is 3}

b $ab - 2bc$
$= a \times b - 2 \times b \times c$
$= b(a - 2c)$ {HCF is b}

With practice the middle line is not necessary.

Example 18

Fully factorise: **a** $8x^2 + 12x$ **b** $3y^2 - 6xy$

a $8x^2 + 12x$
$= 2 \times 4 \times x \times x + 3 \times 4 \times x$
$= 4x(2x + 3)$ {HCF is $4x$}

b $3y^2 - 6xy$
$= 3 \times y \times y - 2 \times 3 \times x \times y$
$= 3y(y - 2x)$ {HCF is $3y$}

Example 19

Fully factorise: **a** $-2a + 6ab$ **b** $-2x^2 - 4x$

a $-2a + 6ab$
$= 6ab - 2a$ {Write with $6ab$ first}
$= 2 \times 3 \times a \times b - 2 \times a$
$= 2a(3b - 1)$ {HCF is $2a$}

b $-2x^2 - 4x$
$= -2 \times x \times x + -2 \times 2 \times x$
$= -2x(x + 2)$ {HCF is $-2x$}

Example 20

Fully factorise:
a $2(x + 3) + x(x + 3)$ **b** $x(x + 4) - (x + 4)$

a $2(x + 3) + x(x + 3)$ {HCF is $(x + 3)$}
$= (x + 3)(2 + x)$

b $x(x + 4) - (x + 4)$ {HCF is $(x + 4)$}
$= x(x + 4) - 1(x + 4)$
$= (x + 4)(x - 1)$

Example 21

Fully factorise $(x-1)(x+2) + 3(x-1)$

$(x-1)(x+2) + 3(x-1)$ {HCF is $(x-1)$}
$= (x-1)[(x+2) + 3]$
$= (x-1)(x+5)$

Notice the square brackets in the second line. This helps to distinguish between the sets of brackets.

EXERCISE 5G

1 Copy and complete:
  a $2x + 4 = 2(x + ...)$
  b $3a - 12 = 3(a - ....)$
  c $15 - 5p = 5(.... - p)$
  d $18x + 12 = 6(.... + 2)$
  e $4x^2 - 8x = 4x(x - ....)$
  f $2m + 8m^2 = 2m(.... + 4m)$

2 Copy and complete:
  a $4x + 16 = 4(.... + ...)$
  b $10 + 5d = 5(.... + ...)$
  c $5c - 5 = 5(.... - ....)$
  d $cd + de = d(.... + ...)$
  e $6a + 8ab = ...(3 + 4b)$
  f $6x - 2x^2 = ...(3 - x)$
  g $7ab - 7a = ...(b - 1)$
  h $4ab - 6bc = ...(2a - 3c)$

You can check your factorisations by expanding back out!

3 Fully factorise:
  a $3a + 3b$
  b $8x - 16$
  c $3p + 18$
  d $28 - 14x$
  e $7x - 14$
  f $12 + 6x$
  g $ac + bc$
  h $12y - 6a$
  i $5a + ab$
  j $bc - 6cd$
  k $7x - xy$
  l $xy + y$
  m $a + ab$
  n $xy - yz$
  o $3pq + pr$
  p $cd - c$

4 Fully factorise:
  a $x^2 + 2x$
  b $5x - 2x^2$
  c $4x^2 + 8x$
  d $14x - 7x^2$
  e $6x^2 + 12x$
  f $x^3 + 9x^2$
  g $x^2y + xy^2$
  h $4x^3 - 6x^2$
  i $9x^3 - 18xy$
  j $a^3 + a^2 + a$
  k $2a^2 + 4a + 8$
  l $3a^3 - 6a^2 + 9a$

5 Fully factorise:
  a $-9a + 9b$
  b $-3 + 6b$
  c $-8a + 4b$
  d $-7c + cd$
  e $-a + ab$
  f $-6x^2 + 12x$
  g $-5x + 15x^2$
  h $-2b^2 + 4ab$
  i $-a + a^2$

6 Fully factorise:
  a $-6a - 6b$
  b $-4 - 8x$
  c $-3y - 6z$
  d $-9c - cd$
  e $-x - xy$
  f $-5x^2 - 20x$
  g $-12y - 3y^2$
  h $-18a^2 - 9ab$
  i $-16x^2 - 24x$

7 Fully factorise:
  a $2(x - 7) + x(x - 7)$
  b $a(x + 3) + b(x + 3)$
  c $4(x + 2) - x(x + 2)$
  d $x(x + 9) + (x + 9)$
  e $a(b + 4) - (b + 4)$
  f $a(b + c) + d(b + c)$
  g $a(m + n) - b(m + n)$
  h $x(x + 3) - x - 3$

8 Fully factorise:

   a $(x+3)(x-5) + 4(x+3)$ **b** $5(x-7) + (x-7)(x+2)$

   c $(x+6)(x+4) - 8(x+6)$ **d** $(x-2)^2 - 6(x-2)$

   e $(x+2)^2 - (x+2)(x+1)$ **f** $5(a+b) - (a+b)(a+1)$

   g $3(a-2)^2 - 6(a-2)$ **h** $(x+4)^2 + 3(x+4)(x-1)$

   i $x(x-1) - 6(x-1)(x-5)$ **j** $3(x+5) - 4(x+5)^2$

Review set 5A

1 Expand and simplify:

   a $3(x-4)$ **b** $-5(3+y)$ **c** $2(y^2 - z)$

   d $x(x+1)$ **e** $3x(x-2)$ **f** $-3x(x-5)$

2 Solve for x:

   a $2(x+4) = 3 - x$ **b** $\dfrac{x}{4} = \dfrac{4}{9}$ **c** $\dfrac{5x+4}{3} = \dfrac{x}{2}$

3 Expand and simplify:

   a $(x+3)(x-8)$ **b** $(x-2)(x+5)$ **c** $(4-x)(x-1)$

   d $(x+3)^2$ **e** $(x+5)(x-5)$ **f** $(2x-4)(x+3)$

4 Oil comes in 3 l and 5 l cans. If 42 cans contain 152 l of oil, how many of the cans hold 5 l?

5 Expand and simplify:

   a $(x-6)(x+6)$ **b** $(4x+1)(4x-1)$ **c** $(4x+1)(3x-2)$

   d $(x+3)(x-1) - (3-x)(x+4)$

6 Find the HCF of:

   a $6c$ and $15c^2$ **b** $4pq$ and $8p$ **c** $18r^2s$ and $15rs^2$

7 Fully factorise:

   a $6a + 8$ **b** $3x^2 - 12x$ **c** $15x - 6x^2$

   d $-4x - 2xy$ **e** $2(x-3) + (x+1)(x-3)$ **f** $(x+2)^2 - 3(x+2)$

Review set 5B

1 Expand and simplify:

   a $4(x-2)$ **b** $7(4-x)$ **c** $x(8+x)$

   d $t(r-s)$ **e** $5 - (x+1)$ **f** $2(x+3) + 4x$

2 Solve for x:

   a $3(1-x) = x + 2$ **b** $\dfrac{5}{3} = \dfrac{x}{5}$ **c** $\dfrac{3x-7}{2} = \dfrac{2x+2}{3}$

3 Expand and simplify:

   a $(x-7)(x+1)$ **b** $(x+6)(x+2)$ **c** $(3-x)(x+5)$

   d $(x-4)^2$ **e** $(x-1)(x+1)$ **f** $(2x-5)(4-x)$

4 Expand and simplify:
   a $(x+4)(x-4)$ **b** $(2-3d)(2+3d)$ **c** $(4x+y)(4x-y)$

5 Half of a class have black hair, and two fifths of the class have brown hair. There are 3 other students in the class.
   a Write this information as an algebraic equation.
   b How many students have black hair?

6 Find the missing factor:
   a $3x \times \square = 12x$ **b** $\square \times 5y = 15y$ **c** $7x \times \square = 14x^2$

7 Fully factorise:
   a $24 + 6x$ **b** $7x - 7$
   c $-12x + 4$ **d** $5x^2 - 4x$
   e $x(x+5) - 11(x+5)$ **f** $(x-2)(x+9) + (x+9)(x+5)$

8 When one quarter of a number is subtracted from one third of the number, the result is 7. Find the number.

Review set 5C

1 Expand and simplify:
   a $3(7 + 2a)$ **b** $5(7x + y)$ **c** $-2a(b - a)$
   d $4a(m - n^2)$ **e** $3(x - 4) + 5(2 - x)$ **f** $2x(x - 4) + 8(x + 3)$

2 Solve for x:
   a $9 - 4x = 2x - (1 - x)$ **b** $\dfrac{2}{5} = \dfrac{3x}{8}$ **c** $\dfrac{x+5}{2} - \dfrac{x-2}{3} = \dfrac{4x}{5}$

3 Expand and simplify:
   a $(x+6)(x-3)$ **b** $(x-11)(x-2)$ **c** $(4-x)(x+3)$
   d $(2x-5)(x+1)$ **e** $(x+7)^2$ **f** $(x+6)(4x-3)$

4 Expand and simplify:
   a $(x+5)(x-5)$ **b** $(1-7x)(1+7x)$ **c** $(8+q)(8-q)$
   d $2(x+3)(x+2) - 3(x+2)(x-1)$

5 **a** Use the difference of two squares expansion to show that $13 \times 17 = 15^2 - 2^2$.
   b Evaluate 33×27 without using a calculator.

6 Fully factorise:
   a $9k - 6$ **b** $15x + 12x^2$ **c** $-8a^2 - 4a$
   d $5ab + 10b^2$ **e** $(2-x)(x+3) + (x+3)$ **f** $4(x-7) - (x-2)(x-7)$

7 Inna has only 5-cent and 20-cent coins. She has 27 coins, with total value €3.15. How many 5-cent coins does Inna have?

8 Clara, Dean and Elaine were candidates in an election in which 1000 people voted. Elaine won the election, receiving 95 more votes than Dean, and 186 more votes than Clara. How many votes did Dean receive?

Graphs, charts, and tables

6

Contents:

A	Interpreting graphs and tables	[11.1]
B	Types of graphs	[11.3]
C	Graphs which compare data	[11.3]
D	Using technology to graph data	[11.3]

Opening problem

Amon and Maddie were practicing their golf drives on a driving range. Amon hit 20 drives, which travelled the following distances in metres:

152 183 194 172 160 148 177 159 192 188
165 174 181 191 188 165 180 174 147 191

Maddie suggested that Amon should have a try with her driver. While using Maddie's driver, Amon's drives travelled the following distances:

150 152 169 195 189 177 188 196 182 175
180 167 174 182 179 197 180 168 178 194

Things to think about:

a Just by looking at the data, is there a noticeable difference between the data sets?

b How can we represent the data in a way that makes it easier to compare the data sets?

When we conduct a **statistical investigation**, we collect information called **data**. We might investigate the traffic levels on a road, the effectiveness of a medicine, or the sales records of a shop. In this chapter, we look at some different ways to present data that make it easier to understand and use.

A INTERPRETING GRAPHS AND TABLES [11.1]

Magazines and newspapers frequently contain graphs and tables which display information. It is important that we interpret this information correctly. We often use **percentages** in our analysis.

Example 1

A survey was carried out amongst retired people to see if they were worried about global warming. The results were collated and a bar chart drawn.

a How many retired people were not concerned about global warming?

b How many retired people were surveyed?

c What percentage of retired people were:
  i a little concerned
  ii very worried about global warming?

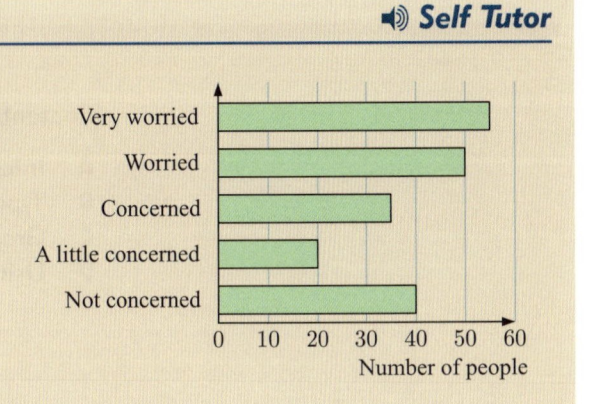

---

a 40 retired people were not concerned about global warming.

b $40 + 20 + 35 + 50 + 55 = 200$ retired people were surveyed.

c **i** The percentage 'a little concerned'
$$= \frac{20}{200} \times 100\%$$
$$= 10\%$$

ii The percentage 'very worried'
$$= \frac{55}{200} \times 100\%$$
$$= 27.5\%$$

To display data more clearly, we sometimes truncate axes. This means we skip over a part of the graph where all the columns are present.

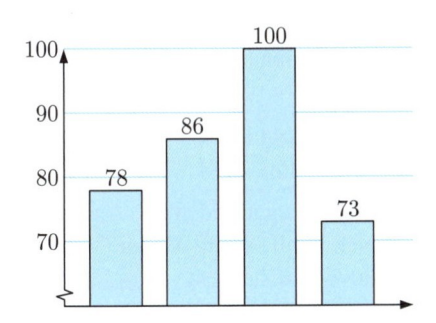

EXERCISE 6A

1 The graph alongside shows the number of days' supply of blood for various blood groups available in a major hospital. We can see that for blood type B^+ there is enough blood for transfusions within the next 5 days of normal usage.

   a How many blood groups are there?
   b What blood type is in greatest supply?
   c If supply for 2 or less days is 'critical', what blood types are in critical supply?

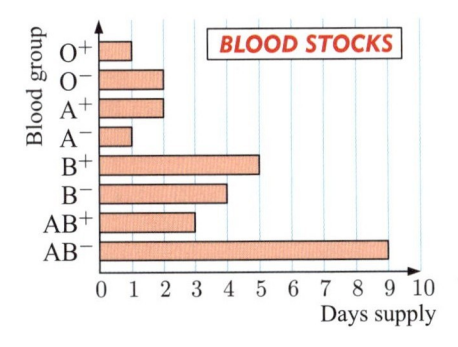

Graphs, charts, and tables (Chapter 6)

2 **Children with diabetes**

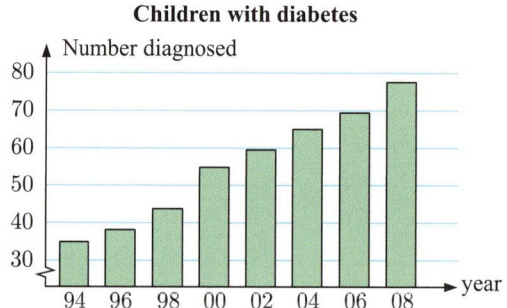

The number of children diagnosed with diabetes in a large city over time is illustrated in the graph alongside.

a How many children were diagnosed in:
   i 1996   ii 2006?

b Find the percentage increase in diagnosis of the disease from:
   i 1996 to 2006   ii 2000 to 2008.

3 The graph shows the change in temperature at the 'Weather Centre' from 6 am to 6 pm on a particular day.

a What was the temperature at:
   i 6 am   ii 6 pm   iii noon?

b Over what period was the temperature:
   i decreasing   ii increasing?

c What was the maximum temperature and at what time did it occur?

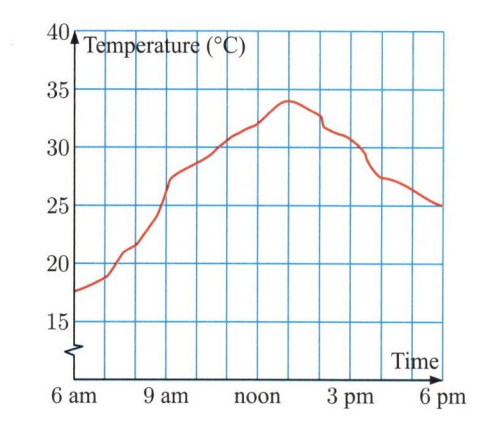

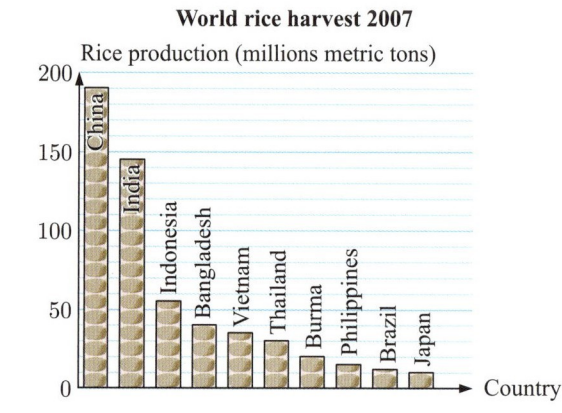

4 **World rice harvest 2007**

The graph shows the world's largest rice growers and the quantity of rice they harvested in 2007.

a In 2007, what tonnage of rice was harvested in:
   i Vietnam   ii Burma?

b What was the total tonnage harvested from the countries included?

c What percentage of the total rice harvest was grown in China?

d What percentage of rice does India grow compared with China?

5 At a school, the year 11 students were asked to nominate their favourite fruit. The following data was collected:

a How many year 11 students were there?

b What was the most popular fruit?

c What percentage of year 11 students chose mandarins as their favourite fruit?

d The school canteen sells apples, bananas and pears. What percentage of year 11 students will be able to order their favourite fruit?

Type of fruit	Frequency
Apple	20
Banana	24
Grapes	3
Orange	11
Mandarin	10
Nectarine	7
Pear	2
Peach	3

6 The table below displays the percentage of people with each blood type, categorised by country.

Blood Type	O⁺	O⁻	A⁺	A⁻	B⁺	B⁻	AB⁺	AB⁻
Austria	30%	7%	33%	8%	12%	3%	6%	1%
Canada	39%	7%	36%	7%	8%	1%	2%	1%
France	36%	6%	37%	7%	9%	1%	3%	1%
Hong Kong	40%	0.3%	26%	0.3%	27%	0.2%	6%	0.2%
South Korea	27%	0.3%	34%	0.3%	27%	0.3%	11%	0.1%
United Kingdom	37%	7%	35%	7%	8%	2%	3%	1%
USA	37%	7%	36%	6%	9%	1%	3%	1%

    a What percentage of Canadians have type B⁺ blood?
    b In which countries is A⁺ the most common blood type?
    c Which of the countries listed has the highest percentage of population with type AB⁺ blood?
    d Which blood type is the fourth most common in the USA?
    e In which country is B⁺ more common than A⁺?

7

Telling Statistics — Crashes by age

Age	All Casualties	Fatalities
under 20	59 099	567
20 - 29	60 129	726
30 - 39	46 034	500
40 - 49	36 983	398
50 - 59	23 537	283
60 - 69	13 155	202
70 - 79	8277	230
80+	4802	257
unreported	6388	9

[1] *Road Casualties Great Britain: 2006 Annual Report*,
© Crown copyright 2007. Reproduced under the terms of the Click-Use Licence.

The table shows road casualties by age group in 2006 in Great Britain.[1]

    a Which age group has:
        i the most fatalities   **ii** the least casualties?
    b **i** How many fatalities were in the 30 - 39 age group?
        ii What percentage of the casualties in the 30 - 39 age group were fatalities?
    c What percentage of casualties does the 50 - 59 age group have compared with:
        i the under 20 age group   **ii** all age groups?

8 The graph alongside shows the distance June travels on her morning jog. Use the graph to determine:
    a the distance she jogs
    b the time taken for her jog
    c the distance travelled after 15 minutes
    d the time taken to jog the first 6 km
    e the average speed for the whole distance.

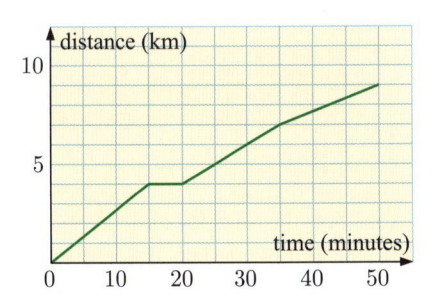

9 Use the chart on the next page to answer the following:
    a How far is it from:
        i London to Aberdeen   **ii** Cambridge to Oxford?
    b How far would you need to travel to complete the circuit from Glasgow to Cardiff to Oxford and back to Glasgow?
    c If you could average 85 km/h on a trip from Cardiff to London, how long would it take, to the nearest 5 minutes?

Graphs, charts, and tables   (Chapter 6)   143

Distances are in kilometres.

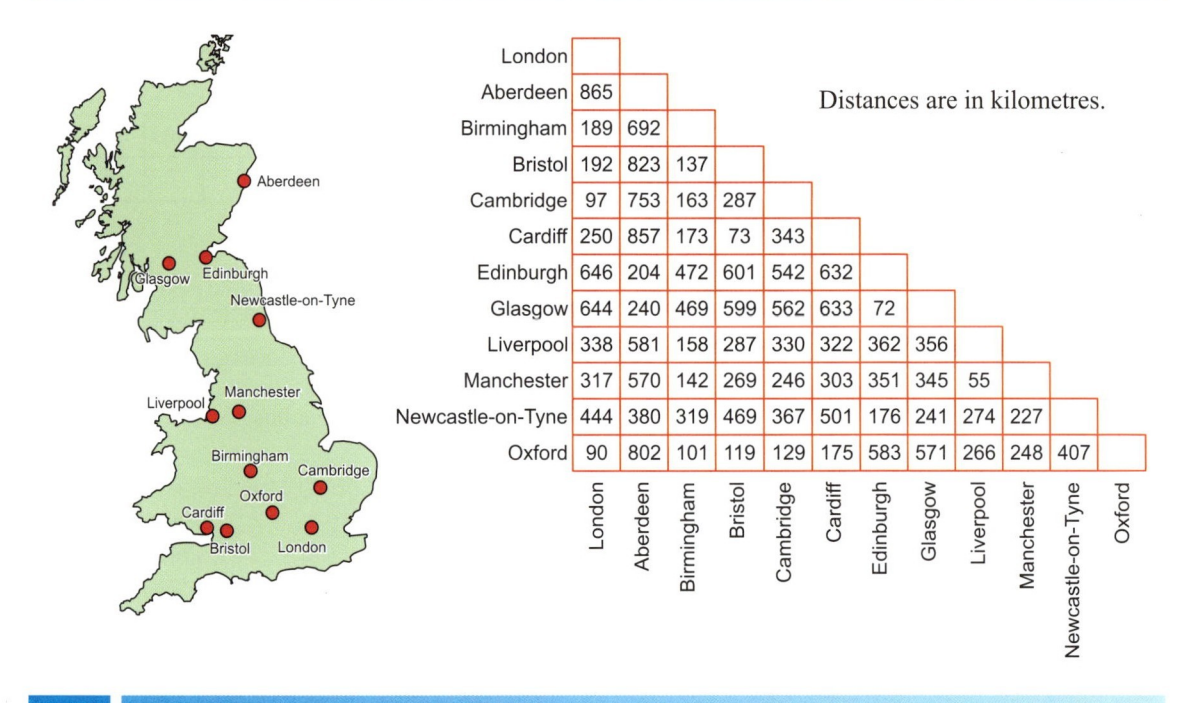

	London	Aberdeen	Birmingham	Bristol	Cambridge	Cardiff	Edinburgh	Glasgow	Liverpool	Manchester	Newcastle-on-Tyne
Aberdeen	865										
Birmingham	189	692									
Bristol	192	823	137								
Cambridge	97	753	163	287							
Cardiff	250	857	173	73	343						
Edinburgh	646	204	472	601	542	632					
Glasgow	644	240	469	599	562	633	72				
Liverpool	338	581	158	287	330	322	362	356			
Manchester	317	570	142	269	246	303	351	345	55		
Newcastle-on-Tyne	444	380	319	469	367	501	176	241	274	227	
Oxford	90	802	101	119	129	175	583	571	266	248	407

B   TYPES OF GRAPHS   [11.3]

There are several different types of data that we can collect:

Categorical data is data which is sorted into categories.

Numerical data is data which can be written in numerical form. It can either be **discrete** or **continuous**.
Discrete data takes exact number values, and is often a result of **counting**.
Continuous data takes numerical values within a continuous range, and is usually a result of **measuring**.

Graphs and charts are used to display data in a form that is not only more visually appealing, but also easier to understand.

Different kinds of graphs and charts are used to represent different kinds of data. We will see that categorical data is usually displayed using a **bar chart** or a **pie chart**, and numerical data is usually displayed using a **line graph** or a **stem-and-leaf plot**.

BAR CHART

A **bar chart** is a popular method of displaying statistical data and is probably the easiest statistical graph to construct. The information may be displayed either vertically or horizontally. The height (if vertical) or length (if horizontal) of each bar is proportional to the quantity it represents. All bars are of the same width. If the data is discrete then the bars are separated by a space.

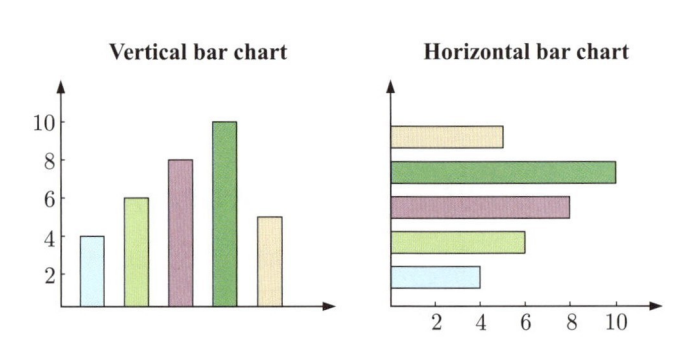

Example 2

Teachers at a local school were asked what mode of transport they used that day to travel to school. The results are summarised in the table:

Mode of transport	Car	Bicycle	Bus	Walk
Number of teachers	15	3	7	5

a Display the data on a vertical bar chart.

b What percentage of teachers used a bus that morning?

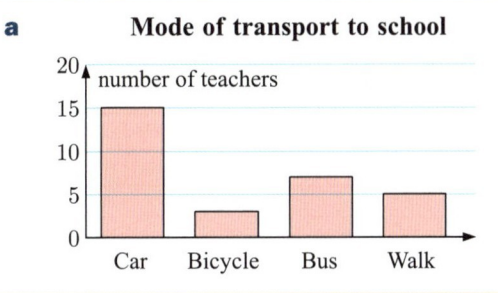

a Mode of transport to school

b Total number of teachers
$= 15 + 3 + 7 + 5$
$= 30$

Percentage who used a bus
$= \frac{7}{30} \times 100\%$
$\approx 23.3\%$

PIE CHART

A **pie chart** presents data in a circle. The circle is divided into sectors which represent the categories. The size of each sector is proportional to the quantity it represents, so its sector angle can be found as a fraction of $360°$.

Example 3

For the data on teachers' mode of transport in **Example 2**:

a calculate the sector angles

b construct a pie chart.

a For car, $\quad \frac{15}{30} \times 360° = 180°$.

For bicycle, $\quad \frac{3}{30} \times 360° = 36°$.

For bus, $\quad \frac{7}{30} \times 360° = 84°$.

For walk, $\quad \frac{5}{30} \times 360° = 60°$.

b Mode of transport to school

SCATTER DIAGRAM AND LINE GRAPH

We are often given data which shows how one quantity *varies* with another. The data will be given as ordered pairs which we can plot on a set of axes.

If the data is *discrete*, it does not make sense to join the points, and we have a **scatter diagram**.

Graphs, charts, and tables (Chapter 6)

For example, if each apple at a market stall costs 20 pence, we obtain the scatter diagram shown. It does not make sense to buy a part of an apple, so we do not join the points.

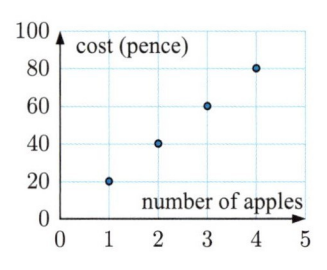

If the data is *continuous* we can join the points with straight lines to form a **line graph**. We often obtain line graphs when we observe a quantity that varies with time. You will see this in the following example.

Example 4 ◀) Self Tutor

The temperature at Geneva airport was measured each hour and the results recorded in the table below. Draw a line graph to illustrate this data.

Time	0800	0900	1000	1100	1200	1300	1400	1500	1600	1700	1800	1900
Temperature (°C)	5	8	11	12	15	16	18	14	12	11	11	9

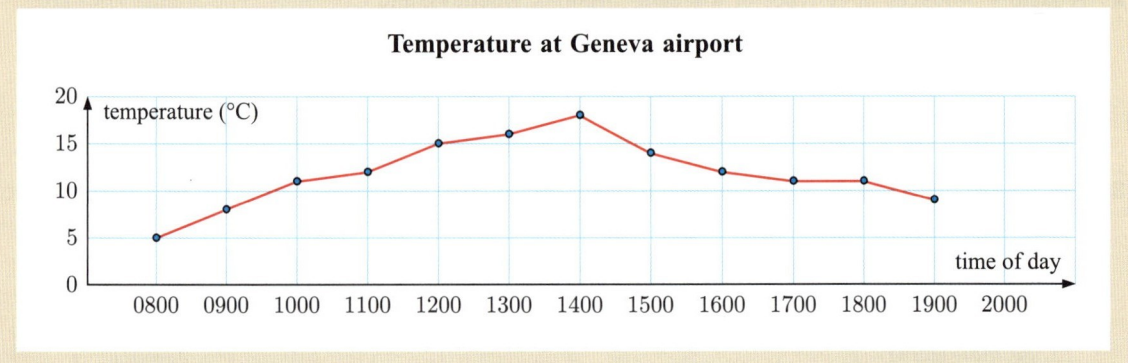

Temperature at Geneva airport

STEM-AND-LEAF PLOTS

A **stem-and-leaf plot** (often called a stem-plot) is a way of writing down the data in groups, and is used for small data sets. It shows actual data values and gives a visual comparison of frequencies.

For numbers with two digits, the first digit forms part of the **stem** and the second digit forms a **leaf**.

For example, for the data value 17, 1 would be recorded on the stem, and the 7 would be a leaf.

An **ordered** stem-plot arranges all data from smallest to largest.

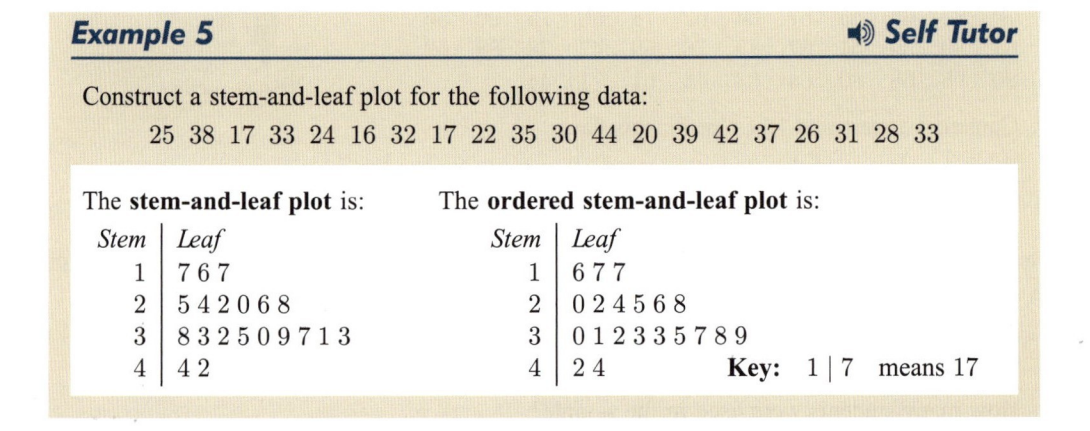

Example 5 ◀) Self Tutor

Construct a stem-and-leaf plot for the following data:

25 38 17 33 24 16 32 17 22 35 30 44 20 39 42 37 26 31 28 33

The **stem-and-leaf plot** is:

Stem	Leaf
1	7 6 7
2	5 4 2 0 6 8
3	8 3 2 5 0 9 7 1 3
4	4 2

The **ordered stem-and-leaf plot** is:

Stem	Leaf
1	6 7 7
2	0 2 4 5 6 8
3	0 1 2 3 3 5 7 8 9
4	2 4

Key: 1 | 7 means 17

Notice the following features of the stem-and-leaf plot:

- All the actual data is shown.
- The minimum (smallest) data value is 16.
- The maximum (largest) data value is 44.
- The 'thirties' interval (30 to 39) occurred most often, and is the **modal class**.
- The key indicates the place value of the stem. For example, on a different data set we might have the key 1 | 7 means 1.7.

EXERCISE 6B

1 Of the 30 teachers in a school, 6 teach Maths, 7 teach English, 4 teach Science, 5 teach Humanities subjects, 4 teach Modern Languages, 2 teach Theatre Arts, and 2 teach Physical Education.
   a Draw a vertical bar chart to display this information.
   b What percentage of the teachers teach Maths or Science?

2 A factory produces three types of toy cars: Astons, Bentleys, and Corvettes. The annual sales are:

Toy car make	Aston	Bentley	Corvette
Sales (thousands of £)	65	30	25

   a Find the sector angles for each category.
   b Construct a pie chart for the data.

3 The midday temperature and daily rainfall were measured every day for one week in Kingston. The results are summarised in the table below:

Day	Sunday	Monday	Tuesday	Wednesday	Thursday	Friday	Saturday
Temperature (°C)	23	20	18	25	27	24	26
Rainfall (mm)	8	4	2	12	10	9	1

Draw a vertical bar chart to illustrate the temperature readings, and a horizontal bar chart to illustrate the rainfall readings.

4 a Draw a stem-and-leaf plot using stems 2, 3, 4, and 5 for the following data:
       29, 27, 33, 30, 46, 40, 35, 24, 21, 58, 27, 34, 25, 36, 57, 34, 42, 51, 50, 48
   b Redraw the stem-and-leaf plot from a to make it ordered.

5 The data set below is the test scores (out of 100) for a Science test for 50 students.

```
92  29  78  67  68  58  80  89  92  69  66  56  88
81  70  73  63  55  67  64  62  74  56  75  90  56
59  64  89  39  51  87  89  76  59  47  38  88  62
72  80  95  68  80  64  53  43  61  71  44
```

   a Construct a stem-and-leaf plot for this data.
   b What percentage of the students scored 80 or more for the test?
   c What percentage of students scored less than 50 for the test?

6 In a pie chart on *leisure activities* the sector angle for *ice skating* is 34°. This sector represents 136 students.
   a The sector angle for *watching television* is 47°. How many students watch television for leisure?
   b If 38 students *visit friends*, what sector angle would represent them?
   c How many students were used in the sample?

Graphs, charts, and tables (Chapter 6) 147

7 The length of the shadow cast by a tree was measured at hourly intervals:

Time	0800	0900	1000	1100	1200	1300	1400	1500	1600
Shadow length (m)	30	20	12	6	2	5	10	17	25

    a Is it more appropriate to use a scatter diagram or a line graph to display this data?
    b Display the data on your chosen graph.

8 For the ordered stem-and-leaf plot given, find:
    a the minimum value
    b the maximum value
    c the number of data with a value greater than 25
    d the number of data with a value of at least 40
    e the percentage of the data which is less than 15.

Stem	Leaf
0	1 3 7
1	0 3 4 7 8 8 9
2	0 0 1 2 2 3 5 5 6 8 9
3	2 4 4 5 8 9
4	3

Key: 3 | 2 means 32

9 Following weekly lessons, Guy's golf scores on successive Saturdays were:
        98 96 92 93 89 90 88 85 and 84
    a Which is more appropriate to draw for this data, a line graph or scatter diagram?
    b Graph the data appropriately.

10 A reviewer gives scores out of 6 for a group of 45 films:

        3.4 3.7 4.4 5.1 5.3 3.9 3.3 5.8 4.0 4.2 4.3 4.3 4.7 3.7 3.5
        4.1 4.3 4.8 5.0 5.5 4.4 4.4 5.2 5.4 5.9 3.9 3.1 2.9 4.4 5.7
        4.5 3.4 2.9 2.7 1.8 4.9 4.1 4.2 3.7 4.2 4.3 4.3 4.5 3.4 5.1

    a Construct a stem-and-leaf plot for this data using 0, 1, 2, 3, 4, and 5 as the stems.
    b Redraw the stem-and-leaf plot so that it is ordered.
    c What advantage does a stem-and-leaf plot have over a frequency table?
    d What is the   **i** highest   **ii** lowest   film review score?
    e If a 'must see' rating is awarded to films that score 5.0 or more, what percentage of films achieve a 'must see' rating?
    f What percentage of films scored less than half marks in the review?

C   GRAPHS WHICH COMPARE DATA   [11.3]

Two distributions can be compared by using:

- side-by-side bar charts or **compound bar charts**
- back-to-back bar charts
- back-to-back stem-and-leaf plots

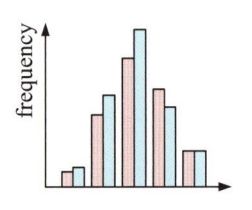

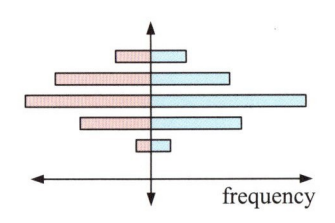

	6	1
2 0	7	0 5 6
7 5 3 2 1	8	2 2 4 5 8
9 8 7 6 6 5 3 3 2 0	9	0 3 4 5 5 7 9
7 1	10	6 7 8 8
4	11	2 3 7
	12	6

Key: 6 | 1   means 61

Suppose two machines A and B in a factory were tested each day for 60 days to see how many faulty screw caps they produced. The results are summarised in the frequency table alongside.

Machine A

Number faulty	Frequency
2	1
3	0
4	4
5	16
6	24
7	6
8	5
9	2
10	0
11	0
12	1
13	1

Machine B

Number faulty	Frequency
3	2
4	3
5	5
6	5
7	10
8	11
9	20
10	3
11	1

We can compare the data for the two machines using a compound bar chart or back-to-back bar chart:

Compound bar chart of screw cap data

Back-to-back bar chart of screw cap data

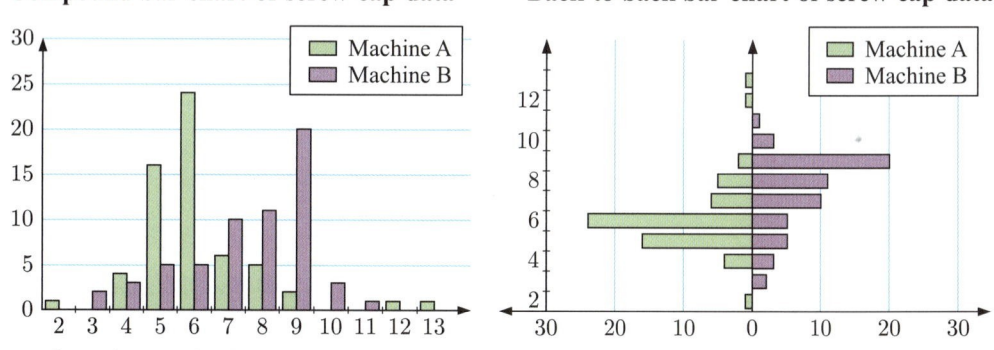

We can see from the graphs that machine B generally produces more faulty screw caps than machine A.

Example 6   ◀)) Self Tutor

15 students were examined in Geography and Mathematics. The results were:

| Geography | 65 | 70 | 56 | 67 | 49 | 82 | 79 | 88 | 47 | 76 | 69 | 58 | 90 | 45 | 82 |
| Mathematics | 75 | 67 | 81 | 88 | 84 | 66 | 77 | 72 | 60 | 58 | 67 | 71 | 74 | 82 | 89 |

Use an ordered back-to-back stem-and-leaf plot to compare the results.

Before ordering:

```
   Geography      Mathematics
       5 7 9 | 4 |
         8 6 | 5 | 8
       9 7 5 | 6 | 7 6 0 7
       6 9 0 | 7 | 5 7 2 1 4
       2 8 2 | 8 | 1 8 4 2 9
           0 | 9 |      Key:  8 | 2 means 82
```

After ordering:

```
   Geography      Mathematics
       9 7 5 | 4 |
         8 6 | 5 | 8
       9 7 5 | 6 | 0 6 7 7
       9 6 0 | 7 | 1 2 4 5 7
       8 2 2 | 8 | 1 2 4 8 9
           0 | 9 |      Key:  8 | 2 means 82
```

We observe that:
- the Geography marks are more spread than those for Mathematics
- the Mathematics marks are generally higher than those for Geography.

Graphs, charts, and tables (Chapter 6)

EXERCISE 6C

1 In each of the following graphs, two data sets of the same size are compared. What can be deduced from each graph?

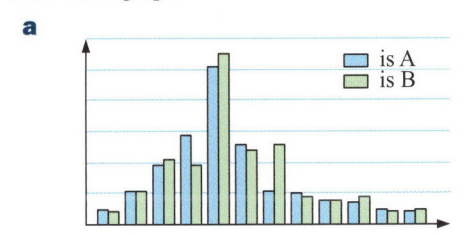

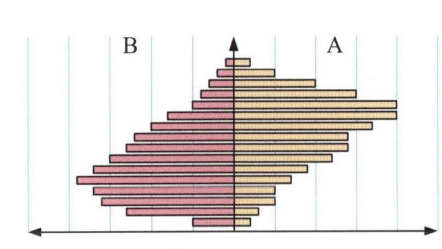

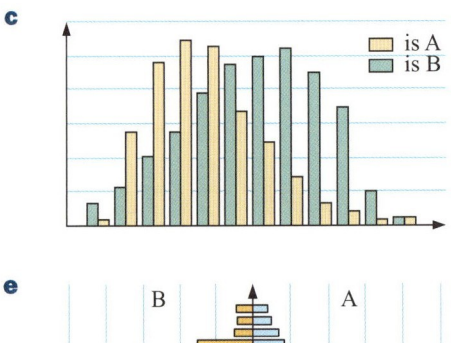

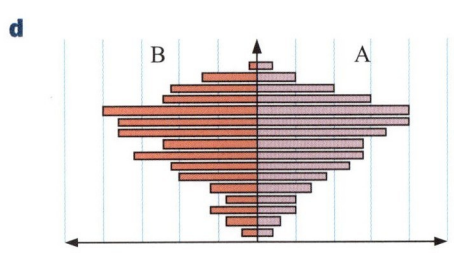

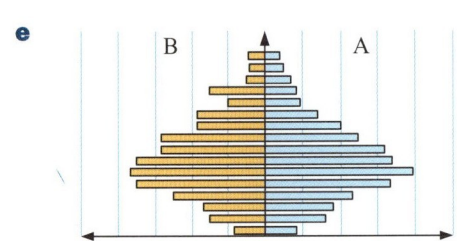

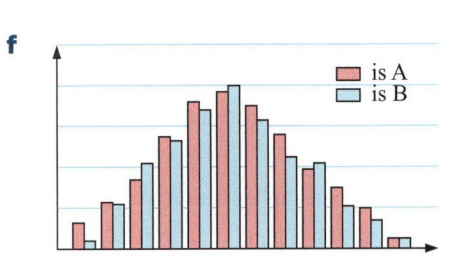

a □ is A □ is B

b B | A

c □ is A □ is B

d B | A

e B | A

f □ is A □ is B

2 Pedro sells small ceramic items on an internet auction site. He lives in the USA and sells within his country and overseas. He uses the standard postal service for local deliveries and a private freight company for international ones. Pedro records the number of items that are broken each month over a 70 month period. Which delivery service is Pedro happier with? Explain your answer.

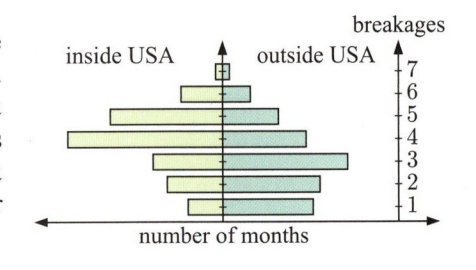

inside USA | outside USA — breakages 1–7, number of months

3 This stem-and-leaf plot shows the One Day International cricket scores for a batsman in the 2009 and 2010 seasons.

a In which season was the batsman more consistent?

b In which season did the batsman score more runs?

Season 2009		Season 2010
4 3 0	0	
8 8 6 1	1	4
9 6 5 5	2	0 6
9 7 6 2 0	3	1 3 3 6 9
7 4	4	2 2 4 5 8 9
7	5	2 3 6 7
2	6	1 1

Key: 2 | 0 means 20 runs

4 The house sales of a real estate agency for 2009 and 2010 are summarised in the table below:

	Jan	Feb	Mar	Apr	May	Jun	Jul	Aug	Sep	Oct	Nov	Dec
2009	2	8	8	11	25	26	31	34	28	13	10	4
2010	5	3	6	14	21	25	28	29	15	13	7	3

a Construct a back-to-back bar chart of the data.
   b Compare the sales in the two years.

5 Two brothers living together travel by different means to university; Alex travels by train and Stan travels by bus. Over a three week period, their travel times in minutes were:

| Alex | 17 | 22 | 34 | 60 | 41 | 15 | 55 | 30 | 36 | 23 | 27 | 48 | 34 | 25 | 45 |
| Stan | 31 | 19 | 28 | 42 | 24 | 18 | 30 | 36 | 34 | 25 | 38 | 31 | 22 | 29 | 32 |

   a Construct a back-to-back stem-and-leaf plot of the data.
   b Which mode of transport is more reliable? Explain your answer.

6 a Construct a side-by-side stem-and-leaf plot for the data in the **Opening Problem** on page **139**.
   b Is there a noticeable difference between the data sets?

D USING TECHNOLOGY TO GRAPH DATA [11.3]

Many special computer programs are used to help us organise and graph data.

STATISTICS PACKAGE

Click on the icon to run the statistical graphing software.
Change the data in the table and see the effect on the graph.

- Notice that the graph's heading and the labels on the axes can be changed.
- The type of graph can be changed by clicking on the icon to give the type that you want.

Experiment with the package and use it whenever possible.

Discovery   Spreadsheets for graphing data

The colours of cars in a supermarket car park are recorded alongside. Suppose you want to draw a frequency bar chart of this data.

Colour	white	red	blue	green	other
Frequency	38	27	19	18	11

The following steps using a computer spreadsheet enable you to do this quickly and easily.

   Step 1: Start a new spreadsheet, type in the table, and then highlight the area as shown.

   Step 2: Click the Insert tab. Home Insert Page Layout

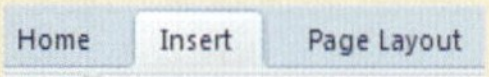

	A	B
1	Colour	Frequency
2	white	38
3	red	27
4	blue	19
5	green	18
6	other	11

SPREADSHEET

   Step 3: Select Column  and choose the first 2-D column option.

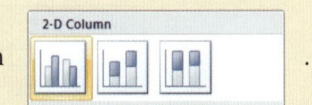

Graphs, charts, and tables (Chapter 6)

You should get:

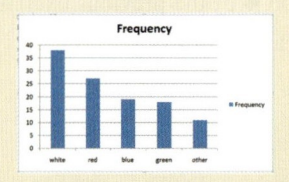

Frequency bar chart

This demonstration takes you through all the steps.

DEMO

Now suppose the colours of cars in the neighbouring car park were also recorded. The results are summarised in the following table.

Colour	white	red	blue	green	other
Frequency 1	38	27	19	18	11
Frequency 2	15	18	21	9	3

Step 4: Type the *Frequency 2* data into the C column, and highlight the three columns as shown.

Step 5: Click the Insert tab.

	A	B	C	D
1	Colour	Frequency 1	Frequency 2	
2	white	38	15	
3	red	27	18	
4	blue	19	21	
5	green	18	9	
6	other	11	3	
7				

Step 6: Select Column and choose the first 2-D column option.

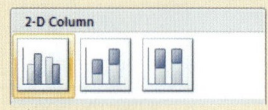

Step 7: Experiment with other types of graphs and data.

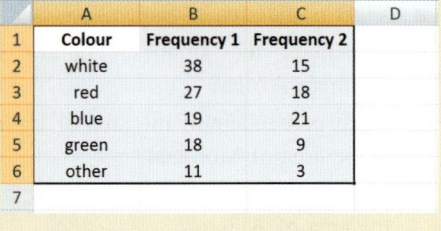

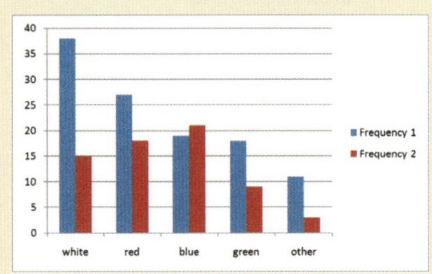

What to do:

1 Gather statistics of your own or use data from questions in the previous exercise. Use the spreadsheet to draw an appropriate statistical graph of the data.

2 Find out how to adjust labels, scales, legends, and other features of the graph.

EXERCISE 6D

Use technology to answer the following questions. Make sure each graph is fully labelled.

1 Draw a pie chart for this data:

Favourite colour	Frequency
Green	38
Blue	34
Red	29
Purple	21
Other	34

2 After leaving school, four graduates compare their weekly incomes in dollars at 5 year intervals. Their incomes are shown in the table alongside.

	After 5 years	After 10 years
Kaylene	685	2408
Harry	728	1345
Wei	820	2235
Matthew	1056	1582

  a Draw side-by-side bar charts to represent the data.

  b Draw back-to-back bar charts to represent the data.

  c Find the percentage increase for each person for the data given.

  d Two of the four gained university qualifications. Which ones are they likely to be?

3 Consider again the real estate agency data from question **4** of the previous exercise.
  a Construct: **i** a side-by-side bar chart   **ii** a back-to-back bar chart   for the data.
  b Which chart provides a better means of comparing the two data sets?

Review set 6A

1 The graph alongside shows the areas of the countries classified by the UN as Northern Africa.
  a What is the area of Sudan?
  b Which is the smallest country in Northern Africa?
  c What percentage of the area of Egypt is the area of Morocco?
  d What percentage of Northern Africa is the area of Algeria?

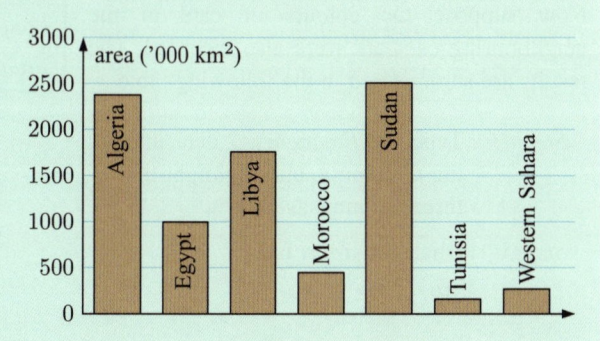

2 The table alongside shows the money spent by a business over the course of a year.
  a How much did the business spend?
  b Calculate the sector angle for each category.
  c Construct a pie chart to display the data.

Administration	£144 000
Production	£200 000
Marketing	£180 000
Distribution	£120 000
Advertising	£76 000

3 Farmer Jane owns the assortment of animals shown in the table alongside.
  a Display this data on a vertical bar chart.
  b What percentage of animals on the farm are chickens?
  c Name the three most common animals on the farm.

Animal	Number
Chickens	12
Cows	35
Dogs	4
Ducks	10
Geese	5
Goats	24
Llamas	11
Sheep	19

4 The table alongside shows the number of males and females participating in a school's drama class each year for the last five years.

	2006	2007	2008	2009	2010
Males	10	8	5	10	14
Females	15	18	17	20	18

  a Display the data on a side-by-side bar chart.
  b In which year was there the greatest difference between the number of males and females?

5 For the given data on calf weights:
  a Explain what 5 | 1 means.
  b Find the minimum calf weight.
  c Find the maximum calf weight.
  d Find which weight occurs most frequently.

Weight of calves (kg)

```
2 | 8
3 | 1 4 9
4 | 0 3 3 6 7
5 | 1 4 4 4 5 5 8
6 | 3 5        Key:  6 | 3  means 63 kg
```

6 Huw owns a flower shop. The table below shows the total cost of supplying, as well as the sales for each flower type, for the past year.

Flower	Roses	Carnations	Tulips	Orchids	Azaleas	Lilies
Cost (£)	17 000	15 000	8000	7000	5000	8000
Sales (£)	35 000	25 000	16 000	15 000	15 000	14 000

  a Draw two pie charts to display the data.
  b Which two flower types account for more than half of the total costs?
  c Which two flower types account for half of the total sales?
  d Huw needs to reduce his workload, so he decides to stop selling one type of flower. Which flower type would you recommend he stop selling? Explain your answer.

7 To determine if a weight-loss program is effective, a group of 25 men trialled the program for three months. Their weights in kilograms before starting the program were:

  95   104   93   86   82   111   100   125   117   121   119   97   120
  104   132   111   98   83   123   79   101   135   114   99   122

Their weights after completing the program were:

  79   92   84   78   68   99   85   106   99   107   102   83   110
  93   125   96   79   74   113   68   89   122   95   83   106

  a Construct a back-to-back stem-and-leaf plot of the data.
  b Would you say that the weight-loss program is effective? Explain your answer.

Review set 6B

1 **Estimated quantity of crops harvested**

United Kingdom   Thousand tonnes

	2000	2001	2002	2003	2004	2005	2006	2007	2008	2009
Wheat	16 704	11 580	15 973	14 282	15 468	14 863	14 735	13 221	17 227	14 379
Barley	6492	6660	6128	6360	5799	5495	5239	5079	6144	6769
Oats	640	621	753	749	626	532	728	712	784	757
Potatoes	6636	6649	6966	5918	6316	5979	5727	5564	6145	6423
Brussel sprouts	78.5	67.3	54.8	42.7	55.8	45.1	46.1	44.8	43.3	43.6
Cauliflowers	172.4	156.1	107.4	116.5	126.3	168.3	133.2	123.7	122.1	108.5
Carrots	673.2	725.8	760.0	718.4	602.4	671.1	710.1	701.3	735.4	671.0
Onion, dry bulb	391.4	392.7	374.9	283.4	373.6	340.9	413.6	358.8	303.8	354.9
Lettuce	155.2	135.8	123.9	109.9	125.6	140.9	131.7	126.4	109.0	110.6
Tomatoes	116.6	113.0	109.1	100.9	75.6	78.5	78.8	84.1	85.6	86.8

Extracted from *Annual Abstract of Statistics, 2010 Edition*, © Crown copyright 2010.   Source: Agricultural Departments: 01904455332
Reproduced under the terms of the Click-Use Licence.

The above table shows the approximate harvest of some crops in the UK in the decade 2000 - 2009.
  a What weight of carrots was harvested in 2004?
  b Which year was the best for potato growers?
  c Which crops had larger yields at the end of the decade than the beginning?

d What percentage of the year 2000 lettuce harvest was the year 2008 lettuce harvest?

e What percentage of the decade's cauliflower harvest was produced in 2005?

2 The number of drivers caught speeding in each month last year were:

Jan	Feb	Mar	Apr	May	Jun	Jul	Aug	Sep	Oct	Nov	Dec
80	65	60	95	50	85	70	40	55	80	60	90

Display this data on a vertical bar chart.

3 The prices of IBM shares over a 10 day period were:

Day	1	2	3	4	5	6	7	8	9	10
Share Price ($)	116.00	116.50	118.00	116.80	116.50	117.00	118.40	118.50	118.50	119.80

a Is a line graph or a scatter diagram more appropriate for this data?

b Display the data on your chosen graph. Use a range of $115 to $120 on the vertical axis.

c On what day was the share price: **i** highest   **ii** lowest?

4 The weights of 16 new-born babies in kilograms are:

2.3, 3.1, 3.8, 4.1, 3.6, 3.5, 4.2, 2.8, 3.4, 3.9, 4.0, 5.1, 4.4, 3.9, 4.0, 3.3

Draw a stem-and-leaf plot for this data.

5 Over the course of a 35 game season, basketballers Rhys and Evan kept a record of the number of rebounds they made each game. The results were:

Rhys	Evan
8 6 4 9 6 10 9 9 8	7 7 6 8 6 7 6 6 8
7 5 7 8 7 4 7 8 5	6 5 7 7 8 5 6 6 5
8 9 6 3 9 10 8 7 10	7 9 7 6 6 5 8 7 7
9 7 8 8 10 9 6 8	8 5 7 7 6 8 7 8

a Construct a back-to-back bar chart for the data.

b Which player was more consistent?

c Which player generally collected the most rebounds?

6 A pet store owner wants to know whether men or women own more pets. He surveys 50 men and 50 women, each of whom live by themselves, and collects data on how many pets they own. The results are as follows:

a Display the data on a side-by-side bar chart.

b In general, do men or women own more pets?

Men		Women	
No. of pets	Frequency	No. of pets	Frequency
0	15	0	7
1	20	1	10
2	10	2	15
3	3	3	10
4	2	4	5
5	0	5	3

7 A selection of students in their final year of high school were asked what they planned to do next year. The responses are displayed in the table alongside:

Use technology to construct a pie chart for this data.

Response	Frequency
Work	89
Apprenticeship	47
University	71
Travel	38

Exponents

7

A	Exponent or index notation	[1.4, 1.9]
B	Exponent or index laws	[1.9, 2.4]
C	Zero and negative indices	[1.9, 2.4]
D	Standard form	[1.9]

Opening problem

Amadeo Avogadro (1776-1856) first proposed that the volume of a gas, at a given pressure and temperature, is proportional to the number of atoms or molecules present, regardless of the nature of the gas. Johann Josef Loschmidt later estimated that one gram of hydrogen contains 6.02×10^{23} atoms, and this number was named in honour of Avogadro.

Things to think about:

- How can we write this number as an ordinary number?
- How many atoms would be in one tonne of hydrogen gas?
- Can you find the mass of 10^{30} atoms of hydrogen?

A EXPONENT OR INDEX NOTATION [1.4, 1.9]

The use of **exponents**, also called **powers** or **indices**, allows us to write products of factors and also to write very large or very small numbers quickly.

We have seen previously that $2 \times 2 \times 2 \times 2 \times 2$ can be written as 2^5.

2^5 reads "two to the power of five" or "two with index five".

In this case 2 is the **base** and 5 is the **exponent**, **power**, or **index**.

We say that 2^5 is written in **exponent** or **index notation**.

2^5 ← exponent, power, or index
← base

Example 1

Find the integer equal to: **a** 3^4 **b** $2^4 \times 3^2 \times 7$

a 3^4
$= 3 \times 3 \times 3 \times 3$
$= 81$

b $2^4 \times 3^2 \times 7$
$= 2 \times 2 \times 2 \times 2 \times 3 \times 3 \times 7$
$= 16 \times 9 \times 7$
$= 1008$

Example 2

Write as a product of prime factors in index form:
a 144   **b** 4312

a

2	144
2	72
2	36
2	18
3	9
3	3
	1

$\therefore 144 = 2^4 \times 3^2$

b

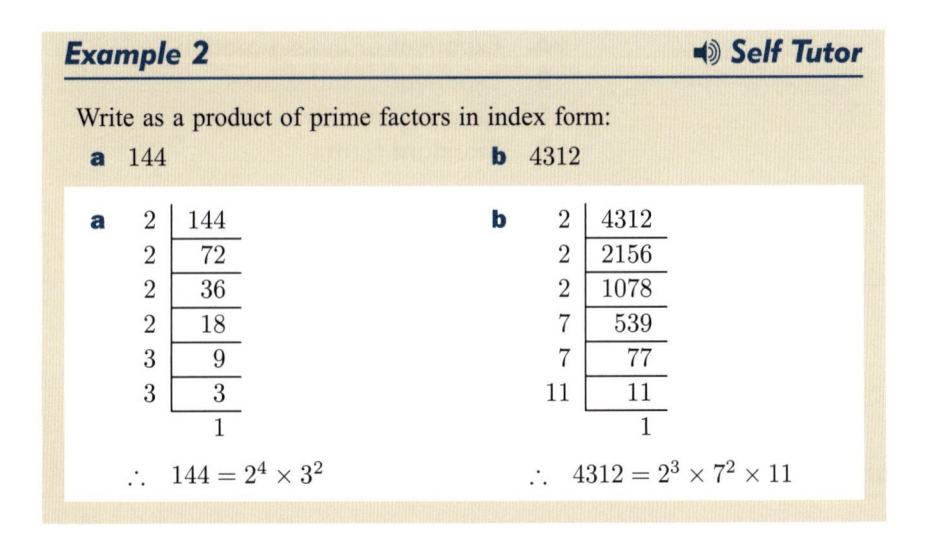

2	4312
2	2156
2	1078
7	539
7	77
11	11
	1

$\therefore 4312 = 2^3 \times 7^2 \times 11$

EXERCISE 7A.1

1 Find the integer equal to:
  a 2^3
  b 3^3
  c 2^5
  d 5^3
  e $2^3 \times 3$
  f $3^2 \times 5^3$
  g $2^2 \times 7^2$
  h 5×11^4
  i $2^2 \times 3^3 \times 5$
  j $2^3 \times 3 \times 7^2$
  k $3^2 \times 5^2 \times 13$
  l $2^4 \times 5^2 \times 11$

2 By dividing continuously by the primes 2, 3, 5, 7, ..., write as a product of prime factors in index form:
  a 12
  b 15
  c 28
  d 24
  e 50
  f 98
  g 108
  h 360
  i 1128
  j 784
  k 952
  l 6500

3 The following numbers can be written in the form 2^n. Find n.
  a 32
  b 256
  c 4096

4 The following numbers can be written in the form 3^n. Find n.
  a 27
  b 729
  c 59 049

5 By considering $3^1, 3^2, 3^3, 3^4, 3^5$ .... and looking for a pattern, find the last digit of 3^{33}.

6 What is the last digit of 7^{77}?

7 Find n if:
  a $5^4 = n$
  b $n^3 = 343$
  c $11^n = 161\,051$
  d $(0.6)^n = 0.046\,656$

Historical note

Nicomachus of Gerasa lived around 100 AD. He discovered an interesting number pattern involving cubes and sums of odd numbers:

$$1 = 1^3$$
$$3 + 5 = 8 = 2^3$$
$$7 + 9 + 11 = 27 = 3^3 \quad \text{etc.}$$

NEGATIVE BASES

So far we have only considered **positive** bases raised to a power.

We will now briefly look at **negative** bases. Consider the statements below:

$(-1)^1 = -1$ $\qquad$ $(-2)^1 = -2$
$(-1)^2 = -1 \times -1 = 1$ $\qquad$ $(-2)^2 = -2 \times -2 = 4$
$(-1)^3 = -1 \times -1 \times -1 = -1$ $\qquad$ $(-2)^3 = -2 \times -2 \times -2 = -8$
$(-1)^4 = -1 \times -1 \times -1 \times -1 = 1$ $\qquad$ $(-2)^4 = -2 \times -2 \times -2 \times -2 = 16$

From the pattern above it can be seen that:

- a **negative** base raised to an **odd** power is **negative**
- a **negative** base raised to an **even** power is **positive**.

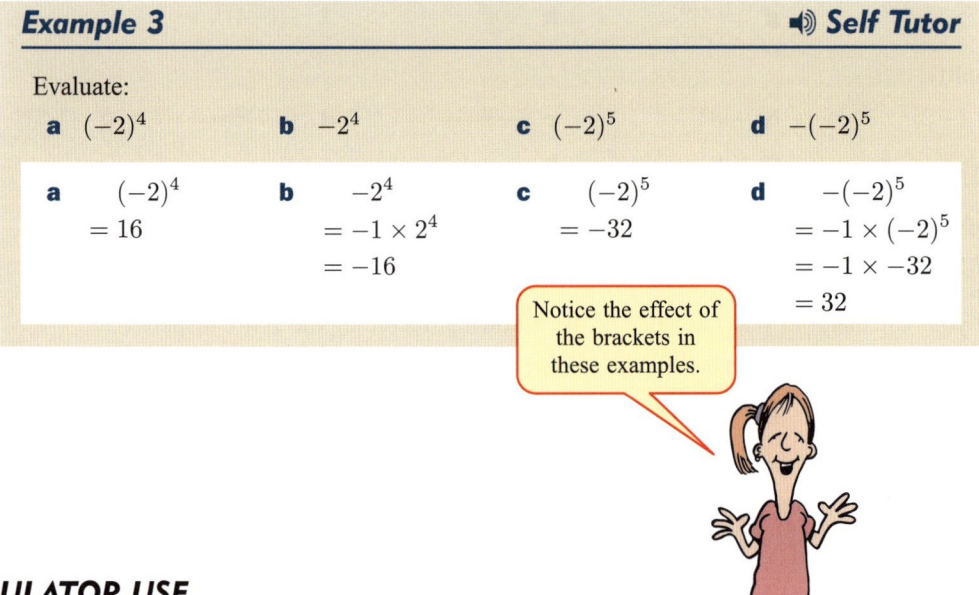

Example 3 ◀ϧ Self Tutor

Evaluate:

a $(-2)^4$ $\qquad$ **b** -2^4 $\qquad$ **c** $(-2)^5$ $\qquad$ **d** $-(-2)^5$

a $(-2)^4$
$= 16$

b -2^4
$= -1 \times 2^4$
$= -16$

c $(-2)^5$
$= -32$

d $-(-2)^5$
$= -1 \times (-2)^5$
$= -1 \times -32$
$= 32$

Notice the effect of the brackets in these examples.

CALCULATOR USE

Different calculators have different keys for entering powers, but in general they perform raising to powers in a similar manner.

Power keys

$\boxed{x^2}$ $\quad$ squares the number in the display.

$\boxed{\wedge}$ $\quad$ raises the number in the display to whatever power is required. On some calculators this key is $\boxed{y^x}$, $\boxed{a^x}$, or $\boxed{x^y}$.

Example 4   ◀) Self Tutor

Find, using your calculator: **a** 6^5 **b** $(-5)^4$ **c** -7^4

> Not all calculators will use these key sequences. If you have problems, refer to the calculator instructions on page **14**.

			Answer
a	Press:	6 [^] 5 [ENTER]	7776
b	Press:	[(] [(−)] 5 [)] [^] 4 [ENTER]	625
c	Press:	[(−)] 7 [^] 4 [ENTER]	−2401

EXERCISE 7A.2

1 Simplify:

   a $(-1)^4$ **b** $(-1)^5$ **c** $(-1)^6$ **d** $(-1)^{10}$ **e** $(-1)^{15}$

   f $(-1)^8$ **g** -1^8 **h** $-(-1)^8$

2 Simplify:

   a $(-3)^3$ **b** -3^3 **c** $-(-3)^3$ **d** $(-6)^2$ **e** -6^2

   f $-(-6)^2$ **g** $(-4)^3$ **h** -4^3 **i** $-(-4)^3$

3 Simplify:

   a $(-2)^5$ **b** -3^4 **c** -2^6 **d** $(-7)^2$ **e** $(-3)^3$

   f $-(-2)^3$ **g** -6^4 **h** $-(-5)^4$

4 Simplify:

   a $2^3 \times 3^2 \times (-1)^5$ **b** $(-1)^4 \times 3^3 \times 2^2$ **c** $(-2)^3 \times (-3)^4$

5 Use your calculator to find the value of the following, recording the entire display:

   a 2^8 **b** $(-5)^4$ **c** -3^5 **d** 7^4 **e** 8^3

   f $(-7)^6$ **g** -7^6 **h** 1.05^{12} **i** -0.623^{11} **j** $(-2.11)^{17}$

B   EXPONENT OR INDEX LAWS   [1.9, 2.4]

Notice that:

- $2^3 \times 2^4 = 2 \times 2 \times 2 \times 2 \times 2 \times 2 \times 2 = 2^7$

- $\dfrac{2^5}{2^2} = \dfrac{2 \times 2 \times 2 \times \cancel{2} \times \cancel{2}}{\cancel{2} \times \cancel{2}} = 2^3$

- $(2^3)^2 = 2 \times 2 \times 2 \times 2 \times 2 \times 2 = 2^6$

- $(3 \times 5)^2 = 3 \times 5 \times 3 \times 5 = 3 \times 3 \times 5 \times 5 = 3^2 \times 5^2$

- $\left(\dfrac{2}{5}\right)^3 = \dfrac{2}{5} \times \dfrac{2}{5} \times \dfrac{2}{5} = \dfrac{2 \times 2 \times 2}{5 \times 5 \times 5} = \dfrac{2^3}{5^3}$

Exponents (Chapter 7)

These examples can be generalised to the exponent or index laws:

- $a^m \times a^n = a^{m+n}$ To **multiply** numbers with the **same base**, keep the base and **add** the indices.
- $\dfrac{a^m}{a^n} = a^{m-n}, \quad a \neq 0$ To **divide** numbers with the **same base**, keep the base and **subtract** the indices.
- $(a^m)^n = a^{m \times n}$ When **raising** a **power** to a **power**, keep the base and **multiply** the indices.
- $(ab)^n = a^n b^n$ The power of a product is the product of the powers.
- $\left(\dfrac{a}{b}\right)^n = \dfrac{a^n}{b^n}, \quad b \neq 0$ The power of a quotient is the quotient of the powers.

Example 5   ◆)) Self Tutor

Simplify using the laws of indices:

a $2^3 \times 2^2$ **b** $x^4 \times x^5$

a $2^3 \times 2^2 = 2^{3+2}$
$= 2^5$
$= 32$

b $x^4 \times x^5 = x^{4+5}$
$= x^9$

> To multiply, keep the base and add the indices.

Example 6   ◆)) Self Tutor

Simplify using the index laws: **a** $\dfrac{3^5}{3^3}$ **b** $\dfrac{p^7}{p^3}$

a $\dfrac{3^5}{3^3} = 3^{5-3}$
$= 3^2$
$= 9$

b $\dfrac{p^7}{p^3} = p^{7-3}$
$= p^4$

> To divide, keep the base and subtract the indices.

Example 7   ◆)) Self Tutor

Simplify using the index laws:

a $(2^3)^2$ **b** $(x^4)^5$

a $(2^3)^2$
$= 2^{3 \times 2}$
$= 2^6$
$= 64$

b $(x^4)^5$
$= x^{4 \times 5}$
$= x^{20}$

> To raise a power to a power, keep the base and multiply the indices.

> Each factor within the brackets has to be raised to the power outside them.

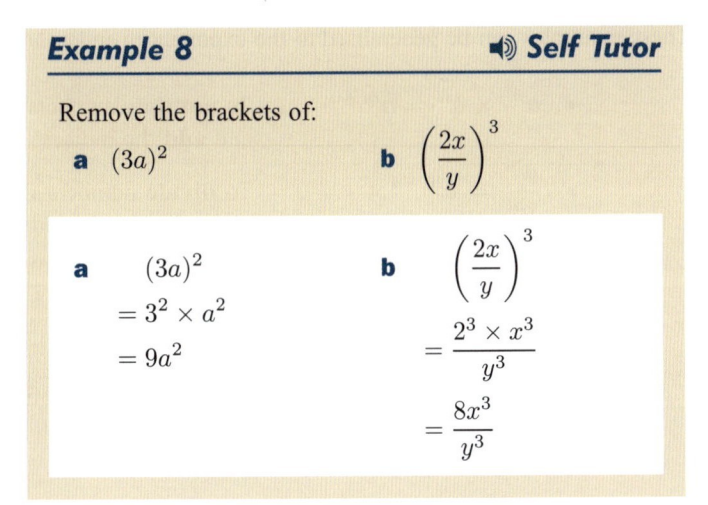

Example 8 •⟩ **Self Tutor**

Remove the brackets of:

a $(3a)^2$
b $\left(\dfrac{2x}{y}\right)^3$

a $(3a)^2$
$= 3^2 \times a^2$
$= 9a^2$

b $\left(\dfrac{2x}{y}\right)^3$
$= \dfrac{2^3 \times x^3}{y^3}$
$= \dfrac{8x^3}{y^3}$

EXERCISE 7B

1 Simplify using the index laws:
  a $2^3 \times 2^1$
  b $2^2 \times 2^2$
  c $3^5 \times 3^4$
  d $5^2 \times 5^3$
  e $x^2 \times x^4$
  f $a^3 \times a$
  g $n^4 \times n^6$
  h $b^3 \times b^5$

2 Simplify using the index laws:
  a $\dfrac{2^4}{2^3}$
  b $\dfrac{3^5}{3^2}$
  c $\dfrac{5^7}{5^3}$
  d $\dfrac{4^9}{4^5}$
  e $\dfrac{x^6}{x^3}$
  f $\dfrac{y^7}{y^4}$
  g $a^8 \div a^7$
  h $b^9 \div b^5$

3 Simplify using the index laws:
  a $(2^2)^3$
  b $(3^4)^3$
  c $(2^3)^6$
  d $(10^2)^5$
  e $(x^3)^2$
  f $(x^5)^3$
  g $(a^5)^4$
  h $(b^6)^4$

4 Simplify using the index laws:
  a $\dfrac{3^6}{3^2}$
  b $5^4 \times 5^2$
  c $\dfrac{7^5}{7^3}$
  d $(2^4)^2$
  e $2^2 \times 2^4$
  f $11^3 \div 11^2$
  g $(3^2)^3$
  h $(5^2)^3$

5 Simplify using the index laws:
  a $a^5 \times a^2$
  b $n^3 \times n^5$
  c $a^7 \div a^3$
  d $a^5 \times a$
  e $b^9 \div b^4$
  f $(a^3)^6$
  g $a^n \times a^5$
  h $(b^2)^4$
  i $b^6 \div b^3$
  j $m^4 \times m^3 \times m^7$
  k $(a^3)^3 \times a$
  l $(g^2)^4 \times g^3$

6 Remove the brackets of:
  a $(ab)^3$
  b $(ac)^4$
  c $(bc)^5$
  d $(abc)^3$
  e $(2a)^4$
  f $(5b)^2$
  g $(3n)^4$
  h $(2bc)^3$
  i $\left(\dfrac{2}{p}\right)^3$
  j $\left(\dfrac{a}{b}\right)^3$
  k $\left(\dfrac{m}{n}\right)^4$
  l $\left(\dfrac{2c}{d}\right)^5$

Exponents (Chapter 7)

C   ZERO AND NEGATIVE INDICES [1.9, 2.4]

Consider $\dfrac{2^3}{2^3} = \dfrac{8}{8}$ which is 1.

Using the exponent law for division, $\dfrac{2^3}{2^3} = 2^{3-3} = 2^0$.

We therefore conclude that $2^0 = 1$.

In general, we can state the **zero index law**: $a^0 = 1$ for all $a \neq 0$.

Now consider $\dfrac{2^4}{2^7}$ which is $\dfrac{2 \times 2 \times 2 \times 2}{2 \times 2 \times 2 \times 2 \times 2 \times 2 \times 2} = \dfrac{1}{2^3}$

Using the exponent law for division, $\dfrac{2^4}{2^7} = 2^{4-7} = 2^{-3}$

Consequently, $2^{-3} = \dfrac{1}{2^3}$. $\dfrac{1}{2^3}$ is the **reciprocal** of 2^3, which means that 2^{-3} and 2^3 are reciprocals of each other.

In general, we can state the **negative index law**:

> If a is any non-zero number and n is an integer, then $a^{-n} = \dfrac{1}{a^n}$.
>
> This means that a^n and a^{-n} are **reciprocals** of one another.
>
> In particular, notice that $a^{-1} = \dfrac{1}{a}$.

Using the negative index law, $\left(\dfrac{2}{3}\right)^{-4} = \dfrac{1}{\left(\dfrac{2}{3}\right)^4} = 1 \div \left(\dfrac{2}{3}\right)^4$ {division}

$= 1 \div \dfrac{2^4}{3^4}$ {exponent law}

$= 1 \times \dfrac{3^4}{2^4}$ {division of fractions}

$= \left(\dfrac{3}{2}\right)^4$ {exponent law}

So, in general we can see that: $\left(\dfrac{a}{b}\right)^{-n} = \left(\dfrac{b}{a}\right)^n$ provided $a \neq 0$, $b \neq 0$.

Example 9   ◀)) Self Tutor

Simplify, giving answers in simplest rational form:

a 7^0 **b** 3^{-2} **c** $3^0 - 3^{-1}$ **d** $\left(\dfrac{5}{3}\right)^{-2}$

a $7^0 = 1$

b $3^{-2} = \dfrac{1}{3^2} = \dfrac{1}{9}$

c $3^0 - 3^{-1} = 1 - \dfrac{1}{3} = \dfrac{2}{3}$

d $\left(\dfrac{5}{3}\right)^{-2} = \left(\dfrac{3}{5}\right)^2 = \dfrac{9}{25}$

EXERCISE 7C

1 Simplify, giving answers in simplest rational form:
- **a** 3^0
- **b** 6^{-1}
- **c** 4^{-1}
- **d** 5^0
- **e** 3^2
- **f** 3^{-2}
- **g** 5^3
- **h** 5^{-3}
- **i** 7^2
- **j** 7^{-2}
- **k** 10^3
- **l** 10^{-3}

2 Write as a fraction:
- **a** x^{-1}
- **b** k^{-1}
- **c** t^{-3}
- **d** r^{-5}

3 Simplify, giving answers in simplest rational form:
- **a** $(\frac{1}{2})^0$
- **b** $\frac{5^4}{5^4}$
- **c** $2t^0$
- **d** $(2t)^0$
- **e** 7^0
- **f** 3×4^0
- **g** $\frac{5^3}{5^5}$
- **h** $\frac{2^6}{2^{10}}$
- **i** $(\frac{1}{4})^{-1}$
- **j** $(\frac{3}{8})^{-1}$
- **k** $(\frac{2}{3})^{-1}$
- **l** $(\frac{1}{5})^{-1}$
- **m** $2^0 + 2^1$
- **n** $5^0 - 5^{-1}$
- **o** $3^0 + 3^1 - 3^{-1}$
- **p** $(\frac{1}{3})^{-2}$
- **q** $(\frac{2}{3})^{-3}$
- **r** $(1\frac{1}{2})^{-3}$
- **s** $(\frac{4}{5})^{-2}$
- **t** $(2\frac{1}{2})^{-2}$

4 Write the following without brackets or negative indices:
- **a** $(3b)^{-1}$
- **b** $3b^{-1}$
- **c** $7a^{-1}$
- **d** $(7a)^{-1}$
- **e** $\left(\frac{1}{t}\right)^{-2}$
- **f** $(4t)^{-2}$
- **g** $(5t)^{-2}$
- **h** $(5t^{-2})^{-1}$
- **i** xy^{-1}
- **j** $(xy)^{-1}$
- **k** xy^{-3}
- **l** $(xy)^{-3}$
- **m** $(3pq)^{-1}$
- **n** $3(pq)^{-1}$
- **o** $3pq^{-1}$
- **p** $\frac{(xy)^3}{y^{-2}}$

5 Write as powers of 2, 3 or 5:
- **a** 25
- **b** $\frac{1}{25}$
- **c** 27
- **d** $\frac{1}{27}$
- **e** 16
- **f** $\frac{1}{16}$
- **g** $\frac{2}{3}$
- **h** $\frac{3}{5}$
- **i** $\frac{9}{125}$
- **j** $\frac{32}{81}$
- **k** $2\frac{2}{5}$
- **l** $9\frac{3}{8}$

6 Write as powers of 10:
- **a** 1000
- **b** 0.01
- **c** 100 000
- **d** 0.000 001

D STANDARD FORM [1.9]

Consider the pattern alongside. Notice that each time we divide by 10, the **exponent** or **power** of 10 decreases by one.

$\div 10$: $10\,000 = 10^4$ -1
$\div 10$: $1000 = 10^3$ -1
$\div 10$: $100 = 10^2$ -1
$\div 10$: $10 = 10^1$ -1
$\div 10$: $1 = 10^0$ -1
$\div 10$: $\frac{1}{10} = 10^{-1}$ -1
$\div 10$: $\frac{1}{100} = 10^{-2}$ -1
$\div 10$: $\frac{1}{1000} = 10^{-3}$

Exponents (Chapter 7) 163

We can use this pattern to simplify the writing of very large and very small numbers.

For example,
$$5\,000\,000 \qquad \text{and} \qquad 0.000\,003$$
$$= 5 \times 1\,000\,000 \qquad\qquad\qquad = \dfrac{3}{1\,000\,000}$$
$$= 5 \times 10^6 \qquad\qquad\qquad\qquad = \dfrac{3}{1} \times \dfrac{1}{1\,000\,000}$$
$$\qquad\qquad\qquad\qquad\qquad\qquad = 3 \times 10^{-6}$$

STANDARD FORM

> **Standard form** (or **scientific notation**) involves writing any given number as *a number between 1 and 10*, multiplied by an *integer power of* 10. It has the form
> $$a \times 10^n \quad \text{where} \quad 1 \leqslant a < 10 \quad \text{and} \quad n \in \mathbb{Z}.$$

Example 10 ◀) Self Tutor

Write in standard form: **a** 37 600 **b** 0.000 86

a $37\,600 = 3.76 \times 10\,000$ {shift decimal point 4 places to the left and $\times 10\,000$}
$\qquad\quad\, = 3.76 \times 10^4$

b $0.000\,86 = 8.6 \div 10^4$ {shift decimal point 4 places to the right and $\div 10\,000$}
$\qquad\qquad\, = 8.6 \times 10^{-4}$

Example 11 ◀) Self Tutor

Write as an ordinary number: **a** 3.2×10^2 **b** 5.76×10^{-5}

a $\quad 3.2 \times 10^2$ **b** $\quad 5.76 \times 10^{-5}$
$\quad = 3.20 \times 100 \qquad\qquad = 000005.76 \div 10^5$
$\quad = 320 \qquad\qquad\qquad\,\, = 0.000\,057\,6$

Example 12 ◀) Self Tutor

Simplify the following, giving your answer in standard form:
a $(5 \times 10^4) \times (4 \times 10^5)$ **b** $(8 \times 10^5) \div (2 \times 10^3)$

a $\quad (5 \times 10^4) \times (4 \times 10^5)$ **b** $\quad (8 \times 10^5) \div (2 \times 10^3)$
$\quad = 5 \times 4 \times 10^4 \times 10^5 \qquad\qquad = \dfrac{8 \times 10^5}{2 \times 10^3}$
$\quad = 20 \times 10^{4+5}$
$\quad = 2 \times 10^1 \times 10^9 \qquad\qquad\quad\, = \dfrac{8}{2} \times \dfrac{10^5}{10^3}$
$\quad = 2 \times 10^{1+9}$
$\quad = 2 \times 10^{10} \qquad\qquad\qquad\quad = \tfrac{8}{2} \times 10^{5-3}$
$\qquad\qquad\qquad\qquad\qquad\qquad = 4 \times 10^2$

To help write numbers in standard form:

- If the original number is > 10, the power of 10 is **positive** $(+)$.
- If the original number is < 1, the power of 10 is **negative** $(-)$.
- If the original number is between 1 and 10, leave it as it is and multiply it by 10^0.

EXERCISE 7D.1

1 Write the following as powers of 10:
- **a** 100
- **b** 1000
- **c** 10
- **d** 100 000
- **e** 0.1
- **f** 0.01
- **g** 0.0001
- **h** 100 000 000

2 Express the following in standard form:
- **a** 387
- **b** 38 700
- **c** 3.87
- **d** 0.0387
- **e** 0.003 87
- **f** 20.5
- **g** 205
- **h** 0.205
- **i** 20 500
- **j** 20 500 000
- **k** 0.000 205

3 Express the following in standard form:
- **a** The circumference of the Earth is approximately 40 075 kilometres.
- **b** The distance from the Earth to the Sun is 149 500 000 000 m.
- **c** Bacteria are single cell organisms, some of which have a diameter of 0.0004 mm.
- **d** There are typically 40 million bacteria in a gram of soil.
- **e** The probability that your six numbers will be selected for Lotto on Saturday night is 0.000 000 141 62.
- **f** Superfine sheep have wool fibres as low as 0.01 mm in diameter.

4 Write as an ordinary decimal number:
- **a** 3×10^2
- **b** 2×10^3
- **c** 3.6×10^4
- **d** 9.2×10^5
- **e** 5.6×10^6
- **f** 3.4×10^1
- **g** 7.85×10^6
- **h** 9×10^8

5 Write as an ordinary decimal number:
- **a** 3×10^{-2}
- **b** 2×10^{-3}
- **c** 4.7×10^{-4}
- **d** 6.3×10^{-5}
- **e** 1.7×10^0
- **f** 9.5×10^{-4}
- **g** 3.49×10^{-1}
- **h** 7×10^{-6}

6 Write as an ordinary decimal number:
- **a** The wavelength of visible light is 9×10^{-7} m.
- **b** In 2007, the world population was approximately 6.606×10^9.
- **c** The diameter of our galaxy, the Milky Way, is 1×10^5 light years.
- **d** The smallest viruses are 1×10^{-5} mm in size.
- **e** 1 atomic mass unit is approximately 1.66×10^{-27} kg.

7 Write in standard form:
- **a** 18.17×10^6
- **b** 0.934×10^{11}
- **c** 0.041×10^{-2}

Exponents (Chapter 7)

8 Simplify the following, giving your answer in standard form:

   a $(8 \times 10^3) \times (2 \times 10^4)$ **b** $(8 \times 10^3) \times (4 \times 10^5)$

   c $(5 \times 10^4) \times (3 \times 10^5)$ **d** $(2 \times 10^3)^3$

   e $(6 \times 10^3)^2$ **f** $(7 \times 10^{-2})^2$

   g $(9 \times 10^4) \div (3 \times 10^3)$ **h** $(8 \times 10^5) \div (4 \times 10^6)$

STANDARD FORM ON A CALCULATOR

Scientific and graphics calculators are able to display very large and very small numbers in standard form.

If you perform $2\,300\,000 \times 400\,000$ your calculator might display $\boxed{9.2\,\text{E}+11}$ or $\boxed{9.2^{11}}$ or $\boxed{9.2\,\text{E}\,11}$, all of which actually represent 9.2×10^{11}.

Likewise, if you perform $0.0024 \div 10\,000\,000$ your calculator might display $\boxed{2.4^{-10}}$ or $\boxed{2.4\,\text{E}\,\text{-}10}$, which actually represent 2.4×10^{-10}.

You will find instructions for graphics calculators on page **15**.

EXERCISE 7D.2

1 Write each of the following as it would appear on the display of *your* calculator:

   a $4\,650\,000$ **b** $0.000\,051\,2$ **c** 5.99×10^{-4}

   d 3.761×10^{10} **e** $49\,500\,000$ **f** $0.000\,008\,44$

2 Calculate each of the following, giving your answers in standard form. The decimal part should be correct to 2 decimal places.

   a $0.06 \times 0.002 \div 4000$ **b** $426 \times 760 \times 42\,000$ **c** $627\,000 \times 74\,000$

   d $320 \times 600 \times 51\,400$ **e** $0.004\,28 \div 120\,000$ **f** $0.026 \times 0.00\,42 \times 0.08$

Example 13   Self Tutor

Use your calculator to find:

   a $(1.42 \times 10^4) \times (2.56 \times 10^8)$ **b** $(4.75 \times 10^{-4}) \div (2.5 \times 10^7)$

Instructions are given for the **Casio fx-9860G**:   *Answer:*

   a 1.42 [EXP] 4 [×] 2.56 [EXP] 8 [EXE] 3.6352×10^{12}

   b 4.75 [EXP] [(−)] 4 [÷] 2.5 [EXP] 7 [EXE] 1.9×10^{-11}

---

3 Find, in standard form, with decimal part correct to 2 places:

   a $(5.31 \times 10^4) \times (4.8 \times 10^3)$ **b** $(2.75 \times 10^{-3})^2$ **c** $\dfrac{8.24 \times 10^{-6}}{3 \times 10^4}$

   d $(7.2 \times 10^{-5}) \div (2.4 \times 10^{-6})$ **e** $\dfrac{1}{4.1 \times 10^4}$ **f** $(3.2 \times 10^3)^2$

4 For the following, give answers in standard form correct to 3 significant figures:
  a How many millimetres are there in 479.8 kilometres?
  b How many seconds are there in one year?
  c How many seconds are there in a millennium?
  d How many kilograms are there in 0.5 milligrams?

5 If a missile travels at 3600 km/h, how far will it travel in:
  a 1 day **b** 1 week **c** 2 years?

  Give your answers in standard form with decimal part correct to 2 places. Assume that 1 year = 365 days.

6 Light travels at a speed of 3×10^8 metres per second. How far will light travel in:
  a 1 minute **b** 1 day **c** 1 year?

  Give your answers in standard form with decimal part correct to 2 decimal places. Assume that 1 year = 365 days.

Review set 7A

1 Find the integer equal to: **a** 3^4 **b** 5×2^3

2 Write as a product of primes in index form: **a** 36 **b** 242

3 Simplify:
  a $(-2)^3$
  b $-(-1)^8$
  c $(-1)^3 \times (-2)^2 \times -3^3$

4 Simplify, giving your answers in simplest rational form:
  a 3^{-3}
  b $\left(\frac{4}{3}\right)^{-2}$
  c $3^0 - 3^1$

5 Write $\frac{1}{16}$ as a power of 2.

6 Simplify, using the exponent laws:
  a $5^6 \times 5$
  b $b^7 \div b^2$
  c $(x^4)^3$

7 Express in simplest form, without brackets:
  a $(5x)^2$
  b $(3mn)^3$
  c $\left(\frac{p}{2q}\right)^4$

8 Write in standard form:
  a 9
  b 34 900
  c 0.0075

9 Write as an ordinary decimal number:
  a 2.81×10^6
  b 2.81×10^0
  c 2.81×10^{-3}

10 Simplify, giving your answer in standard form:
  a $(6 \times 10^3) \times (7.1 \times 10^4)$
  b $(2.4 \times 10^6) \div (4 \times 10^2)$

11 The Earth orbits around the Sun at a speed of approximately 1.07×10^5 km/h. How far does the Earth move, relative to the Sun, in:

　a 1 day　　　　　　　　**b** 1 week　　　　　　　　**c** 1 year?

Give your answers in standard form with decimal part correct to 2 decimal places. Assume that 1 year = 365 days.

Review set 7B

1 Find the integer equal to:　**a** 7^3　**b** $3^2 \times 5^2$

2 Write as a product of primes in index form:　**a** 42　**b** 144

3 Simplify:

　a $-(-1)^7$　　　　　**b** -4^3　　　　　**c** $(-2)^5 \times (-3)^2$

4 Simplify, giving your answers in simplest rational form:

　a 6^{-2}　　　　　**b** $\left(1\tfrac{1}{2}\right)^{-1}$　　　　　**c** $\left(\tfrac{3}{5}\right)^{-2}$

5 Simplify, using the exponent laws:

　a $3^2 \times 3^6$　　　　　**b** $a^5 \div a^5$　　　　　**c** $(y^3)^5$

6 Write as powers of 2, 3 or 5:

　a $\tfrac{16}{25}$　　　**b** $\tfrac{40}{81}$　　　**c** 180　　　**d** $11\tfrac{1}{9}$

7 Express in simplest form, without brackets or negative indices:

　a $(5c)^{-1}$　　　　　**b** $7k^{-2}$　　　　　**c** $(4d^2)^{-3}$

8 Write in standard form:

　a 263.57　　　　　**b** 0.000 511　　　　　**c** 863 400 000

9 Write as an ordinary decimal number:

　a 2.78×10^0　　　　**b** 3.99×10^7　　　　**c** 2.081×10^{-3}

10 Simplify, giving your answer in standard form:

　a $(8 \times 10^3)^2$　　　　　**b** $(3.6 \times 10^5) \div (6 \times 10^{-2})$

11 How many kilometres are there in 0.21 millimetres? Give your answer in standard form.

Activity   Astronomical distances

Astronomers often have to deal with extremely large distances. They measure things like the distance between stars, and the size of galaxies. Because of the large numbers, astronomers have their own set of units.

1. One **astronomical unit** (AU) is the distance between the Earth and the Sun, which is about 150 million kilometres. Write this number in standard form.

2. One **light year** is 9.5×10^{12} km. How many AU is this?

3. For longer distances, astronomers use a unit called a **parsec**, which is about 3.26 light years. Write this number in standard form, in:
   a AU
   b km

4. The distance from Earth to a star can be calculated using the formula $d = 2 \times p^{-1}$, where
   - d is the distance in parsecs, and
   - p is the *parallax* of the star (found through a series of other measurements).

   Copy and complete the following table:

Star	Parallax	Distance from Earth (parsecs)
Alpha Centauri	1.494 46	
Polaris	0.015 12	
Deneb	4.58×10^{-3}	

Formulae and inequalities

8

Contents:

A	Formula substitution	[2.5]
B	Formula rearrangement	[2.5]
C	Formula derivation	[2.5]
D	Interpreting linear inequalities	[2.1]
E	Solving linear inequalities	[2.2]

Opening problem

Dinesh weighs d kg. He has an older brother named Mandar who weighs m kg, and a younger brother named Ravi who weighs r kg.

a Write a formula for the total weight T kg of the brothers.

b Dinesh is heavier than Ravi but lighter than Mandar. If Mandar weighs 87 kg and Ravi weighs 63 kg, represent the possible values of d using an inequality.

The equations we have solved so far in the book have had only one variable. In this chapter we will consider equations with more than one variable. We also consider inequalities, where the LHS and RHS are not balanced.

A FORMULA SUBSTITUTION [2.5]

A **formula** is an equation which connects two or more variables.
The plural of formula is **formulae** or **formulas**.

For example, the speed formula $s = \dfrac{d}{t}$ relates the three variable quantities speed (s), distance travelled (d), and time taken (t).

We usually write formulae with one variable on its own on the left hand side. The other variable(s) and constants are written on the right hand side.

The variable on its own is called the **subject** of the formula.

So, in $s = \dfrac{d}{t}$, s is the subject of the formula.

If a formula contains two or more variables and we know the value of all but one of them, we can **substitute** the known values into the formula and hence find the value of the unknown variable.

> Step 1: Write down the formula.
> Step 2: State the values of the known variables.
> Step 3: Substitute into the formula to form a one variable equation.
> Step 4: Solve the equation for the unknown variable.

Example 1 ◀) Self Tutor

When a stone is dropped from a cliff into the sea, the total distance fallen, D metres, is given by the formula $D = \tfrac{1}{2}gt^2$ where t is the time of fall in seconds and g is the gravitational constant of 9.8 m/s². Find:

a the distance fallen after 4 seconds

b the time (to the nearest $\tfrac{1}{100}$th second) taken for the stone to fall 200 metres.

a $D = \tfrac{1}{2}gt^2$ where $g = 9.8$ and $t = 4$

$\therefore \ D = \tfrac{1}{2} \times 9.8 \times 4^2$ Calculator:

        $= 78.4$ 0.5 × 9.8 × 4 x^2 ENTER

$\therefore$ the stone has fallen 78.4 metres.

b $D = \tfrac{1}{2}gt^2$ where $D = 200$ and $g = 9.8$

$\therefore \ \tfrac{1}{2} \times 9.8 \times t^2 = 200$

$\therefore \ 4.9t^2 = 200$

$\therefore \ t^2 = \dfrac{200}{4.9}$ Calculator:

                      TI: √ 200 ÷ 4.9) ENTER

$\therefore \ t = \pm\sqrt{\dfrac{200}{4.9}}$ or

                      Casio: √ (200 ÷ 4.9) EXE

$\therefore \ t \approx 6.39$ {as $t > 0$}

$\therefore$ the time taken is about 6.39 seconds.

EXERCISE 8A

1 The formula for finding the circumference C of a circle with radius r is $C = 2\pi r$. Find:

   a the circumference of a circle of radius 4.2 cm

   b the radius of a circle with circumference 112 cm

   c the diameter of a circle with circumference 400 metres.

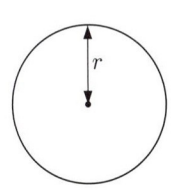

Formulae and inequalities (Chapter 8)

2 When a stone is dropped from the top of a cliff, the total distance fallen is given by the formula $D = \frac{1}{2}gt^2$ where D is the distance in metres and t is the time taken in seconds. Given that $g = 9.8$ m/s^2, find:
   a the total distance fallen in the first 2 seconds of fall
   b the height of the cliff, to the nearest metre, if the stone takes 4.8 seconds to hit the ground.

3 When a car travels a distance d kilometres in time t hours, the average speed for the journey is given by the formula $s = \dfrac{d}{t}$ km/h. Find:
   a the average speed of a car which travels 250 km in $3\frac{1}{2}$ hours
   b the distance travelled by a car in $2\frac{3}{4}$ hours if its average speed is 80 km/h
   c the time taken, to the nearest minute, for a car to travel 790 km at an average speed of 95 km/h.

4 A circle's area A is given by $A = \pi r^2$ where r is the length of its radius. Find:
   a the area of a circle of radius 6.4 cm
   b the radius of a circular swimming pool which has an area of 160 m^2.

5 Scuba divers experience decompression sickness if they stay under water too long. The recommended maximum length of a dive is given by the formula $t = \dfrac{17\,500}{d^2}$, where t is the dive time in minutes and d is the depth in metres. Find:
   a the maximum dive time of a 35 m deep dive
   b the recommended maximum depth for a diver who wants to spend 45 minutes under water.

6 A cylinder of radius r and height h has volume given by $V = \pi r^2 h$. Find:
   a the volume of a cylindrical tin can of radius 8 cm and height 21.2 cm
   b the height of a cylinder of radius 6 cm and volume 120 cm^3
   c the radius, in mm, of a copper pipe with volume 470 cm^3 and length 6 m.

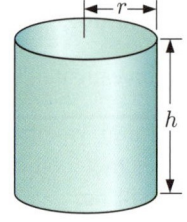

7 A child's final height can be estimated using the formula $H = \dfrac{M + D}{2} + k$ cm, where M is the mother's height in cm, D is the father's height in cm, and k is $+4.5$ cm if the child is male or -2.5 cm if the child is female. Estimate:
   a the final height of a boy with mother 158 cm and father 167 cm tall
   b the final height of a girl with mother 175 cm and father 180 cm tall
   c the height of the mother of a woman 166 cm tall whose father was 182 cm tall.

8 The formula $D = 3.56\sqrt{h}$ km gives the approximate distance to the horizon which can be seen by a person with eye level h metres above sea level. Find:
   a the distance to the horizon when a person's eye level is 20 m above sea level
   b how far above sea level a person's eye must be for the person to be able to see for 25 km.

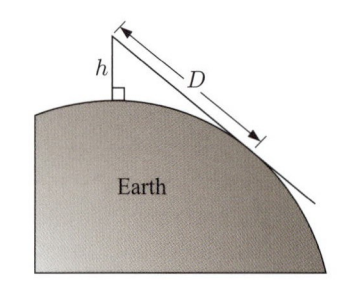

9 The *period* or time taken for one complete swing of a simple pendulum is given approximately by $T = \frac{1}{5}\sqrt{l}$ seconds, where l is the length of the pendulum in cm. Find:

   a the time for one complete swing of the pendulum if its length is 45 cm

   b the length of a pendulum which has a period of 1.8 seconds.

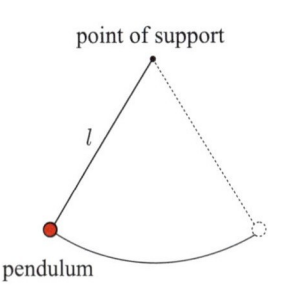

Activity   *Pizza pricing*

Luigi's Pizza Parlour is famous for its 'Seafood Special' pizza.

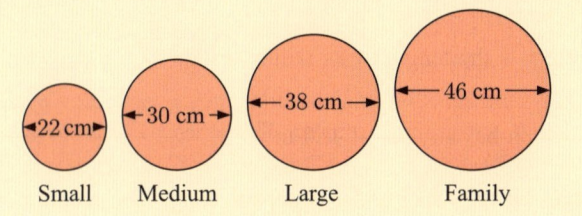

LUIGI'S PIZZAS	*Seafood Special*	
	Small	€8.00
	Medium	€10.60
Free Delivery!	Large	€14.00
	Family	€18.20

Small 22 cm, Medium 30 cm, Large 38 cm, Family 46 cm

Sasha, Enrico and Bianca decide to find Luigi's formula for the price €P for each size pizza. Letting r cm be the radius of a pizza, the formulae they worked out were:

Sasha: $P = \dfrac{17r - 27}{20}$ Enrico: $P = \sqrt{\dfrac{33r - 235}{2}}$ Bianca: $P = 5 + \dfrac{r^2}{40}$.

What to do:

1 Investigate the suitability of each formula.

2 Luigi is introducing a Party size pizza of diameter 54 cm. What do you think his price will be?

B FORMULA REARRANGEMENT   [2.5]

In the formula $D = xt + p$, D is expressed in terms of the other variables, x, t and p. We therefore say that D is the **subject** of the formula.

We can rearrange a formula to make one of the other variables the subject. However, we must do this carefully to ensure the formula is still true.

> We **rearrange** formulae using the same processes which we use to solve equations. Anything we do to one side we must also do to the other.

Example 2

Make y the subject of $2x + 3y = 12$.

$2x + 3y = 12$
$\therefore\ 2x + 3y - 2x = 12 - 2x$ $\{-2x$ from both sides$\}$
$\therefore\ 3y = 12 - 2x$
$\therefore\ \dfrac{3y}{3} = \dfrac{12 - 2x}{3}$ $\{\div$ both sides by $3\}$
$\therefore\ y = \dfrac{12}{3} - \dfrac{2x}{3}$
$= 4 - \tfrac{2}{3}x$

Example 3

Make y the subject of $x = 5 - cy$.

$x = 5 - cy$
$\therefore\ x + cy = 5 - cy + cy$ $\{+ cy$ to both sides$\}$
$\therefore\ x + cy = 5$
$\therefore\ x + cy - x = 5 - x$ $\{-x$ from both sides$\}$
$\therefore\ cy = 5 - x$
$\therefore\ \dfrac{cy}{c} = \dfrac{5 - x}{c}$ $\{\div$ both sides by $c\}$
$\therefore\ y = \dfrac{5 - x}{c}$

Example 4

Make z the subject of $c = \dfrac{m}{z}$.

$c = \dfrac{m}{z}$
$\therefore\ c \times z = \dfrac{m}{z} \times z$ $\{\times$ both sides by $z\}$
$\therefore\ cz = m$
$\therefore\ \dfrac{cz}{c} = \dfrac{m}{c}$ $\{\div$ both sides by $c\}$
$\therefore\ z = \dfrac{m}{c}$

EXERCISE 8B.1

1 Make y the subject of:
  a $2x + 5y = 10$ **b** $3x + 4y = 20$ **c** $2x - y = 8$
  d $2x + 7y = 14$ **e** $5x + 2y = 20$ **f** $2x - 3y = -12$

2 Make x the subject of:
  a $p + x = r$ **b** $xy = z$ **c** $3x + a = d$
  d $5x + 2y = d$ **e** $ax + by = p$ **f** $y = mx + c$
  g $2 + tx = s$ **h** $p + qx = m$ **i** $6 = a + bx$

3 Make y the subject of:
   a $mx - y = c$
   b $c - 2y = p$
   c $a - 3y = t$
   d $n - ky = 5$
   e $a - by = n$
   f $p = a - ny$

4 Make z the subject of:
   a $az = \dfrac{b}{c}$
   b $\dfrac{a}{z} = d$
   c $\dfrac{3}{d} = \dfrac{2}{z}$
   d $\dfrac{z}{2} = \dfrac{a}{z}$
   e $\dfrac{b}{z} = \dfrac{z}{n}$
   f $\dfrac{m}{z} = \dfrac{z}{a-b}$

5 Make:
   a a the subject of $F = ma$
   b r the subject of $C = 2\pi r$
   c d the subject of $V = ldh$
   d K the subject of $A = \dfrac{b}{K}$
   e h the subject of $A = \dfrac{bh}{2}$
   f T the subject of $I = \dfrac{PRT}{100}$
   g m the subject of $E = mc^2$
   h a the subject of $M = \dfrac{a+b}{2}$

REARRANGEMENT AND SUBSTITUTION

In the previous section on formula substitution, the variables were replaced by numbers and then the equation was solved.

However, we sometimes need to substitute several values for the unknowns and solve the equation for each case. In this situation it is quicker to **rearrange** the formula **before substituting**.

Example 5 ◆) Self Tutor

The circumference of a circle is given by $C = 2\pi r$, where r is the circle's radius. Rearrange this formula to make r the subject, and hence find the radius when the circumference is: **a** 10 cm **b** 20 cm **c** 50 cm.

$2\pi r = C$, so $r = \dfrac{C}{2\pi}$

a When $C = 10$, $r = \dfrac{10}{2\pi} \approx 1.59$ ∴ the radius is about 1.59 cm.

b When $C = 20$, $r = \dfrac{20}{2\pi} \approx 3.18$ ∴ the radius is about 3.18 cm.

c When $C = 50$, $r = \dfrac{50}{2\pi} \approx 7.96$ ∴ the radius is about 7.96 cm.

EXERCISE 8B.2

1 The equation of a straight line is $5x + 3y = 18$.
   Rearrange this formula into the form $y = mx + c$.
   Hence, state the value of: **a** the gradient m **b** the y-intercept c.

2 **a** Make a the subject of the formula $K = \dfrac{d^2}{2ab}$.
   b Find the value of a when:
      i $K = 112$, $d = 24$, $b = 2$
      ii $K = 400$, $d = 72$, $b = 0.4$.

Formulae and inequalities (Chapter 8)

3 When a car travels a distance d kilometres in time t hours, the average speed s for the journey is given by the formula $s = \dfrac{d}{t}$ km/h.

  a Make d the subject of the formula. Hence find the distance travelled by a car if:
  - **i** the average speed is 60 km/h and the time travelled is 3 hours
  - **ii** the average speed is 80 km/h and the time travelled is $1\tfrac{1}{2}$ hours
  - **iii** the average speed is 95 km/h and the time travelled is 1 h 20 min.

  b Make t the subject of the formula. Hence find the time required for a car to travel:
  - **i** 180 km at an average speed of 60 km/h
  - **ii** 140 km at an average speed of 35 km/h
  - **iii** 220 km at an average speed of 100 km/h.

4 The simple interest $\$I$ paid on an investment of $\$P$ is determined by the annual rate of interest r (as a decimal) and the duration of the investment, n years. The interest is given by the formula $I = P \times r \times n$.

  a Make n the subject of the formula.
  b **i** Find the time required to generate $\$1050$ interest on an investment of $\$6400$ at an interest rate of 8% per annum.
  ii Find the time required for an investment of $\$1000$ to double at an interest rate of 10% per annum.

C FORMULA DERIVATION [2.5]

When we construct or **derive** a formula it is often useful to first consider an example with numbers. We can then generalise the result.

For example, the perimeter of the rectangle is given by

$P = 3 + 6 + 3 + 6$ metres

$\therefore \ P = (2 \times 3) + (2 \times 6)$ metres

$\therefore \ P$ is double the width plus double the length.

We now consider a rectangle which is a wide and b long.

In this case, $P = 2a + 2b$
or $P = 2(a+b)$.

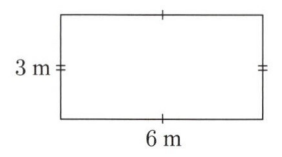

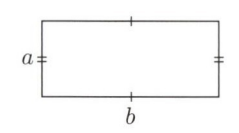

Example 6

Write the formula for the total cost RM C of a taxi trip given a fixed charge of:

a RM 3, plus RM 0.55 per km for 12 km
b RM 3, plus RM 0.55 per km for k km
c RM 3, plus RM d per km for k km
d RM F, plus RM d per km for k km.

a $C = 3 + (0.55 \times 12)$

b $C = 3 + (0.55 \times k)$
$\therefore \ C = 3 + 0.55k$

c $C = 3 + d \times k$
$\therefore \ C = 3 + dk$

d $C = F + dk$

Example 7

Write a formula for the amount A in a person's bank account if initially the balance was:

a $5000, and $200 was withdrawn each week for 10 weeks
b $5000, and $200 was withdrawn each week for w weeks
c $5000, and x was withdrawn each week for w weeks
d B, and x was withdrawn each week for w weeks.

a $A = 5000 - 200 \times 10$

b $A = 5000 - 200 \times w$
$\therefore A = 5000 - 200w$

c $A = 5000 - x \times w$
$\therefore A = 5000 - xw$

d $A = B - x \times w$
$\therefore A = B - xw$

EXERCISE 8C

1 Write a formula for the amount €A in a bank account if the initial balance was:
  a €2000, and then €150 was deposited each week for 8 weeks
  b €2000, and then €150 was deposited each week for w weeks
  c €2000, and then €d was deposited each week for w weeks
  d €P, and then €d was deposited each week for w weeks.

2 Write a formula for the water usage, W litres, of a household given a weekly usage of:
  a 3500 l over 16 weeks   **b** 3500 l over n weeks   **c** H l over n weeks.

3 Write a formula for the cost C of a mobile phone plan if the joining fee was:
  a $20, and then $29 was charged each month for 24 months
  b $20, and then $29 was charged each month for n months
  c $20, and then m was charged each month for n months
  d s, and then m was charged each month for n months.

4 Write a formula for the current weight W of Naomi if initially she weighed:
  a 100 kg, and she lost 0.5 kg per week for 12 weeks
  b 100 kg, and she lost 0.5 kg per week for n weeks
  c 100 kg, and she lost k kg per week for n weeks
  d I kg, and she lost k kg per week for n weeks.

5 Katie has made a large pot of marmalade, and is storing it in jars. Write a formula for the amount M ml of marmalade left in her stockpot, if she initially had:
  a 8000 ml, and she fills up 10 jars of 350 ml each
  b 8000 ml, and she fills up j jars of 350 ml each
  c 8000 ml, and she fills up j jars of c ml each
  d L ml, and she fills up j jars of c ml each.

6 Write a formula for the hire cost £H of a fancy dress costume given a fixed charge of:
  a £35, plus £15 per day for 6 days   **b** £35, plus £15 per day for d days
  c £B, plus £15 per day for d days   **d** £B, plus £C per day for d days.

Formulae and inequalities (Chapter 8) 177

7 The perimeter of a polygon is the sum of the lengths of its sides. Write a formula for the perimeter P of the following shapes:

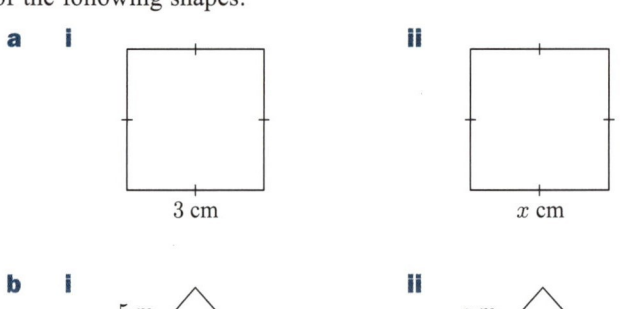

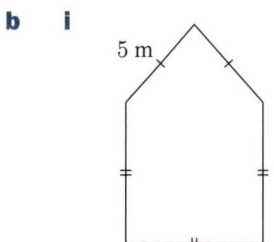

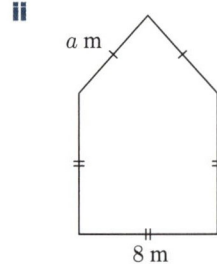

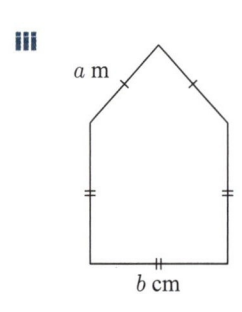

a **i** square with side 3 cm **ii** square with side x cm

b **i** pentagon (house shape) with slant sides 5 m and base 8 m **ii** pentagon with slant sides a m and base 8 m **iii** pentagon with slant sides a m and base b cm

D INTERPRETING LINEAR INEQUALITIES [2.1]

Many rides at theme parks have a rule that people must be at least 120 cm tall to use the ride. This can be written as a **linear inequality** using the variable h to represent a person's height in cm.

$h \geqslant 120$ reads 'h is greater than or equal to 120'.

We can represent allowable heights on a **number line**:

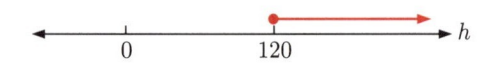

The number line shows that any height of 120 cm or more is an acceptable height to go on the ride. We say that these are **solutions** of the inequality.

REPRESENTING INEQUALITIES ON A NUMBER LINE

Suppose our solution to an inequality is $x \geqslant 4$, so *every* number which is 4 or greater than 4 is a possible value for x. We could represent this on a number line by:

The filled-in circle indicates that 4 **is** included.

The arrowhead indicates that all numbers on the number line in this direction are included.

If our solution is $x < 5$, our representation would be:

The hollow circle indicates that 5 **is not** included.

Example 8

Represent the following inequalities on a number line:

a $1 \leqslant x < 5$　　　　**b** $x < 0$ or $x \geqslant 4$

EXERCISE 8D

1 Represent the following inequalities on a number line:

- **a** $x > 5$
- **b** $x \geqslant 1$
- **c** $x \leqslant 2$
- **d** $x < -1$
- **e** $-2 \leqslant x \leqslant 2$
- **f** $-3 < x \leqslant 4$
- **g** $1 \leqslant x < 6$
- **h** $-1 < x < 0$
- **i** $x < 0$ or $x \geqslant 3$
- **j** $x \leqslant -1$ or $x \geqslant 2$
- **k** $x < 2$ or $x > 5$
- **l** $x \leqslant -2$ or $x > 0$

2 Write down the inequality used to describe the set of numbers:

Formulae and inequalities (Chapter 8)

E   SOLVING LINEAR INEQUALITIES   [2.2]

Notice that $5 > 3$ and $3 < 5$,
and that $-3 < 2$ and $2 > -3$.

This suggests that if we **interchange** the LHS and RHS of an inequality, then we must **reverse** the inequality sign. $>$ is the reverse of $<$, $\geqslant$ is the reverse of $\leqslant$.

You may also remember from previous years that:
- If we **add** or **subtract** the same number to both sides, the inequality sign is *maintained*.
  For example, if $5 > 3$ then $5 + 2 > 3 + 2$.
- If we **multiply** or **divide** both sides by a **positive** number, the inequality sign is *maintained*.
  For example, if $5 > 3$ then $5 \times 2 > 3 \times 2$.
- If we **multiply** or **divide** both sides by a **negative** number, the inequality sign is *reversed*.
  For example, if $5 > 3$ then $5 \times -1 < 3 \times -1$.

The method of solution of linear inequalities is thus identical to that of linear equations with the exceptions that:

> - **interchanging** the sides **reverses** the inequality sign
> - **multiplying** or **dividing** both sides by a **negative** number **reverses** the inequality sign.

Example 9   ◆) Self Tutor

Solve for x and graph the solutions: **a** $3x - 4 \leqslant 2$ **b** $3 - 2x < 7$

a $3x - 4 \leqslant 2$
$\therefore$ $3x - 4 + 4 \leqslant 2 + 4$ {adding 4 to both sides}
$\therefore$ $3x \leqslant 6$
$\therefore$ $\dfrac{3x}{3} \leqslant \dfrac{6}{3}$ {dividing both sides by 3}
$\therefore$ $x \leqslant 2$

Check: If $x = 1$ then $3x - 4 = 3 \times 1 - 4 = -1$ and $-1 \leqslant 2$ is true.

b $3 - 2x < 7$
$\therefore$ $3 - 2x - 3 < 7 - 3$ {subtracting 3 from both sides}
$\therefore$ $-2x < 4$
$\therefore$ $\dfrac{-2x}{-2} > \dfrac{4}{-2}$ {dividing both sides by -2, so reverse the sign}
$\therefore$ $x > -2$

Check: If $x = 3$ then $3 - 2x = 3 - 2 \times 3 = -3$,
       and $-3 < 7$ is true.

*We reverse the inequality sign in **b** when we divide by -2.*

Example 10

Solve for x and graph the solutions: $-5 < 9 - 2x$

$$-5 < 9 - 2x$$
$$\therefore \quad -5 + 2x < 9 - 2x + 2x \quad \text{\{adding } 2x \text{ to both sides\}}$$
$$\therefore \quad 2x - 5 < 9$$
$$\therefore \quad 2x - 5 + 5 < 9 + 5 \quad \text{\{adding 5 to both sides\}}$$
$$\therefore \quad 2x < 14$$
$$\therefore \quad \frac{2x}{2} < \frac{14}{2} \quad \text{\{dividing both sides by 2\}}$$
$$\therefore \quad x < 7$$

Check: If $x = 5$ then $-5 < 9 - 2 \times 5$, and $-5 < -1$ which is true.

Example 11

Solve for x and graph the solutions: $3 - 5x \geqslant 2x + 7$

$$3 - 5x \geqslant 2x + 7$$
$$\therefore \quad 3 - 5x - 2x \geqslant 2x + 7 - 2x \quad \text{\{subtracting } 2x \text{ from both sides\}}$$
$$\therefore \quad 3 - 7x \geqslant 7$$
$$\therefore \quad 3 - 7x - 3 \geqslant 7 - 3 \quad \text{\{subtracting 3 from both sides\}}$$
$$\therefore \quad -7x \geqslant 4$$
$$\therefore \quad \frac{-7x}{-7} \leqslant \frac{4}{-7} \quad \text{\{dividing both sides by } -7 \text{, so reverse the sign\}}$$
$$\therefore \quad x \leqslant -\tfrac{4}{7}$$

Check: If $x = -1$ then $3 - 5 \times (-1) \geqslant 2 \times (-1) + 7$. Simplifying gives $8 \geqslant 5$ which is true.

EXERCISE 8E

1 Solve for x and graph the solutions:

a $4x \leqslant 12$
b $-3x < 18$
c $-5x \geqslant -35$
d $3x + 2 < 0$
e $5x - 7 > 2$
f $2 - 3x \geqslant 1$
g $5 - 2x \leqslant 11$
h $2(3x - 1) < 4$
i $5(1 - 3x) \geqslant 8$

2 Solve for x and graph the solutions:

a $7 \geqslant 2x - 1$
b $-13 < 3x + 2$
c $20 > -5x$
d $-3 \geqslant 4 - 3x$
e $3 < 5 - 2x$
f $2 \leqslant 5(1 - x)$

Formulae and inequalities (Chapter 8)

3 Solve for x and graph the solutions:

    a $3x + 2 > x - 5$ **b** $2x - 3 < 5x - 7$ **c** $5 - 2x \geqslant x + 4$

    d $7 - 3x \leqslant 5 - x$ **e** $3x - 2 > 2(x - 1) + 5x$ **f** $1 - (x - 3) \geqslant 2(x + 5) - 1$

4 Solve for x:

    a $3x + 1 > 3(x + 2)$ **b** $5x + 2 < 5(x + 1)$ **c** $2x - 4 \geqslant 2(x - 2)$

    d Comment on your solutions to **a**, **b** and **c**.

Review set 8A

1 The formula for the density D of a substance with mass M and volume V is $D = \dfrac{M}{V}$.

    a Find the density of lead if 350 g of lead occupies 30.7 cm^3.

    b Find the mass of a lump of uranium with density 18.97 g/cm^3 and volume 2 cm^3.

    c Find the volume of a piece of pine timber with mass 6 kg and density 650 kg/m^3.

2 Make t the subject of: **a** $3t - s = 13$ **b** $\dfrac{t}{r} = \dfrac{4}{t}$

3 Write down the inequality used to describe the set of numbers:

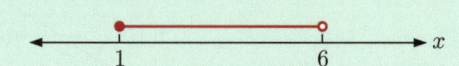

4 **a** A trough is initially empty. Write a formula for the volume of water V in the trough if:

    i six 8-litre buckets of water are poured into it

    ii n 8-litre buckets of water are poured into it

    iii n l-litre buckets of water are poured into it.

    b A trough contains 25 litres of water. Write a formula for the volume of water V in the trough if n buckets of water, each containing l litres, are poured into it.

5 Represent the following inequalities on a number line:

    a $-2 < x < 2$ **b** $x \leqslant -5$ or $x \geqslant -1$

6 Solve for x and show the solutions on a number line:

    a $3(x - 4) \leqslant x + 6$ **b** $7 - 2(x - 3) > 5(3 - 2x)$

7 The formula for the surface area of a solid cone with radius r and slant height l, is $A = \pi r l + \pi r^2$.

    a Rearrange this formula to make l the subject.

    b Find the slant height of a solid cone with surface area 30π cm^2, and radius 3 cm.

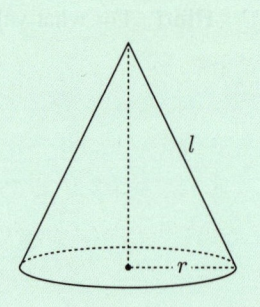

Review set 8B

1 The formula for the volume of a sphere is $V = \frac{4}{3}\pi r^3$, where r is the radius. Find:
  a the volume of a sphere of radius 3.4 cm
  b the radius of a sphere of volume 7.2 m³.

2 Make j the subject of: **a** $l = 2jk - 3$ **b** $\dfrac{pRj}{d} = s$

3 Write down the inequality used to describe the set of numbers:

[number line with open circle at -1 arrow left, closed circle at 4 arrow right, labelled x]

4 Write a formula for the total cost £C of packing parcels of books for dispatch if the charge is:
  a £2 per parcel plus £1.20 for one book
  b £2 per parcel plus £1.20 per book for 5 books
  c £p per parcel plus £1.20 per book for b books
  d £p per parcel plus £x per book for b books.

5 Write down a formula for the perimeter P of:
  a [triangle with sides 4 cm, 7 cm, and marked side]
  b [triangle with sides n, m, and marked side]

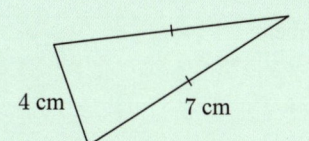

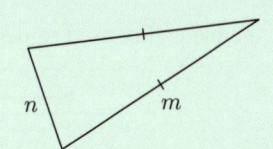

6 Represent the following inequalities on a number line:
  a $-1 \leqslant x < 3$ **b** $x < 0$ or $x \geqslant 3$

7 Solve for x and show the solutions on a number line:
  a $2x + 7 < 22 - 3x$ **b** $5(x + 4) \geqslant 5 - 2(3 - x)$

Challenge

1 Solve for x: $(x + 2)(2 - x) \geqslant x(6 - x)$

2 Solve for x: $\sqrt{x + 3} \geqslant \sqrt{3 - x}$
   Hint: For what values of x does $\sqrt{3 - x}$ have meaning?

Simultaneous equations

9

Contents:

A	Equating values of y	[2.6]
B	Solution by substitution	[2.6]
C	Solution by elimination	[2.6]
D	Problem solving	[2.6]

Opening problem

Toby owns a fleet of trucks, and the trucks come in two sizes. The small trucks can carry a maximum of 3 tonnes, while the large trucks can carry a maximum of 5 tonnes.

There are 25 trucks in Toby's fleet, and the trucks can carry a combined total of 95 tonnes.

How many trucks of each size does Toby own?

In the **Opening Problem**, there are *two* unknowns: the number of small trucks, and the number of large trucks. There is also enough information for two equations: one for the total number of trucks, and one for the total tonnage.

There are many truck combinations which give a total of 25 trucks, and there are many combinations which carry a total of 95 tonnes. However, we need a solution that satisfies *both* of these conditions.

The values of the variables that satisfy both equations at the same time are called the **simultaneous solution** to the pair of equations.

Discovery

The coin problem

In my pocket I have 8 coins. They are $1 and $2 coins, and their total value is $11. How many of each type of coin do I have?

What to do:

1 Copy and complete the following table:

Number of $1 coins	0	1	2	3	4	5	6	7	8
Value of $1 coins									
Number of $2 coins	8	7							
Value of $2 coins									
Total value of coins									

2 Use the table to find the solution to the problem.

3 Suppose I have x $1 coins and y $2 coins in my pocket.
  a By considering the total number of coins, explain why $x + y = 8$.
  b By considering the total value of the coins, explain why $x + 2y = 11$.

4 You should have found that there were five $1 coins and three $2 coins.
  a Substitute $x = 5$ and $y = 3$ into $x + y = 8$. What do you notice?
  b Substitute $x = 5$ and $y = 3$ into $x + 2y = 11$. What do you notice?

5 My friend has 12 coins in her pocket. They are all either £1 or £2. If the total value of her coins is £17, how many of each type does she have? Can you find the solution by algebraic means?

In this course we will consider **linear simultaneous equations** containing two unknowns, usually x and y. There are infinitely many values of x and y which satisfy the first equation. Likewise, there are infinitely many values of x and y which satisfy the second equation. In general, however, only one combination of values for x and y satisfies **both** equations at the same time.

We sometimes use a brace $\{$ to show the equations are related.

For example, consider the simultaneous equations $\begin{cases} x + y = 9 \\ 2x + 3y = 21 \end{cases}$.

If $x = 6$ and $y = 3$ then:
- $x + y = (6) + (3) = 9$ ✓   The first equation is satisfied
- $2x + 3y = 2(6) + 3(3) = 12 + 9 = 21$ ✓   The second equation is satisfied.

So, $x = 6$ and $y = 3$ is the **solution** to the simultaneous equations $\begin{cases} x + y = 9 \\ 2x + 3y = 21 \end{cases}$.

Simultaneous equations (Chapter 9)

The solutions to linear simultaneous equations can be found by **trial and error** as in the **Discovery**, but this can be quite tedious. They may also be found by drawing **graphs**, which we investigate in **Chapter 24**, but this can be slow and also inaccurate.

We thus consider **algebraic methods** for finding the simultaneous solution.

A EQUATING VALUES OF y [2.6]

If both equations are given with y as the **subject**, we can find the simultaneous solution by equating the right hand sides of the equations.

Example 1

Find the simultaneous solution to the equations: $y = 2x - 1$, $y = x + 3$

If $y = 2x - 1$ and $y = x + 3$, then

$\qquad 2x - 1 = x + 3$ {equating ys}

$\therefore \quad 2x - 1 - x = x + 3 - x$ {subtracting x from both sides}

$\therefore \quad x - 1 = 3$

$\therefore \quad x = 4$ {adding 1 to both sides}

and so $y = 4 + 3$ {using $y = x + 3$}

$\therefore \quad y = 7$

So, the simultaneous solution is $x = 4$ and $y = 7$.

Check: In $y = 2x - 1$, $y = 2 \times 4 - 1 = 8 - 1 = 7$ ✓

In $y = x + 3$, $y = 4 + 3 = 7$ ✓

Always check your solution in both equations.

EXERCISE 9A

1 Find the simultaneous solution to the following pairs of equations:

a $y = x - 2$
$\quad y = 3x + 6$

b $y = x + 2$
$\quad y = 2x - 3$

c $y = 6x - 6$
$\quad y = x + 4$

d $y = 2x + 1$
$\quad y = x - 3$

e $y = 5x + 2$
$\quad y = 3x - 2$

f $y = 3x - 7$
$\quad y = 3x - 2$

g $y = 3x + 2$
$\quad y = 2x + 3$

h $y = 3x + 1$
$\quad y = 3x + 5$

i $y = 5x - 2$
$\quad y = 10x - 4$

2 Find the simultaneous solution to the following pairs of equations:

a $y = x + 4$
$\quad y = 5 - x$

b $y = x + 1$
$\quad y = 7 - x$

c $y = 2x - 5$
$\quad y = 3 - 2x$

d $y = x - 4$
$\quad y = -2x - 4$

e $y = 3x + 2$
$\quad y = -2x - 3$

f $y = 4x + 6$
$\quad y = 6 - 2x$

B SOLUTION BY SUBSTITUTION   [2.6]

The method of **solution by substitution** is used when at least one equation is given with either x or y as the **subject** of the formula, or if it is easy to make x or y the subject.

Example 2

Solve simultaneously, by substitution: $y = 9 - x$
$2x + 3y = 21$

> We substitute $9 - x$ for y in the other equation.

$y = 9 - x$ .... (1) $2x + 3y = 21$ .... (2)

Since $y = 9 - x$, then $2x + 3(9 - x) = 21$
$\therefore \quad 2x + 27 - 3x = 21$
$\therefore \quad 27 - x = 21$
$\therefore \quad x = 6$

Substituting $x = 6$ into (1) gives $y = 9 - 6 = 3$.

The solution is: $x = 6$, $y = 3$.

Check: (1) $3 = 9 - 6$ ✓   (2) $2(6) + 3(3) = 12 + 9 = 21$ ✓

Example 3

Solve simultaneously, by substitution: $2y - x = 2$
$x = 1 + 8y$

> x is the subject of the second equation, so we substitute $1 + 8y$ for x in the first equation.

$2y - x = 2$ .... (1) $x = 1 + 8y$ .... (2)

Substituting (2) into (1) gives $2y - (1 + 8y) = 2$
$\therefore \quad 2y - 1 - 8y = 2$
$\therefore \quad -6y = 3$
$\therefore \quad y = -\frac{1}{2}$

Substituting $y = -\frac{1}{2}$ into (2) gives $x = 1 + 8 \times -\frac{1}{2} = -3$

The solution is: $x = -3$, $y = -\frac{1}{2}$.

Check: (1) $2(-\frac{1}{2}) - (-3) = -1 + 3 = 2$ ✓
(2) $1 + 8(-\frac{1}{2}) = 1 - 4 = -3$ ✓

Simultaneous equations (Chapter 9)

EXERCISE 9B

1 Solve simultaneously, using substitution:

    a $y = 3 + x$
       $5x - 2y = 0$

    b $y = x - 2$
       $x + 3y = 6$

    c $y = 5 - x$
       $4x + y = 5$

    d $y = 2x - 1$
       $3x - y = 6$

    e $2x + 3y = 12$
       $y = 3x + 4$

    f $y = 5 - 2x$
       $5x - 2y = 8$

2 Use the substitution method to solve simultaneously:

    a $x = y + 2$
       $3x - 2y = 9$

    b $x = -1 + 5y$
       $x = 3 - 5y$

    c $x = 6 - 3y$
       $3x - 3y = 2$

    d $2x + 3y = 4$
       $x = 1 - 2y$

    e $x = -4 - 2y$
       $2y - 3x = 8$

    f $2x - 4y = 5$
       $x = -y - 8$

3   **a** Try to solve by substitution: $y = 2x + 5$ and $y = 2x + 7$.

    b What is the simultaneous solution for the equations in **a**? Explain your answer.

4   **a** Try to solve by substitution: $y = 4x + 3$ and $2y = 8x + 6$.

    b How many simultaneous solutions do the equations in **a** have? Explain your answer.

C   SOLUTION BY ELIMINATION   [2.6]

In most problems which require the simultaneous solution of linear equations, each equation will be of the form $ax + by = c$. Solution by substitution is often tedious in such situations, and the method of **elimination** of one of the variables is preferred.

One method is to make the coefficients of x (or y) the **same size** but **opposite in sign** and then **add** the equations. This has the effect of **eliminating** one of the variables.

Example 4   ◀) Self Tutor

Solve simultaneously, by elimination: $4x + 3y = 2$ .... (1)
                                              $x - 3y = 8$ .... (2)

Notice that coefficients of y are the same size but opposite in sign.

We **add** the LHSs and the RHSs to get an equation which contains x only.

$$\begin{aligned} 4x + 3y &= 2 \\ +\quad x - 3y &= 8 \\ \hline 5x &= 10 \end{aligned}$$ {adding the equations}

$\therefore \quad x = 2$ {dividing both sides by 5}

Substituting $x = 2$ into (1) gives $4(2) + 3y = 2$
                               $\therefore \quad 8 + 3y = 2$
                               $\therefore \quad 3y = -6$
                               $\therefore \quad y = -2$

The solution is $x = 2$ and $y = -2$.

Check: in (2): $(2) - 3(-2) = 2 + 6 = 8$ ✓

In problems where the coefficients of x (or y) are **not** the **same size** or **opposite in sign**, we may first have to **multiply** each equation by a number.

Example 5

Solve simultaneously, by elimination: $\quad 3x + 2y = 7$
$\qquad\qquad\qquad\qquad\qquad\qquad\qquad\qquad 2x - 5y = 11$

$3x + 2y = 7 \ \ ....\ (1) \qquad 2x - 5y = 11 \ \ ....\ (2)$

We can eliminate y by multiplying (1) by 5 and (2) by 2.

$\therefore \quad 15x + 10y = 35$
$+ \quad\ 4x - 10y = 22$

$\qquad 19x \qquad\ \ = 57 \qquad$ {adding the equations}
$\qquad \therefore \quad x = 3 \qquad\ \ \ $ {dividing both sides by 19}

Substituting $x = 3$ into equation (1) gives

$\quad 3(3) + 2y = 7$
$\therefore \quad 9 + 2y = 7$
$\therefore \qquad 2y = -2$
$\therefore \qquad\ y = -1$

So, the solution is: $\ x = 3, \ y = -1$.

Check: $\ 3(3) + 2(-1) = 9 - 2 = 7 \ \checkmark \qquad 2(3) - 5(-1) = 6 + 5 = 11 \ \checkmark$

Example 6

Solve by elimination: $\quad 3x + 4y = 14$
$\qquad\qquad\qquad\qquad\ \ 4x + 5y = 17$

$\qquad\qquad 3x + 4y = 14 \ \ ....\ (1)$
$\qquad\qquad 4x + 5y = 17 \ \ ....\ (2)$

To eliminate x, multiply both sides of

(1) by 4: $\quad 12x + 16y = 56 \quad\ ....\ (3)$
(2) by -3: $\ -12x - 15y = -51 \ \ ....\ (4)$
$\qquad\qquad\qquad\quad y = 5 \quad\ $ {adding (3) and (4)}

Substituting $y = 5$ into (2) gives

$\qquad\qquad 4x + 5(5) = 17$
$\qquad \therefore \quad 4x + 25 = 17$
$\qquad \therefore \qquad 4x = -8$
$\qquad \therefore \qquad\ x = -2$

Thus $x = -2$ and $y = 5$.

Check:
(1) $\ 3(-2) + 4(5) = (-6) + 20 = 14 \ \checkmark$
(2) $\ 4(-2) + 5(5) = (-8) + 25 = 17 \ \checkmark$

Simultaneous equations (Chapter 9)

WHICH VARIABLE TO ELIMINATE

There is always a choice whether to eliminate x or y, so our choice depends on which variable is easier to eliminate.

In **Example 6**, try to solve by multiplying (1) by 5 and (2) by -4. This eliminates y rather than x. The final solution should be the same.

EXERCISE 9C

1 What equation results when the following are added vertically?

- **a** $3x + 4y = 6$
  $8x - 4y = 5$
- **b** $2x - y = 7$
  $-2x + 5y = 5$
- **c** $7x - 3y = 2$
  $2x + 3y = 7$
- **d** $6x - 11y = 12$
  $3x + 11y = -6$
- **e** $-7x + 2y = 5$
  $7x - 3y = 6$
- **f** $2x - 3y = -7$
  $-2x - 8y = -4$

2 Solve the following using the method of elimination:

- **a** $5x - y = 4$
  $2x + y = 10$
- **b** $3x - 2y = 7$
  $3x + 2y = -1$
- **c** $-5x - 3y = 14$
  $5x + 8y = -29$
- **d** $4x + 3y = -11$
  $-4x - 2y = 6$
- **e** $2x - 5y = 14$
  $4x + 5y = -2$
- **f** $-6x - y = 17$
  $6x + 5y = -13$

3 Give the equation that results when both sides of the equation:

- **a** $2x + 5y = 1$ are multiplied by 5
- **b** $3x - y = 4$ are multiplied by -1
- **c** $x - 7y = 8$ are multiplied by 3
- **d** $5x + 4y = 9$ are multiplied by -2
- **e** $-3x - 2y = 2$ are multiplied by 6
- **f** $4x - 2y = 3$ are multiplied by -4

4 Solve the following using the method of elimination:

- **a** $2x + y = 8$
  $x - 3y = 11$
- **b** $3x + 2y = 7$
  $x + 3y = 7$
- **c** $5x - 2y = 17$
  $3x - y = 9$
- **d** $2x + 3y = 13$
  $3x + 2y = 17$
- **e** $4x - 3y = 1$
  $2x + 5y = 7$
- **f** $2x + 5y = 14$
  $5x - 3y + 27 = 0$
- **g** $7x - 2y = 20$
  $4x + 3y = -1$
- **h** $3x - 2y = 5$
  $5x - 3y = 8$
- **i** $3x - 4y = -15$
  $2x + 3y = 7$
- **j** $4x + 3y = 14$
  $5x - 2y = 29$
- **k** $2x - 3y = 1$
  $5x + 7y = 3$
- **l** $8x - 5y = -9$
  $3x + 4y = -21$
- **m** $3x + 8y + 34 = 0$
  $5x - 4y = 0$
- **n** $5x - 6y = 8$
  $6x - 7y - 9 = 0$
- **o** $2x - 7y - 18 = 0$
  $3x - 5y - 5 = 0$

5 Use the method of elimination to attempt to solve:

- **a** $2x - y = 3$
  $4x - 2y = 6$
- **b** $3x + 4y = 6$
  $6x + 8y = 7$

Comment on your results.

D PROBLEM SOLVING [2.6]

Many problems can be described mathematically by a **pair of linear equations**, or two equations of the form $ax + by = c$, where x and y are the two variables or unknowns.

We have already seen an example of this in the **Discovery** on page **184**.

Once the equations are formed, they can then be solved simultaneously and thus the original problem solved. The following method is recommended:

> *Step 1:* Decide on the two unknowns; call them x and y, say. Do not forget appropriate units.
> *Step 2:* Write down **two** equations connecting x and y.
> *Step 3:* Solve the equations simultaneously.
> *Step 4:* Check your solutions with the original data given.
> *Step 5:* Give your answer in sentence form.

The form of the original equations will help you decide whether to use the substitution method, or the elimination method.

Example 7 ◀ Self Tutor

Two numbers have a sum of 45 and a difference of 13. Find the numbers.

Let x and y be the unknown numbers, where $x > y$.

Then $x + y = 45$ .... (1) {'sum' means add}
and $x - y = 13$ .... (2) {'difference' means subtract}
$\therefore \quad 2x = 58$ {adding (1) and (2)}
$\therefore \quad x = 29$ {dividing both sides by 2}

Substituting into (1) gives: $29 + y = 45$
$\therefore \quad y = 16$

The numbers are 29 and 16.

Check: (1) $29 + 16 = 45$ ✓   (2) $29 - 16 = 13$ ✓

When solving problems with simultaneous equations we must find two equations containing two unknowns.

Example 8 ◀ Self Tutor

When shopping in Jamaica, 5 coconuts and 14 bananas cost me $8.70, and 8 coconuts and 9 bananas cost $9.90. Find the cost of each coconut and each banana.

Let each coconut cost x cents and each banana cost y cents.

$\therefore \quad 5x + 14y = 870$ .... (1)
$ 8x + 9y = 990$ .... (2)

To eliminate x, we multiply (1) by 8 and (2) by -5.

The units must be the same on both sides of each equation.

$$\therefore \quad 40x + 112y = 6960 \quad \ldots (3)$$
$$\underline{-40x - 45y = -4950} \quad \ldots (4)$$
$$67y = 2010 \quad \{\text{adding (3) and (4)}\}$$
$$\therefore \quad y = 30 \quad \{\text{dividing both sides by 67}\}$$

Substituting in (2) gives $8x + 9 \times 30 = 990$
$$\therefore \quad 8x = 990 - 270$$
$$\therefore \quad 8x = 720$$
$$\therefore \quad x = 90 \quad \{\text{dividing both sides by 8}\}$$

Check: $5 \times 90 + 14 \times 30 = 450 + 420 = 870$ ✓
$8 \times 90 + 9 \times 30 = 720 + 270 = 990$ ✓

Thus coconuts cost 90 cents each and bananas cost 30 cents each.

Example 9 ◀) Self Tutor

In my pocket I have only 5-cent and 10-cent coins. How many of each type of coin do I have if I have 24 coins altogether and their total value is $1.55?

Let x be the number of 5-cent coins and y be the number of 10-cent coins.

$\therefore \quad x + y = 24 \quad \ldots (1) \quad \{\text{the total number of coins}\}$
and $\quad 5x + 10y = 155 \quad \ldots (2) \quad \{\text{the total value of coins}\}$

Multiplying (1) by -5 gives $\quad -5x - 5y = -120 \quad \ldots (3)$
$$\underline{5x + 10y = 155} \quad \ldots (2)$$
$$\therefore \quad 5y = 35 \quad \{\text{adding (3) and (2)}\}$$
$$\therefore \quad y = 7 \quad \{\text{dividing both sides by 5}\}$$

Substituting into (1) gives $\quad x + 7 = 24$
$$\therefore \quad x = 17$$

Check: $17 + 7 = 24$ ✓
$5 \times 17 + 10 \times 7 = 85 + 70 = 155$ ✓

Thus I have 17 five-cent coins and 7 ten-cent coins.

EXERCISE 9D

1 The sum of two numbers is 49 and their difference is 19. Find the numbers.

2 The average of two numbers is 43 and their difference is 16. Find the numbers.

3 The average of two numbers is 20. If one of the numbers is doubled and the other is trebled, the average increases to 52. Find the numbers.

4 Four nectarines and three peaches cost £2.90, and three nectarines and a peach cost £1.90. Find the cost of each fruit.

5 A visit to the cinemas costs €64 for a group of 2 adults and 5 children, and €68 for a group of 3 adults and 4 children. Find the cost of each adult ticket and each children's ticket.

6 Answer the **Opening Problem** on page **183**.

7 Martin collects 20-cent and 50-cent coins. He has 37 coins, and the total value of the coins is $11.30. How many coins of each type does Martin have?

8 A tailor made costumes for students in a school play. Each male costume took 2 hours and cost $40 to make. Each female costume took 3 hours and cost $80 to make. In total the tailor spent 30 hours and $680 on the costumes. How many male costumes and how many female costumes did the tailor make?

9 For the parallelogram alongside, find x and y.

(Parallelogram with sides 19 cm, 11 cm, $(x+3y)$ cm, and $(3x+2y)$ cm)

10 Ron the painter charges an hourly fee, as well as a fixed call-out fee, for his work. He charges $165 for a 2 hour job, and $345 for a 5 hour job. Find Ron's call-out fee and hourly rate.

11 On the **Celsius** temperature scale, ice melts at $0\,°C$ and water boils at $100\,°C$. On the **Fahrenheit** temperature scale, ice melts at $32\,°F$ and water boils at $212\,°F$.
There is a linear relationship between temperature in degrees Celsius (C) and temperature in degrees Fahrenheit (F). It has the form $C = aF + b$ where a and b are constants.

  a Find the values of a and b in simplest fractional form.
  b Convert $77\,°F$ to degrees Celsius.

Review set 9A

1 Solve simultaneously, by substitution:
  a $y - 5x = 8$ and $y = 3x + 6$
  b $3x + 2y = 4$ and $2x - y = 5$.

2 Solve simultaneously: $y = 4x - 1$ and $3x - 2y = -8$.

3 Solve simultaneously:
  a $2x + 3y = 5$
     $3x - y = -9$
  b $4x - 3y - 2 = 0$
     $5x - 2y = 13$

4 3 sausages and 4 chops cost $12.40, and 5 sausages and 3 chops cost $11.50. Find the cost of each item.

5 Drivers are fined £200 for exceeding the speed limit by up to 15 km/h, and £450 for exceeding the speed limit by more than 15 km/h. In one night, a policeman gave out 22 speeding fines worth a total of £6650. How many drivers were caught exceeding the speed limit by more than 15 km/h?

6 The largest of three consecutive even numbers is 20 less than double the smallest number. What are the numbers?

Review set 9B

1. Solve simultaneously:
   a. $y = 3x + 4$ and $y = -2x - 6$
   b. $y = 3x - 4$ and $2x - y = 8$

2. Solve simultaneously: $2x - 5y = -9$ and $y = 3x - 3$

3. Solve the following using the method of elimination: $3x - 2y = 3$ and $4x + 3y = 4$.

4. The larger of two numbers is 2 more than three times the smaller number. If their difference is 12, find the numbers.

5. Eric and Jordan were each given $8 to spend at a candy store. Eric bought 2 chocolate bars and 5 lolly bags, while Jordan bought 4 chocolate bars and 2 lolly bags. Neither child had any money left over. Find the cost of a chocolate bar.

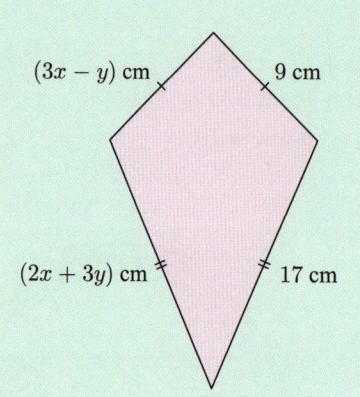

6. For the kite given alongside, find x and y.

   (sides labelled: $(3x - y)$ cm, 9 cm, $(2x + 3y)$ cm, 17 cm)

Challenge

1 Pat thinks of three numbers. Adding them in pairs he obtains answers of 11, 17, and 22. What are the numbers?

2 Solve for x: $373x + 627y = 2492$
$627x + 373y = 3508$

Hint: There is no need to use the technique of 'elimination'. Look at the two equations carefully.

3 Find a, b and c given that: $ab = c$
$bc = a$
$ca = b$

4 How many four digit numbers can be found in which

- the first digit is three times the last digit
- the second digit is the sum of the first and third digits
- the third digit is twice the first digit?

5 What can be deduced about a, b and c if $a + b = 2c$ and $b + c = 2a$?

6 Find x, y and z if:

  a $x + y - z = 10$
$x - y + z = -4$
$2x + y + 3z = 5$

  b $x + y - z = 8$
$2x + y + z = 9$
$x + 3y + z = 10$

7 If $a + b = 1$ and $a^2 + b^2 = 3$, find the value of ab.

8 A model train set has two concentric circular tracks which cross over at a bridge. Train A is 0.4 m long and train B is 0.6 m long as shown. Train A travels faster than train B. They leave from the same point on the track, but in opposite directions. Each time they pass each other on the track it takes 2.5 seconds. After their first loop, the trains pass each other 0.5 m away from their starting point. If the track is 25 m long, find the speed of each train.

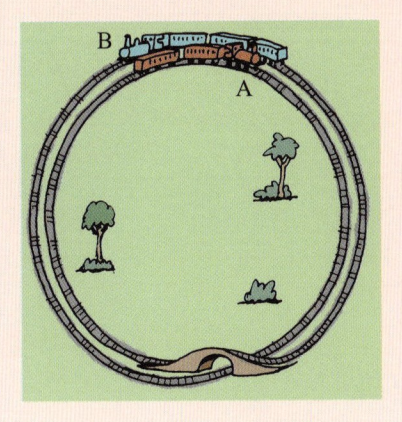

The theorem of Pythagoras

10

Contents:

  A   Pythagoras' theorem   [4.6]
  B   Problem solving   [4.6]
  C   Circle problems   [4.6, 4.7]

Opening problem

Water flows through a pipe of radius 35 cm. The water has a maximum depth of 20 cm. What is the widest object that can float down the pipe?

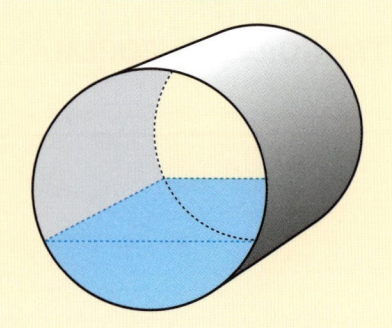

Right angles (90° angles) are used when constructing buildings and dividing areas of land into rectangular regions.

The ancient **Egyptians** used a rope with 12 equally spaced knots to form a triangle with sides in the ratio $3:4:5$.

This triangle has a right angle between the sides of length 3 and 4 units.

In fact, this is the simplest right angled triangle with sides of integer length.

The Egyptians used this procedure to construct their right angles:

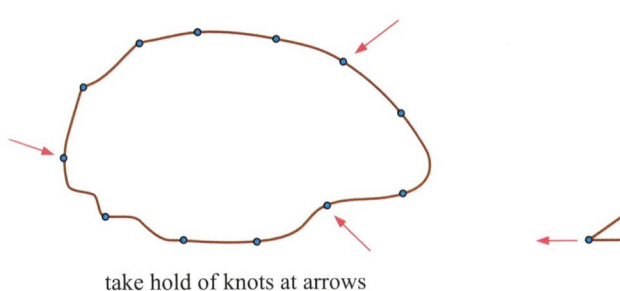

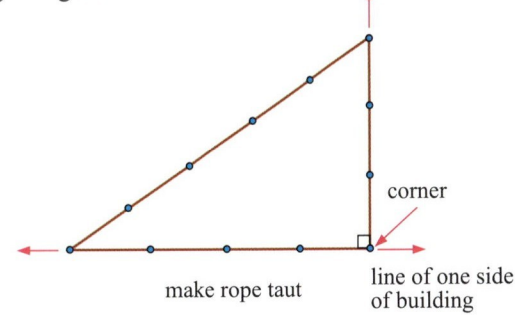

take hold of knots at arrows   make rope taut   line of one side of building / corner

A   PYTHAGORAS' THEOREM   [4.6]

A **right angled triangle** is a triangle which has a right angle as one of its angles.

The side **opposite** the **right angle** is called the **hypotenuse** and is the **longest** side of the triangle.

The other two sides are called the **legs** of the triangle.

Around 500 BC, the Greek mathematician **Pythagoras** described a rule which connects the lengths of the sides of all right angled triangles. It is thought that he discovered the rule while studying tessellations of tiles on floors. Such patterns, like the one illustrated, were common on interior walls and floors in ancient **Greece**.

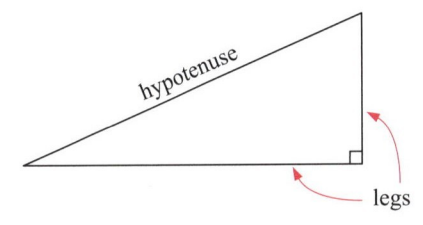

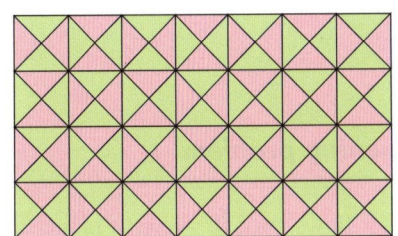

PYTHAGORAS' THEOREM

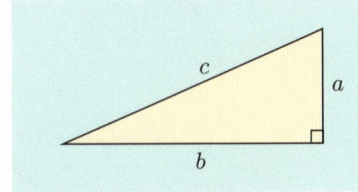

In a right angled triangle with hypotenuse c and legs a and b,
$$c^2 = a^2 + b^2.$$

By looking at the tile pattern above, can you see how Pythagoras may have discovered the rule?

In geometric form, **Pythagoras' theorem** is:

In any right angled triangle, the area of the square on the hypotenuse is equal to the sum of the areas of the squares on the other two sides.

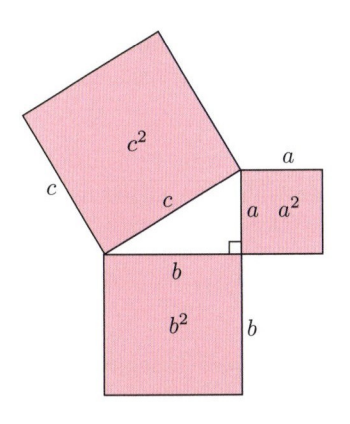

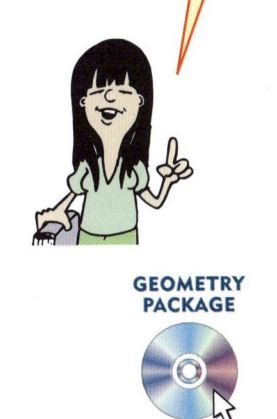

GEOMETRY PACKAGE

The theorem of Pythagoras   (Chapter 10)

There are over 370 different proofs of Pythagoras' theorem. Here is one of them:

On a square we draw 4 identical (congruent) right angled triangles, as illustrated. A smaller square is formed in the centre.

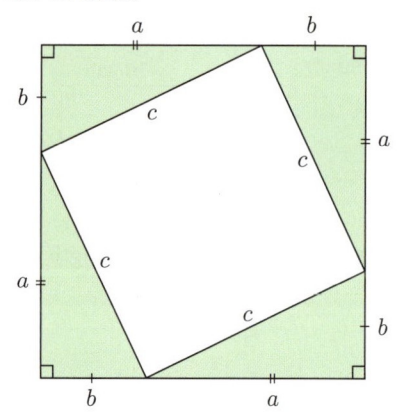

Suppose the legs are of length a and b and the hypotenuse has length c.

The total area of the large square
$= 4 \times$ area of one triangle $+$ area of smaller square

$$\therefore \quad (a+b)^2 = 4(\tfrac{1}{2}ab) + c^2$$
$$\therefore \quad a^2 + 2ab + b^2 = 2ab + c^2$$
$$\therefore \quad a^2 + b^2 = c^2$$

Example 1 ◀)) Self Tutor

Find the length of the hypotenuse in:

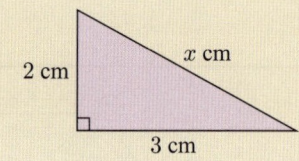

The hypotenuse is opposite the right angle and has length x cm.

$$\therefore \quad x^2 = 3^2 + 2^2$$
$$\therefore \quad x^2 = 9 + 4$$
$$\therefore \quad x^2 = 13$$
$$\therefore \quad x = \sqrt{13} \quad \{\text{as } x > 0\}$$

$\therefore$ the hypotenuse is about 3.61 cm long.

If $x^2 = k$, then $x = \pm\sqrt{k}$, but we reject $-\sqrt{k}$ as lengths must be positive.

Example 2 ◀)) Self Tutor

Find the length of the third side of this triangle:

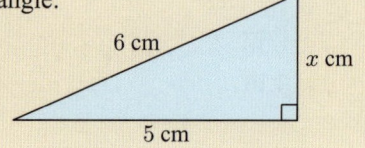

The hypotenuse has length 6 cm.

$$\therefore \quad x^2 + 5^2 = 6^2 \quad \{\text{Pythagoras}\}$$
$$\therefore \quad x^2 + 25 = 36$$
$$\therefore \quad x^2 = 11$$
$$\therefore \quad x = \sqrt{11} \quad \{\text{as } x > 0\}$$

$\therefore$ the third side is about 3.32 cm long.

Example 3

Find x:

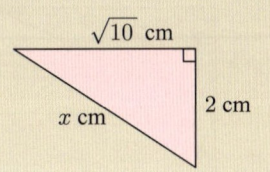

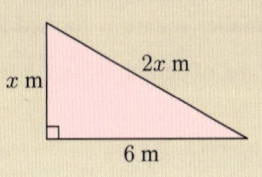

a The hypotenuse has length x cm.

$\therefore x^2 = 2^2 + (\sqrt{10})^2$ {Pythagoras}
$\therefore x^2 = 4 + 10$
$\therefore x^2 = 14$
$\therefore x = \sqrt{14}$ {as $x > 0$}
$\therefore x \approx 3.74$

b $(2x)^2 = x^2 + 6^2$ {Pythagoras}
$\therefore 4x^2 = x^2 + 36$
$\therefore 3x^2 = 36$
$\therefore x^2 = 12$
$\therefore x = \sqrt{12}$ {as $x > 0$}
$\therefore x \approx 3.46$

Example 4

Find the value of y, giving your answer correct to 3 significant figures.

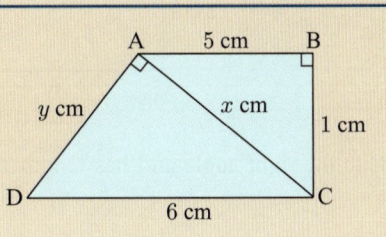

In triangle ABC, the hypotenuse is x cm.

$\therefore x^2 = 5^2 + 1^2$ {Pythagoras}
$\therefore x^2 = 26$
$\therefore x = \sqrt{26}$ {as $x > 0$}

In triangle ACD, the hypotenuse is 6 cm.

$\therefore y^2 + (\sqrt{26})^2 = 6^2$ {Pythagoras}
$\therefore y^2 + 26 = 36$
$\therefore y^2 = 10$
$\therefore y = \sqrt{10}$ {as $y > 0$}
$\therefore y \approx 3.16$

Since we must find the value of y, we leave x in square root form. Rounding it will reduce the accuracy of our value for y.

EXERCISE 10A.1

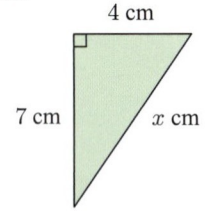

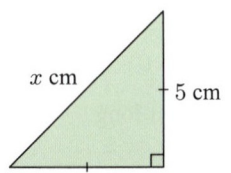

1 Find the length of the hypotenuse in the following triangles, giving your answers correct to 3 significant figures:

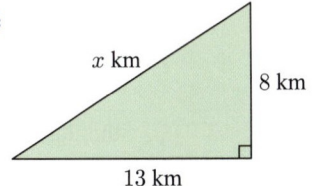

2 Find the length of the third side of these triangles, giving your answers correct to 3 significant figures:

a Triangle with legs 6 cm and x cm, hypotenuse 11 cm.

b Right triangle with legs 2.8 km and 1.9 km, hypotenuse x km.

c Right-angled isosceles triangle with two equal sides x cm and hypotenuse 9.5 cm.

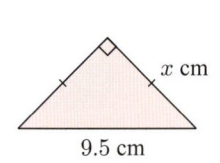

3 Find x in the following:

a Right triangle with legs 3 cm and $\sqrt{2}$ cm, hypotenuse x cm.

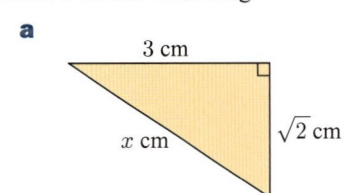

b Right triangle with legs $\sqrt{7}$ cm and $\sqrt{5}$ cm, hypotenuse x cm.

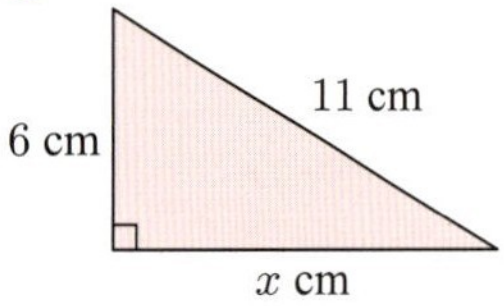

c Right-angled isosceles triangle with two equal sides x cm and hypotenuse $\sqrt{10}$ cm.

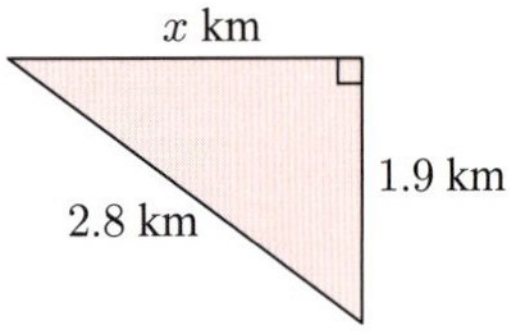

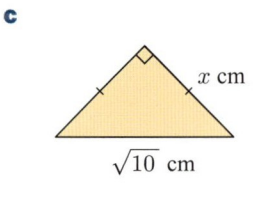

4 Solve for x:

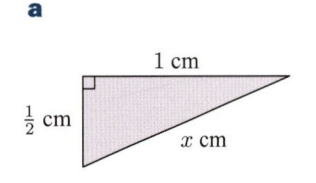

a Right triangle with legs $\frac{1}{2}$ cm and 1 cm, hypotenuse x cm.

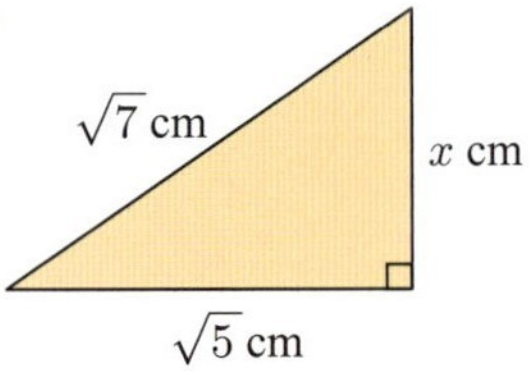

b Right triangle with legs $\frac{1}{2}$ cm and $\frac{3}{2}$ cm, hypotenuse x cm.

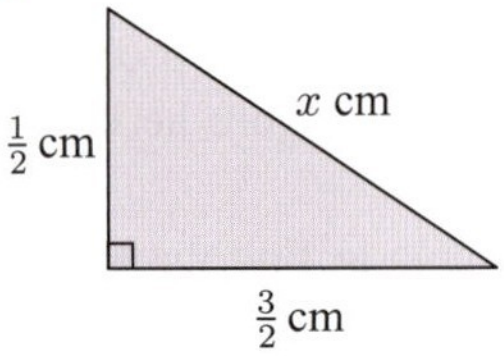

c Right triangle with legs $\frac{\sqrt{3}}{2}$ m and 1 m, hypotenuse x m.

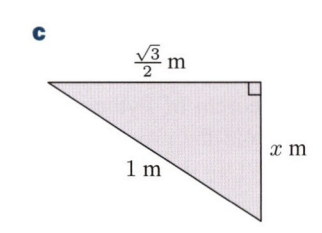

5 Find the values of x, giving your answers correct to 3 significant figures:

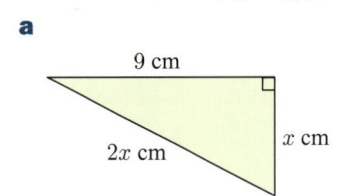

a Right triangle with legs 9 cm and x cm, hypotenuse $2x$ cm.

b Right triangle with legs $3x$ cm and $2x$ cm, hypotenuse 26 cm.

c Right triangle with legs $2x$ m and $3x$ m, hypotenuse $\sqrt{20}$ m.

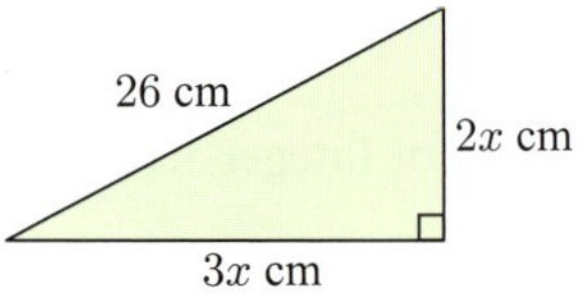

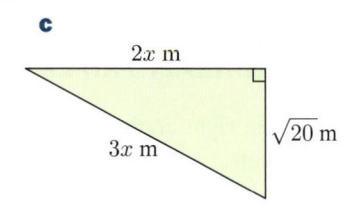

6 Find the values of any unknowns:

a Figure with sides 2 cm, 3 cm, y cm, x cm.

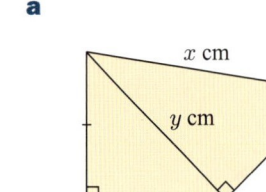

b Figure with sides 2 cm, 4 cm, 7 cm, y cm, x cm.

c Figure with sides 1 cm, 3 cm, 2 cm, x cm, y cm.

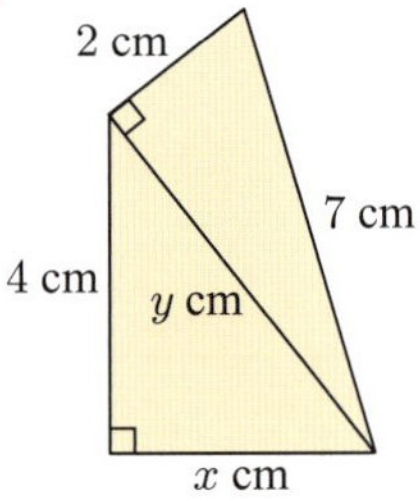

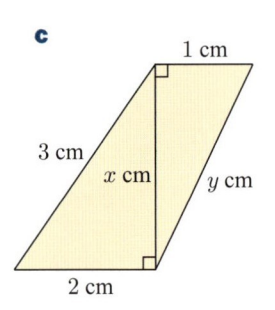

7 Find x, correct to 3 significant figures:

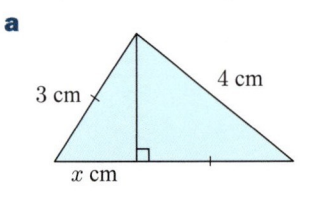

a Triangle with sides 3 cm, 4 cm, base x cm, with altitude.

b Right triangle with legs 5 cm and $(x-2)$ cm, hypotenuse 13 cm.

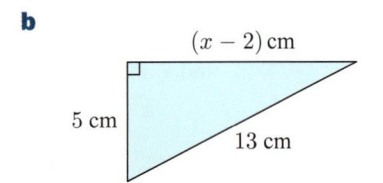

8 Find the length of side AC correct to 3 significant figures:

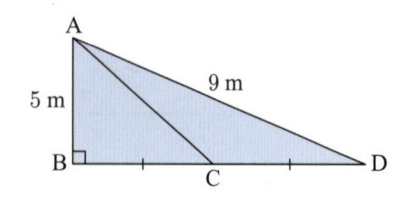

9 Find the distance AB in the following:

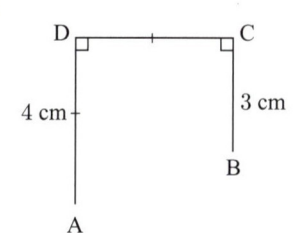

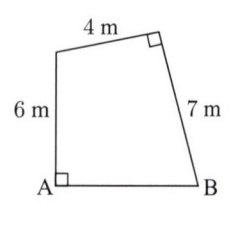

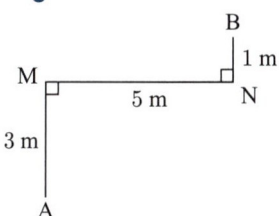

  a   **b**   **c**

Challenge

10 In 1876, President Garfield of the USA published a proof of the theorem of Pythagoras. Alongside is the figure he used. Write out the proof.

  Hint: Use the area of a trapezium formula to find the area of ABED.

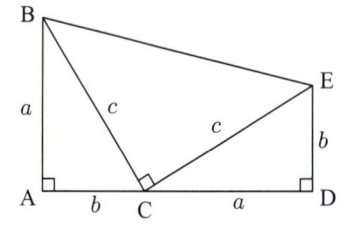

PYTHAGOREAN TRIPLES

The simplest right angled triangle with sides of **integer** length is the **3-4-5 triangle**.

The numbers 3, 4, and 5 satisfy the rule $3^2 + 4^2 = 5^2$.

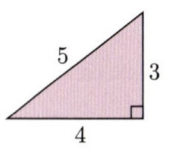

> The set of positive integers $\{a, b, c\}$ is a **Pythagorean triple** if it obeys the rule $a^2 + b^2 = c^2$.

Other examples are: $\{5, 12, 13\}$, $\{7, 24, 25\}$, $\{8, 15, 17\}$.

Example 5   ◀)) Self Tutor

Show that $\{5, 12, 13\}$ is a Pythagorean triple.

We find the square of the **largest** number first.

$$13^2 = 169$$
$$\text{and } 5^2 + 12^2 = 25 + 144 = 169$$
$$\therefore 5^2 + 12^2 = 13^2$$

So, $\{5, 12, 13\}$ is a Pythagorean triple.

The theorem of Pythagoras (Chapter 10)

Example 6 · Self Tutor

Find k if $\{9, k, 15\}$ is a Pythagorean triple.

Let $9^2 + k^2 = 15^2$ {Pythagoras}
$\therefore \quad 81 + k^2 = 225$
$\therefore \quad k^2 = 144$
$\therefore \quad k = \sqrt{144}$ {as $k > 0$}
$\therefore \quad k = 12$

EXERCISE 10A.2

1 Determine if the following are Pythagorean triples:
   a $\{8, 15, 17\}$
   b $\{6, 8, 10\}$
   c $\{5, 6, 7\}$
   d $\{14, 48, 50\}$
   e $\{1, 2, 3\}$
   f $\{20, 48, 52\}$

2 Find k if the following are Pythagorean triples:
   a $\{8, 15, k\}$
   b $\{k, 24, 26\}$
   c $\{14, k, 50\}$
   d $\{15, 20, k\}$
   e $\{k, 45, 51\}$
   f $\{11, k, 61\}$

3 Explain why there are infinitely many Pythagorean triples of the form $\{3k, 4k, 5k\}$ where $k \in \mathbb{Z}^+$.

Discovery — Pythagorean triples spreadsheet

Well known Pythagorean triples include $\{3, 4, 5\}$, $\{5, 12, 13\}$, $\{7, 24, 25\}$ and $\{8, 15, 17\}$.

SPREADSHEET

Formulae can be used to generate Pythagorean triples.

An example is $2n + 1$, $2n^2 + 2n$, $2n^2 + 2n + 1$ where n is a positive integer.

A spreadsheet can quickly generate sets of Pythagorean triples using such formulae.

What to do:

1 Open a new spreadsheet and enter the following:
   a in column A, the values of n for $n = 1, 2, 3, 4, 5, \ldots$
   b in column B, the values of $2n + 1$
   c in column C, the values of $2n^2 + 2n$
   d in column D, the values of $2n^2 + 2n + 1$.

	A	B	C	D
1	n	a	b	c
2	1	=2*A2+1	=2*A2^2+2*A2	=C2+1
3	=A2+1			
4				
5	↓	↓ fill down ↓		↓

2 Highlight the appropriate formulae and **fill down** to Row 11 to generate the first 10 sets of triples.

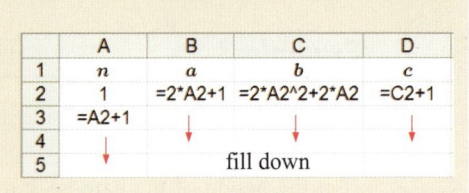

	A	B	C	D
1	n	a	b	c
2	1	3	4	5
3	2	5	12	13
4	3	7	24	25
5	4	9	40	41

3 Check that each set of numbers is indeed a triple by adding columns to find $a^2 + b^2$ and c^2.

4 Research some other formulae that generate Pythagorean triples.

B   PROBLEM SOLVING   [4.6]

Many practical problems involve triangles. We can apply Pythagoras' theorem to any triangle that is right angled.

SPECIAL GEOMETRICAL FIGURES

The following special figures contain right angled triangles:

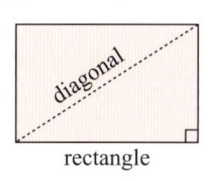

In a **rectangle**, right angles exist between adjacent sides.

Construct a **diagonal** to form a right angled triangle.

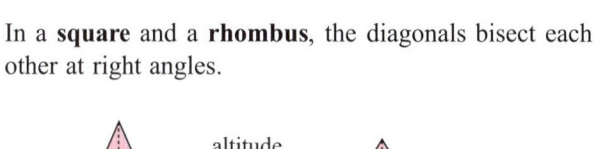

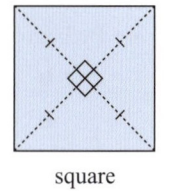

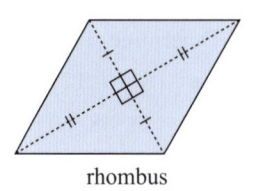

In a **square** and a **rhombus**, the diagonals bisect each other at right angles.

In an **isosceles triangle** and an **equilateral triangle**, the altitude bisects the base at right angles.

Things to remember

- Draw a neat, clear diagram of the situation.
- Mark on known lengths and right angles.
- Use a symbol such as x to represent the unknown length.
- Write down Pythagoras' theorem for the given information.
- Solve the equation.
- Where necessary, write your answer in sentence form.

Example 7

A rectangular gate is 3 m wide and has a 3.5 m diagonal. How high is the gate?

Let the height of the gate be x m.

Now $(3.5)^2 = x^2 + 3^2$ {Pythagoras}
$\therefore\ 12.25 = x^2 + 9$
$\therefore\ 3.25 = x^2$
$\therefore\ x = \sqrt{3.25}$ {as $x > 0$}
$\therefore\ x \approx 1.80$

The gate is approximately 1.80 m high.

The theorem of Pythagoras (Chapter 10)

Example 8

A rhombus has diagonals of length 6 cm and 8 cm. Find the length of its sides.

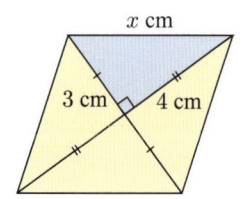

The diagonals of a rhombus bisect at right angles.
Let each side of the rhombus have length x cm.

$\therefore \quad x^2 = 3^2 + 4^2 \qquad$ {Pythagoras}
$\therefore \quad x^2 = 25$
$\therefore \quad x = \sqrt{25} \qquad$ {as $x > 0$}
$\therefore \quad x = 5$

The sides are 5 cm in length.

Example 9

Two towns A and B are illustrated on a grid which has grid lines 5 km apart. How far is it from A to B?

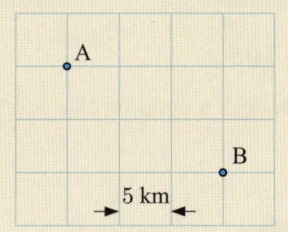

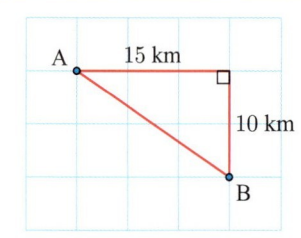

$AB^2 = 15^2 + 10^2 \qquad$ {Pythagoras}
$\therefore \quad AB^2 = 225 + 100 = 325$
$\therefore \quad AB = \sqrt{325} \qquad$ {as $AB > 0$}
$\therefore \quad AB \approx 18.0$

A and B are about 18.0 km apart.

Example 10

An equilateral triangle has sides of length 6 cm. Find its area.

The altitude bisects the base at right angles.
$\therefore \quad a^2 + 3^2 = 6^2 \qquad$ {Pythagoras}
$\therefore \quad a^2 + 9 = 36$
$\therefore \quad a^2 = 27$
$\therefore \quad a = \sqrt{27} \qquad$ {as $a > 0$}

Now, area $= \frac{1}{2} \times$ base $\times$ height
$= \frac{1}{2} \times 6 \times \sqrt{27}$
$= 3\sqrt{27}$ cm^2
≈ 15.6 cm^2

So, the area is about 15.6 cm^2.

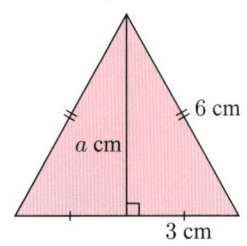

Example 11

A helicopter travels from base station S for 112 km to outpost A. It then turns 90° to the right and travels 134 km to outpost B. How far is outpost B from base station S?

Let SB be x km.

We are given that $S\hat{A}B = 90°$.

Now $x^2 = 112^2 + 134^2$ {Pythagoras}
∴ $x^2 = 30\,500$
∴ $x = \sqrt{30\,500}$ {as $x > 0$}
∴ $x \approx 175$

So, outpost B is 175 km from base station S.

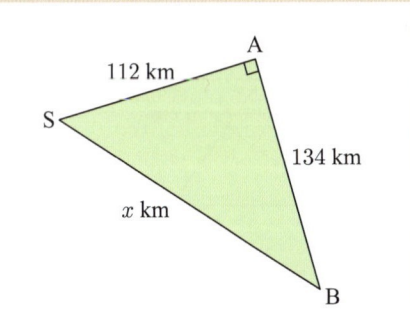

EXERCISE 10B

1 How high does a child on this seesaw go?

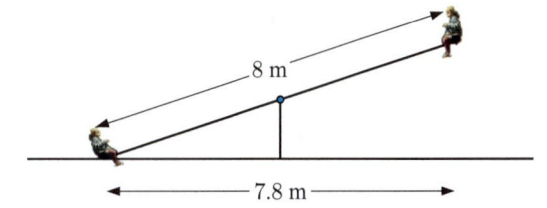

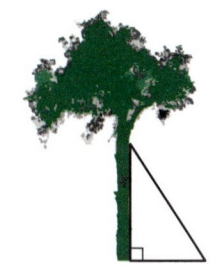

2 A stage carpenter designs a tree supported by a wooden strut. The vertical plank is 1.8 m long, and the base is 45 cm long. How long is the strut?

3 A large boat has its deck 1.6 m above a pier. Its gangplank is 7 m long. How close to the pier must the boat get for passengers to disembark?

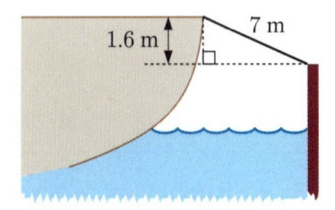

4 A rectangle has sides of length 8 cm and 3 cm. Find the length of its diagonals.

5 The longer side of a rectangle is three times the length of the shorter side. If the length of the diagonal is 10 cm, find the dimensions of the rectangle.

6 A rectangle with diagonals of length 20 cm has sides in the ratio 2 : 1. Find the:
    a perimeter   **b** area of the rectangle.

7 A rhombus has sides of length 6 cm. One of its diagonals is 10 cm long. Find the length of the other diagonal.

8 A square has diagonals of length 10 cm. Find the length of its sides.

9 A rhombus has diagonals of length 8 cm and 10 cm. Find its perimeter.

10 A yacht sails 5 km due west and then 8 km due south. How far is it from its starting point?

The theorem of Pythagoras (Chapter 10)

11 On the grid there are four towns A, B, C and D. The grid lines are 5 km apart. How far is it from:
  a A to B
  b B to C
  c C to D
  d D to A
  e A to C
  f B to D?

  Give all answers correct to 3 significant figures.

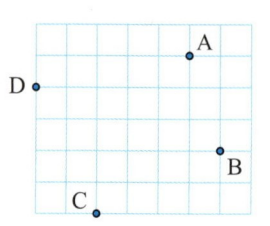

12 A street is 8 m wide, and there are street lights positioned either side of the street every 20 m. How far is street light X from street light:
  a A
  b B
  c C
  d D?

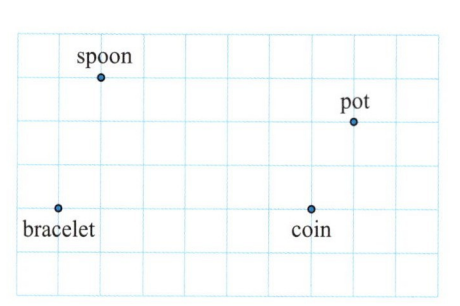

13 An archaeological team mark out a grid with grid lines 2 m apart. During the dig they find the objects shown. How far is:
  a the pot from the spoon
  b the coin from the spoon
  c the bracelet from the pot?

14 An equilateral triangle has sides of length 12 cm. Find the length of one of its altitudes.

15 The area of a triangle is given by the formula $A = \frac{1}{2}bh$.
  An isosceles triangle has equal sides of length 8 cm and a base of length 6 cm. Find the area of the triangle.

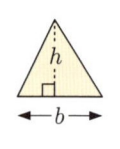

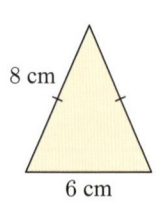

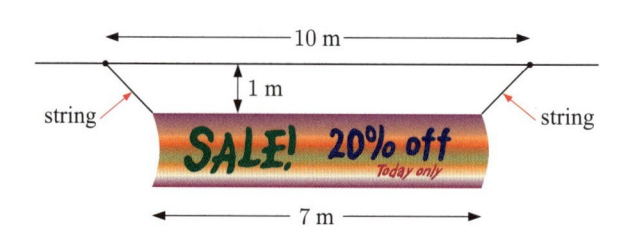

16 Heather wants to hang a 7 m long banner from the roof of her shop. The hooks for the strings are 10 m apart, and Heather wants the top of the banner to hang 1 m below the roof. How long should each of the strings be?

17 Two bushwalkers set off from base camp at the same time, walking at right angles to one another. One walks at an average speed of 5 km/h, and the other at an average speed of 4 km/h. Find their distance apart after 3 hours.

18 To get to school from her house, Ella walks down Bernard Street, then turns 90° and walks down Thompson Road until she reaches her school gate. She walks twice as far along Bernard Street as she does along Thompson Road. If Ella's house is 2.5 km in a straight line from her school gate, how far does Ella walk along Bernard Street?

19 Boat A is 10 km east of boat B. Boat A travels 6 km north, and boat B travels 2 km west. How far apart are the boats now?

C CIRCLE PROBLEMS [4.6, 4.7]

There are several properties of circles which involve right angles. In these situations we can apply Pythagoras' theorem. The properties themselves will be examined in more detail in **Chapter 27**.

ANGLE IN A SEMI-CIRCLE

> The angle in a semi-circle is a right angle.

No matter where C is placed on the arc AB, $\widehat{ACB}$ is always a right angle.

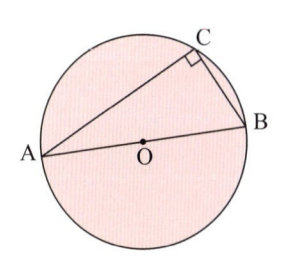

Example 12

A circle has diameter XY of length 13 cm. Z is a point on the circle such that XZ is 5 cm. Find the length YZ.

From the angle in a semi-circle theorem, we know $X\widehat{Z}Y$ is a right angle.
Let the length YZ be x cm.

$\therefore \ 5^2 + x^2 = 13^2$ {Pythagoras}
$\therefore \ x^2 = 169 - 25 = 144$
$\therefore \ x = \sqrt{144}$ {as $x > 0$}
$\therefore \ x = 12$

So, YZ has length 12 cm.

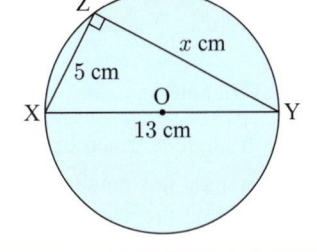

A CHORD OF A CIRCLE

> The line drawn from the centre of a circle at right angles to a chord bisects the chord.

This follows from the **isosceles triangle theorem**.

The construction of radii from the centre of the circle to the end points of the chord produces two right angled triangles.

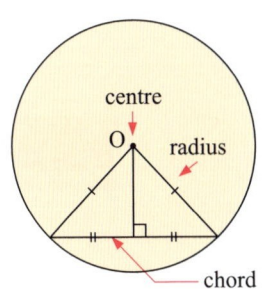

Example 13

A circle has a chord of length 10 cm. If the radius of the circle is 8 cm, find the shortest distance from the centre of the circle to the chord.

The shortest distance is the 'perpendicular distance'. The line drawn from the centre of a circle, perpendicular to a chord, bisects the chord.

The theorem of Pythagoras (Chapter 10) 207

$$\therefore \quad AB = BC = 5 \text{ cm}$$
In $\triangle AOB$, $5^2 + x^2 = 8^2$ {Pythagoras}
$$\therefore \quad x^2 = 64 - 25 = 39$$
$$\therefore \quad x = \sqrt{39} \quad \{\text{as } x > 0\}$$
$$\therefore \quad x \approx 6.24$$

So, the shortest distance is about 6.24 cm.

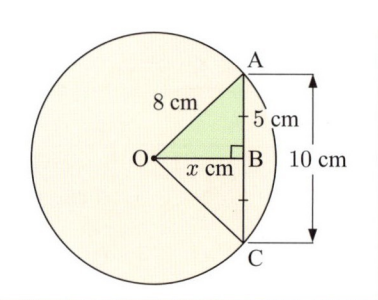

TANGENT-RADIUS PROPERTY

A tangent to a circle and a radius at the point of contact meet at right angles.

Notice that we can now form a right angled triangle.

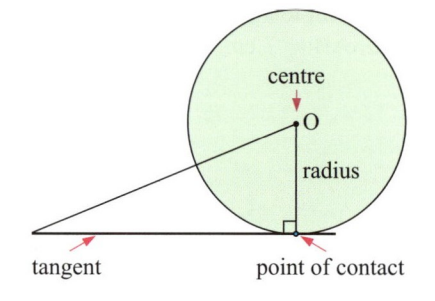

Example 14 ◀) Self Tutor

A tangent of length 10 cm is drawn to a circle with radius 7 cm. How far is the centre of the circle from the end point of the tangent?

Let the distance be d cm.
$$\therefore \quad d^2 = 7^2 + 10^2 \quad \{\text{Pythagoras}\}$$
$$\therefore \quad d^2 = 149$$
$$\therefore \quad d = \sqrt{149} \quad \{\text{as } d > 0\}$$
$$\therefore \quad d \approx 12.2$$

So, the centre is 12.2 cm from the end point of the tangent.

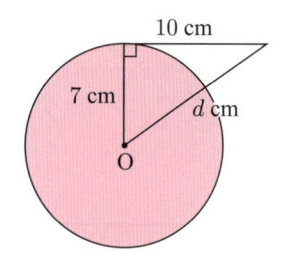

Example 15 ◀) Self Tutor

Two circles have a common tangent with points of contact at A and B. The radii are 4 cm and 2 cm respectively. Find the distance between the centres given that AB is 7 cm.

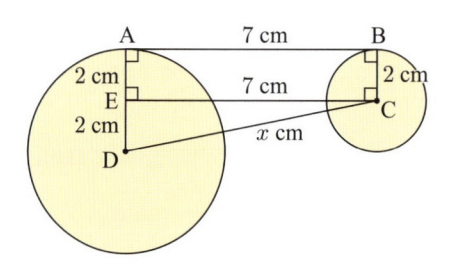

For centres C and D, we draw BC, AD, and CD.

We draw CE parallel to AB, so ABCE is a rectangle.
$$\therefore \quad CE = 7 \text{ cm} \quad \{\text{as } CE = AB\}$$
and $DE = 4 - 2 = 2$ cm
Now $x^2 = 2^2 + 7^2$ {Pythagoras in $\triangle DEC$}
$$\therefore \quad x^2 = 53$$
$$\therefore \quad x \approx 7.28 \quad \{\text{as } x > 0\}$$

$\therefore$ the distance between the centres is about 7.28 cm.

EXERCISE 10C

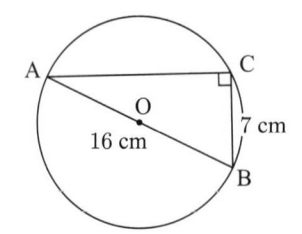

1 A circle has diameter AB of length 16 cm. C is a point on the circle such that BC = 7 cm. Find the length of AC.

2 AT is a tangent to a circle with centre O. The circle has radius 5 cm and AB = 7 cm. Find the length of the tangent.

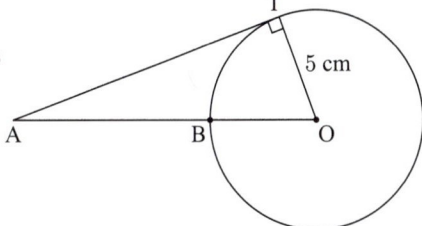

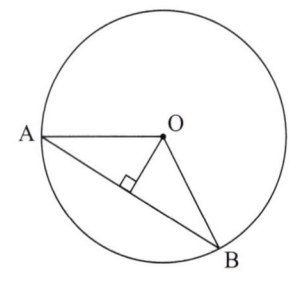

3 A circle has centre O and a radius of 8 cm. Chord AB is 13 cm long. Find the shortest distance from the chord to the centre of the circle.

4 A rectangle with side lengths 11 cm and 6 cm is inscribed in a circle. Find the radius of the circle.

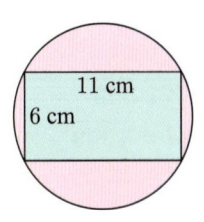

5 A circle has diameter AB of length 10 cm. C is a point on the circle such that AC is 8 cm. Find the length BC.

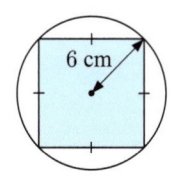

6 A square is inscribed in a circle of radius 6 cm. Find the length of the sides of the square, correct to 3 significant figures.

7 A chord of a circle has length 3 cm. If the circle has radius 4 cm, find the shortest distance from the centre of the circle to the chord.

8 A chord of length 6 cm is 3 cm from the centre of a circle. Find the length of the circle's radius.

9 A chord is 5 cm from the centre of a circle of radius 8 cm. Find the length of the chord.

10 A circle has radius 3 cm. A tangent is drawn to the circle from point P which is 9 cm from O, the circle's centre. How long is the tangent?

11 Find the radius of a circle if a tangent of length 12 cm has its end point 16 cm from the circle's centre.

The theorem of Pythagoras (Chapter 10)

12 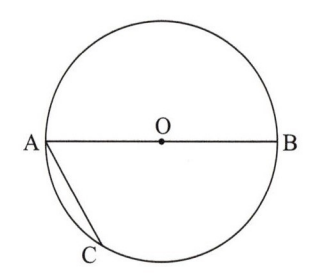 AB is a diameter of a circle and AC is half the length of AB. If BC is 12 cm long, what is the radius of the circle?

13 Two circular plates of radius 15 cm are placed in opposite corners of a rectangular table as shown. Find the distance between the centres of the plates.

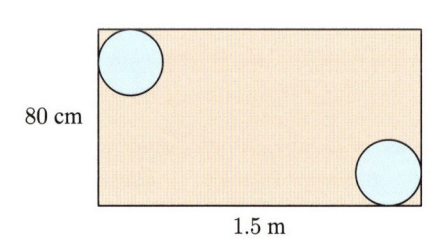

80 cm

1.5 m

14 10 m

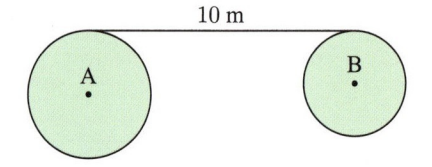

A and B are the centres of two circles with radii 4 m and 3 m respectively. The illustrated common tangent has length 10 m. Find the distance between the centres correct to 2 decimal places.

15 Two circles are drawn so they do not intersect. The larger circle has radius 6 cm. A common tangent is 10 cm long and the centres are 11 cm apart. Find the radius of the smaller circle, correct to 3 significant figures.

10 cm

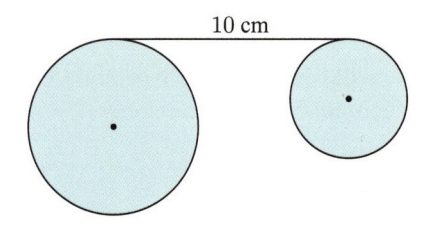

16 Answer the **Opening Problem** on page **195**.

Review set 10A

1 Find the lengths of the unknown sides in the following triangles. Give your answers correct to 3 significant figures.

a 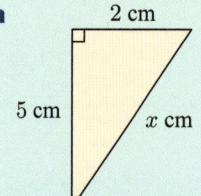 2 cm, 5 cm, x cm

b 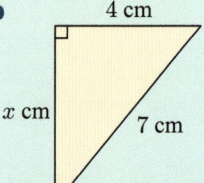 4 cm, x cm, 7 cm

c 8 cm, $2x$ cm, x cm

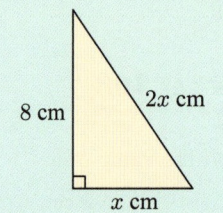

2 Amber is furnishing her new apartment. She buys a TV cabinet with a widescreen TV compartment measuring 100 cm by 65 cm. Will her 115 cm widescreen TV fit in the compartment?
(**Hint**: TVs are measured on the diagonal.)

3 Show that $\{5, 11, 13\}$ is not a Pythagorean triple.

4 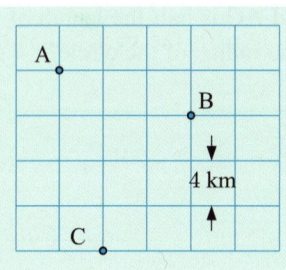 Find, correct to 3 significant figures, the distance from:

    a A to B   **b** B to C   **c** A to C

5 A rhombus has diagonals of length 12 cm and 18 cm. Find the length of its sides.

6 A circle has a chord of length 10 cm. The shortest distance from the circle's centre to the chord is 5 cm. Find the radius of the circle.

7 Kay is making a new window for her house. The window will be a regular octagon with sides 20 cm long. To make it, Kay plans to buy a square piece of glass and then cut the corners off, as shown.

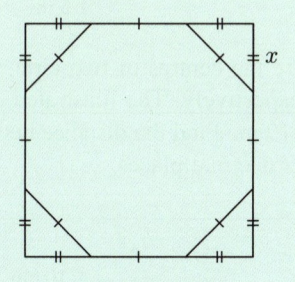

    a Find x.

    b Hence find the dimensions of the piece of glass that Kay needs to buy (to the nearest cm).

8 Find the values of the unknowns:

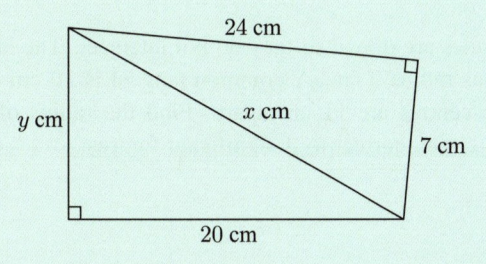

9 Find x, correct to 3 significant figures:

    a   **b**

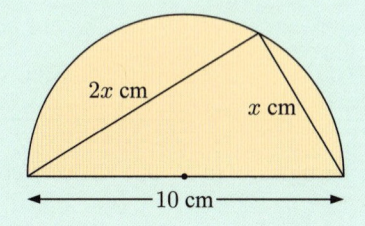

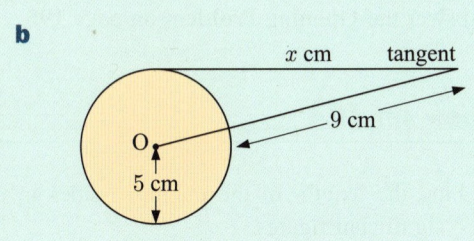

Review set 10B

1 Find the value of x:

    a   **b** 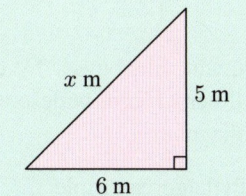   **c**

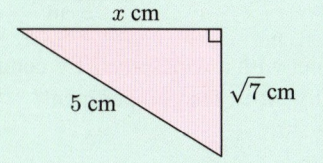

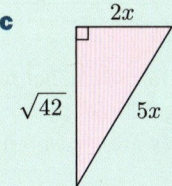

2 Paulo's high school is 6 km west and 3.5 km north of his home. What is the straight line distance from Paulo's house to school?

3 Find k if $\{20, k, 29\}$ is a Pythagorean triple.

4 The grid lines on the map are 3 km apart. A, B and C are farm houses. How far is it from:

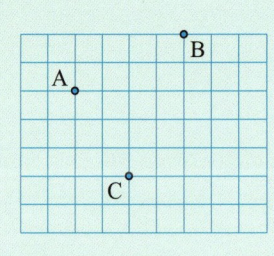

    a A to B   **b** B to C   **c** C to A?

5 If the diameter of a circle is 20 cm, find the shortest distance from a chord of length 16 cm to the centre of the circle.

6 Find the length of plastic coated wire required to make this clothes line:

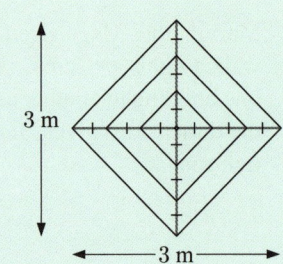

7 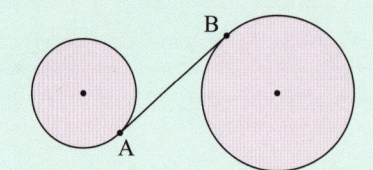 The circles illustrated have radii of length 5 cm and 7 cm respectively.

Their centres are 18 cm apart. Find the length of the common tangent AB.

8 The WM Keck Observatory at Mauna Kea, Hawaii, has a spherical dome with the cross-section shown. Find the width w of the floor.

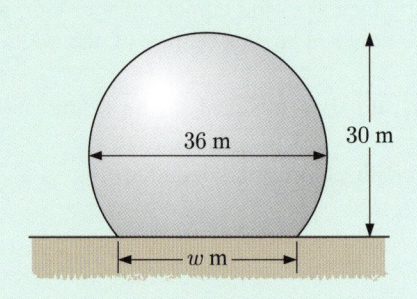

9 Find y in the following, giving your answers correct to 3 significant figures:

    a   **b**

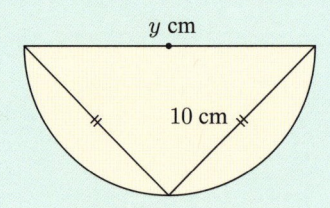

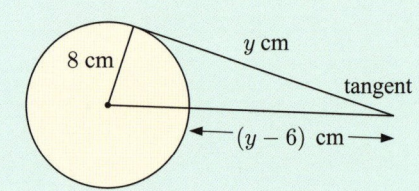

Challenge

1 A cubic die has sides of length 2 cm. Find the distance between opposite corners of the die.

Leave your answer in surd form.

2 A room is 5 m by 4 m and has a height of 3 m. Find the distance from a corner point on the floor to the opposite corner of the ceiling.

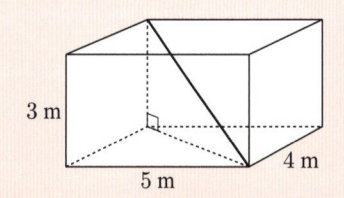

3 Marvin the Magnificent is attempting to walk a tightrope across an intersection from one building to another as illustrated. Using the dimensions given, find the length of the tightrope.

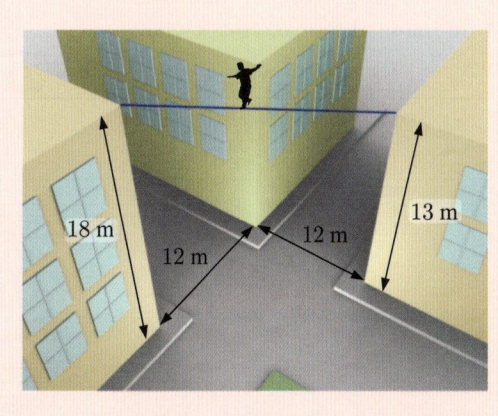

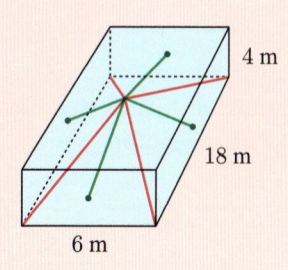

4 A 6 m by 18 m by 4 m hall is to be decorated with streamers for a party.

4 streamers are attached to the corners of the floor, and 4 streamers are attached to the centres of the walls as illustrated.

All 8 streamers are then attached to the centre of the ceiling.

Find the total length of streamers required.

Mensuration (length and area)

11

Contents:

A	Length	[6.1]
B	Perimeter	[6.2]
C	Area	[6.1, 6.2, 6.5]
D	Circles and sectors	[6.3, 6.5]

Opening problem

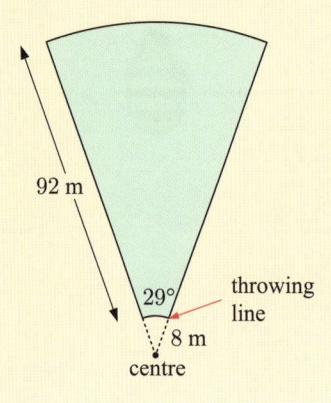

A javelin throwing arena is illustrated alongside. It has the shape of a sector of a circle of radius 100 m. The throwing line is 8 m from the centre. A white line is painted on the two 92 m straights and on the two circular arcs.

a Find the total length of the painted white line.

b If the shaded landing area is grassed, what is the total area of grass?

The measurement of **length**, **area**, **volume** and **capacity** is of great importance.

Constructing a tall building or a long bridge across a river, joining the circuits of a microchip, and rendezvousing in space to repair a satellite all require the use of measurement with skill and precision.

Builders, architects, engineers, and manufacturers all need to measure the sizes of objects to considerable accuracy.

The most common system of measurement is the **Système International (SI)**.

Important units that you should be familiar with include:

Measurement of	Unit	What it means
Length	metre	How long or how far.
Mass	kilogram	How heavy an object is.
Capacity	litre	How much liquid or gas is contained.
Time	hours, minutes, seconds	How long it takes.
Temperature	degrees Celsius and Fahrenheit	How hot or cold.
Speed	metres per second (m/s)	How fast it is travelling.

The SI uses prefixes to indicate an increase or decrease in the size of a unit.

Prefix	Symbol	Meaning	Prefix	Symbol	Meaning
tera	T	1 000 000 000 000	centi	c	0.01
giga	G	1 000 000 000	milli	m	0.001
mega	M	1 000 000	micro	μ	0.000 001
kilo	k	1000	nano	n	0.000 000 001
hecto	h	100	pico	p	0.000 000 000 001

In this course we will work primarily with the prefixes kilo, centi, and milli.

A LENGTH [6.1]

The base unit of length in the SI is the **metre** (m). Other units of length based on the metre are:

- **millimetres** (mm)   used to measure   the length of a bee
- **centimetres** (cm)   used to measure   the width of your desk
- **kilometres** (km)   used to measure   the distance between two cities.

The table below summarises the connection between these units of length:

> 1 **kilometre** (km) = 1000 **metres** (m)
> 1 **metre** (m) = 100 **centimetres**
> 1 **centimetre** (cm) = 10 **millimetres** (mm)

LENGTH UNITS CONVERSIONS

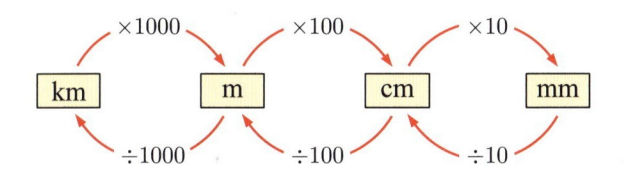

So, to convert cm into km we ÷ 100 and then ÷ 1000.

Notice that, when converting from:

- smaller units to larger units we **divide** by the conversion factor
- larger units to smaller units we **multiply** by the conversion factor.

Example 1

Convert: a 4.5 km to m   b 1.25 m to mm

a 4.5 km
$= (4.5 \times 1000)$ m
$= 4500$ m

b 1.25 m
$= (1.25 \times 100)$ cm
$= (1.25 \times 100 \times 10)$ mm
$= 1250$ mm

Example 2

Convert: a 350 cm to m   b 23 000 mm to m

a 350 cm
$= (350 \div 100)$ m
$= 3.5$ m

b 23 000 mm
$= (23\,000 \div 10)$ cm
$= (23\,000 \div 10 \div 100)$ m
$= 23$ m

EXERCISE 11A

1 Suggest an appropriate unit of length for measuring the following:
  a the length of a baby
  b the width of an eraser
  c the distance from London to Cambridge
  d the height of an old oak tree
  e the length of an ant
  f the length of a pen

2 Estimate the following and then check by measuring:
  a the length of your desk
  b the width of your pencil case
  c the height of a friend
  d the dimensions of your classroom
  e the length of a tennis court
  f the width of a hockey pitch

3 Convert:
  a 52 km to m
  b 115 cm to mm
  c 1.65 m to cm
  d 6.3 m to mm
  e 0.625 km to cm
  f 8.1 km to mm

4 Convert:
  a 480 cm to m
  b 54 mm to cm
  c 5280 m to km
  d 2000 mm to m
  e 580 000 cm to km
  f 7 000 000 mm to km

5 Convert the following lengths:
  a 42.1 km to m
  b 210 cm to m
  c 75 mm to cm
  d 1500 m to km
  e 1.85 m to cm
  f 42.5 cm to mm
  g 2.8 km to cm
  h 16 500 mm to m
  i 0.25 km to mm

6 A packet contains 120 wooden skewers, each of which is 15 cm long. If the skewers are placed in a line end to end, how far will the line stretch?

7 The length of a marathon is about 42 km. If the distance around your school's track is 400 m, how many laps must you complete to run the length of a marathon?

8 When Lucy walks, the length of her stride is 80 cm. Every morning she walks 1.7 km to school. How many steps does she take?

9 The height of a pack of 52 cards is 1.95 cm. Find:
- **a** the thickness, in millimetres, of a single card
- **b** the height, in metres, of 60 packs stacked on top of one another
- **c** the number of cards required to form a stack 12 cm high.

B PERIMETER [6.2]

The **perimeter** of a figure is the measurement of the distance around its boundary.

For a **polygon**, the perimeter is obtained by adding the lengths of all sides.

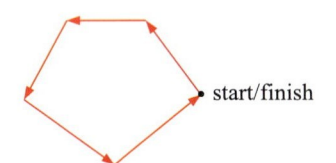

One way of thinking about perimeter is to imagine walking around a property. Start at one corner and walk around the boundary. When you arrive back at your starting point the **perimeter** is the distance you have walked.

You should remember from previous years these perimeter formulae:

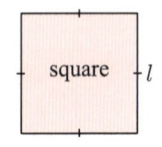

Square

$P = 4l$

Rectangle

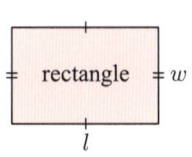

$P = 2l + 2w$
or $P = 2(l + w)$

Example 3

Find the perimeter of:

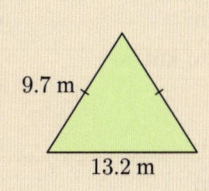

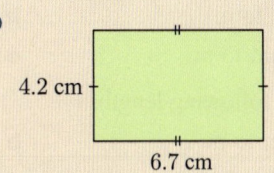

a triangle with sides 9.7 m, 9.7 m, 13.2 m

b rectangle 4.2 cm by 6.7 cm

a Perimeter $= 2 \times 9.7 + 13.2$
$= 32.6$ m

b $P = 2 \times 4.2 + 2 \times 6.7$
$= 8.4 + 13.4$
$= 21.8$ cm

Mensuration (length and area) (Chapter 11)

EXERCISE 11B

1 Measure with your ruler the lengths of the sides of each given figure and then find its perimeter.

   a   **b** 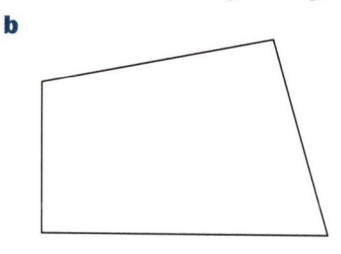   **c**

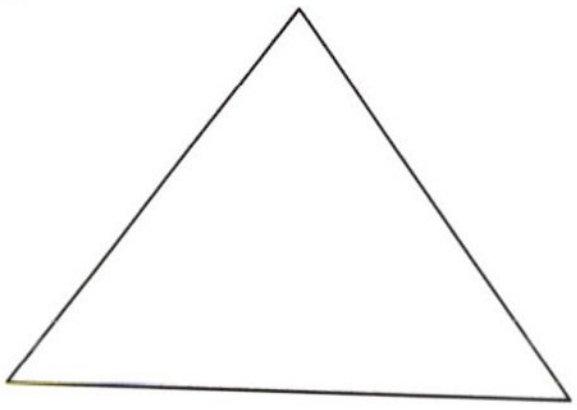

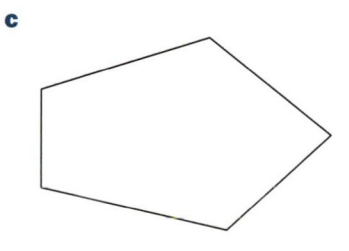

2 Find the perimeter of:

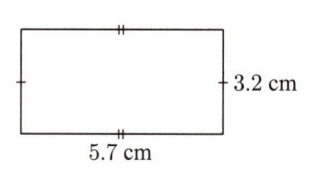

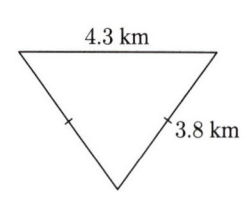

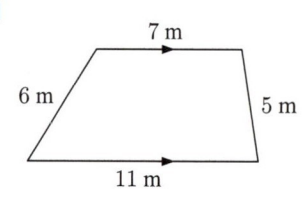

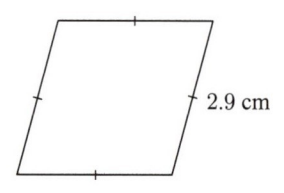

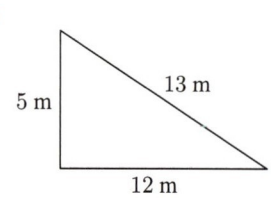

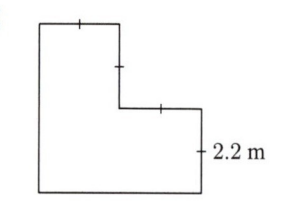

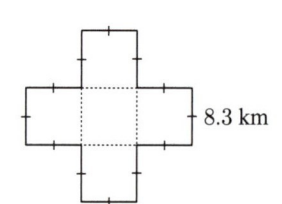

   a square with side 9.7 cm

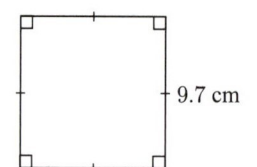

   b rectangle 5.7 cm by 3.2 cm

   c isosceles triangle with base 4.3 km and equal sides 3.8 km

   d trapezium with sides 7 m, 5 m, 11 m, 6 m

   e rhombus with side 2.9 cm

   f right triangle with sides 5 m, 12 m, 13 m

   g L-shape with side 2.2 m

   h plus/cross shape with side 8.3 km

   i pentagon with sides 4.1 m and 3.4 m

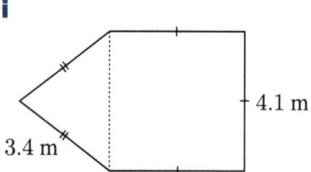

3 Find a formula for the perimeter P of:

   a rectangle with sides a and b

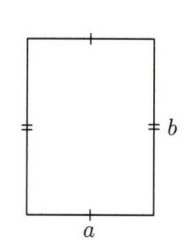

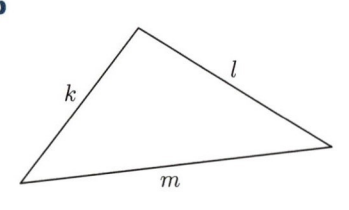

   b triangle with sides k, l, m

   c right triangle with legs $4a$ and $3a$

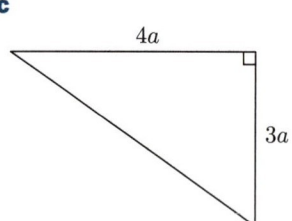

4 An isosceles triangle has a perimeter of 30 cm. If the base is 7.8 cm long, find the length of the equal sides.

5 A rectangle has one side of length 11.2 m and its perimeter is 39.8 m. Find the width of the rectangle.

6 A rectangle is 16.4 cm by 11.8 cm and has the same perimeter as an equilateral triangle. Find the length of the sides of the triangle.

7 Find the perimeter of the house in the plan alongside.

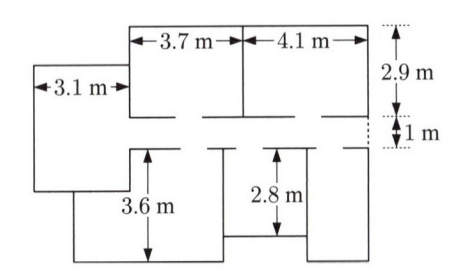

8 An octagonal area of lawn is created by removing 2 m by 2 m corners from a rectangular area. Find the new perimeter of the lawn.

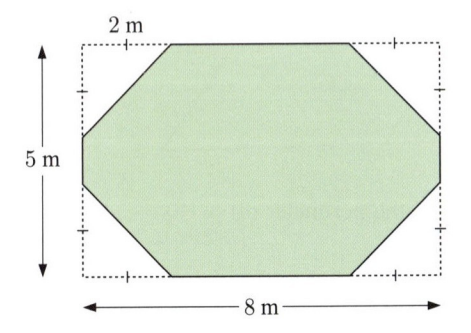

9 Calculate the length of wire required to construct the frame for the model house illustrated alongside.

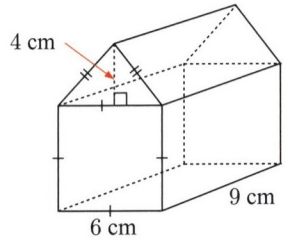

C   AREA   [6.1, 6.2, 6.5]

All around us we see surfaces such as walls, ceilings, paths and ovals. All of these surfaces have boundaries that help to define the surface.

> An **area** is the amount of *surface* within specified boundaries.
>
> The **area** of the surface of a closed figure is measured in terms of the number of square units it encloses.

UNITS OF AREA

Area can be measured in square millimetres, square centimetres, square metres and square kilometres; there is also another unit called a hectare (ha).

Since 1 m = 100 cm, the squares below have the same area.

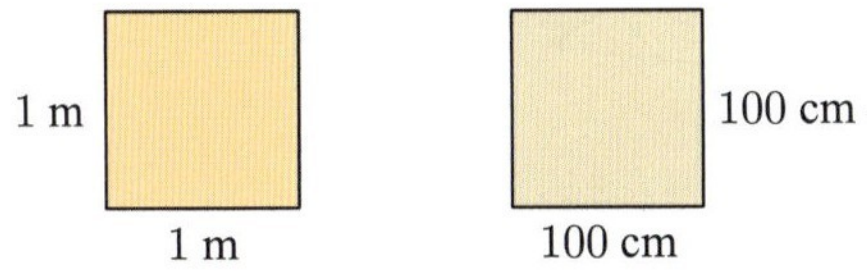

So, $1 \text{ m}^2 = 100 \text{ cm} \times 100 \text{ cm}$
         $= 10\,000 \text{ cm}^2$

> $1 \text{ mm}^2 = 1 \text{ mm} \times 1 \text{ mm}$
> $1 \text{ cm}^2 = 10 \text{ mm} \times 10 \text{ mm} \quad = 100 \text{ mm}^2$
> $1 \text{ m}^2 = 100 \text{ cm} \times 100 \text{ cm} \quad = 10\,000 \text{ cm}^2$
> $1 \text{ ha} = 100 \text{ m} \times 100 \text{ m} \quad = 10\,000 \text{ m}^2$
> $1 \text{ km}^2 = 1000 \text{ m} \times 1000 \text{ m} \quad = 1\,000\,000 \text{ m}^2 \text{ or } 100 \text{ ha}$

Mensuration (length and area) (Chapter 11)

AREA UNITS CONVERSIONS

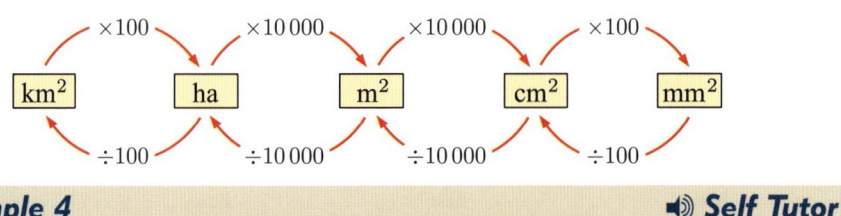

km² ×100→ ha ×10 000→ m² ×10 000→ cm² ×100→ mm²
km² ←÷100 ha ←÷10 000 m² ←÷10 000 cm² ←÷100 mm²

Example 4 ◆)) Self Tutor

Convert: **a** 6 m² to cm²   **b** 18 500 m² to ha

a 6 m² = (6 × 10 000) cm²
= 60 000 cm²

b 18 500 m² = (18 500 ÷ 10 000) ha
= 18 500. ÷ 10 000 ha
= 1.85 ha

EXERCISE 11C.1

1 Suggest an appropriate area unit for measuring the following:
  a the area of a postage stamp
  b the area of your desktop
  c the area of a vineyard
  d the area of your bedroom floor
  e the area of Ireland
  f the area of a toe-nail

2 Convert:
  a 23 mm² to cm²
  b 3.6 ha to m²
  c 726 cm² to m²
  d 7.6 m² to mm²
  e 8530 m² to ha
  f 0.354 ha to cm²
  g 13.54 cm² to mm²
  h 432 m² to cm²
  i 0.004 82 m² to mm²
  j 3 km² into m²
  k 0.7 km² into ha
  l 660 ha into m²
  m 660 ha into km²
  n 0.05 m² into cm²
  o 25 cm² into m²
  p 5.2 mm² into cm²
  q 0.72 km² into mm²

3 Calculate the area of the following rectangles:
  a 50 cm by 0.2 m in cm²
  b 0.6 m by 0.04 m in cm²
  c 30 mm by 4 mm in cm²
  d 0.2 km by 0.4 km in m²

Make sure you change both length units into the units required in the answer.

4 A 2 ha block of land is to be divided into 32 blocks of equal size. Find the area for each block in m².

5 The area of a square coaster is 64 cm². How many coasters can be made from a sheet of wood with area 4 m²?

AREA FORMULAE

You should remember these area formulae from previous years:

Rectangles

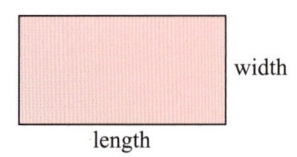

width
length

Area = length × width

Triangles

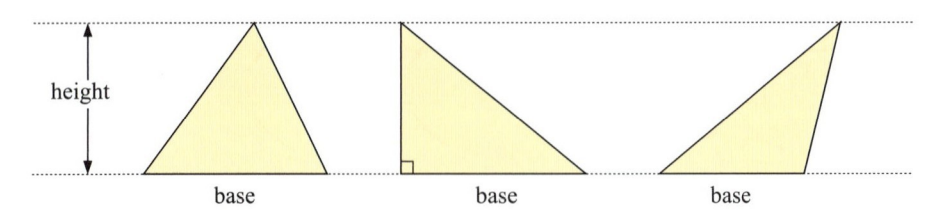

$$\text{Area} = \tfrac{1}{2} (\text{base} \times \text{height})$$

Parallelograms

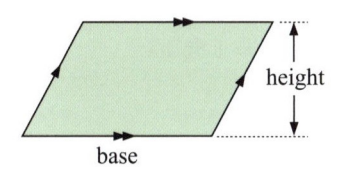

$$\text{Area} = \text{base} \times \text{height}$$

Trapezia

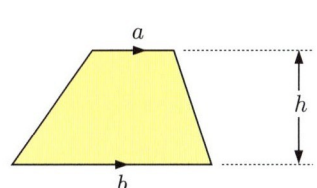

$$\text{Area} = \begin{bmatrix} \text{The average of the} \\ \text{lengths of the two} \\ \text{parallel sides} \end{bmatrix} \times \begin{bmatrix} \text{the distance between} \\ \text{the parallel sides} \end{bmatrix}$$

$$A = \left(\frac{a+b}{2}\right) \times h \quad \text{or} \quad A = \tfrac{1}{2}(a+b) \times h$$

Example 5 ◀)) Self Tutor

Find the area of:

a (triangle with base 12 m, height 5 m)

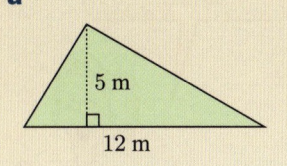

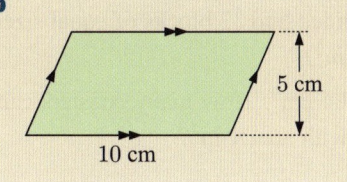

b (parallelogram with base 10 cm, height 5 cm)

c (trapezium with parallel sides 11 m and 16 m, height 4 m)

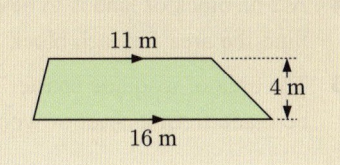

a Area
$= \tfrac{1}{2} \text{ base} \times \text{height}$
$= \tfrac{1}{2} \times 12 \times 5$
$= 30 \text{ m}^2$

b Area
$= \text{base} \times \text{height}$
$= 10 \times 5$
$= 50 \text{ cm}^2$

c Area
$= \left(\dfrac{a+b}{2}\right) \times h$
$= \left(\dfrac{11+16}{2}\right) \times 4$
$= 54 \text{ m}^2$

Mensuration (length and area) (Chapter 11)

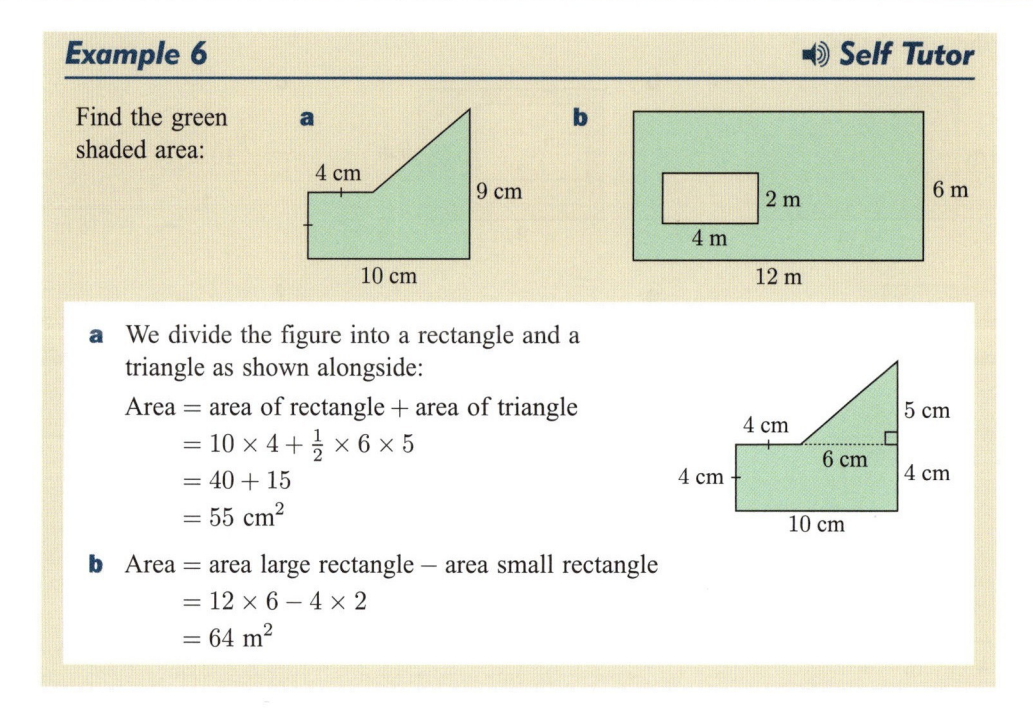

Example 6 ◆》 Self Tutor

Find the green shaded area:

a (figure: composite shape with 4 cm, 9 cm, 10 cm)

b (figure: rectangle 12 m × 6 m with inner rectangle 4 m × 2 m removed)

a We divide the figure into a rectangle and a triangle as shown alongside:

Area = area of rectangle + area of triangle
$= 10 \times 4 + \frac{1}{2} \times 6 \times 5$
$= 40 + 15$
$= 55$ cm^2

b Area = area large rectangle − area small rectangle
$= 12 \times 6 - 4 \times 2$
$= 64$ m^2

EXERCISE 11C.2

1 Find the area of the shaded region:

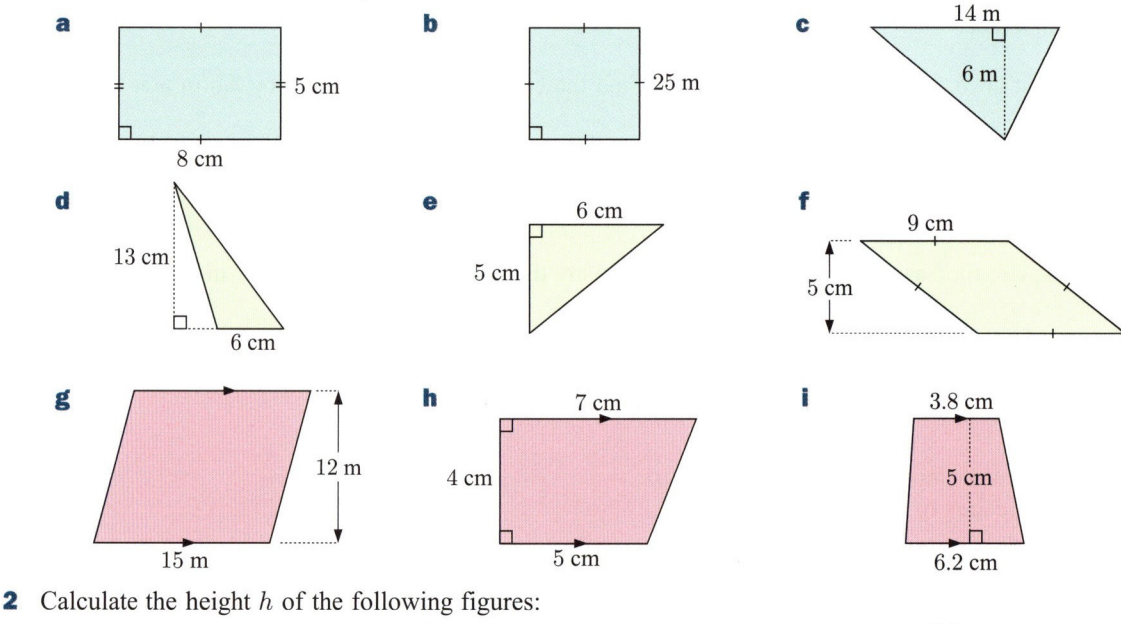

a rectangle 8 cm × 5 cm

b square 25 m × 25 m

c triangle with base 14 m and height 6 m

d triangle with height 13 cm and base 6 cm

e right triangle with legs 5 cm and 6 cm

f parallelogram with side 9 cm and height 5 cm

g parallelogram with base 15 m and height 12 m

h trapezium with parallel sides 7 cm and 5 cm, height 4 cm

i trapezium with parallel sides 3.8 cm and 6.2 cm, height 5 cm

2 Calculate the height h of the following figures:

a triangle, base 8 cm, height h cm, Area = 24 cm^2

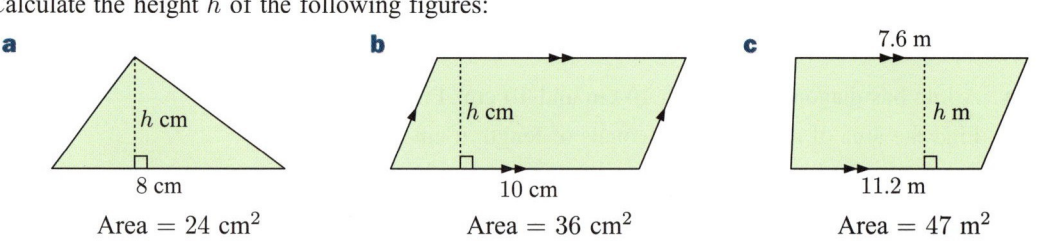

b parallelogram, base 10 cm, height h cm, Area = 36 cm^2

c parallelogram, base 11.2 m (top 7.6 m), height h m, Area = 47 m^2

3 Find the area shaded:

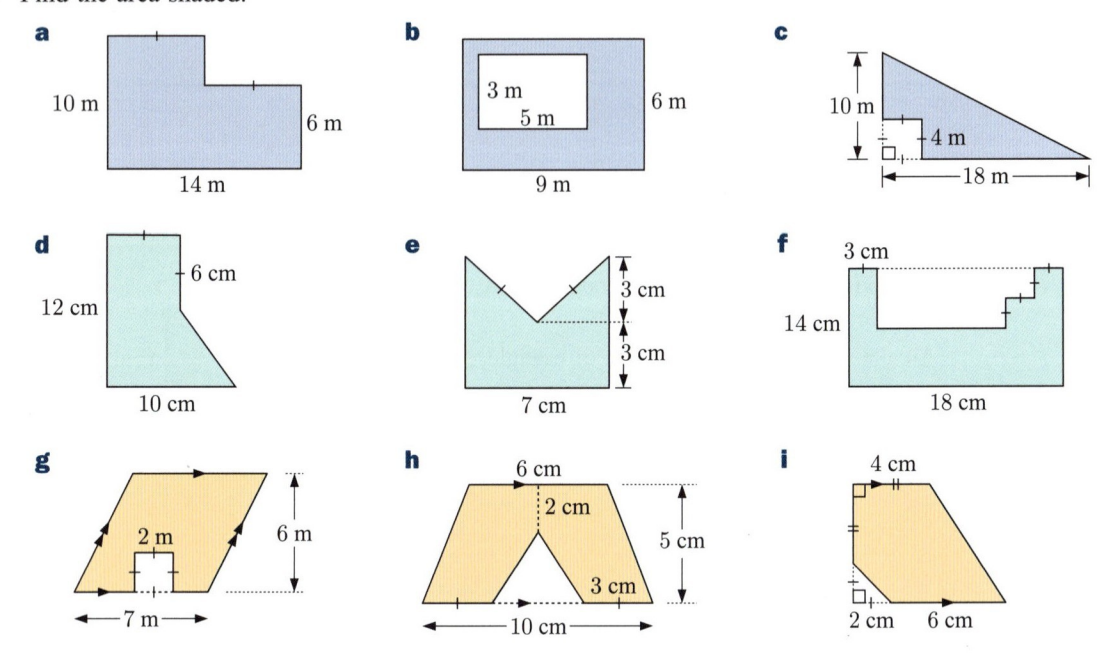

a [composite shape: 10 m by 14 m with 6 m by (14−?) cutout, stepped, labeled 10 m, 14 m, 6 m]

b Rectangle 9 m by 6 m with inner rectangle 3 m by 5 m

c Right triangle with heights 10 m and 4 m, base 18 m

d Shape with 6 cm top, 12 cm left side, 10 cm bottom

e M-shape, 7 cm wide, 3 cm + 3 cm

f Shape 14 cm by 18 cm with stepped cutout, 3 cm

g Parallelogram with 7 m, 2 m, 6 m

h Shape with 6 cm, 2 cm, 10 cm, 5 cm, 3 cm

i Shape with 4 cm, 2 cm, 6 cm

4 A photograph is 6 cm by 4 cm and its border is 12 cm by 10 cm. Calculate the visible area of the border.

5 A triangular face of a roof measures 2.4 m from tip to base, and has base length 8.1 m. Find the area of this face.

6 Instant lawn costs $15 per square metre. Find the cost of covering a 5.2 m by 3.6 m area with instant lawn.

7 A 4.2 m by 3.5 m tablecloth is used to cover a square table with sides of length 3.1 m. Find the area of the tablecloth which overhangs the edges.

8 A square tile has an area of 256 cm². How many tiles are needed for a floor 4 m × 2.4 m?

9 a Find the area of a rhombus which has diagonals of length 12 cm and 8 cm.
 b One diagonal of a rhombus is twice as long as the other diagonal. If the rhombus has area 32 cm², find the length of the shorter diagonal.

10 The area of trapezium ABCD is 204 cm². Find the area of triangle DBC.

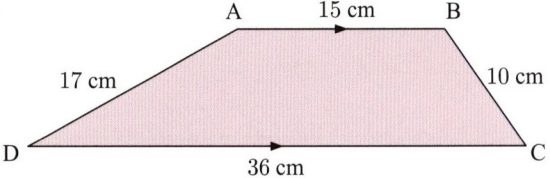

[Trapezium with AB = 15 cm, BC = 10 cm, DA = 17 cm, DC = 36 cm]

11 a A kite has diagonals of length 16 cm and 10 cm. Find its area.
 b Find the area of a kite with diagonals of length a cm and b cm.

12 Parallelogram ABCD has AB = 10 cm and diagonal DB = 15 cm. If the shortest distance from C to line AB is 8 cm, find the shortest distance from A to DB.

Mensuration (length and area) (Chapter 11) 223

13 The dimensions of the 'Bermuda Triangle' are shown alongside. North Caicos Island is where the altitude from Bermuda meets the Miami-San Juan line.

  a Find the distance from Bermuda to North Caicos Island.

  b Find the area of the Bermuda Triangle.

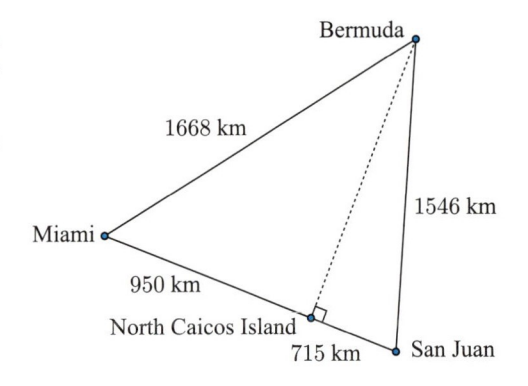

D CIRCLES AND SECTORS [6.3, 6.5]

You need to be familiar with these terms relating to circles:

A **circle** is the set of all points a fixed distance from a point called the circle's **centre**.

A line segment from the centre to any point on the circle is called a **radius**. We denote the length of the radius by r.

The perimeter of a circle is called its **circumference**.

A line segment which joins any two points on the circle is called a **chord**.

A chord which passes through the centre of the circle is called a **diameter**. We denote the length of the diameter by d.

An **arc** is a continuous part of the circle. The length of an arc is called its **arclength**.

Every arc has a corresponding **sector**, which is the portion of the circle subtended by the same angle θ as the arc.

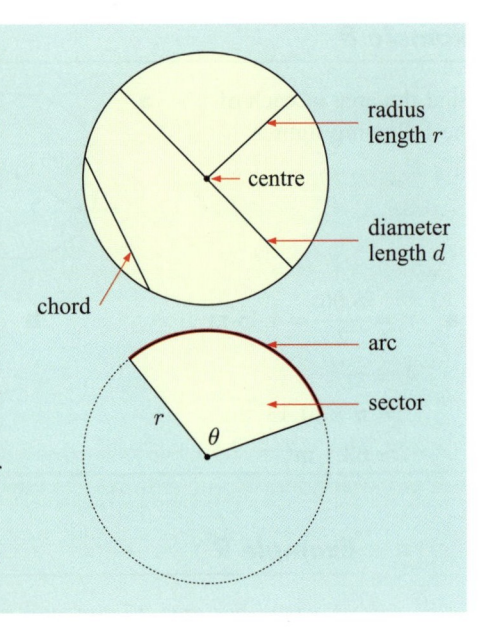

The formulae for the circumference and area of a circle both involve the number π or "pi". π is an irrational number, and $\pi \approx 3.14$.

Circle		Circumference $C = \pi d$ or $C = 2\pi r$ Area $A = \pi r^2$
Sector		Arclength $s = \left(\frac{\theta}{360}\right) \times 2\pi r$ Area $A = \left(\frac{\theta}{360}\right) \times \pi r^2$

Example 7

Find the perimeter of:

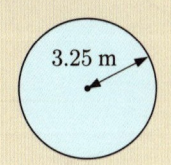

a (circle with radius 3.25 m)

b (sector with angle 60°, radius 12 cm)

The length of an arc is a fraction of the circumference of a circle.

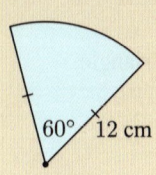

a Perimeter
$= 2\pi r$
$= 2 \times \pi \times 3.25$ m
≈ 20.4 m

b Perimeter
$= 12 + 12 +$ length of arc
$= 24 + \left(\frac{60}{360}\right) \times 2 \times \pi \times 12$
≈ 36.6 cm

Example 8

Find the area of each of the following figures:

a (circle with diameter 8.96 m)

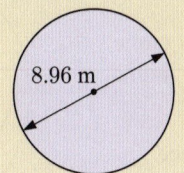

b (sector with angle 60°, radius 8 cm)

The area of a sector is a fraction of the area of a circle.

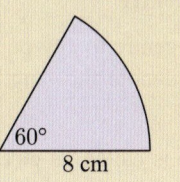

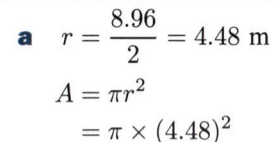

a $r = \dfrac{8.96}{2} = 4.48$ m

$A = \pi r^2$
$= \pi \times (4.48)^2$
≈ 63.1 m^2

b Area $= \left(\dfrac{\theta}{360}\right) \times \pi r^2$
$= \dfrac{60}{360} \times \pi \times 8^2$
≈ 33.5 cm^2

Example 9

A sector has area 25 cm² and radius 6 cm. Find the angle subtended at the centre.

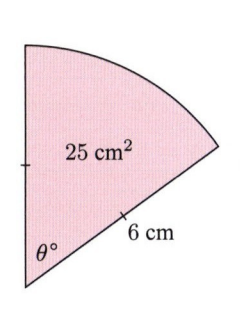

Area $= \left(\dfrac{\theta}{360}\right) \times \pi r^2$

$\therefore \quad 25 = \dfrac{\theta}{360} \times \pi \times 6^2$

$\therefore \quad 25 = \dfrac{\theta \pi}{10}$

$\therefore \quad \dfrac{250}{\pi} = \theta$

$\therefore \quad \theta \approx 79.6$

$\therefore$ the angle measures $79.6°$.

Mensuration (length and area) (Chapter 11)

EXERCISE 11D

1 Find, to 3 significant figures, the **i** perimeter and **ii** area of the following figures:

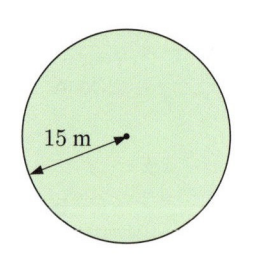

a 7 cm (radius)

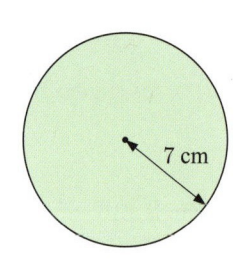

b 15 m (radius)

c 18 mm (diameter)

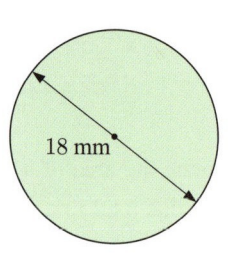

2 Calculate, correct to 3 significant figures, the circumference of a circle with:
  a radius 8 cm
  b radius 0.54 m
  c diameter 11 cm.

3 Calculate, correct to 3 significant figures, the area of a circle with:
  a radius 10 cm
  b radius 12.2 m
  c diameter 9.7 cm.

4 For the following circle sectors, calculate the **i** arc length and **ii** perimeter.
Give your answers to 4 significant figures.

a semicircle, 6 cm

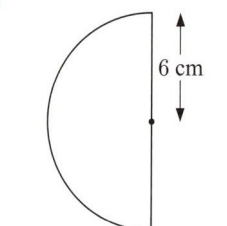

b quarter circle, 3 cm

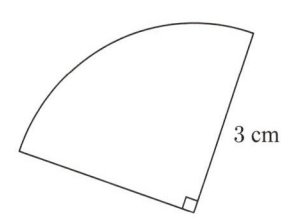

c 24 mm, 120°

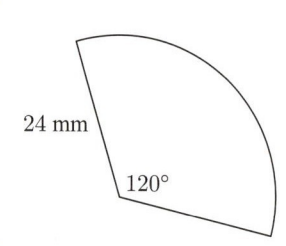

d 40°, 5 m

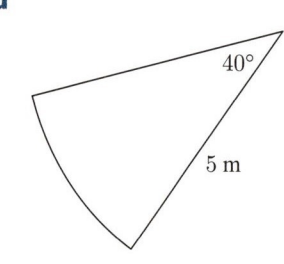

e 12.6 cm

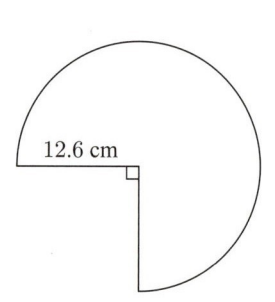

f 3.2 km, 70°

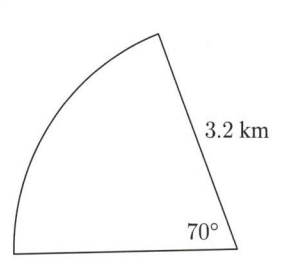

5 Calculate the length of the arc of a circle if:
  a the radius is 12.5 cm and the angle at the centre is 60°
  b the radius is 8.4 m and the angle at the centre is 120°.

6 Find the area shaded:

a 7 cm

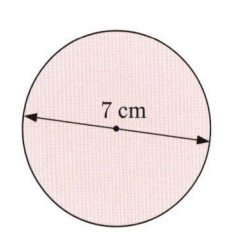

b 12 m

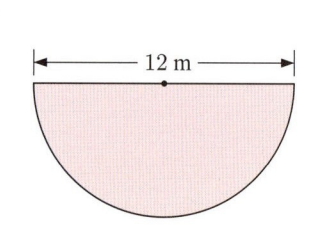

c 4 cm

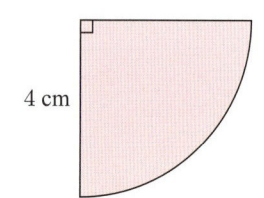

d 120°, 5 m

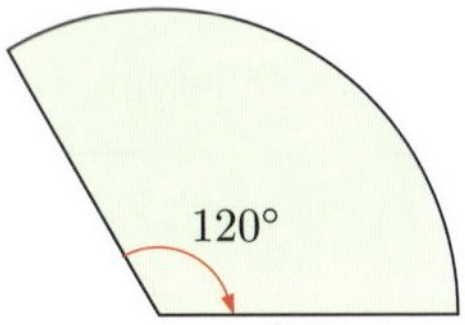

e 36°, 9.8 cm

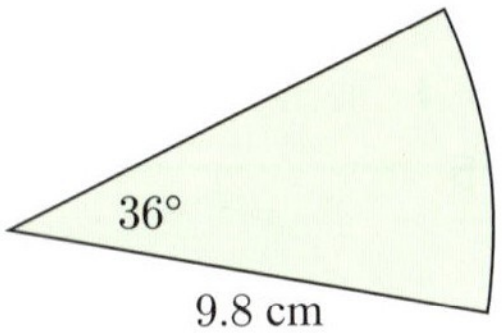

f 15°, 38 mm

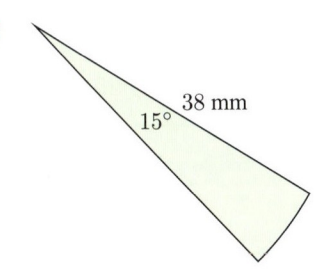

7 Calculate the area of a sector of:
  a radius 5.62 m and angle 80°
  b radius 8.7 cm and angle 210°.

8 **a** Find the circumference of a circle of radius 13.4 cm.
  b Find the length of an arc of a circle of radius 8 cm and angle 120°.
  c Find the perimeter of a sector of a circle of radius 9 cm and sector angle 80°.

9 Calculate the radius of a circle with:
  a circumference 20 cm
  b area 20 cm^2
  c area 9π m^2.

10 Find, in terms of π:
  a the length of arc AB
  b the perimeter of sector OAB
  c the area of sector OAB.

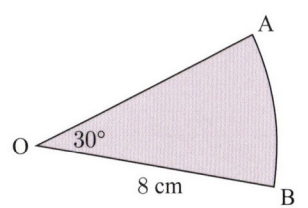

11 Find:
  a the arclength of a sector of radius 4.8 m and angle 200°
  b the area of a sector of radius 27.6 cm and angle 115°
  c the perimeter of a sector of radius 73.5 cm and angle 65°.

12 A sector of angle 300° has area 28 cm^2. Find the diameter of the circle the sector comes from.

13 A sector has a radius of 4.5 m and an arc length of 18.85 m. Find:
  a the subtended angle
  b the area of the sector.

14 Find the perimeter and area of the following shapes:

  a 80 m, 100 m

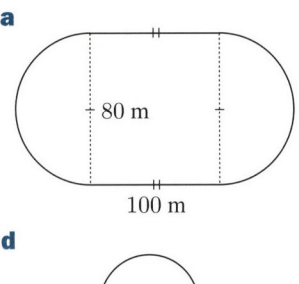

  b 4 cm, 10 cm

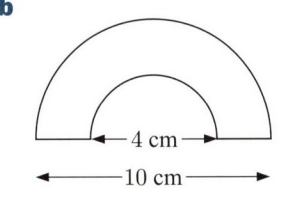

  c 50 m, 100 m

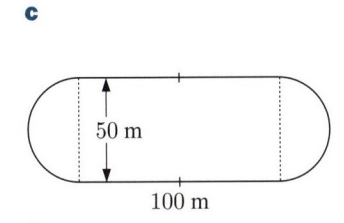

  d 5 cm, 6 cm

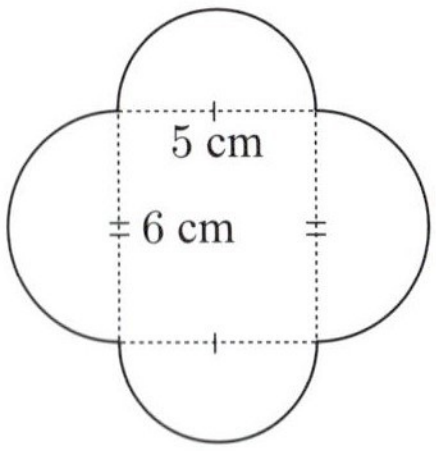

  e 6 cm, 5 squares

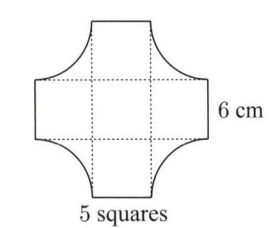

  f 10 cm

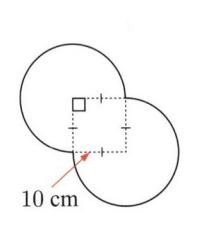

Mensuration (length and area) (Chapter 11) 227

g 5 cm, 3 cm

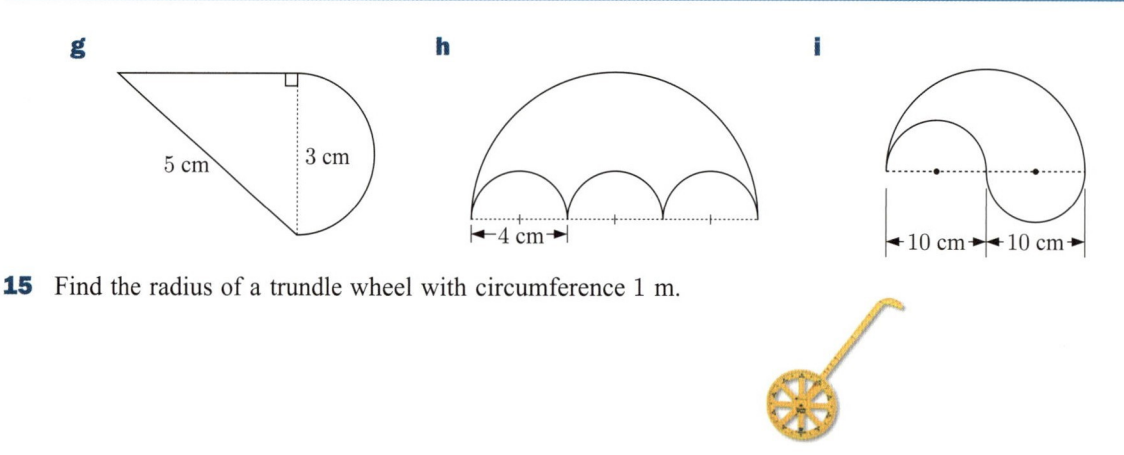

h 4 cm

i 10 cm, 10 cm

15 Find the radius of a trundle wheel with circumference 1 m.

16 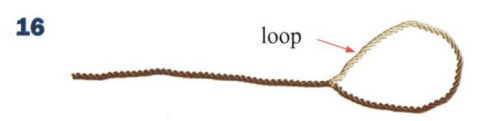 loop — A lasso is made from a rope that is 10 m long. The loop of the lasso has a radius of 0.6 m when circular. Find the length of the rope that is not part of the loop.

17 A circular golfing green has a diameter of 20 m. The pin must be positioned on the green at least 3 metres from its edge. Find the area of the green on which the pin is allowed to be positioned.

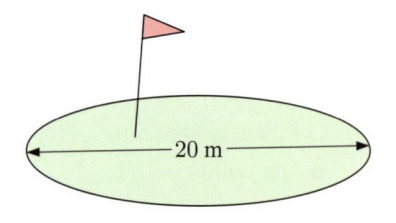

20 m

18 The second hand of a clock is 10 cm long. How far does the tip of the second hand travel in 20 seconds?

19 Neil cuts a slice from a pizza of diameter 30 cm. If the angle of his slice is $50°$, what area of pizza does Neil have?

20 Answer the questions in the **Opening Problem** on page **213**.

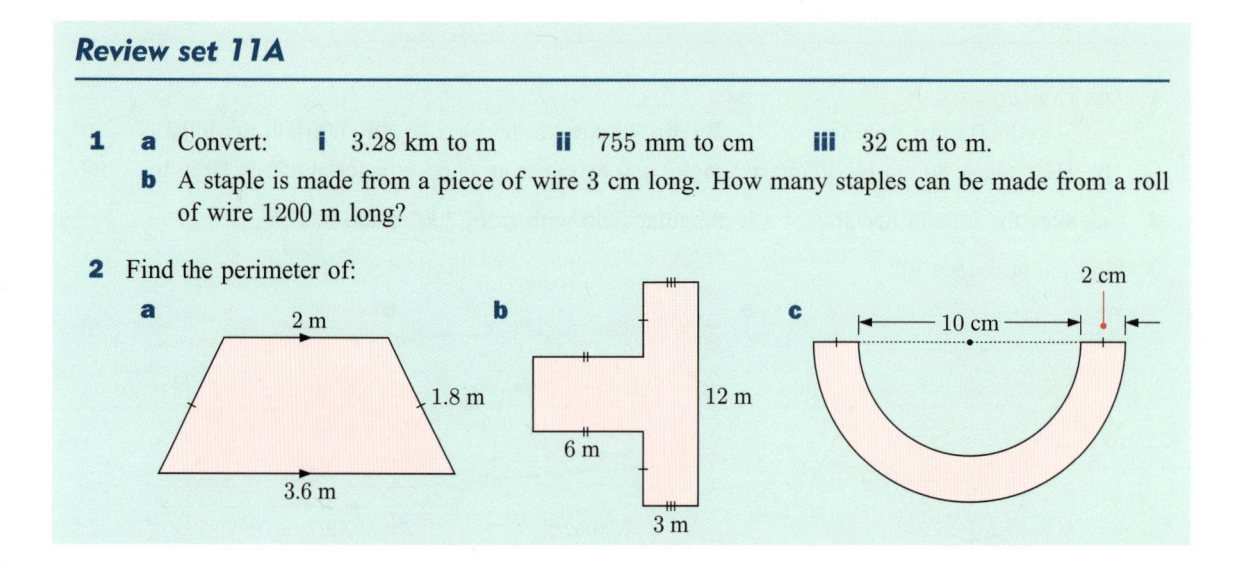

Review set 11A

1 a Convert: **i** 3.28 km to m **ii** 755 mm to cm **iii** 32 cm to m.
  b A staple is made from a piece of wire 3 cm long. How many staples can be made from a roll of wire 1200 m long?

2 Find the perimeter of:

a 2 m, 1.8 m, 3.6 m

b 12 m, 6 m, 3 m

c 10 cm, 2 cm

3 Find the area of:

a ![triangle with base 8 cm and height 5 cm]

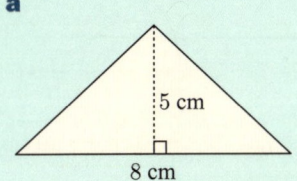

b ![quarter circle with radius 5 m]

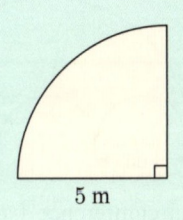

c ![right trapezium with parallel sides 6 m and 3 m, and height 5 m]

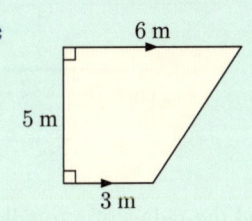

4 The diameter of a car tyre is 50 cm.
   a How far does the car need to travel for the tyre to complete one revolution?
   b How many revolutions does the tyre complete if the car travels 2 km?

5 Determine the angle of a sector with arc length 32 cm and radius 7 cm.

6 Find a formula for the   i perimeter P ii area A of:

   a ![L-shaped figure with sides z, x, y]

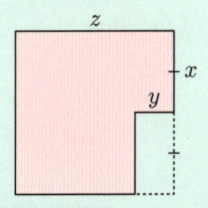

   b ![parallelogram-like quadrilateral with sides a, b, c, d]

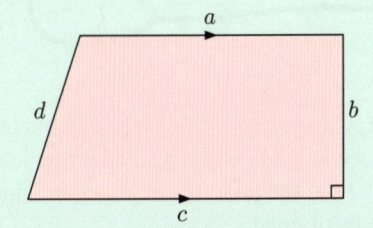

7 A circle has area 8 m². Find:
   a its radius
   b its circumference.

8 ![right triangle ABC with AB = 5 cm, BC = 12 cm, AC = 13 cm, and altitude d cm from B to AC]

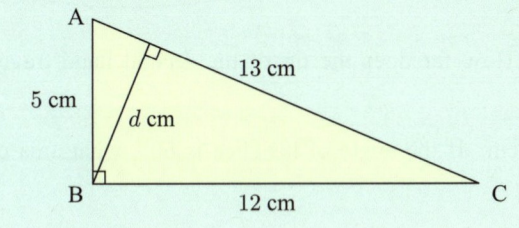

By finding the area of triangle ABC in two different ways, show that $d = \frac{60}{13}$.

Review set 11B

1 a Convert:
   i 3000 mm² to cm²   ii 40 000 cm² to m²   iii 600 000 m² to ha.

   b How many 80 cm by 40 cm rectangles can be cut from curtain material that is 10 m by 2 m?

2 Calculate the area in hectares of a rectangular field with sides 300 m and 0.2 km.

3 Find the perimeter of:

   a ![parallelogram with sides 7 cm and 8 cm]

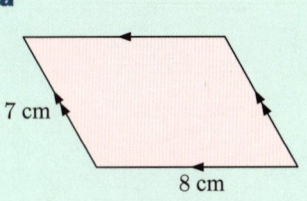

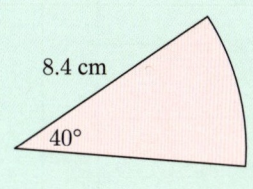

   b ![sector with radius 8.4 cm and angle 40°]

   c ![shape with 16 cm height, 6 cm and 20 cm horizontal segments]

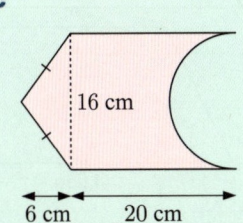

Mensuration (length and area) **(Chapter 11)**

4 Find the area of:

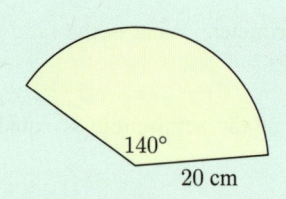

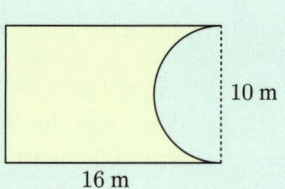

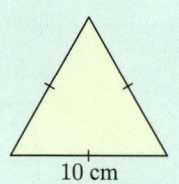

   a   **b**   **c**

(sector: 140°, 20 cm)   (rectangle 16 m wide with semicircle of diameter 10 m cut out)   (isosceles triangle, base 10 cm)

5 A sector of a circle has radius 12 cm and angle 135°.
  a What fraction of a whole circle is this sector?
  b Find the perimeter of the sector.
  c Find the area of the sector.

6 A circle has circumference of length 40.8 m. Find its:
  a radius   **b** area.

7 Find the formula for the area A of:

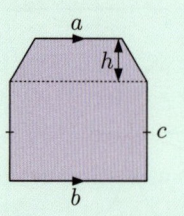

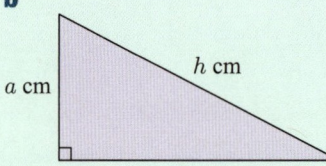

  a (pentagon with top a, height h, width c, base b)   **b** (right triangle with vertical side a cm and horizontal side h cm)

8 Alongside is a diagram of the national flag of Djibouti. Find the area of each colour, given the star has area 71.8 cm².

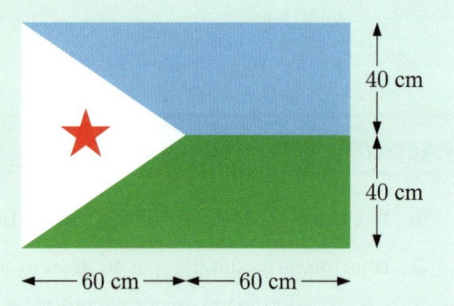

Challenge

1 A regular hexagon and an equilateral triangle have the same perimeter. What is the ratio of their areas?

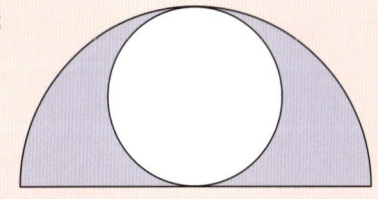

2 Prove that the shaded area of the semi-circle is equal to the area of the inner circle.

3 Show that the two shaded regions have equal areas.

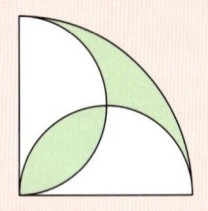

4 Find in terms of π the perimeter and area of the shaded region.

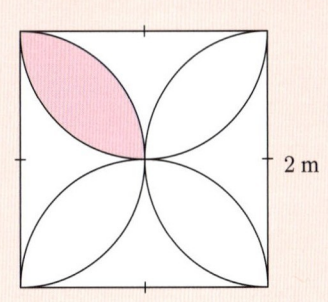

2 m

Activity

1 Jill has a number of 2×1 tiles. In how many ways can she tile a 4×4 grid?

2 6 points are equally spaced around a circle.
- **a** If each point is connected to every other point by a straight line, how many lines will be drawn?
- **b** By choosing any 3 distinct points, a triangle is formed. In how many ways can this be done?

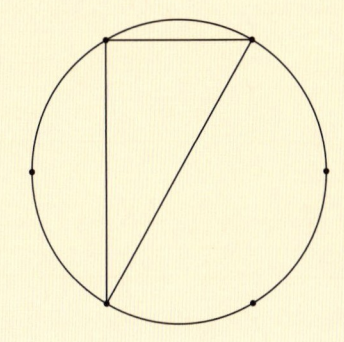

Topics in arithmetic

12

Contents:

A	Percentage	[1.8]
B	Profit and loss	[1.8]
C	Simple interest	[1.8]
D	Multipliers and chain percentage	[1.8]
E	Compound growth	[1.8]
F	Speed, distance and time	[1.13]
G	Travel graphs	[1.13]

Opening problem

80% of the profits from a cake stall will be given to charity.

The ingredients for the cakes cost £100, and the total value of the cakes sold was £275.

a How much profit did the cake stall make?
b How much will be given to charity?

A PERCENTAGE [1.8]

You should have seen percentages in previous years, and in particular that:

- $x\%$ means $\dfrac{x}{100}$.
- $x\%$ of a quantity is $\dfrac{x}{100} \times$ the quantity.

EXERCISE 12A

1. Write as a percentage:
   a $\frac{7}{10}$
   b $\frac{13}{50}$
   c $\frac{3}{25}$
   d $\frac{11}{200}$
   e 2
   f 0.2
   g 0.05
   h 1
   i 0.98
   j 0.003

2. Write as a fraction in simplest form and also as a decimal:
   a 75%
   b 7%
   c 1.5%
   d 160%
   e 113%

3. Express as a percentage:
   a 35 marks out of 50 marks
   b 3 km out of 20 km
   c 8 months out of 2 years
   d 40 min out of 2.5 hours

4. Tomas reduces his weight from 85.4 kg to 78.7 kg. What was his percentage weight loss?

5. If 17% of Helen's assets amount to €43 197, find:
   a 1% of her assets
   b the total value of all her assets.

6. Find:
   a 20% of 3 kg
   b 4.2% of $26 000
   c 105% of 80 kg
   d $1\frac{1}{4}$% of 2000 litres
   e 0.7% of 2670 tonnes
   f 46.7% of £35 267.20

7. Alex scored 72% for an examination out of 150 marks. How many marks did Alex score?

8. a A marathon runner starts a race with a mass of 72.0 kg. Despite continual rehydration he loses 3% of this mass during the race. Calculate his mass at the end of the race.
   b Another runner had a starting mass of 68.3 kg and a finishing mass of 66.9 kg. Calculate her percentage loss in mass.

9. Petra has a monthly income of £4700. She does not have to pay any tax on the first £2400 she earns, but she has to pay 15% of the remainder as tax.
   a How much tax does Petra have to pay?
   b How much does Petra have left after tax?
   c What percentage of the £4700 does Petra actually pay in tax?

10. If 3 students in a class of 24 are absent, what percentage are present?

11. After 2 hours a walker completed 8 km of a journey of 11.5 km. Calculate the percentage of the journey which remains.

12. The side lengths of the rectangle are increased by 20%. What is the percentage increase in the area of the rectangle?

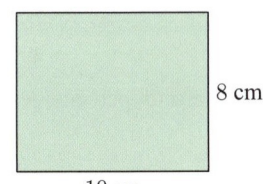

13. A circle's radius is increased by 10%. By what percentage does its area increase?

14. Answer the **Opening Problem** on page **231**.

B PROFIT AND LOSS [1.8]

We use money nearly every day, so we need to understand profit, loss and discount.

Profit is an example of an **increase**. Loss and discount are examples of a **decrease**.

> A **profit** occurs if the selling price is *higher* than the cost price.
>
> **Profit = selling price − cost price**
>
> A **loss** occurs if the selling price is *lower* than the cost price.
>
> **Loss = cost price − selling price**

MARK UP AND MARK DOWN

If a purchase price is **marked up** then it is increased, and a *profit* will be made.

If a purchase price is **marked down** then it is decreased, and a *loss* will be made.

Example 1 ◀) Self Tutor

A camera is purchased for €650 and is marked up by 20%.
Find: **a** the profit **b** the selling price.

a Profit = 20% of cost price
= 20% of €650
= $\frac{20}{100}$ × €650
= €130

b Selling price
= cost price + profit
= €650 + €130
= €780

Marked up by 20% means increased by 20%.

Example 2 ◀) Self Tutor

A pair of board shorts was bought for $35. They were marked down by 20% and sold in an end-of-summer clearance. Find:
a the loss **b** the selling price.

a Loss
= 20% of cost price
= 20% of $35
= $\frac{20}{100}$ × $35
= $7

b Selling price
= cost price − loss
= $35 − $7
= $28

Marked down 20% means decreased by 20%.

EXERCISE 12B.1

1 Estelle bakes loaves of bread for her bakery. If a loaf of bread costs €1.40 to make, and sells for €2.90, find her profit on the sale.

2 Greg built a wooden table which he sold for €148. He calculated that the cost of building the table was €176. Find his profit or loss on the sale.

3 Brad bought an old car for £600. He spent £1038 restoring it and sold it for £3500. Find his profit or loss on the sale.

4 Ed bought 180 caps at $10 each to sell at a baseball game. Unfortunately he only sold 128 caps at $15 each. Find his profit or loss on the sale of the caps.

5 Find **i** the profit **ii** the selling price   for the following items:
  a a shirt is purchased for $20 and marked up 10%
  b a DVD player is purchased for $250 and marked up 80%
  c a rugby ball is purchased for £50 and sold at a 15% profit
  d a house is purchased for €255 000 and sold at a 21% profit.

6 Find **i** the loss **ii** the selling price   for the following items:
  a a jumper is purchased for €55 and marked down 30% as it is shop-soiled
  b a heater is purchased for £175 and marked down 35% as winter is almost over
  c a microwave is purchased for $105 and is sold at a 25% loss in a stock-clearance
  d a car is purchased for €9600 and sold at a 14% loss as the car dealer has too many used cars.

7 A contractor buys his materials from a wholesaler and sells them at a 12% mark up. For one particular job the materials cost him $920. What profit does he make on the materials?

8 A pair of shoes has a marked price of $160. However, the store is having a clearance sale, so a 28% discount is offered.
  a How much discount will be deducted? **b** What is the selling price of the shoes?
  c If a 12.5% sales tax must be paid on the selling price, what will be the final price paid by the customer?

PERCENTAGE PROFIT AND LOSS

Sometimes it is important for a retailer to express profit or loss as a **percentage of the cost price**.

Profit and loss correspond to a percentage increase or decrease in the price respectively.

Example 3   ◀)) Self Tutor

A bicycle was bought for $240 and sold for $290.
Find the profit as a percentage of cost price.

Profit = $290 − $240 = $50

∴ profit as a *percentage* of cost price $= \dfrac{\text{profit}}{\text{cost price}} \times 100\%$

$= \dfrac{50}{240} \times 100\%$

$\approx 20.8\%$

We are really calculating the percentage increase in the price!

Example 4

Monika bought shares in Tescos at €21.00 per share but was forced to sell them at €18.60 each.
Find: **a** her loss per share   **b** the loss per share as a percentage of the cost price.

a   Loss
$= \text{cost price} - \text{selling price}$
$= €21.00 - €18.60$
$= €2.40$
$\therefore$ the loss made was €2.40 per share.

b   Loss as a percentage of the cost price
$= \dfrac{\text{loss}}{\text{cost price}} \times 100\%$
$= \dfrac{€2.40}{€21.00} \times 100\%$
$\approx 11.4\%$

EXERCISE 12B.2

1 A tennis racquet bought for €95 was then sold for €132. Find the profit as a percentage of the cost price.

2 A 25 m roll of carpet was bought wholesale for $435. If the whole roll is sold at $32.50 per metre, find:
   a the selling price   **b** the profit
   c the profit as a percentage of the wholesale (cost) price.

3 Athos bought a crate of apricots for $17.60. There were 11 kg of apricots in the crate. He sold the apricots in his shop in 1 kilogram bags for $2.85 each.
   a How much did 1 kg of apricots cost Athos?
   b What was his profit per kilogram?
   c Find his profit as a percentage of his cost price.

4 A furniture store has a clearance sale. If a sofa costing €1450 is marked down to €980, find:
   a the loss made on the sale
   b the loss as a percentage of the cost price.

We are really calculating the percentage decrease in the price!

5 Felipe pays £18 200 for a boat, but because of financial difficulties he is soon forced to sell it for £13 600.
   a Find the loss on this sale.   **b** Express this loss as a percentage of the cost price.

6 Sue bought a concert ticket for $55 but was unable to go to the concert. She sold the ticket to a friend for $40, as that was the best price she could get.
   a Find her loss.   **b** Express her loss as a percentage of her cost price.

7 A newly married couple purchased a two-bedroom unit for £126 000. They spent another £14 300 putting in a new kitchen and bathroom. Two years later they had twins and were forced to sell the unit so they could buy a bigger house. Unfortunately, due to a down-turn in the market they received only £107 500 for the sale. What was:
   a the total cost of the unit   **b** the loss on the sale
   c the loss as a percentage of their total costs?

C SIMPLE INTEREST   [1.8]

Whenever money is lent, the person lending the money is known as the **lender** and the person receiving the money is known as the **borrower**. The amount borrowed from the lender is called the **principal**.

The lender usually charges a fee called **interest** to the borrower. This fee represents the cost of using the other person's money. The borrower has to repay the principal borrowed plus the interest charged for using that money.

The amount of interest charged on a loan depends on the **principal**, the **time** the amount is borrowed for, and the **interest rate**.

SIMPLE INTEREST

Under the simple interest method, interest is calculated on the initial amount borrowed for the entire period of the loan.

Example 5   Self Tutor

Calculate the simple interest on a $4000 loan at a rate of 7% per annum over 3 years. Hence find the total amount to be repaid.

$$\begin{aligned}\text{The interest payable for 1 year} &= 7\% \text{ of } \$4000 \\ &= 0.07 \times \$4000 \\ \therefore \text{ the interest payable over 3 years} &= 0.07 \times \$4000 \times 3 \\ &= \$840 \\ \text{So, the total amount to be repaid} &= \$4000 + \$840 \\ &= \$4840 \end{aligned}$$

Example 6   Self Tutor

John wants to earn £2000 in interest on a 4 year loan of £15 000. What rate of simple interest will he need to charge?

The interest needed each year = £2000 ÷ 4 = £500

$$\therefore \text{ the interest rate} = \frac{£500}{£15\,000} \times 100\%$$
$$= \tfrac{10}{3}\%$$

∴ the rate would need to be $3\tfrac{1}{3}\%$ p.a.

p.a. reads per annum or per year.

Example 7   Self Tutor

How long would it take a €12 000 loan to generate €3000 simple interest if it is charged at a rate of 8.2% p.a.?

Topics in arithmetic (Chapter 12)

> The interest each year
> $= 8.2\%$ of €12 000
> $= 0.082 \times €12\,000$
> $= €984$
>
> $\therefore$ the period $= \dfrac{3000}{984}$ years
> ≈ 3.0488 years
> ≈ 3 years and 18 days.

EXERCISE 12C.1

1. Calculate the simple interest on a:
   a. $8500 loan at 6.8% simple interest p.a. for 3 years
   b. $17 250 loan at 7.5% simple interest p.a. for 1 year 3 months.

2. Calculate the total amount to be repaid on a loan of:
   a. $2250 at 5.7% p.a. simple interest for 5 years
   b. €5275 at 7.9% p.a. simple interest for 240 days.

3. Find the rate of simple interest per annum charged on a loan if:
   a. $368 is charged on a $4280 loan over 17 months
   b. £1152 is charged on an £11 750 loan over $3\tfrac{1}{2}$ years.

4. How long will it take to earn:
   a. €2500 on a loan of €20 000 at 6.7% p.a. simple interest
   b. £4000 on a loan of £16 000 at 8.3% p.a. simple interest?

THE SIMPLE INTEREST FORMULA

In **Example 5**, the interest payable on a $4000 loan at 7% p.a. simple interest for 3 years was $\$4000 \times 0.07 \times 3$.

From this observation we construct the **simple interest formula**:

$I = Prn$ where I is the **simple interest**
  P is the **principal** or amount borrowed
  r is the **rate of interest per annum** as a **decimal**
  n is the **time** or **duration** of the loan in **years**.

You need to memorise this formula.

Example 8 ◀) Self Tutor

Calculate the simple interest on a $6000 loan at a rate of 8% p.a. over 4 years. Hence find the total amount to be repaid.

$P = 6000$ Now $I = Prn$
$r = 8 \div 100 = 0.08$ $\therefore I = 6000 \times 0.08 \times 4$
$n = 4$ $\therefore I = \$1920$

The total amount to be repaid is $\$6000 + \$1920$
  $= \$7920$

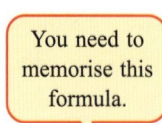

Example 9

If you wanted to earn $5000 in interest on a 4 year loan of $17 000, what rate of simple interest per annum would you need to charge?

$I = 5000$
$n = 4$
$P = 17\,000$

Now $I = Prn$
$\therefore \quad 5000 = 17\,000 \times r \times 4$
$\therefore \quad 68\,000r = 5000$
$\therefore \quad r = \dfrac{5000}{68\,000}$ {dividing both sides by 68 000}
$\therefore \quad r \approx 0.0735$

$\therefore$ you would need to charge a rate of 7.35% p.a. simple interest.

Example 10

How long would it take to earn interest of $4000 on a loan of $15 000 if a rate of 7.5% p.a. simple interest is charged?

$I = 4000$
$P = 15\,000$
$r = 7.5 \div 100 = 0.075$

Now $I = Prn$
$\therefore \quad 4000 = 15\,000 \times 0.075 \times n$
$\therefore \quad 4000 = 1125n$
$\therefore \quad n \approx 3.56$

So, it would take 3 years 7 months to earn the interest.

EXERCISE 12C.2

1 Calculate the simple interest on a loan of:
   a $2000 at a rate of 6% p.a. over 4 years
   b £9600 at a rate of 7.3% p.a. over a 17 month period
   c $30 000 at a rate of 6.8% p.a. over a 5 year 4 month period
   d €7500 at a rate of 7.6% p.a. over a 278 day period.

2 Which loan charges less simple interest?
   £25 000 at a rate of 7% p.a. for 4 years   or   £25 000 at a rate of 6.75% p.a. for $4\frac{1}{2}$ years

3 What rate of simple interest per annum must be charged if you want to earn:
   a $800 after 5 years on $6000   **b** €1000 after 20 months on €8800?

4 What rate of simple interest per annum would need to be charged on a loan of £20 000 if you wanted to earn £3000 in interest over 2 years?

5 Monique wants to buy a television costing $1500 in 18 months' time. She has already saved $1300 and deposits this in an account that pays simple interest. What annual rate of interest must the account pay to enable Monique to reach her target?

6 How long would it take to earn interest of:

    a $3000 on a loan of $10 000 at a rate of 8% p.a. simple interest

    b ¥82 440 on a loan of ¥229 000 at a rate of 6% p.a. simple interest?

7 If you deposited $8000 in an investment account that paid a rate of 7.25% p.a. simple interest, how long would it take to earn $1600 in interest?

Activity   *Simple interest calculator*

Click on the icon to obtain a simple interest calculator.

SIMPLE INTEREST

What to do:

Use the software to check the answers to **Examples 5** to **10**.

D   MULTIPLIERS AND CHAIN PERCENTAGE   [1.8]

In Susan's Casualwear business she buys items at a certain price and has to increase this price by 40% to make a profit and pay tax.

Suppose she buys a pair of slacks for $80. At what price should she mark them for sale?

One method is to find 40% of $80 and add this on to $80,

    40% of $80 = $\frac{40}{100}$ × $80 = $32

    So, the marked price would be $80 + $32 = $112.

This method needs **two steps**.

A **one-step** method is to use a **multiplier**.

    Increasing by 40% is the same as multiplying by 100% + 40% or 140%.

    So, $80 × 140% = $80 × 1.4 = $112

Example 11   ◀⑴ Self Tutor

What multiplier corresponds to:

  a a 25% increase   **b** a 15% decrease?

  a 100% + 25% = 125%   ∴ multiplier is 1.25

  b 100% − 15% = 85%   ∴ multiplier is 0.85

> A **multiplier** is a **one-step** method for increasing or decreasing quantities.

Example 12

A house is bought for €120 000 and soon after is sold for €156 000. What is the percentage increase on the investment?

Method 1:

multiplier
$= \dfrac{\text{new value}}{\text{old value}}$
$= \dfrac{156\,000}{120\,000}$
$= 1.30$
$= 130\%$
$\therefore$ a 30% increase occurred

Method 2:

percentage increase
$= \dfrac{\text{increase}}{\text{original}} \times 100\%$
$= \dfrac{156\,000 - 120\,000}{120\,000} \times 100\%$
$= \dfrac{36\,000}{120\,000} \times 100\%$
$= 30\%$
$\therefore$ a 30% increase occurred

> percentage change $= \dfrac{\text{change}}{\text{original}} \times 100\%$

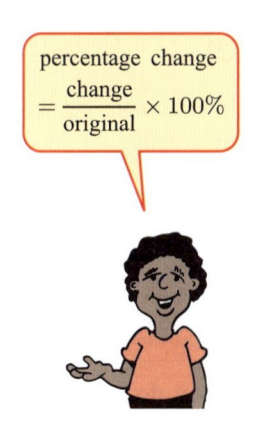

EXERCISE 12D.1

1 What multiplier corresponds to a:
  a 10% increase
  b 10% decrease
  c 33% increase
  d 21% decrease
  e 7.2% increase
  f 8.9% decrease?

2 Use a multiplier to calculate the following:
  a increase $80 by 6%
  b increase £68 by 20%
  c increase 50 kg by 14%
  d decrease €27 by 15%
  e decrease £780 by 16%
  f decrease 35 m by 10%

3
  a Jason was being paid a wage of €25 per hour. His employer agreed to increase his wage by 4%. What is Jason's new wage per hour?
  b At the school athletics day Sadi increased her previous best javelin throw of 29.5 m by 8%. How far did she throw the javelin?
  c The lawn in Oscar's back garden is 8.7 cm high. When Oscar mows the lawn he reduces its height by 70%. How high is the lawn now?

4 Find the percentage change that occurs when:
  a $80 increases to $120
  b £9000 decreases to £7200
  c €95 reduces to €80
  d €90 increases to €118
  e 16 kg increases to 20 kg
  f 8 m reduces to 6.5 m

5 A block of land is bought for €75 000 and sold later for €110 000. Calculate the percentage increase in the investment.

6 A share trader buys a parcel of shares for $4250 and sells them for $3800. Calculate the percentage decrease in the investment.

7 Terry found that after a two week vacation his weight had increased from 85 kg to 91 kg. What percentage increase in weight was this?

8 Frederik left a wet piece of timber, originally 3.80 m long, outside to dry. In the sun it shrank to a length of 3.72 m. What percentage reduction was this?

9 Shelley was originally farming 250 ha of land. However, she now farms 270 ha. What percentage increase is this?

Topics in arithmetic (Chapter 12)

CHAIN PERCENTAGE PROBLEMS

When two or more percentage changes occur in succession, we have a **chain percentage**.

For example, Brad owns an antique lamp worth £220. After a year, the value has increased by 10%, and after cleaning and polishing the value increases another 7%.

> Increasing by 10% has a multiplier of $110\% = 1.1$.
> So, after a year the lamp is worth $£220 \times 1.1 = £242$.
> Increasing by 7% has a multiplier of $107\% = 1.07$.
> So, the final value of the lamp after cleaning and polishing is $£242 \times 1.07 = £258.94$.

However, we can save time by applying both multipliers at once:

> Final value $= £220 \times 1.1 \times 1.07$
> $= £258.94$ ✓

Using the chain percentage method we can calculate the effect of two, three, four or more multipliers at the same time.

Note: A common mistake to avoid is *adding* the percentages. In Brad's case, a *wrong* method to calculate the answer is to say $10\% + 7\% = 17\%$, so use a multiplier of $117\% = 1.17$.

In this case the final result would be $£220 \times 1.17 = £257.40$ ✗

Example 13   ◀) Self Tutor

Increase $3500 by 10% and then decrease the result by 14%.

Increasing by 10% has a multiplier of $110\% = 1.1$
Decreasing by 14% has a multiper of $86\% = 0.86$
So, the final amount $= \$3500 \times 1.1 \times 0.86$
$= \$3311$

Example 14   ◀) Self Tutor

A 1.25 litre soft drink is bought by a deli for $0.80. The deli owner adds 60% mark up then 15% goods tax. What price does the customer pay (to the nearest 5 cents)?

A 60% mark up means we multiply by $160\% = 1.6$
A 15% goods tax indicates we multiply by a further $115\% = 1.15$
$\therefore$ cost to customer $= \$0.80 \times 1.6 \times 1.15$
$= \$1.472$
$\approx \$1.45$ {to the nearest 5 cents}

EXERCISE 12D.2

1. **a** Increase $2000 by 20% and then by 20%.
   b Increase £3000 by 10% and then decrease the result by 15%.
   c Decrease €4000 by 9% and then decrease the result by 11%.
   d Decrease $5000 by 6% and then increase the result by 10%.

2 True or false?

"If we increase an amount by a certain percentage and then decrease the result by the same percentage, we get back to the original amount."

3 Jarrod buys a wetsuit for $55 to be sold in his shop. He adds 40% for profit and also adds 12% goods tax. What price will he write on the sales tag?

4 Game consoles are bought by an electronics store owner for £120. They are marked up by 55% in order for profit to be made. After a few weeks a discount of 10% is given to encourage more sales. A goods tax of 8% is applied at the point of sale. What does the customer now pay?

Example 15   ◆) Self Tutor

An investment of ¥600 000 attracts interest rates of 6.8%, 7.1% and 6.9% over 3 successive years. What is it worth at the end of this period?

A 6.8% increase uses a multiplier of $106.8\% = 1.068$
A 7.1% increase uses a multiplier of $107.1\% = 1.071$
A 6.9% increase uses a multiplier of $106.9\% = 1.069$

$\therefore$ the final value $= ¥600\,000 \times 1.068 \times 1.071 \times 1.069$
$\phantom{\therefore \text{the final value }} = ¥733\,651$

---

5 A motorcycle today costs £3750. The inflation rates over the next three years are predicted to be 3%, 4%, and 5%. If this occurs, what is the expected cost of the motorcycle at the end of this period?

6 If the rate of inflation is expected to remain constant at 3% per year for the next 5 years, what would you expect a €35 000 car to cost in 5 years' time?

7 An investment of $30 000 is left to accumulate interest over a 3-year period. During the first year the interest paid was 8.7%. In successive years the rates paid were 8.4% and 5.9%. Find the value of the investment after 3 years.

Example 16   ◆) Self Tutor

Over a three year period the value of housing increases by 6%, decreases by 5%, and then increases by 8%. What is the overall effect of these changes?

Let x be the original value of a house.

$\therefore$ value after one year $= \$x \times 1.06$ {6% increase}
value after two years $= \$x \times 1.06 \times 0.95$ {5% decrease}
value after three years $= \$x \times 1.06 \times 0.95 \times 1.08$ {8% increase}
$= \$x \times 1.087\,56$
$\approx \$x \times 108.76\%$

So, an 8.76% increase has occurred.

---

8 Find the overall effect of:
    a increases of 8% and 12% over two consecutive years
    b decreases of 3%, 8% and 6% over three consecutive years
    c an increase of 5% over three consecutive years.

Topics in arithmetic (Chapter 12)   243

9 Joshua's wages increase by 3.2%, 4.8% and 7.5% over three consecutive years. What is his overall percentage increase over this period?

10 Jasmin's income increases by 11%, decreases by 7%, and then increases by 14% over three consecutive years. What is her overall percentage increase for this three year period?

11 A cutlery set costs a retail shop €65. In order to make a profit, a 45% mark up is made. As the item does not sell, two months later the price is reduced by 30%. When it is sold a goods tax of 17.5% is added. What price is paid by the customer, to the nearest euro?

E COMPOUND GROWTH [1.8]

If you bank $1000, then you are actually lending the money to the bank. The bank in turn uses your money to lend to other people. While banks pay you interest to encourage your custom, they charge interest to borrowers at a higher rate. That way the banks make a profit.

If you leave the money in the bank for a period of time, the interest is automatically added to your account and so the principal is increased. The next lot of interest will then be calculated on the higher principal. This creates a **compounding** effect on the interest as you are getting **interest on interest**.

Consider an investment of $1000 with interest of 6% p.a. paid each year and compounded.

After year	Interest paid	Value
0		$1000.00
1	6% of $1000.00 = $60.00	$1000.00 + $60.00 = $1060.00
2	6% of $1060.00 = $63.60	$1060.00 + $63.60 = $1123.60
3	6% of $1123.60 = $67.42	$1123.60 + $67.42 = $1191.02

We can use **chain percentage increases** to calculate the account balance after 3 years.

Each year, the account balance is 106% of its previous value.

$\therefore$ future value after 3 years $= \$1000 \times 1.06 \times 1.06 \times 1.06$
$= \$1000 \times (1.06)^3$
$= \$1191.02$

Example 17   ◀) Self Tutor

$5000 is invested at 8% p.a. compound interest with interest calculated annually.
   a What will it amount to after 3 years?   **b** Find the interest earned.

   a The multiplier is $108\% = 1.08$
   $\therefore$ value after 3 years $= \$5000 \times (1.08)^3$
   $= \$6298.56$

   b Interest earned $= \$6298.56 - \$5000$
   $= \$1298.56$

> **Example 18** ◀) *Self Tutor*
>
> An investment of £5500 amounted to £8000 after 4 years of compound growth. What was the annual rate of growth?
>
> If the annual multiplier was x, then $5500 \times x^4 = 8000$
>
> $\therefore \quad x^4 = \dfrac{8000}{5500}$
>
> $\therefore \quad x = \sqrt[4]{\dfrac{8000}{5500}} \approx 1.098\,201$
>
> $\therefore \quad x \approx 109.82\%$
>
> So, the annual growth rate was 9.82%.

EXERCISE 12E

1. Find the final value of a compound interest investment of:
    a. $2500 after 3 years at 6% p.a. with interest calculated annually
    b. £4000 after 4 years at 7% p.a. with interest calculated annually
    c. €8250 after 4 years at 8.5% p.a. with interest calculated annually.

2. Find the total interest earned for the following compound interest investments:
    a. €750 after 2 years at 6.8% p.a. with interest calculated annually
    b. $3350 after 3 years at 7.25% p.a. with interest calculated annually
    c. £12 500 after 4 years at 8.1% p.a. with interest calculated annually.

3. Xiao Ming invests 12 000 yuan into an account which pays 7% p.a. compounded annually. Find:
    a. the value of her account after 2 years
    b. the total interest earned after 2 years.

4. Kiri places $5000 in a fixed term investment account which pays 5.6% p.a. compounded annually.
    a. How much will she have in her account after 3 years?
    b. What interest has she earned over this period?

5. Jian invests $34 000 in a fund which accumulates interest at 8.4% per annum. If the money is left in the fund for a 6-year period, what will be its maturing value?

6. Which investment would earn you more interest on an 8000 peso investment for 5 years:
    one which pays 8% p.a. simple interest   or   one which pays 7.5% p.a. compound interest?

7. Calculate the rate at which compound interest is paid if:
    a. $1000 becomes $1123.60 after 2 years
    b. €5000 becomes €7178.15 after 5 years.

8. Molly invests $6000 at 5% p.a. fixed *simple* interest. Max invests $6000 at 4.5% p.a. fixed *compound* interest.
    a. Which is the better investment for 4 years and by how much?
    b. Which investment is better after 30 years and by how much?

9. The value of a car halves in 3 years. Find its annual rate of *depreciation* or loss in value.

10 After 4 years a tractor purchased for €58 500 has a resale value of €35 080. Find its annual rate of depreciation.

F SPEED, DISTANCE AND TIME [1.13]

We are all familiar with the concept of speed, or how fast something is moving.

> The **average speed** s is calculated by dividing the total distance travelled d by the total time taken t. It is the distance travelled *per unit of time*.
>
> $$s = \frac{d}{t}$$

For example, if I cycle 60 km in 3 hours then $d = 60$ km and $t = 3$ hours, and my average speed $s = \frac{60 \text{ km}}{3 \text{ h}} = 20$ km/h.

Notice that $s = \frac{d}{t}$ can be rearranged to $t = \frac{d}{s}$ and $d = st$.

The following triangle may help you with these rearrangements:

Cover the variable you are trying to find to see how it can be expressed in terms of the other two variables.

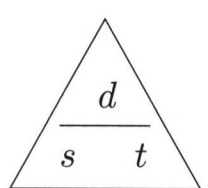

Example 19 ◀)) Self Tutor

Clark runs a 42.2 km marathon in 3 hours 5 mins and 17 s. Find his average speed in km/h.

3 hours 5 min 17 s $= 3 + \frac{5}{60} + \frac{17}{3600}$ hours

$\approx 3.088\,056$ hours

$\therefore \quad s = \frac{d}{t} \approx \frac{42.2 \text{ km}}{3.088\,056 \text{ h}} \approx 13.7$ km/h

Clark's average speed is about 13.7 km/h.

Example 20 ◀)) Self Tutor

Taylor serves a tennis ball at 130 km/h.
  a Write this speed in m/s.
  b The ball travels 24 m before reaching her opponent. How long does this take?

a 130 km/h $= \frac{130 \text{ km}}{1 \text{ hour}}$

$= \frac{130 \times 1000 \text{ m}}{1 \times 60 \times 60 \text{ s}}$

≈ 36.1 m/s

b $t = \frac{d}{s}$

$\approx \frac{24 \text{ m}}{36.1 \text{ m/s}}$

≈ 0.665 s

So, it takes 0.665 s for the ball to reach Taylor's opponent.

Example 21

Biathlete Jo cycles 60 km at a speed of 30 km/h, and then runs another 15 km at a speed of 10 km/h. Find:
  a the total time
  b the average speed for Jo's training session.

a 1st leg: $t = \dfrac{d}{s}$ 2nd leg: $t = \dfrac{d}{s}$

$\phantom{\text{1st leg: } t} = \dfrac{60 \text{ km}}{30 \text{ km/h}}$ $\phantom{\text{2nd leg: } t} = \dfrac{15 \text{ km}}{10 \text{ km/h}}$

$\phantom{\text{1st leg: } t} = 2 \text{ hours}$ $\phantom{\text{2nd leg: } t} = 1.5 \text{ hours}$

$\therefore$ total time $= 2$ hours $+ 1.5$ hours $= 3.5$ hours

b Total distance travelled $= 60$ km $+ 15$ km $= 75$ km

$\therefore$ average speed $s = \dfrac{d}{t}$

$\phantom{\therefore \text{ average speed } s} = \dfrac{75 \text{ km}}{3.5 \text{ h}}$

$\phantom{\therefore \text{ average speed } s} \approx 21.4$ km/h

EXERCISE 12F

1 A car travels for 2 h 20 min at an average speed of 65 km/h. Calculate the distance travelled.

2 An Olympic sprinter runs 100 m in 10.05 seconds. Calculate his average speed in:
  a m/s
  b km/h

3 How long does it take, in seconds, for a 160 m long train to enter a tunnel when the train is travelling at 170 km/h?

4 Jane can run 11.4 km in 49 min 37 sec. Calculate her average speed in km/h.

5 Find the time taken, to the nearest second, to:
  a drive 280 km at an average speed of 95 km/h
  b run 10 000 m at an average speed of 11 km/h.

6 Find the distance travelled when:
  a walking at an average speed of 3.5 km/h for 2 h 15 min
  b flying at an average speed of 840 km/h for 6 h 35 min.

7 A student walks for 2 hours at 3.5 km/h and then for 1 hour at 2 km/h. Find:
  a the total distance walked
  b the average speed.

8 In a 42.2 km marathon, Kuan runs the first 35 km at an average speed of 11 km/h. He walks the next 6 km at 4.5 km/h, and staggers the final 1.2 km at 1.5 km/h. Find Kuan's average speed for the marathon.

9 A family drives 775 km for their holiday. The first part of the trip is 52 km and takes 1 h 10 min. The remainder is covered at an average speed of 100 km/h. Find the average speed for the whole journey.

10 Convert:
  a 15 m/s into km/h
  b 120 km/h into m/s.

Topics in arithmetic (Chapter 12)   247

11 Two cyclists are travelling side by side along a long straight cycle track, one at 30 km/h and the other at 31 km/h. The faster cyclist wishes to overtake the slower one, and will need to gain 8 m relative to the slower cyclist in order to do this safely. Find:

   a the time taken for the faster cyclist to overtake the slower cyclist

   b the distance travelled by the faster cyclist in this time.

G   TRAVEL GRAPHS   [1.13]

It is often helpful to draw a graph of a journey. We put time on the horizontal axis and distance on the vertical axis.

Suppose a car travels 150 kilometres in 1.5 hours. A graph of the journey is shown alongside.

The average speed for the journey $= \dfrac{\text{distance}}{\text{time}}$

$= \dfrac{150}{1.5} = 100$ km/h

Notice that the point A on the graph indicates we have travelled 100 km in one hour. This matches our calculated average speed.

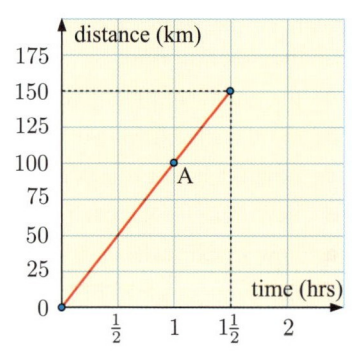

When we have two similar journeys, we can draw them on the same set of axes to compare them. For example, we could compare Ella's trips to work on Monday and Tuesday, or the progress of Evan and Robbie in a race.

Example 22   ◀)) Self Tutor

The graph alongside indicates the distance a homing pigeon travelled from its point of release until it reached its home. Use the graph to determine:

  a the total length of the flight
  b the time taken for the pigeon to reach home
  c the time taken to fly the first 200 km
  d the time taken to fly from the 240 km mark to the 400 km mark
  e the average speed for the first 4 hours.

  a Length of flight is 480 km.
  b Time to reach home is 10 hours.
  c Time for first 200 km is $2\tfrac{1}{2}$ hours.
  d It takes 3 hours to fly 240 km. It takes $6\tfrac{1}{2}$ hours to fly 400 km.
     ∴ it takes $3\tfrac{1}{2}$ hours to fly from 240 km to 400 km.
  e In the first 4 hours it flies 320 km.   ∴   average speed $= \dfrac{320}{4} = 80$ km/h.

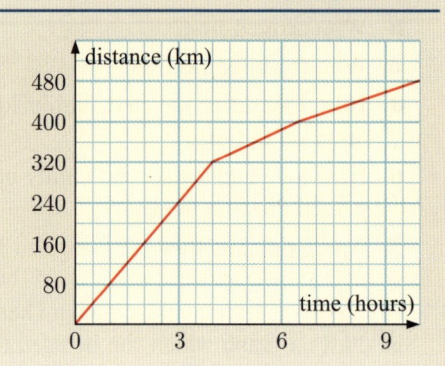

EXERCISE 12G

1 The graph alongside shows the distance Frances walks to work. Use the graph to determine:
  a the distance to work
  b the time taken to get to work
  c the distance walked after
   i 12 minutes   **ii** 20 minutes
  d the time taken to walk
   i 0.4 km   **ii** 1.3 km
  e the average speed for the whole distance.

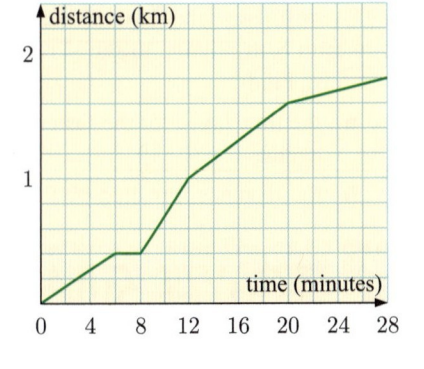

2 Two cyclists took part in a handicap time trial. The distance-time graph indicates how far each has travelled. Use the graph to find:
  a the handicap time given to cyclist B
  b the distance travelled by each cyclist
  c how far both cyclists had travelled when A caught B
  d how long it took each cyclist to travel 80 km
  e how much faster A completed the time trial than B
  f the average speed of each cyclist.

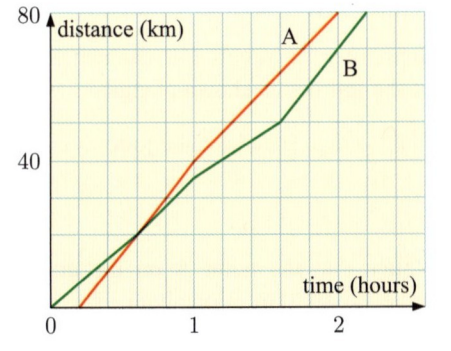

3 The Reynolds and Smith families live next door to each other in San Francisco. They are taking a vacation to their favourite beach, 150 km from where they live.
  a Who left first?
  b Who arrived first?
  c Who travelled fastest?
  d How long after the first family left did they pass each other on the road?
  e How long had the second family been driving when they passed the first family?
  f Approximately how far from San Francisco is this "passing point"?

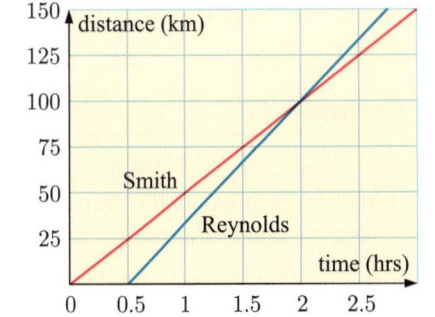

4 Patricia drives from home to pick up her children from school. She draws a graph which can be used to explain her journey. The vertical axis shows her distance from home in kilometres. The horizontal axis measures the time from when she left home in minutes. Her first stop is at traffic lights.
  a When did she stop for the red traffic light?
  b How long did the light take to change?
  c How long did she spend at the school?
  d How far away is the school from her home?
  e When was her rate of travel (speed) greatest?

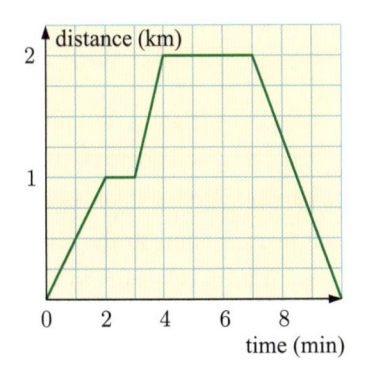

Review set 12A

1. What multiplier corresponds to:
   a a 13% decrease
   b a 10.9% increase?

2. a Increase $2500 by 16%.
   b Decrease 65 kg by 10%.

3. In the long jump, Tran jumps 5.65 m and Lim beats this distance by 7%. How far did Lim jump?

4. Eito purchases a pair of shoes for ¥6100 and marks them up 45% for sale. What is:
   a the selling price
   b the profit?

5. Moira bought a car for £4500 but had to sell it for £4000 a few weeks later. What was her:
   a loss
   b percentage loss?

6. A store has an item for $80 and discounts it by 15%. Find:
   a the discount
   b the sale price.

7. David purchased a stamp collection for €860. Two years later it was valued at €2410. Calculate the percentage increase in the value of the investment.

8. A publisher sells a book for $20 per copy to a retailer. The retailer marks up the price by 75% and then adds 10% for a goods tax. What price does the customer pay?

9. The annual rate of inflation is predicted to be 3% next year, then 3.5% in the year after that. What will be the cost in two years' time of an item that currently costs $50 if the cost rises in line with inflation?

10. How much is borrowed if a simple interest rate of 8% p.a. results in an interest charge of $3600 after 3 years?

11. A person wants to earn £3000 interest on an investment of £17 000 over 3 years. What is the minimum simple interest rate that will achieve this target?

12. How long would it take to earn €5000 interest on an investment of €22 500 at a rate of 9.5% p.a. simple interest?

13. Calculate the simple interest on a $6000 loan at a rate of 8.5% p.a. over 3 years.

14. Find the final value of a compound interest investment of $20 000 after 3 years at 7.5% p.a. with interest calculated annually.

15. Which of the following would earn more interest on a $7500 investment for 4 years:
    • 9% p.a. simple interest calculated annually   or
    • 8% p.a. compounded interest calculated annually?

16. Find the time taken to drive 305 km at an average speed of 70 km/h.

17. A motorist drives for 30 minutes at 90 km/h, and then for 1 hour at 60 km/h. Find:
    a the total distance travelled
    b the average speed for the whole trip.

Review set 12B

1. What multiplier corresponds to:
   a. a 10% increase
   b. an 11.7% decrease?

2. a. Increase £3625 by 8%.
   b. Decrease 387 km by 1.8%.

3. Adam bought a bicycle for €165 and sold it soon after for €130. What was Adam's:
   a. loss
   b. percentage loss?

4. A furniture store bought a chair for €380, marked it up by 35% and then discounted it by 15%. What was:
   a. the marked-up price
   b. the discounted price?

5. A company cut its advertising budget by 12%. If the company previously spent $80 000 on advertising, what was the new advertising budget?

6. A toaster is sold to a retailer for €38. The retailer marks it up by 40%, discounts it by 15%, and then sells it to a customer after adding on a goods tax of 16%. What did the customer pay?

7. For the next three years the annual inflation rate is predicted to be 3.2%, 4.1% and 4.8%. If this occurs, what should be the value of a house currently at $325 000?

8. What simple interest is earned on an investment of $6500 for 4 years at 6.8% p.a.?

9. How much is borrowed if a simple interest rate of 7.2% p.a. results in an interest charge of $216 after $2\frac{1}{2}$ years?

10. How long would it take for a loan of €45 000 to earn €15 120 interest at a rate of 8% p.a. simple interest?

11. An investment of $25 000 is made for 4 years at 8.2% p.a. compounded yearly. Find:
    a. the final value of the investment
    b. the interest earned.

12. €8000 is invested for 10 years at 8% p.a. compound interest. Find:
    a. the final value of the investment
    b. the amount of interest earned
    c. the simple interest rate needed to be paid for the same return on the investment.

13. Find the distance travelled by flying at an average speed of 780 km/h for 1 hour 40 minutes.

14. The graph shows the distance travelled by two families between New York and Washington DC. Use the graph to find:
    a. the distance from New York to Washington DC
    b. how much quicker the Maple family completed the trip than the Johnson family
    c. the average speed for each family over the first two hours
    d. the average speed for the Johnsons over the whole trip.

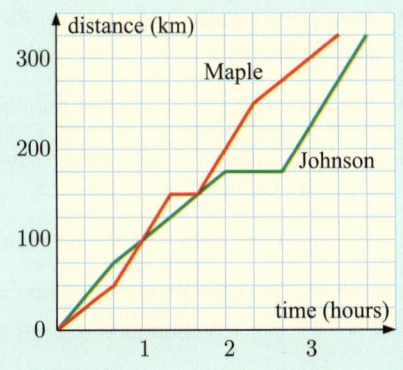

15. After 5 years a house costing $175 000 was sold for $240 000. What was the annual rate of compound growth?

16. Jimmy is driving 200 km to his holiday destination. He drives the first 100 km at 60 km per hour, and the next 100 km at 100 km per hour. Find his average speed for the whole journey.

Mensuration (solids and containers)   13

Contents:

- **A** Surface area — [6.4]
- **B** Volume — [6.1, 6.4]
- **C** Capacity — [6.1, 6.4]
- **D** Mass — [6.1]
- **E** Compound solids — [6.5]

Opening problem

Chun's roof is leaking. 10 ml of water is dripping onto her floor every minute. She places a 10 cm by 8 cm by 3 cm container under the leak to catch the drops.

How often will Chun need to empty the container?

In this chapter we deal with measurements associated with 3-dimensional objects. These may be solids which have **mass**, **surface area**, and **volume**, or containers which can hold a certain **capacity**.

The shapes we deal with include **prisms** and **pyramids** which have all flat or **plane faces**, and **cylinders**, **cones** and **spheres** which have **curved surfaces**.

A   SURFACE AREA   [6.4]

SOLIDS WITH PLANE FACES

The **surface area** of a three-dimensional figure with plane faces is the sum of the areas of the faces.

To help find the surface area of a solid, it is often helpful to draw a **net**. This is a two-dimensional plan which can be folded to construct the solid.

Software that demonstrates **nets** can be found at *http://www.peda.com/poly/*

Example 1

Find the total surface area of the rectangular box:

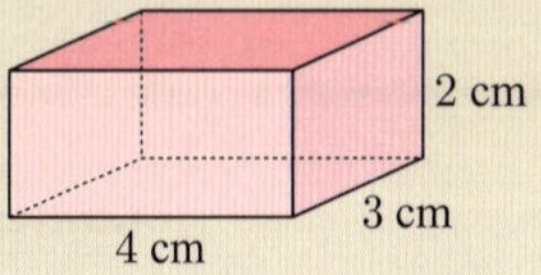

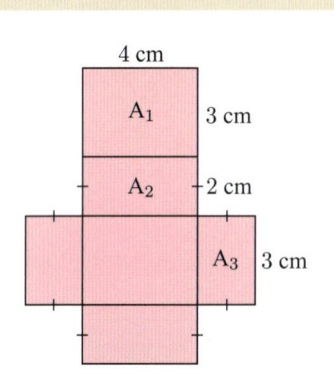

$A_1 = 4 \times 3 = 12$ cm²   (bottom and top)

$A_2 = 4 \times 2 = 8$ cm²   (front and back)

$A_3 = 2 \times 3 = 6$ cm²   (sides)

$\therefore$ total surface area $= 2 \times A_1 + 2 \times A_2 + 2 \times A_3$
$= 2 \times 12 + 2 \times 8 + 2 \times 6$
$= 52$ cm²

So, the total surface area of the box is 52 cm².

Example 2

What is the total surface area of this wedge?

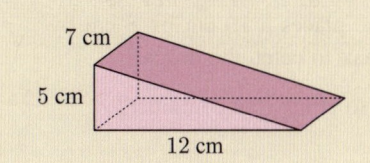

Sometimes we need to use Pythagoras' theorem to find a missing length.

Let the length of the slant be h cm.

$h^2 = 12^2 + 5^2$ {Pythagoras}
$\therefore h^2 = 169$
$\therefore h = 13$ {as $h > 0$}

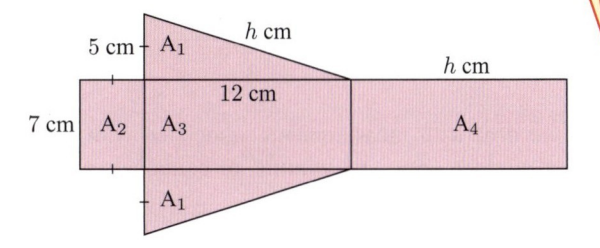

Now, $A_1 = \frac{1}{2}$(base × height)
$= \frac{1}{2} \times 12 \times 5$
$= 30$ cm²

$A_2 = 7 \times 5$
$= 35$ cm²

$A_3 = 12 \times 7$
$= 84$ cm²

$A_4 = 13 \times 7$
$= 91$ cm²

$\therefore$ total surface area $= 2 \times A_1 + A_2 + A_3 + A_4$
$= 2 \times 30 + 35 + 84 + 91$
$= 270$ cm²

Mensuration (solids and containers)   (Chapter 13)

Example 3   ◀) Self Tutor

Find the surface area of the square-based pyramid:

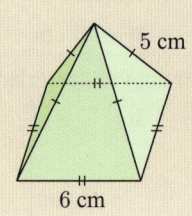

The figure has:
- 1 square base 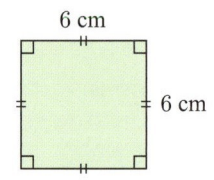
- 4 triangular faces

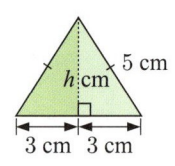

$h^2 + 3^2 = 5^2$ {Pythagoras}
$\therefore \quad h^2 + 9 = 25$
$\therefore \quad h^2 = 16$
$\therefore \quad h = 4$ {as $h > 0$}

Total surface area $= 6 \times 6 \ + \ 4 \times (\frac{1}{2} \times 6 \times 4)$
$\phantom{\text{Total surface area }} = 36 + 48$
$\phantom{\text{Total surface area }} = 84 \text{ cm}^2$

Example 4   ◀) Self Tutor

Find the cost of erecting a 6 m by 4 m rectangular garden shed that is 2 m high if the metal sheeting costs $15 per square metre.

The shed: Net:

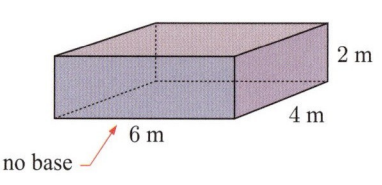

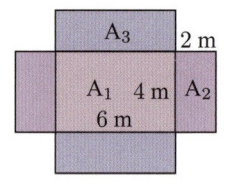

no base

$A_1 = 6 \times 4$ $A_2 = 4 \times 2$ $A_3 = 6 \times 2$
$ = 24 \text{ m}^2$ $ = 8 \text{ m}^2$ $ = 12 \text{ m}^2$

$\therefore \ $ total surface area $= A_1 + 2 \times A_2 + 2 \times A_3$
$\phantom{\therefore \ \text{total surface area }} = 24 + 2 \times 8 + 2 \times 12$
$\phantom{\therefore \ \text{total surface area }} = 64 \text{ m}^2$

$\therefore \ $ cost $= 64 \times \$15$
$\phantom{\therefore \ \text{cost }} = \$960$

EXERCISE 13A.1

1 Find the surface area of a cube with sides:
  a 3 cm
  b 4.5 cm
  c 9.8 mm

2 Find the surface area of the following rectangular prisms:
  a 4 cm, 10 cm, 7 cm
  b 40 mm, 16 mm, 50 mm
  c 42 m, 95 m, 3 m

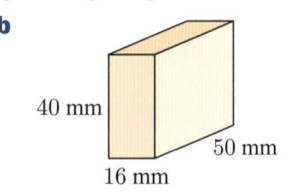

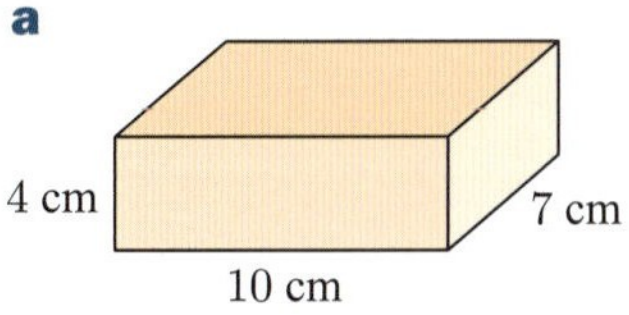

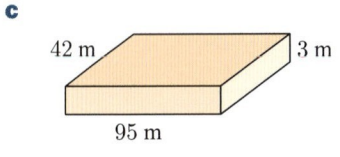

3 Find the surface area of the following triangular prisms:
  a 10 m, 2 m, 8 m
  b 6 cm, 8 cm, 20 cm
  c 4 cm, 6 cm, 9 cm

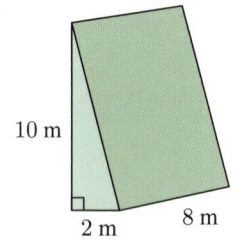

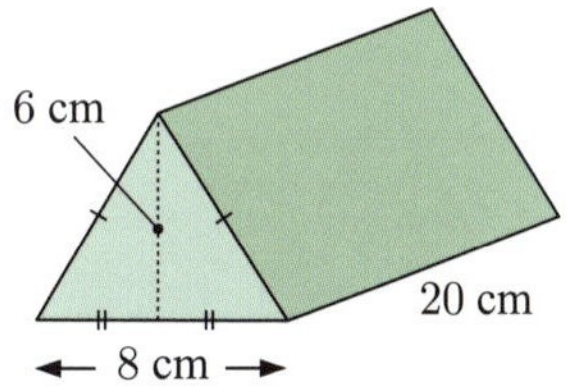

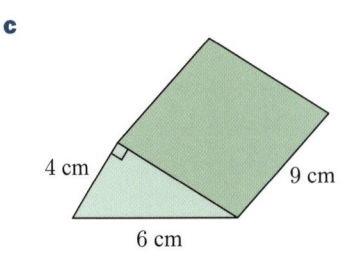

4 Find the surface area of the following square-based pyramids:
  a 9 cm, 12 cm
  b 13 m, 10 m
  c 60 cm

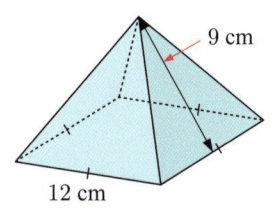

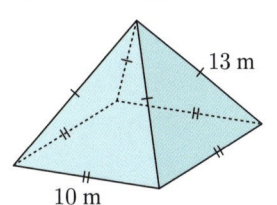

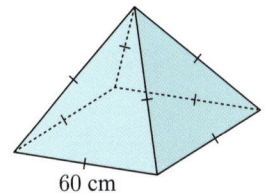

5 Find the surface area of the following prisms:
  a 4 cm, 8 cm, 16 cm
  b 3 m, 5 m, 5 m, 8 m, 10 m
  c 25 m, 12 m, 2 m, 4 m

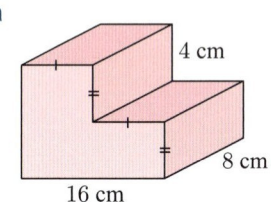

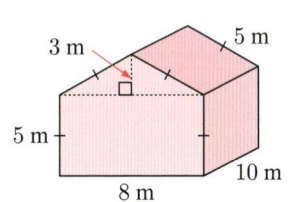

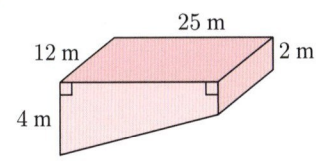

6 A metal pencil box is 20 cm by 15 cm by 8 cm high. Find the total area of metal used to make the pencil box.

7 [bookend diagram: 12 cm, 10 cm, 4 cm, 5 cm]
Tracy owns 8 wooden bookends like the one illustrated.
  a Calculate the total surface area of each bookend.
  b If 50 ml of varnish covers an area of 2000 cm², how much varnish is needed to coat all 8 bookends?

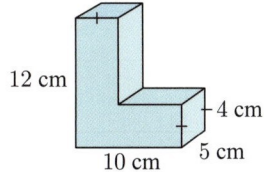

8 Calculate the area of material needed to make this tent. Do not forget the floor. [2 m, 3 m, 3.5 m]

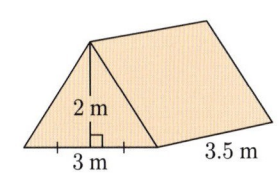

Mensuration (solids and containers) (Chapter 13)

9 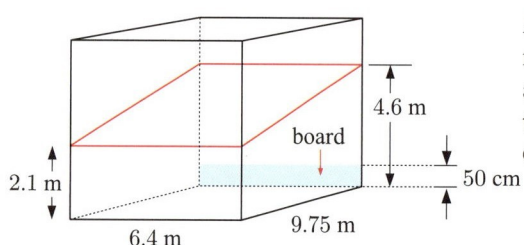 A squash court has the dimensions given. Each shot may strike the floor, or the walls below the red line and excluding the board on the front wall. Calculate the total surface playing area of the walls and the floor. Give your answer correct to 4 significant figures.

Dimensions: 2.1 m, 6.4 m, 4.6 m, 9.75 m, 50 cm (board)

10 Find a formula for the surface area A of the following solids:

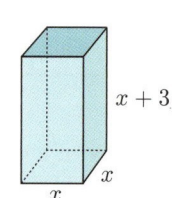

a Rectangular box with dimensions $4x$, x, x.

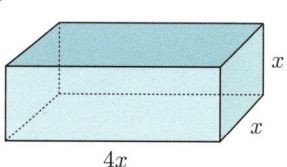

b Rectangular prism with dimensions x, x, $x+3$.

c Triangular prism with dimensions x, $2x$, $x+2$.

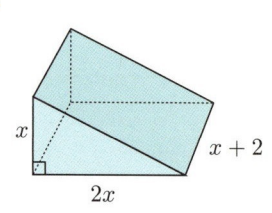

SOLIDS WITH CURVED SURFACES

Not all objects have all flat surfaces. We consider the outer surface area of three common solids which have *curved* surfaces. These are **cylinders**, **cones** and **spheres**.

Cylinders

Consider the cylinder shown below. If the cylinder is cut, opened out and flattened onto a plane, it takes the shape of a rectangle.

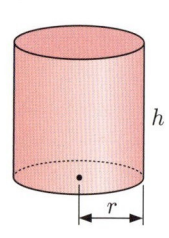

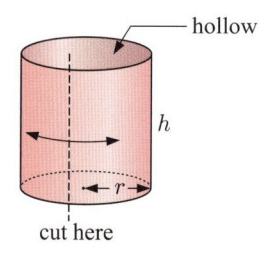

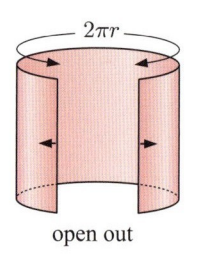

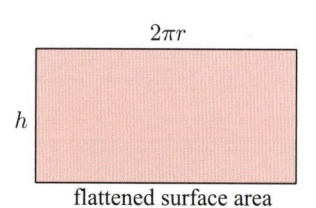

The length of the rectangle is the same as the circumference of the cylinder. You can check that the curved surface produces a rectangle by peeling the label off a cylindrical can and noticing the shape when the label is flattened.

So, for a hollow cylinder, the outer surface area A = area of rectangle

$\therefore A$ = length $\times$ width

$\therefore A = 2\pi r \times h$

$\therefore A = 2\pi r h$

Object	Figure	Outer surface area
Hollow cylinder	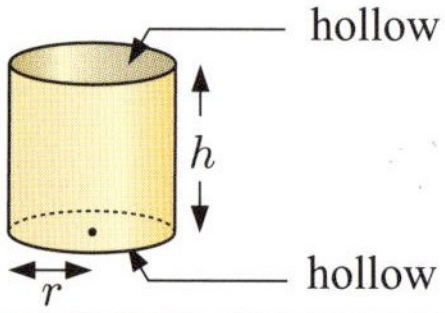 hollow, h, r, hollow	$A = 2\pi r h$ (no ends)

Object	Figure	Outer surface area	
Hollow can	hollow, h, r, solid	$A = 2\pi rh + \pi r^2$	(one end)
Solid cylinder	solid, h, r, solid	$A = 2\pi rh + 2\pi r^2$	(two ends)

Cones

The curved surface of a cone is made from a sector of a circle. The radius of the sector is the slant height of the cone. The arc length of the sector is the circumference of the base of the cone.

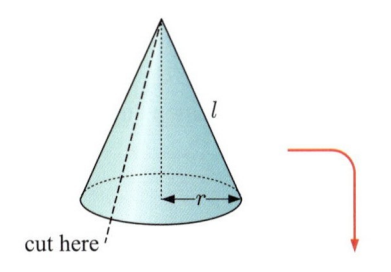

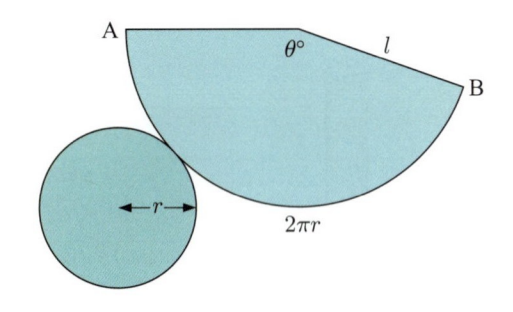

$$\text{arc AB} = \left(\frac{\theta}{360}\right) 2\pi l$$

But arc AB $= 2\pi r$

$$\therefore \left(\frac{\theta}{360}\right) 2\pi l = 2\pi r$$

$$\therefore \frac{\theta}{360} = \frac{r}{l}$$

The area of curved surface $=$ area of sector

$$= \left(\frac{\theta}{360}\right) \pi l^2$$

$$= \left(\frac{r}{l}\right) \pi l^2$$

$$= \pi r l$$

The area of the base $= \pi r^2$

$\therefore$ the total area $= \pi r l + \pi r^2$

Object	Figure	Outer surface area	
Hollow cone	r, l	$A = \pi r l$	(no base)
Solid cone	r, l	$A = \pi r l + \pi r^2$	(solid)

Mensuration (solids and containers) (Chapter 13)

Spheres

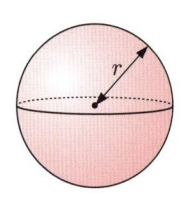

Surface area $A = 4\pi r^2$

The mathematics required to prove this formula is beyond the scope of this course.

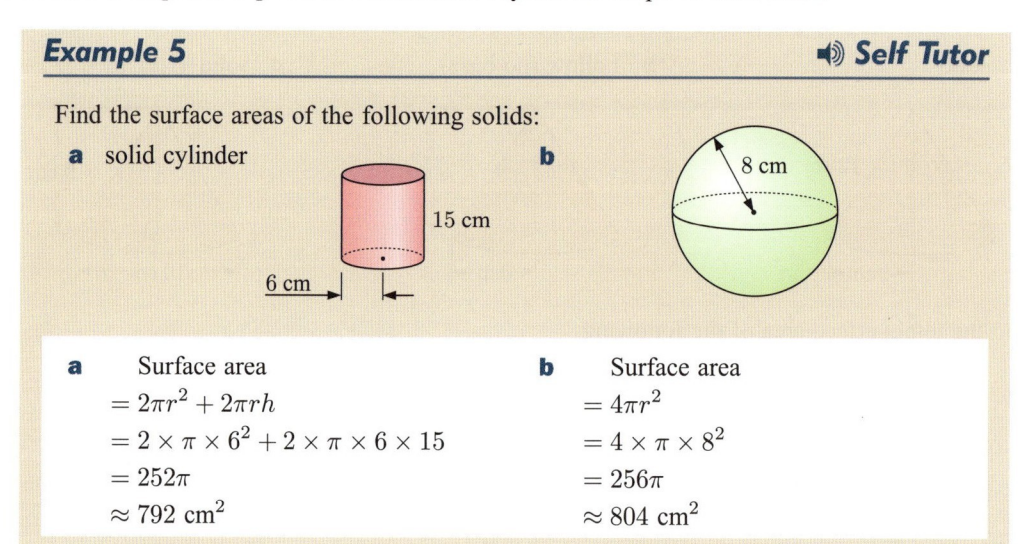

Example 5

Find the surface areas of the following solids:

a solid cylinder (6 cm, 15 cm)

b sphere (8 cm)

a Surface area
$= 2\pi r^2 + 2\pi rh$
$= 2 \times \pi \times 6^2 + 2 \times \pi \times 6 \times 15$
$= 252\pi$
≈ 792 cm^2

b Surface area
$= 4\pi r^2$
$= 4 \times \pi \times 8^2$
$= 256\pi$
≈ 804 cm^2

Example 6

Find the surface area of a solid cone of base radius 5 cm and height 12 cm.

Let the slant height be l cm.

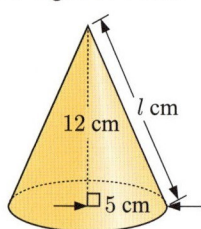

$l^2 = 5^2 + 12^2$ {Pythagoras}
$\therefore \ l^2 = 169$
$\therefore \ l = \sqrt{169} = 13$ {as $l > 0$}

Now $A = \pi r^2 + \pi rl$
$\therefore \ A = \pi \times 5^2 + \pi \times 5 \times 13$
$\therefore \ A = 90\pi$
$\therefore \ A \approx 283$

The surface area is approximately 283 cm^2.

EXERCISE 13A.2

1 Find the outer surface area of the following:

a solid (8 cm, 3 cm)

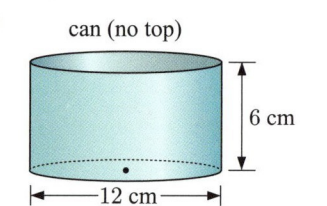

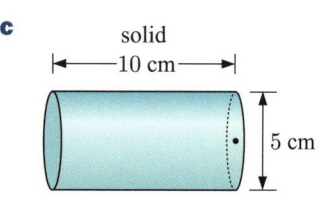

b can (no top) (6 cm, 12 cm)

c solid (10 cm, 5 cm)

d tank (no top) 3.8 m height, 3.8 m diameter

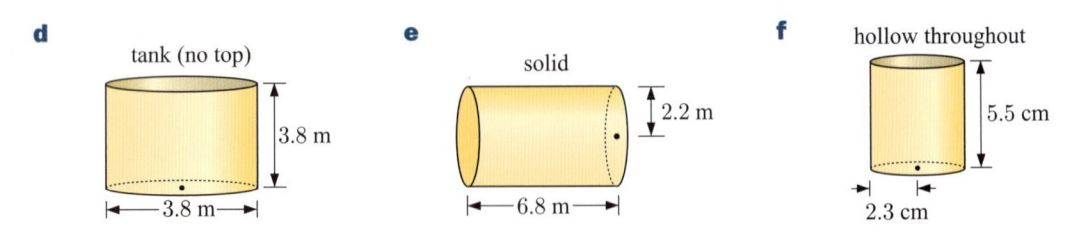

e solid 2.2 m diameter, 6.8 m length

f hollow throughout 5.5 cm height, 2.3 cm diameter

2 Find the total surface area of the following cones, giving your answers in terms of π:
  a solid — 12 cm height, 4 cm radius
  b hollow (no base) — 8 m height, 6 m radius
  c solid — 9 cm height, 10 cm radius

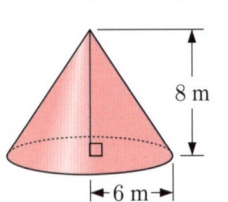

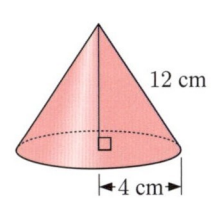

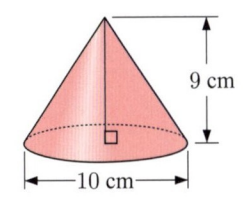

3 Find the total surface area of the following:
  a sphere of radius 20 cm
  b sphere of diameter 6.8 km
  c hemisphere of height 3 cm

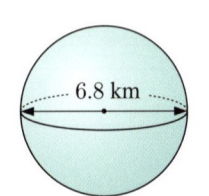

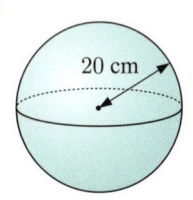

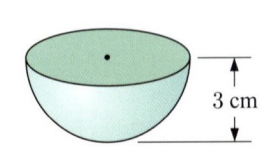

4 Find the total surface area of:
  a a cylinder of base radius 9 cm and height 20 cm
  b a cone of base radius and perpendicular height both 10 cm
  c a sphere of radius 6 cm
  d a hemisphere of base radius 10 m.

5 A ball bearing has a radius of 1.2 cm. Find the surface area of the ball bearing.

6 Find the area of metal required to make the can illustrated alongside. Include the top and bottom in your answer.

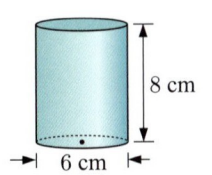

(cylinder: 8 cm height, 6 cm diameter)

7 How many spheres of 15 cm diameter can be covered by 10 m² of material?

8 A conical piece of filter paper has a base radius of 2 cm, and is 5 cm high.
Find the surface area of the filter paper, correct to 3 significant figures.

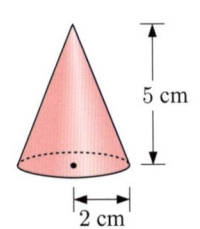

(cone: 5 cm height, 2 cm radius)

9 The Earth's radius is 6371 km. Find its surface area.

10 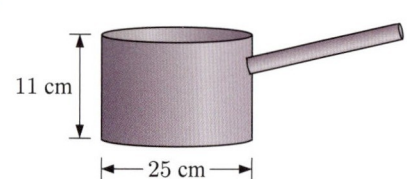 What area of sheet metal is needed to make the saucepan alongside, excluding the handle?

(11 cm, 25 cm)

11 A bicycle horn has a rubber sphere attached to a plastic conical horn. Both the sphere and the cone have diameter 7 cm, and the cone has slant length 12 cm. Calculate the required area of:
  a rubber   **b** plastic.

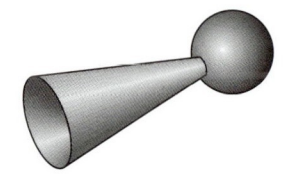

12 Find: **a** the radius of a sphere of surface area 400 m^2
  b the height of a solid cylinder of radius 10 cm and surface area 2000 cm^2
  c the slant height of a solid cone of base radius 8 m and surface area 850 m^2.

13 Find a formula for the surface area A of the following solids:

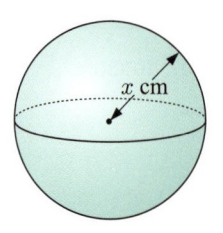

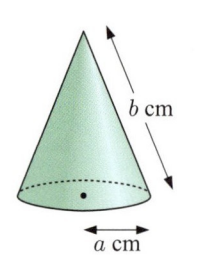

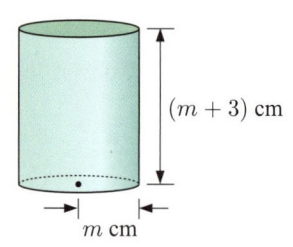

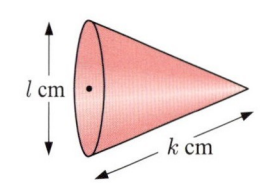

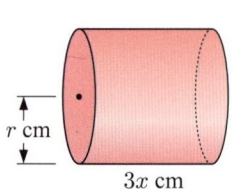

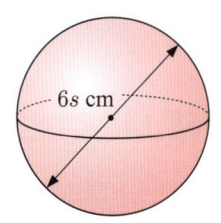

  a sphere, radius x cm
  b cone, slant length b cm, base radius a cm
  c cylinder, height $(m+3)$ cm, radius m cm
  d cone, height l cm, base radius k cm
  e cylinder, radius r cm, height $3x$ cm
  f sphere, diameter $6s$ cm

B VOLUME   [6.1, 6.4]

The **volume** of a solid is the amount of space it occupies. It is measured in *cubic* units.

UNITS OF VOLUME

Volume can be measured in cubic millimetres, cubic centimetres or cubic metres.

Since $1 \text{ cm} = 10 \text{ mm}$, we can see that:

1 cm^3
$= 10 \text{ mm} \times 10 \text{ mm} \times 10 \text{ mm}$
$= 1000 \text{ mm}^3$

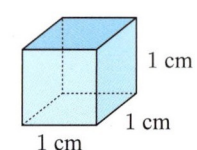

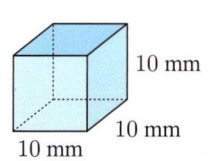

Likewise, since 1 m = 100 cm, we can see that:

$$1 \text{ m}^3$$
$$= 100 \text{ cm} \times 100 \text{ cm} \times 100 \text{ cm}$$
$$= 1\,000\,000 \text{ cm}^3$$

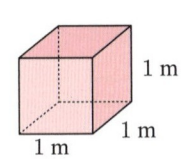

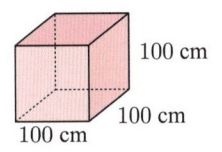

VOLUME UNITS CONVERSIONS

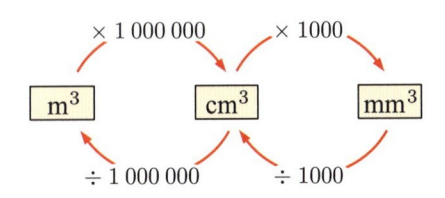

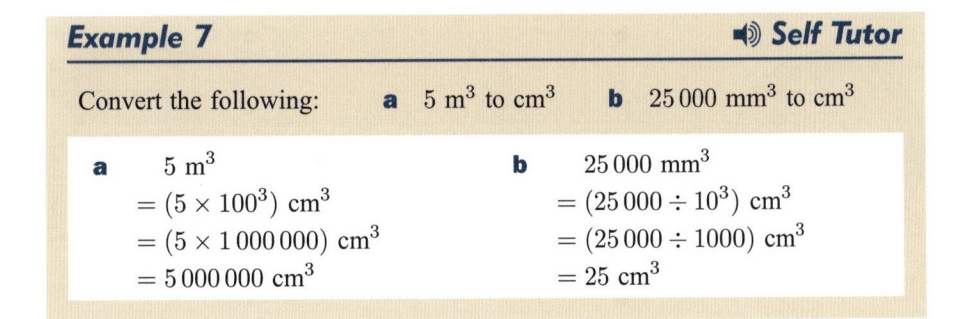

m^3 ×1 000 000 → cm^3 ×1000 → mm^3

m^3 ← ÷1 000 000 cm^3 ← ÷1000 mm^3

Example 7

Convert the following: **a** 5 m³ to cm³   **b** 25 000 mm³ to cm³

a 5 m^3
$= (5 \times 100^3) \text{ cm}^3$
$= (5 \times 1\,000\,000) \text{ cm}^3$
$= 5\,000\,000 \text{ cm}^3$

b $25\,000 \text{ mm}^3$
$= (25\,000 \div 10^3) \text{ cm}^3$
$= (25\,000 \div 1000) \text{ cm}^3$
$= 25 \text{ cm}^3$

EXERCISE 13B.1

1 Convert the following:

   a 8.65 cm³ to mm³   **b** 86 000 mm³ to cm³   **c** 300 000 cm³ to m³

   d 124 cm³ to mm³   **e** 300 mm³ to cm³   **f** 3.7 m³ to cm³

2 1.85 cm³ of copper is required to make one twenty-cent coin. How many twenty-cent coins can be made from a cubic metre of copper?

3 A toy store has 400 packets of marbles on display, and each packet contains 80 marbles. There are 850 mm³ of glass in each marble. Find the total volume of glass in the marbles on display. Give your answer in cm³.

VOLUME FORMULAE

Rectangular prism or cuboid

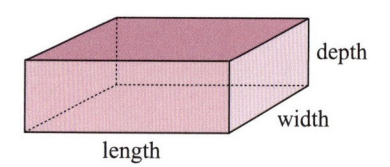

Volume = length × width × depth

Solids of uniform cross-section

Consider the triangular prism alongside. Notice that vertical slices parallel to the front triangular face will all be the same size and shape as that face. We say that solids like this are solids of *uniform cross-section*. The cross-section in this case is a triangle.

Another example is the hexagonal prism shown opposite.

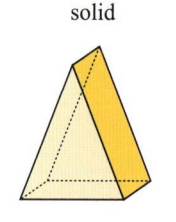

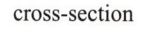

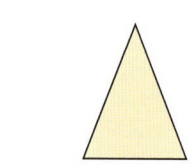

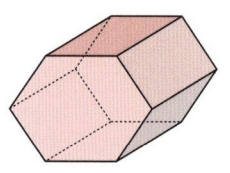

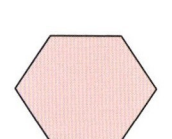

For any solid of uniform cross-section:

Volume = area of cross-section × length

In particular, for a **cylinder**, the cross-section is a circle.

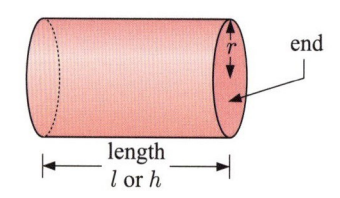

Volume = area of circle × length
$= \pi r^2 \times l$

So, $V = \pi r^2 l$ or $V = \pi r^2 h$

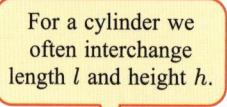

For a cylinder we often interchange length l and height h.

PYRAMIDS AND CONES

These **tapered solids** have a flat base and come to a point called the **apex**. They **do not** have identical cross-sections. The cross-sections always have the same shape, but not the same size.

For example,

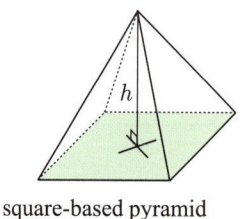

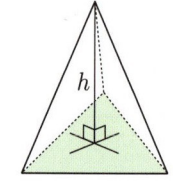

square-based pyramid   triangular-based pyramid   cone

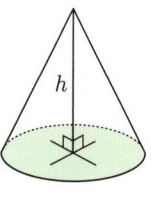

Volume = $\frac{1}{3}$ (area of base × height)

A formal proof of this formula is beyond the scope of this course. However, it may be demonstrated using water displacement. Compare tapered solids with solids of uniform cross-section with identical bases and the same heights.

For example:
- a cone and a cylinder
- a square-based pyramid and a square-based prism.

SPHERES

The Greek philosopher **Archimedes** was born in Syracuse in 287 BC. Amongst many other important discoveries, he found that the volume of a sphere is equal to two thirds of the volume of the smallest cylinder which encloses it.

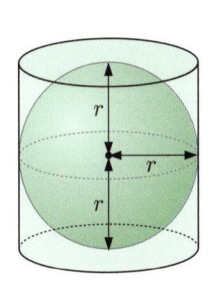

$$\text{Volume of cylinder} = \pi r^2 \times h$$
$$= \pi r^2 \times 2r$$
$$= 2\pi r^3$$
$$\therefore \text{ volume of sphere} = \tfrac{2}{3} \times \text{volume of cylinder}$$
$$= \tfrac{2}{3} \times 2\pi r^3$$
$$= \tfrac{4}{3}\pi r^3$$

Thus $\boxed{V = \tfrac{4}{3}\pi r^3}$

Archimedes' tomb was marked by a sphere inscribed in a cylinder.

SUMMARY

Object	Figure	Formula
Solids of uniform cross-section	height, end (cylinder and prism)	**Volume of uniform solid = area of end × height**
Pyramids and cones	height, base (pyramid and cone)	**Volume of a pyramid or cone = $\tfrac{1}{3}$(area of base × height)**
Spheres	sphere with radius r	**Volume of a sphere = $\tfrac{4}{3}\pi r^3$**

Mensuration (solids and containers) (Chapter 13)

Example 8

Find, correct to 3 significant figures, the volume of the following solids:

a

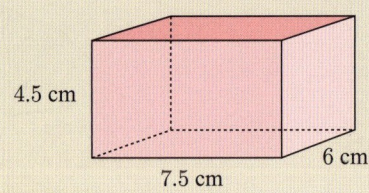

4.5 cm, 7.5 cm, 6 cm

b

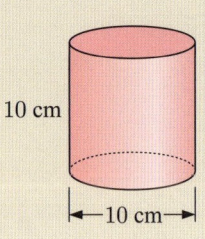

10 cm, 10 cm (diameter)

a   Volume
= length × width × depth
= 7.5 cm × 6 cm × 4.5 cm
≈ 203 cm³

b   Volume
= area of cross-section × height
= $\pi r^2 \times h$
= $\pi \times 5^2 \times 10$
≈ 785 cm³

Example 9

Find the volumes of these solids:

a 12 cm, 10 cm (square pyramid)

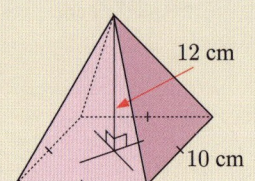

b 10 cm height, 6 cm radius (cone)

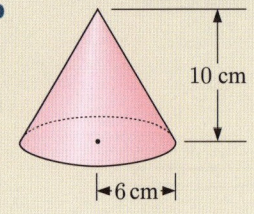

a   Volume
= $\frac{1}{3}$ × area of base × height
= $\frac{1}{3} \times 10 \times 10 \times 12$
= 400 cm³

b   Volume
= $\frac{1}{3}$ × area of base × height
= $\frac{1}{3} \times \pi \times 6^2 \times 10$
≈ 377 cm³

Example 10

Find the volume of the sphere in cubic centimetres, to the nearest whole number:

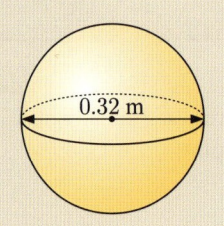

0.32 m

First, convert 0.32 m to cm.

0.32 m = 32 cm

$V = \frac{4}{3}\pi r^3$

∴ $V = \frac{4}{3}\pi \times 16^3$

∴ $V \approx 17\,157$ cm³

Change the units to centimetres before calculating the volume.

EXERCISE 13B.2

1 Find the volume of the following:

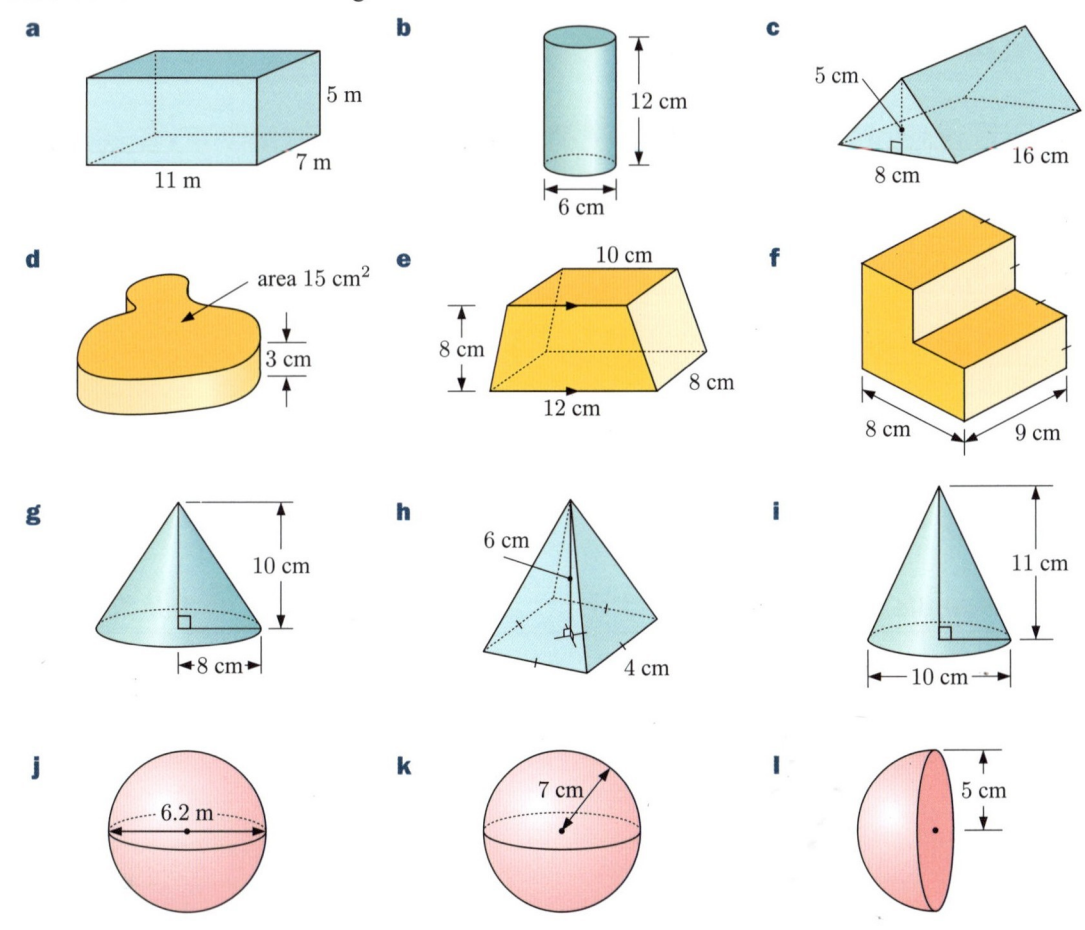

a Rectangular prism: 11 m × 7 m × 5 m

b Cylinder: diameter 6 cm, height 12 cm

c Triangular prism: 5 cm, 8 cm, length 16 cm

d Prism with cross-sectional area 15 cm², height 3 cm

e Trapezoidal prism: parallel sides 10 cm and 12 cm, height 8 cm, length 8 cm

f Stepped solid: 8 cm × 9 cm (with steps)

g Cone: radius 8 cm, height 10 cm

h Square-based pyramid: base 6 cm × 4 cm

i Cone: radius 10 cm, height 11 cm

j Sphere: diameter 6.2 m

k Sphere: radius 7 cm

l Hemisphere: radius 5 cm

2 A beach ball has a diameter of 1.2 m. Find the volume of air inside the ball.

3 A new road tunnel will have a cross-sectional area of 33 m², and will be 2.35 km long. What volume of soil must be excavated to build the tunnel?

4 The roof timber at the end of a building has the dimensions given. If the timber is 10 cm thick, find the volume of timber used for making one end.

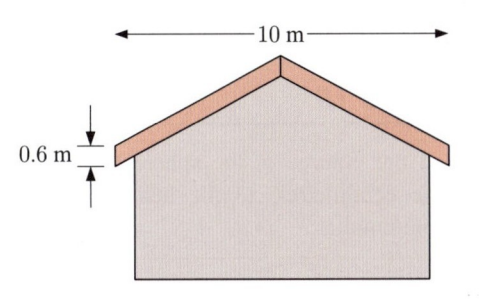

(10 m wide, 0.6 m thick at base)

5 The conservatory for tropical plants at the Botanic gardens is a square-based pyramid with sides 30 metres long and height 15 metres. Calculate the volume of air in this building.

Mensuration (solids and containers) (Chapter 13) 265

6 Calculate the volume of wood needed to make the podium illustrated.

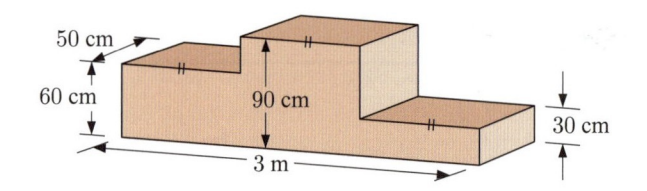

7 A conical heap of gravel is 1.4 m high and has a diameter of 2.6 m. What volume of gravel is in the heap?

8 Find formulae for the volume V of the following objects:

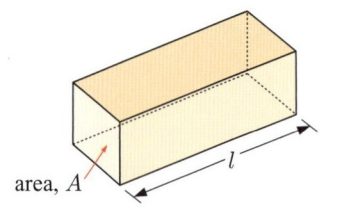

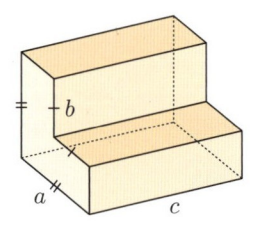

   a area, A, l

   b a, b, c

9 How many spherical fishing sinkers with diameter 1 cm could be made by melting a rectangular block of lead 20 cm by 5 cm by 6 cm and casting the molten product?

10 Find the volume of the British penny, which has diameter 20.32 mm and thickness 1.65 mm.

11 A sphere and a cone have the same volume, and the same radius r.
Find the height h of the cone, in terms of r.

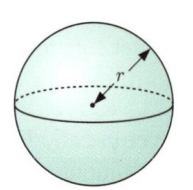

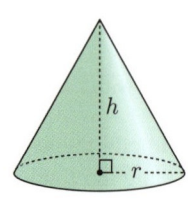

C CAPACITY [6.1, 6.4]

The **capacity** of a container is the quantity of fluid or gas used to fill it.

The basic unit of capacity is the litre.

$$1 \text{ centilitre (cl)} = 10 \text{ millilitres (ml)}$$
$$1 \text{ litre} = 1000 \text{ millilitres (ml)}$$
$$1 \text{ litre} = 100 \text{ centilitres (cl)}$$
$$1 \text{ kilolitre (kl)} = 1000 \text{ litres}$$

To avoid confusion with the number 1, we write out the full word litre.

CAPACITY UNITS CONVERSION

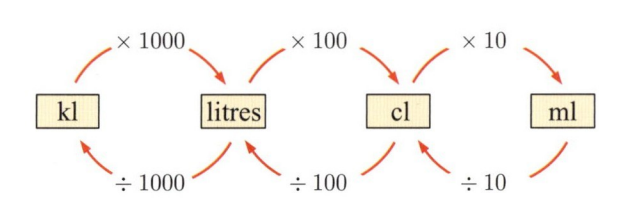

kl —×1000→ litres —×100→ cl —×10→ ml

ml —÷10→ cl —÷100→ litres —÷1000→ kl

Example 11

Convert:
  a   4.2 litres to ml   **b**   36 800 litres to kl   **c**   25 cl to litres

a   4.2 litres
$= (4.2 \times 1000)$ ml
$= 4200$ ml

b   36 800 litres
$= (36\,800 \div 1000)$ kl
$= 36.8$ kl

c   25 cl
$= (25 \div 100)$ litres
$= 0.25$ litres

EXERCISE 13C.1

1   Give the most appropriate units of capacity for measuring the amount of water in a:
    a   test tube   **b**   small drink bottle   **c**   swimming pool
    d   laundry tub   **e**   ice cream container   **f**   medicine glass

2   Convert:
    a   68 cl into ml   **b**   3.76 litres into cl   **c**   375 ml into cl
    d   47 320 litres into kl   **e**   3.5 kl into litres   **f**   0.423 litres into ml
    g   0.054 kl into litres   **h**   58 340 cl into kl

3   An evaporative air conditioner runs on water. It needs 12 litres to run effectively. How many 80 cl jugs of water are needed to run the air conditioner?

4   In one city the average driver uses 30 litres of petrol per week. If there are 700 000 drivers in the city, calculate the total petrol consumption of the city's drivers in a 52 week year. Give your answer in kl.

CONNECTING VOLUME AND CAPACITY

1 millilitre (ml) of fluid fills a container of size 1 cm^3.

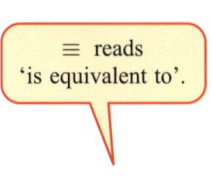

We say: 1 ml $\equiv$ 1 cm^3,   1 litre $\equiv$ 1000 cm^3 and   1 kl $=$ 1000 litres $\equiv$ 1 m^3.

$\equiv$ reads 'is equivalent to'.

Example 12

How many kl of water would a 3 m by 2.4 m by 1.8 m tank hold when full?

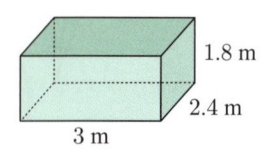

V = area of cross-section $\times$ height
$= (3 \times 2.4) \times 1.8$ m^3
$= 12.96$ m^3

$\therefore$ capacity is 12.96 kl.

Example 13

Water pours into a cylindrical tank of diameter 4 m at a constant rate of 1 kl per hour. By how much does the water level rise in 5 hours (to the nearest mm)?

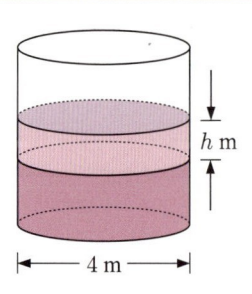

In 5 hours the capacity of water that flows in
$= 1$ kl per hour $\times 5$ hours $= 5$ kl

Since 1 kl $\equiv 1$ m^3, the volume of water that flows in is 5 m^3.

Let the height increase by h m.

Then the volume of water that has entered the tank is:
$$V = \pi r^2 h$$
$$\therefore \ V = \pi \times 2^2 \times h$$
$$\therefore \ V = 4\pi h$$
$$\therefore \ 4\pi h = 5 \qquad \{\text{equating volumes}\}$$
$$\therefore \ h = \frac{5}{4\pi} \approx 0.398 \quad \{\text{dividing both sides by } 4\pi\}$$

$\therefore$ the water level rises 0.398 m.

EXERCISE 13C.2

1 The size of a car engine is often given in litres. Convert the following into cubic centimetres:
 a 2.3 litres **b** 0.8 litres **c** 1.8 litres **d** 3.5 litres

2 a Find the capacity (in ml) of a bottle of volume 25 cm^3.
 b Find the volume of a tank (in m^3) if its capacity is 3200 kl.
 c How many litres are there in a tank of volume 7.32 m^3?

3 Find the capacity (in kl) of the following tanks:
 a 2.1 m, 2.5 m, 4.2 m
 b 2.6 m, 3.4 m
 c 3.2 m, 8.6 m

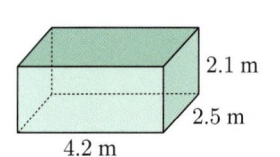

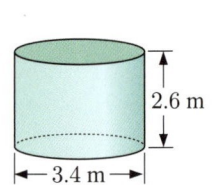

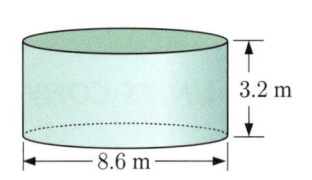

4 A spherical snow globe is made of glass that is 1 cm thick. If the outer diameter of the globe is 12 cm, find the capacity of its interior.

5 How many cylindrical bottles 12 cm high and with 6 cm diameter could be filled from a tank containing 125 litres of detergent?

6 A 1 litre cylindrical can of paint has a base radius of 5 cm. Find the height of the can.

7 The area of the bottom of a pool is 20 m^2, and the pool is 1.5 m deep. A hose fills the pool at a rate of 50 litres per minute. How long will it take to fill the pool?

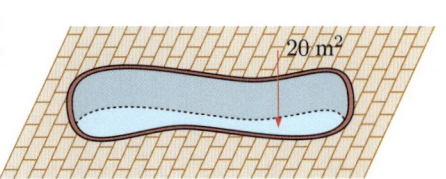

8 Rachael is drinking orange juice from a cylindrical glass with base diameter 6 cm. She takes a sip, drinking 30 ml. By how much does the level of the juice in her glass fall?

9 Consider the following 3 containers:

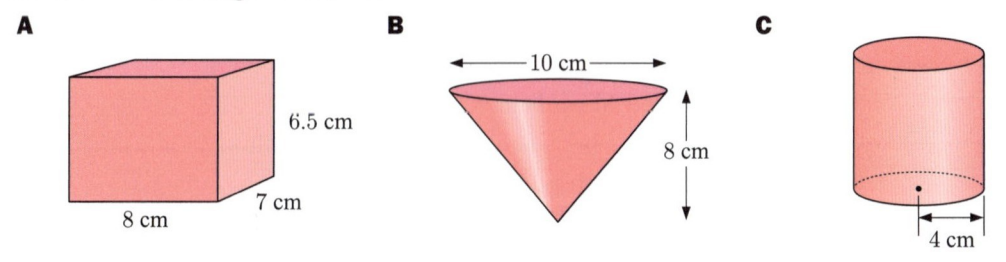

A
6.5 cm
7 cm
8 cm

B
10 cm
8 cm

C
4 cm

Container A is filled with water. The water from container A is then poured into container B until it is full, and the remainder is poured into container C. Find the height of the water level in container C.

10 Answer the **Opening Problem** on page **251**.

D MASS [6.1]

The **mass** of an object is the amount of matter in it.

The SI base unit of mass is the **kilogram**. Other units of mass are connected in the following way:

1 **gram** (g) is the mass of 1 ml of pure water.	1 g = 1000 mg
1 **kilogram** (kg) is the mass of 1 litre of pure water.	1 kg = 1000 g
1 **tonne** (t) is the mass of 1 kl of pure water.	1 t = 1000 kg

MASS UNITS CONVERSION

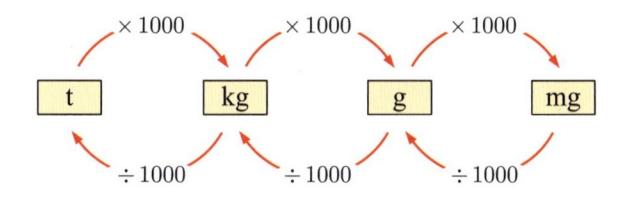

t ×1000→ kg ×1000→ g ×1000→ mg
t ←÷1000 kg ←÷1000 g ←÷1000 mg

DENSITY

The **density** of an object is its mass divided by its volume.

$$\text{density} = \frac{\text{mass}}{\text{volume}}$$

For example, water has a density of 1 g per cm^3.

Example 14

a Find the density of a 430 g brass bell of volume 50 cm^3.

b Pure gold has density 19 300 kg/m^3. Find the volume of a 1.24 kg gold ingot.

a density = $\dfrac{\text{mass}}{\text{volume}}$

= $\dfrac{430 \text{ g}}{50 \text{ cm}^3}$

= 8.6 g/cm^3

∴ the brass bell has density 8.6 g/cm^3.

b density = $\dfrac{\text{mass}}{\text{volume}}$

∴ volume = $\dfrac{\text{mass}}{\text{density}}$

= $\dfrac{1.24 \text{ kg}}{19\,300 \text{ kg/m}^3}$

≈ 0.000 064 2 m^3

≈ 64.2 cm^3

∴ the ingot has volume 64.2 cm^3.

EXERCISE 13D

1 Convert:

  a 3200 g to kg
  b 1.87 t to kg
  c 47 835 mg to kg
  d 4653 mg to g
  e 2.83 t to g
  f 0.0632 t to g
  g 74 682 g to t
  h 1.7 t to mg
  i 91 275 g to kg

2 Kelly has 1200 golf balls each weighing 45 grams. What is the total weight of the balls in kilograms?

3 Estia has 75 kg of timber. She wants to cut the timber into cubes for a children's game. Each cube is to weigh 8 g. If 20% of the timber is wasted due to saw cuts, how many cubes can be made?

4 Calculate:
  a the density of 5.2 cm^3 of stainless steel with mass 40 g
  b the mass of 12 m^3 of willow, which has density 420 kg/m^3
  c the volume of 7 t of aluminium, which has density 2700 kg/m^3.

5 Tim puts 38 l of petrol in his car. If the petrol has density 0.737 g/cm^3, find the mass of the added petrol.

6 Find the densities of these objects in g per cm^3:

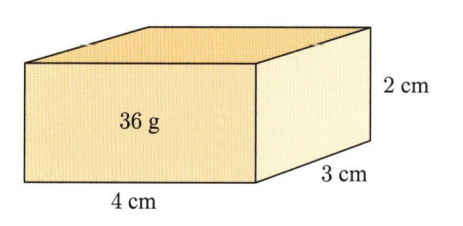

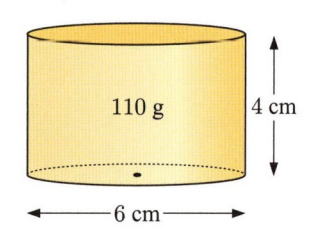

  a rectangular block: 4 cm × 3 cm × 2 cm, 36 g
  b cylinder: diameter 6 cm, height 4 cm, 110 g

7 Laura buys a 1 kg packet of flour. Her rectangular canister is 12 cm by 10 cm by 15 cm high. If flour weighs 0.53 grams per cm^3, will the flour fit in the canister?

8 A cubic centimetre of liquid has mass 1.05 grams. Calculate, in kilograms, the mass of 1 litre of liquid.

9 A rectangular block of metal measures 40 cm by 20 cm by 20 cm. It has a density of 4.5 g/cm^3. Calculate the mass of the block in kilograms.

E COMPOUND SOLIDS [6.5]

We can find the surface area and volume of more complicated solids by separating the shape into objects that we are familiar with.

Example 15

The diagram consists of a cone joined to a cylinder.

Find, in terms of π:
a the surface area of the solid
b the volume of the solid.

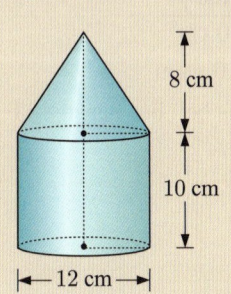

a $l^2 = 6^2 + 8^2$ {Pythagoras}
$\therefore \ l^2 = 100$
$\therefore \ l = 10$

Total area = area of cone + area of cylinder + area of base
$= \pi r l + 2\pi r h + \pi r^2$
$= \pi \times 6 \times 10 + 2\pi \times 6 \times 10 + \pi \times 6^2$
$= 60\pi + 120\pi + 36\pi$
$= 216\pi$ cm^2

b Volume = volume of cone + volume of cylinder
$= \frac{1}{3}\pi r^2 h_{\text{cone}} + \pi r^2 h_{\text{cyl}}$
$= \frac{1}{3} \times \pi \times 6^2 \times 8 + \pi \times 6^2 \times 10$
$= 96\pi + 360\pi$
$= 456\pi$ cm^3

Example 16

A concrete tank has an external diameter of 10 m and an internal height of 3 m. If the walls and bottom of the tank are 30 cm thick, how many cubic metres of concrete are required to make the tank?

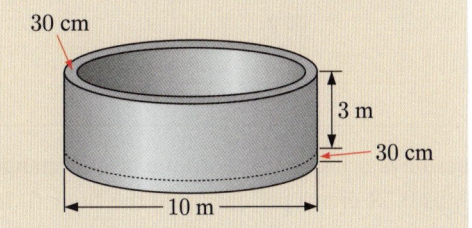

The tank's walls form a hollow cylinder with outer radius 5 m and inner radius 4.7 m. Its bottom is a cylinder with radius 5 m and height 30 cm.

walls of tank: volume = base area × height
$$= [\pi \times 5^2 - \pi \times (4.7)^2] \times 3$$
$$\approx 27.43 \text{ m}^3$$

bottom of tank: volume = base area × height
$$= \pi \times 5^2 \times 0.3$$
$$\approx 23.56 \text{ m}^3$$

Total volume of concrete required $\approx (27.43 + 23.56)$ m$^3 \approx 51.0$ m^3.

EXERCISE 13E

1 Find the surface area and volume of the following:

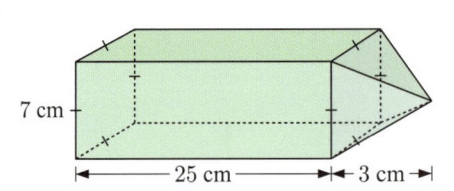

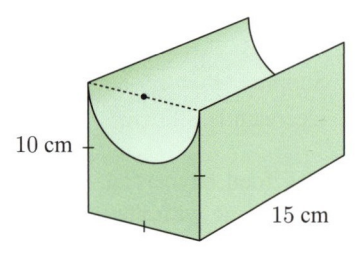

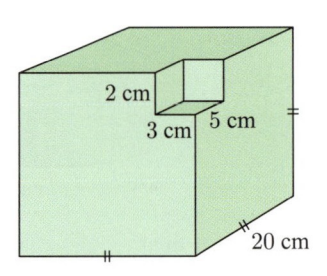

a 7 cm, 25 cm, 3 cm

b 10 cm, 15 cm

c 2 cm, 3 cm, 5 cm, 20 cm

2 A chimney consists of a rectangular prism with two open cubes on top. Find the external surface area of the chimney.

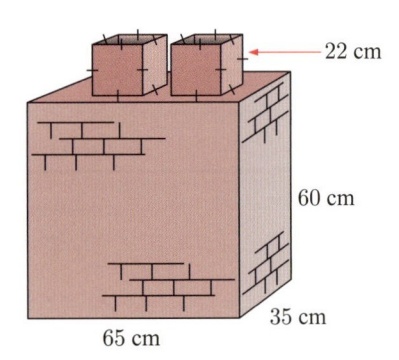

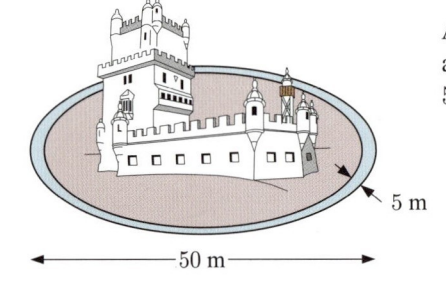

(22 cm, 60 cm, 35 cm, 65 cm)

3 A castle is surrounded by a circular moat which is 5 m wide and 2 m deep. The diameter of the outer edge of the moat is 50 m. Find, in kilolitres, the quantity of water in the moat.

4 a Find the volume of the dumbbell illustrated.
b If the material used to make the dumbbell weighs 2.523 g per cm^3, find the total mass of the dumbbell.

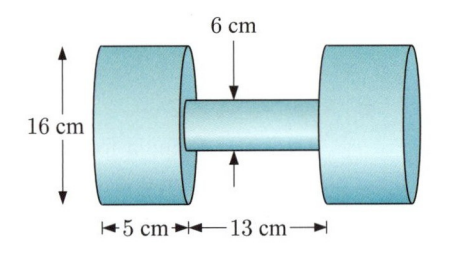

(6 cm, 16 cm, 5 cm, 13 cm)

5 For the given solid, calculate the:
  a surface area
  b volume
  c mass given a density of 6.7 g per cm³.

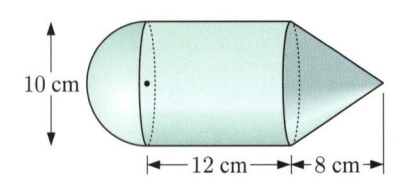

6 **a** Consider the icecream cone opposite, filled with icecream:
     Suppose $r = 3.3$ cm and $h = 10.5$ cm. Find, correct to 3 significant figures, the total:
     i surface area   **ii** volume of the icecream.
  b Suppose $r = 2.9$ cm and the volume is 130 cm³. Find h.
  c Suppose $h = 3r$ and the volume is 115 cm³. Find r.
  d Suppose $r = 4.5$ cm and the total surface area of the cone and icecream is 320 cm². Find the slant length of the cone.

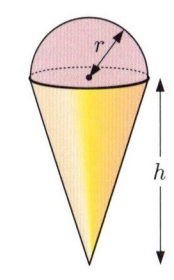

7 This dog food bowl is made in the shape of a 'truncated cone', which is a cone with the top cut off. Find:
  a the slant height of the original cone
  b the surface area of the original cone
  c r
  d the area of plastic required to make the dog food bowl.

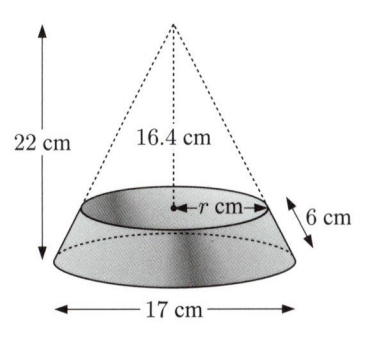

8 Assuming these solids have a density of d g per cm³, find formulae for their:
     i surface area A **ii** volume V **iii** mass M.
  a 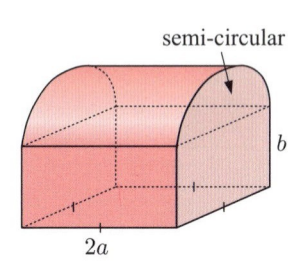
  b

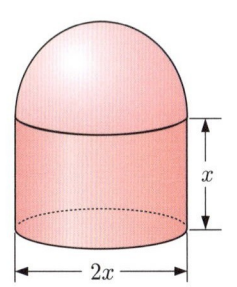

9 An observatory is built as a cylinder with a hemisphere above it.
  a Suppose $r = 4$ m and $h = 5$ m. Find, to 3 significant figures, the observatory's:
     i above ground surface area
     ii volume.
  b Suppose $h = 2r$.
     i Find a formula for the volume of the solid in simplest form.
     ii If the volume is 1944π, find r.
     iii If the above ground surface area is 384π, find r.

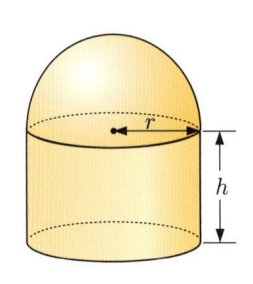

Mensuration (solids and containers) (Chapter 13) 273

10 A cylindrical container with radius 12 cm is partly filled with water. Two spheres with radii 3 cm and 4 cm are dropped into the water and are fully submerged. Find the *exact* increase in height of water in the cylinder.

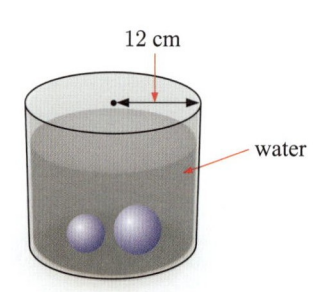

Discovery — Making cylindrical bins

Your business has won a contract to make 40 000 cylindrical bins, each to contain $\frac{1}{20}$ m^3.

To minimise costs (and therefore maximise profits) you need to design the bin of minimum surface area.

What to do:

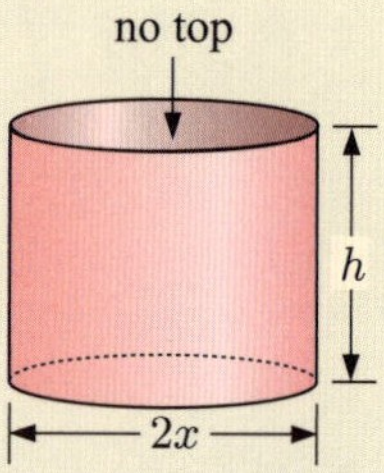

1 Find the formula for the volume V and the outer surface area A in terms of the base radius x and the height h.

2 Convert $\frac{1}{20}$ m^3 into cm^3.

3 Show that the surface area can be written as
$$A = \pi x^2 + \frac{100\,000}{x} \text{ cm}^2.$$

4 Use the **graphing package** or a **graphics calculator** to obtain a sketch of the function $Y = \pi X^2 + 100\,000/X$.
Find the minimum value of Y and the value of X when this occurs.

5 Draw the bin made from a minimum amount of material. Make sure you fully label your diagram.

6 Investigate the dimensions of a cylindrical can which is to hold exactly 500 ml of soft drink. Your task is to minimise the surface area of material required. Remember your container will need two ends.

Review set 13A

1 Convert:
  a 2600 mm^3 to cm^3
  b 8 000 000 cm^3 to m^3
  c 1.2 m^3 to cm^3
  d 5.6 litres to ml
  e 250 litres to kl
  f 56 cm^3 to ml

2 Find the surface area of the following solids:
  a **b** 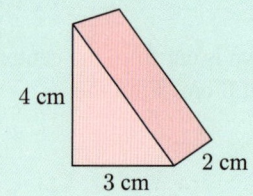 **c**

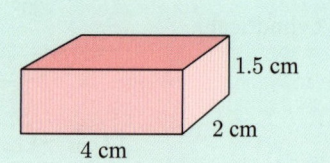

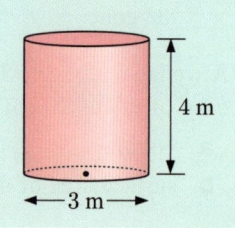

3 A concreting plant manufactures 20 m³ of concrete per hour. The concrete is used to make bollards of volume 216 000 cm³. How many bollards per hour can be made?

4 Find the volume of the following, correct to 2 decimal places:

a 28 cm, 32 cm

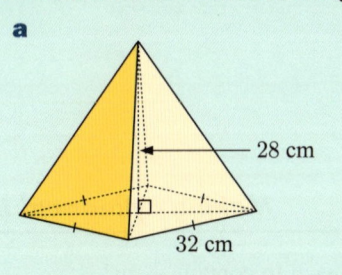

b 4.8 cm, 5.7 cm

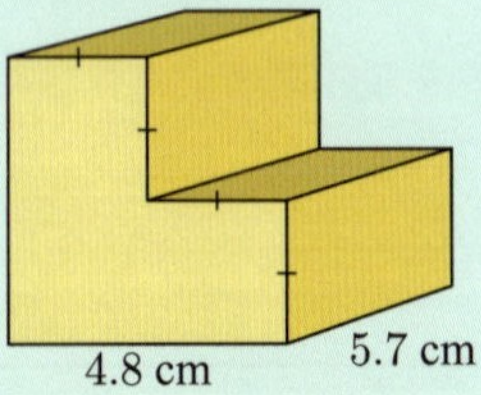

c 5 m, 6 m

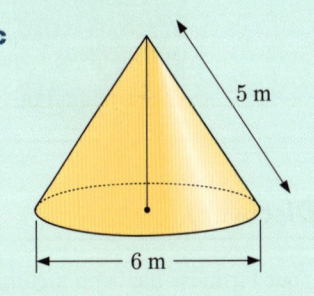

5 2 cm, 2 cm, 3 cm, 3 cm

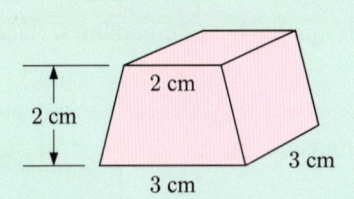

An ice block with uniform cross-section has the dimensions shown on the left. Find:

a the surface area of the ice block

b the volume of the ice block

c the amount of water (in ml) needed to make the ice block

d the number of complete ice blocks that can be made from a 2 l jug of water.

6 Find the density of these objects in g per cm³.

a 72 g, 6 cm, 5 cm

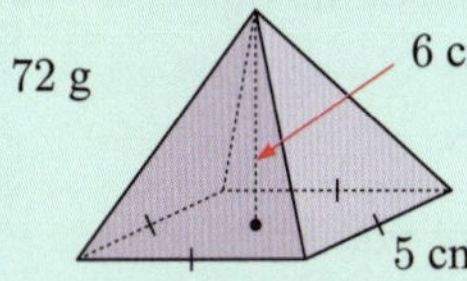

b 85 g, 8 cm

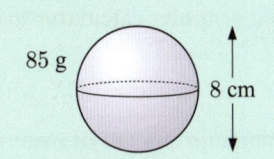

7 Marie has bought a plant which she needs to transfer from its cylindrical pot to the ground. The pot has diameter 10 cm and is 20 cm high. Marie needs to dig a hole 4 cm wider and 5 cm deeper than the pot. She then inserts the plant, and fills in the rest of the hole with extra soil.

  a Find the volume of the hole Marie needs to dig.

  b Before inserting the plant, Marie fills the hole with water. How much water will she need, assuming none of it soaks away?

  c Once the water soaks in, she puts the plant in the hole. How much extra soil will she need to fill the hole?

20 cm, 10 cm

8 **a** Find the radius of a sphere with surface area 200 cm².

  b A solid cone has a base radius of 2 m and a surface area of 10π m². Find the slant length of the cone.

9 A wedge with angle 20° as shown is cut from the centre of a cylindrical cake of radius 13 cm and height 6 cm. Find the:

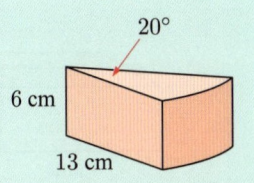

  a volume

  b surface area of the wedge.

20°, 6 cm, 13 cm

Review set 13B

1 Convert:
   a 350 mg to g
   b 250 kg to t
   c 16.8 kg to g
   d 150 ml to litres
   e 260 litres to cl
   f 0.8 litres to ml

2 Find the surface area of the following solids:
   a (cube/rectangular prism: 59 cm, 31 cm)
   b (cylinder: 3.4 m high, 1.5 m diameter)
   c (pyramid: slant 27 mm, base 8 mm × 8 mm)

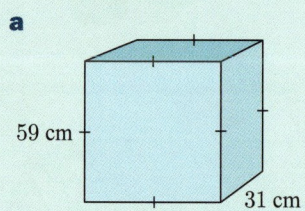

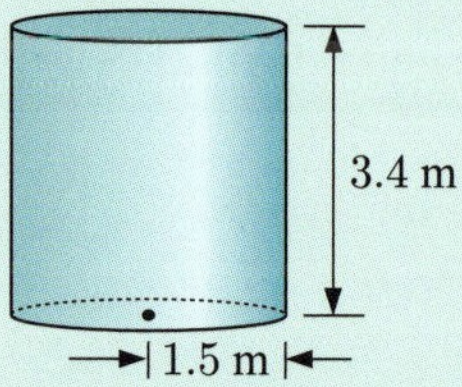

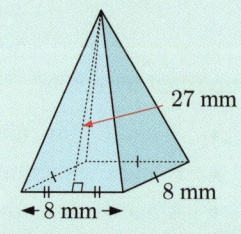

3 Li has a 10 cm × 8 cm × 5 cm block of clay. She wants to mould 50 clay spheres to use as heads for her figurines. Assuming there is no wastage, find the radius of the spheres Li should make.

4 A teapot contains 1.3 litres of tea. 4 cups measuring 270 ml each are poured from the teapot. How much tea remains in the teapot?

5 Find the volume of the following, correct to 2 decimal places:
   a (cylinder: 15 m high, 2.4 m diameter)
   b (cone: 67 cm high, 72 cm diameter)
   c (sphere: 42 cm radius)

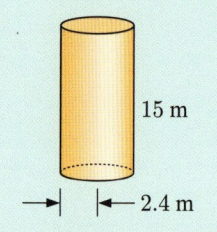

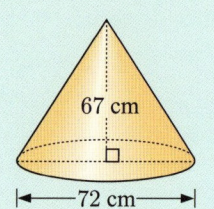

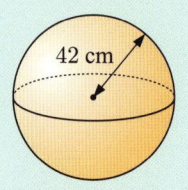

6 A sphere has radius 11.4 cm and density 5.4 g per cm^3. Calculate the mass of the sphere in kg.

7 Gavin uses a cylindrical bucket to water his plants. The bucket is 30 cm wide and 30 cm high. If Gavin fills his bucket 8 times to water his plants, how much water does he use?

8 Calculate the volume of wood in the model train tunnel illustrated. (10 cm, 6 cm, 1 cm, 25 cm)

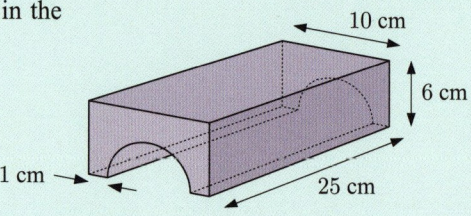

9 A clock tower has the dimensions shown. On each side of the tower there is a clock which is 2 m in diameter. The highest point of the tower is 24 m above ground level.
   a Find the height of the roof pyramid.
   b Find the volume of the tower.
   c The whole tower, excluding the clock faces, is to be painted. Find, correct to 3 significant figures, the surface area to be painted.

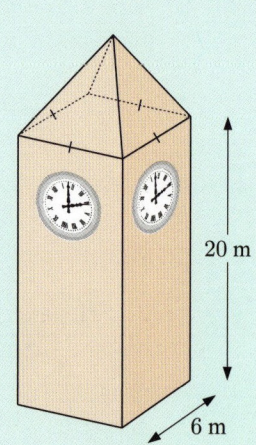

   (tower: 20 m, 6 m)

Challenge

1 You have one 3 litre bucket and one 5 litre bucket.

   a How can you measure exactly 4 litres from the tap?

   b How can you measure exactly 7 litres from the tap?

   5 litres
   3 litres

2 Three pipes A, B, and C, lead into a dam. The dam can be filled by letting:

   - A and C flow for 3 days, *or*
   - B and C flow for 4 days, *or*
   - A and B flow for 6 days.

   Assume that each pipe has water flowing at a constant rate which is not affected by the flow in the other pipes. How long will it take to fill the dam if all 3 pipes are flowing?

Coordinate geometry

14

Contents:

A	Plotting points	[7.1]
B	Distance between two points	[7.1, 7.2]
C	Midpoint of a line segment	[7.3]
D	Gradient of a line segment	[7.1, 7.4]
E	Parallel lines	[7.5]
F	Using coordinate geometry	[7.2 - 7.5]

Opening problem

On the given map, Peta's house is located at point P, and Russell lives at point R.

a State ordered pairs of numbers which exactly specify the positions of P and R.

b State the coordinates of the eastern end of the oval.

c Find the shortest distance from Peta's house to Russell's house.

d Locate the point which is midway between Peta's house and Russell's house.

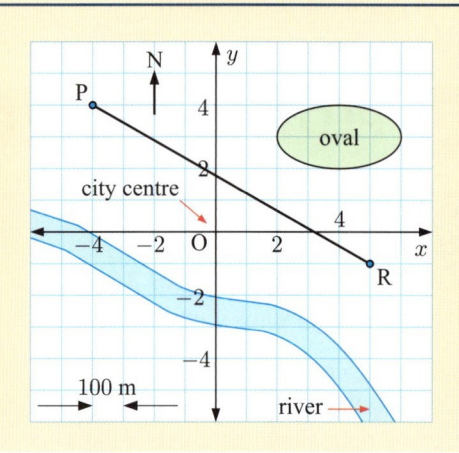

Historical note

History now shows that the two Frenchmen René Descartes and Pierre de Fermat arrived at the idea of **analytical geometry** at about the same time. Descartes' work "*La Geometrie*", however, was published first, in 1637, while Fermat's "*Introduction to Loci*" was not published until after his death.

René Descartes    **Pierre de Fermat**

The initial approaches used by these mathematicians were quite opposite. Descartes began with a line or curve and then found the equation which described it. Fermat, to a large extent, started with an equation and investigated the shape of the curve it described. This interaction between algebra and geometry shows the power of **analytical geometry** as a branch of mathematics.

THE NUMBER PLANE

We start with an origin O. Two perpendicular axes are drawn through O.

The x-**axis** is horizontal and the y-**axis** is vertical. This forms the **number plane**.

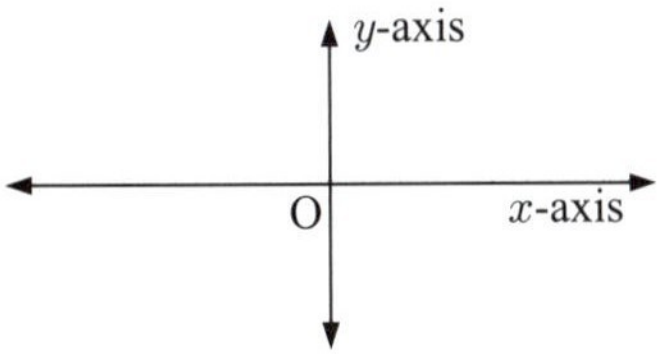

The **number plane** is also known as either:
- the **2-dimensional plane**, or
- the **Cartesian plane**, named after **René Descartes**.

The position of any point in the number plane can be specified in terms of an **ordered pair** of numbers (x, y), where:
- x is the **horizontal step** from a fixed point or **origin** O
- y is the **vertical step** from O.

In the diagram, the point P is at (a, b).
 a and b are referred to as the **coordinates** of P.
 a is called the x-**coordinate**, and
 b is called the y-**coordinate**.

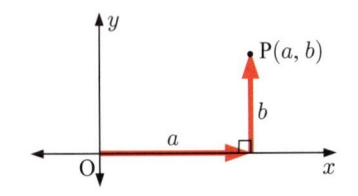

A PLOTTING POINTS   [7.1]

To plot the point A(3, 4):
- start at the origin O
- move right along the x-axis 3 units
- then move upwards 4 units.

To plot the point B(5, −2):
- start at the origin O
- move right along the x-axis 5 units
- then move downwards 2 units.

To plot the point C(−4, 1):
- start at the origin O
- move left along the x-axis 4 units
- then move upwards 1 unit.

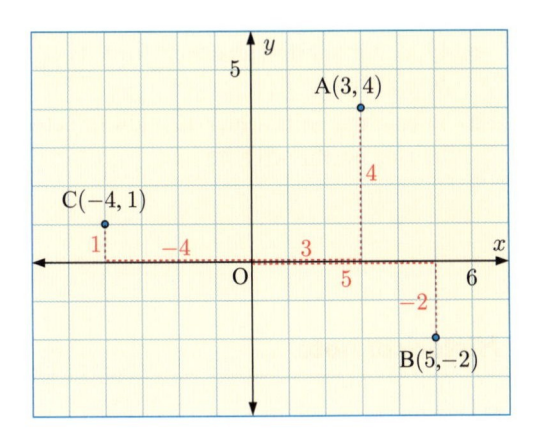

The x-coordinate is always given first. It indicates the movement away from the origin in the horizontal direction.

For A(3, 4) we say that:
3 is the x-**coordinate** of A.
4 is the y-**coordinate** of A.

Coordinate geometry (Chapter 14)

QUADRANTS

The x- and y-axes divide the Cartesian plane into four regions referred to as **quadrants**. These quadrants are numbered in an **anti-clockwise direction** as shown alongside.

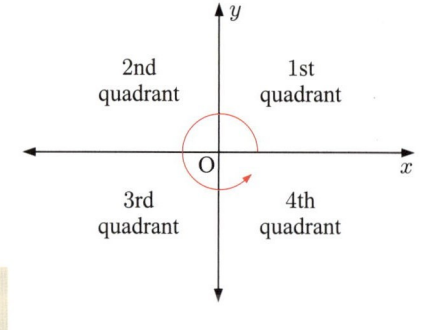

2nd quadrant | 1st quadrant
3rd quadrant | 4th quadrant

Example 1 ◀)) Self Tutor

Plot the points A(3, 5), B(−1, 4), C(0, −3), D(−3, −2) and E(4, −2) on the same set of axes.

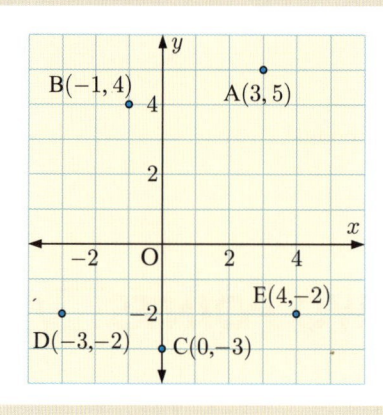

Start at O and move horizontally first, then vertically.
→ is positive
← is negative
↑ is positive
↓ is negative.

Example 2 ◀)) Self Tutor

On a Cartesian plane, show all the points with positive x-coordinate and negative y-coordinate.

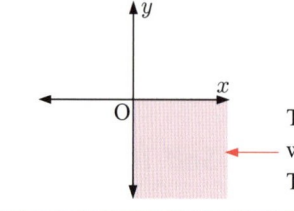

This shaded region contains all points where x is positive and y is negative. The points on the axes are not included.

EXERCISE 14A

1 State the coordinates of the points J, K, L, M and N:

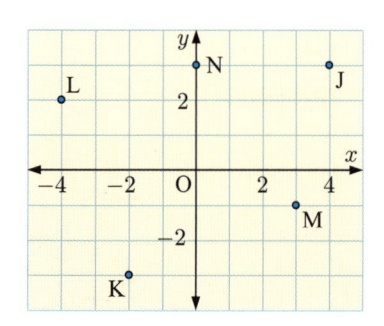

2 On the same set of axes plot the following points:
- **a** P(2, 1)
- **b** Q(2, −3)
- **c** R(−3, −1)
- **d** S(−2, 3)
- **e** T(−4, 0)
- **f** U(0, −1)
- **g** V(−5, −3)
- **h** W(4, −2)

3 State the quadrant in which each of the points in question **2** lies.

4 On different sets of axes show all points with:
- **a** x-coordinate equal to -2
- **b** y-coordinate equal to -3
- **c** x-coordinate equal to 0
- **d** y-coordinate equal to 0
- **e** negative x-coordinate
- **f** positive y-coordinate
- **g** negative x and y-coordinates
- **h** positive x and negative y-coordinates

5 On separate axes plot the following sets of points:
- **a** $\{(0, 0), (1, -1), (2, -2), (3, -3), (4, -4)\}$
- **b** $\{(-2, 3), (-1, 1), (0, -1), (1, -3), (2, -5)\}$
    - **i** Are the points collinear?
    - **ii** Do any of the following rules fit the set of points?
        - **A** $y = 2x + 1$
        - **B** $y = 2x - 1$
        - **C** $y = x$
        - **D** $y = -2x - 1$
        - **E** $x + y = 0$

B DISTANCE BETWEEN TWO POINTS   [7.1, 7.2]

Consider the points A(1, 3) and B(4, 1). We can join the points by a straight line segment of length d units. Suppose we draw a right angled triangle with hypotenuse AB and with sides parallel to the axes.

It is clear that $d^2 = 3^2 + 2^2$ {Pythagoras}
$\therefore d^2 = 13$
$\therefore d = \sqrt{13}$ {as $d > 0$}
$\therefore d = 3.61$

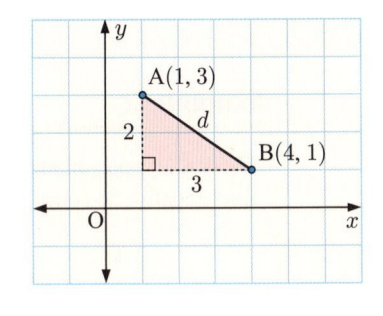

$\therefore$ the distance from A to B is approximately 3.61 units.

Example 3   ◀)) Self Tutor

Find the distance between P(−2, 1) and Q(3, 3).

We construct a right angled triangle with shorter sides on the grid lines.

$PQ^2 = 5^2 + 2^2$ {Pythagoras}
$\therefore PQ^2 = 29$
$\therefore PQ = \sqrt{29}$ units   {PQ > 0}
$\therefore PQ \approx 5.39$ units

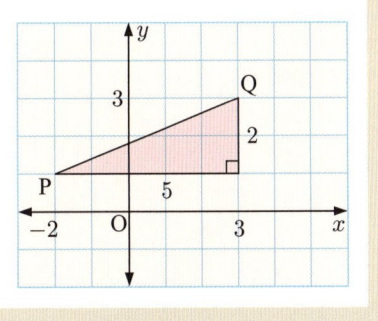

With practice you will not need to use grid paper. A neat sketch will do.

Coordinate geometry (Chapter 14)

EXERCISE 14B.1

1 If necessary, use Pythagoras' theorem to find the distance between:
- **a** A and B
- **b** A and D
- **c** C and A
- **d** F and C
- **e** G and F
- **f** C and G
- **g** E and C
- **h** E and D
- **i** B and G.

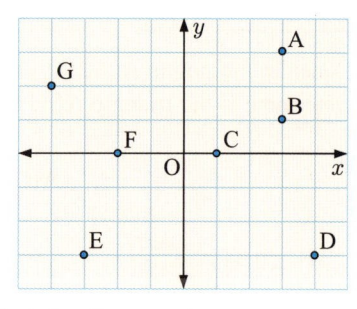

2 Plot the following pairs of points and use Pythagoras' theorem to find the distances between them. Give your answers correct to 3 significant figures:
- **a** $A(3, 5)$ and $B(2, 6)$
- **b** $P(2, 4)$ and $Q(-3, 2)$
- **c** $R(0, 6)$ and $S(3, 0)$
- **d** $L(2, -7)$ and $M(1, -2)$
- **e** $C(0, 5)$ and $D(-4, 0)$
- **f** $A(5, 1)$ and $B(-1, -1)$
- **g** $P(-2, 3)$ and $Q(3, -2)$
- **h** $R(3, -4)$ and $S(-1, -3)$
- **i** $X(4, -1)$ and $Y(3, -3)$.

THE DISTANCE FORMULA

To avoid drawing a diagram each time we wish to find a distance, a **distance formula** can be developed.

In going from $A(x_1, y_1)$ to $B(x_2, y_2)$, the x-step $= x_2 - x_1$, and the y-step $= y_2 - y_1$.

Using Pythagoras' theorem,

$(AB)^2 = (x\text{-step})^2 + (y\text{-step})^2$

$\therefore \quad AB = \sqrt{(x\text{-step})^2 + (y\text{-step})^2} \qquad \{AB > 0\}$

$\therefore \quad d = \sqrt{(x_2 - x_1)^2 + (y_2 - y_1)^2}$.

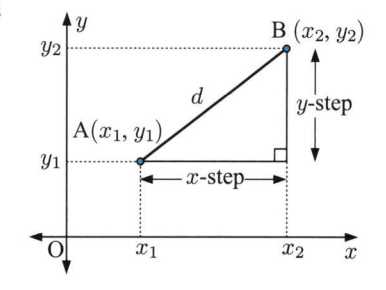

If $A(x_1, y_1)$ and $B(x_2, y_2)$ are two points in a plane, then the distance between these points is given by:

$$AB = \sqrt{(x_2 - x_1)^2 + (y_2 - y_1)^2}$$

or $\quad d = \sqrt{(x\text{-step})^2 + (y\text{-step})^2}$.

The distance formula saves us having to graph the points each time we want to find a distance. However, you can still use a sketch and Pythagoras if you need.

Example 4 ◢) Self Tutor

Find the distance between $A(-2, 1)$ and $B(3, 4)$.

$A(-2, 1) \quad B(3, 4)$
$x_1 y_1 x_2 y_2$

$AB = \sqrt{(x_2 - x_1)^2 + (y_2 - y_1)^2}$
$= \sqrt{(3 - -2)^2 + (4 - 1)^2}$
$= \sqrt{5^2 + 3^2}$
$= \sqrt{25 + 9}$
$= \sqrt{34}$ units
≈ 5.83 units

Example 5

Consider the points A(−2, 0), B(2, 1) and C(1, −3).
Determine if the triangle ABC is equilateral, isosceles or scalene.

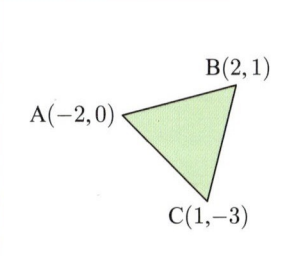

$AB = \sqrt{(2 - -2)^2 + (1 - 0)^2}$
$= \sqrt{4^2 + 1^2}$
$= \sqrt{17}$ units

$BC = \sqrt{(1 - 2)^2 + (-3 - 1)^2}$
$= \sqrt{(-1)^2 + (-4)^2}$
$= \sqrt{17}$ units

$AC = \sqrt{(1 - -2)^2 + (-3 - 0)^2}$
$= \sqrt{3^2 + (-3)^2}$
$= \sqrt{18}$ units

As AB = BC, triangle ABC is isosceles.

EXERCISE 14B.2

1 Find the distance between the following pairs of points:
  a A(3, 1) and B(5, 3)
  b C(−1, 2) and D(6, 2)
  c O(0, 0) and P(−2, 4)
  d E(8, 0) and F(2, 0)
  e G(0, −2) and H(0, 5)
  f I(2, 0) and J(0, −1)
  g R(1, 2) and S(−2, 3)
  h W(5, −2) and Z(−1, −5).

2 Classify triangle ABC as either equilateral, isosceles or scalene:
  a A(3, −1), B(1, 8), C(−6, 1)
  b A(1, 0), B(3, 1), C(4, 5)
  c A(−1, 0), B(2, −2), C(4, 1)
  d A($\sqrt{2}$, 0), B(−$\sqrt{2}$, 0), C(0, −$\sqrt{5}$)
  e A($\sqrt{3}$, 1), B(−$\sqrt{3}$, 1), C(0, −2)
  f A(a, b), B(−a, b), C(0, 2).

C MIDPOINT OF A LINE SEGMENT   [7.3]

THE MIDPOINT FORMULA

If point M is halfway between points A and B then M is the **midpoint** of AB.

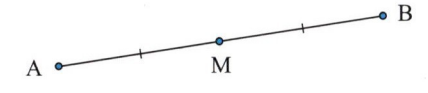

Consider the points A(1, 2) and B(7, 4).

It is clear from the diagram alongside that the midpoint M of AB is (4, 3).

We notice that: $\frac{1+7}{2} = 4$ and $\frac{2+4}{2} = 3$.

So, the x-coordinate of M is the *average* of the x-coordinates of A and B,
and the y-coordinate of M is the *average* of the y-coordinates of A and B.

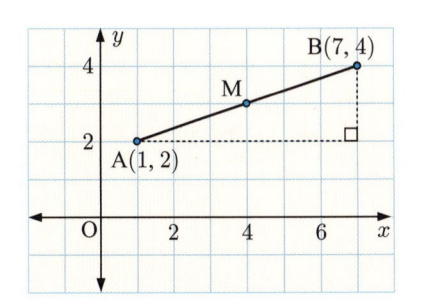

Coordinate geometry (Chapter 14)

If $A(x_1, y_1)$ and $B(x_2, y_2)$ are two points then the **midpoint** M of AB has coordinates

$$\left(\frac{x_1 + x_2}{2}, \frac{y_1 + y_2}{2}\right).$$

We also notice that there are equal steps in coordinates from A to M to B.

For example, consider $A(1, 2)$, $M(4, 3)$ and $B(7, 4)$.

$$\underset{x_1}{1} \xrightarrow{+3} \underset{x_M}{4} \xrightarrow{+3} \underset{x_2}{7} \qquad \underset{y_1}{2} \xrightarrow{+1} \underset{y_M}{3} \xrightarrow{+1} \underset{y_2}{4}$$

Example 6 ◆) Self Tutor

Find the coordinates of the midpoint of AB for $A(-1, 3)$ and $B(4, 7)$.

x-coordinate of midpoint	y-coordinate of midpoint
$= \dfrac{-1+4}{2}$	$= \dfrac{3+7}{2}$
$= \dfrac{3}{2}$	$= 5$
$= 1\dfrac{1}{2}$	

$\therefore$ the midpoint of AB is $(1\tfrac{1}{2}, 5)$.

You may also be able to find the midpoint from a sketch.

Example 7 ◆) Self Tutor

M is the midpoint of AB. Find the coordinates of B if A is $(1, 3)$ and M is $(4, -2)$.

Let B be (a, b).

$\therefore \dfrac{a+1}{2} = 4$ and $\dfrac{b+3}{2} = -2$

$\therefore a + 1 = 8$ and $b + 3 = -4$

$\therefore a = 7$ and $b = -7$

$\therefore$ B is $(7, -7)$.

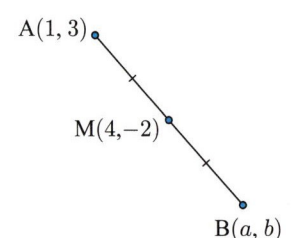

Example 8 ◆) Self Tutor

Suppose A is $(-2, 4)$ and M is $(3, -1)$, where M is the midpoint of AB. Use *equal steps* to find the coordinates of B.

x-step: $-2 \xrightarrow{+5} 3 \xrightarrow{+5} 8$

y-step: $4 \xrightarrow{-5} -1 \xrightarrow{-5} -6$

$\therefore$ B is $(8, -6)$.

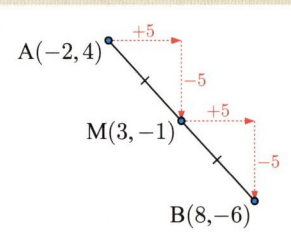

EXERCISE 14C

1 Use this diagram only to find the coordinates of the midpoint of the line segment: 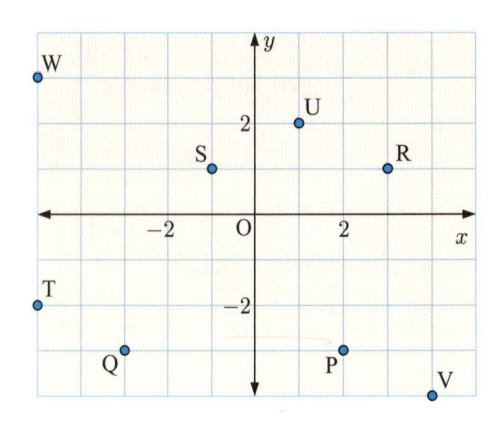
- **a** SR
- **b** QS
- **c** QR
- **d** RU
- **e** SP
- **f** WT
- **g** PV
- **h** VR

2 Find the coordinates of the midpoint of the line segment joining the pairs of points:
- **a** $(8, 1)$ and $(2, 5)$
- **b** $(2, -3)$ and $(0, 1)$
- **c** $(3, 0)$ and $(0, 6)$
- **d** $(-1, 4)$ and $(1, 4)$
- **e** $(5, -3)$ and $(-1, 0)$
- **f** $(-2, 4)$ and $(4, -2)$
- **g** $(5, 9)$ and $(-3, -4)$
- **h** $(3, -2)$ and $(1, -5)$.

3 M is the midpoint of AB. Find the coordinates of B for:
- **a** $A(6, 4)$ and $M(3, -1)$
- **b** $A(-5, 0)$ and $M(0, -1)$
- **c** $A(3, -2)$ and $M(1\frac{1}{2}, 2)$
- **d** $A(-1, -2)$ and $M(-\frac{1}{2}, 2\frac{1}{2})$
- **e** $A(7, -3)$ and $M(0, 0)$
- **f** $A(3, -1)$ and $M(0, -\frac{1}{2})$.

Check your answers using the *equal steps* method given in **Example 8**.

4 T is the midpoint of PQ. Find the coordinates of P for:
- **a** $T(-3, 4)$ and $Q(3, -2)$
- **b** $T(2, 0)$ and $Q(-2, -3)$.

5 AB is the diameter of a circle with centre C. A is $(3, -2)$ and B is $(-1, -4)$. Find the coordinates of C.

6 PQ is a diameter of a circle with centre $(3, -\frac{1}{2})$. Find the coordinates of P given that Q is $(-1, 2)$.

7 The diagonals of parallelogram PQRS bisect each other at X. Find the coordinates of S.

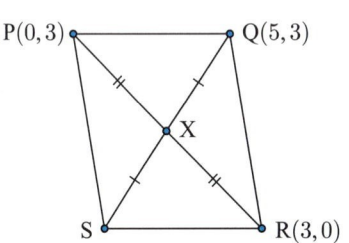

8 Triangle ABC has vertices $A(-1, 3)$, $B(1, -1)$, and $C(5, 2)$. Find the length of the line segment from A to the midpoint of BC.

D GRADIENT OF A LINE SEGMENT [7.1, 7.4]

When looking at line segments drawn on a set of axes, it is clear that different line segments are inclined to the horizontal at different angles. Some appear to be *steeper* than others.

The **gradient** of a line is a measure of its steepness.

The gradient is a comparison between vertical and horizontal movement.

Coordinate geometry (Chapter 14)

If we choose any two distinct (different) points on the line, the **horizontal step** and **vertical step** between them may be determined.

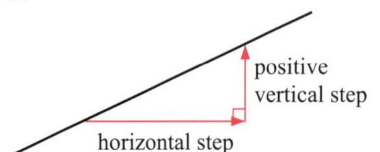

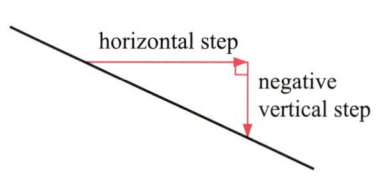

Case 1: *Case 2:*

The **gradient** of a line is found by using: $\dfrac{\text{vertical step}}{\text{horizontal step}}$ or $\dfrac{y\text{-step}}{x\text{-step}}$ or $\dfrac{\text{rise}}{\text{run}}$.

We can see that:
- in *Case 1* both steps are positive and so the gradient is positive
- in *Case 2* the steps are opposite in sign and so the gradient is negative.

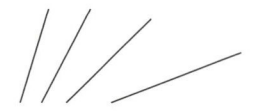

Lines like   are forward sloping and have **positive gradients**.

Lines like   are backward sloping and have **negative gradients**.

Since gradient is a *ratio* of vertical and horizontal change, we can calculate it using any points we choose.

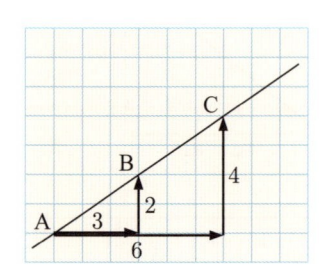

For example, consider the line shown.

Using points A and B, the gradient $= \frac{2}{3}$.

Using points A and C, the gradient $= \frac{4}{6} = \frac{2}{3}$ also.

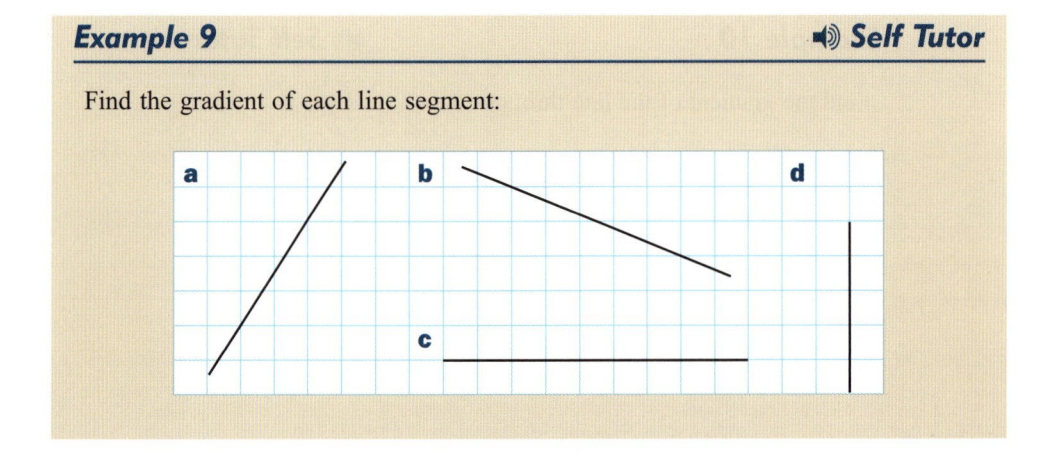

Example 9   ◀)) Self Tutor

Find the gradient of each line segment:

a   b   c   d

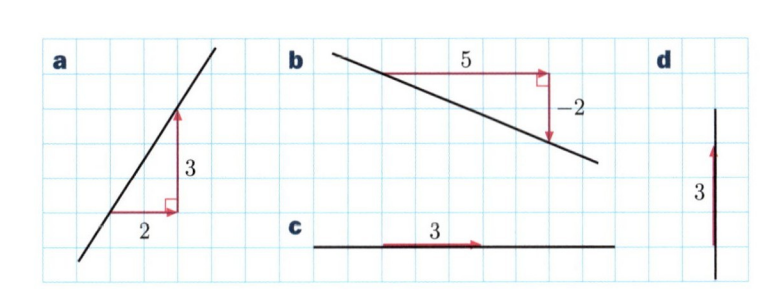

a gradient = $\frac{3}{2}$

b gradient = $\frac{-2}{5} = -\frac{2}{5}$

c gradient = $\frac{0}{3} = 0$

d gradient = $\frac{3}{0}$ which is undefined

We can see that:

> The gradient of any **horizontal** line is **0**, since the vertical step (numerator) is 0. This makes sense because a horizontal line has no gradient.
>
> The gradient of any **vertical** line is **undefined**, since the horizontal step (denominator) is 0.

THE GRADIENT FORMULA

If A is (x_1, y_1) and B is (x_2, y_2), the **gradient** of AB is $\dfrac{y_2 - y_1}{x_2 - x_1}$.

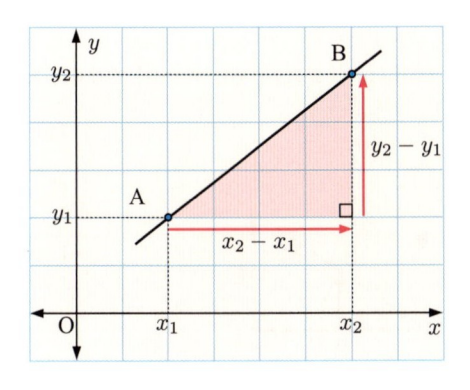

Example 10 ◀) Self Tutor

Find the gradient of the line through $(3, -2)$ and $(6, 4)$.

$(3, -2)$ $(6, 4)$
$\;\;x_1\;\;y_1\;\;\;\;x_2\;y_2$

gradient = $\dfrac{y_2 - y_1}{x_2 - x_1}$

= $\dfrac{4 - -2}{6 - 3}$

= $\dfrac{6}{3}$

= 2

Coordinate geometry (Chapter 14)

Example 11

Draw a line with gradient $-\frac{2}{3}$ through $(2, 4)$.

Plot the point $(2, 4)$.

gradient $= \dfrac{y\text{-step}}{x\text{-step}} = \dfrac{-2}{3}$

$\therefore$ let y-step $= -2$, x-step $= 3$.

Use these steps to find another point, and draw the line through these points.

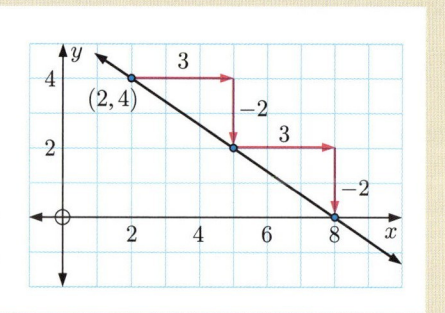

It is a good idea to use a positive x-step.

EXERCISE 14D.1

1 Find the gradient of each line segment:

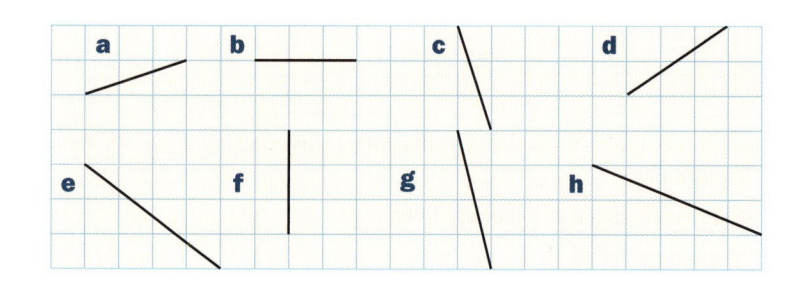

2 On grid paper, draw a line segment with gradient:
  a $\frac{3}{4}$ **b** $-\frac{1}{2}$ **c** 2 **d** -3 **e** 0 **f** $-\frac{2}{5}$

3 Find the gradient of the line segment joining the pair of points:
  a $(2, 3)$ and $(7, 4)$
  b $(5, 7)$ and $(1, 6)$
  c $(1, -2)$ and $(3, 6)$
  d $(5, 5)$ and $(-1, 5)$
  e $(3, -1)$ and $(3, -4)$
  f $(5, -1)$ and $(-2, -3)$
  g $(-5, 2)$ and $(2, 0)$
  h $(0, -1)$ and $(-2, -3)$.

4 On the same set of axes, draw lines through $(1, 2)$ with gradients of $\frac{3}{4}$, $\frac{1}{2}$, 1, 2 and 3.

5 On the same set of axes, draw lines through $(-2, -1)$ with gradients of 0, $-\frac{1}{2}$, -1 and -3.

USING GRADIENTS

In real life gradients occur in many situations, and can be interpreted in a variety of ways.

For example, the sign alongside would indicate to motor vehicle drivers that there is an uphill climb ahead. However, we also use gradients for things that are not physical slopes.

Consider the situation in the graph alongside where a motor vehicle travels at a constant speed for a distance of 600 km in 8 hours.

The gradient of the line $= \dfrac{\text{vertical step}}{\text{horizontal step}} = \dfrac{600}{8} = 75$

But also, speed $= \dfrac{\text{distance}}{\text{time}} = \dfrac{600 \text{ km}}{8 \text{ hours}} = 75$ km/h.

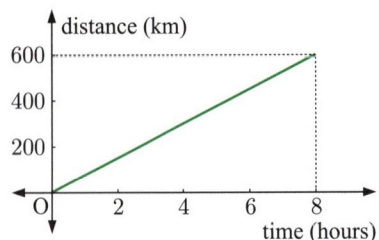

So, for a graph of distance against time, the *gradient* can be interpreted as the *speed*.

In the following exercise we will consider a number of problems where gradient can be interpreted as a rate.

EXERCISE 14D.2

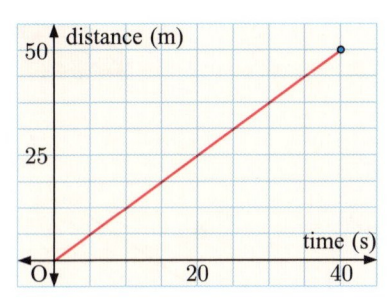

1 The graph alongside indicates the distances and corresponding times as Tan walks a distance of 50 metres.

  a Find the gradient of the line.

  b Interpret the gradient found in **a**.

  c Is the speed of the walker constant or variable? What evidence do you have for your answer?

2 The graph alongside indicates the distances travelled by a train. Determine:

  a the average speed for the whole trip

  b the average speed from

  i A to B **ii** B to C

  c the time interval over which the speed was greatest.

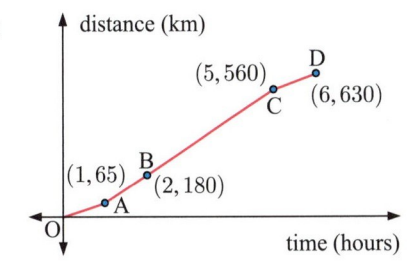

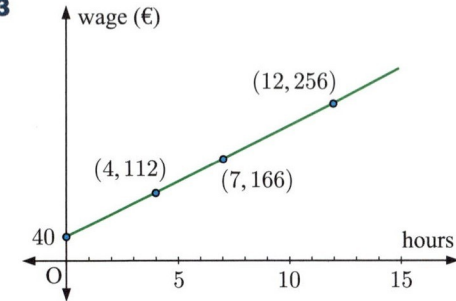

3 The graph alongside indicates the wages paid to security guards.

  a What does the intercept on the vertical axis mean?

  b Find the gradient of the line. What does this gradient mean?

  c Determine the wage for working:

  i 6 hours **ii** 15 hours.

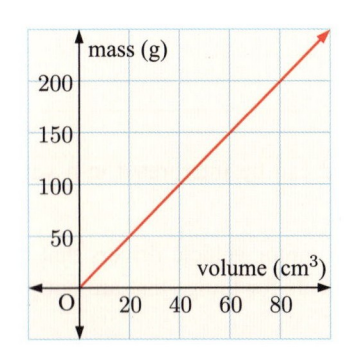

4 The graph alongside shows the mass of different volumes of glass.

  a Calculate the gradient of the graph.

  b Interpret the gradient.

  c Find the volume of 750 g of glass.

Coordinate geometry (Chapter 14)

5 The graphs alongside indicate the fuel consumption and distance travelled at speeds of 60 km/h (graph A) and 90 km/h (graph B).

  a Find the gradient of each line.
  b What do these gradients mean?
  c If fuel costs $1.40 per litre, how much more would it cost to travel 1000 km at 90 km/h compared with 60 km/h?

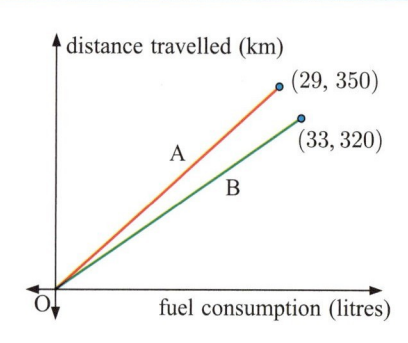

6 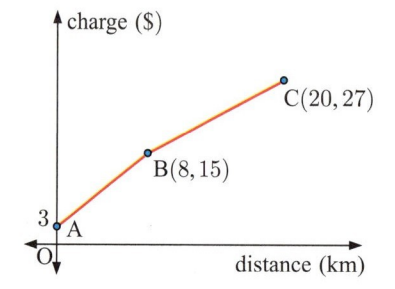 The graph alongside indicates the courier charge for different distances travelled.

  a What does the value at A indicate?
  b Find the gradients of the line segments AB and BC. What do these gradients indicate?
  c If a straight line segment was drawn from A to C, find its gradient. What would this gradient mean?

E PARALLEL LINES   [7.5]

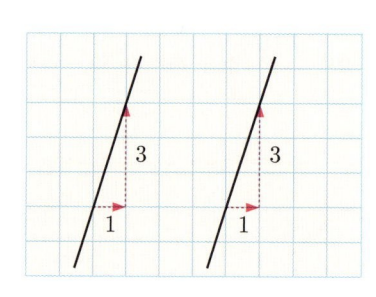

The lines shown are parallel. We can see that both of them have a gradient of 3.

In fact:

- if two lines are **parallel**, then they have **equal gradient**
- if two lines have **equal gradient**, then they are **parallel**.

Example 12   ◀) Self Tutor

Find the gradient of all lines parallel to a line:

  a with gradient $\frac{2}{3}$
  b through A(5, 6) and B(8, −2).

  a Parallel lines always have the same gradient.
  ∴ since the original line has gradient $\frac{2}{3}$, all lines parallel to it also have gradient $\frac{2}{3}$.

  b gradient of AB $= \dfrac{-2 - 6}{8 - 5} = \dfrac{-8}{3} = -\dfrac{8}{3}$

  ∴ all lines parallel to AB will have gradient $-\frac{8}{3}$.

Example 13

The line joining A(2, 3) to B(a, −1) is parallel to a line with gradient −2. Find a.

gradient of AB $= -2$ {parallel lines have equal gradient}

$\therefore \dfrac{-1-3}{a-2} = -2$

$\therefore \dfrac{-4}{a-2} = \dfrac{-2}{1}$

$\therefore \dfrac{-4}{a-2} = \dfrac{-2}{1}\left(\dfrac{a-2}{a-2}\right)$ {achieving a common denominator}

$\therefore -4 = -2(a-2)$ {equating numerators}

$\therefore -4 = -2a + 4$

$\therefore 2a = 8$

$\therefore a = 4$

EXERCISE 14E.1

1 Find the gradient of all lines parallel to a line:
  a with gradient −2
  b through A(2, −5) and B(4, 1)
  c through C(−4, 3) and D(3, 1)
  d through Z(−4, −5) and the origin
  e with gradient $\frac{12}{17}$
  f through P(0, −4) and Q(−3, 8).

2 Identify all pairs of parallel lines:
  A the line through A(−2, 5) and B(1, −1)
  C the line through I(−3, −2) and J(4, −2)
  D the line through the origin and L(12, −9)
  E a line with gradient −2
  F the line through P(6, −5) and Q(−2, 1)
  G the x-axis.

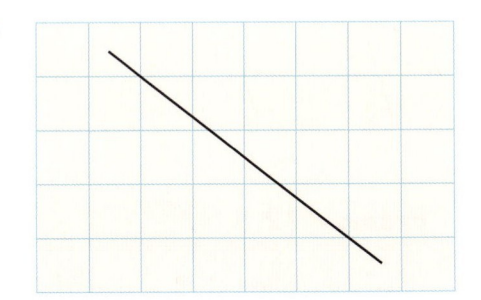

3 Find a given that the line joining:
  a A(1, 3) and B(3, a) is parallel to a line with gradient 3
  b P(a, −3) and Q(4, −2) is parallel to a line with gradient $\frac{1}{3}$
  c M(3, a) and N(a, 5) is parallel to a line with gradient $-\frac{2}{5}$.

4 Consider the points A(1, 4), B(−1, 0), C(6, 3), and D(t, −1). Find t if:
  a AB is parallel to CD
  b AC is parallel to DB.

Coordinate geometry (Chapter 14)

COLLINEAR POINTS

> Three or more points are **collinear** if they lie on the same straight line.

If three points A, B and C are collinear, the gradient of AB is equal to the gradient of BC and also the gradient of AC.

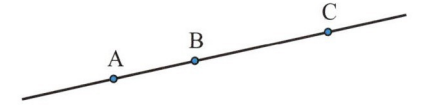

Example 14 ◀) Self Tutor

Show that the following points are collinear: A(1, −1), B(6, 9), C(3, 3).

$$\text{gradient of AB} = \frac{9 - -1}{6 - 1} \qquad \text{gradient of BC} = \frac{3 - 9}{3 - 6}$$
$$= \frac{10}{5} \qquad\qquad\qquad\qquad = \frac{-6}{-3}$$
$$= 2 \qquad\qquad\qquad\qquad\quad = 2$$

∴ AB is parallel to BC, and as point B is common to both line segments, A, B and C are *collinear*.

EXERCISE 14E.2

1 Determine whether or not the following sets of three points are collinear:
  a A(1, 2), B(4, 6) and C(−4, −4)
  b P(−6, −6), Q(−1, 0) and R(4, 6)
  c R(5, 2), S(−6, 5) and T(0, −4)
  d A(0, −2), B(−1, −5) and C(3, 7).

2 Find c given that:
  a A(−4, −2), B(0, 2) and C(c, 5) are collinear
  b P(3, −2), Q(4, c) and R(−1, 10) are collinear.

F USING COORDINATE GEOMETRY [7.2 - 7.5]

Coordinate geometry can be used:
- to **check** the truth of a geometrical fact
- to **prove** a geometrical fact by using general cases.

In these problems we find distances, midpoints, and gradients either from a sketch or by using the appropriate formulae.

Example 15 ◀) Self Tutor

P(3, −1), Q(1, 7) and R(−1, 5) are the vertices of a triangle.
M is the midpoint of PQ and N is the midpoint of PR.
  a Find the coordinates of M and N.
  b Find the gradients of MN and QR.
  c What can be deduced from **b**?
  d Find distances MN and QR.
  e What can be deduced from **d**?

a M is $\left(\dfrac{3+1}{2}, \dfrac{-1+7}{2}\right)$ which is $(2, 3)$.   N is $\left(\dfrac{3+-1}{2}, \dfrac{-1+5}{2}\right)$ which is $(1, 2)$.

b gradient of MN $= \dfrac{2-3}{1-2}$ gradient of QR $= \dfrac{5-7}{-1-1}$
$\phantom{\text{gradient of MN}} = 1$ $\phantom{\text{gradient of QR}} = 1$

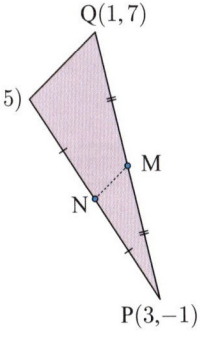

c Equal gradients implies that MN is parallel to QR.

d MN $= \sqrt{(1-2)^2 + (2-3)^2}$ QR $= \sqrt{(-1-1)^2 + (5-7)^2}$
$ = \sqrt{1+1}$ $ = \sqrt{4+4}$
$ = \sqrt{2}$ $ = \sqrt{8}$
$ \approx 1.41$ units $ = 2\sqrt{2}$
 $ \approx 2.83$ units

e From **d**, QR is twice as long as MN. $\{2\sqrt{2}$ compared with $\sqrt{2}\}$

> We can write MN ∥ QR to say "MN is parallel to QR".

EXERCISE 14F

1 Given $A(0, 4)$, $B(5, 6)$ and $C(4, 1)$, where M is the midpoint of AB and N is the midpoint of BC:
  a Illustrate the points A, B, C, M and N on a set of axes.
  b Show that MN is parallel to AC, using gradients.
  c Show that MN is half the length of AC.

2 Given $K(2, 5)$, $L(6, 7)$, $M(4, 1)$:
  a Illustrate the points on a set of axes.
  b Show that triangle KLM is isosceles.
  c Find the midpoint P of LM. Mark it on your sketch.
  d What can be said about lines KP and LM?

> For figures named ABCD, etc. the labelling is in cyclic order.

3 Given $A(3, 4)$, $B(5, 8)$, $C(13, 5)$ and $D(11, 1)$:
  a Plot A, B, C and D on a set of axes.
  b Use gradients to show that:
    i AB is parallel to DC   **ii** BC is parallel to AD.
  c What kind of figure is ABCD?
  d Check that $AB = DC$ and $BC = AD$ using the distance formula.
  e Find the midpoints of diagonals: **i** AC **ii** BD.
  f What property of parallelograms has been checked in **e**?

4 Given $A(3, 5)$, $B(8, 5)$, $C(5, 1)$ and $D(0, 1)$:
  a Plot A, B, C and D on a set of axes.   **b** Show that ABCD is a rhombus.
  c Find the midpoints of AC and BD.

5 Given P(−6, −1), A(2, −5), B(4, 1), and C(5, 4):
  a Plot P, A, B and C on a set of axes.
  b Show that A, B and C are collinear.
  c Find the midpoints of PA, PB and PC.
  d Show that the points found in **c** are also collinear.

6 Consider the points A(−3, 7), B(1, 8), C(4, 0) and D(−7, −1). P, Q, R and S are the midpoints of AB, BC, CD and DA respectively.
  a Find the coordinates of: **i** P **ii** Q **iii** R **iv** S.
  b Find the gradient of: **i** PQ **ii** QR **iii** RS **iv** SP.
  c What can be deduced about quadrilateral PQRS from **b**?

Review set 14A

1 Plot the following points on the number plane:
  A(1, 3)   B(−2, 0)   C(−2, −3)   D(2, −1)

2 Find the distance between the following sets of points:
  a P(4, 0) and Q(0, −3)
  b R(2, −5) and S(−1, −3)

3 Find the coordinates of the midpoint of the line segment joining A(8, −3) and B(2, 1).

4 Find the gradients of the lines in the following graphs:
  a 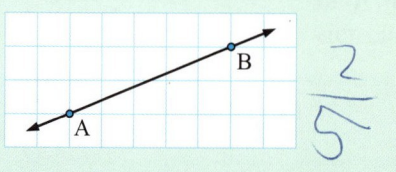
  b

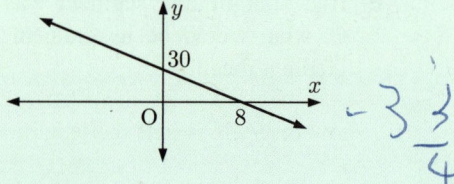

5 The graph alongside shows the distance travelled by a train over a 2 hour journey between two cities.
  a Find the average speed from: 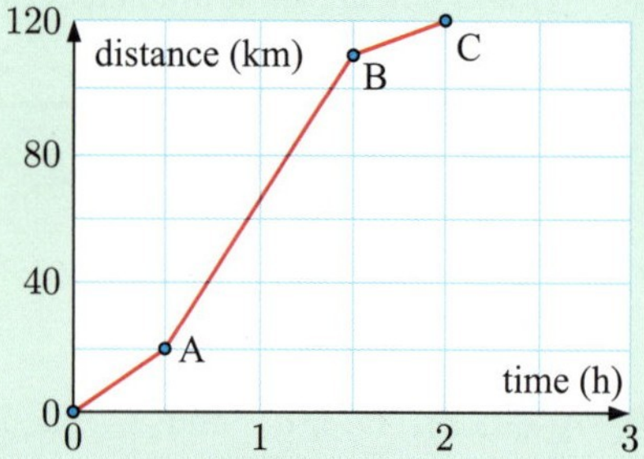
    i O to A   **ii** A to B   **iii** B to C
  b Compare your answers to **a** with the gradients of the line segments:
    i OA   **ii** AB   **iii** BC
  c Find the average speed for the whole journey.

6 Given A(2, −1), B(−5, 3), C(3, 4), classify triangle ABC as equilateral, isosceles or scalene.

7 The line joining X(2, −3) and Y(−1, k) is parallel to a line with gradient $\frac{1}{2}$. Find k.

8 Show that A(1, −2), B(4, 4) and C(5, 6) are collinear.

9 Find b given that A(−6, 2), B(b, 0) and C(3, −4) are collinear.

10 Given A(−3, 1), B(1, 4) and C(4, 0): 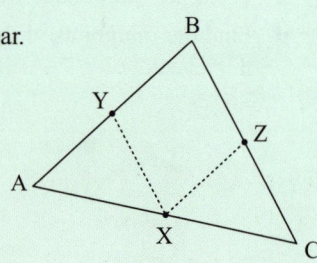
  a Show that triangle ABC is isosceles.
  b Find the midpoints X, Y and Z of the three sides.
  c Show that XY = XZ.
  d What type of quadrilateral is BYXZ?

Review set 14B

1 **a** Find the midpoint of the line segment joining $A(-2, 3)$ to $B(-4, 3)$.
   b Find the distance from $C(-3, -2)$ to $D(0, 5)$.
   c Find the gradient of all lines parallel to a line with gradient $-\frac{3}{2}$.

2 On different sets of axes, show all points with:
   a x-coordinates equal to -3
   b y-coordinates equal to 5
   c positive x-coordinates and negative y-coordinates.

3 Find the distance between $K(-3, 2)$ and $L(3, 7)$.

4 If $M(1, -1)$ is the midpoint of AB, and A is $(-3, 2)$, find the coordinates of B.

5 Find the gradient of the line segment joining:
   a $(5, -1)$ and $(-2, 6)$
   b $(5, 0)$ and $(5, -2)$

6 The graph alongside shows the amount charged by a plumber according to the time he takes to do a job.
   a What does the value at A indicate?
   b Find the gradients of the line segments AB and BC. What do these gradients indicate?
   c If a straight line segment was drawn from A to C, what would be its gradient? What would this gradient mean?

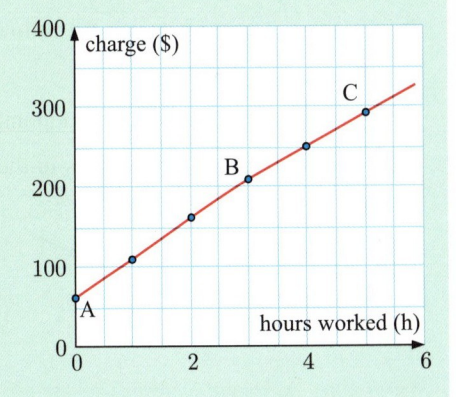

7 AB and CD are both diameters of the circle. Find:
   a the coordinates of D
   b the radius of the circle.

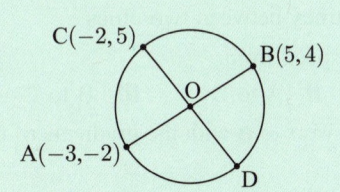

   $C(-2, 5)$, $B(5, 4)$, $A(-3, -2)$

8 $A(-1, 2)$, $B(3, a)$ and $C(-3, 7)$ are collinear. Find a.

9 Given $A(-3, 2)$, $B(2, 3)$, $C(4, -1)$ and $D(-1, -2)$ are the vertices of quadrilateral ABCD:
   a Find the gradient of AB and DC.
   b Find the gradient of AD and BC.
   c What do you deduce from your answers to **a** and **b**?
   d Find the midpoints of the diagonals of the quadrilateral. What property of parallelograms does this check?

Analysis of discrete data

15

Contents:

A	Variables used in statistics	[11.2]
B	Organising and describing discrete data	[11.2, 11.3]
C	The centre of a discrete data set	[11.4]
D	Measuring the spread of discrete data	[11.4]
E	Data in frequency tables	[11.4]
F	Grouped discrete data	[11.4]
G	Statistics from technology	[11.8]

Opening problem

A stretch of highway was notoriously dangerous, being the site of a large number of accidents each month.

In an attempt to fix this problem, the road was resurfaced, and the speed limit was reduced.

To determine if the upgrade has made a difference, data was analysed for the number of accidents occurring each month for the three years before and the three years after the upgrade.

Before upgrade

8 4 9 7   11 10 8 8   6 10 10 9
5 9 6 7   5 7 7 9   8 6 5 7
8 7 2 6   9 7 10 6   8 7 10 8

After upgrade

4 7 8 3   8 4 6 7   8 4 7 7
9 8 6 5   6 8 6 7   7 3 5 5
9 7 8 7   6 6 7 8   8 9 7 4

Things to think about:

- Can you state clearly the problem that needs to be solved?
- What is the best way of organising this data?
- What are suitable methods for displaying the data?
- How can we best indicate what happens in a typical month on the highway?
- How can we best indicate the spread of the data?
- Can a satisfactory conclusion be made?

Historical note

- Florence Nightingale (1820-1910), the famous "lady with the lamp", developed and used graphs to represent data relating to hospitals and public health.

- Today about 92% of all nations conduct a census at regular intervals. The UN gives assistance to developing countries to help them with census procedures, so that accurate and comparable worldwide statistics can be collected.

STATISTICS

Statistics is the art of solving problems and answering questions by collecting and analysing data.

The facts or pieces of information we collect are called **data**. Data is the plural of the word *datum*, which means a single piece of information.

A list of information is called a **data set**. When it is first collected and is not in an organised form, it is called **raw data**.

The process of **statistical enquiry** (or **investigation**) includes the following steps:

Step 1: Examining a problem which may be solved using data and posing the correct question(s).
Step 2: Collecting data.
Step 3: Organising the data.
Step 4: Summarising and displaying the data.
Step 5: Analysing the data, making a conclusion in the form of a conjecture.
Step 6: Writing a report.

CENSUS OR SAMPLE

The two ways to collect data are by census or sample.

A **census** is a method which involves collecting data about every individual in a *whole population*.

The individuals in a population may be people or objects. A census is detailed and accurate but is expensive, time consuming, and often impractical.

A **sample** is a method which involves collecting data about a *part of the population* only.

A sample is cheaper and quicker than a census, but is not as detailed or as accurate. Conclusions drawn from samples always involve some error.

A sample must truly reflect the characteristics of the whole population. It must therefore be **unbiased** and **sufficiently large**.

A **biased sample** is one in which the data has been unfairly influenced by the collection process, and is not truly representative of the whole population.

Analysis of discrete data (Chapter 15) 297

A VARIABLES USED IN STATISTICS [11.2]

There are two types of variables that we commonly deal with: **categorical** variables and **quantitative** variables.

> A **categorical variable** is one which describes a particular quality or characteristic.
> It can be divided into **categories**. The information collected is called **categorical data**.

Examples of categorical variables are:

- *Getting to school*: the categories could be train, bus, car and walking.
- *Colour of eyes*: the categories could be blue, brown, hazel, green, and grey.

We saw examples of categorical variables in **Chapter 6**.

> A **quantitative variable** is one which has a numerical value, and is often called a **numerical variable**.
> The information collected is called **numerical data**.

Quantitative variables can be either **discrete** or **continuous**.

> A **quantitative discrete variable** takes exact number values and is often a result of **counting**.

Examples of discrete quantitative variables are:

- *The number of people in a household*: the variable could take the values 1, 2, 3, ...
- *The score out of 30 for a test*: the variable could take the values 0, 1, 2, 3, ..., 30.
- *The times on a digital watch*: `12:15`

> A **quantitative continuous variable** takes numerical values within a certain continuous range. It is usually a result of **measuring**.

Examples of quantitative continuous variables are:

- *The weights of newborn babies*: the variable could take any positive value on the number line, but is likely to be in the range 0.5 kg to 7 kg.
- *The heights of Year 10 students*: the variable could be measured in centimetres. A student whose height is recorded as 145 cm could have exact height anywhere between 144.5 cm and 145.5 cm.
- *The times on an analogue watch*:

In this chapter we will focus on **discrete** variables. Continuous variables will be covered in **Chapter 19**.

INTERNET STATISTICS

There are thousands of sites worldwide which display statistics for everyone to see. Sites which show statistics that are important on a global scale include:

- *www.un.org*   for the United Nations
- *www.who.int*   for the World Health Organisation

EXERCISE 15A

1. Classify the following variables as either categorical or numerical:
   - **a** the brand of shoes a person is wearing
   - **b** the number of cousins a person has
   - **c** voting intention at the next election
   - **d** the number of cars in a household
   - **e** the temperature of coffee in a mug
   - **f** favourite type of apple
   - **g** the town or city where a person was born
   - **h** the cost of houses on a street

2. Write down the possible categories for the following categorical variables:
   - **a** gender
   - **b** favourite football code
   - **c** hair colour

3. State whether a census or a sample would be used for these investigations:
   - **a** the reasons for people using taxis
   - **b** the heights of the basketballers at a particular school
   - **c** the percentage of people in a city who suffer from asthma
   - **d** the resting pulse rates of members of your favourite sporting team
   - **e** the number of pets in Canadian households
   - **f** the amount of daylight each month where you live

4. Discuss any possible bias in the following situations:
   - **a** Only Year 12 students are interviewed about changes to the school uniform.
   - **b** Motorists stopped in peak hour are interviewed about traffic problems.
   - **c** A phone poll where participants must vote by text message.
   - **d** A 'who will you vote for' survey at an expensive city restaurant.

5. For each of the following possible investigations, classify the variable as either quantitative discrete or quantitative continuous:
   - **a** the number of clocks in each house
   - **b** the weights of the members of a basketball team
   - **c** the number of kittens in each litter
   - **d** the number of bread rolls bought each week by a family
   - **e** the number of leaves on a rose plant stem
   - **f** the amount of soup in each can
   - **g** the number of people who die from heart attacks each year in a given city
   - **h** the amount of rainfall in each month of the year
   - **i** the stopping distances of cars travelling at 80 km/h
   - **j** the number of cars passing through an intersection each hour

B ORGANISING AND DESCRIBING DISCRETE DATA [11.2, 11.3]

In the **Opening Problem** on page **295**, the quantitative discrete variable is *the number of accidents per month*.

To organise the data a **tally-frequency table** could be used. We count the data systematically and use a '|' to indicate each data value. We use |||| to represent 5.

Analysis of discrete data (Chapter 15)

Below is the table for *Before upgrade*:

No. of accidents/month	Tally	Frequency
2	|	1
3		0
4	|	1
5					3
6							5
7										8
8									7
9							5
10							5
11	|	1
	Total	36

A **vertical bar chart** could be used to display this data:

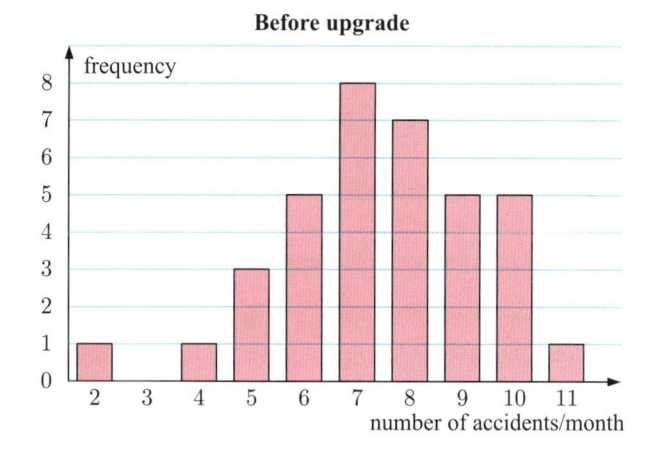

Before upgrade

DESCRIBING THE DISTRIBUTION OF A DATA SET

The **mode** of a data set is the most frequently occurring value(s). Many data sets show **symmetry** or **partial symmetry** about the mode.

If we place a curve over the vertical bar chart we see that this curve shows symmetry. We say that we have a **symmetrical distribution**.

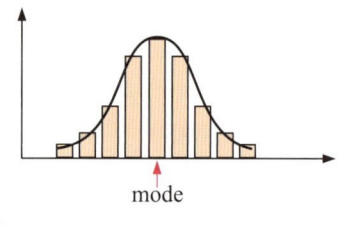

The distribution alongside is said to be **negatively skewed**. By comparison with the symmetrical distribution, it has been 'stretched' on the left (or negative) side of the mode.

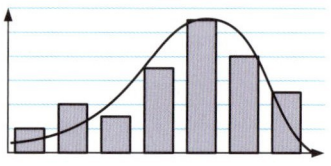

So, we have:

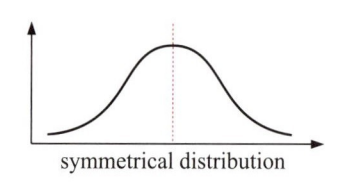

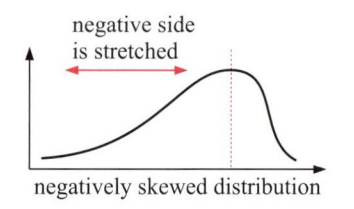

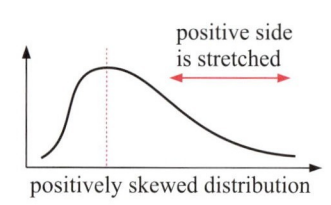

symmetrical distribution   negatively skewed distribution   positively skewed distribution

EXERCISE 15B.1

1 20 students were asked "How many pets do you have in your household?" and the following data was collected: 2 1 0 3 1 2 1 3 4 0 0 2 2 0 1 1 0 1 0 1

  a What is the variable in this investigation?
  b Is the data discrete or continuous? Why?
  c Construct a vertical bar chart to display the data. Use a heading for the graph, and add an appropriate scale and label to each axis.
  d How would you describe the distribution of the data? Is it symmetrical, positively skewed, or negatively skewed?
  e What percentage of the households had no pets?
  f What percentage of the households had three or more pets?

2 A randomly selected sample of shoppers was asked, 'How many times did you shop at a supermarket in the past week?' A column graph was constructed for the results.

  a How many shoppers gave data in the survey?

  b How many of the shoppers shopped once or twice?

  c What percentage of the shoppers shopped more than four times?

  d Describe the distribution of the data. Interpret this result.

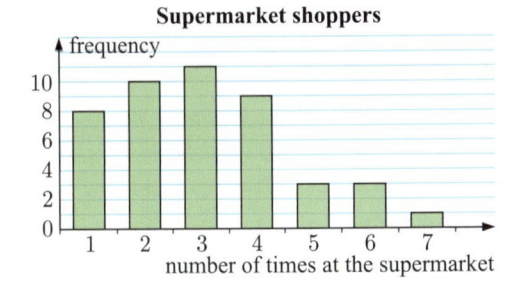

3 The number of toothpicks in a box is stated as 50 but the actual number of toothpicks has been found to vary. To investigate this, the number of toothpicks in a box was counted for a sample of 60 boxes:

50 52 51 50 50 51 52 49 50 48 51 50 47 50 52 48 50 49 51 50
49 50 52 51 50 50 52 50 53 48 50 51 50 50 49 48 51 49 52 50
49 49 50 52 50 51 49 52 52 50 49 50 49 51 50 50 51 50 53 48

  a What is the variable in this investigation?

  b Is the data continuous or discrete?

  c Construct a frequency table for this data.

  d Display the data using a bar chart.

  e Describe the distribution of the data.

  f What percentage of the boxes contained exactly 50 toothpicks?

4 Revisit the **Opening Problem** on page **295**.

  a Organise the *After upgrade* data in a tally-frequency table.

  b Is the *After upgrade* data skewed?

  c Draw a side-by-side vertical bar chart of the data. (Use the graph on page **299** to help.)

  d What evidence is there that the safety upgrade has made a difference?

GROUPED DISCRETE DATA

In situations where there are lots of different numerical values recorded, it may not be practical to use an ordinary tally-frequency table. In these cases, it is often best to **group** the data into **class intervals**. We can then display the grouped data in a bar chart.

For example, a local hardware store is interested in the number of people visiting the store at lunch time.

Over 30 consecutive weekdays they recorded the following data:

37 30 17 13 46 23 40 28 38 24 23 22 18 29 16
35 24 18 24 44 32 54 31 39 32 38 41 38 24 32

In this case we group the data into class intervals of length 10. The tally-frequency table is shown below. We then use the table to construct a vertical bar chart.

The first column represents the values from 10 to 19, the second from 20 to 29, and so on.

Analysis of discrete data (Chapter 15)

Number of people	Tally	Frequency
10 to 19	|||||	5
20 to 29	||||| ||||	9
30 to 39	||||| |||||		11
40 to 49	||||	4
50 to 59			1
	Total	30

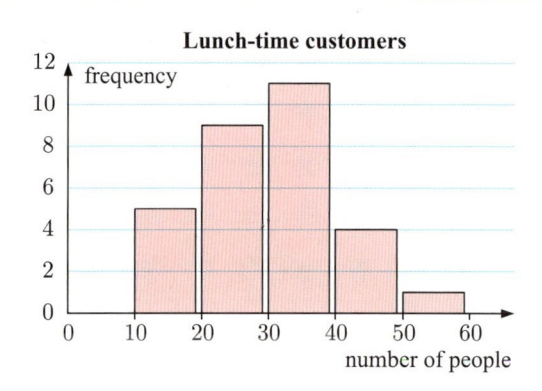

Lunch-time customers

EXERCISE 15B.2

1 Forty students were asked to count the number of red cars they saw on the way to school one morning. The results are shown alongside.

```
23  7 15 32 13 44 28 15 20 48
16 34 32  5 22 11 31 10 24 16
33 45 20 24 13  9 24 16  5 47
37 23 27 19 21 29 37 11 30 28
```

  a Construct a tally-frequency table for this data using class intervals 0 - 9, 10 - 19, ..., 40 - 49.
  b Display the data on a vertical bar chart.
  c How many students saw less than 20 red cars?
  d What percentage of students saw at least 30 red cars?
  e What is the modal class for the data?

2 The data gives the number of chairs made each day by a furniture production company over 26 days:

```
38 27 29 33 18 22 42 27 36 30 16 23 34
22 19 37 28 44 37 25 33 40 22 16 39 25
```

  a Construct a tally and frequency table for this data.
  b Draw a vertical bar chart to display the data.
  c On what percentage of days were less than 40 chairs made?
  d On how many days were at least 30 chairs made?
  e Find the modal class for the data.

3 Over a 6 week period, a museum keeps a record of the number of visitors it receives each day. The results are:

```
515 432 674 237 445 510 585 411 605 332 196
432 527 421 318 570 640 298 554 611 458 322
584 232 674 519 174 377 543 630 490 501
139 549 322 612 222 625 582 381 459 609
```

  a Construct a tally and frequency table for this data using class intervals 0 - 99, 100 - 199, 200 - 299, ..., 600 - 699.
  b Draw a vertical bar chart to display the data.
  c On how many days did the museum receive at least 500 visitors?
  d What is the modal class for the data?
  e Describe the distribution of the data. Interpret your results.

4 Thirty high schools were surveyed to find out how many Year 12 students there were at each school. The following data was collected:

```
82 57 75 71 66 80 92 74 89 70
74 60 98 70 83 55 67 85 78 62
83 71 77 69 62 83 94 88 64 75
```

  a Construct a tally and frequency table for this data.
  b Draw a vertical bar chart to display the data.

c How many schools have at least 80 Year 12 students?
d What percentage of the schools have less than 70 Year 12 students?
e Find the modal class for the data.
f Describe the distribution of the data.

C THE CENTRE OF A DISCRETE DATA SET [11.4]

We can get a better understanding of a data set if we can locate the **middle** or **centre** of the data and get an indication of its **spread**. Knowing one of these without the other is often of little use.

There are *three statistics* that are used to measure the **centre** of a data set.
These are: the **mean**, the **median** and the **mode**.

THE MEAN

> The **mean** of a data set is the statistical name for the arithmetic average.
>
> $$\text{mean} = \frac{\text{the sum of all data values}}{\text{the number of data values}}$$
>
> or $\bar{x} = \dfrac{\sum x}{n}$ where $\bar{x}$ is the mean
> $\sum x$ is the sum of the data
> n is the number of data values in the data set.

The mean gives us a single number which indicates a centre of the data set. It is not necessarily a member of the data set.

For example, a mean test mark of 67% tells us that there are several marks below 67% and several above it. 67% is at the centre, but it does not show that one of the students scored 67%.

THE MEDIAN

> The **median** is the *middle value* of an ordered data set.

An ordered data set is obtained by listing the data, usually from smallest to largest.

The median splits the data in halves. Half of the data are less than or equal to the median, and half are greater than or equal to it.

For example, if the median mark for a test is 67% then you know that half the class scored less than or equal to 67%, and half scored greater than or equal to 67%.

For an **odd number** of data, the median is one of the data.

For an **even number** of data, the median is the average of the two middle values, and may not be one of the original data.

> If there are n data values, calculate $\dfrac{n+1}{2}$.
>
> The median is the $\left(\dfrac{n+1}{2}\right)$th data value.

Analysis of discrete data (Chapter 15)

For example:

If there are 13 data values, $n = 13$,

$\therefore \dfrac{n+1}{2} = \dfrac{13+1}{2} = 7$, and so the median is the 7th ordered data value.

If there are 14 data values, $n = 14$,

$\therefore \dfrac{n+1}{2} = \dfrac{14+1}{2} = 7.5$, and so the median is the average of the 7th and 8th ordered data values.

THE MODE

> The **mode** is the most frequently occurring value in the data set.

If a data set has two modes, we say it is **bimodal**.

If a data set has three or more modes, we do not use the mode as a measure of the middle.

Example 1 ◀)) **Self Tutor**

The numbers of small aeroplanes flying in to a remote airstrip over a 15-day period is   5 7 0 3 4 6 4 0 5 3 6 9 4 2 8.   For this data set, find:

a the mean   **b** the median   **c** the mode.

a mean $= \dfrac{5+7+0+3+4+6+4+0+5+3+6+9+4+2+8}{15}$ ⟵ $\dfrac{\Sigma x}{n}$

$= \dfrac{66}{15}$

$= 4.4$ aeroplanes

b The ordered data set is: 0 0 2 3 3 4 4 4 5 5 6 6 7 8 9   {as $n = 15$, $\dfrac{n+1}{2} = 8$}

$\therefore$ median $= 4$ aeroplanes

c 4 is the score which occurs the most often $\therefore$ mode $= 4$ aeroplanes

---

Suppose that on the next day, 6 aeroplanes land on the airstrip in **Example 1**. We need to recalculate the measures of the centre to see the effect of this new data value.

We expect the mean to rise as the new data value is greater than the old mean.

In fact, since n is now 16, the new mean $= \dfrac{66+6}{16} = \dfrac{72}{16} = 4.5$ aeroplanes.

The new ordered data set is: 0 0 2 3 3 4 4 4 5 5 6 6 6 7 8 9   {as $n = 16$, $\dfrac{n+1}{2} = 8.5$}

two middle scores

$\therefore$ median $= \dfrac{4+5}{2} = 4.5$ aeroplanes

This new data set has two modes, 4 and 6 aeroplanes, so the data set is bimodal.

Note that equal or approximately equal values of the mean, mode, and median *may* indicate a **symmetrical distribution** of data. However, we should always check using a graph before calling a data set symmetric.

Example 2

Solve the following problems:
a The mean of six scores is 78.5. What is the sum of the scores?
b Find x if 10, 7, 3, 6 and x have a mean of 8.

a $\dfrac{\text{sum}}{6} = 78.5$

$\therefore$ sum $= 78.5 \times 6$
$= 471$

$\therefore$ the sum of the scores is 471.

b There are 5 scores.

$\therefore \dfrac{10 + 7 + 3 + 6 + x}{5} = 8$

$\therefore \dfrac{26 + x}{5} = 8$

$\therefore 26 + x = 40$

$\therefore x = 14$

EXERCISE 15C

1 Find the **i** mean **ii** median **iii** mode for each of the following data sets:
  a 12, 17, 20, 24, 25, 30, 40
  b 8, 8, 8, 10, 11, 11, 12, 12, 16, 20, 20, 24
  c 7.9, 8.5, 9.1, 9.2, 9.9, 10.0, 11.1, 11.2, 11.2, 12.6, 12.9
  d 427, 423, 415, 405, 445, 433, 442, 415, 435, 448, 429, 427, 403, 430, 446, 440, 425, 424, 419, 428, 441

2 Consider the following two data sets:
  Data set A: 5, 6, 6, 7, 7, 7, 8, 8, 9, 10, 12   Data set B: 5, 6, 6, 7, 7, 7, 8, 8, 9, 10, 20
  a Find the mean for each data set.
  b Find the median for each data set.
  c Explain why the mean of *Data set A* is less than the mean of *Data set B*.
  d Explain why the median of *Data set A* is the same as the median of *Data set B*.

3 The selling prices of nine houses are:
  $158 000, $290 000, $290 000, $1.1 million, $900 000, $395 000,
  $925 000, $420 000, $760 000
  a Find the mean, median, and modal selling prices.
  b Explain why the mode is an unsatisfactory measure of the middle in this case.
  c Is the median a satisfactory measure of the middle of this data set?

4 The following raw data is the daily rainfall (to the nearest millimetre) for the month of February 2007 in a city in China: 0, 4, 1, 0, 0, 0, 2, 9, 3, 0, 0, 0, 8, 27, 5, 0, 0, 0, 0, 8, 1, 3, 0, 0, 15, 1, 0, 0
  a Find the mean, median and mode for the data.
  b Give a reason why the median is not the most suitable measure of centre for this set of data.
  c Give a reason why the mode is not the most suitable measure of centre for this set of data.

Analysis of discrete data (Chapter 15)

5 A basketball team scored 38, 52, 43, 54, 41, and 36 points in their first six matches.
  a Find the mean number of points scored for the first six matches.
  b What score does the team need to shoot in their next match to maintain the same mean score?
  c The team scores only 20 points in the seventh match. What is the mean number of points scored for the seven matches?
  d If the team scores 42 points in their eighth and final match, will their previous mean score increase or decrease? Find the mean score for all eight matches.

6 The mean of 12 scores is 8.8. What is the sum of the scores?

7 While on a camping holiday, Lachlan drove an average of 214 km per day for a period of 8 days. How far did Lachlan drive in total while on holiday?

8 The mean monthly sales for a CD store are $216 000. Calculate the total sales for the store for the year.

9 Find x if 7, 15, 6, 10, 4, and x have a mean of 9.

10 Find a, given that 10, a, 15, 20, a, a, 17, 7, and 15 have a mean of 12.

11 Over a semester, Jamie did 8 science tests. Each was marked out of 30, and Jamie averaged 25. However, when checking his files, he could only find 7 of the 8 tests. For these he scored 29, 26, 18, 20, 27, 24 and 29. Determine how many marks he scored for the eighth test.

12 A sample of 12 measurements has a mean of 8.5, and a sample of 20 measurements has a mean of 7.5. Find the mean of all 32 measurements.

13 In the United Kingdom, the months of autumn are September, October, and November. If the mean temperature was $S°C$ for September, $O°C$ for October, and $N°C$ for November, find an expression for the mean temperature $A°C$ for the whole of autumn.

14 The mean, median, and mode of seven numbers are 8, 7, and 6 respectively. Two of the numbers are 8 and 10. If the smallest of the seven numbers is 4, find the largest of the seven numbers.

D MEASURING THE SPREAD OF DISCRETE DATA [11.4]

Knowing the middle of a data set can be quite useful. However, for a more accurate picture of the data set we also need to know its **spread**, or how much variation there is in the data.

For example, the following two data sets both have a mean value of 6:   2, 3, 4, 5, 6, 7, 8, 9, 10
4, 5, 5, 6, 6, 6, 7, 7, 8.

However, the first data set is more widely *spread* than the second one.

Three commonly used statistics that indicate the spread of a set of data are the

  • **range**   • **interquartile range**   • **standard deviation**.

The standard deviation, which is a measure of the spread about the mean, will not be covered in this course.

THE RANGE

> The **range** is the difference between the **maximum** (largest) data value and the **minimum** (smallest) data value.
>
> range = maximum data value − minimum data value

Example 3 ◀)) Self Tutor

Find the range of the data set: 5, 3, 8, 4, 9, 7, 5, 6, 2, 3, 6, 8, 4.

range = maximum value − minimum value = 9 − 2 = 7

THE QUARTILES AND THE INTERQUARTILE RANGE

The **median** divides an ordered data set into halves, and these halves are divided in half again by the **quartiles**.

The middle value of the lower half is called the **lower quartile**. One quarter (or 25%) of the data have values less than or equal to the lower quartile. 75% of the data have values greater than or equal to the lower quartile.

The middle value of the upper half is called the **upper quartile**. One quarter (or 25%) of the data have values greater than or equal to the upper quartile. 75% of the data have values less than or equal to the upper quartile.

The **interquartile range** is the range of the middle half (50%) of the data.

> interquartile range = upper quartile − lower quartile

The data is thus divided into quarters by the lower quartile Q_1, the median Q_2, and the upper quartile Q_3.

So, the interquartile range, $IQR = Q_3 - Q_1$.

Example 4 ◀)) Self Tutor

For the data set: 7, 3, 4, 2, 5, 6, 7, 5, 5, 9, 3, 8, 3, 5, 6   find the:
a median **b** lower and upper quartiles **c** interquartile range.

The ordered data set is: 2 3 3 3 4 5 5 5 6 6 7 7 8 9 (15 of them)

a As $n = 15$, $\dfrac{n+1}{2} = 8$ ∴ the median = 8th score = 5

b As the median is a data value, we now ignore it and split the remaining data into two:

  lower   upper
  2 3 3 3 4 5 5   5 6 6 7 7 8 9

  Q_1 = median of lower half = 3
  Q_3 = median of upper half = 7

c $IQR = Q_3 - Q_1 = 7 - 3 = 4$

Analysis of discrete data (Chapter 15)

Example 5 ◀)) Self Tutor

For the data set: 6, 10, 7, 8, 13, 7, 10, 8, 1, 7, 5, 4, 9, 4, 2, 5, 9, 6, 3, 2 find the:
a median **b** lower and upper quartiles **c** interquartile range.

> The ordered data set is: 1 2 2 3 4 4 5 5 6 6 7 7 7 8 8 9 9 10 10 13   (20 of them)
>
> **a** As $n = 20$, $\dfrac{n+1}{2} = 10.5$
>
> $\therefore$ median $= \dfrac{\text{10th value} + \text{11th value}}{2} = \dfrac{6+7}{2} = 6.5$
>
> **b** As the median is not a data value we split the data into two:
>
> $$\underbrace{1\ 2\ 2\ 3\ \underbrace{4\ 4}_{Q_1 = 4}\ 5\ 5\ 6\ 6}_{\text{lower}}\quad \underbrace{7\ 7\ 7\ 8\ \underbrace{8\ 9}_{Q_3 = 8.5}\ 9\ 10\ 10\ 13}_{\text{upper}}$$
>
> **c** IQR $= Q_3 - Q_1$ **Note:** Some computer packages (for example, **MS Excel**)
> $= 8.5 - 4$ calculate quartiles in a different way from this example.
> $= 4.5$

EXERCISE 15D

1 For each of the following data sets, make sure the data is ordered and then find:
  i the median
  ii the upper and lower quartiles
  iii the range
  iv the interquartile range.
  a 5, 6, 6, 6, 7, 7, 7, 8, 8, 8, 8, 9, 9, 9, 9, 9, 10, 10, 11, 11, 11, 12, 12
  b 11, 13, 16, 13, 25, 19, 20, 19, 19, 16, 17, 21, 22, 18, 19, 17, 23, 15
  c 23.8, 24.4, 25.5, 25.5, 26.6, 26.9, 27, 27.3, 28.1, 28.4, 31.5

2 The times spent (in minutes) by 24 people in the checkout queue at a supermarket were:

1.4 5.2 2.4 2.8 3.4 3.8 2.2 1.5
0.8 0.8 3.9 2.3 4.5 1.4 0.5 0.1
1.6 4.8 1.9 0.2 3.6 5.2 2.7 3.0

  a Find the median waiting time and the upper and lower quartiles.
  b Find the range and interquartile range of the waiting times.
  c Copy and complete the following statements:
   i "50% of the waiting times were greater than ...... minutes."
   ii "75% of the waiting times were less than ...... minutes."
   iii "The minimum waiting time was ...... minutes and the maximum waiting time was ...... minutes. The waiting times were spread over ...... minutes."

3 For the data set given, find:
- **a** the minimum value
- **b** the maximum value
- **c** the median
- **d** the lower quartile
- **e** the upper quartile
- **f** the range
- **g** the interquartile range.

Stem	Leaf
2	0 1 2 2
3	0 0 1 4 4 5 8
4	0 2 3 4 6 6 9
5	1 1 4 5 8

5 | 1 represents 51

E DATA IN FREQUENCY TABLES [11.4]

When the same data appears several times we often summarise it in a **frequency table**. For convenience we denote the data values by x and the frequencies of these values by f.

Consider the data set displayed alongside.

The mode

There are 14 of data value 6 which is more than any other data value.

The mode is therefore 6.

Data value	Frequency	Product
3	1	$1 \times 3 = 3$
4	2	$2 \times 4 = 8$
5	4	$4 \times 5 = 20$
6	14	$14 \times 6 = 84$
7	11	$11 \times 7 = 77$
8	6	$6 \times 8 = 48$
9	2	$2 \times 9 = 18$
Total	40	258

The mean

A 'Product' column helps to add all scores.

We know the mean $= \dfrac{\text{the sum of all data values}}{\text{the number of data values}}$, so for data in a frequency table, $\bar{x} = \dfrac{\sum fx}{\sum f}$

In this case the mean $= \dfrac{\sum fx}{\sum f} = \dfrac{258}{40} = 6.45$.

The median

There are 40 data values, an even number, so there are *two* middle data values.

As the sample size $n = 40$, $\dfrac{n+1}{2} = \dfrac{41}{2} = 20.5$

$\therefore$ the median is the average of the 20th and 21st data values.

In the table, the blue numbers show us accumulated values.

Remember that the median is the middle of the ordered data set.

Data Value (x)	Frequency (f)		
3	1	1 ←	one number is 3
4	2	3 ←	3 numbers are 4 or less
5	4	7 ←	7 numbers are 5 or less
6	14	21 ←	21 numbers are 6 or less
7	11	32 ←	32 numbers are 7 or less
8	6		
9	2		
Total	40		

We can see that the 20th and 21st data values (in order) are both 6s.

$\therefore$ median $= \dfrac{6+6}{2} = 6$.

Analysis of discrete data (Chapter 15)

Example 6

Each student in a class of 20 is assigned a number between 1 and 10 to indicate his or her fitness.

Calculate the:
- **a** mean
- **b** median
- **c** mode
- **d** range

of the scores.

Score	Number of students
5	1
6	2
7	4
8	7
9	4
10	2
Total	20

a

Score (x)	Frequency (f)	Product (fx)
5	1	$5 \times 1 = 5$
6	2	$6 \times 2 = 12$
7	4	$7 \times 4 = 28$
8	7	$8 \times 7 = 56$
9	4	$9 \times 4 = 36$
10	2	$10 \times 2 = 20$
Total	20	157

The mean score $= \dfrac{\sum fx}{\sum f}$

$= \dfrac{157}{20}$

$= 7.85$

STATISTICS PACKAGE

b There are 20 scores, and so the median is the average of the 10th and 11th.

Score	Number of students	
5	1	← 1st student
6	2	← 2nd and 3rd student
7	4	← 4th, 5th, 6th and 7th student
8	7	← 8th, 9th, **10th, 11th**, 12th, 13th, 14th student
9	4	
10	2	

The 10th and 11th students both scored 8 ∴ median = 8.

c Looking down the 'number of students' column, the highest frequency is 7. This corresponds to a score of 8, so the mode = 8.

d The range = highest data value − lowest data value = 10 − 5 = 5

EXERCISE 15E

1 A class of students was asked how many times they were sunburnt over the school holidays. The results are shown alongside.

  a Copy the table, adding a product column.
  b Find the:
  i mean
  ii median
  iii mode.

Number of sunburns	Frequency
0	2
1	10
2	8
3	6
4	2
5	1
6	1

2 The members of a school band were each asked how many musical instruments they played. The results were:

Number of instruments	Frequency
1	18
2	14
3	6
4	4
Total	42

Calculate the: **a** mode **b** median **c** mean **d** range.

3 The following frequency table records the number of books read in the last year by 50 fifteen-year-olds.

Number of books	Frequency
0	2
1	4
2	7
3	4
4	2
5	0
6	1
7	8
8	13
9	7
10	2

a For this data, find the:
  i mean **ii** median **iii** mode **iv** range.
b Construct a vertical bar chart for the data. Indicate the measures of centre (mean, median and mode) on the horizontal axis.
c Describe the distribution of the data.
d Why is the mean smaller than the median for this data?
e Which measure of centre would be most suitable for this data set?

4 Hui breeds ducks. The number of ducklings surviving for each pair after one month is recorded in the table.

Number of survivors	Frequency
0	1
1	2
2	5
3	9
4	20
5	30
6	9
Total	76

a Calculate the:
  i mean **ii** mode **iii** median.
b Calculate the range of the data.
c Is the data skewed?
d How does the skewness of the data affect the measures of the middle of the distribution?

5 Participants in a survey were asked how many foreign countries they had visited. The results are displayed in the vertical bar chart alongside:

a Construct a frequency table from the graph.
b How many people took part in the survey?
c Calculate the:
  i mean **ii** median
  iii mode **iv** range of the data.

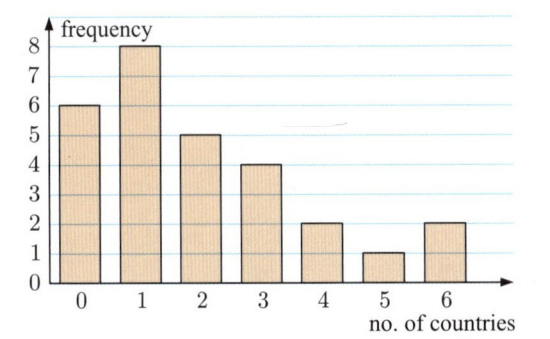

F GROUPED DISCRETE DATA   [11.4]

One issue to consider when grouping data into class intervals is that the original data is lost. This means that calculating the exact mean and median becomes impossible. However, we can still *estimate* these values, and in general this is sufficient.

Analysis of discrete data (Chapter 15)

THE MEAN

When information has been grouped in classes, we use the **midpoint** of the class to represent all scores within that interval.

We are assuming that the scores within each class are evenly distributed throughout that interval. The mean calculated will therefore be an **estimate** of the true value.

Example 7 ◀⑴ Self Tutor

The table summarises the marks received by students for a Physics examination out of 50.

a Estimate the mean mark.
b What is the modal class?
c Can the range of the data be found?

Class interval	Frequency
0 - 9	2
10 - 19	31
20 - 29	73
30 - 39	85
40 - 49	26

Class interval	f	Mid-point (x)	fx
0 - 9	2	4.5	9.0
10 - 19	31	14.5	449.5
20 - 29	73	24.5	1788.5
30 - 39	85	34.5	2932.5
40 - 49	26	44.5	1157.0
Totals	217		6336.5

a Mean $= \dfrac{\sum fx}{\sum f}$

$= \dfrac{6336.5}{217}$

≈ 29.2

b The modal class is 30 - 39 marks.
c No, as we do not know the smallest and largest score.

EXERCISE 15F

1 40 students receive marks out of 100 for an examination in Chemistry. The results were:

70 65 50 40 58 72 39 85 90 65 53 75 83 92 66 78 82 88 56 68
43 90 80 85 78 72 59 83 71 75 54 68 75 89 92 81 77 59 63 80

a Find the exact mean of the data.
b Group the data into the classes 0 - 9, 10 - 19, 20 - 29, ..., 90 - 99, forming a frequency table. Include columns for the midpoint (x), and fx.
c Estimate the mean from the grouped data in **b**.
d How close is your answer in **c** to the exact value in **a**?

2 A sample of 100 students was asked how many times they bought lunch from the canteen in the last four weeks. The results were:

Number of lunches	0-5	6-10	11-15	16-20
Frequency	28	45	15	12

a Estimate the mean number of bought lunches for each student.
b What is the modal class?

3 The percentage marks for boys and girls in a science test are given in the table:

a Estimate the mean mark for the girls.
b Estimate the mean mark for the boys.
c What can you deduce by comparing **a** and **b**?

Marks	Girls	Boys
21 - 30	2	0
31 - 40	6	5
41 - 50	10	8
51 - 60	8	11
61 - 70	4	5
71 - 80	5	6
81 - 90	3	4
91 - 100	1	0

G STATISTICS FROM TECHNOLOGY [11.8]

GRAPHICS CALCULATOR

A **graphics calculator** can be used to find descriptive statistics and to draw some types of graphs.

Consider the data set: 5 2 3 3 6 4 5 3 7 5 7 1 8 9 5 $\bar{x}$ is the mean

No matter what brand of calculator you use you should be able to:

- Enter the data as a list.
- Enter the statistics calculation part of the menu and obtain the descriptive statistics like these shown.

Instructions for these tasks can be found in the **Graphics Calculator Instructions** section, on page 22.

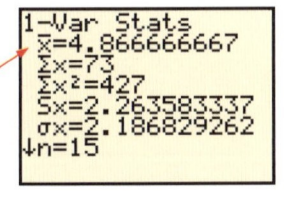

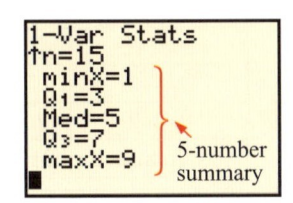

COMPUTER PACKAGE

Various statistical packages are available for computer use, but many are expensive and often not easy to use. Click on the icon to use the statistics package on the CD.

Enter the data sets: Set 1:   5 2 3 3 6 4 5 3 7 5 7 1 8 9 5

Set 2:   9 6 2 3 5 5 7 5 6 7 6 3 4 4 5 8 4

Examine the side-by-side bar charts.

Click on the Statistics tab to obtain the descriptive statistics.

Select Print... from the File menu to print all of these on one sheet of paper.

EXERCISE 15G

1 Helen and Jessica both play for the Lightning Basketball Club. The numbers of points scored by each of them over a 12-game period were:

Helen: 20, 14, 0, 28, 38, 25, 26, 17, 24, 24, 6, 3
Jessica: 18, 20, 22, 2, 18, 31, 7, 15, 17, 16, 22, 29

a Calculate the mean and median number of points for both of them.
b Calculate the range and interquartile range for both of them.
c Which of the girls was the higher scorer during the 12-game period?
d Who was more consistent?

2 Enter the **Opening Problem** data on page **295** for the *Before upgrade* data in Set 1 and the *After upgrade* data in Set 2 of the computer package. Print out the page of graphs and descriptive statistics. Write a brief report on the effect of the safety upgrade.

3 Use your graphics calculator to check the answers to **Example 6** on page **309**.

4 Use your graphics calculator to check the answers to **Example 7** on page **311**.

5 A group of Alzheimer's patients participated in a memory test where they were asked to memorise and recite a series of words. The results are shown alongside.

Use your calculator to find the:

- **a** mean
- **b** median
- **c** range
- **d** lower quartile
- **e** upper quartile
- **f** interquartile range.

Longest word series memorised	Frequency
2	5
3	7
4	12
5	16
6	9
7	6
8	1
9	0
10	1

6 The heights (to the nearest centimetre) of boys and girls in a Year 10 class in Norway are as follows:

Boys: 165 171 169 169 172 171 171 180 168 168 166 168 170 165 171 173 187 181 175 174 165 167 163 160 169 167 172 174 177 188 177 185 167 160

Girls: 162 171 156 166 168 163 170 171 177 169 168 165 156 159 165 164 154 171 172 166 152 169 170 163 162 165 163 168 155 175 176 170 166

- **a** Use your calculator to find measures of centre (mean and median) and spread (range and IQR) for each data set.
- **b** Write a brief comparative report on the height differences between boys and girls in the class.

7

Sales	Frequency
75 - 99	42
100 - 124	61
125 - 149	63
150 - 174	46
175 - 199	15
200 - 224	18
225 - 249	37
250 - 274	16

A bookshop tracks its sales per day over a year.

- **a** Use your calculator to find the mean of the data.
- **b** Estimate the total book sales for the year.
- **c** Draw a graph of the sales figures.
- **d** Comment on the shape of the distribution, and suggest a reason for this shape.

Review set 15A

1 Classify the following numerical variables as either discrete or continuous:
- **a** the number of oranges on each orange tree
- **b** the heights of seedlings after two weeks
- **c** the scores of team members in a darts competition.

2 A randomly selected sample of small businesses were asked, "How many full-time employees are there in your business?". A bar chart has been constructed from the results.

a How many small businesses gave data in the survey?

b How many of the businesses had only one or two full-time employees?

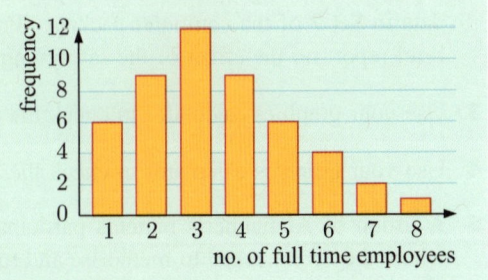

c What percentage of the businesses had five or more full-time employees?

d Describe the distribution of the data.

e Find the mean of the data.

3 The data alongside are the number of call-outs each day for a city fire department over a period of 25 days:

```
29  14  23  32  28  30   9  24  31
30  18  22  27  15  32  26  22  19
16  23  38  12   8  22  31
```

a Construct a tally and frequency table for the data using class intervals 0 - 9, 10 - 19, 20 - 29, and 30 - 39.

b Display the data on a vertical bar chart.

c On how many days were there at least 20 call-outs?

d On what percentage of days were there less than 10 call-outs?

e Find the modal class for the data.

4 For the following data set of the number of points scored by a rugby team, find:

a the mean   **b** the mode   **c** the median   **d** the range

e the upper and lower quartiles   **f** the interquartile range.

28, 24, 16, 6, 46, 34, 43, 16, 36, 49, 30, 28, 4, 31, 47, 41, 26, 25, 20, 29, 42

5 The test score out of 40 marks was recorded for a group of 30 students:

```
25  18  35  32  34  28  24  39  29  33
22  34  39  31  36  35  36  33  35  27
26  25  20  18   9  19  32  23  28  27
```

a Construct a tally and frequency table for this data.

b Draw a bar chart to display the data.

c How many students scored less than 20 for the test?

d If an 'A' was awarded to students who scored 30 or more for the test, what percentage of students scored an 'A'?

6 Eight scores have an average of six. Scores of 15 and x increase the average to 7. Find x.

7 Using the bar chart alongside:

a construct a frequency table

b determine the total number of:

  i games played   **ii** goals scored

c find the:

  i mean   **ii** median

  iii mode   **iv** range.

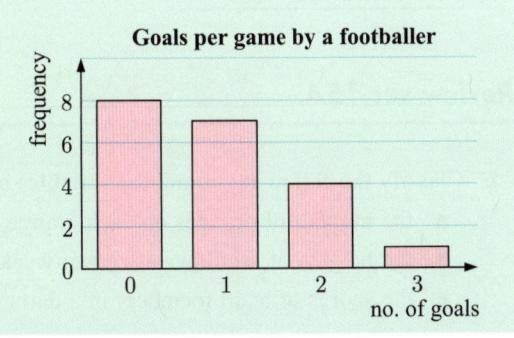

Analysis of discrete data (Chapter 15) 315

8 For the data set given, find the:
- **a** minimum value
- **b** maximum value
- **c** median
- **d** lower quartile
- **e** upper quartile
- **f** range
- **g** interquartile range.

Stem	Leaf
1	2 4 4 6 8
2	2 3 7 7 7 9 9
3	0 0 2 4 5 8
4	0 2 3

4 | 0 represents 40

9 The number of potatoes growing on each of 100 potato plants was recorded and summarised in the table below:

No. of potatoes	0 - 2	3 - 5	6 - 8	9 - 11	12 - 14	15 - 17
Frequency	7	11	25	40	15	2

Estimate the mean number of potatoes per plant.

10 Use technology to find the
- **a** mean
- **b** median
- **c** lower quartile
- **d** upper quartile

of the following data set:

```
147  152  164  159  174  140  155  166  180  177
156  182  174  168  170  165  143  185  126  148
138  141  156  142  130  182  156  182  141  158
```

Review set 15B

1 A class of 20 students was asked "How many children are there in your household?" and the following data was collected:

1 2 3 3 2 4 5 4 2 3 8 1 2 1 3 2 1 2 1 2

- **a** What is the variable in the investigation?
- **b** Is the data discrete or continuous? Explain your answer.
- **c** Construct a frequency table for the data.
- **d** Construct a vertical bar chart to display the data.
- **e** How would you describe the distribution of the data? Is it symmetrical, positively skewed, or negatively skewed?
- **f** What is the mode of the data?

2 A class of thirty students were asked how many emails they had sent in the last week.
The results were: 12 6 21 15 18 4 28 32 17 44 9 32 26 18 11
24 31 17 52 7 42 37 19 6 20 15 27 8 36 28

- **a** Construct a tally and frequency table for this data, using intervals 0 - 9, 10 - 19, ..., 50 - 59.
- **b** Draw a vertical bar chart to display the data.
- **c** Find the modal class.
- **d** What percentage of students sent at least 30 emails?
- **e** Describe the distribution of the data.

3 A sample of 15 measurements has a mean of 14.2 and a sample of 10 measurements has a mean of 12.6. Find the mean of the total sample of 25 measurements.

4 Determine the mean of the numbers 7, 5, 7, 2, 8 and 7. If two additional numbers, 2 and x, reduce the mean by 1, find x.

5 The local transport authority recorded the number of vehicles travelling along a stretch of road each day for 40 days. The data is displayed in the bar chart alongside:

  a On how many days were there at least 180 vehicles?
  b On what percentage of days were there less than 160 vehicles?
  c What is the modal class?
  d Estimate the mean number of vehicles on the stretch of road each day.

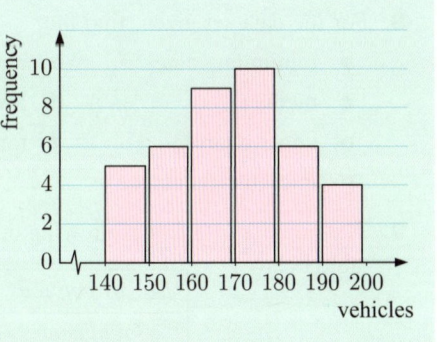

6 Jenny's golf scores for her last 20 rounds were:

90 106 84 103 112 100 105 81 104 98
107 95 104 108 99 101 106 102 98 101

  a Find the median, lower quartile and upper quartile of the data set.
  b Find the interquartile range of the data set and explain what it represents.

7 For the data displayed in the stem-and-leaf plot find the:

  a mean   **b** median
  c lower quartile **d** upper quartile
  e range   **f** interquartile range

Stem	Leaf
3	8 9
4	2 2 5
5	0 1 1 7 9
6	1 3 4
7	0

7 | 0 represents 70

8 The given table shows the distribution of scores for a Year 10 spelling test in Austria.

  a Calculate the: **i** mean   **ii** mode
                        iii median **iv** range of the scores.
  b The average score for all Year 10 students across Austria in this spelling test was 6.2. How does this class compare to the national average?
  c The data set is skewed. Is the skewness positive or negative?

Score	Frequency
6	2
7	4
8	7
9	12
10	5
Total	30

9 Sixty people were asked: "How many times have you been to the cinema in the last twelve months?". The results are given in the table alongside.

Estimate the mean of the data.

No. of times	Frequency
0 - 4	19
5 - 9	24
10 - 14	10
15 - 19	5
20 - 24	2

10 The data below shows the number of pages contained in a random selection of books from a library:

295 612 452 182 335 410 256 715 221 375
508 310 197 245 411 162 95   416 372 777
411 236 606 192 487

  a Use technology to find the:
      i mean   **ii** median
      iii lower quartile **iv** upper quartile
  b Find the range and interquartile range for the data.

Straight lines

16

Contents:

A	Vertical and horizontal lines	[7.6]
B	Graphing from a table of values	
C	Equations of lines	[7.6]
D	Graphing lines from equations	[7.6]
E	Lines of symmetry	[7.8]

Opening problem

On the coordinate axes alongside, three lines are drawn.

Things to think about:

- How can we use algebra to describe the set of all points on:
  ▸ line (1)   ▸ line (2)   ▸ line (3)?
- What forms do our descriptions of a line take when the line is:
  ▸ vertical   ▸ horizontal?

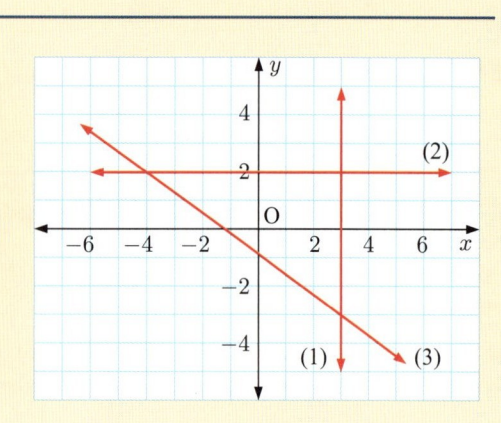

In **Chapter 14** we learnt how to find the gradient of a line segment. In this chapter we will see how the gradient can be used to find the **equation** of a line.

The **equation of a line** is an equation which connects the x and y values for every point on the line.

A VERTICAL AND HORIZONTAL LINES [7.6]

To begin with we consider horizontal and vertical lines which are parallel to either the x or y-axis.

Discovery 1 — Vertical and horizontal lines

What to do:

1. Using graph paper, plot the following sets of points on the Cartesian plane. Rule a line through each set of points.
    a $(3, 4)$, $(3, 2)$, $(3, 0)$, $(3, -2)$, $(3, -4)$
    b $(6, -1)$, $(6, -3)$, $(6, 1)$, $(6, 5)$, $(6, 3)$
    c $(0, -5)$, $(0, -2)$, $(0, 1)$, $(0, 4)$, $(0, -3)$
    d $(-3, -1)$, $(5, -1)$, $(-1, -1)$, $(4, -1)$, $(0, -1)$
    e $(-2, 6)$, $(-2, -3)$, $(-2, 0)$, $(-2, -2)$, $(-2, 2)$
    f $(4, 0)$, $(0, 0)$, $(7, 0)$, $(-1, 0)$, $(-3, 0)$

2. Can you state the gradient of each line? If so, what is it?
3. What do all the points on a vertical line have in common?
4. What do all the points on a horizontal line have in common?
5. Can you state the equation of each line?

VERTICAL LINES

All **vertical** lines have **equations** of the form $x = a$, where a is a constant.

The gradient of a vertical line is **undefined**.

A sketch of the vertical lines $x = -2$ and $x = 1$ is shown alongside.

For all points on a vertical line, regardless of the value of the y-coordinate, the value of the x-coordinate is always the same.

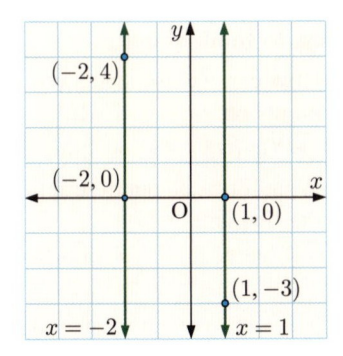

HORIZONTAL LINES

All **horizontal** lines have **equations** of the form $y = b$, where b is a constant.

The gradient of a horizontal line is **zero**.

A sketch of the horizontal lines $y = -3$ and $y = 2$ is shown alongside.

For all points on a horizontal line, regardless of the value of the x-coordinate, the value of the y-coordinate is always the same.

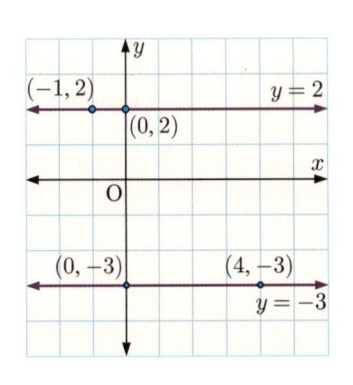

Straight lines (Chapter 16)

EXERCISE 16A

1 Identify as either a vertical or horizontal line and hence plot the graph of:
  a $y = 6$ **b** $x = -3$ **c** $x = 2$ **d** $y = -4$

2 Identify as either a vertical or horizontal line:
  a a line with zero gradient
  b a line with undefined gradient.

3 Find the equation of:
  a the x-axis
  b the y-axis
  c a line parallel to the x-axis and three units below it
  d a line parallel to the y-axis and 4 units to the right of it.

4 Find the equation of:
  a the line with zero gradient that passes through $(-1, 3)$
  b the line with undefined gradient that passes through $(4, -2)$.

B GRAPHING FROM A TABLE OF VALUES

In this section we will graph some straight lines from tables of values. Our aim is to identify some features of the graphs and determine which part of the equation of the line controls them.

GRAPHING FROM A TABLE OF VALUES

Consider the equation $y = 2x + 1$. We can choose any value we like for x and use our equation to find the corresponding value for y.

We can hence construct a **table of values** for points on the line.

For example:

When $x = -3$,   When $x = 2$,
  $y = 2 \times -3 + 1$ $y = 2 \times 2 + 1$
  $= -6 + 1$ $= 4 + 1$
  $= -5$ $= 5$

x	-3	-2	-1	0	1	2	3
y	-5	-3	-1	1	3	5	7

From this table we plot the points $(-3, -5)$, $(-2, -3)$, $(-1, -1)$, $(0, 1)$, $(1, 3)$, $(2, 5)$, and $(3, 7)$ on the Cartesian plane. We see that they all lie in a straight line.

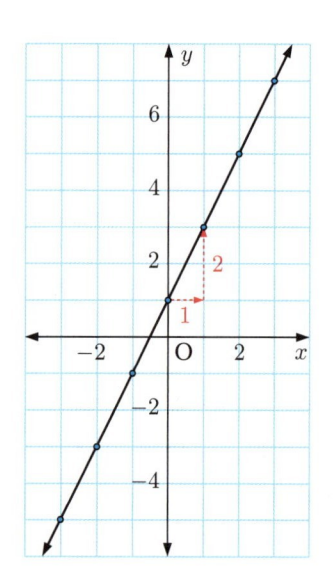

We can use the techniques from **Chapter 14** to find the gradient of the line. Using the points $(0, 1)$ and $(1, 3)$, the gradient is $\frac{y\text{-step}}{x\text{-step}} = \frac{2}{1} = 2$.

AXES INTERCEPTS

The **x-intercept** of a line is the value of x where the line meets the x-axis.

The **y-intercept** of a line is the value of y where the line meets the y-axis.

We can see that for the graph of $y = 2x + 1$, the x-intercept is $-\frac{1}{2}$ and the y-intercept is 1.

Example 1 ◀) Self Tutor

Consider the equation $y = x - 2$.

a Construct a table of values using $x = -3, -2, -1, 0, 1, 2$ and 3.
b Draw the graph of $y = x - 2$.
c Find the gradient and axes intercepts of the line.

a

x	-3	-2	-1	0	1	2	3
y	-5	-4	-3	-2	-1	0	1

c Using the points $(0, -2)$ and $(2, 0)$,

the gradient $= \dfrac{y\text{-step}}{x\text{-step}} = \dfrac{2}{2} = 1$.

The x-intercept is 2.
The y-intercept is -2.

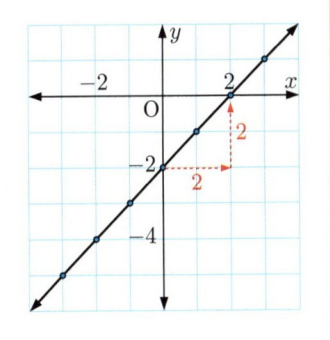

EXERCISE 16B

1 For each of the following equations:
  i construct a table of values for values of x from -3 to 3
  ii plot the graph of the line
  iii find the gradient and axes intercepts of the line.

  a $y = x$ **b** $y = 3x$ **c** $y = \frac{1}{3}x$ **d** $y = -3x$
  e $y = 2x + 1$ **f** $y = -2x + 1$ **g** $y = \frac{1}{2}x + 3$ **h** $y = -\frac{1}{2}x + 3$

2 Look at your graphs of $y = x$, $y = 3x$, and $y = \frac{1}{3}x$.
  a Arrange the graphs in order of steepness from least to greatest.
  b What part of the equation controls the degree of steepness of a line?

3 Look at your graphs of $y = 3x$ and $y = -3x$.
What part of the equation controls whether the graph is forward sloping or backward sloping?

4 Look at your graphs of $y = 3x$, $y = 2x + 1$, and $y = \frac{1}{2}x + 3$.
What part of the equation controls where the graph cuts the y-axis?

Straight lines (Chapter 16)

C EQUATIONS OF LINES [7.6]

Discovery 2 Graphs of the form $y = mx + c$

The use of a graphics calculator or suitable graphing package is recommended for this **Discovery**.

What to do:

1 On the same set of axes, graph the family of lines of the form $y = mx$:

   a where $m = 1, 2, 4, \frac{1}{2}, \frac{1}{5}$ **b** where $m = -1, -2, -4, -\frac{1}{2}, -\frac{1}{5}$

GRAPHING PACKAGE

2 What are the gradients of the lines in question **1**?

3 What is your interpretation of m in the equation $y = mx$?

4 On the same set of axes, graph the family of lines of the form $y = 2x + c$ where $c = 0, 2, 4, -1, -3$.

5 What is your interpretation of c for the equation $y = 2x + c$?

> $y = mx + c$ is the **gradient-intercept form** of the equation of a line with gradient m and y-intercept c.

For example:

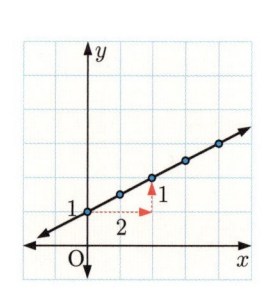

The illustrated line has gradient $m = \dfrac{y\text{-step}}{x\text{-step}} = \frac{1}{2}$

and y-intercept $c = 1$.

$\therefore$ its equation is $y = \frac{1}{2}x + 1$.

We can find the equation of a line if we are given:
- its gradient and the coordinates of one point on the line, **or**
- the coordinates of two points on the line.

Example 2 ◀) Self Tutor

Find the equations of these lines:

a

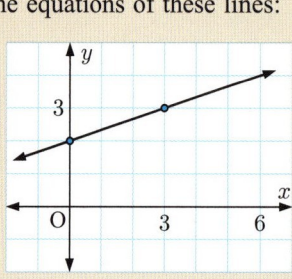

b

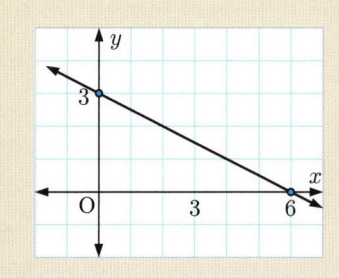

a

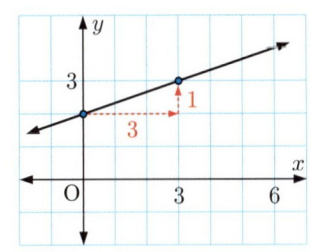

The gradient $m = \dfrac{y\text{-step}}{x\text{-step}} = \dfrac{1}{3}$.

The y-intercept $c = 2$.

$\therefore$ the equation is $y = \tfrac{1}{3}x + 2$

b

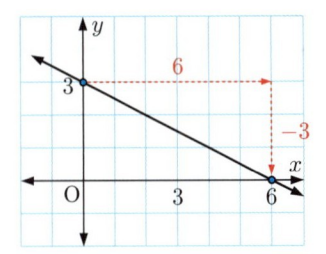

The gradient $m = \dfrac{y\text{-step}}{x\text{-step}} = \dfrac{-3}{6} = -\tfrac{1}{2}$.

The y-intercept $c = 3$.

$\therefore$ the equation is $y = -\tfrac{1}{2}x + 3$

Example 3 ◀)) Self Tutor

Find the equation of a line:
a with gradient 2 and y-intercept 5
b with gradient $\tfrac{2}{3}$ which passes through $(6, -1)$.

a $m = 2$ and $c = 5$, so the equation is $y = 2x + 5$.

b $m = \tfrac{2}{3}$ so the equation is $y = \tfrac{2}{3}x + c$

But when $x = 6$, $y = -1$ {the point $(6, -1)$ lies on the line}

$\therefore \quad -1 = \tfrac{2}{3}(6) + c$

$\therefore \quad -1 = 4 + c$

$\therefore \quad -5 = c$

So, the equation is $y = \tfrac{2}{3}x - 5$.

Example 4 ◀)) Self Tutor

Find the equation of a line passing through $(-1, 5)$ and $(3, -2)$.

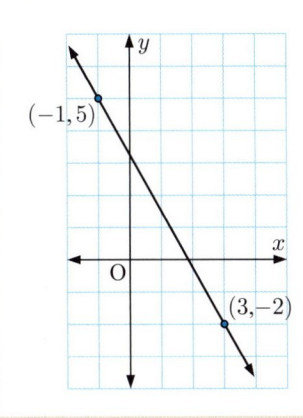

The gradient of the line $m = \dfrac{-2 - 5}{3 - -1} = -\tfrac{7}{4}$

$\therefore$ the equation is $y = -\tfrac{7}{4}x + c$

But when $x = -1$, $y = 5$

$\therefore \quad 5 = -\tfrac{7}{4}(-1) + c$

$\therefore \quad 5 = \tfrac{7}{4} + c$

$\therefore \quad \tfrac{20}{4} = \tfrac{7}{4} + c$

$\therefore \quad c = \tfrac{13}{4}$

So, the equation is $y = -\tfrac{7}{4}x + \tfrac{13}{4}$.

Straight lines (Chapter 16)

EXERCISE 16C

1 Find the equation of a line:
   a with gradient 3 and y-intercept -2
   b with gradient -4 and y-intercept 8
   c with gradient $\frac{1}{2}$ and y-intercept $\frac{2}{3}$
   d with gradient $-\frac{2}{3}$ and y-intercept $\frac{3}{4}$.

2 Find the gradient and y-intercept of a line with equation:
   a $y = 3x + 11$
   b $y = -2x + 6$
   c $y = \frac{1}{2}x$
   d $y = -\frac{1}{3}x - 2$
   e $y = 3$
   f $x = 8$
   g $y = 3 - 2x$
   h $y = -1 + \frac{1}{2}x$
   i $y = \dfrac{3x + 1}{2}$
   j $y = \dfrac{2x - 1}{3}$
   k $y = \dfrac{1 - x}{4}$
   l $y = \dfrac{3 - 2x}{5}$

3 Find the equations of these lines:

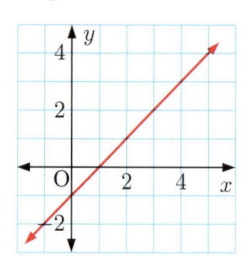

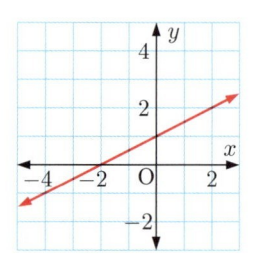

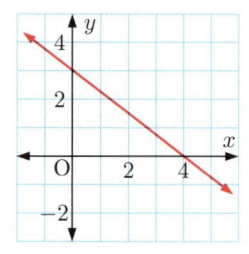

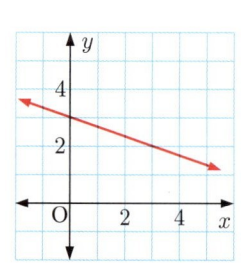

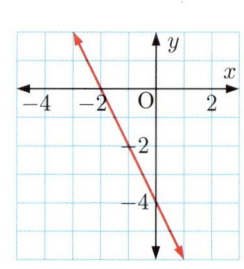

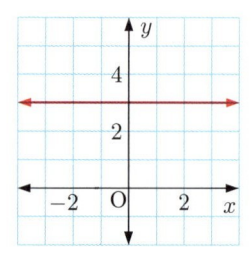

4 Find the equation of a line with:
   a gradient 2 which passes through the point $(1, 4)$
   b gradient -3 which passes through the point $(3, 1)$
   c gradient $\frac{2}{3}$ which passes through the point $(3, 0)$
   d gradient $-\frac{1}{4}$ which passes through the point $(2, -3)$
   e gradient $\frac{4}{5}$ which passes through the point $(10, -4)$
   f gradient $-\frac{1}{6}$ which passes through the point $(-12, -5)$.

5 Find the equation of a line passing through:
   a $(-1, 1)$ and $(2, 7)$
   b $(2, 0)$ and $(6, 2)$
   c $(-3, 3)$ and $(6, 0)$
   d $(-1, 7)$ and $(2, -2)$
   e $(5, 2)$ and $(-1, 2)$
   f $(3, -1)$ and $(3, 4)$
   g $(3, -1)$ and $(0, 4)$
   h $(2, 6)$ and $(-2, 1)$
   i $(4, -1)$ and $(-1, -2)$
   j $(3, 4)$ and $(-1, -3)$
   k $(4, -5)$ and $(-3, 1)$
   l $(-1, 3)$ and $(-2, -2)$.

6 Find the equation connecting the variables given:

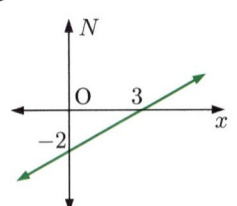

a Line through origin and (something), with M on vertical axis, t on horizontal axis, y-intercept 4, gradient $\frac{1}{3}$.

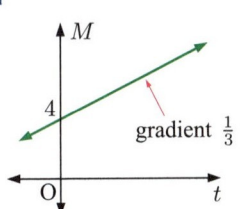

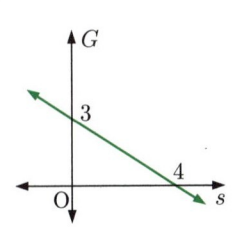

b N on vertical axis, x on horizontal axis, passes through (0, -2) and (3, 0).

c G on vertical axis, s on horizontal axis, passes through (0, 3) and (4, 0).

d H on vertical axis, g on horizontal axis, passes through (0, 2) and (4, -2).

e F on vertical axis, x on horizontal axis, passes through (0, 5) and (10, 8).

f P on vertical axis, t on horizontal axis, passes through (0, -2) and (6, -4).

Notice the variable on each axis.

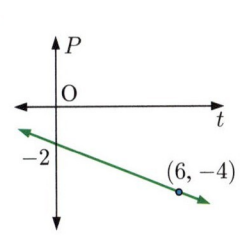

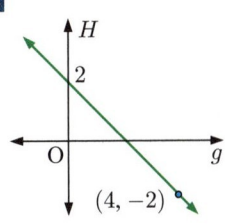

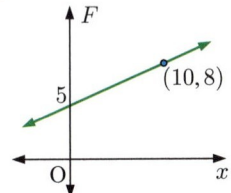

7 Find the equation of a line:

  a which has gradient $\frac{1}{2}$ and cuts the y-axis at 3

  b which is parallel to a line with gradient 2, and passes through the point $(-1, 4)$

  c which cuts the x-axis at 5 and the y-axis at -2

  d which cuts the x-axis at -1, and passes through $(-3, 4)$

  e which is parallel to a line with gradient $-\frac{4}{3}$, and cuts the x-axis at 5

  f which has x-intercept $-\frac{1}{2}$ and y-intercept -1.

Example 5   ◀) Self Tutor

A line has equation $y = 3x - 4$.

  a Does $(2, 1)$ lie on the line?   **b** Find a given that $(a, 3)$ lies on the line.

  a Substituting $x = 2$ into the equation of the line,
  $y = 3(2) - 4$
  $= 6 - 4$
  $= 2$
  So, $(2, 2)$ lies on the line, but $(2, 1)$ does not.

  b Substituting $(a, 3)$ into the equation of the line,
  $3 = 3(a) - 4$
  $\therefore 7 = 3a$
  $\therefore a = \frac{7}{3}$

---

8 Does:

  a $(1, 3)$ lie on $y = -x + 4$ **b** $(-2, 5)$ lie on $y = 3x + 7$

  c $y = \frac{1}{2}x - 4$ pass through $(2, 2)$ **d** $y = 3 - 2x$ pass through $(5, -7)$?

9 Find a given that:

   a $(3, a)$ lies on $y = \frac{1}{2}x + \frac{1}{2}$
   b $(-2, a)$ lies on $y = -3x + 7$
   c $(a, 4)$ lies on $y = 2x - 6$
   d $(a, -1)$ lies on $y = -x + 3$.

D GRAPHING LINES FROM EQUATIONS [7.6]

Lines with equations given in the gradient-intercept form are easily graphed by finding two points on the graph.

The easiest point to find is the y-intercept. The other can be found by substitution or using the gradient.

Example 6 ◀)) Self Tutor

Graph the line with equation $y = \frac{1}{3}x + 2$.

Method 1 (using substitution):

The y-intercept is 2.

When $x = 3$, $y = 1 + 2 = 3$.

$\therefore$ $(0, 2)$ and $(3, 3)$ lie on the line.

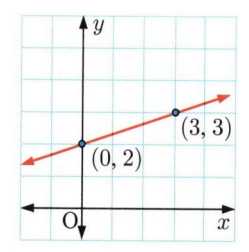

Method 2 (using gradient):

The y-intercept is 2 and the gradient $= \frac{1}{3}$ ← y-step
                                                  ↖ x-step

We start at $(0, 2)$, then find another point by moving across 3, then up 1.

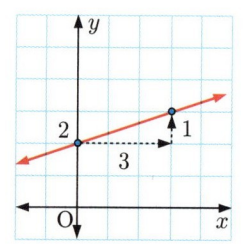

EXERCISE 16D

1 Graph the line with equation:

   a $y = 2x + 3$
   b $y = \frac{1}{2}x - 3$
   c $y = -x + 5$
   d $y = -4x - 2$
   e $y = -\frac{1}{3}x$
   f $y = -3x + 4$
   g $y = \frac{3}{4}x$
   h $y = \frac{1}{3}x - 1$
   i $y = -\frac{3}{2}x + 2$

2 **a** The line with equation $y = 2x - 1$ is reflected in the x-axis.
     i Graph the line and draw its image.
     ii Find the gradient and y-intercept of the image.
     iii Find the equation of the reflected line.

   b The line with equation $y = \frac{1}{2}x + 2$ is reflected in the y-axis.
     i Graph the line and draw its image.
     ii Find the gradient and y-intercept of the image.
     iii Find the equation of the reflected line.

E LINES OF SYMMETRY [7.8]

Many geometrical shapes have **lines of symmetry**. If the shape is drawn on the Cartesian plane, we can use the information learnt in this chapter to find the equations of the lines of symmetry.

Example 7   ◀) Self Tutor

Consider the points A(1, 3), B(6, 3) and C(6, 1).

  a Plot the points, then locate D such that ABCD is a rectangle.
  b State the coordinates of D.
  c Write down the equations of any lines of symmetry.

a

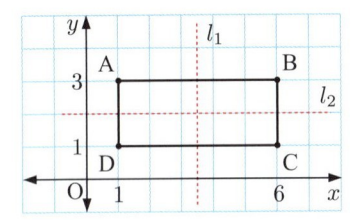

c l_1 is a vertical line with x-coordinate midway between 1 and 6.

$\therefore$ its equation is $x = \frac{1+6}{2} = 3.5$

l_2 is a horizontal line with y-coordinate midway between 1 and 3.

$\therefore$ its equation is $y = \frac{3+1}{2} = 2$.

So, the lines of symmetry have equations $x = 3.5$ and $y = 2$.

b D is at (1, 1).

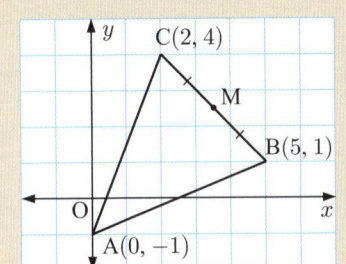

Example 8   ◀) Self Tutor

A(0, −1), B(5, 1) and C(2, 4) are the coordinates of isosceles triangle ABC.

  a Show that AB and AC have equal length.
  b Find the coordinates of M, the midpoint of line segment BC.
  c Find the equation of the line of symmetry of triangle ABC.

a $AB = \sqrt{(5-0)^2 + (1--1)^2}$
       $= \sqrt{5^2 + 2^2}$
       $= \sqrt{29}$ units

$AC = \sqrt{(2-0)^2 + (4--1)^2}$
    $= \sqrt{2^2 + 5^2}$
    $= \sqrt{29}$ units

So, AB and AC have equal length.

b The midpoint of BC is

$M\left(\frac{5+2}{2}, \frac{1+4}{2}\right)$.

So, M is $\left(\frac{7}{2}, \frac{5}{2}\right)$.

c The line of symmetry is the line through A and M.

The gradient of the line is $m = \dfrac{\frac{5}{2} - -1}{\frac{7}{2} - 0}$

$= \dfrac{\frac{7}{2}}{\frac{7}{2}} = 1$

The y-intercept is $c = -1$ (at A).

$\therefore$ its equation is $y = x - 1$.

Straight lines (Chapter 16)

EXERCISE 16E

1 Find the equations of the lines of symmetry of the following:

a, **b**, 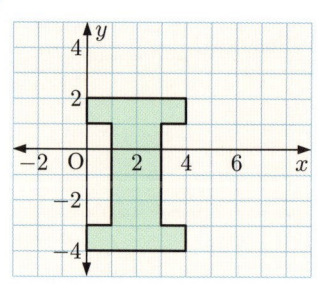 **c**

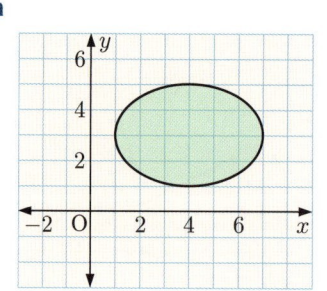

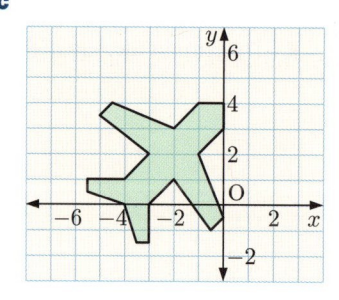

2 **a** Plot the points A(1, 0), B(9, 0), C(8, 3) and D(2, 3).
   b Classify the figure ABCD.
   c Find the equations of any lines of symmetry of ABCD.

3 **a** Plot the points A(−1, 2), B(3, 2), C(3, −2) and D(−1, −2).
   b Classify the figure ABCD.
   c Find the equations of any lines of symmetry of ABCD.

4 P, Q, R and S are the vertices of a rectangle. Given P(1, 3), Q(7, 3) and S(1, −2) find:
   a the coordinates of R
   b the midpoints of line segments PR and QS
   c the equations of the lines of symmetry.
   d What geometrical fact was verified by **b**?

5 Plot the points O(0, 0), A(1, 4), B(9, 2) and C(8, −2).
   a Prove that line segments OA and BC are parallel, and OA = BC.
   b Given that OAB is a right angle, what can you say about OABC?
   c Find the midpoints of OA and AB.
   d Find the equations of any lines of symmetry of OABC.

6 OABC is a quadrilateral with A(5, 0), B(8, 4) and C(3, 4).
   a Plot the points A, B and C and complete the figure OABC.
   b Find the equation of line segment BC.
   c Using lengths, show that OABC is a rhombus.
   d Find the midpoints of line segments OB and AC.
   e What has been verified in **d**?
   f Find the equations of any lines of symmetry.

Review set 16A

1. Find the equation of a vertical line through $(-1, 5)$.

2. Determine the equation of the illustrated line:

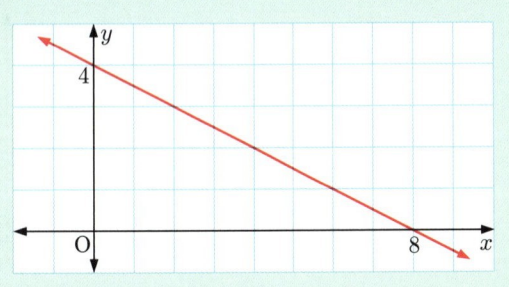

3. Find the equation of the line through $(1, -2)$ and $(3, 4)$.

4. Find the equation of the line with gradient -2 and y-intercept 3.

5. Find the equation of the line with:

   a gradient $\frac{2}{3}$ which passes through $(-3, 4)$ **b** zero gradient that passes through $(5, -4)$.

6. Does $y = \frac{4}{5}x + \frac{2}{5}$ pass through $(3, 3)$?

7. Draw the graph of the line with equation: **a** $y = \frac{3}{4}x - 2$ **b** $y = -2x + 5$.

8. Given $A(-3, 1)$, $B(1, 4)$ and $C(4, 0)$:

   a Show that triangle ABC is isosceles.

   b Find the midpoint X of line segment AC.

   c Find the equations of any lines of symmetry of triangle ABC.

9. Consider the points $A(3, -2)$, $B(8, 0)$, $C(6, 5)$ and $D(1, 3)$.

   a Prove that line segments AB and DC are parallel and equal in length.

   b Line segments AB and BC are perpendicular. Prove they are equal in length.

   c Classify the quadrilateral ABCD.

   d Find the equations of all lines of symmetry of ABCD.

Review set 16B

1. **a** Find the equation of the x-axis.

   b Write down the gradient and y-intercept of the line with equation $y = 5 - 2x$.

2. Determine the equation of the illustrated line:

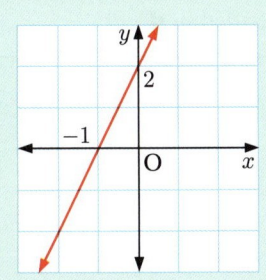

3 Find, in gradient-intercept form, the equation of a line:
   a with gradient -2 and y-intercept 7
   b passing through $(-1, 3)$ and $(2, 1)$
   c parallel to a line with gradient $\frac{3}{2}$ and passing through $(5, 0)$.

4 Does $(-3, 5)$ lie on $y = -4x - 7$?

5 Find the equation connecting the variables for the graph given.

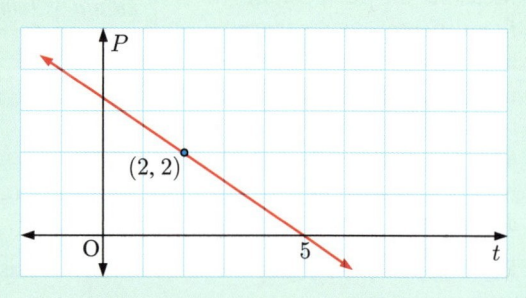

6 Find k if:
   a $(-2, k)$ lies on $y = 3x - 8$
   b $(k, 4)$ lies on $y = -\frac{1}{2}x + 5$.

7 Find the equations of the following graphs:
   a   **b**   **c**

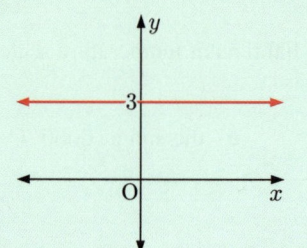

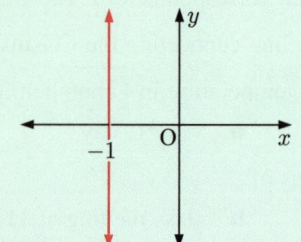

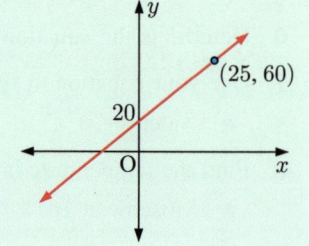

8 Draw the graph of the line with equation $y = -2x + 7$.

9 Consider the points $A(-11, 2)$, $B(-5, -6)$, $C(3, 0)$ and $D(-3, 8)$.
   a Plot A, B, C and D on a set of axes.
   b Show that all the sides of quadrilateral ABCD are equal in length.
   c Given that line segment AB is perpendicular to line segment BC, classify ABCD.
   d ABCD has four lines of symmetry. Find their equations.
   e Find the midpoint of line segment AC.
   f Check that each of the lines of symmetry passes through the point found in **e**.

Activity

Fahrenheit and Celsius

In this experiment you will determine the relationship between the Celsius and Fahrenheit temperature scales.

What to do:

1. Measure the temperature of five different liquids (such as hot water and iced water) using a thermometer that measures in both Fahrenheit and Celsius. Record the results in a table like the one alongside.

Liquid	Temperature in Celsius	Temperature in Fahrenheit

2. Plot the points on a graph with °C on the x-axis and °F on the y-axis.
3. Is there a linear relationship between °F and °C?
4. Where does the graph pass through the y-axis?
5. What temperature in Fahrenheit corresponds to 0°C?
6. Determine the equation of the line connecting the Celsius and Fahrenheit temperature scales.
7. Use your equation to find the temperature in Fahrenheit of:
    a water at 70°C
    b a 36°C day
    c the sun at 6000°C.
8. Find the temperature in Celsius of:
    a Moscow at 16°F
    b glass melting at 1148°F.
9. At what temperature in degrees Celsius does the temperature in degrees Fahrenheit become negative?

Trigonometry

17

Contents:

A	Labelling sides of a right angled triangle	[8.1]
B	The trigonometric ratios	[8.1]
C	Problem solving	[8.1]
D	True bearings	[8.7]

Opening problem

For the safety of users, wheelchair access ramps must not have an angle of incline θ exceeding $5°$.

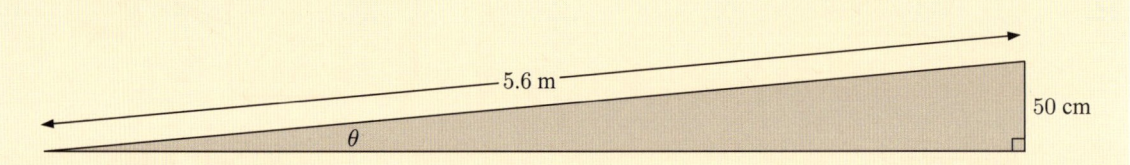

A ramp outside a post office is 5.6 m long, with a vertical rise of 50 cm. Does this ramp comply with the safety regulations?

Trigonometry is a branch of mathematics that deals with triangles. In particular, it considers the relationship between their side lengths and angles.

We can apply trigonometry in engineering, astronomy, architecture, navigation, surveying, the building industry, and in many other branches of applied science.

In this course we consider only the trigonometry of right angled triangles. However, the principles do extend to all triangles, increasing greatly the applications of trigonometry in the real world.

A LABELLING SIDES OF A RIGHT ANGLED TRIANGLE   [8.1]

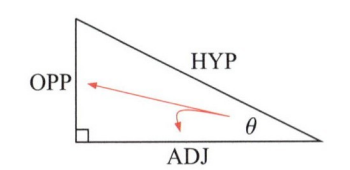

For the right angled triangle with angle θ:

- the **hypotenuse (HYP)** is the longest side
- the **opposite (OPP)** side is opposite θ
- the **adjacent (ADJ)** side is adjacent to θ.

Given a right angled triangle ABC with angles of θ and ϕ:

For angle θ,   BC is the **opposite side**
AB is the **adjacent side**.

For angle ϕ,   AB is the **opposite side**
BC is the **adjacent side**.

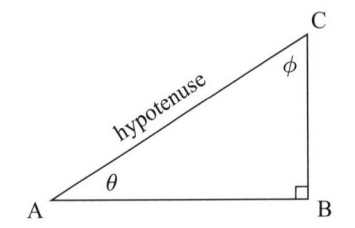

Example 1   ◀)) Self Tutor

For the triangle shown, name the:

a   hypotenuse
b   side opposite θ
c   side adjacent to θ.

a   The hypotenuse is QR.
{the longest side, opposite the right angle}
b   PQ
c   PR

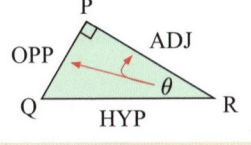

In any right angled triangle, locate the hypotenuse first. Then locate the opposite side for the angle you are working with.

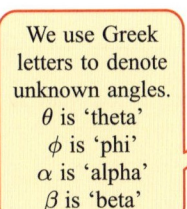

We use Greek letters to denote unknown angles.
θ is 'theta'
ϕ is 'phi'
α is 'alpha'
β is 'beta'

Example 2   ◀)) Self Tutor

For this triangle name the:

a   hypotenuse
b   side opposite angle α
c   side adjacent α
d   side opposite β
e   side adjacent β

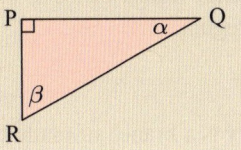

a   QR   (opposite the right angle)
b   PR
c   PQ 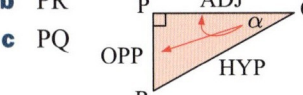
d   PQ
e   PR

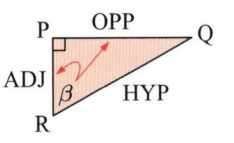

Trigonometry (Chapter 17)

EXERCISE 17A

1 For the triangles given, name the:
  i hypotenuse
  ii side opposite angle θ
  iii side adjacent to θ

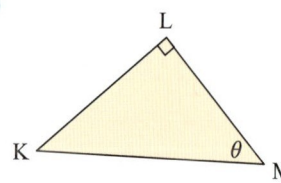

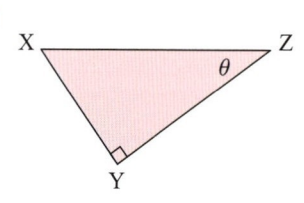

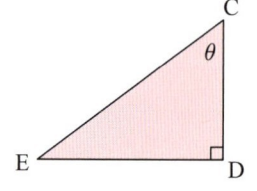

a Triangle ABC, right angle at A, angle θ at B.

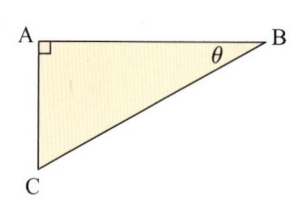

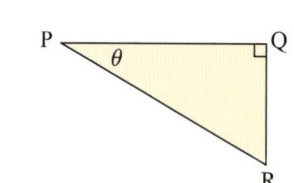

b Triangle KLM, right angle at L, angle θ at M.

c Triangle PQR, right angle at Q, angle θ at P.

d Triangle XYZ, right angle at Y, angle θ at X.

e Triangle CDE, right angle at D, angle θ at C.

f Triangle RST, right angle at R, angle θ at T.

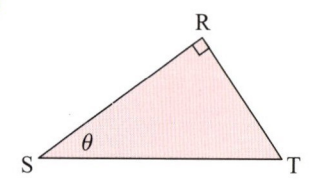

2 For the triangle given, name the:
  i hypotenuse
  ii side opposite α
  iii side adjacent to α
  iv side opposite β
  v side adjacent to β

a Triangle PQR, right angle at Q, α at P, β at R.

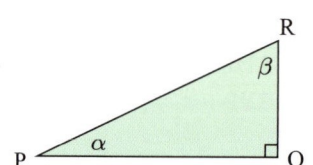

b Triangle ABC, right angle at B, β at A, α at C.

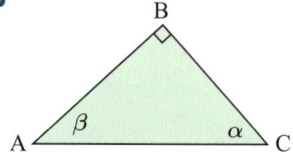

B THE TRIGONOMETRIC RATIOS [8.1]

Discovery 1 — Ratio of sides of right angled triangles

In this **Discovery** we will find the ratios $\dfrac{\text{OPP}}{\text{HYP}}$, $\dfrac{\text{ADJ}}{\text{HYP}}$ and $\dfrac{\text{OPP}}{\text{ADJ}}$ in a series of triangles which are enlargements of each other.

What to do:

1 Consider four right angled triangles ABC. $\widehat{CAB}$ is $30°$ in each case but the sides vary in length.

By accurately measuring to the nearest millimetre, complete a table like the one following.

Notice that $\dfrac{AB}{AC} = \dfrac{ADJ}{HYP}$, $\dfrac{BC}{AC} = \dfrac{OPP}{HYP}$,

and $\dfrac{BC}{AB} = \dfrac{OPP}{ADJ}$.

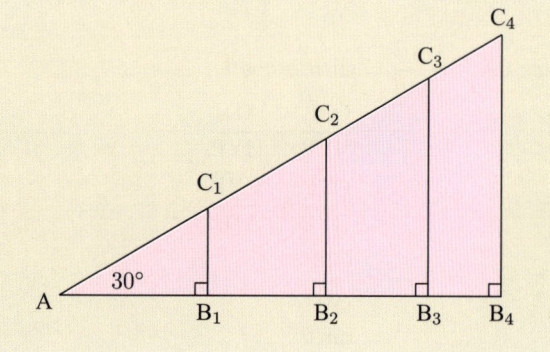

Triangle	AB	BC	AC	$\dfrac{AB}{AC}$	$\dfrac{BC}{AC}$	$\dfrac{BC}{AB}$
1						
2						
3						
4						

Convert all fractions to 2 decimal places.

PRINTABLE WORKSHEET

2 Repeat **1** for the set of triangles alongside.

3 What have you discovered from **1** and **2**?

From the **Discovery** you should have found that:

> For a fixed angled right angled triangle, the ratios $\dfrac{\text{OPP}}{\text{HYP}}$, $\dfrac{\text{ADJ}}{\text{HYP}}$ and $\dfrac{\text{OPP}}{\text{ADJ}}$ are constant no matter how much the triangle is enlarged.

These ratios have the traditional names **sine**, **cosine** and **tangent** respectively.

We abbreviate them to **sin**, **cos** and **tan**.

> In any right angled triangle with an angle θ:
>
> $\sin\theta = \dfrac{\text{OPP}}{\text{HYP}}$, $\quad \cos\theta = \dfrac{\text{ADJ}}{\text{HYP}}$, $\quad \tan\theta = \dfrac{\text{OPP}}{\text{ADJ}}$

Notice that
$$\begin{aligned}\dfrac{\sin\theta}{\cos\theta} &= \sin\theta \div \cos\theta \\ &= \dfrac{\text{OPP}}{\text{HYP}} \div \dfrac{\text{ADJ}}{\text{HYP}} \\ &= \dfrac{\text{OPP}}{\text{HYP}} \times \dfrac{\text{HYP}}{\text{ADJ}} \\ &= \dfrac{\text{OPP}}{\text{ADJ}} \\ &= \tan\theta\end{aligned}$$

So, $\quad \tan\theta = \dfrac{\sin\theta}{\cos\theta}$

Trigonometry (Chapter 17)

FINDING TRIGONOMETRIC RATIOS

Example 3

For the given triangle find $\sin \theta$, $\cos \theta$ and $\tan \theta$.

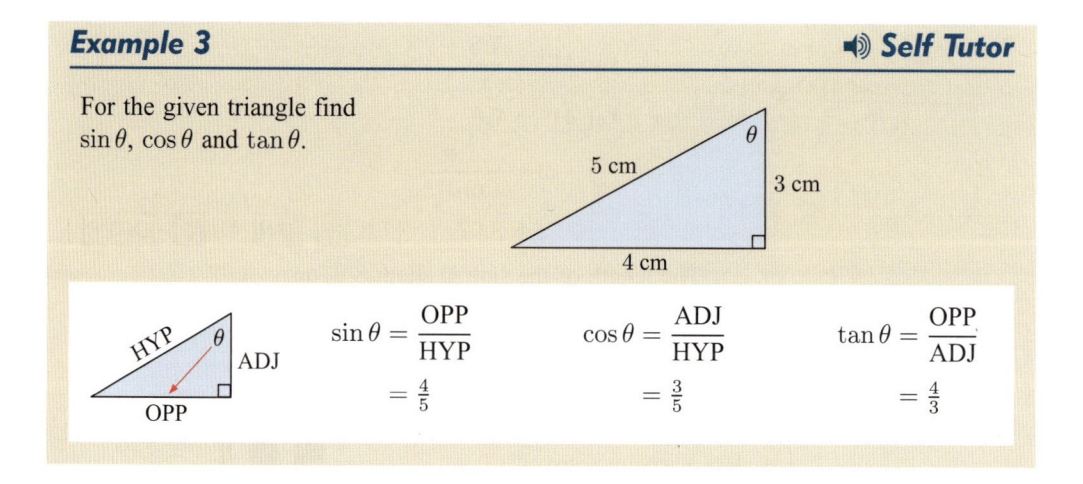

(Triangle with hypotenuse 5 cm, adjacent 4 cm, opposite 3 cm, angle θ at top)

$$\sin \theta = \frac{\text{OPP}}{\text{HYP}} = \frac{4}{5} \qquad \cos \theta = \frac{\text{ADJ}}{\text{HYP}} = \frac{3}{5} \qquad \tan \theta = \frac{\text{OPP}}{\text{ADJ}} = \frac{4}{3}$$

We can use these ratios to find unknown sides and angles of right angled triangles. When solving for unknowns, we can use a calculator to evaluate the trigonometric ratios.

FINDING SIDES

In a right angled triangle, if we are given another angle and a side we can find:

- the third angle using 'the angle sum of a triangle is $180°$'
- the other sides using trigonometry.

Step 1: Redraw the figure and mark on it HYP, OPP, ADJ relative to the given angle.
Step 2: Choose the correct trigonometric ratio and use it to set up an equation.
Step 3: Solve to find the unknown.

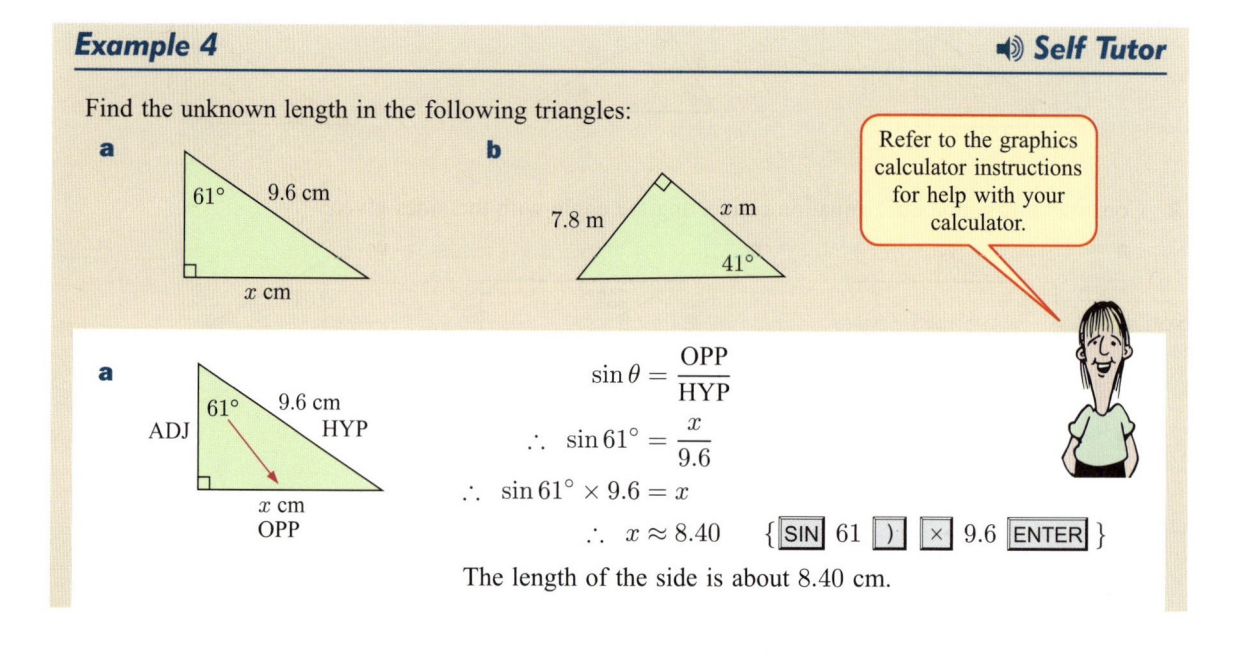

Example 4

Find the unknown length in the following triangles:

a (Triangle with angle 61°, hypotenuse 9.6 cm, opposite side x cm)

b (Triangle with side 7.8 m, angle 41°, side x m)

Refer to the graphics calculator instructions for help with your calculator.

a (Redrawn triangle with 61°, HYP 9.6 cm, OPP x cm, ADJ)

$$\sin \theta = \frac{\text{OPP}}{\text{HYP}}$$

$$\therefore \sin 61° = \frac{x}{9.6}$$

$$\therefore \sin 61° \times 9.6 = x$$

$$\therefore x \approx 8.40 \qquad \{\boxed{\text{SIN}}\ 61\ \boxed{)}\ \boxed{\times}\ 9.6\ \boxed{\text{ENTER}}\}$$

The length of the side is about 8.40 cm.

b

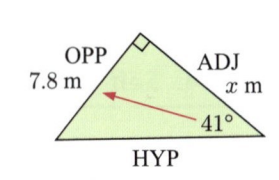

$$\tan\theta = \frac{\text{OPP}}{\text{ADJ}}$$

$$\therefore \tan 41° = \frac{7.8}{x}$$

$$\therefore x \times \tan 41° = 7.8$$

$$\therefore x = \frac{7.8}{\tan 41°}$$

$$\therefore x \approx 8.97 \quad \{7.8 \div \boxed{\text{TAN}}\ 41\ \boxed{)}\ \boxed{\text{ENTER}}\}$$

The length of the side is about 8.97 m.

Unless otherwise stated, all lengths should be given correct to 3 significant figures and all angles correct to 1 decimal place.

EXERCISE 17B.1

1 For each of the following triangles find:

  i $\sin\theta$ **ii** $\cos\theta$ **iii** $\tan\theta$ **iv** $\sin\phi$ **v** $\cos\phi$ **vi** $\tan\phi$

a **b** 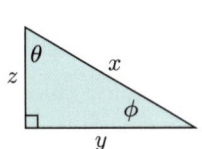 **c**

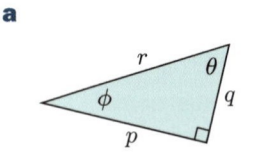

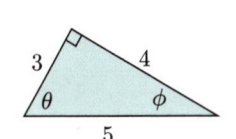

d 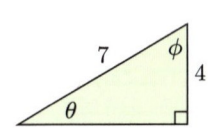 **e** 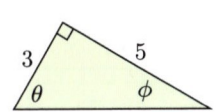 **f**

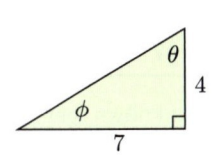

2 Construct a trigonometric equation connecting the angle with the sides given:

a **b** 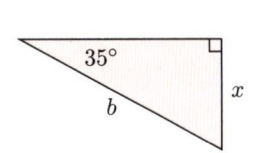 **c**

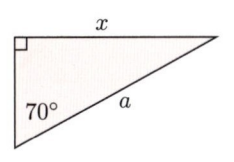

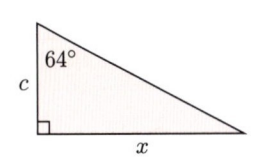

d 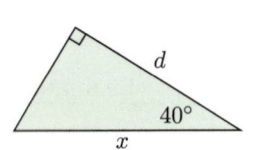 **e** 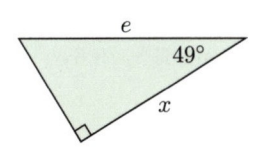 **f**

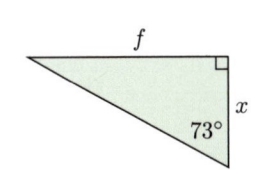

Trigonometry (Chapter 17)

g triangle with angle 54°, side x, side g

h triangle with angle 30°, side x, side h

i triangle with angle 68°, side i, side x

3 Find, correct to 2 decimal places, the value of x in:

a right triangle with 76° angle, side 16 cm adjacent, x cm opposite

b right triangle with 30° angle, 15 cm, and x cm

c right triangle with 64° angle, 4.8 m, and x m

d right triangle with 5 km, 42° angle, x km

e right triangle with 8 m, 34° angle, x m

f right triangle with 80 cm, 74° angle, x cm

g right triangle with 28° angle, 52 m, x m

h right triangle with 45 km, 68° angle, x km

i right triangle with x mm, 27° angle, 11 mm

j right triangle with 5.6 cm, 70° angle, x cm

k right triangle with 50° angle, x m, 27 m

l right triangle with 12 km, x km, 49° angle

4 Find *all* the unknown angles and sides of:

a right triangle with a cm, 28° angle, b cm, 12 cm, θ

b right triangle with 15 m, θ, a m, 63°, b m

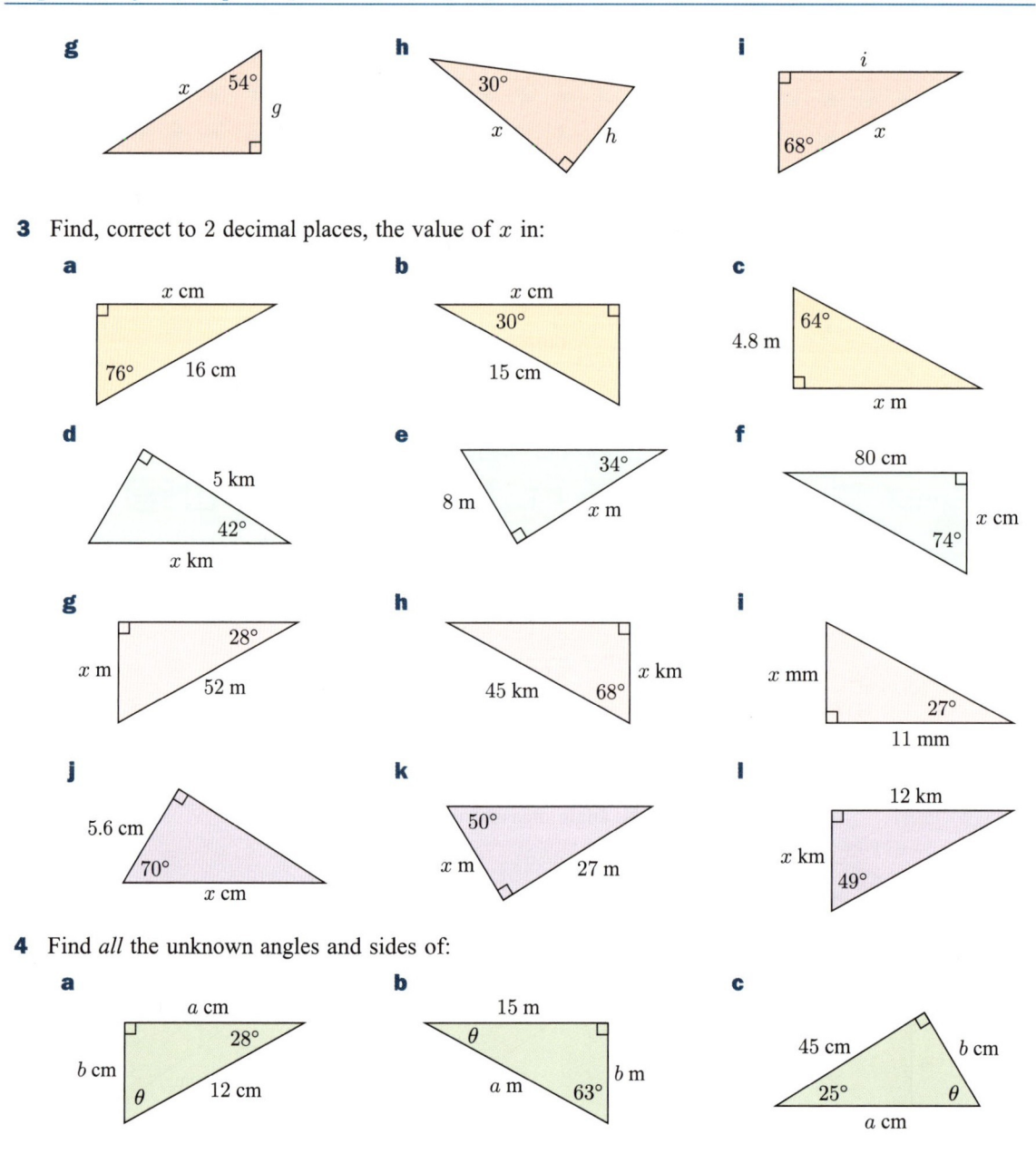

c triangle with 45 cm, b cm, 25°, a cm, θ

FINDING ANGLES

In the right angled triangle shown, $\sin \theta = \frac{3}{5}$.

So, we are looking for the angle θ with a sine of $\frac{3}{5}$.

If $\sin^{-1}(....)$ reads "the angle with a sine of ....", we can write $\theta = \sin^{-1}(\frac{3}{5})$.

Another way of describing this is to say "θ is the *inverse sine* of $\frac{3}{5}$".

> If $\sin \theta = x$ then θ is the **inverse sine** of x.

We can define **inverse cosine** and **inverse tangent** in a similar way.

You can find graphics calculator instructions for finding these inverse trigonometric functions on page **16**.

Example 5

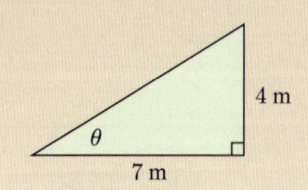

Find the measure of the angle marked θ in:

a *(right triangle with legs 7 m (adjacent to θ) and 4 m (opposite))*

b *(right triangle with hypotenuse 5.92 km and side 2.67 km adjacent to θ)*

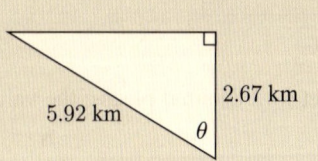

a

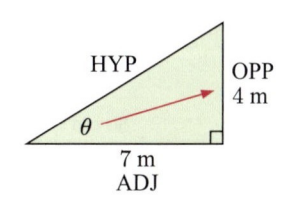

$$\tan \theta = \frac{\text{OPP}}{\text{ADJ}}$$

$\therefore \ \tan \theta = \frac{4}{7}$

$\therefore \ \theta = \tan^{-1}\left(\frac{4}{7}\right)$

$\therefore \ \theta \approx 29.7°$ { SHIFT tan (4 ÷ 7) EXE }

So, the angle measure is about 29.7°.

b

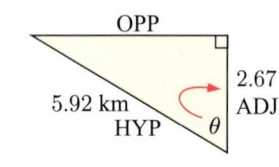

$$\cos \theta = \frac{\text{ADJ}}{\text{HYP}}$$

$\therefore \ \cos \theta = \frac{2.67}{5.92}$

$\therefore \ \theta = \cos^{-1}\left(\frac{2.67}{5.92}\right)$

$\therefore \ \theta \approx 63.2°$ { SHIFT cos (2.67 ÷ 5.92) EXE }

So, the angle measure is about 63.2°.

EXERCISE 17B.2

1 Find the measure of the angle marked θ in:

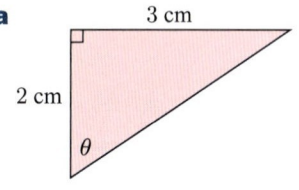

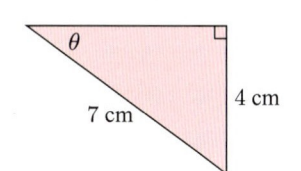

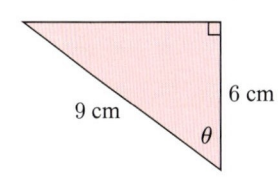

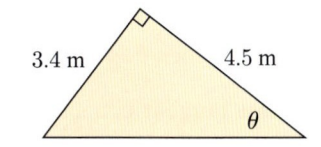

a right triangle with legs 3 cm and 2 cm, θ at the 3 cm–hypotenuse vertex

b right triangle with legs 7 cm and 4 cm, θ at top

c right triangle with legs 9 cm and 6 cm, θ at the 9 cm–hypotenuse vertex

d right triangle with legs 3.2 m and 5.6 m, θ shown

e right triangle with sides 3.1 km and 2.7 km, θ at top

f right triangle with legs 3 m and 4 m, θ shown

g right triangle with 5.2 km and 4.7 km, θ shown

h right triangle with 3.4 m and 4.5 m, θ at bottom

i right triangle with 7.2 mm and 12.4 mm, θ shown

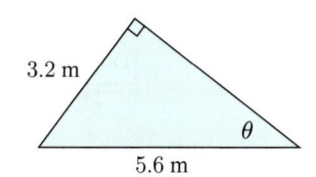

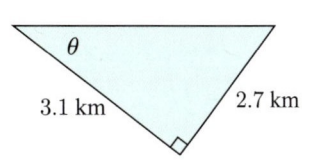

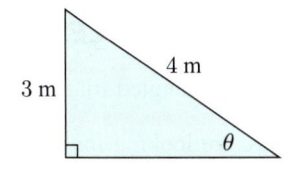

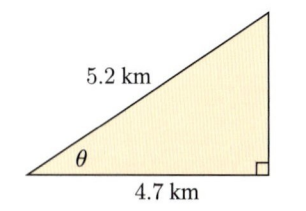

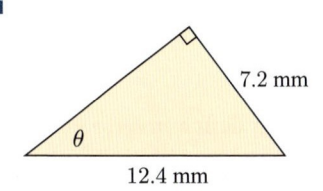

Trigonometry (Chapter 17)   339

2 Find all the unknown sides and angles in the following:

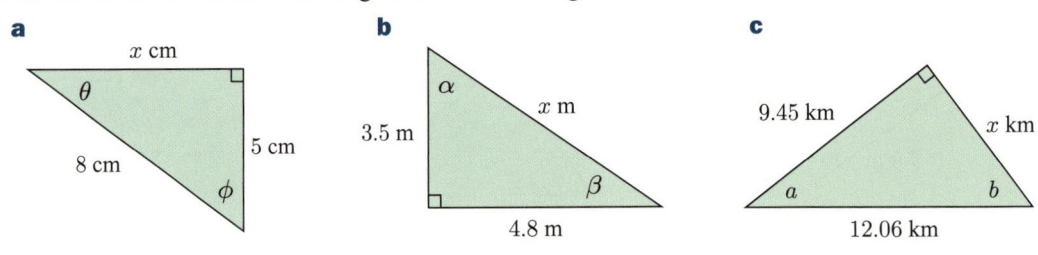

a Triangle with x cm (top), 5 cm (right), 8 cm (hypotenuse), angles θ and ϕ.

b Triangle with α (top), x m, 3.5 m (left), 4.8 m (bottom), angle β.

c Triangle with 9.45 km, x km, 12.06 km, angles a and b.

3 Check your answers for x in question **2** using Pythagoras' theorem.

4 Find the unknowns correct to 3 significant figures:

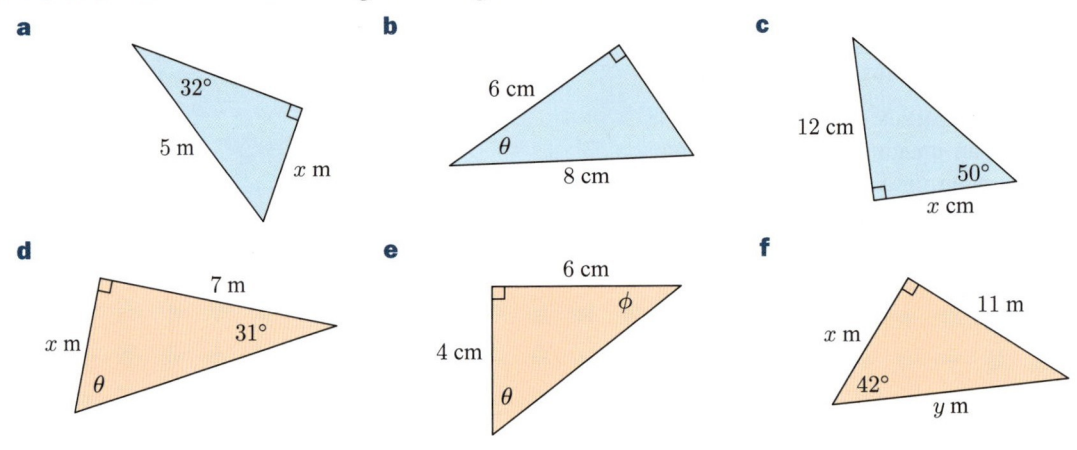

a Triangle: 32°, 5 m, x m.

b Triangle: 6 cm, 8 cm, angle θ.

c Triangle: 12 cm, 50°, x cm.

d Triangle: 7 m, 31°, x m, angle θ.

e Triangle: 6 cm, 4 cm, angles ϕ and θ.

f Triangle: 11 m, 42°, x m, y m.

5 Find the unknowns correct to 3 significant figures:

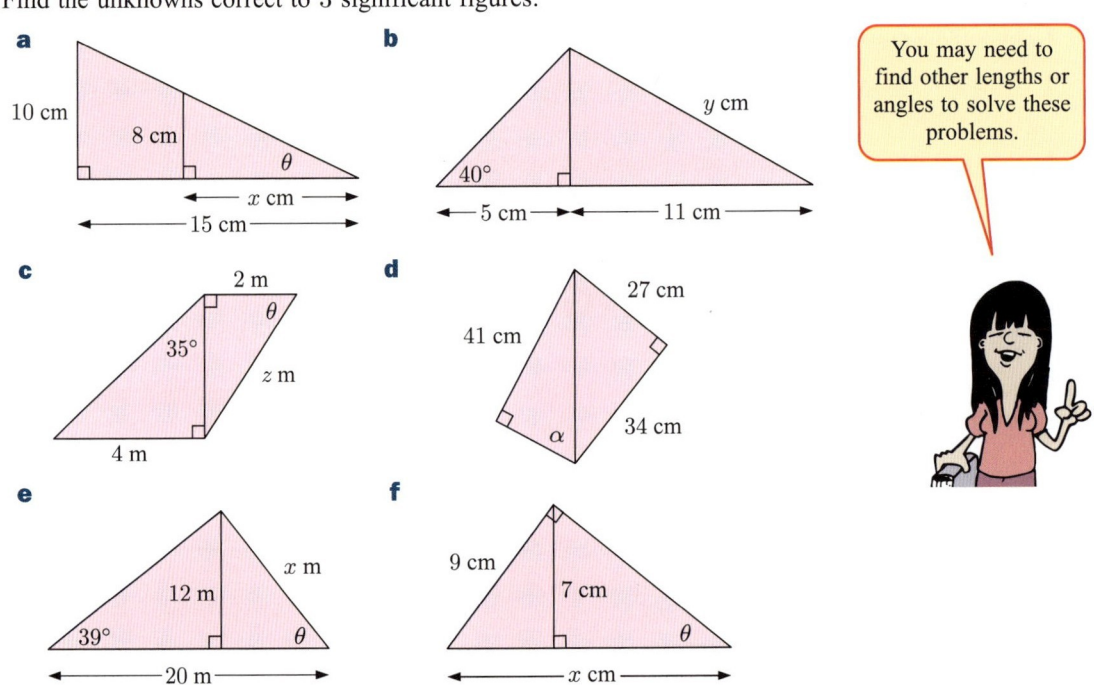

a 10 cm, 8 cm, x cm, 15 cm, angle θ.

b y cm, 40°, 5 cm, 11 cm.

c 2 m, 35°, z m, 4 m, angle θ.

d 27 cm, 41 cm, 34 cm, angle α.

e 39°, 12 m, 20 m, x m, angle θ.

f 9 cm, 7 cm, x cm, angle θ.

> You may need to find other lengths or angles to solve these problems.

6 Try to find θ using trigonometry. What conclusion can you draw about each triangle?

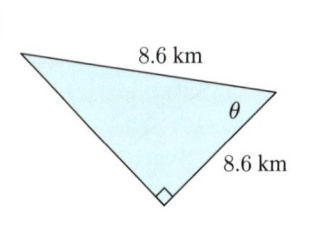

a 8.1 m, 7.9 m, θ

b 14 mm, 12 mm, θ

c 8.6 km, 8.6 km, θ

Discovery 2 — Hipparchus and the universe

Hipparchus was a Greek astronomer and mathematician born in Nicaea in the 2nd century BC. He is considered among the greatest astronomers of antiquity. In this **Discovery** we see how Hipparchus measured the radius of the moon.

From the earth's surface, the angle between an imaginary line to the centre of the moon, and an imaginary line to the edge of the moon (a tangent to the moon) is about $0.25°$.

The average distance from the earth to the moon is about $384\,403$ km.

Hipparchus made several estimations of this distance over his life.

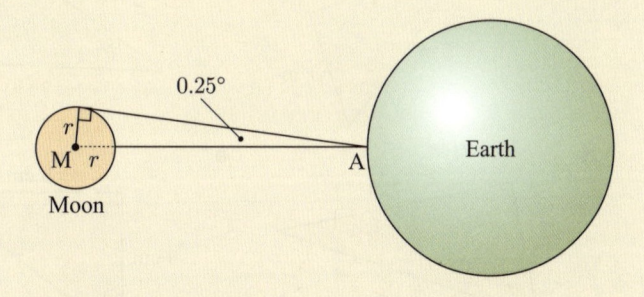

What to do:

1 Confirm from the diagram that $\sin 0.25° = \dfrac{r}{r + 384\,403}$.

2 Solve this equation to find r, the radius of the moon.

3 Research the actual radius of the moon, and if possible find out how it was calculated. How does your answer to **2** compare?

4 Reserach Hipparchus' other astronomical achievements.

C PROBLEM SOLVING [8.1]

The trigonometric ratios can be used to solve a wide variety of problems involving right angled triangles. When solving such problems it is important to follow the steps below:

Step 1: Read the question carefully.

Step 2: Draw a diagram, not necessarily to scale, with the given information clearly marked.

Step 3: If necessary, label the vertices of triangles in the figure.

Trigonometry (Chapter 17)

Step 4: State clearly any assumptions you make which will enable you to use right angled triangles or properties of other geometric figures.

Step 5: Choose an appropriate trigonometric ratio. Use it to generate an equation connecting the quantities. On some occasions more than one equation may be needed.

Step 6: Solve the equation(s) to find the unknown.

Step 7: Answer the question in words.

ANGLES OF ELEVATION AND DEPRESSION

The angle between the horizontal and your line of sight is called the **angle of elevation** if you are looking upwards, or the **angle of depression** if you are looking downwards.

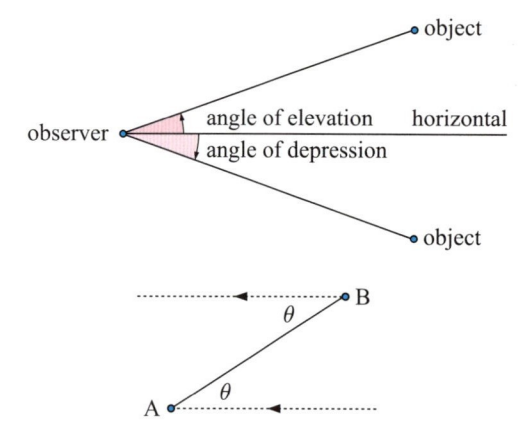

If the angle of elevation from A to B is θ, then the angle of depression from B to A is also θ.

When using trigonometry to solve problems we often use:

- the properties of isosceles and right angled triangles
- the properties of circles and tangents
- angles of elevation and depression.

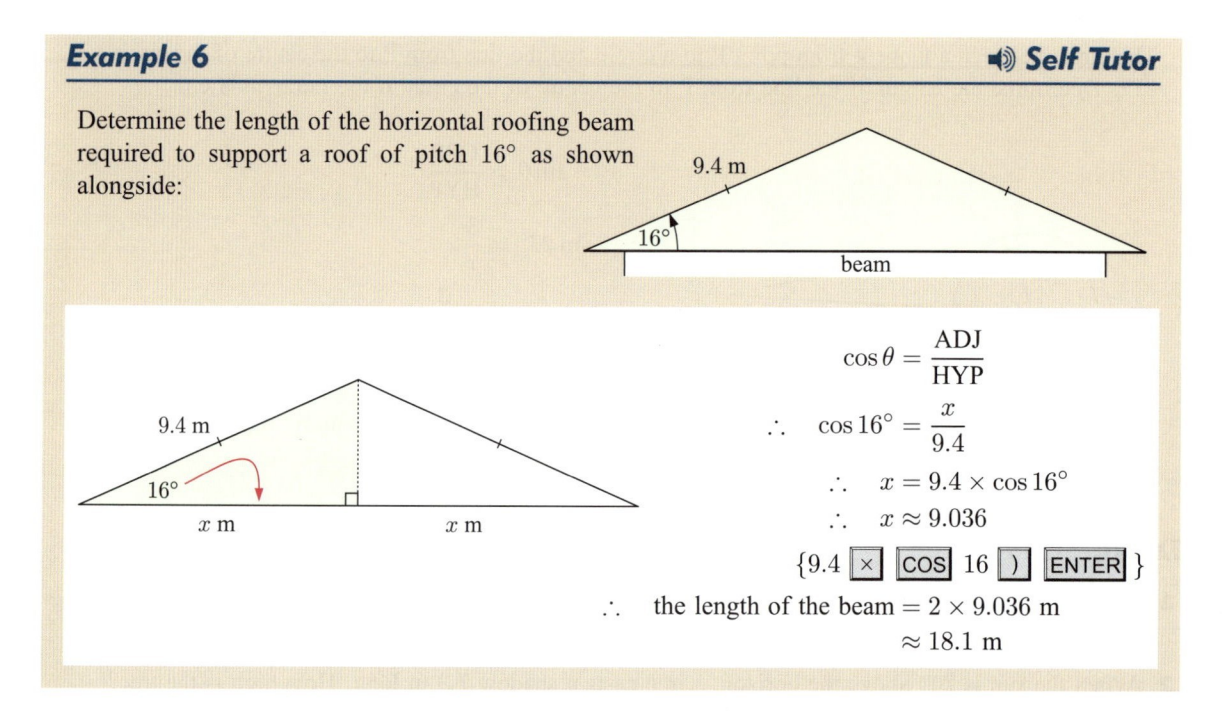

Example 6 ◀》 Self Tutor

Determine the length of the horizontal roofing beam required to support a roof of pitch 16° as shown alongside:

$$\cos \theta = \frac{\text{ADJ}}{\text{HYP}}$$

$$\therefore \quad \cos 16° = \frac{x}{9.4}$$

$$\therefore \quad x = 9.4 \times \cos 16°$$

$$\therefore \quad x \approx 9.036$$

{9.4 [×] [COS] 16 [)] [ENTER] }

$\therefore$ the length of the beam $= 2 \times 9.036$ m
≈ 18.1 m

Example 7

A ladder 4.1 m in length rests against a vertical wall and reaches 3.5 m up from ground level. Find:
a the angle the ladder makes with the ground
b the distance from the foot of the ladder to the wall using trigonometry.

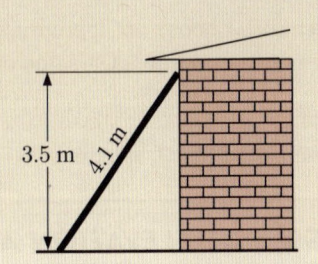

a $\sin \theta = \dfrac{\text{OPP}}{\text{HYP}} = \dfrac{3.5}{4.1}$

$\therefore \theta = \sin^{-1}\left(\dfrac{3.5}{4.1}\right)$

$\therefore \theta \approx 58.6°$ { SHIFT sin (3.5 ÷ 4.1) EXE }

$\therefore$ the ladder makes an angle of about 58.6° with the ground.

b $\cos \theta = \dfrac{\text{ADJ}}{\text{HYP}}$

$\therefore \cos 58.61° = \dfrac{x}{4.1}$

$\therefore 4.1 \times \cos 58.61° = x$

$\therefore 2.14 \approx x$ $\therefore$ the foot of the ladder is about 2.14 m from the wall.

Example 8

The angle between a tangent from point P to a circle and the line from P to the centre of the circle is 27°. Determine the length of the line from P to the centre of the circle if the radius is 3 cm.

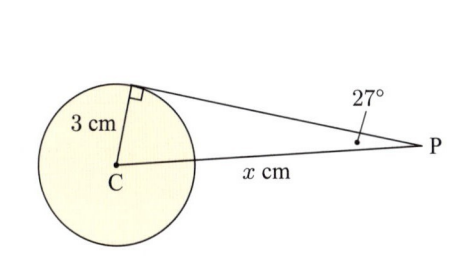

$\sin \theta = \dfrac{\text{OPP}}{\text{HYP}}$

$\therefore \sin 27° = \dfrac{3}{x}$

$\therefore x = \dfrac{3}{\sin 27°}$

$\therefore x \approx 6.61$

$\therefore$ CP has length approximately 6.61 cm.

EXERCISE 17C

1 From a point 235 m from the base of a cliff, the angle of elevation to the cliff top is 25°. Find the height of the cliff.

2 When the sun is 24° above the horizon, a tree casts a shadow 7.3 m long. How high is the tree?

Trigonometry (Chapter 17)

3 A new road is to be constructed as shown alongside. Find θ, the diversion angle from the current road.

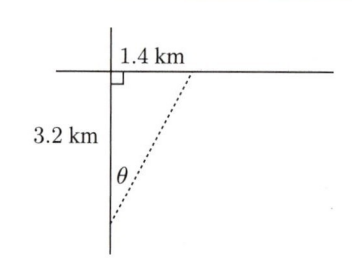

4 What angle will a 5 m ladder make with a wall if it reaches 4.2 m up the wall?

5 The angle of elevation from a fishing boat to the top of a lighthouse 25 m above sea-level is $6°$. Calculate the horizontal distance from the boat to the lighthouse.

6 A rectangular gate has a diagonal strut of length 3 m. The angle between the diagonal and a side is $28°$. Find the length of the longer side of the gate.

7 A model helicopter takes off from the horizontal ground with a constant vertical speed of 5 m/s. After 10 seconds the angle of elevation from Sam to the helicopter is $62°$. Sam is 1.8 m tall. How far is Sam's head from the helicopter at this time?

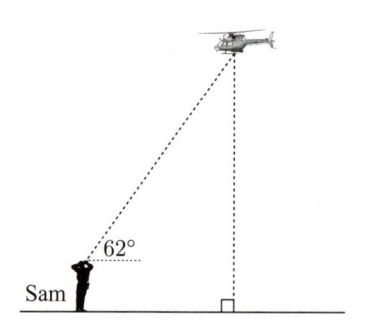

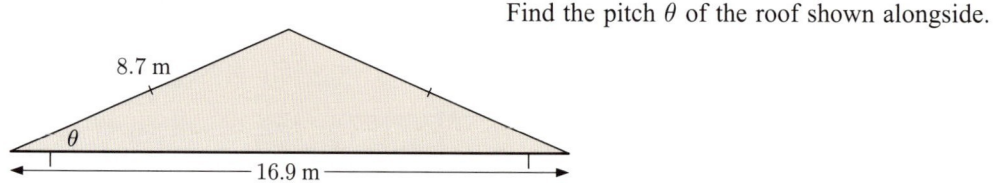

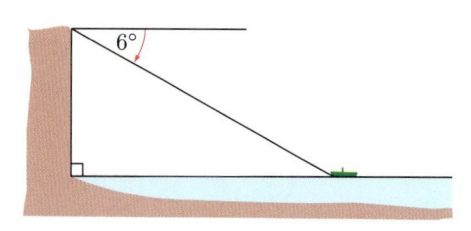

8 Find the pitch θ of the roof shown alongside.

9 From a vertical cliff 80 m above sea level, a fishing boat is observed at an angle of depression of $6°$. How far out to sea is the boat?

10 A railway line goes up an incline of constant angle $4°$ over a horizontal distance of 4 km. How much altitude has the train gained by the end of the incline?

11 A kite is attached to a 50 m long string. The other end of the string is secured to the ground. If the kite is flying 35 m above ground level, find the angle θ that the string makes with the ground.

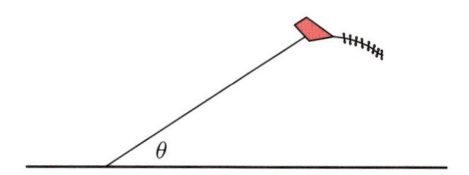

12 Antonio drew a margin along the edge of his 30 cm long page. At the top of the page the margin was 2 cm from the edge of the page, but at the bottom the margin was 3 cm from the edge of the page. How many degrees off parallel was Antonio's margin?

13 A goal post was hit by lightning and snapped in two. The top of the post is now resting 15 m from its base at an angle of 25°. Find the height of the goal post before it snapped.

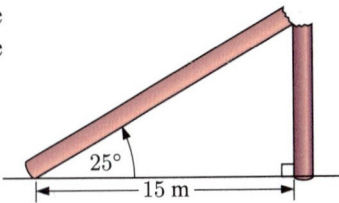

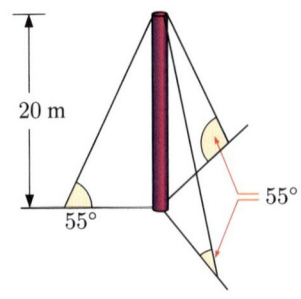

14 Three strong cables are used to brace a 20 m tall pole against movement due to the wind. Each rope is attached so that the angle of elevation to the top of the pole is 55°. Find the total length of cable.

15 A rectangle has length 6 m and width 4 m. Find the acute angle formed where the diagonals intersect.

16 A tangent from point P to a circle of radius 4 cm is 10 cm long. Find:
  a the distance of P from the centre of the circle
  b the size of the angle between the tangent and the line joining P to the centre of the circle.

17 AB is a chord of a circle with centre O and radius of length 5 cm. AB has length 8 cm. Find the size of angle $A\hat{O}B$, which is the angle AB *subtends* at the centre of the circle.

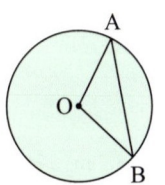

18 Find the area of the parallelogram:

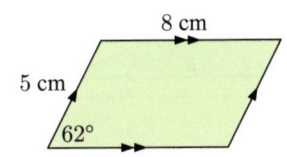

19 A rhombus has sides of length 10 cm, and the angle between two adjacent sides is 76°. Find the length of the longer diagonal of the rhombus.

20 For the circle given, find:
  a the radius of the circle
  b the distance between A and B.

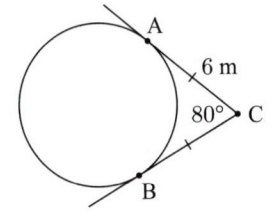

21 An aeroplane takes off from the ground at an angle of 27° and its average speed in the first 10 seconds is 200 km/h. What is the altitude of the plane at the end of this time?

22 Find the size of angle ABC.

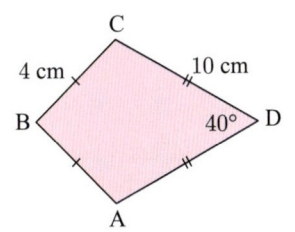

Trigonometry (Chapter 17) 345

23 The angle of elevation from a point on level ground to the top of a building 100 m high is 22°.
   a Find the distance of the point from the base of the building.
   b The point is moved towards the building until the angle of elevation is 40°. How far is the point moved?

24 From a point A which is 30 m from the base of a building B, the angle of elevation to the top of the building C is 56°, and to the top of the flag pole CD is 60°.
Find the length of the flag pole.

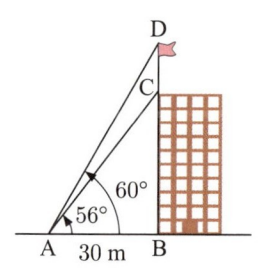

25 Find the shortest distance between the two parallel lines.

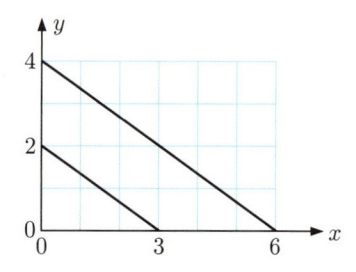

D TRUE BEARINGS   [8.7]

We can measure a direction by comparing it with the **true north direction**. We call this a **true bearing**. Measurements are always taken in the **clockwise** direction.

Imagine you are standing at point A, facing north. You turn **clockwise** through an angle until you face B. The **bearing of B from A** is the angle through which you have turned.

So, the bearing of B from A is the clockwise measure of the angle between the 'north' line through A, and AB.

In the diagram above, the bearing of B from A is 72° from true north. We write this as 072°.

To find the true **bearing of A from B**, we place ourselves at point B and face north. We then measure the clockwise angle through which we have to turn so that we face A. The true bearing of A from B is 252°.

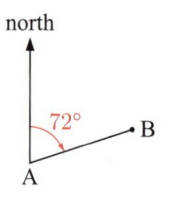

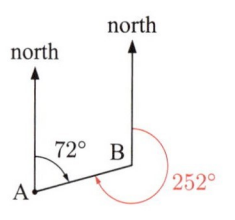

Note:
 • A true bearing is always written using three digits.
   For example, we write 072° rather than 72°.
 • The bearings of A from B and B from A always differ by 180°.
   You should be able to explain this using angle pair properties for parallel lines.

Example 9

An aeroplane departs A and flies on a 143° course for 368 km. It then changes direction to a 233° course and flies a further 472 km to town C. Find:
  a the distance of C from A
  b the bearing of C from A.

First, we draw a fully labelled diagram of the flight. On the figure, we show angles found using parallel lines.

The aeroplane turns $(233° - 143°)$ which is 90°.

∴ angle ABC measures 90°.

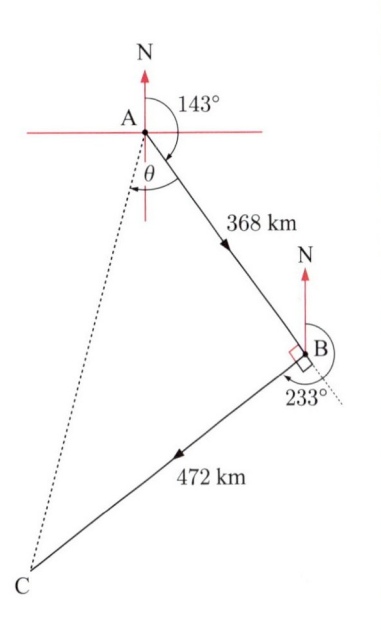

a $AC^2 = AB^2 + BC^2$

  ∴ $AC = \sqrt{368^2 + 472^2}$ {Pythagoras}

  ≈ 598.5

  So, C is about 599 km from A.

b To find the required angle we first need to find θ.

  Now $\tan \theta = \dfrac{\text{OPP}}{\text{ADJ}} = \dfrac{472}{368}$

  ∴ $\theta = \tan^{-1}\left(\dfrac{472}{368}\right)$

  ∴ $\theta \approx 52.1°$

  The required angle is $143° + 52.1° \approx 195.1°$

  ∴ the bearing of C from A is about 195.1°.

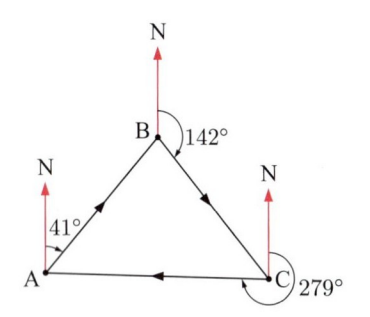

EXERCISE 17D

1 Draw diagrams to represent bearings from O of:
  a 136°   **b** 240°   **c** 051°   **d** 327°

2 Find the bearing of Q from P if the bearing of P from Q is:
  a 054°   **b** 113°   **c** 263°   **d** 304°

3 A, B and C are the checkpoints of a triangular orienteering course. For each of the following courses, find the bearing of:
  i B from A   **ii** C from B   **iii** B from C
  iv C from A   **v** A from B   **vi** A from C.

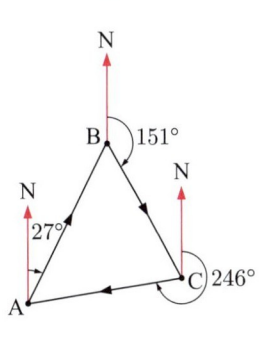

Trigonometry (Chapter 17)

4 A bushwalker walks 14 km east and then 9 km south. Find the bearing of his finishing position from his starting point.

5 Lighthouse L is 3 km north and 5 km west of lighthouse M. Find the bearing of:
   a lighthouse L from lighthouse M
   b lighthouse M from lighthouse L.

6 Runner A runs at 10 km/h due north. Runner B leaves the same spot and runs at 12 km/h due east. Find the distance and bearing of runner B from runner A after 30 minutes.

7 A hiker walks in the direction 153° and stops when she is 9 km south of her starting point. How far did she walk?

8 A ship sails for 60 km on a bearing of 040°. How far east of its starting point is the ship?

9 Natasha is 50 m due east of Michelle. Natasha walks 20 m due north, and Michelle walks 10 m due south. Find the distance and bearing of Michelle from Natasha now.

10 An aeroplane travels on a bearing of 295° so that it is 200 km west of its starting point. How far has it travelled on this bearing?

11 A fishing trawler sails from port P in the direction 024° for 30 km, and then in the direction 114° for 20 km.
Calculate:
   a the distance and bearing of the trawler from P
   b the direction in which the trawler must sail in order to return to P.

12 A search and rescue team travel 73 km on a bearing of 243°. They then need to go a further 2 km in the direction 153° to reach the missing vessel.
   a How far away was the vessel?
   b What initial direction would have led the team straight to the vessel?

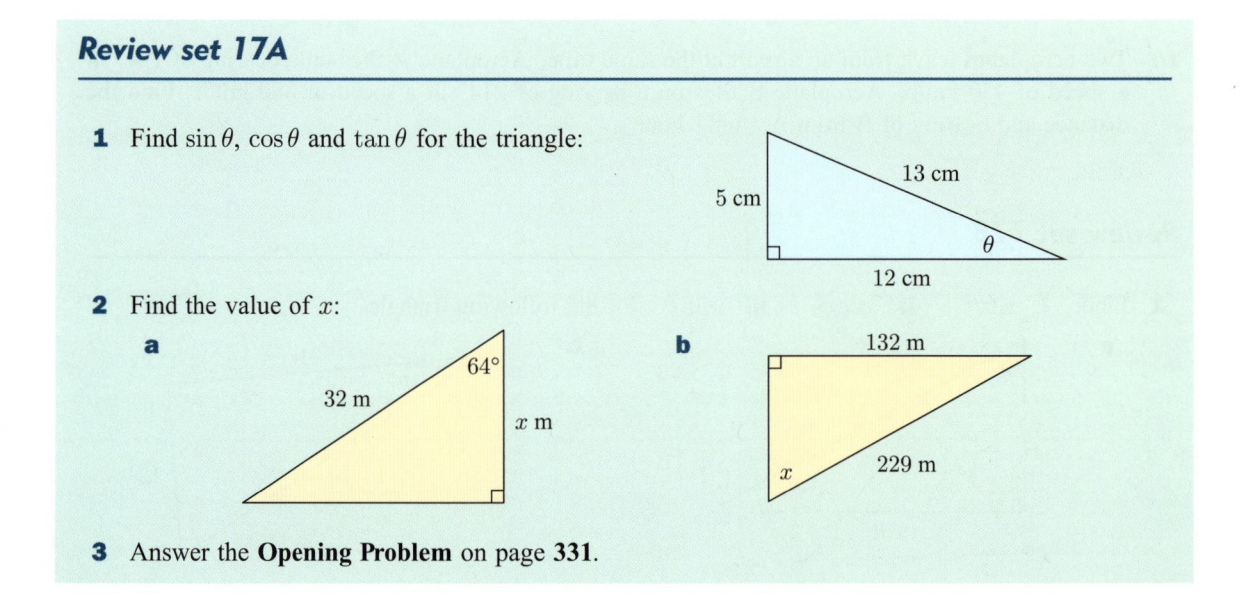

Review set 17A

1 Find $\sin\theta$, $\cos\theta$ and $\tan\theta$ for the triangle:

2 Find the value of x:
   a (triangle with 32 m, 64°, x m)
   b (triangle with 132 m, 229 m, x)

3 Answer the **Opening Problem** on page **331**.

4 Find the measure of all unknown sides and angles in triangle CDE:

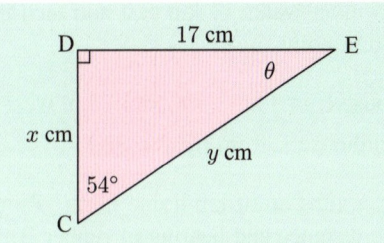

5 From a point 120 m horizontally from the base of a building, the angle of elevation to the top of the building is 34°. Find the height of the building.

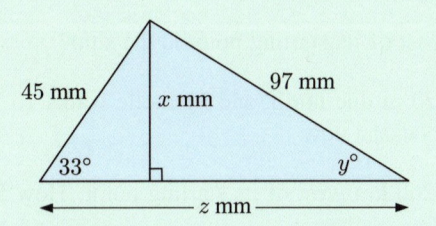

6 Find the size of the unknowns.

7 A rectangular patio has a diagonal of 17.9 m. The diagonal makes an angle of 56 degrees to the house. Find the dimensions of the patio (to the nearest cm).

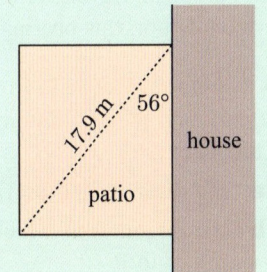

8 Find the diameter of this circle.

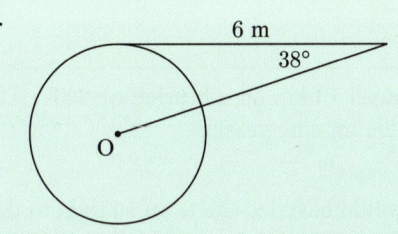

9 A ship sails 40 km on the bearing 056°. How far is it north of its starting point?

10 Two aeroplanes leave from an airport at the same time. Aeroplane A flies on a bearing of 124° at a speed of 450 km/h. Aeroplane B flies on a bearing of 214° at a speed of 380 km/h. Find the distance and bearing of B from A after 1 hour.

Review set 17B

1 Find: **i** $\sin\theta$ **ii** $\cos\phi$ **iii** $\tan\theta$ for the following triangles:

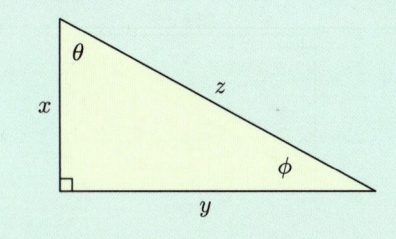

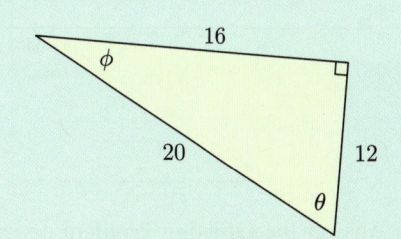

a

b

2 Find the value of θ in the following:

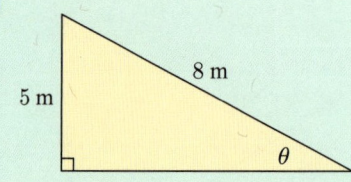

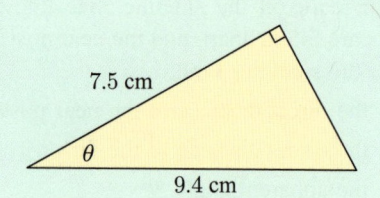

a [triangle with sides 5 m, 8 m, angle θ]

b [triangle with sides 7.5 cm, 9.4 cm, angle θ]

3 Find the measure of all unknown sides and angles in triangle KLM:

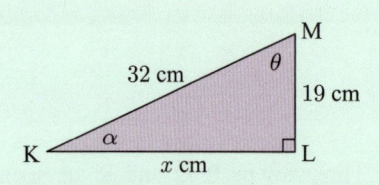

[triangle KLM with KM = 32 cm, ML = 19 cm, KL = x cm, angle at M = θ, angle at K = α, right angle at L]

4 The angle of elevation from a point 2 km from the base of the vertical cliff to the top of the cliff is 17.7°. Find the height of the cliff, in metres.

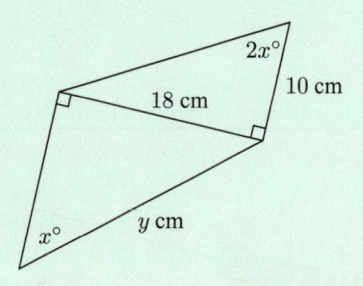

5 Find the unknowns in the diagram alongside.

[quadrilateral with sides 18 cm, 10 cm, y cm, angles $2x°$ and $x°$]

6 A truck lifts one end of a felled tree trunk 80 cm off the ground. If the trunk is 35 m long, what angle with the ground does it make?

7 Find:
  a the diameter of the circle
  b the distance BC.

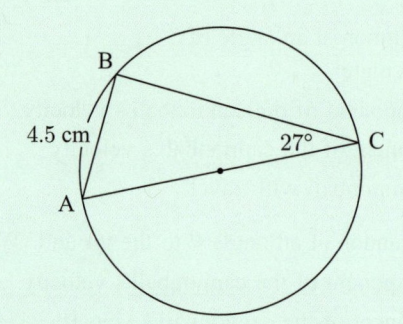

[circle with chord AB = 4.5 cm, angle at C = 27°, AC is diameter]

8 Two cyclists depart from A at the same time. X cycles in a direction 145° for two hours at a speed of 42 km per hour. Y cycles due east and at the end of the two hours is directly north of X.
  a How far did X travel in 2 hours?
  b How far did Y travel in 2 hours?
  c Determine the average speed at which Y cycled.

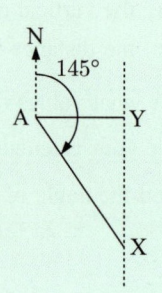

9 A rugby player is taking a penalty kick from the 22 m mark on the sideline. He knows that the posts are 5.5 m apart, and the near post is 31.25 m from the sideline. Find:
  a the direct distance to the near post
  b the direct distance to the far post
  c the apparent angle, θ.

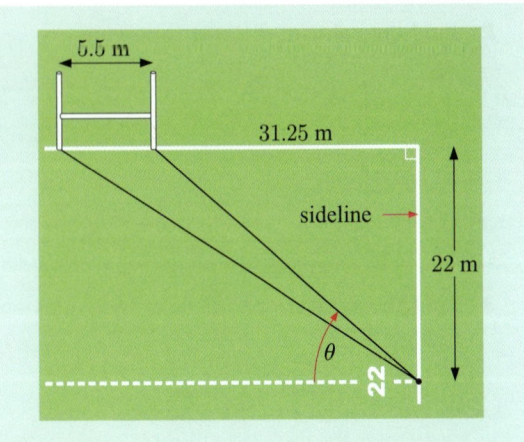

10 Three towns P, Q and R are located such that Q is 10.8 km southeast of P, and R is 15.4 km southwest of P.
  a Draw a labelled diagram of the situation.
  b Find the distance from R to Q.
  c Find the bearing of Q from R.

Challenge

Adam and Jamie are firing a cannon. They know the cannonball will travel at 55 m/s. Its velocity can be separated into a horizontal component h and a vertical component v.

The distance that the cannonball will travel is given by the formula $d = \dfrac{hv}{4.9}$.

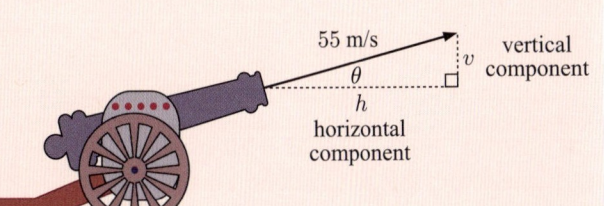

1 Suppose they fire the cannon at an angle of 30° to the ground. Calculate:
  a the horizontal component of the cannonball's velocity
  b the vertical component of the cannonball's velocity
  c the distance the cannonball will travel.

2 Suppose they fire the cannon at an angle θ to the ground. Write in terms of θ:
  a the horizontal component of the cannonball's velocity
  b the vertical component of the cannonball's velocity
  c the distance the cannonball will travel.

3 For what values of θ are the formulae in **2** valid?

4 Use your calculator to draw a graph of the function in **2 c**. Use the domain from **3**.

5 Find the angle of trajectory for which the cannonball travels furthest.

Algebraic fractions

18

Contents:

- **A** Simplifying algebraic fractions [2.9]
- **B** Multiplying and dividing algebraic fractions [2.9]
- **C** Adding and subtracting algebraic fractions [2.9]

Opening problem

Consider this right angled triangle.

a Write expressions for $\cos\theta$, $\sin\theta$, and $\tan\theta$ in terms of a and b.

b Use your expressions in **a** to simplify $\sin\theta \div \cos\theta$.

c Use Pythagoras' theorem to help simplify $\cos\theta \times \cos\theta + \sin\theta \times \sin\theta$.

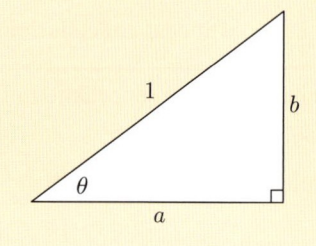

Fractions which involve unknowns are called **algebraic fractions**.

Algebraic fractions occur in many areas of mathematics. In particular, we often see them in problems involving trigonometry and similar triangles.

A SIMPLIFYING ALGEBRAIC FRACTIONS [2.9]

We have observed previously that number fractions can be simplified by **cancelling common factors**.

For example, $\dfrac{12}{28} = \dfrac{\overset{1}{\cancel{4}} \times 3}{\underset{1}{\cancel{4}} \times 7} = \dfrac{3}{7}$. In this case we cancelled the common factor 4.

The same principle can be applied to algebraic fractions:

> If the numerator and denominator of an algebraic fraction are both written in factored form and common factors are found, we can simplify by **cancelling the common factors**.

For example,
$$\frac{4ab}{2a} = \frac{2 \times \cancel{2}^{1} \times \cancel{a}^{1} \times b}{_{1}\cancel{2} \times \cancel{a}_{1}} \quad \{\text{fully factorised}\}$$
$$= \frac{2b}{1} \quad \{\text{after cancellation}\}$$
$$= 2b$$

For algebraic fractions, check both the numerator and denominator to see if they can be expressed as the product of factors, then look for common factors which can be cancelled.

If you have cancelled out correctly, the final expression will be equal to the initial expression for any values you substitute in for the variables.

In the above example, suppose $a = 3$ and $b = 5$.

$$\text{LHS} = \frac{4ab}{2a} = \frac{4 \times 3 \times 5}{2 \times 3} = \frac{60}{6} = 10.$$

$$\text{RHS} = 2b = 2 \times 5 = 10. \checkmark$$

ILLEGAL CANCELLATION

Take care with fractions such as $\frac{a+3}{3}$.

When cancelling in algebraic fractions, only factors can be cancelled, not terms.

The expression in the numerator, $a + 3$, **cannot** be written as the product of factors other than $1 \times (a+3)$. a and 3 are *terms* of the expression, not factors.

A typical **error** of **illegal cancellation** is: $\frac{a + \cancel{3}^{1}}{_{1}\cancel{3}} = \frac{a+1}{1} = a + 1.$

You can check that this cancellation of terms is incorrect by substituting a non-zero value for a.

For example, if $a = 3$ then $\text{LHS} = \frac{a+3}{3} = \frac{3+3}{3} = 2$,

whereas $\text{RHS} = a + 1 = 4.$ ✗

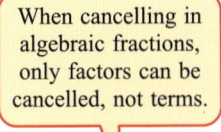

Example 1 ◂)) Self Tutor

Simplify: **a** $\dfrac{2x^2}{4x}$ **b** $\dfrac{6xy}{3x^3}$ **c** $\dfrac{x+y}{x}$

a $\dfrac{2x^2}{4x}$

$= \dfrac{\cancel{2}^{1} \times \cancel{x}^{1} \times x}{_{2}\cancel{4} \times \cancel{x}_{1}}$

$= \dfrac{x}{2}$

b $\dfrac{6xy}{3x^3}$

$= \dfrac{^{2}\cancel{6} \times \cancel{x}^{1} \times y}{_{1}\cancel{3} \times \cancel{x} \times x \times x}$

$= \dfrac{2y}{x^2}$

c $\dfrac{x+y}{x}$

cannot be simplified as $x + y$ is a sum, not a product.

Algebraic fractions (Chapter 18)

Example 2

Simplify: a $\dfrac{(x+3)(x-2)}{4(x+3)}$ b $\dfrac{2(x+3)^2}{x+3}$

> In these examples $(x+3)$ is the common factor.

a $\dfrac{{}^1\cancel{(x+3)}(x-2)}{4\cancel{(x+3)}_1}$

$= \dfrac{x-2}{4}$

b $\dfrac{2(x+3)^2}{x+3}$

$= \dfrac{2(x+3)(x+3)^1}{\cancel{(x+3)}_1}$

$= 2(x+3)$

EXERCISE 18A.1

1 Simplify if possible:

a $\dfrac{6a}{3}$ b $\dfrac{10b}{5}$ c $\dfrac{3}{6x}$ d $\dfrac{8t}{t}$ e $\dfrac{t+2}{t}$

f $\dfrac{k}{4k}$ g $\dfrac{x^2}{x}$ h $\dfrac{3y}{6y}$ i $\dfrac{8a^2}{4a}$ j $\dfrac{2b}{4b^2}$

k $\dfrac{a}{a-5}$ l $\dfrac{2x^2}{x^2}$ m $\dfrac{4a}{12a^3}$ n $\dfrac{4x^2}{8x}$ o $\dfrac{a^5}{a^2}$

p $\dfrac{t^2+8}{t}$ q $\dfrac{a^2b}{ab^2}$ r $\dfrac{a+b}{a-c}$ s $\dfrac{15x^2y^3}{3xy^4}$ t $\dfrac{8abc^2}{4bc}$

u $\dfrac{(2a)^2}{a}$ v $\dfrac{(2a)^2}{4a^2}$ w $\dfrac{(3a^2)^2}{3a}$ x $\dfrac{(3a^2)^2}{9a^2}$ y $\dfrac{(3a^2)^2}{18a^3}$

2 Split the following expressions into two parts and simplify if possible.

For example, $\dfrac{x+9}{x} = \dfrac{x}{x} + \dfrac{9}{x} = 1 + \dfrac{9}{x}$.

a $\dfrac{x+3}{3}$ b $\dfrac{4a+1}{2}$ c $\dfrac{a+b}{c}$ d $\dfrac{a+2b}{b}$

e $\dfrac{2a+4}{2}$ f $\dfrac{3a+6b}{3}$ g $\dfrac{4m+8n}{4}$ h $\dfrac{4m+8n}{2m}$

3 Which of the expressions in **2** could be simplified and which could not? Explain why this is so.

4 Simplify:

a $\dfrac{3(x+2)}{3}$ b $\dfrac{4(x-1)}{2}$ c $\dfrac{7(b+2)}{14}$ d $\dfrac{2(n+5)}{12}$

e $\dfrac{10}{5(x+2)}$ f $\dfrac{15}{5(3-a)}$ g $\dfrac{6(x+2)}{(x+2)}$ h $\dfrac{x-4}{2(x-4)}$

i $\dfrac{2(x+2)}{x(x+2)}$ j $\dfrac{x(x-5)^2}{3(x-5)}$ k $\dfrac{(x+2)(x+3)}{2(x+2)^2}$ l $\dfrac{(x+2)(x+5)}{5(x+5)}$

m $\dfrac{(x+2)(x-1)}{(x-1)(x+3)}$ n $\dfrac{(x+5)(2x-1)}{3(2x-1)}$ o $\dfrac{(x+6)^2}{3(x+6)}$ p $\dfrac{x^2(x+2)}{x(x+2)(x-1)}$

q $\dfrac{(x+2)^2(x+1)}{4(x+2)}$ r $\dfrac{(x+2)^2(x-1)^2}{(x-1)^2x^2}$

FACTORISATION AND SIMPLIFICATION

It is often necessary to factorise either the numerator or denominator before simplification can be done.

Example 3

Simplify: **a** $\dfrac{4a+8}{4}$ **b** $\dfrac{3}{3a-6b}$

a $\dfrac{4a+8}{4}$
$= \dfrac{\cancel{4}^{1}(a+2)}{\cancel{4}_{1}}$
$= \dfrac{(a+2)}{1}$
$= a+2$

b $\dfrac{3}{3a-6b}$
$= \dfrac{\cancel{3}^{1}}{\cancel{3}_{1}(a-2b)}$
$= \dfrac{1}{a-2b}$

Example 4

Simplify: **a** $\dfrac{ab-ac}{b-c}$ **b** $\dfrac{2x^2-4x}{4x-8}$

a $\dfrac{ab-ac}{b-c}$
$= \dfrac{a\cancel{(b-c)}^{1}}{\cancel{b-c}_{1}}$
$= \dfrac{a}{1}$
$= a$

b $\dfrac{2x^2-4x}{4x-8}$
$= \dfrac{\cancel{2}^{1}x\cancel{(x-2)}^{1}}{\cancel{4}_{2}\cancel{(x-2)}_{1}}$
$= \dfrac{x}{2}$

It is sometimes useful to use the property: $\boxed{b-a = -1(a-b)}$

Example 5

Simplify: **a** $\dfrac{3a-3b}{b-a}$ **b** $\dfrac{ab^2-ab}{1-b}$

a $\dfrac{3a-3b}{b-a}$
$= \dfrac{3\cancel{(a-b)}^{1}}{-1\cancel{(a-b)}_{1}}$
$= -3$

b $\dfrac{ab^2-ab}{1-b}$
$= \dfrac{ab\cancel{(b-1)}^{1}}{-1\cancel{(b-1)}_{1}}$
$= -ab$

Algebraic fractions (Chapter 18)

EXERCISE 18A.2

1 Simplify by cancelling common factors:

a $\dfrac{6}{2(x+2)}$
b $\dfrac{2x+6}{2}$
c $\dfrac{3x+12}{3}$
d $\dfrac{3x+6}{6}$

e $\dfrac{5x+20}{10}$
f $\dfrac{3a+12}{9}$
g $\dfrac{xy+xz}{x}$
h $\dfrac{xy+xz}{z+y}$

i $\dfrac{ab+bc}{ab-bc}$
j $\dfrac{3x-12}{6(x-4)^2}$
k $\dfrac{(x+3)^2}{6x+18}$
l $\dfrac{2(x-y)^2}{6(x-y)}$

2 Simplify:

a $\dfrac{4x+8}{2x+4}$
b $\dfrac{mx+nx}{2x}$
c $\dfrac{mx+nx}{m+n}$
d $\dfrac{x+y}{mx+my}$

e $\dfrac{2x+4}{2}$
f $\dfrac{x^2+2x}{x}$
g $\dfrac{x^2+2x}{x+2}$
h $\dfrac{x}{bx+cx}$

i $\dfrac{3x^2+6x}{x+2}$
j $\dfrac{2x^2+6x}{2x}$
k $\dfrac{2x^2+6x}{x+3}$
l $\dfrac{ax^2+bx}{ax+b}$

3 Simplify, if possible:

a $\dfrac{2a-2b}{b-a}$
b $\dfrac{3a-3b}{6b-6a}$
c $\dfrac{a-b}{b-a}$
d $\dfrac{a+b}{a-b}$

e $\dfrac{x-2y}{4y-2x}$
f $\dfrac{3m-6n}{2n-m}$
g $\dfrac{3x-3}{x-x^2}$
h $\dfrac{xy^2-xy}{3-3y}$

i $\dfrac{6x^2-3x}{1-2x}$
j $\dfrac{4x+6}{4}$
k $\dfrac{12x-6}{2x-x^2}$
l $\dfrac{5x-10}{4-2x}$

B MULTIPLYING AND DIVIDING ALGEBRAIC FRACTIONS [2.9]

The rules for multiplying and dividing algebraic fractions are identical to those used with numerical fractions. These are:

To **multiply** two or more fractions, we multiply the numerators to form the new numerator, and we multiply the denominators to form the new denominator.

$$\dfrac{a}{b} \times \dfrac{c}{d} = \dfrac{a \times c}{b \times d} = \dfrac{ac}{bd}$$

To **divide** by a fraction we multiply by its reciprocal.

$$\dfrac{a}{b} \div \dfrac{c}{d} = \dfrac{a}{b} \times \dfrac{d}{c} = \dfrac{ad}{bc}$$

MULTIPLICATION

Step 1: Multiply numerators and multiply denominators.
Step 2: Separate the factors.
Step 3: Cancel any common factors.
Step 4: Write in simplest form.

For example, $\dfrac{n^2}{3} \times \dfrac{6}{n} = \dfrac{n^2 \times 6}{3 \times n}$ {Step 1}

$= \dfrac{n \times n \times 2 \times 3}{3 \times n}$ {Step 2}

$= \dfrac{n \times \not{n}^1 \times 2 \times \not{3}^1}{{}_1\not{3} \times \not{n}_1}$ {Step 3}

$= \dfrac{2n}{1}$

$= 2n$ {Step 4}

Example 6 ◀) Self Tutor

Simplify: **a** $\dfrac{4}{d} \times \dfrac{d}{8}$ **b** $\dfrac{5}{g} \times g^3$

a $\dfrac{4}{d} \times \dfrac{d}{8} = \dfrac{{}^1\not{4} \times \not{d}^1}{{}_1\not{d} \times \not{8}_2}$

$= \tfrac{1}{2}$

b $\dfrac{5}{g} \times g^3 = \dfrac{5}{g} \times \dfrac{g^3}{1}$

$= \dfrac{5 \times \not{g}^1 \times g \times g}{\not{g}^1}$

$= 5g^2$

DIVISION

Step 1: To divide by a fraction, multiply by its reciprocal.

Step 2: Multiply numerators and multiply denominators.

Step 3: Cancel any common factors.

Step 4: Write in simplest form.

For example,

$\dfrac{m}{2} \div \dfrac{n}{6} = \dfrac{m}{2} \times \dfrac{6}{n}$ {Step 1}

$= \dfrac{m \times 6}{2 \times n}$ {Step 2}

$= \dfrac{m \times \not{6}^3}{{}_1\not{2} \times n}$ {Step 3}

$= \dfrac{3m}{n}$ {Step 4}

Example 7 ◀) Self Tutor

Simplify: **a** $\dfrac{6}{x} \div \dfrac{2}{x^2}$ **b** $\dfrac{8}{p} \div 2$

a $\dfrac{6}{x} \div \dfrac{2}{x^2} = \dfrac{6}{x} \times \dfrac{x^2}{2}$

$= \dfrac{3 \times \not{2}^1 \times \not{x}^1 \times x}{{}_1\not{x} \times \not{2}_1}$

$= 3x$

b $\dfrac{8}{p} \div 2 = \dfrac{8}{p} \times \dfrac{1}{2}$

$= \dfrac{{}^4\not{8} \times 1}{p \times \not{2}_1}$

$= \dfrac{4}{p}$

Algebraic fractions (Chapter 18) 357

EXERCISE 18B

1 Simplify:

- **a** $\dfrac{a}{2} \times \dfrac{b}{3}$
- **b** $\dfrac{x}{4} \times \dfrac{2}{x}$
- **c** $\dfrac{c}{4} \times \dfrac{2}{c}$
- **d** $\dfrac{a}{2} \times \dfrac{a}{3}$
- **e** $\dfrac{a}{b} \times \dfrac{x}{y}$
- **f** $\dfrac{x}{y} \times \dfrac{y}{x}$
- **g** $\dfrac{x}{3} \times x$
- **h** $\dfrac{x}{4} \times \dfrac{8}{y}$
- **i** $\dfrac{n}{2} \times \dfrac{1}{n^2}$
- **j** $\dfrac{6}{p} \times \dfrac{p}{2}$
- **k** $\dfrac{m}{x} \times \dfrac{x}{n}$
- **l** $x \times \dfrac{2}{x}$
- **m** $\dfrac{5}{t} \times t^2$
- **n** $\left(\dfrac{x}{y}\right)^2$
- **o** $\left(\dfrac{4}{d}\right)^2$
- **p** $\dfrac{a}{b} \times \dfrac{b}{c} \times \dfrac{c}{a}$

2 Simplify:

- **a** $\dfrac{x}{3} \div \dfrac{x}{2}$
- **b** $\dfrac{3}{y} \div \dfrac{6}{y}$
- **c** $3 \div \dfrac{1}{x}$
- **d** $6 \div \dfrac{2}{y}$
- **e** $\dfrac{3}{p} \div \dfrac{1}{p}$
- **f** $\dfrac{c}{n} \div n$
- **g** $d \div \dfrac{5}{d}$
- **h** $x \div \dfrac{x}{3}$
- **i** $1 \div \dfrac{a}{b}$
- **j** $\dfrac{3}{d} \div 2$
- **k** $\dfrac{4}{x} \div \dfrac{x^2}{2}$
- **l** $\dfrac{4}{x} \div \dfrac{8}{x^2}$
- **m** $a \div \dfrac{a^2}{3}$
- **n** $\dfrac{x}{y} \div \dfrac{x^2}{y}$
- **o** $\dfrac{5}{a} \div \dfrac{a}{2}$
- **p** $\dfrac{a^2}{5} \div \dfrac{a}{3}$

3

- **a** $\dfrac{x}{3} \times \dfrac{6}{x}$
- **b** $\dfrac{b}{a} \div \dfrac{b}{2}$
- **c** $\dfrac{4b}{a} \div \dfrac{2a}{b^2}$
- **d** $\dfrac{r}{3s} \times \dfrac{2t}{u}$
- **e** $\dfrac{2n}{m} \div \dfrac{3n}{m^2}$
- **f** $\dfrac{5p}{q^3} \times \dfrac{2q}{15}$
- **g** $\dfrac{w}{6x} \div \dfrac{3y}{2z}$
- **h** $\left(\dfrac{k}{4}\right)^2$

C   ADDING AND SUBTRACTING ALGEBRAIC FRACTIONS   [2.9]

The rules for addition and subtraction of algebraic fractions are identical to those used with numerical fractions.

To **add** two or more fractions we obtain the *lowest common denominator* and then add the resulting numerators.

$$\dfrac{a}{c} + \dfrac{b}{c} = \dfrac{a+b}{c}$$

To **subtract** two or more fractions we obtain the *lowest common denominator* and then subtract the resulting numerators.

$$\dfrac{a}{c} - \dfrac{d}{c} = \dfrac{a-d}{c}$$

To find the lowest common denominator, we look for the **lowest common multiple of the denominators**.

For example: when adding $\frac{3}{4} + \frac{2}{3}$,   the lowest common denominator is 12,

when adding $\frac{2}{3} + \frac{1}{6}$,   the lowest common denominator is 6.

To find $\frac{3}{4} + \frac{2}{3}$, we notice the LCD is 12.

$$\frac{3}{4} + \frac{2}{3} = \frac{3 \times 3}{4 \times 3} + \frac{2 \times 4}{3 \times 4} \quad \{\text{LCD} = 12\}$$

$$= \frac{9}{12} + \frac{8}{12} \quad \{\text{simplifying}\}$$

$$= \frac{17}{12} \quad \{\text{adding the numerators}\}$$

To find $\frac{x}{2} + \frac{3x}{5}$, we notice the LCD is 10. We then proceed in the same manner as for ordinary fractions:

$$\frac{x}{2} + \frac{3x}{5} = \frac{x \times 5}{2 \times 5} + \frac{3x \times 2}{5 \times 2} \quad \{\text{LCD} = 10\}$$

$$= \frac{5x}{10} + \frac{6x}{10} \quad \{\text{simplifying}\}$$

$$= \frac{11x}{10} \quad \{\text{adding the numerators}\}$$

Example 8 ◀)) Self Tutor

Simplify: **a** $\dfrac{x}{3} + \dfrac{5x}{6}$ **b** $\dfrac{3b}{4} - \dfrac{2b}{3}$

a
$$\dfrac{x}{3} + \dfrac{5x}{6}$$
$$= \dfrac{x \times 2}{3 \times 2} + \dfrac{5x}{6} \quad \{\text{LCD } = 6\}$$
$$= \dfrac{2x}{6} + \dfrac{5x}{6}$$
$$= \dfrac{2x + 5x}{6}$$
$$= \dfrac{7x}{6}$$

b
$$\dfrac{3b}{4} - \dfrac{2b}{3}$$
$$= \dfrac{3b \times 3}{4 \times 3} - \dfrac{2b \times 4}{3 \times 4} \quad \{\text{LCD } = 12\}$$
$$= \dfrac{9b}{12} - \dfrac{8b}{12}$$
$$= \dfrac{b}{12}$$

Example 9 ◀)) Self Tutor

Simplify: **a** $\dfrac{b}{3} + 1$ **b** $\dfrac{a}{4} - a$

a
$$\dfrac{b}{3} + 1 = \dfrac{b}{3} + \dfrac{3}{3}$$
$$= \dfrac{b+3}{3}$$

b
$$\dfrac{a}{4} - a = \dfrac{a}{4} - \dfrac{a \times 4}{1 \times 4}$$
$$= \dfrac{a}{4} - \dfrac{4a}{4}$$
$$= \dfrac{-3a}{4} \text{ or } -\dfrac{3a}{4}$$

Algebraic fractions (Chapter 18)

EXERCISE 18C

1 Simplify by writing as a single fraction:

a $\dfrac{x}{2} + \dfrac{x}{5}$
b $\dfrac{x}{3} - \dfrac{x}{6}$
c $\dfrac{x}{4} + \dfrac{3x}{5}$
d $\dfrac{x}{2} - \dfrac{x}{5}$

e $\dfrac{2t}{3} - \dfrac{7t}{12}$
f $\dfrac{11n}{21} - \dfrac{n}{7}$
g $\dfrac{a}{2} + \dfrac{a}{3}$
h $\dfrac{a}{2} + \dfrac{b}{4}$

i $\dfrac{n}{3} + \dfrac{2n}{15}$
j $\dfrac{5g}{6} - \dfrac{g}{3}$
k $\dfrac{4s}{5} - \dfrac{2s}{3}$
l $a - \dfrac{3a}{5}$

m $\dfrac{x}{3} + \dfrac{x}{2} + \dfrac{x}{6}$
n $\dfrac{y}{2} + \dfrac{y}{4} - \dfrac{y}{3}$
o $\dfrac{z}{4} + \dfrac{z}{6} - \dfrac{z}{3}$
p $2q - \dfrac{q}{3} + \dfrac{2q}{7}$

2 Simplify:

a $\dfrac{x}{3} + 2$
b $\dfrac{m}{2} - 1$
c $\dfrac{a}{3} + a$
d $\dfrac{b}{5} - 2$

e $\dfrac{x}{6} - 3$
f $3 + \dfrac{x}{4}$
g $5 - \dfrac{x}{6}$
h $2 + \dfrac{3}{x}$

i $6 - \dfrac{3}{x}$
j $b + \dfrac{3}{b}$
k $\dfrac{5}{x} + x$
l $\dfrac{y}{6} - 2y$

3 Simplify:

a $\dfrac{x}{3} + \dfrac{3x}{5}$
b $\dfrac{3x}{5} - \dfrac{2x}{7}$
c $\dfrac{x}{10} + 3$
d $4 - \dfrac{x}{3}$

e $\dfrac{3b}{5} + \dfrac{b}{4}$
f $4 + \dfrac{2x}{3}$
g $\dfrac{a}{5} - 3a$
h $\dfrac{5b}{3} - \dfrac{3b}{5}$

4 Answer the **Opening Problem** on page **351**.

Review set 18A

1 Simplify:

a $\dfrac{6x^2}{2x}$
b $6 \times \dfrac{n}{2}$
c $\dfrac{x}{2} \div 3$
d $\dfrac{8x}{(2x)^2}$

2 Simplify, if possible:

a $\dfrac{8}{4(c+3)}$
b $\dfrac{3x+8}{4}$
c $\dfrac{4x+8}{4}$
d $\dfrac{x(x+1)}{3(x+1)(x+2)}$

3 Write as a single fraction:

a $\dfrac{2x}{3} + \dfrac{3x}{5}$
b $\dfrac{2x}{3} \times \dfrac{3x}{5}$
c $\dfrac{2x}{3} \div \dfrac{3x}{5}$
d $\dfrac{2x}{3} - \dfrac{3x}{5}$

4 Simplify by factorisation:

a $\dfrac{4x+8}{x+2}$
b $\dfrac{5-10x}{2x-1}$
c $\dfrac{4x^2+6x}{2x+3}$

Review set 18B

1 Simplify:

a $\dfrac{4a}{6a}$ b $\dfrac{x}{3} \times 6$ c $3 \div \dfrac{1}{n}$ d $\dfrac{12x^2}{6x}$

2 Simplify, if possible:

a $\dfrac{3x+15}{5}$ b $\dfrac{3x+15}{3}$ c $\dfrac{2(a+4)}{(a+4)^2}$ d $\dfrac{abc}{2ac(b-a)}$

3 Write as a single fraction:

a $\dfrac{3x}{4} + 2x$ b $\dfrac{3x}{4} - 2x$ c $\dfrac{3x}{4} \times 2x$ d $\dfrac{3x}{4} \div 2x$

4 Simplify by factorisation:

a $\dfrac{3-x}{x-3}$ b $\dfrac{5x+10}{2x+4}$ c $\dfrac{3x^2-9x}{ax-3a}$

Challenge

In the **Opening Problem** we considered a right angled triangle with hypotenuse of length 1.

We now suppose the hypotenuse has length c.

1 Write expressions for $\cos\theta$, $\sin\theta$, and $\tan\theta$ in terms of a, b, and c.

2 Use your expressions in **1** to simplify $\sin\theta \div \cos\theta$.

3 Use Pythagoras' theorem to help simplify $\cos\theta \times \cos\theta + \sin\theta \times \sin\theta$.

4 Show that the area of the triangle is given by $A = \tfrac{1}{2}ac\sin\theta$.

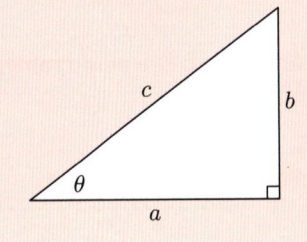

Continuous data

19

Contents:

A	The mean of continuous data	[11.5]
B	Cumulative frequency	[11.7]

Opening problem

Andriano collected data for the rainfall from the last month for 90 towns in Argentina. The results are displayed in the frequency table alongside:

Rainfall (r mm)	Frequency
$50 \leqslant r < 60$	7
$60 \leqslant r < 70$	20
$70 \leqslant r < 80$	32
$80 \leqslant r < 90$	22
$90 \leqslant r < 100$	9
Total	90

Things to think about:

- Is the data discrete or continuous?
- What does the interval $60 \leqslant r < 70$ actually mean?
- How can the shape of the distribution be described?
- Is it possible to calculate the exact mean of the data?

In **Chapter 15** we saw that a **continuous numerical variable** can theoretically take any value on part of the number line. A continuous variable is usually **measured** so that data can be recorded.

Examples of continuous numerical variables are:

The height of year 10 students: the variable can take any value from about 100 cm to 200 cm.

The speed of cars on a stretch of highway: the variable can take any value from 0 km/h to the fastest speed that a car can travel, but is most likely to be in the range 50 km/h to 150 km/h.

Since a continuous variable can take any value on an interval, it is rare for two measurements to be exactly the same. This means that we always group continuous data.

Continuous data is placed into **class intervals** which are usually represented by **inequalities**.

For example, for heights from 140 cm to 150 cm, we could write $140 \leqslant h < 150$.

GRAPHING CONTINUOUS VARIABLES

In **Chapter 15** we used a vertical bar chart to display data from a discrete variable. We can do the same thing for a continuous variable. However, because a continuous variable can take a value anywhere in an interval right up to the edge of the next interval, we do not leave gaps between the columns. We call this graph a **frequency histogram**.

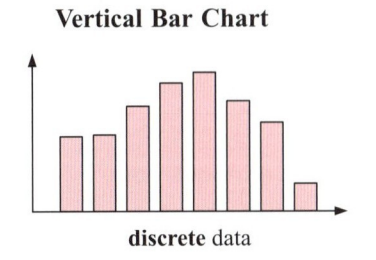

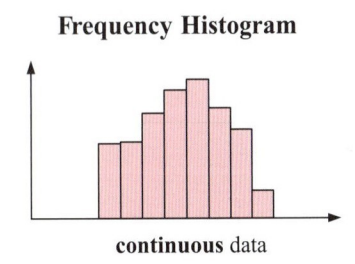

Vertical Bar Chart

discrete data

Frequency Histogram

continuous data

A THE MEAN OF CONTINUOUS DATA   [11.5]

To find the mean of continuous data, we use the same method as for grouped discrete data described in **Chapter 15** section **F**.

Since the data is given in intervals, our answer will only be an *estimate* of the mean.

Example 1

◀)) **Self Tutor**

The heights of students (h cm) in a hockey training squad were measured and the results tabled:

a Draw a frequency histogram of the data.
b Estimate the mean height.
c State the modal class.

Height (h cm)	Frequency (f)
$130 \leqslant h < 140$	2
$140 \leqslant h < 150$	4
$150 \leqslant h < 160$	12
$160 \leqslant h < 170$	20
$170 \leqslant h < 180$	9
$180 \leqslant h < 190$	3

a

b

Height (h cm)	Mid-value (x)	Freq. (f)	fx
$130 \leqslant h < 140$	135	2	270
$140 \leqslant h < 150$	145	4	580
$150 \leqslant h < 160$	155	12	1860
$160 \leqslant h < 170$	165	20	3300
$170 \leqslant h < 180$	175	9	1575
$180 \leqslant h < 190$	185	3	555
Total		50	8140

$$\text{Mean} = \frac{\sum fx}{\sum f} \approx \frac{8140}{50} \approx 163 \text{ cm}$$

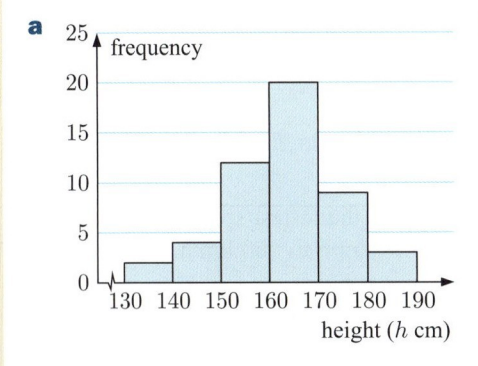

c The modal class is $160 \leqslant h < 170$.

Continuous data (Chapter 19)

EXERCISE 19A

1 A frequency table for the weights of a volleyball squad is given alongside.

Weight (kg)	Frequency
$75 \leqslant w < 80$	2
$80 \leqslant w < 85$	5
$85 \leqslant w < 90$	8
$90 \leqslant w < 95$	7
$95 \leqslant w < 100$	5
$100 \leqslant w < 105$	1

   a Explain why 'weight' is a continuous variable.
   b What is the modal class? Explain what this means.
   c Draw a frequency histogram of the data.
   d Describe the distribution of the data.

2 40 tests are done across a region to find the variation in soil pH. The results are shown below.

Soil pH (x)	$4.5 \leqslant x < 5$	$5 \leqslant x < 5.5$	$5.5 \leqslant x < 6$	$6 \leqslant x < 6.5$	$6.5 \leqslant x < 7$
Frequency	8	9	11	7	5

   a Draw a frequency histogram of the data.
   b What is the modal class?
   c What percentage of the region has soil with pH between:
      i 5 and 5.5   **ii** 6 and 7?

3 A plant inspector takes a random sample of ten week old plants from a nursery and measures their height in millimetres.
The results are shown in the table alongside.

Height (h mm)	Frequency
$20 \leqslant h < 40$	4
$40 \leqslant h < 60$	17
$60 \leqslant h < 80$	15
$80 \leqslant h < 100$	8
$100 \leqslant h < 120$	2
$120 \leqslant h < 140$	4

   a What is the modal class?
   b Estimate the mean height.
   c How many of the seedlings are 40 mm or more?
   d What percentage of the seedlings are between 60 and 80 mm?
   e If the total number of seedlings in the nursery is 857, estimate the number which measure:
      i less than 100 mm   **ii** between 40 and 100 mm.

4 The distances travelled to school by a random sample of students were:

Distance (km)	$0 \leqslant d < 1$	$1 \leqslant d < 2$	$2 \leqslant d < 3$	$3 \leqslant d < 4$	$4 \leqslant d < 5$
Number of students	76	87	54	23	5

   a Draw a frequency histogram of the distances travelled to school.
   b What is the modal class?
   c Estimate the mean distance travelled by the students.
   d What percentage of the students travelled at least 2 km to school?
   e If there are 28 students in Josef's class, estimate the number who travel less than 1 km to school.

5 The times taken in minutes for players to finish a computer game were:

Time (t)	$5 \leqslant t < 10$	$10 \leqslant t < 15$	$15 \leqslant t < 20$	$20 \leqslant t < 25$	$25 \leqslant t < 30$	$30 \leqslant t < 35$
Frequency	2	8	16	20	24	10

   a What percentage of the players finished the game in less than 20 minutes?
   b Estimate the mean time to finish the game.
   c If 2589 other people play the game, estimate the number who will complete it in less than 25 minutes.

6 The duration of calls to a centre one morning are given in the table.

Call duration (t min)	Frequency
$0 \leqslant t < 1$	37
$1 \leqslant t < 2$	68
$2 \leqslant t < 3$	73
$3 \leqslant t < 4$	41
$4 \leqslant t < 5$	26
$5 \leqslant t < 6$	13

a Draw a frequency histogram to display the data.
b Describe the distribution of the data.
c Estimate the mean call time.
d If there are 340 calls to the centre in the afternoon, estimate the number that will last no more than 3 minutes.

7 This table displays the number of stars of various *apparent magnitudes* visible above Greater New York one night. Apparent magnitude measures the brightness of a star, with lower numbers representing brighter stars.

a Describe and interpret the distribution of the data.
b Estimate the mean apparent magnitude of the visible stars this night.
c Midtown Manhattan in New York City has light pollution that blocks out all stars with an apparent magnitude of 2 or more. How many stars can be seen from Midtown Manhattan this night?

Apparent magnitude (M)	Frequency
$-2 \leqslant M < -1$	1
$-1 \leqslant M < 0$	1
$0 \leqslant M < 1$	6
$1 \leqslant M < 2$	8
$2 \leqslant M < 3$	33
$3 \leqslant M < 4$	194

B CUMULATIVE FREQUENCY [11.7]

We are often interested in how many scores lie above or below a particular value.

For example, we may wish to know how many newborn babies weighed less than 2.5 kg, or how many Canadian companies had over $500 million revenue.

To answer questions like these, we construct a **cumulative frequency distribution table** and a **cumulative frequency graph** to represent the data.

> The **cumulative frequency** gives a *running total* of the scores up to a particular value.
> It is the total frequency up to a particular value.

Starting with a frequency table, we can add a cumulative frequency column and then graph this data on a **cumulative frequency curve**. The cumulative frequencies are plotted on the vertical axis.

From the cumulative frequency graph we can find the three values which divide the ordered data into quarters:

- The **median** Q_2 splits the data into two halves. It lies 50% of the way through the data.
- The **first quartile** Q_1 is the score value 25% of the way through the data.
- The **third quartile** Q_3 is the score value 75% of the way through the data.

Example 2

The data shown gives the weights of 80 male basketball players.
a Construct a cumulative frequency distribution table.
b Represent the data on a cumulative frequency graph.
c Use your graph to estimate the:
  i median weight
  ii upper quartile
  iii number of men weighing less than 83 kg
  iv number of men weighing more than 92 kg.

Weight (w kg)	Frequency
$65 \leqslant w < 70$	1
$70 \leqslant w < 75$	2
$75 \leqslant w < 80$	8
$80 \leqslant w < 85$	16
$85 \leqslant w < 90$	21
$90 \leqslant w < 95$	19
$95 \leqslant w < 100$	8
$100 \leqslant w < 105$	3
$105 \leqslant w < 110$	1
$110 \leqslant w < 115$	1

a
Weight (w kg)	Frequency	Cumulative Frequency
$65 \leqslant w < 70$	1	1
$70 \leqslant w < 75$	2	3 ← this is $1 + 2$
$75 \leqslant w < 80$	8	11 ← this is $1 + 2 + 8$
$80 \leqslant w < 85$	16	27
$85 \leqslant w < 90$	21	48 ← this 48 means that there are 48 players who weigh less than 90 kg, so (90, 48) is a point on the cumulative frequency graph.
$90 \leqslant w < 95$	19	67
$95 \leqslant w < 100$	8	75
$100 \leqslant w < 105$	3	78
$105 \leqslant w < 110$	1	79
$110 \leqslant w < 115$	1	80

b **Cumulative frequency graph of basketballers' weights**

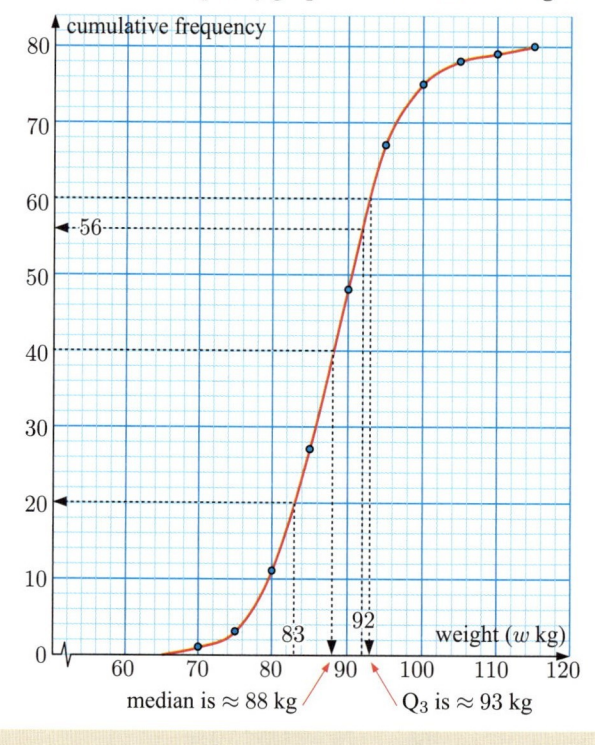

c
  i 50% of 80 = 40,
    $\therefore$ median ≈ 88 kg
  ii 75% of 80 = 60,
    $\therefore Q_3 \approx 93$ kg
  iii There are 20 men who weigh less than 83 kg.
  iv There are $80 - 56 = 24$ men who weigh more than 92 kg.

Example 3

The heights of 100 14-year-old girls and 100 14-year-old boys were measured and the results tabled.

a Draw, on the same axes, the cumulative frequency curve for both the boys and the girls.

b Estimate for both the boys and the girls:
  i the median
  ii the interquartile range (IQR).

c Compare the two distributions.

Freq. (girls)	Height (h cm)	Freq. (boys)
5	$140 \leqslant h < 145$	2
10	$145 \leqslant h < 150$	5
15	$150 \leqslant h < 155$	10
30	$155 \leqslant h < 160$	13
20	$160 \leqslant h < 165$	20
10	$165 \leqslant h < 170$	30
8	$170 \leqslant h < 175$	15
2	$175 \leqslant h < 180$	5

a

CF (girls)	Freq. (girls)	Height (h cm)	Freq. (boys)	CF (boys)
5	5	$140 \leqslant h < 145$	2	2
15	10	$145 \leqslant h < 150$	5	7
30	15	$150 \leqslant h < 155$	10	17
60	30	$155 \leqslant h < 160$	13	30
80	20	$160 \leqslant h < 165$	20	50
90	10	$165 \leqslant h < 170$	30	80
98	8	$170 \leqslant h < 175$	15	95
100	2	$175 \leqslant h < 180$	5	100

Cumulative frequency graph of boys' and girls' heights

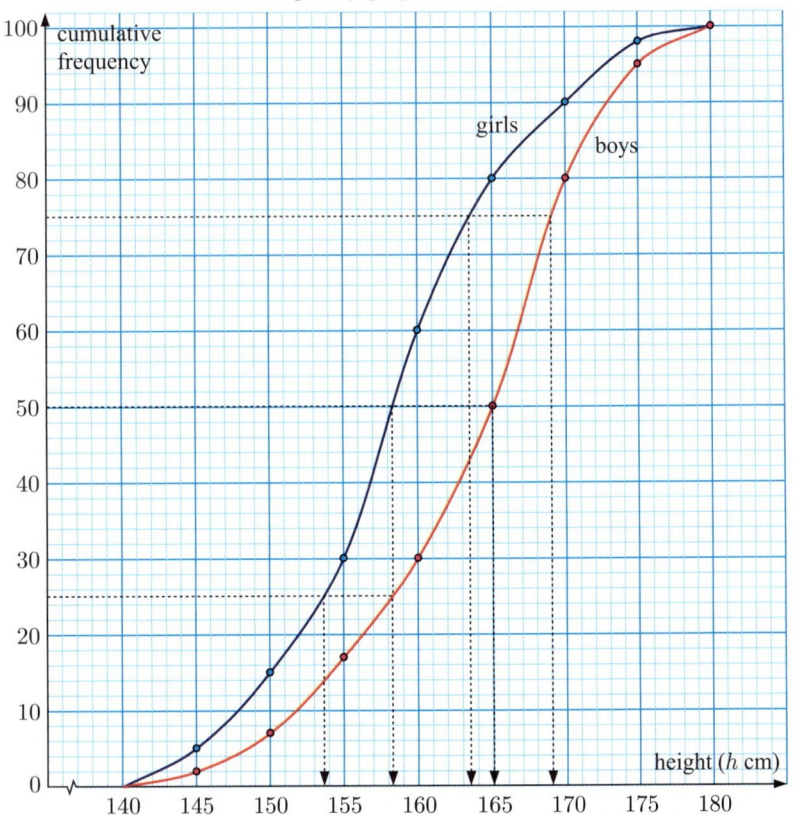

b Since there are 100 girls (and 100 boys), 50% is the 50th height, Q_1 is the 25th height, and Q_3 is the 75th height.

For girls:
    i median ≈ 158 cm
    ii IQR $= Q_3 - Q_1$
              $\approx 163.5 - 153.7$
              ≈ 10 cm

For boys:
    i median ≈ 165 cm
    ii IQR $= Q_3 - Q_1$
              $\approx 169 - 158$
              ≈ 11 cm

c The two distributions are similar in shape, but the boys' heights are further right than the girls'. The median height for the boys is 7 cm more than for the girls. So, the boys are considerably taller.

Since the IQRs are nearly the same, the spread of heights is similar for each gender.

EXERCISE 19B

1 A waste management company records the total mass of rubbish per month for a number of houses in a region. The data is summarised below:

Mass (m kg)	$10 \leqslant m < 20$	$20 \leqslant m < 30$	$30 \leqslant m < 40$	$40 \leqslant m < 50$	$50 \leqslant m < 60$
Number of houses	15	21	47	33	4

  a Construct a cumulative frequency table for this data.
  b How many houses did the company keep a record of?
  c Draw a cumulative frequency graph to display the data.
  d Estimate how many households threw away:
    i less than 25 kg of waste
    ii more than 55 kg of waste.
  e Estimate the:
    i median
    ii lower quartile
    iii upper quartile.

2 In a running race, the times (in minutes) of 160 competitors were recorded as follows:

Draw a cumulative frequency graph of the data and use it to estimate:

  a the median time
  b the approximate number of runners whose time was not more than 32 minutes
  c the approximate time in which the fastest 40 runners completed the course
  d the interquartile range.

Times (t min)	Frequency
$20 \leqslant t < 25$	18
$25 \leqslant t < 30$	45
$30 \leqslant t < 35$	37
$35 \leqslant t < 40$	33
$40 \leqslant t < 45$	19
$45 \leqslant t < 50$	8

3 The lengths of 30 trout (l cm) were measured. The following data was obtained:

Length (cm)	$30 \leqslant l < 32$	$32 \leqslant l < 34$	$34 \leqslant l < 36$	$36 \leqslant l < 38$	$38 \leqslant l < 40$	$40 \leqslant l < 42$	$42 \leqslant l < 44$
Frequency	1	1	3	7	11	5	2

  a Construct a cumulative frequency curve for the data.
  b Estimate the percentage of trout with length less than 39 cm.
  c Estimate the median length of trout caught.
  d Estimate the interquartile range of trout length and explain what this represents.
  e Use a calculator to estimate the mean of the data.
  f Comment on the shape of the distribution of trout lengths.

4 The cumulative frequency curve shows the weights of Sam's goat herd in kilograms.

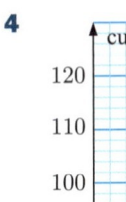

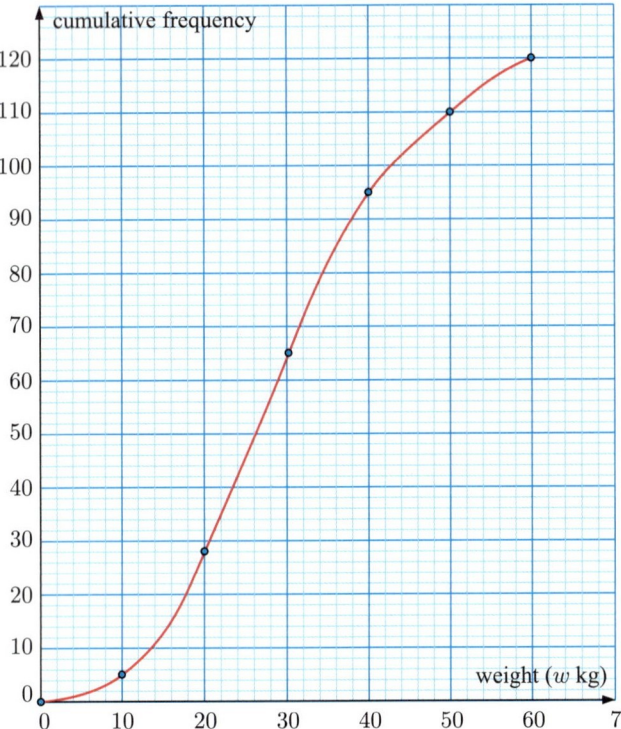

  a How many goats does Sam have?
  b Estimate the median goat weight.
  c Any goats heavier than 32 kg will go to market. How many goats will go to market?
  d What is the IQR for Sam's herd?

5 The weights of cabbages grown by two brothers on separate properties were measured for comparison. The results are shown in the table:

  a Draw, on the same axes, cumulative frequency curves for both cabbage samples.
  b Estimate for each brother:
      i the median weight
      ii the IQR
  c Compare the two distributions.

Frequency (Alan)	Weight (w grams)	Frequency (John)
4	$400 \leqslant w < 550$	4
32	$550 \leqslant w < 700$	48
44	$700 \leqslant w < 850$	56
52	$850 \leqslant w < 1000$	48
44	$1000 \leqslant w < 1150$	28
24	$1150 \leqslant w < 1300$	16
200	Totals	200

6 The times taken for trampers to climb Ben Nevis were recorded and the results tabled.

Time (t min)	$175 \leqslant t < 190$	$190 \leqslant t < 205$	$205 \leqslant t < 220$	$220 \leqslant t < 235$	$235 \leqslant t < 250$
Frequency	11	35	74	32	8

  a Construct a cumulative frequency curve for the walking times.
  b Estimate the median time for the walk.
  c Estimate the IQR and explain what it means.
  d Guides on the walk say that anyone who completes the walk in 3 hours 15 min or less is extremely fit. Estimate the number of extremely fit trampers.
  e Comment on the shape of the distribution of walking times.

7

Cumulative frequency curve of watermelon weight data

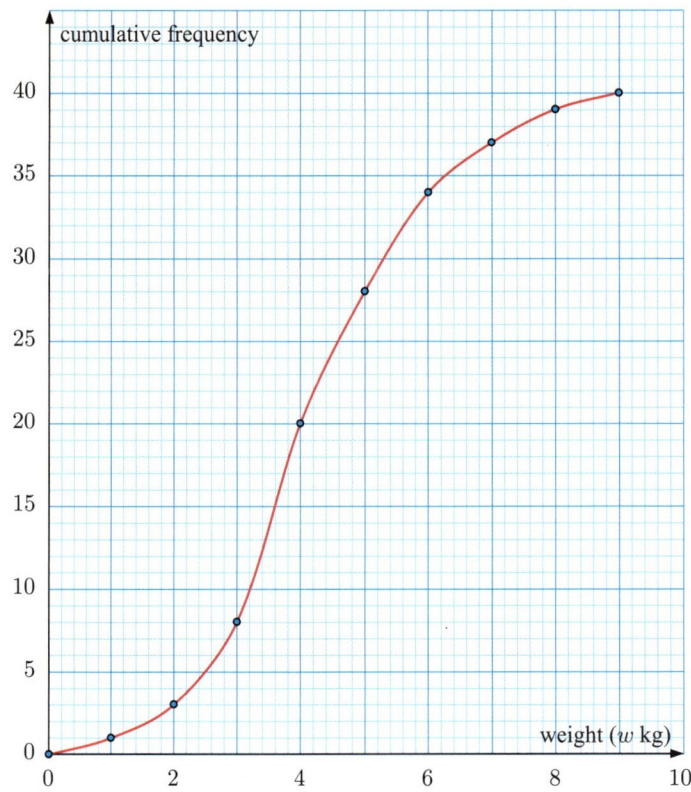

The given graph describes the weight of 40 watermelons.

  a Estimate the:
    i median weight
    ii IQR

    for the weight of the watermelons.

  b Construct a cumulative frequency table for the data including a frequency column.

  c Estimate the mean weight of the watermelons.

Review set 19A

1 A frequency table for the masses of eggs (m grams) in a carton marked '50 g eggs' is given below.

  a Explain why 'mass' is a continuous variable.
  b What is the modal class? Explain what this means.
  c Estimate the mean of the data.
  d Describe the distribution of the data.

Mass (g)	Frequency
$48 \leqslant m < 49$	1
$49 \leqslant m < 50$	1
$50 \leqslant m < 51$	16
$51 \leqslant m < 52$	4
$52 \leqslant m < 53$	3

2 The speeds of vehicles (v km/h) travelling along a stretch of road are recorded over a 60 minute period. The results are given in the table alongside.

  a Estimate the mean speed of the vehicles.
  b Draw a frequency histogram of the data.
  c Find the modal class.
  d What percentage of drivers exceeded the speed limit of 60 km/h?
  e Describe the distribution of the data.

Speed (v km/h)	Frequency
$40 \leqslant v < 45$	14
$45 \leqslant v < 50$	22
$50 \leqslant v < 55$	35
$55 \leqslant v < 60$	38
$60 \leqslant v < 65$	25
$65 \leqslant v < 70$	10

3 The weekly wages of employees in a factory are recorded in the table below.

Weekly wage (£w)	$0 \leqslant w < 400$	$400 \leqslant w < 800$	$800 \leqslant w < 1200$	$1200 \leqslant w < 1600$	$1600 \leqslant w < 2000$
Frequency	20	60	120	40	10

a Draw a cumulative frequency graph to illustrate this information.
b Use the graph to estimate:
  i the median wage
  ii the number of employees earning less than £750 per week.

4 The cumulative frequency curve shows the time spent by people in a supermarket on a given day.

a Construct a cumulative frequency table for the data, using the intervals $0 \leqslant t < 5$, $5 \leqslant t < 10$, and so on.
b Use the graph to estimate:
  i the median time
  ii the IQR.
c Copy and complete:
  i 50 people spent less than .... minutes in the supermarket.
  ii .... people spent more than 40 minutes in the supermarket.

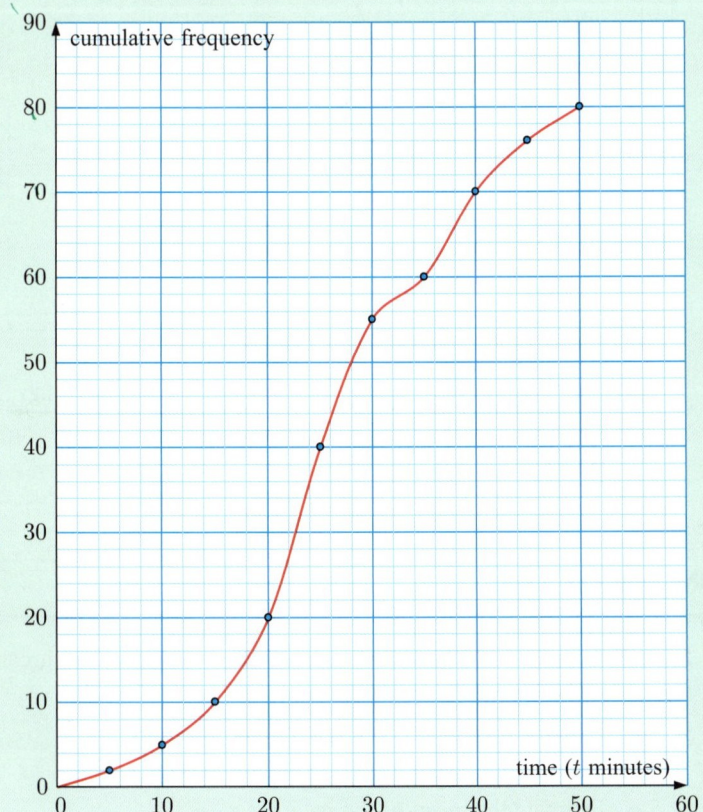

Review set 19B

1 The table alongside summarises the masses of 50 domestic cats chosen at random.

Mass (m kg)	Frequency
$0 \leqslant m < 2$	5
$2 \leqslant m < 4$	18
$4 \leqslant m < 6$	12
$6 \leqslant m < 8$	9
$8 \leqslant m < 10$	5
$10 \leqslant m < 12$	1

a What is the length of each class interval?
b What is the modal class?
c Find the approximate mean.
d Draw a frequency histogram of the data.
e From a random selection of 428 cats, how many would you expect to weigh at least 8 kg?

2 The table alongside summarises the best times of 100 swimmers who swim 50 m.

    a Estimate the mean time.

    b What is the modal class?

Time (t s)	Frequency
$25 \leqslant t < 30$	5
$30 \leqslant t < 35$	17
$35 \leqslant t < 40$	34
$40 \leqslant t < 45$	29
$45 \leqslant t < 50$	15

3 The percentage scores in a test were recorded. The results were categorised by gender.

    a Check that the same number of boys and girls took the test.

    b Draw the cumulative frequency graphs for boys and girls on the same set of axes.

    c Estimate the median and interquartile range of each data set.

    d Compare the distributions.

Frequency (boys)	Percentage score (s)	Frequency (girls)
5	$0 \leqslant s < 10$	0
8	$10 \leqslant s < 20$	5
12	$20 \leqslant s < 30$	10
10	$30 \leqslant s < 40$	12
30	$40 \leqslant s < 50$	20
50	$50 \leqslant s < 60$	30
20	$60 \leqslant s < 70$	50
10	$70 \leqslant s < 80$	13
5	$80 \leqslant s < 90$	6
0	$90 \leqslant s < 100$	4

4 In a one month period at a particular hospital the lengths of newborn babies were recorded. The results are shown in the table given.

    a Represent the data on a frequency histogram.

    b How many babies are 52 cm or more?

    c What percentage of babies have lengths in the interval 50 cm $\leqslant l <$ 53 cm?

    d Construct a cumulative frequency distribution table.

    e Represent the data on a cumulative frequency graph.

    f Use your graph to estimate the:

        i median length

        ii number of babies with length less than 51.5 cm.

Length (l cm)	Frequency
$48 \leqslant l < 49$	1
$49 \leqslant l < 50$	3
$50 \leqslant l < 51$	9
$51 \leqslant l < 52$	10
$52 \leqslant l < 53$	16
$53 \leqslant l < 54$	4
$54 \leqslant l < 55$	5
$55 \leqslant l < 56$	2

Activity

In this activity you will collect data from your class, and use the knowledge gained in this chapter to analyse the data.

What to do:

1 Measure the height of each student in your class. Copy and complete the table given, showing your results.

Height (h cm)	Freq (boys)	Freq (girls)	Freq total
$140 \leqslant h < 145$			
$145 \leqslant h < 150$			
$\vdots$			

2 Draw a cumulative frequency graph for the total frequency.

On a second graph, on the same set of axes, draw the cumulative frequency graphs for both the boys and the girls.

3 What do you notice about the graph of the total frequency compared with the graphs for each gender?

4 Use the total frequency graph to estimate:
    a the median   **b** the interquartile range (IQR).

5 Using the cumulative frequency graph for each gender, estimate for both boys and girls:
    a the median   **b** the IQR.

6 Compare the values obtained in **4** and **5**. Discuss why the values may be different.

Similarity

20

Contents:

A	Similarity	[4.5]
B	Similar triangles	[4.5]
C	Problem solving	[4.5]

Opening problem

Jacob makes cylindrical tanks of different sizes. His smallest tank has a height of 2 m and a radius of 0.8 m. He wants to manufacture another tank in the same proportions, but with a base radius of 1 m.

What height should the new tank have?

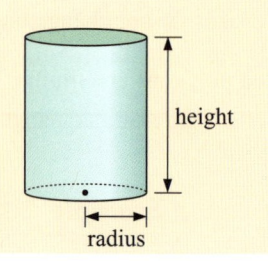

We have seen previously that two figures are **congruent** if they are identical in every respect apart from position. In this chapter we discuss **similarity**, which deals with figures that differ in size but have the same **proportions**.

A   SIMILARITY   [4.5]

Two figures are **similar** if one is an enlargement of the other, regardless of their orientation.

The corresponding sides of the figures must be *in proportion*, but the figures may be on a different rotation, or be reflected.

For any two similar figures, the side length will be increased (or decreased) by the same ratio from one figure to the next. This ratio is called the **scale factor** of the enlargement.

Discussion

- Discuss whether the following pairs of figures are similar:

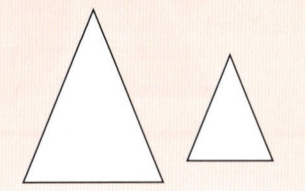

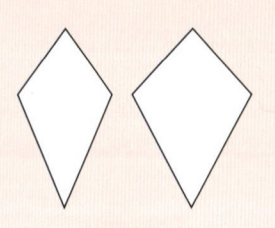

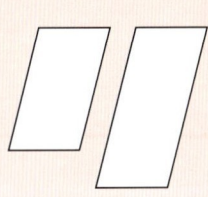

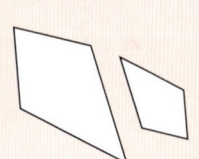

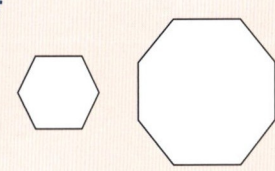

  a b c

  d e f

- Are congruent figures similar?

Consider the enlargement alongside for which the scale factor k is 1.5.

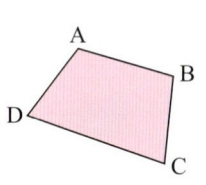

We often label the image of A as A′, the image of B as B′, etc.

Since $k = 1.5$, notice that $\dfrac{A'B'}{AB} = \dfrac{B'C'}{BC} = \dfrac{C'D'}{CD} = \dfrac{D'A'}{DA} = \dfrac{B'D'}{BD} = ... = 1.5$

Angle sizes do not change under enlargements.

If two polygons are **similar** then:
- the figures are equiangular **and** • the corresponding sides are *in proportion*.

Example 1 ◀) Self Tutor

These figures are similar.
Find x correct to 2 decimal places.

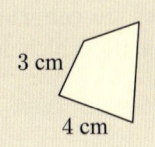

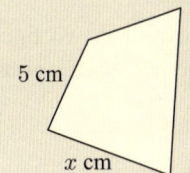

3 cm   5 cm
4 cm x cm

Since the figures are similar, their corresponding sides are in the same ratio.

$\therefore \quad \dfrac{x}{4} = \dfrac{5}{3}$

$\therefore \quad x = \tfrac{5}{3} \times 4$

$\therefore \quad x = \tfrac{20}{3}$

$\therefore \quad x \approx 6.67$

Similarity (Chapter 20)

EXERCISE 20A

1 Solve for x:

   a $x : 6 = 2 : 15$ **b** $x : 4 = 3 : 10$

   c $x : 5 = 7 : 31$ **d** $x : 8 = 9 : 102$

You can revise ratios in **Chapter 1**.

2 Find x given that the figures are similar:

   a 4 cm, 3 cm, x cm, 6 cm

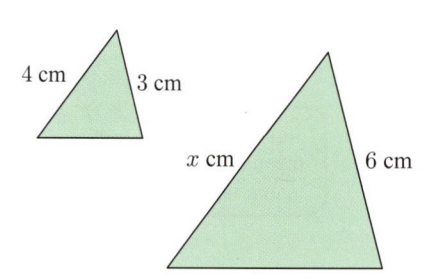

   b 4 cm, 5 cm, 7 cm, x cm

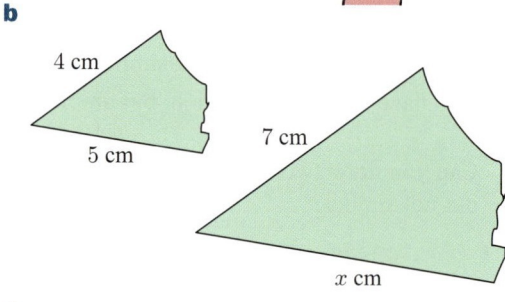

   c 5 cm, 3 cm, x cm, 8 cm

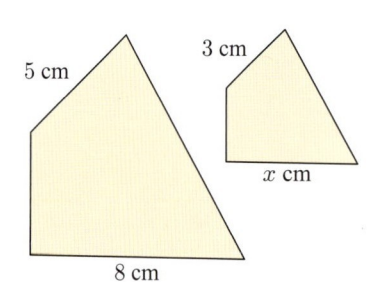

   d x m, 7 m, 5 m, 11 m

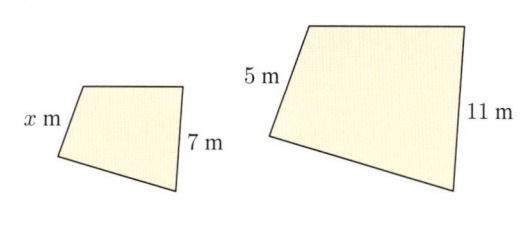

3 **a** If a line of length 2 cm is enlarged with scale factor 3, find its new length.

    b A 3 cm length has been enlarged to 4.5 cm. Find the scale factor k.

4 Rectangles ABCD and FGHE are similar. Find the length of FG.

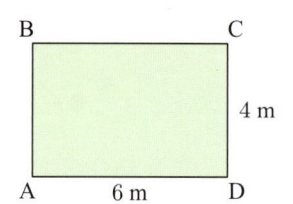

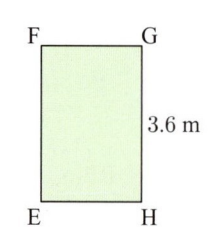

   ABCD: 6 m × 4 m; FGHE: 3.6 m

5 Comment on the truth of the following statements. For any statement which is false you should justify your answer with an illustration.

   a All circles are similar.   **b** All ellipses are similar.

   c All squares are similar.   **d** All rectangles are similar.

6 The diagram shows a 2 m wide path around a 12 m by 8 m swimming pool.

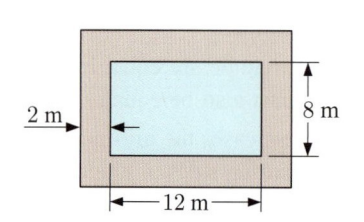

Are the two rectangles similar? Justify your answer.

7 Find x given that triangle ABC is similar to triangle A'B'C':

a

b

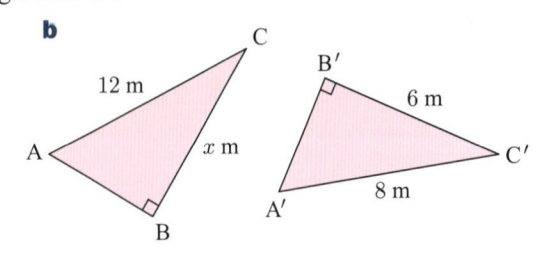

8 Sketch two polygons that:
  a are equiangular, but not similar
  b have sides in proportion, but are not similar.

9 Can you draw two triangles which are equiangular but not similar?

'In proportion' means 'in the same ratio'.

B SIMILAR TRIANGLES   [4.5]

In the previous exercise, you should have found that:

> If two triangles are equiangular then they are **similar**.
> Similar triangles have corresponding sides in the same ratio.

If two triangles are equiangular then one of them must be an enlargement of the other.

For example, $\triangle$ABC is *similar* to $\triangle$PQR.

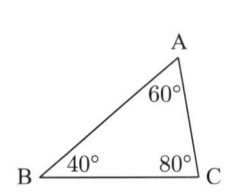

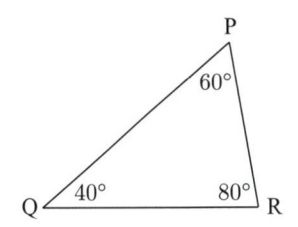

So, $\dfrac{QR}{BC} = \dfrac{RP}{CA} = \dfrac{PQ}{AB}$ where each fraction equals the scale factor of the enlargement.

> To establish that two triangles are **similar**, we need to show that they are **equiangular** *or* that their **sides are in proportion**.

You should note:
- Either of these properties is sufficient to prove that two triangles are similar.
- Since the angles of any triangle add up to $180°$, if two angles of one triangle are equal in size to two angles of another triangle, then the remaining angles of the triangles must also be equal.
- In examinations, many diagrams are labelled 'NOT TO SCALE'. In these cases the information marked on the diagram is correct, but we cannot find more information by measuring sides or angles, or relying on the appearance of the diagram.

Similarity (Chapter 20)

Example 2

Show that the following figures possess similar triangles:

a

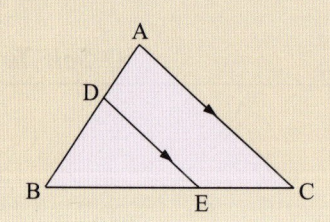

b

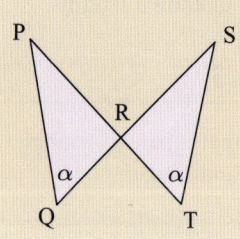

a

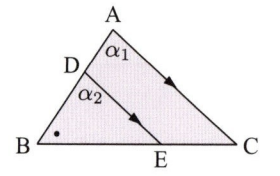

△s ABC and DBE are equiangular as:
- $\alpha_1 = \alpha_2$ {equal corresponding angles}
- angle B is common to both triangles

∴ the triangles are similar.

b

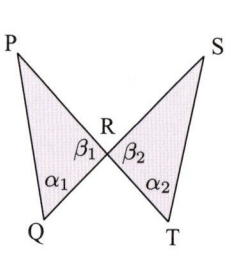

△s PQR and STR are equiangular as:
- $\alpha_1 = \alpha_2$ {given}
- $\beta_1 = \beta_2$ {vertically opposite angles}

∴ the triangles are similar.

EXERCISE 20B.1

1 Show that the following figures possess similar triangles:

a

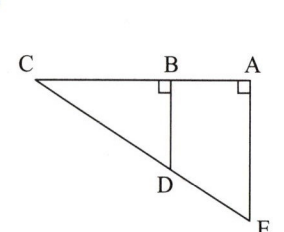

b

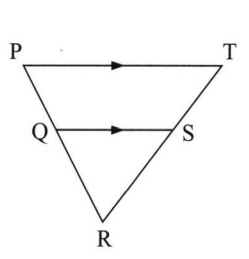

c

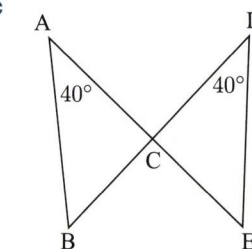

d

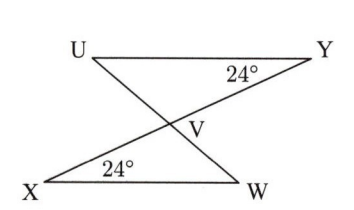

e

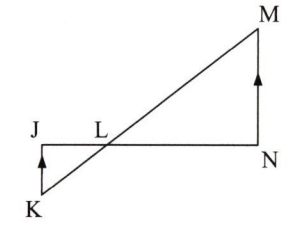

f

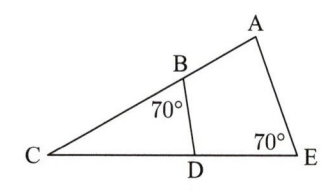

FINDING SIDE LENGTHS

Once we have established that two triangles are similar, we may use the fact that corresponding sides are in the same ratio to find unknown lengths.

Example 3   ◀) Self Tutor

Establish that a pair of triangles is similar and find x:

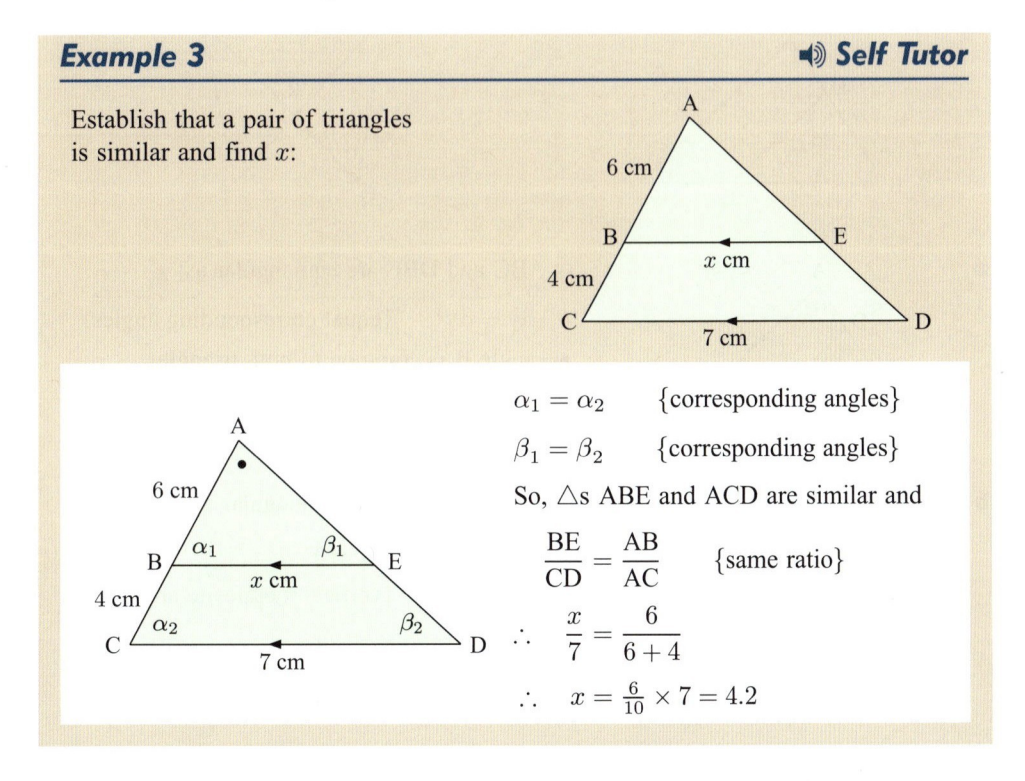

$\alpha_1 = \alpha_2$ {corresponding angles}

$\beta_1 = \beta_2$ {corresponding angles}

So, △s ABE and ACD are similar and

$$\frac{BE}{CD} = \frac{AB}{AC} \quad \text{\{same ratio\}}$$

$$\therefore \quad \frac{x}{7} = \frac{6}{6+4}$$

$$\therefore \quad x = \tfrac{6}{10} \times 7 = 4.2$$

When solving similar triangle problems, it may be useful to use the following method, written in the context of the example above:

Step 1: Label equal angles.

Step 2: Show that the triangles are equiangular, and hence similar.

Step 3: Put the information in a table, showing the equal angles and the sides opposite these angles.

Step 4: Use the columns to write down the equation for the ratio of the corresponding sides.

Step 5: Solve the equation.

	α	β	•	
-	6	x		small △
-	10	7		large △

from which $\dfrac{6}{10} = \dfrac{x}{7}$

$\therefore \quad x = 4.2$

Example 4   ◀) Self Tutor

In the figure alongside, BD = 20 cm.

Establish that a pair of triangles is similar, then find x.

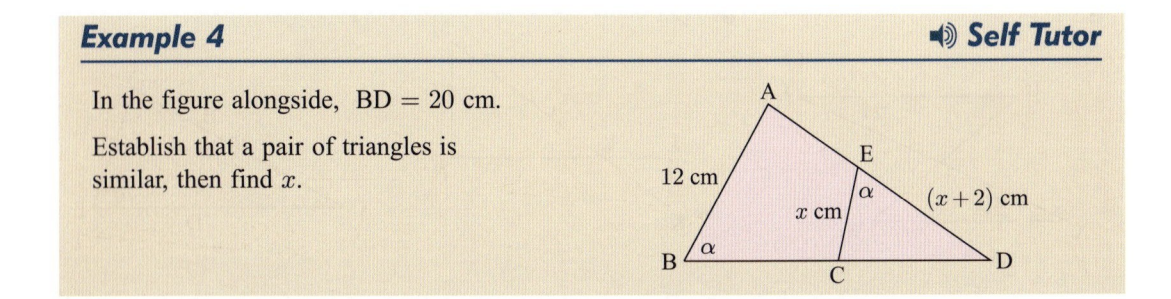

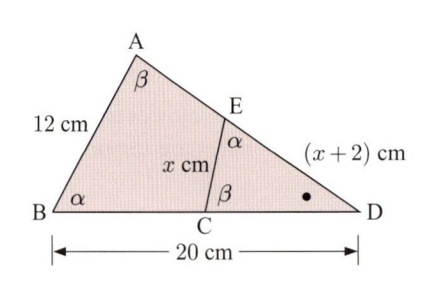

Triangles CED and ABD are equiangular since:
- $\widehat{CED} = \widehat{ABD}$
- angle D is common

$\therefore$ the triangles are similar.

$\therefore \widehat{BAD} = \widehat{ECD}$, and we call this angle β.

α	β	$\bullet$	
-	$x+2$	x	small $\triangle$
-	20	12	large $\triangle$

$\therefore \quad \dfrac{x+2}{20} = \dfrac{x}{12} \quad$ {same ratio}

$\therefore \quad 12(x+2) = 20x$
$\therefore \quad 12x + 24 = 20x$
$\therefore \quad 24 = 8x$
$\therefore \quad x = 3$

EXERCISE 20B.2

1 In each of the following, establish that a pair of triangles is similar. Then, find x:

a, **b**, 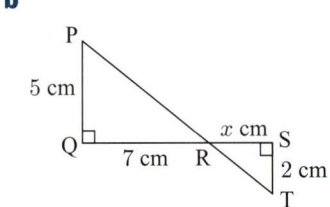 **c**, 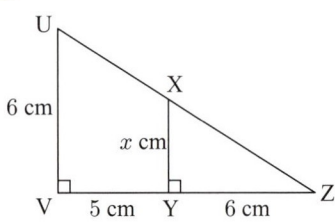 **d**, 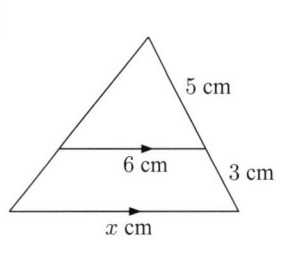 **e**, 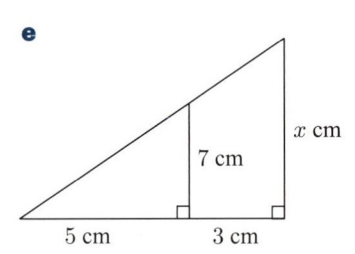 **f**, 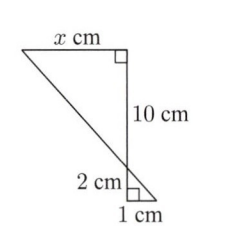 **g**, 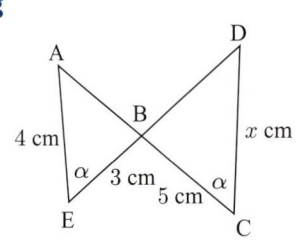 **h**, 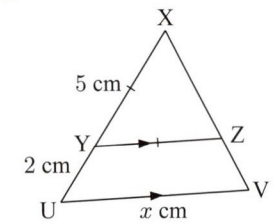 **i**

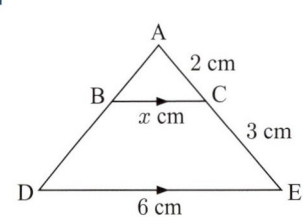

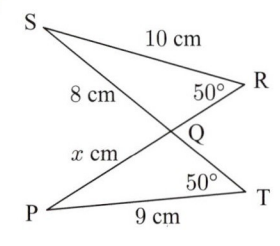

C PROBLEM SOLVING [4.5]

The properties of similar triangles have been known since ancient times. However, even with the technologically advanced measuring instruments available today, similar triangles are important for finding heights and distances which would otherwise be difficult to measure.

Step 1: Read the question carefully. Draw a sketch showing all the given information.

Step 2: Introduce a variable such as x, for the unknown quantity to be found.

Step 3: Set up an equation involving the variable, and then solve to find its value.

Step 4: Answer the question in a sentence.

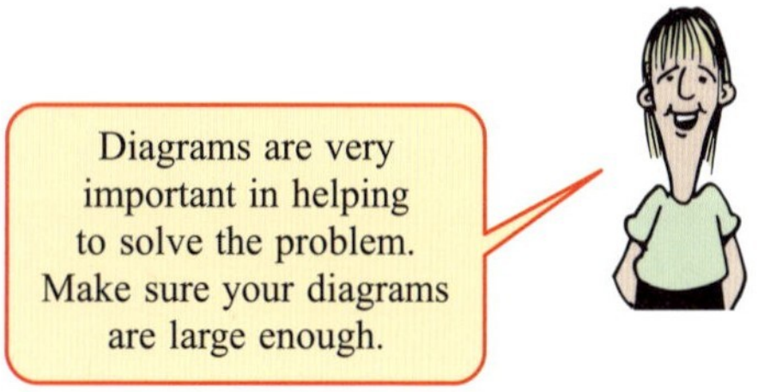

Diagrams are very important in helping to solve the problem. Make sure your diagrams are large enough.

Example 5   ◀) Self Tutor

When a 30 cm stick is stood vertically on the ground it casts a 24 cm shadow. At the same time a man casts a shadow of length 152 cm. How tall is the man?

The sun shines at the same angle on both. We suppose the sun is angle α to horizontal. Let the man be h cm tall.

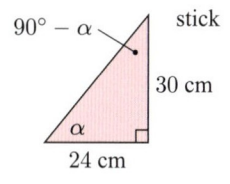

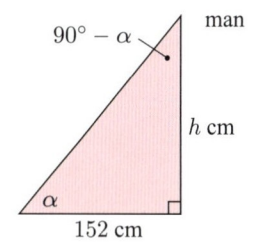

The triangles are equiangular and $\therefore$ similar.

$\therefore \quad \dfrac{h}{30} = \dfrac{152}{24}$ {same ratio}

$\therefore \quad h = \dfrac{152}{24} \times 30$

$\therefore \quad h = 190$ So, the man is 190 cm tall.

	α	$90° - \alpha$	$90°$	
	30 cm	24 cm	-	small $\triangle$
	h cm	152 cm	-	large $\triangle$

EXERCISE 20C

1 Find the height of the pine tree:

a 1 m stick, 1.2 m shadow, 8.4 m

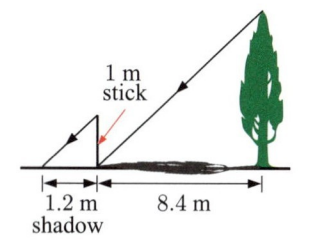

b 1 m stick, 2.4 m shadow, 18 m

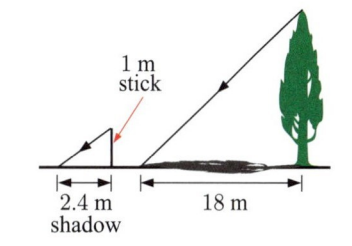

Similarity (Chapter 20) 381

Example 6

Hester places a small mirror on the ground 15 m from a tree. She stands where she can just see the top of the tree in the mirror. Hester is now 4 m from the mirror, and her eyes are 160 cm off the ground. How tall is the tree?

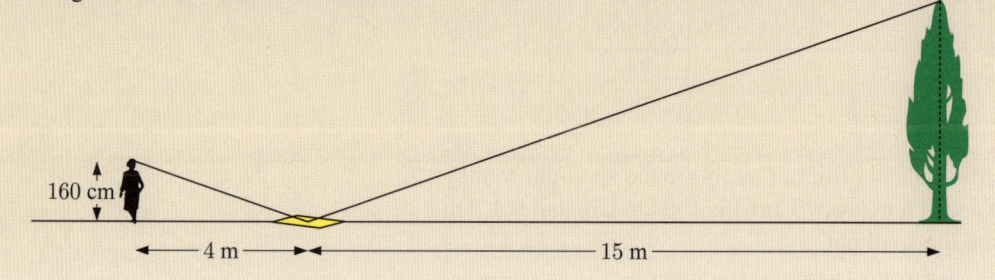

The reflection of the tree comes off the mirror at equal angles. We call these α.

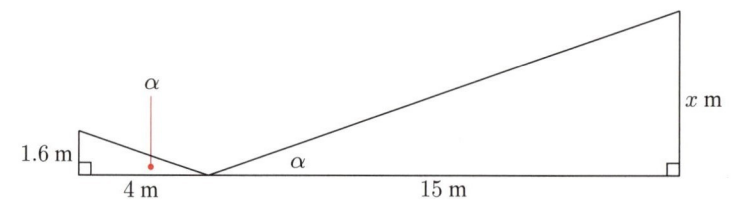

The two triangles are equiangular and so they are similar.

$\therefore \quad \dfrac{x}{1.6} = \dfrac{15}{4}$ {same ratio}

$\therefore \quad x = \dfrac{15}{4} \times 1.6$

$\therefore \quad x = 6$

So, the tree is 6 m high.

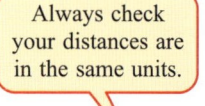

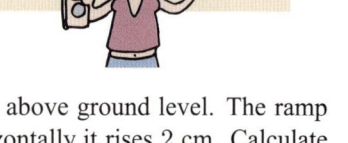

Always check your distances are in the same units.

2 A ramp is built to enable wheelchair access to a building that is 24 cm above ground level. The ramp has a constant slope of 2 in 15, which means that for every 15 cm horizontally it rises 2 cm. Calculate the length of the base of the ramp.

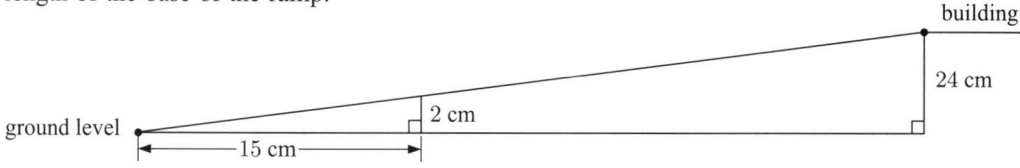

3 A piece of timber leaning against a wall, just touches the top of a fence, as shown. Find how far up the wall the timber reaches.

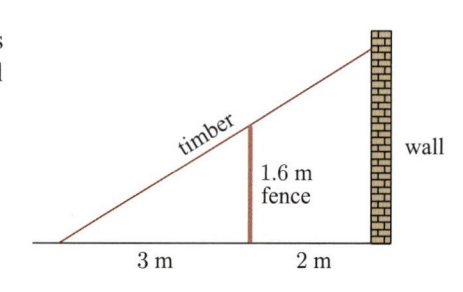

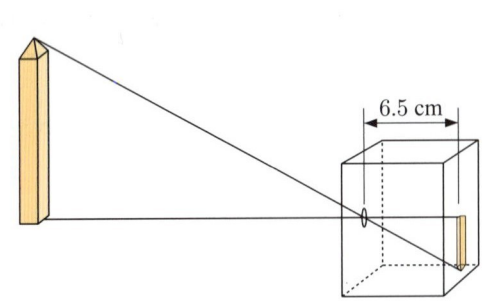

4 A pinhole camera displays an image on a screen as shown alongside. The monument shown is 21 m tall and its image is 3.5 cm high. The distance from the pinhole to the image is 6.5 cm.

How far is the pinhole from the monument?

5 Curtis walks in front of an in-ground spotlight shining on a wall 5 m away. Curtis is 156 cm tall, and is 1.2 m from the spotlight.

How tall is his shadow?

6 Narelle is drawing a floorplan of her house. Her bedroom is a rectangle 3.9 m long by 3.6 m wide. She decides to draw her room 7 cm long on her floorplan. How wide will it be?

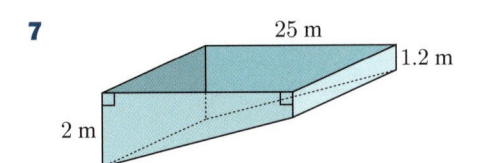

7 A swimming pool is 1.2 m deep at one end, and 2 m deep at the other end. The pool is 25 m long. Isaac jumps into the pool 10 metres from the shallow end. How deep is the pool at this point?

8 Ryan is standing on the edge of the shadow cast by a 5 m tall building. Ryan is 4 m from the building, and is 1.8 m tall. How far must Ryan walk towards the building to be completely shaded from the sun?

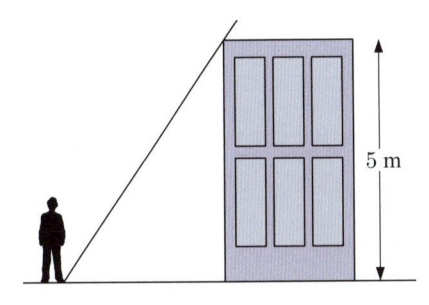

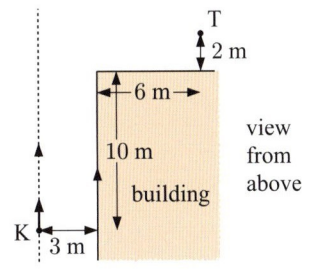

9 Kalev is currently at K. He is walking at 1 m/s, parallel to the side of a building. A flag pole is located at T. How long will it be before Kalev will be able to see the flag pole?

10 A, B, C and D are pegs on the bank of a canal which has parallel straight sides. C and D are directly opposite each other. AB = 30 m and BC = 140 m.

When I walk from A directly away from the bank, I reach a point E, 25 m from A, where E, B and D line up. How wide is the canal?

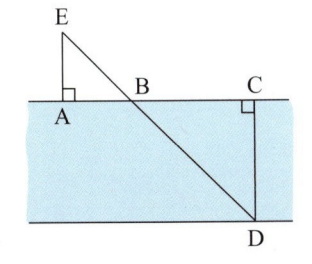

Similarity (Chapter 20)

11 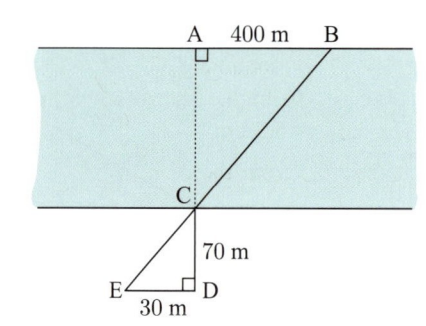 An engineer was asked to construct a bridge across a river. When surveying the site, he started at C and walked 70 m away from the river to D, then 30 m parallel to the river to E. He noticed that C and E formed a straight line with a statue at B.

The bridge must span the river and extend 40 m from the river bank in both directions. How long must the bridge be?

Give your answer correct to the nearest metre.

12 The dimensions of a tennis court are given in the diagram alongside.

Samantha hits a shot from the base line corner at S. The ball passes over her service line at T such that UT = 1.92 m.

The ball then travels over the net and lands on the opposite baseline AD.

   a Find the length of SU and BC.

   b A ball landing on the baseline is "in" if it lands between points B and C.

   Assuming the ball continues along the same trajectory, will it land "in"?

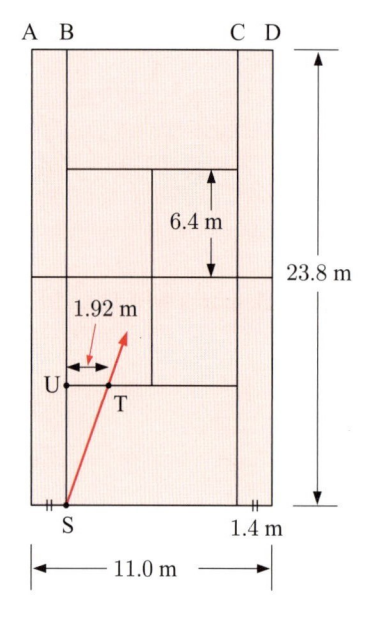

Review set 20A

1 Draw two equiangular quadrilaterals which are not similar.

2 Find the value of x:

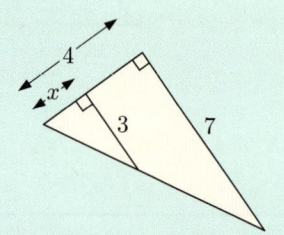

   a 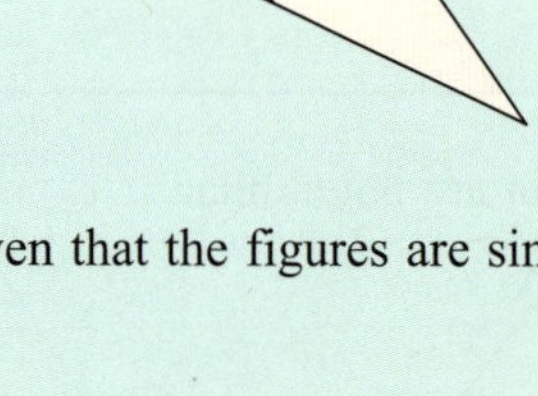

   b

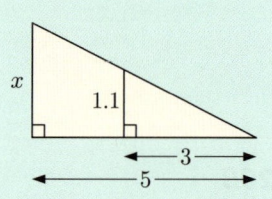

3 Find x, given that the figures are similar:

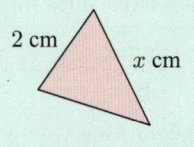

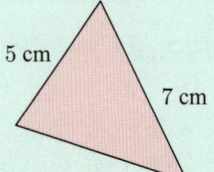

4 Show that the following figures possess similar triangles.

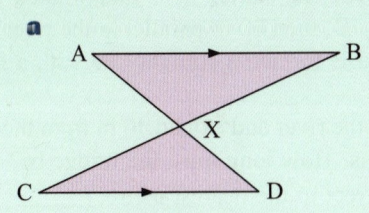

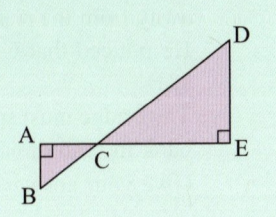

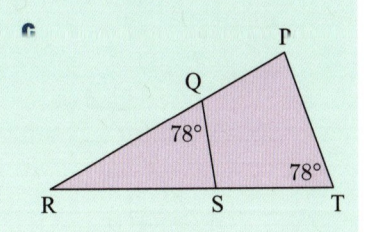

a
b
c

5 Find the value of the unknown in:

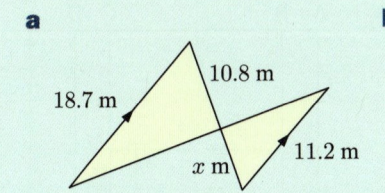

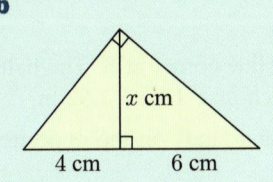

a
b

6 Parallelograms ABCD and EFGH are similar. Find x.

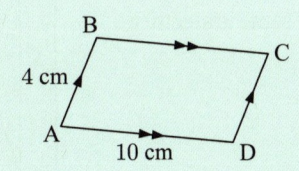

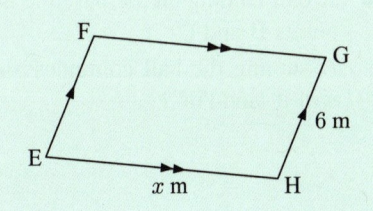

7 P and Q are markers on the banks of a canal which has parallel sides. R and S are telegraph poles which are directly opposite each other. PQ = 30 m and QR = 100 m.
When I walked 20 m from P directly away from the bank, I reached the point T such that T, Q and S lined up.
How wide is the canal?

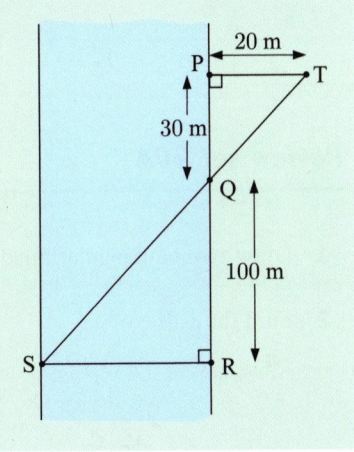

Review set 20B

1 Draw two quadrilaterals which have sides in proportion but are not similar.

2 Triangles ABC and PQR are similar. Find x.

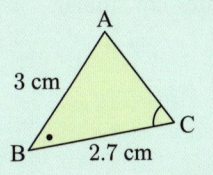

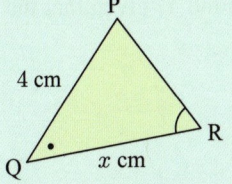

Similarity (Chapter 20)

3 In the following figures, establish that a pair of similar triangles exists, and hence find x:

a Triangle with A at top, B and C on sides with BC = 3 cm, AB = x cm, AD = 5 cm, DE = 8 cm.

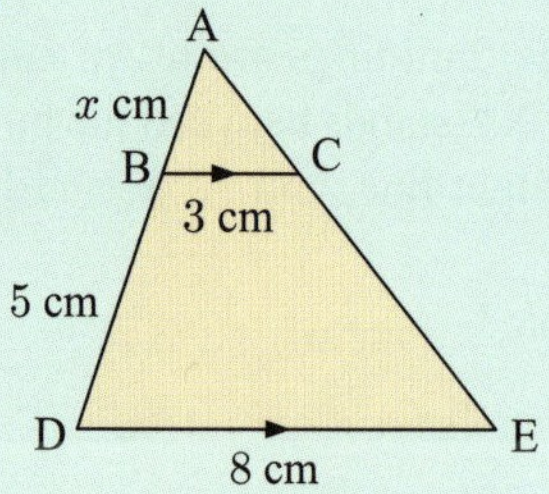

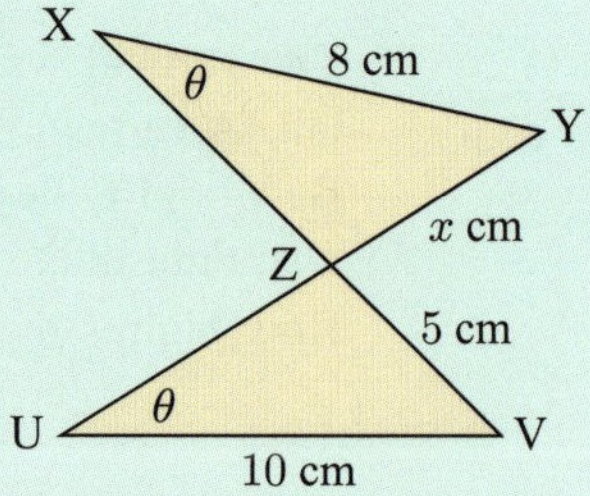

b Crossed triangles: XY = 8 cm, ZV = 5 cm, UV = 10 cm, YZ = x cm, angles θ at X and V.

c Triangle PTR with PT = 8 cm, PQ = 4 cm, QR = 6 cm, TS = x cm, angles α at P and at S.

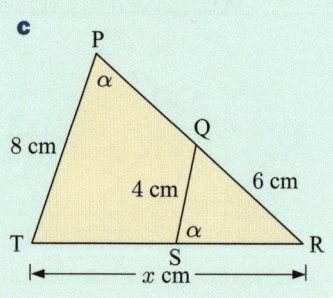

4 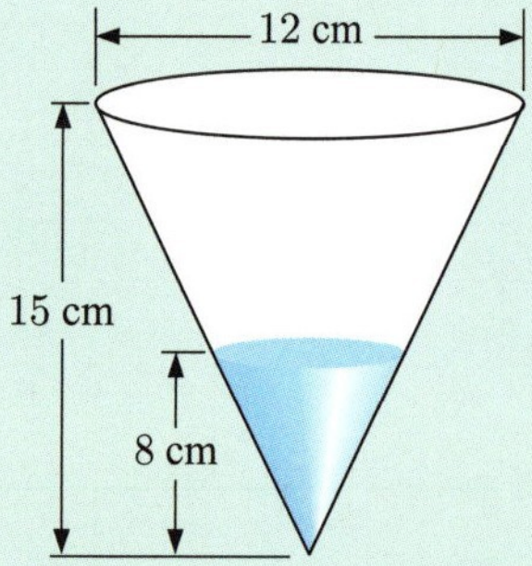 A conical flask has height 15 cm and base diameter 12 cm. Water is poured into the flask to a depth of 8 cm.

a Show that triangles ABC and MNC are similar.

b Hence, show that $x = 3.2$.

c Find the diameter of the surface of the water.

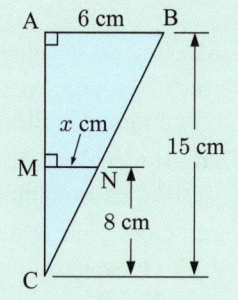

(Diagram: cone with top diameter 12 cm, height 15 cm, water depth 8 cm; right-side diagram shows triangle ABC with AB = 6 cm, BC = 15 cm, and MN = x cm at height 8 cm from C.)

5
a Explain why triangles ABE and ACD are similar.
b Find the length of CD given that BE has length 4 cm.

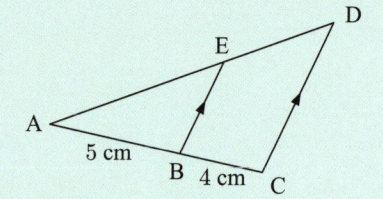

(Diagram: triangle ACD with E on AD, B on AC, AB = 5 cm, BC = 4 cm.)

6 Rectangles ABCD and EFGH are similar. Find the dimensions of rectangle EFGH.

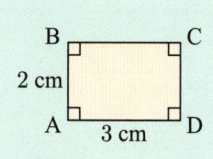

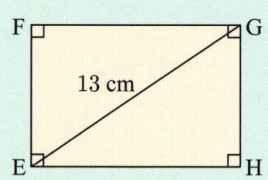

(Rectangle ABCD: AB = 2 cm, AD = 3 cm. Rectangle EFGH with diagonal FH = 13 cm.)

7 Francis holds a ruler 50 cm away from his eye, and measures a ship in the distance. It appears to be 1.6 cm long. Francis knows the ship is really 50 m long. How far away is it?

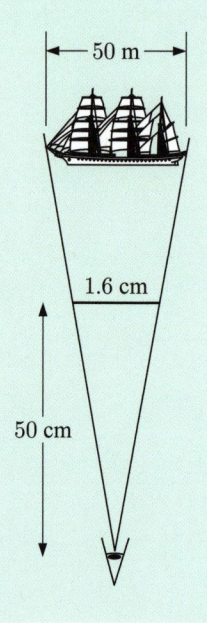

(Diagram shows ship 50 m long, ruler image 1.6 cm at 50 cm from eye.)

Challenge

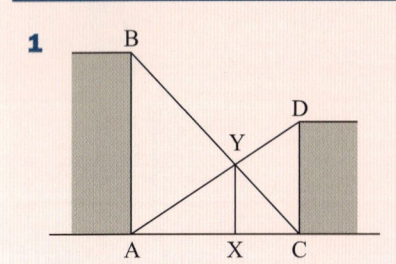

1 The vertical walls of two buildings are 40 m and 30 m tall. A vertical flag pole XY stands between the buildings. B, Y, and C lie in a straight line, and A, Y, and D lie in a straight line.

How high is the flag pole?

2 All circles are similar, since they are enlargements of one another.

   a Copy and complete the table opposite for the areas of different circles. Leave your answers in terms of π.

   b If a circle is enlarged with scale factor k, by what value is the area multiplied?

   c Does your result in **b** work for other figures? Test it using:

      i squares   **ii** rectangles

      iii right angled triangles.

Radius (cm)	Area (cm²)
1	
2	
3	
4	

Introduction to functions

Contents:

A	Mapping diagrams	[3.1]
B	Functions	[3.1, 3.6]
C	Function notation	[3.1, 3.6]
D	Reciprocal functions	[3.5]

Opening problem

Émile buys a baguette 72 cm long. He considers slicing it up into different numbers of slices, and wonders how long each piece will be if they are all the same length. To keep track of all his calculations, Émile makes a table:

Number of slices	2	3	6	12	18
Slice length (cm)	36	24	12	6	4

a What slice lengths result from cutting the baguette into 4, 8, or 9 equal pieces?
b Draw a graph of the data. Put 'number of slices' on the x-axis.
c Describe the shape of the graph. What happens as x gets very small? What happens when x gets very large?
d Write down an equation linking the 'number of slices' (x) with the 'slice length' (y).

In this chapter we look at how the variables can be related. The value of one variable is dependent on the value of the other. In some cases we can write an expression for one variable in terms of the other. We call this a **function**.

A MAPPING DIAGRAMS [3.1]

Consider the family of Mr and Mrs Schwarz. Their sons are Hans and Gert and their daughter is Alex.

There are many relationships between members of the family. For example, "is a brother of", "is older than", "is the parent of", and so on.

Introduction to functions (Chapter 21)

Here is a **mapping diagram** which maps the set of children C onto the set of parents P.

The connection for this mapping is: "is a child of".

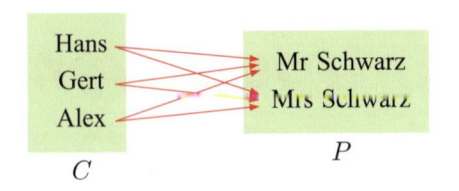

Hans, Gert, Alex → Mr Schwarz, Mrs Schwarz

C → P

A **mapping** is used to map the members or **elements** of one set called the **domain**, onto the members of another set called the **range**.

In particular we can define:

- The **domain** of a mapping is the set of elements which are to be mapped.
- The **range** of a mapping is the set of elements which are the result of mapping the elements of the domain.

Consider these two mappings:

mapping '$y = x + 3$'

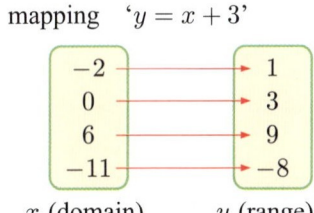

$-2 \to 1$
$0 \to 3$
$6 \to 9$
$-11 \to -8$

x (domain) y (range)

mapping '$y = x^2 + 1$'

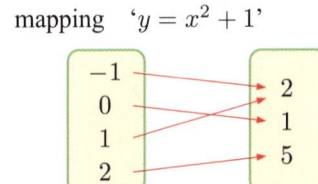

$-1 \to 2$
$0 \to 1$
$1 \to 5$
2

x (domain) y (range)

$y = x + 3$ or 'add 3 onto x' is called a **one-one** mapping because every element in the domain maps onto one and only one element in the range.

$y = x^2 + 1$ or 'square x and then add 1' is called a **many-one** mapping because more than one element in the domain maps onto the same element in the range.

In the previous example "is a child of", the mapping is **many-many**.

EXERCISE 21A.1

1 Copy and complete the following 'sets and mappings' diagrams:

  a mapping 'y is the number of wheels on x'   **b** mapping 'x eats y'.

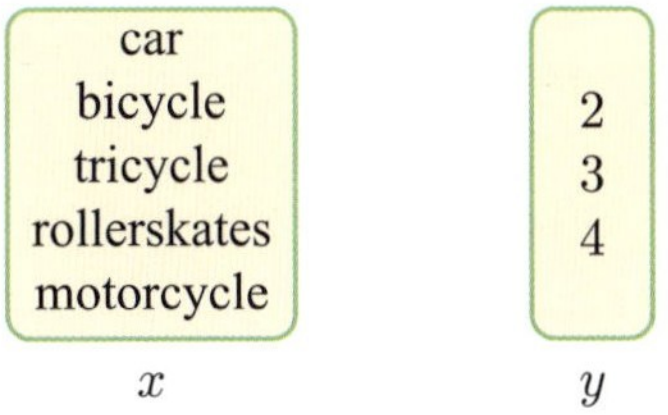

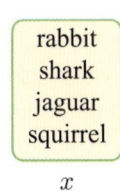

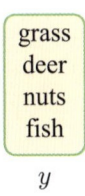

  { car, bicycle, tricycle, rollerskates, motorcycle }   { 2, 3, 4 }
  x y

  { rabbit, shark, jaguar, squirrel }   { grass, deer, nuts, fish }
  x y

2 Copy and complete the following 'sets and mappings' diagrams. State whether the mapping is one-one, many-one, one-many, or many-many.

  a mapping '$y = 2x - 5$'   **b** mapping 'is not equal to' 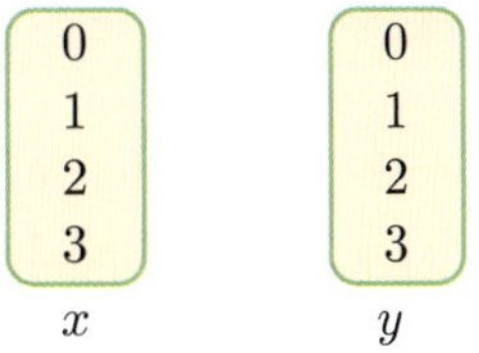   **c** mapping '$y^2 = x$'

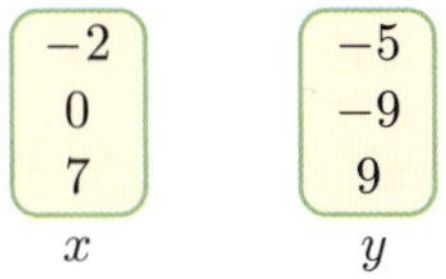

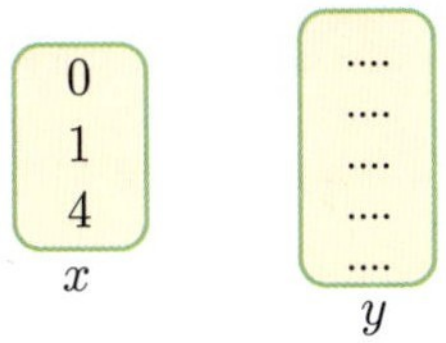

  { -2, 0, 7 }   { -5, -9, 9 }
  x y

  { 0, 1, 2, 3 }   { 0, 1, 2, 3 }
  x y

  { 0, 1, 4 }   { ...., ..., ..., ... }
  x y

Introduction to functions (Chapter 21)

d mapping 'is greater than'

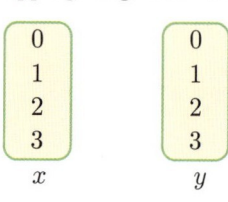

x: {0, 1, 2, 3} y: {0, 1, 2, 3}

e mapping 'add 1'

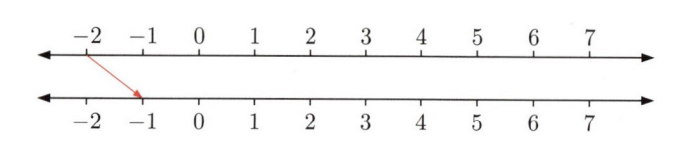

3 For these domains and mappings, describe the corresponding range:

a domain {real numbers}   mapping: 'subtract 20'
b domain {odd numbers}   mapping: 'double'
c domain {positive real numbers}   mapping: 'find the square root'
d domain {real numbers $\geqslant 0$}   mapping: 'add 10'
e domain {even numbers}   mapping: 'divide by 2'

SET NOTATION

Example 1   ◀) *Self Tutor*

Consider the set $\{0, \pm 1, \pm 2, \pm 3\}$ under the mapping 'square the number'.

a Draw a 'sets and mappings' diagram of this mapping.
b Find the domain and range of this mapping.

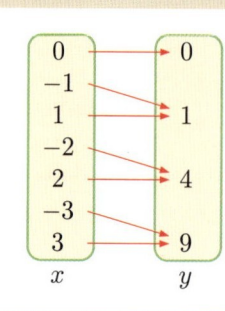

a x: {0, -1, 1, -2, 2, -3, 3} → y: {0, 1, 4, 9}

b $\{0, \pm 1, \pm 2, \pm 3\}$ maps onto $\{0, 1, 4, 9\}$

The domain is $\{0, \pm 1, \pm 2, \pm 3\}$
and the range is $\{0, 1, 4, 9\}$.

We could write this mapping as $x \mapsto x^2$.

We can also write mappings as a set of *ordered pairs* (x, y). The first element of each ordered pair is mapped to the second element.

For example, consider the mapping described by the set $\{(1, 3), (2, 5), (3, -4), (4, 3), (5, -4)\}$.

The ordered pair $(1, 3)$ tells us that 1 is mapped to 3.

The ordered pair $(2, 5)$ tells us that 2 is mapped to 5.

A complete diagram for this mapping is:

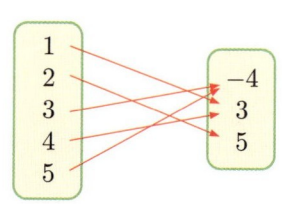

{1, 2, 3, 4, 5} → {-4, 3, 5}

EXERCISE 21A.2

1. For the following mappings:
   - **i** draw a 'sets and mappings' diagram
   - **ii** state the domain and range.
   - **a** the set $\{-2, -1, 0, 1, 2\}$ under the mapping 'multiply by 3'
   - **b** the set $\{1, 2, 3, 4, 5\}$ under the mapping $x \mapsto x - 3$
   - **c** the mapping $y = 6 - 2x$, where x is from the set $\{-5, -3, 0, 2, 4\}$.

2. The following sets of ordered pairs describe a mapping. For each set:
   - **i** draw a diagram
   - **ii** state if the mapping is one-one, many-one, one-many, or many-many.
   - **a** $\{(-2, 3), (-1, 5), (0, -2), (1, 4), (2, -1)\}$
   - **b** $\{(1, 3), (2, 1), (3, 3), (4, 1), (5, 3)\}$
   - **c** $\{(1, 1), (1, 2), (2, -2), (3, 0), (2, -1)\}$

B FUNCTIONS [3.1, 3.6]

The mapping in **Example 1** is a many-one mapping, and is an example of a *function*.

A **function** is a mapping in which each element of the domain maps onto *exactly one* element of the range.

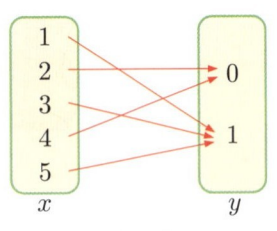

is a **many-one** mapping and is a function.

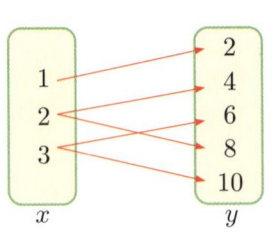

is a **one-many** mapping and is **not a function**.

We can see that functions can only be one-one or many-one mappings. One-many and many-many mappings are *not* functions.

Suppose a function maps set A onto set B. We say that:
- A is the **domain** of the function
- B is the **range** of the function.

Example 2

For the domain $\{0, 1, 2, 3\}$ and the function 'subtract 2', find the range.

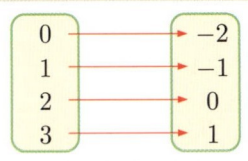

So, the range is $\{-2, -1, 0, 1\}$.

Introduction to functions (Chapter 21)

To help describe the domain and range of a function, we can use interval notation:

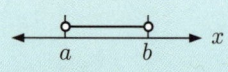

For numbers *between* a and b we write '$a < x < b$'.

For numbers '*outside*' a and b we write '$x < a$ or $x > b$'.

A filled in circle indicates the inclusion of the end point.
An open circle indicates the non-inclusion of that point.

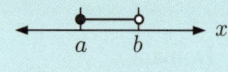

would be written as '$a \leqslant x < b$'.

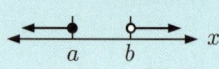

would be written as '$x \leqslant a$ or $x > b$'.

Consider these examples:

- All values of x and y are possible.
  $\therefore$ the domain is $\{x \mid x \in \mathbb{R}\}$
  and the range is $\{y \mid y \in \mathbb{R}\}$.

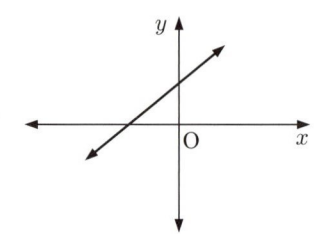

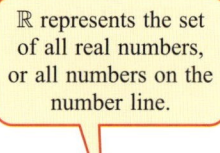

$\mathbb{R}$ represents the set of all real numbers, or all numbers on the number line.

- All values of $x < 2$ are possible.
  $\therefore$ the domain is $\{x \mid x < 2, \ x \in \mathbb{R}\}$.
  All values of $y > -1$ are possible.
  $\therefore$ the range is $\{y \mid y > -1, \ y \in \mathbb{R}\}$.

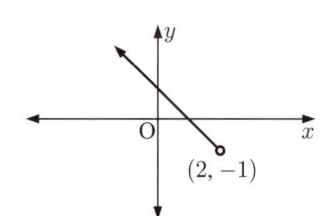

- x can take any value.
  $\therefore$ the domain is $\{x \mid x \in \mathbb{R}\}$.
  y cannot be < -2.
  $\therefore$ the range is $\{y \mid y \geqslant -2, \ y \in \mathbb{R}\}$.

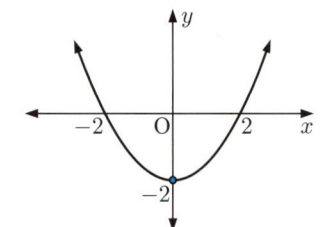

- x can take all values except $x = 0$.
  $\therefore$ the domain is $\{x \mid x \neq 0, \ x \in \mathbb{R}\}$.
  y can take all values except $y = 0$.
  $\therefore$ the range is $\{y \mid y \neq 0, \ y \in \mathbb{R}\}$.

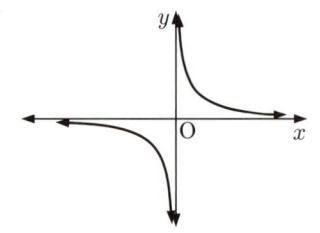

Example 3

For each of the following graphs, state the domain and range:

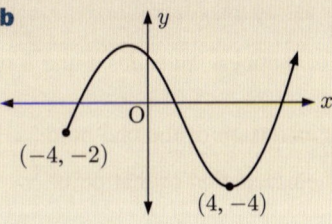

a (parabola with vertex (3, 4), opening down)

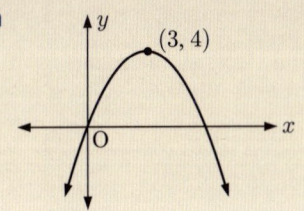

b (curve through (−4, −2) going right, with minimum at (4, −4))

c (line segment from (−1, −2) to (4, 3), open circle at (4, 3))

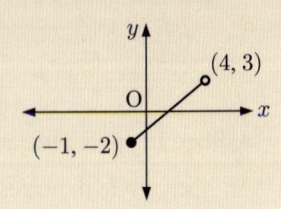

a Domain:
$\{x \mid x \in \mathbb{R}\}$.
Range:
$\{y \mid y \leqslant 4, \ y \in \mathbb{R}\}$.

b Domain:
$\{x \mid x \geqslant -4, \ x \in \mathbb{R}\}$.
Range:
$\{y \mid y \geqslant -4, \ y \in \mathbb{R}\}$.

c Domain:
$\{x \mid -1 \leqslant x < 4, \ x \in \mathbb{R}\}$.
Range:
$\{y \mid -2 \leqslant y < 3, \ y \in \mathbb{R}\}$.

It is common practice when dealing with graphs on the Cartesian plane to assume the domain and range are real. So, it is common to write $\{x \mid x \leqslant 3, \ x \in \mathbb{R}\}$ as just $\{x \mid x \leqslant 3\}$.

EXERCISE 21B.1

1 State the domain and range for these sets of points:
   a $\{(-1, 5), (-2, 3), (0, 4), (-3, 8), (6, -1), (-2, 3)\}$
   b $\{(5, 4), (-3, 4), (4, 3), (2, 4), (-1, 3), (0, 3), (7, 4)\}$.

2 For each of the following graphs, find the domain and range.

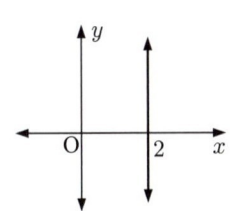

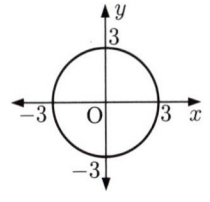

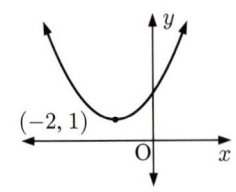

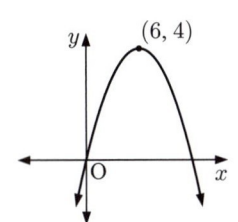

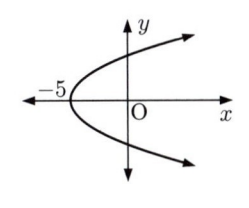

a (line with open circle at (−4, −2))

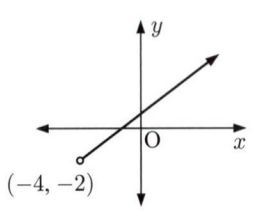

b (vertical line at $x = 2$)

c (circle centered at O with radius 3)

d (parabola opening down with vertex at origin)

e (horizontal line at $y = -5$)

f (parabola opening up with vertex (−2, 1))

g (parabola opening down with vertex (6, 4))

h (sideways parabola opening right with vertex at $x = -5$)

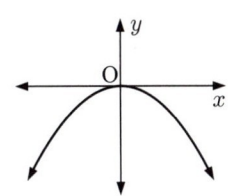

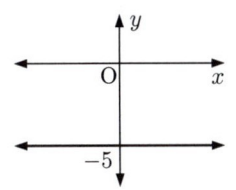

i (hyperbola with vertical asymptote at $x = 1$)

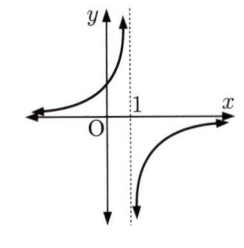

Introduction to functions (Chapter 21)

3 Find the range for the functions with domain D:

   a $D = \{-1, 0, 2, 7, 9\}$, function: 'add 3'.

   b $D = \{-2, -1, 0, 1, 2\}$, function: 'square and then divide by 2'.

   c $D = \{x \mid -2 < x < 2\}$, function: 'multiply x by 2 then add 1'.

   d $D = \{x \mid -3 \leqslant x \leqslant 4\}$, function: 'cube x'.

> In **3 c** and **3 d** we assume that $x \in \mathbb{R}$.

4 For each of these functions:

     i use a graphics calculator to help sketch the function

     ii find the range.

   a $y = 3x + 1$ on the domain $\{x \mid -2 \leqslant x \leqslant 2\}$

   b $y = x^2$ on the domain $\{x \mid -3 \leqslant x \leqslant 4\}$

   c $y = 4x - 1$ on the domain $\{x \mid -2 \leqslant x \leqslant 3\}$

   d $y = \dfrac{1}{x - 1}$ on the domain $\{x \mid 0 \leqslant x \leqslant 3, \ x \neq 1\}$

   e $y = x + \dfrac{1}{x}$ on the domain $\{x \mid -4 \leqslant x \leqslant 4, \ x \neq 0\}$

   f $y = x^2 + 1$ on the domain $\{x \mid x \in \mathbb{R}\}$

   g $y = x^3$ on the domain $\{x \mid x \in \mathbb{R}\}$

GEOMETRIC TEST FOR FUNCTIONS: "VERTICAL LINE TEST"

If we draw all possible vertical lines on the graph of a relation:

- the relation is a function if each line cuts the graph no more than once
- the relation is *not* a function if *any* line cuts the graph more than once.

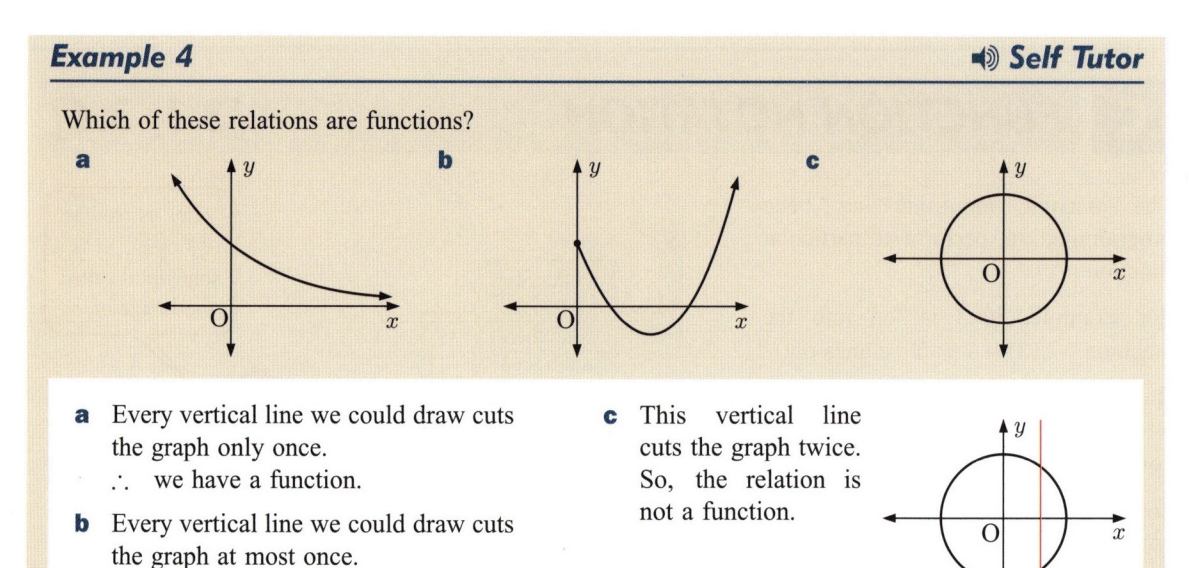

Example 4   ◆)) Self Tutor

Which of these relations are functions?

a   **b**   **c**

  a Every vertical line we could draw cuts the graph only once.
∴ we have a function.

  b Every vertical line we could draw cuts the graph at most once.
∴ we have a function.

  c This vertical line cuts the graph twice. So, the relation is not a function.

EXERCISE 21B.2

1 Which of the following sets of ordered pairs are functions? Give reasons for your answers.
   a $\{(1, 1), (2, 2), (3, 3), (4, 4)\}$
   b $\{(-1, 2), (-3, 2), (3, 2), (1, 2)\}$
   c $\{(2, 5), (-1, 4), (-3, 7), (2, -3)\}$
   d $\{(3, -2), (3, 0), (3, 2), (3, 4)\}$
   e $\{(-7, 0), (-5, 0), (-3, 0), (-1, 0)\}$
   f $\{(0, 5), (0, 1), (2, 1), (2, -5)\}$

2 Use the vertical line test to determine which of the following are graphs of functions:

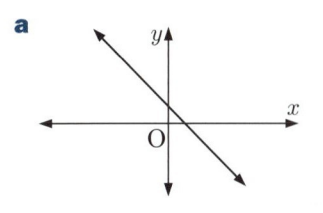

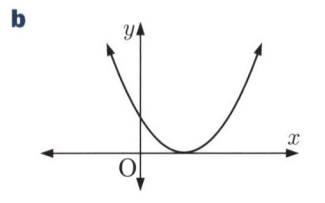

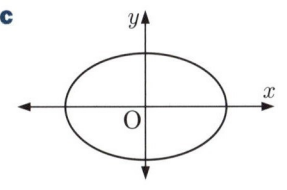

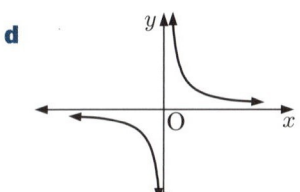

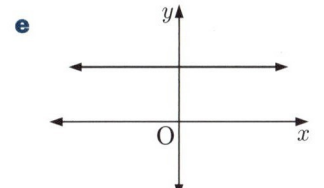

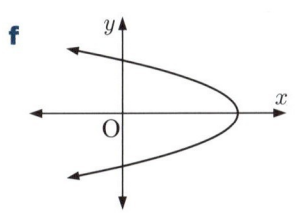

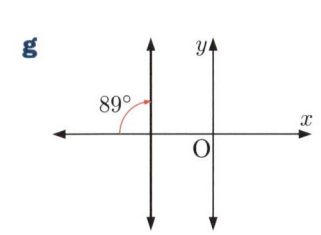

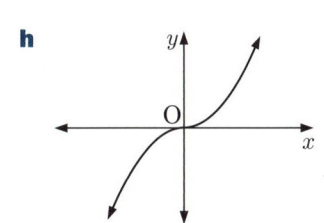

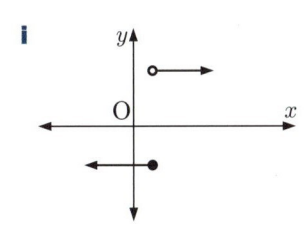

   a b c
   d e f
   g h i

3 Will the graph of a straight line always be a function? Give evidence for your answer.

C FUNCTION NOTATION [3.1, 3.6]

The machine alongside has been programmed to perform a particular function.

For example, if 3 is fed into the machine, $2(3) - 1 = 5$ comes out.

If f is used to represent this function, we say that 'f is the function that will convert x into $2x - 1$'.

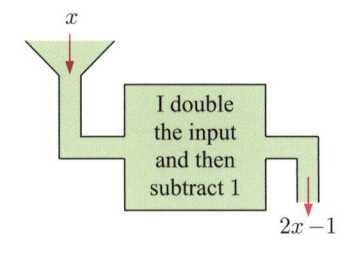

So, f would convert 2 into $2(2) - 1 = 3$ and -4 into $2(-4) - 1 = -9$.

I double the input and then subtract 1

$2x - 1$

$f(x)$ is read as 'f of x'. It is sometimes called the **image** of x.

This function can be written as: $f : x \mapsto 2x - 1$ or as $f(x) = 2x - 1$.

function f such that x maps onto $2x - 1$

Introduction to functions (Chapter 21)

If $f(x)$ is the value of y for a given value of x, then $y = f(x)$.

For $f(x) = 2x - 1$, $f(2) = 2(2) - 1 = 3$

This indicates that the point $(2, 3)$ lies on the graph of the function.

Likewise, $f(-4) = 2(-4) - 1 = -9$. This indicates that the point $(-4, -9)$ also lies on the graph.

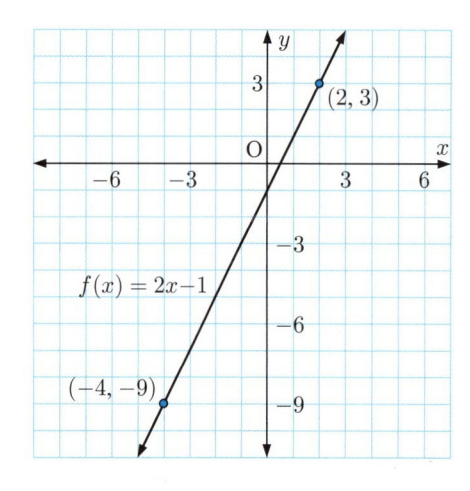

Example 5 ◆⟩ Self Tutor

If $f : x \mapsto 3x^2 - 4x$, find and interpret: **a** $f(2)$ **b** $f(-5)$

a $f(2)$
$= 3(2)^2 - 4(2)$ {replacing x by (2)}
$= 3 \times 4 - 8 = 4$

This indicates that $(2, 4)$ lies on the graph of the function.

b $f(-5)$
$= 3(-5)^2 - 4(-5)$ {replacing x by (-5)}
$= 3(25) + 20 = 95$

This indicates that $(-5, 95)$ lies on the graph of the function.

Example 6 ◆⟩ Self Tutor

If $f(x) = 4 - 3x - x^2$, find in simplest form: **a** $f(t)$ **b** $f(-x)$ **c** $f(x+2)$

a $f(t)$
$= 4 - 3t - t^2$
{replacing x by t}

b $f(-x)$
$= 4 - 3(-x) - (-x)^2$
{replacing x by $(-x)$}
$= 4 + 3x - x^2$

c $f(x+2)$
$= 4 - 3(x+2) - (x+2)^2$
{replacing x by $(x+2)$}
$= 4 - 3x - 6 - (x^2 + 4x + 4)$
$= -2 - 3x - x^2 - 4x - 4$
$= -x^2 - 7x - 6$

EXERCISE 21C

1 **a** If $f(x) = 3x - 7$, find and interpret $f(5)$.
b If $g : x \mapsto x - x^2$, find and interpret $g(3)$.
c If $H(x) = \dfrac{2x + 5}{x - 1}$, find and interpret $H(4)$.

2 **a** If $f(x) = 5 - 4x$, find:
    i $f(0)$ **ii** $f(3)$ **iii** $f(-4)$ **iv** $f(100)$

  b If $E(x) = 2(3 - x)$, find:
    i $E(0)$ **ii** $E(1)$ **iii** $E(5)$ **iv** $E(-2)$

  c If $h : x \mapsto \dfrac{x}{x-3}$, find:
    i $h(2)$ **ii** $h(5)$ **iii** $h(10)$ **iv** $h(-7)$

3 **a** If $f : x \mapsto 2x - 3$, find: **i** $f(4)$ **ii** x so that $f(x) = 1$.

  b If $g(x) = \dfrac{x+1}{10}$, find: **i** $g(4)$ **ii** a so that $g(a) = 2$.

  c If $m(x) = \tfrac{1}{2}x + 5$, find: **i** $m(-2)$ **ii** x so that $m(x) = 1$.

4 Suppose $f(x) = 3x + 5$ and $g(x) = 2x - 3$. Find x so that $f(x) = g(x)$.

5 The value of a car t years after purchase is given by $V(t) = 28\,000 - 4000t$ dollars.

  a Find $V(4)$ and state what this value means.

  b Find t when $V(t) = 8000$ and explain what this represents.

  c Find the original purchase price of the car.

  d Do you think this formula is valid for all $t > 0$?

6 Suppose $f(x) = 2x - 1$ on the domain $\{x \mid -3 \leqslant x \leqslant 1\}$.

  a Sketch the graph of $y = f(x)$, labelling the axes intercepts.

  b State the range of this function.

7 Suppose $g(x) = 6 - 5x$ on the domain $\{x \mid -2 \leqslant x \leqslant 2\}$.

  a Sketch the graph of $y = g(x)$, labelling the axes intercepts.

  b State the range of this function.

8 The graph of a function is given alongside. Use the graph to:

  a find $f(2)$

  b estimate the values of x, to 1 decimal place, when $f(x) = -3$.

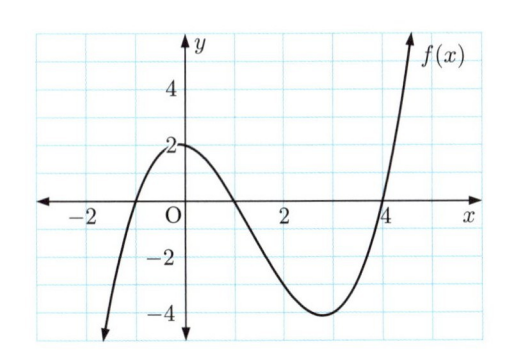

9 If $f(x) = 3x + 4$, find in simplest form:
  a $f(t)$ **b** $f(-t)$ **c** $f(x+2)$ **d** $f(x-1)$ **e** $f(4x)$

10 If $f(x) = 5 - 2x$, find in simplest form:
  a $f(a)$ **b** $f(-a)$ **c** $f(a+1)$ **d** $f(x-3)$ **e** $f(2x)$

11 If $P(x) = x^2 + 4x - 3$, find in simplest form:
  a $P(x+2)$ **b** $P(1-x)$ **c** $P(-x)$ **d** $P(x^2)$ **e** $P(x^2+1)$

Introduction to functions (Chapter 21)   397

Discovery 1   *Fluid filling functions*

When water is added to a container, the depth of water is given by a function of time. If the water is added at a *constant rate*, the volume of water added is directly proportional to the time taken to add it.

DEMO

So, for a container with a uniform cross-section, the graph of depth against time is a straight line, or *linear*. We can see this in the depth-time graph alongside.

The question arises:
'How does the shape of the container affect the appearance of the graph?'

For example, consider the graph shown for a vase of conical shape.

The depth increases more quickly when the vase is narrow, and slows down as the vase widens. The graph is therefore a curve as shown.

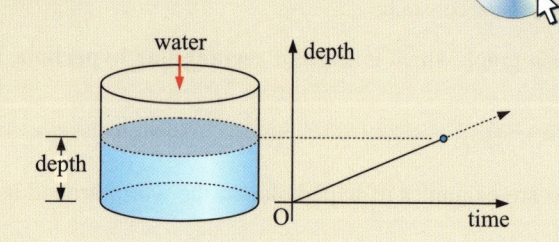

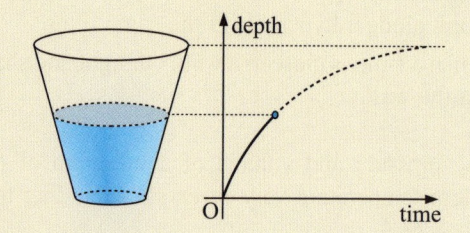

What to do:

1 For each of the following containers, draw a depth-time graph as water is added at a constant rate.

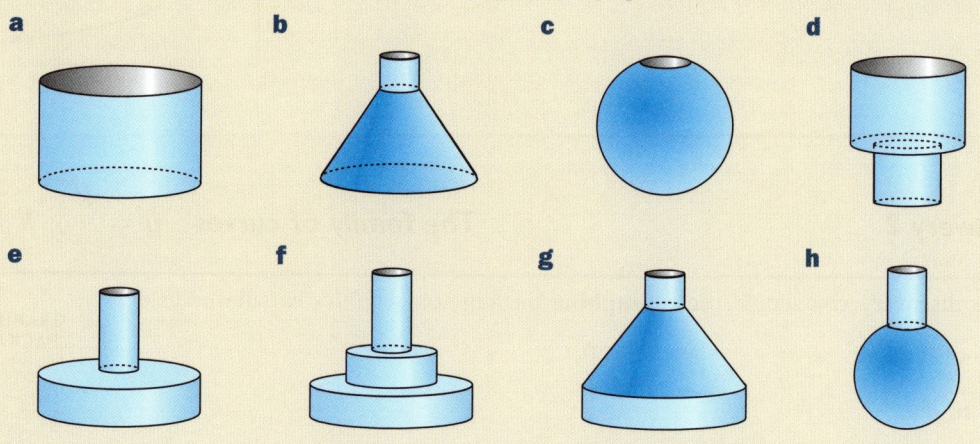

   a   **b**   **c**   **d**

   e   **f**   **g**   **h**

2 Use the water filling demonstration to check your answers to question **1**.

D RECIPROCAL FUNCTIONS [3.5]

A **reciprocal function** has an equation of the form $y = \dfrac{k}{x}$ where k is a constant.

It has a graph which is called a **rectangular hyperbola**.

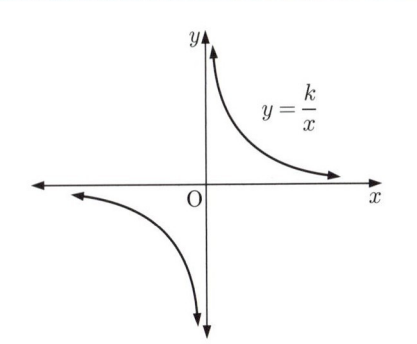

There are examples of hyperbolae in the world around us.

For example:

- when an aeroplane breaks the sound barrier, the sonic boom reaches every point along a hyperbola at the same time
- when a lamp is close to a wall, the light and shadow form part of a hyperbola on the wall.

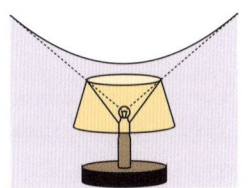

- the pressure and volume of a kilogram of oxygen gas at room temperature vary *inversely* according to the equation $P = \dfrac{77.4}{V}$.

  If P is graphed against V, the curve is one branch of a hyperbola.

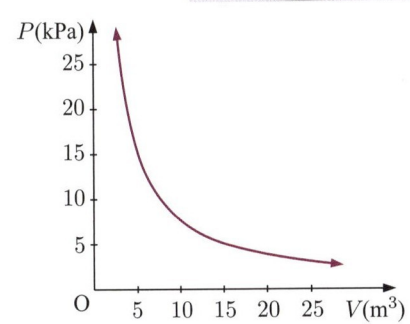

Discovery 2   The family of curves $y = \dfrac{k}{x}$, $k \neq 0$

In this discovery you should use a **graphing package** or **graphics calculator** to draw curves of the form $y = \dfrac{k}{x}$ where $k \neq 0$.

What to do:

1. On the same set of axes, draw the graphs of $y = \dfrac{1}{x}$, $y = \dfrac{4}{x}$, and $y = \dfrac{8}{x}$.
2. Describe the effect of the value of k on the graph for $k > 0$.
3. Repeat **1** for $y = \dfrac{-1}{x}$, $y = \dfrac{-4}{x}$, and $y = \dfrac{-8}{x}$.
4. Comment on the change in shape of the graph in **3**.
5. Explain why there is no point on the graph when $x = 0$.
6. Explain why there is no point on the graph when $y = 0$.

Introduction to functions (Chapter 21)

You should have noticed that functions of the form $y = \dfrac{k}{x}$ are undefined when $x = 0$.

On the graph we see that the function is defined for values of x getting closer and closer to $x = 0$, but the function never reaches the line $x = 0$. We say that $x = 0$ is a **vertical asymptote**.

Likewise, as the values of x get larger, the values of y get closer to 0, but never quite reach 0. We say that $y = 0$ is a **horizontal asymptote**.

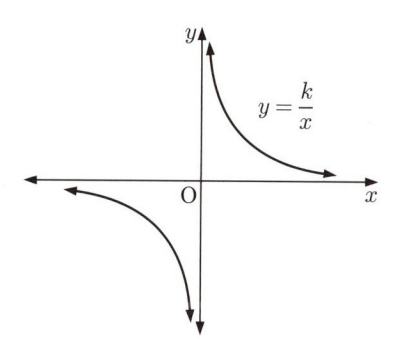

> An **asymptote** is a line which a graph approaches, but never quite reaches.

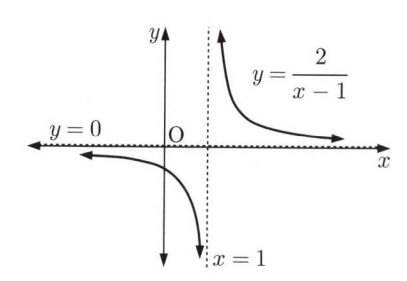

The graph of $y = \dfrac{2}{x-1}$ alongside is undefined when $x - 1 = 0$, which is when $x = 1$. It has the vertical asymptote $x = 1$.

As the values of x get larger, the values of y approach 0, but never quite reach it. So, the graph has the horizontal asymptote $y = 0$.

EXERCISE 21D

1 Consider the function $y = \dfrac{5}{x}$, which can be written as $xy = 5$.

  a Explain why both x and y can take all real values except 0.

  b What are the asymptotes of the function $y = \dfrac{5}{x}$?

  c Find y when: **i** $x = 500$ **ii** $x = -500$
  d Find x when: **i** $y = 500$ **ii** $y = -500$

  e By plotting points or by using technology, graph $y = \dfrac{5}{x}$.

  f Without calculating new values, sketch the graph of $y = \dfrac{-5}{x}$.

2 Kate has to make 40 invitations for her birthday party. How fast she can make the invitations will affect how long the job takes her.

Suppose Kate can make n invitations per hour and the job takes her t hours.

  a Complete this table of values, adding 4 more columns:

Invitations per hour (n)	4	8	12	....
Time taken (t)				

  b Draw a graph of n versus t with n on the horizontal axis.

  c Is it reasonable to draw a smooth curve through the points plotted in **b**? If you did, what shape would the curve have?

  d State a formula for the relationship between n and t.

3 Consider the function $y = \dfrac{3}{x-2}$.

  a Use technology to graph the function. Label the axes intercepts.
  b Find the equations of any vertical or horizontal asymptotes.

4 Consider the function $y = \dfrac{2}{x+1}$.

  a Use technology to graph the function. Label the axes intercepts.
  b Find the equations of any vertical or horizontal asymptotes.

5 Consider the function $y = \dfrac{1}{x-3} + 1$.

  a Use technology to graph the function. Label the axes intercepts.
  b Find the equations of any vertical or horizontal asymptotes.

Instructions for graphing a function can be found on page 23.

Review set 21A

1 Consider the mapping $\{(-2, -4), (-1, -2), (-2, 0), (-1, 2), (-2, 4)\}$.

  a Draw a 'sets and mappings' diagram of the mapping.
  b State the domain and range of the mapping.
  c Is the mapping one-one, many-one, one-many, or many-many?
  d Is the mapping a function?

2 For these functions, find the domain and range:

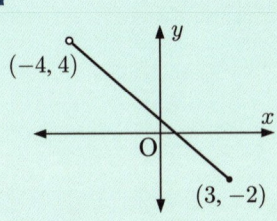

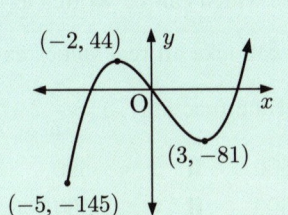

  a [graph showing line through $(-4, 4)$ and $(3, -2)$]
  b [graph with points $(-2, 44)$, $(3, -81)$, $(-5, -145)$]
  c [graph of a hyperbola-like curve]

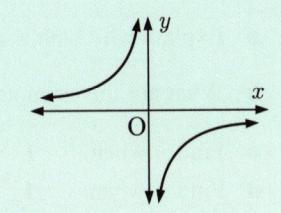

3 **a** If $f(x) = 5x + 2$, find and interpret $f(-3)$.
   b Given $f : x \mapsto 4 - 3x$, find: **i** $f(2)$ **ii** $f(-5)$ **iii** $f(x+1)$.

4 For the following graphs, find the domain and range, and decide whether it is the graph of a function:

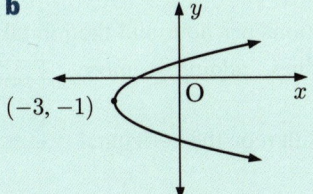

  a [horizontal line $y = 2$]
  b [sideways parabola with vertex $(-3, -1)$]
  c [line through $(-2, 2)$ and $(1, -3)$]

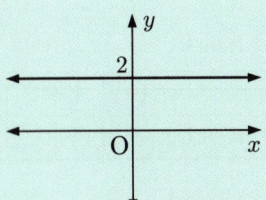

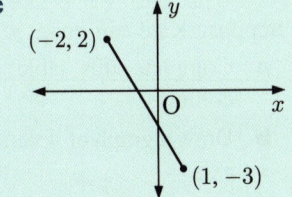

5 If $f(x) = 5x - 4$, find:

  a $f(-3)$ **b** $f(x-1)$ **c** x so that $f(x) = 3$

Review set 21B

1 **a** Copy and complete the mapping diagram alongside.
   b State whether the mapping is one-one, many-one, one-many, or many-many.
   c Is the mapping a function?

mapping '$y = x^2 - 2$'

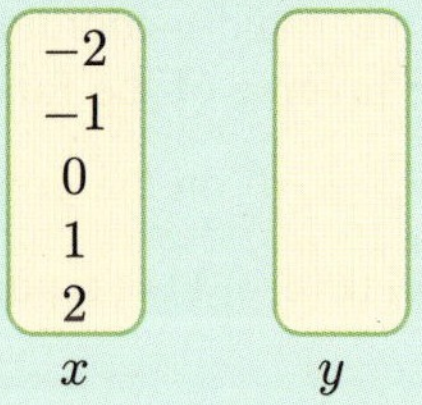

x: $-2, -1, 0, 1, 2$

2 For the following graphs, determine:
   i the range and domain
   ii whether it is the graph of a function.

a (line through $(-6, 0)$ area, passing through $(0, 2)$, open circle at lower end)

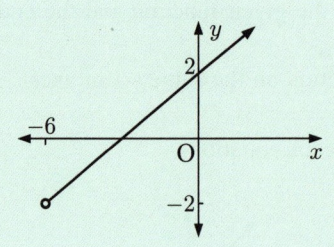

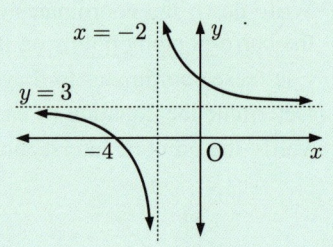

b ($x = -2$ vertical asymptote, $y = 3$ horizontal asymptote, passes through -4)

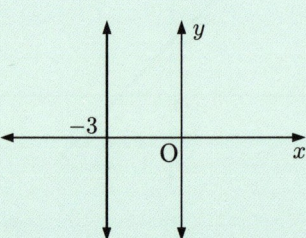

c (vertical line $x = -3$)

d (sideways parabola with vertex at $(1, -3)$)

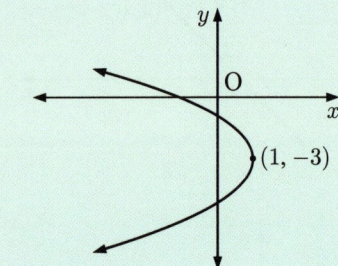

3 If $f(x) = \tfrac{1}{3}x + 5$, find in simplest form:
   a $f(-3)$
   b $f(-x)$
   c $f(x+1)$

4 Sketch the graph of $y = 3 - 2x$ on the domain $\{x \mid -3 \leqslant x \leqslant 3\}$. State the range of this function.

5 Consider the function $f(x) = \dfrac{4}{x+3} - 1$.
   a Use technology to graph $f(x)$.
   b Find the equations of any vertical or horizontal asymptotes.

Challenge

A linear function has a graph which is a straight line.

If we swap the x and y-coordinates of each point on the graph, we obtain another straight line. It is the graph of the **inverse** of the function.

For any point (a, b) on the graph of the function, the point (b, a) will lie on the graph of its inverse.

For example, if $(4, -1)$ is a point on the graph of a function, then $(-1, 4)$ is a point on the graph of its inverse.

1 For each of the following linear functions:

   i Copy the graph given onto a set of axes.
   ii Write down the coordinates of two points on the given function and the coordinates of the corresponding points on its inverse.
   iii Use these coordinates to draw the inverse function on the same set of axes.
   iv Determine the equation of each line.
   v Verify the point of intersection using simultaneous equations.

a

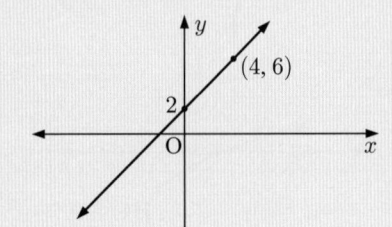

b

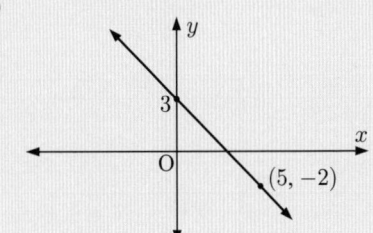

c

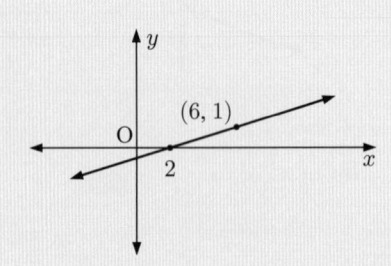

d

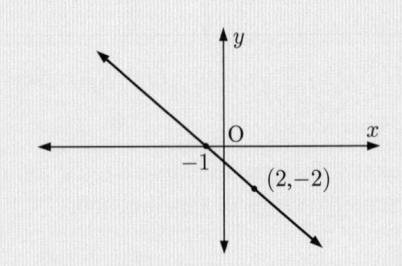

2 a What do you notice about the graph of each function and its inverse?
   b Draw the mirror line where the graphs reflect.
   c Find the equation of the mirror line.

Transformation geometry

22

Contents:

A	Directed line segments	[5.1]
B	Component form	[5.1]
C	Translations	[5.4]
D	Rotations	[5.4]
E	Reflections	[5.4]
F	Enlargements and reductions	[5.4]
G	Transforming functions	[3.8]
H	Miscellaneous transformations	[5.4, 3.8]

Opening problem

Consider the triangles on the illustrated plane.
- **a** What transformation would map the red triangle onto:
  - **i** triangle A
  - **ii** triangle B
  - **iii** triangle C
  - **iv** triangle D?
- **b** What single transformation would map triangle A onto triangle C?

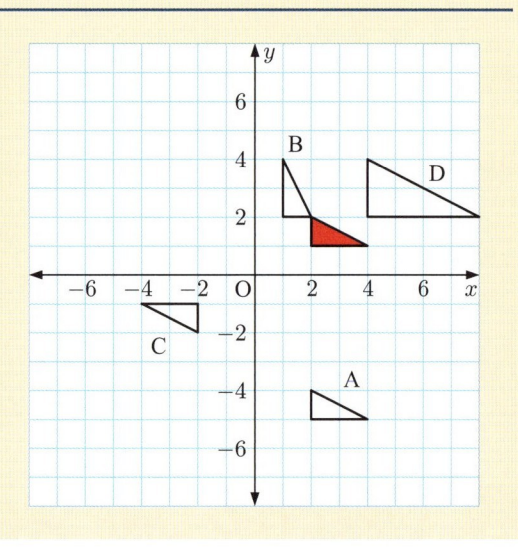

TRANSFORMATIONS

A change in the size, shape, orientation, or position of an object is called a **transformation**.

For example, many trees, plants, flowers, animals, and insects are **symmetrical** in some way. Such symmetry results from a **reflection**.

Reflections, rotations, translations and enlargements are all examples of transformations. We can describe these transformations mathematically using **transformation geometry**.

In **transformation geometry**, figures are changed (or transformed) in size, shape, orientation, or position according to certain rules.

The original figure is called the **object** and the new figure is called the **image**.

We will consider the following **transformations**:

- **Translations** where every point moves a fixed distance in a given direction
- **Reflections** or mirror images
- **Rotations** about a point through a given angle
- **Enlargements** and **reductions** about a point with a given factor.

Here are some examples:

translation (slide)

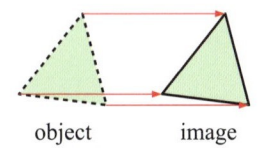

reflection

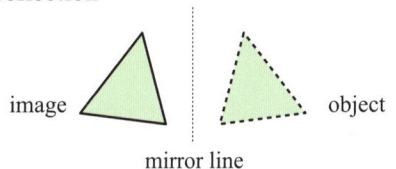

rotation about O through angle θ

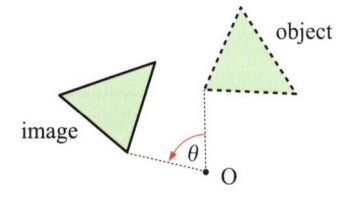

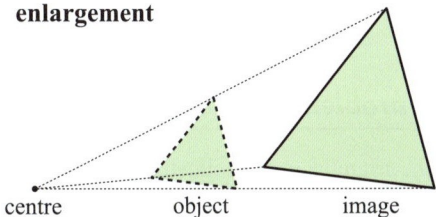

enlargement

reduction $(k = \frac{1}{2})$

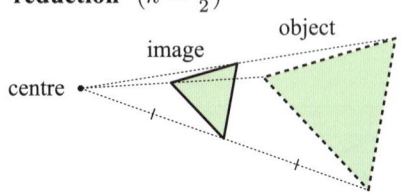

Click on the icon to obtain computer demonstrations of these transformations.

A · DIRECTED LINE SEGMENTS · [5.1]

In earlier chapters we measured various properties of objects, for example the width of a box, the length of a field, or the mass of a ball. These values all have **size** or **magnitude**.

Now consider a bus travelling at 100 km/h in a south east direction. To completely describe the motion of the bus, we need both the speed (100 km/h) *and* the direction (south east).

Transformation geometry (Chapter 22)

To achieve this we use quantities called **vectors**. Vectors have both magnitude and direction.

> Quantities which only have magnitude are called **scalars**.
>
> Quantities which have both magnitude and direction are called **vectors**.

For example, **velocity** is a vector since it deals with speed (a scalar) in a particular direction. Other examples of vector quantities are acceleration, force, displacement, and momentum.

REPRESENTING VECTORS

Consider again the bus travelling at 100 km/h in a south east direction.

A good way of representing this situation is to use an arrow on a scale diagram.

The **length of the arrow** represents the size or magnitude of the velocity, and the **arrowhead** shows the direction of travel.

Vectors are always in a straight line.

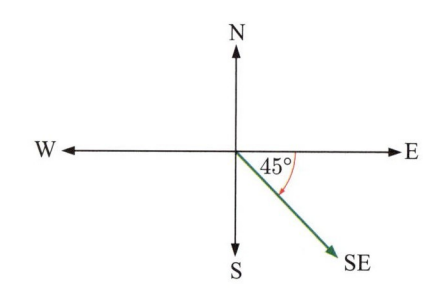

Scale: 1 cm represents 50 km/h

> Consider the vector represented by the line segment from O to A. 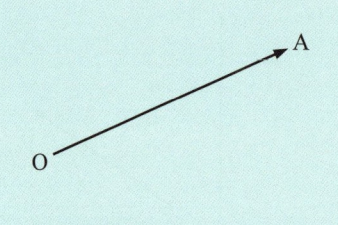
>
> We represent this **vector** by $\overrightarrow{OA}$.
>
> The **magnitude** or **length** of the vector is represented by $|\overrightarrow{OA}|$ or OA. 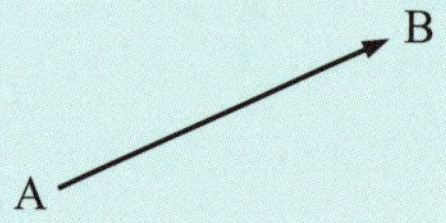
>
> $\overrightarrow{AB}$ is the vector which starts or **emanates** from A and ends or **terminates** at B. We say that $\overrightarrow{AB}$ is the **position vector** of B relative to A.

Example 1 ◀)) Self Tutor

On a scale diagram, sketch the vector which represents a velocity of:

  a 15 m/s in a westerly direction   **b** 40 m/s on a bearing 075°.

  a *Scale:* 1 cm ≡ 10 m/s   **b** *Scale:* 1 cm ≡ 10 m/s

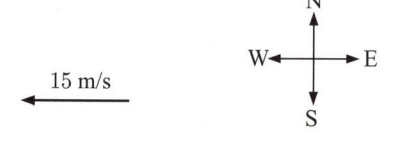

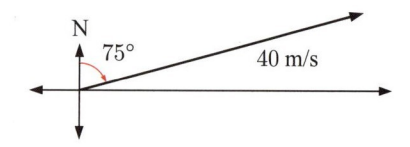

EXERCISE 22A

1 Using a scale of 1 cm to represent 10 units, sketch a vector to represent:
   a 40 km/h in a SW direction
   b 35 m/s in a northerly direction
   c a displacement of 25 m in a direction 120°
   d an aeroplane taking off at an angle of 12° to the runway, with a speed of 60 m/s.

2 If ⟶ represents a force of 45 Newtons due east, draw a directed line segment representing a force of:
   a 75 N due west
   b 60 N south west.

3 Draw a scaled arrow diagram representing the following vectors:
   a a velocity of 60 km/h in a NE direction
   b a momentum of 45 kg m/s in the direction 250°
   c a displacement of 25 km in the direction 055°
   d an aeroplane taking off at an angle of 10° to the runway, at a speed of 90 km/h.

B COMPONENT FORM [5.1]

When vectors are drawn on a coordinate grid, we can describe them in terms of their **components** in the x and y directions.

$\begin{pmatrix} x \\ y \end{pmatrix}$ is a **column vector** written in **component form**.

For example, given $\begin{pmatrix} -1 \\ 2 \end{pmatrix}$ we could draw

where -1 is the x-component or x-step
and 2 is the y-component or y-step.

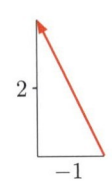

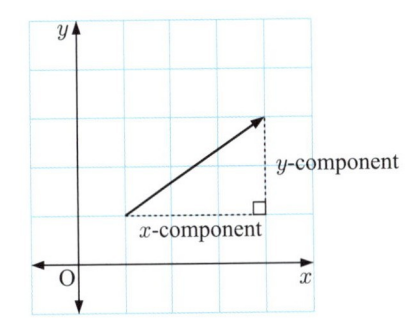

Example 2   ◉ Self Tutor

L(-2, 3) and M(4, 1) are two points. Find a $\overrightarrow{LM}$ b $\overrightarrow{ML}$.

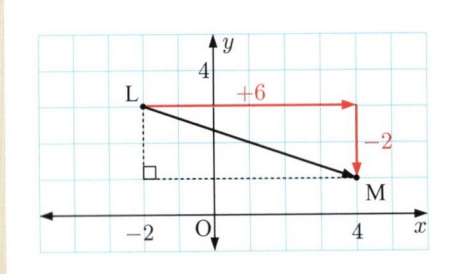

a The x-component goes from -2 to 4, which is $+6$.
   The y-component goes from 3 to 1, which is -2.

   $\therefore \overrightarrow{LM} = \begin{pmatrix} 6 \\ -2 \end{pmatrix}$

b $\overrightarrow{ML} = \begin{pmatrix} -6 \\ 2 \end{pmatrix}$

Transformation geometry (Chapter 22)

Instead of plotting points as in **Example 2**, we can also find a vector using a formula.

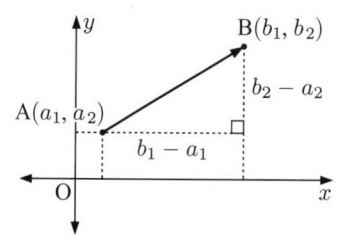

If A is (a_1, a_2) and B is (b_1, b_2) then

$$\overrightarrow{AB} = \begin{pmatrix} b_1 - a_1 \\ b_2 - a_2 \end{pmatrix} \quad \begin{matrix} \leftarrow x\text{-step} \\ \leftarrow y\text{-step} \end{matrix}$$

Example 3 ◀ Self Tutor

If A is at $(2, -3)$ and B at $(4, 2)$, find: **a** $\overrightarrow{AB}$ **b** $\overrightarrow{BA}$

a $\overrightarrow{AB} = \begin{pmatrix} 4-2 \\ 2--3 \end{pmatrix} = \begin{pmatrix} 2 \\ 5 \end{pmatrix}$

b $\overrightarrow{BA} = \begin{pmatrix} 2-4 \\ -3-2 \end{pmatrix} = \begin{pmatrix} -2 \\ -5 \end{pmatrix}$

EXERCISE 22B

1 Draw arrow diagrams to represent the vectors:

a $\begin{pmatrix} 4 \\ 2 \end{pmatrix}$ **b** $\begin{pmatrix} 0 \\ 3 \end{pmatrix}$ **c** $\begin{pmatrix} -2 \\ 5 \end{pmatrix}$ **d** $\begin{pmatrix} 3 \\ 4 \end{pmatrix}$

2 Write the illustrated vectors in component form:

a **b** 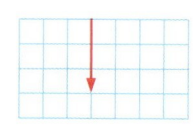 **c**

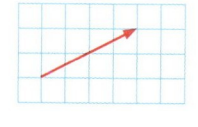

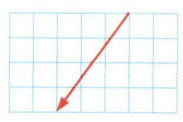

d 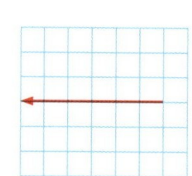 **e** 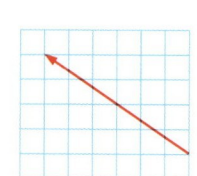 **f**

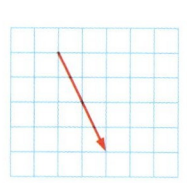

3 Write in component form:

a $\overrightarrow{BA}$ **b** $\overrightarrow{CA}$ **c** $\overrightarrow{CD}$
d $\overrightarrow{DA}$ **e** $\overrightarrow{BD}$ **f** $\overrightarrow{DC}$
g $\overrightarrow{AB}$ **h** $\overrightarrow{AC}$ **i** $\overrightarrow{DB}$

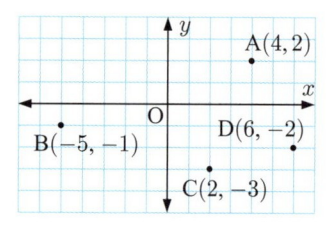

A(4, 2), B(-5, -1), C(2, -3), D(6, -2)

4 Suppose A is at $(3, 4)$, B is at $(-1, 2)$, and C is at $(2, -1)$. Find:

a $\overrightarrow{OA}$ **b** $\overrightarrow{AB}$ **c** $\overrightarrow{CO}$ **d** $\overrightarrow{BC}$ **e** $\overrightarrow{CA}$

Plot A, B and C on a grid and check your answers.

5 A is $(2, -3)$ and $\overrightarrow{AB}$ is $\begin{pmatrix} -1 \\ 5 \end{pmatrix}$. Find the coordinates of B.

O refers to the origin $(0, 0)$.

C TRANSLATIONS [5.4]

A **translation** moves an object from one place to another. Every point on the object moves the same distance in the same direction. Since the movement involves both distance *and* direction, we can describe it using a **vector**.

Suppose point P is at (2, 3). If we translate P using the **translation vector** $\binom{3}{-1}$, we move P with x-step 3 and y-step -1.

	P		P'
x-coordinate	2	+3 →	5
y-coordinate	3	−1 →	2

The image point P' is at (5, 2).

We write P(2, 3) $\xrightarrow{\binom{3}{-1}}$ P'(5, 2).

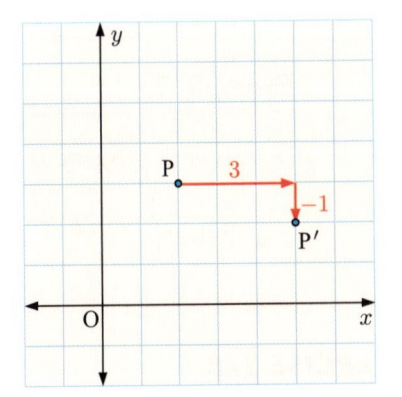

Example 4   ◀)) Self Tutor

Point A is at (1, 3).

a Find the image point B when A is translated through $\binom{2}{-1}$.

b Find the translation vector when A is translated to C(4, 5).

c Illustrate the translations on a grid.

a

	A		B
x-coordinate	1	+2 →	3
y-coordinate	3	−1 →	2

∴ B is at (3, 2).

b

	A		C
x-coordinate	1	+3 →	4
y-coordinate	3	+2 →	5

∴ the translation vector is $\binom{3}{2}$.

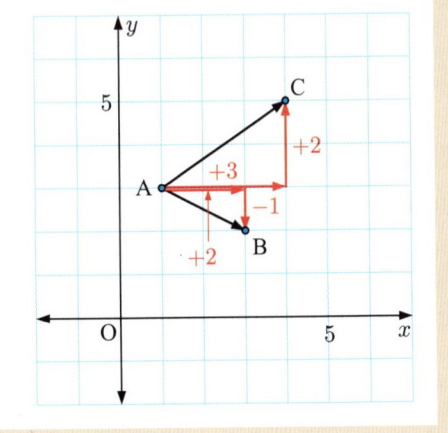

EXERCISE 22C

1 Find the image point when:

a (2, −1) is translated through $\binom{3}{4}$

b (5, 2) is translated through $\binom{-1}{4}$

c (−3, 4) is translated through $\binom{2}{-1}$

d (−1, −3) is translated through $\binom{6}{-2}$.

2 Find the translation vector when:

  a $(3, -2)$ is translated to $(3, 1)$
  b $(0, 4)$ is translated to $(-2, -3)$
  c $(1, 4)$ is translated to $(3, 4)$
  d $(-3, -2)$ is translated to $(-1, -3)$.

3 What point has image $(-3, 2)$ under the translation $\begin{pmatrix} -3 \\ 1 \end{pmatrix}$?

4 Find the translation vector which maps:

  a A onto E
  b E onto A
  c A onto C
  d C onto A
  e B onto E
  f D onto E
  g E onto C
  h E onto D
  i D onto B
  j A onto D.

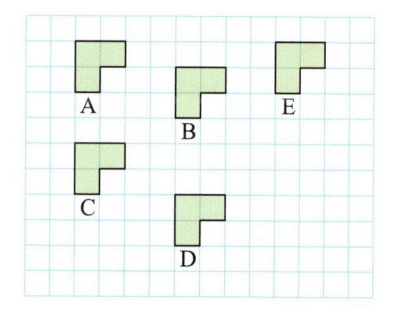

Example 5   ◀)) Self Tutor

Triangle OAB has vertices O(0, 0), A(2, 3), and B(−1, 2).

Find the image vertices when the triangle is translated $\begin{pmatrix} 3 \\ 2 \end{pmatrix}$.

Illustrate the object and image on a set of axes.

O(0, 0) $\xrightarrow{\begin{pmatrix} 3 \\ 2 \end{pmatrix}}$ O'(3, 2)

A(2, 3) $\xrightarrow{\begin{pmatrix} 3 \\ 2 \end{pmatrix}}$ A'(5, 5)

B(−1, 2) $\xrightarrow{\begin{pmatrix} 3 \\ 2 \end{pmatrix}}$ B'(2, 4)

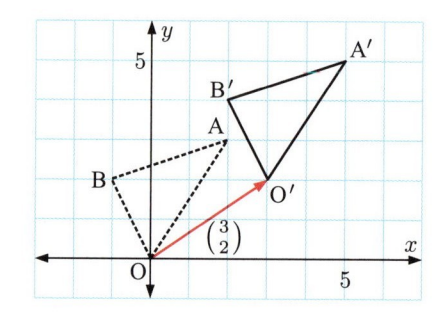

5 Triangle ABC has vertices A(−1, 3), B(4, 1), and C(0, −2).

  a Draw triangle ABC on a set of axes.
  b Translate the figure by the translation vector $\begin{pmatrix} 4 \\ -2 \end{pmatrix}$.
  c State the coordinates of the image vertices A', B' and C'.
  d Through what distance has each point moved?

When we translate point A, we often label its image A'.

D ROTATIONS [5.4]

In the diagram, P(x, y) moves under a **rotation** about O, through an angle of θ, to a new position P'(x', y'). We see that OP = OP' and $\widehat{POP'} = \theta$ where **positive** θ is measured **anticlockwise**.

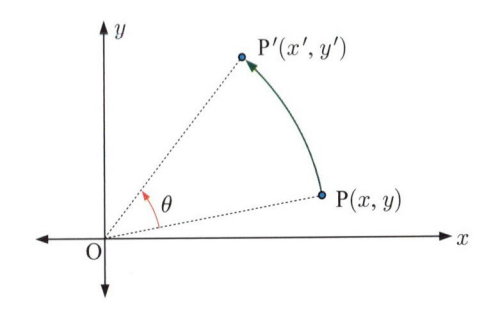

O is the only point which does not move under the rotation.

In this course we will concentrate on rotations of 90° (both clockwise and anticlockwise) and 180°.

To illustrate a rotation, we draw a sector or circle with centre at the **centre of rotation**, and which goes through the object point. We then measure the required angle and mark the image point.

Example 6

Find the image of the point (3, 1) under a rotation about O(0, 0) which is:
- **a** 90° anticlockwise
- **b** 90° clockwise
- **c** 180°.

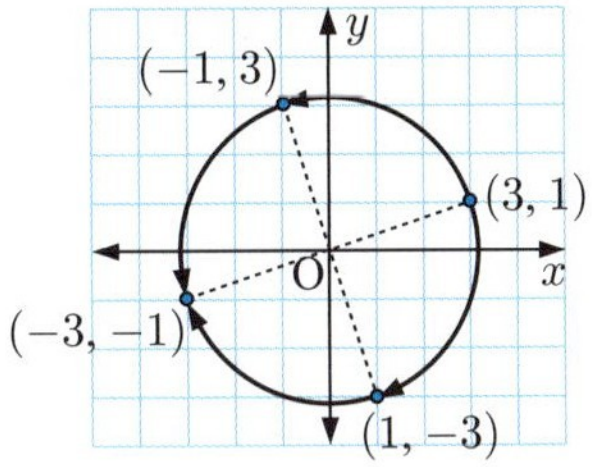

a (3, 1) → (−1, 3)

b (3, 1) → (1, −3)

c (3, 1) → (−3, −1)

We can also rotate objects around points other than the origin.

Example 7

Triangle ABC has vertices A(−1, 2), B(−1, 5) and C(−3, 5). It is rotated clockwise through 90° about (−2, 0). Draw the image of triangle ABC and label it A'B'C'.

A(−1, 2) → A'(0, −1)

B(−1, 5) → B'(3, −1)

C(−3, 5) → C'(3, 1)

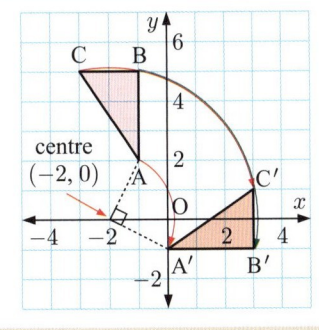

Transformation geometry (Chapter 22)

EXERCISE 22D

1 Find the image of the point $(-2, 3)$ under these rotations about the origin $O(0, 0)$:
   a clockwise through $90°$
   b anticlockwise through $90°$
   c through $180°$.

2 Find the image of $(4, -1)$ under these rotations about $(0, 2)$:
   a $90°$ anticlockwise
   b through $180°$
   c $90°$ clockwise.

3 Find the image of $(-3, 1)$ under these rotations:
   a $180°$ about $(-4, 3)$
   b $90°$ anticlockwise about $(1, 2)$.

4 Triangle ABC has vertices $A(2, 4)$, $B(4, 1)$, and $C(1, -1)$. It is rotated anticlockwise through $90°$ about $(0, 3)$.
   a Draw triangle ABC and its image $A'B'C'$.
   b Write down the coordinates of the vertices of triangle $A'B'C'$.

5 Triangle PQR with $P(3, -2)$, $Q(1, 4)$ and $R(-1, 1)$ is rotated about R through $180°$.
   a Draw triangle PQR and its image $P'Q'R'$.
   b Write down the coordinates of P', Q' and R'.

Discovery 1 — Rotations

In this discovery we generalise some special rotations of a point about the origin $O(0, 0)$.

What to do:

1 Have a close look at the solution to **Example 6**, and your answers to question **1** of the exercise above.

2 Predict the image of the point $P(x, y)$ under these rotations about $O(0, 0)$:
   a $90°$ anticlockwise
   b $90°$ clockwise
   c $180°$.

3 Check your prediction by performing the three rotations on a point of your choosing.

4 Compare your results with other students in your class.

E REFLECTIONS [5.4]

To **reflect** a point P in a **mirror line**, we first draw a line through P perpendicular to the mirror line. The image P' lies on this perpendicular line, on the other side of the mirror line, the same distance away as P.

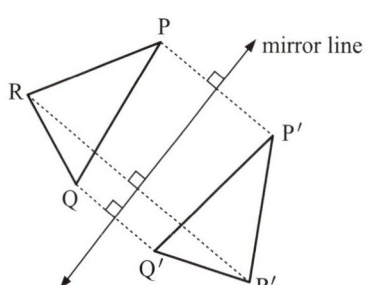

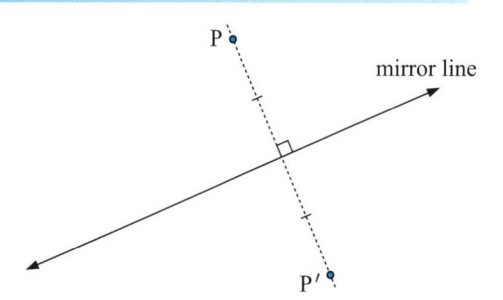

To reflect an object, we reflect each point in the object in the mirror line. For simple shapes it is easier to just reflect key points, such as corners, and then draw in the sides.

We will concentrate on reflections:
- in the x-axis or y-axis
- in lines parallel to the axes
- in the lines $y = x$ and $y = -x$.

Example 8

Find the image of the point $(3, 1)$ under a reflection in:
  a the x-axis   **b** the y-axis   **c** $y = x$ **d** $y = -x$

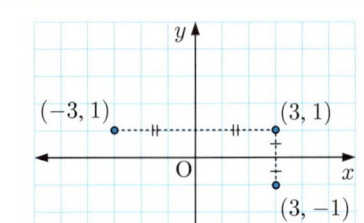

a $(3, 1) \to (3, -1)$
b $(3, 1) \to (-3, 1)$

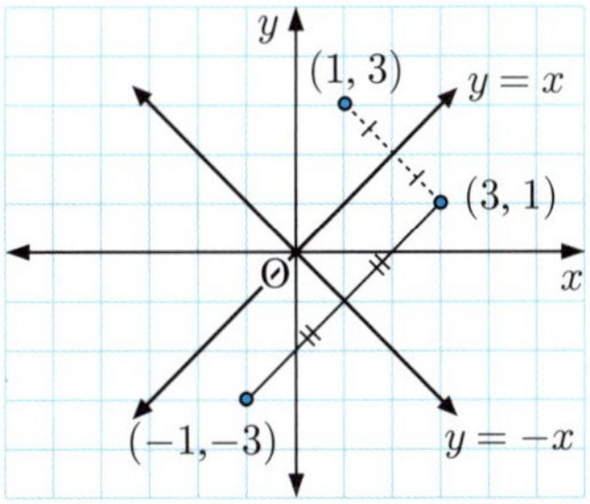

c $(3, 1) \to (1, 3)$
d $(3, 1) \to (-1, -3)$

EXERCISE 22E

1 Copy and reflect in the given line:

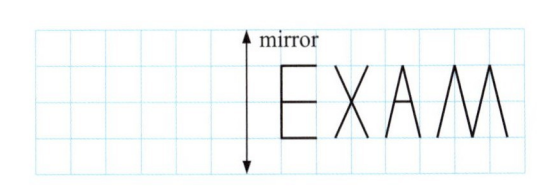

2 Find, by graphical means, the image of the point $(4, -1)$ under a reflection in:
  a the x-axis   **b** the y-axis   **c** the line $y = x$ **d** the line $y = -x$.

3 Find, by graphical means, the image of the point $(-1, -3)$ under a reflection in:
  a the y-axis   **b** the line $y = -x$ **c** the line $x = 2$ **d** the line $y = -1$
  e the x-axis   **f** the line $x = -3$ **g** the line $y = x$ **h** the line $y = 2$.

4 Copy the graph given onto a grid with both axes going from -6 to 6. Reflect T in:
  a the y-axis and label it U
  b the line $y = -1$ and label it V
  c the line $y = -x$ and label it W.

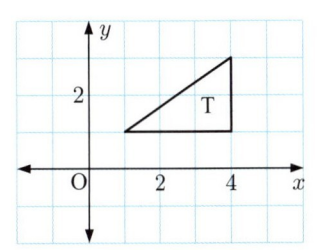

Transformation geometry (Chapter 22)

5 Copy and complete the following table:

Point	Mirror line			
	x-axis	y-axis	$y = x$	$y = -x$
(3, 2)				
(1, −2)				
(−2, 4)				
(a, b)				

6 Copy the graph given. Reflect the quadrilateral:
  a in the x-axis, labelling the image B
  b in the line $y = -x$, labelling the image C.

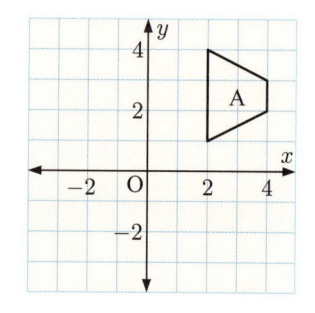

F ENLARGEMENTS AND REDUCTIONS [5.4]

The diagram alongside shows the **enlargement** of triangle PQR with centre point C and scale factor $k = 3$.

P′, Q′ and R′ are located such that CP′ = 3 × CP, CQ′ = 3 × CQ, and CR′ = 3 × CR.

The image P′Q′R′ has sides which are 3 times longer than those of the object PQR.

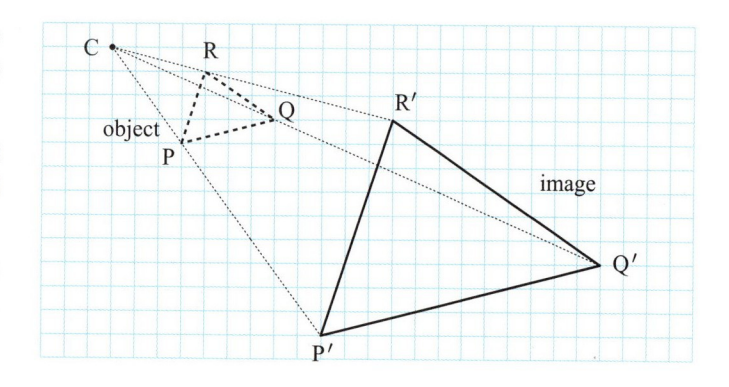

Alongside is a **reduction** of triangle KLM with centre C and scale factor $k = \frac{1}{2}$.

To obtain the image, the distance from C to each point on the object is halved.

The image K′L′M′ has sides which are half the length of the side of the object KLM.

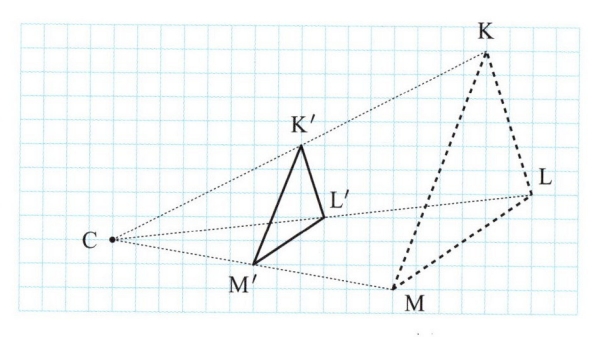

The **scale factor** of an enlargement or reduction is the ratio of lengths in the image to those in the object.

ENLARGEMENTS WITH CENTRE THE ORIGIN

Suppose we use the origin O as the centre of an enlargement.

P(x, y) moves to P$'(x', y')$ such that P$'$ lies on the line OP. OP$' = k$OP, for some value of k.

We call this **an enlargement with centre O(0, 0) and scale factor k**.

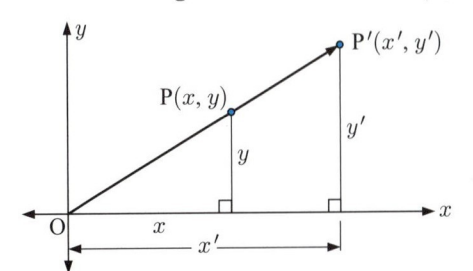

From the similar triangles,

$$\frac{x'}{x} = \frac{y'}{y} = \frac{OP'}{OP} = k$$

$\therefore \quad x' = kx \quad \text{and} \quad y' = ky$

Under an enlargement with centre O(0, 0) and scale factor k, $(x, y) \rightarrow (kx, ky)$.

Example 9 ◀) Self Tutor

Consider the triangle ABC with vertices A(1, 1), B(4, 1) and C(1, 4).
Find the position of the image of △ABC under:
- **a** an enlargement with centre O(0, 0) and scale factor $k = 2$
- **b** a reduction with centre O(0, 0) and scale factor $k = \frac{1}{2}$.

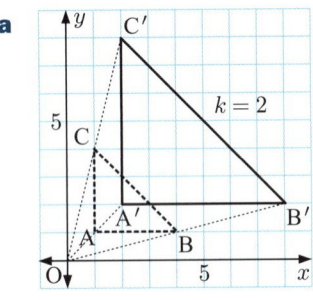

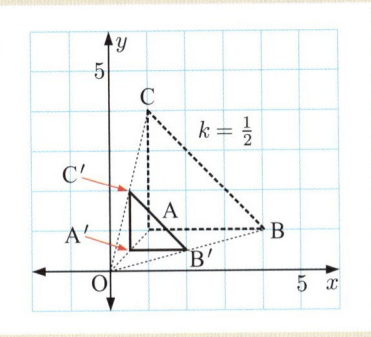

We can see from the examples above that:

If $k > 1$, the image figure is an **enlargement** of the object.

If $0 < k < 1$, the image figure is a **reduction** of the object.

EXERCISE 22F

1 Copy each diagram onto squared paper. Enlarge or reduce with centre C and the scale factor k given:

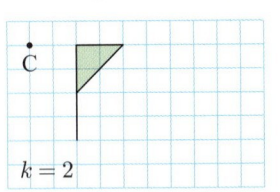

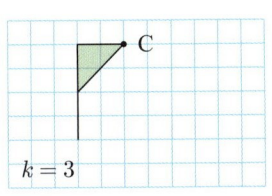

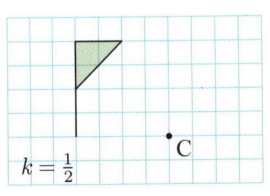

- **a** $k = 2$
- **b** $k = 3$
- **c** $k = \frac{1}{2}$

Transformation geometry (Chapter 22)

2 Copy triangle T onto squared paper.
   a Enlarge T about centre C(7, 2) with scale factor $k = 3$.
   b Reduce T about centre D(4, −3) with scale factor $k = \frac{1}{2}$.

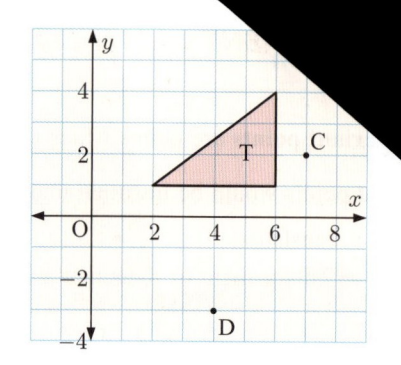

3 Copy quadrilateral Q onto squared paper.
   a Reduce Q about centre O(0, 0) with scale factor $\frac{1}{2}$.
   b Enlarge Q about centre C(9, −3) with scale factor 2.

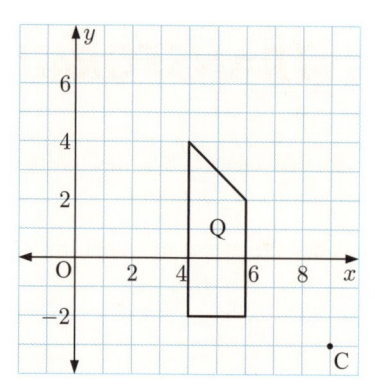

4 Find the scale factor k in each of the following enlargements or reductions:
   a
   b

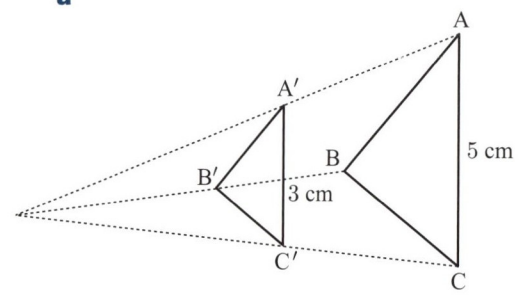

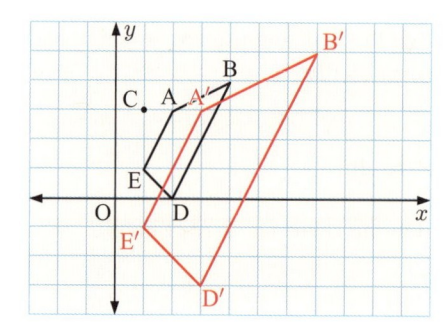

5 Find the coordinates of the centre of enlargement:

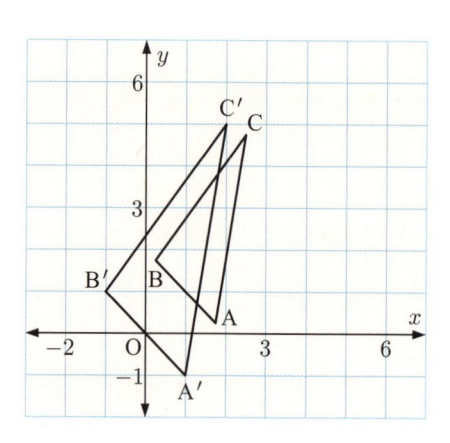

6 Find the image of the point:
   a (3, 4) under an enlargement with centre O(0, 0) and scale factor $k = 1\frac{1}{2}$.
   b (−1, 4) under a reduction with centre C(2, −2) and scale factor $k = \frac{2}{3}$.

Transformation geometry (Chapter 22)

Invariant points

...s which do not move under a transformation.

...ariant under:
- a rotation about O(0, 0)
- a reflection in a mirror line
- an enlargement... ...eduction about O(0, 0) with scale factor k?

G TRANSFORMING FUNCTIONS [3.8]

So far in this chapter we have looked at transformations of points and shapes. We now consider the transformations of functions.

We consider the effect of transforming the graph of $y = f(x)$ into $y = f(x) + k$ and $y = f(x + k)$, where $k \in \mathbb{Z}$, $k \neq 0$.

Discovery 2

In this discovery we will graph many different functions. To help with this you can either click on the icon and use the graphing package, or else follow the instructions on page 23 for your calculator.

GRAPHING PACKAGE

What to do:

1. On the same set of axes graph:

   a $y = \dfrac{1}{x}$ **b** $y = \dfrac{1}{x} + 2$ **c** $y = \dfrac{1}{x} - 3$ **d** $y = \dfrac{1}{x} + 5$

   What transformation maps $y = \dfrac{1}{x}$ onto $y = \dfrac{1}{x} + k$?

2. On the same set of axes graph:

   a $y = \dfrac{1}{x}$ **b** $y = \dfrac{1}{x+2}$ **c** $y = \dfrac{1}{x-3}$ **d** $y = \dfrac{1}{x+4}$

   What transformation maps $y = \dfrac{1}{x}$ onto $y = \dfrac{1}{x+k}$?

You should have discovered that:

- $y = f(x)$ maps onto $y = f(x) + k$ under a **vertical translation** of $\begin{pmatrix} 0 \\ k \end{pmatrix}$.
- $y = f(x)$ maps onto $y = f(x + k)$ under a **horizontal translation** of $\begin{pmatrix} -k \\ 0 \end{pmatrix}$.

Transformation geometry (Chapter 22)

Example 10

On each of the following, $f(x)$ is mapped onto $g(x)$ using a single transformation.

i Describe the transformation fully.   **ii** Write $g(x)$ in terms of $f(x)$.

a

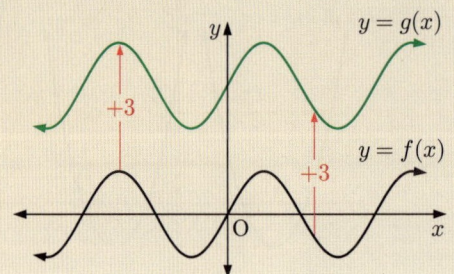

b

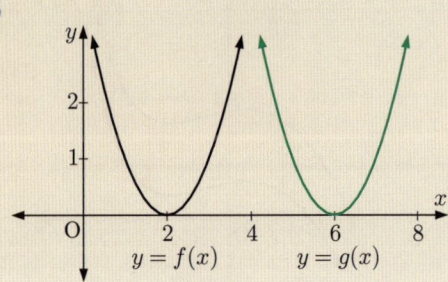

a **i** The graph of $f(x)$ has been moved up 3 units.
∴ $f(x)$ has undergone a vertical translation of $\binom{0}{3}$ to produce $g(x)$.
ii $g(x) = f(x) + 3$

b **i** The graph of $f(x)$ has moved 4 units to the right.
∴ $f(x)$ has undergone a horizontal translation of $\binom{4}{0}$ to produce $g(x)$.
ii $g(x) = f(x - 4)$

Example 11

Consider $f(x) = \frac{1}{2}x + 1$. On separate sets of axes graph:

a $y = f(x)$ and $y = f(x + 2)$ **b** $y = f(x)$ and $y = f(x) + 2$

$y = \frac{1}{2}x + 1$ has gradient $\frac{1}{2}$ and y-intercept 1.

a $y = f(x + 2)$ indicates a horizontal translation of $\binom{-2}{0}$, so $f(x)$ is translated 2 units to the left.

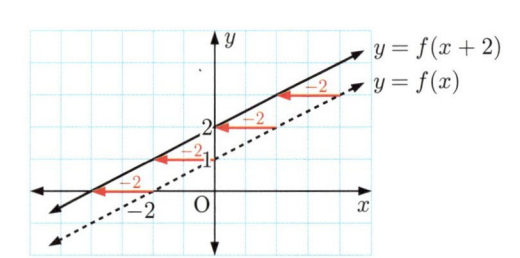

b $y = f(x) + 2$ indicates a vertical translation of $\binom{0}{2}$, so $f(x)$ is translated 2 units upwards.

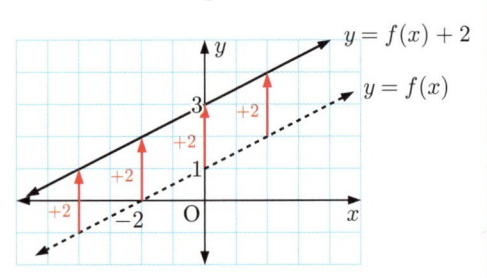

To help draw the graphs in the following exercise, you may wish to use the **graphing package** or your **graphics calculator**.

GRAPHING PACKAGE

EXERCISE 22G

1 In each of the following, $f(x)$ is mapped onto $g(x)$ using a single transformation.

    i Describe the transformation fully.
    ii Write $g(x)$ in terms of $f(x)$.

a

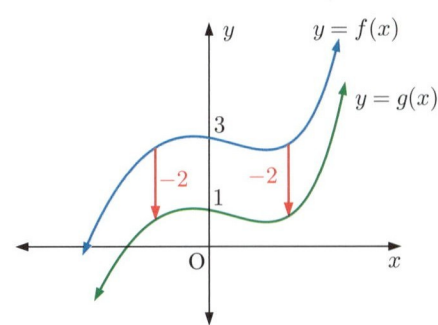

b

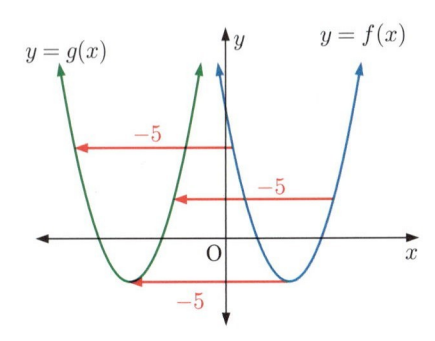

c

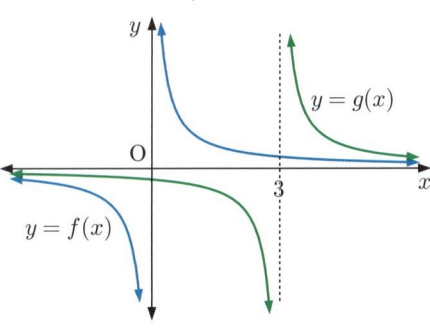

2 Consider $f(x) = 3x - 2$. On separate sets of axes, graph:

    a $y = f(x)$ and $y = f(x) + 4$
    b $y = f(x)$ and $y = f(x + 4)$.

3 Consider $f(x) = 2^x$.

    a Use technology to sketch $y = f(x)$.
    b On the same grid, graph $y = f(x) - 1$ and $y = f(x - 3)$. Label each graph.

4 Consider $g(x) = \left(\frac{1}{2}\right)^x$.

    a Use technology to graph $y = g(x)$.
    b On the same set of axes, graph $y = g(x)$ and $y = g(x) - 1$.
    c Write down the equation of the asymptote of $y = g(x) - 1$.
    d Now graph $h(x) = \left(\frac{1}{2}\right)^{x-1}$. What transformation shifts $y = g(x)$ to $y = h(x)$?

> An asymptote is a line the graph approaches but never reaches.

5 Consider $f(x) = 2x + 3$.

    a Graph $y = f(x)$ and $y = f(x - 2)$ on the same set of axes.
    b Find algebraically an expression for $f(x - 2)$.
    c Use coordinate geometry and your answer to **a** to find the equation of the line $y = f(x - 2)$. Compare your equation with your answer to **b**.

6 Consider $g(x) = \frac{1}{2}x^3$.

    a Graph $y = g(x)$, $y = g(x) + 4$, and $y = g(x) - 1$ on the same set of axes.
    b What transformation shifts $y = g(x) - 1$ to $y = g(x) + 4$?

Transformation geometry (Chapter 22)

7 What transformation shifts $f(x)$ to $g(x)$?

a

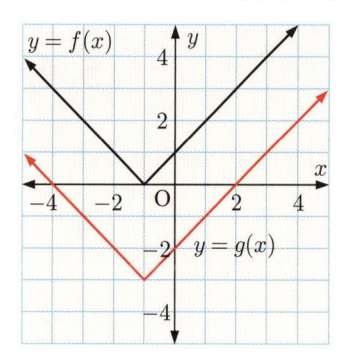

b

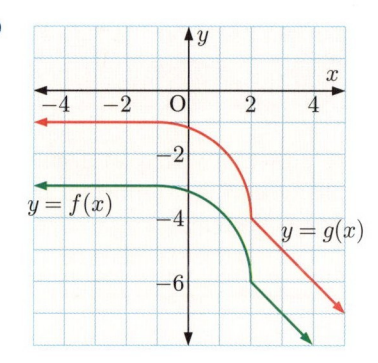

c

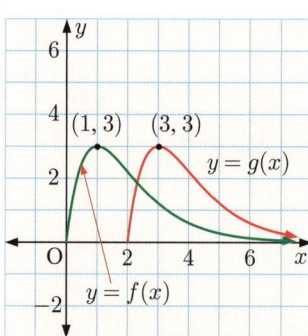

8 Copy each of the following, and draw the required function:

a sketch $y = f(x-2)$

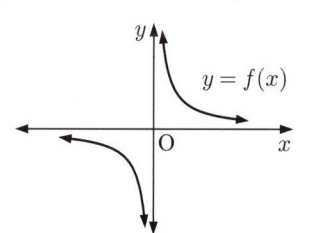

b sketch $y = f(x) + 2$

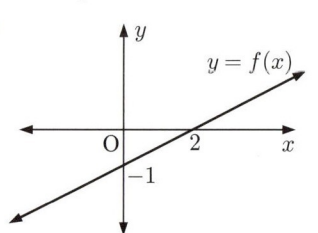

c sketch $y = f(x) + 3$

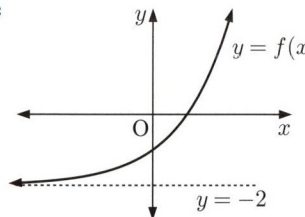

d sketch $y = f(x+1)$

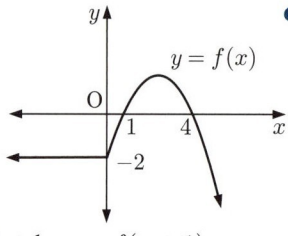

e sketch $y = f(x) - 1$

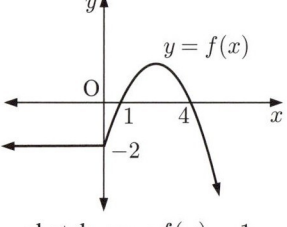

f sketch $y = f(x-4)$

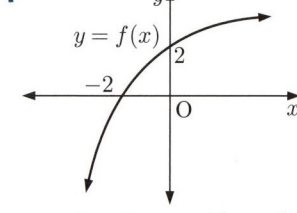

9 The graph of $y = f(x)$ is shown alongside. On the same set of axes, graph:

   a $y = f(x)$ **b** $y = f(x) + 2$
   c $y = f(x-2)$

Label each graph clearly.

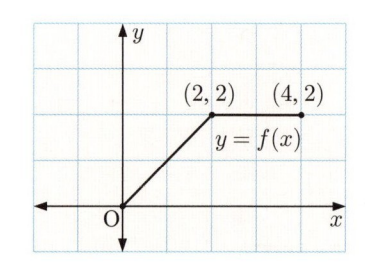

H MISCELLANEOUS TRANSFORMATIONS

[5.4, 3.8]

In this section we present a variety of geometric transformations, without saying what type they are. You need to identify the type of transformation and state its key features, such as the equation of the mirror line or the scale of an enlargement.

The following flowchart may prove useful when identifying transformations of shapes:

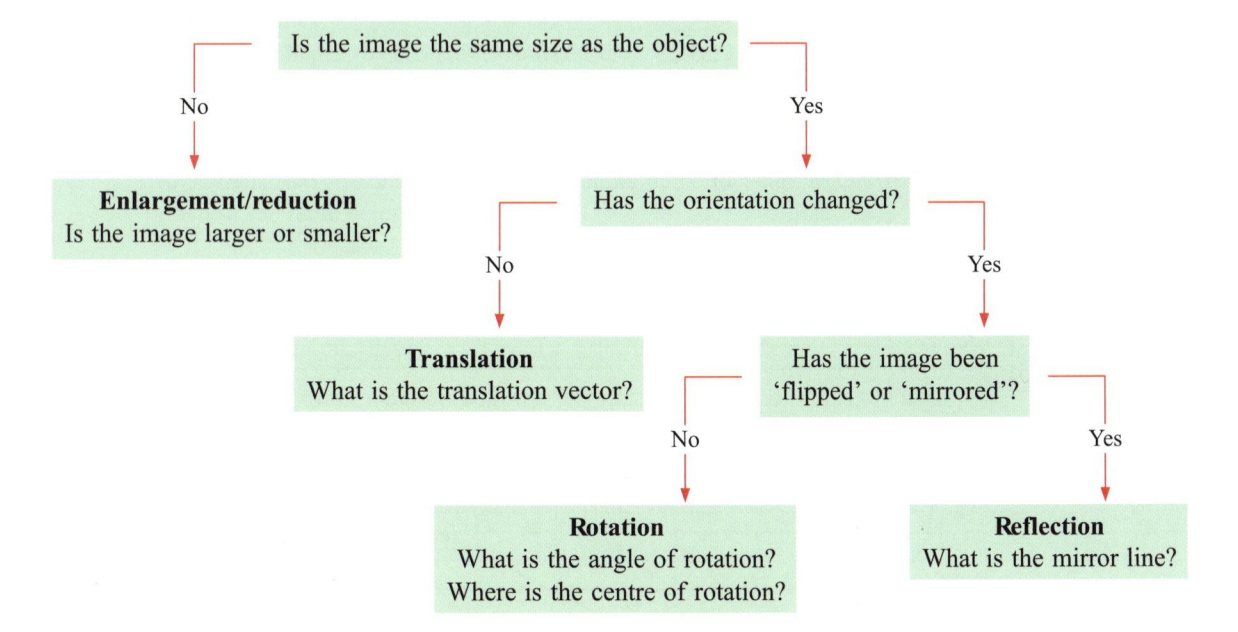

- Is the image the same size as the object?
  - **No** → **Enlargement/reduction** Is the image larger or smaller?
  - **Yes** → Has the orientation changed?
    - **No** → **Translation** What is the translation vector?
    - **Yes** → Has the image been 'flipped' or 'mirrored'?
      - **No** → **Rotation** What is the angle of rotation? Where is the centre of rotation?
      - **Yes** → **Reflection** What is the mirror line?

EXERCISE 22H

1 Identify the following transformations, stating all key features:

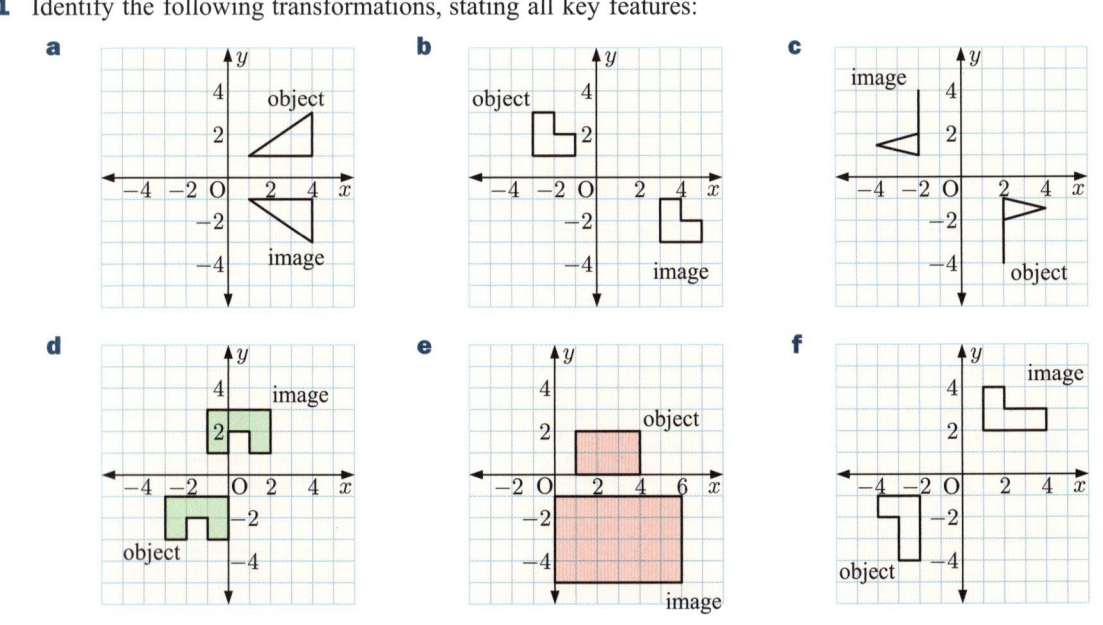

a, b, c, d, e, f

Transformation geometry (Chapter 22) 421

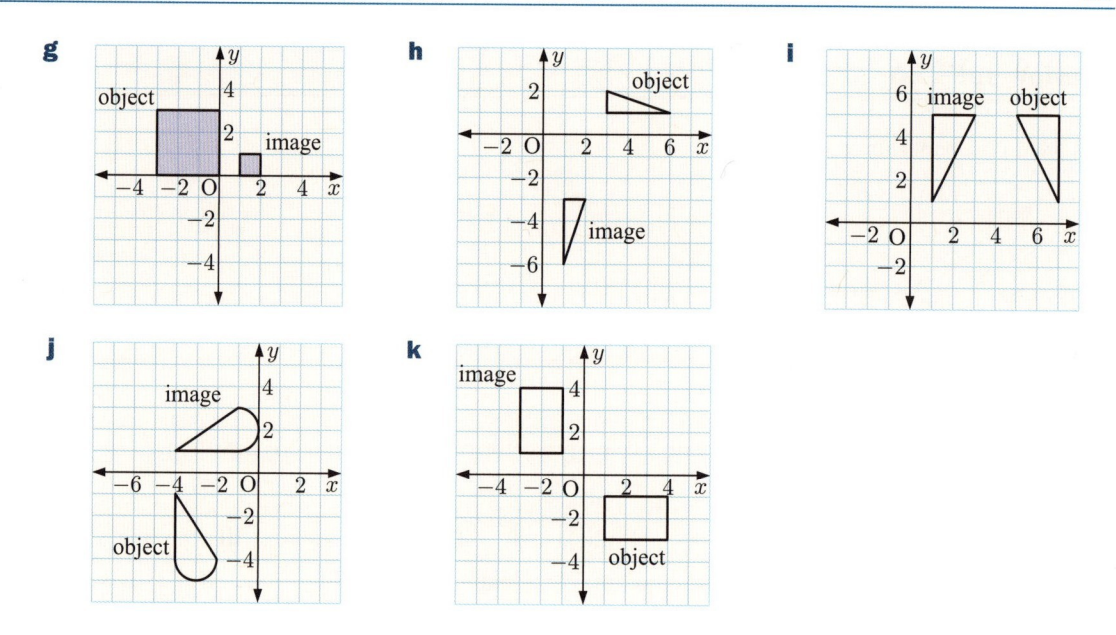

g, **h**, **i**, **j**, **k** (diagrams of objects and their images on coordinate grids)

2 For the following graphs:

  i Find the translation vector that shifts $f(x)$ to $g(x)$.

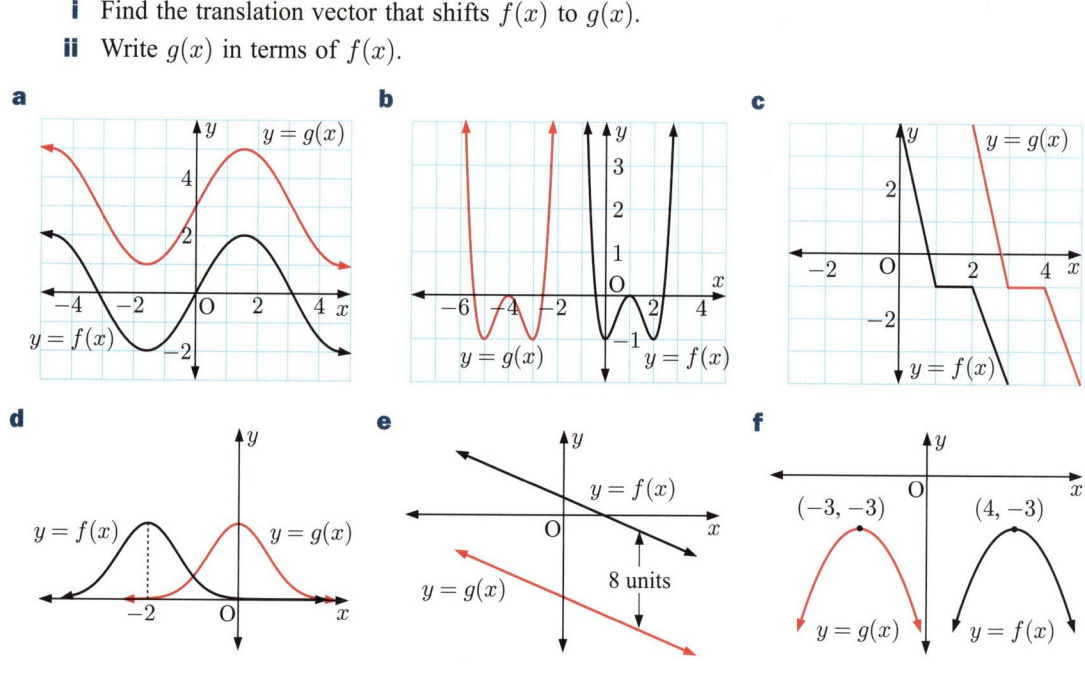

  ii Write $g(x)$ in terms of $f(x)$.

a, **b**, **c**, **d**, **e**, **f** (graphs showing $y = f(x)$ and $y = g(x)$)

In **e**, the translation is 8 units.

In **f**, points $(-3, -3)$ and $(4, -3)$ are marked on $y = g(x)$ and $y = f(x)$ respectively.

3 Answer the questions in the **Opening Problem** on page **403**.

Review set 22A

1 On grid paper draw the vectors:

   a $\begin{pmatrix} -2 \\ 3 \end{pmatrix}$ **b** $\begin{pmatrix} 1 \\ 4 \end{pmatrix}$ **c** $\begin{pmatrix} -3 \\ -5 \end{pmatrix}$

2 Write in the form $\begin{pmatrix} x \\ y \end{pmatrix}$:

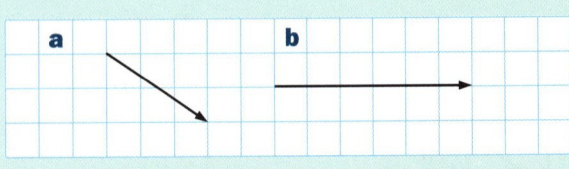

3 Draw a vector diagram to represent a velocity vector of 50 km/h in a NE direction.

4 Find the image of:

   a $(2, -5)$ under a reflection in   **i** the x-axis   **ii** the line $y = x$ **iii** the line $x = 3$

   b $(-1, 4)$ under a clockwise rotation of $90°$ about   **i** $O(0, 0)$ **ii** $A(2, 1)$

   c $(5, -2)$ under a translation of $\begin{pmatrix} -3 \\ 4 \end{pmatrix}$.

5 Find the image of quadrilateral Q when reflected in the line $y = -x$.

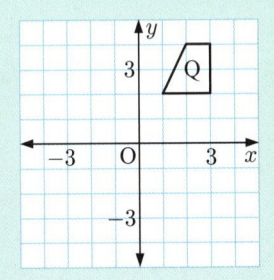

6 **a** Draw triangle ABC with $A(1, -2)$, $B(1, -4)$, and $C(2, -4)$.

   b Rotate triangle ABC anticlockwise through $90°$ about the origin.

7 Copy this diagram and then enlarge the figure F with centre C and scale factor $k = 2$.

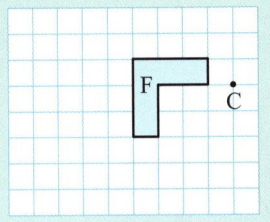

8 Fully describe the transformation shown:

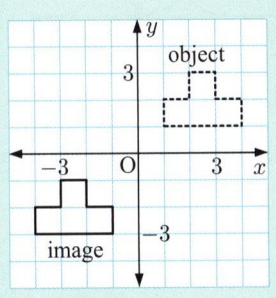

9 Consider $f(x) = 2x - 1$. On separate axes, graph:

   a $y = f(x)$ and $y = f(x - 2)$ **b** $y = f(x)$ and $y = f(x) - 2$.

10 Copy the graph alongside.
Draw on the same axes, the graphs of:
  a $y = f(x) + 3$
  b $y = f(x + 2)$.

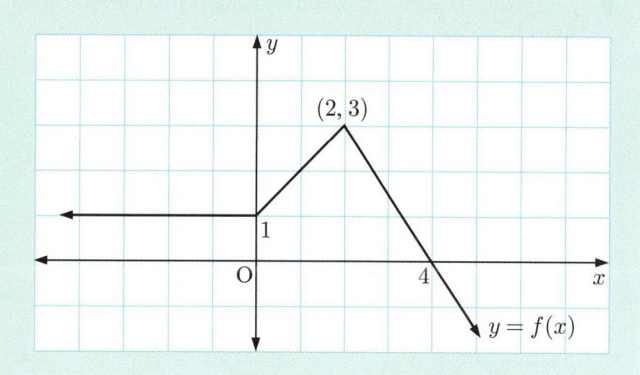

Review set 22B

1 On grid paper draw the vectors:

  a $\begin{pmatrix} 1 \\ 4 \end{pmatrix}$ **b** $\begin{pmatrix} -3 \\ -1 \end{pmatrix}$ **c** $\begin{pmatrix} 5 \\ -2 \end{pmatrix}$

2 Write in the form $\begin{pmatrix} x \\ y \end{pmatrix}$:

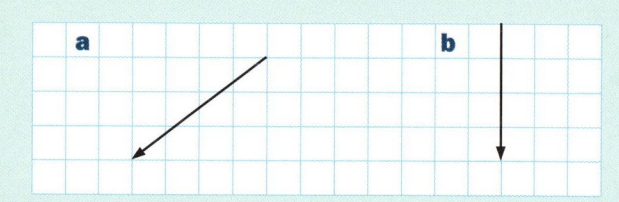

3 Draw a vector diagram to represent a displacement of 200 km in a westerly direction.

4 Find the image of $(3, -2)$ under a reflection in:
  a the x-axis   **b** the line $y = -x$ **c** the line $y = 4$.

5 Find the image of $(3, -7)$ under:
  a a translation of $\begin{pmatrix} 2 \\ -4 \end{pmatrix}$ **b** a rotation through $90°$ clockwise with centre $C(-1, -3)$.

6 Copy the diagram onto grid paper, and then translate figure F by $\begin{pmatrix} 6 \\ -2 \end{pmatrix}$.

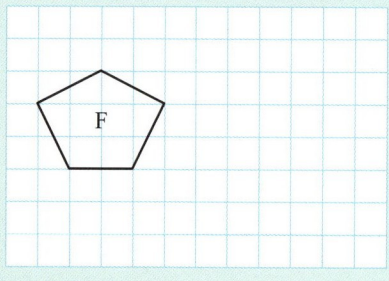

7 Rectangle R has coordinates $A(1, 0)$, $B(1, 3)$, $C(2, 3)$, and $D(2, 0)$.
  a Draw rectangle R on a set of axes.
  b Enlarge rectangle R with centre $O(0, 0)$ and scale factor 3.

8 Fully describe the geometric transformation that maps the object onto the image.

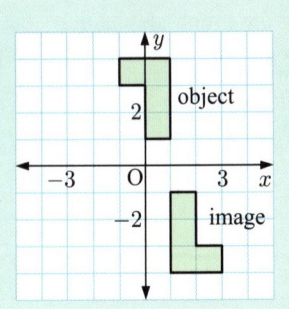

9 What transformation does the diagram alongside describe?

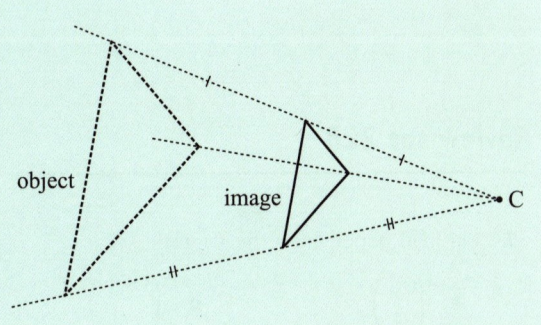

10 Consider $f(x) = \frac{1}{2}x + 3$. On separate axes, graph:
   a $y = f(x)$ and $y = f(x+1)$
   b $y = f(x)$ and $y = f(x) + 1$

11 For the following pairs of graphs:
   i fully describe the transformation that takes $f(x)$ to $g(x)$
   ii write $g(x)$ in terms of $f(x)$.

a

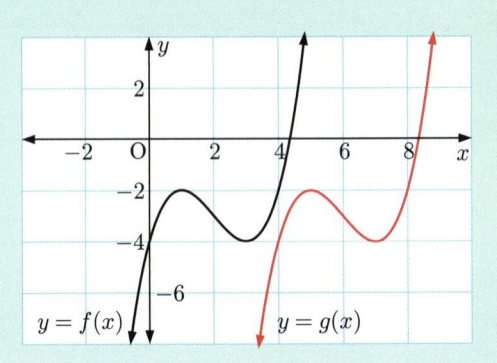

b

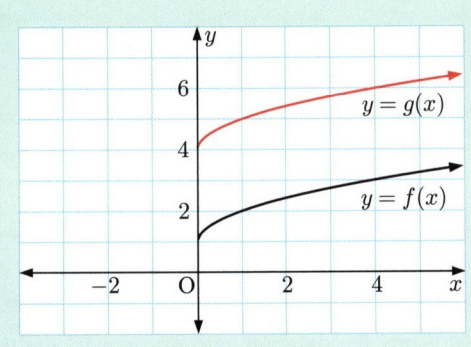

Two variable analysis

23

Contents:

A	Correlation	[11.9]
B	Line of best fit by eye	[11.9]

Opening problem

The relationship between the *height* and *weight* of members of a football team is to be investigated. The raw data for each player is given below:

Player	Height	Weight
1	203	106
2	189	93
3	193	95
4	187	86
5	186	85
6	197	92

Player	Height	Weight
7	180	78
8	186	84
9	188	93
10	181	84
11	179	86
12	191	92

Player	Height	Weight
13	178	80
14	178	77
15	186	90
16	190	86
17	189	95
18	193	89

Things to think about:
- Are the variables categorical or quantitative?
- What is the dependent variable?
- What would the scatter diagram look like? Are the points close to being linear?
- Does an increase in the independent variable generally cause an increase or a decrease in the dependent variable?
- How can we indicate the strength of the linear connection between the variables?
- How can we find the equation of the 'line of best fit' and how can we use it?

TWO VARIABLE ANALYSIS

We often want to know how two variables are **associated** or **related**. We want to know whether an increase in one variable results in an increase or a decrease in the other, or if it makes no difference.

To analyse the relationship between two variables, we first need to decide which is the **dependent** variable and which is the **independent** variable.

The independent variable is the one we think causes the other. So, the value of the dependent variable *depends* on the value of the independent variable.

Next we plot collected data on a **scatter diagram**. The independent variable is placed on the horizontal axis, and the dependent variable is placed on the vertical axis.

Consider the following two typical scatter diagrams:

In the first scatter diagram the points are quite random. It is hard to tell how they could be related.

In the second scatter diagram the points are all close to the red line shown. We say that there is a strong linear connection or **linear correlation** between these two variables. The red line is called the **line of best fit** because it best represents the data.

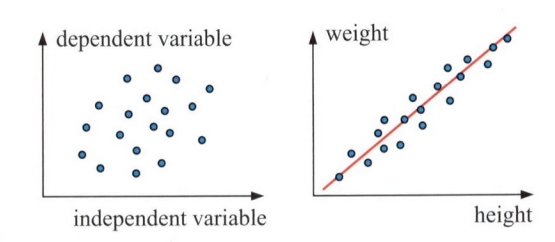

The scatter diagram for the **Opening Problem** is drawn alongside. *Height* is the independent variable and is represented on the horizontal axis. We see that in general, as the height increases, the weight increases also.

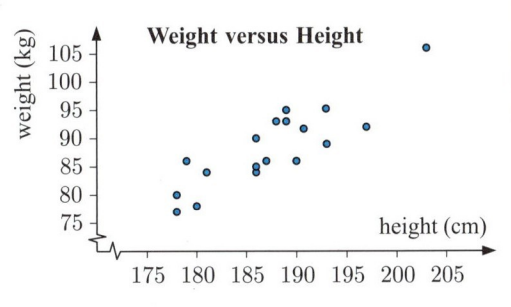

The weight of a person is usually **dependent** on their height.

A   CORRELATION   [11.9]

Correlation is a measure of the strength and direction of the relationship or association between two variables.

When we analyse the correlation between two variables, we should follow these steps:

Step 1:   Look at the scatter diagram for any **pattern**.

For a generally *upward* shape we say that the correlation is **positive**.
As the independent variable increases, the dependent variable generally increases.

For a generally *downward* shape we say that the correlation is **negative**.
As the independent variable increases, the dependent variable generally decreases.

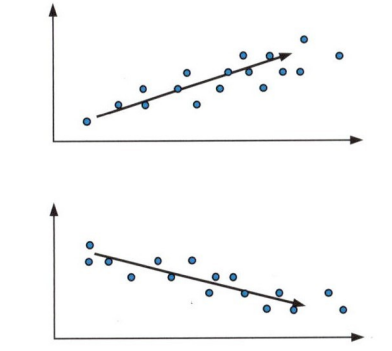

Two variable analysis (Chapter 23) 427

For *randomly scattered* points with no upward or downward trend, we say there is **no correlation**.

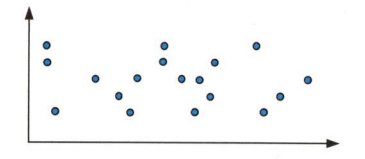

Step 2: Look at the pattern of points to see if the relationship is **linear**.

The relationship is approximately linear.   The relationship is not linear.

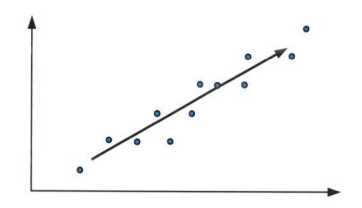

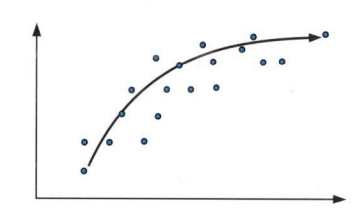

Step 3: Look at the spread of points to make a judgement about the **strength** of the correlation. For **positive relationships** we would classify the following scatter diagrams as:

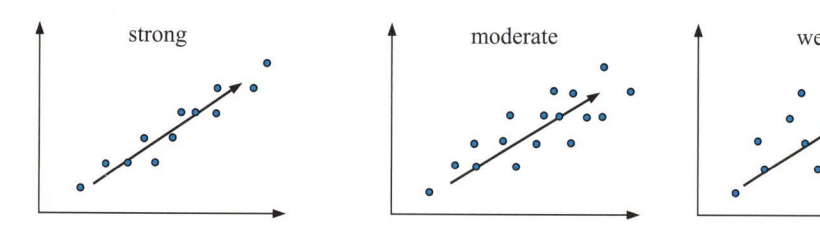

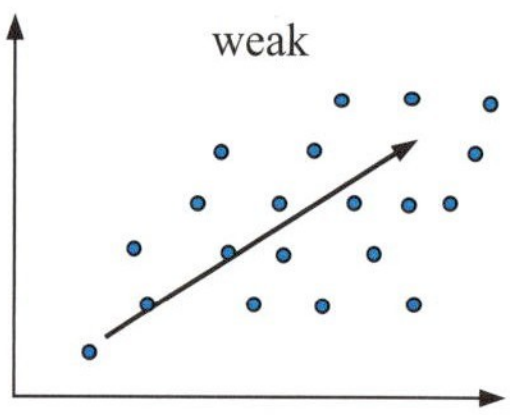

strong   moderate   weak

We classify the strengths for **negative relationships** in the same way:

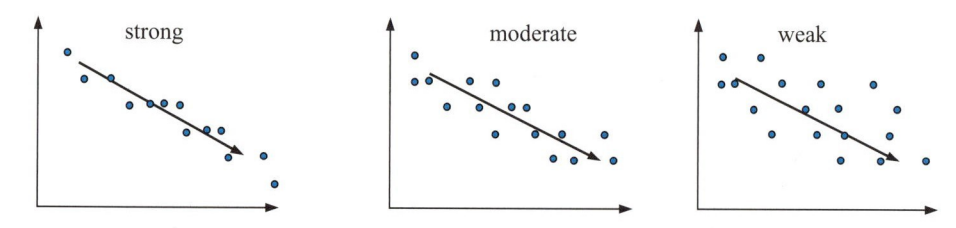

strong   moderate   weak

In the scatter diagram for the **Opening Problem** data, there appears to be a moderate positive correlation between the footballers' heights and weights. The relationship appears to be linear.

EXERCISE 23A

1 For each of the scatter diagrams below state:

    i whether there is positive, negative, or no association between the variables
    ii whether the relationship between the variables appears to be linear
    iii the strength of the association (zero, weak, moderate or strong).

a   **b**   **c**

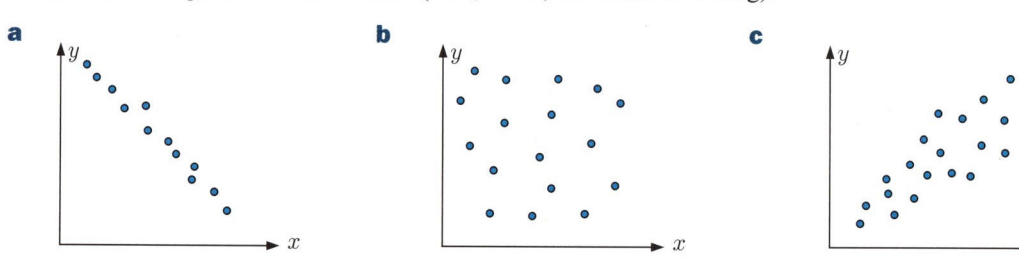

d

e

f

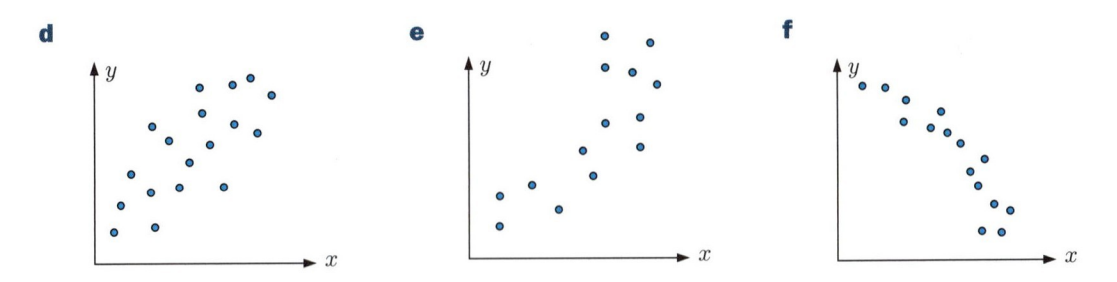

2 Copy and complete the following:
  a If there is a positive association between the variables x and y, then as x increases, y ......
  b If there is a negative correlation between the variables T and d, then as T increases, d ......
  c If there is no association between two variables then the points on the scatter diagram are ....

3 a 10 students were asked for their exam marks in Physics and Mathematics. Their percentages are given in the table below.

Student	A	B	C	D	E	F	G	H	I	J
Physics	75	83	45	90	70	78	88	50	55	95
Maths	68	70	50	65	60	72	75	40	45	80

  i Draw a scatter diagram with the Physics marks on the horizontal axis.
  ii Comment on the relationship between the Physics and Mathematics marks.

  b The same students were asked for their Art exam results. These were:

Student	A	B	C	D	E	F	G	H	I	J
Art	75	70	80	85	82	70	60	75	78	65

Draw a scatter diagram to see is there is any relationship between the Physics marks and the Art marks of each student.

4 The following table shows the sales of soft drinks in a shop each month, along with the average daily temperature for the month.

Month	Jan	Feb	Mar	Apr	May	Jun	Jul	Aug	Sep	Oct	Nov	Dec
Temperature (°C)	7	10	11	13	15	19	22	25	23	18	11	8
Sales (thousands £)	12	8	10	15	16	18	22	25	20	15	16	12

Draw a scatter diagram with the independent variable temperature along the horizontal axis. Comment on the relationship between the sales and the temperature.

5 Students were asked to measure their height in centimetres and their shoe size. The results are recorded in the table below:

Height (cm)	165	155	140	145	158	148	160	164	160	155	150	160
Shoe size	6.5	4.5	4	5.5	6	5.5	6	6.5	5.5	5	5	5.5

Comment on any relationship between height and shoe size.

B LINE OF BEST FIT BY EYE   [11.9]

Consider again the **Opening Problem**.

The scatter diagram for this data is shown alongside. We can see there is a moderate positive linear correlation between the variables, so it is reasonable to use a line of best fit to model the data.

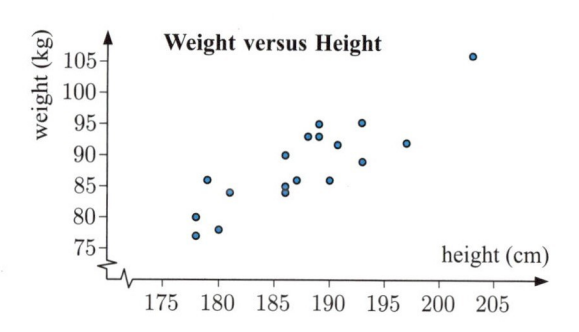

One way to do this is to draw a straight line through the data points which:

- includes the **mean point** $(\overline{x}, \overline{y})$
- has about as many points above the line as are below it.

For the **Opening Problem**, the mean point is approximately $(187, 88)$.

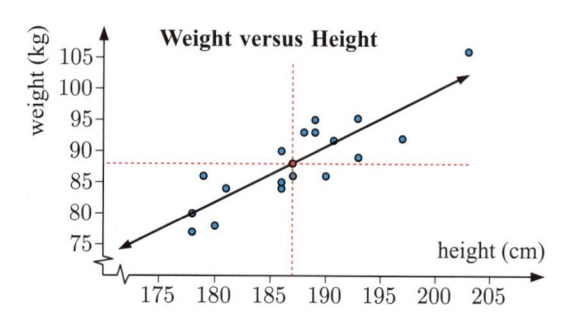

After plotting the mean on the scatter diagram, we draw in the line of best fit by eye.

As this line is an estimate only, lines drawn by eye will vary from person to person.

Having found our line of best fit, we can then use this linear model to estimate a value of y for any given value of x.

Example 1   ◀)) Self Tutor

Ten students were surveyed to find the number of marks they received in a pre-test for a module of work, and a test after it was completed.

The results were:

Pre-test (x)	40	79	60	65	30	73	56	67	45	85
Post-test (y)	48	91	70	71	50	85	65	75	60	95

a Find the mean point $(\overline{x}, \overline{y})$.

b Draw a scatter diagram of the data. Mark the point $(\overline{x}, \overline{y})$ on the scatter diagram and draw in the line of best fit.

c Estimate the mark for another student who was absent for the post-test but scored 70 for the pre-test.

a $\overline{x} = \dfrac{40 + 79 + 60 + \ldots + 85}{10} = 60$

$\overline{y} = \dfrac{48 + 91 + 70 + \ldots + 95}{10} = 71$ So, $(\overline{x}, \overline{y})$ is $(60, 71)$.

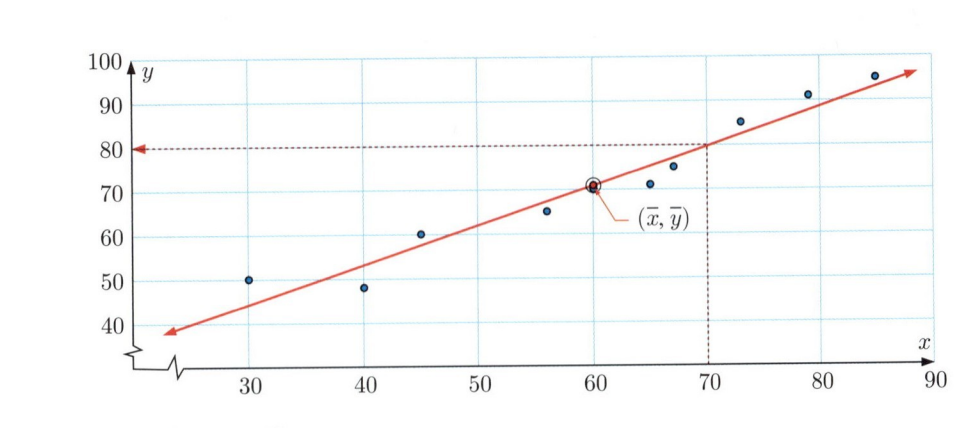

b

[Scatter diagram with line of best fit passing through $(\bar{x}, \bar{y})$; dashed lines showing when $x = 70$, $y \approx 80$.]

c When $x = 70$, $y \approx 80$.

∴ we estimate the post-test score to be 80.

EXERCISE 23B.1

1 A class of 13 students was asked to record their times spent preparing for a test. The table below gives their recorded preparation times and the scores that they achieved for the test.

Minutes spent preparing	75	30	35	65	110	60	40	80	56	70	50	110	18
Test score	25	31	30	38	55	20	39	47	35	45	32	33	34

a Which of the two variables is the independent variable?

b Calculate the mean time $\bar{x}$ and the mean score $\bar{y}$.

c Construct a scatter diagram for the data.

d Comment on the correlation between the variables.

e Copy and complete the following statements about the scatter diagram:
There appears to be a ......, ... correlation between the *minutes spent preparing* and the *test score*. This means that as the time spent preparing increases, the scores ....

f Plot $(\bar{x}, \bar{y})$ on the scatter diagram.

g Draw the line of best fit on the scatter diagram.

h If another student spent 25 minutes preparing for the test, what would you predict his test score to be?

2 The table alongside shows the *percentage of unemployed adults* and the *number of major thefts per day* in eight large cities.

a Find the mean percentage $\bar{x}$ and the mean number of thefts $\bar{y}$.

b Draw a scatter diagram for this data.

c Describe the association between the *percentage of unemployed adults* and the *number of major thefts per day*.

d Plot $(\bar{x}, \bar{y})$ on the scatter diagram.

e Draw the line of best fit on the scatter diagram.

f Another city has 8% unemployment. Estimate the number of major thefts per day for that city.

City	Percentage	Number
A	7	113
B	6	67
C	10	117
D	7	82
E	9	120
F	6	32
G	3	61
H	7	76

3 A café manager believes that during April the *number of people wanting dinner* is related to the *temperature at noon*. Over a 13 day period, the number of diners and the noon temperature were recorded.

Temperature ($x\,°C$)	18	20	23	25	25	22	20	23	27	26	28	24	22
Number of diners (y)	63	70	74	81	77	65	75	87	91	75	96	82	88

a Find the mean point $(\bar{x}, \bar{y})$.
b Draw a scatter diagram for this data.
c Comment on the correlation between the variables.
d Plot $(\bar{x}, \bar{y})$ on the scatter diagram.
e Draw the line of best fit on the scatter diagram.
f Estimate the number of diners at the café when it is April and the temperature is:
  i 19°C **ii** 29°C.

INTERPOLATION AND EXTRAPOLATION

Suppose we have gathered data to investigate the association between two variables. We obtain the scatter diagram shown below. The data values with the lowest and highest values of x are called the **poles**.

We find the mean point and estimate the line of best fit. We can use the line of best fit to estimate the value of one variable given a value for the other.

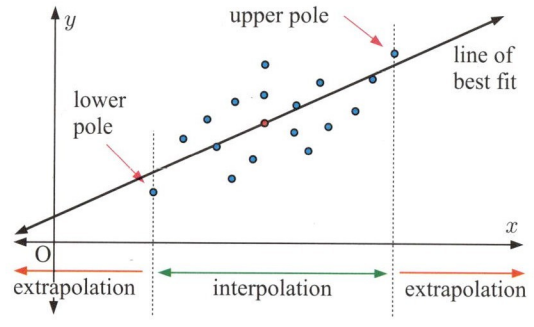

If we use values of x **in between** the poles, we say we are **interpolating** between the poles.

If we use values of x **outside** the poles, we say we are **extrapolating** outside the poles.

The accuracy of an *interpolation* depends on how linear the original data was. Strongly correlated data leads to good estimates, but if the data has weak correlation we would expect an estimate to be less accurate.

The accuracy of an *extrapolation* depends not only on how linear the original data was, but also on the assumption that the linear trend will continue past the poles. The validity of this assumption depends greatly on the situation under investigation. Because we have no data outside the poles, we do not know if there will be a change in trend for those values of the variables.

As a general rule, it is reasonable to interpolate between the poles, but unreliable to extrapolate outside them.

CARE MUST BE TAKEN WHEN EXTRAPOLATING

We need to be careful when extrapolating.

For example, in the years prior to the 1968 Mexico City Olympic Games, there was a steady, regular increase in the long jump world record. However, due to the high altitude and a perfect jump, the USA competitor Bob Beamon shattered the record by a huge amount, not in keeping with previous increases.

Example 2

The table below shows the income for Mandy's Clothing Alterations, established in 1990.

Year	1991	1993	1996	1998	1999	2002	2005	2008	2009	2010
Income ($10 000s)	0.9	2.2	3.6	6.1	6.3	7.7	10.8	13.4	15.1	15.5

a Draw a scatter diagram to illustrate this data.
b Calculate the mean point and add it to the scatter diagram.
c Draw a line of best fit for this data.
d Predict the income of Mandy's business for the year:
   i 1997   **ii** 2015.
e Comment on the reliability of your answers to **d**.

a - c Let x be the number of years since 1990, and y be the income in $10 000s.

x	1	3	6	8	9	12	15	18	19	20
y	0.9	2.2	3.6	6.1	6.3	7.7	10.8	13.4	15.1	15.5

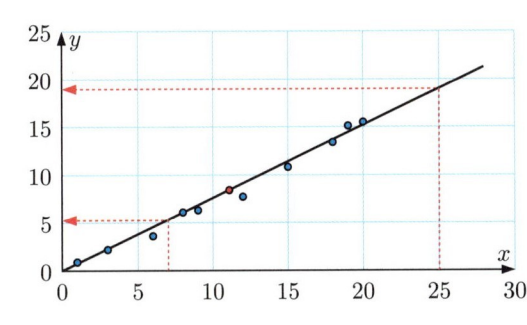

$$\overline{x} = \frac{1 + 3 + 6 + \ldots + 20}{10}$$
$$= 11.1$$

$$\overline{y} = \frac{0.9 + 2.2 + 3.6 + \ldots + 15.5}{10}$$
$$\approx 8.2$$

d   **i** When $x = 7$, $y \approx 5$ $\therefore$ we estimate the income in 1997 to be $50 000.
   ii When $x = 25$, $y \approx 19$ $\therefore$ we estimate the income in 2015 to be $190 000.

e   **i** The estimate for 1997 is an interpolation, and the data has a strong correlation. So, we expect the estimate of $50 000 to be fairly reliable.
   ii The estimate for 2015 is an extrapolation. So, it will only be reasonable if the trend we see from 1990 to 2010 continues.

EXERCISE 23B.2

1 A "triadic patent family" is a patent that has been filed at the European, Japan, and United States Patent Offices. The number of triadic patent families filed from Canada over a number of years is shown below.

Year	1992	1994	1996	1998	2000	2002	2004
Triadic patent families	273	355	438	590	609	686	766

  a Draw a scatter diagram of this information.
  b Find and plot the mean point.
  c Estimate a line of best fit for this data.

Two variable analysis (Chapter 23) 433

  d Use your line of best fit to estimate the number of triadic patent families filed from Canada in the year:
     i 1999
     ii 2007.
  e Comment on the reliability of your results in **d**.

2 The table below shows the number of gold medals from the total number of medals won by various countries at the 2008 Beijing Olympics.

Gold Medals	51	36	23	19	14	9	7	5	4
Total Medals	100	110	72	47	46	25	40	18	7

  a Draw a scatter diagram displaying this data.
  b Find and plot the mean point.
  c Draw the line of best fit on your scatter diagram.
  d Germany won 16 gold medals at the Beijing Olympics. Estimate the total number of medals that Germany won.
  e Mexico won 2 gold medals. How many medals would you estimate Mexico won in total?
  f How accurate do you expect your answers to **d** and **e** to be?

  Put Gold Medals on the x-axis.

3 The following table shows the price (in pounds) and weight (in carats) of some Colombian emeralds.

Weight (carats)	0.9	0.76	0.82	0.91	0.97	1.02	1.06	1.21	0.28	1.09	0.51
Price (£)	360	342	328	819	825	612	1060	726	168	872	306

  a Plot these points on a scatter diagram.
  b Add the mean point and line of best fit to your graph.
  c Comment on the correlation of the data.
  d Estimate the price of a Colombian emerald weighing:
     i 0.64 carats
     ii 1.7 carats.
  e Would you expect your answers to **d** to be accurate? Explain why or why not.

4 After sliding down a slope, a sled slows down along a flat area of snow. The table below shows the speed of the sled after various time intervals.

Time (x s)	0	1	2	3	4
Speed (s km/h)	30	26.6	23.1	19.6	15.9

  a Putting time on the horizontal axis, draw a scatter diagram for this data.
  b Calculate the mean point and add it to your graph.
  c Draw the line of best fit.
  d Find the x-intercept of the line of best fit. What does this represent?
  e Estimate the speed of the sled after 12 seconds. Comment on the reliability of this prediction.

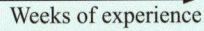

Review set 23A

1 The scatter diagram shows the number of defective items made in a week by each employee of a factory, plotted against the employee's number of weeks of experience. 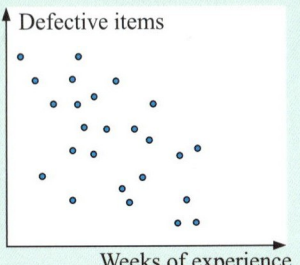
   a What are the independent and dependent variables?
   b Is the association between the variables:
      i weak or strong
      ii positive or negative?

2 The maximum speed of a Chinese dragonboat with different numbers of paddlers is recorded in the table below:

Number of paddlers, x	4	6	10	18	30
Maximum speed, y km/h	8	11	13	16	25

   a Draw a scatter diagram for the data.
   b Find $\bar{x}$ and $\bar{y}$.
   c Plot the point $(\bar{x}, \bar{y})$ on the scatter diagram.
   d Draw the line of best fit by eye on the scatter diagram.
   e Predict the maximum speed of a dragonboat with 24 paddlers.

3 Strawberry plants are sprayed with a pesticide-fertiliser mix. The data below give the yield of strawberries per plant for various spray concentrations:

Spray concentration (x ml per litre)	0	2	4	5	8
Yield of strawberries per plant (y)	8	10	21	20	35

   a Draw a scatter diagram for the data.
   b Comment on the correlation between the variables.
   c What is the significance of your answer to b?
   d Find the mean point and add it to your graph.
   e Draw the line of best fit.
   f Predict the number of strawberries per plant if the spray concentration is:
      i 3 ml per litre
      ii 10 ml per litre.
   g Give one reason why your answer to f ii may be invalid.

4 Ben and his friends form a soccer team called the 'Awkward Turtles'. They are not very good, but improve over the season. The following table shows the week number (x) and how many goals they lost by (y) that week.

x	1	2	3	4	5	6	7	8	9
y	9	7	6	7	5	5	4	4	2

   a Display this information on a scatter diagram.
   b Find and plot the point $(\bar{x}, \bar{y})$.
   c Add the line of best fit to the scatter diagram.
   d Find the x-intercept of the line of best fit. What does this represent?
   e Explain why extrapolating a long way is unreasonable for this data.

Review set 23B

1 Traffic controllers want to find the association between the *average speed* of cars in a city and the *age of drivers*. Devices for measuring average speed were fitted to the cars of drivers participating in a survey.

   The results are shown in the scatter diagram.

   a What is the independent variable?

   b Describe the association between the variables.

   c Is it sensible to find the line of best fit for these variables? Why or why not?

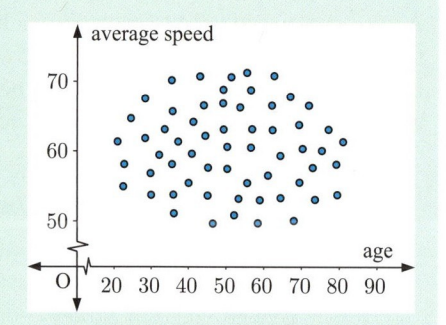

2 Following an outbreak of the *Ebola* virus, a rare and deadly haemorrhagic fever, medical authorities begin taking records of the number of cases of the fever. Their records are shown below.

Days after outbreak, n	2	3	4	5	6	7	8	9	10	11
Diagnosed cases, d	8	14	33	47	80	97	118	123	139	153

   a Produce a scatter diagram for d against n. Does a linear model seem appropriate for this data?

   b Find $\bar{n}$ and $\bar{d}$.

   c Plot the point $(\bar{n}, \bar{d})$ on the scatter diagram.

   d Draw the line of best fit by eye.

   e Use the graph to predict the number of diagnosed cases on day 14. Is this predicted value reliable? Give reasons for your answer.

3 The following table gives peptic ulcer rates per 1000 people for differing family incomes in the year 1998.

Income (I €1000s)	10	15	20	25	30	40	50	60	80
Peptic ulcer rate (R)	8.3	7.7	6.9	7.3	5.9	4.7	3.6	2.6	1.2

   a Draw a scatter diagram for the data.

   b Add a line of best fit by eye through the mean point.

   c Estimate the peptic ulcer rate in families with an income of €45 000.

   d Explain why the model is inadequate for families with income in excess of €100 000.

   e Later it is realised that one of the figures was written incorrectly. Which is it likely to be? Explain your answer.

4 Some people collect rare coins and will pay far more for them than they were originally worth.

   The average value of a circulated 1930 Australian penny sold at auction over the period from 1962 to 2006 is shown in dollars in the table below.

Year	1962	1972	1977	1985	1991	1996	2002	2006
Value	120	335	615	1528	2712	4720	8763	16 250

   Suppose x is the number of years *since* 1962 and V is the value of the penny in dollars.

   a Draw a scatter diagram of V against x.

   b Comment on the association between the variables.

   c Explain why drawing a line of best fit through the mean point would not be useful here.

Discussion

Two variable surveys

Across the world, social networking has become part of a teenager's everyday routine. However, some studies have indicated that there is a **correlation** between hours spent on social networking sites and academic achievement at school.

1 Suppose you are to conduct a study to determine if there is a correlation between social networking and achievement at school.

    a Explain how you will conduct your survey by stating:
        i who you will survey
        ii what questions you will ask
        iii what data you will collate.

    b What outcome do you expect from your survey?

2 In a recent survey, each student was asked: "How many hours do you spend on the computer each day?" and "What did you get for your last maths test?".

    a Is this a fair survey? Why or why not?   **b** How can the survey be improved?

3 A survey of 50 university students asked: "How many hours a day (on average) do you spend on social networking sites?" and "What is your current grade point average?".

The results are displayed on the scatter diagram alongside.

    a Describe the correlation between the variables.
    b Suggest reasons why the data has this correlation.

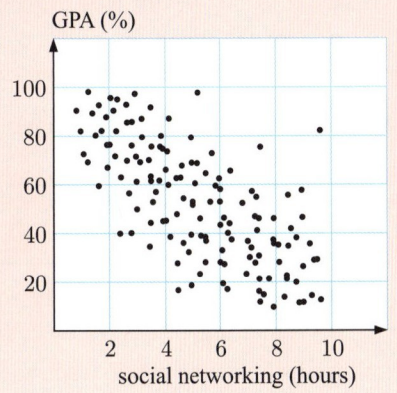

Further functions

24

Contents:

A	Unfamiliar functions	[3.6]
B	Solving equations graphically	[2.6, 2.11, 3.6]
C	Problem solving	[3.6]

Opening problem

In a wildlife conservation program, some pairs of red squirrels and water voles were released onto an island. Their numbers were monitored for several years, allowing the research team to calculate equations to describe the populations.

After x years, there were:

$$S = \frac{400}{1 + 9 \times 0.56^x} \quad \text{pairs of squirrels, and}$$

$$V = \frac{1000}{1 + 199 \times 0.27^x} \quad \text{pairs of water voles.}$$

a Sketch graphs of these two equations on the same pair of axes.
b What are the y-intercepts of these graphs, and what do these values represent?
c When are there equal numbers of squirrels and voles?
d What happens to the populations after a long period of time?

A UNFAMILIAR FUNCTIONS [3.6]

So far in this course, we have only examined a few of the many types of functions that exist. Other functions are interesting for a variety of reasons, and many are useful for describing real world situations. In this chapter, we will use technology to investigate functions that we do not know how to deal with using algebra.

We can use a graphics calculator to obtain:

- a table of values for a function
- a sketch of the function
- the **zeros** or **x-intercepts** of the function
- the **y-intercept** of the function
- any **asymptotes** of the function
- the turning points of the function where it is a **local maximum** or **local minimum**
- the points of intersection of two functions.

Instructions for using your calculator are found beginning on page **23**.

Example 1

Consider $f(x) = 2x^2 - 3x - 4$.

Using your graphics calculator:

a complete the table of values alongside

b sketch $y = f(x)$ on a pair of axes

c find the axes intercepts

d find the minimum of $f(x)$.

Mark the features from **c** and **d** on your sketch.

x	$f(x)$
-3	
-2	
-1	
0	
1	
2	
3	

a

x	$f(x)$
-3	23
-2	10
-1	1
0	-4
1	-5
2	-2
3	5

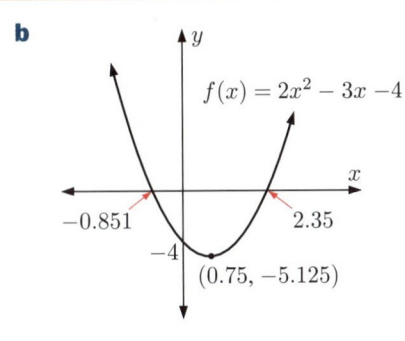

b $f(x) = 2x^2 - 3x - 4$, with x-intercepts at -0.851 and 2.35, y-intercept at -4, and minimum at $(0.75, -5.125)$.

c The y-intercept is -4.
The x-intercepts are -0.851 and 2.351.

d The minimum point is $(0.75, -5.125)$.
So, the minimum value of $f(x)$ is -5.125.

QUADRATIC FUNCTIONS

Quadratic functions are functions with the form $f(x) = ax^2 + bx + c$, where a, b and c are constants and $a \neq 0$.

The function $f(x) = 2x^2 - 3x - 4$ in **Example 1** is a quadratic function.

Every quadratic has a maximum or a minimum point called its **vertex**.

A quadratic function may have 0, 1, or 2 **zeros**, values of x for which $f(x) = 0$.

Further functions (Chapter 24)

TURNING POINTS

Consider the function on the right.

Point A is higher than all the points around it, but it is not as high as C. We say A is a **local maximum** because it is higher than every point *locally*, or nearby. C is also a local maximum because it is higher than every point near to it. It is also the **global maximum**, as it is the highest point of $f(x)$.

Similarly, B is a **local minimum** because it is lower than all the points around it. The function does not have a global minimum because the function keeps getting lower forever.

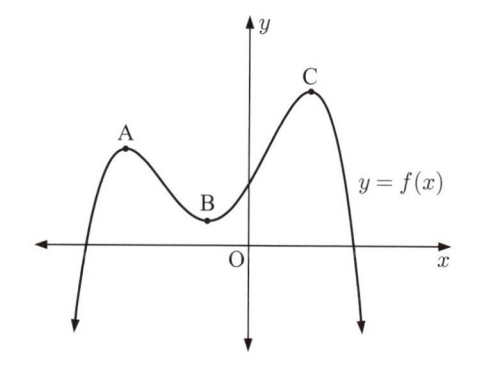

> A **local maximum (minimum)** of a function is a point higher (lower) than every other point nearby.
>
> A **global maximum (minimum)** of a function is a point higher (lower) than every other point on the function.

Collectively, these points are known as the **turning points** of the function.

Example 2
◀)) Self Tutor

Consider $f(x) = \dfrac{3x - 9}{x^2 - x - 2}$.

a Use your graphics calculator to help sketch the function.
b State the equations of the asymptotes of the function.
c State the axes intercepts of the function.
d Describe the turning points of the function.

Include all of the information on your sketch.

Make sure you have a good view window.

a

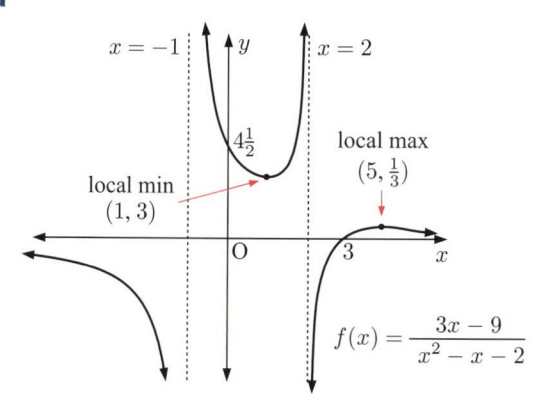

[Sketch showing vertical asymptotes $x = -1$ and $x = 2$, y-intercept at $4\tfrac{1}{2}$, local min $(1, 3)$, local max $(5, \tfrac{1}{3})$, x-intercept at 3, with $f(x) = \dfrac{3x-9}{x^2-x-2}$]

b horizontal asymptote is $y = 0$
vertical asymptotes are $x = -1$, $x = 2$

c x-intercept is 3, y-intercept is $4\tfrac{1}{2}$

d local maximum $(5, \tfrac{1}{3})$, local minimum $(1, 3)$

EXERCISE 24A

1 For these quadratic functions, find:

    i the turning point (vertex)   **ii** the y-intercept   **iii** the x-intercepts

  a $y = x^2 - 3$ **b** $f(x) = 2x^2 - 2x - 1$ **c** $f(x) = 9x^2 + 6x - 4$

2 For the following quadratics, use your graphics calculator to:

    i sketch the graph of the function
    ii find the coordinates of the vertex
    iii find the axes intercepts.

  Label your sketch with the information found in **ii** and **iii**.

  a $f(x) = x^2 - 4$ **b** $y = 2x^2 - 3x + 1$ **c** $f(x) = -x^2 - 9x - 8$

  d $y = \frac{1}{2}x^2 - 4x + 5$ **e** $g(x) = 6 - 4x^2$ **f** $h(x) = 23 + 17x - \frac{1}{3}x^2$

3 Consider $f(x) = x^3 - 4x^2 + 5x - 3$ for $-1 \leqslant x \leqslant 4$.

  a Sketch the graph with help from your graphics calculator.
  b Find the x- and y-intercepts of the graph.
  c Find and classify any turning points of the function.
  d State the range of the function.
  e Create a table of values for $f(x)$ on $-1 \leqslant x \leqslant 4$ with x-steps of 0.5.

4 Consider $f(x) = x^4 - 3x^3 - 10x^2 - 7x + 3$ for $-4 \leqslant x \leqslant 6$.

  a Set your calculator window to show y from -150 to 350. Hence sketch the graph of $f(x)$.
  b Find the largest zero of $f(x)$.
  c Find the turning point of the function near $x = 4$.
  d Adjust the window to $-2 \leqslant x \leqslant 1$, $-2 \leqslant y \leqslant 7$. Hence sketch the function for $-2 \leqslant x \leqslant 1$.
  e Find the other two turning points and classify them.
  f Make a table of values for $f(x)$ on $0 \leqslant x \leqslant 1$ with x-steps of 0.1.

5 For each of these functions:

    i use your graphics calculator to help sketch the function
    ii state the equations of any asymptotes
    iii find the axes intercepts
    iv find and classify any turning points.

Vertical asymptotes can be found by letting the denominator be 0.

  a $f(x) = \dfrac{4}{x-2}$ **b** $f(x) = 2 - \dfrac{3}{x+1}$

  c $f(x) = 2^x - 3$ **d** $f(x) = 2x + \dfrac{1}{x}$

  e $f(x) = \dfrac{4x}{x^2 - 4x - 5}$ **f** $f(x) = 3^{-x} + 2$

  g $f(x) = \dfrac{x^2 - 1}{x^2 + 1}$ **h** $f(x) = \dfrac{x^2 + 1}{x^2 - 1}$

  i $f(x) = \dfrac{2^x + 3}{2^x + 1}$

Further functions (Chapter 24)

6 Consider $f(x) = 2^x - x^2$.
   a Find the values of $f(x)$ for $x = -2, -1, 0, 1, 2, 3, 4, 5$.
   b Use **a** to set a suitable window on your graphics calculator, and hence sketch $f(x)$ on $-2 \leqslant x \leqslant 5$.
   c Find the zeros of $f(x)$.
   d Find the turning points of $f(x)$.
   e Find the range of $f(x)$ on the domain in **b**.

7 Suppose $f(x) = 2^x$, $g(x) = x^2 - 1$, and $h(x) = \dfrac{x-1}{2x+1}$.

Copy and complete the table, giving your answers correct to 3 decimal places where necessary.

x	$f(x)$	$g(x)$	$h(x)$
-2			
-1.5			
-0.5			
0			
0.5			
1			
2			
2.7			
3.61			

8 Consider $f(x) = \dfrac{x^2}{2^x}$.
   a Use your graphics calculator to sketch $y = f(x)$.
   b Find the axes intercepts of the function.
   c Find the turning points of the function.
   d Write down the equation of the horizontal asymptote.
   e Explain why the function does not have a vertical asymptote.

B SOLVING EQUATIONS GRAPHICALLY
[2.6, 2.11, 3.6]

In **Chapter 9** we learned how to solve linear simultaneous equations like $\begin{cases} y + 3x = 4 \\ 3y - 2x = 23. \end{cases}$

We used the *substitution method* and the *elimination method*. Using our knowledge of straight lines from **Chapter 16**, we now introduce a third way, which is the *graphical method*.

$y + 3x = 4$ and $3y - 2x = 23$ are both equations of straight lines. The line represents all points where the equation is true. So, any point where the lines meet satisfies *both* equations. This point is a **simultaneous solution** to the equations.

> To solve simultaneous equations using the graphical method:
> *Step 1:* Write both equations with y as the subject.
> *Step 2:* Graph the two equations using your graphics calculator. Sketch the graph.
> *Step 3:* Use your calculator to find the intersection of the lines.

Instructions for using your calculator to find the intersection are on page **24**.

Example 3

Solve these simultaneous equations graphically: $\begin{cases} y + 3x = 4 \\ 3y - 2x = 23. \end{cases}$

Step 1: $y + 3x = 4$ .... (1) $\qquad$ $3y - 2x = 23$ .... (2)
$\therefore\ y = 4 - 3x$ $\qquad\qquad\qquad \therefore\ 3y = 23 + 2x$
$\qquad\qquad\qquad\qquad\qquad\qquad\quad \therefore\ y = \dfrac{23 + 2x}{3}$

Step 2:

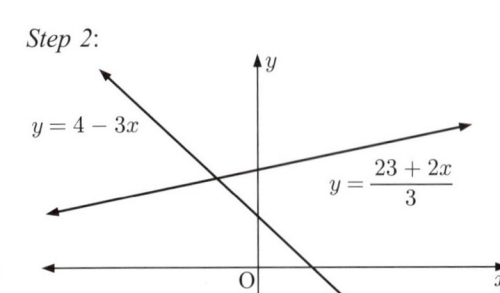

Step 3: Using a graphics calculator, we find that the intersection point is $(-1, 7)$.

$\therefore$ the simultaneous solution is $x = -1,\ y = 7$.

Check:
in (1), $\quad 7 + 3(-1) = 7 - 3 = 4$ ✓
in (2), $\quad 3(7) - 2(-1) = 21 + 2 = 23$ ✓

EXERCISE 24B.1

1 Solve these simultaneous equations graphically:

a $\begin{cases} y = 6 - 4x \\ y = x + 1 \end{cases}$ $\qquad$ **b** $\begin{cases} y = 3x - 2 \\ y - 2x = 1 \end{cases}$ $\qquad$ **c** $\begin{cases} 4x - y = -9 \\ y - x = 6 \end{cases}$

d $\begin{cases} 3x + y = 8 \\ 5y - x = -16 \end{cases}$ $\qquad$ **e** $\begin{cases} 2x + 3y = 11 \\ 3x - y = 5 \end{cases}$ $\qquad$ **f** $\begin{cases} 4y - 3x = -11 \\ 7x - 3y = -8 \end{cases}$

2 a Try to solve using the method of elimination: $\begin{cases} 3x - 2y = 5 \\ 9x - 6y = 7. \end{cases}$

$\quad$ **b** Graph the two equations from **a**. Comment on what you find.

3 a Try to solve using the method of elimination: $\begin{cases} x + 2y = -3 \\ 4y = -2x - 6. \end{cases}$

$\quad$ **b** Graph the two equations from **a**. Comment on what you find.

SOLVING UNFAMILIAR EQUATIONS

Technology also allows us to solve equations with expressions we are unfamiliar with.

Suppose we are given an equation of the form $f(x) = g(x)$.

There are two different approaches we can take to find solutions:

Method 1: Graph $y = f(x)$ and $y = g(x)$ on the same set of axes, and find the x-coordinates where they meet.

Method 2: If we subtract $g(x)$ from both sides, we have $f(x) - g(x) = 0$. We can therefore graph $y = f(x) - g(x)$ and find the x-intercepts.

Further functions (Chapter 24)

For example, consider the equation $\quad 2x^3 - 3x^2 - 2x = \frac{1}{3}x^2 + x - 2$.

To solve this, we let $\quad f(x) = 2x^3 - 3x^2 - 2x \quad$ and $\quad g(x) = \frac{1}{3}x^2 + x - 2$.

Method 1:

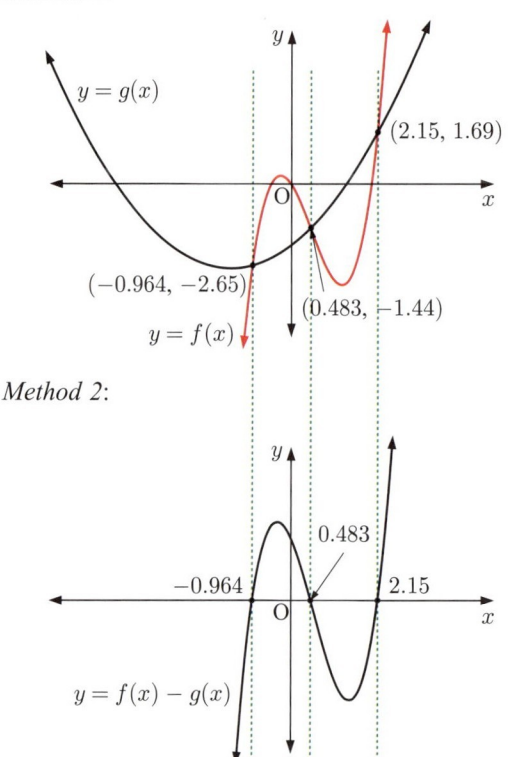

We graph $y = f(x)$ and $y = g(x)$ and find the points of intersection. These are $(-0.964, -2.65)$, $(0.483, -1.44)$, and $(2.15, 1.69)$.

So, the solutions of the equation are $x = -0.964$, 0.483, 2.15.

Method 2:

$y = f(x) - g(x)$
$= (2x^3 - 3x^2 - 2x) - (\frac{1}{3}x^2 + x - 2)$
$= 2x^3 - 3x^2 - 2x - \frac{1}{3}x^2 - x + 2$
$= 2x^3 - \frac{10}{3}x^2 - 3x + 2$

So we plot $y = f(x) - g(x)$ and find the x-intercepts.

These are -0.964, 0.483, and 2.15.

So, the solutions of the equation are $x = -0.964$, 0.483, 2.15.

Note: Many calculators have a 'Solver' mode which can be used to solve equations like these. However, 'Solver' will only give *one* answer where there may be more than one. It is therefore better to stick with the graphical method.

Example 4   ◀) Self Tutor

Solve $2^x = 4 - x$ by graphing $y = 2^x$ and $y = 4 - x$ on the same set of axes.

Give your answer correct to 3 significant figures.

Let $Y_1 = 2^x$ and $Y_2 = 4 - x$

Using a graphics calculator, we find that they meet when $x \approx 1.39$.

$\therefore$ the solution is $x \approx 1.39$

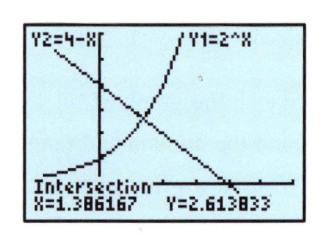

Example 5

Solve $2^x = 4 - x$ by drawing one graph. Give your answer correct to 3 significant figures.

$$2^x = 4 - x$$
$$\therefore \quad 2^x - 4 + x = 0$$

We graph $y = 2^x - 4 + x$ using a graphics calculator to help.

The x-intercept is ≈ 1.39

$\therefore$ the solution is $x \approx 1.39$

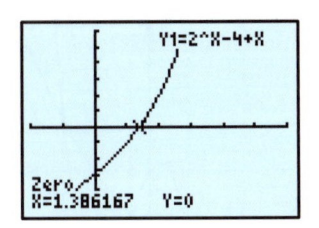

EXERCISE 24B.2

1 Use technology to solve:

   a $-2x^2 = x - 3$ **b** $\frac{1}{2}x^2 = x + 2$ **c** $x(x - 2) = 3 - x$

   d $(x + 2)(x - 1) = 2 - 3x$ **e** $(2x + 1)^2 = 3 - x$ **f** $(x - 2)^2 = 1 + x$

2 Use *Method 1* to solve, correct to 3 significant figures:

   a $2^x = 3x$ **b** $\sqrt{x} = 3 - x$ **c** $x^2 = \sqrt{x + 2}$

   d $3^x = 5$ **e** $3^x = x^2$ **f** $x^3 + 2 = 3x - x^2$

3 Use *Method 2* to solve, correct to 3 significant figures:

   a $x^3 - x + 3 = 0$ **b** $5 - x = \sqrt{x}$ **c** $3^x = x^3 + 1$

   d $x^2 - 3 = \sqrt[3]{x}$ **e** $3x^2 + 1 = \dfrac{12}{x - 4}$ **f** $\dfrac{x + 7}{x - 3} = 2^{-x}$

4 Find the coordinates of the points, correct to 2 decimal places, where these graphs meet:

   a $y = x^2 + 2x - 3$ and $y = \dfrac{4}{x}$ **b** $y = x^3$ and $y = 5^x$

   c $y = \dfrac{5}{x}$ and $y = \dfrac{1}{\sqrt{x}} + 1$ **d** $y = 2^x - 1$ and $y = \dfrac{1}{x^3}$

5 a Use your graphics calculator to draw, on the same axes, the functions $f(x) = x - \dfrac{1}{x}$ and $g(x) = 2^{-x} - 1$.

   b State the equations of the asymptotes of $f(x)$.

   c Find the coordinates of any points where $y = f(x)$ and $y = g(x)$ meet.

6 Consider $f(x) = \dfrac{x^2 + 4}{x^2 + 1}$.

   a Sketch the graph of $y = f(x)$.

   b Find the domain and range of $f(x)$.

   c Write down the equations of any asymptotes of $y = f(x)$.

   d Find the coordinates of any points where $y = f(x)$ meets $y = 5$.

   e Suppose $y = f(x)$ meets $y = k$ at exactly two points. What possible values could k have?

Further functions (Chapter 24) 445

7 Consider $f(x) = \dfrac{x+2}{x-1}$ and $g(x) = 2^x$.

  a Sketch the graphs of $y = f(x)$ and $y = g(x)$ on the same set of axes for $-5 \leqslant x \leqslant 5$.
  b Find the coordinates of the points of intersection of the two graphs.
  c Find the values of x for which $2^x > \dfrac{x+2}{x-1}$.

C PROBLEM SOLVING [3.6]

We can use technology to investigate functions found in real life situations.

Example 6 ◀) Self Tutor

During a locust plague, the area of land eaten is given by $A = 8000 \times 2^{0.5n}$ hectares, where n is the number of weeks after the initial observation.

  a Find the size of the area initially eaten.
  b Find the size of the area eaten after: **i** 1 week **ii** 4 weeks.
  c Graph A against n.
  d How long would it take for the area eaten to reach $50\,000$ hectares?

a Initially, $n = 0$ $\therefore$ $A = 8000 \times 2^0$
  $\therefore$ $A = 8000$ hectares

b Using the table function:
  i when $n = 1$, $A \approx 11\,313$ So, $11\,313$ hectares have been eaten
  ii when $n = 4$, $A = 32\,000$ So, $32\,000$ hectares have been eaten.

c

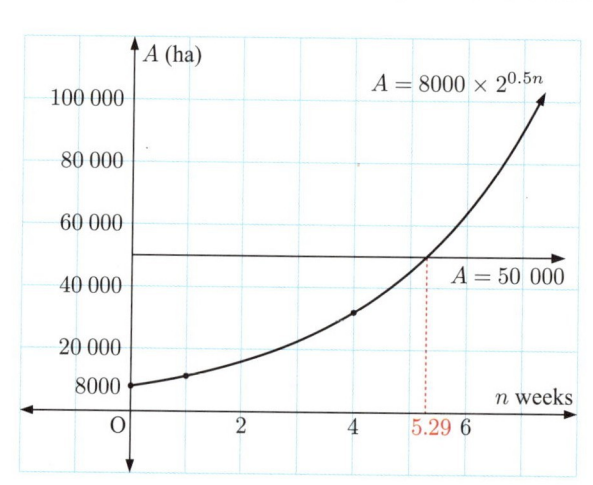

d We plot $Y_1 = 8000 \times 2^{0.5X}$ and $Y_2 = 50\,000$ on the same axes.
  The graphs meet when $X \approx 5.29$
  $\therefore$ it takes approximately 5.29 weeks for the area eaten to reach $50\,000$ hectares.

EXERCISE 24C

1. A local zoo starts a breeding program to ensure the survival of a species of mongoose. From a previous program, the expected population in n years' time is given by $P = 40 \times 2^{0.2n}$.
   a. What is the initial population purchased by the zoo?
   b. What is the expected population after:
      i. 3 years
      ii. 5 years
      iii. 10 years?
   c. Graph P against n.
   d. How long will it take for the population to reach 100?

2. A new drug is undergoing trials to test its effectiveness. The amount in a patient's bloodstream t hours after administration is modelled by $A = 25t \times 0.641^t$ units.
   a. Find the amount of the drug in the patient after:
      i. 0 hours
      ii. 1 hour
      iii. 2 hours
      iv. 5 hours.
   b. Graph A against t.
   c. When is the level of the drug at a maximum? What amount is this?
   d. The patient feels the effects of the drug when its level is over 5 units. Over what time period is this?

3. A nursery finds that the profit from selling s shrubs a day is given by the function
   $P(s) = -\frac{2}{3}s^2 + \frac{40}{3}s - 34$ pounds.
   a. Draw a graph of the profit against the number of shrubs sold.
   b. What are the horizontal axis intercepts? What do they represent?
   c. What is the maximum profit and when does it occur?

4. An enclosed box has length x cm, height 5 cm, and volume 400 cm³. The surface area of the box is given by
   $y = 160 + 10x + \dfrac{800}{x}$ cm².
   a. Graph the surface area function for $0 \leqslant x \leqslant 30$.
   b. State the equation of the vertical asymptote.
   c. Find the minimum surface area of the box. How long is the box when this occurs?

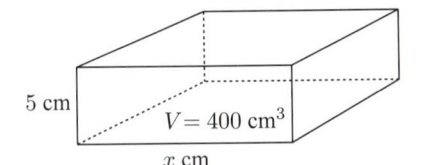

5. The temperature of a cake fresh out of the oven is modelled by $T = 20 + 60 \times 0.96^x$ °C, where x is the number of minutes after it is removed.
   a. What temperature was the cake when it came out of the oven?
   b. Find the temperature of the cake after:
      i. 20 minutes
      ii. 45 minutes
      iii. 1 hour.
   c. Draw a graph of the cake's temperature over time.
   d. What temperature is the cake heading towards?
   e. If the cake is ready to eat when its temperature is 50 °C, when does this occur?

6. Answer the questions in the **Opening Problem** on page 437.

Further functions (Chapter 24)

Review set 24A

1 For the function $y = x^2 - 2$ on $-3 \leqslant x \leqslant 4$:
   a copy and complete the table of values:

x	-3	-2	-1	0	1	2	3	4
y								

   b sketch the function on a pair of axes
   c write down its zeros
   d find the coordinates of the minimum value
   e state the range.

2 Consider the function $f(x) = \dfrac{x+3}{x-5}$.
   a Graph $y = f(x)$.
   b Find the asymptotes of $f(x)$.
   c Find the axes intercepts.
   d Add the features in **b** and **c** to your graph.

3 Use graphical methods to find the simultaneous solution of $\begin{cases} y - 2x = 3 \\ 3x + 5y = -17. \end{cases}$

4 Solve for x, correct to 3 significant figures:
   a $7^x = 50$
   b $5x^3 = 12 + \sqrt{x}$

5 Find the coordinates of the points of intersection for:
   a $y = 2^{-x}$ and $y = 1.5x^2 - 3$
   b $y = \sqrt{x} + 3$ and $y = x^2 - 7x + 8$

6 Suppose $f(x) = \dfrac{x^2 + 4}{x^2 - 1}$.
   a Use technology to sketch the graph of $y = f(x)$.
   b Find the equations of the three asymptotes.
   c Find the domain and range of $f(x)$.
   d If $\dfrac{x^2 + 4}{x^2 - 1} = k$ has 2 solutions, find the range of possible values of k.

7 A small herd of elands is introduced to an island where there are no other animals competing for food. The population is given by the function $p(t) = -\dfrac{x^4}{81} + \dfrac{7x^2}{3} + 80$, where t is the number of years since the colony's introduction.
   a What was the initial size of the herd introduced to the island?
   b What is the maximum population of the herd and when does this occur?
   c Sketch the function, showing your answers to **a** and **b**.
   d When will the elands become extinct on this island? Explain your answer.

Review set 24B

1 Let $f(x) = \left(\tfrac{1}{4}\right)^x$.
   a Find the values of $f(x)$ for $x = -2, -1, 0, 1, 2, 3$.
   b What is the y-intercept of $y = f(x)$?

c Draw $y = f(x)$ on a set of axes.

d Write the equation of the asymptote of $f(x)$.

2 Consider $y = 5x - 2x^2 - x^3$ on $-4 \leqslant x \leqslant 2$.

a Sketch a graph of this function.

b Write down the coordinates of any local maxima or minima.

c Find the x-intercepts of this function.

d What is the range of $y = 5x - 2x^2 - x^3$ on this domain?

3 Solve simultaneously using a graph: $\begin{cases} y = 7 + 2x \\ x + 3y = 4. \end{cases}$

4 Consider $f(x) = \dfrac{x-3}{x^2 + 3x - 4}$.

a Use a graphics calculator to help graph the function.

b State the equations of any asymptotes.

c Find the axes intercepts.

d Find and classify any turning points.

5 Solve for x, correct to 3 significant figures:

a $3^x = 11$ **b** $x^3 - 6x = 5 + x^2$ **c** $5^x = x^2 + 2$

6 Find the coordinates of the points of intersection for:

a $y = x^3$ and $y = \dfrac{5}{x} - 2$ **b** $y = 3^x + 2$ and $y = \dfrac{1}{x^2}$

7 Suppose $f(x) = (1.2)^{\frac{x}{10}}$ and $g(x) = (0.8)^{\frac{x}{10}}$

a Copy and complete the table of values alongside.

b For $-10 \leqslant x \leqslant 20$, write down the largest and smallest values of $f(x)$ and $g(x)$.

c Use technology and parts **a** and **b** to sketch $y = f(x)$ and $y = g(x)$ on the same set of axes.

d Find the point of intersection of $f(x)$ and $g(x)$.

x	$f(x)$	$g(x)$
-10	0.833	1.25
-5		
0		
5		
10		
15		
20		

8 A doughnut shop sells doughnuts in bulk. The price they charge per doughnut is given by the function $P = \dfrac{d + 2.5}{d}$, where P is the price in euros, and d is the number of doughnuts bought.

a Find the cost per doughnut if you buy:

i 1 doughnut **ii** a 6-pack **iii** a 24-pack.

b Graph P against d, for $d > 0$.

c A charity wishes to get some doughnuts for fundraising. If they want to pay at most €1.05 per doughnut, how many doughnuts will they need to buy?

d Find and interpret the horizontal asymptote of this function.

Probability

25

Contents:

A	Introduction to probability	[10.1]
B	Estimating probability	[10.2, 10.6]
C	Probabilities from two-way tables	[10.2, 10.6]
D	Expectation	[10.3]
E	Representing combined events	[10.5, 10.6]
F	Theoretical probability	[10.4, 10.6]
G	Compound events	[10.4]
H	Using tree diagrams	[10.5]
I	Sampling with and without replacement	[10.5]
J	Mutually exclusive and non-mutually exclusive events	[10.4]
K	Miscellaneous probability questions	[10.4 - 10.6]

Opening problem

Jenaro and Marisa are playing a game at the local fair. They are each given a bag containing an equal number of red balls and blue balls, and must each draw one ball from the bag at the same time. Before doing so, they must try to guess whether the balls they select will be the same colour or different colours.

Jenaro thinks it is more than likely that the balls will be the same colour. Marisa thinks it is more likely that the balls will be different colours. Their friend Pia thinks that both outcomes are equally likely.

Who is correct?

A INTRODUCTION TO PROBABILITY [10.1]

Consider these statements:

> "The Wildcats will probably beat the Tigers on Saturday."
> "It is unlikely that it will rain today."
> "I will probably make the team."
> "It is almost certain that I will understand this chapter."

Each of these statements indicates a **likelihood** or **chance** of a particular event happening.

We can indicate the likelihood of an event happening in the future by using a percentage.

> 0%   indicates we believe the event **will not occur**.
> 100% indicates we believe the event **is certain to occur**.

All events can therefore be assigned a percentage between 0% and 100% (inclusive).

A number close to 0% indicates the event is **unlikely** to occur, whereas a number close to 100% means that it is **highly likely** to occur.

In mathematics, we usually write probabilities as either decimals or fractions rather than percentages. However, as 100% = 1, comparisons or conversions from percentages to fractions or decimals are very simple.

> A **probability value** is a measure of the chance of a particular event happening.
>
> An **impossible** event which has 0% chance of happening is assigned a probability of 0.
>
> A **certain** event which has 100% chance of happening is assigned a probability of 1.
>
> All other events can be assigned a probability between 0 and 1.

For example, when tossing a coin the probability that it falls 'heads' is 50% or $\frac{1}{2}$ or 0.5.

We can write P(head) = $\frac{1}{2}$ or P(H) = $\frac{1}{2}$, both of which read 'the probability of getting a head is one half'.

The assigning of probabilities is usually based on either:
- observing past data or the results of an experiment (experimental probability), or
- what we expect to happen because of symmetry (theoretical probability).

If A is an event with probability P(A) then $0 \leqslant P(A) \leqslant 1$.

If P(A) = 0, the event cannot occur.

If P(A) = 1, the event is certain to occur.

If P(A) is very close to 1, it is highly likely that the event will occur.

If P(A) is very close to 0, it is highly unlikely that the event will occur.

> The probability of an event cannot be **negative**, or **greater than 1**. It does not make sense to be "less than impossible" or "more than certain".

Probability (Chapter 25)

The probability line below shows words which can be used to describe the chance of an event occurring.

```
    0                                    1/2                                1
    •─────────────────────────────────────•─────────────────────────────────•
impossible  extremely  very unlikely   unlikely   equally   likely   very likely  extremely  certain
            unlikely                              likely                          likely
```

EXERCISE 25A

1 Describe these probabilities using words from the probability line above:

    a 0   **b** 0.51   **c** $\frac{1}{1000}$ **d** 0.23   **e** 1   **f** $\frac{1}{2}\%$

    g 0.77   **h** 0.999   **i** $\frac{15}{26}$ **j** $\frac{500}{1999}$ **k** 0.002   **l** $\frac{17}{20}$

2 Suppose that $P(A) = \frac{1}{3}$, $P(B) = 60\%$ and $P(C) = 0.54$.
Which event is: **a** most **b** least likely?

3 Use words to describe the probability that:
    a the maximum temperature in London tomorrow will be negative
    b you will sleep in the next 48 hours
    c Manchester United will win its next football match
    d you will be eaten by a dinosaur
    e it will rain in Singapore some time this week.

B   ESTIMATING PROBABILITY   [10.2, 10.6]

In an ideal situation, we could find the exact probability of an event occurring. However, often we can only estimate the probability by experimentation, or by using data that has been collected over time.

In a probability experiment:

- The **number of trials** is the total number of times the experiment is repeated.
- The **outcomes** are the different results possible for one trial of the experiment.
- The **frequency** of a particular outcome is the number of times that this outcome is observed.
- The **relative frequency** of an outcome is the frequency of that outcome divided by the total number of trials.

$$\text{relative frequency} = \frac{\text{frequency}}{\text{number of trials}}$$

For example, when tossing a tin can in the air 250 times, it comes to rest on an end 37 times. We say:

- the number of trials is 250
- the outcomes are *landing on an end* and *landing on a side*
- the frequency of *landing on an end* is 37
- the frequency of *landing on a side* is 213
- the relative frequency of *landing on an end* $= \frac{37}{250} \approx 0.148$
- the relative frequency of *landing on a side* $= \frac{213}{250} \approx 0.852$.

The **relative frequency** of an event is an estimate of its **probability**.

We write estimated P(end) ≈ 0.148 and estimated P(side) ≈ 0.852.

Suppose in one year an insurance company receives 9573 claims from its 213 829 clients. The probability of a client making a claim in the next year can be predicted by the relative frequency:
$$\tfrac{9537}{213\,829} \approx 0.0446 \approx 4.46\%.$$

Knowing this result will help the company calculate its charges or premiums for the following year.

Activity — Rolling a pair of dice

In this experiment you will roll a pair of dice and add the numbers on the uppermost faces. When this is repeated many times the sums can be recorded in a table like this one:

Sum	2	3	4	5	6	7	8	9	10	11	12
Frequency											
Relative Frequency											

What to do:

1. Roll two dice 100 times and record the results in a table.

2. Calculate the relative frequency for each possible outcome.

3. Combine the results of everyone in your class. Calculate the overall relative frequency for each outcome.

4. Discuss your results.

The larger the number of trials, the more confident we are that the estimated probability obtained is accurate.

Example 1 — Self Tutor

Estimate the probability of:
- **a** tossing a head with one toss of a coin if it falls heads 96 times in 200 tosses
- **b** rolling a *six* with a die given that when it was rolled 300 times, a *six* occurred 54 times.

a   Estimated P(getting a head)
= relative frequency of getting a head
= $\tfrac{96}{200}$
= 0.48

b   Estimated P(rolling a *six*)
= relative frequency of rolling a *six*
= $\tfrac{54}{300}$
= 0.18

Example 2

A marketing company surveys 80 randomly selected people to discover what brand of shoe cleaner they use. The results are shown in the table alongside:

Brand	Frequency
Shine	27
Brite	22
Cleano	20
No scuff	11

a Based on these results, estimate the probability of a community member using:

  i Brite **ii** Cleano.

b Would you classify the estimates in **a** as very good, good, or poor? Why?

a We start by calculating the relative frequency for each brand.

  i Estimated P(Brite) = 0.275
  ii Estimated P(Cleano) = 0.250

b Poor, as the sample size is very small.

Brand	Frequency	Relative Frequency
Shine	27	0.3375
Brite	22	0.2750
Cleano	20	0.2500
No scuff	11	0.1375

EXERCISE 25B

1 Estimate the probability of rolling *an odd number* with a die, if *an odd number* occurred 33 times when the die was rolled 60 times.

2 Clem fired 200 arrows at a target and hit the target 168 times. Estimate the probability of Clem hitting the target.

3 Ivy has free-range hens. Out of the first 123 eggs that they laid, she found that 11 had double-yolks. Estimate the probability of getting a double-yolk egg from her hens.

4 Jackson leaves for work at the same time each day. Over a period of 227 working days, on his way to work he had to wait for a train at the railway crossing on 58 days. Estimate the probability that Jackson has to wait for a train on his way to work.

5 Ravi has a circular spinner marked P, Q, and R on 3 equal sectors. The spinner was twirled 417 times and finished on Q on 138 occasions. Estimate the probability of getting a Q on the next spin.

6 Each time Claude shuffled a pack of cards before a game, he recorded the suit of the top card of the pack. His results for 140 games were 34 hearts, 36 diamonds, 38 spades and 32 clubs. Estimate the probability that the top card of a shuffled pack is:

  a a heart **b** a club or diamond.

7 Estimate probabilities from these observations:

  a Our team has won 17 of its last 31 games.
  b There are 23 two-child families in our street of 64 families.

8 A marketing company was commissioned to investigate brands of products usually found in the bathroom. The results of a soap survey are shown alongside:

  a How many people were randomly selected in this survey?
  b Calculate the relative frequency of use of each brand of soap, correct to 3 significant figures.

Brand	Freq.	Rel. Freq.
Silktouch	125	
Super	107	
Just Soap	93	
Indulgence	82	
Total		

c Using the results obtained by the marketing company, estimate the probability that the soap used by a randomly selected person is:
  i Just Soap **ii** Indulgence **iii** Silktouch.

9 Two coins were tossed 489 times and the *number of heads* occurring at each toss was recorded. The results are shown opposite:
  a Copy and complete the table given.
  b Estimate the chance of the following events occurring:
    i 0 heads **ii** 1 head **iii** 2 heads.

Outcome	Freq.	Rel. Freq.
0 heads	121	
1 head		
2 heads	109	
Total		

10 At the Annual Show the toffee apple vendor estimated that three times as many people preferred red toffee apples to green toffee apples.
  a If 361 people wanted green toffee apples, estimate how many wanted red.
  b Copy and complete the table given.
  c Estimate the probability that the next customer will ask for:
    i a green toffee apple **ii** a red toffee apple.

Colour	Freq.	Rel. Freq.
Green	361	
Red		
Total		

11 The tickets sold for a tennis match were recorded as people entered the stadium. The results are shown opposite:
  a How many tickets were sold in total?
  b Copy and complete the table given.
  c A person in the stadium is selected at random. Estimate the probability that the person bought a Concession ticket.

Ticket Type	Freq.	Rel. Freq.
Adult	3762	
Concession	1084	
Child	389	
Total		

12 The results of a local Council election are shown in the table. It is known that 6000 people voted in the election.
  a Copy and complete the table given.
  b Estimate the chance that a randomly selected person from this electorate voted for a female councillor.

Councillor	Freq.	Rel. Freq.
Mr Tony Trimboli	2167	
Mrs Andrea Sims	724	
Mrs Sara Chong	2389	
Mr John Henry		
Total		

C PROBABILITIES FROM TWO-WAY TABLES [10.2, 10.6]

Two-way tables are tables which compare two categorical variables. They usually result from a survey.

For example, the year 10 students in a small school were tested to determine their ability in mathematics. The results are summarised in the two-way table shown:

	Boy	Girl
Good at maths	17	19
Not good at maths	8	12

There are 12 girls who are not good at maths.

In this case the variables are *ability in maths* and *gender*.

Probability (Chapter 25)

We can use two-way tables to estimate probabilities:

Example 3

To investigate the breakfast habits of teenagers, a survey was conducted amongst the students of a high school. The results were:

	Male	Female
Regularly eats breakfast	87	53
Does not regularly eat breakfast	68	92

Use this table to estimate the probability that a randomly selected student from the school:

a is male
b is male *and* regularly eats breakfast
c is female *or* regularly eats breakfast
d is male, given that the student regularly eats breakfast
e regularly eats breakfast, given that the student is female.

We extend the table to include totals:

	Male	Female	Total
Regularly eats breakfast	87	53	140
Does not regularly eat breakfast	68	92	160
Total	155	145	300

a There are 155 males out of the 300 students surveyed.
∴ P(male) $= \frac{155}{300} \approx 0.517$

b 87 of the 300 students are male and regularly eat breakfast.
∴ P(male *and* regularly eats breakfast) $= \frac{87}{300} \approx 0.29$

c $53 + 92 + 87 = 232$ out of the 300 are female or regularly eat breakfast.
∴ P(female *or* regularly eats breakfast) $= \frac{232}{300} \approx 0.773$

d Of the 140 students who regularly eat breakfast, 87 are male.
∴ P(male given that regularly eats breakfast) $= \frac{87}{140} \approx 0.621$

e Of the 145 females, 53 regularly eat breakfast
∴ P(regularly eats breakfast, given female) $= \frac{53}{145} \approx 0.366$

In probability, "A or B" means A, B, or both.

EXERCISE 25C

1 310 students at a high school were surveyed on the question "Do you like watching basketball being played on TV?". The results are shown in the two-way table alongside.

	Like	Dislike
Junior students	87	38
Senior students	129	56

a Copy and complete the table to include 'totals'.
b Estimate the probability that a randomly selected student:
  i likes watching basketball on TV and is a junior student
  ii likes watching basketball on TV and is a senior student
  iii likes watching basketball on TV, given that the student is a senior
  iv is a senior, given that the student likes watching basketball on TV.

2 A survey investigated the issue of equal wage levels for men and women doing the same job. Adult workers were asked if they had a problem with this issue. The results are summarised in the two-way table shown.

	Problem	No Problem
Men	146	175
Women	188	134

Assuming that the results are representative of the whole community, estimate the probability that the next randomly chosen adult worker:

  a is a woman
  b has a problem with the issue
  c is a male with no problem with the issue
  d is a female, given the person has a problem with the issue
  e has no problem with the issue, given that the person is female.

3 The two-way table shows the students who can and cannot swim in three different year groups at a school.

	Can swim	Cannot swim
Year 4	215	85
Year 7	269	31
Year 10	293	7

If a student is randomly selected from these year groups, estimate the probability that:

  a the student can swim
  b the student cannot swim
  c the student is from year 7
  d the student is from year 7 and cannot swim
  e the student is from year 7 or cannot swim
  f the student cannot swim, given that the student is from year 7 or 10
  g the student is from year 4, given that the student cannot swim.

D EXPECTATION [10.3]

Suppose we repeat an experiment many times. If we know in advance the probability of an event occurring in each trial, we can predict the total number of times the event will occur.

For example, when rolling an ordinary die, the probability of rolling a '4' is $\frac{1}{6}$.

If we roll the die 120 times, we expect $120 \times \frac{1}{6} = 20$ of the outcomes to be '4's.

> Suppose the probability of an event occurring is p. If the trial is repeated n times, the **expectation** of the event, or the number of times we expect it to occur, is np.

Example 4   Self Tutor

In one week, 79 out of 511 trains were late to the station at Keswick. In the next month, 2369 trains are scheduled to pass through the station. How many of these would you expect to be late?

We estimate the probability of a train being late to be $p = \frac{79}{511}$.

We expect $2369 \times \frac{79}{511} \approx 366$ trains to be late.

Probability (Chapter 25)

EXERCISE 25D

1. In a particular region in Africa, the probability that it will rain on any one day is 0.177. On how many days of the year would you expect it to rain?

2. At practice, Tony kicked 53 out of 74 goals from the penalty goal spot. If he has 18 attempts to kick penalty goals through the season, how many is he expected to score?

3. A certain type of drawing pin, when tossed 400 times, landed on its back 144 times.
   a. Estimate the probability that it will land on its back if it is tossed once.
   b. If the drawing pin is tossed 72 times, how many "backs" would you expect?

4. A bag contains 5 red and 3 blue discs. A disc is chosen at random and then replaced. This is repeated 200 times. How many times would you expect a red disc to be chosen?

5. A die has the numbers 0, 1, 2, 2, 3 and 4 on its faces. The die is rolled 600 times. How many times might we expect a result of:
   a. 0
   b. 2
   c. 1, 2 or 3
   d. not a 4?

6. A test has 20 multiple choice questions with 4 options for each question. What mark would a student who guessed every question expect to get?

7. On the last occasion Annette threw darts at the target shown, she hit the inner circle 17% of the time and the outer circle 72% of the time.
   a. Estimate the probability of Annette completely missing the target with her next throw.
   b. Suppose Annette throws the dart 100 times at the target. She receives 100 points when she hits the inner circle and 20 points when she hits the outer circle. Find:
      i. the number of "inners", "outers", and "misses" you would expect her to get
      ii. the total number of points you would expect her to get
      iii. the mean number of points you would expect per throw.

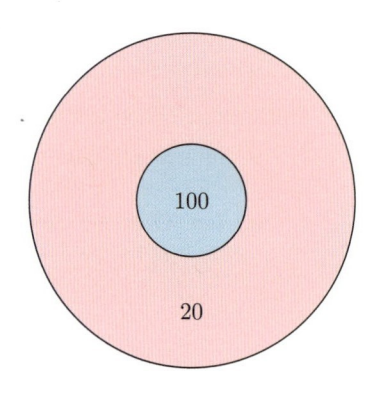

E REPRESENTING COMBINED EVENTS [10.5, 10.6]

The possible outcomes for tossing two coins are listed below:

two heads   head and tail   tail and head   two tails

These results are the **combination** of two events: tossing coin 1 and tossing coin 2.

If H represents a 'head' and T represents a 'tail', the sample space of possible outcomes is HH, HT, TH, and TT.

> A **sample space** is the set of all possible outcomes of an experiment.

Possible ways of representing sample spaces are:
- listing them
- using a 2-dimensional grid
- using a tree diagram
- using a Venn diagram.

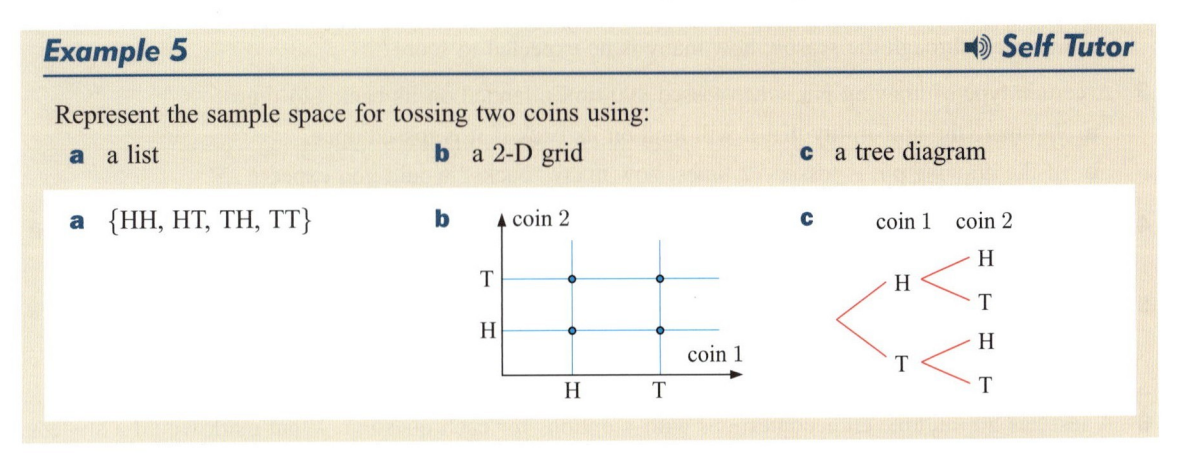

Example 5

Represent the sample space for tossing two coins using:
- **a** a list
- **b** a 2-D grid
- **c** a tree diagram

a {HH, HT, TH, TT}

b 2-D grid with coin 1 on horizontal axis (H, T) and coin 2 on vertical axis (H, T), showing four points.

c Tree diagram:
coin 1 → coin 2
H → H, T
T → H, T

Example 6

Two marbles are drawn from a bag containing several marbles of different colours.

Illustrate, using a tree diagram, the possible outcomes if the bag contains:
- **a** orange and blue marbles
- **b** red, green, and yellow marbles.

a Let O be the event of getting an orange
B be the event of getting a blue.

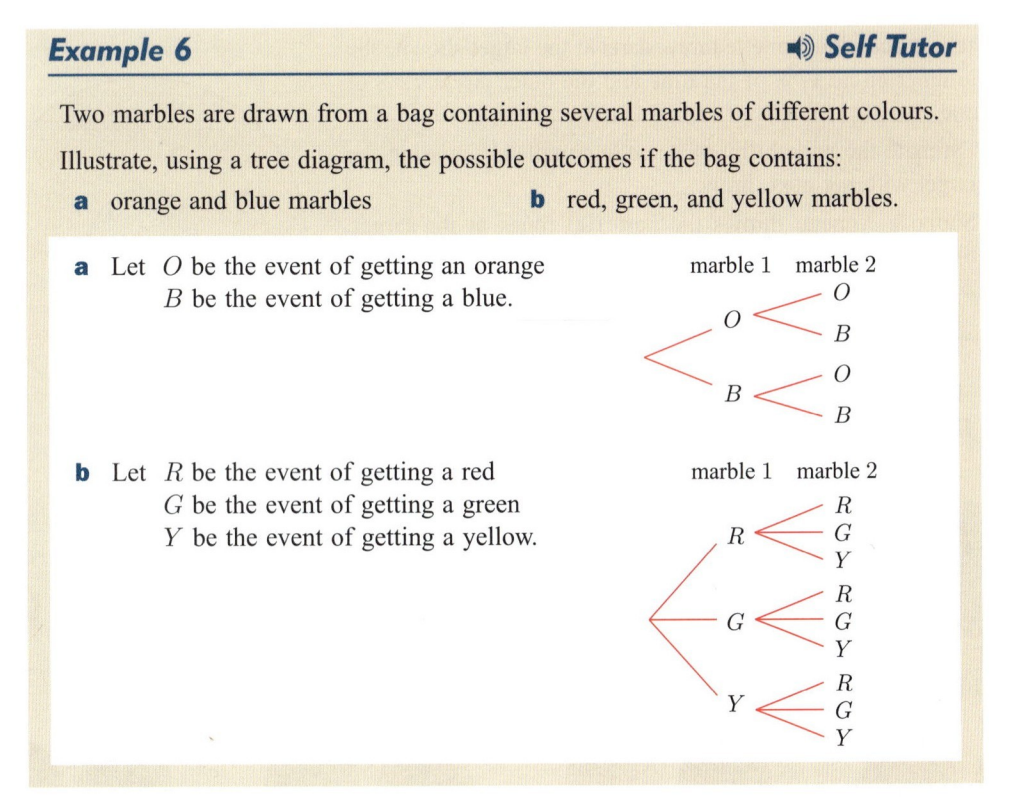

marble 1 → marble 2
O → O, B
B → O, B

b Let R be the event of getting a red
G be the event of getting a green
Y be the event of getting a yellow.

marble 1 → marble 2
R → R, G, Y
G → R, G, Y
Y → R, G, Y

We have already seen Venn diagrams in **Chapter 2**.

If two events have common outcomes, a Venn diagram may be a suitable way to display the sample space.

For example, the Venn diagram opposite shows that of the 27 students in a class, 11 play tennis, 17 play basketball, and 3 play neither of these sports.

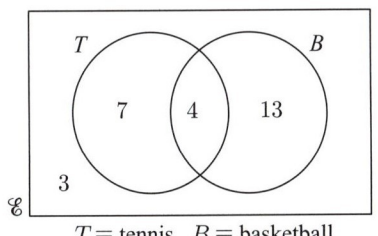

Venn diagram: T circle contains 7, intersection contains 4, B circle contains 13, outside (in $\mathcal{E}$) contains 3.

$T \equiv$ tennis $B \equiv$ basketball

Probability (Chapter 25) 459

EXERCISE 25E

1 List the sample space for the following:
   a twirling a square spinner labelled A, B, C, D
   b the sexes of a 2-child family
   c the order in which 4 blocks A, B, C, and D can be lined up
   d the sexes of the 8 different 3-child families
   e tossing a coin   **i** twice   **ii** three times   **iii** four times.

2 Illustrate on a 2-dimensional grid, the sample space for:
   a rolling a die and tossing a coin simultaneously
   b rolling two dice
   c rolling a die and spinning a spinner with sides A, B, C, D
   d twirling two square spinners: one labelled A, B, C, D, and the other 1, 2, 3, 4.

3 Illustrate on a tree diagram, the sample space for:
   a tossing a 5-cent and 10-cent coin simultaneously
   b tossing a coin and twirling an equilateral triangular spinner labelled A, B, and C
   c twirling two equilateral triangular spinners labelled 1, 2, and 3, and X, Y, and Z
   d drawing two tickets from a hat containing a number of pink, blue, and white tickets
   e drawing two beads from a bag containing 3 red and 4 blue beads.

4 Draw a Venn diagram to show a class of 20 students where 10 study History, 15 study Geography, and 2 study neither subject.

F THEORETICAL PROBABILITY   [10.4, 10.6]

From the methods of showing sample spaces in the previous section, we can find the probabilities of combined events.

These are theoretical probabilities which are calculated using

$$P(\text{event happens}) = \frac{\text{number of ways the event can happen}}{\text{total number of possible outcomes}}.$$

For example, say we are tossing two coins. We have seen already that the sample space is {HH, HT, TH, TT}.

There are 4 possible outcomes, of which only one (HH) gives two heads.

So, the probability of getting two heads is $P(2 \text{ heads}) = \frac{1}{4}$.

However, the probability of getting one head is $P(1 \text{ head}) = \frac{2}{4} = \frac{1}{2}$, as there are *two* ways of getting one head: HT and TH.

Example 7

Three coins are tossed. Write down a list of all possible outcomes. Find the probability of getting:
- **a** 3 heads
- **b** at least one head
- **c** 3 heads if it is known that there is at least one head.

We list the outcomes in a systematic way.

The sample space is: HHH HHT TTH TTT
  HTH THT
  THH HTT

a $P(3 \text{ heads}) = \frac{1}{8}$

b $P(\text{at least one H}) = \frac{7}{8}$ {all except TTT}

c $P(\text{HHH knowing at least one H}) = \frac{1}{7}$
{The sample space now excludes TTT}

Example 8

A die has the numbers 0, 0, 1, 1, 4 and 5. It is rolled *twice*. Illustrate the sample space using a 2-D grid. Hence find the probability of getting:
- **a** a total of 5
- **b** two numbers which are the same.

2-D grid:

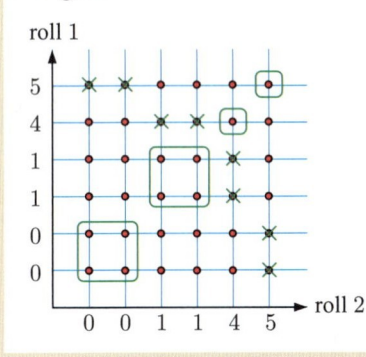

(roll 1 vs roll 2 grid with values 0, 0, 1, 1, 4, 5 on each axis)

There are $6 \times 6 = 36$ possible outcomes.

a $P(\text{total of 5})$
$= \frac{8}{36}$ {those with a ×}
$= \frac{2}{9}$

b $P(\text{same numbers})$
$= \frac{10}{36}$ {those circled}
$= \frac{5}{18}$

Example 9

In a class of 30 students, 19 play sport, 8 play the piano, and 3 both play sport and the piano. Display this information on a Venn diagram, and hence determine the probability that a randomly selected class member plays:
- **a** both sport and the piano
- **b** at least one of sport and the piano
- **c** sport, but not the piano
- **d** exactly one of sport and the piano
- **e** neither sport nor the piano
- **f** the piano if it is known that the student plays sport.

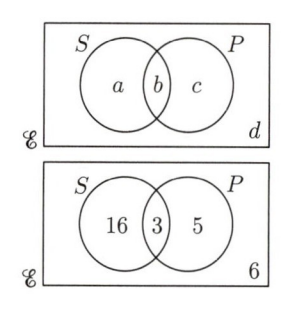

Let S represent the event of 'playing sport',
and P represent the event of 'playing the piano'.
Now $a + b = 19$ {as 19 play sport}
$b + c = 8$ {as 8 play the piano}
$b = 3$ {as 3 play both}
$a + b + c + d = 30$ {as there are 30 in the class}
$\therefore b = 3, \quad a = 16, \quad c = 5, \quad d = 6.$

a   P(S and P)
$= \frac{3}{30}$
$= \frac{1}{10}$

b   P(at least one of S and P)
$= \frac{16+3+5}{30}$
$= \frac{24}{30}$ (or $\frac{4}{5}$)

c   P(S but not P)
$= \frac{16}{30}$
$= \frac{8}{15}$

d   P(exactly one of S and P)
$= \frac{16+5}{30}$
$= \frac{7}{10}$

In **f**, since we know that the student plays sport, we look only at the sport set S.

e   P(neither S nor P)
$= \frac{6}{30}$
$= \frac{1}{5}$

f   P(P given S)
$= \frac{3}{16+3}$
$= \frac{3}{19}$

EXERCISE 25F

1   **a**   List all possible orderings of the letters O, D, and G.
     b   If these three letters are placed at random in a row, what is the probability of:
         i   spelling DOG   **ii**   O appearing first
         iii   O not appearing first   **iv**   spelling DOG or GOD?

2   The Venn diagram shows the sports played by boys at the local high school.
A student is chosen at random.
Find the probability that he:

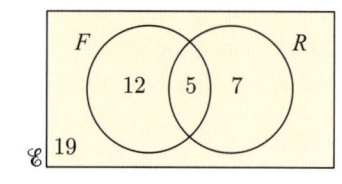

     a   plays football
     b   plays both codes
     c   plays football or rugby
     d   plays exactly one of these sports
     e   plays neither of these sports
     f   plays football, given that he is in at least one team
     g   plays rugby, given that he plays football.

3   Draw the grid of the sample space when a 10-cent and a 50-cent coin are tossed simultaneously. Hence determine the probability of getting:

     a   two heads   **b**   two tails
     c   exactly one head   **d**   at least one head.

4 A coin and a pentagonal spinner with sectors 1, 2, 3, 4, and 5 are tossed and spun respectively.
   a Draw a grid to illustrate the sample space of possible outcomes.
   b How many outcomes are possible?
   c Use your grid to determine the chance of getting:
      i a head and a 4
      ii a tail and an odd number
      iii an even number
      iv a tail or a 3.

5 List the six different orders in which Alex, Bodi, and Kek may sit in a row. If the three of them sit randomly in a row, determine the probability that:
   a Alex sits in the middle
   b Alex sits at the left end
   c Alex sits at the right end
   d Bodi and Kek are seated together.

6 a List the 8 possible 3-child families, according to the gender of the children. For example, BGB means *"the first is a boy, the second is a girl, and the third is a boy"*.
   b Assuming that each of these is equally likely to occur, determine the probability that a randomly selected 3-child family consists of:
      i all boys
      ii all girls
      iii boy, then girl, then girl
      iv two girls and a boy
      v a girl for the eldest
      vi at least one boy.

7 In a class of 24 students, 10 take Biology, 12 take Chemistry, and 5 take neither Biology nor Chemistry. Find the probability that a student picked at random from the class takes: 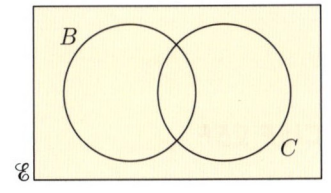
   a Chemistry but not Biology
   b Chemistry or Biology.

8 a List, in systematic order, the 24 different orders in which four people P, Q, R, and S may sit in a row.
   b Hence, determine the probability that when the four people sit at random in a row:
      i P sits on one end
      ii Q sits on one of the two middle seats
      iii P and Q are seated together
      iv P, Q, and R are seated together, not necessarily in that order.

9 A pair of dice is rolled. 
   a Show that there are 36 members in the sample space of possible outcomes by displaying them on a grid.
   b Hence, determine the probability of a result with:
      i the dice showing a 4 and the other a 5
      ii both dice showing the same result
      iii at least one die showing a result of 3
      iv either a 4 or 6 being displayed
      v both dice showing even numbers
      vi the sum of the values being 7.

10 60 married men were asked whether they gave their wife flowers or chocolates for their last birthday. The results were: 26 gave chocolates, 21 gave flowers, and 5 gave both chocolates and flowers. If one of the married men was chosen at random, determine the probability that he gave his wife:
   a flowers but not chocolates
   b neither chocolates nor flowers
   c chocolates or flowers.

Probability (Chapter 25) 463

11 List the possible outcomes when four coins are tossed simultaneously. Hence determine the probability of getting:

   a all heads   **b** two heads and two tails   **c** more tails than heads

   d at least one tail   **e** exactly one head.

12 **a** Copy and complete the grid alongside for the sample space of drawing one card from an ordinary pack.

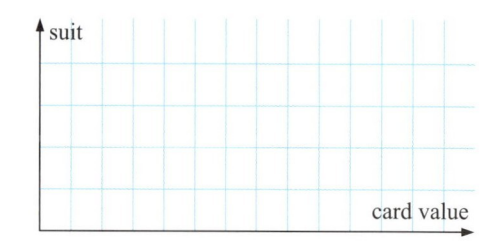

   b Use your grid to determine the probability of getting:

     i a Queen   **ii** the Jack of hearts   **iii** a spade

     iv a picture card   **v** a red 7   **vi** a diamond or a club

     vii a King or a heart   **viii** a Queen and a 3.

13 The medical records for a class of 28 children show whether they had previously had measles or mumps. The records show 22 have had measles, 13 have had measles and mumps, and 27 have had measles or mumps. If one child from the class is selected at random, determine the probability that he or she has had:

   a measles   **b** mumps but not measles   **c** neither mumps nor measles.

G COMPOUND EVENTS   [10.4]

We have previously used two-dimensional grids to represent sample spaces and hence find answers to certain probability problems.

Consider again a simple example of tossing a coin and rolling a die simultaneously.

To determine the probability of getting a head and a '5', we can illustrate the sample space on the two-dimensional grid shown. We can see that there are 12 possible outcomes but only one with the property that we want, so the answer is $\frac{1}{12}$.

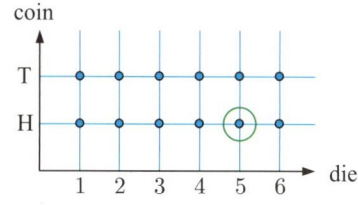

However, notice that $P(\text{a head}) = \frac{1}{2}$, $P(\text{a '5'}) = \frac{1}{6}$ and $\frac{1}{2} \times \frac{1}{6} = \frac{1}{12}$.

This means that $P(\text{a head and a '5'}) = P(\text{a head}) \times P(\text{a '5'})$.

In other words, to find the combined probability, we can multiply the separate probabilities.

INDEPENDENT EVENTS

If A and B are two events for which the occurrence of each one does not affect the occurrence of the other, then $P(A \text{ and } B) = P(A) \times P(B)$.

The two events 'getting a head' and 'rolling a 5' are events with this property, as the occurrence or non-occurrence of either one of them cannot affect the occurrence of the other. We say these events are **independent**.

If two events A and B are **independent** then $P(A \text{ and } B) = P(A) \times P(B)$.

Example 10 ◀) Self Tutor

A coin is tossed and a die rolled simultaneously. Find the probability that a tail and a '2' result.

'Getting a tail' and 'rolling a 2' are independent events.

$\therefore$ P(a tail **and** a '2') = P(a tail) $\times$ P(a '2')
$= \frac{1}{2} \times \frac{1}{6}$
$= \frac{1}{12}$

COMPLEMENTARY EVENTS

Two events are **complementary** if exactly one of them *must* occur.

The probabilities of complementary events sum to 1.

The **complement** of event E is denoted E'. It is the event when E fails to occur.

For any event E with **complementary** event E',
$P(E) + P(E') = 1$ or $P(E') = 1 - P(E)$.

Example 11 ◀) Self Tutor

Sunil has probability $\frac{4}{5}$ of hitting a target and Monika has probability $\frac{5}{6}$.
If they both fire simultaneously at the target, determine the probability that:
a they both hit it **b** they both miss it.

Let S be the event of Sunil hitting and M be the event of Monika hitting.

a P(both hit)
$= P(S \text{ and } M)$
$= P(S) \times P(M)$
$= \frac{4}{5} \times \frac{5}{6}$
$= \frac{2}{3}$

b P(both miss)
$= P(S' \text{ and } M')$
$= P(S') \times P(M')$
$= \frac{1}{5} \times \frac{1}{6}$
$= \frac{1}{30}$

EXERCISE 25G.1

1 A coin and a pentagonal spinner with edges marked A, B, C, D, and E are tossed and twirled simultaneously. Find the probabilities of getting:
  a a head and a D
  b a tail and either an A or a D.

Probability (Chapter 25)

2 A spinner with 6 equal sides has 3 red, 2 blue, and 1 yellow edge. A second spinner with 7 equal sides has 4 purple and 3 green edges. Both spinners are twirled simultaneously. Find the probability of getting:
   a a red and a green
   b a blue and a purple.

3 Janice and Lee take set shots at a netball goal from 3 m. From past experience, Janice throws a goal on average 2 times in every 3 shots, whereas Lee throws a goal 4 times in every 7. If they both shoot for goals, determine the probability that:
   a both score a goal
   b both miss
   c Janice scores a goal but Lee misses.

4 When a nut was tossed 400 times it finished on its edge 84 times and on its side for the rest. Use this information to estimate the probability that when two identical nuts are tossed:
   a they both fall on their edges
   b they both fall on their sides.

   edge   side

5 Tei has probability $\frac{1}{3}$ of hitting a target with an arrow, while See has probability $\frac{2}{5}$. If they both fire at the target, determine the probability that:
   a both hit the target
   b both miss the target
   c Tei hits the target and See misses
   d Tei misses the target and See hits.

6 A certain brand of drawing pin was tossed into the air 600 times. It landed on its back ⊥ 243 times and on its side ⋏ for the remainder. Use this information to estimate the probability that:
   a one drawing pin, when tossed, will fall on its   **i** back   **ii** side
   b two drawing pins, when tossed, will both fall on their backs
   c two drawing pins, when tossed, will both fall on their sides.

DEPENDENT EVENTS

Suppose a cup contains 4 red and 2 green marbles. One marble is randomly chosen, its colour is noted, and it is then put aside. A second marble is then randomly selected. What is the chance that it is red?

$$\text{If the first marble was red,} \quad \text{P(second is red)} = \frac{3}{5} \quad \begin{matrix} \text{3 reds remaining} \\ \text{5 to choose from} \end{matrix}$$

$$\text{If the first marble was green,} \quad \text{P(second is red)} = \frac{4}{5} \quad \begin{matrix} \text{4 reds remaining} \\ \text{5 to choose from} \end{matrix}$$

So, the probability of the second marble being red **depends** on what colour the first marble was. We therefore have **dependent events**.

> Two or more events are **dependent** if they are **not independent**.
>
> **Dependent** events are events for which the occurrence of one of the events *does affect* the occurrence of the other event.

For compound events which are dependent, a similar product rule applies as to that for independent events:

> If A and B are dependent events then   P(A **then** B) = P(A) × P(B given that A has occurred).

Example 12

A box contains 4 blue and 3 yellow buttons of the same size. Two buttons are randomly selected from the box without replacement. Find the probability that:
- **a** both are yellow
- **b** the first is yellow and the second is blue.

a P(both are yellow)
= P(first is yellow *and* second is yellow)
= P(first is yellow) × P(second is yellow given that the first is yellow)
= $\frac{3}{7} \times \frac{2}{6}$ ← 2 yellows remaining / 6 to choose from
= $\frac{1}{7}$

b P(first is Y and second is B)
= P(first is Y) × P(second is B given that the first is Y)
= $\frac{3}{7} \times \frac{4}{6}$ ← 4 blues remaining / 6 to choose from
= $\frac{2}{7}$

EXERCISE 25G.2

1 A packet contains 8 identically shaped jelly beans. 5 are green and 3 are yellow. Two jelly beans are randomly selected without replacing the first before the second is drawn.
- **a** Determine the probability of getting:
  - **i** two greens
  - **ii** a green then a yellow
  - **iii** a yellow then a green
  - **iv** two yellows.
- **b** Why do your answers in **a** add up to 1?

2 A pocket in a golf bag contains 6 white and 4 yellow golf balls. Two of them are selected at random without replacement.
- **a** Determine the probability that:
  - **i** both are white
  - **ii** the first is white and the second is yellow
  - **iii** one of each colour is selected.
- **b** Why do your answers in **a** not add up to 1?

3 A container has 4 purple, 3 blue, and 1 gold ticket. Three tickets are selected without replacement. Find the probability that:
- **a** all are purple
- **b** all are blue
- **c** the first two are purple and the third is gold.

4 A sewing box contains 6 black, 3 brown, and 5 red buttons. Two buttons are selected without replacement. Find the probability that:
- **a** both are black
- **b** neither is red
- **c** they have different colours.

Probability (Chapter 25) 467

H USING TREE DIAGRAMS   [10.5]

Tree diagrams can be used to illustrate sample spaces, provided that the alternatives are not too numerous. Once the sample space is illustrated, the tree diagram can be used for determining probabilities.

Consider **Example 11** again. The tree diagram for this information is:

S means Sunil hits
M means Monika hits

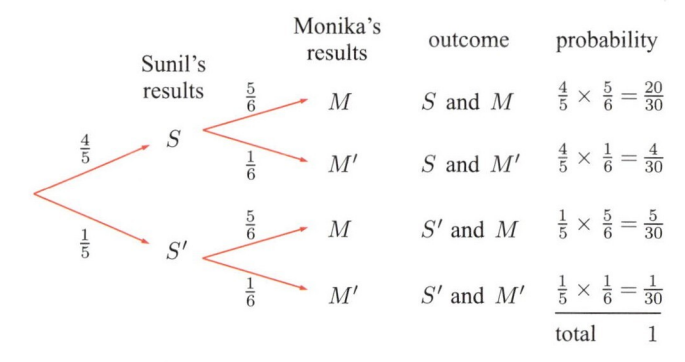

	Sunil's results	Monika's results	outcome	probability
	$\frac{4}{5}$ S	$\frac{5}{6}$ M	S and M	$\frac{4}{5} \times \frac{5}{6} = \frac{20}{30}$
		$\frac{1}{6}$ M'	S and M'	$\frac{4}{5} \times \frac{1}{6} = \frac{4}{30}$
	$\frac{1}{5}$ S'	$\frac{5}{6}$ M	S' and M	$\frac{1}{5} \times \frac{5}{6} = \frac{5}{30}$
		$\frac{1}{6}$ M'	S' and M'	$\frac{1}{5} \times \frac{1}{6} = \frac{1}{30}$
			total	1

Notice that:

- The probabilities for hitting and missing are marked on the branches.
- There are *four* alternative paths and each path shows a particular outcome.
- All outcomes are represented.
- The probability of each outcome is obtained by **multiplying** the probabilities along its path.

Example 13   ◀)) Self Tutor

Stephano is having problems. His desktop computer will only boot up 90% of the time and his laptop will only boot up 70% of the time.

a Draw a tree diagram to illustrate this situation.
b Use the tree diagram to determine the chance that:
  i both will boot up
  ii Stephano has no choice but to use his desktop computer.

a D = desktop computer boots up
L = laptop boots up

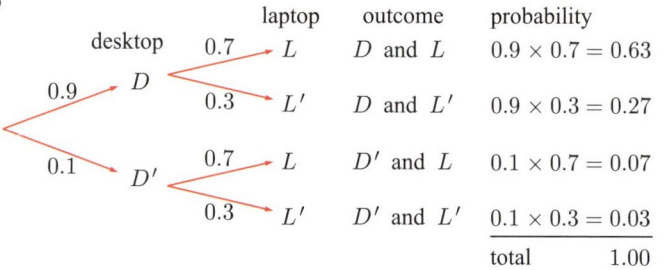

	desktop	laptop	outcome	probability
	0.9 D	0.7 L	D and L	$0.9 \times 0.7 = 0.63$
		0.3 L'	D and L'	$0.9 \times 0.3 = 0.27$
	0.1 D'	0.7 L	D' and L	$0.1 \times 0.7 = 0.07$
		0.3 L'	D' and L'	$0.1 \times 0.3 = 0.03$
			total	1.00

b i   P(both boot up)
    = P(D and L)
    = 0.9×0.7
    = 0.63

ii   P(desktop boots up but laptop does not)
    = P(D and L')
    = 0.9×0.3
    = 0.27

Example 14

Bag A contains 4 red jelly beans and 1 yellow jelly bean. Bag B contains 2 red and 3 yellow jelly beans. A bag is randomly selected by tossing a coin, and one jelly bean is removed from it. Determine the probability that it is yellow.

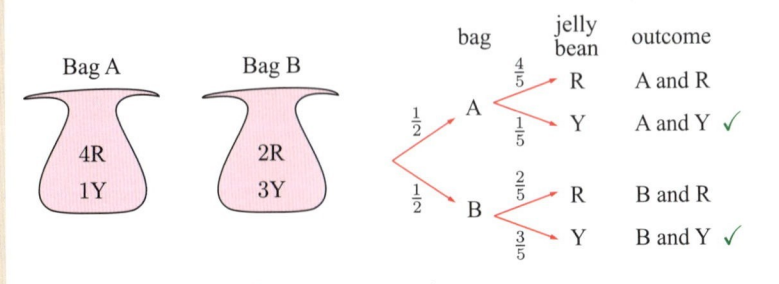

To get a yellow we take either the first branch ticked **or** the second one ticked. We **add** the probabilities for these outcomes.

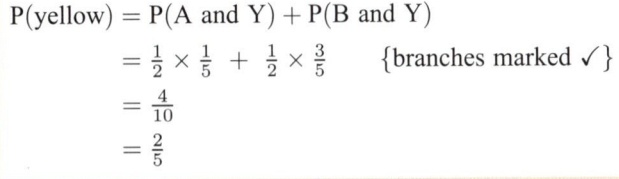

$$P(\text{yellow}) = P(A \text{ and } Y) + P(B \text{ and } Y)$$
$$= \tfrac{1}{2} \times \tfrac{1}{5} + \tfrac{1}{2} \times \tfrac{3}{5} \quad \{\text{branches marked } \checkmark\}$$
$$= \tfrac{4}{10}$$
$$= \tfrac{2}{5}$$

EXERCISE 25H

1 Suppose this spinner is spun twice:

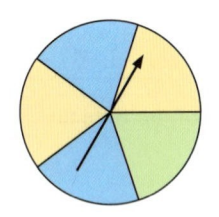

   a Copy and complete the branches on the tree diagram shown.
   b What is the probability that blue appears on both spins? 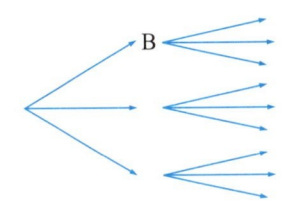
   c What is the probability that green appears on both spins?
   d What is the probability that different colours appear on both spins?
   e What is the probability that blue appears on *either* spin?

2 The probability of the race track being muddy next week is estimated to be $\tfrac{1}{4}$. If it is muddy, the horse Rising Tide will start favourite with probability $\tfrac{2}{5}$ of winning. If it is dry he has a $\tfrac{1}{20}$ chance of winning.

   a Display the sample space of possible results on a tree diagram.
   b Determine the probability that Rising Tide will win next week.

3 Sylke has bad luck with the weather when she takes her summer holidays. She estimates that it rains 60% of the time and it is cold 70% of the time.

   a Draw a tree diagram to illustrate this situation.
   b Use the tree diagram to determine the chance that for Sylke's holidays:
      i it is cold and raining
      ii it is fine and cold.

Probability (Chapter 25) 469

4 Machine A cans 60% of the fruit at a factory. Machine B cans the rest. Machine A spoils 3% of its product, while Machine B spoils 4%. Determine the probability that the next can inspected at this factory will be spoiled.

5 Box A contains 2 blue and 3 red blocks and Box B contains 5 blue and 1 red block. A box is chosen at random (by the flip of a coin) and one block is taken at random from it. Determine the probability that the block is red.

6

A: 4B, 3R
B: 3B, 4R
C: 5B, 2R

Three bags contain different numbers of blue and red tickets. A bag is selected using a die which has three A faces, two B faces, and one C face.
One ticket is selected randomly from the chosen bag. Determine the probability that it is: **a** blue **b** red.

I SAMPLING WITH AND WITHOUT REPLACEMENT [10.5]

Sampling is the process of selecting one object from a large group and inspecting it for some particular feature. The object is then either **put back** (sampling **with replacement**) or **put to one side** (sampling **without replacement**).

Sometimes the inspection process makes it impossible to return the object to the large group.
Such processes include:

- Is the chocolate hard- or soft-centred? Bite it or squeeze it to see.
- Does the egg contain one or two yolks? Break it open and see.
- Is the object correctly made? Pull it apart to see.

The sampling process is used for quality control in industrial processes.

Example 15 ◄⏵ Self Tutor

A bin contains 4 blue and 5 green marbles. A marble is selected from this bin and its colour is noted. It is then *replaced*. A second marble is then drawn and its colour is noted. Determine the probability that:

a both are blue
b the first is blue and the second is green
c there is one of each colour.

Tree diagram:
B = blue
G = green

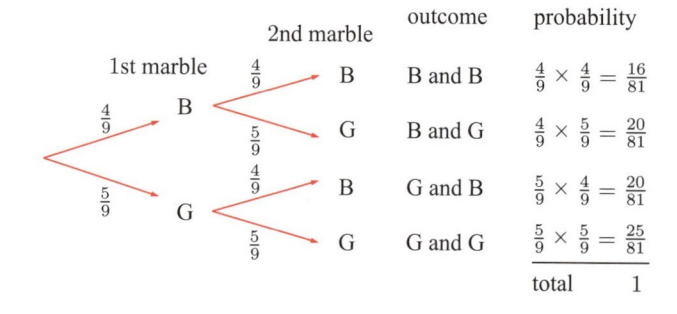

1st marble	2nd marble	outcome	probability
B ($\frac{4}{9}$)	B ($\frac{4}{9}$)	B and B	$\frac{4}{9} \times \frac{4}{9} = \frac{16}{81}$
	G ($\frac{5}{9}$)	B and G	$\frac{4}{9} \times \frac{5}{9} = \frac{20}{81}$
G ($\frac{5}{9}$)	B ($\frac{4}{9}$)	G and B	$\frac{5}{9} \times \frac{4}{9} = \frac{20}{81}$
	G ($\frac{5}{9}$)	G and G	$\frac{5}{9} \times \frac{5}{9} = \frac{25}{81}$
		total	1

a	P(both blue)	b	P(first is B and second is G)	c	P(one of each colour)
	$= \frac{4}{9} \times \frac{4}{9}$		$= \frac{4}{9} \times \frac{5}{9}$		$= P(\text{B then G or G then B})$
	$= \frac{16}{81}$		$= \frac{20}{81}$		$= P(\text{B then G}) + P(\text{G then B})$
					$= \frac{4}{9} \times \frac{5}{9} + \frac{5}{9} \times \frac{4}{9}$
					$= \frac{40}{81}$

EXERCISE 25I

1 A box contains 6 red and 3 yellow tickets. Two tickets are drawn at random (the first being *replaced* before the second is drawn). Draw a tree diagram to represent the sample space and use it to determine the probability that:

   a both are red
   b both are yellow
   c the first is red and the second is yellow
   d one is red and the other is yellow.

2 7 tickets numbered 1, 2, 3, 4, 5, 6 and 7 are placed in a hat. Two of the tickets are taken from the hat at random *without replacement*. Determine the probability that:

   a both are odd
   b both are even
   c the first is even and the second is odd
   d one is even and the other is odd.

3 Jessica has a bag of 9 acid drops which are all identical in shape. 5 are raspberry flavoured and 4 are orange flavoured. She selects one acid drop at random, eats it, and then takes another, also at random. Determine the probability that:

   a both acid drops were orange flavoured
   b both acid drops were raspberry flavoured
   c the first was raspberry and the second was orange
   d the first was orange and the second was raspberry.

   Add your answers to **a**, **b**, **c** and **d**. Explain why this sum is 1.

4 A cook selects an egg at random from a carton containing 7 ordinary eggs and 5 double-yolk eggs. She cracks the egg into a bowl and sees whether it has two yolks or not. She then selects another egg at random from the carton and checks it.
Let S represent "a single yolk egg" and D represent "a double yolk egg".

   a Draw a tree diagram to illustrate this sampling process.
   b What is the probability that both eggs had two yolks?
   c What is the probability that both eggs had only one yolk?

5 Freda selects a chocolate at random from a box containing 8 hard-centred and 11 soft-centred chocolates. She bites it to see whether it is hard-centred or not. She then selects another chocolate at random from the box and checks it.
Let H represent "a hard-centred chocolate" and S represent "a soft-centred chocolate".

   a Draw a tree diagram to illustrate this sampling process.
   b What is the probability that both chocolates have hard centres?
   c What is the probability that both chocolates have soft centres?

6 In a particular board game there are nine tiles: five are green and the remainder are brown. The tiles start face down on the table so they all look the same.

   a If a player is required to pick a tile at random, determine the probability that it is:

     i green   **ii** brown.

   b Suppose a player has to pick two tiles in a row, replacing the first and shuffling them before the second is selected. Copy and complete the tree diagram illustrating the possible outcomes.

   c Using **b**, determine the probability that:

     i both tiles are green   **ii** both tiles are brown

    iii tile 1 is brown and tile 2 is green

    iv one tile is brown and the other is green.

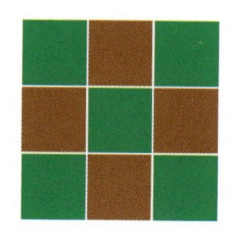

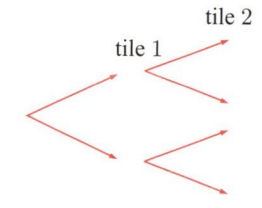

7 A sporting club runs a raffle in which 200 tickets are sold. There are two winning tickets which are drawn at random, in succession, without replacement. If Adam bought 8 tickets in the raffle, determine the probability that he:

   a wins first prize   **b** does not win first prize   **c** wins both prizes

   d wins neither prize   **e** wins second prize *given that* he did not win first prize.

8 In the manufacturing of transformers for electric lights, there is a 3% chance that any transformer made is faulty. Benny leaves for a job with 3 transformers in his van. He is to install 2 new lights.

   a When selecting a transformer, is this sampling with or without replacement?

   b Draw a tree diagram to illustrate this sampling process.

   c Find the probability that Benny will not be able to finish the job with the transformers on board.

J   MUTUALLY EXCLUSIVE AND NON-MUTUALLY EXCLUSIVE EVENTS   [10.4]

- If two events have no common outcomes we say they are **mutually exclusive** or **disjoint**.
- If two events have common outcomes they are **not mutually exclusive**.

Suppose we select a card at random from a normal pack of 52 playing cards. Consider carefully these events:

   Event X: the card is a heart   *Event Y:*   the card is an ace   *Event Z:*   the card is a 7

Notice that Y and Z do not have a common outcome, so they are *mutually exclusive* events.

We see that $P(Y \text{ or } Z) = P(\text{ace or seven}) = \frac{8}{52}$ and $P(\text{ace}) + P(\text{seven}) = \frac{4}{52} + \frac{4}{52} = \frac{8}{52}$

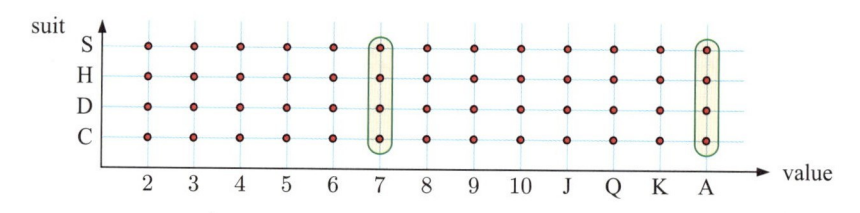

If two events A and B are **mutually exclusive** then $P(A \text{ or } B) = P(A) + P(B)$

In contrast, X and Z do have a common outcome: the 7 of hearts. They are *not* mutually exclusive events.

We see that $P(X \text{ or } Z) = P(\text{heart or seven}) = \frac{16}{52}$ and $P(\text{heart}) + P(\text{seven}) = \frac{13}{52} + \frac{4}{52} = \frac{17}{52}$.

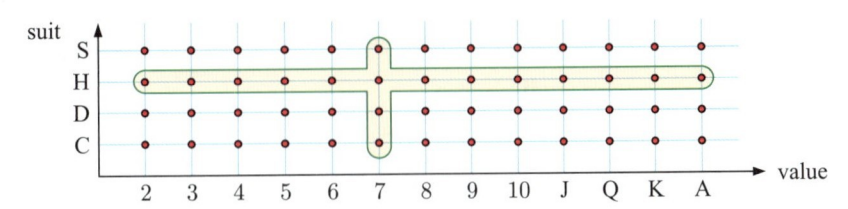

Actually, $P(\text{heart or seven}) = P(\text{heart}) + P(\text{seven}) - P(\text{heart and seven})$.

If two events A and B are **not mutually exclusive** then $P(A \text{ or } B) = P(A) + P(B) - P(A \text{ and } B)$.

EXERCISE 25J

1 An ordinary die with faces 1, 2, 3, 4, 5, and 6 is rolled once. Consider these events:
  A: getting a 1 B: getting a 3 C: getting an odd number
  D: getting an even number E: getting a prime number F: getting a result greater than 3.
  a List all possible pairs of events which are mutually exclusive.
  b Find: **i** $P(B \text{ or } D)$ **ii** $P(D \text{ or } E)$ **iii** $P(A \text{ or } E)$
              iv $P(B \text{ or } E)$ **v** $P(C \text{ or } D)$ **vi** $P(A \text{ or } B \text{ or } F)$.

2 A committee consists of 4 accountants, 2 managers, 5 lawyers, and 6 engineers. A chairperson is randomly selected. Find the probability that the chairperson is:
  a a lawyer   **b** a manager or an engineer   **c** an accountant or a manager

3 A jar contains 3 red balls, 2 green balls, and 1 yellow ball. Two balls are selected at random from the jar without replacement. Find the probability that the balls are either both red or both green.

4 A coin and an ordinary die are tossed simultaneously.
  a Draw a grid showing the 12 possible outcomes.
  b Find the probability of getting: **i** a head and a 5   **ii** a head or a 5.
  c Check that: $P(H \text{ or } 5) = P(H) + P(5) - P(H \text{ and } 5)$.

5 Two ordinary dice are rolled.
  a Draw a grid showing the 36 possible outcomes.
  b Find the probability of getting: **i** a 3 and a 4   **ii** a 3 or a 4.
  c Check that: $P(3 \text{ or } 4) = P(3) + P(4) - P(3 \text{ and } 4)$.

K   MISCELLANEOUS PROBABILITY QUESTIONS [10.4 – 10.6]

In this section you will encounter a variety of probability questions. You will need to select the appropriate technique for each problem, and are encouraged to use tools such as tree and Venn diagrams.

Probability (Chapter 25)

EXERCISE 25K

1 A team of 3 males and 5 females randomly chooses a 'captain' and an 'organiser'. The one person may have both roles. Find the probability that:
   a the captain is female
   b both positions are taken by males
   c one male and one female get the positions.

2 A survey of a neighbourhood investigates the incidence of arthritis in various age groups. The results are shown alongside.

	Age		
	< 15	15 - 64	≥ 65
arthritis	4	42	28
not arthritis	80	237	22

   a Find the probability that a randomly selected individual:
   i has arthritis and is over 64 years old
   ii does not have arthritis
   iii is less than 65 years old
   iv has arthritis given they are at least 15 years old.
   b In a population of 30 000 people, how many would you expect to be of working age (between 15 and 64 inclusive) and without arthritis?

3 50 students went on a 'thrill seekers' holiday. 40 went white-water rafting, 21 went paragliding, and each student did at least one of these activities.
   a From a Venn diagram, find how many students did both activities.
   b If a student from this group is randomly selected, find the probability that he or she:
   i went white-water rafting but not paragliding
   ii went paragliding given that he or she went white-water rafting.

4 A bag contains 7 red and 3 blue balls. Two balls are randomly selected without replacement. Find the probability that:
   a the first is red and the second is blue
   b the balls are different in colour.

5 In a class of 25 students, 19 have fair hair, 15 have blue eyes, and 22 have fair hair, blue eyes or both. A child is selected at random. Determine the probability that the child has:
   a fair hair and blue eyes
   b neither fair hair nor blue eyes
   c fair hair but not blue eyes
   d blue eyes given that the child has fair hair.

6 Abdul cycles to school and must pass through a set of traffic lights. The probability that the lights are red is $\frac{1}{4}$. When they are red, the probability that Abdul is late for school is $\frac{1}{10}$. When they are not red the probability is $\frac{1}{50}$.
   a Calculate the probability that Abdul is late for school.
   b There are 200 days in the school year. How many days in the school year would you expect Abdul to be late?

7 28 students go tramping. 23 get sunburn, 8 get blisters, and 5 get both sunburn and blisters. Determine the probability that a randomly selected student:
   a did not get blisters
   b either got blisters or sunburn
   c neither got blisters nor sunburn
   d got blisters, given that the student was sunburnt
   e was sunburnt, given that the student did not get blisters.

8 A company puts a small toy in some of its breakfast cereal packets. A tester randomly selects one packet from a row of 10, checks if it has a toy, and returns the packet. Later, another tester runs the same test on the same row of 10. Three of the ten packets have a toy. Find the probability that:
   a both testers found a toy   **b** only one tester found a toy.

9 An examination in French has two parts: aural and written. When 30 students sit for the examination, 25 pass aural, 26 pass written, and 3 fail both parts. Determine the probability that a student who:
   a passed aural also passed written   **b** passed aural, failed written.

10 Three coins are tossed. Find the probability that:
   a all of them are tails   **b** two are heads and the other is a tail.

11 On a tour of the Musée d'Orsay, there are 5 people from Paris, 12 from the rest of France, 4 from Germany, 3 from Canada, and 2 from the USA. Someone asks the guide a question. Find the probability that the questioner is:
   a German   **b** from France   **c** not from France.

12 Marius has 2 bags of peaches. Bag A has 4 ripe and 2 unripe peaches, and bag B has 5 ripe and 1 unripe peaches. Ingrid selects a bag by tossing a coin, and takes a peach from that bag.
   a Determine the probability that the peach is ripe.
   b Given that the peach is ripe, what is the probability it came from B?

Review set 25A

1 Use words to describe the probability:
   a $\frac{2}{5}$ **b** of a woman having quadruplets   **c** 98%.

2 Donna kept records of the number of clients she interviewed over a period of consecutive days.
   a For how many days did the survey last?
   b Estimate Donna's chances of interviewing:
      i no clients on a day
      ii four or more clients on a day
      iii less than three clients on a day.

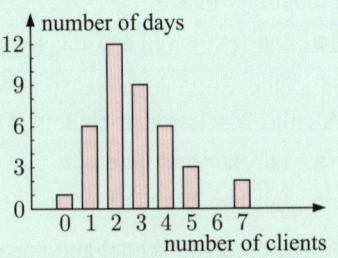

3 Illustrate on a 2-dimensional grid the possible outcomes when a coin and a pentagonal spinner with sides labelled A, B, C, D, and E are tossed and spun simultaneously.

4 University students were surveyed to find who owns a motor vehicle (MV) and who owns a computer. The results are shown in the two-way table.
Estimate the probability that a randomly selected university student has:

	MV	no MV
computer	124	168
no computer	16	22

   a a computer   **b** a motor vehicle   **c** a computer and a motor vehicle
   d a motor vehicle given that the student does not have a computer.

5 What is meant by saying that two events are "independent"?

6 Use a tree diagram to illustrate the sample space for the possible four-child families. Hence determine the probability that a randomly chosen four-child family:
   a is all boys   **b** has exactly two boys   **c** has more girls than boys.

7 In a shooting competition, Louise has 80% chance of hitting her target and Kayo has 90% chance of hitting her target. If they both have a single shot, determine the probability that:
  a both hit their targets
  b neither hits her target
  c at least one hits her target
  d only Kayo hits her target.

8 Two fair six-sided dice are rolled simultaneously. Determine the probability that the result is a 'double', which means both dice show the same number.

9 A bag contains 4 green and 3 red marbles. Two marbles are randomly selected from the bag without replacement. Determine the probability that:
  a both are green
  b they are different in colour.

10 A circle is divided into 5 sectors with equal angles at the centre. It is made into a spinner, and the sectors are numbered 1, 2, 3, 4, and 5. A coin is tossed and the spinner is spun.
  a Use a 2-dimensional grid to show the sample space.
  b What is the chance of getting: **i** a head and a 5   **ii** a head or a 5?

11 Bag X contains three white and two red marbles. Bag Y contains one white and three red marbles. A bag is randomly chosen and two marbles are drawn from it. Illustrate the given information on a tree diagram and hence determine the probability of drawing two marbles of the same colour.

12 At a local girls school, 65% of the students play netball, 60% play tennis, and 20% play neither sport. Display this information on a Venn diagram, and hence determine the likelihood that a randomly chosen student plays:
  a netball   **b** netball but not tennis   **c** at least one of these two sports
  d exactly one of these two sports   **e** tennis, given that she plays netball.

Review set 25B

1 In his last 37 attempts, Mr Smith has completed the daily crossword 28 times. Mr Davey has a 72% crossword completion record. Who is more likely to finish today's crossword?

2 Pierre conducted a survey to determine the ages of people walking through a shopping mall. The results are shown in the table alongside. Estimate, to 3 decimal places, the probability that the next person Pierre meets in the shopping mall is:
  a between 20 and 39 years of age
  b less than 40 years of age   **c** at least 20 years of age.

Age	Frequency
0 - 19	22
20 - 39	43
40 - 59	39
60+	14

3 **a** List the sample space of possible results when a tetrahedral die with four faces labelled A, B, C, and D is rolled and a 20-cent coin is tossed simultaneously.
  b Use a tree diagram to illustrate the sample spaces for the following:
    i Bags A, B, and C contain green or yellow tickets. A bag is selected and then a ticket taken from it.
    ii Martina and Justine play tennis. The first to win three sets wins the match.

4 When a box of drawing pins was dropped onto the floor, it was observed that 49 pins landed on their backs and 32 landed on their sides. Estimate, to 2 decimal places, the probability of a drawing pin landing:
  a on its back   **b** on its side.

5 The letters A, B, C, D, ..., N are put in a hat.

  a Determine the probability of drawing a vowel (A, E, I, O, or U) if one of the letters is chosen at random.

  b If two letters are drawn without replacement, copy and complete the following tree diagram including all probabilities:

  c Use your tree diagram to determine the probability of drawing:

  i a vowel and a consonant   **ii** at least one vowel.

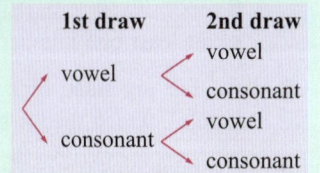

6 A farmer fences his rectangular property into 9 rectangular paddocks as shown alongside.

If a paddock is selected at random, what is the probability that it has:

  a no fences on the boundary of the property

  b one fence on the boundary of the property

  c two fences on the boundary of the property?

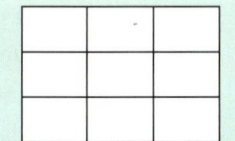

7 Bag X contains 3 black and 2 red marbles. Bag Y contains 4 black and 1 red marble. A bag is selected at random and then two marbles are selected without replacement. Determine the probability that: **a** both marbles are red   **b** two black marbles are picked from Bag Y.

8 Two dice are rolled simultaneously. Illustrate this information on a 2-dimensional grid. Determine the probability of getting:

  a two 5s   **b** at least one 4   **c** a sum greater than 9   **d** a sum of 7 or 11.

9 A class consists of 25 students. 15 have blue eyes, 9 have fair hair, and 3 have both blue eyes and fair hair. Represent this information on a Venn diagram.

Hence find the probability that a randomly selected student from the class:

  a has neither blue eyes nor fair hair   **b** has blue eyes, but not fair hair

  c has fair hair given that he or she has blue eyes

  d does not have fair hair given that he or she does not have blue eyes.

10 The two-way table alongside shows the results from asking the question "Do you like the school uniform?".

If a student is randomly selected from these year groups, estimate the probability that the student:

	Likes	Dislikes
Year 8	129	21
Year 9	108	42
Year 10	81	69

  a likes the school uniform   **b** dislikes the school uniform

  c is in year 8 and dislikes the uniform   **d** is in year 9 given the student likes the uniform

  e likes the uniform given the student is in year 10.

11 The probability of a delayed flight on a foggy day is $\frac{9}{10}$. When it is not foggy the probability of a delayed flight is $\frac{1}{12}$. The probability of a foggy day is $\frac{1}{20}$. Construct a tree diagram with this information. Hence find the probability of:

  a a foggy day and a delayed flight

  b a delayed flight

  c a flight which is not delayed.

  d Comment on your answers to **b** and **c**.

Sequences

26

Contents:

A	Number sequences	[2.12]
B	Algebraic rules for sequences	[2.12]
C	The difference method for sequences	[2.12]

Opening problem

In Henry's city, the streets are laid out in a square grid.

To get between two points A and B, Henry walks along the streets so that he is always moving North or East.

For a 2 × 1 journey,
Henry can choose between 3 different routes.

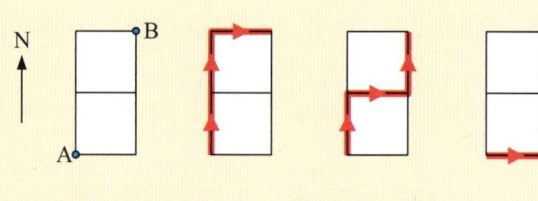

For a 2 × 2 journey,
Henry has 6 options:

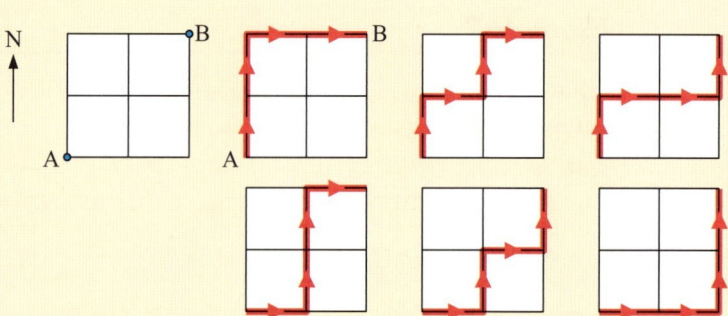

a How many different paths are there for a:
  i 2 × 3 journey **ii** 2 × 4 journey **iii** 2 × 5 journey?
b How many different paths are there for a 2 × 50 journey?
c Is there an easy way of finding the answer to **b**?

A NUMBER SEQUENCES [2.12]

A **number sequence** is a set of numbers listed in a specific order, where the numbers can be found by a specific rule.

The first term is denoted by u_1, the second by u_2, the third by u_3, and so on.

The **nth term** is written as u_n.

We often describe a number sequence in words, giving a rule which connects each term with previous terms.

For example, $15, 11, 7, 3, -1, ...$ can be described by the rule:

  Start with 15 and each term thereafter is 4 less than the previous one.

  The next two terms are $u_6 = -1 - 4 = -5$
  and $u_7 = -5 - 4 = -9$.

We say that this sequence is **linear** because each term differs from the previous one by a constant value.

Example 1   ◀) Self Tutor

Write down a rule to describe the sequence and hence find its next two terms:

  a $3, 7, 11, 15, 19, ...$ **b** $2, 6, 18, 54, ...$ **c** $0, 1, 1, 2, 3, 5, 8, ...$

  a Start with 3 and each term thereafter is 4 more than the previous term.
      $u_6 = 23$ and $u_7 = 27$.
  b Start with 2 and each term thereafter is 3 times the previous term.
      $u_5 = 54 \times 3 = 162$ and $u_6 = 162 \times 3 = 486$.
  c The first two terms are 0 and 1, and each term thereafter is the sum of the previous two terms.
      $u_8 = 5 + 8 = 13$ and $u_9 = 8 + 13 = 21$.

Example 2   ◀) Self Tutor

Draw the next two matchstick figures in these sequences and write the number of matchsticks used as a number sequence:

  a

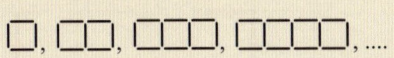

  b

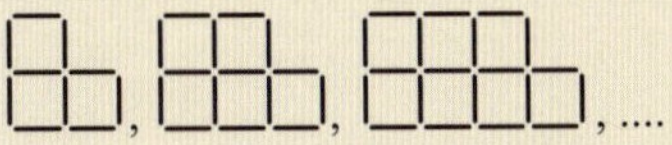

  a

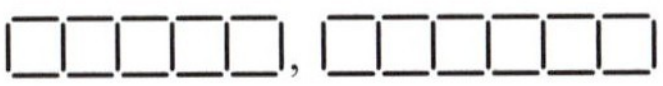

  $4, 7, 10, 13, 16, 19, ...$

  b

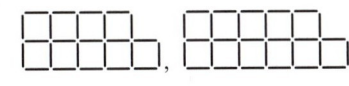

  $10, 15, 20, 25, 30, ...$

Sequences (Chapter 26)

EXERCISE 26A

1 Find the next two terms of:
 a 4, 8, 12, 16, 20, ...
 b 9, 6, 3, 0, −3, ...
 c 11, 13, 15, 17, 19, ...
 d 4, $6\frac{1}{2}$, 9, $11\frac{1}{2}$, 14, ...
 e 12, 5, −2, −9, −16, ...
 f 47, 43, 39, 35, 31, ...

2 Write down a rule to describe the sequence and hence find its next two terms:
 a 5, 8, 11, 14, 17, ...
 b 2, 9, 16, 23, 30, ...
 c 8, 19, 30, 41, 52, ...
 d 38, 34, 30, 26, 22, ...
 e 3, −2, −7, −12, −17, ...
 f $\frac{1}{2}$, 2, $3\frac{1}{2}$, 5, $6\frac{1}{2}$, ...

3 Write down a rule to describe the sequence and hence find its next two terms:
 a 3, 6, 12, 24, 48, ...
 b 1, 2, 4, 8, 16, ...
 c 2, 10, 50, 250, ...
 d 36, 18, 9, $4\frac{1}{2}$, ...
 e 162, 54, 18, 6, ...
 f 405, 135, 45, 15, ...

4 Find the next two terms of:
 a 0, 1, 4, 9, 16, ...
 b 1, 4, 9, 16, 25, ...
 c 0, 1, 8, 27, 64, ...
 d $\frac{1}{4}$, $\frac{1}{9}$, $\frac{1}{16}$, $\frac{1}{25}$, ...
 e 0, 1, 3, 6, 10, ...
 f 2, 6, 12, 20, 30, ...

5 Write down a rule to describe the sequences and hence find its next three terms:
 a 1, 1, 2, 3, 5, 8, ...
 b 1, 3, 4, 7, 11, ...
 c 2, 3, 5, 7, 11, 13, ...

6 Draw the next two matchstick figures in these sequences and write the number of matchsticks used as a number sequence:

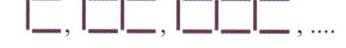

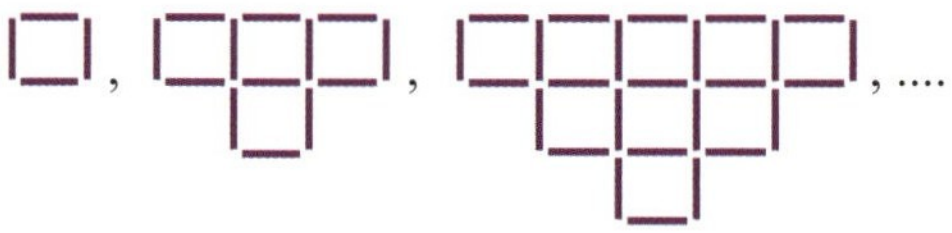

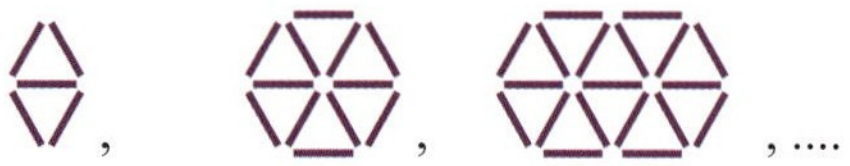

7 Draw the next two figures in these sequences and write the number of dots used as a number sequence:

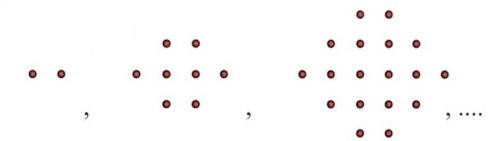

B ALGEBRAIC RULES FOR SEQUENCES   [2.12]

An alternative way to describe a sequence is to write an algebraic rule or formula for its nth term u_n.

For example: $u_n = 3n + 2$, $u_n = n^2 + n$,   or $u_n = \dfrac{1}{n}$

Since these are general formulae for all terms of their sequences, u_n is often called the **general term**.

The possible substitutions for n are: $n = 1, 2, 3, 4, 5, 6, ...$ so an algebraic rule for u_n is valid for $n \in \mathbb{Z}^+$ only.

Example 3   ◀) Self Tutor

Find the first 5 terms of the sequence with the rule:

a $u_n = 5n - 3$ **b** $u_n = n(n+2)$ **c** $u_n = 3 \times 2^n$

a $u_1 = 5(1) - 3 = 2$
$u_2 = 5(2) - 3 = 7$
$u_3 = 5(3) - 3 = 12$
$u_4 = 5(4) - 3 = 17$
$u_5 = 5(5) - 3 = 22$
The sequence is:
2, 7, 12, 17, 22, ...

b $u_1 = 1(3) = 3$
$u_2 = 2(4) = 8$
$u_3 = 3(5) = 15$
$u_4 = 4(6) = 24$
$u_5 = 5(7) = 35$
The sequence is:
3, 8, 15, 24, 35, ...

c $u_1 = 3 \times 2^1 = 6$
$u_2 = 3 \times 2^2 = 12$
$u_3 = 3 \times 2^3 = 24$
$u_4 = 3 \times 2^4 = 48$
$u_5 = 3 \times 2^5 = 96$
The sequence is:
6, 12, 24, 48, 96, ...

Discussion   *Properties of sequences*

- Consider the sequence in **Example 3** part **a**. The sequence is *linear* because each term differs from the previous one by the same constant 5.
  What part of the formula for u_n indicates this fact?
- What can be said about the formula for a linear sequence where each term differs from the previous one by: **a** 7   **b** -4?
- Consider the sequence in **Example 3** part **c**. Notice that each term is double the previous term. What part of the formula for u_n causes this?

Example 4   ◀) Self Tutor

a Find an expression for the nth term u_n of 3, 6, 9, 12, 15, ... Use the expression to find the next two terms of the sequence.

b *Hence* find a formula for the nth term of:
   i 4, 7, 10, 13, 16, ...   **ii** 1, 4, 7, 10, 13, ...   **iii** $\tfrac{1}{5}, \tfrac{1}{8}, \tfrac{1}{11}, \tfrac{1}{14}, ...$

a $u_1 = 3 \times 1$, $u_2 = 3 \times 2$, $u_3 = 3 \times 3$, $u_4 = 3 \times 4$, $u_5 = 3 \times 5$
∴ $u_n = 3 \times n = 3n$
∴ $u_6 = 3 \times 6 = 18$ and $u_7 = 3 \times 7 = 21$.

b **i** $u_1 = 3+1$, $u_2 = 6+1$, $u_3 = 9+1$, $u_4 = 12+1$, $u_5 = 15+1$

Each term is 1 more than in the sequence in **a**.

∴ the nth term is $3n + 1$

ii $u_1 = 3-2$, $u_2 = 6-2$, $u_3 = 9-2$, $u_4 = 12-2$, $u_5 = 15-2$

Each term is 2 less than in the sequence in **a**.

∴ the nth term is $3n - 2$

iii $u_1 = \dfrac{1}{3+2}$, $u_2 = \dfrac{1}{6+2}$, $u_3 = \dfrac{1}{9+2}$, $u_4 = \dfrac{1}{12+2}$, $u_5 = \dfrac{1}{15+2}$

By comparison with the sequence in **a**, the nth term is $\dfrac{1}{3n+2}$

EXERCISE 26B

1 Find the first four terms of the sequence with nth term:

   a $u_n = 2n + 3$ **b** $u_n = 2n + 5$ **c** $u_n = 3n + 2$

   d $u_n = 3n + 5$ **e** $u_n = -2n + 1$ **f** $u_n = -2n + 3$

   g $u_n = 6 - 3n$ **h** $u_n = 17 - 4n$ **i** $u_n = 76 - 7n$

2 Find the first four terms of the sequence with nth term:

   a $u_n = n^2 + 1$ **b** $u_n = n^2 - 1$ **c** $u_n = n^2 + n$

   d $u_n = n(n+2)$ **e** $u_n = n^3 + 1$ **f** $u_n = n^3 + 2n^2 - 1$

3 **a** Find a formula for the nth term of the sequence: 2, 4, 6, 8, 10, 12, ...

   b *Hence* find a formula for the nth term of:

      i 4, 6, 8, 10, 12, 14, ...   **ii** 1, 3, 5, 7, 9, ...

4 **a** Find a formula for the nth term of: 5, 10, 15, 20, 25, ...

   b *Hence* find a formula for the nth term of:

      i 6, 11, 16, 21, 26, ...   **ii** 3, 8, 13, 18, 23, ...

5 Find a formula for the nth term of:

   a 2, 5, 8, 11, 14, ...   **b** 17, 19, 21, 23, 25, ...   **c** 30, 25, 20, 15, 10, ...

   d 7, 5, 3, 1, −1, ...   **e** −7, −3, 1, 5, 9, ...   **f** −1, −4, −7, −10, −13, ...

6 **a** Find a formula for the nth term of: 2, 4, 8, 16, 32, ...

   b *Hence* find a formula for the nth term of: 6, 12, 24, 48, 96, ...

7 **a** Find a formula for the nth term of: 1, 2, 3, 4, 5, 6, ...

   b *Hence* find a formula for the nth term of:

      i 2, 3, 4, 5, 6, 7, ...   **ii** 3, 4, 5, 6, 7, 8, ...

      iii $\frac{1}{1}, \frac{1}{2}, \frac{1}{3}, \frac{1}{4}, \frac{1}{5}$, ...   **iv** $\frac{1}{2}, \frac{1}{3}, \frac{1}{4}, \frac{1}{5}, \frac{1}{6}$, ...

      v $\frac{1}{2}, \frac{2}{3}, \frac{3}{4}, \frac{4}{5}, \frac{5}{6}$, ...   **vi** $\frac{3}{1}, \frac{4}{2}, \frac{5}{3}, \frac{6}{4}, \frac{7}{5}, \frac{8}{6}$, ...

      vii $1 \times 2, 2 \times 3, 3 \times 4, 4 \times 5$, ...   **viii** $2 \times 3, 3 \times 4, 4 \times 5, 5 \times 6$, ...

      ix $1 \times 3, 2 \times 4, 3 \times 5, 4 \times 6$, ...

8 **a** Find a formula for the nth term of: 1, 4, 9, 16, 25, ...

   b *Hence* find a formula for the nth term of:

      i 4, 9, 16, 25, 36, ...   **ii** 0, 3, 8, 15, 24, ...   **iii** $\frac{1}{1}, \frac{1}{4}, \frac{1}{9}, \frac{1}{16}, \frac{1}{25}$, ...

9 Find a formula for the nth term of:
   a 1, 8, 27, 64, 125, ...
   b 0, 7, 26, 63, 124, ...
   c 3, 6, 12, 24, 48, ...
   d 24, 12, 6, 3, $1\frac{1}{2}$, ...

C THE DIFFERENCE METHOD FOR SEQUENCES [2.12]

We have seen that a **linear** sequence is one in which each term differs from the previous term by the same constant. The general term will have the form $u_n = an + b$ where a and b are constants. You should notice how this form compares with that of a linear function.

Another common type of sequence is a **quadratic** sequence, which has nth term $u_n = an^2 + bn + c$, where a, b, and c are constants.

For example, $u_n = 2n^2 - 7n + 3$ is a quadratic sequence.

Its first few terms are:
$$u_1 = 2 \times 1^2 - 7 \times 1 + 3 = -2$$
$$u_2 = 2 \times 2^2 - 7 \times 2 + 3 = -3$$
$$u_3 = 2 \times 3^2 - 7 \times 3 + 3 = 0$$
$$u_4 = 2 \times 4^2 - 7 \times 4 + 3 = 7$$

So, $2n^2 - 7n + 3$ describes the sequence $-2, -3, 0, 7, ...$

In order to find the formula for one of these sequences, we use a technique called the **difference method**.

Discovery   The difference method

Part 1: Linear sequences

Consider the linear sequence $u_n = 3n + 2$ where $u_1 = 5$, $u_2 = 8$, $u_3 = 11$, $u_4 = 14$, and $u_5 = 17$.

We construct a **difference table** to display the sequence, and include a row for the **first difference** $\Delta 1$. This is the difference between successive terms of the sequence.

The symbol Δ is the Greek letter 'delta'. It often means 'difference'.

n	1	2	3	4	5
u_n	5	8	11	14	17
$\Delta 1$		3	3	3	3

What to do:

1 Construct a difference table for the sequence defined by:
   a $u_n = 4n + 3$
   b $u_n = -3n + 7$

2 Copy and complete:
   For the linear sequence $u_n = an + b$ the values of $\Delta 1$ are ....

3 Copy and complete the difference table for the general linear sequence $u_n = an + b$:

n	1	2	3	4	5
u_n	$(a+b)$	$2a+b$	$3a+b$	☐	☐
$\Delta 1$		a	☐	☐	☐

$(2a+b) - (a+b) = a$

4 The circled elements of the difference table in **3** can be used to find the formula for u_n.
For example, in the original example above, $a = 3$ and $a + b = 5$.
$\therefore\ a = 3$, $b = 2$, and hence $u_n = 3n + 2$.
Use the difference method to find $u_n = an + b$ for the sequence:

a 4, 11, 18, 25, 32, 39, ...
b 41, 37, 33, 29, 25, 21, ...

Part 2: Quadratic sequences

Now consider the quadratic sequence defined by $u_n = 2n^2 - n + 3$.

Its terms are: $u_1 = 4$, $u_2 = 9$, $u_3 = 18$, $u_4 = 31$, $u_5 = 48$, $u_6 = 69$.

We again construct a difference table, and this time we include another row for the **second difference** $\Delta 2$. This is the difference between the terms of the first difference.

n	1	2	3	4	5	6
u_n	4	9	18	31	48	69
$\Delta 1$		5	9	13	17	21
$\Delta 2$			4	4	4	4

Notice that although $\Delta 1$ is not constant, $\Delta 2$ is constant.

What to do:

5 Construct a difference table for the quadratic sequence defined by:

a $u_n = n^2 + 2n + 3$ **b** $u_n = -n^2 + 5n + 4$ **c** $u_n = 3n^2 - 8n + 1$

6 Copy and complete:
For the quadratic sequence $u_n = an^2 + bn + c$, the values of $\Delta 2$ are ....

7 Copy and complete the difference table for the general quadratic sequence $u_n = an^2 + bn + c$:

n	1	2	3	4	5	6
u_n	$(a+b+c)$	$4a+2b+c$	$9a+3b+c$	☐	☐	☐
$\Delta 1$		$(3a+b)$	$5a+b$	☐	☐	☐
$\Delta 2$			$(2a)$	☐	☐	☐

$(4a+2b+c) - (a+b+c) = 3a+b$ $(5a+b) - (3a+b) = 2a$

8 Describe how the circled elements in **7** can be used to find the formula for u_n.

9 Use the difference method to find $u_n = an^2 + bn + c$ for the sequence:

a 2, 0, 0, 2, 6, ... **b** -5, 4, 19, 40, 67, ...

You should have discovered that:

- For the **linear sequence** $u_n = an + b$, the **first differences** are constant and equal to a.
  The general difference table is:

n	1	2	3	4	5
u_n	$a+b$	$2a+b$	$3a+b$	$4a+b$	$5a+b$
$\Delta 1$	a	a	a	a	

  We use $\Delta 1$ to find a, and the first term of u_n to find b.

- For the **quadratic sequence** $u_n = an^2 + bn + c$, the **second differences** are constant and equal to $2a$.
  The general difference table is:

n	1	2	3	4
u_n	$a+b+c$	$4a+2b+c$	$9a+3b+c$	$16a+4b+c$
$\Delta 1$	$3a+b$	$5a+b$	$7a+b$	
$\Delta 2$		$2a$	$2a$	

  We use the circled terms to find a, b and c.

This means we can determine if a sequence is linear or quadratic by constructing a difference table and seeing which row gives constant differences.

> You should not memorise these tables but learn to quickly generate them when you need.

Example 5 ◀) Self Tutor

Find a formula for the nth term of: 6, 13, 20, 27, 34, 41, ...

The difference table is:

n	1	2	3	4	5	6
u_n	6	13	20	27	34	41
$\Delta 1$	7	7	7	7	7	

The $\Delta 1$ values are constant, so the sequence is linear.

$$u_n = an + b \text{ with } a = 7 \text{ and } a + b = 6$$
$$\therefore 7 + b = 6$$
$$\therefore b = -1$$

$\therefore$ the nth term is $u_n = 7n - 1$

Sequences (Chapter 26) 485

Example 6   ◀) Self Tutor

Examine the dot sequence:

○ ,   ○ ○ ,   ○ ○ ○ ,   ○ ○ ○ ○ ,   ○ ○ ○ ○ ○ , ...

a How many dots are in the next *two* figures?
b Find a formula for u_n, the number of dots in the nth figure.

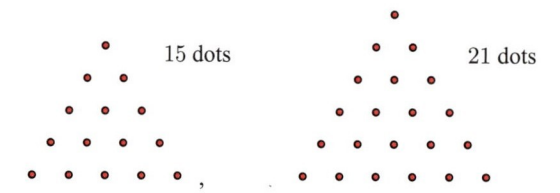

a   15 dots   21 dots

b $u_1 = 1$, $u_2 = 3$, $u_3 = 6$, $u_4 = 10$, $u_5 = 15$, $u_6 = 21$

The difference table is:

n	1	2	3	4	5	6
u_n	1	3	6	10	15	21
$\Delta 1$		2	3	4	5	6
$\Delta 2$			1	1	1	1

The $\Delta 2$ values are constant, so the sequence is quadratic with general term $u_n = an^2 + bn + c$.

$2a = 1$, so $a = \frac{1}{2}$

$3a + b = 2$, so $\frac{3}{2} + b = 2$ and $\therefore b = \frac{1}{2}$

$a + b + c = 1$, so $\frac{1}{2} + \frac{1}{2} + c = 1$ and $\therefore c = 0$

$\therefore$ the nth term is $u_n = \frac{1}{2}n^2 + \frac{1}{2}n$

EXERCISE 26C

1 Use the method of differences to find the nth term of:
  a 1, 5, 9, 13, 17, 21, ...
  b 17, 14, 11, 8, 5, 2, ...
  c 2, 6, 12, 20, 30, 42, ...
  d 0, 6, 14, 24, 36, 50, ...

2 Consider the sequence: 2, 12, 30, 56, 90, 132, ...
  a Use the difference method to find the nth term.
  b Suggest an alternative formula for u_n by considering $u_1 = 1 \times 2$, $u_2 = ... \times ....$, $u_3 = ... \times ....$, and so on.

3 Consider the dot pattern:
  a Find u_n for $n = 1, 2, 3, 4, 5, 6$, and 7.
  b Find a formula for the nth term.
  c How many dots are needed to make up the 30th figure in the pattern?

4 These diagrams represent the hand-shakes between one person (A), two people (A and B), three people (A, B, and C), four people (A, B, C, and D), and so on.

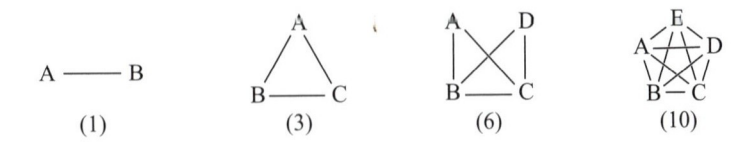

a Draw diagrams showing hand-shakes for 6, 7, and 8 people.

b When you are sure that you have counted them correctly, find the formula for the nth term of the sequence 0, 1, 3, 6, 10, ...

c 179 delegates attend a conference. If every person shakes hands with every other person, how many hand-shakes take place?

5 Consider the matchstick pattern:

a Find u_n for $n = 1, 2, 3, 4, 5$, and 6.

b Find a formula for the nth term.

c How many matchsticks are needed to make up the 50th figure in the pattern?

6 Consider the sequence u_n where:
$u_1 = 1 \times 1$
$u_2 = 2 \times 3$
$u_3 = 3 \times 5$
$u_4 = 4 \times 7$
$u_5 = 5 \times 9$ and so on.

a Find the values of the first 8 terms.

b Use the difference method to find a formula for u_n.

c Hence, find the value of u_{50}.

7 Answer the questions in the **Opening Problem** on page **477**.

Review set 26A

1 Write down a rule for the sequence and find its next two terms:
  a 6, 10, 14, 18, 22, ...
  b 250, 220, 190, 160, ...
  c 1, 4, 9, 16, 25, ...

2 Draw the next *two* matchstick figures in the pattern and write down the number of matchsticks used as a number sequence:

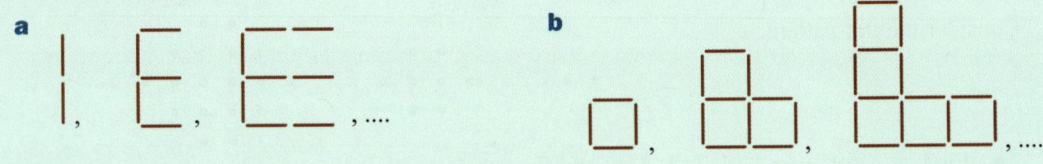

a

b

3 Find the first four terms of the sequence with nth term:
  a $u_n = 6n - 1$
  b $u_n = n^2 + 5n - 2$

Sequences (Chapter 26)

4 **a** Find a formula for the nth term of the sequence: 4, 8, 12, 16, ...

   b *Hence* find u_n for:

   i 1, 5, 9, 13, ...   **ii** $\frac{1}{3}, \frac{1}{7}, \frac{1}{11}, \frac{1}{15}, ...$

   c Find the 20th term for each of the sequences in **b**.

5 List the first four terms of the sequence defined by:

   a $u_n = 2 \times 3^n$ **b** $u_n = 5 \times (-2)^{n-1}$

6 Use the method of differences to find the nth term of:

   a 5, 12, 19, 26, 33, ...   **b** -1, 6, 15, 26, 39, 54, ...

7 Consider the figures:

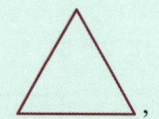

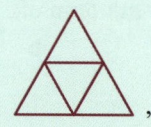

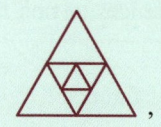

Suppose u_n is the number of triangles in the nth figure, so $u_1 = 1$ and $u_2 = 5$ (4 small triangles and 1 large triangle).

   a Find u_n for $n = 3, 4, 5$.

   b Use the method of differences to find a formula for u_n.

   c How many triangles are in the 50th figure?

8 Sarah has baked a cake, and wishes to divide it into pieces using straight line cuts.

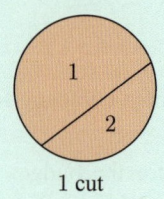

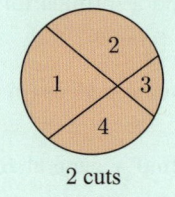

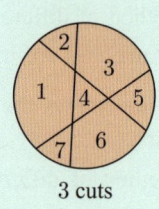

1 cut   2 cuts   3 cuts

Suppose u_n is the maximum number of pieces which can be made from n cuts, so $u_1 = 2$, $u_2 = 4$, $u_3 = 7$.

   a Find u_n for $n = 4$ and 5.

   b Use the method of differences to find a formula for u_n.

   c If Sarah makes 10 cuts, what is the maximum number of pieces she can make?

Review set 26B

1 Write down a rule for the sequence and find its next two terms:

   a 17, 12, 7, 2, ...   **b** 2, 4, 8, 16, ...   **c** $-5, -3, -1, 1, ...$

2 Draw the next *two* figures and write down the number of dots used as a number sequence:

   a   **b**

3 Find the first four terms of the sequence with nth term:

   a $u_n = -4n + 5$ **b** $u_n = (n+2)(n-1)$

4 **a** Find a formula for the nth term of the sequence: 6, 12, 18, 24, ...

   b *Hence* find u_n for:

     i 10, 16, 22, 28, ...   **ii** $\frac{5}{7}, \frac{11}{13}, \frac{17}{19}, \frac{23}{25}, ...$

   c Find the 15th term for each of the sequences in **b**.

5 List the first *four* terms of the sequence defined by:

   a $u_n = 48 \times \left(\frac{1}{4}\right)^n$ **b** $u_n = n^3 - 4n$

6 Use the method of differences to find the nth term of:

   a 43, 34, 25, 16, 7, ...   **b** 4, 12, 22, 34, 48, ...

7 Consider the sequence of figures:

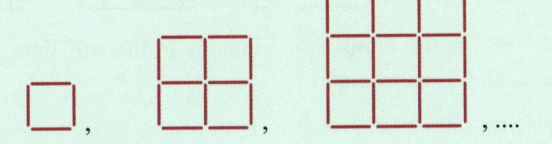

Suppose u_n is the number of matchsticks required to make the nth figure, so $u_1 = 4$ and $u_2 = 12$.

   a Find u_n for $n = 3, 4, 5, 6$.

   b Use the method of differences to find a formula for u_n.

   c How many matches are in the 10th figure?

8 The table alongside shows the photocopying budget (in euros) of a company for the last five years.

   a Use the method of differences to find a general formula for the budget in year n.

   b Predict the photocopying budget in year 10.

n	u_n
1	2356
2	2533
3	2710
4	2887
5	3064

Circle geometry

27

Contents:

A Circle theorems [4.7]
B Miscellaneous right angle problems
[4.6, 4.7, 8.7]

Opening problem

While driving along a straight highway, a car receives radio signal along a 30 km stretch. The radio tower nearby transmits signal for a radius of 18 km. How far is the tower from the road?

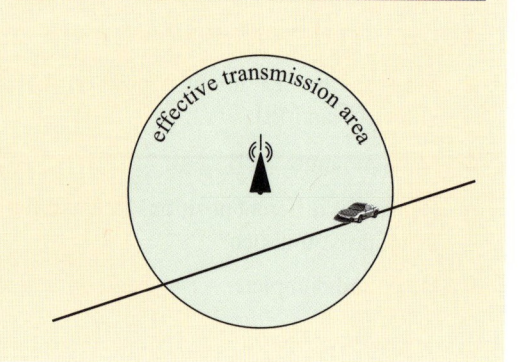

A CIRCLE THEOREMS [4.7]

Before we can talk about the properties and theorems of circles, we need to learn the appropriate language for describing them.

- A **circle** is the set of all points which are equidistant from a fixed point called the **centre**.

- The **circumference** is the distance around the entire circle boundary.

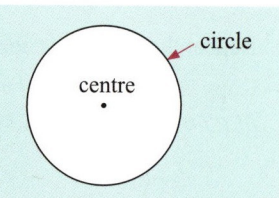

- An **arc** of a circle is any continuous part of the circle.

- A **chord** of a circle is a line segment joining any two points on the circle.

- A **semi-circle** is a half of a circle.

- A **diameter** of a circle is any chord passing through its centre.

- A **radius** of a circle is any line segment joining its centre to any point on the circle.

- A **tangent** to a circle is any line which touches the circle in exactly one point.

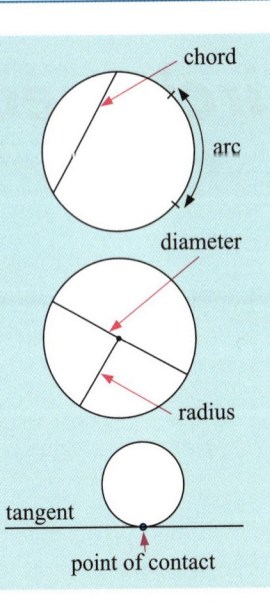

Discovery — Properties of circles

This discovery is best attempted using the **computer package** on the CD.

However, you can also use a compass, ruler and protractor.

Part 1: The angle in a semi-circle

What to do:

1. Draw a circle and construct a diameter. Label it as shown.
2. Mark any point P not at A or B on the circle. Draw AP and PB.
3. Measure angle APB.
4. Repeat for different positions of P and for different circles. What do you notice?
5. Copy and complete: *The angle in a semi-circle is ......*

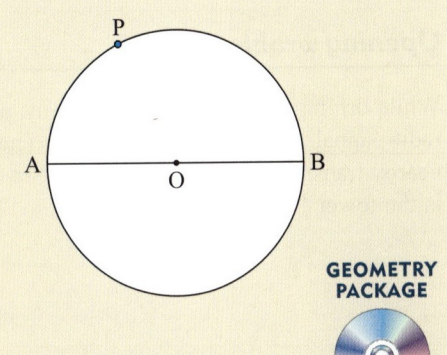

Part 2: Chords of a circle theorem

What to do:

1. Draw a circle with centre C. Construct any chord AB.
2. Construct the perpendicular from C to AB which cuts the chord at M.
3. Measure the lengths of AM and BM. What do you notice?
4. Repeat the procedure above with another circle and chord.
5. Copy and complete: *The perpendicular from the centre of a circle to a chord ......*

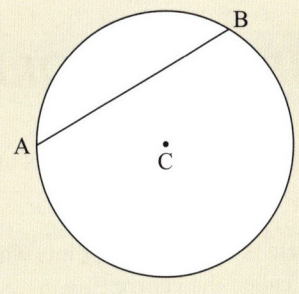

Circle geometry (Chapter 27)

Part 3: Radius-tangent theorem

What to do:

1. Use a compass to draw a circle with centre O, and mark on it a point A.

2. Draw at A, as accurately as possible, a tangent TA.

3. Draw the radius OA.

4. Measure the angle OAT with a protractor.

5. Repeat the procedure above with another circle and tangent.

6. Copy and complete: *The tangent to a circle is ...... to the radius at the point ......*

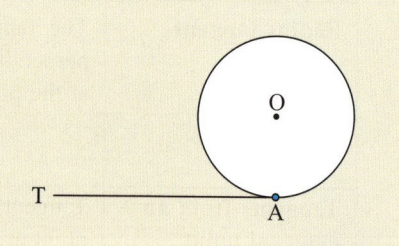

Part 4: Tangents from an external point

What to do:

1. Use your compass to draw a circle, centre O.

2. From an external point P draw the two tangents to the circle to meet it at A and B.

3. Measure AP and BP.

4. Repeat with another circle of different size.

5. Copy and complete:
   Tangents from an external point to a circle are ......

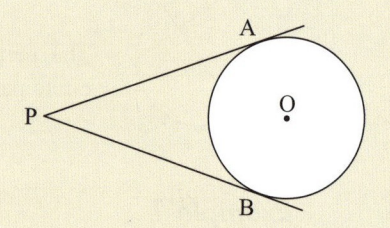

You should have discovered the following **circle theorems**:

Name of theorem	Statement	Diagram
Angle in a semi-circle	The angle in a semi-circle is a right angle.	$A\hat{B}C = 90°$
Chords of a circle	The perpendicular from the centre of a circle to a chord bisects the chord.	$AM = BM$

Name of theorem	Statement	Diagram
Radius-tangent	The tangent to a circle is perpendicular to the radius at the point of contact.	$\widehat{OAT} = 90°$ 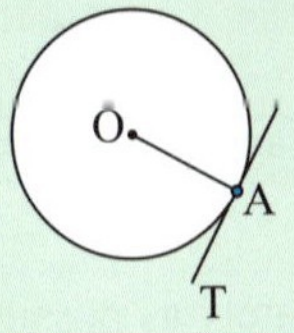
Tangents from an external point	Tangents from an external point are equal in length.	$AP = BP$ 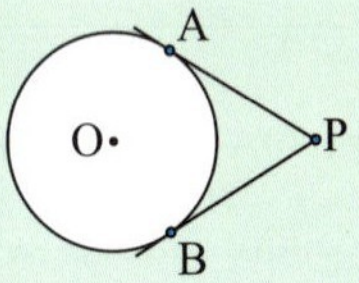

Two useful **converses** are:

- If line segment AB subtends a right angle at C then the circle through A, B and C has diameter AB.

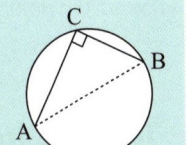

- The perpendicular bisector of a chord of a circle passes through its centre.

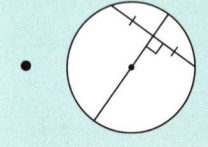

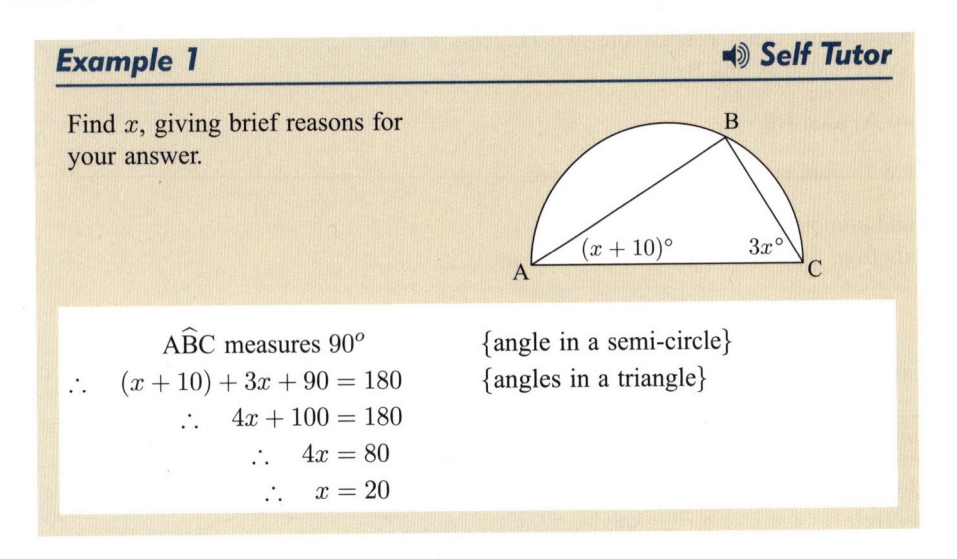

Example 1

Find x, giving brief reasons for your answer.

$\widehat{ABC}$ measures $90°$ {angle in a semi-circle}
$\therefore \ (x + 10) + 3x + 90 = 180$ {angles in a triangle}
$\therefore \ 4x + 100 = 180$
$\therefore \ 4x = 80$
$\therefore \ x = 20$

EXERCISE 27A

1 Find the value of any unknowns, giving brief reasons for your answers:

a $53°$, $x°$

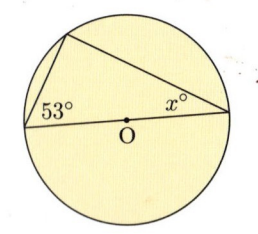

b $x°$, $(2x)°$

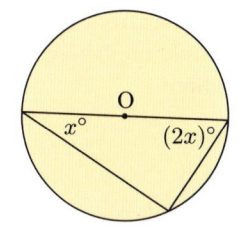

c $(2x)°$, $(3x)°$

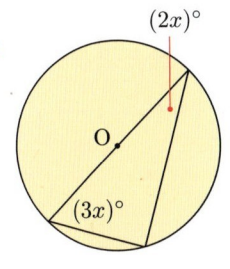

Circle geometry (Chapter 27)

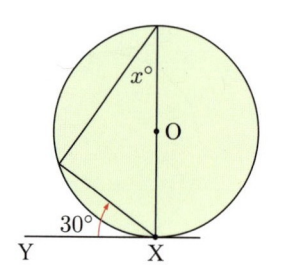

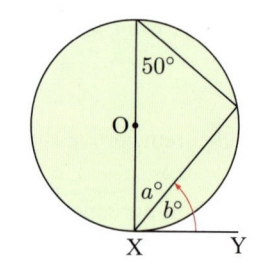

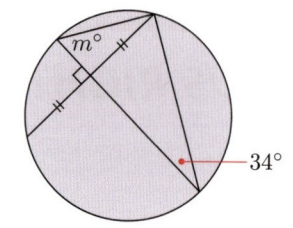

d (circle with $x°$ at center, $30°$ at Y, tangent at X)

e ($50°$ at top, $a°$ and $b°$ at X, tangent XY)

f ($40°$ and $30°$ at O, $a°$ and $b°$ at tangent point)

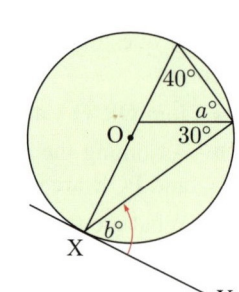

g 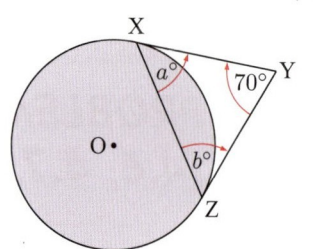 XY and YZ are tangents from point Y ($a°$ at X, $70°$ at Y, $b°$ at Z)

h ($m°$, $34°$, chord bisector)

i ($n°$ at O, $82°$ at A, tangents from A and C)

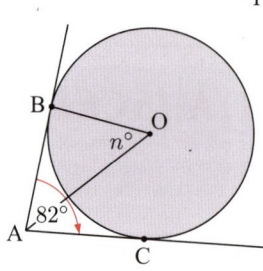

2 A circle is drawn and four tangents to it are constructed as shown below.

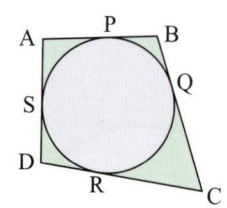

Deduce that $AB + CD = BC + AD$.

3 Find the radius of the circle which touches the three sides of the triangle as shown. (3 cm, 4 cm)

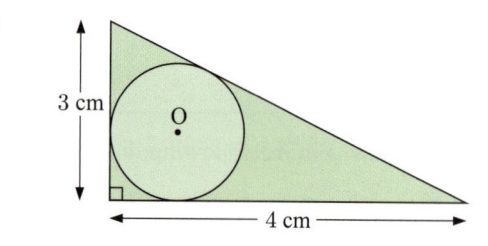

4 A circle is inscribed in a right angled triangle. The radius of the circle is 3 cm, and BC has length 8 cm. Find the perimeter of the triangle ABC.

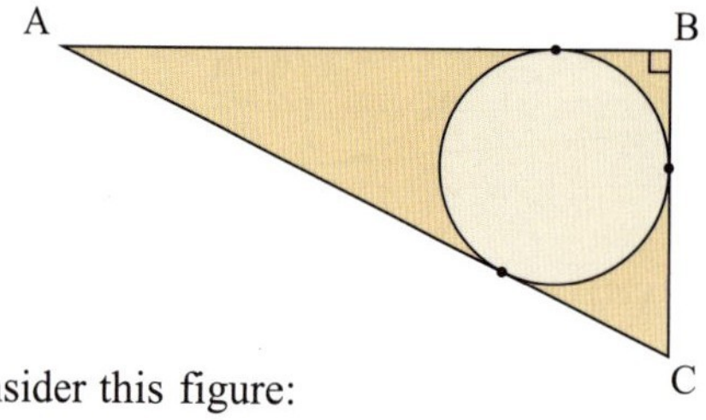

5 Consider this figure:

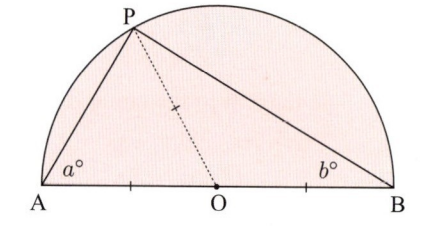

a What can be deduced about:

  i $A\widehat{P}O$ **ii** $B\widehat{P}O$?

b Using $\triangle APB$, explain why $2a + 2b = 180$ and hence that $a + b = 90$.

c What theorem have you proven?

6 In this question we prove the *chords of a circle* theorem.

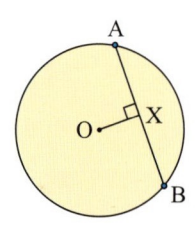

a For the given figure join OA and OB and classify $\triangle OAB$.

b Apply the isosceles triangle theorem to triangle OAB. What geometrical facts result?

7 In this question we prove the *tangents from an external point* theorem.

  a Join OP, OA and OB.

  b Assuming the *tangent-radius* theorem, prove that $\triangle$s POA and POB are congruent.

  c What are the consequences of the congruence in **b**?

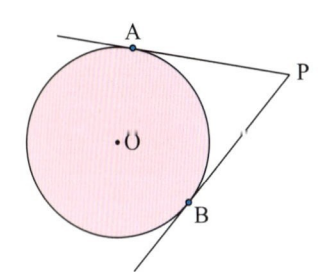

B MISCELLANEOUS RIGHT ANGLE PROBLEMS [4.6, 4.7, 8.7]

In this course, we have examined a number of properties of right angled triangles. Pythagoras' theorem and trigonometry can both be applied to the right angles that appear in circle problems. This section presents questions that combine these topics. Think carefully about where the important right angles are, and which rules you should be using.

Example 2   ◀) Self Tutor

Find the unknowns in the following diagrams:

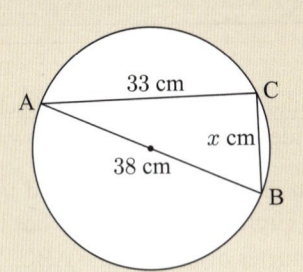

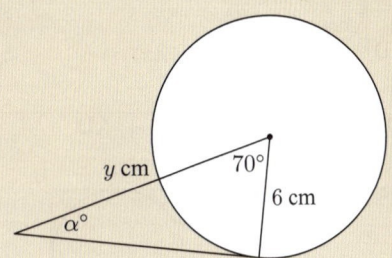

a   (circle with A, C, B; AC = 33 cm, AB = 38 cm, CB = x cm)

b   (circle of radius 6 cm, tangent forming external angle $\alpha°$, y cm hypotenuse, 70° at centre)

a The triangle is right angled at C   {angle in a semi-circle}
$$\therefore \ 33^2 + x^2 = 38^2 \quad \text{\{Pythagoras\}}$$
$$\therefore \ x = \sqrt{38^2 - 33^2} \quad \text{\{as } x > 0\text{\}}$$
$$\therefore \ x \approx 18.8$$

b The tangent to the circle forms a right angle at the point of contact.
$$\therefore \ \alpha + 70 + 90 = 180 \quad \text{\{angles in a } \triangle\text{\}}$$
$$\therefore \ \alpha = 20$$
$$\cos 70° = \frac{6}{y} \quad \left\{\cos\theta = \frac{\text{ADJ}}{\text{HYP}}\right\}$$
$$\therefore \ y = \frac{6}{\cos 70°}$$
$$\therefore \ y \approx 17.5$$

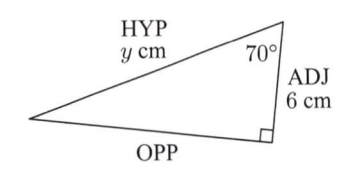

(right triangle: HYP = y cm, ADJ = 6 cm, 70° angle, OPP opposite)

Circle geometry (Chapter 27)

EXERCISE 27B

1 Find the unknowns:

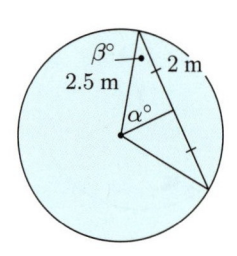

a x mm, 19 mm, 47 mm

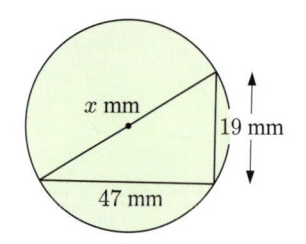

b 8 cm, 25°, y cm, z cm

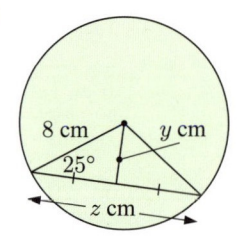

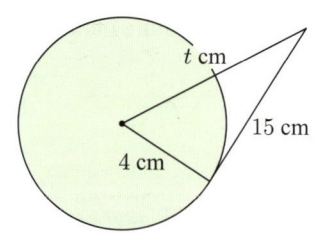

c t cm, 4 cm, 15 cm

d $\beta°$, 2.5 m, 2 m, $\alpha°$

e e km, f km, 75°, 3 km, d km

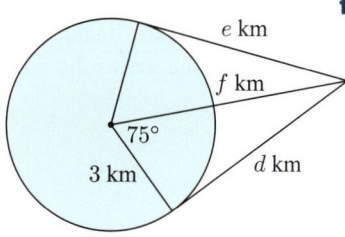

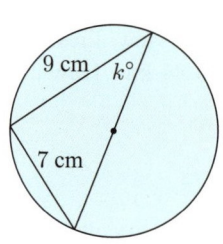

f 9 cm, $k°$, 7 cm

g 31 mm, b mm, 140°

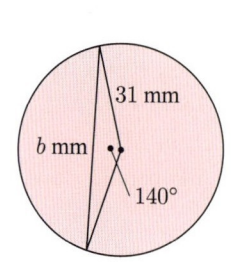

h 33°, d cm, c cm, 14 cm

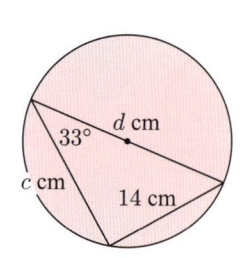

i 17°, 11 cm, x cm

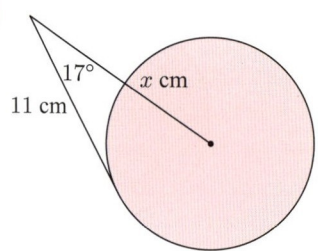

2 Find the length of the diameter of each of these circles:

a 9 cm, 15 cm

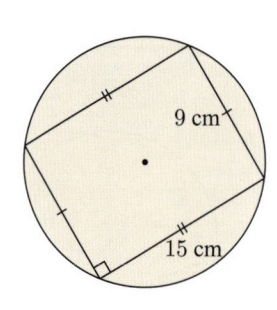

b 7 cm

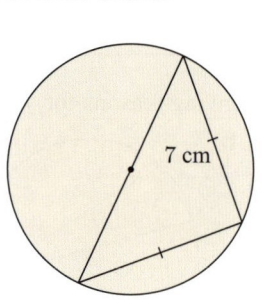

c 36°, 28 cm

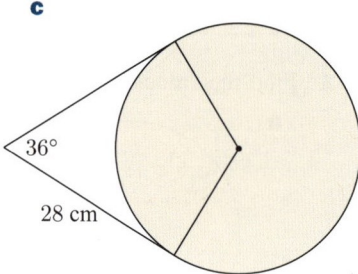

3

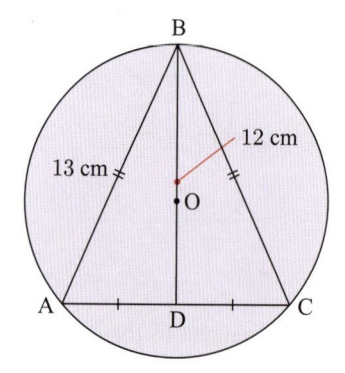

Circle with points A, B, C on the circumference, D on AC, and centre O. BD = 12 cm, AB = 13 cm.

The circle shown has centre O.

a Explain why $B\hat{D}A$ is a right angle.
b Evaluate the length AD.
c Calculate the size of angle ABD.
d Join OA, and state the size of $O\hat{A}B$.
e Find the measure of angle OAD.
f Find the length of the radius of this circle.
g Describe a quicker way of finding the radius.

4 The circles alongside pass through each other's centre. The chord AB is 10 cm long.

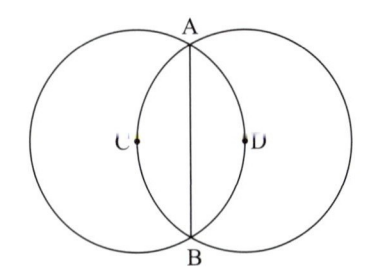

  a Explain why $\widehat{ACD} = 60°$.
  b Find the radius of the circles.

5 Can a wooden plank with rectangular cross section $20 \text{ mm} \times 107 \text{ mm}$ be cut from a circular log of radius 5.5 cm?

6 A radar operates with a 50 km radius. An aeroplane enters its field of view, flies in a straight line, and exits again, having flown 84 km. How close did the aeroplane get to the radar?

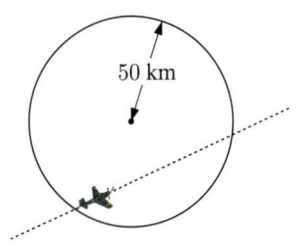

7 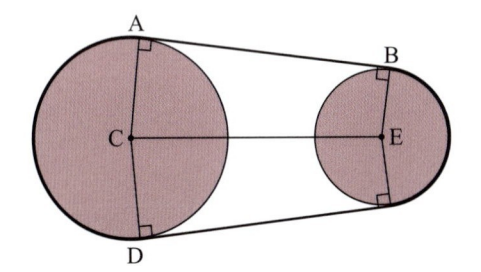 A chain goes around two sprockets as shown. The centres of the sprockets are 45 cm apart. The larger sprocket has radius 12 cm, and the smaller has radius 4 cm. Find:

  a the length of chain AB
  Hint: Draw EF parallel to AB meeting AC at F.
  b reflex angle ACD
  c the total length of chain required.

Review set 27A

1 Find the values of any unknowns, giving reasons for your answers.

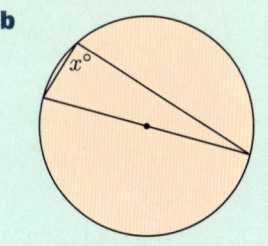

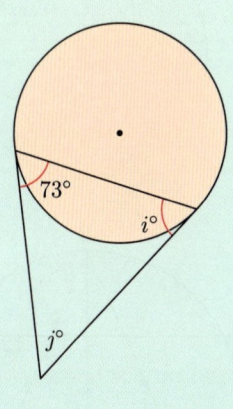

  a $30°$, $a°$
  b $x°$
  c $73°$, $i°$
  d $28°$, $a°$
  e $40°$, $a°$, $b°$, $c°$ — DE is a tangent to the circle.
  $j°$

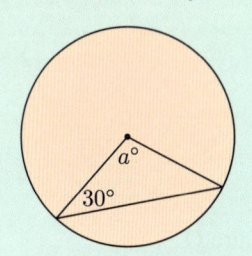

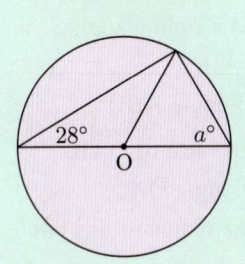

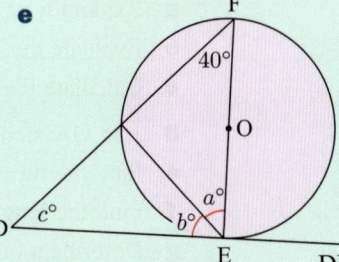

Circle geometry (Chapter 27)

2 Copy and complete:
Triangle OAC is isosceles {as AO = ...}
∴ A$\hat{C}$O = ... {.....}
Likewise, triangle BOC is .....
∴ B$\hat{C}$O = ... {.....}
Thus the angles of triangle ABC measure $a°$, $b°$ and .....
∴ $2a + 2b$ = ... {.....}
∴ $a + b$ = ...
and so A$\hat{C}$B = ...

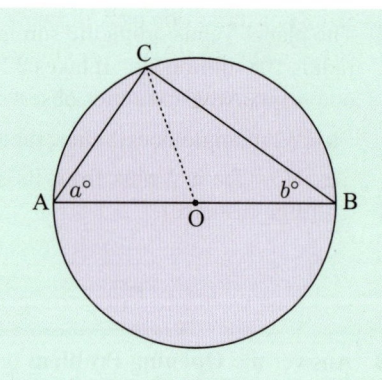

3

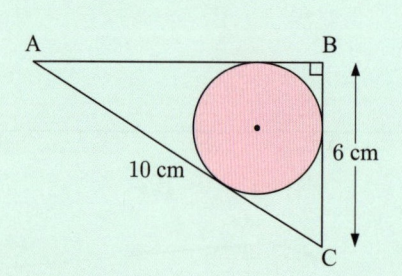

Find:
 a the length of side AB
 b the length of the radius of the circle.

4 AB and CM are common tangents to two circles. Show that:
 a M is the midpoint of AB
 b A$\hat{C}$B is a right angle.

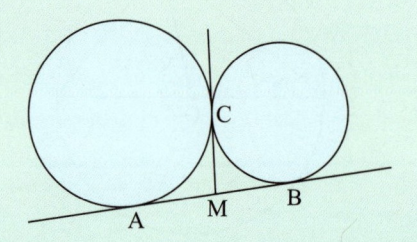

5 Find the value of x:
 a 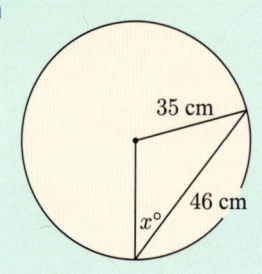
 b 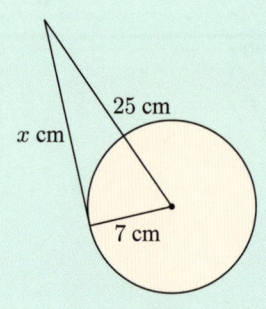
 c

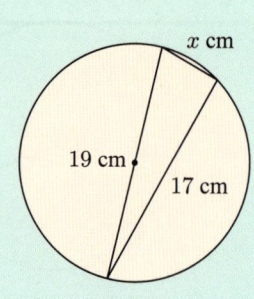

6

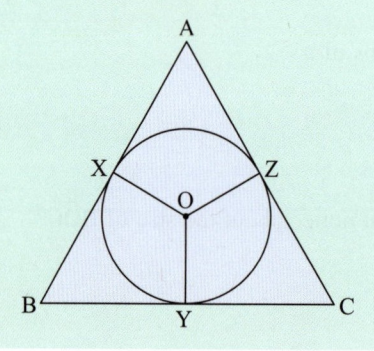

Triangle ABC is an equilateral triangle, with sides of length $2\sqrt{3}$ cm. A circle is inscribed within the triangle as shown.
Find the radius of the circle.

7 The planet Venus orbits the sun in a near-circular orbit of radius 108 million km. It takes 225 earth days to complete one orbit. An astronomer observes Venus for 40 days.

  a What angle does Venus subtend in the 40 days?
  b How far is Venus from its starting point? (straight line distance)

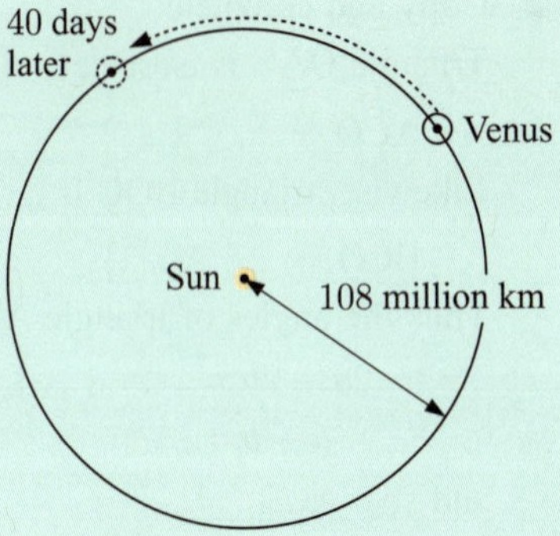

8 Answer the **Opening Problem** on page **489**.

Review set 27B

1 Find the values of the unknowns. State your reasoning.

  a [circle with centre O, diameter drawn, angle 48° at one end, $x°$ at the other]

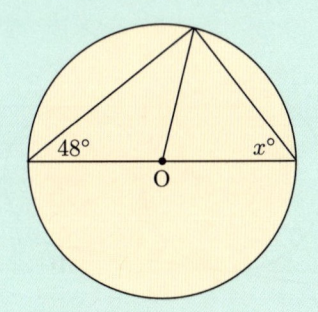

  b [circle with centre O, angle 140° at O; XZ and YZ are tangents from point Z, angle $x°$ at Z]

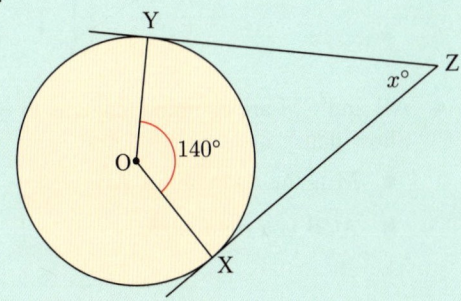

  XZ and YZ are tangents from point Z.

  c [circle with centre O, tangent at A, T outside, angle 20° at T, angle $x°$ at O between OA and OC]

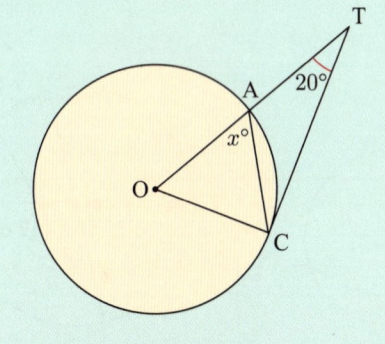

  d [circle with centre O (diameter), angles $6x°$, $y°$, and $2x°$ marked in triangle]

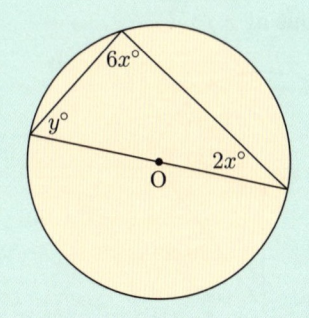

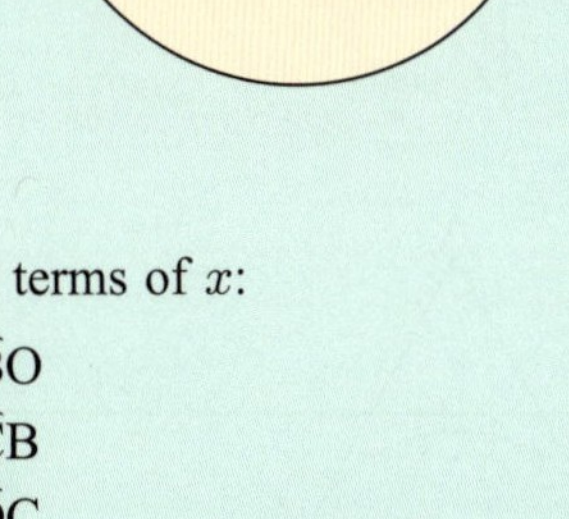

2 Consider the following figure:

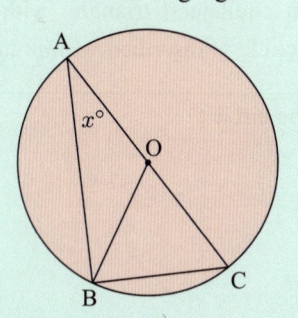

  [circle with centre O, triangle ABC inscribed, angle $x°$ at A, radii OA, OB, OC drawn]

  a Find, in terms of x:
   i $\widehat{ABO}$
   ii $\widehat{ACB}$
   iii $\widehat{BOC}$.

  b What do you notice about the size of $\widehat{BOC}$?

Circle geometry (Chapter 27)

3 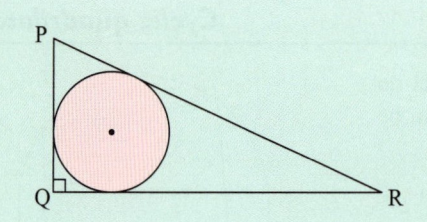 The circle inscribed in triangle PQR has radius of length 3 cm.
PQ has length 7 cm.
Find the perimeter of triangle PQR.

4 In triangle PQR, PQ = PR. A circle is drawn with diameter PQ, and the circle cuts QR at S.
Show that S is the midpoint of QR.

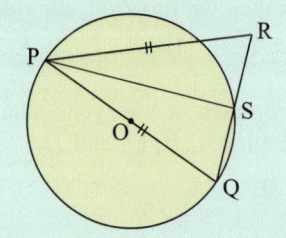

5 Find any unknowns:

a 40 m, 9 m, $b°$, a m

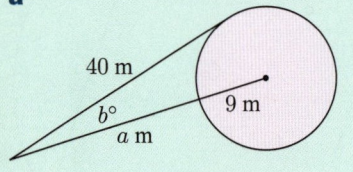

b 14 cm, 25°, c cm

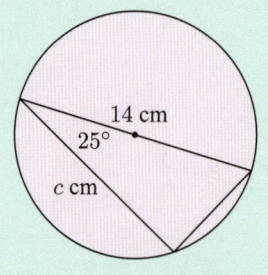

c r mm, 84 mm, 100°

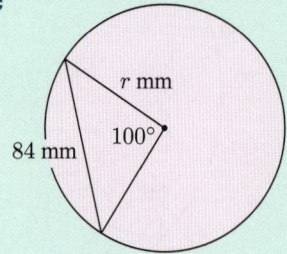

6 A circle with centre O has tangents at A and B meeting at external point P. The circle has radius 5 m. AB has length 6 m. Find OP.

7 An undersea earthquake had 'moderate' effect for a radius of 20 km. Along a straight stretch of coastline, an area 35 km long felt a moderate effect. How far offshore was the earthquake's epicentre?

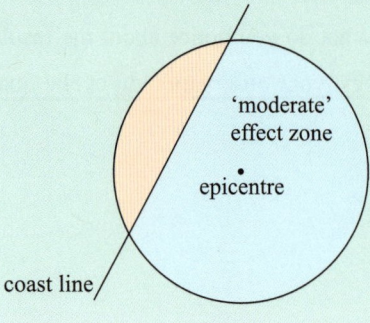

Activity

Cyclic quadrilaterals

We can always draw a circle through any three points that do not lie in a straight line. However, a circle may or may not be drawn through any four points in a plane.

If we can draw a circle through four points, we say that the points are **concyclic**. If we join each point to the adjacent points then we form a **cyclic quadrilateral**.

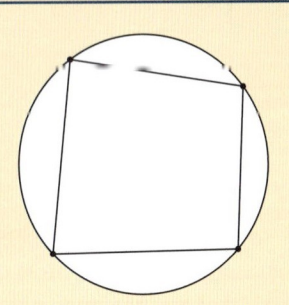

1 For each of the cyclic quadrilaterals below, measure the angles A, B, C, and D.

a

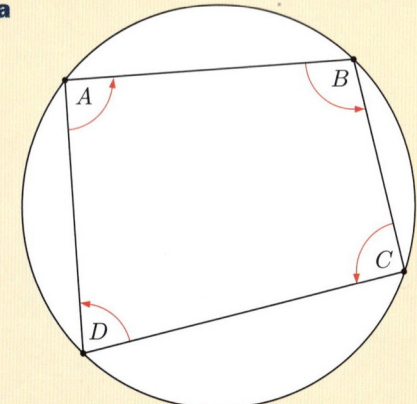

b

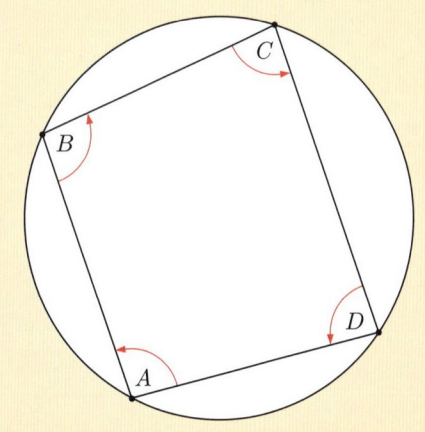

2 For each case in **1**, find the sums $A + C$ and $B + D$.

3 What do you notice about the results in **2**?

4 Test your observation on cyclic quadrilaterals of your own choosing.

Multi-topic questions

28

The following questions are classified as multi-topic as they consist of questions from at least two different parts of the syllabus.

For example, this question involves **trigonometry**, **mensuration**, **circle theorems** and **percentages**.

11 November 2002, Paper 3

In triangle LMN, angle LNM = 90°,
angle MLN = 28°, and LM = 10 cm.

  a Calculate:

    i MN   **ii** LN

    iii the area of triangle LMN.

  b A circle is drawn with LM as its diameter.

    i Find the area of the circle.

    ii Write the area of triangle LMN as a percentage of the area of the circle.

    iii Explain why the point N is on the circle.

Many of the questions in **Chapters 28** and **29** are adapted from past examination papers for IGCSE Mathematics 0580 by permission of Cambridge International Examinations. The 0580 course is a different syllabus from that followed by students of the 0607 course, but has many features in common. These questions are certainly appropriate for practising mathematical techniques and applications relevant to the 0607 curriculum, but do not necessarily represent the style of question that will be encountered on the 0607 examination papers. Teachers are referred to the specimen papers of the 0607 syllabus and past examination papers from 2009 onwards for a more representative group of questions. Cambridge International Examinations bears no responsibility for the example answers to questions taken from its past question papers which are contained in this publication.

MULTI-TOPIC QUESTIONS

1 May 2001, Paper 3

In basketball, a basket scored in open play earns two points, and a basket scored from a free throw earns one point.

   a **i** Larry scored 7 baskets in open play and 4 baskets from free throws.
What was the total number of points he scored?

      ii Mike scored x baskets in open play and y baskets from free throws.
Write an expression involving x and y for the total number of points that he scored.

      iii Naresh scored a total of 11 points.
Copy and complete the table to show all the possible ways that he could score 11 points.
(One possible way has been shown for you.)

Baskets in open play (2 points)	0					
Baskets from free throws (1 point)	11					

   b The basketball team has six players.
In one match the total number of points scored by the team was 72, made up as follows.

         Larry   18   Naresh   11   Pete   16
         Mike   15   Oathur   6   Quentin   6

     i Display this information in a pie chart.
     ii Find the median score.
     iii Work out the mean score.

   c In one season the team scored a total of 882 points in all its matches.
The mean score per match was 63 points.
How many matches did the team play?

2 May 2001, Paper 3

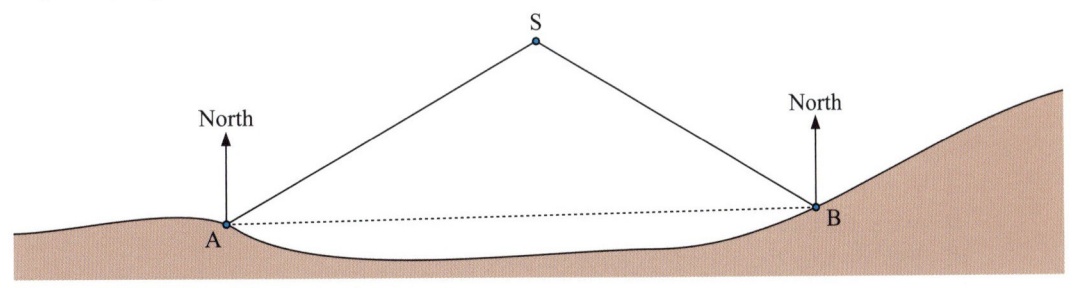

A and B are two points on a coastline. B is directly to the east of A.
A ship S can be seen from both A and B.
The bearing of S from A is 054°. The bearing of S from B is 324°.

   a Find the number of degrees in:
      i angle SAB   **ii** angle SBA.

   b Use your answers to **a** to show that angle ASB = 90°.
   c The straight line distance AB is 6 kilometres.
Work out the distance of the ship:
      i from A   **ii** from B.

d

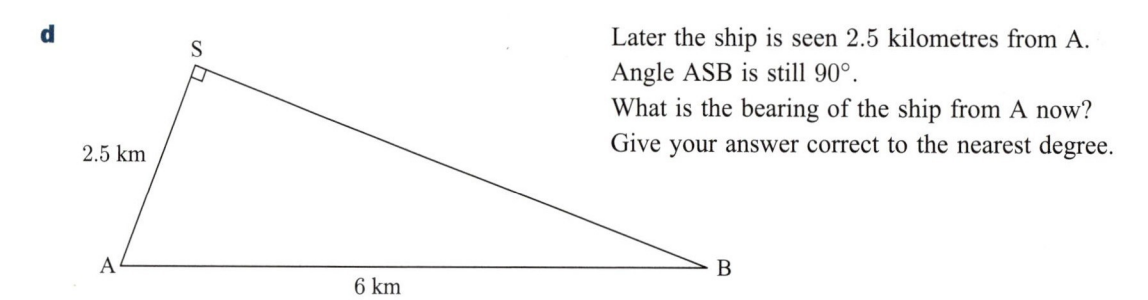

2.5 km, S, A, 6 km, B (triangle with right angle at S)

Later the ship is seen 2.5 kilometres from A. Angle ASB is still 90°.

What is the bearing of the ship from A now? Give your answer correct to the nearest degree.

3 a Fully describe the transformation that takes parallelogram A to:

  i B **ii** C
  iii D.

  b Find the value of θ.
  c Find α.

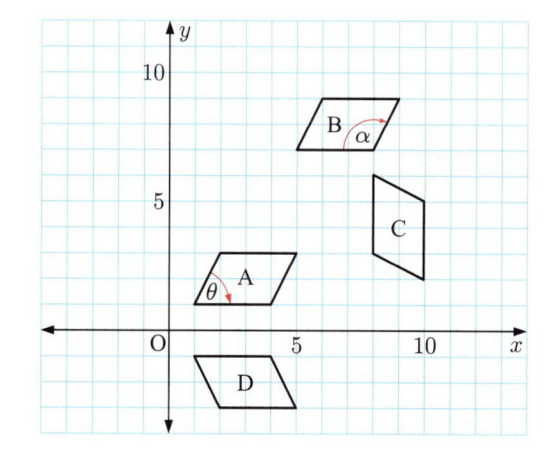

4 Adapted from November 2001, Paper 3

The diagram shows two methods, A and B, of paying for units of electricity.

  a Use the graph for Method A to find the cost of using 180 units.
  b Use the graph for Method B to find the cost per unit for:

   i the first 40 units
   ii the remaining units.

  c How many units cost $34 when paying by Method B?
  d Find the number of units which cost the same when paying by Method A or Method B. 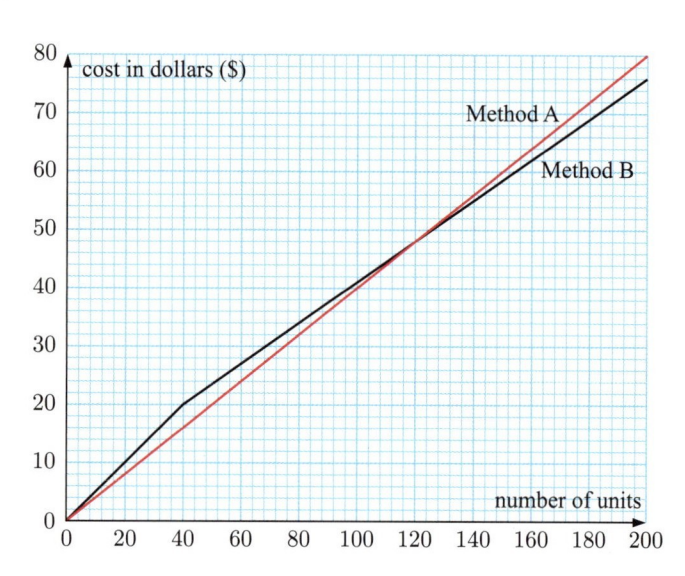
  e How much is saved by Method B when paying for 200 units?
  f Find the number of units used if $2 is saved when paying by Method B.
  g A customer's bill was $65. Find how much they must pay after 12% tax has been added.

5 May 2001, Paper 3

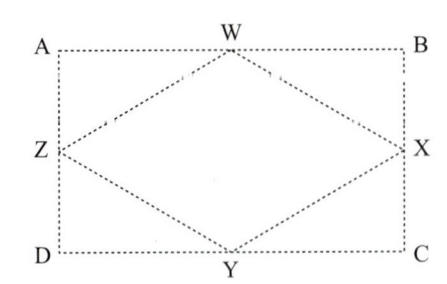

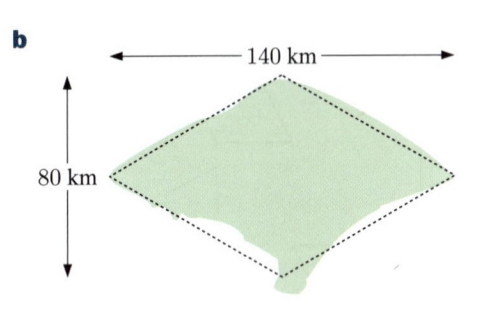

a ABCD is a rectangle.
AB = 140 mm and BC = 80 mm.
W, X, Y, and Z are the midpoints of AB, BC, CD, and DA respectively.
Calculate the area of:
  i triangle AWZ
  ii rhombus WXYZ.

b The shape of the island of Bali is approximately a rhombus, as shown in the diagram.
It is 140 km long and 80 km wide.
Estimate the area of Bali.

c A guide book says that the population of Bali is 3 million. It also says that there are 520 people to every square kilometre of the island.
Use this information to calculate another approximation for the area of Bali.

6 Adapted from November 2001, Paper 3

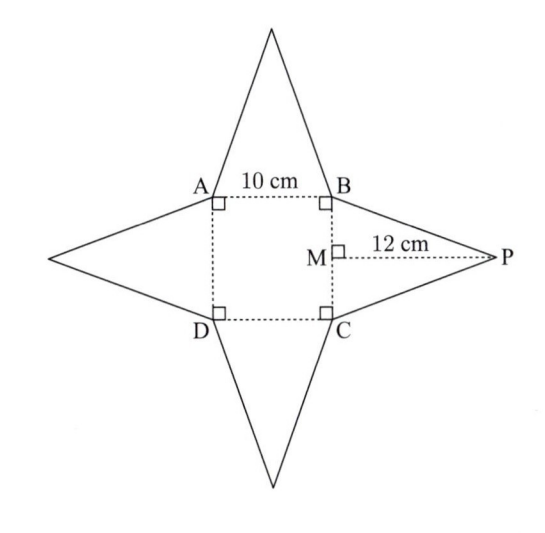

The diagram is a sketch of a net. It shows a square and four congruent triangles.
AB = 10 cm, MP = 12 cm, and BP = PC.

a
  i What special name is given to each of the four triangles in the net?
  ii Calculate the length of BP.
  iii Calculate the perimeter of the net.

b What is the order of rotational symmetry of the net?

c A solid can be made from the net.
  i Write down the name of this solid.
  ii Calculate the sum of the lengths of the edges of the solid.
  iii The base of the solid is ABCD and its height is 10.9 cm.
  The volume V of the solid is given by
  $V = \frac{1}{3} \times$ area of base $\times$ height.
  Calculate the volume of the solid.

Multi-topic questions (Chapter 28)

7 Adapted from May 2002, Paper 3

a Pencils cost p cents each and erasers cost e cents each.
Farah buys 7 pencils and 3 erasers.
  i Write down the total cost in cents, in terms of p and e.
  ii If Farah pays $1.85 in total, write an equation connecting p and e.
  iii When James buys 5 pencils and 6 erasers from the same store, he pays $1.90. Write a second equation connecting p and e.
  iv Solve the equations simultaneously to find p and e.

b Zak starts with $1. Each day the money he has doubles. After 1 day he has $2, after 2 days he has $4 and so on.
How much money does he have after:
  i 4 days   ii 7 days   iii d days? (Give your answer in its simplest form.)

8 November 2001, Paper 3

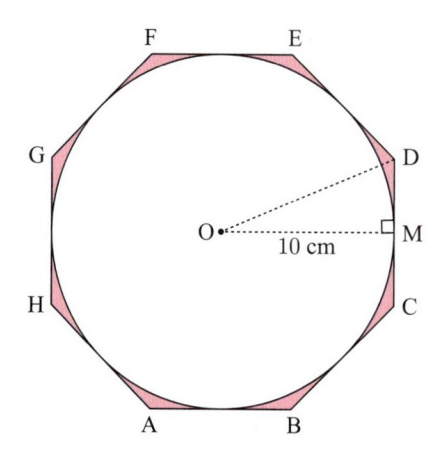

ABCDEFGH is a regular octagon.
A circle with centre O and radius 10 cm, touches the sides of the octagon at their midpoints.

a Show that angle CDE is 135°.
b Find: i angle ODM   ii angle DOM.
c Using trigonometry, calculate the length of MD.
d Calculate the area of:
  i triangle DOM   ii the octagon
  iii the circle.
e Calculate the total shaded area.
f What percentage of the area of the octagon is shaded? Give your answer to the nearest whole number.

9 November 2002, Paper 3

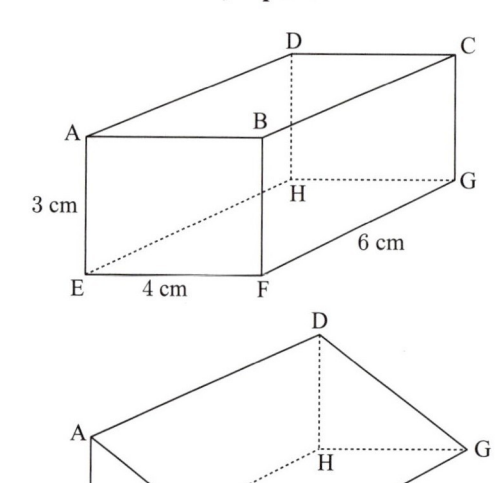

The cuboid shown has EF = 4 cm, FG = 6 cm, and AE = 3 cm.

a Calculate:
  i the volume of the cuboid
  ii the surface area of the cuboid.

b The cuboid is divided into two equal triangular prisms. One of them is shown in the diagram.
  i Write down the volume of the triangular prism.
  ii Find the area of the rectangle AFGD.

10 November 2002, Paper 3

At 0900, Ian and Joe start to dig a garden. They both dig at the same rate.

a When they are half-way through the job, what fraction of the garden has Ian dug?

b Keith arrives at 1000 to help. At this time the job is half done. All three dig at the same rate until the job is finished.

   i What fraction of the garden does Ian dig after Keith arrives?
   ii What fraction of the garden does Ian dig altogether?
   iii At what time is the job finished?

11 November 2002, Paper 3

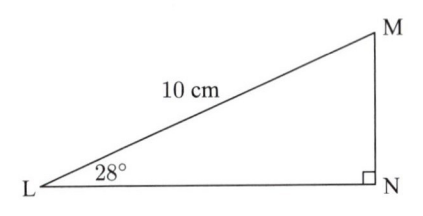

In triangle LMN, angle LNM $= 90°$, angle MLN $= 28°$, and LM $= 10$ cm.

a Calculate:
   i MN   **ii** LN   **iii** the area of triangle LMN.

b A circle is drawn with LM as its diameter.
   i Find the area of the circle.
   ii Write the area of triangle LMN as a percentage of the area of the circle.
   iii Explain why the point N is on the circle.

12 Adapted from November 2002, Paper 3

A group of students are trying to find the best price at which to sell their school newspaper. After trialling several prices, they construct the following graph:

a At what price will no-one buy the newspaper?

b At what price will 150 newspapers be sold?

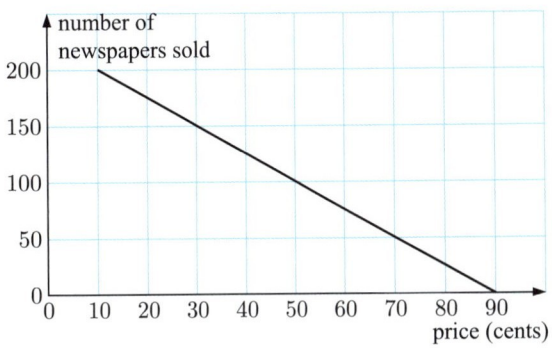

c The printing cost for n newspapers is $\$(20 + \frac{n}{10})$.

Copy and complete the table:

Price (cents)	Number of newspapers sold	Money received (cents)	Printing cost (cents)	Profit (cents)
10	200	2000	4000	-2000
20	175	3500	3750	-250
30				
40				
50				
60	75	4500	2750	1750
70				
80				
90				

d What price brings the maximum profit for the group? How many newspapers are sold, and what is the profit?

Multi-topic questions   (Chapter 28)

13 **May 2003, Paper 3**

Fifty students take part in a quiz. The table shows the results.

Number of correct answers	5	6	7	8	9	10	11	12
Number of students	4	7	8	7	10	6	5	3

  a How many students had 6 correct answers?

  b How many students had less than 11 correct answers?

  c Find:

    i the mode   **ii** the median   **iii** the mean number of correct answers.

  d A bar chart is drawn to show the results. The height of the bar for the number of students who had 5 correct answers is 2 cm. What is the height of the bar for the number of students who had 9 correct answers?

  e A pie chart is drawn to show the results. What is the sector angle for the number of students who had 11 correct answers?

  f The students who had the most correct answers shared a prize of £225. How much did each of these students receive?

  g Work out the percentage of students who had less than 7 correct answers.

  h A student is chosen at random from the fifty students. What is the probability that this student had:

    i exactly 10 correct answers   **ii** at least 10 correct answers

    iii more than 1 correct answer?

14 **November 2003, Paper 3**

A dentist recorded the number of fillings that each of a group of 30 children had in their teeth. The results were:

    2 4 0 5 1 1 3 2 6 0 2 2 3 2 1
    4 3 0 1 6 1 4 1 6 5 1 0 3 4 2

  a Copy and complete the frequency table shown alongside.

  b Find the:

    i modal number of fillings

    ii median number of fillings

    iii mean number of fillings.

Number of fillings	Frequency
0	
1	
2	
3	
4	
5	
6	

  c One of these children is chosen at random. Find the probability that the child has:

    i exactly one filling   **ii** more than three fillings.

  d These 30 children were chosen from a larger group of 300 children. Estimate how many children in the larger group have no fillings in their teeth.

15 **Adapted from May 2003, Paper 3**

  a Bottles of water cost 25 cents each.

    i Find the cost of 7 bottles.

    ii Write down an expression for the cost of b bottles, in cents.

    iii Convert your answer to **i** into dollars.

    iv Write down an expression for the cost of b bottles, in dollars.

  b The total cost T of n bars of chocolate is given by $T = nc$.

    i Write c in terms of T and n.   **ii** What does c represent?

c **i** The total cost of 8 books is $36. Find the average cost of the books.
ii One of the 8 books is removed. Its value was $6.60. Find the average value of the remaining books.
iii The total cost of x books is $$y$. Find the average cost of the books.
iv One of the x books is removed. Its value was $$z$. Find the average value of the remaining books in terms of x, y, and z.

16 Adapted from November 2003, Paper 3

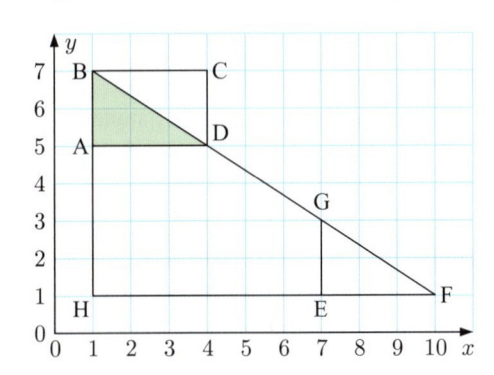

a Triangle ABD is translated onto triangle EGF by the vector $\begin{pmatrix} a \\ b \end{pmatrix}$.
Write down the values of a and b.

b Describe fully the single transformation which maps triangle ABD onto:
i triangle CDB   **ii** triangle HBF.

c **i** Work out the area of triangle ABD.
ii What is the ratio
area of triangle ABD : area of triangle HBF?
Give your answer in its lowest terms.

d **i** Find the gradient of the line BF.
ii Hence find the equation of this line.

17 May 2001, Paper 3

a The following list shows the marks gained by a group of 10 students in an examination.
65, 51, 35, 34, 12, 51, 50, 75, 48, 39

i Write down the mode.   **ii** Find the median of the scores.
iii Find the mean of the scores.

b The table alongside shows the number of students in the whole school awarded different grades in the examination.

Grade	Number of students	Angle on a pie chart
A	5	
B	15	
C	40	
D	20	
E	10	
Totals	90	

i Copy and complete the table alongside by calculating the angles required to draw a pie chart of the data.
ii Draw an accurate pie chart to show the data in the table. Label the sectors A, B, C, D, and E.
iii What is the probability that a student chosen at random was awarded the grade:
(1) C   **(2)** D or E?

18 November 2003, Paper 3

a The perimeter P of a triangle is given by the formula $P = 6x + 3$.
i Find the value of P when $x = 4$.   **ii** Find the value of x when $P = 39$.
iii Rearrange the formula to write x in terms of P.

b The perimeter of another triangle is $(9x + 4)$ centimetres.
Two sides of this triangle have lengths $2x$ centimetres and $(3x + 1)$ centimetres.
i Write an expression, in terms of x, for the length of the third side.
ii The perimeter of this triangle is 49 cm. Find the length of each side.

Multi-topic questions (Chapter 28)

19 May 2004, Paper 3

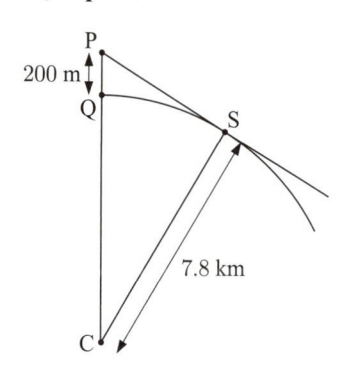

Q and S lie on a circle with radius 7.8 kilometres and centre C.
CQ is extended by 200 metres to P.
PS is a tangent to the circle at S.

a Explain why angle PSC is a right angle.
b Write down the length of PC in kilometres.
c Calculate the length of PS in kilometres.
d Calculate the area of triangle PSC. Give your answer correct to 2 significant figures.
e Calculate angle QCS.

20 May 2004, Paper 3

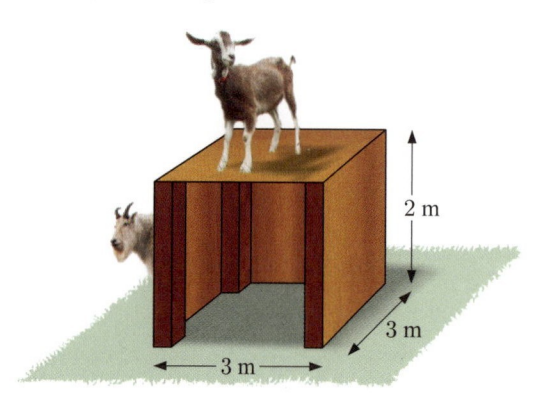

The diagram shows a shelter that Vudnella plans to build for her goats. The shelter will stand on level ground with four identical vertical posts at the corners. Three walls will be made by attaching rectangular wooden planks to the posts. The front will be left open. The shelter will have a square roof, 3 metres by 3 metres. The shelter will be 2 metres high.

a Calculate the area of the roof.
b **i** Calculate the area of one wall.
    ii Write down the total area of the three walls.

c The planks used for the walls are 3 metres long and 20 centimetres wide.
  i Calculate the area, in square metres, of one of the planks.
  ii Calculate the total number of planks Vudnella will need to build the three walls of the shelter.
d The four corner posts are each 2 metres high and 10 centimetres by 10 centimetres in cross-section. Calculate the volume, in cubic metres, of one post.
e To build the shelter, Vudnella will need 1.5 kilograms of nails. Copy and complete the table below:

Item		Total cost of item
Posts	at €1.20 each	
Planks	at €0.30 each	
Roof material	at €1.60 per m²	
Nails	at €1.40 per kg	
	Total cost of shelter	

Multi-topic questions (Chapter 28)

21 **May 2005, Paper 3**

Juana is travelling by plane from Spain to England.

- **a** Her case weighs 17.2 kilograms. The maximum weight allowed is 20 kilograms. By how much is the weight of her case below the maximum allowed?
- **b** She changes 150 euros (€) into pounds (£). The exchange rate is €1 = £0.71. Calculate how much she receives.
- **c** She travels from her home to the airport by train. She catches a train at 0955 and the journey takes 45 minutes.
    - **i** At what time does she arrive at the airport?
    - **ii** She has to wait until 1210 to get on her plane. For how long does she have to wait?
- **d** The plane takes off at 1240 Spanish time, which is 1140 English time. The flight takes $2\frac{1}{4}$ hours. What is the time in England when she arrives?
- **e** The plane has seats for 420 passengers. 15% of the seats are empty. How many passengers are on the plane?

22 **May 2006, Paper 3**

- **a** Simplify the expression $5p - 2q - (p + q)$.
- **b** Solve the equation $3(2x - 5) = 27$.
- **c** A kite has sides of length j cm and k cm. 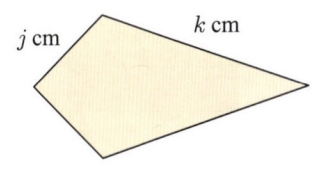
    - **i** Write an expression for the perimeter of the kite in terms of j and k.
    - **ii** The perimeter of the kite is 72 centimetres. Write down an equation connecting j and k.
    - **iii** If $k = 2j$, find the value of k.
- **d** **i** Use the formula $w = \dfrac{s-t}{r}$ to find the value of w when $s = \frac{5}{6}$, $t = \frac{2}{3}$, and $r = \frac{1}{2}$.
    - **ii** Rearrange the formula in **d i** to write s in terms of w, r, and t.

23 **May 2005, Paper 3**

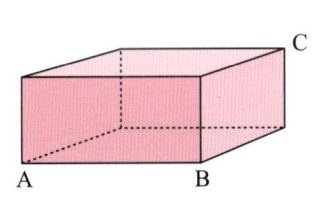

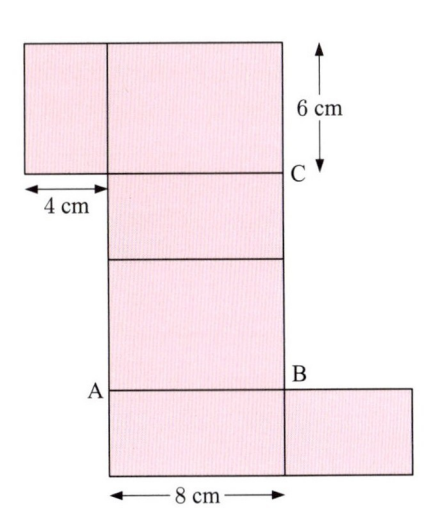

The diagram above shows a cuboid and its net.

- **a** Calculate the total surface area of the cuboid.
- **b** Calculate the volume of the cuboid.
- **c** An ant walks directly from A to C on the surface of the cuboid.
    - **i** Calculate the length of the ant's journey.   **ii** Calculate the size of angle CAB on the net.

Multi-topic questions (Chapter 28)

24 **May 2007, Paper 3**

Marguerite earns £336 per month after tax. She divides her earnings between bills, food, savings, and personal spending.

  a Her bills take $\frac{2}{7}$ of her earnings. Show that £240 is left for her other items.
  b She divides the £240 between food, savings, and personal spending in the ratio 5 : 3 : 4.
    i Calculate how much she spends on food.
    ii Marguerite saves the same amount each month. Show that she saves £720 in one year.
    iii She invests the £720 in a bank which pays 6% per year compound interest. How much will this be worth after 2 years?

25 **Adapted from November 2005, Paper 3**

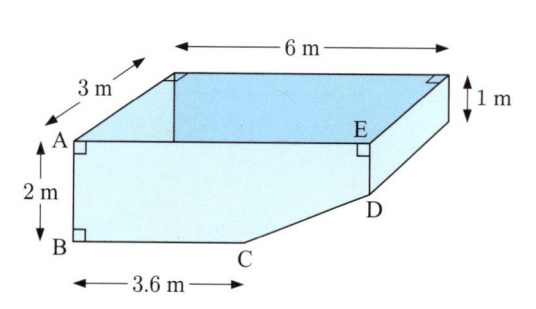

The diagram shows a swimming pool with cross-section ABCDE. The pool is 6 metres long and 3 metres wide. AB = 2 m, ED = 1 m, and BC = 3.6 m.

  a **i** Calculate the area of the cross-section ABCDE.
    ii Calculate the capacity of the pool. Give your answer in litres. (1 cubic metre is 1000 litres.)
    iii One litre of water evaporates every hour for each square metre of the water surface. If the pool is initially full, how many litres of water will evaporate in 2 hours?

  b The tank at a school holds 61 500 litres of water. Water flows out of the tank at 1000 litres per hour.
    i Calculate how long it takes for the tank to empty. Give your answer in hours and minutes.
    ii Convert 61 500 litres to gallons. Give your answer to the nearest gallon. (4.55 litres = 1 gallon.)
    iii Every 10 000 gallons of water needs 2.5 litres of purifier. How many litres of purifier does the school need for the tank?
    iv The purifier is sold in 1 litre bottles. How many bottles of purifier will the school need?

26 **Adapted from May 2007, Paper 3**

  a Find the value of:
    i 5^0 **ii** the square root of 64
    iii the cube root of 64   **iv** the integer closest in value to $(1.8)^3$.
  b **i** List the sets $A = \{\text{factors of } 18\}$ and $B = \{\text{factors of } 27\}$.
    ii Display the sets A and B on a Venn diagram with universal set $\mathscr{E} = \{x \mid 1 \leqslant x \leqslant 30, \ x \in \mathbb{Z}\}$.
    iii Find: **(1)** $A \cap B$ **(2)** $A \cup B$ **(3)** $n(A \cup B)$
  c **i** Two of the factors of 2007 are square numbers. One of these is 1. Find the other factor which is a square number.
    ii Write down the two factors of 2007 which are prime.

27 **Adapted from May 2006, Paper 3**

A wax candle is a cylinder with radius 1.5 centimetres and height 20 centimetres.

   a Calculate, correct to the nearest cubic centimetre, the volume of wax in the candle.
(The volume of a cylinder with radius r and height h is $\pi r^2 h$.)

   b The candle burns 0.8 cm^3 of wax every minute. How long, in hours and minutes, will it last? Write your answer correct to the nearest minute.

   c The candles are stored neatly in boxes which measure x cm by 24 cm by 20 cm. Each box contains 96 candles. Calculate the value of x.

   d A shopkeeper pays \$25 for one box of 96 candles. He sells all of the candles for 35 cents each.
      i How much profit does he make?
      ii Calculate his profit as a percentage of the cost price.
      iii 22% of the profit must be paid as tax. How much does this amount to?

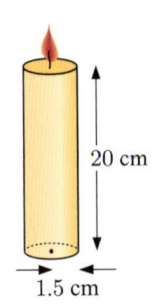

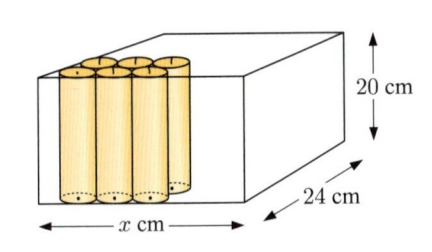

28 **May 2007, Paper 3**

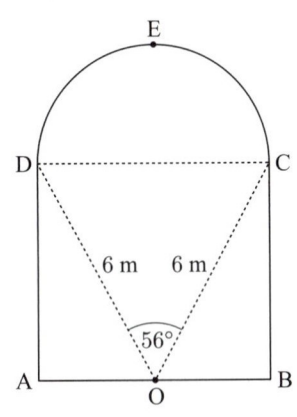

ABCED is the cross-section of a tunnel.
ABCD is a rectangle and DEC is a semi-circle.
O is the midpoint of AB.
OD = OC = 6 m and angle DOC = 56°.

   a   **i** Show that angle COB = 62°.
      ii Calculate the length of OB.
      iii Write down the width of the tunnel, AB.
      iv Calculate the length of BC.

   b Calculate the area of:
      i rectangle ABCD   **ii** semi-circle DEC
      iii the cross-section of the tunnel.

   c The tunnel is 500 metres long.
      i Calculate the volume of earth excavated in the construction of the tunnel.
      ii A car travels through the tunnel at a constant speed of 60 kilometres per hour. How many seconds does it take to pass through the tunnel?

29 **May 2007, Paper 3**

   a Kinetic energy E is related to mass m and speed v by the formula $E = \frac{1}{2}mv^2$.
      i Calculate E when $m = 5$ and $v = 12$.
      ii Calculate v when $m = 8$ and $E = 225$.
      iii Make m the subject of the formula.

   b Factorise completely: $xy^2 - x^2 y$.

   c Solve the equation $3(x-5) + 2(14 - 3x) = 7$.

   d Solve the simultaneous equations $\begin{cases} 4x + y = 13 \\ 2x + 3y = 9 \end{cases}$

Multi-topic questions   (Chapter 28) 513

30 **November 2006, Paper 3**

 a A builder estimates the number of bricks in a wall by dividing the area of the wall by the area of the face of a brick. The brick wall is 10 metres long and 1.5 metres high. Each brick is 20 centimetres long and 10 centimetres high. How many bricks does the builder estimate are in the wall?
 b The builder mixes sand and cement in the ratio 5 : 2 to make mortar. He wants 14 buckets of mortar.
   i How many buckets of sand and how many buckets of cement does he need?
   ii One bag of cement fills 3.5 buckets. How many bags of cement must the builder buy?
 c A kitchen floor requires 720 tiles. The builder adds an extra 5% to this number to allow for mistakes.
   i Calculate how many tiles the builder needs to buy.
   ii Tiles are sold in packs of 100 which can not be split. How many packs should the builder buy?

31 **November 2007, Paper 3**

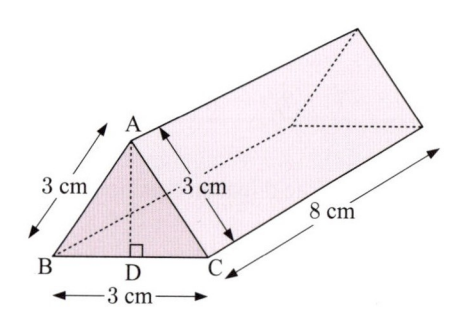

A physics teacher uses a set of identical triangular glass prisms in a lesson. Their cross-section is an equilateral triangle with sides of length 3 cm.

 a   **i** Calculate the length of AD.
   ii Calculate the area of triangle ABC.
   iii The length of the prism is 8 cm. Calculate the volume of the prism.

 b After the lesson, the glass prisms are put into a plastic box, which is also a triangular prism. Its cross-section is an equilateral triangle with sides of length 9 cm. The length of the box is 16 cm.
   i Work out the largest number of glass prisms that can fit into the box.
   ii Sketch a net of the box.
   iii Calculate the surface area of the box.
   iv The plastic for the box cost 6 cents per square centimetre. 540 cm² of plastic was used in the manufacturing process. Calculate the total cost of the plastic, giving your answer in dollars.

32 **May 2008, Paper 3**

Alphonse, his wife, and their child fly from Madrid to the Olympic Games in Beijing. The adult plane fare is 450 euros. The child fare is 68% of the adult fare.

a Show that the total plane fare for the family is 1206 euros.

b The ratio of the money spent on plane fares : accommodation : tickets = 6 : 5 : 3. Calculate the total cost of the holiday.

c Alphonse changes 500 euros into Chinese yuan at a rate of 1 euro = 9.91 Chinese yuan. How many Chinese yuan does he receive?

d The plane leaves Madrid at 0545. The journey takes 11 hours 35 minutes. Beijing time is 7 hours ahead of Madrid time. Find the time in Beijing when they arrive.

33 **Adapted from November 2008, Paper 3**

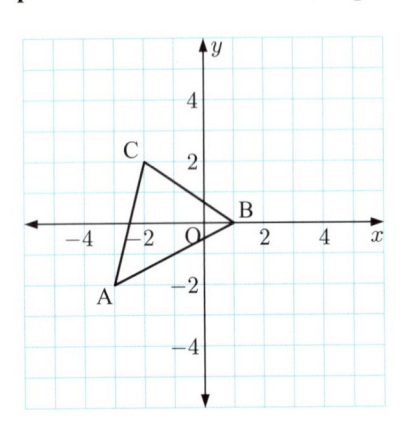

Triangle ABC is drawn on the grid.

a **i** Write down the coordinates of A.
  ii Write $\overrightarrow{AB}$ and $\overrightarrow{BC}$ in component form.

b Translate triangle ABC by $\binom{4}{-3}$. Label the image T.

c Enlarge triangle ABC with centre A and scale factor 2. Label the image E.

d Rotate triangle ABC through 180° about the midpoint of the side AB. Label the image R.

34 **May 2008, Paper 3**

a Solve the equations:

  i $3x - 4 = 14$ **ii** $\dfrac{y+1}{5} = 2$ **iii** $3(2z - 7) - 2(z - 3) = -9$

b Donna sent p postcards and q letters to her friends.

  i The total number of postcards and letters she sent was 12. Write down an equation connecting p and q.
  ii A stamp for a postcard costs 25 cents. A stamp for a letter costs 40 cents. Donna spent 375 cents on stamps altogether. Write down another equation connecting p and q.
  iii Solve your equations simultaneously to find the values of p and q.

35 **Adapted from November 2008, Paper 3**

Aida, Bernado and Cristiano need €30 000 to start a business.

a **i** If the trio borrows $\frac{2}{5}$ of this amount, show that they still need €18 000.
  ii They provide the €18 000 themselves in the ratio Aida : Bernado : Cristiano = 5 : 4 : 3. Calculate the amount each of them provides.

b **i** Office equipment costs 35% of the €30 000. Calculate the cost of the equipment.
  ii General office expenses cost another €6500. Write this as a fraction of €30 000. Give your answer in simplest form.
  iii The remainder of the €30 000 covers rent for their office for a year. How much rent do they need to pay each month?

Multi-topic questions (Chapter 28)

36 May 2008, Paper 3

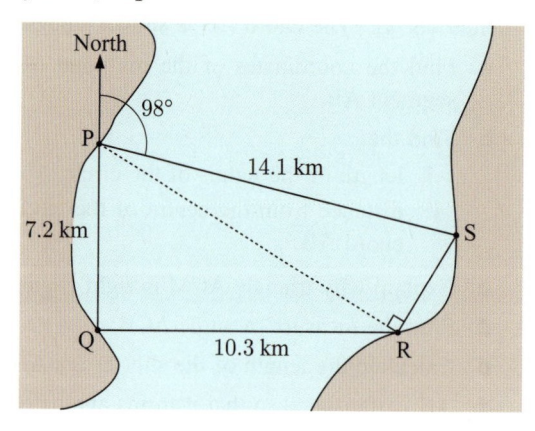

P, Q, R, and S are ports on a wide bay. A ferry sails from P, stopping at Q, R, and S, before returning to P.

Q is 7.2 kilometres due south of P.
R is 10.3 kilometres due east of Q.
The bearing of S from P is $098°$.
Angle PRS $= 90°$ and SP $= 14.1$ km.

(Diagram shows: North arrow at P, angle $98°$ from North, SP $= 14.1$ km, PQ $= 7.2$ km, QR $= 10.3$ km, S to the east, right angle at R.)

  a Show that angle QPR $\approx 55°$.
  b Write down the bearing of R from P.
  c Explain why angle RPS $= 27°$.
  d Calculate the distance RS.
  e Find the total distance the ferry sails.
  f The total sailing time for the ferry is 4 hours 30 minutes. Calculate the average sailing speed, in kilometres per hour, for the whole journey.

37 The population of insects t days after colonising a new habitat is given by
$P = 22\,000 - 21\,600 \times 2^{-0.1t}$ insects.
  a Comment on the domain of this function.
  b What is the population after 50 days? Give your answer in standard form.
  c Sketch a graph of the function for $0 \leqslant t \leqslant 365$ days.
  d What asymptote does the graph have? Explain the significance of this result.
  e State the range of the function for the domain $0 \leqslant t \leqslant 365$ days.
  f At what point does the function meet the line $P = 15\,000$ insects? Explain the significance of this result.

38 Consider the set $\{2, 3, 4, 6\}$. The members of the set are each written on a card, and the cards are placed in a hat. Two cards are randomly selected from the hat, without replacement.
  a Draw a tree diagram to illustrate the possible outcomes.
  b Find the probability that:
    i both of the cards drawn have even numbers
    ii the HCF of the numbers drawn is also a member of the set
    iii the LCM of the number drawn is *not* a member of the set.

39 Consider the function $f(x) = \frac{1}{2}x^3 + 2x^2 - 2x - 1$ on the domain $-6 \leqslant x \leqslant 2$.
  a Find the:
    i axes intercepts   **ii** local maxima and minima   **iii** range of $f(x)$.
  b Draw a graph of $y = f(x)$, displaying the features found in **a**.
  c $g(x) = f(x - 3)$.   Draw $g(x)$ on your graph.
  d $h(x) = -\dfrac{7}{x}$. Find the points of intersection of $f(x)$ and $h(x)$.

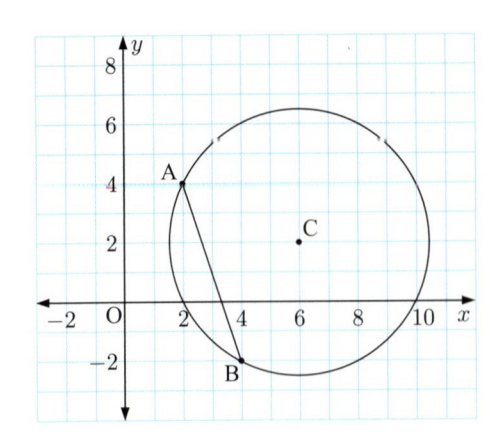

40 A(2, 4) and B(4, −2) lie on a circle which has centre (6, 2). The chord AB is shown alongside.

  a Find the coordinates of the midpoint M of line segment AB.

  b Find the:

   i length of the radius of the circle

   ii distance from the centre of the circle to the chord AB.

  c Explain why triangle ACM is right angled.

  d Find the measure of angle ACB.

  e Calculate the length of the shorter arc AB.

  f AB is translated so that it forms another chord of the circle. What translation vector does this?

41 The sum of the lengths of any two sides of a triangle must be longer than the third side.

So, for example, $\dfrac{x}{3} + 1 > \dfrac{x+1}{2}$.

  a Write two other inequations involving x.

  b Solve all three inequations for x.

  c Illustrate the solutions to the three inequations on the same number line.

  d The actual values that x may take must satisfy all three inequations. What range of values can x take?

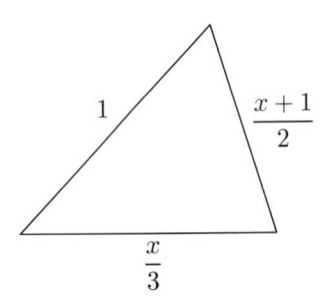

42 Consider the line $y = 6 - x$.

  a Copy and complete the table of values alongside for points on the line.

  b For each of the points in the table in **a**, calculate the area of the rectangle whose diagonal is from the point to the origin.

  c Write the areas found in **b** as a sequence. Use the method of differences to show that this sequence is quadratic.

x	1	2	3	4	5
y					

Investigation questions 29

Many of the questions in **Chapters 28** and **29** are adapted from past examination papers for IGCSE Mathematics 0580 by permission of Cambridge International Examinations. The 0580 course is a different syllabus from that followed by students of the 0607 course, but has many features in common. These questions are certainly appropriate for practising mathematical techniques and applications relevant to the 0607 curriculum, but do not necessarily represent the style of question that will be encountered on the 0607 examination papers. Teachers are referred to the specimen papers of the 0607 syllabus and past examination papers from 2009 onwards for a more representative group of questions. Cambridge International Examinations bears no responsibility for the example answers to questions taken from its past question papers which are contained in this publication.

Investigation 1

Adapted from November 1993, Paper 3 and May 1998, Paper 3

1 The two digit number $\boxed{8\,|\,6}$ is $8 \times 10 + 6$.

   a Copy and complete these statements:

   i $27 = 2 \times \ldots + 7$

   ii $38 = \ldots \times 10 + \ldots$

   iii $67 = \ldots \times \ldots + \ldots$

   b Write the two digit number $\boxed{A\,|\,B}$ in terms of A and B.

   c Show that $\boxed{P\,|\,Q} - \boxed{Q\,|\,P} = 9(P - Q)$.

   d Explain why $\boxed{P\,|\,Q} - \boxed{Q\,|\,P}$ can never equal 4.

   e Find all the two digit numbers $\boxed{P\,|\,Q}$ such that $\boxed{P\,|\,Q} - \boxed{Q\,|\,P}$ equals:

   i 27   **ii** 72   **iii** -36

   f Show that the difference $\boxed{P\,|\,Q}^2 - \boxed{Q\,|\,P}^2$ is always divisible by 99.

2 Consider the following procedure:

   Step 1: Using digits from 1 to 9, write down a three digit number.

   Step 2: Make a second three digit number by reversing the digits of the first number.

   Step 3: Subtract the second number from the first.

   a Carry out ten different calculations using the rule.

   b What do you notice about your answers?

   c How many possible results from using the rule are there?

Investigation questions (Chapter 29)

Investigation 2

1 Consider the pattern:

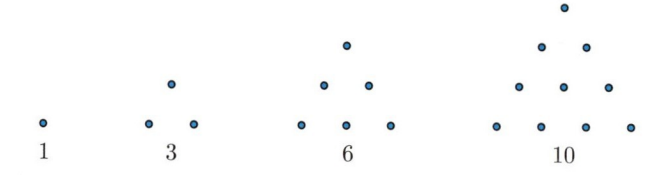

```
                                          •
                           •             • •
              •           • •           • • •
  •          • •         • • •         • • • •
  1           3            6              10
```

  a Draw the next two diagrams in the pattern, and write down the number of dots in each.

  b Explain in words how many dots are added to the pattern each time.

  c The nth diagram in the pattern contains $\dfrac{n(n+1)}{2}$ dots.

  Check this formula is correct for the first 6 diagrams.

  d Find the number of dots in the:

  i 10th **ii** 50th **iii** $(n+1)$th diagram.

  e Which member of the pattern contains:

  i 2211 **ii** $\dfrac{(n+3)(n+4)}{2}$ **iii** $\dfrac{n^2-n}{2}$ dots?

2 Consider the pattern:

$$1^3 = 1 = 1^2$$
$$1^3 + 2^3 = 9 = 3^2$$
$$1^3 + 2^3 + 3^3 = \ldots = \ldots$$
$$1^3 + 2^3 + 3^3 + 4^3 = \ldots = \ldots$$

  a Copy and complete the pattern.

  b Write down the next two rows of the pattern.

  c Using **1**, write down the sum in the nth row of the pattern.

  d Find the sum of the first 9 cubes.

  e The sum of the first x cubes is 14 400. Find the value of x.

Investigation 3

Adapted from May 1994, Paper 3 and May 1999, Paper 3

The number 21 can be written as $4 \times 0 + 7 \times 3$.

The number 22 can be written as $4 \times 2 + 7 \times 2$.

1 Write each of the numbers below in the form $4a + 7b$, where a and b are non-negative integers.

$$20 = 4 \times \ldots + 7 \times \ldots$$
$$21 = 4 \times 0 + 7 \times 3$$
$$22 = 4 \times 2 + 7 \times 2$$
$$23 = 4 \times \ldots + 7 \times \ldots$$
$$24 = 4 \times \ldots + 7 \times \ldots$$
$$25 = \ldots$$
$$26 = \ldots$$
$$27 = \ldots$$
$$28 = \ldots$$

2 The number 43 can be written as $4 \times 9 + 7 \times 1$
    or $4 \times 2 + 7 \times 5$.

  a Write 40 in the form $4a + 7b$ in two different ways.

  b Write 72 in the form $4a + 7b$ in *three* different ways.

3 The table shows the values of $4a + 7b$ for different values of a and b.

		b				
		0	1	2	3	4
a	0	0	7	14	21	....
	1	4	11	18	....	32
	2	8	15	....	29	36
	3	12	19	....	33	
	4	16	....	30		

  a Fill in the missing values in the table. You could use **1** to help you.

  b Most of the values from 0 to 20 appear in the table. List the numbers which will not appear.

  c What is the largest number that cannot be written in the form $4a + 7b$, where a and b are non-negative integers?

4 **a** Describe the pattern of numbers you can see in any diagonal down the table with direction:

  i right to left (↙)   **ii** left to right (↘).

  b Explain why this occurs.

5 If we allow a and b to be negative whole numbers, $4a + 7b$ can equal any whole number.
  For example, 10 is not in the table but $4a + 7b = 10$ for $a = -1$ and $b = 2$.

  a Find values of a and b so that $4a + 7b$ equals any three of the numbers you listed in **3b**.

  b Find two more ways $4a + 7b$ can equal 0, if negative values for a and b are allowed. How many ways do you think there are?

Investigation questions (Chapter 29)

Investigation 4

1 A team of archaeologists is setting up to explore a new site. They construct a square grid using pegs and string so they can record where each object is found. The size of the grid determines the number of pegs they need, and the number of squares created.

Grid size	1	2	3	4
Number of stringlines	4	6	8	10
Number of pegs	4	8	12	16
Number of squares	1	4	9	16

    a Draw a diagram for the grid of size 5. Find the number of:
        i stringlines   **ii** pegs   **iii** squares.

    b Draw a diagram for the grid of size 6. Find the number of:
        i stringlines   **ii** pegs   **iii** squares.

    c For the grid of size n, write a formula for the number of:
        i stringlines   **ii** pegs   **iii** squares.

    d For a grid with 81 squares, find the number of:
        i stringlines   **ii** pegs.

    e For a grid with 48 pegs, find the number of:
        i stringlines   **ii** squares.

    f A grid has twice as many squares as pegs. How many stringlines does it have?

2 A second archaeological survey is performed using a rectangular grid of squares.
The grid opposite is an example of such a grid. It has 4 squares in one direction and 3 squares in the other.

    a If there are 4 squares in one direction and 3 squares in the other, find the total number of:
        i stringlines   **ii** pegs   **iii** squares.

    b If there are x squares in one direction and y squares in the other, find the total number of:
        i stringlines   **ii** pegs   **iii** squares.

Investigation 5

Adapted from May 2003, Paper 3

The table below gives the temperature $T\,°C$ of a cup of tea, x minutes after it was made.

Time (x minutes)	0	2	4	6	8	10	12	14	16	18	20
Temperature ($T\,°C$)	84	65	52	43	36	31	28	26	24	23	22

1. Graph the information in the table on a grid like the one shown:

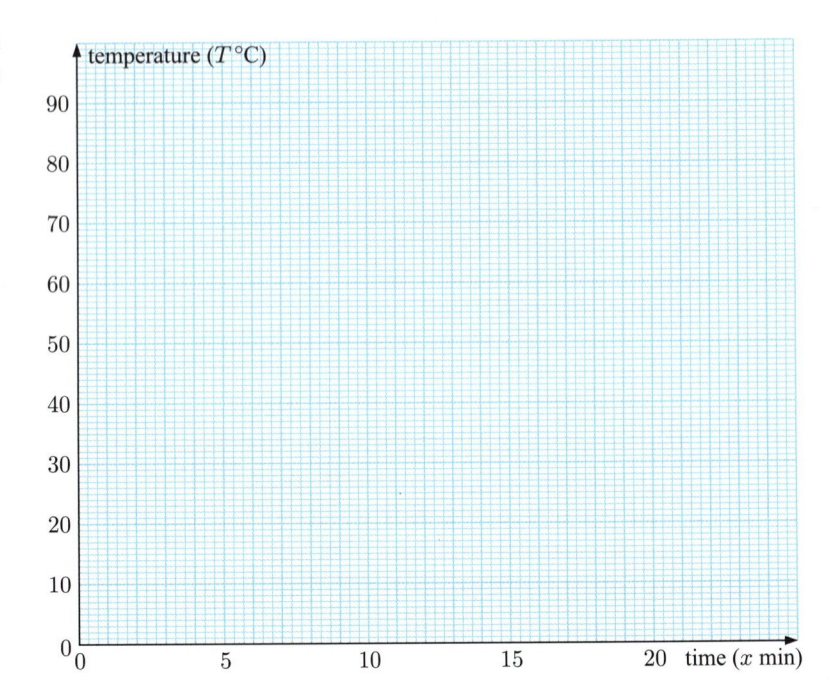

2. What is the temperature of the tea after:
   a 5 minutes
   b 15 minutes?

3. After how many minutes is its temperature 30°C?

4. By how much has its temperature gone down between 4 minutes and 8 minutes?

5. a Copy and complete the table which shows falls in temperature.

Time	0 to 4 mins	4 to 8 mins	8 to 12 mins	12 to 16 mins
Fall in temperature				

   b What pattern do you notice about these falls in temperature?

6. How hot will the tea be after half an hour?

7. Estimate the room temperature.

Investigation questions (Chapter 29)

Investigation 6

1 Consider the following pattern of rectangles:

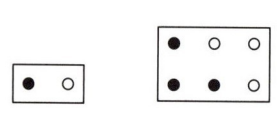

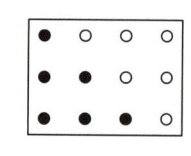

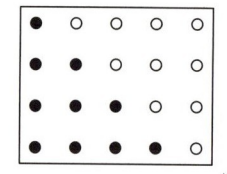

a Copy and complete the table below:

Rectangle	Number of rows	Number of columns	Total number of dots	Number of black dots	Number of white dots
1	1	2	2	1	1
2	2	3	6	3	
3	3				
4					

b Draw the 5th rectangle, and add the 5th row to your table.

c For the nth rectangle, find the number of:
  i rows **ii** columns **iii** dots **iv** black dots.

d Copy and complete:
$$1 = 1$$
$$1 + 2 = 3$$
$$1 + 2 + 3 = ...$$
$$1 + 2 + 3 + 4 = ...$$
$$1 + 2 + 3 + 4 + 5 = ...$$
$$1 + 2 + 3 + 4 + ... + n = ...$$

2 Consider the following pattern of squares:

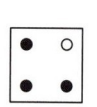

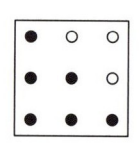

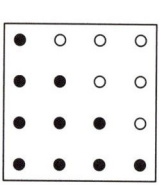

a Copy and complete the table below:

Square	Total number of dots	Number of black dots	Number of white dots
1	1	1	0
2	4	3	
3	9		
4			

b Draw the 5th square in the pattern and hence add the next row to your table.

c For the nth square, find the total number of:
  i dots **ii** black dots **iii** white dots.

d Suppose a dot is chosen at random.
  i Find the probability that the dot is black for square:
    a 1 **b** 2 **c** 3 **d** 4 **e** 5
  ii Show that the probability that the dot is black for square n is $\frac{1}{2} + \frac{1}{2n}$.

Investigation 7

1

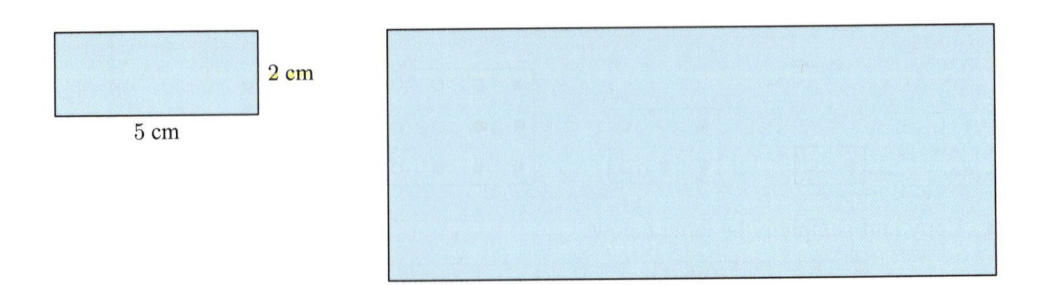

The smaller rectangle has been enlarged with scale factor 3 to produce the larger rectangle.
Find:
  a the side lengths of the image rectangle
  b the area of both rectangles
  c the ratio   object area : image area.

2 Consider enlarging this rectangle with scale factor 3:

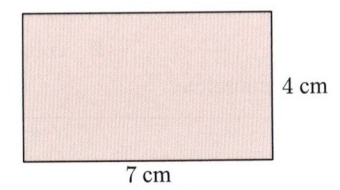

Find:
  a the side lengths of the image rectangle
  b the area of both rectangles
  c the ratio   object area : image area.

3 Now consider a rectangle a units long and b units wide. Enlarge the rectangle with scale factor 3. Hence explain your results in **1 c** and **2 c**.

4 Consider again a rectangle a units long and b units wide. This time we enlarge it with different scale factors.
  a Investigate the   object area : image area   ratio for rectangles under:
      i an enlargement with scale factor 4
      ii a reduction with scale factor $\frac{1}{2}$.
  b Explain your results in general terms.
  c Use an enlargement or reduction with scale factor k on a rectangle a units long and b units wide to prove your general result.

5 Extend your investigation to triangles or circles. How does an enlargement or reduction with scale factor k change the area of any planar shape?

Investigation questions (Chapter 29)

Investigation 8

Adapted from June 1997, Paper 3

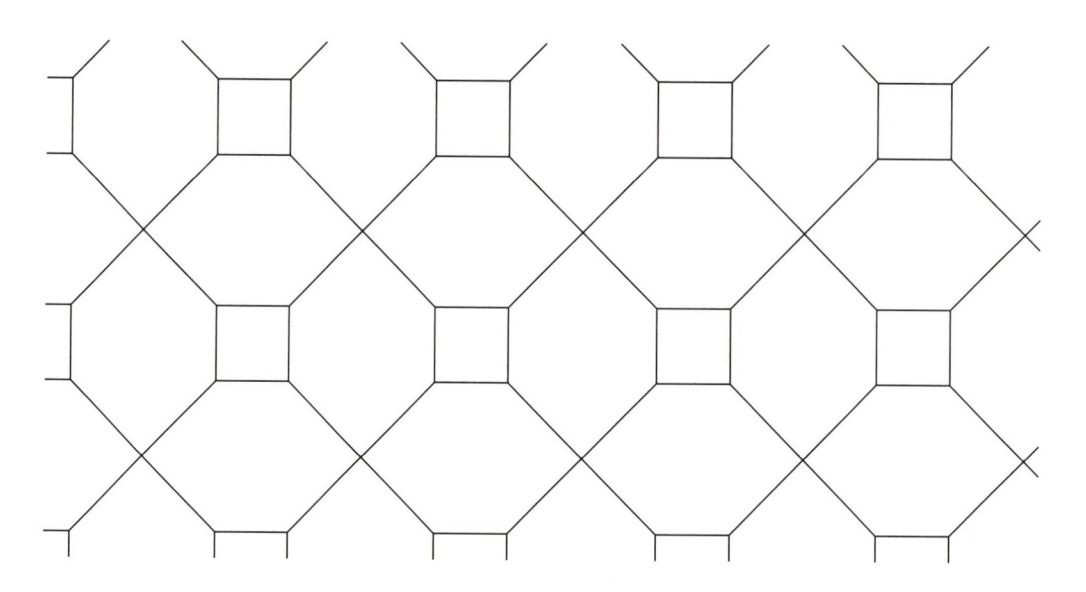

The three shapes shown below can be found within the above tiling pattern.

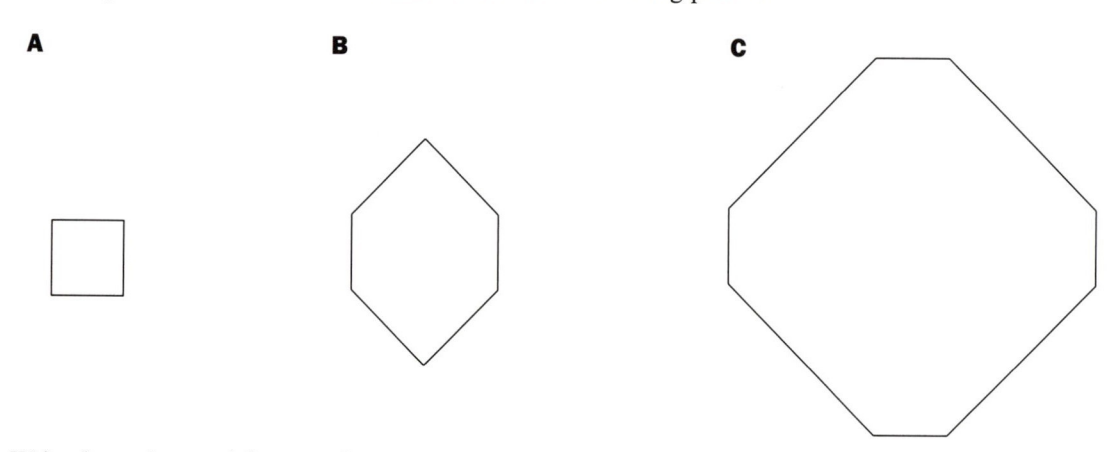

A   **B**   **C**

1. Write down the special name of each shape.
2. Copy the three shapes **A**, **B** and **C** shown above and on each diagram draw the lines of symmetry.
3. Find the sizes of all the interior angles of each shape.
4. Which one of the three shapes is a **regular** polygon?
5. Explain briefly why the other two shapes are not regular polygons.
6. The area of shape **A** is 1 cm^2 and the area of shape **C** is 17 cm^2. Calculate the area of shape **B**.
7. Using shape **B** only, investigate other possible tiling patterns. You may choose any side lengths you wish, but keep the angles constant.

Investigation 9

1 Tamie buys 3 kg of plums and 5 kg of cherries for a total cost of £31.
  a Write an equation that describes this information, using x to represent the cost per kg of plums and y to represent the cost per kg of cherries.
  b Make y the subject of your equation.
  c Graph y against x on a set of coordinate axes.
  d Your line should go through the point $(4, 3.8)$. What does this represent?
  e What can you say about the maximum and minimum possible prices of the fruits?
  f If you know that both fruits cost a whole number of pounds per kg, what possible prices are there?
  g Steph buys 4 kg of plums and 3 kg of cherries for £23.
   i Write an equation that describes this information.
   ii Rearrange the equation and hence add the equation to your graph.
   iii What information does this give you?
  h Check your results by solving your equations from **a** and **g** simultaneously.

2 The next day, Tamie buys 5 kg of blueberries and 1 kg of pears. The total cost is £34.
Steph buys 3 kg each of blueberries and pears, and pays £30.
Use graphing techniques to find the prices of these fruits.

3 It takes a few weeks for Tamie and Steph to eat all of this fruit. When they next go shopping, the prices have changed. Tamie buys 3 kg of plums and 1 kg of cherries for £15, while Steph buys 6 kg of plums and 2 kg of cherries for £30.
  a Write down equations for these purchases.
  b Graph these equations on a new set of coordinate axes.
  c What do you notice from your graph? What does this mean?
  d What are some possible prices of these fruits?
  e Later that day, Arthur buys 3 kg of plums and 1 kg of cherries. By this time, the plums are discounted at 25% off, so the total cost is £12. What price are the cherries now?

Investigation 10

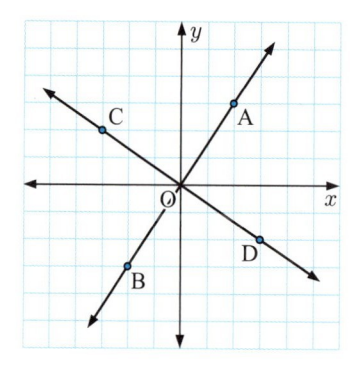

1 Lines AB and CD are perpendicular.
  a Find the gradient of each line.
  b Multiply the gradients in **a**.

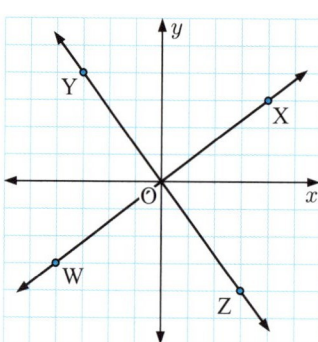

2 Lines WX and YZ are perpendicular.
  a Find the gradient of each line.
  b Multiply the gradients in **a**.

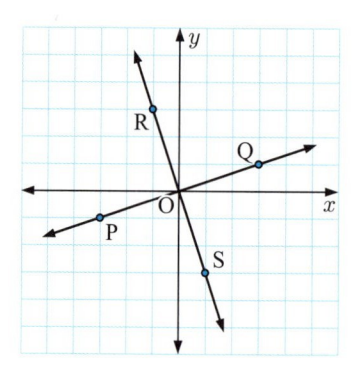

3 Lines PQ and RS are perpendicular.
  a Find the gradient of each line.
  b Multiply the gradients in **a**.

4 Use the evidence in **1**, **2**, and **3** to make a statement about the gradients of two perpendicular lines.

5 Consider the lines $y = \frac{5}{2}x + 1$ and $y = mx - 3$.
  a Write down the gradient of each line.
  b Find m if the lines are: **i** parallel **ii** perpendicular.

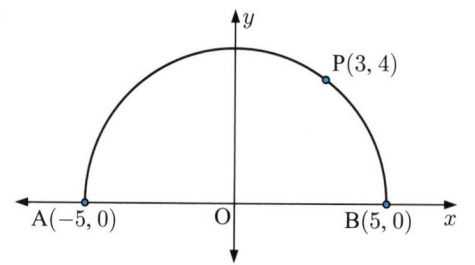

6
  a Find the gradients of line segments AP and BP.
  b Is angle APB a right angle? Give evidence for your answer.
  c Find the lengths of AB, BP, and AP, giving your answers in square root form.
  d Show that $AP^2 + BP^2 = AB^2$.
  e Explain the significance of the result in **d**.

7 Points: A(0, 0), B(5, 0), C(8, 4), D(3, 4)

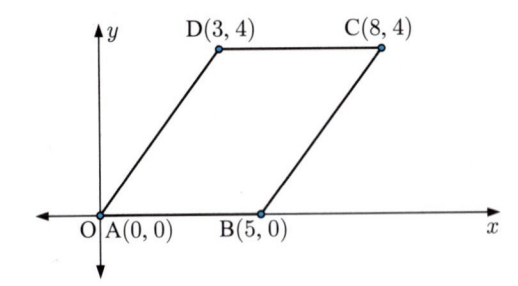

a Find the lengths of AB, BC, CD, and AD.
b Hence describe the quadrilateral ABCD.
c Find the gradients of line segments AC and BD.
d Explain the significance of the result in **c**.

Investigation questions (Chapter 29)

Investigation 11

When you go to the stationery shop, there are many different sizes of paper you can buy. The sizes are often chosen in *series* so that all the page sizes in the series are mathematically **similar**.

One common series of paper sizes is called the *A-series*. The largest page size in the A-series is an A0 page, which has an area of 1 m².

If we cut the A0 page across its long side, we make two A1 pages. Their sides are in the same ratio as the A0 page, and their area is a half of the area of the A0 page.

If we cut the A1 pages across their long sides, we make A2 pages. We do the same again to produce A3 pages, and so on to produce smaller and smaller sheets, but always with the same ratio of side lengths.

This process is illustrated below:

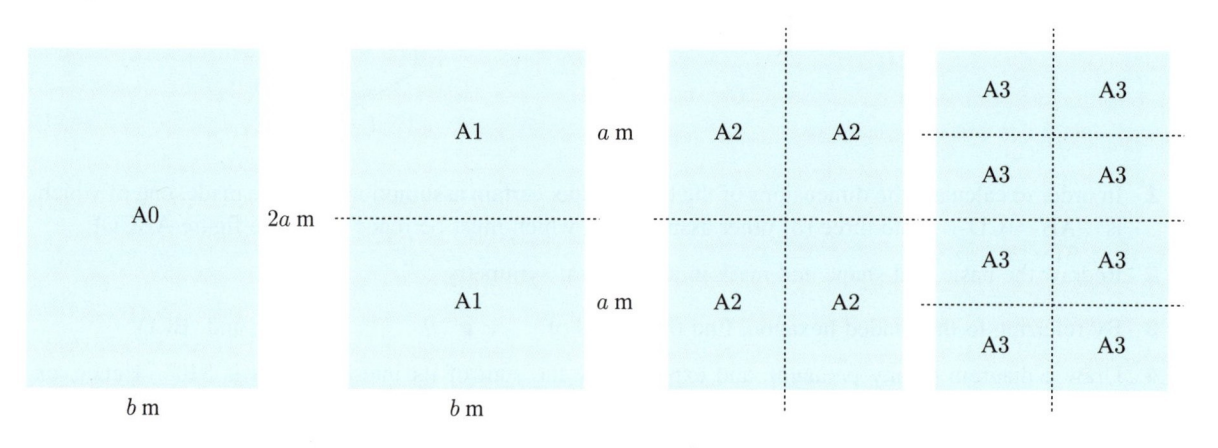

1 From one A0 sheet, how many sheets can be cut which have size:
   a A1   **b** A2   **c** A3   **d** A4   **e** A5?

2 Find the area of a sheet of size:
   a A1   **b** A2   **c** A3   **d** A4   **e** A5.

3 Suppose the A0 sheet is $2a$ m long and b m wide. Write down the dimensions of the A1 sheet, in terms of a and b.

4 Explain why $\dfrac{2a}{b} = \dfrac{b}{a}$.

5 From **4**, show that $b = \sqrt{2}a$.

6 Write the area of the A0 sheet in terms of a only.

7 Show that $a = \sqrt{\dfrac{1}{2\sqrt{2}}}$. Hence calculate the dimensions of an A1 page, correct to the nearest mm.

8 Find the dimensions of an A4 sheet, correct to the nearest mm.

9 A new T-series of paper sizes is about to be introduced. T0 will have area 2 m², and the remainder of the series will be cut in the same way as the A-series. Find the dimensions of the pages known as:
   a T0   **b** T1   **c** T2.

Investigation 12

The diagram given shows part of a tessellation pattern used on a seat cover. Each basic unit is to have this shape:

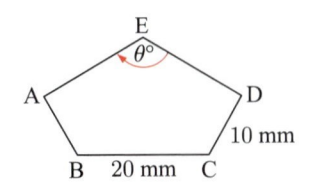

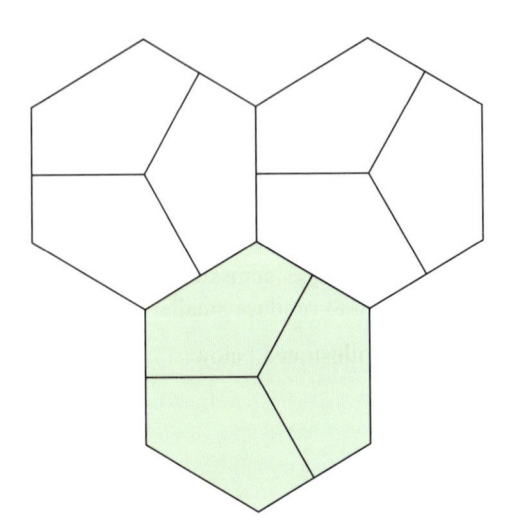

1 In order to calculate the dimensions of the basic shape, certain assumptions must be made, one of which is "AB = CD". State three (3) other assumptions which must be made about the figure ABCDE.

2 Redraw the basic unit shape and mark in any axes of symmetry.

3 By referring to the shaded hexagon, find the values of: **a** θ **b** $A\widehat{B}C$ and $B\widehat{C}D$.

4 Draw a diagram of any pentagon and explain why the sum of its interior angles is 540°. Hence, or otherwise, find the size of the interior angles at A and D.

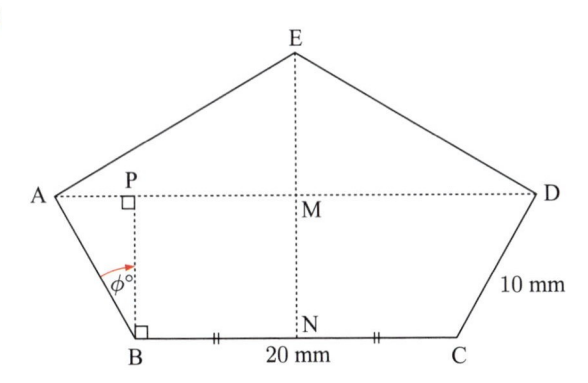

5 In the given figure:
   a find the value of ϕ
   b use trigonometry to find the length of AP
   c find the length of AM
   d find the length of AE correct to 1 decimal place.

6 Charlie wants to know how many pentagons are in 1 m² of seat cover material. He splits the figure into triangle ADE and trapezium ABCD.
   a Find the length ME.
   b Find the distance MN.
   c Calculate the area of each pentagon.
   d Answer Charlie's question, giving your answer to the nearest 100 pentagons.

Investigation questions (Chapter 29)

Investigation 13

From time to time all motor vehicle drivers must brake as rapidly as possible in order to stop the vehicle.

The **reaction time** of the driver is the time taken between seeing a problem and starting the braking. Reaction times vary from one person to another, and depend on physical fitness, age, tiredness, and the presence of medicines or drugs in the body.

The **reaction distance** is the distance travelled during the reaction time.

The **braking distance** is the distance travelled from where the driver first applies the brakes to where the car stops.

The **stopping distance** is found by adding the distance travelled while reacting to the distance travelled while braking.

$$\text{stopping distance} = \text{reaction distance} + \text{braking distance}$$

1 The reaction distance R is calculated using the formula $R = \dfrac{sr}{3.6}$ metres,

where $s = $ the speed of the vehicle in km/h, and
$r = $ the reaction time of the driver in seconds.

a The reaction time of a driver is 1.2 seconds. Find the reaction distance travelled by the car if the car is travelling at:
   i 60 km/h   **ii** 100 km/h.

b A driver is tired and her reaction time is 3.2 seconds. What is the reaction distance if she is travelling at 90 km/h?

2 Braking distance depends on the speed of the vehicle and the road surface. The braking distance B can be calculated using the formula $B = \dfrac{s^2}{210f}$ metres,

where $s = $ the speed of the vehicle in km/h, and
$f = $ the surface factor of the road.

Some surface factors for common road materials are given in the table below:

Dry bitumen	Wet bitumen	Loose gravel	Ice
0.8	0.45	0.55	0.1

a Find the braking distance of a car if:
   i the speed is 60 km/h and the surface is loose gravel
   ii the speed is 20 km/h and the surface is ice.

b A car is travelling at 80 km/h and the braking distance was recorded at about 70 metres. Which surface do you think the driver was travelling on?

3 What is the total stopping distance for a car travelling at 50 km/h if:
a the driver's reaction time is 0.9 seconds and the surface is wet bitumen
b the driver was distracted and reacted after 3 seconds, and the surface was ice?

4 Matt wants to know whether the reaction distance or the braking distance forms the greater part of the total stopping distance. His reaction time is 0.75 seconds, and he is initially interested in dry bitumen conditions only.

   a Use your calculator's table function to help copy and complete this table:

Speed (km/h)	Reaction distance (m)	Braking distance (m)
10		
20		
30		
40		
50		
60		
70		
80		
90		
100		

   b i For these conditions, estimate the speed at which the reaction distance and braking distance are the same.

      ii Use the equations for reaction distance and braking distance to find the exact non-zero value where these distances are equal.

   c For dry bitumen conditions, how would you answer Matt?

   d How would you answer Matt for other road surface conditions?

Investigation questions (Chapter 29)

Investigation 14

The perfect doughnut shape is called a **torus**.

1. If the torus is viewed from above, what mathematical shape is seen?
2. Draw the view seen from the side of the torus.

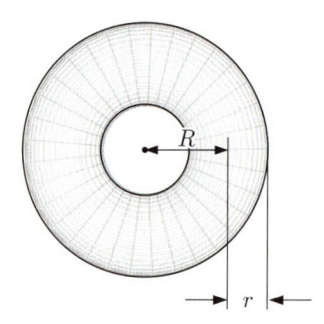

3. The volume of a doughnut can be calculated using the formula $V = 2\pi^2 R r^2$.

   a Find the volume of a doughnut where $R = 7$ cm and $r = 2$ cm.

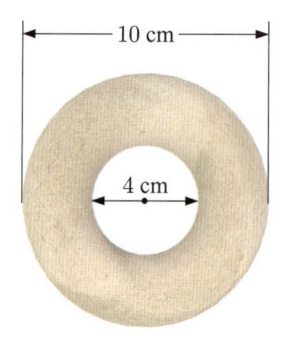

   b Anna makes doughnuts with the dimensions shown.

   i Find R and r.

   ii Find the volume of one of Anna's doughnuts.

4. Now consider a metal washer which has the dimensions shown. Its thickness is 4 mm.

   a Find the cross-sectional area of the washer.

   b Find the volume of the washer.

   c Could 1500 washers be made from a block of iron measuring 10 cm by 10 cm by 10 cm? Give reasons for your answer.

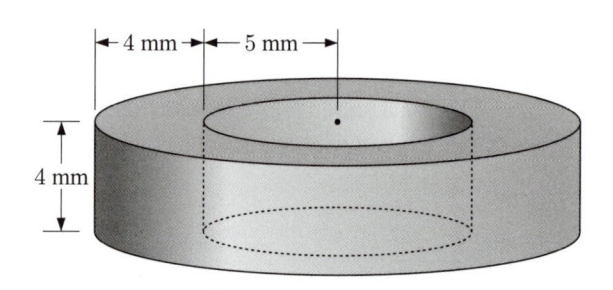

5 In this section we establish the formula for the volume of a doughnut.

a Start with a washer which has a square radial cross-section as shown in pink. The larger circle has radius $R + r$ and the square radial cross-section is $2r$ by $2r$.

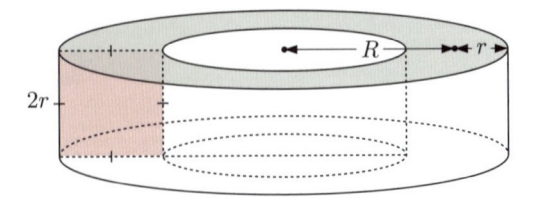

    i Find the radius of the inner circle.
    ii Explain why the shaded area of the upper surface of the washer can be calculated using $A = \pi(R+r)^2 - \pi(R-r)^2$.
    iii Show that the formula in **ii** simplifies to $A = 4\pi R r$.
    iv Explain why the washer has volume $V = 8\pi R r^2$.

b A vertical knife cut through the centre of a doughnut will expose two identical circular radial cross-sectional shapes. So, the doughnut is like the washer in **a**, but has a circular cross-section.

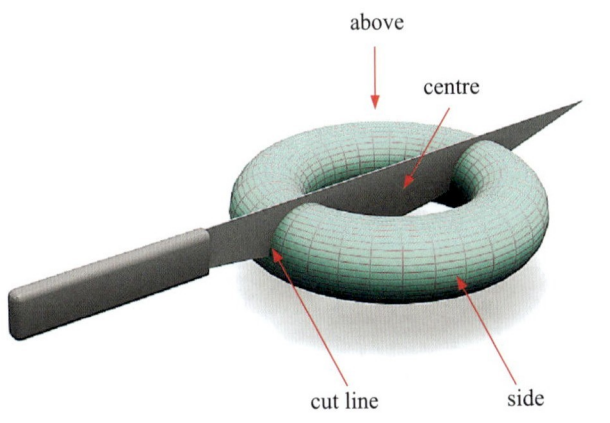

    i Find the area of the square cross-section in terms of r.
    ii What fraction of the square is occupied by the largest circle which can be drawn inside it?

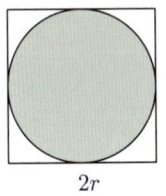

c Now replace the square cross-section by this largest circle.
    i What solid is now formed?
    ii Explain why this solid has volume $V = 2\pi^2 R r^2$.

Investigation questions (Chapter 29)

Investigation 15

The following graph shows the height of the tide above the bottom of a short shipping channel for a 24-hour period.

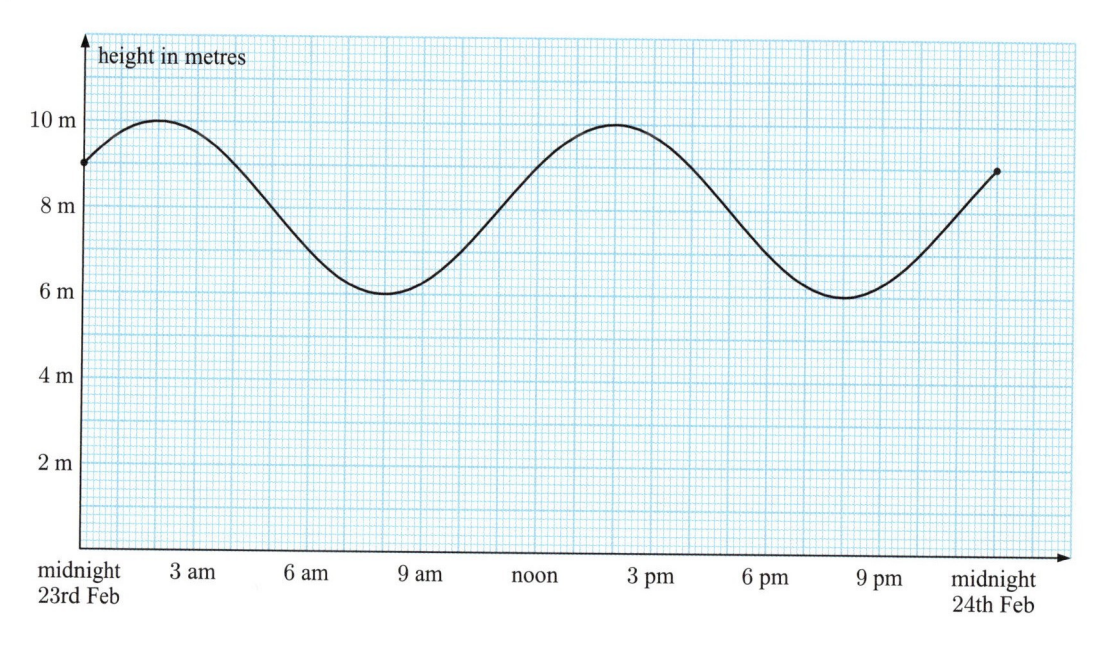

1 At what times was the tide: **a** highest   **b** lowest?
2 What was the average tide height?
3 At what times was the tide 8 m?
4 Estimate the time when the tide was 7 m.
5 A ferry sits in the water so its bottom is 5 m below water level. When can the ferry safely move along the channel?
6 A container vessel sits with its bottom 8 m below water level.
   a When can the container vessel move safely along the channel?
   b If the ship arrives at 8 am, how long will it have to wait to enter the channel?
   c Suppose the ship arrives at a random time of day. Find the probability that it will have to wait before moving through the channel.
7 The channel is dredged to make it 2 m deeper.
   a Describe in mathematical terms what happens to the graph of the tide.
   b Recalculate the probability from **6 c**.
   c Comment on the effectiveness of the dredging.

Investigation 16

Adapted from June 1989, Paper 6

Consider the figures **P** to **T**.

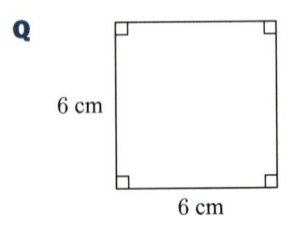

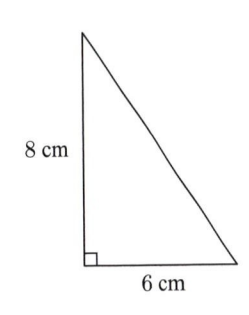

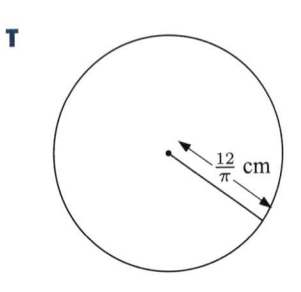

P — rectangle 8 cm × 4 cm

Q — square 6 cm × 6 cm

R — right-angled triangle, height 8 cm, base 6 cm

S — L-shaped figure with dimensions 3 cm, 2 cm, 4 cm, 6 cm

T — circle with radius $\frac{12}{\pi}$ cm

1. Calculate the perimeter of each of these figures. Write your results in the table.
   Comment on your results.

2. Find the area of each of these figures, and hence complete the table.

3. The regular hexagon **H** with side length 4 cm, has area ≈ 41.57 cm^2.
   Using the letters **P, Q, R, S, T**, and **H**, list the areas in order of size, starting with the smallest.

4. Explain any conclusion you arrive at.

Figure	Perimeter (cm)	Area (cm^2)
P		
Q		
R		
S		
T		
H	24	41.57

Investigation questions (Chapter 29)

Investigation 17

Adapted from November 1997, Paper 4

1. A tin of soup is 11 cm high and has a radius of 4 cm. Calculate the volume of the tin.

2. The tins are packed tightly in boxes of 12, as seen from above in the diagram opposite. The height of each box is 11 cm.
   a. Write down the diameter of each tin.
   b. Write down the length and the width of the box.
   c. Calculate the percentage of the volume of the box which is not occupied by the tins.

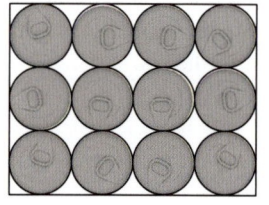

3. A shopkeeper buys the tins of soup for $0.90 each, and sells them for $1.20 each. For a box of 12 tins, find the:
   a. cost price
   b. selling price.

4. The shopkeeper tries to increase sales by offering a box of 12 tins for $12.98. At this price:
   a. how much does a customer save by buying a box of 12 tins
   b. what profit does the shopkeeper make on each box of 12 tins
   c. what *percentage* profit does the shopkeeper make on each box of 12 tins?

Investigation 18

Adapted from June 1997, Paper 4

Maria thinks of 3 possible savings schemes for her baby son.

Scheme A: save $10 on his 1st birthday, $20 on his 2nd birthday, $30 on his 3rd birthday, $40 on his 4th birthday, ...

Scheme B: save $1 on his 1st birthday, $2 on his 2nd birthday, $4 on his 3rd birthday, $8 on his 4th birthday, ...

Scheme C: save $1 on his 1st birthday, $4 on his 2nd birthday, $9 on his 3rd birthday, $16 on his 4th birthday, ...

1 The table alongside shows the amount saved with each scheme for the son's first four birthdays. Complete the table for his 5th, 6th, and 7th birthdays.

Scheme	\multicolumn{7}{c	}{Birthday}
	1st	2nd	3rd	4th	5th	6th	7th
A	$10	$20	$30	$40			
B	$1	$2	$4	$8			
C	$1	$4	$9	$16			

2 For each of the Schemes A, B, and C, write an expression for the amount to be saved on his nth birthday.

3 The formulae for the *total* amount saved up to and including his nth birthday are as follows:

$$\text{Scheme A:} \quad \text{total} = \$5n(n+1)$$
$$\text{Scheme B:} \quad \text{total} = \$(2^n - 1)$$
$$\text{Scheme C:} \quad \text{total} = \$\frac{n(n+1)(2n+1)}{6}$$

a For *each* of the schemes A, B, and C, find the total amount saved up to and including his 10th birthday.

b Which scheme gives the smallest total amount of savings up to and including his 18th birthday?

c Find the birthday when the scheme you have selected in **b** *first* gives the smallest total amount of savings.

Investigation questions (Chapter 29)

Investigation 19

The numbers in the **Fibonacci sequence** are called **Fibonacci numbers**.

The sequence is: 1, 1, 2, 3, 5, 8, ...

A **Fibonacci rectangle** is one in which the sides are consecutive Fibonacci numbers.

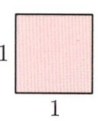

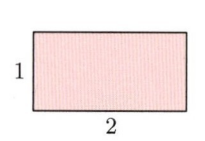

1 Write down the next four terms of the Fibonacci sequence.

2 Describe in words how each term is found from the previous two terms.

3 Draw examples of the next 3 Fibonacci rectangles.

4 Complete the following table where n is the position of the Fibonacci number in the sequence.

n	Fibonacci number	Fibonacci rectangle	Area of rectangle
1	1	1×1	1
2	1	1×2	
3	2	2×3	
4			
5			
6			
7			
8			
9			
10			

5 Add an extra column to your table which is the sum of the areas of the first n Fibonacci rectangles. You should find that the sum of the areas of the first ten Fibonacci rectangles is 7920.

6 Transfer the information from the *even* rows of your table to the table alongside.

n	Fibonacci number	Sum of areas of first n rectangles
2	1	
4		
6		
8		
10		

Hence, for *even* n, write an expression for the sum of the areas of the first n rectangles, in terms of n.

7 Transfer the information from the *odd* rows of your table to the table alongside.

n	Fibonacci number	Sum of areas of first n rectangles
1	1	
3	2	
5		
7		
9		

Hence, for *odd* n, write an expression for the sum of the areas of the first n rectangles, in terms of n.

Investigation questions (Chapter 29)

Investigation 20

In this investigation we discover relationships between the vertices, edges, regions, and faces, of **planar shapes** and **polyhedra**.

Part I: Planar shapes

Consider the figure alongside:

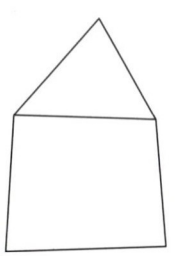

We can see that there are:

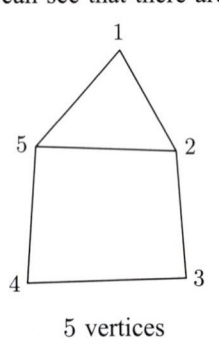

5 vertices 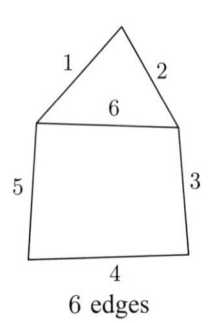   6 edges 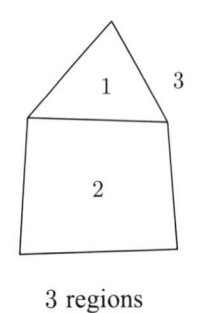   3 regions (outside the figure counts as a region)

1 Look at the following figures:

a

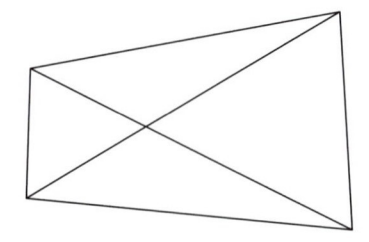

b

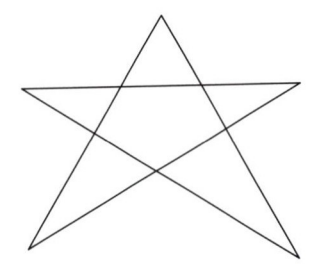

c

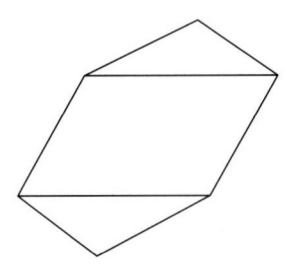

d

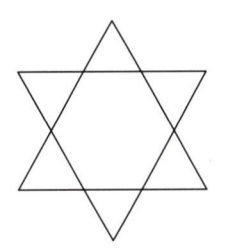

Copy and complete:

Figure	Vertices (V)	Regions (R)	Edges (E)
a			
b			
c			
d			

Investigation questions (Chapter 29)

2. Draw four more diagrams similar to those above.
3. Extend the table to include the example given at the top, and the four other diagrams that you have drawn in **2**.
4. For each diagram, find the value of $V + R$.
5. Find a relationship between V, R, and E. This relationship is one of **Euler's rules**.
6. Use the rules you have found to determine the number of:
   a. vertices in a figure with 7 edges and 3 regions
   b. edges in a figure with 5 vertices and 4 regions
   c. regions of a figure with 10 edges and 8 vertices.
7. Draw two *different* figures which have 5 vertices and 7 edges.

Part II: Polyhedra

The diagrams of four *polyhedra* are shown below. There is a relationship between the number of edges E, the number of faces F, and the number of vertices V for all solids bounded by planes.

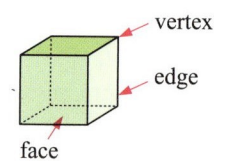

8. Copy and complete the following table for the solids labelled **a**, **b**, **c**, and **d**.

   a   **b** 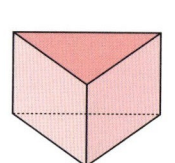   **c** 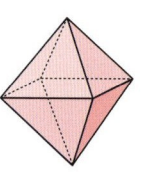   **d**

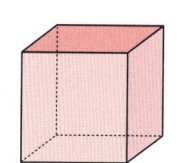

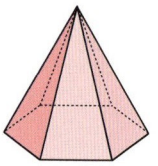

   e and **f** are for solids of your choosing.

Figure	F	V	F + V	E
a				
b				
c				
d				
e				
f				

9. Look carefully at the last two columns of your table. Can you see the relationship? This is **Euler's rule** for polyhedra.
10. Does Euler's rule apply for a solid with cut off corners?
11. Use Euler's rule for polyhedra to determine the number of:
    a. vertices if there are 9 edges and 5 faces
    b. edges if there are 8 faces and 12 vertices.
12. Dan believes he has discovered a polyhedron which has 8 vertices and 9 edges. Show that Dan has made an error in counting.

Answers

EXERCISE 1A

1.
Number	$\mathbb{N}$	$\mathbb{Z}$	$\mathbb{Q}$	$\mathbb{R}$
19	✓	✓	✓	✓
$-\frac{2}{3}$	×	×	✓	✓
$\sqrt{7}$	×	×	×	✓
5.6389	×	×	✓	✓
$\sqrt{16}$	✓	✓	✓	✓
2π	×	×	×	✓
-11	×	✓	✓	✓
$\frac{6}{0}$	×	×	×	×
$\sqrt{-2}$	×	×	×	×

2. **a** 1, 2, 5, 10 **b** 1, 2, 4, 8, 16 **c** 1, 2, 3, 4, 6, 12 **d** 1, 2, 3, 6, 9, 18 **e** 1, 17 **f** 1, 2, 4, 5, 10, 20 **g** 1, 2, 4, 8, 16, 32 **h** 1, 3, 7, 9, 21, 63 **i** 1, 2, 3, 4, 6, 9, 12, 18, 36 **j** 1, 2, 3, 6, 7, 14, 21, 42 **k** 1, 2, 4, 8, 16, 32, 64 **l** 1, 2, 4, 5, 10, 20, 25, 50, 100

3. **a** 49 **b** 125 **c** 11 **d** 169 **e** 13 **f** 216

4. **a** $16 = 4^2$, $529 = 23^2$, $20\,802\,721 = 4561^2$
   b $27 = 3^3$, $343 = 7^3$, $13\,824 = 24^3$
   c $\sqrt{11} \approx 3.32$
   $11 \div 2 = 5.5$
   $11 \div 3 = 3.\overline{6}$ So, 11 is a prime.
   $\sqrt{17} \approx 4.12$
   $17 \div 2 = 8.5$
   $17 \div 3 = 5.\overline{6}$ So, 17 is a prime.
   $\sqrt{97} \approx 9.85$
   $97 \div 2 = 48.5$
   $97 \div 3 = 32.\overline{3}$
   $97 \div 5 = 19.4$
   $97 \div 7 \approx 13.8$ So, 97 is a prime.
   d $64 = 8^2$ and $64 = 4^3$
   $729 = 27^2$ and $729 = 9^3$

5. 53, 59, 61, 67

6. 1 does not have two different factors.

7. $\sqrt{263} \approx 16.2$
   $263 \div 2 = 131.5$
   $263 \div 3 = 87.\overline{6}$
   $263 \div 5 = 52.6$
   $263 \div 7 \approx 37.6$
   $263 \div 11 \approx 23.9$
   $263 \div 13 \approx 20.2$ So, 263 is a prime.

EXERCISE 1B

1. **a** 10 **b** 2 **c** -8 **d** 10 **e** 6 **f** 6 **g** 24 **h** 24
2. **a** 37 **b** 43 **c** 3 **d** 24 **e** 6 **f** 19 **g** 12 **h** 10 **i** 6 **j** 16 **k** 20 **l** 2
3. **a** 17 **b** 13 **c** 1 **d** 9 **e** 69 **f** 9 **g** 43 **h** 7 **i** 25 **j** 3 **k** 16 **l** -2
4. **a** 4 **b** 21 **c** 13 **d** 92 **e** 10 **f** 15 **g** 108 **h** 4 **i** 7
5. **a** 5 **b** 3 **c** $\frac{1}{2}$ **d** 5 **e** 7 **f** 18 **g** 1 **h** $-\frac{1}{4}$
6. **a** 15 **b** 3 **c** -42 **d** $-\frac{1}{2}$ **e** 4 **f** 7 **g** 21 **h** 4 **i** 17 **j** 13 **k** $1\frac{1}{2}$ **l** $1\frac{1}{4}$
7. **a** 438 **b** 874 **c** 33 **d** 8 **e** -1053 **f** 4 **g** -6 **h** -83 **i** -8
8. **a** 4.75 m **b** £6.62 **c** 4510 km **d** 11.8 kg **e** 75 hours

EXERCISE 1C

1. **a** 6, 12, 18, 24, 30 **b** 11, 22, 33, 44, 55 **c** 13, 26, 39, 52, 65 **d** 29, 58, 87, 116, 145
2. **a** 3 **b** 4 **c** 6 **d** 13 **e** 1 **f** 5 **g** 9 **h** 24
3. **a** 198 **b** 493 **4** **a** 306 **b** 8004
5. **a** 24 **b** 24 **c** 42 **d** 72 **e** 30 **f** 28 **g** 30 **h** 36
6. **a** 36 **b** 75 **7** 60 seconds

EXERCISE 1D

1. **a** $\frac{12}{13}$ **b** $\frac{11}{16}$ **c** $\frac{5}{8}$ **d** $\frac{17}{30}$ **e** $4\frac{3}{7}$ **f** $2\frac{1}{6}$ **g** $3\frac{1}{2}$ **h** $6\frac{1}{6}$
2. **a** $\frac{4}{11}$ **b** $\frac{1}{6}$ **c** $\frac{1}{9}$ **d** $\frac{5}{8}$ **e** $1\frac{3}{4}$ **f** $1\frac{1}{10}$ **g** $1\frac{5}{6}$ **h** $2\frac{2}{21}$
3. **a** $\frac{1}{9}$ **b** $\frac{2}{7}$ **c** $1\frac{1}{2}$ **d** $4\frac{2}{3}$ **e** $1\frac{1}{7}$ **f** $\frac{1}{2}$ **g** $6\frac{1}{4}$ **h** $2\frac{10}{27}$
4. **a** $\frac{6}{7}$ **b** $\frac{11}{16}$ **c** $\frac{2}{3}$ **d** $\frac{1}{10}$ **e** $1\frac{2}{3}$ **f** $3\frac{5}{9}$ **g** $\frac{4}{9}$ **h** $1\frac{7}{20}$
5. **a** $5\frac{8}{35}$ **b** $1\frac{5}{6}$ **c** $2\frac{1}{2}$ **d** $\frac{2}{5}$ **e** 12 **f** $1\frac{1}{11}$ **g** $4\frac{2}{3}$ **h** $\frac{1}{2}$ **i** $1\frac{1}{6}$ **j** $\frac{3}{5}$ **k** $2\frac{3}{5}$ **l** $\frac{1}{10}$ **m** 11 **n** $1\frac{1}{4}$ **o** $4\frac{2}{5}$
6. **a** 35 goals **b** £240.00 **c** $\frac{7}{12}$ remains **d** **i** $\frac{2}{3}$ **ii** €610.00 **e** $\frac{1}{4}$
7. **a** 36 points **b** ¥7 560 000
8. **a** $\frac{8}{15}$ **b** $\frac{13}{21}$ **c** $\frac{19}{56}$ **d** $\frac{5}{12}$ **e** $\frac{3}{5}$ **f** $\frac{8}{21}$ **g** $\frac{12}{35}$ **h** $2\frac{7}{10}$ **i** $4\frac{1}{8}$ **j** $4\frac{5}{28}$ **k** $1\frac{6}{11}$

EXERCISE 1E

1. **a** 2, 4, 8, 16, 32, 64, 128, 256 **b** 3, 9, 27, 81, 243 **c** 4, 16, 64, 256 **d** 5, 25, 125, 625
2. **a** 5 **b** 2 **c** 2 **d** 3 **e** 3 **f** 5 **g** 4 **h** 5 **i** 10 **j** $1\frac{1}{2}$
3. **a** 4 **b** 2401 **c** 16 384 **d** 9 **e** 2.6 **f** 4.1 **g** 0.571 787 **h** 0.71 **i** 1.0 **j** 84.64 **k** 1.169 858 56 **l** 64.363 43 **m** 81 **n** -81 **o** 20.003 76

EXERCISE 1F.1

1. **a** 9 : 7 **b** 11 : 13 **c** **i** 8 : 9 **ii** 8 : 5 **iii** 5 : 9 **iv** 9 : 5

Answers

2 a 8 : 3   **b** 3 : 7   **c** 35 : 45   **d** 300 : 50
  e 500 : 3000   **f** 400 : 2500   **g** 9000 : 150
  h 12 : 8000   **i** 240 : 40

EXERCISE 1F.2

1 a 3 : 4   **b** 2 : 1   **c** 1 : 3   **d** 3 : 5
  e 1 : 2   **f** 7 : 4   **g** 1 : 2   **h** 3 : 4
  i 5 : 4   **j** 1 : 2 : 3   **k** 20 : 1   **l** 1 : 2 : 4
2 a 5 : 2   **b** 3 : 7   **c** 3 : 2   **d** 2 : 1
  e 7 : 12   **f** 1 : 4   **g** 4 : 1   **h** 1 : 20
3 a 1 : 2   **b** 3 : 1   **c** 3 : 1   **d** 3 : 5
  e 2 : 3   **f** 8 : 15   **g** 8 : 39   **h** 39 : 50
  i 2 : 1   **j** 1 : 2   **k** 4 : 1   **l** 6 : 4 : 3
4 a 1 : 4   **b** 3 : 1   **c** 1 : 5   **d** 5 : 7
  e 8 : 1   **f** 1 : 5   **g** 8 : 3

EXERCISE 1F.3

1 a $x = 12$ **b** $x = 3$ **c** $x = 10$ **d** $x = 28$ **e** $x = 35$
  f $x = 42$ **g** $x = 96$ **h** $x = 56$ **i** $x = 36$
2 a $x = 15$ **b** $x = 6$ **c** $x = 15$ **d** $x = 9$
  e $x = 3$ **f** $x = 16$
3 18 litres   **4** 1 kg (= 1 litre)   **5** €52
6 350 pencils   **7** 1.25 l
8 a **i** £480   **ii** £300   **iii** £800
  b **i** 3 m   **ii** 10 m   **iii** 0.9 m

EXERCISE 1F.4

1 23.04 cm   **2** £17 880   **3** 30.771 km/h   **4** 710 km
5 2212 HKD   **6 a** **i** 4.2 m   **ii** 1.32 m   **b** 3.55 mm
7 $9.92   **8** 15 : 16

EXERCISE 1F.5

1 a 5   **b** 5   **c** 16   **d** 17   **e** 13   **f** 19   **g** 11   **h** 19
2 a 60 m : 60 m   **b** 90 m : 30 m   **c** 48 m : 72 m
  d 52 m : 68 m
3 a £10 : £50   **b** $30 : $35   **c** €21.60 : €14.40
4 a €20 000   **b** €15 000   **5** 472 nurses
6 a $28.70   **b** 205 : 82
  c Bill gets 7.143 kg and Bob gets 2.857 kg.
7 Barry - £1 500 000, Robin - £1 000 000, Maurice - £3 500 000
8 a 7.2 kg   **b** 1.5 kg
9 a 24 Vauxhalls   **b** 8 Fords   **c** 12 Audis

EXERCISE 1G

1 a $0.65 = \frac{13}{20} = 65\% = 13 : 20$
  b $60\% = \frac{3}{5} = 0.6 = 3 : 5$ **c** $2 : 5 = \frac{2}{5} = 0.4 = 40\%$
  d $\frac{5}{8} = 0.625 = 5 : 8 = 62.5\%$

Decimal	Fraction	Ratio	Percentage
0.25	$\frac{1}{4}$	1 : 4	25%
0.85	$\frac{17}{20}$	17 : 20	85%
0.36	$\frac{9}{25}$	9 : 25	36%
0.8	$\frac{4}{5}$	4 : 5	80%
$0.\overline{2}$	$\frac{2}{9}$	2 : 9	$22.\overline{2}\%$
1.25	$1\frac{1}{4}$	5 : 4	125%
2	$\frac{2}{1}$	2 : 1	200%
5.5	$5\frac{1}{2}$	11 : 2	550%

EXERCISE 1H

1 a 70%   **b** 15%   **c** 0.9%   **d** $13.8\overline{3}\%$
2 7.85%   **3 a** €2541   **b** €254 100
4 a 0.6 kg   **b** $1092   **c** 84 kg   **d** 25 litres
  e 18.69 tonnes   **f** £16 469.78
5 108 marks   **6 a** 69.84 kg   **b** 2.05%
7 a £345   **b** £4355   **c** 7.34%
8 87.5%   **9** 30.4%   **10** 44%

EXERCISE 1I.1

1 a 1   **b** 7   **c** 8   **d** 12   **e** 128
2 a 2.4   **b** 3.6   **c** 4.9   **d** 6.4   **e** 4.3
3 a 4.24   **b** 2.73   **c** 5.63   **d** 4.38   **e** 6.52
4 a 0.2   **b** 0.18   **c** 0.184   **d** 0.1838
5 a 4.3   **b** 9.13   **c** 11.2   **d** 0.05   **e** 0.73
  f 0.025   **g** 0.5   **h** 6.17   **i** 2.429
6 7.45 cm ≈ 7.5 cm   is correct, however Julie should have used the original value of 7.45 cm to round to the nearest integer, i.e., 7.45 cm ≈ 7 cm.

EXERCISE 1I.2

1 a 42   **b** 6.24   **c** 0.046   **d** 0.25   **e** 440   **f** 2100
  g 31 000   **h** 10.3   **i** 1   **j** 1.0   **k** 264 000
  l 0.037 64   **m** 3699   **n** 0.0076   **o** 30 000   **p** 70
2 a **i** 30 000 people   **ii** 26 000 people   **b** 26 000 people
3 2549 people   **4** probably 133 000

EXERCISE 1I.3

1 a 320   **b** 400   **c** 420   **d** 3000   **e** 6400   **f** 14 000
2 a 2400   **b** 4200   **c** 9000   **d** 15 000   **e** 28 000
  f 150 000   **g** 90 000   **h** 360 000   **i** 720 000
3 a 100   **b** 1000   **c** 10 000   **d** 300   **e** 2000
  f 200   **g** 75   **h** 250   **i** 2000

EXERCISE 1J.1

1 a 300 minutes   **b** 4320 minutes   **c** 3780 minutes
  d 37 minutes
2 a 52 days   **b** 16 days   **c** 1095 days   **d** 0.25 days
3 a 2100 seconds   **b** 11 940 seconds
  c 432 000 seconds   **d** 777 600 seconds
4 a 5 h 8 min   **b** 7 h 11 min 10 sec
  c 4 h 5 min   **d** 2 h 35 min
5 54 hours
6 a 2 h 25 min   **b** 7 h 44 min   **c** 5 h 48 min
  d 6 h 35 min
7 1 h 14 min   **8 a** 42 hours   **b** €378
9 a 11.16 am   **b** 8.45 am   **c** 3.45 pm   **d** 9.48 am
10 3.15 pm   **11** 129.6 km

EXERCISE 1J.2

1 a 0957   **b** 1106   **c** 1600   **d** 1425   **e** 0800
  f 0106   **g** 2058   **h** 1200   **i** 0002
2 a 11.40 am   **b** 3.46 am   **c** 4.34 pm   **d** 7.00 pm
  e 8.00 am   **f** 11.30 pm   **g** 12.23 pm   **h** 8.40 pm

3

	Departure	Travelling Time	Arrival
a	0520	6 h 20 min	1140
b	0710	6 h 55 min	1405
c	0931	56 min	1027
d	1229	4 h 23 min	1652
e	2012	8 h 35 min	0447 (next day)

REVIEW SET 1A

1

Number	$\mathbb{N}$	$\mathbb{Z}$	$\mathbb{Q}$	$\mathbb{R}$
17.3	×	×	✓	✓
-5	×	✓	✓	✓
$\frac{4}{0}$	×	×	×	×
$\sqrt{6}$	×	×	×	✓
12	✓	✓	✓	✓

2 a 14   **b** $\frac{1}{4}$ **c** -33 **3** 14   **4** 390
5 a $\frac{34}{35}$ **b** 8   **6** 45 m   **7 a** 125   **b** 4
8 a 2 : 5   **b** 3 : 20   **9 a** 90 kg   **b** 28 kg
10 6 adults   **11** $220 000, $132 000, $88 000
12 a $0.75 = \frac{3}{4} = 75\% = 3 : 4$ **b** $\frac{2}{3} = 0.\overline{6} = 2 : 3 = 66.7\%$
13 35.34 kg   **14 a** 96   **b** 2.71   **15** 5 h 46 min

REVIEW SET 1B

1 Yes, 47 is a prime number.   **2** £83.08
3 1, 3, 5, 9, 15, 45   **4** 30   **5 a** $\frac{9}{10}$ **b** $\frac{1}{6}$ **c** $6\frac{1}{3}$
6 a 279 936   **b** 2.65   **7 a** 3 : 1   **b** 4 : 3 : 9
8 a $x = 20$ **b** $x = 40$ **9** 36.50 euros
10 2.6 kg   **11** 125 males   **12** 65.5%
13 a 457.27   **b** 35 000   **14 a** 8.05 pm   **b** 2005

EXERCISE 2A

1 a 5   **b i** true   **ii** false
   c i false   **ii** true   **iii** true   **iv** false
2 a i 12   **ii** 5   **b** $S' = \{1, 3, 5, 6, 8, 10, 12\}$
   iii 2 $T' = \{1, 2, 3, 5, 6, 7, 8, 9, 10, 12\}$
   c i true   **ii** false   **iii** true   **d i** false   **ii** true
   e $x = 2$ **f** finite as it contains a finite number of elements
3 a $\varnothing$, $\{a\}$
   b $\varnothing$, $\{a\}$, $\{b\}$, $\{c\}$, $\{a, b\}$, $\{b, c\}$, $\{a, c\}$, $\{a, b, c\}$
   c 16   (For a set with 1 element, 2 subsets;
       for a set with 2 elements, 4 subsets;
       for a set with 3 elements, 8 subsets.)
4 $\varnothing$, $\{2\}$, $\{4\}$, $\{7\}$, $\{9\}$, $\{2, 4\}$, $\{2, 7\}$, $\{2, 9\}$, $\{4, 7\}$, $\{4, 9\}$,
$\{7, 9\}$, $\{2, 4, 7\}$, $\{2, 4, 9\}$, $\{2, 7, 9\}$, $\{4, 7, 9\}$ (15 of them)
5 a $S = \{1, 2, 3, 6\}$ **b** $S = \{6, 12, 18, 24, \ldots\}$
   c $S = \{1, 17\}$ **d** $S = \{17, 34, 51, 68, \ldots\}$
   e $S = \{2, 3, 5, 7, 11, 13, 17, 19\}$
   f $S = \{12, 14, 15, 16, 18, 20, 21, 22, 24, 25, 26, 27, 28\}$
6 a 4   **b** is infinite   **c** 2   **d** is infinite   **e** 8   **f** 13
7 a $A = \{23, 29\}$, $B = \{22, 24, 26, 28\}$,
   $C = \{21, 22, 24, 25, 26, 27, 28\}$, $D = \varnothing$
   b i 2   **ii** 0   **c i** A and D **ii** B and D
   d i false   **ii** true   **iii** false
8 a i 7   **ii** 4   **iii** 3   **iv** 2   **v** 5
   b $n(S) + n(S') = n(\mathscr{E})$
9 $n(\varnothing) = 0$
10 If sets A and B are equal, this means the elements of A are
identical to the elements of B, so $n(A) = n(B)$.

EXERCISE 2B

1 a true   **b** true   **c** true   **d** true
   e false   **f** false   **g** true   **h** true
2 a, b, c, d, f, g, h are rational;   **e** is irrational
3 a $0.\overline{7} = \frac{7}{9}$ **b** $0.\overline{41} = \frac{41}{99}$ **c** $0.\overline{324} = \frac{12}{37}$
4 a 0.527 can be written as $\frac{527}{1000}$, and 527, 1000 are integers
   b $0.\overline{9} = 1$
5 a e.g., $\sqrt{2} + (-\sqrt{2}) = 0$ which is rational
   b e.g., $\sqrt{2} \times \sqrt{50} = \sqrt{100} = 10$ which is rational
6 a true   **b** false   **c** true
7 $\mathbb{Q}'$ represents all of the irrational numbers such as $\sqrt{3}$.

EXERCISE 2C

1 a The set of all real x such that x is greater than 4.
   b The set of all real x such that x is less than or equal to 5.
   c The set of all real y such that y lies between 0 and 8.
   d The set of all real x such that x lies between 1 and 4 or is equal to 1 or 4.
   e The set of all real t such that t lies between 2 and 7.
   f The set of all real n such that n is less than or equal to 3 or n is greater than 6.
2 a $\{2, 3, 4, 5, 6\}$ **b** $\{5, 6, 7, 8, 9, \ldots\}$
   c $\{\ldots, -4, -3, -2, -1, 0, 1, 2\}$ **d** $\{0, 1, 2, 3, 4, 5\}$
   e $\{-4, -3, -2, -1, 0, 1, 2, 3, \ldots\}$ **f** $\{1, 2, 3, 4, 5, 6\}$
3 a $\{x \mid -5 \leqslant x \leqslant -1, \ x \in \mathbb{Z}\}$
   There are other correct answers.
   b $\{x \mid x \leqslant 5, \ x \in \mathbb{N}\}$ There are other correct answers.
   c $\{x \mid x \geqslant 4, \ x \in \mathbb{Z}\}$ There are other correct answers.
   d $\{x \mid x \leqslant 1, \ x \in \mathbb{Z}\}$ There are other correct answers.
   e $\{x \mid -5 \leqslant x \leqslant 1, \ x \in \mathbb{Z}\}$
   There are other correct answers.
   f $\{x \mid x \leqslant 44, \ x \in \mathbb{Z}\}$ There are other correct answers.
4 a $\{x \mid x > 3\}$ **b** $\{x \mid 2 < x \leqslant 5\}$
   c $\{x \mid x \leqslant -1 \text{ or } x \geqslant 2\}$ **d** $\{x \mid -1 \leqslant x \leqslant 4, \ x \in \mathbb{Z}\}$
   e $\{x \mid 0 \leqslant x \leqslant 6, \ x \in \mathbb{N}\}$ **f** $\{x \mid x < 0\}$
5 a [number line from 4 to 8]   **b** [number line from −5 to 4]
c [number line open at −3, closed at 5]   **d** [number line from −5 to 0, integer points]
e [number line ≤ 6]   **f** [number line −5 to 0]
6 a finite   **b** infinite   **c** infinite   **d** finite
   e finite   **f** infinite

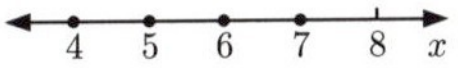

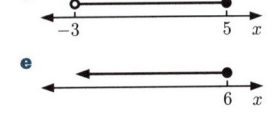

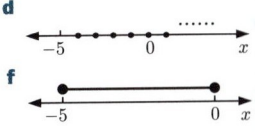

EXERCISE 2D

1 a [Venn diagram with $A = \{2, 3, 5, 7\}$; outside: 1, 4, 6, 8]
   $A = \{2, 3, 5, 7\}$
   b $A' = \{1, 4, 6, 8\}$
   c $n(A) = 4$, $n(A') = 4$
2 a [Venn diagram with $V = \{a, e, i, o, u\}$; outside: other letters]

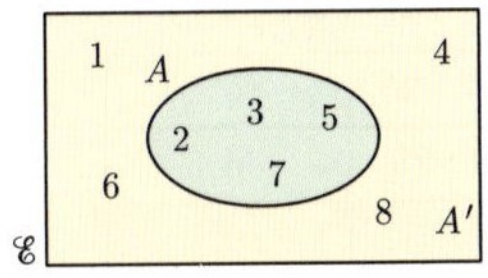

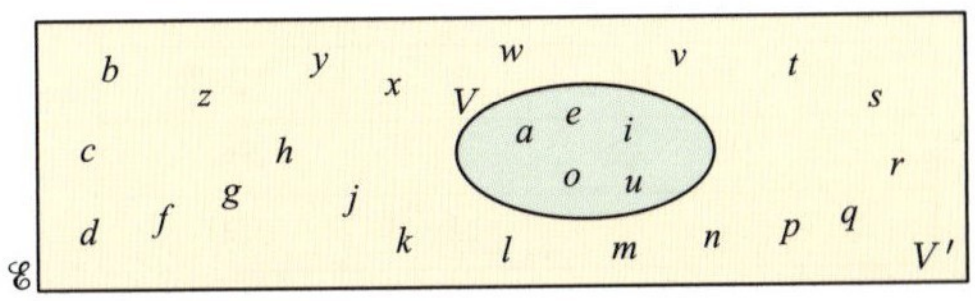

b $V' = \{b, c, d, f, g, h, j, k, l, m, n, p, q, r, s, t, v, w, x, y, z\}$

3 a i $\mathcal{E} = \{1, 2, 3, 4, 5, 6, 7, 8, 9, 10\}$
  ii $N = \{3, 8\}$ **iii** $M = \{1, 3, 4, 7, 8\}$
b $n(N) = 2$, $n(M) = 5$ **c** No, $N \nsubseteq M$.

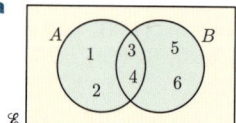

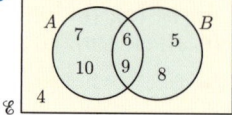

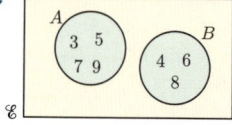

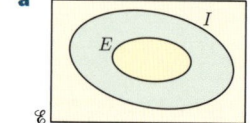

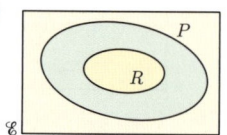

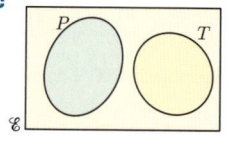

4
Venn diagram with sets S and L: S contains dolphins, whales; intersection contains otters, penguins, crocodiles; L contains cockroaches, parrots; outside: earthworms.

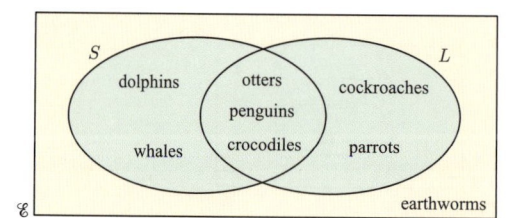

5 a Venn diagram A contains 1, 2; intersection 3, 4; B contains 5, 6.
b Venn diagram A contains 7, 10; intersection 6, 9; B contains 5, 8; outside 4.
c A contains 3, 5, 7, 9; B contains 4, 6, 8 (disjoint).

6 a E inside I.   **b** R inside P.
c P and T disjoint.   **d** H inside P.

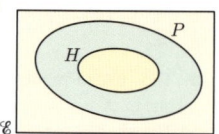

7 a/b Nested diagram: innermost N contains 0, 10; next $\mathbb{Z}$ contains -5; next $\mathbb{Q}$ contains $0.\overline{3}$, $\frac{1}{2}$, $5\frac{1}{4}$; outside $\mathbb{Q}'$: $0.2137005618.....$, $\sqrt{2}$.

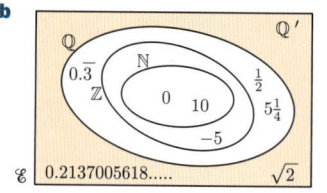

c i true   **ii** true   **iii** true
d (shaded section of diagram alongside)

EXERCISE 2E.1

1 a i $C = \{1, 3, 7, 9\}$ **ii** $D = \{1, 2, 5\}$
  iii $\mathcal{E} = \{1, 2, 3, 4, 5, 6, 7, 8, 9\}$ **iv** $C \cap D = \{1\}$
  v $C \cup D = \{1, 2, 3, 5, 7, 9\}$
b i $n(C) = 4$ **ii** $n(D) = 3$ **iii** $n(\mathcal{E}) = 9$
  iv $n(C \cap D) = 1$ **v** $n(C \cup D) = 6$

2 a i $A = \{2, 7\}$ **ii** $B = \{1, 2, 4, 6, 7\}$
  iii $\mathcal{E} = \{1, 2, 3, 4, 5, 6, 7, 8\}$ **iv** $A \cap B = \{2, 7\}$
  v $A \cup B = \{1, 2, 4, 6, 7\}$
b i $n(A) = 2$ **ii** $n(B) = 5$ **iii** $n(\mathcal{E}) = 8$
  iv $n(A \cap B) = 2$ **v** $n(A \cup B) = 5$

3 a Venn diagram: A contains 7, 4; intersection 2, 11, 9; B contains 1, 5, 6, 12; outside 3, 8; also 10 in A.

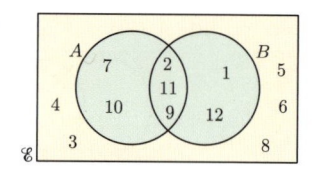

b i $A \cap B = \{2, 9, 11\}$
  ii $A \cup B = \{1, 2, 7, 9, 10, 11, 12\}$
  iii $B' = \{3, 4, 5, 6, 7, 8, 10\}$
c i $n(A) = 5$ **ii** $n(B') = 7$
  iii $n(A \cap B) = 3$ **iv** $n(A \cup B) = 7$

4 a $A \cap B = \{1, 3, 9\}$
b $A \cup B = \{1, 2, 3, 4, 6, 7, 9, 12, 18, 21, 36, 63\}$

5 a $X \cap Y = \{B, M, T, Z\}$
b $X \cup Y = \{A, B, C, D, M, N, P, R, T, W, Z\}$

6 a i $n(A) = 8$ **ii** $n(B) = 10$
  iii $n(A \cap B) = 3$ **iv** $n(A \cup B) = 15$
b $n(A) + n(B) - n(A \cap B) = 8 + 10 - 3 = 15 = n(A \cup B)$

7 a $n(A) + n(B) - n(A \cap B) = (a + b) + (b + c) - b$
$= a + b + c = n(A \cup B)$
b $A \cap B = \varnothing$, $\therefore n(A \cap B) = 0$

8 a $\varnothing$ **b** $\mathcal{E}$ **c** $\varnothing$

EXERCISE 2E.2

1 a not in A - shaded pink 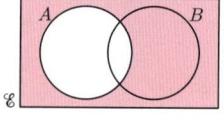 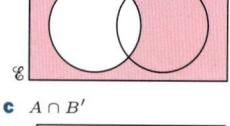
b in both A and B 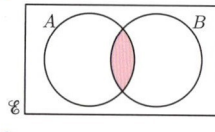
c $A \cap B'$ 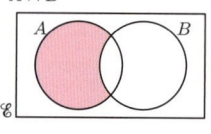
d in either A or B
e $A \cup B'$ 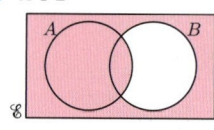
f $(A \cup B)'$
g $(A \cap B)'$ 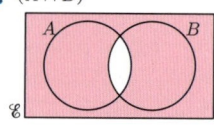
h in exactly one of A or B

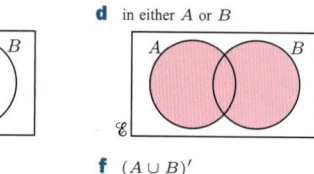

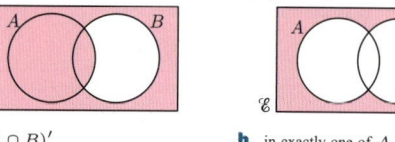

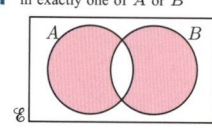

2 a the complement of 'in X'   **b** in X but not in Y
c the complement of 'in exactly one of X and Y'

3 a A' **b** $A' \cap B$

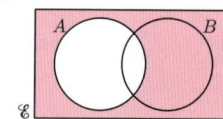

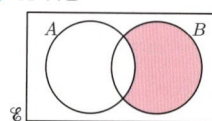

c $A' \cup B$ **d** $A' \cap B'$

4 a A **b** B'

c $A \cup B$ **d** $A \cap B$

5 a

▨ represents $A \cap B$
▩ represents $(A \cap B)'$

▨ represents A'
▩ represents B'
whole shaded region is $A' \cup B'$

b

▨ represents $A \cap B$
▩ represents $A' \cap B$
whole shaded region represents $(A \cap B) \cup (A' \cap B)$

▨ represents B

EXERCISE 2F

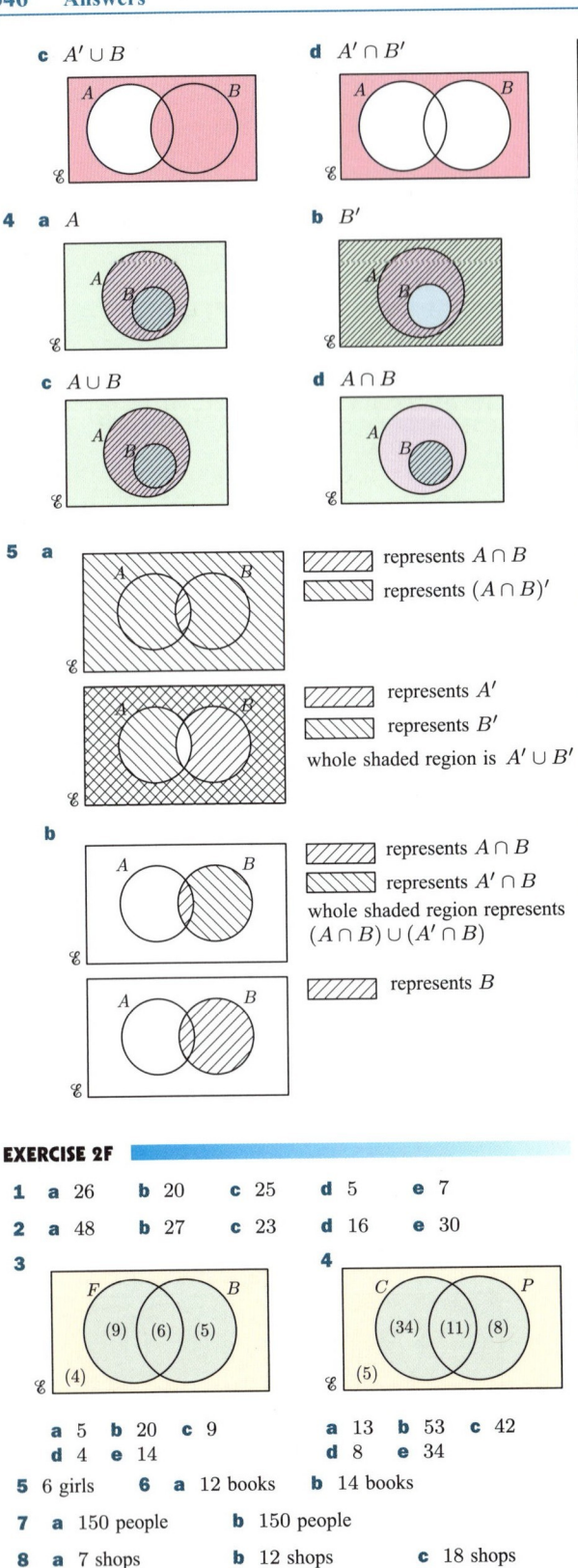

1 a 26 **b** 20 **c** 25 **d** 5 **e** 7
2 a 48 **b** 27 **c** 23 **d** 16 **e** 30

3 F (9) (6) (5) B (4)

a 5 **b** 20 **c** 9
d 4 **e** 14

4 C (34) (11) (8) P (5)

a 13 **b** 53 **c** 42
d 8 **e** 34

5 6 girls **6 a** 12 books **b** 14 books
7 a 150 people **b** 150 people
8 a 7 shops **b** 12 shops **c** 18 shops
9 14 cars **10** 39 people attended **11** 7% of them
12 1 worker uses both

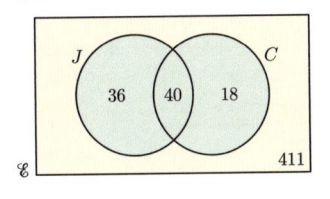

REVIEW SET 2A

1 a 1.3 can be written as $\frac{13}{10}$, and 13, 10 are integers
  b false **c** $\{23, 29, 31, 37\}$
  d The set of all real t such that t lies between -1 and 3, including -1.
  e $\{x \mid 0 < x \leqslant 5\}$ **f** [number line from -2 to 3]

2 a [Venn diagram with set A containing 3, 6, 9, 12; outside: 1, 2, 5, 4, 11, 10, 8, 7; A']

  b $A' = \{1, 2, 4, 5, 7, 8, 10, 11\}$ **c** $n(A') = 8$ **d** false

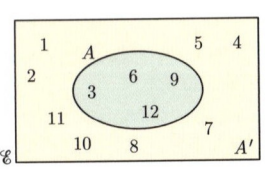

3 $\varnothing, \{1\}, \{3\}, \{6\}, \{8\}, \{1,3\}, \{1,6\}, \{1,8\}, \{3,6\}, \{3,8\}, \{6,8\}, \{1,3,6\}, \{1,3,8\}, \{1,6,8\}, \{3,6,8\}$ (15 of them)

4 a false **b** false

5 a i $A = \{1, 2, 3, 4, 5\}$ **ii** $B = \{1, 2, 7\}$
  iii $\mathcal{E} = \{1, 2, 3, 4, 5, 6, 7\}$
  iv $A \cup B = \{1, 2, 3, 4, 5, 7\}$ **v** $A \cap B = \{1, 2\}$
  b i $n(A) = 5$ **ii** $n(B) = 3$ **iii** $n(A \cup B) = 6$

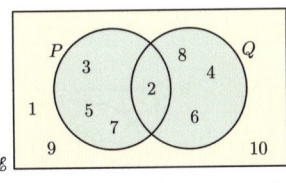

6 a [Venn diagram: P contains 3, 5, 7; intersection 2; Q contains 8, 4, 6; outside 1, 9, 10]

  b i $P \cap Q = \{2\}$ **ii** $P \cup Q = \{2, 3, 4, 5, 6, 7, 8\}$
  iii $Q' = \{1, 3, 5, 7, 9, 10\}$
  c i $n(P') = 6$ **ii** $n(P \cap Q) = 1$ **iii** $n(P \cup Q) = 7$
  d true

7 a The shaded region is the complement of X, i.e., everything not in X.
  b The shaded region represents 'in exactly one of X or Y but not both'.
  c The shaded region represents everything in X or in neither set.

8 [Venn diagram: J contains 36, intersection 40, C contains 18; outside 411] So, 505 took part.

REVIEW SET 2B

1 a i false **ii** false **b** $0.\overline{51} = \frac{51}{99}$, and 51, 99 are integers
  c $\{t \mid t \leqslant -3 \text{ or } t > 4\}$ **d** [number line]

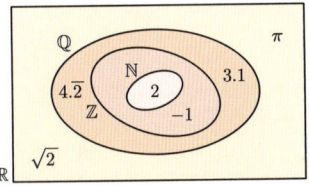

2 [Venn diagram with $\mathbb{R}$, $\mathbb{Q}$ containing 4.2, $\mathbb{Z}$ containing -1, $\mathbb{N}$ containing 2; π, 3.1 outside, $\sqrt{2}$ in $\mathbb{R}$]

Answers 547

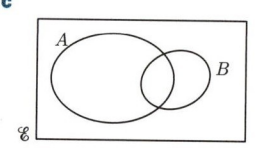

3 a [Venn diagram: A contains 10, 14; intersection 12; B contains 11, 13; outside 15]
b [Venn diagram: R with S inside, S shaded]
c [Venn diagram: A and B overlapping, no shading]

4 a $A \cap B = \{1, 2, 3, 6\}$
b $A \cup B = \{1, 2, 3, 4, 6, 8, 9, 12, 18, 24\}$

5 a [Venn diagram: A contains 2, 4, 6; intersection 3, 5, 7; B contains 1, 9; outside 8, 10]
b i $A' = \{1, 4, 6, 8, 9, 10\}$ **ii** $A \cap B = \{3, 5, 7\}$
c i false **ii** true **d i** 4 **ii** 5 **iii** 6

6 a B' **b** in A and in B
c $(A \cup B)'$

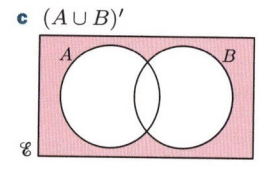

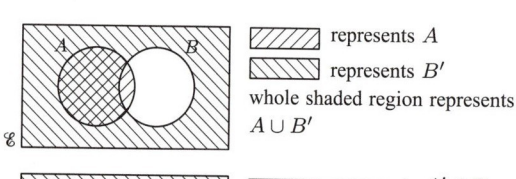

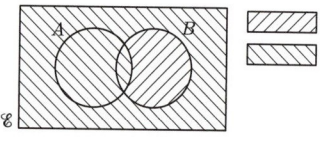

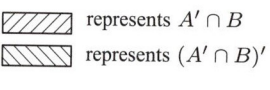

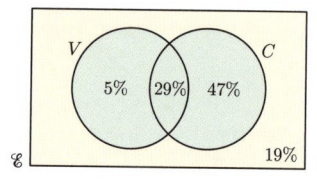

7 [Venn diagrams with shaded regions]
hatched represents A
cross-hatched represents B'
whole shaded region represents $A \cup B'$

hatched represents $A' \cap B$
cross-hatched represents $(A' \cap B)'$

[Venn diagram V, C with 5%, 29%, 47%, outside 19%]
So, 5% volunteered only.

CHALLENGE

4 people did not like any of the three bands.

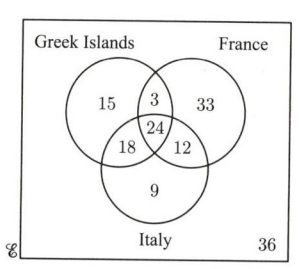

2 a [Venn diagram: Greek Islands 15, France 33, Italy 9; pairwise 3, 18, 12; centre 24; outside 36]
b i 15 people
ii 9 people
iii 36 people

EXERCISE 3A
1 5   **2** 14   **3** 28   **4** 7   **5** 12
6 18   **7** 32   **8** 13   **9** 9 and 10
10 a 4   **b** 7   **c** 10   **d** 31

EXERCISE 3B
1 a false, $z + 9$ is an expression   **b** true
c true   **d** false, $K = 4 + 5v$ is an equation
e false, $5p + 5y - 5$ has 3 terms   **f** true
g false, the coefficient of y in $3x - 2y - 4$ is -2
h false, the constant term in $5a + b - 4$ is -4
i false, the constant term in $7 + 3s + t$ is 7

2 a 3   **b** 5   **c** 6   **d** 2   **e** 1   **f** -3 **g** -1
h 1   **i** $-\frac{1}{2}$

3 a 1   **b** 2   **c** 2   **d** 3   **e** 2   **f** 3   **g** 2
h 2   **i** 2

4 a 4   **b** -3 **c** $2y$ and $4y$ **d** -5

5 a x and $3x$ **b** $2z$ and $4z$ **c** $-y$ and $4y$ **d** 2 and 8
e $-5x$ and $2x$; 3 and -1 **f** $3xy$ and $4xy$

6 a C   **b** A   **c** D   **d** B

EXERCISE 3C
1 a 21   **b** 18   **c** 17   **d** 0   **e** 2   **f** 6
g 13   **h** 15   **i** 4   **j** 15   **k** 6   **l** 15

2 a 10   **b** -7 **c** 16   **d** 15   **e** 12   **f** 24
g 8   **h** 3

3 a 7   **b** 0   **c** 0   **d** -36 **e** 64   **f** 31
g -96 **h** 16

4 a 5   **b** 9   **c** 19   **d** 49   **e** 20   **f** 4
g 5   **h** 10

5 a -24 **b** 4   **c** -3 **d** 45   **e** $-\frac{11}{7}$ **f** 38
g 14   **h** 43

EXERCISE 3D.1
1 a 7   **b** $2 + x$ **c** $y + z$ **d** $m + n + o$
2 a 40   **b** $6a$ **c** $2bc$ **d** eiu
3 a $\frac{7}{3}$ **b** $\frac{5}{t}$ **c** $\frac{k}{6l}$ **d** $\frac{f+g}{r}$
4 a $9 - 6$ **b** $r - 2$ **c** $x - y$
5 a $a + 3k$ **b** $2z - 5s$ **c** $\frac{b^2}{7}$ **d** $3d - 6$
e xy **f** $l + 2m + n$ **g** $r \times \frac{s}{2}$ **h** $\frac{w}{\sqrt{h}}$

EXERCISE 3D.2
1 a 540 pence   **b** $90c$ pence   **c** cy pence
2 a 24 kg   **b** $3t$ kg   **c** mt kg
3 a €2600   **b** €$(5000 - 200p)$ **c** €$(5000 - pq)$

548 Answers

4 **a** €5   **b** $€\left(\dfrac{40}{a}\right)$ **c** $€\left(\dfrac{b}{a}\right)$

5 $130 + k$ cm   6 $x + z + 13$ lines

7 **a** $14 - 8v$ litres   **b** $14 - bv$ litres

8 **a** 12 km   **b** kt km   **c** $\dfrac{s}{5}$ km/h   9 $4c + 7g$ euros

10 $12a + b + 250$ cents   11 $\dfrac{f+g+h}{3}$ grams

12 **a** $x+2$ **b** $x-6$ **c** $3x$ **d** $\dfrac{x}{5}$
    e $7x$ **f** $x+6$ **g** $2x+3$ **h** $\dfrac{x}{4}-9$

13 **a** .... $x - 5$.   **b** .... $100 - y$ m to go.
    c .... $2e$ chickens.   **d** .... $3a$.   **e** .... $j + 1$.
    f .... $u - 1, u - 2$.   **g** .... $17 - m$.   **h** .... $o + 2$.

14 **a** $s + s + 1 + s + 2$ **b** $k + k + 2$, where k is odd
    c $5x + 20(x+3)$ cents   **d** $5g + 4(20-g)$ euros
    e $23x + 15(17-x)$ pounds

EXERCISE 3E.1

1 **a** $x=-11$ **b** $x=-3$ **c** $x=-7$ **d** $x=-3$
   e $x=5$ **f** $x=9$ **g** $x=1$ **h** $x=-5$
   i $x=-2$ **j** $x=3$ **k** $x=-1\tfrac{1}{2}$ **l** $x=-6$

2 **a** $x=11$ **b** $x=-5\tfrac{1}{2}$ **c** $x=-4$ **d** $x=3\tfrac{1}{2}$
   e $x=1$ **f** $x=11$ **g** $x=-6$ **h** $x=11$
   i $x=-\tfrac{1}{2}$ **j** $x=-2$ **k** $x=4$ **l** $x=-9$

3 **a** $x=28$ **b** $x=-15$ **c** $x=-16$ **d** $x=-12$
   e $x=19$ **f** $x=-11$ **g** $x=10$ **h** $x=24$

4 **a** $x=-5\tfrac{1}{2}$ **b** $x=-3$ **c** $x=17$ **d** $x=-7$
   e $x=3$ **f** $x=8\tfrac{1}{2}$

EXERCISE 3E.2

1 **a** $x=6$ **b** $x=-3$ **c** $x=1\tfrac{1}{5}$ **d** $x=-3$
   e $x=-3\tfrac{1}{2}$ **f** $x=-4$ **g** $x=-3$ **h** $x=-\tfrac{1}{2}$
   i $x=-2\tfrac{1}{2}$

2 **a** $x=3$ **b** $x=2$ **c** $x=2$ **d** $x=6\tfrac{1}{2}$
   e $x=1$ **f** $x=6$ **g** $x=1\tfrac{1}{2}$ **h** $x=-2$
   i $x=-1\tfrac{1}{2}$

EXERCISE 3F

1 **a** $x=\pm 7$ **b** $x=\pm 11$ **c** $x=\pm 2\sqrt{14}$
   d $x=\pm\sqrt{46}$ **e** no solution as x^2 is never negative
   f no solution as x^2 is never negative   **g** $x=\pm\sqrt{23}$
   h $x=0$ **i** $x=\pm\sqrt{17}$

2 **a** $x=\pm 5$ **b** $x=\pm 4$ **c** $x=\pm 2$
   d $x=\pm 3$ **e** no solution as x^2 is never negative
   f $x=\pm\sqrt{6}$ **g** no solution as x^2 is never negative
   h $x=\pm 10$ **i** no solution as x^2 is never negative

EXERCISE 3G

1 **a** $x+6=13$ **b** $x-5=-4$ **c** $2x+7=1$
   d $\dfrac{x-1}{2}=45$ **e** $3x=17-x$ **f** $5x=x+2$

2 **a** $x+(x+1)=33$ **b** $x+(x+1)+(x+2)=102$
   c $x+(x+2)=52$ **d** $x+(x+2)+(x+4)=69$

3 **a** $40t + 25(10-t) = 280$ **b** $40p + 70(p-3) = 340$
   c $250t + 720t = 2910$

EXERCISE 3H

1 13   2 12   3 7   4 37 and 38
5 33   6 31   7 20   8 13   9 34
10 7 m   11 €27   12 85 cm per year

REVIEW SET 3A

1 **a** false   **b** false   **c** false   **d** true
2 **a** -12 **b** -11 **c** 0   **d** -12
3 **a** $x-5$ **b** $c+d+e^2$ 4 **a** $x=2$ **b** $x=8\tfrac{1}{2}$
5 **a** $x=\pm\sqrt{17}$ **b** no solution as x^2 is never negative
6 $x + 80(x+15) = 6240$
7 **a** 38   **b** 46, 47, and 48   **c** 124 pages

REVIEW SET 3B

1 **a** expression   **b** 4 terms   **c** -5 **d** 7   **e** $2x$ and $3x$
2 **a** -4 **b** 7   **c** $3\tfrac{1}{2}$ **d** 361   3 $9x + 3(2x)$ dollars
4 **a** $x=-4$ **b** $x=14$ 5 **a** $x=\pm 2$ **b** $x=0$
6 **a** $53-3x=29$ **b** $x+x+2=20$
7 **a** 11   **b** \$6.80   **c** \$12.50

EXERCISE 4A

1 **a**, **b**,  **c**, 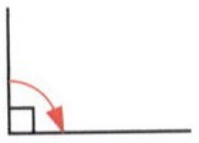 **d**, 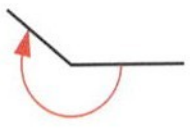 **e** (diagrams)

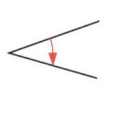

2 **a** acute   **b** reflex   **c** straight   **d** obtuse
   e reflex   **f** straight   **g** acute   **h** obtuse

3 **a** acute   **b** obtuse   **c** revolution   **d** reflex
   e acute   **f** right angle   **g** obtuse   **h** straight
   i reflex   **j** acute   **k** reflex   **l** obtuse

4 **a** 59°   **b** 48°   **c** 85°   **d** 74°   **e** 121°   **f** 133°

5 $\widehat{\text{KLM}}$

EXERCISE 4B

1 **a** ...... are collinear.   **b** ...... is a line segment.
   c ...... is line DF.   **d** ...... are concurrent at D.

2 **a**, **b**, 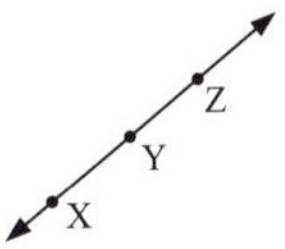 **c**, 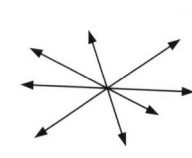 **d** (diagrams; **d** transversal)

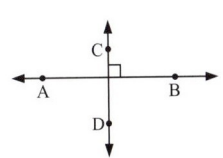

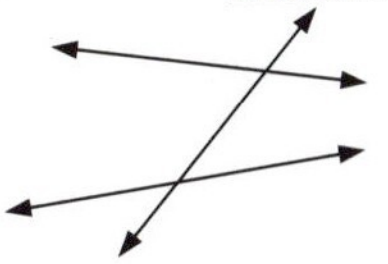

Answers 549

3

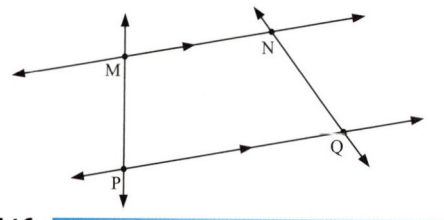

EXERCISE 4C

1
a right angled, scalene
b obtuse angled, isosceles
c obtuse angled, scalene
d equilateral
e acute angled, isosceles
f right angled, isosceles

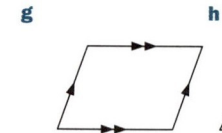

2 a b c d 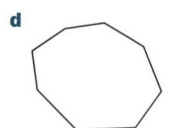 e 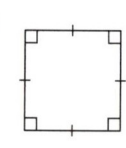 f 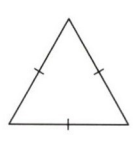 g h 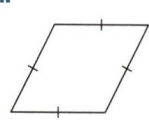 i

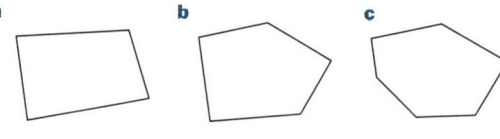

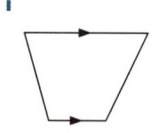

3 a
- Opposite sides are parallel.
- Opposite sides are equal in length.
- Opposite angles are equal in size.
- Diagonals bisect each other.

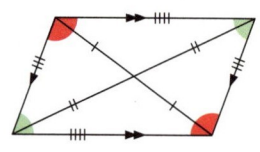

b
- All sides are equal in length.
- Opposite sides are parallel.
- Opposite angles are equal in size.
- Diagonals bisect each other at right angles.
- Diagonals bisect the angles at each vertex.

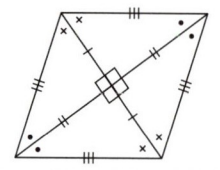

EXERCISE 4D

1 a 2 b 4 c 2 d 4 e 2 f 0 as is not a rhombus
g 10 h infinite i 3 j 5 k 1 l 3

2 A, B, C, D, E, H, I, K, M, O, T, U, V, W, X, Y

3 a b 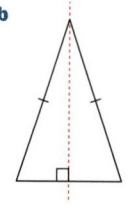 c

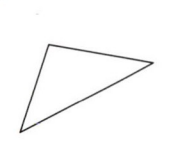

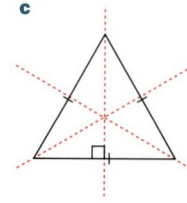

4 a 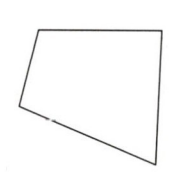 b 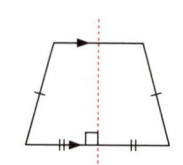 c 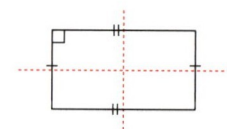 d

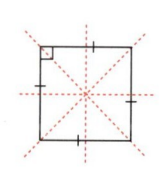

5 a 4 b 2 c 3 d 2 e 8 f 4
6 5   **7** H, I, N, O, S, X, Z

EXERCISE 4E

1 A and D; B and E   **2** A and O; E, I and M; F and H

3 a i FG   ii $F\hat{G}H$ b i ON   ii $O\hat{N}M$
c i QR   ii $Q\hat{R}P$ d i TS   ii $T\hat{S}R$
e i ON   ii $O\hat{N}M$ f i FE   ii $F\hat{E}D$

EXERCISE 4F

1 a $y = 44$ b $x = 122$ c $x = 141$ d $y = 180$
e $y = 99$ f $x = y = 90$

2 a $y = 55$ {angles in right angle}
b $f = 117$ {co-interior angles}
c $c = 102$ {co-interior angles}
d $y = 65$ {alternate angles}
e $x = 100$ {corresponding angles}
f $x = 49$ {co-interior angles}
g $x = 112$ {vertically opposite angles}
h $x = 45$ {angles at a point}
i $d = 333$ {angles at a point}
j $a = 116$ {corresponding angles}
k $x = 138$ {angles on a line}
l $b = 108$ {alternate angles}
m $a = 65$ {angles on a line}, $b = 65$ {corresponding angles}
n $a = 57$ {vert. opp. angles},
  $b = 57$ {corresponding angles}
o $a = 102$ {co-interior angles}, $b = 102$ {co-interior angles}
p $c = 90$ {angles on a line}
q $a = 59$ {angles on a line}, $b = 59$ {corresponding angles}
r $i = 218$ {angles at a point}
s $a = 122$ {vert. opp. angles}, $b = 58$ {co-interior angles}
  $c = 58$ {corresponding angles}, $d = 122$ {angles on a line}
t $b = 137$ {angles at a point}
u $r = 81$, $s = 81$ {corresponding angles}

3 a $d = 125$ {angles at a point}
b $e = 120$ {angles at a point}
c $f = 45$ {angles at a point}
d $h = 36$ {angles on a line}
e $g = 60$ {corresponding angles/angles on a line}
f $x = 85$ {co-interior angles}
g $x = 45$ {angles on a line}
h $x = 15$ {angles in right angle}
i $x = 42$ {angles at a point}

4 **a** KL ∥ MN {alternate angles equal}
  b KL ∦ MN {co-interior angles not supplementary}
  c KL ∥ MN {corresponding angles equal}
5 **a** $x = 60$, $y = 60$ **b** $a = 90$, $b = 35$
  c $p = 90$, $q = 25$, $r = 25$

EXERCISE 4G

1 **a** $a = 62$ {angles of a triangle}
  b $b = 91$ {angles of a triangle}
  c $c = 109$ {angles of a triangle}
  d $d = 128$ {exterior angle of a triangle}
  e $e = 136$ {exterior angle of a triangle}
  f $f = 58$ {exterior angle of a triangle}
2 **a** AB **b** AC **c** BC **d** AC and BC **e** BC
  f BC **g** BC **h** BC **i** AB
3 **a** true **b** false **c** false **d** false **e** true
4 **a** $a = 20$ {angles of a triangle}
  b $b = 60$ {angles of a triangle}
  c $c = 56$ {angles of a triangle}
  $d = 76$ {corresponding angles}
  d $a = 84$ {vert. opp. angles}, $b = 48$ {angles of a triangle}
  e $a = 60$ {angles on a line}
  $b = 100$ {ext. angle of a triangle}
  f $a = 72$, $b = 65$ {vertically opposite angles}
  $c = 137$ {ext. angle of triangle}
  $d = 43$ {angles on a line}
5 $46.5°$, $34.5°$ and $99°$

EXERCISE 4H

1 **a** $x = 36$ {isosceles triangle theorem/angles of a triangle}
  b $x = 55$ {isosceles triangle theorem/angles of a triangle}
  c $x = 36$ {isosceles triangle theorem/angles of a triangle}
  d $x = 73$ {isosceles triangle theorem}
  e $x = 60$ {angles on a line/isos. △ theorem/angles of a △}
  f $x = 32.5$ {isos. △ theorem/angles on a line/angles of a △}
2 **a** $x = 16$ {isosceles triangle theorem}
  b $x = 9$ {isosceles triangle theorem}
  c $x = 90$ {isosceles triangle theorem/
      line from apex to midpoint of base}
3 **a** equilateral **b** isosceles **c** equilateral **d** isosceles
  e equilateral **f** isosceles
4 **a** $x = 52$ **b** △ABC is isosceles (BA = BC)
5 **a** $\theta = 72$ **b** $\phi = 54$ **c** $\widehat{ABC} = 108°$
6 **a** $\theta = 36$ **b** $\phi = 72$ **c** $\widehat{ABC} = 144°$

EXERCISE 4I

1 **a** $360°$ **b** $540°$ **c** $720°$ **d** $1080°$
2 **a** $x = 87$ **b** $x = 43$ **c** $x = 52.5$ **d** $a = 108$
  e $a = 120$ **f** $a = 65$
3 **a** $x = 60$ {angles of a pentagon}
  b $x = 72$ {angles of a hexagon}
  c $x = 120$ {angles of a hexagon}
  d $x = 60$ {angles of a hexagon}
  e $x = 125$ {angles of a heptagon}
  f $x = 135$ {angles of an octagon}
4 $135°$ **5** **a** $108°$ **b** $120°$ **c** $135°$ **d** $144°$
6 12 angles **7** No such polygon exists.

8

Regular Polygon	No. of sides	No. of angles	Size of each angle
equilateral triangle	3	3	$60°$
square	4	4	$90°$
pentagon	5	5	$108°$
hexagon	6	6	$120°$
octagon	8	8	$135°$
decagon	10	10	$144°$

9 • $180(n-2)°$ • $\theta = \dfrac{180(n-2)°}{n}$
10 **a** Yes, these are all $30°$. **b** Yes, the two inner ones.
11 **a** $128\frac{4}{7}°$ **b** $\alpha = 25\frac{5}{7}$, $\beta = 102\frac{6}{7}$, $\gamma = 77\frac{1}{7}$, $\delta = 51\frac{3}{7}$
12 $\alpha = 60$, $\beta = 80$
13 We must be able to find integers k such that
  $k\left[\dfrac{(n-2) \times 180}{n}\right] = 360$ {angles at a point}
  $\therefore \ k = \dfrac{2n}{n-2}$ where $n = 3, 4, 5, 6, ...$
  The only possibilities are:
  $k = 6$, $n = 3$; $k = 4$, $n = 4$; $k = 3$, $n = 6$
  So, only equilateral triangles, squares and regular hexagons tessellate.
14 **a**   **b**

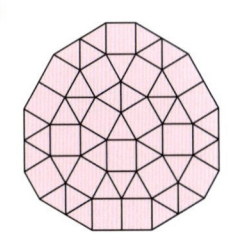

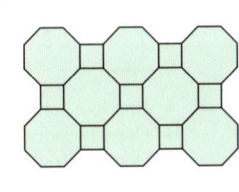

EXERCISE 4J

1 **a** $x = 120$ **b** $x = 95$ **c** $x = 60$
2 **a** $108°$ **b** $135°$ **c** $144°$ **d** $162°$ **e** $176.4°$
  f $\left(180 - \dfrac{360}{n}\right)°$
3 **a** 8 sides **b** 24 sides **c** 180 sides **d** 720 sides
4 **a** 6 sides **b** 12 sides **c** 72 sides **d** 360 sides

REVIEW SET 4A

1 **a** $\widehat{TPS}$ and $\widehat{TPQ}$ **b** $\widehat{PTS}$ and $\widehat{PST}$ **c** $\widehat{TPS}$
  d △QPU and △SPR
2 **a** rectangle **b** square **c** parallelogram
3 **a** 2 **b** 0 **c** 4
4 **a** ...... are equal in size.
  b ...... are supplementary (add to $180°$).
5 **a** $x = 72$ {corr. angles} **b** $x = 20$ {angles on a line}
  c $x = 242$ {angles at a point}
  d $x = 65$ {angles on a line/alternate angles}
  e $x = 40$ {vertically opposite/co-interior angles}
6 yes {angles on a line/alternate angles equal}
7 **a** $x = 62$ **b** $x = 152$ **c** $x = 68$
8 △ABC is isosceles since $\widehat{ACB} = \widehat{ABC} = 62°$
  {angles on a line/angles in a triangle/isosceles triangle theorem}
9 **a** $x = 122$ {angles in a quadrilateral}
  b $x = 60$ {opposite angles of parallelogram}
  $y = 5$ {opposite sides of parallelogram}

Answers

c Must be a parallelogram and so a rectangle. {equal opposite sides and one angle a right angle} $x = 35$, $y = 55$ {alternate angles}

10

Polygon	Number of sides	Sum of interior angles
pentagon	5	540°
hexagon	6	720°
octagon	8	1080°

11 **a** $x = 110$ {angles of a pentagon}
  b $x = 120$ {angles of a hexagon}
  c $x = 100$ {exterior angles of a polygon}
  d $x = 75$ {exterior angles of a polygon}

REVIEW SET 4B

1 **a** AK or BJ or CF
  b $D\hat{E}B$ or $H\hat{E}F$ or $K\hat{H}B$ or $J\hat{H}I$ or $G\hat{H}E$ or $J\hat{H}D$
  c GI, JB, and AK   **d** CF and GI
  e CF and AK, or GI and AK

2

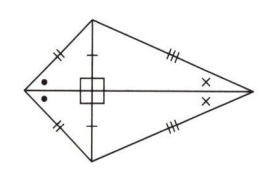

3 square, rhombus 4 **a** 5 **b** 6 **c** none
5 **a** $a = 73$ {angles on a line} **b** $b = 90$ {angles on a line}
  c $c = 56$ {vert. opp. angles}
  d $a = 110$ {alternate angles}, $b = 110$ {vert. opp. angles}
  e $x = 40$ {angles on a line}
6 **a** $x = 60$ {angles in a $\triangle$} **b** $a = 131$ {ext. angle of a $\triangle$}
  c $x = 2$ {equal sides of equilateral triangle}
7 $x = 96$ {corr. angles/isosceles $\triangle$ theorem/angles in a $\triangle$},
  $y = 96$ {corr. angles}
8 **a** right angled scalene **b** obtuse angled scalene
  c obtuse angled isosceles
9 **a** $x = 56$ {angles on a line/angles in a quadrilateral}
  b $a = 44$ {angles in a triangle}, $b = 46$ {alternate angles},
  $c = 88$ {isosceles triangle theorem/angles in a triangle}
10 **a** 150° **b** 160°
11 **a** $x = 100$ {vert. opp. angles/angles of a pentagon}
   b $x = 140$ {angles of a regular nonagon}

CHALLENGE

1 **a** sum = 180°
  b Sum always seems to be 180° (or close to it).
  c The sum of the angles of all '5-point stars' is 180°.
  d Hint: $B\hat{E}I + E\hat{B}I = J\hat{I}D$
2 **a** No, not regular, as not all angles are equal. **b**
  c 3
  d 262 cm

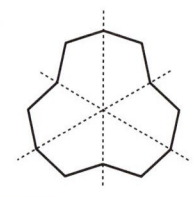

EXERCISE 5A

1 **a** $3x + 3$ **b** $10 - 2x$ **c** $-x - 2$ **d** $x - 3$
  e $4a + 8b$ **f** $6x + 3y$ **g** $5x - 5y$ **h** $-6x^2 + 6y^2$
  i $-2x - 8$ **j** $-6x + 3$ **k** $x^2 + 3x$ **l** $2x^2 - 10x$
  m $-3x - 6$ **n** $-4x + 12$ **o** $2x - 7$ **p** $-2x + 2y$
  q $a^2 + ab$ **r** $ab - a^2$ **s** $2x^2 - x$ **t** $2x^3 - 2x^2 - 4x$

2 **a** $2x + 5$ **b** $1 - 4x$ **c** $3x - 1$ **d** $2 - 4x$ **e** x^2
  f $6x - x^2$ **g** $2ab + a^2$ **h** $7x - 3x^2$ **i** $2x^2 - 10x$
3 **a** $5x - 2$ **b** $3a - 2b$ **c** $a + 2b$ **d** $15 - 3y$ **e** $-6y - 10$
  f $15x - 8$ **g** $a + 5b$ **h** $x^2 + 6x - 6$ **i** $x^2 + 2x + 6$
  j $2x^2 - x$ **k** $-2x^2 + 2x$ **l** $x^2 - y^2$ **m** $5 - 3x$
  n $8x - 8$ **o** $6x^2 - 22x$

EXERCISE 5B

1 **a** $x = 9$ **b** $x = -12$ **c** $x = 1$ **d** $x = -2$
  e $x = 2\frac{2}{3}$ **f** $x = -3$
2 **a** $x = -3$ **b** $x = 6$ **c** $x = 2$ **d** $x = 3$
  e $x = 2$ **f** $x = 1$
3 **a** $x = 0$ **b** $x = 2$ **c** $x = 3$ **d** $x = 3$
  e $x = -1$ **f** $x = -\frac{7}{9}$ **g** $x = -5$ **h** $x = 6$
  i $x = 3\frac{1}{2}$
4 **a** No solution as equation becomes $0 = 13$ which is never true.
  b An infinite number of solutions exist as equation becomes $6x - 12 = 6x - 12$ which is true for all x.
5 -2 6 50 7 9 8 13
9 17 five cent and 23 ten cent 10 5 roses
11 16 of 6-pack, 9 of 10-pack 12 650 litres

EXERCISE 5C

1 **a** $x = 3\frac{1}{3}$ **b** $x = 6$ **c** $x = \frac{2}{5}$ **d** $x = \frac{8}{27}$
  e $x = \frac{24}{25}$ **f** $x = 0$
2 **a** $x = -\frac{1}{4}$ **b** $x = -18$ **c** $x = -5$ **d** $x = 18$
  e $x = -1$ **f** $x = -\frac{1}{5}$ **g** $x = -1$ **h** $x = -5$
  i no solution
3 **a** $x = 12$ **b** $x = -\frac{36}{5}$ **c** $x = -\frac{16}{5}$ **d** $x = \frac{13}{7}$
  e $x = 16$ **f** $x = \frac{40}{7}$ **g** $x = \frac{16}{3}$ **h** $x = \frac{11}{5}$
  i $x = \frac{55}{28}$ **j** $x = \frac{4}{5}$ **k** $x = -\frac{6}{5}$ **l** $x = \frac{17}{24}$

EXERCISE 5D

1 **a** $A_1 = ac$ **b** $A_2 = ad$ **c** $A_3 = bc$ **d** $A_4 = bd$
  e $A = (a+b)(c+d)$
  $(a+b)(c+d) = ac + ad + bc + bd$
2 **a** $x^2 + 10x + 21$ **b** $x^2 + x - 20$ **c** $x^2 + 3x - 18$
  d $x^2 - 4$ **e** $x^2 - 5x - 24$ **f** $6x^2 + 11x + 4$
  g $1 + 2x - 8x^2$ **h** $12 + 5x - 2x^2$ **i** $6x^2 - x - 2$
  j $25 - 10x - 3x^2$ **k** $7 + 27x - 4x^2$ **l** $25x^2 + 20x + 4$
3 **a** $x^2 - 4$ **b** $a^2 - 25$ **c** $16 - x^2$ **d** $4x^2 - 1$
  e $25a^2 - 9$ **f** $16 - 9a^2$
4 **a** $x^2 + 6x + 9$ **b** $x^2 - 4x + 4$ **c** $9x^2 - 12x + 4$
  d $1 - 6x + 9x^2$ **e** $9 - 24x + 16x^2$ **f** $25x^2 - 10xy + y^2$
5 $A = (x + 6)(x + 4) = x^2 + 10x + 24$

EXERCISE 5E

1 **a** $x^2 - 4$ **b** $x^2 - 4$ **c** $4 - x^2$ **d** $4 - x^2$
  e $x^2 - 1$ **f** $1 - x^2$ **g** $x^2 - 49$ **h** $c^2 - 64$
  i $d^2 - 25$ **j** $x^2 - y^2$ **k** $16 - d^2$ **l** $25 - e^2$
2 **a** $4x^2 - 1$ **b** $9x^2 - 4$ **c** $16y^2 - 25$
  d $4y^2 - 25$ **e** $9x^2 - 1$ **f** $1 - 9x^2$
  g $4 - 25y^2$ **h** $9 - 16a^2$ **i** $16 - 9a^2$

3 **a** $4a^2 - b^2$ **b** $a^2 - 4b^2$ **c** $16x^2 - y^2$
  d $16x^2 - 25y^2$ **e** $4x^2 - 9y^2$ **f** $49x^2 - 4y^2$

4 **a** **i** 43×37 **ii** 24×26
  $= (40+3)(40-3)$ $= (25-1)(25+1)$
  $= 40^2 - 3^2$ $= 25^2 - 1^2$

  b **i** 396 **ii** 2499 **iii** 9991

EXERCISE 5F

1 **a** 3×5 **b** $3 \times x$ **c** $2 \times y$ **d** $x \times y$
  e $3 \times 13 \times x$ **f** $a \times a$
  g $5 \times 5 \times b \times b$ **h** $c \times c \times d$ **i** $7 \times x \times y$
  j $3 \times m \times m \times n$ **k** $2 \times 3 \times 7 \times p \times q \times q$
  l $2 \times 2 \times 3 \times 3 \times i \times j \times k \times k$

2 **a** $2a$ **b** $5b$ **c** $4xy$ **d** $4x$ **e** x **f** $-2x$
  g $-b$ **h** $4a$ **i** $-3xy$

3 **a** 2 **b** c **c** 1 **d** k **e** $3a$ **f** $5x$
  g $5x$ **h** $8y$ **i** 18

4 **a** ab **b** abc **c** $12a$ **d** a **e** r **f** q
  g $3b$ **h** dp **i** $4r$ **j** $3pq$ **k** $2ab$ **l** $6xy$
  m 5 **n** $12wz$ **o** $12pqr$

5 **a** $(x+2)$ **b** $2(x+5)$ **c** x **d** $2(x+1)$
  e $2(x+3)$ **f** $2x(x-3)$

EXERCISE 5G

1 **a** $2(x+2)$ **b** $3(a-4)$ **c** $5(3-p)$
  d $6(3x+2)$ **e** $4x(x-2)$ **f** $2m(1+4m)$

2 **a** $4(x+4)$ **b** $5(2+d)$ **c** $5(c-1)$ **d** $d(c+e)$
  e $2a(3+4b)$ **f** $2x(3-x)$ **g** $7a(b-1)$ **h** $2b(2a-3c)$

3 **a** $3(a+b)$ **b** $8(x-2)$ **c** $3(p+6)$ **d** $14(2-x)$
  e $7(x-2)$ **f** $6(2+x)$ **g** $c(a+b)$ **h** $6(2y-a)$
  i $a(5+b)$ **j** $c(b-6d)$ **k** $x(7-y)$ **l** $y(x+1)$
  m $a(1+b)$ **n** $y(x-z)$ **o** $p(3q+r)$ **p** $c(d-1)$

4 **a** $x(x+2)$ **b** $x(5-2x)$ **c** $4x(x+2)$
  d $7x(2-x)$ **e** $6x(x+2)$ **f** $x^2(x+9)$
  g $xy(x+y)$ **h** $2x^2(2x-3)$ **i** $9x(x^2-2y)$
  j $a(a^2+a+1)$ **k** $2(a^2+2a+4)$ **l** $3a(a^2-2a+3)$

5 **a** $9(b-a)$ **b** $3(2b-1)$ **c** $4(b-2a)$
  d $c(d-7)$ **e** $a(b-1)$ **f** $6x(2-x)$
  g $5x(3x-1)$ **h** $2b(2a-b)$ **i** $a(a-1)$

6 **a** $-6(a+b)$ **b** $-4(1+2x)$ **c** $-3(y+2z)$
  d $-c(9+d)$ **e** $-x(1+y)$ **f** $-5x(x+4)$
  g $-3y(4+y)$ **h** $-9a(2a+b)$ **i** $-8x(2x+3)$

7 **a** $(x-7)(2+x)$ **b** $(x+3)(a+b)$ **c** $(x+2)(4-x)$
  d $(x+9)(x+1)$ **e** $(b+4)(a-1)$ **f** $(b+c)(a+d)$
  g $(m+n)(a-b)$ **h** $(x+3)(x-1)$

8 **a** $(x+3)(x-1)$ **b** $(x-7)(x+7)$ **c** $(x+6)(x-4)$
  d $(x-2)(x-8)$ **e** $x+2$ **f** $(a+b)(4-a)$
  g $3(a-2)(a-4)$ **h** $(x+4)(4x+1)$
  i $5(x-1)(6-x)$ **j** $-(x+5)(4x+17)$

REVIEW SET 5A

1 **a** $3x-12$ **b** $-15-5y$ **c** $2y^2-2z$
  d x^2+x **e** $3x^2-6x$ **f** $-3x^2+15x$

2 **a** $x=-1\tfrac{2}{3}$ **b** $x=1\tfrac{7}{9}$ **c** $x=-1\tfrac{1}{7}$

3 **a** $x^2-5x-24$ **b** $x^2+3x-10$ **c** $-x^2+5x-4$
  d x^2+6x+9 **e** x^2-25 **f** $2x^2+2x-12$

4 13 cans

5 **a** x^2-36 **b** $16x^2-1$ **c** $12x^2-5x-2$
  d $2x^2+3x-15$

6 **a** $3c$ **b** $4p$ **c** $3rs$

7 **a** $2(3a+4)$ **b** $3x(x-4)$ **c** $3x(5-2x)$
  d $-2x(2+y)$ **e** $(x-3)(x+3)$ **f** $(x+2)(x-1)$

REVIEW SET 5B

1 **a** $4x-8$ **b** $28-7x$ **c** $8x+x^2$ **d** $rt-st$
  e $4-x$ **f** $6x+6$

2 **a** $x=\tfrac{1}{4}$ **b** $x=8\tfrac{1}{3}$ **c** $x=5$

3 **a** x^2-6x-7 **b** $x^2+8x+12$ **c** $-x^2-2x+15$
  d $x^2-8x+16$ **e** x^2-1 **f** $-2x^2+13x-20$

4 **a** x^2-16 **b** $4-9d^2$ **c** $16x^2-y^2$

5 **a** $\dfrac{n}{2}+\dfrac{2n}{5}+3=n$, where n is the total number of students in the class
  b 15 students

6 **a** 4 **b** 3 **c** $2x$

7 **a** $6(4+x)$ **b** $7(x-1)$ **c** $-4(3x-1)$
  d $x(5x-4)$ **e** $(x+5)(x-11)$ **f** $(x+9)(2x+3)$

8 84

REVIEW SET 5C

1 **a** $21+6a$ **b** $35x+5y$ **c** $2a^2-2ab$
  d $4am-4an^2$ **e** $-2x-2$ **f** $2x^2+24$

2 **a** $x=1\tfrac{3}{7}$ **b** $x=1\tfrac{1}{15}$ **c** $x=5$

3 **a** $x^2+3x-18$ **b** $x^2-13x+22$ **c** $-x^2+x+12$
  d $2x^2-3x-5$ **e** $x^2+14x+49$ **f** $4x^2+21x-18$

4 **a** x^2-25 **b** $1-49x^2$ **c** $64-q^2$
  d $-x^2+7x+18$

5 **a** $13 \times 17 = (15-2)(15+2)$ **b** 891
  $= 15^2 - 2^2$

6 **a** $3(3k-2)$ **b** $3x(5+4x)$ **c** $-4a(2a+1)$
  d $5b(a+2b)$ **e** $-(x+3)(x-3)$ **f** $-(x-7)(x-6)$

7 fifteen 5cent coins **8** 332 votes

EXERCISE 6A

1 **a** 8 **b** AB$^-$ **c** O$^+$, O$^-$, A$^+$, A$^-$

2 **a** **i** 38 **ii** 69 **b** **i** 81.6% **ii** 43%

3 **a** **i** 17.5 °C **ii** 25 °C **iii** 32 °C
  b **i** 1 pm to 6 pm **ii** 6 am to 1 pm **c** 34 °C at 1 pm

4 **a** **i** 35 000 000 t **ii** 20 000 000 t
  b $\approx$ 552 000 000 t **c** $\approx$ 34.5% **d** $\approx$ 76.3%

5 **a** 80 students **b** banana **c** 12.5% **d** 57.5%

6 **a** 8% **b** Austria, France, South Korea
  c South Korea **d** O$^-$ **e** Hong Kong

7 **a** **i** 20 - 29 **ii** 80+ **b** **i** 500 **ii** 1.09%
  c **i** 39.8% **ii** 9.11%

8 **a** 9 km **b** 50 min **c** 4 km **d** 30 min **e** 10.8 km/h

9 **a** **i** 865 km **ii** 129 km **b** 1379 km **c** 2 h 55 min

Answers

EXERCISE 6B

1 a Subjects taught by teachers in a school (bar chart: Maths 6, English 7, Science 4, Humanities 5, Mod. Languages 4, Theatre Arts 2, PE 2)

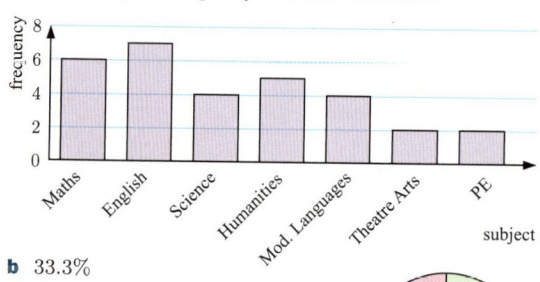

b 33.3%

2 a Aston 195°, Bentley 90°, Corvette 75°   **b** Toy car makes (pie chart)

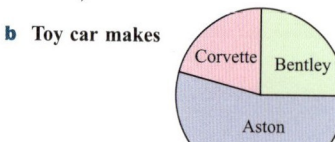

3 Midday temperature in Kingston (bar chart: Su 23, Mo 20, Tu 18, We 25, Th 27, Fr 24, Sa 26)

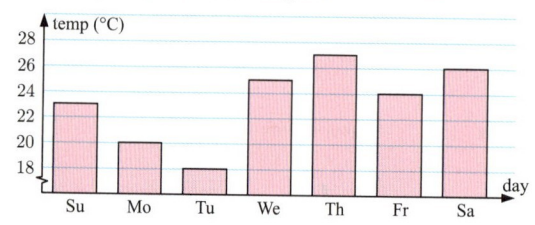

Rainfall in Kingston (bar chart: Su 8, Mo 4, Tu 2, We 11, Th 10, Fr 9, Sa 1)

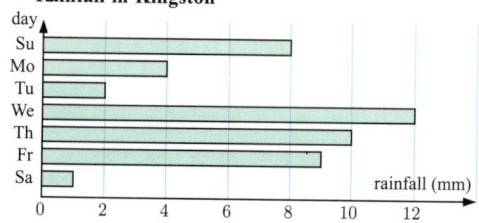

4 a
Stem	Leaf
2	9 7 4 1 7 5
3	3 0 5 4 6 4
4	6 0 2 8
5	8 7 1 0

b
Stem	Leaf
2	1 4 5 7 7 9
3	0 3 4 4 5 6
4	0 2 6 8
5	0 1 7 8

Key: 5 | 8 means 58

5 a Science Test results
2	9
3	8 9
4	3 4 7
5	1 3 5 6 6 6 8 9 9
6	1 2 2 3 4 4 4 6 7 7 8 8 9
7	0 1 2 3 4 5 6 8
8	0 0 0 1 7 8 8 9 9 9
9	0 2 2 5

Key: 2 | 9 means 29

b 28% **c** 12%

6 a 188 students **b** 9.5° **c** 1440 students

7 a The data is continuous. Therefore we use a line graph.

b Shadow length over time data (line graph)

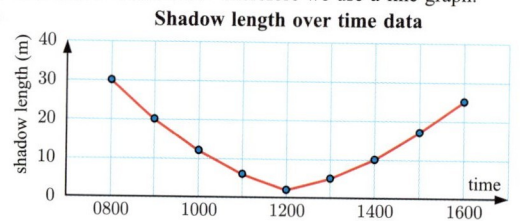

8 a 1 **b** 43 **c** 10 **d** 1 **e** 21.4%

9 a A scatter diagram as the data is discrete.

b Golf score data for Guy (scatter plot)

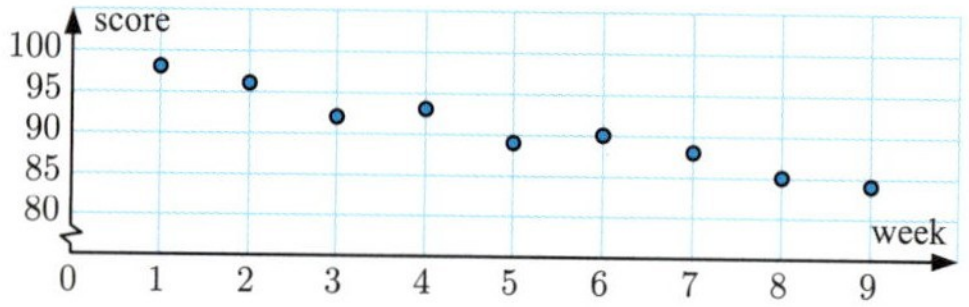

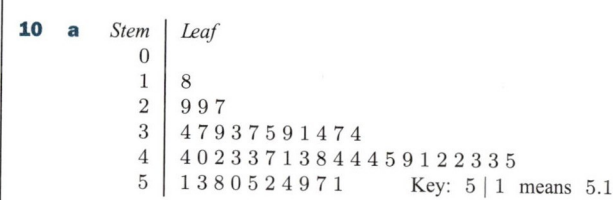

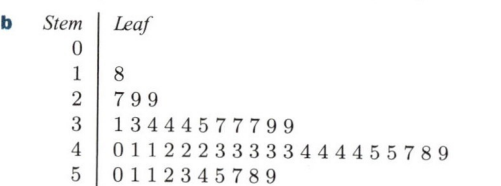

10 a
Stem	Leaf
0	
1	8
2	9 9 7
3	4 7 9 3 7 5 9 1 4 7 4
4	4 0 2 3 3 7 1 3 8 4 4 4 4 5 9 1 2 2 3 3 5
5	1 3 8 0 5 2 4 9 7 1

Key: 5 | 1 means 5.1

b
Stem	Leaf
0	
1	8
2	7 9 9
3	1 3 4 4 4 5 7 7 7 9 9
4	0 1 1 2 2 2 3 3 3 3 3 4 4 4 4 5 5 7 8 9
5	0 1 1 2 3 4 5 7 8 9

c The stem-and-leaf plot shows all the actual data values.

d i 5.9 **ii** 1.8 **e** 22.2% **f** 8.9%

EXERCISE 6C

1 a A and B are very similar, with minor variations.
b The values of A are generally higher than the values of B.
c The values of B are generally higher than the values of A.
d A and B are very similar. **e** A and B are very similar.
f A and B are very similar.

2 'Outside USA' service makes Pedro happier than 'Inside USA' service. This is because there are generally fewer breakages with the private company.

3 a In 2010 as the scores are more closely grouped.
b In 2010, 842 compared with 559 in 2009.

4 a Real estate sales data 09-10 (back-to-back bar chart 2009 vs 2010)

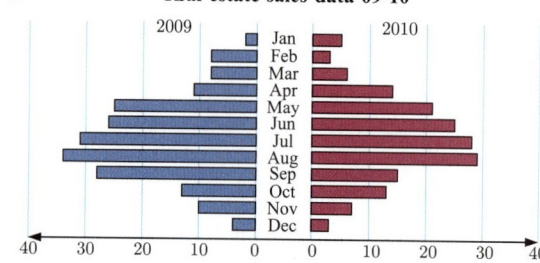

b The sales each month are quite similar for both years although more houses were sold in total in 2009. (This is Northern hemisphere data as more houses sell in warmer weather.)

5 a Travel times to university

Alex (train)		Stan (bus)
7 5	1	8 9
7 5 3 2	2	2 4 5 8 9
6 4 4 0	3	0 1 1 2 4 6 8
8 5 1	4	2
5	5	
0	6	

Key: 4 | 2 means 42 min

b As the bus data is less spread out, travelling by bus is more reliable.

6 a

```
        Golf driving distances
   Amon              Maddie
    8 7  | 14 |
    9 2  | 15 | 0 2
    5 5 0 | 16 | 7 8 9
  7 4 4 2 | 17 | 4 5 7 8 9
  8 8 3 1 0 | 18 | 0 0 2 2 8 9
  4 2 1 1 | 19 | 4 5 6 7    Key: 17 | 4 means 174 m
```

b Yes, shots with Maddie's driver are less spread out and therefore more consistent. They are also generally longer hits.

EXERCISE 6D

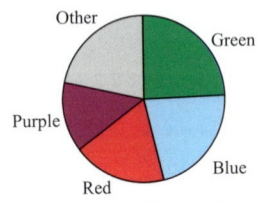

1 Pie chart with sectors: Other, Green, Blue, Red, Purple.

2 a Comparison of weekly incomes (column graph: after 5 years and after 10 years for Kaylene, Harry, Wei, Matthew).

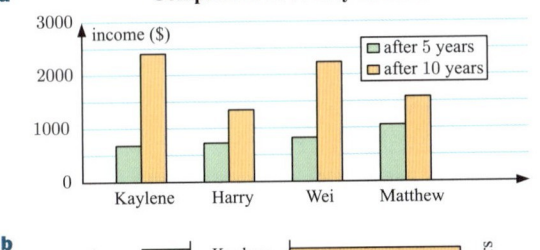

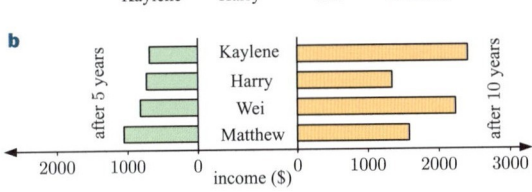

b Horizontal bar graph comparing after 5 years and after 10 years for Kaylene, Harry, Wei, Matthew.

c

Graduate	% increase
Kaylene	252
Harry	84.8
Wei	173
Matthew	49.8

d Kaylene and Wei

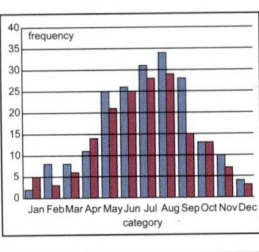

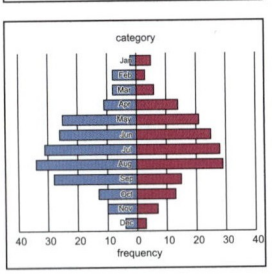

3 a i Frequency column graph by month (Jan–Dec).

ii Horizontal back-to-back bar graph by month.

b Either; a personal preference.

REVIEW SET 6A

1 a $2\,500\,000$ km^2 **b** Tunisia   **c** 45%   **d** 27.9%

2 a £720 000
b Admin. 72°, Production 100°, Marketing 90°, Distribution 60°, Advert. 38°
c Business expenses (pie chart): Marketing 25%, Production 27.8%, Admin 20%, Advertising 10.6%, Distribution 16.7%

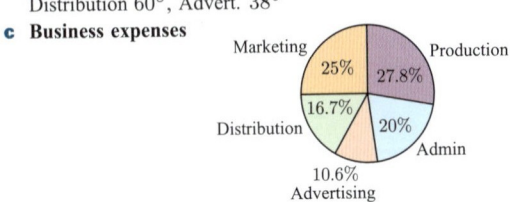

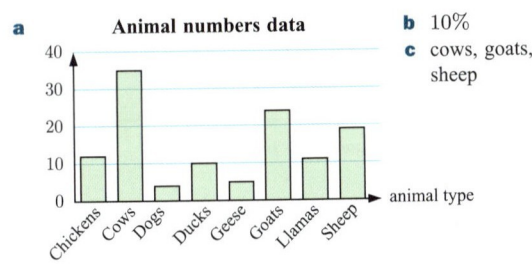

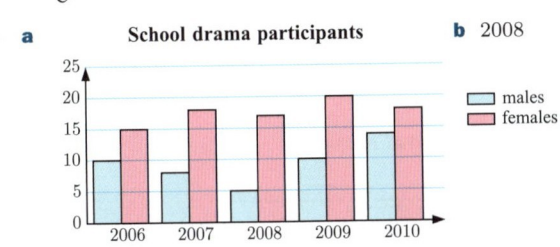

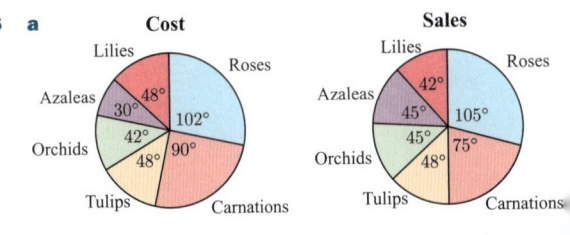

3 a Animal numbers data (column graph: Chickens, Cows, Dogs, Ducks, Geese, Goats, Llamas, Sheep)
b 10%   **c** cows, goats, sheep

4 a School drama participants (column graph by year 2006–2010, males and females)   **b** 2008

5 a 5 | 1 means 51 kg   **b** 28 kg   **c** 65 kg   **d** 54 kg

6 a Cost pie chart: Lilies 48°, Roses 102°, Carnations 90°, Tulips 48°, Orchids 42°, Azaleas 30°.
Sales pie chart: Lilies 42°, Roses 105°, Carnations 75°, Tulips 48°, Orchids 45°, Azaleas 45°.

b Roses and Carnations   **c** Roses and Carnations
d Lilies as he makes least profit (only £6000).

7 a

```
     Weights of men data
    Before            After
              | 6  | 8 8
          9   | 7  | 4 8 9 9
        6 3 2 | 8  | 3 3 4 5 9
      9 8 7 5 3 | 9  | 2 3 5 6 9 9
        4 4 1 0 | 10 | 2 6 6 7
        9 7 4 1 1 | 11 | 0 3
        5 3 2 1 0 | 12 | 2 5
              5 2 | 13 |
              Key: 10 | 2 means 102 kg
```

b Yes, the 'After' weights are significantly less than the 'Before' weights as a group.

REVIEW SET 6B

1 a 602 400 t   **b** 2002   **c** barley, oats
d 70.2%   **e** 12.6%

Answers 555

2 Speeding driver data (bar chart, Jan–Dec, frequency)

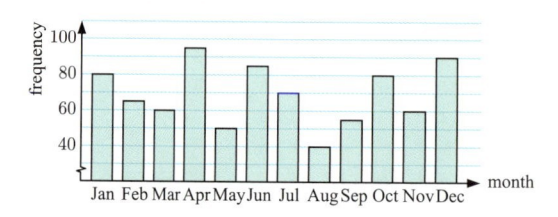

3 a A line graph.
b IBM share price data (scatter/line graph, days 1–10, prices 115–119)
c i Day 10 **ii** Day 1

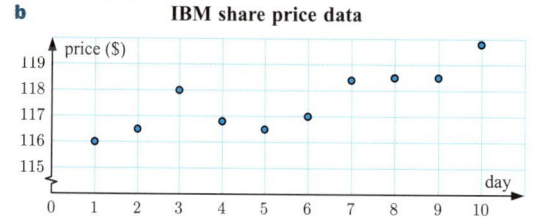

4 Weights of new-born babies

Stem	Leaf
2	3 8
3	1 3 4 5 6 8 9 9
4	0 0 1 2 4
5	1

Key: 5 | 1 means 5.1 kg

5 a Rebounds (back-to-back bar chart for Rhys and Evan)
b Evan, as his data is more closely grouped. **c** Rhys

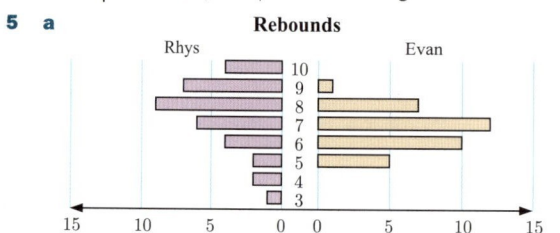

6 a Pet owner data (bar chart of men and women by number of pets 0–5)
b Women own more pets.

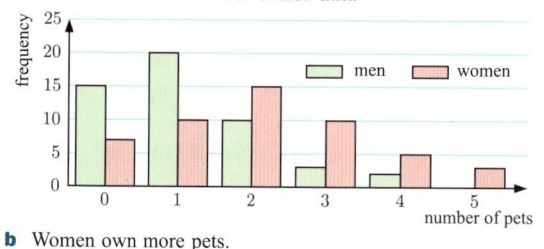

7 Pie chart: Travel 15.5%, Work 36.3%, Apprenticeship 19.2%, University 29.0%

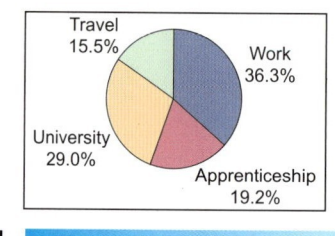

EXERCISE 7A.1

1 a 8 **b** 27 **c** 32 **d** 125
  e 24 **f** 1125 **g** 196 **h** 73 205
  i 540 **j** 1176 **k** 2925 **l** 4400

2 a $12 = 2^2 \times 3$ **b** $15 = 3 \times 5$ **c** $28 = 2^2 \times 7$
  d $24 = 2^3 \times 3$ **e** $50 = 2 \times 5^2$ **f** $98 = 2 \times 7^2$
  g $108 = 2^2 \times 3^3$ **h** $360 = 2^3 \times 3^2 \times 5$
  i $1128 = 2^3 \times 3 \times 47$ **j** $784 = 2^4 \times 7^2$
  k $952 = 2^3 \times 7 \times 17$ **l** $6500 = 2^2 \times 5^3 \times 13$

3 a $n = 5$ **b** $n = 8$ **c** $n = 12$
4 a $n = 3$ **b** $n = 6$ **c** $n = 10$ **5** 3 **6** 7
7 a $n = 625$ **b** $n = 7$ **c** $n = 5$ **d** $n = 6$

EXERCISE 7A.2

1 a 1 **b** -1 **c** 1 **d** 1 **e** -1 **f** 1
  g -1 **h** -1

2 a -27 **b** -27 **c** 27 **d** 36 **e** -36 **f** -36
  g -64 **h** -64 **i** 64

3 a -32 **b** -81 **c** -64 **d** 49 **e** -27
  f 8 **g** -1296 **h** -625

4 a -72 **b** 108 **c** -648

5 a 256 **b** 625 **c** -243 **d** 2401 **e** 512
  f 117 649 **g** $-117\,649$ **h** 1.795 856 326
  i $-0.005\,487\,423\,936$ **j** $-325\,687.9871$

EXERCISE 7B

1 a $2^4 = 16$ **b** $2^4 = 16$ **c** $3^9 = 19\,683$
  d $5^5 = 3125$ **e** x^6 **f** a^4 **g** n^{10} **h** b^8

2 a $2^1 = 2$ **b** $3^3 = 27$ **c** $5^4 = 625$
  d $4^4 = 256$ **e** x^3 **f** y^3 **g** a **h** b^4

3 a $2^6 = 64$ **b** $3^{12} = 531\,441$ **c** $2^{18} = 262\,144$
  d $10^{10} = 10\,000\,000\,000$ **e** x^6 **f** x^{15} **g** a^{20}
  h b^{24}

4 a $3^4 = 81$ **b** $5^6 = 15\,625$ **c** $7^2 = 49$
  d $2^8 = 256$ **e** $2^6 = 64$ **f** 11
  g $3^6 = 729$ **h** $5^6 = 15\,625$

5 a a^7 **b** n^8 **c** a^4 **d** a^6 **e** b^5 **f** a^{18}
  g a^{n+5} **h** b^8 **i** b^3 **j** m^{14} **k** a^{10} **l** g^{11}

6 a a^3b^3 **b** a^4c^4 **c** b^5c^5 **d** $a^3b^3c^3$
  e $16a^4$ **f** $25b^2$ **g** $81n^4$ **h** $8b^3c^3$
  i $\dfrac{8}{p^3}$ **j** $\dfrac{a^3}{b^3}$ **k** $\dfrac{m^4}{n^4}$ **l** $\dfrac{32c^5}{d^5}$

EXERCISE 7C

1 a 1 **b** $\dfrac{1}{6}$ **c** $\dfrac{1}{4}$ **d** 1 **e** 9 **f** $\dfrac{1}{9}$
  g 125 **h** $\dfrac{1}{125}$ **i** 49 **j** $\dfrac{1}{49}$ **k** 1000 **l** $\dfrac{1}{1000}$

2 a $\dfrac{1}{x}$ **b** $\dfrac{1}{k}$ **c** $\dfrac{1}{t^3}$ **d** $\dfrac{1}{r^5}$

3 a 1 **b** 1 **c** 2 **d** 1 **e** 1 **f** 3 **g** $\dfrac{1}{25}$
  h $\dfrac{1}{16}$ **i** 4 **j** $\dfrac{8}{3}$ **k** $\dfrac{3}{2}$ **l** 5 **m** 3 **n** $\dfrac{4}{5}$
  o $\dfrac{11}{3}$ **p** 9 **q** $\dfrac{27}{8}$ **r** $\dfrac{8}{27}$ **s** $\dfrac{25}{16}$ **t** $\dfrac{4}{25}$

4 a $\dfrac{1}{3b}$ **b** $\dfrac{3}{b}$ **c** $\dfrac{7}{a}$ **d** $\dfrac{1}{7a}$ **e** t^2 **f** $\dfrac{1}{16t^2}$
  g $\dfrac{1}{25t^2}$ **h** $\dfrac{t^2}{5}$ **i** $\dfrac{x}{y}$ **j** $\dfrac{1}{xy}$ **k** $\dfrac{x}{y^3}$ **l** $\dfrac{1}{x^3y^3}$
  m $\dfrac{1}{3pq}$ **n** $\dfrac{3}{pq}$ **o** $\dfrac{3p}{q}$ **p** x^3y^5

5 a 5^2 **b** 5^{-2} **c** 3^3 **d** 3^{-3}
  e 2^4 **f** 2^{-4} **g** $2^1 3^{-1}$ **h** $3^1 5^{-1}$
  i $3^2 5^{-3}$ **j** $2^5 3^{-4}$ **k** $2^2 3^1 5^{-1}$ **l** $3^1 5^2 2^{-3}$

6 a 10^3 **b** 10^{-2} **c** 10^5 **d** 10^{-6}

EXERCISE 7D.1

1 **a** 10^2 **b** 10^3 **c** 10^1 **d** 10^5 **e** 10^{-1}
 f 10^{-2} **g** 10^{-4} **h** 10^8
2 **a** 3.87×10^2 **b** 3.87×10^4 **c** 3.87×10^0
 d 3.87×10^{-2} **e** 3.87×10^{-3} **f** 2.05×10^1
 g 2.05×10^2 **h** 2.05×10^{-1} **i** 2.05×10^4
 j 2.05×10^7 **k** 2.05×10^{-4}
3 **a** 4.0075×10^4 km **b** 1.495×10^{11} m
 c 4×10^{-4} mm **d** 4×10^7 bacteria
 e 1.4162×10^{-7} **f** 1×10^{-2} mm
4 **a** 300 **b** 2000 **c** 36 000 **d** 920 000
 e 5 600 000 **f** 34 **g** 7 850 000 **h** 900 000 000
5 **a** 0.03 **b** 0.002 **c** 0.000 47 **d** 0.000 063
 e 1.7 **f** 0.000 95 **g** 0.349 **h** 0.000 007
6 **a** 0.000 000 9 m **b** 6 606 000 000 **c** 100 000 light years
 d 0.000 01 mm **e** 0.000......00 1 66 kg
                  26 zeros
7 **a** 1.817×10^7 **b** 9.34×10^{10} **c** 4.1×10^{-4}
8 **a** 1.6×10^8 **b** 3.2×10^9 **c** 1.5×10^{10} **d** 8×10^9
 e 3.6×10^7 **f** 4.9×10^{-3} **g** 3×10^1 **h** 2×10^{-1}

EXERCISE 7D.2

1 **a** 4.65^{06} **b** 5.12^{-05} **c** 5.99^{-04}
 d 3.761^{10} **e** 4.95^{07} **f** 8.44^{-06}
2 **a** 3×10^{-8} **b** 1.36×10^{10} **c** 4.64×10^{10}
 d 9.87×10^9 **e** 3.57×10^{-8} **f** 8.74×10^{-6}
3 **a** 2.55×10^8 **b** 7.56×10^{-6} **c** 2.75×10^{-10}
 d 3×10^1 **e** 2.44×10^{-5} **f** 1.02×10^7
4 **a** 4.80×10^8 mm **b** 3.15×10^7 seconds
 c 3.15×10^{10} seconds **d** 5×10^{-7} kg
5 **a** 8.64×10^4 km **b** 6.05×10^5 km **c** 6.31×10^7 km
6 **a** 1.8×10^{10} m **b** 2.59×10^{13} m **c** 9.46×10^{15} m

REVIEW SET 7A

1 **a** 81 **b** 40 2 **a** $36 = 2^2 \times 3^2$ **b** $242 = 2 \times 11^2$
3 **a** -8 **b** -1 **c** 108 4 **a** $\frac{1}{27}$ **b** $\frac{9}{16}$ **c** -2
5 2^{-4} 6 **a** $5^7 = 78\,125$ **b** b^5 **c** x^{12}
7 **a** $25x^2$ **b** $27m^3n^3$ **c** $\frac{p^4}{16q^4}$
8 **a** 9×10^0 **b** 3.49×10^4 **c** 7.5×10^{-3}
9 **a** 2 810 000 **b** 2.81 **c** 0.002 81
10 **a** 4.26×10^8 **b** 6×10^3
11 **a** 2.57×10^6 km **b** 1.80×10^7 km **c** 9.37×10^8 km

REVIEW SET 7B

1 **a** 343 **b** 225
2 **a** $42 = 2 \times 3 \times 7$ **b** $144 = 2^4 \times 3^2$
3 **a** 1 **b** -64 **c** -288 4 **a** $\frac{1}{36}$ **b** $\frac{2}{3}$ **c** $2\frac{7}{9}$
5 **a** $3^8 = 6561$ **b** 1 **c** y^{15}
6 **a** $2^4 5^{-2}$ **b** $2^3 5^1 3^{-4}$ **c** $2^2 3^2 5^1$ **d** $2^2 5^2 3^{-2}$
7 **a** $\frac{1}{5c}$ **b** $\frac{7}{k^2}$ **c** $\frac{1}{64d^6}$
8 **a** 2.6357×10^2 **b** 5.11×10^{-4} **c** 8.634×10^8
9 **a** 2.78 **b** 39 900 000 **c** 0.002 081
10 **a** 6.4×10^7 **b** 6×10^6 11 2.1×10^{-7} km

EXERCISE 8A

1 **a** 26.4 cm **b** 17.8 cm **c** 127.3 m
2 **a** 19.6 m **b** 112.9 m
3 **a** 71.4 km/h **b** 220 km **c** 8 h 19 min
4 **a** 128.7 cm^2 **b** 7.14 m
5 **a** 14 min 17 s **b** 19.7 m
6 **a** 4263 cm^3 **b** 1.06 cm **c** 4.99 mm
7 **a** 167 cm **b** 175 cm **c** 155 cm
8 **a** 15.9 km **b** 49.3 m 9 **a** 1.34 sec **b** 81 cm

EXERCISE 8B.1

1 **a** $y = 2 - \frac{2}{5}x$ **b** $y = 5 - \frac{3}{4}x$ **c** $y = 2x - 8$
 d $y = 2 - \frac{2}{7}x$ **e** $y = 10 - \frac{5}{2}x$ **f** $y = \frac{2}{3}x + 4$
2 **a** $x = r - p$ **b** $x = \frac{z}{y}$ **c** $x = \frac{d-a}{3}$
 d $x = \frac{d-2y}{5}$ **e** $x = \frac{p-by}{a}$ **f** $x = \frac{y-c}{m}$
 g $x = \frac{s-2}{t}$ **h** $x = \frac{m-p}{q}$ **i** $x = \frac{6-a}{b}$
3 **a** $y = mx - c$ **b** $y = \frac{c-p}{2}$ **c** $y = \frac{a-t}{3}$
 d $y = \frac{n-5}{k}$ **e** $y = \frac{a-n}{b}$ **f** $y = \frac{a-p}{n}$
4 **a** $z = \frac{b}{ac}$ **b** $z = \frac{a}{d}$ **c** $z = \frac{2d}{3}$
 d $z = \pm\sqrt{2a}$ **e** $z = \pm\sqrt{bn}$ **f** $z = \pm\sqrt{m(a-b)}$
5 **a** $a = \frac{F}{m}$ **b** $r = \frac{C}{2\pi}$ **c** $d = \frac{V}{lh}$ **d** $K = \frac{b}{A}$
 e $h = \frac{2A}{b}$ **f** $T = \frac{100I}{PR}$ **g** $m = \frac{E}{c^2}$ **h** $a = 2M - b$

EXERCISE 8B.2

1 $y = -\frac{5}{3}x + 6$ **a** $-\frac{5}{3}$ **b** 6
2 **a** $a = \frac{d^2}{2bK}$ **b** **i** 1.29 **ii** 16.2
3 **a** $d = st$ **i** 180 km **ii** 120 km **iii** 126.7 km
 b $t = \frac{d}{s}$ **i** 3 hours **ii** 4 hours **iii** 2 hours 12 mins
4 **a** $n = \frac{I}{Pr}$ **b** **i** 2.05 years **ii** 10 years

EXERCISE 8C

1 **a** $A = 2000 + 150 \times 8$ **b** $A = 2000 + 150w$
 c $A = 2000 + dw$ **d** $A = P + dw$
2 **a** $W = 3500 \times 16$ **b** $W = 3500n$ **c** $W = Hn$
3 **a** $C = 20 + 29 \times 24$ **b** $C = 20 + 29n$
 c $C = 20 + mn$ **d** $C = s + mn$
4 **a** $W = 100 - 0.5 \times 12$ **b** $W = 100 - 0.5n$
 c $W = 100 - kn$ **d** $W = I - kn$
5 **a** $M = 8000 - 10 \times 350$ **b** $M = 8000 - 350j$
 c $M = 8000 - cj$ **d** $M = L - cj$
6 **a** $H = 35 + 15 \times 6$ **b** $H = 35 + 15d$
 c $H = B + 15d$ **d** $H = B + Cd$
7 **a** **i** $P = 4 \times 3$ cm **ii** $P = 4x$ cm
 b **i** $P = 2 \times 5 + 3 \times 8$ m **ii** $P = 2a + 3 \times 8$ m
 iii $P = 2a + 3b$ m

Answers

EXERCISE 8D

1 Number line diagrams for parts **a** through **l**:
- **a** open circle at 5, arrow right
- **b** closed circle at 1, arrow left
- **c** closed circle at 2, arrow left
- **d** open circle at −1, arrow left
- **e** closed circles at −2 and 2
- **f** open circles at −3 and 4
- **g** closed circle at 1, open circle at 6
- **h** open circle at −1, closed circle at 0
- **i** open circle at 0, closed circle at 3
- **j** closed circle at −1, open circle at 2
- **k** open circles at 2 and 5
- **l** open circle at −2, closed circle at 0

2 a $x > 0$ **b** $x \leqslant -2$ **c** $x \geqslant 100$
d $x < 0.2$ **e** $-1 \leqslant x \leqslant 4$ **f** $3 \leqslant x < 10$
g $-5 < x < 5$ **h** $7 < x \leqslant 20$
i $x < 2$ or $x \geqslant 7$ **j** $x < -3$ or $x > 0$
k $x \leqslant 4$ or $x \geqslant 17$ **l** $x \leqslant 21$ or $x > 33$

EXERCISE 8E

1 a $x \leqslant 3$ **b** $x > -6$ **c** $x \leqslant 7$
d $x < -\frac{2}{3}$ **e** $x > \frac{9}{5}$ **f** $x \leqslant \frac{1}{3}$
g $x \geqslant -3$ **h** $x < 1$ **i** $x \leqslant -\frac{1}{5}$

2 a $x \leqslant 4$ **b** $x > -5$ **c** $x > -4$
d $x \geqslant \frac{7}{3}$ **e** $x < 1$ **f** $x \leqslant \frac{3}{5}$

3 a $x > -\frac{7}{2}$ **b** $x > \frac{4}{3}$ **c** $x \leqslant \frac{1}{3}$
d $x \geqslant 1$ **e** $x < 0$ **f** $x \leqslant -\frac{5}{3}$

4 a No solutions as $1 \not> 6$. **b** True for all real x, i.e., $x \in \mathbb{R}$.
c True for all real x, i.e., $x \in \mathbb{R}$.
d No solutions in **a**, an infinite number of solutions for **b**, and an infinite number of solutions in **c** when $2x - 4 = 2(x - 2)$.

REVIEW SET 8A

1 a 11.4 g/cm³ **b** 37.9 g **c** 9230.8 cm³
2 a $t = \dfrac{s + 13}{3}$ **b** $t = \pm 2\sqrt{r}$ **3** $1 \leqslant x < 6$
4 a **i** $V = 6 \times 8$ **ii** $V = 8n$ **iii** $V = ln$
   b $V = 25 + ln$
5 a open circles at −2 and 2 **b** closed circles at −5 and −1

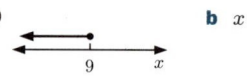

6 a $x \leqslant 9$ **b** $x > \frac{1}{4}$

7 a $l = \dfrac{A - \pi r^2}{\pi r}$ **b** 7 cm

REVIEW SET 8B

1 a 164.6 cm³ **b** 1.20 m
2 a $j = \dfrac{l + 3}{2k}$ **b** $j = \dfrac{sd}{pR}$ **3** $x < -1$ or $x \geqslant 4$
4 a $C = 2 + 1.20$ **b** $C = 2 + 1.20 \times 5$
  c $C = p + 1.20b$ **d** $C = p + bx$
5 a $P = 2 \times 7 + 4$ cm **b** $P = 2 \times m + n$
6 a open circle at −1, closed circle at 3 **b** closed circle at 0, open circle at 3
7 a $x < 3$ **b** $x \geqslant -7$

CHALLENGE

1 $x \leqslant \frac{2}{3}$ **2** $0 \leqslant x \leqslant 3$

EXERCISE 9A

1 a $x = -4, y = -6$ **b** $x = 5, y = 7$ **c** $x = 2, y = 6$
  d $x = -4, y = -7$ **e** $x = -2, y = -8$ **f** no solution
  g $x = 1, y = 5$ **h** no solution **i** $x = \frac{2}{5}, y = 0$

2 a $x = \frac{1}{2}, y = 4\frac{1}{2}$ **b** $x = 3, y = 4$ **c** $x = 2, y = -1$
  d $x = 0, y = -4$ **e** $x = -1, y = -1$ **f** $x = 0, y = 6$

EXERCISE 9B

1 a $x = 2, y = 5$ **b** $x = 3, y = 1$ **c** $x = 0, y = 5$
  d $x = 5, y = 9$ **e** $x = 0, y = 4$ **f** $x = 2, y = 1$

2 a $x = 5, y = 3$ **b** $x = 1, y = \frac{2}{5}$
  c $x = 2, y = 1\frac{1}{3}$ **d** $x = 5, y = -2$
  e $x = -3, y = -\frac{1}{2}$ **f** $x = -4\frac{1}{2}, y = -3\frac{1}{2}$

3 a reduces to $5 = 7$ which is never true
  b no solution - the two lines they represent are parallel (same gradient)
     $\therefore$ they never intersect

4 a reduces to $8x + 6 = 8x + 6$ which is always true
  b infinite number of solutions - the lines they represent are coincident

EXERCISE 9C

1 a $11x = 11$ **b** $4y = 12$ **c** $9x = 9$ **d** $9x = 6$
  e $-y = 11$ **f** $-11y = -11$

2 a $x = 2, y = 6$ **b** $x = 1, y = -2$
  c $x = -1, y = -3$ **d** $x = 1, y = -5$
  e $x = 2, y = -2$ **f** $x = -3, y = 1$

3 a $10x + 25y = 5$ **b** $-3x + y = -4$
  c $3x - 21y = 24$ **d** $-10x - 8y = -18$
  e $-18x - 12y = 12$ **f** $-16x + 8y = -12$

4 a $x = 5, y = -2$ **b** $x = 1, y = 2$
  c $x = 1, y = -6$ **d** $x = 5, y = 1$
  e $x = 1, y = 1$ **f** $x = -3, y = 4$
  g $x = 2, y = -3$ **h** $x = 1, y = -1$
  i $x = -1, y = 3$ **j** $x = 5, y = -2$
  k $x = \frac{16}{29}, y = \frac{1}{29}$ **l** $x = -3, y = -3$

m $x = -\frac{34}{13}$, $y = -\frac{85}{26}$ **n** $x = -2$, $y = -3$
o $x = -5$, $y = -4$

5 a infinite number of solutions, lines are coincident
b no solution, lines are parallel

EXERCISE 9D
1 34 and 15 **2** 51 and 35 **3** 16 and 24
4 nectarines 56 pence, peaches 22 pence
5 adults €12, children €8
6 15 small trucks and 10 large trucks
7 24 twenty cent coins and 13 fifty cent coins
8 9 male and 4 female costumes **9** $x = 5$, $y = 2$
10 $45 call out and $60 an hour
11 a $a = \frac{5}{9}$, $b = -\frac{160}{9}$ **b** $25\,°C$

REVIEW SET 9A
1 a $x = -1$, $y = 3$ **b** $x = 2$, $y = -1$
2 $x = 2$, $y = 7$ **3 a** $x = -2$, $y = 3$ **b** $x = 5$, $y = 6$
4 A sausage costs $0.80 and a chop $2.50. **5** 9 drivers
6 24, 26, and 28

REVIEW SET 9B
1 a $x = y = -2$ **b** $x = -4$, $y = -16$
2 $x = \frac{24}{13}$, $y = \frac{33}{13}$ **3** $x = 1$, $y = 0$
4 5 and 17 **5** $1.50 **6** $x = 4$, $y = 3$

CHALLENGE
1 3, 8, and 14 **2** $x = 5$, $y = 1$

3
a	0	1	-1	-1	1
b	0	1	-1	1	-1
c	0	1	1	-1	-1

4 only 3961 **5** $a = b = c$
6 a $x = 3$, $y = 5$, $z = -2$ **b** $x = 4$, $y = 2\frac{1}{2}$, $z = -1\frac{1}{2}$
7 $ab = -1$
8 train A ≈ 20.4 cm/s, train B ≈ 19.6 cm/s

EXERCISE 10A.1
1 a 8.06 cm **b** 7.07 cm **c** 15.3 km
2 a 9.22 cm **b** 2.06 km **c** 6.72 cm
3 a $x = \sqrt{11}$ **b** $x = \sqrt{2}$ **c** $x = \sqrt{5}$
4 a $x = \sqrt{\frac{5}{4}}$ or $\frac{1}{2}\sqrt{5}$ **b** $x = \sqrt{\frac{10}{4}}$ or $\frac{1}{2}\sqrt{10}$ **c** $x = \frac{1}{2}$
5 a $x \approx 5.20$ **b** $x \approx 7.21$ **c** $x = 2$
6 a $x = \sqrt{17}$, $y = 2\sqrt{2}$ **b** $x = \sqrt{29}$, $y = 3\sqrt{5}$
c $x = \sqrt{5}$, $y = \sqrt{6}$
7 a $x \approx 1.41$ **b** $x = 14$ **8** AC ≈ 6.24 m
9 a AB $= \sqrt{17}$ cm **b** AB $= \sqrt{29}$ m **c** AB $= \sqrt{41}$ m
10 Area of trapezium $= \left(\dfrac{a+b}{2}\right)(a+b)$
Sum of areas of triangles $= \frac{1}{2}ab + \frac{1}{2}c^2 + \frac{1}{2}ab$
Equate these, etc.

EXERCISE 10A.2
1 a, b, d, f are Pythagorean triples.
2 a $k = 17$ **b** $k = 10$ **c** $k = 48$ **d** $k = 25$
e $k = 24$ **f** $k = 60$
3 $(3k)^2 + (4k)^2 = 9k^2 + 16k^2 = 25k^2 = (5k)^2$
∴ there are infinitely many Pythagorean triples as k takes infinitely many values.

EXERCISE 10B
1 1.78 m **2** 1.86 m **3** 6.81 m **4** 8.54 cm
5 3.16 cm × 9.49 cm **6 a** 53.7 cm **b** 160 cm²
7 6.63 cm **8** 7.07 cm **9** 25.6 cm **10** 9.43 km
11 a 15.8 km **b** 22.4 km **c** 22.4 km **d** 25.5 km
e 29.2 km **f** 31.6 km
12 a 21.5 m **b** 8 m **c** 21.5 m **d** 40.8 m
13 a 12.2 m **b** 11.7 m **c** 14.6 m
14 10.4 cm **15** 22.2 cm² **16** 1.80 m
17 19.2 km **18** $\sqrt{5} \approx 2.24$ km **19** 13.4 km

EXERCISE 10C
1 14.4 cm **2** 10.9 cm **3** 4.66 cm
4 $\frac{1}{2}\sqrt{157} \approx 6.26$ cm **5** 6 cm
6 $2\sqrt{18} \approx 8.49$ cm **7** 3.71 cm **8** 4.24 cm
9 12.5 cm **10** 8.49 cm **11** 10.6 cm
12 $4\sqrt{3}$ cm or 6.93 cm **13** 1.3 m **14** 10.05 m
15 ≈ 1.42 cm **16** 63.2 cm

REVIEW SET 10A
1 a $\sqrt{29} \approx 5.39$ cm **b** $\sqrt{33} \approx 5.74$ cm
c $\sqrt{\frac{64}{3}} \approx 4.62$ cm, $2\sqrt{\frac{64}{3}} \approx 9.24$ cm
2 Yes, diagonal of TV compartment measures 119.3 cm which is > 115 cm.
3 $5^2 + 11^2 = 146 \neq 13^2$.
4 a $4\sqrt{10} \approx 12.6$ units **b** $4\sqrt{13} \approx 14.4$ units
c $4\sqrt{17} \approx 16.5$ units
5 $3\sqrt{13} \approx 10.8$ cm **6** radius is $5\sqrt{2}$ cm ≈ 7.07 cm
7 a $x = 10\sqrt{2} \approx 14.1$ cm **b** 48 cm × 48 cm square
8 $x = 25$, $y = 15$
9 a $x = 2\sqrt{5} \approx 4.47$ **b** $x = \sqrt{171} \approx 13.1$

REVIEW SET 10B
1 a $x = \sqrt{18}$ **b** $x = \sqrt{61}$ **c** $x = \sqrt{2}$
2 6.95 km **3** $k = 21$
4 a $6\sqrt{5} \approx 13.4$ km **b** $3\sqrt{29} \approx 16.2$ km
c $3\sqrt{13} \approx 10.8$ km
5 6 cm **6** $12\sqrt{2} \approx 17.0$ m **7** $6\sqrt{5} \approx 13.4$ cm
8 $12\sqrt{5} \approx 26.8$ m **9 a** $y = 10\sqrt{2} \approx 14.1$ **b** $y = 15$

CHALLENGE
1 $2\sqrt{3}$ cm **2** $5\sqrt{2} \approx 7.07$ m **3** $\sqrt{313} \approx 17.7$ m
4 ≈ 66.8 m

EXERCISE 11A
1 a cm **b** mm **c** km **d** m **e** mm **f** cm
3 a 52 000 m **b** 1150 mm **c** 165 cm **d** 6300 mm
e 62 500 cm **f** 8 100 000 mm
4 a 4.8 m **b** 5.4 m **c** 5.28 km **d** 2 m
e 5.8 km **f** 7 km
5 a 42 100 m **b** 2.1 m **c** 7.5 cm **d** 1.5 km
e 185 cm **f** 425 mm **g** 280 000 cm
h 16.5 m **i** 250 000 mm
6 18 m **7** 105 laps **8** 2125 steps
9 a 0.375 mm **b** 1.17 m **c** 320 cards

Answers

EXERCISE 11B
1 **a** $P = 103$ mm **b** $P = 118$ mm **c** $P = 103$ mm

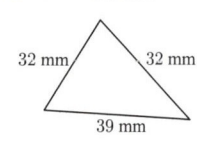

2 **a** 38.8 cm **b** 17.8 cm **c** 11.9 km **d** 29 m **e** 11.6 cm **f** 30 m **g** 17.6 m **h** 99.6 km **i** 19.1 m

3 **a** $P = 2a + 2b$ or $P = 2(a + b)$ **b** $P = k + l + m$ **c** $P = 12a$

4 11.1 cm **5** 8.7 m **6** 18.8 cm **7** 38.4 m **8** $10 + 8\sqrt{2} \approx 21.3$ m **9** 113 cm

EXERCISE 11C.1
1 **a** cm^2 **b** m^2 **c** ha **d** m^2 **e** km^2 **f** mm^2

2 **a** 0.23 cm^2 **b** 36 000 m^2 **c** 0.0726 m^2 **d** 7 600 000 mm^2 **e** 0.853 ha **f** 35 400 000 cm^2 **g** 1354 mm^2 **h** 4 320 000 cm^2 **i** 4820 mm^2 **j** 3 000 000 m^2 **k** 70 ha **l** 6 600 000 m^2 **m** 6.6 km^2 **n** 500 cm^2 **o** 0.0025 m^2 **p** 0.052 cm^2 **q** 720 000 000 000 mm^2

3 **a** 1000 cm^2 **b** 240 cm^2 **c** 1.2 cm^2 **d** 80 000 cm^2

4 625 m^2 **5** 625 coasters

EXERCISE 11C.2
1 **a** 40 cm^2 **b** 625 m^2 **c** 42 m^2 **d** 39 cm^2 **e** 15 cm^2 **f** 45 cm^2 **g** 180 m^2 **h** 24 cm^2 **i** 25 cm^2

2 **a** $h = 6$ **b** $h = 3.6$ **c** $h = 5$

3 **a** 112 m^2 **b** 39 m^2 **c** 74 m^2 **d** 84 cm^2 **e** 31.5 cm^2 **f** 189 cm^2 **g** 38 m^2 **h** 34 cm^2 **i** 34 cm^2

4 96 cm^2 **5** 9.72 m^2 **6** $280.80 **7** 5.09 m^2 **8** 375 tiles **9** **a** 48 cm^2 **b** $4\sqrt{2} \approx 5.66$ cm **10** 144 cm^2 **11** **a** 80 cm^2 **b** $\frac{1}{2}ab$ cm^2 **12** $5\frac{1}{3}$ cm **13** **a** 1371 km **b** 1 141 383 km^2

EXERCISE 11D
1 **a** **i** 44.0 cm **ii** 154 cm^2 **b** **i** 94.2 m **ii** 707 m^2 **c** **i** 56.5 mm **ii** 254 mm^2

2 **a** 50.3 cm **b** 3.39 m **c** 34.6 cm

3 **a** 314 cm^2 **b** 468 m^2 **c** 73.9 cm^2

4 **a** **i** 18.85 cm **ii** 30.85 cm
  b **i** 4.712 cm **ii** 10.71 cm
  c **i** 50.27 mm **ii** 98.27 mm
  d **i** 3.491 m **ii** 13.49 m
  e **i** 59.38 cm **ii** 84.58 cm
  f **i** 3.910 km **ii** 10.31 km

5 **a** 13.1 cm **b** 17.6 m
6 **a** 38.5 cm^2 **b** 56.5 m^2 **c** 12.6 cm^2 **d** 26.2 m^2 **e** 30.2 cm^2 **f** 189 mm^2
7 **a** 22.1 m^2 **b** 139 cm^2
8 **a** 84.2 cm **b** 16.8 cm **c** 30.6 cm
9 **a** $r = \frac{10}{\pi} \approx 3.18$ cm **b** 2.52 cm **c** 3 m
10 **a** $\frac{4}{3}\pi$ cm **b** $16 + \frac{4}{3}\pi$ cm **c** $\frac{16}{3}\pi$ cm^2
11 **a** 16.8 m **b** 764 cm^2 **c** 230 cm
12 6.54 cm **13** **a** 240° **b** 42.4 m^2
14 **a** 451 m, 13 000 m^2 **b** 28.0 cm, 33.0 cm^2 **c** 357 m, 6960 m^2 **d** 34.6 cm, 77.9 cm^2 **e** 61.7 cm, 211 cm^2 **f** 94.2 cm, 571 cm^2 **g** 13.7 cm, 9.53 cm^2 **h** 37.7 cm, 37.7 cm^2 **i** 62.8 cm, 157 cm^2

15 15.9 cm **16** 6.23 m **17** 154 m^2 **18** 20.9 cm
19 98.2 cm^2 **20** **a** 239 m **b** 2515 m^2

REVIEW SET 11A
1 **a** **i** 3280 m **ii** 75.5 cm **iii** 0.32 m **b** 40 000 staples
2 **a** 9.2 m **b** 42 m **c** 41.7 cm
3 **a** 20 cm^2 **b** 19.6 m^2 **c** 22.5 m^2
4 **a** 157 cm **b** 1273 revolutions **5** 262°
6 **a** **i** $P = 4x + 2z$ **ii** $A = 2xz - xy$
  b **i** $P = a + b + c + d$ **ii** $A = \frac{a+c}{2} \times b$
7 **a** 1.60 m **b** 10.0 m
8 Area $= \frac{1}{2} \times 5 \times 12$ or $\frac{1}{2} \times 13 \times d$, etc.

REVIEW SET 11B
1 **a** **i** 30 cm^2 **ii** 4 m^2 **iii** 60 ha **b** 62 rectangles
2 6 ha **3** **a** 30 cm **b** 22.7 cm **c** 85.1 cm
4 **a** 489 cm^2 **b** 121 m^2 **c** $25\sqrt{3} \approx 43.3$ cm^2
5 **a** $\frac{3}{8}$ **b** 52.3 cm **c** 170 cm^2
6 **a** 6.49 m **b** 132 m^2
7 **a** $A = \left(\frac{a+b}{2}\right)h + bc$ **b** $A = \frac{1}{2}a\sqrt{h^2 - a^2}$ cm^2
8 blue - 3600 cm^2, green - 3600 cm^2, white - 2328.2 cm^2

CHALLENGE
1 $3:2$ **4** π m, $\frac{\pi}{2} - 1$ m^2

EXERCISE 12A
1 **a** 70% **b** 26% **c** 12% **d** 5.5% **e** 200% **f** 20% **g** 5% **h** 100% **i** 98% **j** 0.3%
2 **a** $\frac{3}{4} = 0.75$ **b** $\frac{7}{100} = 0.07$ **c** $\frac{3}{200} = 0.015$ **d** $1\frac{3}{5} = 1.6$ **e** $1\frac{13}{100} = 1.13$
3 **a** 70% **b** 15% **c** $33\frac{1}{3}$% **d** $26\frac{2}{3}$%
4 7.85% **5** **a** €2541 **b** €254 100
6 **a** 600 g **b** $1092 **c** 84 kg **d** 25 litres **e** 18.7 tonnes **f** £16 469.78
7 108 marks **8** **a** 69.8 kg **b** 2.05% loss
9 **a** £345 **b** £4355 **c** 7.34%
10 87.5% **11** 30.4% **12** 44% **13** 21%
14 **a** £175 **b** £140

Answers

EXERCISE 12B.1

1 €1.50   2 €28 loss   3 £1862 profit   4 $120 profit
5 a i $2   ii $22   b i $200   ii $450
   c i £7.50   ii £57.50   d i €53 550 ii €308 550
6 a i €16.50 ii €38.50   b i £61.25   ii £113.75
   c i $26.25 ii $78.75   d i €1344   ii €8256
7 $110.40   8 a $44.80   b $115.20   c $129.60

EXERCISE 12B.2

1 38.9%   2 a $812.50   b $377.50   c 86.8%
3 a $1.60   b $1.25   c 78.1%
4 a €470   b 32.4% loss   5 a £4600   b 25.3%
6 a $15   b 27.3%
7 a £140 300   b £32 800   c 23.4%

EXERCISE 12C.1

1 a $1734   b $1617.19   2 a $2891.25   b €5549.01
3 a 6.07% p.a.   b 2.80% p.a.
4 a ≈ 1.87 years = 1 year 45 weeks
   b ≈ 3.01 years = 3 years 4 days

EXERCISE 12C.2

1 a $480   b £992.80   c $10 880   d €434.14
2 The first one, £7000 compared with £7593.75 for the second.
3 a 2.67% p.a.   b 6.82% p.a.   4 7.5% p.a.
5 10.3% p.a.   6 a 3 years 9 months   b 6 years
7 ≈ 2 years 9 months

EXERCISE 12D.1

1 a 1.1   b 0.9   c 1.33   d 0.79   e 1.072   f 0.911
2 a $84.80   b £81.60   c 57 kg   d €22.95
   e £655.20   f 31.5 m
3 a €26 per hour   b 31.86 m   c 2.61 cm
4 a 50% increase   b 20% decrease   c 15.8% decrease
   d 31.1% increase   e 25% increase   f 18.8% decrease
5 46.7% increase   6 10.6% decrease   7 7.06% increase
8 2.11% decrease   9 8% increase

EXERCISE 12D.2

1 a $2880   b £2805   c €3239.60   d $5170
2 False, e.g., $1000 increased by 10% is $1100,
   $1100 decreased by 10% is $990, not $1000.
3 $86.24 (including tax)   4 £180.79   5 £4217.85
6 €40 575   7 $37 434.85
8 a 21.0% increase   b 16.1% decrease   c 15.8% increase
9 16.3%   10 17.7% increase   11 €78

EXERCISE 12E

1 a $2977.54   b £5243.18   c €11 433.33
2 a €105.47   b $782.73   c £4569.19
3 a 13 738.80 yuan   b 1738.80 yuan
4 a $5887.92   b $887.92   5 $55 163.86
6 1st plan earns 3200 pesos, 2nd plan earns 3485 pesos
   $\therefore$ plan 2.
7 a 6% p.a.   b 7.5% p.a.
8 a Molly's, as it earns $44.89 more.
   b Max's, as it earns $7471.91 more.
9 ≈ 20.6% p.a.   10 12% p.a.

EXERCISE 12F

1 $151\frac{2}{3} \approx 152$ km   2 a 9.95 m/s   b 35.8 km/h
3 3.39 seconds   4 13.8 km/h
5 a 2 h 56 min 51 s   b 54 min 33 s
6 a 7.875 km   b 5530 km
7 a 9 km   b 3 km/h   8 7.94 km/h   9 92.3 km/h
10 a 54 km/h   b $33\frac{1}{3}$ m/s   11 a 28.8 sec   b 248 m

EXERCISE 12G

1 a 1.8 km   b 28 min   c i 1 km   ii 1.6 km
   d i 6 min   ii 16 min   e 3.86 km/h
2 a 12 min   b 80 km   c 20 km
   d A: 1 h 48 min, B: 2 h 12 min   e 24 min
   f A: 44.4 km/h, B: 36.4 km/h
3 a the Smith family   b the Reynolds family
   c the Reynolds family   d 2 hours   e $1\frac{1}{2}$ hours
   f 100 km
4 a after 2 min   b 1 min   c 3 min
   d 2 km   e between the 3 and 4 minute marks

REVIEW SET 12A

1 a 0.87   b 1.109   2 a $2900   b 58.5 kg
3 6.05 m   4 a ¥8845   b ¥2745
5 a £500   b 11.1%   6 a $12   b $68
7 180% increase   8 $38.50   9 $53.30   10 $15 000
11 5.88% p.a.   12 ≈ 2 years 4 months   13 $1530
14 $24 845.94
15 Plan 1: $2700, Plan 2: $2703.67
    $\therefore$ Plan 2 earns more interest.
16 4 h 21 min 26 sec   17 a 105 km   b 70 km/h

REVIEW SET 12B

1 a 1.1   b 0.883   2 a £3915   b ≈ 380 km
3 a €35   b 21.2%   4 a €513   b €436.05
5 $70 400   6 €52.46   7 $365 911   8 $1768
9 $1200   10 4.2 years, i.e., 4 years 73 days
11 a $34 264.87   b $9264.87
12 a €17 271.40   b €9271.40   c 11.6% p.a.   13 1300 km
14 a 325 km   b 20 min
    c Johnson: 87.5 km/h, Maple: 100 km/h   d 88.6 km/h
15 6.52% p.a.   16 75 km/h

EXERCISE 13A.1

1 a 54 cm^2 b 121.5 cm^2 c 576.24 mm^2
2 a 276 cm^2 b 6880 mm^2 c 8802 m^2
3 a ≈ 198 m^2 b ≈ 496 cm^2 c ≈ 148 cm^2
4 a 360 cm^2 b 340 m^2 c ≈ 9840 cm^2
5 a 576 cm^2 b 384 m^2 c ≈ 823 m^2 6 1160 cm^2
7 a 364 cm^2 b 72.8 ml   8 34 m^2 9 167.4 m^2
10 a $A = 18x^2$ b $A = 6x^2 + 12x$
    c $A = 5x^2 + 6x + x\sqrt{5}(x+2)$

EXERCISE 13A.2

1. **a** ≈ 207 cm² **b** ≈ 339 cm² **c** ≈ 196 cm² **d** ≈ 56.7 m² **e** ≈ 124 m² **f** ≈ 79.5 cm²
2. **a** 64π cm² **b** 60π m² **c** $5\pi(5+\sqrt{106})$ cm²
3. **a** ≈ 5030 cm² **b** ≈ 145 km² **c** ≈ 84.8 cm²
4. **a** ≈ 1640 cm² **b** ≈ 758 cm² **c** ≈ 452 cm² **d** ≈ 942 m²
5. ≈ 18.1 cm² 6. ≈ 207 cm² 7. 141 spheres
8. ≈ 33.8 cm² 9. $\approx 510\,000\,000$ km²
10. ≈ 1350 cm² 11. **a** ≈ 154 cm² **b** ≈ 132 cm²
12. **a** ≈ 5.64 m **b** ≈ 21.8 cm **c** ≈ 25.8 m
13. **a** $A = 4\pi x^2$ cm² **b** $A = \pi a^2 + \pi ab$ cm²
    c $A = 2\pi m^2 + 2\pi m(m+3)$ cm²
    d $A = \frac{\pi}{4}l^2 + \frac{\pi}{2}kl$ cm² **e** $A = 2\pi r^2 + 6\pi rx$ cm²
    f $A = 36\pi s^2$ cm²

EXERCISE 13B.1

1. **a** 8650 mm³ **b** 86 cm³ **c** 0.3 m³ **d** 124 000 mm³ **e** 0.3 cm³ **f** 3 700 000 cm³
2. 540 540 coins 3. 27 200 cm³

EXERCISE 13B.2

1. **a** 385 m³ **b** ≈ 339 cm³ **c** 320 cm³ **d** 45 cm³ **e** 704 cm³ **f** 432 cm³ **g** ≈ 670 cm³ **h** 32 cm³ **i** ≈ 288 cm³ **j** ≈ 125 m³ **k** ≈ 1440 cm³ **l** ≈ 262 cm³
2. ≈ 0.905 m³ 3. 77 550 m³ 4. 0.6 m³
5. 4500 m³ 6. 0.9 m³ 7. ≈ 2.48 m³
8. **a** $V = Al$ **b** $V = (a^2 - b^2)c$ 9. 1145 sinkers
10. ≈ 535 mm³ 11. $h = 4r$

EXERCISE 13C.1

1. **a** ml **b** ml or cl **c** kl **d** litres **e** litres **f** ml
2. **a** 680 ml **b** 376 cl **c** 37.5 cl **d** 47.32 kl **e** 3500 litres **f** 423 ml **g** 54 litres **h** 0.5834 kl
3. 15 jugs 4. 1 092 000 kl

EXERCISE 13C.2

1. **a** 2300 cc **b** 800 cc **c** 1800 cc **d** 3500 cc
2. **a** 25 ml **b** 3200 m³ **c** 7320 litres
3. **a** 22.05 kl **b** ≈ 23.6 kl **c** ≈ 186 kl
4. ≈ 524 ml 5. 368 bottles 6. 12.7 cm 7. 10 hours
8. 1.06 cm 9. 3.07 cm 10. every 24 min

EXERCISE 13D

1. **a** 3.2 kg **b** 1870 kg **c** 0.047 835 kg **d** 4.653 g **e** 2 830 000 g **f** 63 200 g **g** 0.074 682 t **h** 1 700 000 000 mg **i** 91.275 kg
2. 54 kg 3. 7500 cubes
4. **a** ≈ 7.69 g/cm³ **b** 5040 kg **c** ≈ 2.59 m³
5. ≈ 28.0 kg 6. **a** 1.5 g/cm³ **b** 0.973 g/cm³
7. No, as there is 1887 cm³ of flour and the capacity of the canister is 1800 cm³.
8. 1.05 kg 9. 72 kg

EXERCISE 13E

1. **a** $A = 791$ cm², $V = 1274$ cm³
   b $A \approx 807$ cm², $V \approx 911$ cm³
   c $A = 2400$ cm², $V \approx 7970$ cm³
2. 17 179 cm² 3. ≈ 1410 kl 4. **a** 2378 cm³ **b** 6 kg
5. **a** ≈ 682 cm² **b** ≈ 1410 cm³ **c** ≈ 9.47 kg
6. **a** i ≈ 183 cm² ii ≈ 195 cm³
   b $h \approx 8.96$ cm **c** $r \approx 2.80$ cm **d** ≈ 13.6 cm
7. **a** ≈ 23.6 cm **b** ≈ 857 cm² **c** $r \approx 6.35$
   d ≈ 506 cm²
8. **a** i $A = (4+3\pi)a^2 + 8ab$ ii $V = a^2(4b + \pi a)$
      iii $M = a^2d(4b + \pi a)$
   b i $A = 5\pi x^2$ ii $V = \frac{5}{3}\pi x^3$ iii $M = \frac{5}{3}\pi dx^3$
9. **a** i 226 m² ii 385 m³
   b i $V = \frac{8}{3}\pi r^3$ ii $r = 9$ iii $r = 8$
10. $\frac{91}{108}$ cm

REVIEW SET 13A

1. **a** 2.6 cm³ **b** 8 m³ **c** 1 200 000 cm³ **d** 5600 ml **e** 0.25 kl **f** 56 ml
2. **a** 34 cm² **b** 36 cm² **c** ≈ 51.8 m²
3. 92 bollards
4. **a** ≈ 9557.33 cm³ **b** ≈ 98.50 cm³ **c** ≈ 37.70 m³
5. **a** ≈ 37.4 cm² **b** 15 cm³ **c** 15 ml **d** 133 ice blocks
6. **a** 1.44 g/cm³ **b** 0.317 g/cm³
7. **a** ≈ 3850 cm³ **b** ≈ 3.85 litres **c** ≈ 2280 cm³
8. **a** 3.99 cm **b** 3 m 9. **a** ≈ 177 cm³ **b** ≈ 242 cm²

REVIEW SET 13B

1. **a** 0.35 g **b** 0.25 t **c** 16 800 g **d** 0.15 litres **e** 26 000 cl **f** 800 ml
2. **a** $\approx 14\,300$ cm² **b** ≈ 46.2 m² **c** 496 mm²
3. 1.24 cm 4. 220 ml
5. **a** ≈ 271.43 m³ **b** $\approx 90\,930.26$ cm³
   c $\approx 310\,339.09$ cm³
6. ≈ 33.5 kg 7. ≈ 170 litres 8. ≈ 872 cm³
9. **a** 4 m **b** 768 m³ **c** ≈ 527 m²

CHALLENGE

1. For example:
   a Fill the 5 litre bucket, then empty 3 litres into the 3 litre bucket, leaving 2 litres in the 5 litre bucket. Pour these 2 litres into an empty container. Repeat the procedure but this time combine the 2 remaining litres from the 5 litre bucket with the 2 litres poured into the empty container previously. There will now be 4 litres in this container.
   b Fill the 5 litre bucket, then empty all 5 litres into an empty container. Repeat this procedure so there are now 10 litres set aside. Now fill the 3 litre bucket using 3 litres from the 10 litres set aside. There will be 7 litres remaining in this container.
2. $2\frac{2}{3}$ days

Answers

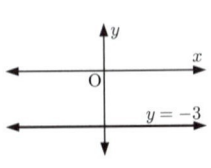

EXERCISE 14A
1. J(4, 3), K(−2, −3), L(−4, 2), M(3, −1), N(0, 3)
2. 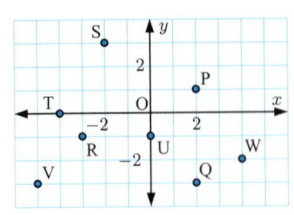
3. **a** 1st **b** 4th **c** 3rd **d** 2nd
   e None, it is on the negative x-axis.
   f None, it is on the negative y-axis.
   g 3rd **h** 4th
4. **a** $x = -2$ **b** $y = -3$ **c** $x = 0$ **d** $y = 0$ **e**, 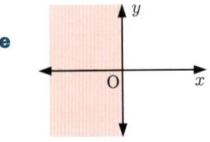 **f**, 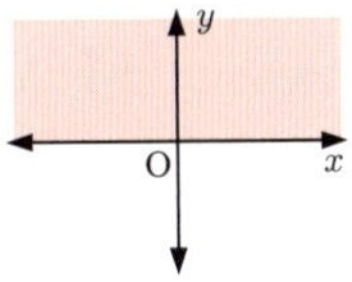 **g**, 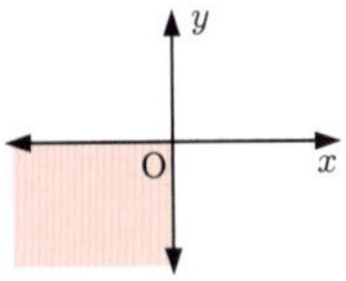 **h** (shaded regions)
5. **a** 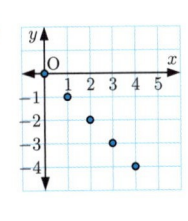 **i** yes **ii** E **b** **i** yes **ii** D

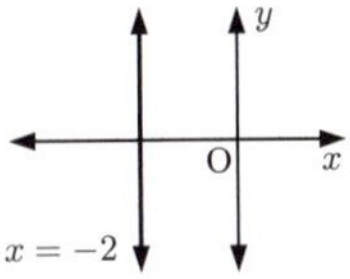

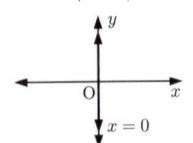

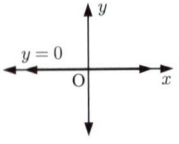

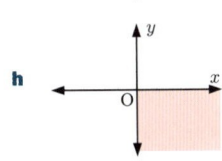

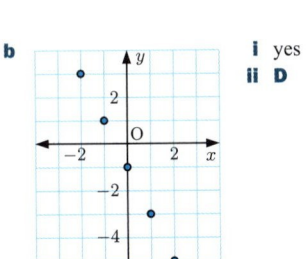

EXERCISE 14B.1
1. **a** 2 units **b** $\sqrt{37}$ units **c** $\sqrt{13}$ units
   d 3 units **e** $2\sqrt{2}$ units **f** $\sqrt{29}$ units
   g 5 units **h** 7 units **i** $5\sqrt{2}$ units
2. **a** 1.41 units **b** 5.39 units **c** 6.71 units
   d 5.10 units **e** 6.40 units **f** 6.32 units
   g 7.07 units **h** 4.12 units **i** 2.24 units

EXERCISE 14B.2
1. **a** $2\sqrt{2}$ units **b** 7 units **c** $2\sqrt{5}$ units **d** 6 units
   e 7 units **f** $\sqrt{5}$ units **g** $\sqrt{10}$ units **h** $3\sqrt{5}$ units
2. **a** isosceles (AB = AC) **b** scalene
   c isosceles (AB = BC) **d** isosceles (AC = BC)
   e equilateral
   f isosceles (AC = BC), equilateral when $b = 2 \pm a\sqrt{3}$

EXERCISE 14C
1. **a** (1, 1) **b** (−2, −1) **c** (0, −1) **d** (2, 1½)
   e (½, −1) **f** (−5, ½) **g** (3, −3½) **h** (3½, −1½)
2. **a** (5, 3) **b** (1, −1) **c** (1½, 3) **d** (0, 4)
   e (2, −1½) **f** (1, 1) **g** (1, 2½) **h** (2, −3½)
3. **a** B(0, −6) **b** B(5, −2) **c** B(0, 6) **d** B(0, 7)
   e B(−7, 3) **f** B(−3, 0)
4. **a** P(−9, 10) **b** P(6, 3) **5** C(1, −3)
6. P(7, −3) **7** S(−2, 0) **8** $\frac{\sqrt{89}}{2}$ units

EXERCISE 14D.1
1. **a** $\frac{1}{3}$ **b** 0 **c** −3 **d** $\frac{2}{3}$ **e** $-\frac{3}{4}$ **f** undefined
   g −4 **h** $-\frac{2}{5}$
2. **a**, **b**, 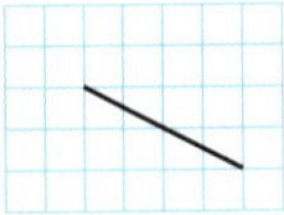 **c**, 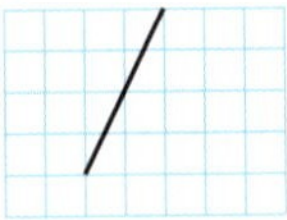 **d**, 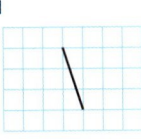 **e**, **f** (diagrams)
3. **a** $\frac{1}{5}$ **b** $\frac{1}{4}$ **c** 4 **d** 0 **e** undefined
   f $\frac{2}{7}$ **g** $-\frac{2}{7}$ **h** 1
4. (diagram with $m = 3$, $m = 2$, $m = 1$, $m = \frac{3}{4}$, $m = \frac{1}{2}$ through (1, 2))
5. (diagram with $m = -3$, $m = 0$, $m = -\frac{1}{2}$, $m = -1$ through (−2, −1))

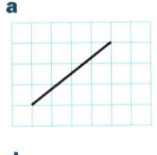

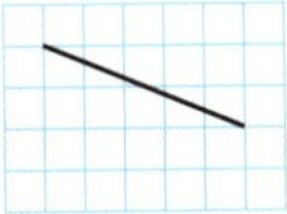

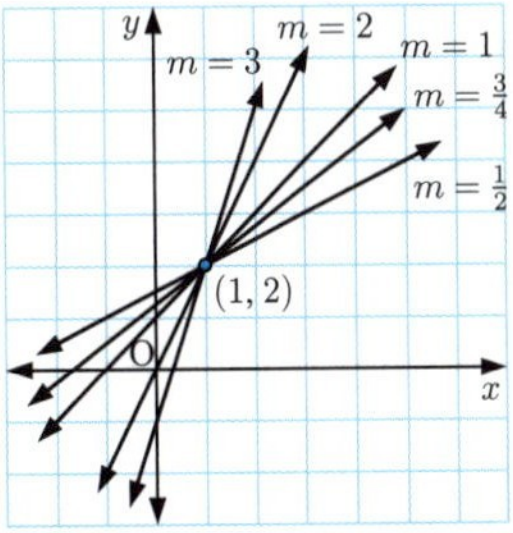

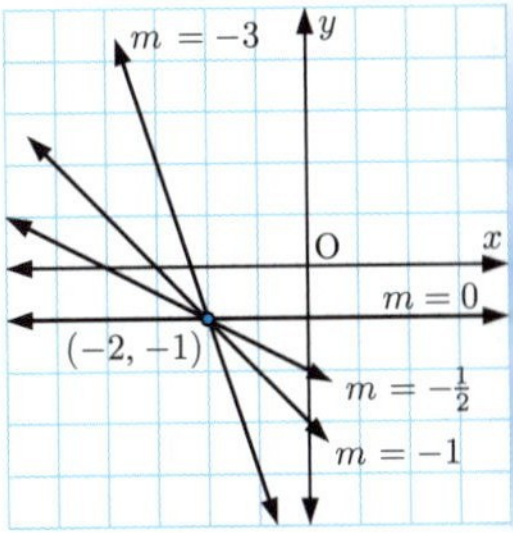

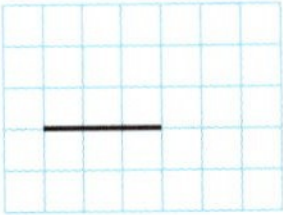

EXERCISE 14D.2
1. **a** $1\frac{1}{4}$ **b** Tan walks at $1\frac{1}{4}$ metres per second.
   c Constant as the gradient is constant.
2. **a** 105 km/h **b** **i** 115 km/h **ii** 126.7 km/h
   c From time 2 hours until time 5 hours.
3. **a** The y-intercept (0, 40) indicates that security guards earn a base rate of €40 before doing any work.
   b The gradient of 18 means that a taxi driver earns €18 per hour of work.
   c **i** €148 **ii** €310
4. **a** $2\frac{1}{2}$
   b One cubic centimetre of glass has a mass of 2.5 g. Thus, the density of glass is 2.5 g/cm³.
   c 300 cm³

5 a A has gradient $\frac{350}{29} \approx 12.1$; B has gradient $\frac{320}{33} \approx 9.70$
  b A travels 12.1 km per litre of fuel; B travels 9.70 km per litre of fuel.
  c $28.38

6 a $3 base charge
  b AB has gradient $1\frac{1}{2}$; BC has gradient 1. These gradients indicate the charge per kilometre travelled.
  c AC has gradient $1\frac{1}{5}$ which means that the average charge is $1.20 per kilometre travelled.

EXERCISE 14E.1

1 a -2 **b** 3 **c** $-\frac{2}{7}$ **d** $1\frac{1}{4}$ **e** $\frac{12}{17}$ **f** -4

2 A and E; B, D, and F; C and G

3 a $a = 9$ **b** $a = 1$ **c** $a = 6\frac{1}{3}$ **4 a** $t = 4$ **b** $t = 4$

EXERCISE 14E.2

1 a not collinear **b** collinear **c** not collinear **d** collinear

2 a $c = 3$ **b** $c = -5$

EXERCISE 14F

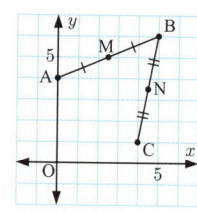

1 a
  b gradient of MN $= -\frac{3}{4}$
  gradient of AC $= -\frac{3}{4}$
  c MN $= 2\frac{1}{2}$ units and AC $= 5$ units

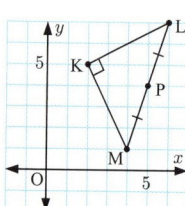

2 a
  b KL $=$ KM $= 2\sqrt{5}$ units
  $\therefore$ $\triangle$KLM is isosceles
  c P(5, 4)
  d gradient of KP $= -\frac{1}{3}$
  gradient of LM $= 3$,
  $\therefore$ KP is perpendicular to LM.

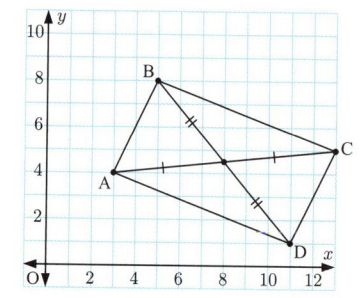

3 a
  b i gradient of AB $= 2$
  gradient of DC $= 2$, $\therefore$ AB $\parallel$ DC
  ii gradient of BC $= -\frac{3}{8}$
  gradient of AD $= -\frac{3}{8}$, $\therefore$ BC $\parallel$ AD
  c a parallelogram
  d AB $=$ DC $= 2\sqrt{5}$ units
  BC $=$ AD $= \sqrt{73}$ units
  e i midpoint of AC is $(8, 4\frac{1}{2})$
  ii midpoint of BD is $(8, 4\frac{1}{2})$
  f Diagonals bisect each other.

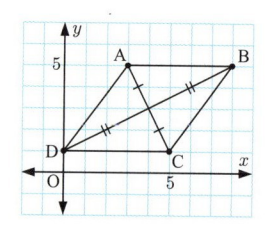

4 a
  b AB $=$ BC $=$ DC $=$ DA $= 5$ units
  $\therefore$ ABCD is a rhombus.
  c midpoint of AC is $(4, 3)$; midpoint of BD is $(4, 3)$

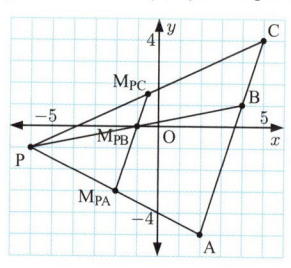

5 a
  b gradient of AB = gradient of BC = 3
  So, AB is parallel to BC, and since B is common to both line segments, then A, B, and C are collinear.
  c midpoint of PA is $M_{PA}(-2, -3)$,
  midpoint of PB is $M_{PB}(-1, 0)$,
  midpoint of PC is $M_{PC}(-\frac{1}{2}, 1\frac{1}{2})$
  d gradient of $M_{PA}M_{PB} = 3$
  gradient of $M_{PB}M_{PC} = 3$
  So, $M_{PA}M_{PB}$ is parallel to $M_{PB}M_{PC}$, and since M_{PB} is common to both line segments, then M_{PA}, M_{PB}, and M_{PC} are collinear.

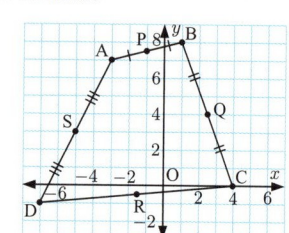

6 a i $P(-1, 7\frac{1}{2})$
  ii $Q(2\frac{1}{2}, 4)$
  iii $R(-1\frac{1}{2}, -\frac{1}{2})$
  iv $S(-5, 3)$

  b i -1 **ii** $\frac{9}{8}$ **iii** -1 **iv** $\frac{9}{8}$
  c Opposite sides are parallel and so it is a parallelogram.

REVIEW SET 14A

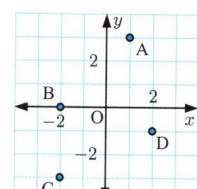

1
2 a 5 units **b** $\sqrt{13}$ units
3 $(5, -1)$
4 a $\frac{2}{5}$ **b** $-3\frac{3}{4}$

5 a i 40 km/h **ii** 90 km/h **iii** 20 km/h
  b i 40 **ii** 90 **iii** 20
  The gradients are the same as the average speeds in **a**.
  c 60 km/h

6 AB $=$ BC $= \sqrt{65}$ units, AC $= \sqrt{26}$ units
  $\therefore$ $\triangle$ABC is isosceles

7 $k = -4\frac{1}{2}$

8 gradient of AB = gradient of BC = 2   and B is common

9 $b = -3$

10 **a** AB = BC = 5 units
   b X($\frac{1}{2}$, $\frac{1}{2}$), Y(-1, $2\frac{1}{2}$), Z($2\frac{1}{2}$, 2)   **c** XY = $\frac{5}{2}$ = XZ
   d AB = BC   {from **a**}
      ∴ YB = BZ = $\frac{5}{2}$ {half lengths of each side}
      Also, XY = XZ = $\frac{5}{2}$
      ∴ BZ = ZX = XY = YB = $\frac{5}{2}$
      So, BYZX is a rhombus.

REVIEW SET 14B

1 **a** $(-3, 3)$ **b** $\sqrt{58}$ units   **c** $-\frac{3}{2}$

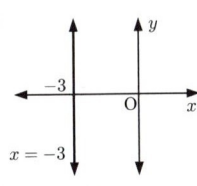

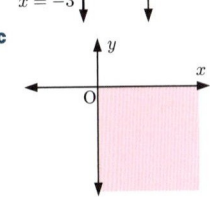

2 **a** [graph: $x = -3$]   **b** [graph: $y = 5$]   **c** [graph]

3 $\sqrt{61}$ units   **4** B is $(5, -4)$ **5** **a** -1 **b** undefined

6 **a** The value of 60 at A indicates that the plumber charges a call-out fee of $60.
   b AB has gradient 50; BC has gradient 40
      These gradients indicate the average hourly charge for the time intervals $0 \leqslant h \leqslant 3$ (AB) or $h > 3$ (BC).
   c AC has gradient 46 which means that the plumber charges an average of $46 per hour for a job lasting 5 hours.

7 **a** D(4, -3)   **b** 5 units   **8** $a = -8$

9 **a** gradient AB = gradient DC = $\frac{1}{5}$
   b gradient AD = gradient BC = -2
   c AB ∥ DC and AD ∥ BC ∴ ABCD is a parallelogram.
   d ($\frac{1}{2}$, $\frac{1}{2}$); diagonals bisect each other

EXERCISE 15A

1 **a** categorical   **b** numerical   **c** categorical
   d numerical   **e** numerical   **f** categorical
   g categorical   **h** numerical

2 **a** male, female
   b soccer, gridiron, AFL, rugby league, rugby union, Gaelic
   c black, blond, brown, grey, red, white

3 **a** sample   **b** census   **c** sample   **d** census   **e** sample
   f sample

5 **a** quantitative discrete   **b** quantitative continuous
   c quantitative discrete   **d** quantitative discrete
   e quantitative discrete   **f** quantitative continuous
   g quantitative discrete   **h** quantitative continuous
   i quantitative continuous   **j** quantitative discrete

EXERCISE 15B.1

1 **a** number of pets in a household
   b Discrete, since you can't have part of a pet.

c [Bar graph: Number of household pets — frequencies 6, 7, 4, 2, 1 for 0, 1, 2, 3, 4 pets]

d positively skewed   **e** 30%   **f** 15%

2 **a** 45 shoppers   **b** 18 shoppers   **c** 15.6%
   d Positively skewed - most shoppers shopped 1 - 4 times per week, whilst few shoppers shopped 5 - 7 times per week.

3 **a** number of toothpicks in a box   **b** discrete

c

No. of toothpicks	Tally	Freq.
47	|	1
48							5
49												10
50																									23
51												10
52											9
53				2
Total		60

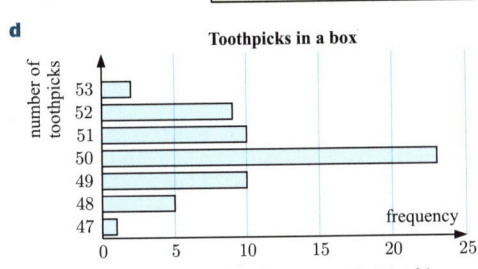

d [Bar graph: Toothpicks in a box]

e approximately symmetrical   **f** 38.3%

4 **a**

No. of accidents/month	Tally	Freq.
3				2
4						4
5					3
6								6
7												10
8										8
9					3
Total		36

b Yes, slightly negatively skewed.

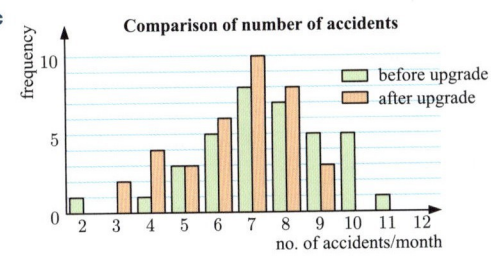

c [Bar graph: Comparison of number of accidents, before upgrade and after upgrade]

d The distribution seems to have shifted towards the lower end. Before there were 11 times when 9 or more accidents/month occurred, now only 3 times.

Answers

EXERCISE 15B.2

1 a

Number of red cars	Tally	Frequency
0 - 9	IIII	4
10 - 19	HHT HHT I	11
20 - 29	HHT HHT III	13
30 - 39	HHT III	8
40 - 49	IIII	4
	Total	40

b Red car data (histogram)

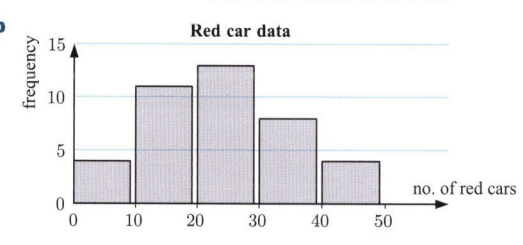

c 15 students **d** 30% **e** 20 - 29 red cars

2 a

Number of chairs made per day	Tally	Frequency
10 - 19	IIII	4
20 - 29	HHT HHT	10
30 - 39	HHT IIII	9
40 - 49	III	3
	Total	26

b Production of chairs (histogram)

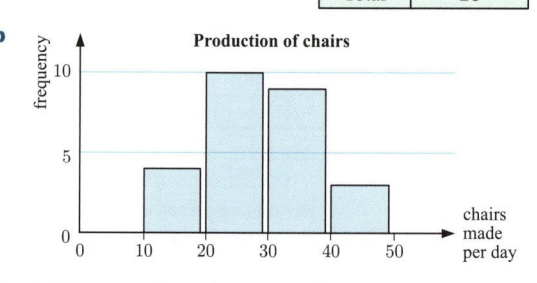

c 88.5% **d** 12 days **e** 20 - 29 chairs/day

3 a

Number of visitors each day	Tally	Frequency
0 - 99		0
100 - 199	III	3
200 - 299	IIII	4
300 - 399	HHT I	6
400 - 499	HHT III	8
500 - 599	HHT HHT II	12
600 - 699	HHT IIII	9
	Total	42

b Museum visitors (histogram)

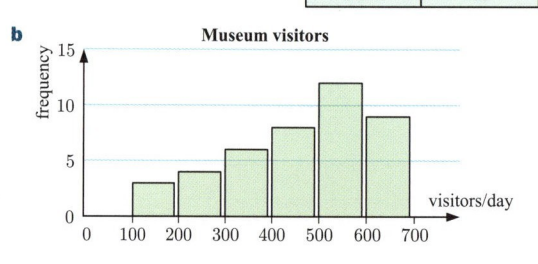

c 21 days **d** 500 - 599 visitors
e Negatively skewed - there are relatively few days on which the number of visitors is low.

4 a

Year 12 students	Tally	Frequency
50 - 59	II	2
60 - 69	HHT II	7
70 - 79	HHT HHT	10
80 - 89	HHT III	8
90 - 99	III	3
	Total	30

b Year 12 student enrolments (histogram)

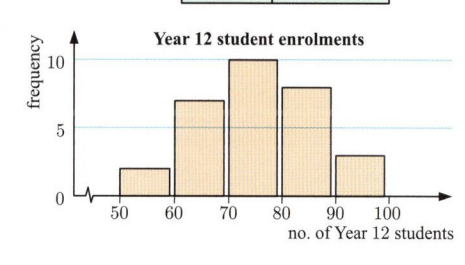

c 11 schools **d** 30% **e** 70 - 79 students
f a symmetrical distribution

EXERCISE 15C

1 a **i** 24 **ii** 24 **iii** no mode
  b **i** 13.3 **ii** 11.5 **iii** 8
  c **i** 10.3 **ii** 10.0 **iii** 11.2
  d **i** 428.6 **ii** 428 **iii** 415 and 427

2 a A: 7.73, B: 8.45   **b** A: 7, B: 7
  c The data sets are the same except for the last value, and the last value of A is less than the last value of B, so the mean of A is less than the mean of B.
  d The middle value of the data sets is the same, so the median is the same.

3 a mean: $582 000, median: $420 000, mode: $290 000
  b The mode is the second lowest value, so does not take the higher values into account.
  c No, since the data is not evenly distributed, the median is not in the centre.

4 a mean: 3.11 mm, median: 0 mm, mode: 0 mm
  b The data is very positively skewed so the median is not in the centre.
  c The mode is the lowest value so does not take the higher values into account.

5 a 44 **b** 44 points **c** 40.6 **d** increase mean to 40.75
6 105.6 **7** 1712 km **8** $2 592 000 **9** $x = 12$
10 $a = 8$ **11** 27 marks **12** 7.875
13 $A = \dfrac{30S + 31O + 30N}{91}$ **14** 15

EXERCISE 15D

1 a **i** 9 **ii** $Q_1 = 7$, $Q_3 = 10$ **iii** 7 **iv** 3
  b **i** 18.5 **ii** $Q_1 = 16$, $Q_3 = 20$ **iii** 14 **iv** 4
  c **i** 26.9 **ii** $Q_1 = 25.5$, $Q_3 = 28.1$ **iii** 7.7 **iv** 2.6

2 a median = 2.35, $Q_1 = 1.4$, $Q_3 = 3.7$
  b range = 5.1, IQR = 2.3
  c **i** ...... greater than 2.35 minutes
    ii ...... less than 3.7 minutes
    iii The minimum waiting time was 0.1 minutes and the maximum waiting time was 5.2 minutes. The waiting times were spread over 5.1 minutes.

3 a 20 **b** 58 **c** 40 **d** 30 **e** 49 **f** 38 **g** 19

EXERCISE 15E

1 a

Number of sunburns (x)	Frequency (f)	Product (fx)
0	2	0
1	10	10
2	8	16
3	6	18
4	2	8
5	1	5
6	1	6
Total	30	63

b i 2.1 **ii** 2 **iii** 1

2 a 1 **b** 2 **c** ≈ 1.90 **d** 3

3 a i 5.74 **ii** 7 **iii** 8 **iv** 10
c bimodal

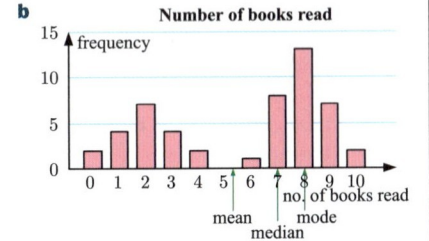

d The mean takes into account the full range of numbers of books read and is affected by extreme values. Also the values which are lower than the median are well below it.
e median

4 a i 4.25 **ii** 5 **iii** 5 **b** 6 **c** Yes, negatively skewed.
d The mean is less than the mode and median.

5 a

Foreign countries visited	Frequency
0	6
1	8
2	5
3	4
4	2
5	1
6	2

b 28 people
c i ≈ 1.96 **ii** 1.5 **iii** 1 **iv** 6

EXERCISE 15F

1 a 71.225 **c** 71.5 **d** very close

b

Chem. exam mark	f	x	fx
30 - 39	1	34.5	34.5
40 - 49	2	44.5	89.0
50 - 59	7	54.5	381.5
60 - 69	6	64.5	387.0
70 - 79	10	74.5	745.0
80 - 89	10	84.5	845.0
90 - 99	4	94.5	378.0
	40		2860

2 a 8.41 **b** 6 - 10 lunches
3 a ≈ 55.2 **b** ≈ 58.3
c For this test the boys performed better than the girls.

EXERCISE 15G

1 a Helen: mean ≈ 18.8, median $= 22$
   Jessica: mean ≈ 18.1, median $= 18$
b Helen: range $= 38$, IQR $= 15.5$
   Jessica: range $= 29$, IQR $= 6.5$
c Helen, but not by much.
d Jessica: smaller range and IQR.

5 a ≈ 4.96 **b** 5 **c** 8 **d** 4 **e** 6 **f** 2

6 a Boys: mean ≈ 171, median $= 170.5$
   range $= 28$, IQR $= 7$
   Girls: mean ≈ 166, median $= 166$
   range $= 25$, IQR $= 7.5$
b The distributions show that in general, the boys are taller than the girls but there is little variation between the distributions of their heights.

7 a ≈ 155 **b** $\approx 46\,200$ sales
c Bookshop sales for one year

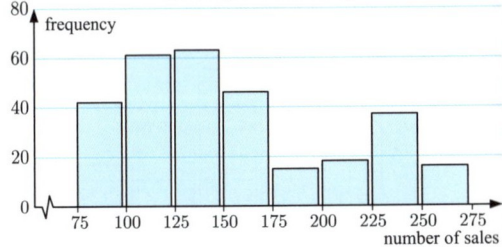

d The distribution is bimodal which could be due to the popularity of a particular book boosting sales during the period of 37 days.

REVIEW SET 15A

1 a discrete **b** continuous **c** discrete
2 a 49 **b** 15 **c** 26.5% **d** positively skewed
e ≈ 3.51 employees

3 a

No. call-outs/day	Tally	Frequency
0 - 9	||	2
10 - 19	||||| |	6
20 - 29	||||| |||||	10
30 - 39	||||| ||	7
Total		25

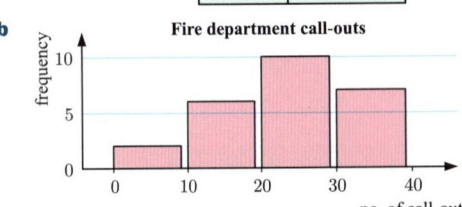

b Fire department call-outs

c 17 days **d** 8% **e** 20 - 29 call-outs/day
4 a $\bar{x} \approx 29.6$ **b** 16 and 28 **c** 29 **d** 45
e $Q_1 = 22$, $Q_3 = 41.5$ **f** 19.5

5 a

Test scores	Tally	Frequency
0 - 9	|	1
10 - 19	|||	3
20 - 29	||||| ||||| ||	12
30 - 39	||||| ||||| ||||	14
Total		30

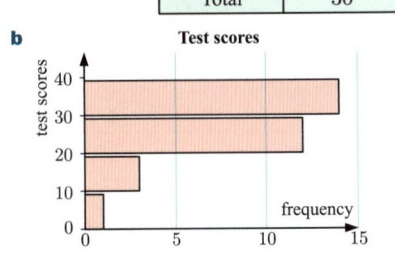

b Test scores
c 4 students
d 46.7%

Answers 567

6 $x = 7$

7 a

Goals/game	Frequency
0	8
1	7
2	4
3	1
Total	20

b i 20 games **ii** 18 goals
c i 0.9 goals **ii** 1 goal **iii** 0 goals **iv** 3 goals

8 a 12 **b** 43 **c** 29 **d** 20 **e** 34.5 **f** 31 **g** 14.5

9 8.53 potatoes per plant

10 a $\bar{x} \approx 159$ **b** 157 **c** 143 **d** 174

REVIEW SET 15B

1 a The number of children per household.
b discrete - as we cannot have part of a child
c

Number of children	Tally	Frequency
0		0
1	ЖТ	5
2	ЖТ II	7
3	IIII	4
4	II	2
5	I	1
6		0
7		0
8	I	1
Total		20

d Number of children in a household (histogram)

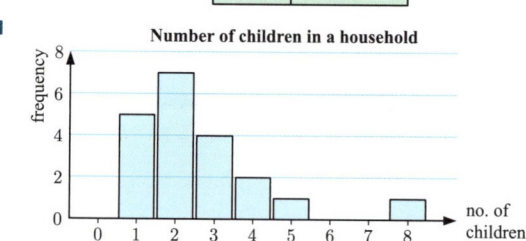

e positively skewed **f** mode = 2

2 a

Emails sent last week	Tally	Frequency
0 - 9	ЖТ I	6
10 - 19	ЖТ IIII	9
20 - 29	ЖТ II	7
30 - 39	ЖТ	5
40 - 49	II	2
50 - 59	I	1
Total		30

b Emails data (histogram)

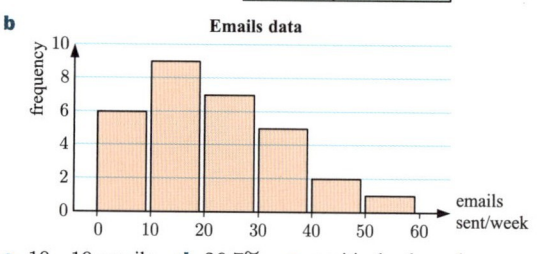

c 10 - 19 emails **d** 26.7% **e** positively skewed

3 ≈ 13.56 **4** mean = 6, $x = 2$

5 a 10 days **b** 27.5% **c** 170 - 179 vehicles **d** $\bar{x} \approx 169$

6 a median = 101.5, $Q_1 = 98$, $Q_3 = 105.5$
b IQR = 7.5. The middle 50% of her golf scores lie between 98 and 105.5. This is an interval of length 7.5 scores.

7 a $\bar{x} \approx 52.3$ **b** 51 **c** $Q_1 = 42$
d $Q_3 = 61$ **e** 32 **f** IQR = 19

8 a i $\bar{x} \approx 8.47$ **ii** 9 **iii** 9 **iv** 4
b The class performed well above average. **c** negative

9 $\bar{x} \approx 7.58$

10 a i $\bar{x} \approx 371$ **ii** 372 **iii** 228.5 **iv** 469.5
b range = 682, IQR = 241

EXERCISE 16A

1 a horizontal line **b** vertical line 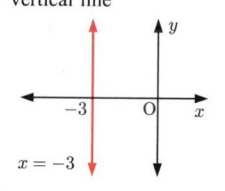
c vertical line 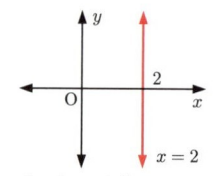 **d** horizontal line

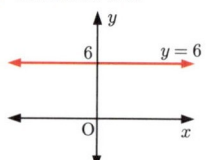

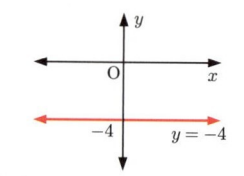

2 a horizontal line **b** vertical line
3 a $y = 0$ **b** $x = 0$ **c** $y = -3$ **d** $x = 4$
4 a $y = 3$ **b** $x = 4$

EXERCISE 16B

1 a i

x	-3	-2	-1	0	1	2	3
y	-3	-2	-1	0	1	2	3

ii (graph of $y = x$)

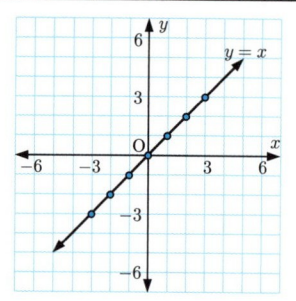

iii gradient = 1, x- and y-intercepts are both 0

b i

x	-3	-2	-1	0	1	2	3
y	-9	-6	-3	0	3	6	9

ii (graph of $y = 3x$)

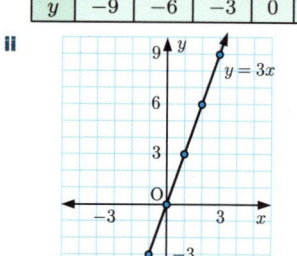

iii gradient = 3, x- and y-intercepts are both 0

c i

x	-3	-2	-1	0	1	2	3
y	-1	$-\frac{2}{3}$	$-\frac{1}{3}$	0	$\frac{1}{3}$	$\frac{2}{3}$	1

ii graph of $y = \frac{1}{3}x$

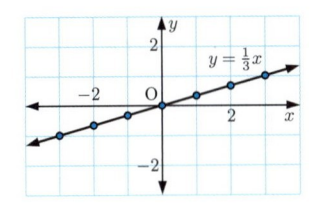

iii gradient $= \frac{1}{3}$, x- and y-intercepts are both 0

d i

x	-3	-2	-1	0	1	2	3
y	9	6	3	0	-3	-6	-9

ii graph of $y = -3x$

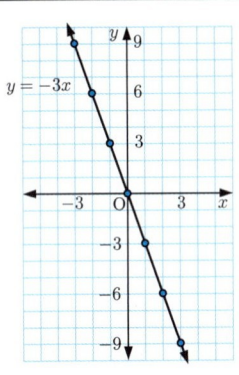

iii gradient $= -3$, x- and y-intercepts are both 0

e i

x	-3	-2	-1	0	1	2	3
y	-5	-3	-1	1	3	5	7

ii graph of $y = 2x + 1$

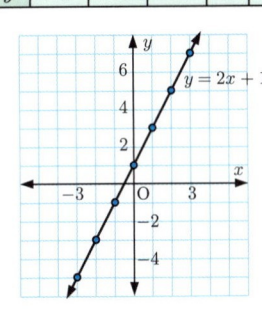

iii gradient $= 2$, x-intercept is $-\frac{1}{2}$, y-intercept is 1

f i

x	-3	-2	-1	0	1	2	3
y	7	5	3	1	-1	-3	-5

ii graph of $y = -2x + 1$

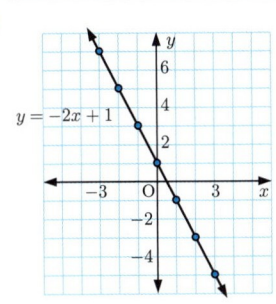

iii gradient -2, x-intercept is $\frac{1}{2}$, y-intercept is 1

g i

x	-3	-2	-1	0	1	2	3
y	$1\frac{1}{2}$	2	$2\frac{1}{2}$	3	$3\frac{1}{2}$	4	$4\frac{1}{2}$

ii graph of $y = \frac{1}{2}x + 3$

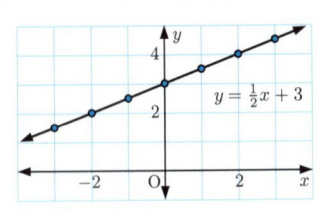

iii gradient $= \frac{1}{2}$, x-intercept is -6, y-intercept is 3

h i

x	-3	-2	-1	0	1	2	3
y	$4\frac{1}{2}$	4	$3\frac{1}{2}$	3	$2\frac{1}{2}$	2	$1\frac{1}{2}$

ii graph of $y = -\frac{1}{2}x + 3$

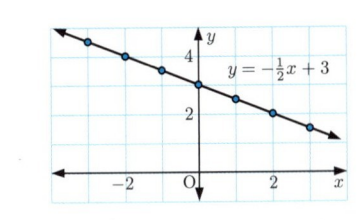

iii gradient $= -\frac{1}{2}$, x-intercept is 6, y-intercept is 3

2 a $y = \frac{1}{3}x$, $y = x$, $y = 3x$ (from least to most steep)
b coefficient of x

3 the sign of the coefficient of x

4 the constant term of the equation

EXERCISE 16C

1 a $y = 3x - 2$ **b** $y = -4x + 8$ **c** $y = \frac{1}{2}x + \frac{2}{3}$
d $y = -\frac{2}{3}x + \frac{3}{4}$

2 a $m = 3,\ c = 11$ **b** $m = -2,\ c = 6$ **c** $m = \frac{1}{2},\ c = 0$
d $m = -\frac{1}{3},\ c = -2$ **e** $m = 0,\ c = 3$
f m is undefined, no y-intercept **g** $m = -2,\ c = 3$
h $m = \frac{1}{2},\ c = -1$ **i** $m = \frac{3}{2},\ c = \frac{1}{2}$ **j** $m = \frac{2}{3},\ c = -1$
k $m = -\frac{1}{4},\ c = \frac{1}{4}$ **l** $m = -\frac{2}{5},\ c = \frac{3}{5}$

3 a $y = x - 1$ **b** $y = \frac{1}{2}x + 1$ **c** $y = -\frac{3}{4}x + 3$
d $y = -\frac{1}{3}x + 3$ **e** $y = -2x - 4$ **f** $y = 3$

4 a $y = 2x + 2$ **b** $y = -3x + 10$ **c** $y = \frac{2}{3}x - 2$
d $y = -\frac{1}{4}x - 2\frac{1}{2}$ **e** $y = \frac{4}{5}x - 12$ **f** $y = -\frac{1}{6}x - 7$

5 a $y = 2x + 3$ **b** $y = \frac{1}{2}x - 1$ **c** $y = -\frac{1}{3}x + 2$
d $y = -3x + 4$ **e** $y = 2$ **f** $x = 3$
g $y = -\frac{5}{3}x + 4$ **h** $y = \frac{5}{4}x + 3\frac{1}{2}$ **i** $y = \frac{1}{5}x - 1\frac{4}{5}$
j $y = \frac{7}{4}x - 1\frac{1}{4}$ **k** $y = -\frac{6}{7}x - 1\frac{4}{7}$ **l** $y = 5x + 8$

6 a $M = \frac{1}{3}t + 4$ **b** $N = \frac{2}{3}x - 2$ **c** $G = -\frac{3}{4}s + 3$
d $H = -g + 2$ **e** $F = \frac{3}{10}x + 5$ **f** $P = -\frac{1}{3}t - 2$

7 a $y = \frac{1}{2}x + 3$ **b** $y = 2x + 6$ **c** $y = \frac{2}{5}x - 2$
d $y = -2x - 2$ **e** $y = -\frac{4}{3}x + 6\frac{2}{3}$ **f** $y = -2x - 1$

8 a yes **b** no **c** no **d** yes

9 a $a = 2$ **b** $a = 13$ **c** $a = 5$ **d** $a = 4$

Answers 569

EXERCISE 16D

1 a $y = 2x+3$ (graph)
b $y = \frac{1}{2}x - 3$ (graph)
c $y = -x+5$ (graph)
d $y = -4x-2$ (graph)
e $y = -\frac{1}{3}x$ (graph), $(3, -1)$
f $y = -3x+4$ (graph), $1\frac{1}{3}$
g $y = \frac{3}{4}x$ (graph), $(4, 3)$
h $y = \frac{1}{3}x - 1$ (graph)
i $y = -\frac{3}{2}x + 2$ (graph), $1\frac{1}{3}$

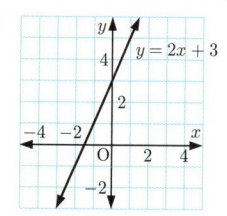

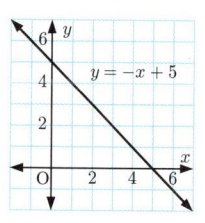

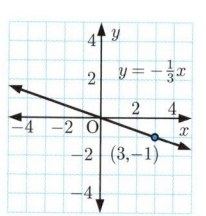

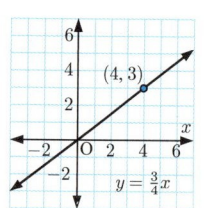

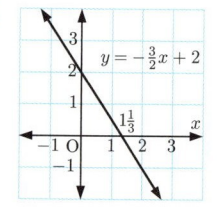

2 a i $y = 2x - 1$, $y = -2x + 1$ (graph)
ii gradient $= -2$, y-intercept $= 1$
iii $y = -2x + 1$

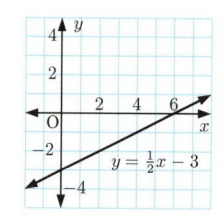

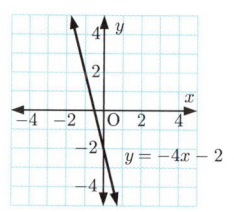

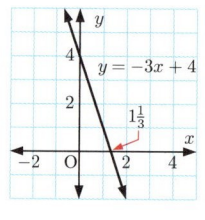

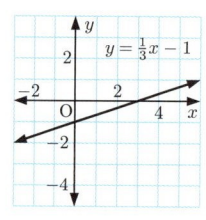

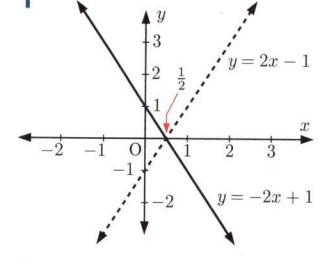

b i $y = \frac{1}{2}x + 2$, $y = -\frac{1}{2}x + 2$ (graph)
ii gradient $= -\frac{1}{2}$, y-intercept $= 2$
iii $y = -\frac{1}{2}x + 2$

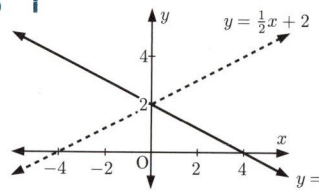

EXERCISE 16E

1 a $x = 4$, $y = 3$ b $x = 2$, $y = -1$ c $y = x + 4$

2 a (graph showing trapezium with vertices D, C, A, B)
b a trapezium
c $x = 5$

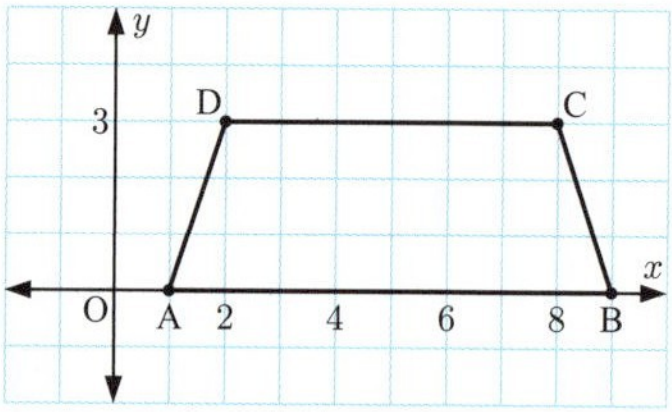

3 a (graph showing square with vertices A, B, C, D)
b a square
c $x = 1$, $y = 0$, $y = x - 1$, $y = -x + 1$

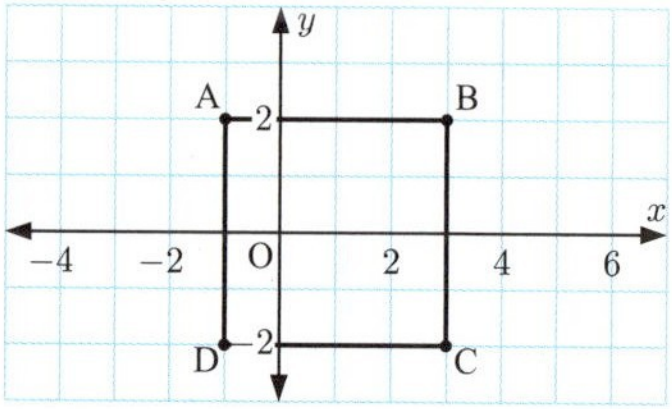

4 a R is at $(7, -2)$
b midpt of PR is $(4, \frac{1}{2})$ and midpt of QS is $(4, \frac{1}{2})$
c $x = 4$, $y = \frac{1}{2}$
d The diagonals of a rectangle bisect each other.

5 (graph with vertices O, A, B, C)
a gradient of OA $= 4$, gradient of BC $= 4$ $\therefore$ OA $\parallel$ BC
   OA $=$ BC $= \sqrt{17}$ units
b From **a**, a pair of opposite sides are parallel and equal in length, $\therefore$ OABC is a parallelogram.
   Since angle OAB is a right angle {given} then the parallelogram is a rectangle.
c $(\frac{1}{2}, 2)$ and $(5, 3)$
d $y = -\frac{1}{4}x + 2\frac{1}{8}$ and $y = 4x - 17$

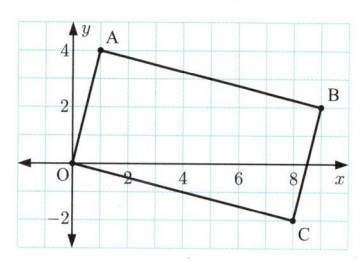

6 a (graph showing parallelogram with vertices O, A, B, C)
b $y = 4$, $3 \leqslant x \leqslant 8$
c OA $=$ AB $=$ BC $=$ CO $= 5$ units
   $\therefore$ OABC is a rhombus
d midpt of OB $= (4, 2)$ and midpt of AC $= (4, 2)$
e Diagonals of a rhombus bisect each other.
f $y = \frac{1}{2}x$ and $y = -2x + 10$

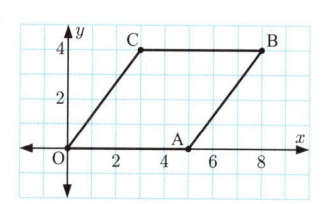

REVIEW SET 16A

1 $x = -1$ **2** $y = -\frac{1}{2}x + 4$ **3** $y = 3x - 5$
4 $y = -2x + 3$ **5** a $y = \frac{2}{3}x + 6$ b $y = -4$ **6** no

570 Answers

7 a

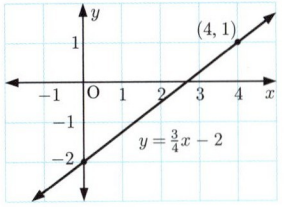

b

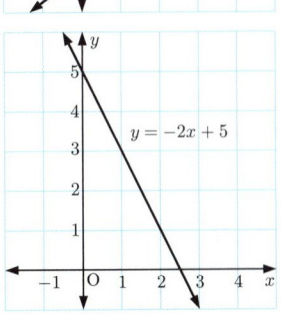

8

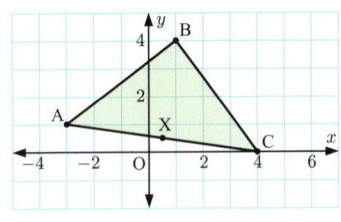

a AB = BC = 5 units ∴ △ABC is isosceles
b X is at $(\frac{1}{2}, \frac{1}{2})$
c BX is a line of symmetry with equation $y = 7x - 3$.

9

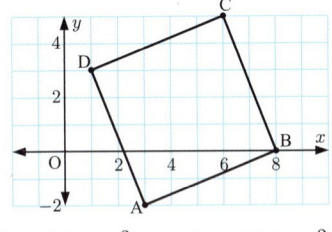

a gradient of AB = $\frac{2}{5}$, gradient of DC = $\frac{2}{5}$, ∴ AB ∥ DC.
Also AB = CD = $\sqrt{29}$ units
b AB = BC = $\sqrt{29}$ units   **c** ABCD is a square
d $y = \frac{2}{5}x - \frac{3}{10}$, $y = -\frac{5}{2}x + 12\frac{3}{4}$, $y = -\frac{3}{7}x + 3\frac{3}{7}$,
$y = \frac{7}{3}x - 9$

REVIEW SET 16B

1 a $y = 0$ **b** gradient = -2, y-intercept = 5
2 $y = 2x + 2$
3 a $y = -2x + 7$ **b** $y = -\frac{2}{3}x + 2\frac{1}{3}$ **c** $y = \frac{3}{2}x - 7\frac{1}{2}$
4 yes   **5** $P = -\frac{2}{3}t + 3\frac{1}{3}$ **6 a** $k = -14$ **b** $k = 2$
7 a $y = 3$ **b** $x = -1$ **c** $y = \frac{8}{5}x + 20$
8

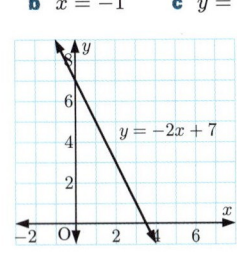

9 a

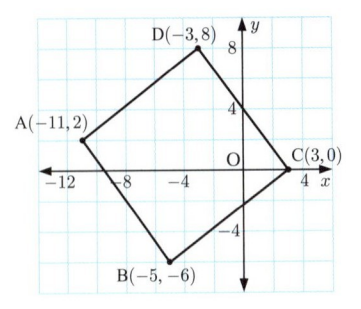

b AB = BC = CD = DA = 10 units
c From **b**, ABCD is a rhombus and since AB is perpendicular to BC {given}, then one angle is a right angle.
∴ ABCD is a square.
d $y = -\frac{4}{3}x - 4\frac{1}{3}$, $y = \frac{3}{4}x + 4$, $y = -\frac{1}{7}x + \frac{3}{7}$, $y = 7x + 29$
e midpoint is $(-4, 1)$
f $-\frac{4}{3}x - 4\frac{1}{3} = -\frac{4}{3}(-4) - 4\frac{1}{3} = 1$ ✓
$\frac{3}{4}x + 4 = \frac{3}{4}(-4) + 4 = 1$ ✓
$-\frac{1}{7}x + \frac{3}{7} = -\frac{1}{7}(-4) + \frac{3}{7} = 1$ ✓
$7x + 29 = 7(-4) + 29 = 1$ ✓

EXERCISE 17A

1 a **i** BC **ii** AC **iii** AB   **b** **i** KM **ii** KL **iii** LM
  c **i** PR **ii** QR **iii** PQ   **d** **i** XZ **ii** XY **iii** YZ
  e **i** CE **ii** DE **iii** CD   **f** **i** ST **ii** RT **iii** RS
2 a **i** PR **ii** QR **iii** PQ **iv** PQ **v** QR
  b **i** AC **ii** AB **iii** BC **iv** BC **v** AB

EXERCISE 17B.1

1 a **i** $\frac{p}{r}$ **ii** $\frac{q}{r}$ **iii** $\frac{p}{q}$ **iv** $\frac{q}{r}$ **v** $\frac{p}{r}$ **vi** $\frac{q}{p}$
  b **i** $\frac{y}{x}$ **ii** $\frac{z}{x}$ **iii** $\frac{y}{z}$ **iv** $\frac{z}{x}$ **v** $\frac{y}{x}$ **vi** $\frac{z}{y}$
  c **i** $\frac{4}{5}$ **ii** $\frac{3}{5}$ **iii** $\frac{4}{3}$ **iv** $\frac{3}{5}$ **v** $\frac{4}{5}$ **vi** $\frac{3}{4}$
  d **i** $\frac{4}{7}$ **ii** $\frac{\sqrt{33}}{7}$ **iii** $\frac{4}{\sqrt{33}}$ **iv** $\frac{\sqrt{33}}{7}$ **v** $\frac{4}{7}$ **vi** $\frac{\sqrt{33}}{4}$
  e **i** $\frac{5}{\sqrt{34}}$ **ii** $\frac{3}{\sqrt{34}}$ **iii** $\frac{5}{3}$ **iv** $\frac{3}{\sqrt{34}}$ **v** $\frac{5}{\sqrt{34}}$ **vi** $\frac{3}{5}$
  f **i** $\frac{7}{\sqrt{65}}$ **ii** $\frac{4}{\sqrt{65}}$ **iii** $\frac{7}{4}$ **iv** $\frac{4}{\sqrt{65}}$ **v** $\frac{7}{\sqrt{65}}$ **vi** $\frac{4}{7}$
2 a $\sin 70° = \frac{x}{a}$ **b** $\sin 35° = \frac{x}{b}$ **c** $\tan 64° = \frac{x}{c}$
  d $\cos 40° = \frac{d}{x}$ **e** $\cos 49° = \frac{x}{e}$ **f** $\tan 73° = \frac{f}{x}$
  g $\cos 54° = \frac{g}{x}$ **h** $\tan 30° = \frac{h}{x}$ **i** $\sin 68° = \frac{i}{x}$
3 a $x \approx 15.52$ **b** $x \approx 12.99$ **c** $x \approx 9.84$
  d $x \approx 6.73$ **e** $x \approx 11.86$ **f** $x \approx 22.94$
  g $x \approx 24.41$ **h** $x \approx 16.86$ **i** $x \approx 5.60$
  j $x \approx 16.37$ **k** $x \approx 22.66$ **l** $x \approx 10.43$
4 a $\theta = 62°$, $a \approx 10.6$, $b \approx 5.63$
  b $\theta = 27°$, $a \approx 16.8$, $b \approx 7.64$
  c $\theta = 65°$, $a \approx 49.7$, $b \approx 21.0$

EXERCISE 17B.2

1 a 56.3°   **b** 34.8°   **c** 48.2°   **d** 34.8°   **e** 41.1°
  f 48.6°   **g** 25.3°   **h** 37.1°   **i** 35.5°

Answers 571

2 a $x \approx 6.24$, $\theta \approx 38.7°$, $\phi \approx 51.3°$ **3** All check ✓
  b $x \approx 5.94$, $\alpha \approx 53.9°$, $\beta \approx 36.1°$
  c $x \approx 7.49$, $a \approx 38.4°$, $b \approx 51.6°$
4 a $x \approx 2.65$ **b** $\theta \approx 41.4°$
  c $x \approx 10.1$ **d** $x \approx 4.21$, $\theta = 59°$
  e $\theta \approx 56.3°$, $\phi \approx 33.7°$ **f** $x \approx 12.2$, $y \approx 16.4$
5 a $x = 12$, $\theta \approx 33.7°$ **b** $y \approx 11.8$
  c $z \approx 6.05$, $\theta \approx 70.7°$ **d** $\alpha \approx 70.8°$
  e $x \approx 13.1$, $\theta \approx 66.6°$ **f** $x \approx 14.3$, $\theta \approx 38.9°$
6 The 3 triangles do not exist.
  a $\sin\theta > 1$ **b** $\cos\theta > 1$ **c** $\theta = 0°$

EXERCISE 17C

1 110 m   **2** 3.25 m   **3** $\theta \approx 23.6°$ **4** 32.9°
5 238 m   **6** 2.65 m   **7** 54.6 m   **8** $\theta \approx 13.8°$
9 761 m   **10** 280 m   **11** $\theta \approx 44.4°$ **12** 1.91°
13 23.5 m   **14** 73.2 m   **15** 67.4°
16 a 10.8 cm   **b** 21.8°   **17** 106°   **18** 35.3 cm^2
19 15.8 cm   **20 a** ≈ 5.03 m   **b** AB ≈ 7.71 m
21 252 m   **22** $\approx 118°$ **23 a** 248 m   **b** 128 m
24 7.48 m   **25** 1.66 units

EXERCISE 17D

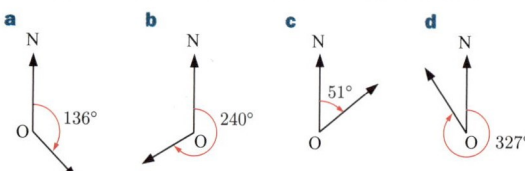

1 a N, 136°   **b** N, 240°   **c** N, 51°   **d** N, 327°
2 a 234°   **b** 293°   **c** 083°   **d** 124°
3 a i 041°   **ii** 142°   **iii** 322°   **iv** 099°   **v** 221°
  vi 279°
  b i 027°   **ii** 151°   **iii** 331°   **iv** 066°   **v** 207°
  vi 246°
4 123°   **5 a** 301°   **b** 121°   **6** 7.81 km, 130°
7 10.1 km   **8** 38.6 km   **9** 58.3 m, 239°
10 221 km   **11 a** 36.1 km, 057.7°   **b** 238°
12 a 73.0 km   **b** 241°

REVIEW SET 17A

1 $\sin\theta = \frac{5}{13}$, $\cos\theta = \frac{12}{13}$, $\tan\theta = \frac{5}{12}$
2 a $x \approx 14.0$ **b** $x \approx 35.2°$
3 $\theta \approx 5.12°$ which is $> 5°$
  $\therefore$ the ramp does not comply with the safety regulations.
4 $\theta = 36°$, $x \approx 12.4$, $y \approx 21.0$ **5** 80.9 m
6 $x \approx 24.5$, $y \approx 14.6$, $z \approx 132$ **7** 14.84 m × 10.01 m
8 ≈ 9.38 m   **9** ≈ 22.4 km   **10** ≈ 589 km on bearing 264°

REVIEW SET 17B

1 a i $\frac{y}{z}$ **ii** $\frac{y}{z}$ **iii** $\frac{y}{x}$ **b i** 0.8   **ii** 0.8   **iii** $\frac{4}{3}$
2 a $\theta \approx 38.7°$ **b** $\theta \approx 37.1°$
3 $x \approx 25.7$, $\alpha \approx 36.4°$, $\theta \approx 53.6°$ **4** ≈ 638 m
5 $x \approx 30.5$, $y \approx 35.5$ **6** 1.31°
7 a 9.91 cm   **b** BC ≈ 8.83 cm
8 a 84 km   **b** ≈ 48.2 km   **c** ≈ 24.1 km/h
9 a 38.2 m   **b** 42.8 m   **c** $\theta \approx 35.1°$

10 a Diagram: N, 45°, 45°, P, W–E, 15.4 km, 10.8 km, S, R, Q
  b 18.8 km   **c** 080.0°

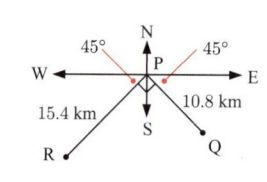

CHALLENGE

1 a $h \approx 47.6$ m/s   **b** $v = 27.5$ m/s   **c** $d \approx 267$ m
2 a $h = 55\cos\theta$ m/s   **b** $v = 55\sin\theta$ m/s
  c $d = \dfrac{3025\cos\theta\sin\theta}{4.9}$ m
3 $0° < \theta < 90°$
4 graph of d (m) vs θ, maximum at $(45, 308.67)$, $d = \dfrac{3025\cos\theta\sin\theta}{4.9}$
5 45°

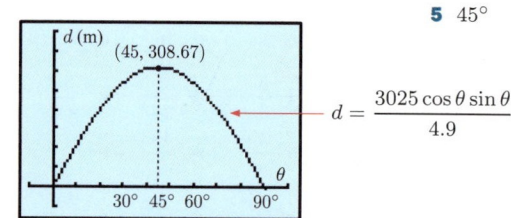

EXERCISE 18A.1

1 a $2a$ **b** $2b$ **c** $\dfrac{1}{2x}$ **d** 8   **e** cannot be simplified
  f $\frac{1}{4}$ **g** x **h** $\frac{1}{2}$ **i** $2a$ **j** $\dfrac{1}{2b}$
  k cannot be simplified   **l** 2   **m** $\dfrac{1}{3a^2}$ **n** $\dfrac{x}{2}$
  o a^3 **p** cannot be simplified   **q** $\dfrac{a}{b}$
  r cannot be simplified   **s** $\dfrac{5x}{y}$ **t** $2ac$ **u** $4a$
  v 1   **w** $3a^3$ **x** a^2 **y** $\dfrac{a}{2}$
2 a $\dfrac{x}{3} + 1$ **b** $2a + \frac{1}{2}$ **c** $\dfrac{a}{c} + \dfrac{b}{c}$ **d** $\dfrac{a}{b} + 2$
  e $a + 2$ **f** $a + 2b$ **g** $m + 2n$ **h** $2 + \dfrac{4n}{m}$
3 e, f and **g** produce simplified answers. They have common factors in the numerator and denominator.
4 a $x + 2$ **b** $2(x - 1)$ **c** $\dfrac{b + 2}{2}$ **d** $\dfrac{n + 5}{6}$ **e** $\dfrac{2}{x + 2}$
  f $\dfrac{3}{3 - a}$ **g** 6   **h** $\frac{1}{2}$ **i** $\dfrac{2}{x}$ **j** $\dfrac{x(x - 5)}{3}$
  k $\dfrac{x + 3}{2(x + 2)}$ **l** $\dfrac{x + 2}{5}$ **m** $\dfrac{x + 2}{x + 3}$ **n** $\dfrac{x + 5}{3}$
  o $\dfrac{x + 6}{3}$ **p** $\dfrac{x}{x - 1}$ **q** $\dfrac{(x + 2)(x + 1)}{4}$ **r** $\dfrac{(x + 2)^2}{x^2}$

EXERCISE 18A.2

1 a $\dfrac{3}{x + 2}$ **b** $x + 3$ **c** $x + 4$ **d** $\dfrac{x + 2}{2}$
  e $\dfrac{x + 4}{2}$ **f** $\dfrac{a + 4}{3}$ **g** $y + z$ **h** x
  i $\dfrac{a + c}{a - c}$ **j** $\dfrac{1}{2(x - 4)}$ **k** $\dfrac{x + 3}{6}$ **l** $\dfrac{x - y}{3}$
2 a 2   **b** $\dfrac{m + n}{2}$ **c** x **d** $\dfrac{1}{m}$ **e** $x + 2$ **f** $x + 2$
  g x **h** $\dfrac{1}{b + c}$ **i** $3x$ **j** $x + 3$ **k** $2x$ **l** x

572 Answers

3 a -2 **b** $-\frac{1}{2}$ **c** -1 **d** cannot be simplified
e $-\frac{1}{2}$ **f** -3 **g** $-\frac{3}{x}$ **h** $-\frac{xy}{3}$ **i** $-3x$ **j** $\frac{2x+3}{2}$
k cannot be simplified **l** $-\frac{5}{2}$

EXERCISE 18B

1 a $\frac{ab}{6}$ **b** $\frac{1}{2}$ **c** $\frac{1}{2}$ **d** $\frac{a^2}{6}$ **e** $\frac{ax}{by}$ **f** 1
  g $\frac{x^2}{3}$ **h** $\frac{2x}{y}$ **i** $\frac{1}{2n}$ **j** 3 **k** $\frac{m}{n}$ **l** 2
  m $5t$ **n** $\frac{x^2}{y^2}$ **o** $\frac{16}{d^2}$ **p** 1

2 a $\frac{2}{3}$ **b** $\frac{1}{2}$ **c** $3x$ **d** $3y$ **e** 3 **f** $\frac{c}{n^2}$
  g $\frac{d^2}{5}$ **h** 3 **i** $\frac{b}{a}$ **j** $\frac{3}{2d}$ **k** $\frac{8}{x^3}$ **l** $\frac{x}{2}$
  m $\frac{3}{a}$ **n** $\frac{1}{x}$ **o** $\frac{10}{a^2}$ **p** $\frac{3a}{5}$

3 a 2 **b** $\frac{2}{a}$ **c** $\frac{2b^3}{a^2}$ **d** $\frac{2rt}{3su}$ **e** $\frac{2m}{3}$ **f** $\frac{2p}{3q^2}$
  g $\frac{wz}{9xy}$ **h** $\frac{k^2}{16}$

EXERCISE 18C

1 a $\frac{7x}{10}$ **b** $\frac{x}{6}$ **c** $\frac{17x}{20}$ **d** $\frac{3x}{10}$ **e** $\frac{t}{12}$ **f** $\frac{8n}{21}$
  g $\frac{5a}{6}$ **h** $\frac{2a+b}{4}$ **i** $\frac{7n}{15}$ **j** $\frac{g}{2}$ **k** $\frac{2s}{15}$
  l $\frac{2a}{5}$ **m** x **n** $\frac{5y}{12}$ **o** $\frac{z}{12}$ **p** $\frac{41q}{21}$

2 a $\frac{x+6}{3}$ **b** $\frac{m-2}{2}$ **c** $\frac{4a}{3}$ **d** $\frac{b-10}{5}$
  e $\frac{x-18}{6}$ **f** $\frac{12+x}{4}$ **g** $\frac{30-x}{6}$ **h** $\frac{2x+3}{x}$
  i $\frac{6x-3}{x}$ **j** $\frac{b^2+3}{b}$ **k** $\frac{5+x^2}{x}$ **l** $-\frac{11y}{6}$

3 a $\frac{14x}{15}$ **b** $\frac{11x}{35}$ **c** $\frac{x+30}{10}$ **d** $\frac{12-x}{3}$
  e $\frac{17b}{20}$ **f** $\frac{12+2x}{3}$ **g** $\frac{14a}{5}$ **h** $\frac{16b}{15}$

4 a $\cos\theta = a$, **c** $\cos\theta \times \cos\theta + \sin\theta \times \sin\theta$
    $\sin\theta = b$, $= a \times a + b \times b$ {using **a**}
    $\tan\theta = \frac{b}{a}$ $= a^2 + b^2$
                $= 1$ {Pythagoras}
  b $\sin\theta \div \cos\theta = \frac{b}{a}$

REVIEW SET 18A

1 a $3x$ **b** $3n$ **c** $\frac{x}{6}$ **d** $\frac{2}{x}$

2 a $\frac{2}{c+3}$ **b** cannot be simplified **c** $x+2$ **d** $\frac{x}{3(x+2)}$

3 a $\frac{19x}{15}$ **b** $\frac{2x^2}{5}$ **c** $\frac{10}{9}$ **d** $\frac{x}{15}$

4 a 4 **b** -5 **c** $2x$

REVIEW SET 18B

1 a $\frac{2}{3}$ **b** $2x$ **c** $3n$ **d** $2x$

2 a cannot be simplified **b** $x+5$ **c** $\frac{2}{a+4}$ **d** $\frac{b}{2(b-a)}$

3 a $\frac{11x}{4}$ **b** $\frac{-5x}{4}$ **c** $\frac{3x^2}{2}$ **d** $\frac{3}{8}$

4 a -1 **b** $\frac{5}{2}$ **c** $\frac{3x}{a}$

CHALLENGE

1 $\cos\theta = \frac{a}{c}$, $\sin\theta = \frac{b}{c}$, $\tan\theta = \frac{b}{a}$

2 $\sin\theta \div \cos\theta = \frac{b}{a} = \tan\theta$

3 $\cos\theta \times \cos\theta + \sin\theta \times \sin\theta$ **4** $A = \frac{1}{2} \times$ base $\times$ height
   $= \frac{a}{c} \times \frac{a}{c} + \frac{b}{c} \times \frac{b}{c}$ {using **1**} $= \frac{1}{2}ab$
   $= \frac{a^2}{c^2} + \frac{b^2}{c^2}$ $\therefore A = \frac{1}{2}ac\sin\theta$
   $= \frac{a^2+b^2}{c^2}$ {using **1**}
   $= \frac{c^2}{c^2}$ {Pythagoras}
   $= 1$

EXERCISE 19A

1 a The variable can take any value in the continuous range 75 to 105. Weight is measured.
  b $85 \leqslant w < 90$. This class has the highest frequency.
  c Weights of a volleyball squad **d** symmetrical

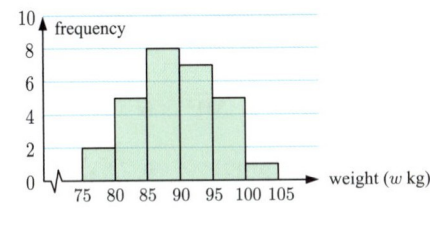

2 a Variation in soil pH **b** $5.5 \leqslant x < 6$
  c **i** 22.5%
      ii 30%

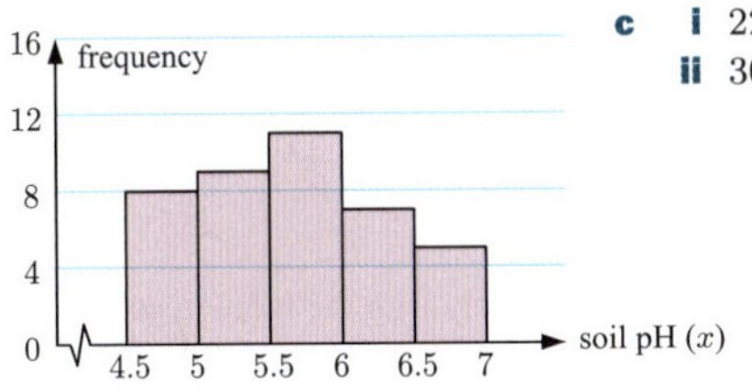

3 a $40 \leqslant h < 60$ mm **b** ≈ 69.6 mm **c** 46 seedlings
  d 30% **e i** ≈ 754 seedlings **ii** ≈ 686 seedlings

4 a Distances travelled to school **b** $1 \leqslant d < 2$ km
  c ≈ 1.66 km
  d 33.5%
  e 9 students

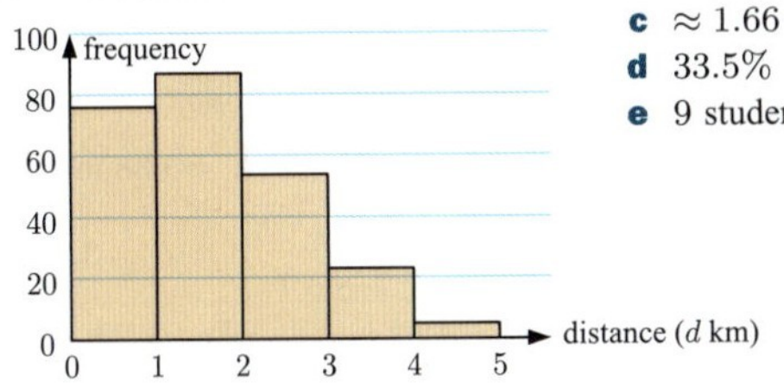

5 a 32.5% **b** ≈ 22.9 min **c** ≈ 1490 people

6 a Call duration

b positively skewed
c ≈ 2.46 min
d ≈ 235 calls

7 a Data is negatively skewed. This means that most of the visible stars were not very bright.
b ≈ 3.19 **c** 16 stars

EXERCISE 19B

1 a

Mass (m kg)	Frequency	Cumulative Frequency
$10 \leqslant m < 20$	15	15
$20 \leqslant m < 30$	21	36
$30 \leqslant m < 40$	47	83
$40 \leqslant m < 50$	33	116
$50 \leqslant m < 60$	4	120

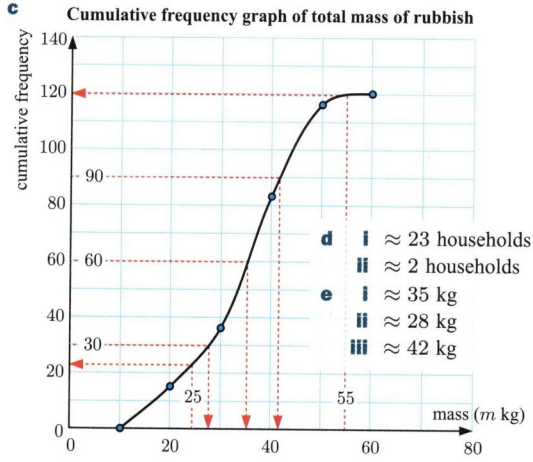

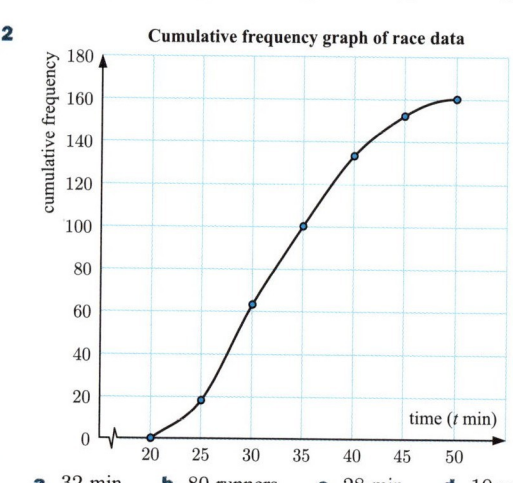

b 120 houses
c Cumulative frequency graph of total mass of rubbish

d i ≈ 23 households
ii ≈ 2 households
e i ≈ 35 kg
ii ≈ 28 kg
iii ≈ 42 kg

2 Cumulative frequency graph of race data

a 32 min **b** 80 runners **c** 28 min **d** 10 min

3 a Cumulative frequency graph of trout length

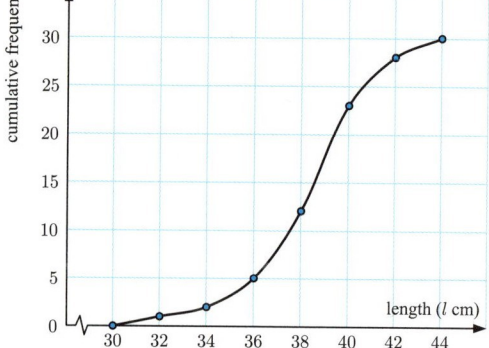

b 57% **c** 38.6 cm **d** 3.0 cm **e** ≈ 38.3 cm
f negatively skewed

4 a 120 goats **b** 29 kg **c** 48 goats **d** 17.5 kg

5 a Cumulative frequency graphs of cabbage weight data

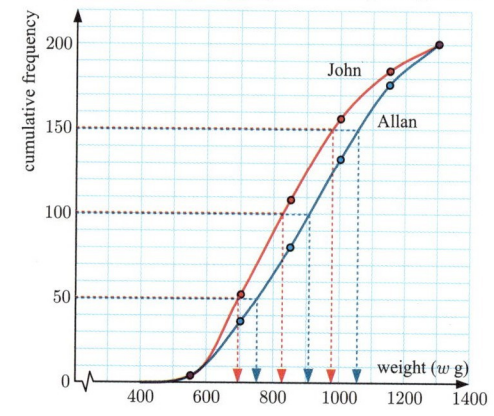

b i Alan, ≈ 910 g; John, ≈ 830 g
  ii Alan, ≈ 310 g; John, ≈ 290 g
c Alan's cabbages are generally heavier than John's. The spread of each data set is about the same.

6 a Cumulative frequency graph of Ben Nevis climb data

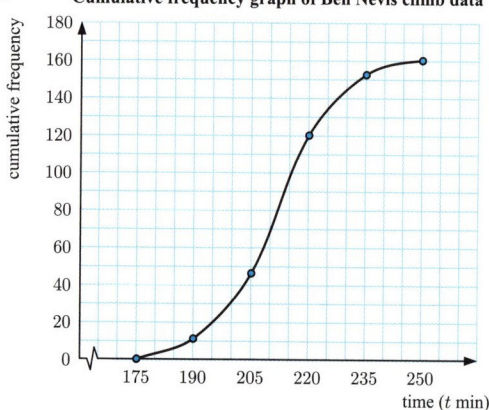

b ≈ 212 min
c $16\frac{1}{2}$ min. This is the length of time in which the middle 50% of the data lies.
d ≈ 20   **e** symmetrical

7 a i 4 kg
  ii 2.1 kg
  c ≈ 4.25 kg

b

Weight (w grams)	Freq.	Cum. Freq.
$0 \leqslant w < 1$	1	1
$1 \leqslant w < 2$	2	3
$2 \leqslant w < 3$	5	8
$3 \leqslant w < 4$	12	20
$4 \leqslant w < 5$	8	28
$5 \leqslant w < 6$	6	34
$6 \leqslant w < 7$	3	37
$7 \leqslant w < 8$	2	39
$8 \leqslant w < 9$	1	40

REVIEW SET 19A

1 a The variable can take any value in the continuous range $48 \leqslant m < 53$ grams. It is measured.
  b $50 \leqslant m < 51$ **c** ≈ 50.8 grams
  d slightly negatively skewed

2 a ≈ 54.9 km/h
  b Speeds of vehicles (histogram)
  c $55 \leqslant v < 60$ **d** ≈ 24.3%   **e** symmetrical

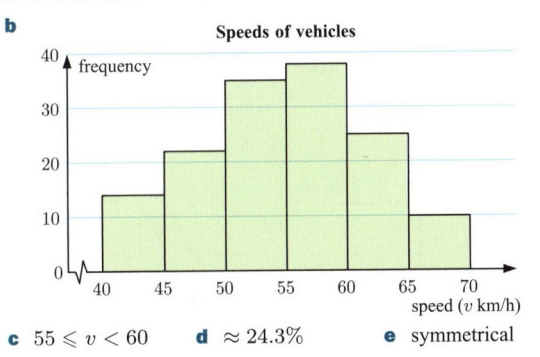

3 a Cumulative frequency graph of wage data 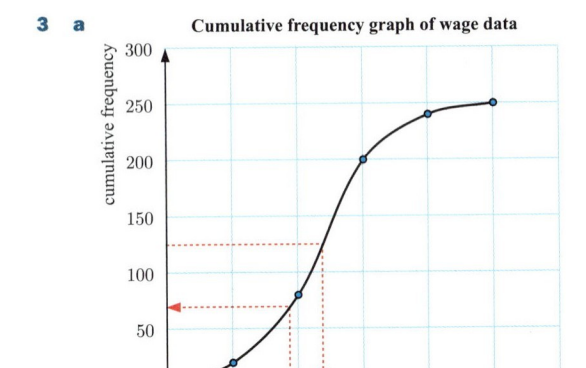
  b i ≈ £950   **ii** ≈ 70 employees

4 a

Time (t min)	Freq.	Cum. Freq.
$0 \leqslant t < 5$	2	2
$5 \leqslant t < 10$	3	5
$10 \leqslant t < 15$	5	10
$15 \leqslant t < 20$	10	20
$20 \leqslant t < 25$	20	40
$25 \leqslant t < 30$	15	55
$30 \leqslant t < 35$	5	60
$35 \leqslant t < 40$	10	70
$40 \leqslant t < 45$	6	76
$45 \leqslant t < 50$	4	80

b i 25 min   **ii** 15 min
c i 27   **ii** 18

REVIEW SET 19B

1 a 2 kg   **b** $2 \leqslant m < 4$ **c** ≈ 4.76
  d Histogram of masses of cats 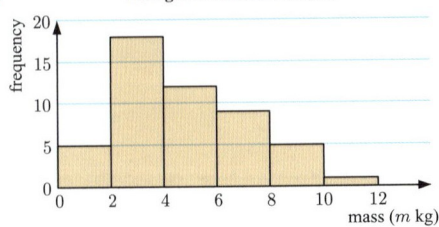
  e 51 of them

2 a ≈ 39.1 sec   **b** $35 \leqslant t < 40$

3 a 150 boys and 150 girls
  b Cumulative frequency graph of test scores 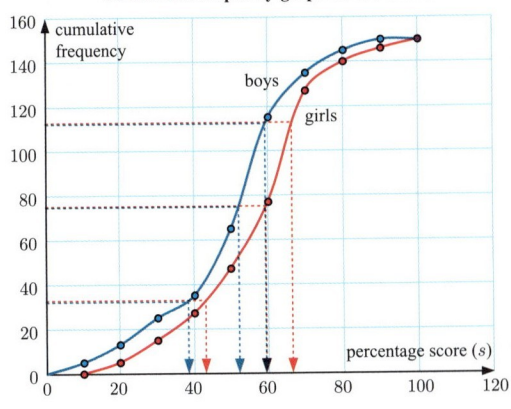
  c For boys: median ≈ 52, IQR ≈ 18
    For girls: median ≈ 59, IQR ≈ 20
  d As the girls graph is further to the right of the boys graph, the girls are outperforming the boys. Both distributions are negatively skewed.

4 a Histogram of newborn babies 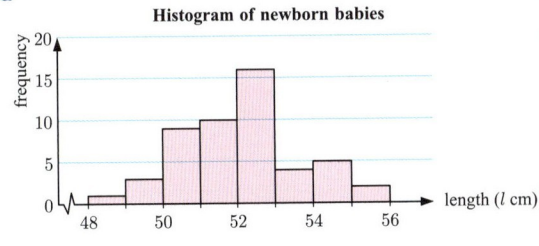
  b 27 babies   **c** 70% of them

d

Upper end point	Cumulative frequency
49	1
50	4
51	13
52	23
53	39
54	43
55	48
56	50

Answers

e Cumulative frequency graph of baby length data

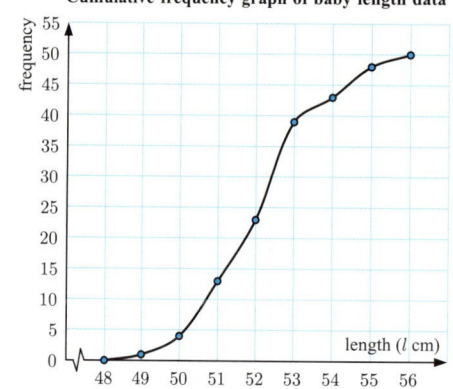

f i ≈ 52.2 cm **ii** 17 babies

EXERCISE 20A

1 a $x = 0.8$ **b** $x = 1.2$ **c** $x \approx 1.13$ **d** $x \approx 0.706$
2 a $x = 8$ **b** $x = 8.75$ **c** $x = 4.8$ **d** $x \approx 3.18$
3 a 6 cm **b** $k = 1.5$
4 $FG = 2.4$ m
5 a true **b** false, e.g.,

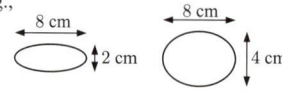

c true **d** false, e.g.,

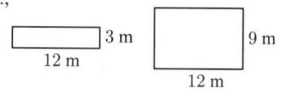

6 They are **not** similar.
Comparing lengths; $k = \frac{16}{12} = \frac{4}{3}$
Comparing widths; $k = \frac{12}{8} = \frac{3}{2}$
and $\frac{4}{3} \neq \frac{3}{2}$.
7 a $x = 4.8$ cm **b** $x = 9$ cm
8 a

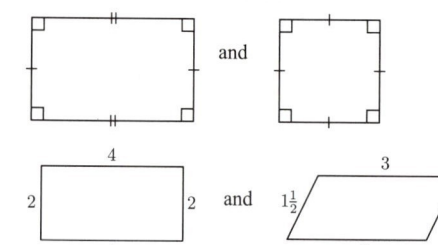

b

9 No, any two equiangular triangles are similar.

EXERCISE 20B.1

1 All of these figures have triangles which can be shown to be equiangular and therefore are similar.
For example, in **a**, $\triangle CBD$ is similar to $\triangle CAE$ as they share an equal angle at C and $\widehat{CBD} = \widehat{CAE} = 90°$.
b $\triangle RQS$ is similar to $\triangle RPT$
c $\triangle BAC$ is similar to $\triangle EDC$
d $\triangle VXW$ is similar to $\triangle VYU$
e $\triangle KJL$ is similar to $\triangle MNL$
f $\triangle CBD$ is similar to $\triangle CEA$

EXERCISE 20B.2

1 a $x = 2.4$ **b** $x = 2.8$ **c** $x \approx 3.27$ **d** $x = 9.6$
e $x = 11.2$ **f** $x = 5$ **g** $x \approx 6.67$ **h** $x = 7$
i $x = 7.2$

EXERCISE 20C

1 a 7 m **b** 7.5 m **2** 1.8 m **3** 2.67 m **4** 39 m
5 6.5 m **6** 6.46 cm **7** 1.52 m **8** 1.44 m
9 9 seconds **10** 117 m **11** 1013 m
12 a $SU = 5.5$ m, $BC = 8.2$ m
b No, the ball's centre is ≈ 11 cm on the D side of C.

REVIEW SET 20A

1 and

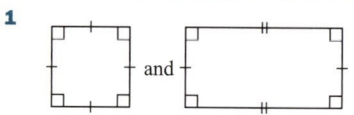

2 a $x \approx 1.71$ **b** $x \approx 1.83$ **3** $x = 2.8$
4 Hint: Carefully show that triangles are equiangular, giving reasons.
5 a $x \approx 6.47$ **b** $x = 2\sqrt{6} \approx 4.90$
6 $x = 15$ **7** ≈ 66.7 m wide

REVIEW SET 20B

1

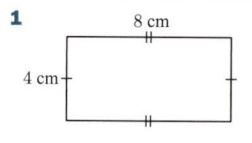

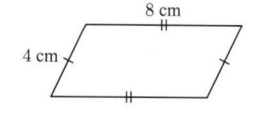

2 $x = 3.6$ **3 a** $x = 3$ **b** $x = 4$ **c** $x = 12$
4 a $\widehat{BAC} = \widehat{NMC} = 90°$ {given}
∠C is common to both ∴ △s ABC and MNC are equiangular, i.e., similar.
b $\frac{x}{8} = \frac{6}{15}$ ∴ $x = \frac{48}{15} = 3.2$ **c** 6.4 cm
5 a Hint: Explain carefully, with reasons, why they are equiangular.
b $CD = 7.2$ cm
6 $2\sqrt{13} \approx 7.21$ cm by $3\sqrt{13} \approx 10.8$ cm **7** 1.5625 km

CHALLENGE

1 ≈ 17.1 m
2 a

Radius (cm)	Area (cm²)
1	π
2	4π
3	9π
4	16π

b k^2

c When a figure is enlarged by k, the area is multiplied by k^2.

EXERCISE 21A.1

1 a

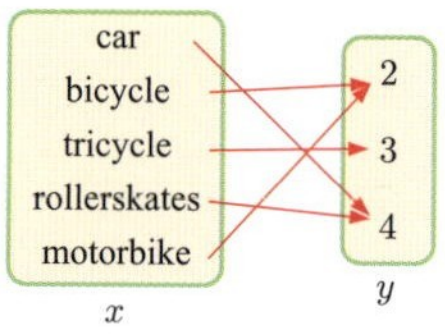

b

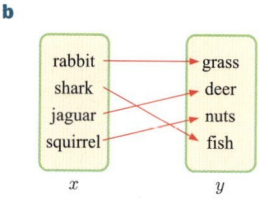

Answers

2 a one-one **b** many-many **c** one-many **d** many-many **e** one–one

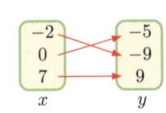

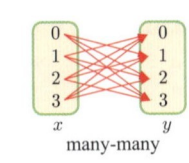

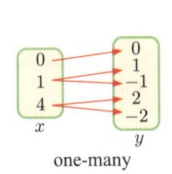

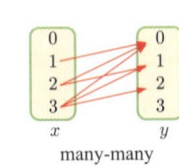

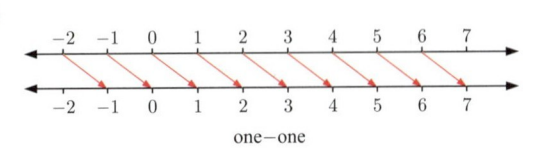

3 a {real numbers}
b {multiples of 2 which are not multiples of 4}
c {positive real numbers} **d** {real numbers $\geqslant 10$}
e {integers}

EXERCISE 21A.2

1 a ii Domain is $\{-2, -1, 0, 1, 2\}$
Range is $\{-6, -3, 0, 3, 6\}$
b ii Domain is $\{1, 2, 3, 4, 5\}$
Range is $\{-2, -1, 0, 1, 2\}$
c ii Domain is $\{-5, -3, 0, 2, 4\}$
Range is $\{-2, 2, 6, 12, 16\}$

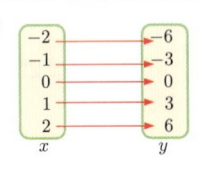

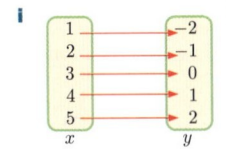

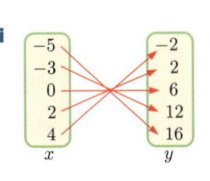

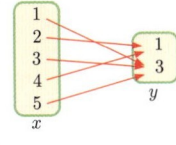

2 a ii one-one **b ii** many-one **c ii** one-many

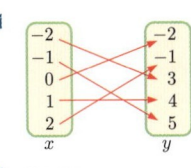

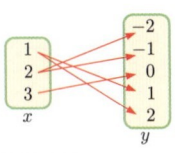

EXERCISE 21B.1

1 a Domain $= \{-3, -2, -1, 0, 6\}$ Range $= \{-1, 3, 4, 5, 8\}$.
b Domain $= \{-3, -1, 0, 2, 4, 5, 7\}$ Range $= \{3, 4\}$.

2 a Domain is $\{x \mid x > -4\}$. Range is $\{y \mid y > -2\}$.
Is a function.
b Domain is $\{x \mid x = 2\}$. Range is $\{y \mid y \in \mathbb{R}\}$.
Is not a function.
c Domain is $\{x \mid -3 \leqslant x \leqslant 3\}$. Range is $\{y \mid -3 \leqslant y \leqslant 3\}$.
Is not a function.
d Domain is $\{x \mid x \in \mathbb{R}\}$. Range is $\{y \mid y \leqslant 0\}$.
Is a function.
e Domain is $\{x \mid x \in \mathbb{R}\}$. Range is $\{y \mid y = -5\}$.
Is a function.
f Domain is $\{x \mid x \in \mathbb{R}\}$. Range is $\{y \mid y \geqslant 1\}$.
Is a function.
g Domain is $\{x \mid x \in \mathbb{R}\}$. Range is $\{y \mid y \leqslant 4\}$.
Is a function.
h Domain is $\{x \mid x \geqslant -5\}$. Range is $\{y \mid y \in \mathbb{R}\}$.
Is not a function.
i Domain is $\{x \mid x \neq 1, x \in \mathbb{R}\}$.
Range is $\{y \mid y \neq 0, y \in \mathbb{R}\}$.
Is a function.

3 a $\{2, 3, 5, 10, 12\}$ **b** $\{0, \frac{1}{2}, 2\}$
c $\{y \mid -3 < y < 5\}$ **d** $\{y \mid -27 \leqslant y \leqslant 64\}$

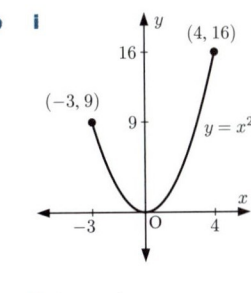

4 a ii Range is $\{y \mid -5 \leqslant y \leqslant 7\}$.
b ii Range is $\{y \mid 0 \leqslant y \leqslant 16\}$.
c ii Range is $\{y \mid -9 \leqslant y \leqslant 11\}$.
d ii Range is $\{y \mid y \leqslant -1 \text{ or } y \geqslant \frac{1}{2}\}$.
e ii Range is $\{y \mid y \leqslant -2 \text{ or } y \geqslant 2\}$.
f ii Range is $\{y \mid y \geqslant 1\}$.

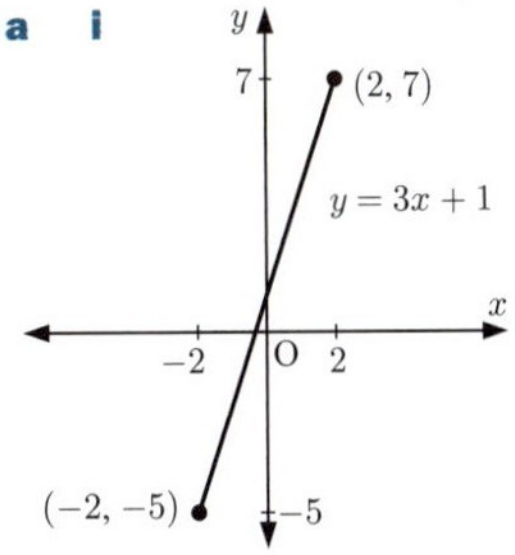

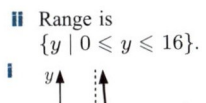

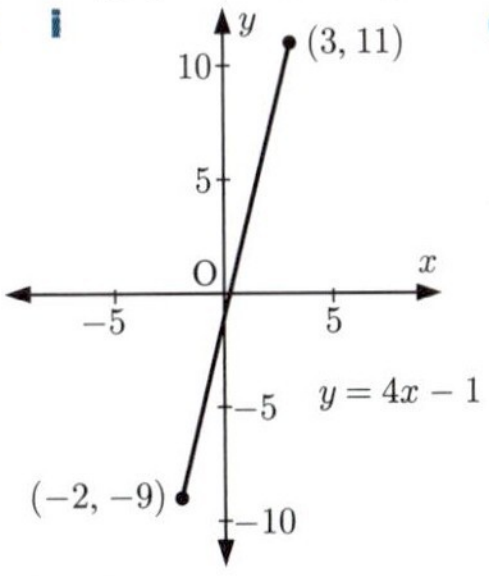

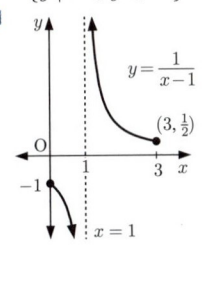

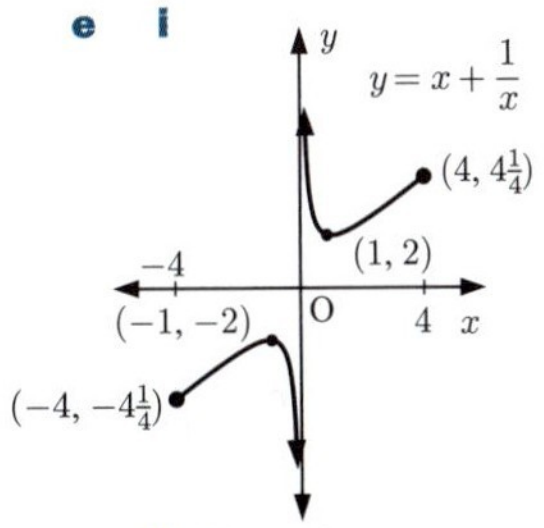

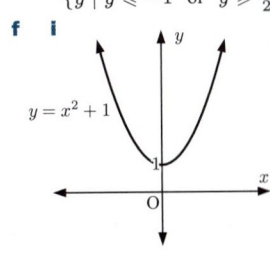

Answers 577

g i

ii Range is $\{y \mid y \in \mathbb{R}\}$

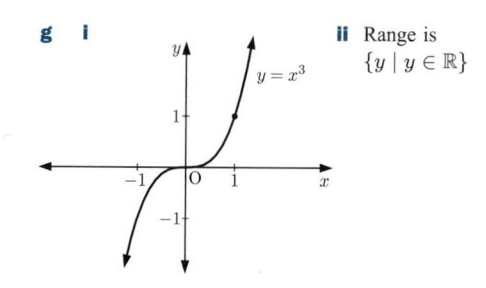

e $y = \dfrac{5}{x}$

f $y = -\dfrac{5}{x}$

EXERCISE 21B.2

1 **a**, **b**, **e** are functions as no two ordered pairs have the same x-coordinate.

2 **a**, **b**, **d**, **e**, **g**, **h**, **i** are functions.

3 No, a vertical line is not a funtion as it does not satisfy the vertical line test.

EXERCISE 21C

1 **a** $f(5) = 8$ which means that 5 is mapped onto 8 and the point $(5, 8)$ lies on the graph of the function f.
 b $g(3) = -6$ which means that 3 is mapped onto -6 and the point $(3, -6)$ lies on the graph of the function g.
 c $H(4) = 4\frac{1}{3}$ which means that 4 is mapped onto $4\frac{1}{3}$ and the point $(4, 4\frac{1}{3})$ lies on the graph of the function H.

2 **a** i 5 ii -7 iii 21 iv -395
 b i 6 ii 4 iii -4 iv 10
 c i -2 ii $2\frac{1}{2}$ iii $1\frac{3}{7}$ iv $\frac{7}{10}$

3 **a** i $f(4) = 5$ ii $x = 2$ **b** i $\frac{1}{2}$ ii $a = 19$
 c i $x = 4$ ii $x = -8$

4 $x = -8$

5 **a** $V(4) = \$12\,000$, the value of the car after 4 years.
 b $t = 5$; the car is worth $\$8000$ after 5 years. **c** $\$28\,000$
 d No, as when $t > 7$, $V(t) < 0$ which is not valid.

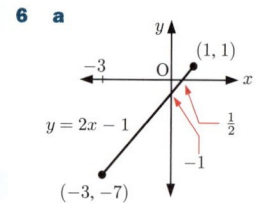

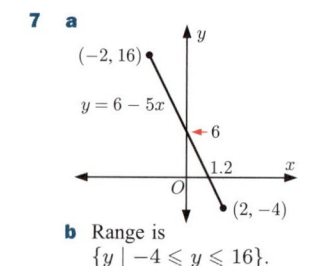

6 **a**

7 **a**

 b Range is $\{y \mid -7 \leqslant y \leqslant 1\}$.
 b Range is $\{y \mid -4 \leqslant y \leqslant 16\}$.

8 **a** $f(2) = -3$ **b** $x \approx -1.4$, 2 or 3.4

9 **a** $3t + 4$ **b** $-3t + 4$ **c** $3x + 10$ **d** $3x + 1$ **e** $12x + 4$

10 **a** $5 - 2a$ **b** $5 + 2a$ **c** $3 - 2a$ **d** $11 - 2x$ **e** $5 - 4x$

11 **a** $x^2 + 8x + 9$ **b** $x^2 - 6x + 2$ **c** $x^2 - 4x - 3$
 d $x^4 + 4x^2 - 3$ **e** $x^4 + 6x^2 + 2$

EXERCISE 21D

1 **a** When x or $y = 0$, $xy = 0$ which is $\neq 5$.
 b vertical asymptote $x = 0$, horizontal asymptote $y = 0$
 c i $y = 0.01$ ii $y = -0.01$
 d i $x = 0.01$ ii $x = -0.01$

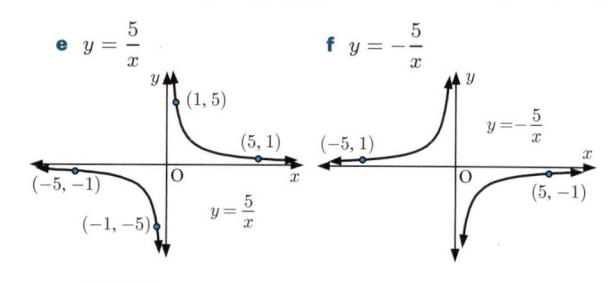

2 **a**

n	4	8	12	16	20	24	28
t	10	5	3.3	2.5	2	1.7	1.4

 b

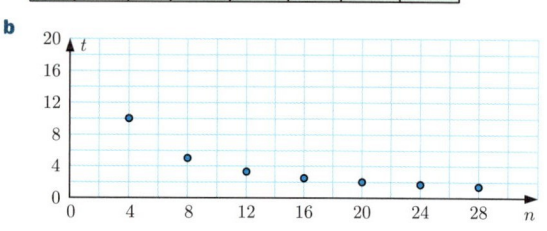

 c Yes, one part of a hyperbola. **d** $t = \dfrac{40}{n}$ or $nt = 40$.

3 **a**

 b vertical asymptote $x = 2$, horizontal asymptote $y = 0$

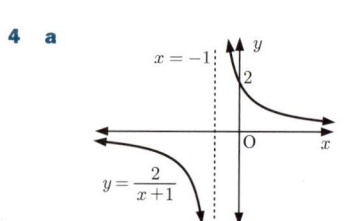

4 **a**

 b vertical asymptote $x = -1$, horizontal asymptote $y = 0$

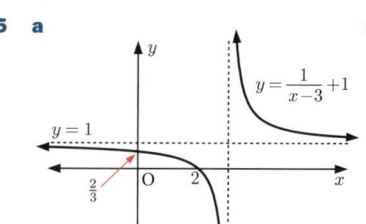

5 **a**

 b vertical asymptote $x = 3$, horizontal asymptote $y = 1$

REVIEW SET 21A

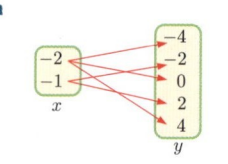

1 **a**

 b Domain is $\{-2, 1\}$ Range is $\{-4, -2, 0, 2, 4\}$
 c one-many
 d no

2 **a** Domain is $\{x \mid -4 < x \leqslant 3\}$. Range is $\{y \mid -2 \leqslant y < 4\}$.
 b Domain is $\{x \mid x \geqslant -5\}$. Range is $\{y \mid y \geqslant -145\}$.
 c Domain is $\{x \mid x \neq 0\}$. Range is $\{y \mid y \neq 0\}$.

3 a -13 This means that -3 maps onto -13, and the point $(-3, -13)$ lies on the graph of the function f.
  b **i** -2 **ii** 19 **iii** $1 - 3x$
4 a Domain is $\{x \mid x \in \mathbb{R}\}$.   Range is $\{y \mid y = 2\}$.
     Is a function.
  b Domain is $\{x \mid x \geqslant -3, \ x \in \mathbb{R}\}$.   Range is $\{y \mid y \in \mathbb{R}\}$.
     Is not a function.
  c Domain is $\{x \mid -2 \leqslant x \leqslant 1\}$.
     Range is $\{y \mid -3 \leqslant y \leqslant 2\}$.   Is a function.
5 a -19 **b** $5x - 9$ **c** $x = \frac{7}{5}$

REVIEW SET 21B

1 a   **b** A many-one function.
      c yes

2 a i Range is $\{y \mid y > -2\}$.   Domain is $\{x \mid x > -6\}$.
    ii function
  b i Range is $\{y \mid y \neq 3\}$.   Domain is $\{x \mid x \neq -2\}$.
    ii function
  c i Range is $\{y \mid y \in \mathbb{R}\}$.   Domain is $\{x \mid x = -3\}$.
    ii not a function
  d i Range is $\{y \mid y \in \mathbb{R}\}$.   Domain is $\{x \mid x \leqslant 1\}$.
    ii not a function

3 a 4 **b** $-\frac{1}{3}x + 5$ **c** $\frac{1}{3}x + \frac{16}{3}$

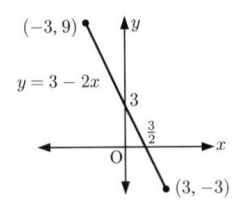

4   Range is $\{y \mid -3 \leqslant y \leqslant 9\}$

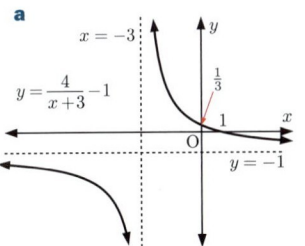

5 a   **b** vertical asymptote $x = -3$, horizontal asymptote $y = -1$

CHALLENGE
Answers on CD.

EXERCISE 22A

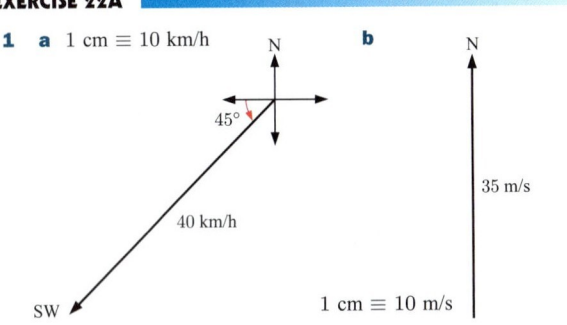

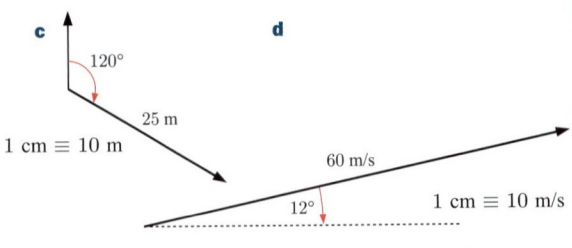

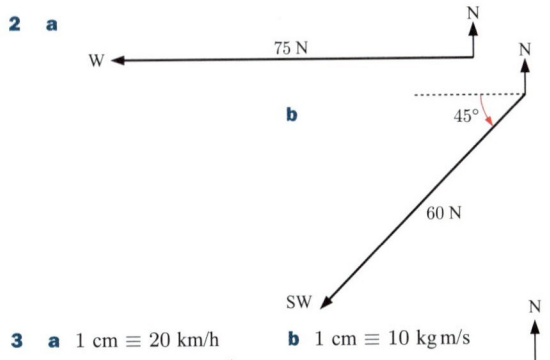

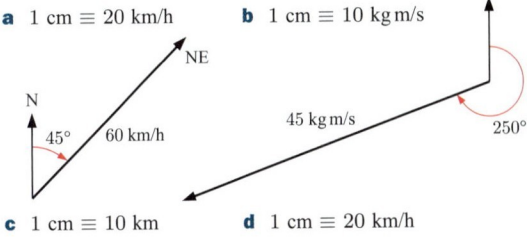

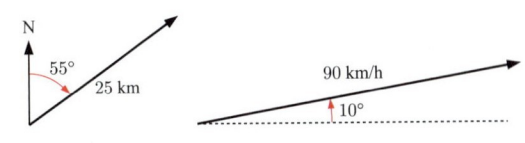

1 a $1 \text{ cm} \equiv 10 \text{ km/h}$ **b**
  c $1 \text{ cm} \equiv 10 \text{ m}$ **d** $1 \text{ cm} \equiv 10 \text{ m/s}$

2 a   **b**

3 a $1 \text{ cm} \equiv 20 \text{ km/h}$ **b** $1 \text{ cm} \equiv 10 \text{ kg m/s}$
  c $1 \text{ cm} \equiv 10 \text{ km}$ **d** $1 \text{ cm} \equiv 20 \text{ km/h}$

EXERCISE 22B

1 a   **b**   **c**   **d**

2 a $\begin{pmatrix} 4 \\ 2 \end{pmatrix}$ **b** $\begin{pmatrix} 0 \\ -3 \end{pmatrix}$ **c** $\begin{pmatrix} -3 \\ -4 \end{pmatrix}$ **d** $\begin{pmatrix} -6 \\ 0 \end{pmatrix}$ **e** $\begin{pmatrix} -6 \\ 4 \end{pmatrix}$ **f** $\begin{pmatrix} 2 \\ -4 \end{pmatrix}$

3 a $\begin{pmatrix} 9 \\ 3 \end{pmatrix}$ **b** $\begin{pmatrix} 2 \\ 5 \end{pmatrix}$ **c** $\begin{pmatrix} 4 \\ 1 \end{pmatrix}$ **d** $\begin{pmatrix} -2 \\ 4 \end{pmatrix}$ **e** $\begin{pmatrix} 11 \\ -4 \end{pmatrix}$
   f $\begin{pmatrix} -4 \\ -1 \end{pmatrix}$ **g** $\begin{pmatrix} -9 \\ 0 \end{pmatrix}$ **h** $\begin{pmatrix} -2 \\ -5 \end{pmatrix}$ **i** $\begin{pmatrix} -11 \\ 4 \end{pmatrix}$

4 a $\begin{pmatrix} 3 \\ 4 \end{pmatrix}$ **b** $\begin{pmatrix} -4 \\ -2 \end{pmatrix}$ **c** $\begin{pmatrix} -2 \\ 1 \end{pmatrix}$ **d** $\begin{pmatrix} 3 \\ -3 \end{pmatrix}$ **e** $\begin{pmatrix} 1 \\ 5 \end{pmatrix}$

5 $B(1, 2)$

EXERCISE 22C

1 a $(5, 3)$ **b** $(4, 6)$ **c** $(-1, 3)$ **d** $(5, -5)$

2 a $\begin{pmatrix} 0 \\ 3 \end{pmatrix}$ **b** $\begin{pmatrix} -2 \\ -7 \end{pmatrix}$ **c** $\begin{pmatrix} 2 \\ 0 \end{pmatrix}$ **d** $\begin{pmatrix} 2 \\ -1 \end{pmatrix}$

3 $(0, 1)$

4 a $\begin{pmatrix} 8 \\ 0 \end{pmatrix}$ **b** $\begin{pmatrix} -8 \\ 0 \end{pmatrix}$ **c** $\begin{pmatrix} 0 \\ -4 \end{pmatrix}$ **d** $\begin{pmatrix} 0 \\ 4 \end{pmatrix}$ **e** $\begin{pmatrix} 4 \\ 1 \end{pmatrix}$
   f $\begin{pmatrix} 4 \\ 6 \end{pmatrix}$ **g** $\begin{pmatrix} -8 \\ -4 \end{pmatrix}$ **h** $\begin{pmatrix} -4 \\ -6 \end{pmatrix}$ **i** $\begin{pmatrix} 0 \\ 5 \end{pmatrix}$ **j** $\begin{pmatrix} 4 \\ -6 \end{pmatrix}$

Answers 579

5 a/b [graph showing triangle ABC and image A'B'C']

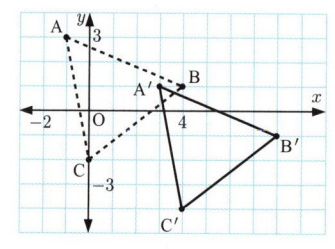

c A'(3, 1), B'(8, −1), C'(4, −4) **d** $\sqrt{20} \approx 4.47$ units

6 [graph showing trapezia A, B, C]

EXERCISE 22D

1 a (3, 2) **b** (−3, −2) **c** (2, −3)
2 a (3, 6) **b** (−4, 5) **c** (−3, −2)
3 a (−5, 5) **b** (−2, −2)
4 a [graph] **b** A'(−1, 5), B'(2, 7), C'(4, 4)
5 a [graph] **b** P'(−5, 4), Q'(−3, −2), R'(−1, 1)

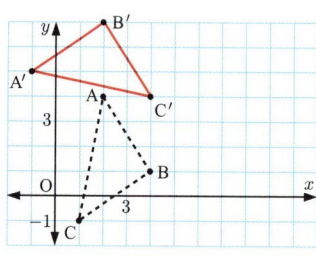

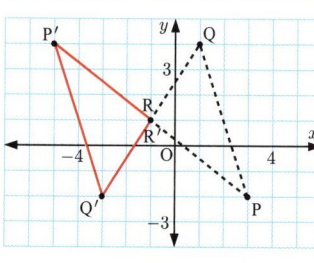

EXERCISE 22E

1 [image: MAX∃ | EXAM with mirror line]

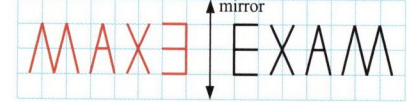

2 a (4, 1) **b** (−4, −1) **c** (−1, 4) **d** (1, −4)
3 a (1, −3) **b** (3, 1) **c** (5, −3) **d** (−1, 1)
  e (−1, 3) **f** (−5, −3) **g** (−3, −1) **h** (−1, 7)

4 [graph with U, T, W, V and lines $y = -1$, $y = -x$]

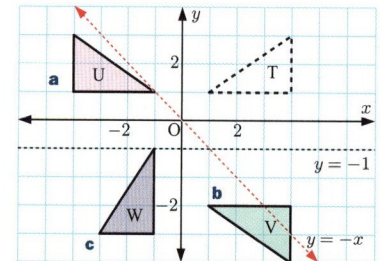

5

Point	Mirror line			
	x-axis	y-axis	$y = x$	$y = -x$
(3, 2)	(3, −2)	(−3, 2)	(2, 3)	(−2, −3)
(1, −2)	(1, 2)	(−1, −2)	(−2, 1)	(2, −1)
(−2, 4)	(−2, −4)	(2, 4)	(4, −2)	(−4, 2)
(a, b)	(a, −b)	(−a, b)	(b, a)	(−b, −a)

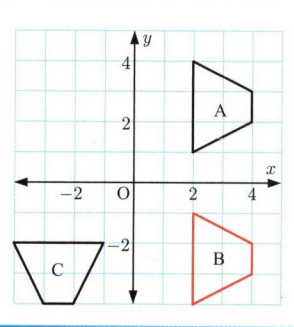

EXERCISE 22F

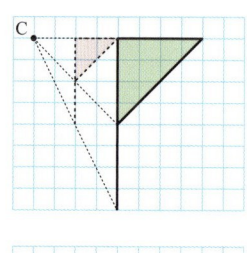

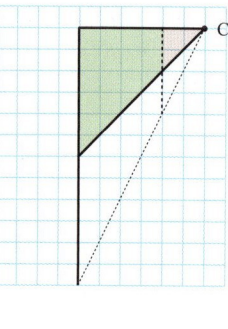

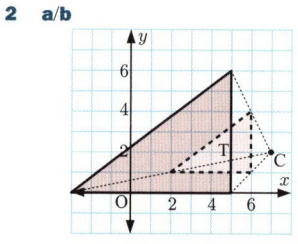

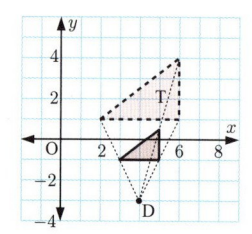

1 a [graph] **b** [graph]
  c [graph]

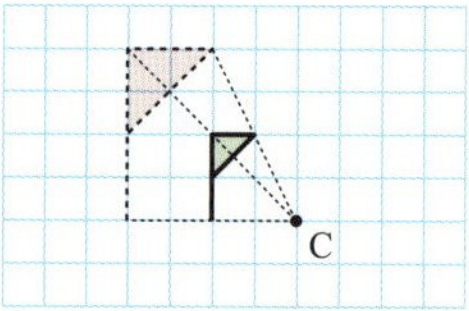

2 a/b [two graphs showing T, C, D]

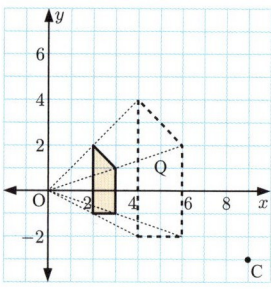

3 a [graph showing Q, C]
  b [graph showing Q, C]

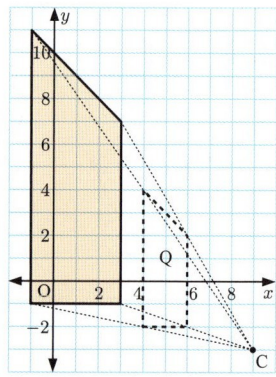

580 Answers

4 a $k = \frac{5}{3}$ **b** $k = 2$ **5** $(4, 4)$

6 a $(4\frac{1}{2}, 6)$ **b** $(0, 2)$

EXERCISE 22G

1 a i Vertical translation of $\begin{pmatrix} 0 \\ -2 \end{pmatrix}$, so $f(x)$ is translated 2 units downwards.
  ii $g(x) = f(x) - 2$

  b i Horizontal translation of $\begin{pmatrix} -5 \\ 0 \end{pmatrix}$, so $f(x)$ is translated 5 units to the left.
  ii $g(x) = f(x + 5)$

  c i Horizontal translation of $\begin{pmatrix} 3 \\ 0 \end{pmatrix}$, so $f(x)$ has moved 3 units to the right.
  ii $g(x) = f(x - 3)$

2 a/b

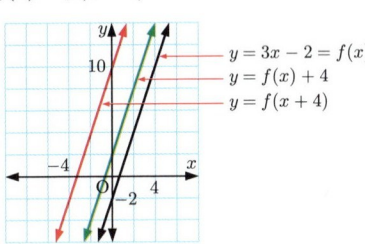

3 a/b

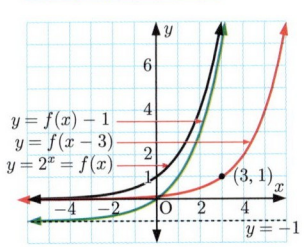

4 a/b

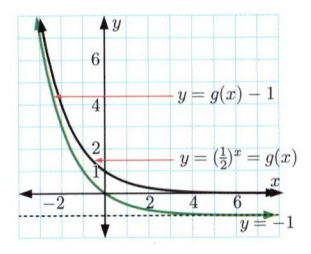

  c $y = -1$

  d A horizontal translation of $\begin{pmatrix} 1 \\ 0 \end{pmatrix}$, so $g(x)$ is translated 1 unit to the right.

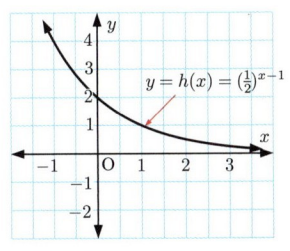

5 a

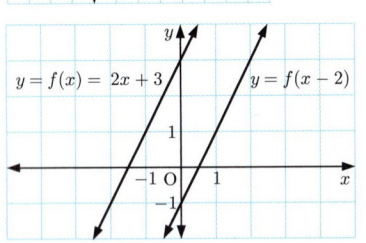

  b $f(x - 2) = 2x - 1$ **c** $y = 2x - 1$

6 a

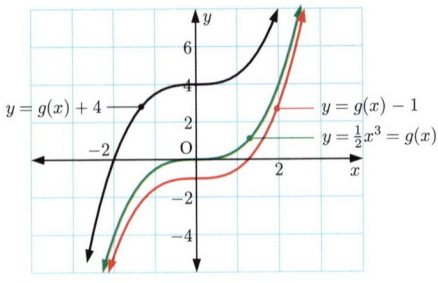

  b $\begin{pmatrix} 0 \\ 5 \end{pmatrix}$

7 a $\begin{pmatrix} 0 \\ -3 \end{pmatrix}$ **b** $\begin{pmatrix} 0 \\ 2 \end{pmatrix}$ **c** $\begin{pmatrix} 2 \\ 0 \end{pmatrix}$

8 a

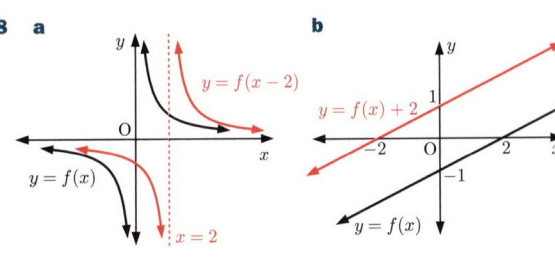

  b

  c

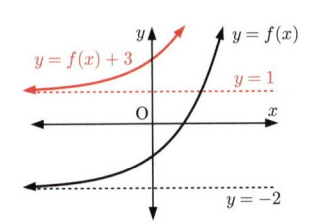

  d

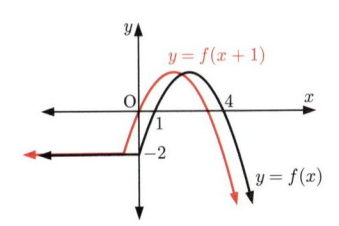

  e

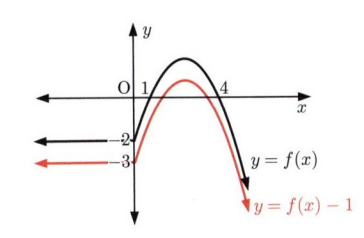

  f

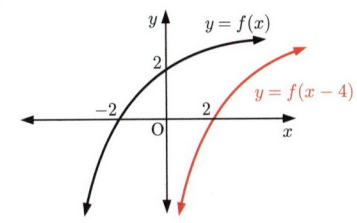

Answers 581

9

5

6 a/b

7

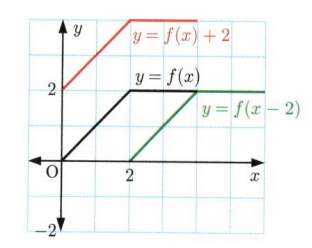

EXERCISE 22H

1 a reflection in x-axis   **b** translation of $\begin{pmatrix} 6 \\ -4 \end{pmatrix}$
   c rotation through $180°$ about $(0, 0)$
   d translation of $\begin{pmatrix} 2 \\ 4 \end{pmatrix}$
   e enlargement with centre $(2, 5)$ and scale factor $k = 2$
   f reflection in $y = -x$
   g reduction with centre $(3, 0)$ and scale factor $k = \frac{1}{3}$
   h rotation clockwise $90°$ about $(0, 0)$
   i reflection in $x = 4$
   j rotation anticlockwise $90°$ about $(-5, 0)$
   k reflection in $y = x$

2 a i $\begin{pmatrix} 0 \\ 3 \end{pmatrix}$ **ii** $g(x) = f(x) + 3$
   b i $\begin{pmatrix} -5 \\ 0 \end{pmatrix}$ **ii** $g(x) = f(x + 5)$
   c i $\begin{pmatrix} 2 \\ 0 \end{pmatrix}$ **ii** $g(x) = f(x - 2)$
   d i $\begin{pmatrix} 2 \\ 0 \end{pmatrix}$ **ii** $g(x) = f(x - 2)$
   e i $\begin{pmatrix} 0 \\ -8 \end{pmatrix}$ **ii** $g(x) = f(x) - 8$
   f i $\begin{pmatrix} -7 \\ 0 \end{pmatrix}$ **ii** $g(x) = f(x + 7)$

3 a i translation of $\begin{pmatrix} 0 \\ -6 \end{pmatrix}$ **ii** reflection in $y = x$
   iii rotation through $180°$ about $(0, 0)$
   iv enlargement with centre $(0, 0)$ and scale factor $k = 2$
   b rotation through $180°$ about $(0, -3)$

REVIEW SET 22A

1 a   **b**   **c**

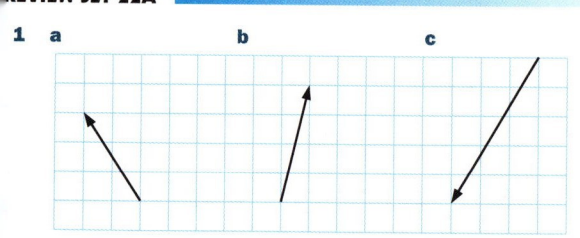

2 a $\begin{pmatrix} 3 \\ -2 \end{pmatrix}$ **b** $\begin{pmatrix} 6 \\ 0 \end{pmatrix}$

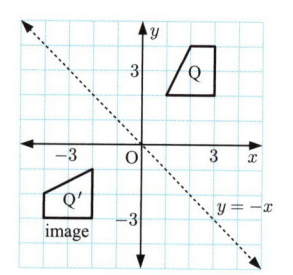

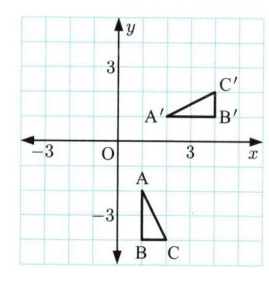

3 1 cm $\equiv 10$ km/h

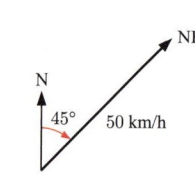

4 a i $(2, 5)$ **ii** $(-5, 2)$ **iii** $(4, -5)$
   b i $(4, 1)$ **ii** $(5, 4)$ **iii** $(2, 2)$

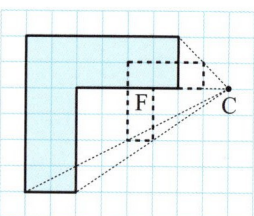

8 translation of $\begin{pmatrix} -5 \\ -4 \end{pmatrix}$

9 a   **b**

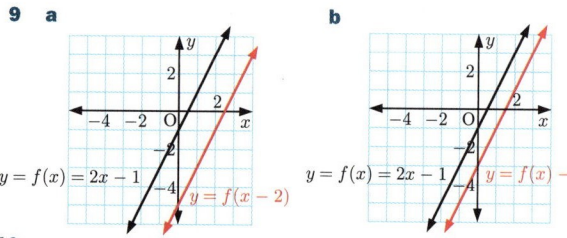

10

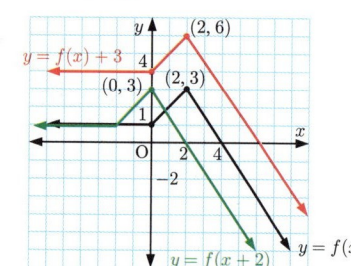

REVIEW SET 22B

1 a   **b**   **c**

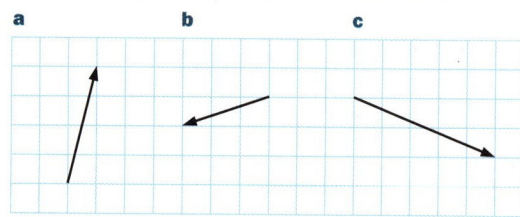

2 a $\begin{pmatrix} -4 \\ -3 \end{pmatrix}$ **b** $\begin{pmatrix} 0 \\ -4 \end{pmatrix}$

3 1 cm ≡ 50 km W ← 200 km

4 a (3, 2) **b** (2, −3) **c** (3, 10)

5 a (5, −11) **b** (−5, −7)

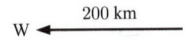

6

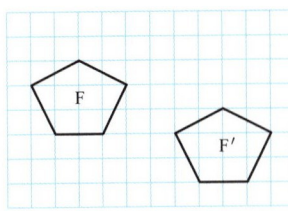

7

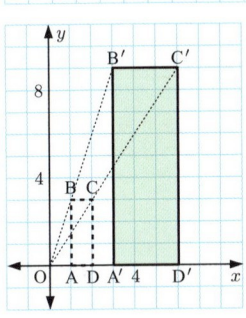

8 rotation through 180° about (1, 0)

9 reduction with centre C and scale factor $k = \frac{1}{2}$

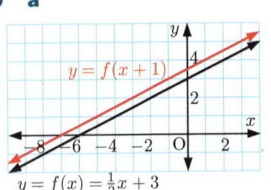

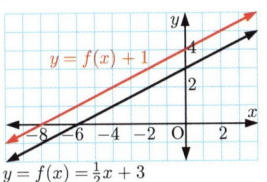

10 a $y = f(x+1)$, $y = f(x) = \frac{1}{2}x + 3$

b $y = f(x) + 1$, $y = f(x) = \frac{1}{2}x + 3$

11 a i $\binom{4}{0}$ **ii** $g(x) = f(x-4)$

b i $\binom{0}{3}$ **ii** $g(x) = f(x) + 3$

EXERCISE 23A

1 a i negative association **ii** linear **iii** strong
b i no association **ii** not linear **iii** zero
c i positive association **ii** linear **iii** moderate
d i positive association **ii** linear **iii** weak
e i positive association **ii** not linear **iii** moderate
f i negative association **ii** not linear **iii** strong

2 a "...... as x increases, y increases"
b "...... as T increases, d decreases"
c "...... randomly scattered"

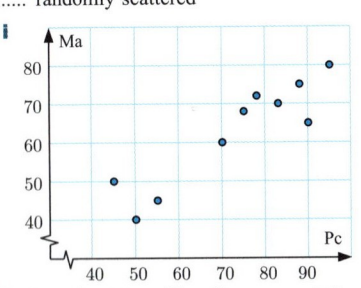

3 a i

ii A moderate, positive, linear association.

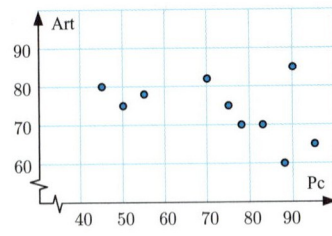

b

A weak, negative, linear association (virtually zero association).

4

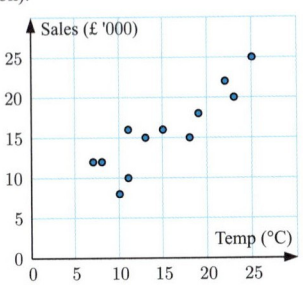

A moderate, positive, linear association exists between *Temperature* and *Sales*.

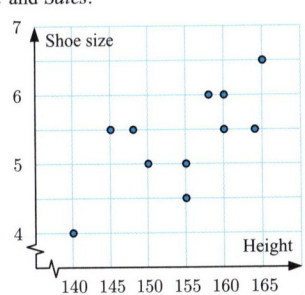

5

A weak, positive, linear association exists between *Shoe size* and *Height*.

EXERCISE 23B.1

1 a Minutes spent preparing (x) **b** $\overline{x} \approx 61.5$, $\overline{y} \approx 35.7$
c

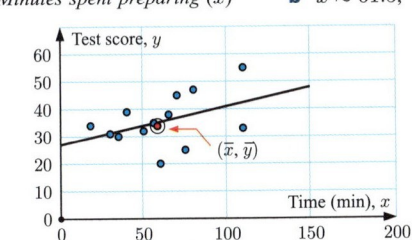

d There is a weak, positive correlation between the variables.
e There appears to be a weak, positive correlation between *minutes spent preparing* and *test score*. This means that as the time preparing increases, the score increases.
f/g On the graph above. **h** ≈ 31 marks

2 a $\overline{x} \approx 6.88$, $\overline{y} = 83.5$
b

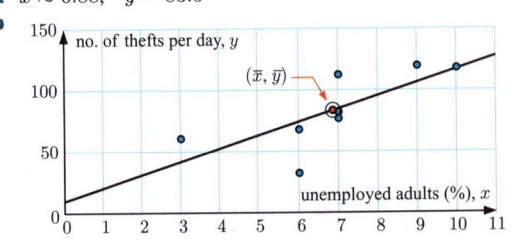

c A moderate, positive correlation between the variables.
d/e On the graph above. **f** About 95 thefts per day.

3 a $(\bar{x}, \bar{y}) \approx (23.3, 78.8)$
b [scatter plot: no. of diners vs temperature (°C)]
c There is a moderate, positive correlation between *number of diners* and *noon temperature*.
d/e On the graph above.
e i ≈ 68 diners **ii** ≈ 93 diners

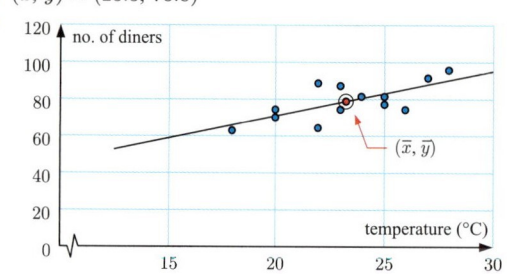

EXERCISE 23B.2

1 a/c [scatter plot: Triadic patent families vs year]
b $(\bar{x}, \bar{y}) = (1998, 531)$ **c** $y \approx 41.3x - 81\,958$
d i ≈ 601 **ii** ≈ 931
e The 1999 estimate is more reliable as we are interpolating.

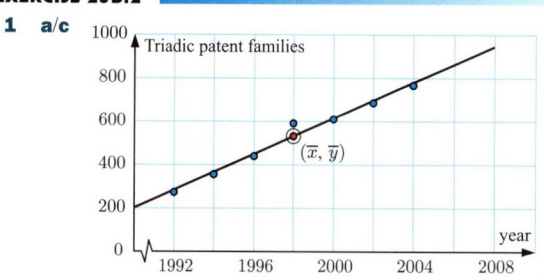

2 a/c [scatter plot: total medals vs gold medals]
b $(18.7, 51.7)$ **d** ≈ 50 medals **e** ≈ 6 medals
f The answers should be reasonably accurate as in **d** we are interpolating and in **e** we are extrapolating fairly close to the pole, and the data is strongly correlated.

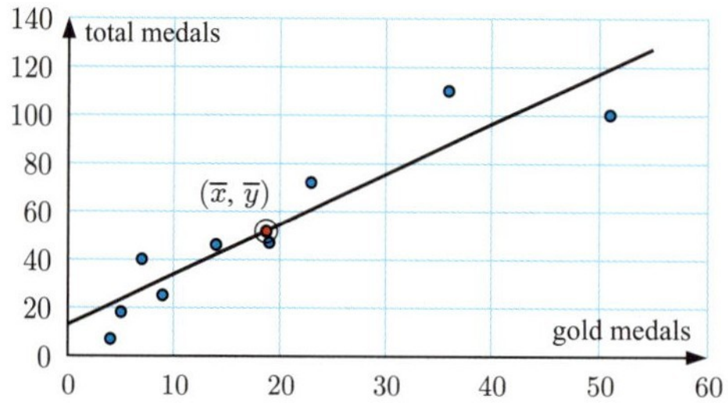

3 a [scatter plot: (£) vs weight (carats)]
b $(0.866, 583)$ **c** weak to moderate
d i $\approx £390$ **ii** £1000
e The answer in **d ii** would not really be accurate as we are extrapolating some distance from the upper pole. The answer in **d i** would be more accurate as here we are interpolating. However the data is only moderately correlated.

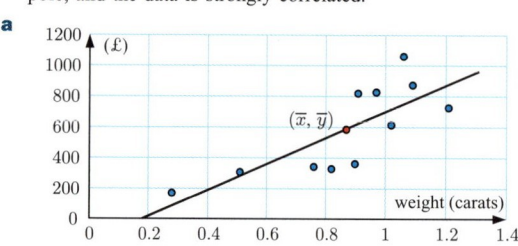

4 a/c [scatter plot: speed (km/h) vs time (s)]
b $(2, 23.0)$
d x-intercept is 9.5. This represents the time taken for the sled to stop completely.
e Estimate at 12 seconds is -12.1 km/h. However, as the sled has already stopped and you cannot have a negative speed, the prediction is unreliable.

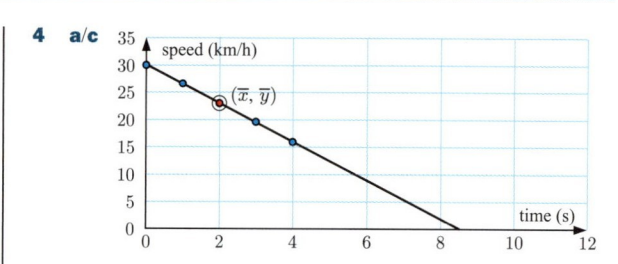

REVIEW SET 23A

1 a The independent variable is *Weeks of experience*. The dependent variable is *Number of defective items*.
b i weak **ii** negative

2 a [scatter plot: y (km/h) vs x]
b $\bar{x} = 13.6$, $\bar{y} = 14.6$ **c/d** On the graph. **e** 21 km/h

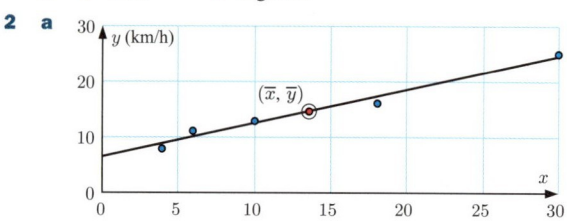

3 a [scatter plot: y (strawberries/plant) vs x (ml/litre)]
b There is a strong, positive correlation between *spray concentration* and *yield of strawberries*.
c This suggests that the higher the spray concentration, the higher the yield of strawberries.
d $(3.8, 18.8)$ **e** $y \approx 3.45x + 5.71$
f i ≈ 16 strawberries/plant **ii** ≈ 40 strawberries/plant
g As 10 lies outside the data range, this involves extrapolation and therefore may not be a reliable prediction.

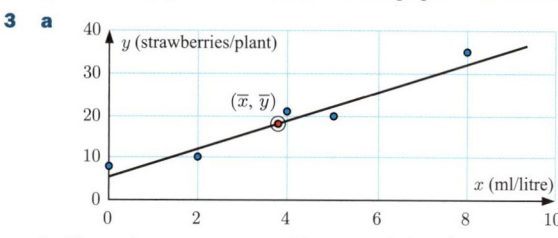

4 a/c [scatter plot: goals lost by vs week number]
b $(\bar{x}, \bar{y}) = (5, 5.44)$
d x-intercept is ≈ 12.6 weeks. This represents the week that the team draws a match.
e The results would be unreliable and the team would not play for a length of time, nor win consistently.

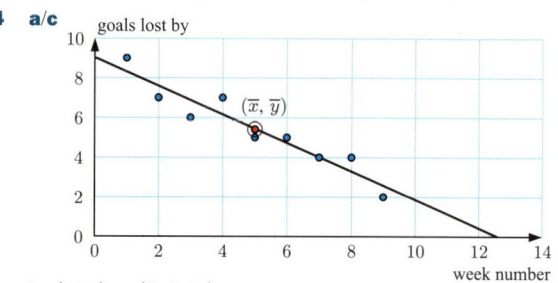

REVIEW SET 23B

1 a The independent variable is *age*. **b** No association exists.
  c It is not sensible to find it as the variables are not linearly related.

2 a

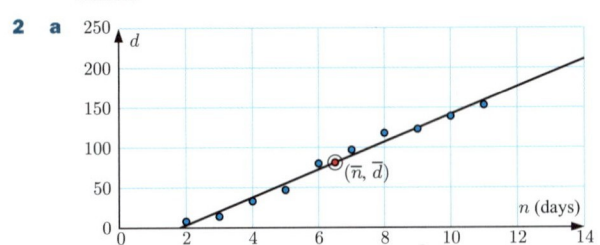

A linear model seems appropriate.

  b $\overline{n} = 6.5$, $\overline{d} = 81.2$ **c/d** On the graph.
  e About 210 diagnosed cases.
  Very unreliable as is outside the poles. The medical team have probably isolated those infected at this stage and there could be a downturn which may be very significant.

3 a, b

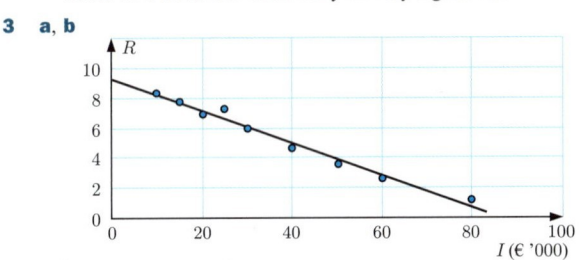

  c 4.5 per 1000 people
  d €100 000 gives a rate of -1.35 which is meaningless, i.e., €100 000 is outside the data range of this model.
  e i $I = 25$, $R = 7.3$ This goes against the trend of decrease in R for increase in I.
     ii b $R \approx -0.104I + 9.08$ **c** 4.4 per 1000 people

4 a

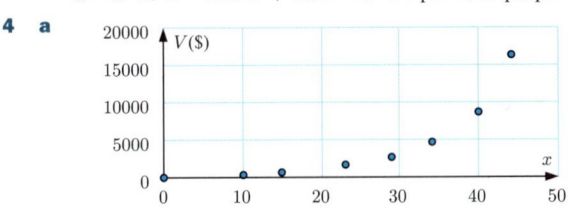

  b A moderate, positive association exists between x and V.
  c The points clearly lie on a curve and not on a straight line. Also, when $x = 0$, $V \approx -3050$ dollars.

EXERCISE 24A

1 a i $(0, -3)$ **ii** -3 **iii** ± 1.73
  b i $(\frac{1}{2}, -\frac{3}{2})$ **ii** -1 **iii** -0.366, 1.366
  c i $(-\frac{1}{3}, -5)$ **ii** -4 **iii** -1.079, 0.412

2 a i

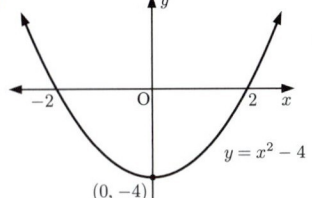

  ii $(0, -4)$
  iii x-intercepts ± 2, y-intercept -4

  b i $y = 2x^2 - 3x + 1$

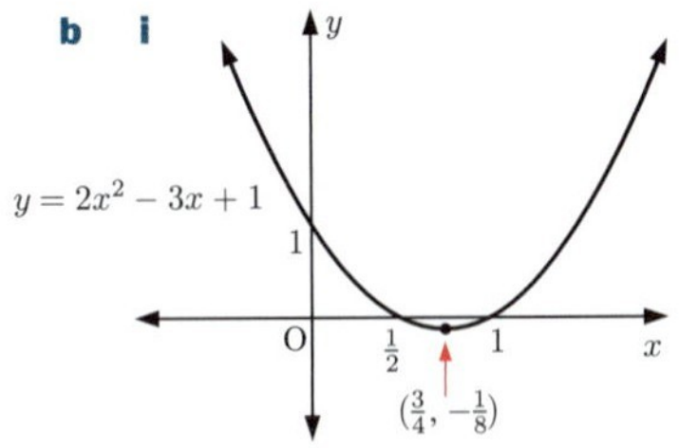

  ii $(\frac{3}{4}, -\frac{1}{8})$
  iii x-intercepts $\frac{1}{2}$, 1, y-intercept 1

  c i $y = -x^2 - 9x - 8$

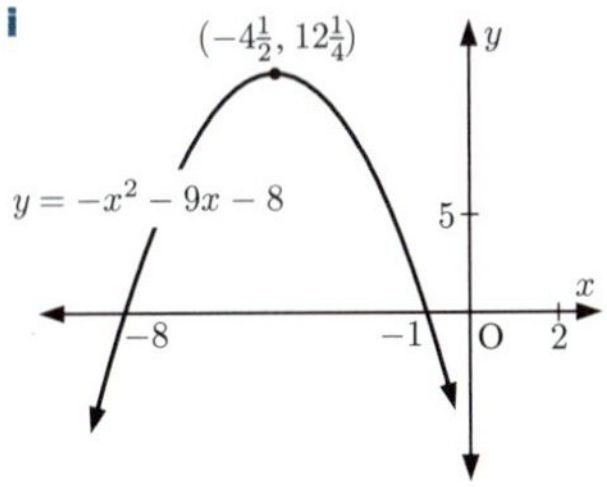

  ii $(-4\frac{1}{2}, 12\frac{1}{4})$
  iii x-intercepts -8, -1, y-intercept -8

  d i $y = \frac{1}{2}x^2 - 4x + 5$

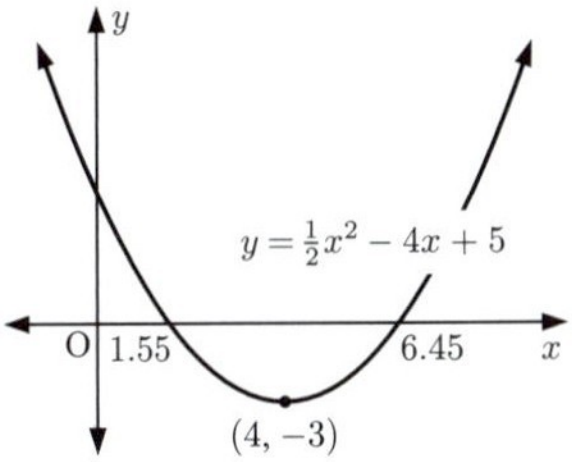

  ii $(4, -3)$
  iii x-intercepts 1.55, 6.45, y-intercept 5

  e i $y = 6 - 4x^2$

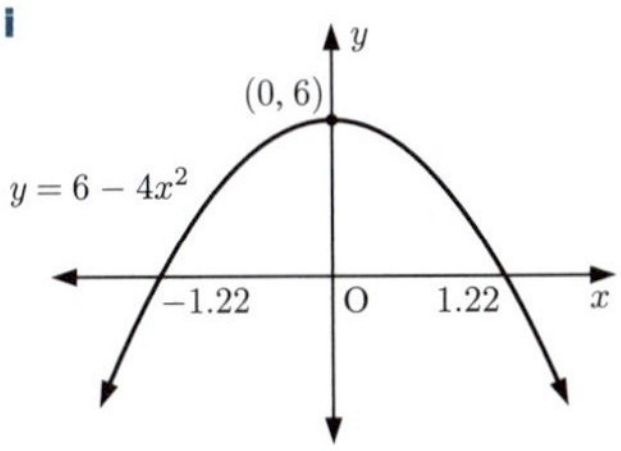

  ii $(0, 6)$
  iii x-intercepts ± 1.22, y-intercept 6

  f i $y = 23 + 17x - \frac{1}{3}x^2$

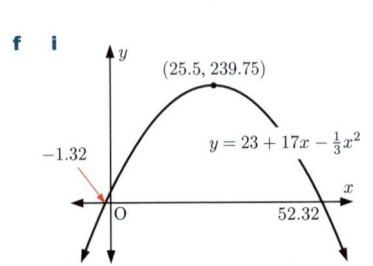

  ii $(25.5, 239.8)$
  iii x-intercepts -1.32, 52.32, y-intercept 23

3 a $f(x) = x^3 - 4x^2 + 5x - 3$, $-1 \leqslant x \leqslant 4$

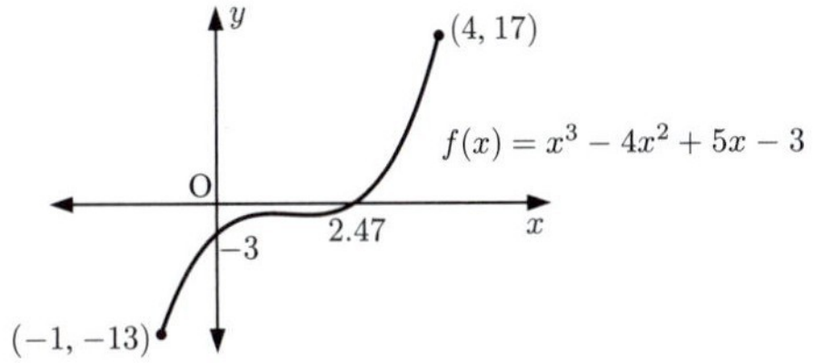

  b x-intercept ≈ 2.47, y-intercept -3
  c local maximum at $(1, -1)$
     local minimum at $\approx (1.67, -1.15)$
  d Range is $\{y \mid -13 \leqslant y \leqslant 17\}$

Answers 585

e
x	y
-1	-13
-0.5	-6.63
0	-3
0.5	-1.38
1	-1
1.5	-1.13

x	y
2	-1
2.5	0.125
3	3
3.5	8.38
4	17

4 a $f(x) = x^4 - 3x^3 - 10x^2 - 7x + 3$, $-4 \leqslant x \leqslant 6$

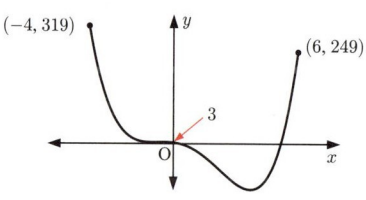

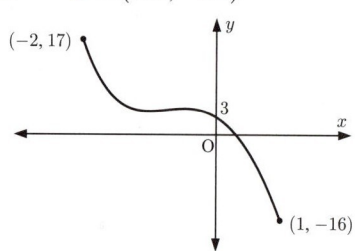

$(-4, 319)$, $(6, 249)$, 3

b ≈ 5.17 **c** $\approx (3.72, -124)$

d $(-2, 17)$, 3, $(1, -16)$

e local maximum at $\approx (-0.470, 4.44)$
local minimum at $(-1, 4)$

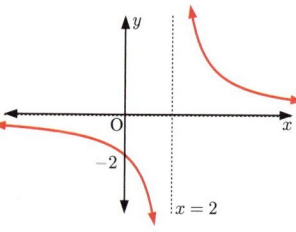

f
x	y
0	3
0.1	2.20
0.2	1.18
0.3	-0.07
0.4	-1.57
0.5	-3.31

x	y
0.6	-5.32
0.7	-7.59
0.8	-10.1
0.9	-12.9
1.0	-16

5 a i $f(x) = \dfrac{4}{x-2}$

ii vertical asymptote $x = 2$, horizontal asymptote $y = 0$
iii no x-intercept, y-intercept -2
iv no turning points exist

b i $f(x) = 2 - \dfrac{3}{x+1}$

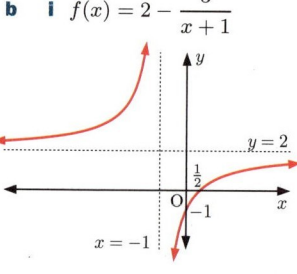

ii vertical asymptote $x = -1$, horizontal asymptote $y = 2$
iii x-intercept $\frac{1}{2}$, y-intercept -1
iv no turning points exist

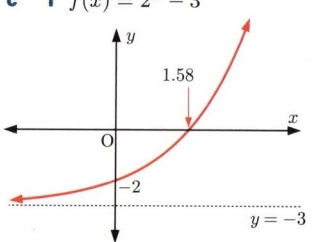

c i $f(x) = 2^x - 3$

ii horizontal asymptote $y = -3$
iii x-intercept ≈ 1.58, y-intercept -2
iv no turning points exist

d i $f(x) = 2x + \dfrac{1}{x}$

ii vertical asymptote $x = 0$, oblique asymptote $y = 2x$
iii no intercepts exist
iv local maximum at $\approx (-0.707, -2.83)$
local minimum at $\approx (0.707, 2.83)$

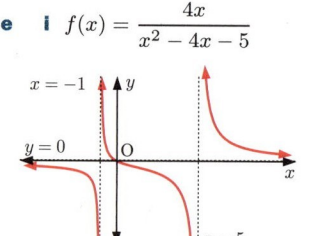

e i $f(x) = \dfrac{4x}{x^2 - 4x - 5}$

ii vertical asymptotes $x = -1$, $x = 5$, horizontal asymptote $y = 0$
iii x- and y-intercepts are both 0
iv no turning points exist

f i $f(x) = 3^{-x} + 2$

ii horizontal asymptote $y = 2$
no vertical asymptote
iii no x-intercepts, y-intercept is 3
iv no turning points exist

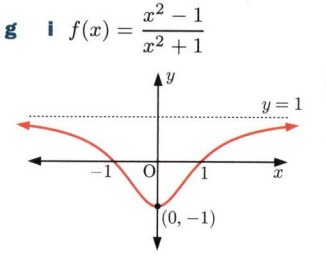

g i $f(x) = \dfrac{x^2 - 1}{x^2 + 1}$

ii horizontal asymptote $y = 1$
iii x-intercepts ± 1, y-intercept -1
iv minimum turning point at $(0, -1)$ (global minimum)

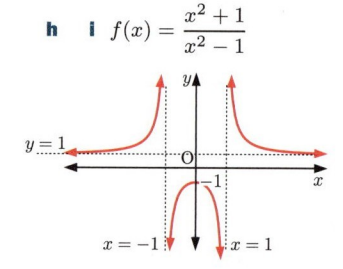

h i $f(x) = \dfrac{x^2 + 1}{x^2 - 1}$

ii vertical asymptotes $x = -1$, $x = 1$, horizontal asymptote $y = 1$
iii no x-intercepts, y-intercept -1
iv local maximum at $(0, -1)$

i i $f(x) = \dfrac{2^x + 3}{2^x + 1}$

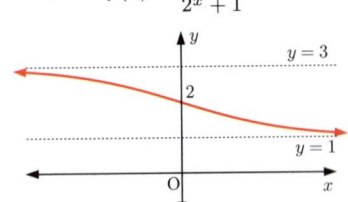

ii horizontal asymptotes $y = 1$, and $y = 3$
iii no x-intercepts, y-intercept 2
iv no turning points exist

3 a $x \approx -1.67$ **b** $x \approx 3.21$
 c $x \approx -0.846$, $x = 0, 2$ **d** $x \approx -1.37$ or 2.07
 e $x \approx 4.22$ **f** no solution
4 a $(-2.56, -1.56)$, $(-1, -4)$ and $(1.56, 2.56)$
 b no solution **c** $(3.21, 1.56)$
 d $(-1.21, -0.57)$ and $(1, 1)$
5 a
 b vertical asymptote $x = 0$, oblique asymptote $y = x$
 c $(-0.725, 0.653)$ and $(0.808, -0.429)$

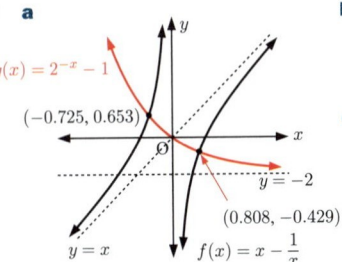

6 a

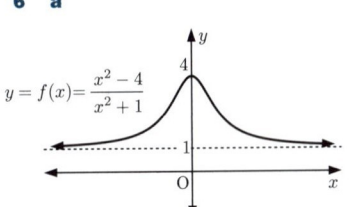

x	$f(x)$
-2	-3.75
-1	-0.5
0	1
1	1
2	0
3	-1
4	0
5	7

b [graph of $f(x) = 2^x - x^2$]

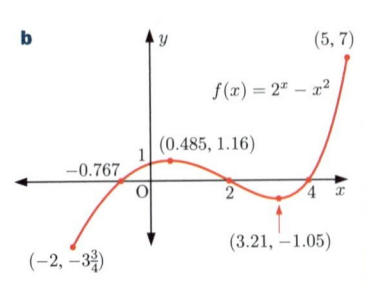

c $\approx -0.767, 2, 4$
d local maximum at $\approx (0.485, 1.16)$
local minimum at $\approx (3.21, -1.05)$
e range $= \{y \mid -3.75 \leqslant y \leqslant 7\}$

6 a [graph of $y = f(x) = \dfrac{x^2 - 4}{x^2 + 1}$]

b Domain is $\{x \mid x \in \mathbb{R}\}$
Range is $\{y \mid 1 < y \leqslant 4\}$
c horizontal asymptote $y = 1$
d It does not meet $y = 5$.
e $1 < k < 4$

7 a [graph with $g(x) = 2^x$ and $f(x) = \dfrac{x + 2}{x - 1}$, point $(2, 4)$, $(-2.60, 0.166)$]

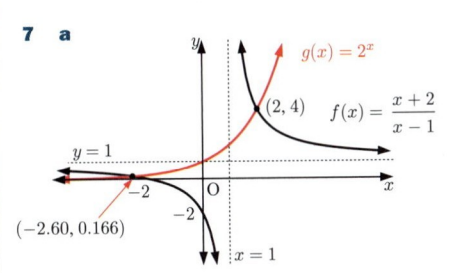

b $(2, 4)$ and $\approx (-2.60, 0.166)$
c For $x > 2$ and for $-2.60 < x < 1$.

7

x	$f(x)$	$g(x)$	$h(x)$
-2	0.25	3	1
-1.5	0.354	1.25	1.25
-0.5	0.707	-0.75	undefined
0	1	-1	-1
0.5	1.414	-0.75	-0.25
1	2	0	0
2	4	3	0.2
2.7	6.498	6.29	0.266
3.61	12.210	12.032	0.318

8 a [graph of $y = \dfrac{x^2}{2^x}$, local max $(2.89, 1.13)$]

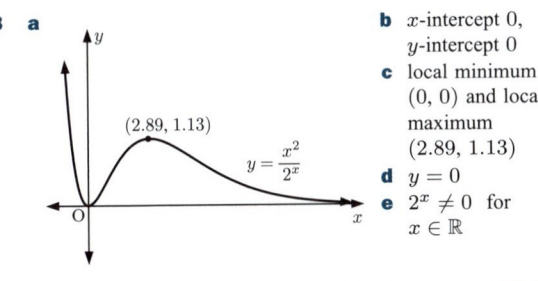

b x-intercept 0, y-intercept 0
c local minimum $(0, 0)$ and local maximum $(2.89, 1.13)$
d $y = 0$
e $2^x \neq 0$ for $x \in \mathbb{R}$

EXERCISE 24C

1 a 40 mongooses
 b i ≈ 61
  ii ≈ 80
  iii 160
 d ≈ 6.61 years
 c [graph $P = 40 \times 2^{0.2n}$]

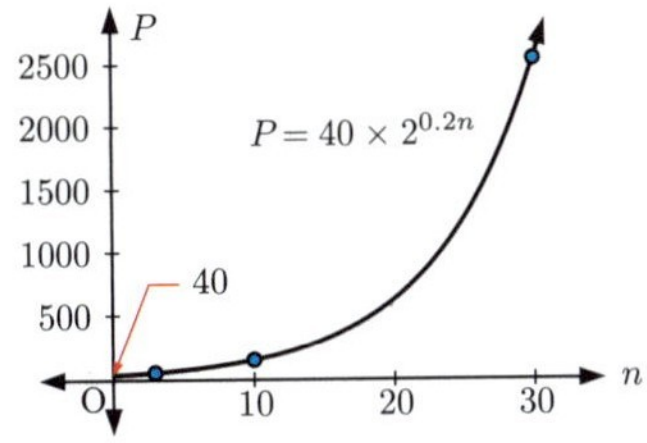

2 a i 0 units **ii** 16.02 units **iii** 20.54 units
  iv 13.53 units
 b [graph $A = 25t \times 0.641^t$, max $(2.25, 20.68)$]
 c At $t \approx 2.25$ hours, max amount 20.68 units.
 d $0.221 < t < 8.41$
 Between 0.221 hours and 8.41 hours.

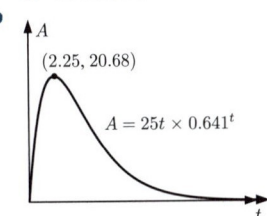

EXERCISE 24B.1

1 a $x = 1$, $y = 2$ **b** $x = 3$, $y = 7$
 c $x = -1$, $y = 5$ **d** $x = 3.5$, $y = -2.5$
 e $x = 2.36$, $y = 2.09$ **f** $x = -3.42$, $y = -5.32$
2 a no solution **b** lines are parallel
3 a infinite solutions **b** they are the same line

EXERCISE 24B.2

1 a $x = -1.5$ or 1 **b** $x \approx -1.24$ or 3.24
 c $x \approx -1.30$ or 2.30 **d** $x \approx -4.83$ or 0.828
 e $x \approx -1.57$ or 0.319 **f** $x \approx 0.697$ or 4.30
2 a $x \approx 0.458$ or 3.31 **b** $x \approx 1.70$
 c $x = -1$ or ≈ 1.35 **d** $x \approx 1.46$
 e $x \approx -0.686$ **f** $x \approx -2.51$

3 a [Graph: $P(£)$ with maximum at $(10, 32.67)$, $P = -\frac{2}{3}s^2 + \frac{40}{3}s - 34$, zeros at 3 and 17]

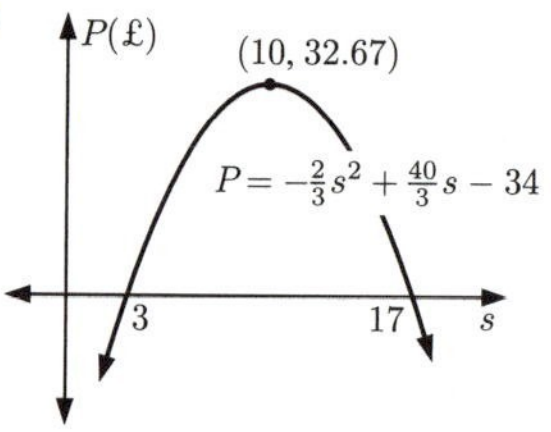

b $x = 3$ and 17
This represents the number of shrubs sold required to break even.
c Max profit is £32.67 when 10 shrubs are sold.

4 a [Graph: $y = 160 + 10x + \frac{800}{x}$ with minimum at $(8.94, 338.9)$]

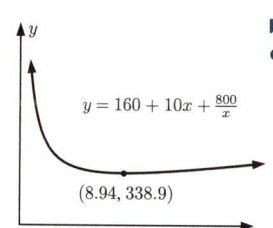

b $x = 0$
c Minimum surface area is 338.9 cm² when the length is 8.94 cm.

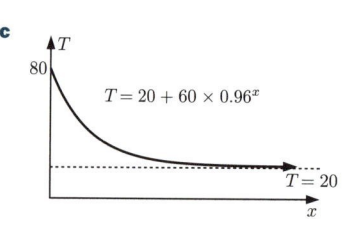

5 a 80 °C
  b i 46.5 °C
    ii 29.6 °C
    iii 25.2 °C
  d 20 °C
  e ≈ 17 minutes

c [Graph: $T = 20 + 60 \times 0.96^x$, asymptote $T = 20$, starting at 80]

6 a [Graph showing $y = V(x) = \frac{1000}{1 + 199 \times 0.27^x}$ and $y = S(x) = \frac{400}{1 + 9 \times 0.56^x}$]

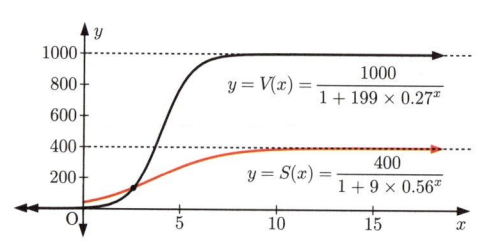

b Squirrels: y-intercept is 40 and water voles: y-intercept is 5.
These represent the initial populations.
c after $x \approx 2.62$ years
d The population of squirrels stabilises at 400 and the population of water voles stabilises at 1000.

REVIEW SET 24A

1 a

x	−3	−2	−1	0	1	2	3	4
y	7	2	−1	−2	−1	2	7	14

b [Graph of $y = x^2 - 2$ through $(-3, 7)$, $(4, 14)$, zeros at ± 1.41]

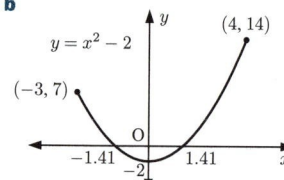

c When $y = 0$, $x = \pm 1.41$, so zeros are ± 1.41
d $(0, -2)$
e $\{y \mid -2 \leqslant y \leqslant 14\}$

2 a [Graph of $y = \frac{x+3}{x-5}$ with asymptotes $y = 1$ and $x = 5$, intercepts -3 and $-\frac{3}{5}$]

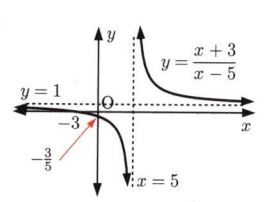

b vertical asymptote $x = 5$
horizontal asymptote $y = 1$
c x-intercept -3 and y-intercept $-\frac{3}{5}$

3 $x \approx -2.46$, $y \approx -1.92$

4 a $x = 2.01$ **b** $x = 1.38$

5 a $(-5.28, 38.8)$, $(-2.30, 4.91)$, and $(1.50, 0.355)$
  b $(0.661, 3.81)$ and $(6.63, 5.58)$

6 a [Graph of $f(x) = \frac{x^2 + 4}{x^2 - 1}$ with asymptotes $x = -1$, $x = 1$, $y = 1$, and point $(0, 4)$]

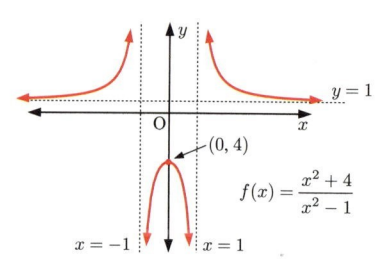

b vertical asymptotes $x = -1$, $x = 1$, horizontal asymptote $y = 1$
c Domain is $\{x \mid x \neq \pm 1, x \in \mathbb{R}\}$
Range is $\{y \mid y \leqslant -4$ or $y > 1\}$
d $k < -4$ or $k > 1$

7 a 80 eland
b 190 eland after 9.72 years
d When $p(t) = 0$, at $t \approx 14.8$ years.

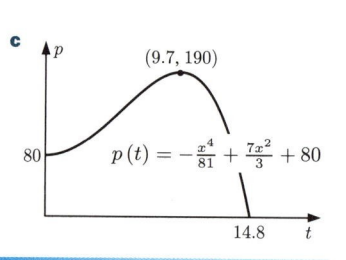

c [Graph of $p(t) = -\frac{x^4}{81} + \frac{7x^2}{3} + 80$ with maximum at $(9.7, 190)$, intercepts 80 and 14.8]

REVIEW SET 24B

1 a

x	−2	−1	0	1	2	3
y	16	4	1	0.25	0.0625	0.015 625

b 1 **c** [Graph of $y = \left(\frac{1}{4}\right)^x$] **d** $y = 0$

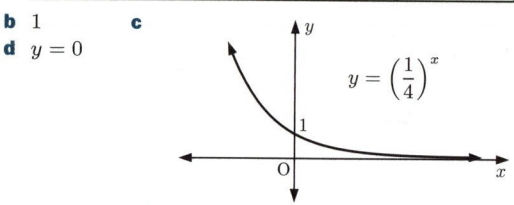

2 a [Graph of $y = 5x - 2x^2 - x^3$ through $(-4, 12)$, $(-3.45, 0)$, local min $(-2.12, -10.1)$, $(0, 0)$, local max $(0.786, 2.21)$, $(1.45, 0)$, $(2, -6)$]

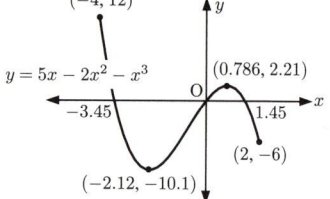

b local minimum $(-2.12, -10.1)$
local maximum $(0.786, 2.21)$
c $x = -3.45$, 0 and 1.45
d $\{y \mid -10.1 \leqslant y \leqslant 12\}$

3 $x \approx -2.43$, $y \approx 2.14$

4 a [Graph of $y = \frac{x-3}{x^2 + 3x - 4}$ with asymptotes $x = -4$, $x = 1$, $y = 0$, intercepts 3 and $\frac{3}{4}$]

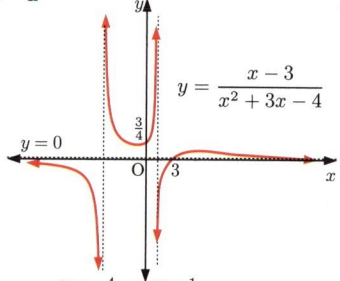

b vertical asymptotes $x = -4$, $x = 1$, horizontal asymptote $y = 0$
c x-intercept is 3
y-intercept is $\frac{3}{4}$
d minimum turning point at $\approx (-0.742, 0.659)$
maximum turning point at $\approx (6.74, 0.0607)$

5 a $x \approx 2.18$ **b** $x \approx 3.29$ **c** $x \approx 0.505$

6 a $\approx (-1.70, -4.94)$ and $(1.26, 1.98)$
  b $\approx (-0.633, 2.50)$ and $(0.516, 3.76)$

7 a

x	$f(x)$	$g(x)$
-10	0.833	1.25
-5	0.913	1.118
0	1	1
5	1.095	0.894
10	1.2	0.8
15	1.315	0.716
20	1.44	0.64

  b for $f(x)$: largest is 1.44, smallest is 0.833
  for $g(x)$: largest is 1.25, smallest is 0.64

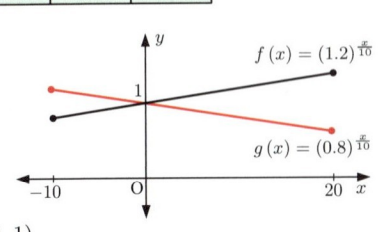

  c graph of $f(x) = (1.2)^{\frac{x}{10}}$ and $g(x) = (0.8)^{\frac{x}{10}}$

  d $(0, 1)$

8 a **i** €3.50 **ii** €1.42 **iii** €1.10
  b graph of $P = \dfrac{d + 2.5}{d}$ with asymptote $P = 1$
  c 50 doughnuts
  d horizontal asymptote $P = 1$. So the price per doughnut approaches €1 as the number of doughnuts bought increases.

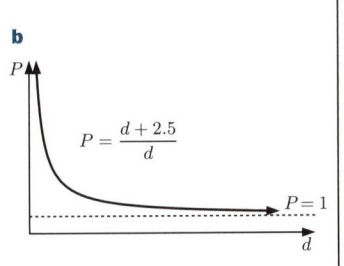

EXERCISE 25A

1 a impossible **b** equally likely
  c extremely unlikely **d** very unlikely **e** certain
  f extremely unlikely **g** very likely
  h extremely likely **i** likely **j** very unlikely
  k extremely unlikely **l** very likely

2 a Event B **b** Event A

3 a unlikely **b** extremely likely **c** likely
  d impossible **e** very likely

EXERCISE 25B

1 0.55 **2** 0.84 **3** ≈ 0.0894 **4** ≈ 0.256 **5** ≈ 0.331
6 a ≈ 0.243 **b** ≈ 0.486
7 a P(winning) ≈ 0.548 **b** P(2 child family) ≈ 0.359

8 a 407 people

Brand	Freq	Rel Freq
Silktouch	125	0.307
Super	107	0.263
Just Soap	93	0.229
Indulgence	82	0.201
Total	407	1.000

  c **i** ≈ 0.229 **ii** ≈ 0.201 **iii** ≈ 0.307

9 a

Outcome	Freq	Rel Freq
0 heads	121	0.247
1 head	259	0.530
2 heads	109	0.223
Total	489	1.000

  b **i** ≈ 0.247 **ii** ≈ 0.530 **iii** ≈ 0.223

10 a 1083 people
  b

Colour	Freq	Rel Freq
Green	361	0.25
Red	1083	0.75
Total	1444	1.00

  c **i** 0.25 **ii** 0.75

11 a 5235 tickets
  b

Ticket Type	Freq	Rel Freq
Adult	3762	0.719
Concession	1084	0.207
Child	389	0.074
Total	5235	1.000

  c ≈ 0.207

12 a

Councillor	Freq	Rel Freq
Mr Tony Trimboli	2167	0.361
Mrs Andrea Sims	724	0.121
Mrs Sara Chong	2389	0.398
Mr John Henry	720	0.12
Total	6000	1.000

  b ≈ 0.519

EXERCISE 25C

1 a

	Like	Dislike	Σ
Junior students	87	38	125
Senior students	129	56	185
Total	216	94	310

  b **i** $\frac{87}{310} \approx 0.281$ **ii** $\frac{129}{310} \approx 0.416$
  iii $\frac{129}{185} \approx 0.697$ **iv** $\frac{129}{216} \approx 0.597$

2 a $\frac{322}{643} \approx 0.501$ **b** $\frac{334}{643} \approx 0.519$ **c** $\frac{175}{643} \approx 0.272$
  d $\frac{188}{334} \approx 0.563$ **e** $\frac{134}{322} \approx 0.416$

3 a $\frac{777}{900} \approx 0.863$ **b** $\frac{123}{900} \approx 0.137$ **c** $\frac{1}{3} \approx 0.333$
  d $\frac{31}{900} \approx 0.0344$ **e** $\frac{392}{900} \approx 0.436$ **f** $\frac{19}{300} \approx 0.0633$
  g $\frac{85}{123} \approx 0.691$

EXERCISE 25D

1 ≈ 65 days **2** ≈ 13 goals **3 a** 0.36 **b** 26 'backs'
4 125 times **5 a** 100 **b** 200 **c** 400 **d** 500
6 5 out of 20
7 a 11%
  b **i** ≈ 17 inners, ≈ 72 outers, ≈ 11 misses
     ii 3140 points **iii** 31.4 points

EXERCISE 25E

1 a {A, B, C, D} **b** {BB, BG, GB, GG}
  c {ABCD, ABDC, ACBD, ACDB, ADBC, ADCB, BACD, BADC, BCAD, BCDA, BDAC, BDCA, CABD, CADB, CBAD, CBDA, CDAB, CDBA, DABC, DACB, DBAC, DBCA, DCAB, DCBA}
  d {GGG, GGB, GBG, BGG, GBB, BGB, BBG, BBB}
  e **i** {HH, HT, TH, TT}
     ii {HHH, HHT, HTH, THH, HTT, THT, TTH, TTT}
     iii {HHHH, HHHT, HHTH, HTHH, THHH, HHTT, HTHT, HTTH, THHT, THTH, TTHH, HTTT, THTT, TTHT, TTTH, TTTT}

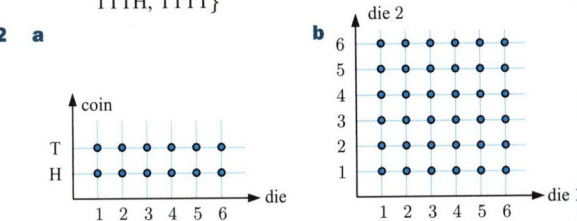

2 a coin/die grid (T, H vs die 1–6)
  b die 2 (1–6) vs die 1 (1–6) grid

Answers 589

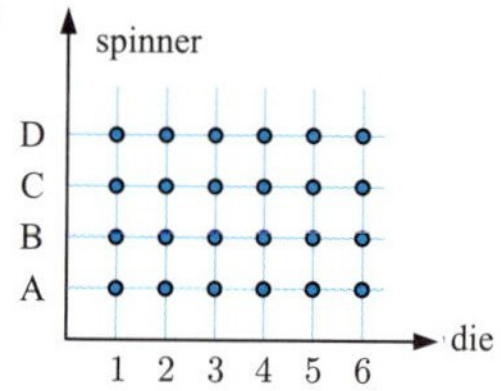

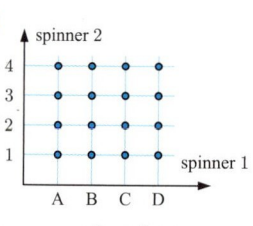

c spinner

(grid: D, C, B, A vs die 1–6)

d spinner 2

(grid: 1–4 vs A, 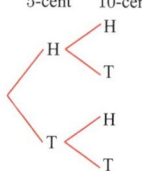 B, 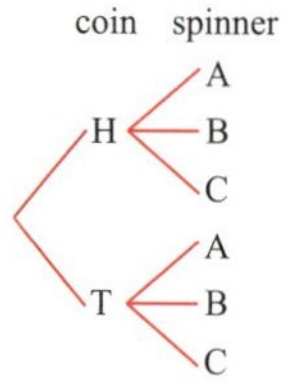 C, 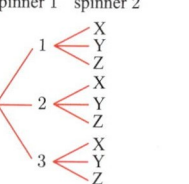 D)

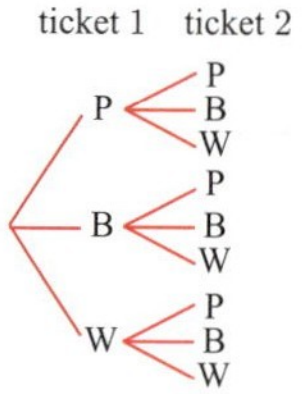

3 a 5-cent, 10-cent tree:
H → H, T
T → H, T

b coin, spinner tree:
H → A, B, C
T → A, B, C

c spinner 1, spinner 2 tree:
1 → X, Y, Z
2 → X, Y, Z
3 → X, Y, Z

d ticket 1, ticket 2 tree:
P → P, B, W
B → P, B, W
W → P, B, W

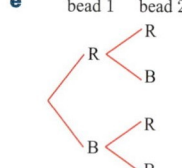

e bead 1, bead 2 tree:
R → R, B
B → R, B

4 Venn diagram: H and G; H only 3, intersection 7, G only 8, outside 2, universal $\mathcal{E}$

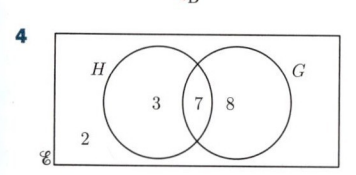

EXERCISE 25F

1 a {ODG, OGD, DOG, DGO, GOD, GDO}
  b i $\frac{1}{6}$ **ii** $\frac{1}{3}$ **iii** $\frac{2}{3}$ **iv** $\frac{1}{3}$

2 a $\frac{17}{43}$ **b** $\frac{5}{43}$ **c** $\frac{24}{43}$ **d** $\frac{19}{43}$ **e** $\frac{19}{43}$ **f** $\frac{17}{24}$ **g** $\frac{5}{17}$

3 50c coin (T, H) vs 10c coin (H, T) grid
  a $\frac{1}{4}$ **b** $\frac{1}{4}$ **c** $\frac{1}{2}$ **d** $\frac{3}{4}$

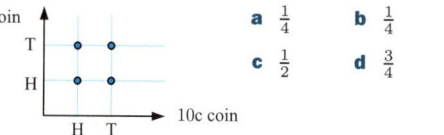

4 a coin (T, H) vs spinner 1–5 grid
  b 10 outcomes **c i** $\frac{1}{10}$ **ii** $\frac{3}{10}$ **iii** $\frac{2}{5}$ **iv** $\frac{3}{5}$

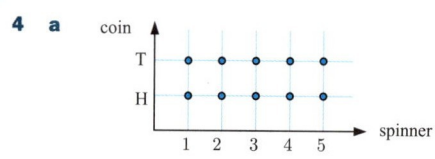

5 {ABK, AKB, BAK, BKA, KAB, KBA}
  a $\frac{1}{3}$ **b** $\frac{1}{3}$ **c** $\frac{1}{3}$ **d** $\frac{2}{3}$

6 a {GGG, GGB, GBG, BGG, GBB, BGB, BBG, BBB}
  b i $\frac{1}{8}$ **ii** $\frac{1}{8}$ **iii** $\frac{1}{8}$ **iv** $\frac{3}{8}$ **v** $\frac{1}{2}$ **vi** $\frac{7}{8}$

7 a $\frac{3}{8}$ **b** $\frac{19}{24}$

8 a {PQRS, PQSR, PRQS, PRSQ, PSQR, PSRQ, QPRS, QPSR, QRPS, QRSP, QSPR, QSRP, RPQS, RPSQ, RQPS, RQSP, RSPQ, RSQP, SPQR, SPRQ, SQPR, SQRP, SRPQ, SRQP}
  b i $\frac{1}{2}$ **ii** $\frac{1}{2}$ **iii** $\frac{1}{2}$ **iv** $\frac{1}{2}$

9 a die 2 (1–6) vs die 1 (1–6) grid
  b i $\frac{1}{18}$ **ii** $\frac{1}{6}$ **iii** $\frac{11}{36}$ **iv** $\frac{5}{9}$ **v** $\frac{1}{4}$ **vi** $\frac{1}{6}$

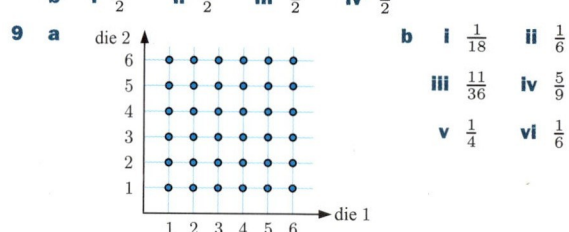

10 a $\frac{4}{15}$ **b** $\frac{3}{10}$ **c** $\frac{7}{10}$

11 {HHHH, HHHT, HHTH, HTHH, THHH, HHTT, HTHT, HTTH, THTH, TTHH, THHT, TTTH, TTHT, THTT, HTTT, TTTT}
  a $\frac{1}{16}$ **b** $\frac{3}{8}$ **c** $\frac{5}{16}$ **d** $\frac{15}{16}$ **e** $\frac{1}{4}$

12 a suit (♥, ♦, ♣, ♠) vs card value (A, 2, 3, 4, 5, 6, 7, 8, 9, 10, J, Q, K) grid
  b i $\frac{1}{13}$ **ii** $\frac{1}{52}$ **iii** $\frac{1}{4}$ **iv** $\frac{3}{13}$ **v** $\frac{1}{26}$ **vi** $\frac{1}{2}$ **vii** $\frac{4}{13}$ **viii** 0

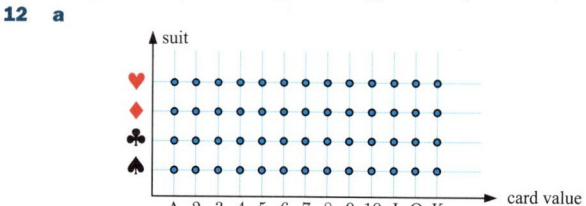

13 a $\frac{11}{14}$ **b** $\frac{5}{28}$ **c** $\frac{1}{28}$

EXERCISE 25G.1

1 a $\frac{1}{10}$ **b** $\frac{1}{5}$ **2 a** $\frac{3}{14}$ **b** $\frac{4}{21}$

3 a $\frac{8}{21}$ **b** $\frac{1}{7}$ **c** $\frac{2}{7}$ **4 a** 0.0441 **b** 0.6241

5 a $\frac{2}{15}$ **b** $\frac{2}{5}$ **c** $\frac{1}{5}$ **d** $\frac{4}{15}$

6 a i $\frac{243}{600} = 0.405$ **ii** $\frac{357}{600} = 0.595$
  b $\frac{6561}{40\,000} \approx 0.164$ **c** $\frac{14\,161}{40\,000} \approx 0.354$

EXERCISE 25G.2

1 a i $\frac{5}{14}$ **ii** $\frac{15}{56}$ **iii** $\frac{15}{56}$ **iv** $\frac{3}{28}$
  b Because these 4 events are the only possible outcomes, one of them must occur, and so their probabilities add to 1.

2 a i $\frac{1}{3}$ **ii** $\frac{4}{15}$ **iii** $\frac{8}{15}$
  b The possibilities are: WW, WY, YW, YY.
  The 3 events do not cover all these possibilities.
  So, the probability sum should not be 1.

3 a $\frac{1}{14}$ **b** $\frac{1}{56}$ **c** $\frac{1}{28}$ **4 a** $\frac{15}{91}$ **b** $\frac{36}{91}$ **c** $\frac{9}{13}$

EXERCISE 25H

1 a Tree: 1st spin, 2nd spin
  B ($\frac{2}{5}$) → B ($\frac{2}{5}$), Y ($\frac{2}{5}$), G ($\frac{1}{5}$)
  Y ($\frac{2}{5}$) → B ($\frac{2}{5}$), Y ($\frac{2}{5}$), G ($\frac{1}{5}$)
  G ($\frac{1}{5}$) → B ($\frac{2}{5}$), Y ($\frac{2}{5}$), G ($\frac{1}{5}$)
  b $\frac{4}{25}$ **c** $\frac{1}{25}$ **d** $\frac{16}{25}$ **e** $\frac{16}{25}$

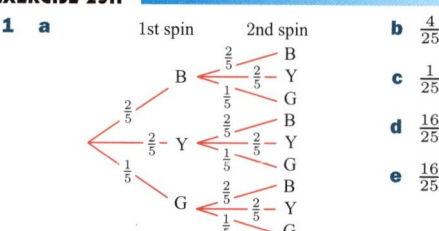

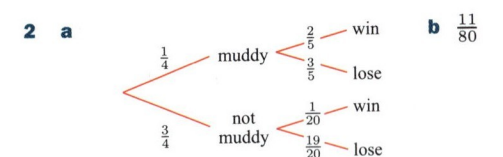

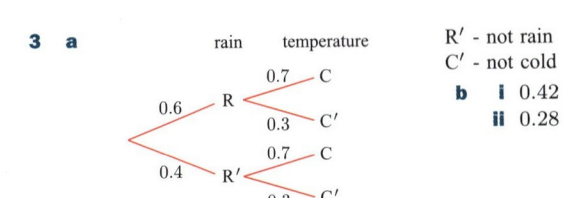

2 a [tree diagram: muddy (1/4) → win (2/5), lose (3/5); not muddy (3/4) → win (1/20), lose (19/20)] **b** $\frac{11}{80}$

3 a [tree diagram: R (0.6) → C (0.7), C' (0.3); R' (0.4) → C (0.7), C' (0.3)] R' - not rain, C' - not cold **b i** 0.42 **ii** 0.28

4 34% **5** $\frac{23}{60}$ **6 a** $\frac{23}{42}$ **b** $\frac{19}{42}$

EXERCISE 25I

1 [tree diagram: 1st ticket R (2/3) → 2nd ticket R (2/3), Y (1/3); Y (1/3) → R (2/3), Y (1/3)] **a** $\frac{4}{9}$ **b** $\frac{1}{9}$ **c** $\frac{2}{9}$ **d** $\frac{4}{9}$

2 a $\frac{2}{7}$ **b** $\frac{1}{7}$ **c** $\frac{2}{7}$ **d** $\frac{4}{7}$

3 a $\frac{1}{6}$ **b** $\frac{5}{18}$ **c** $\frac{5}{18}$ **d** $\frac{5}{18}$
These cases cover all possibilities, so their probabilities must add up to 1.

4 a [tree diagram: 1st egg S (7/12) → 2nd egg S (6/11), D (5/11); D (5/12) → S (7/11), D (4/11)] **b** $\frac{5}{33}$ **c** $\frac{7}{22}$

5 a [tree diagram: 1st chocolate H (8/19) → 2nd chocolate H (7/18), S (11/18); S (11/19) → H (4/9), S (5/9)] **b** $\frac{28}{171}$ **c** $\frac{55}{171}$

6 a i $\frac{5}{9}$ **ii** $\frac{4}{9}$
b [tree diagram: tile 1 G (5/9) → tile 2 G (5/9), B (4/9); B (4/9) → G (5/9), B (4/9)] **c i** $\frac{25}{81}$ **ii** $\frac{16}{81}$ **iii** $\frac{20}{81}$ **iv** $\frac{40}{81}$

7 a $\frac{1}{25}$ **b** $\frac{24}{25}$ **c** $\frac{7}{4975} \approx 0.00141$ **d** $\frac{4584}{4975} \approx 0.921$ **e** $\frac{8}{199}$

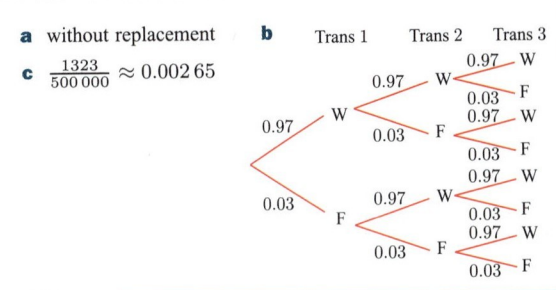

8 a without replacement **c** $\frac{1323}{500\,000} \approx 0.00265$

b [tree diagram: Trans 1, Trans 2, Trans 3; W (0.97) → W (0.97) → W (0.97), F (0.03); F (0.03) → W (0.97), F (0.03); F (0.03) → W (0.97) → W (0.97), F (0.03); F (0.03) → W (0.97), F (0.03)]

EXERCISE 25J

1 a A and B, A and D, A and E, A and F, B and D, B and F, C and D
b i $\frac{2}{3}$ **ii** $\frac{5}{6}$ **iii** $\frac{2}{3}$ **iv** $\frac{1}{2}$ **v** 1 **vi** $\frac{5}{6}$

2 a $\frac{5}{17}$ **b** $\frac{8}{17}$ **c** $\frac{6}{17}$ **3** $\frac{4}{15}$

4 a [grid diagram: coin T/H vs die 1-6] **b i** $\frac{1}{12}$ **ii** $\frac{7}{12}$

c $P(H) + P(5) - P(H \text{ and } 5) = \frac{6}{12} + \frac{2}{12} - \frac{1}{12}$
$= \frac{7}{12} = P(H \text{ or } 5)$

5 a [grid diagram: die 2 (1-6) vs die 1 (1-6)] **b i** $\frac{1}{18}$ **ii** $\frac{5}{9}$

c $P(3) + P(4) - P(3 \text{ and } 4) = \frac{11}{36} + \frac{11}{36} - \frac{2}{36}$
$= \frac{5}{9} = P(3 \text{ or } 4)$

EXERCISE 25K

1 a $\frac{5}{8}$ **b** $\frac{9}{64}$ **c** $\frac{15}{32}$

2 a i $\frac{28}{413} \approx 0.0678$ **ii** $\frac{339}{413} \approx 0.821$
iii $\frac{363}{413} \approx 0.879$ **iv** $\frac{70}{329} \approx 0.213$
b $\approx 17\,215$

3 a 11 students **b i** $\frac{29}{50}$ **ii** $\frac{11}{40}$ **4 a** $\frac{7}{30}$ **b** $\frac{7}{15}$

5 a $\frac{12}{25}$ **b** $\frac{3}{25}$ **c** $\frac{7}{25}$ **d** $\frac{12}{19}$ **6 a** $\frac{1}{25}$ **b** 8 days

7 a $\frac{5}{7}$ **b** $\frac{13}{14}$ **c** $\frac{1}{14}$ **d** $\frac{5}{23}$ **e** $\frac{9}{10}$

8 a 0.09 **b** 0.42 **9 a** $\frac{24}{25}$ **b** $\frac{1}{25}$ **10 a** $\frac{1}{8}$ **b** $\frac{3}{8}$

11 a $\frac{2}{13}$ **b** $\frac{17}{26}$ **c** $\frac{9}{26}$ **12 a** $\frac{3}{4}$ **b** $\frac{5}{9}$

REVIEW SET 25A

1 a unlikely **b** extremely unlikely **c** extremely likely

2 a 39 days **b i** $\frac{1}{39}$ **ii** $\frac{11}{39}$ **iii** $\frac{19}{39}$

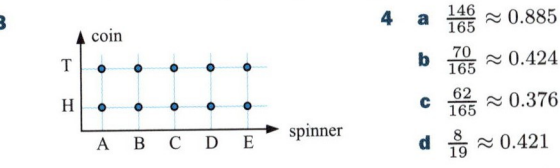

3 [grid diagram: coin T/H vs spinner A-E]

4 a $\frac{146}{165} \approx 0.885$
b $\frac{70}{165} \approx 0.424$
c $\frac{62}{165} \approx 0.376$
d $\frac{8}{19} \approx 0.421$

Answers 591

5 The occurrence of either event does not affect the occurrence of the other event.

6 a $\frac{1}{16}$ **b** $\frac{3}{8}$ **c** $\frac{5}{16}$

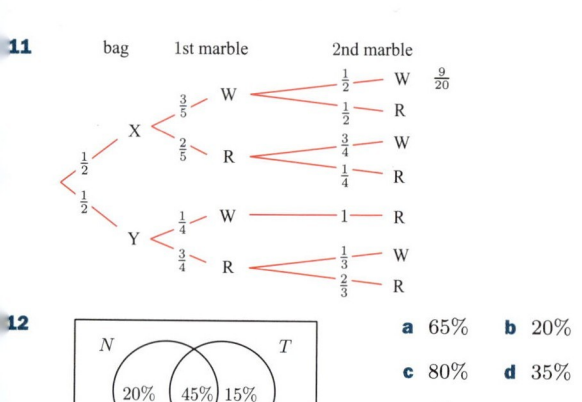

7 a 0.72 **b** 0.02 **c** 0.98 **d** 0.18

8 $\frac{1}{6}$ **9 a** $\frac{2}{7}$ **b** $\frac{4}{7}$

10 a [coin/spinner grid diagram] **b i** $\frac{1}{10}$ **ii** $\frac{3}{5}$

11 [tree diagram: bag X/Y, 1st marble, 2nd marble with probabilities $\frac{1}{2}$, $\frac{3}{5}$, $\frac{2}{5}$, $\frac{1}{4}$, $\frac{3}{4}$, $\frac{1}{2}$, $\frac{1}{2}$, $\frac{3}{4}$, $\frac{1}{4}$, 1, $\frac{1}{3}$, $\frac{2}{3}$; result $\frac{9}{20}$]

12 [Venn diagram N and T: 20%, 45%, 15%, 20%]
 a 65% **b** 20% **c** 80% **d** 35% **e** $\frac{45}{65} \approx 69.2\%$

REVIEW SET 25B

1 Mr Smith **2 a** 0.364 **b** 0.551 **c** 0.814

3 a {AH, BH, CH, DH, AT, BT, CT, DT}
 b i [tree diagram bag A/B/C, ticket G/Y]
 ii [tree diagram sets 1–5 M/J]
 c i $\frac{33}{91}$ **ii** $\frac{36}{91}$

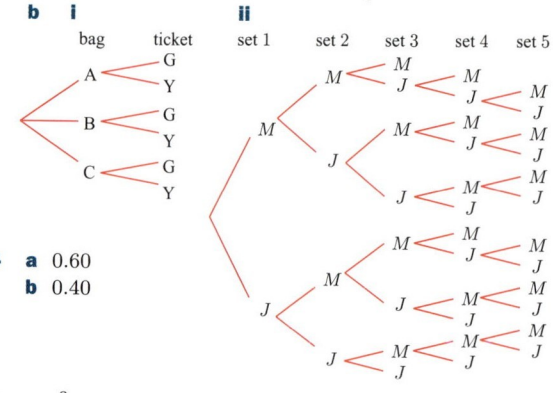

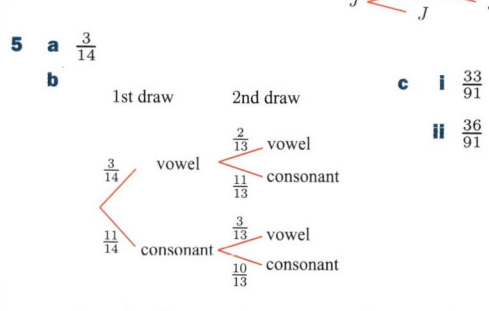

4 a 0.60 **b** 0.40

5 a $\frac{3}{14}$
 b [tree diagram: 1st draw vowel $\frac{3}{14}$, consonant $\frac{11}{14}$; 2nd draw vowel $\frac{2}{13}$, consonant $\frac{11}{13}$, vowel $\frac{3}{13}$, consonant $\frac{10}{13}$]

6 a $\frac{1}{9}$ **b** $\frac{4}{9}$ **c** $\frac{4}{9}$ **7 a** $\frac{1}{20}$ **b** $\frac{3}{10}$

8 [die 1 vs die 2 grid]
 a $\frac{1}{36}$ **b** $\frac{11}{36}$ **c** $\frac{1}{6}$ **d** $\frac{2}{9}$

9 [Venn diagram B and F: 12, 3, 6, 4]
 a $\frac{4}{25}$ **b** $\frac{12}{25}$ **c** $\frac{1}{5}$ **d** $\frac{2}{5}$

10 a ≈ 0.707 **b** ≈ 0.293 **c** ≈ 0.0467 **d** ≈ 0.340
 e 0.54

11 a $\frac{9}{200}$ **b** $\frac{149}{1200}$ **c** $\frac{1051}{1200}$
 d These probabilities add to 1 as the events are complementary.

EXERCISE 26A

1 a 24, 28 **b** $-6, -9$ **c** 21, 23
 d $16\frac{1}{2}, 19$ **e** $-23, -30$ **f** 27, 23

2 a Start with 5 then add 3 each time to get further terms: 20, 23.
 b Start with 2 then add 7 each time to get further terms: 37, 44.
 c Start with 8 then add 11 each time to get further terms: 63, 74.
 d Start with 38 then subtract 4 each time to get further terms: 18, 14.
 e Start with 3 then subtract 5 each time to get further terms: $-22, -27$.
 f Start with $\frac{1}{2}$ then add $1\frac{1}{2}$ each time to get further terms: 8, $9\frac{1}{2}$.

3 a Start with 3 then multiply by 2 each time to get further terms: 96, 192.
 b Start with 1 then multiply by 2 each time to get further terms: 32, 64.
 c Start with 2 then multiply by 5 each time to get further terms: 1250, 6250.
 d Start with 36 then multiply by $\frac{1}{2}$ each time to get further terms: $2\frac{1}{4}, 1\frac{1}{8}$.
 e Start with 162 then multiply by $\frac{1}{3}$ each time to get further terms: $2, \frac{2}{3}$.
 f Start with 405 then multiply by $\frac{1}{3}$ each time to get further terms: $5, 1\frac{2}{3}$.

4 a 25, 36 **b** 36, 49 **c** 125, 216 **d** $\frac{1}{36}, \frac{1}{49}$
 e 15, 21 **f** 42, 56

5 a The first two terms are 1 and 1 and from then on the next term is the sum of the previous two terms: 13, 21, 34.
 b The first two terms are 1 and 3 and from then on the next term is the sum of the previous two terms: 18, 29, 47.
 c The terms are the prime numbers in sequence: 17, 19, 23.

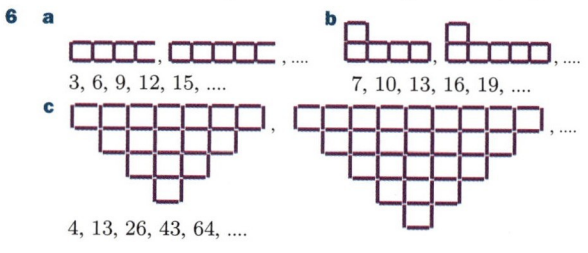

6 a [figures] 3, 6, 9, 12, 15, ...
 b [figures] 7, 10, 13, 16, 19, ...
 c [figures] 4, 13, 26, 43, 64, ...

d 5, 12, 19, 26, 33, ... **e** 6, 11, 16, 21, 26, ...

f 4, 16, 36, 64, 100, ...

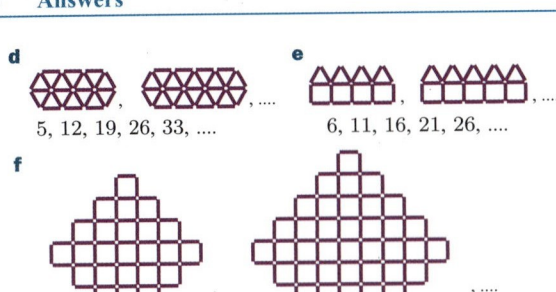

7 a 1, 3, 6, 10, 15, 21, ... **b** 1, 4, 9, 16, 25, 36, ...

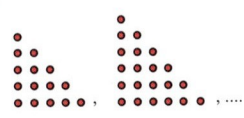

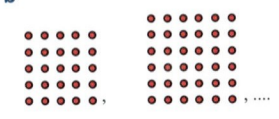

c 1, 4, 9, 16, 25, ... **d** 2, 8, 18, 32, 50, ...

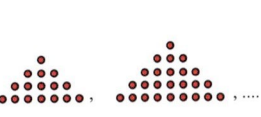

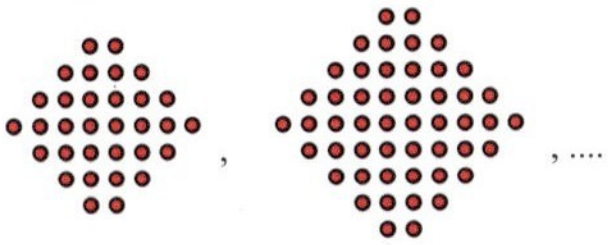

EXERCISE 26B

1 a 5, 7, 9, 11, ... **b** 7, 9, 11, 13, ...
  c 5, 8, 11, 14, ... **d** 8, 11, 14, 17, ...
  e $-1, -3, -5, -7$, ... **f** $1, -1, -3, -5$, ...
  g $3, 0, -3, -6$, ... **h** 13, 9, 5, 1, ...
  i 69, 62, 55, 48, ...

2 a 2, 5, 10, 17, ... **b** 0, 3, 8, 15, ...
  c 2, 6, 12, 20, ... **d** 3, 8, 15, 24, ...
  e 2, 9, 28, 65, ... **f** 2, 15, 44, 95, ...

3 a $u_n = 2n$ **b i** $u_n = 2n + 2$ **ii** $u_n = 2n - 1$
4 a $u_n = 5n$ **b i** $u_n = 5n + 1$ **ii** $u_n = 5n - 2$
5 a $u_n = 3n - 1$ **b** $u_n = 2n + 15$ **c** $u_n = 35 - 5n$
  d $u_n = 9 - 2n$ **e** $u_n = 4n - 11$ **f** $u_n = 2 - 3n$
6 a $u_n = 2^n$ **b** $u_n = 3 \times 2^n$
7 a $u_n = n$
  b i $u_n = n + 1$ **ii** $u_n = n + 2$ **iii** $u_n = \frac{1}{n}$
  iv $u_n = \frac{1}{n+1}$ **v** $u_n = \frac{n}{n+1}$ **vi** $u_n = \frac{n+2}{n}$
  vii $u_n = n(n+1)$ **viii** $u_n = (n+1)(n+2)$
  ix $u_n = n(n+2)$
8 a $u_n = n^2$
  b i $u_n = (n+1)^2$ **ii** $u_n = n^2 - 1$ **iii** $u_n = \frac{1}{n^2}$
9 a $u_n = n^3$ **b** $u_n = n^3 - 1$
  c $u_n = 3 \times 2^{n-1}$ **d** $u_n = 24 \times (\frac{1}{2})^{n-1}$

EXERCISE 26C

1 a $u_n = 4n - 3$ **b** $u_n = 20 - 3n$ **c** $u_n = n^2 + n$
  d $u_n = n^2 + 3n - 4$
2 a $u_n = 4n^2 - 2n$
  b $u_1 = 1 \times 2$, $u_2 = 3 \times 4$, $u_3 = 5 \times 6$, $u_4 = 7 \times 8$, etc
  $\therefore u_n = (2n-1) \times 2n$

3 a $u_1 = 2$, $u_2 = 8$, $u_3 = 18$, $u_4 = 32$, $u_5 = 50$, $u_6 = 72$, $u_7 = 98$
  b $u_n = 2n^2$ **c** $u_{30} = 1800$ dots

4 a (15), (21), (28)

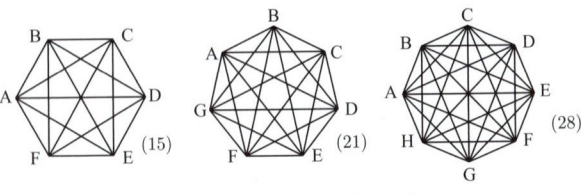

  b $u_n = \frac{1}{2}n^2 - \frac{1}{2}n$ or $u_n = \frac{n(n-1)}{2}$
  c 15 931 handshakes

5 a $u_1 = 5$, $u_2 = 8$, $u_3 = 11$, $u_4 = 14$, $u_5 = 17$, $u_6 = 20$
  b $u_n = 3n + 2$ **c** $u_{50} = 152$

6 a $u_1 = 1$, $u_2 = 6$, $u_3 = 15$, $u_4 = 28$, $u_5 = 45$, $u_6 = 66$, $u_7 = 91$, $u_8 = 120$
  b $u_n = 2n^2 - n$ **c** $u_{50} = 4950$

7 a i 10 paths **ii** 15 paths **iii** 21 paths
  b 1326 paths **c** $u_n = \frac{1}{2}n^2 + \frac{3}{2}n + 1 = \frac{(n+1)(n+2)}{2}$

REVIEW SET 26A

1 a Start with 6, then add 4 each time to get further terms:
  $u_6 = 26$, $u_7 = 30$.
  b Start with 250 then subtract 30 each time to get further terms:
  $u_5 = 130$, $u_6 = 100$.
  c Square the term number: $u_5 = 25$, $u_6 = 36$.

2 a 2, 5, 8, 11, 14, ... **b** 4, 10, 16, 22, 28, ...

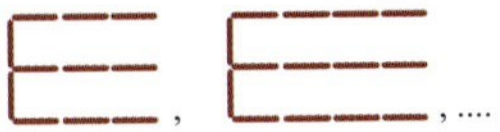

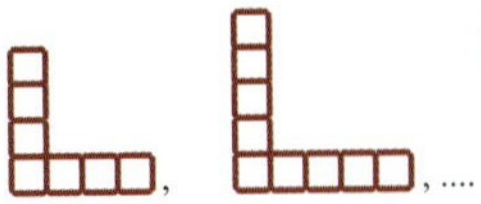

3 a $u_1 = 5$, $u_2 = 11$, $u_3 = 17$, $u_4 = 23$
  b $u_1 = 4$, $u_2 = 12$, $u_3 = 22$, $u_4 = 34$

4 a $u_n = 4n$ **b i** $u_n = 4n - 3$ **ii** $u_n = \frac{1}{4n-1}$
  c i $u_{20} = 77$ **ii** $u_{20} = \frac{1}{79}$

5 a $u_1 = 6$, $u_2 = 18$, $u_3 = 54$, $u_4 = 162$
  b $u_1 = 5$, $u_2 = -10$, $u_3 = 20$, $u_4 = -40$

6 a $u_n = 7n - 2$ **b** $u_n = n^2 + 4n - 6$

7 a $u_3 = 9$, $u_4 = 13$, $u_5 = 17$ **b** $u_n = 4n - 3$
  c $u_{50} = 197$, 197 triangles

8 a $u_4 = 11$, $u_5 = 16$
  b $u_n = \frac{1}{2}n^2 + \frac{1}{2}n + 1$ or $u_n = \frac{n^2 + n + 2}{2}$
  c $u_{10} = 56$, 56 pieces

REVIEW SET 26B

1 a Start with 17 then subtract 5 each time to get further terms:
  $u_5 = -3$, $u_6 = -8$.
  b Start with 2 then multiply each successive term by 2:
  $u_5 = 32$, $u_6 = 64$.
  c Start with -5 then add 2 each time to get further terms:
  $u_5 = 3$, $u_7 = 5$.

2 a 4, 8, 12, 16, 20, ... **b** 3, 8, 15, 24, 35, ...

3 a $u_1 = 1$, $u_2 = -3$, $u_3 = -7$, $u_4 = -11$
  b $u_1 = 0$, $u_2 = 4$, $u_3 = 10$, $u_4 = 18$

4 a $u_n = 6n$ **b i** $u_n = 6n + 4$ **ii** $u_n = \dfrac{6n-1}{6n+1}$
  c i $u_{15} = 94$ **ii** $u_{15} = \dfrac{89}{91}$

5 a $u_1 = 12$, $u_2 = 3$, $u_3 = \frac{3}{4}$, $u_4 = \frac{3}{16}$
  b $u_1 = -3$, $u_2 = 0$, $u_3 = 15$, $u_4 = 48$

6 a $u_n = 52 - 9n$ **b** $u_n = n^2 + 5n - 2$

7 a $u_3 = 24$, $u_4 = 40$, $u_5 = 60$, $u_6 = 84$
  b $u_n = 2n^2 + 2n$ or $u_n = 2n(n+1)$ **c** 220 matches

8 a $u_n = 177n + 2179$ **b** €3949

EXERCISE 27A

1 a $x = 37$ {angles in a triangle, angle in a semi-circle}
  b $x = 30$ {angles in a triangle, angle in a semi-circle}
  c $x = 18$ {angles in a triangle, angle in a semi-circle}
  d $x = 30$ {angle in alternate segment}
  e $a = 40$ {angles in a triangle, angle in a semi-circle}
    $b = 50$ {angle in alternate segment}
  f $a = 60$ {angle in a semi-circle}
    $b = 40$ {angle in alternate segment}
  g $a = b = 55$ {tangents to a point, angles in a triangle}
  h $m = 56$ {chords of a circle, angle in a semi-circle, angles in a triangle}
  i $n = 49$ {tangents to a point, chords of a circle, tangent-radius, angles in a triangle}

3 1 cm **4** 40 cm

5 a i $A\hat{P}O = a°$ **ii** $B\hat{P}O = b°$
  b $A\hat{P}B = a + b$
    $\therefore \ a + a + b + b = 180°$ {angle sum of a $\triangle$} etc.
  c The 'angle in a semi-circle' theorem.

6 a $\triangle OAB$ is isosceles as $OA = OB$ {equal radii}
  b X is the midpoint of chord AB, $O\hat{A}X = O\hat{B}X$,
    $A\hat{O}X = B\hat{O}X$.

7 b The triangles are congruent {RHS} as:
  • $OA = OB$ {equal radii}
  • $O\hat{A}P = O\hat{B}P = 90°$ {tangent property}
  • OP is common
  c Consequences are: • $AP = BP$
    • OP bisects $A\hat{P}B$ and $A\hat{O}B$

EXERCISE 27B

1 a $x \approx 50.7$ **b** $y \approx 3.38$, $z \approx 14.5$ **c** $t \approx 15.5$
  d $\alpha \approx 53.1$, $\beta \approx 36.9$
  e $d \approx 11.2$, $e \approx 11.2$, $f \approx 11.6$ **f** $k \approx 37.5$
  g $b \approx 58.3$ **h** $c \approx 21.6$, $d \approx 25.7$ **i** $x \approx 11.5$

2 a ≈ 17.5 cm **b** ≈ 9.90 cm **c** ≈ 18.2 cm

3 a OD bisects AC
    $\therefore \ B\hat{D}A$ is a right angle {chords of a circle theorem}
  b AD = 5 cm **c** $A\hat{B}D \approx 22.6°$ **d** $O\hat{A}B \approx 22.6°$
  e $O\hat{A}D \approx 44.8°$ **f** radius = 7.04 cm

  g Calculate $A\hat{B}D$. Extend BD to meet the circle at E. Join AE.
    In $\triangle ABE$, $\cos A\hat{B}E = \dfrac{13}{AE}$ etc.

4 a $\triangle ACD$ is an equilateral triangle. $\therefore \ A\hat{C}D = 60°$
  b ≈ 5.77 cm

5 Yes (diagonal of plank ≈ 10.9 cm) **6** ≈ 27.1 km

7 a AB = 44.3 cm **b** reflex $A\hat{C}D = 200.5°$ **c** ≈ 142 cm

REVIEW SET 27A

1 a $a = 120$ {isosceles triangle, angles in a triangle}
  b $x = 90$ {angle in a semi-circle}
  c $i = 73$ {tangents from a point, base angles isosceles triangle}
    $j = 34$ {angles in a triangle}
  d $a = 62$ {angle in a semi-circle, angles in a triangle}
  e $b = 40$ {angle in alternate segment}
    $a = 50$ {radius-tangent}, $c = 50$ {angles in a triangle}

2 AO = OC. .... base angles of isosceles triangle
  .... isosceles .... $(a + b)$ .... 180 .... 90 90

3 a 8 cm **b** 2 cm

5 a $x \approx 48.9$ **b** $x = 24$ **c** $x \approx 8.49$

6 radius = 1 cm **7 a** $64°$ **b** 114 million km

8 ≈ 9.95 km

REVIEW SET 27B

1 a $x = 42$ {angle in a semi-circle, angles in a triangle}
  b $x = 40$ {radius-tangent, angles in a quadrilateral}
  c $x = 55$ {radius-tangent, angles in a triangle, base angles of isosceles triangle}
  d $x = 15$ {angle in a semi-circle}
    $y = 60$ {angles in a triangle}

2 a i $A\hat{B}O = x°$ **ii** $A\hat{C}B = (90 - x)°$ **iii** $B\hat{O}C = 2x°$
  b $B\hat{O}C = 2 \times B\hat{A}C$

3 56 cm

4 Hint: $\triangle PQR$ is isosceles and $P\hat{S}Q = 90°$. Why?

5 a $a = 32$, $b \approx 12.7$ **b** $c \approx 12.7$ **c** $r \approx 54.8$

6 OP = 6.25 m **7** ≈ 9.68 km

CHAPTER 28

Cambridge International Examinations bears no responsibility for the example answers to questions taken from its past question papers which are contained in this publication.

1 a i 18 **ii** $2x + y$

iii

Baskets in open play (2 points)	0	2	4	6	8	10
Baskets from free throws (1 point)	11	9	7	5	3	1

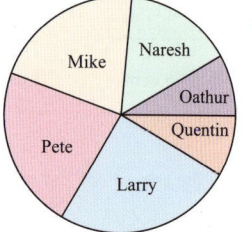

  b i (pie chart showing Mike, Naresh, Oathur, Quentin, Larry, Pete)
    ii 13 points
    iii 12 points

  c 14 matches

Answers

2 a i $36°$ ii $54°$ b **Hint:** Use angle sum of triangle.
  c i ≈ 4.85 km ii ≈ 35.3 km d $025°$

3 a i translation $\begin{pmatrix} 4 \\ 6 \end{pmatrix}$
  ii clockwise rotation $90°$ about $(7, 0)$
  iii reflection about x-axis
  b $\theta \approx 63.4°$ c $\alpha \approx 116.6°$

4 a $72 b i $0.50 per unit ii $0.35 per unit
  c 80 units d 120 units e $4 f 160 units g $72.80

5 a i 1400 mm^2 ii 5600 mm^2 b ≈ 5600 km^2
  c ≈ 5769 km^2

6 a i isosceles ii $BP = 13$ cm iii 104 cm b 4
  c i square-based pyramid ii 92 cm iii 363 cm^3

7 a i $7p + 3e$ cents ii $7p + 3e = 185$
  iii $5p + 6e = 190$ iv $p = 20$, $e = 15$
  b i $16 ii $128 iii 2^d

8 b i $67.5°$ ii $22.5°$ c $MD = 4.14$ cm
  d i ≈ 20.7 cm^2 ii ≈ 331 cm^2 iii ≈ 314 cm^2
  e 17.2 cm^2 f 5.2%

9 a i 72 cm^3 ii 108 cm^2 b i 36 cm^3 ii 30 cm^2

10 a $\frac{1}{4}$ b i $\frac{1}{6}$ ii $\frac{5}{12}$ iii 10.40 am

11 a i $MN = 4.69$ cm ii $LN = 8.83$ cm iii 20.7 cm^2
  b i 78.5 cm^2 ii 26.4%
  iii Angle in a semi-circle is $90°$.

12 a 90 cents b 30 cents each

  c
Price (cents)	Number sold	Money received (cents)	Printing cost (cents)	Profit (cents)
10	200	2000	4000	−2000
20	175	3500	3750	−250
30	150	4500	3500	1000
40	125	5000	3250	1750
50	100	5000	3000	2000
60	75	4500	2750	1750
70	50	3500	2500	1000
80	25	2000	2250	−250
90	0	0	2000	−2000

  d For maximum profit, price is 50 cents per newspaper when 100 newspapers are sold, and the profit is $20.

13 a 7 b 42 c i 9 ii 8 iii 8.3 d 5 cm
  e $36°$ f £75 g 22% h i 0.12 ii 0.28 iii 1

14 a
Number of fillings	Frequency
0	4
1	7
2	6
3	4
4	4
5	2
6	3

  b i 1 ii 2 iii 2.5
  c i $\frac{7}{30}$ ii $\frac{3}{10}$
  d 40 children

15 a i 175 cents ii $25b$ cents iii $1.75
  iv $0.25b$ or $\frac{b}{4}$
  b i $c = \frac{T}{n}$ ii c is the cost of one bar of chocolate.
  c i $4.50 ii $4.20 iii $\left(\frac{y}{x}\right)$ iv $\left(\frac{y-z}{x-1}\right)$

16 a $a = 6$, $b = -4$
  b i a rotation of $180°$ about $(2\frac{1}{2}, 6)$
  ii an enlargement, centre $B(1, 7)$ and scale factor 3
  c i 3 units^2 ii $1:9$ d i $-\frac{2}{3}$ ii $y = -\frac{2}{3}x + 7\frac{2}{3}$

17 a i 51 ii 49 iii 46

  b i
Grade	Number of students	Angle on a pie chart
A	5	$20°$
B	15	$60°$
C	40	$160°$
D	20	$80°$
E	10	$40°$
Totals	90	$360°$

  ii (pie chart with sectors A, B, C, D, E)
  iii (1) $\frac{4}{9}$ (2) $\frac{1}{3}$

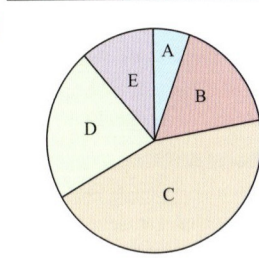

18 a i $P = 27$ ii $x = 6$ iii $x = \frac{P-3}{6}$
  b i $(4x + 3)$ cm
  ii sides have length 10 cm, 16 cm, 23 cm

19 a CS is the radius and PS is the tangent.
  $\therefore \widehat{PSC}$ is a right angle {radius-tangent theorem}
  b $PC = 8$ km c $PS = 1.78$ km d 6.9 km^2
  e $\widehat{QCS} = 12.8°$

20 a 9 m^2
  b i 6 m^2 ii 18 m^2
  c i 0.6 m^2 ii 30 planks
  d 0.02 m^3

  e
Item	Total cost of item
posts	€4.80
planks	€9.00
roof material	€14.40
nails	€2.10
Total cost of shelter	€30.30

21 a 2.8 kg b £106.50 c i 10.40 am ii $1\frac{1}{2}$ hours
  d 1.55 pm e 357 passengers

22 a $4p - 3q$ b $x = 7$
  c i $2j + 2k$ ii $2j + 2k = 72$ iii $k = 24$
  d i $w = \frac{1}{3}$ ii $s = rw + t$

23 a 208 cm^2 b 192 cm^3 c i ≈ 12.8 cm ii $\approx 51.3°$

24 b i £100 iii £808.99

25 a i 10.8 m^2 ii $32\,400$ litres iii 36 litres
  b i 61 hours, 30 mins ii $13\,516$ gallons
  iii 3.4 litres iv 4 bottles

26 a i 1 ii 8 iii 4 iv 6
  b i $A = \{1, 2, 3, 6, 9, 18\}$, $B = \{1, 3, 9, 27\}$
  ii (Venn diagram: ℰ contains 21, 22, 23, 24, 25, 26, 28, 29, 30, 4, 5, 7, 8, 10, 11, 12, 13, 14, 15, 16, 17, 19, 20; A contains 2, 6, 18; A∩B contains 1, 3, 9; B contains 27)

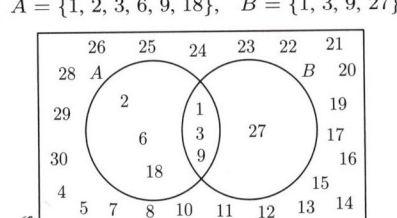

Answers 595

    iii **(1)** $\{1, 3, 9\}$ **(2)** $\{1, 2, 3, 6, 9, 18, 27\}$ **(3)** 7
  c **i** 9   **ii** 3, 223

27 **a** 141 cm³   **b** 2 hrs 57 mins   **c** $x = 36$
  d **i** $8.60   **ii** 34.4%   **iii** $1.89

28 **a** **ii** OB $= 2.82$ m   **iii** AB $= 5.63$ m   **iv** BC $= 5.30$ m
  b **i** 29.8 m²   **ii** 12.5 m²   **iii** 42.3 m²
  c **i** 21 150 m³   **ii** 30 seconds

29 **a** **i** $E = 360$ **ii** $v = 7.5$ **iii** $m = \dfrac{2E}{v^2}$
  b $xy(y - x)$ **c** $x = 2$ **d** $x = 3, y = 1$

30 **a** 750 bricks
  b **i** 10 buckets of sand, 4 of cement   **ii** 2 bags
  c **i** 756 tiles   **ii** 8 packs

31 **a** **i** 2.60 cm   **ii** 3.90 cm²   **iii** 31.2 cm³
  b **i** 18   **ii** (diagram: 16 cm × 9 cm net)
    iii ≈ 502 cm²
    iv $32.40

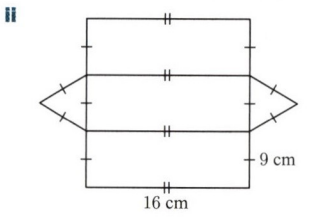

32 **b** 2814 euros   **c** 4955 Chinese yuan
  d 12.20 am the next day

33 **a** **i** $(-3, -2)$ **ii** $\overrightarrow{AB} = \begin{pmatrix}4\\2\end{pmatrix}$, $\overrightarrow{BC} = \begin{pmatrix}-3\\2\end{pmatrix}$
  b (graph)   **c** (graph)
  d (graph)

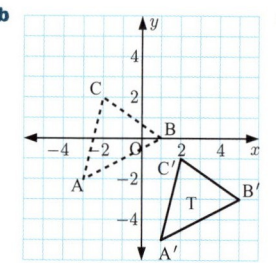

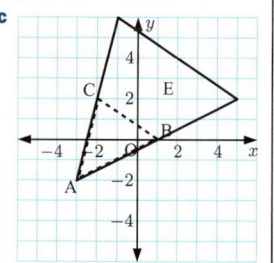

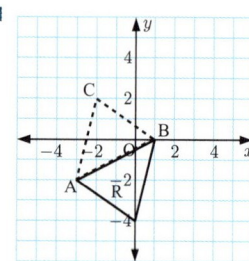

34 **a** **i** $x = 6$ **ii** $y = 9$ **iii** $z = 1.5$
  b **i** $p + q = 12$ **ii** $25p + 40q = 375$
    iii $p = 7, q = 5$

35 **a** **ii** Aida €7500, Bernado €6000, Cristiano €4500
  b **i** €10 500   **ii** $\dfrac{13}{60}$ **iii** €1083.33

36 **b** 125°   **c** angles on a line   **d** RS $= 6.39$ km
  e 38.0 km   **f** 8.44 km/h

37 **a** Domain $\{t \mid t \geqslant 0\}$ **b** $P = 2.1325 \times 10^4$ insects

  c (graph of $P = 22000 - 21600 \times 2^{-0.1t}$, asymptote at $P = 22000$, with 400 and 365 marked)

  d $P = 22000$
    As t increases, the population will approach 22 000.
  e $\{P \mid 400 \leqslant P < 22\,000\}$
  f $\approx (16.3,\ 15\,000)$ After ≈ 16.3 days the population will reach $\approx 15\,000$ insects.

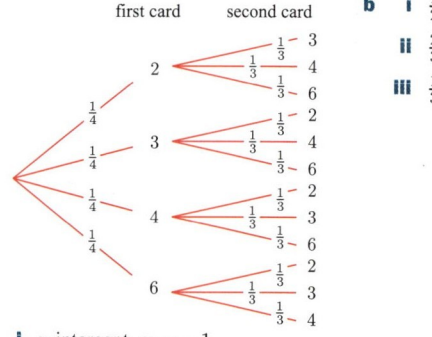

38 **a** (tree diagram: first card 2, 3, 4, 6 each with probability $\frac{1}{4}$; second card branches with probability $\frac{1}{3}$)
  b **i** $\dfrac{1}{2}$ **ii** $\dfrac{2}{3}$ **iii** $\dfrac{1}{3}$

39 **a** **i** y-intercept $y = -1$,
    x-intercept $x \approx -4.75, -0.374, 1.13$
    ii local maximum $(-3.10, 9.52)$,
    local minimum $(0.431, -1.45)$
    iii range $\{y \mid -25 \leqslant y \leqslant 9.52\}$
  b/c (graph showing $y = \tfrac{1}{2}x^3 + 2x^2 - 2x - 1$ and $y = f(x-3)$ with points $(-3.1, 9.52)$, $(2, 7)$, $(5, 7)$, $(-6, -25)$, $(-3, -25)$, $(0.43, -1.45)$)

  d $(-4.63, 1.51)$ and $(-1.48, 4.73)$

40 **a** $M(3, 1)$ **b** **i** 4.47 units   **ii** 3.16 units
  c chords of a circle theorem   **d** $A\widehat{C}B = 90°$
  e ≈ 7.02 units   **f** $\begin{pmatrix}6\\2\end{pmatrix}$

41 **a** $\dfrac{x}{3} + \dfrac{x+1}{2} > 1$, $\dfrac{x+1}{2} + 1 > \dfrac{x}{3}$
  b $x < 3$, $x > \dfrac{3}{5}$, $x > -9$
  c (number line showing -9, $\tfrac{3}{5}$, 3)   **d** $\dfrac{3}{5} < x < 3$

42 **a**

x	1	2	3	4	5
y	5	4	3	2	1

  b $(1, 5)$ area $= 5$ units², $(2, 4)$ area $= 8$ units²,
    $(3, 3)$ area $= 9$ units², $(4, 2)$ area $= 8$ units²,
    $(5, 1)$ area $= 5$ units²

c

n	1	2	3	4	5
u_n	5	8	9	8	5
Δ_1		3	1	-1	-3
Δ_2			-2	-2	-2

Δ_2 is a constant $\therefore$ sequence is a quadratic.

CHAPTER 29

Cambridge International Examinations bears no responsibility for the example answers to questions taken from its past question papers which are contained in this publication.

Investigation 1

1 a   i $27 = 2 \times 10 + 7$ **ii** $38 = 3 \times 10 + 8$
    iii $67 = 6 \times 10 + 7$
 b $A \times 10 + B$ **d** Values can only be multiples of 9.
 e   i 41, 52, 63, 74, 85, and 96   **ii** 91
    iii 15, 26, 37, 48, and 59

 f $\boxed{P\,Q}^2 - \boxed{Q\,P}^2$
$= (\boxed{P\,Q} + \boxed{Q\,P})(\boxed{P\,Q} - \boxed{Q\,P})$

Note $\boxed{P\,Q} + \boxed{Q\,P} = 11(P+Q)$
and $\boxed{P\,Q} - \boxed{Q\,P} = 9(P-Q)$

$\therefore \boxed{P\,Q}^2 - \boxed{Q\,P}^2 = 11(P+Q) \times 9(P-Q)$
$= 99(P+Q)(P-Q)$

$\therefore$ always divisible by 99.

2 c $\boxed{P\,Q\,R} - \boxed{R\,P\,Q} = 99(P-R)$,
and $P - R = 0, \pm 1, \pm 2, ..., \pm 9$
$\therefore$ 17 results
$\{0, \pm 99, \pm 198, \pm 297, \pm 396, \pm 495, \pm 594, \pm 693, \pm 792\}$

Investigation 2

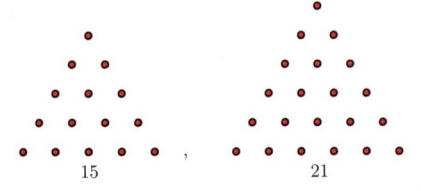

1 a (triangular dot patterns showing 15 and 21)

 b For the fifth member, five dots are added to the previous member.
For the sixth member, six dots are added to the previous member.
For the nth member, n dots are added to the previous member.

 d   i 55 dots   **ii** 1275 dots   **iii** $\dfrac{(n+1)(n+2)}{2}$

 e   i 66th   **ii** $(n+3)$th   **iii** $(n-1)$th

2 a $36 = 6^2$, $100 = 10^2$
 b $1^3 + 2^3 + 3^3 + 4^3 + 5^3 = 225 = 15^2$
$1^3 + 2^3 + 3^3 + 4^3 + 5^3 + 6^3 = 441 = 21^2$

 c $\left(\dfrac{n(n+1)}{2}\right)^2$ **d** 2025   **e** $x = 15$

Investigation 3

1 $20 = 4 \times 5 + 7 \times 0$
$21 = 4 \times 0 + 7 \times 3$
$22 = 4 \times 2 + 7 \times 2$
$23 = 4 \times 4 + 7 \times 1$
$24 = 4 \times 6 + 7 \times 0$
$25 = 4 \times 1 + 7 \times 3$
$26 = 4 \times 3 + 7 \times 2$
$27 = 4 \times 5 + 7 \times 1$
$28 = 4 \times 7 + 7 \times 0$

2 a $40 = 4 \times 10 + 7 \times 0$ **b** $72 = 4 \times 18 + 7 \times 0$
or $40 = 4 \times 3 + 7 \times 4$ $72 = 4 \times 11 + 7 \times 4$
                                    $72 = 4 \times 4 + 7 \times 2$

3 a

			b			
		0	1	2	3	4
	0	0	7	14	21	28
	1	4	11	18	25	32
a	2	8	15	22	29	36
	3	12	19	26	33	
	4	16	23	30		

 b 1, 2, 3, 5, 6, 9, 10, 13, 17   **c** 17

4 a   i decrease by 3   **ii** increase by 11
 b   i Going left, values decrease by 7, and going down, values increase by 4. Overall decrease by 3.
    ii Going right, values increase by 7, and going down, values increase by 4. Overall increase by 11.

5 a $1 = 4 \times 2 + 7 \times -1$ **b** $4 \times -7 + 7 \times 4$
$2 = 4 \times -3 + 7 \times 2$ $4 \times 14 + 7 \times -8$
$3 = 4 \times -1 + 7 \times 1$ There are infinitely many
$5 = 4 \times 3 + 7 \times -1$ solutions.
$6 = 4 \times -2 + 7 \times 2$
$9 = 4 \times 4 + 7 \times -1$
$10 = 4 \times -1 + 7 \times 2$
$13 = 4 \times -2 + 7 \times 3$
$17 = 4 \times -1 + 7 \times 3$

Investigation 4

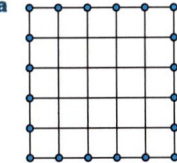

1 a (grid figure)   **b** (grid figure)

    i 12   **ii** 20   **iii** 25   **i** 14   **ii** 24   **iii** 36

 c   i $2n + 2$ **ii** $4n$ **iii** n^2 **d   i** 20   **ii** 36
 e   i 26   **ii** 144   **f** 18 stringlines

2 a   i 9   **ii** 14   **iii** 12
 b   i $x + y + 2$ **ii** $2x + 2y$ **iii** $x \times y$

Answers 597

Investigation 5

1 [graph of temperature T °C vs time x min, decay curve from ~85°C down to ~20°C]

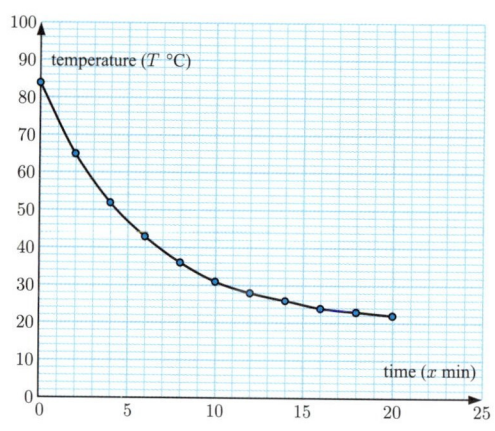

2 a 49 °C **b** 25 °C **3** 11 minutes **4** 16 °C

5 a

Time	0 to 4 mins	4 to 8 mins
Fall in temperature	32 °C	16 °C
Time	8 to 12 mins	12 to 16 mins
Fall in temperature	8 °C	4 °C

b The fall in temperature halves every 4 minutes.

6 $\approx 20.4\,°C$ **7** $\approx 20\,°C$

Investigation 6

1 a/b

Rect.	No. of rows	No. of columns	Total no. of dots	No. of black dots	No. of white dots
1	1	2	2	1	1
2	2	3	6	3	3
3	3	4	12	6	6
4	4	5	20	10	10
5	5	6	30	15	15

b [diagram of 5×6 grid of dots, lower-left triangle black, upper-right triangle white]

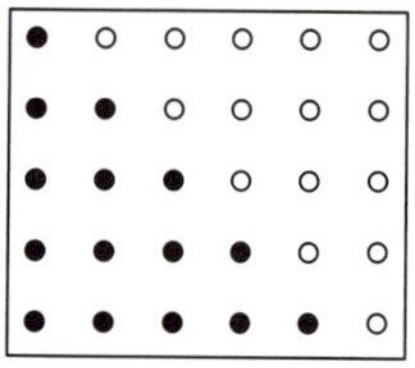

c i n rows **ii** $(n+1)$ columns **iii** $n(n+1)$ dots **iv** $\dfrac{n(n+1)}{2}$ black dots

d
$$1 = 1$$
$$1 + 2 = 3$$
$$1 + 2 + 3 = 6$$
$$1 + 2 + 3 + 4 = 10$$
$$1 + 2 + 3 + 4 + 5 = 15$$
$$1 + 2 + 3 + 4 + \ldots + n = \dfrac{n(n+1)}{2}$$

2 a/b

Square	Total number of dots	Number of black dots	Number of white dots
1	1	1	0
2	4	3	1
3	9	6	3
4	16	10	6
5	25	15	10

b [diagram of 5×5 grid of dots, lower-left triangle including diagonal black, upper-right white]

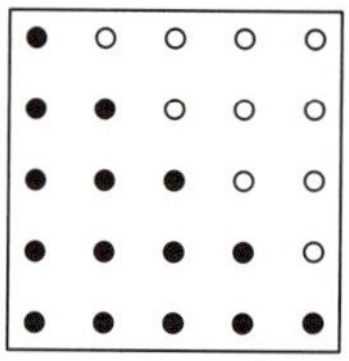

c i n^2 **ii** $\dfrac{n(n+1)}{2}$ **iii** $\dfrac{n(n-1)}{2}$

d i a 1 **b** $\tfrac{3}{4}$ **c** $\tfrac{2}{3}$ **d** $\tfrac{5}{8}$ **e** $\tfrac{3}{5}$

Investigation 7

1 a 6 cm × 15 cm **b** smaller: 10 cm², larger: 90 cm² **c** 1 : 9

2 a 12 cm × 21 cm **b** smaller: 28 cm², larger: 252 cm² **c** 1 : 9

3 Area of object $= ab$
Area of image $= 9ab$
$\therefore$ object area : image area $= 1 : 9$

4 a i 1 : 16 **ii** 4 : 1
b The image area is the object area multiplied by the scale factor squared.
c [two rectangles: smaller with sides a and b; larger with sides ka and kb]

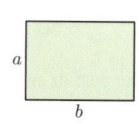

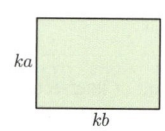

Area of object $= ab$
Area of image $= k^2 ab$
$\therefore$ object area : image area $= 1 : k^2$

5 Image area is object area multiplied by k^2.

Investigation 8

1 A square **B** hexagon **C** octagon

2 A [square with 4 lines of symmetry] **B** [hexagon with 2 lines of symmetry] **C** [octagon with 4 lines of symmetry]

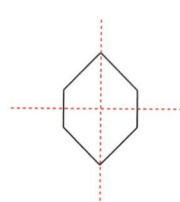

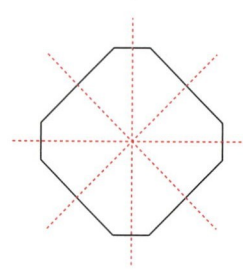

3 A all angles 90° **B** 2 angles 90°, 4 angles 135° **C** all angles 135°

4 A - the square

5 Regular polygons have all lengths of sides equal *and* all angles equal.
B does not have equal angles and **C** does not have equal lengths of sides, therefore they are not regular polygons.

6 4 cm² **7** [tessellation of hexagons]

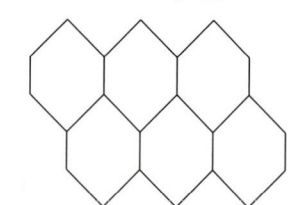

Investigation 9

1. **a** $3x + 5y = 31$
   b $y = \dfrac{31 - 3x}{5}$
   c (graph showing line $y = \dfrac{31-3x}{5}$ with intercepts 6.2 and 10.33)
   d Plums are £4 per kg and cherries are £3.80 per kg.
   e Maximum price of plums is £10.33 and maximum price of cherries is £6.20. Minimum price of both is £0.
   f plums £2 per kg, cherries £5 per kg *or* plums £7 per kg, cherries £2 per kg
   g **i** $4x + 3y = 23$
      ii $y = \dfrac{23 - 4x}{3}$ (graph showing intersection at (2, 5))
      iii The point of intersection is the cost of each fruit per kg. So plums are £2 per kg and cherries are £5 per kg.
   h $x = 2$, $y = 5$

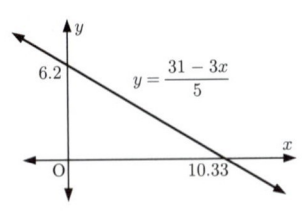

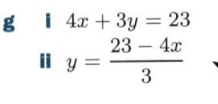

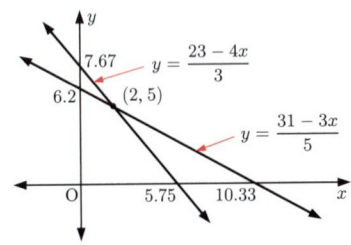

2. blueberries £6 per kg, pears £4 per kg

3. **a** $3x + y = 15$
      $6x + 2y = 30$
   b (graph showing both equations as the same line)
   c The equations represent the same line as Steph bought exactly double of what Tamie purchased.
   d

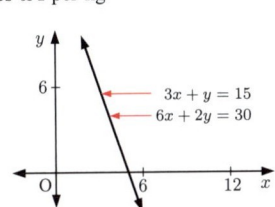

plums £ per kg	1	2	3	4
cherries £ per kg	12	9	6	3

   e plums £4 per kg, cherries £3 per kg

Investigation 10

1. **a** AB has gradient $\tfrac{3}{2}$, CD has gradient $-\tfrac{2}{3}$ **b** -1
2. **a** WX has gradient $\tfrac{3}{4}$, YZ has gradient $-\tfrac{4}{3}$ **b** -1
3. **a** PQ has gradient $\tfrac{1}{3}$, RS has gradient -3 **b** -1
4. The product of the gradients of two perpendicular lines equals -1.
5. **a** $\tfrac{5}{2}$ and m **b** **i** $m = \tfrac{5}{2}$ **ii** $m = -\tfrac{2}{5}$
6. **a** AP has gradient $\tfrac{1}{2}$, BP has gradient -2
   b Yes, $\tfrac{1}{2} \times -2 = -1$ ∴ lines are perpendicular.
   c $AB = 10$, $AP = \sqrt{80}$, $BP = \sqrt{20}$
   e For a semi-circle with diameter AB and point P on the circle, $\triangle APB$ is right angled.
7. **a** $AB = 5$, $BC = 5$, $CD = 5$, $AD = 5$
   b ABCD is a rhombus.
   c AC has gradient $\tfrac{1}{2}$, BD has gradient -2
   d The diagonals of a rhombus are perpendicular.

Investigation 11

1. **a** 2   **b** 4   **c** 8   **d** 16   **e** 32
2. **a** 0.5 m²   **b** 0.25 m²   **c** 0.125 m²
   d 0.0625 m²   **e** 0.031 25 m²
3. a m × b m   4 rectangles are similar   6 $2\sqrt{2}a^2$ m²
7. 841 mm × 595 mm   8 297 mm × 210 mm
9. **a** 1682 mm × 1189 mm   **b** 1189 mm × 841 mm
   c 841 mm × 595 mm

Investigation 12

1. $AE = DE$, $\widehat{BAE} = \widehat{CDE}$, $\widehat{ABC} = \widehat{BCD}$
2. (pentagon diagram with base 20 mm and height 10 mm)
3. **a** $\theta = 120$
   b $\widehat{ABC}$ and $\widehat{BCD} = 120°$
4. $\widehat{BAE} = \widehat{CDE} = 90°$
5. **a** $\phi = 30$ **b** $AP = 5$ mm   **c** $AM = 15$ mm
   d $AE \approx 17.3$ mm
6. **a** $ME \approx 8.66$ mm   **b** $MN \approx 8.66$ mm
   c 346.4 mm²   **d** 2900 pentagons

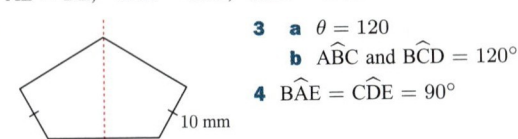

Investigation 13

1. **a** **i** 20 m   **ii** ≈ 33.3 m   **b** 80 m
2. **a** **i** ≈ 31.2 m   **ii** ≈ 19.0 m   **b** wet bitumen
3. **a** ≈ 39 m   **b** ≈ 161 m
4. **a**

Speed (km/h)	Reaction distance (m)	Braking distance (m)
10	2.08	0.60
20	4.17	2.38
30	6.25	5.36
40	8.33	9.52
50	10.42	14.88
60	12.5	21.43
70	14.58	29.17
80	16.67	38.10
90	18.75	48.21
100	20.83	59.52

   b **i** ≈ 35 km/h   **ii** 35 km/h, distance 7.29 m
   c For speeds under 35 km/h, the reaction distance is the greater part of the stopping distance. For speeds greater than 35 km/h, the braking distance is the greater part of the stopping distance.
   d When the speeds are high, the braking distance is the greater part of the stopping distance. At low speeds, the reaction distance is the greater part of the stopping distance.

Investigation 14

1. an annulus   2. (diagram of a stadium-shape)
3. **a** 553 cm³   **b** **i** $R = 3.5$ cm, $r = 1.5$ cm   **ii** 155 cm
4. **a** 176 mm²   **b** 704 mm³
   c No, maximum number of washers is 1420.
5. **a** **i** $R - r$ **iv** **Hint:** volume = area of base × height
   b **i** $A = 4r^2$ **ii** $\tfrac{\pi}{4}$ **c** **i** torus

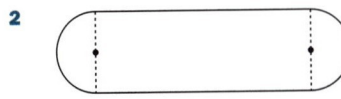

Answers

Investigation 15
1. **a** 2 am and 2 pm   **b** 8 am and 8 pm
2. 8 m   3. 5 am, 11 am, 5 pm, 11 pm
4. 6 am, 10 am, 6 pm, 10 pm   5. all times
6. **a** before 5 am, between 11 am and 5 pm, or after 11 pm
   b 3 hours   **c** $\frac{1}{2}$
7. **a** vertical translation   **b** 1
   c effective as it allows the movement of more ships as the depth is greater

Investigation 16
1/2

Figure	Perimeter (cm)	Area (cm²)
P	24	32
Q	24	36
R	24	24
S	24	30
T	24	45.84
H	24	41.57

The perimeters are all equal.

3. R, S, P, Q, H, T
4. For figures with the same perimeter, as the figure becomes more regular with more sides, the area gets larger with the circle providing maximum area.

Investigation 17
1. 553 cm³   2. **a** 8 cm   **b** 32 cm × 24 cm   **c** 21.4%
3. **a** $10.80   **b** $14.40
4. **a** $1.42   **b** $2.18   **c** 20.2%

Investigation 18
1.

Scheme	1st	2nd	3rd	4th	5th	6th	7th
				Birthday			
A	$10	$20	$30	$40	$50	$60	$70
B	$1	$2	$4	$8	$16	$32	$64
C	$1	$4	$9	$16	$25	$36	$49

2. A - $10n$, B - 2^{n-1}, C - n^2
3. **a** Scheme A: $550
   Scheme B: $1023
   Scheme C: $385
   b Scheme A   **c** 15th birthday

Investigation 19
1. 13, 21, 34, 55
2. The previous two terms are added to get the next term.
3.

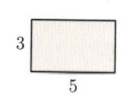

4/5

n	Fibonacci number	Fibonacci rectangle	Area of rectangle	Sum of areas
1	1	1 × 1	1	1
2	1	1 × 2	2	3
3	2	2 × 3	6	9
4	3	3 × 5	15	24
5	5	5 × 8	40	64
6	8	8 × 13	104	168
7	13	13 × 21	273	441
8	21	21 × 34	714	1155
9	34	34 × 55	1870	3025
10	55	55 × 89	4895	7920

6. For even n:

n	Fibonacci number	Sum of areas of first n rectangles
2	1	3
4	3	24
6	8	168
8	21	1155
10	55	7920

7. For odd n:

n	Fibonacci number	Sum of areas of first n rectangles
1	1	1
3	2	9
5	5	64
7	13	441
9	34	3025

If n is even, then the nth Fibonacci number multiplied by the $(n+2)$th Fibonacci number is equal to the area sum of n Fibonacci rectangles.
If n is odd, then the nth Fibonacci number multiplied by the $(n+2)$th Fibonacci number, minus 1 is equal to the area sum of n Fibonacci rectangles.

Investigation 20
1.

Figure	Vertices (V)	Regions (R)	Edges (E)
a	5	5	8
b	10	7	15
c	6	4	8
d	12	8	18

4. **a** 10   **b** 17   **c** 10   **d** 20   5. $V + R - E = 2$
6. **a** 6 vertices   **b** 7 edges   **c** 4 regions
7.

8.

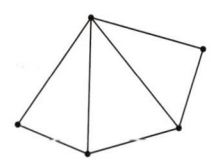

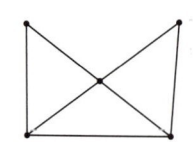

Figure	F	V	F + V	E
a	6	8	14	12
b	5	6	11	9
c	8	6	14	12
d	7	7	14	12

9. $F + V - E = 2$ 10. Yes
11. **a** 6 vertices   **b** 18 edges
12. Dan's polyhedron would have 3 faces, which is impossible.

INDEX

24-hour time	56
acute angle	96
adjacent angles	104
algebraic fraction	351
algebraic product	132
alternate angles	105
angle of depression	341
angle of elevation	341
arc	223
area	218
average speed	245
bar chart	143
BEDMAS	30
biased sample	296
bimodal	303
capacity	265
categorical data	143, 297
census	296
centre of symmetry	101
chain percentage	241
chord	223
circumference	489
class interval	300
coefficient	79
co-interior angles	105
collinear points	97, 291
column vector	406
common factor	34
complement of a set	61
complementary angles	104
complementary events	464
component form	406
composite number	29
compound interest	243
concurrent lines	97
cone	256
congruent figures	103
constant term	79
continuous data	143, 297
corresponding angles	105
cumulative frequency	364
cylinder	255
data set	296
decimal place	50
denominator	35
density	268
dependent events	465
dependent variable	426
diameter	223
difference of two squares	130
discrete data	143, 297
disjoint sets	68
distance formula	281
distributive law	123
domain	388
empty set	61
enlargement	404, 413
equal ratios	41
equation	78
equilateral triangle	99
equivalent fractions	35
expansion	134
exponent	155
expression	78
exterior angle	117
extrapolation	431
factor	29
factorisation	134
finite set	60
formula	169
frequency histogram	362
frequency table	308
function	390
general term	480
global maximum	439
global minimum	439
gradient	284
gradient-intercept form	321
hexagon	98
highest common factor	34
horizontal asymptote	399
horizontal bar chart	143
horizontal line	318
horizontal translation	416
hypotenuse	196
improper fraction	35
independent events	463
independent variable	426
index notation	39
infinite set	28
integer	28
interpolation	431
interquartile range	306
intersection of sets	68
interval notation	64
irrational number	29
isosceles triangle	99, 111
kite	99
like terms	79
line of best fit	426
line segment	97
line symmetry	101
linear correlation	426
linear equation	84
linear inequality	177
local maximum	439
local minimum	439
loss	233
lower quartile	306
lowest common denominator	36
lowest common multiple	34
mapping diagram	388
mass	268
mean	302
median	302
midpoint formula	282
mixed number	35
modal class	146
mode	303
multiple	34
mutually exclusive events	471
natural number	28
negative index law	161
number line	177
number plane	278
number sequence	478
numeral	78
numerator	35
numerical data	143, 297
obtuse angle	96
octagon	98
one figure approximation	52
ordered pair	278
parallel lines	97, 289
parallelogram	99
pentagon	98
percentage	231
perfect cube	28
perfect square	28
perimeter	216
perpendicular lines	97
pie chart	144
polygon	98
position vector	405
positive integer	62
prime factor	33
prime number	29
principal	236
probability value	450
profit	233
pronumeral	78
proper fraction	35
proper subset	60
pyramid	261
Pythagoras' theorem	196
Pythagorean triple	200
quadrant	279
quadratic equation	88
quadratic function	438
quadrilateral	98
radius	223
range	306, 388
ratio	40
rational number	28
raw data	296
real number	29
reciprocal	161
reciprocal function	398
rectangle	99
reduction	404, 413
reflection	404, 411
reflex angle	96
regular polygon	99
relative frequency	451
revolution	96
rhombus	99
right angle	96
right angled triangle	99, 332
rotation	404, 410
rotational symmetry	101
sample	296
sample space	457
scalar	405
scale factor	373, 413
scalene	99
scatter diagram	144
sector	223
semi-circle	490
set	59
significant figure	51
similar figures	373
similar triangles	376
simple interest	236
simultaneous solution	183
skewed distribution	299
sphere	257
square	99
square number	28
square root	28
standard form	163
stem-and-leaf plot	145
straight angle	96
subject	170
subset	60
supplementary angles	104
surface area	251
symmetrical distribution	299
tally-frequency table	299
tangent	207
term	78
three point notation	96
transformation	403
translation	404, 408
transversal	98
trapezium	99
triangle	98, 108
true bearing	345
turning point	439
two-way table	454
undefined gradient	318
union of sets	68
unitary method	44
universal set	60
upper quartile	306
variable	78
vector	405
Venn diagram	65
vertex	438
vertical asymptote	399
vertical bar chart	143
vertical line	318
vertical line test	393
vertical translation	416
vertically opposite angles	104
volume	259
x-intercept	320
y-intercept	320
zero index law	161